D1412741

FLORA

FLORA

VOLUME II
L–Z

THE GARDENER'S BIBLE

CHIEF CONSULTANT: TONY LORD

More than 20,000 garden plants
from around the world

CASSELL

Publisher	Gordon Cheers
Associate publisher	Margaret Olds
Art director	Stan Lamond
Project manager	Kate Etherington
Chief consultant	Tony Lord
Senior consultant	Tony Rodd
Contributors	David Austin, David Banks, Cathy Wilkinson Barash, Matthew Biggs, Don Blaxell, David Bond, Peter Brownless, Geoff Bryant, Kate Bryant, Cole Burrell, Derek Butcher, Jerry Coleby-Williams, Ian Connor, Penny Dunn, Lorraine Flanigan, Jim Folsom, Richard Francis, Jo Ann Gardner, William Grant, Ken Grapes, Sarah Guest, Keith Hammett, Patricia Hanbidge, Ian Hay, Terry Hewitt, Sean Hogan, Geoff Hodge, Mark Kane, Ruth Kiew, Melanie Kinsey, Isobyl la Croix, Todd Lasseigne, David Mabberley, Lawrie Metcalf, Valda Paddison, Helene Pizzi, Lee Reich, Martyn Rix, Tony Rodd, Bruce Rutherford, Stephen Ryan, Donald Schnell, Patrick Seymour, Julie Silk, Geoff Stebbings, Wendy Thomas, David Tomlinson, John Trager, R. G. Turner Jr., Marion Tyree, Rachel Vogan, Scott Williams
Hardiness zone maps	John Frith
Illustrations	Spike Wademan
Managing editors	Janet Parker, Margaret Malone
Editors	Loretta Barnard, Annette Carter, Lynn Cole, Dannielle Doggett, Fiona Doig, Alan Edwards, Janet Healey, Carol Jacobson, Erin King, Scott Lumsden, Heather McNamara, Joy Misrachi, Rob Paratore, Anne Savage, Judith Simpson, Julie Stanton, Marie-Louise Taylor, Michael Wall
Picture research	Gordon Cheers
Photo library	Alan Edwards
Cover design	Stan Lamond
Designer	Joy Eckermann
Picture sizing	Kathy Lamond, Suzanne Potma
Typesetting	Dee Rogers
Index	Loretta Barnard, Scott Lumsden, Heather McNamara, Jan Watson
Production	Bernard Roberts
Publishing assistant	Erin King
Foreign rights	Sarah Minns
Photographers	James Young, David Banks, Chris Bell, Rob Blakers, Lorraine Blyth, Greg Bourke, Ken Brass, Geoff Bryant, Derek Butcher, Claver Carroll, Anna Cheifetz, Leigh Clapp, David Austin Roses, Grant Dixon, Heather Donovan, e-garden Ltd, Bruce Elder, Katie Fallows, Stuart Owen Fox, Richard Francis, Robert Gibson, William Grant, Denise Greig, Barry Griffith, Barry Grossman, Gil Hanly, Ivy Hansen, Dennis Harding, Jack Hobbs, Neil Holmes, Paul Huntley, Richard I'Anson, Ionas Kaltenbach, David Keith Jones, Willie Kempen, Colin Kerr, Robert M. Knight, Carol Knoll, Albert Kuhnigk, Mike Langford, Gary Lewis, Geoff Longford, Stirling Macoboy, John McCann, David McGonigal, Richard McKenna, Ron Moon, Eberhard Morell, Barry Myers-Rice, Steve Newall, Connall Oosterbroek, Larry Pitt, Craig Potton, Janet Price, Geof Prigge, Nick Rains, Christo Reid, Howard Rice, Jamie Robertson, Tony Rodd, Rolf-Ulrich Roesler, Luke Saffigna, Don Skirrow, Raoul Slater, Peter Solness, Ken Stepnell, Warren Steptoe, Oliver Strewe, J. Peter Thoeming, David Titmuss, Wayne Turville, Georg Uebelhart, Sharyn Vanderhorst, Kim Westerskov, Murray White, Vic Widman, Brent Wilson, Geoff Woods, Grant Young

This edition published in 2003 by Cassell,
an imprint of Weidenfeld & Nicolson
Wellington House
125 Strand
London WC2R 0BB

Produced by Global Book Publishing Pty Ltd
Unit 1/181 High Street, Willoughby, NSW 2068, Australia
Ph +61 2 9967 3100 Fax +61 2 9967 5891
Email rightsmanager@globalpub.com.au

All rights reserved. No part of this publication may be reproduced, stored in a retrieval system, or transmitted in any form of by any means, electronic, mechanical, photocopying, recording or otherwise, without the prior written permission of the Publisher.

Photos and illustrations from the Global Photo Library
© Global Book Publishing Pty Ltd 2003
Text © Global Book Publishing Pty Ltd 2003

The Publisher would like to thank Duncan Baird Publishers, London, for permission to re-create in this book the map on page 11 of *The History of the Countryside* by Oliver Rackham.
Thanks also to The Art Archive for use of the following pictures: page 16 (above right), page 19 (below right), page 46 (top centre), page 47 (top right), page 48 (below left), and page 51 (both)

The moral rights of all contributors have been asserted

ISBN 0 30436 435 5

British Library Cataloguing in Publication Data
A catalogue record for this book is available from the British Library

Photographers: The publisher would be pleased to hear from photographers interested in supplying photographs that could be included in new editions of *Flora*. Email photoeditor@globalpub.com.au

Suggestions: The editors would be pleased to hear from plant nurseries, general gardeners, and specialty groups about any plants they feel should be added to future editions of *Flora*. Email editor@globalpub.com.au

Printed in Hong Kong by Sing Cheong Printing Co. Ltd
Film separation Pica Digital Pte Ltd, Singapore

VOLUME I
Page i: *Malus* 'Red Sentinel'
Pages ii–iii: *Magnolia* 'Betty'
Page v: Cobweb in conifer, in the snow
Pages vi–vii: Creative plant combinations offer color and fragrance
Pages viii–ix: *Galanthus nivalis*
Pages xii–xiii: A variety of trees and shrubs provide structure to a garden
Pages 64–65: Aster *novi-belgii* cultivar
Pages 212–213: *Banksia ericifolia*
Pages 274–275: *Camellia reticulata* 'Dali Cha'
Pages 462–463: *Dahlia* 'Tout à Toi'
Pages 520–521: *Echinacea purpurea*
Pages 594–595: *Fritillaria imperialis*
Pages 620–621: *Gaillardia* species
Pages 664–665: *Helianthus annuus*
Pages 724–725: *Iris* 'Marie Caillet'
Pages 762–763: *Kalmia latifolia* 'Ostbo Red'

VOLUME II
Page i: *Bellis perennis* Pomponette Series
Page ii–iii: *Leucospermum* species
Page v: *Lantana* species
Pages vi–vii: *Cotinus coggygria* 'Purpureus'
Pages 784–785: *Lilium* 'Barbaresco'
Pages 846–847: *Moraea villosa*
Pages 910–911: *Narcissus* 'Palmares'
Pages 940–941: *Oenothera* species
Pages 968–969: *Paphiopedilum* species with frog
Pages 1120–1121: *Rosa* 'Cathedral'
Pages 1290–1291: *Sarracenia* × *exornata*
Pages 1394–1395: *Telopea speciosissima* cultivar
Pages 1446–1447: *Vanda* 'Pat Delight'
Pages 1480–1481: *Zinnia elegans* 'Oklahoma Pink'

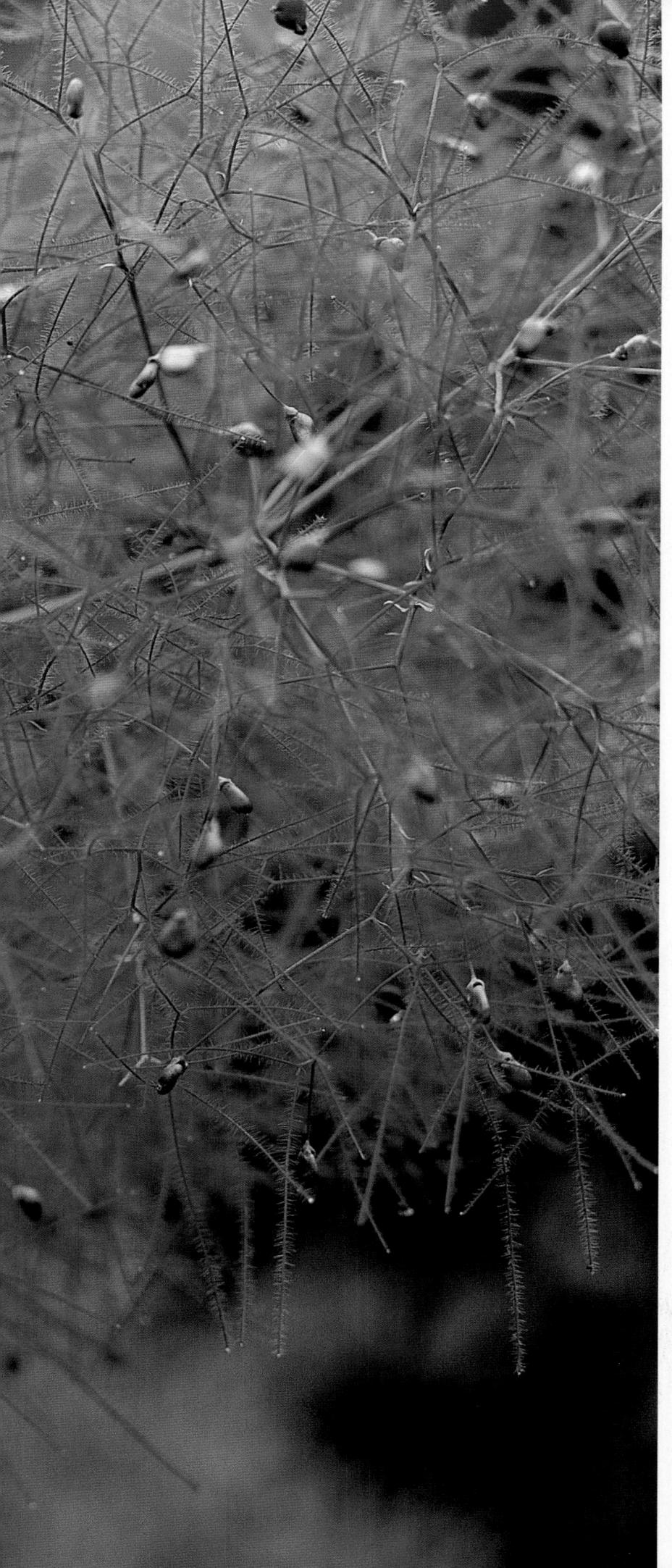

Contents

L

Laburnum alpinum

Lablab purpureus

LABLAB

A genus of a single species in the pea-flower subfamily of the legume (Fabaceae) family, native to Africa but long grown in India, Southeast Asia, Egypt, and Sudan as a vegetable. It must be treated with caution, for most parts of the plant are poisonous; the pods and seeds are edible only after

they have been boiled thoroughly. It is a short-lived herbaceous perennial climber, often treated as a half-hardy annual in colder climates. The leaves consist of 3 triangular leaflets; the pea-flowers occur in various colors and are produced throughout summer, followed by edible pods.

CULTIVATION: Grow in a sunny well-drained site when danger of frost is past. Propagate by seed sown in spring.

Lablab purpureus

syns *Dolichos lablab, Lablab niger*
BANNER BEAN, BLACK BEAN, EGYPTIAN BEAN, HYACINTH BEAN, INDIAN BEAN

☀ ⚘ ↔ 5–10 ft (1.5–3 m)
↑ 12–20 ft (3.5–6 m)

Perennial vine from tropical Africa. Purplish stems; alternate divided leaves, 3 broad oval leaflets. Elongated flowerheads of fragrant white, pink, or purple pea-flowers. Flat, often curved, maroon or purplish seed pods. Most plant parts poisonous; pods and seeds edible if well boiled. 'Darkness', violet-purple flowers, black seeds; 'Daylight', white flowers, white seeds; 'Giganteus', larger form, white flowers. Zones 9–12.

+ LABURNOCYTISUS

Hybrid between the genera *Laburnum* and *Cytisus*, the + sign indicating a graft hybrid. This particular hybrid arose in the French nursery of M. Jean-Louis Adam around 1825. Adam had been grafting the purple broom, *Cytisus purpureus,* onto stems of the common laburnum, *Laburnum anagyroides,* with the object of producing a long-stemmed broom. Most of the resulting plants turned out as expected, but one produced a branch with flowers of a curious brownish color and foliage intermediate between that of the broom and the laburnum. Adam propagated from this plant, producing plants with characteristics of both the parents, which were then named after him to acknowledge his work.

CULTIVATION: Cultivation requirements are the same as for *Laburnum.* The plants grow well in a cool-temperate climate, preferably with uniform annual rainfall. They require moderately fertile soil with good drainage. Seeds germinate readily if they are soaked in warm water for 24 hours before sowing.

+ Laburnocytisus adamii

☀ ❄ ↔ 15 ft (4.5 m) ↑ 25 ft (8 m)
A variable tree, some branches producing the yellow flowers of the laburnum, others with clusters of purple broom flowers, and yet others with muddy beige flowers, in short racemes. The leaves are 3-palmate and dark green; the leaflets about 2 in (5 cm) long. Pea-like flowers appear in late spring. Zones 5–9.

LABURNUM

A genus of only 2 species of small deciduous trees, allied to *Genista* in the pea-flower subfamily of the legume (Fabaceae) family, found in

central and southern Europe. The leaves are trifoliate and alternate. They are widely grown for their long drooping racemes of yellow pea-flowers, produced in spring and early summer. All parts of the plant, especially the seeds, are poisonous.

CULTIVATION: Laburnums grow well in a cool-temperate climate, preferably with uniform annual rainfall; any moderately fertile soil with good drainage will suit them. It may be necessary to carry out some early shaping by way of removing competing leaders, but otherwise very little pruning is required. In larger gardens laburnums are popularly planted to form an arch. The seeds germinate readily if soaked in warm water for 24 hours before sowing. Position where the plants will be sheltered from winter frosts.

Laburnum alpinum

SCOTCH LABURNUM

☀ ❄ ↔ 25 ft (8 m) ↑ 25 ft (8 m)
This is a small spreading tree from mountain regions. The leaflets are deep shiny green above, paler and hairy beneath. Racemes of yellow flowers appear in mid-summer. The seed pods are flattened, smooth, and shiny. 'Pendulum' is a slow-growing form with pendulous branches; 'Pyramidale' has upright branches. Zones 3–9.

Laburnum anagyroides

COMMON LABURNUM, GOLDEN CHAIN TREE

☀ ❄ ↔ 25 ft (8 m) ↑ 25 ft (8 m)
Small tree. Leaves dull green to gray-green, oval to elliptic, to 3 in (8 cm) long, hairy on the undersurface. Drooping racemes of vivid yellow flowers, crowded along the branches, in the late spring to early summer. 'Pendulum' has slender drooping branches. Zones 3–9.

Laburnum anagyroides

Laburnum anagyroides 'Pendulum'

Laburnum × *watereri* 'Vossii'

Laburnum × *watereri*

GOLDEN CHAIN TREE, LABURNUM

☼ ❄ ↔ 25 ft (8 m) ↕ 25 ft (8 m)

This is a hybrid between *L. alpinum* and *L. anagyroides*, which resembles *L. alpinum,* but has leaves and pods that are more densely hairy. Yellow flowers occur in packed racemes. Best-known clonal form, '**Vossii**' ★, has a similar habit to the parent but is more prolific, with longer flower racemes, to 2 ft (0.6 m). Zones 3–9.

LACHENALIA

CAPE COWSLIP

Most of the 110 species of bulbs in this southern African genus, belonging to the hyacinth (Hyacinthaceae) family occur in a small region of Western Cape, with a smaller number in Namibia. They are notable for their interestingly colored, mainly winter- to spring-blooming flowers and highly variable foliage. The leaves are always basal, emerging directly from the bulb, but may be small or large; lance-shaped, heart-shaped, strappy or grassy; matt green, glossy green, plain, or mottled. The flowers come in many colors and are tubular or bell-shaped with 6 petals, the outer 3 forming a fleshy cup, from which the inner 3, often differently colored, protrude. CULTIVATION: These plants are rather frost tender but otherwise easily grown. Plant in full sun in humus-rich well-drained soil. Water and feed during active growth; dry off after flowering. They are suitable for containers. Propagate by offset or by dividing established clumps.

Lachenalia aloides ★

☼/☼ ❄ ↔ 8 in (20 cm) ↕ 12 in (30 cm)

Leaves 2 per bulb, broad, green to blue-green, often darker or maroon-

spotted. The flowers are tubular to funnel-shaped, slightly pendulous, greenish yellow to apricot, and appear from winter through to early summer. Consists of many forms and has been used extensively in hybridization. *L. a.* var. *aurea* produces golden yellow flowers with greenish markings; '**Nelsonii**', densely purple-spotted leaves. *L. a.* '**Pearsonii**', leaves with red-brown spotting on the upper-surface. Zones 9–10.

Lachenalia bulbifera

☼/☼ ❄ ↔ 6–8 in (15–20 cm) ↕ 8–12 in (20–30 cm)

Usually has 1 or 2 densely maroon-spotted leaves per bulb, sometimes developing bulbils along the edges; strong flower stems. The green-tipped, orange-red, tubular flowers are borne in winter–spring. Multiplies freely. Zones 9–10.

Lachenalia contaminata

WILD HYACINTH

☼/☼ ❄ ↔ 8–10 in (20–25 cm) ↕ 6–10 in (15–25 cm)

Forms clump of up to 10 fine grassy leaves per bulb. Dense heads of small, cream, bell-shaped flowers with contrasting dark maroon tips in summer; flower buds with emerald green tips. Zones 9–10.

Lachenalia Hybrid Cultivars

☼/☼ ❄ ↔ 12–16 in (30–40 cm) ↕ 12 in (30 cm)

In modern hybrids the emphasis is mainly on producing many weather-resistant flowers on stocky compact stems. The foliage is also thicker, lusher, and healthier than in wild forms or early hybrids and selections. Typical, among a new range of Dutch-raised hybrids, are: '**Romaud**', faintly marked, broad, strappy leaves, dense heads of soft yellow flowers on short stems; '**Ronina**', similarly colored, with wider-spaced flowers and maroon-spotted leaves and stems. Zones 9–10.

LACTUCA

LETTUCE

Genus of about 75 species of Northern Hemisphere annuals and perennials in

Lachenalia, Hybrid Cultivar, 'Romaud'

Lachenalia, Hybrid Cultivar, 'Ronina'

the daisy (Asteraceae) family, which produce a rosette of entire, lobed, deeply divided, or blistered leaves. Leaf margins are smooth, undulating, serrated, or frilly; leaf color varies from green to brown or red. Masses of tiny flowers, usually white, yellow, or blue, are produced in a tall spike. The seeds are tiny and are white, gray, or black. Some species are spiny or prickly. Only one species, *L. sativa,* is widely cultivated for its edible leaves; the stems of some cultivars are also eaten. The milky sap or juice of lettuces is soporific. CULTIVATION: Lettuces like rich well-drained soil in full sun. They must never be allowed to dry out during the growing period or they will go to seed. Cool conditions are usually needed for germination; the seed can be sown almost year round.

Lachenalia aloides var. *aurea*

Lactuca sativa

COMMON LETTUCE

☀ ❄ ↔ 4–12 in (10–30 cm)
↑ 4–12 in (10–30 cm)

As usually understood, this species is known only in cultivation, but it is thought that it may be an ancient derivative of the wild Mediterranean prickly lettuce, *L. serriola,* now known as a common weed. There are many varieties of lettuce. Leaf shape, size, and color vary, and some are quite attractive. Most are eaten raw, although they can be cooked. All need to be grown quickly to avoid bitterness. *L. s.* var. *augustana* (syn. *L. s.* var. *asparagina),* commonly known as asparagus lettuce, celtuce, or Chinese lettuce, is from Asia. It is a larger plant than the species and grown mainly for its thickened stem, to 3 in (8 cm) in diameter, which is eaten raw or cooked; leaves are usually green, but

there is also a red form. *L. s.* 'Attico', a mini, green, cos-type lettuce with erect smooth-edged leaves, resistant to bolting, tip burn, and downy mildew; **'Australian Yellow Leaf'**, old variety, a gently frilled loose-leaf type with a tender texture and a unique, almost fluorescent yellow-green color, slow to bolt; **'Bubbles'** ★, bred in the UK, a compact green lettuce with notably blistered leaves and a fairly firm sweet head; **'Cocarde'** ★ (arrowhead lettuce), a red oak-leaf type with large arrow-shaped leaves tinged red, tender; **'Cos Verdi'**, a crisp, sweet-flavored, cos-type lettuce with open upright heads and smooth-edged green leaves, reliable; **'Cosmic'**, a cos-type lettuce; **'Crisp Mint'**, a cos-type lettuce with compact tall heads; **'Fortune'**, a butterhead with a medium compact head and green leaves, very quick growing; **'Grandpa Admires'**, an heirloom

butterhead with loose heads of pale green blushing bronze and red, slow to bolt; **'Green Coral'**, a fast-growing loose-leaf type with smooth green leaves that have very frilly margins; **'Green Mignonette'**, a soft-leafed, small, hearting lettuce with blistered leaves and good flavor, hardy; **'Green Oak Leaf'**, an attractive lettuce with green deeply divided leaves similar in shape to those of an oak tree, fast growing; **'Iceberg'** ★, bred in the USA in the 1930s to cope with travel to markets, a large, heavy, hearting lettuce with crisp outer green leaves and a white heart; **'Italian Oak Leaf'**, a medium-sized, green, upright, Italian-style lettuce, very vigorous and resistant to disease; **'Kendo'**, a cos cross with a crisp tight heart, green leaves overlaid with red, yellow heart, very sweet; **'Little Gem'** ★ (syns 'Sugar Cos', 'Sucrine'), a semi-cos, compact, with

dark green crumpled leaves and a firm sweet head; **'Musketeer'**, a large crisphead variety with mid-green leaves, resistant to downy mildew; **'Oak Leaf'**, first listed in France in the 1770s, 3 main colors: green, dark green, and brown, a loose-leaf variety with deeply divided leaves like those of an oak tree (hence the name); **'Purple Oak Leaf'**, a purple-tinged form of the green 'Oak Leaf', withstands heat and cold; **'Red Coral'**, an attractive loose-leaf variety with very frilly red leaves; **'Red Mignonette'**, a butterhead with small red and green heads; **'Red Oak Leaf'**, a red-tinged form of the green 'Oak Leaf'; **'Red Sails'**, a loose-leaf lettuce with bronzy red crinkled leaves, slow to bolt; **'Red Salad Bowl'** ★, a red loose-leaf variety developed from 'Oak Leaf', with long, narrow, serrated leaves; **'Romany'**, a semi-cos with bold, dark green,

Lactuca sativa 'Attico'

L. sativa 'Australian Yellow Leaf'

Lactuca sativa 'Cocarde'

Lactuca sativa 'Cos Verdi'

Lactuca sativa 'Cosmic'

Lactuca sativa 'Bubbles'

Lactuca sativa 'Crisp Mint'

Lactuca sativa 'Fortune'

Lactuca sativa 'Grandpa Admires'

Lactuca sativa 'Green Coral'

L. sativa 'Green Mignonette'

Lactuca sativa 'Green Oak Leaf'

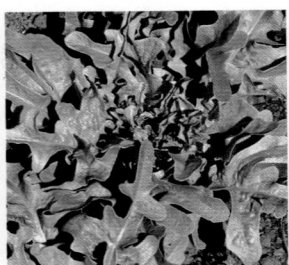

Lactuca sativa 'Italian Oak Leaf'

Lactuca sativa 'Kendo'

Lactuca sativa 'Little Gem'

Lactuca sativa 'Musketeer'

Lactuca sativa 'Purple Oak Leaf'

Lactuca sativa 'Red Coral'

Lactuca sativa 'Red Mignonette'

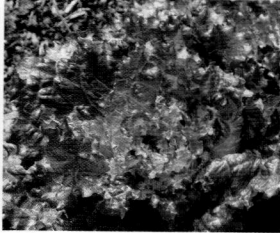

Lactuca sativa 'Red Sails'

Lactuca sativa 'Red Salad Bowl'

Lactuca sativa 'Romany'

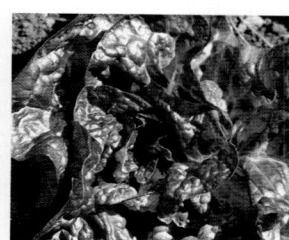

Lactuca sativa 'Sunset'

Lactuca sativa 'Valdor'

Lactuca sativa var. *augustana*

Lactuca watsoniana

Laelia Canariensis

Laelia anceps

upright leaves, a crisp heart, and good flavor, resistant to tip burn and downy mildew; '**Sunset**', a large red butterhead with smooth-edged leaves, good in cool conditions; '**Valdor**' ★, a winter lettuce for growing in an unheated greenhouse or outdoors, which should be sown in the autumn and harvested in the spring, with good resistance to botrytis. Zones 6–11.

Lactuca watsoniana
ALFACINHA

↔ 12–24 in (30–60 cm)
↑ 12–24 in (30–60 cm)

This is a wild species endemic to the grasslands of the Azores, the Canary Islands, and Madeira. Large oval green leaves with a prominent white midrib. Produces a tall spike of small white flowers. Zones 9–11.

LAELIA

This genus from tropical America comprises a very fashionable group of about 60 easily grown, showy, and colorful sympodial orchids (family Orchidaceae). These *Cattleya* relatives are generally lithophytic, although there are a number of epiphytic species. They also differ from that genus by having 8 pollen bundles called pollinia (*Cattleya* have only 4). They are generally smaller plants than the majority of cattleyas, and mostly have 1 leaf per pseudobulb, although there are a few species with 2 leaves. They have been used in numerous artificial hybrids involving a range of related genera, including *Brassavola*, *Broughtonia*, *Cattleya*, *Epidendrum*, and *Sophronitis*.
CULTIVATION: Most species require bright, warm, and moist conditions

during summer while the plants are in active growth, and a cooler dry winter, when most species are dormant. Cultivated plants must have unimpeded drainage, and can be mounted or grown in pots using a coarse bark-based medium. Flowering plants may be enjoyed indoors while in bloom. Propagate by division.

Laelia anceps ★

↔ 8–36 in (20–90 cm)
↑ 8–48 in (20–120 cm)

Native to Mexico. An extremely variable autumn- to winter-flowering species with large somewhat starry flowers, to 5 in (12 cm) across. Up to 5 blooms, on long flattened inflorescences that can grow over 40 in (100 cm) long. Colors range from white through various shades of pink

to deep lavender. Labellum color just as variable, various combinations of white, yellow, orange, purple, and lilac occurring. Also albino (white), bicolored, and splash-petalled forms in cultivation. *L. a.* var. *veitchiana* '**Fort Caroline**', white blooms with a pale lilac labellum in autumn and winter. *L. a.* '**Chamberlain's**', very long inflorescences, often over 40 in (100 cm), purple blooms in autumn and winter. Zones 10–12.

Laelia Canariensis

↔ 8–24 in (20–60 cm)
↑ 8–40 in (20–100 cm)

Popular primary hybrid of *L. anceps* and *L. harpophylla*. Blooms in colors ranging from light purples to orange and yellow tones in winter and spring. Zones 10–12.

Laelia anceps 'Chamberlain's'

L. anceps var. *veitchiana* 'Fort Caroline'

Laelia crispa

Laelia flava

Laelia crispa

☼/☀ ✢ ↔ 8–36 in (20–90 cm)
↕ 8–24 in (20–60 cm)

From Brazil. Growth habit similar to one of the larger *Cattleya* varieties. Up to 7 white blooms, 5 in (12 cm) across, on an upright spike, in late summer. Labellum predominantly purple, with some yellow marks with undulated margins. Zones 10–12.

Laelia flava

☼/☀ ✢ ↔ 4–16 in (10–40 cm)
↕ 8–32 in (20–80 cm)

Native to Brazil. This is a compact rock-growing plant, which produces tall erect spikes of bright yellow flowers in spring–early summer. Blooms are 2 in (5 cm) across, and appear in clusters at the top of the leafless stalk. Zones 10–12.

Laelia milleri

☼/☀ ✢ ↔ 4–16 in (10–40 cm)
↕ 8–27 in (20–70 cm)

From Brazil. A spectacular, compact-growing, lithophytic species with tall spikes of up to 8 orange-red to dark red blooms, 2½ in (6 cm) across, in late spring–summer. Zones 10–12.

Laelia pumila

☀ ✢ ↔ 4–16 in (10–40 cm)
↕ 4–8 in (10–20 cm)

From Brazil. Compact-growing epiphyte. Single pink to dark purple blooms, 3½ in (9 cm) across, produced from the developing new growth, in summer. There are also albino (white) and lilac-colored forms. Prefers more shade than most laelias and may also be grown on slabs of cork or tree-fern. Zones 10–12.

Laelia purpurata

☼/☀ ✢ ↔ 8–36 in (20–90 cm)
↕ 8–36 in (20–90 cm)

National flower of Brazil; has been called the "Queen of the Laelias." Up to 5 blooms, 8 in (20 cm) across, produced off mature pseudobulbs in summer. Tall-growing species; wide range and combination of colors, from pure white through all the shades of pink, purple, and lilac. The flared and trumpet-like labellum comes in a similar color range, with a network of stripes and solid color. There are also albino (pure white), semi-alba, splash-petalled, and bicolored forms. Many varieties have been named, all defining a different color form. Two of the most popular are: *L. p.* var. *carnea* ★, white, with a soft pink labellum; and *L. p.* var. *werkhauseri*, white, with a dark bluish purple labellum and a pleasant fragrance. Zones 10–12.

Laelia tenebrosa

☼/☀ ✢ ↔ 8–36 in (20–90 cm)
↕ 8–32 in (20–80 cm)

From Brazil. Similar growth habit to the closely related *L. purpurata*. Large summer-flowering species with up to 3 blooms, 6 in (15 cm) across. Petals and sepals bronze with a coppery hue; labellum white with very heavy purple veining. Zones 10–12.

Laelia milleri

Laelia purpurata var. *carnea*

Laelia tenebrosa

× *LAELIOCATTLEYA*

An artificial bigeneric group of colorful orchid hybrids (family Orchidaceae) between *Laelia* and *Cattleya*. Generally robust plants with 1 or 2 leaves per pseudobulb. Many of the larger-flowering types are grown commercially for the cut-flower trade. CULTIVATION: Require warmth in winter but will stand cooler winter temperatures for short periods if kept dry while dormant. They enjoy bright light conditions and must have unimpeded drainage and a coarse bark-based medium. Healthy plants will develop an extensive system of thick white roots, long-lived and freely branching. Propagate by division.

× *Laeliocattleya* Hybrids

☀/◐ ✦ ↔ 4–30 in (10–75 cm)
↕ 4–36 in (10–90 cm)

These hybrids come in a wide range of sizes, shapes, and colors, being a combination of 2 genera that are themselves highly variable. Almost all colors may be found, with the exception of black and sky blue. The flower size varies between 2 in (5 cm) and 10 in (25 cm). **C. G. Roebling**, primary hybrid made over a century ago between the "blue-lipped" forms of *Cattleya gaskelliana* and *Laelia purpurata*; **Edgard van Belle 'Edwin Arthur Hausermann'**, bold pink to purple bloom with a strong fragrance; **Mini Purple 'Bette'** ★, popular primary hybrid of compact-growing *Laelia pumila* and *Cattleya walkeriana*, producing pinkish purple flowers; **Myrtle Johnson**, fine "splash-petalled" style, with the labellum colors also appearing on the petals; **Pink Favourite 'Jolly'**, primary hybrid of *Laelia milleri* and *Cattleya walkeriana*; **Tropical Pointer 'Cheetah'**, *Cattleya intermedia* hybrid that gets its spots from one of its ancestors, *C. aclandiae*. Zones 10–12.

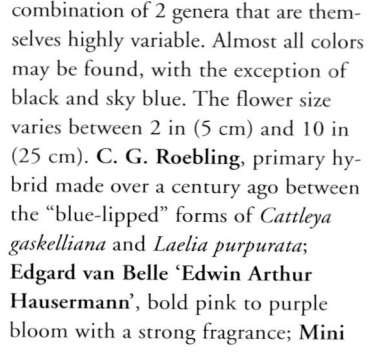

× *Laeliocattleya* Canhamiana 'Coerulea'

× *Laeliocattleya*, H, (× *Laeliocattleya* Blue Ribbon × *Cattleya* Penny Kuroda)

× *Laeliocattleya*, H, C. G. Roebling

× *Laeliocattleya*, H, (*Cattleya* Chocolate Drop × × *Laeliocattleya* Jalapa)

× *L.*, H, (× *L.* Dupreana 'Coerulea' × *Laelia purpurata* var. *werkhauseri*)

× *Laeliocattleya*, Hybrid, Edgard van Belle 'Edwin Arthur Hausermann'

× *Laeliocattleya*, H, Lauren Oko 'Kristy'

× *Laeliocattleya*, H, Mini Purple 'Bette'

× *Laeliocattleya*, Hybrid, Myrtle Johnson

× *Laeliocattleya*, H, Pink Favourite 'Jolly'

× *Laeliocattleya*, Hybrid, Pink Perfume

× *Laeliocattleya*, H, (*Cattleya* Pittiana × leopoldi) × × *Laeliocattleya* Interglossa

× *Laeliocattleya*, Hybrid, (*Laelia* Santa Barbara Sunset × *Cattleya aurantiaca*)

× *Laeliocattleya*, Hybrid, Sallieri

× *Laeliocattleya*, Hybrid, (*Laelia superbiens* × *Cattleya amethystoglossa*)

× *Laeliocattleya*, H, Royal Emperor 'Wade'

× *L.*, Hybrid, Tropical Pointer 'Cheetah'

LAGAROSTROBOS

This genus consists of a single species of evergreen coniferous tree in the plum-pine (Podocarpaceae) family, from Tasmania, Australia. Another species from New Zealand formerly included in it is now placed in the separate genus *Monoao*. *Lagarostrobos* yields a lightly colored, fine-grained, durable wood, highly valued for boat-building and cabinet-work but now rarely obtainable. Growth is very slow, with annual rings in wood often less than a millimeter wide; ages of over 2,000 years have been estimated for some trees. The pale brown to silver-gray bark flakes away, though the trunk remains smooth. The foliage is cypress-like, though the tiny scale-like leaves are arranged spirally, not in opposite pairs as in *Cupressus*. Pollen and seed cones are usually on different trees, the seed cones small and inconspicuous.
CULTIVATION: Grown mainly for their somewhat weeping growth habit, these trees like a cool but near frost-free climate with high humidity and ample rainfall. They prefer deep well-drained soil with plenty of humus.

Lagerstroemia speciosa

Lagerstroemia indica

Although the trees can tolerate full sun when mature, they are best shaded from the hottest summer sun while young. Propagate from seed or half-hardened tip cuttings.

Lagarostrobos franklinii
syn. *Dacrydium franklinii*
HUON PINE
☼ ❋ ↔ 25 ft (8 m) ↑ 100 ft (30 m)
Native to western Tasmania, Australia; rare in the wild. Very slow growing tree with a roughly conical shape, far smaller in cultivation. Branches gracefully arching, drooping, densely clothed with small, scale-like, deep green leaves. Zones 8–9.

LAGENARIA
GOURD
This genus comprises 6 species of annual or perennial vines in the pumpkin (Cucurbitaceae) family, native to tropical regions, that use tendrils to climb. The leaves are heart-shaped or 3- to 5-lobed. The softly scented, white, male and female, bell-shaped flowers may be solitary or in racemes. The fruit may be up to 3 ft (0.9 m)

Lagerstroemia floribunda

Lagarostrobos franklinii, in the wild, Wanderer River, Tasmania, Australia

long and comes in a variety of shapes but is often in the form of a club. The young fruit of some species is edible, though it is bitter, and confined mainly to curries. The mature fruit (gourds) are sometimes cleaned out and their hard dried shells are used as utensils or musical instruments.
CULTIVATION: These strong-growing vines will adapt to most soils in an open sunny position. A tall trellis or similar support should be provided to keep gourds off the ground. Propagate from seed in late spring in temperate climates or at the beginning of the tropical wet season.

Lagenaria siceraria
syns *Lagenaria leucantha, L. vulgaris*
BOTTLE GOURD, CROOKNECK GOURD, TRUMPET GOURD, WHITE-FLOWERED GOURD
☼ ✝ ↔ 10–20 ft (3–6 m) ↑ 10–30 ft (3–9 m)
Widely grown tendril-climbing annual. The leaves are dull green, hairy, oval to heart-shaped, and toothed. Solitary, white, trumpet-shaped flowers are borne in summer. Fruit is variably shaped, greenish yellow, edible, and 3–36 in (8–90 cm) long. Zones 10–12.

LAGERSTROEMIA
CRAPE MYRTLE
Genus in the loosestrife (Lythraceae) family, consisting of 53 species of evergreen or deciduous, small to large trees, occurs from southern and eastern Asia to northern Australia. They have attractive, often peeling bark and simple, variable, usually opposite leaves that in many species provide brilliant autumn color. In summer they bear showy panicles of flowers with crinkled petals and a crape-like texture in differing shades of pink, mauve, and white. For all these reasons, these trees are a popular inclusion in many

Lagenaria siceraria

gardens. The fruit is a capsule. The timber of some species has been used to manufacture bridges, furniture, and railway sleepers.
CULTIVATION: These trees are generally easy to grow, adapting to a wide variety of soils. They grow best in well-drained soil in a sunny position and some tolerate light frosts. Propagate from seed or half-hardened cuttings in summer, or from hardwood cuttings in early winter. Powdery mildew can be a problem, but newer cultivars are more disease resistant.

Lagerstroemia floribunda
☼ ✝ ↔ 15 ft (4.5 m) ↑ 40 ft (12 m)
From Myanmar, southern Thailand, and the Malay Peninsula. Trunk with gray bark; open crown. Leaves broad, somewhat glossy. Mauve-pink flowers, to 2 in (5 cm) across, in few-flowered sprays. Zones 11–12.

Lagerstroemia indica
CRAPE MYRTLE
☼ ❋ ↔ 20 ft (6 m) ↑ 20 ft (6 m)
From China and Japan. Often multi-stemmed deciduous tree, with wide-spreading, flat-topped, open habit when mature. Bark smooth, pinkish gray, mottled. Leaves small, dark green, turning orange-red in autumn. White, pink, mauve, purple, or carmine flowers with crimped petals, in panicles to 8 in (20 cm) long. For cultivars often included here, see Hybrid Cultivars entry. Zones 7–11.

Lagerstroemia speciosa
syn. *Lagerstroemia flos-reginae*
PRIDE OF INDIA, QUEEN CRAPE MYRTLE
☼ ✝ ↔ 30 ft (9 m) ↑ 30–50 ft (9–15 m)
Occurring from India and China to Australia. Deciduous tree with attractive, mottled, smooth, gray-yellow, peeling bark. Leaves dark green, shiny,

duller beneath, turning coppery red in autumn. Erect panicles of white, mauve, purple, or pink flowers in summer–autumn. Zones 10–12.

Lagerstroemia tomentosa

☀ ✦ ↔ 20–30 ft (6–9 m)
↑ 45–75 ft (12–23 m)

From tropical Asia. Deciduous tree with erect branching trunk. Oval to sword-shaped green leaves. Dense panicles of white or purple flowers at branch tips. Zones 11–12.

Lagerstroemia Hybrid Cultivars

CRAPE MYRTLE

☀ ❀ ↔ 8–25 ft (2.4–8 m)
↑ 15–25 ft (4.5–8 m)

Over recent decades the US National Arboretum, Maryland, has released a series of hybrids between *L. indica* and the Japanese species *L. faurei*, combining the flower size of the first with the hardiness, mildew resistance, and bark color of the second. Their given names allude to Native American peoples, and they include the popular '**Natchez**', to about 25 ft (8 m) high, cinnamon bark often mottled with cream, white flowers; '**Tuscarora**', fast growing, to 25 ft (8 m), dark coral pink flowers. An older group of hybrids originated in Australia, reportedly as backcrosses of *L. indica* × *L. speciosa* onto *L. indica*; these are upright and bear large panicles of deep heliotrope flowers. Zones 7–11.

Lagerstroemia, Hybrid Cultivar, 'Natchez'

Lagerstroemia tomentosa

Lagunaria patersonia

LAGUNARIA

This genus comprising a single species in the mallow (Malvaceae) family, native to Norfolk and Lord Howe Islands, off eastern Australia, and a small stretch of coastal Queensland, Australia, was named after Andres de Laguna, a sixteenth-century Spanish physician and botanist. It is an evergreen tree growing to 50 ft (15 m) or more; there are, however, several distinct geographic forms, differing mainly in the quantity of soft downy hairs occurring on the simple alternate leaves. The flowers are hibiscus-like, with a conspicuous staminal column; the fruit is a leathery capsule. It is useful for park and street planting, especially in coastal area, as it can withstand salt-laden winds.

CULTIVATION: This tree grows best in well-drained fertile soil in a warm-temperate or subtropical climate. It requires little or no pruning. Propagate from seeds sown in spring; they germinate very readily in a warm humid atmosphere.

Lagunaria patersonia

syn. *Hibiscus patersonius*

NORFOLK ISLAND HIBISCUS, WHITE OAK

☀ ❀ ↔ 15 ft (4.5 m) ↑ 25–50 ft (8–15 m)

This species was named after William Paterson, who was the second Lieutenant Governor of New South Wales, Australia. Solitary rosy to mauve-pink flowers with golden yellow anthers, are borne in the upper axils, in summer. Contact with the kidney-shaped seeds, enclosed by fine sharp hairs, can cause a skin irritation. '**Royal Purple**' has shiny green leaves and crimson flowers. Zones 10–11.

Lamarckia aurea

Lambertia formosa, in the wild, Blue Mountains, New South Wales, Australia

LAMARCKIA

GOLDEN TOP

A genus of a single species in the grass (Poaceae) family, which is native to the Mediterranean area and the Middle East and naturalized elsewhere. The stems are erect or partly prostrate, the leaves flat, narrow, and strap-like. Spikelets of shining golden yellow flowers, often tinged with purple, are borne in one-sided, dense, feathery, oblong panicles.

CULTIVATION: This grass adapts to most soil types. Propagation is from seed. Position carefully, as this species can become invasive.

Lamarckia aurea

syn. *Chrysurus cynosuroides*

GOLDEN TOP

☀ ❀ ↔ 6–10 in (15–25 cm)
↑ 10–12 in (25–30 cm)

Attractive annual grass with smooth, soft, flat, narrow leaf blades. Spikelets, in groups of 5, of yellow flowers, often purple-tinged when mature, are borne in dense, feathery, 1-sided panicles, in summer. Zones 7–10.

LAMBERTIA

Belonging to the protea (Proteaceae) family, this Australian genus includes about 10 species; 9 from southwestern Western Australia and one from eastern New South Wales. All species are generally upright small to tall shrubs, occasionally small trees. Leaves whorled or opposite, with a spiky point. Flowers, in shades of red, orange, and yellow, are long, narrow, and tubular; clustered in a usually 7-flowered head and in some species surrounded by colorful bracts. Most produce nectar and attract native birds and insects. The woody fruit splits open into 2 halves, each half containing a winged seed.

CULTIVATION: *Lambertia* require well-drained sandy soil in full sun or

Lambertia multiflora

only slight shade and are reasonably frost hardy. Propagate from seed obtained from fruit allowed to dry out after removal from the plant. The fruit may persist on living twigs for some years. Cuttings can be successful, but seed will germinate readily in a couple of weeks.

Lambertia formosa

HONEYFLOWER, MOUNTAIN DEVIL

☀ ❀ ↔ 7 ft (2 m) ↑ 10 ft (3 m)

From around Sydney and the nearby Blue Mountains, New South Wales, Australia. Leaves whorled, to 2½ in (6 cm) long, green above, hairy and whitish below. Flowerheads of 7 reddish flowers surrounded by bracts, borne at stem tips, in spring–summer. Fruit persistent, beaked, horned, and ¾ in (18 mm) long. Zones 8–10.

Lambertia multiflora

HONEYSUCKLE

☀ ❀ ↔ 4 ft (1.2 m) ↑ 5 ft (1.5 m)

From the north and south of Perth, Western Australia. Small shrub with 2 forms: northern populations with pink to pale red flowers, southern populations with yellow flowers. Leaves narrow. Flowers to 1½ in (35 mm) long, in heads of up to 19 though usually 7; fruit smooth with beaks. Zones 8–10.

L

Lamium maculatum 'Pink Pewter'

Lamium maculatum

Lamium maculatum 'Beacon Silver'

Lamium maculatum 'Anne Greenaway'

LAMIUM

DEAD-NETTLE

Type genus for the mint (Lamiaceae) family. This group of about 50 species of low-growing annuals and perennials, which often spreads by rhizomes or runners, occurs naturally in Europe, North Africa, and temperate Asia, but some are also widely naturalized elsewhere and have become weeds. They are known as dead nettles: their opposite pairs of toothed, pointed, heart-shaped leaves resembling those of stinging nettles but lacking the sting. The small flowers, usually yellow, pink, or white, emerge in spring near the stem tips in leafy heads known as verticillasters. Sometimes used in herbal medicines, the leaves can be eaten as a salad vegetable.
CULTIVATION: Very hardy and easily grown in any partly shaded or shaded position in moist, humus-rich, well-drained soil. Variegated forms are common, often needing more light to maintain their color. Propagate at any time from cuttings or by division.

Lamium galeobdolon
syns *Galeobdolon luteum*, *Lamiastrum galeobdolon*
YELLOW ARCHANGEL
☼/☀ ❄ ↔ 48 in (120 cm)
↕ 8–16 in (20–40 cm)
From Eurasia. Vigorous, creeping or scrambling, near-evergreen perennial. Leaves narrow, dark green, elliptical to triangular, to over 2 in (5 cm) long, with deeply toothed edges. Heads of up to 10 yellow flowers, to ¾ in (18 mm) long, in summer. 'Hermann's Pride' ★, narrow leaves with silver streaks and spots; 'Silver Angel', low spreader but stems initially upright, silver-marked leaves. Zones 6–10.

Lamium garganicum
☼/☀ ❄ ↔ 48 in (120 cm)
↕ 8–16 in (20–40 cm)
From Europe, western Asia, and North Africa. A mat-forming, spreading, scrambling, near-evergreen perennial. Leaves broad, dull mid-green, toothed, triangular, to 3 in (8 cm) long. Heads of up to 8 widely spaced purple-pink to red flowers, to over 1 in (25 mm) long, in summer. Zones 6–10.

Lamium maculatum
☼/☀ ❄ ↔ 24–60 in (60–150 cm)
↕ 6–20 in (15–50 cm)
From Europe, western Asia, and North Africa. Spreading, sometimes mounding or scrambling, near-evergreen perennial. Stems long, rooting as they spread, with downy,

Lamium sandrasicum

toothed, pointed oval to triangular, often white-marked leaves, to over 3 in (8 cm) long. Heads of up to 8 widely spaced pinkish red to purple, rarely white, flowers, to ¾ in (18 mm) long, in summer. Many cultivars. 'Album', silver blotched leaves, white flowers; 'Anne Greenaway', tricolor foliage, silver center outlined in dark green on a yellow-green base, light purple flowers; 'Aureum', white-centered yellow-green leaves, pink flowers; 'Beacon Silver', silver leaves with a thin green margin, pink to purplish flowers; 'Pink Nancy', silver leaves with a thin green margin, pale pink flowers; 'Pink Pewter', green leaves overlaid with silver-gray, deep pink flowers; 'White Nancy', silver leaves with a thin green margin, white flowers. Zones 4–10.

Lamium orvala
☼/☀ ❄ ↔ 40 in (100 cm)
↕ 40 in (100 cm)
Found from southern to central Europe. Bushy perennial. Leaves are toothed, pointed oval, to 6 in (15 cm) long. Flowerheads consisting of a few pinkish red to purple flowers, ¾ in (18 mm) long, appear in summer. Zones 6–10.

Lamium sandrasicum
☼/☀ ❄ ↔ 12 in (30 cm) ↕ 4 in (10 cm)
Native to mountainous areas of western Asia. Small creeping perennial with tiny, deeply toothed, heart-shaped leaves. Stems and foliage red-tinted in sun. Pale pink flowers with

red spotting, to 1 in (25 mm) long, held on short stems near ground level, in summer. Zones 4–9.

LAMPRANTHUS

This genus of some 155 species belonging to the iceplant (Aizoaceae) family is found from southern Namibia to South Africa's Eastern Cape; there is also one species possibly native to Australia. They are creeping, sometimes erect subshrubs. The succulent leaves are linear to club-shaped, often triangular in section. The flowers are commonly large and brightly colored and produced profusely over long periods in summer, making them useful for summer bedding and containers in temperate regions. A few are frost hardy, and can be grown all year round in sheltered sites. Some species formerly placed here have now been reclassified as *Oscularia*.
CULTIVATION: These plants need full sun and thrive in poor well-drained soils. They are very easily propagated from stem cuttings, which can be rooted at almost any time of the year.

Lampranthus aurantiacus ★
syn. *Mesembryanthemum aurantiacum*
ICE PLANT
☼ ⚘ ↔ 8–18 in (20–45 cm)
↕ 12–24 in (30–60 cm)
Succulent perennial with upright stems becoming prostrate with age. Leaves bluish green, tapering, minutely rough and spotted. Bears profuse daisy-like

Lampranthus aurantiacus 'Sunman'

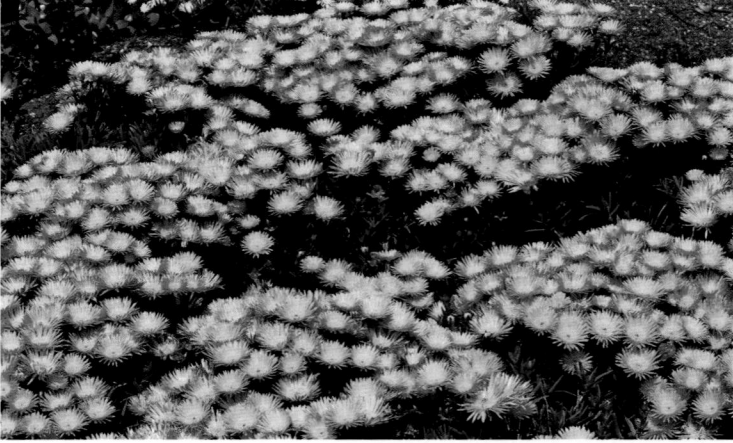

Lampranthus aurantiacus

Lampranthus glaucus

bright yellow or orange flowers in the late spring. '**Sunman**', golden yellow flowers. Zones 9–11.

Lampranthus filicaulis
syn. *Mesembryanthemum filicaule*
TRAILING ICE PLANT
☀ ❄ ↔ 18–36 in (45–90 cm)
↑ 12–24 in (30–60 cm)

Succulent perennial. Weak, delicate, creeping or prostrate stems. Leaves are crowded, tapering, curved, and about 1 in (25 mm) long. Reddish flowers are borne on long stalks. Zones 8–11.

Lampranthus glaucus
NOON FLOWER
☀ ❄ ↔ 12–24 in (30–60 cm)
↑ 12–24 in (30–60 cm)

Bushy, low-spreading, succulent perennial with roughly dotted, flattened, 3-angled, gray-green leaves, to 1 in (25 mm) long. The soft, sulfur yellow, daisy-like flowers appear in late spring. The fruit is a dry capsule. Zones 9–11.

Lampranthus productus
PURPLE ICE PLANT
☀ ❄ ↔ 12–24 in (30–60 cm)
↑ 12–24 in (30–60 cm)

Much-branched succulent perennial with narrow leaves, to 1½ in (35 mm) long, covered with fine dots. Groups of 3 or 5 pale rose pink flowers, each 1 in (25 mm) across. Zones 9–11.

Lampranthus roseus
syn. *Mesembryanthemum roseum*
☀ ❄ ↔ 12–20 in (30–50 cm)
↑ 12–20 in (30–50 cm)

Short-lived, erect, shrubby, succulent perennial, sometimes grown as an annual, with slender branches and narrow curved leaves. Clusters of rose

pink to reddish violet daisy-like flowers, with a slightly peppery smell, in mid-spring–early summer. Zones 9–11.

Lampranthus spectabilis
syn. *Mesembryanthemum spectabile*
ICE PLANT
☀ ❄ ↔ 20–30 in (50–75 cm)
↑ 6–20 in (15–50 cm)

Prostrate, trailing, succulent perennial. Branching stems, mounding spreading habit. Fleshy, bright green to grayish green, curved leaves with reddish tips, keeled and triangular in section. Profuse glossy, pink to purplish red, daisy-like flowers, 2–3 in (5–8 cm) across, in spring–summer. '**Tresco Apricot**', apricot flowers; '**Tresco Brilliant**', magenta flowers; '**Tresco Red**', fiery red flowers. Zones 9–10.

LANTANA

A small genus of about 150 species evergreen shrubs within the vervain (Verbenaceae) family, these plants are mostly found in tropical America. They have scrambling, somewhat prickly stems, simple opposite leaves, rough on both surfaces, and small flowers grouped in dense flattened or hemispherical heads, with the youngest flowers at the center.
CULTIVATION: Lantanas will tolerate quite harsh conditions but are at their best in light fertile soils with free drainage. They flower freely in a sunny open position in a frost-free climate, and although they are generally suitable for coastal areas, they should be given some protection from salt-laden winds. Regular tip pruning when the plants are young will help the formation of a compact shape, but in later years little or no pruning is necessary.

Lantana camara 'Patriot Dove Wings'

Propagate from seed sown in spring or from half-hardened cuttings taken in summer. Soft-tip cuttings can be taken at any time of the year.

Lantana camara
LANTANA
☀ ❄ ↔ 8–30 ft (2.4–9 m)
↑ 4–12 ft (1.2–3.5 m)

Native to the West Indies and Central America. Evergreen shrub. Flowers in shades ranging from creamy white through yellow, orange and pink to brick red, the heads often appearing bicolored owing to florets ageing to another color. Wild forms are particularly invasive colonizers, and proclaimed as noxious weeds in some warm-climate countries, including some States of Australia. Sterile or near-sterile forms available. *L. c.* var. *crocea*, golden yellow to orange flowers. *L. c.* '**Chelsea Gem**', mainly scarlet, and some orange, flowers; '**Orange Carpet**', with trailing habit, orange flowers; '**Patriot Dove Wings**', cascading habit, and pale yellow flowers soon turning white; '**Patriot Rainbow**', compact, about 16 in (40 cm) wide and high, bicolored florets from deep pinkish red to creamy yellow; '**Schloss Ortenburg**', multi-colored florets from yellow to orange or pink; '**Variegata**' (syn. 'Lemon Swirl'), pale green cream-edged leaves, yellow flowers. Zones 9–12.

Lantana camara var. *crocea*

Lantana montevidensis
syn. *Lantana sellowiana*
TRAILING LANTANA
☀ ❄ ↔ 10 ft (3 m) ↑ 3 ft (0.9 m)

Native to the central eastern region of South America. This species is an evergreen trailing shrub. Leaves are dark green, oblong to lance-shaped, and roughly toothed. The rosy lilac flowers, 1 in (25 mm) across, with a bright yellow flush in the throat, are slightly fragrant, and appear in winter and throughout the year. '**Alba**' is a white-flowered cultivar popular in the USA. Zones 9–11.

LAPAGERIA

This genus consists of a single species of evergreen, climbing, woody plants from Chile that twine up trees, trellises, and fences. They are members of the small family Philesiaceae, allied to the sarsaparilla (Smilacaceae) family. Their upright stems need support to climb

Lantana montevidensis

Lantana camara

Lantana camara 'Orange Carpet'

L. camara 'Patriot Rainbow'

L. camara 'Schloss Ortenburg'

Lantana camara 'Variegata'

up and through structures. If there is no support available, the plant will scramble over the ground. The large, oval, dark green leaves are thick and leathery and have distinctive ribbing along the length of the leaf. The large, pendent, bell-shaped flowers have 3 broad waxy outer segments overlapping the 3 narrower inner ones; they are predominantly a rosy red in wild populations, but cultivars can vary in color from deep crimson red to a range of pinks and creams. There have also been some reports of yellow forms of *Lapageria*.

CULTIVATION: Sensitive to frost, these plants need to be in a sheltered spot, away from all-day sun in summer. They like a cool area for their roots, and their branches head toward the light, which helps initiate flower bud development. They need free-draining, open, fertile soil, not waterlogged, with a neutral pH. Propagate from seed in spring; it may take up to 7 years for plants to flower from seed, and flower color may vary in seedlings. They can be grown in a greenhouse.

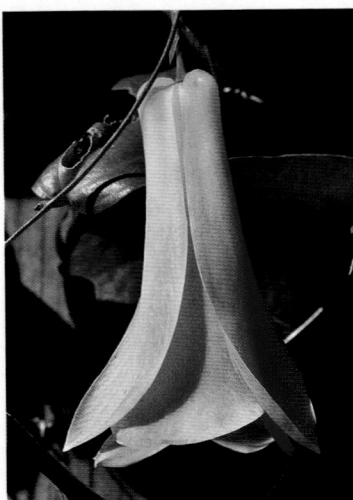

Lapageria rosea 'Angol'

Larix decidua, New Zealand

Lapageria rosea
CHILEAN BELLFLOWER, COPIHUE

☀/☀ ❀ ↔ 3–10 ft (0.9–3 m) ↑ 17 ft (5 m)

Chile's national flower. Leaves, to 5 in (12 cm) long, are held on thin, smooth, rope-like stems. Large rosy red flowers, 4–6 in (10–15 cm) long, are produced in summer–autumn. 'Angol' (perhaps more correctly 'Ongol', though usually sold as 'Angol') has especially large salmon pink flowers; 'Nash Court' bears soft shell pink flowers, the petals marked with dark red stripy mottling. Zones 8–9.

LAPIDARIA

This genus, which comprises a single species native to southern Namibia and neighboring parts of South Africa, belongs to the iceplant (Aizoaceae) family. It is allied to *Dinteranthus* and *Schwantesia*. This compact little-branched plant consists of rosettes of brownish gray leaves. The stems are very short and branch with age, forming mats. There are 6 to 8 leaves per shoot, joined at their bases, with a flat uppersurface and a rounded lower one. The stalked flowers have yellow petals.

CULTIVATION: These plants are grown in the same way as species of *Lithops*. The old bodies do not shrivel for several years, the two halves growing wider apart with the appearance of each new season's body.

Lapidaria margaretae

Larix laricina, in the wild, Ontario, Canada

Lapidaria margaretae
syns *Dinteranthus margaretae*, *Mesembryanthemum margaretae*

KAROO ROSE

☀ ❀ ↔ 6–12 in (15–30 cm)
↑ 3–4 in (8–10 cm)

Native to Namibia. Succulent perennial forming an open spreading mat. Small leaves in pairs, smooth, very thick, almost stone-like, triangular in cross-section, whitish gray-green. Produces golden yellow daisy-like flowers with 6 or 7 stigmas in autumn–winter. Zones 9–11.

LARIX

The larches, members of the pine (Pinaceae) family, comprise the largest genus of deciduous conifers; they are found in northern Europe, over much of Asia from Siberia to as far south as the mountains of northern Myanmar, and in northern North America. They are among the earliest trees to come into leaf in spring, the leaves being carried on both long and short shoots. The upright summer-ripening cones, borne on the shorter shoots, persist on the tree for some time. With age, branches tend to droop in a graceful manner. The leaves are needle-like and usually vivid green, sometimes blue-green in summer, turning butter yellow to old gold in autumn. Some species yield valuable timber that is strong and heavy.

CULTIVATION: Larches are adaptable to most soils, though wet soils are best avoided for all but 1 or 2 species. All larches need plenty of light. Species

Larix decidua 'Pendula'

Larix kaempferi 'Stiff Weeping'

hybridize readily, both in the wild and in cultivation. Propagation from seed is easily achieved.

Larix decidua
syn. *Larix europaea*
EUROPEAN LARCH

☀ ❄ ↔ 12–20 ft (3.5–6 m) ↑ 165 ft (50 m)

Native to mountains of central and eastern Europe; introduced to Britain around 1600. Conical crown becoming broader with age, with some wide-spreading horizontal as well as erect branches. Bark smooth gray, fissured on old trees, coarsely ridged. Leaves tender light green; mature cones yellowish. 'Corley', dwarf spreading tree; 'Pendula', strongly weeping habit, usually grafted on 6–8 ft (1.8–2.4 m) standards. Zones 2–8.

Larix kaempferi
syn. *Larix leptolepis*
JAPANESE LARCH

☀ ❄ ↔ 12–20 ft (4.5–6 m) ↑ 100 ft (30 m)

Common in Japan, less common in cultivation, although it withstands atmospheric pollution. Long low branches sweeping out and up, upper branches sweeping upward; scaly rusty brown bark. Leaves gray-green; female flowers pink or cream; cones brown. 'Pendula' ★ and 'Stiff Weeping' both have pendulous branches. Zones 4–9.

Larix laricina
AMERICAN LARCH, EASTERN LARCH, TAMARACK LARCH

☀ ❄ ↔ 12–20 ft (4.5–6 m) ↑ 60 ft (18 m)

Found across most of northern North America, growing in sphagnum bogs and swamps. Crown open, often with twisted, hooped branches. Bark pink to reddish brown, finely flaking, not fissured. Leaves are short soft needles turning yellow in autumn. Zones 2–8.

Larix lyallii

☼ ❄ ↔6–15 ft (1.8–4.5 m) ↑40 ft (12 m)

From western North America. A small to medium-sized tree, with densely felted young shoots, and 4-angled grayish green leaves. Twigs are densely woolly; the bark thin, furrowed, and scaly. This species is sometimes listed as a subalpine form of *L. occidentalis*. Zones 2–8.

Larix × marschlinsii

syn. *Larix × eurolepis*

DUNKELD LARCH, HYBRID LARCH

☼ ❄ ↔20 ft (6 m) ↑90 ft (27 m)

A hybrid between *L. decidua* and *L. kaempferi*. Intermediate between its parents, differing in having yellow, slightly waxy-bloomed shoots and conical cones. The leaves are long, thin, gray-green, to 1½ in (35 mm) long. 'Varied Directions', pendulous branches. Zones 2–9.

Larix occidentalis

WESTERN LARCH

☼ ❄ ↔15 ft (4.5 m) ↑180 ft (55 m)

Native to North America. Bark purplish gray, deeply and widely fissured; crown rather open, narrowly conical. Leaves bright green on both surfaces. Cones rich purple in summer, with orange and yellow bracts ripening to purple-brown. Zones 3–9.

Larix sibirica

syn. *Larix russica*

SIBERIAN LARCH

☼ ❄ ↔15 ft (4.5 m) ↑100 ft (30 m)

Native to eastern Russia (Siberia), Mongolia, and China's Xinjiang

Lasthenia glabrata

Larrea tridentata

Larix sibirica

Province. Attractive red-brown bark, which becomes furrowed and gnarled with age. The branches sweep down, rising at the tips, preventing snow build-up. The leaves are very narrow, soft bright green in spring, turning gold in autumn. Small scaly cones. Zones 1–8.

LARREA

CREOSOTE BUSH

This genus of 5 species of evergreen shrubs, a member of the twinleaf (Zygophyllaceae) family, occurs from South America to southwestern USA. The suckering jointed stems carry opposite compound leaves with leaflets up to ¾ in (18 mm) long. The flowers are solitary, borne at the branch tips, with 5 unequal sepals and clawed, oblong, yellow petals. The rounded fruits are covered with soft fine hairs. A secretion from the leaves, which gives them a varnished look, has a smell resembling creosote, particularly when wet. These bushes also release toxins that restricts the growth of nearby plants. Plant parts are used by local peoples for their medicinal properties, despite their unpleasant taste. CULTIVATION: All *Larrea* species prefer light, sandy well-drained soil in an open sunny position. Propagation is from seed.

Lasiopetalum macrophyllum

Larix lyallii, in the wild, Yoho National Park, British Columbia, Canada

Larrea tridentata

syn. *Larrea divaricata*

COVILLE, CREOSOTE BUSH

☼ ❄ ↔6–10 ft (1.8–3 m) ↑6–12 ft (1.8–3.5 m)

Found from southwest USA to northern Mexico. Straggly, slow-growing, aromatic, evergreen shrub. Dark gray to black bark. Leaves compound, resinous, dark green to yellowish green, with 2 or 3 oblong to spear-shaped leaflets. Profuse tiny yellow flowers, to ½ in (12 mm) across, in spring and autumn. Zones 7–10.

LASIOPETALUM

Genus of the cacao (Sterculiaceae) family containing 35 species that occur only in Australia. All species are shrubs of various sizes and occur in heaths, woodlands, and forests at low to medium altitudes on a variety of soils. A characteristic feature is the presence of brownish hairs on almost all parts of the plant: stems, leaves, and flowers. The leaves are simple, green or graygreen on the uppersurface, hairy on the undersurface. Flowers are borne in heads or clusters at the branch tips or in the leaf axils; the petals are small and not as obvious as the colored calyx, which can be white, cream, or pink. The fruit is a 3-celled capsule, each cell containing a single black seed. CULTIVATION: Grow in well-drained sandy soils. Seed is not easy to obtain, since the fruit is enclosed in the remains of the calyx when mature and seeds are shed quite soon after ripening. Cuttings seem to be the more successful means of propagation.

Lasiopetalum macrophyllum

SHRUBBY RUSTY PETALS

☼ ◐ ↔5 ft (1.5 m) ↑12 ft (3.5 m)

Varies from almost prostrate in coastal habitats to upright in the forest and

Larix × marschlinsii 'Varied Directions'

woodland. Leaves grayish green, broadly lance-shaped, undersurface densely hairy. Flowers covered in rusty hairs, in spring–summer. Zones 9–11.

LASTHENIA

This genus of annuals and perennials in the daisy (Asteraceae) family consists of 16 species from the Pacific coast of North America and one from central Chile. Their wild habitats include dunes, saline flats, and grasslands. The leaves are opposite, simple or dissected, smooth-surfaced or sometimes hairy. Showy long-stalked flowerheads, borne at the stem tips, have both ray and disc florets, both usually golden yellow, with the rays broad and rounded, forming a neat ring around the broad domed disc. CULTIVATION: *Lasthenia* species are drought and frost tolerant, and adaptable to a wide range of soils and positions. Propagate from seed.

Lasthenia glabrata

GOLDFIELDS

☼ ❄ ↔9–18 in (22.5–45 cm) ↑18–24 in (45–60 cm)

From California, USA. Erect annual. Leaves narrow, toothed, fleshy, 2–6 in (5–15 cm) long. Daisy-like flowerheads with golden or lemon yellow ray florets, to 1½ in (35 mm) across, in summer. Zones 7–10.

Lathyrus odoratus 'All But Blue'

Lathyrus odoratus 'Annie Good'

Lathyrus odoratus 'Anniversary'

LATANIA

There are 3 species in this genus of the palm (Arecaceae) family, all endemic to the Mascarene Islands, east of Madagascar. Once more common in drier parts of the islands' coastal regions, they are now rare owing to the clearing of land for agriculture. Each species is confined to one island. They are tall single-stemmed palms with large fan-shaped fronds. The male and female flowers are borne on separate plants, usually during the wet season. Although all 3 species are similar in general appearance, they differ in the coloration of the leaves. CULTIVATION: The young plants grow quite quickly, but they must be placed in full sun, in well-drained soil, and not exposed to frosts. Propagate from fresh seed, which can take 4 months to germinate after sowing. Seed obtained from plants in cultivation, where there are 2 or 3 species growing near each other, can produce hybrids.

Latania loddigesii ★

BLUE LATAN PALM

☼ ✈ ↔ 12 ft (3.5 m) ↑ 25 ft (8 m)

Native to Mauritius, the middle island of the Mascarene group. Glaucous adult leaves with woolly white bases. Fronds over 15 ft (4.5 m). The flowers, on inflorescences to 6 ft (1.8 m), are borne in summer; male and female are similar in size. The fruit, round and fleshy, turns greenish brown when ripe. Zones 10–12.

Latania verschaffeltii ★

YELLOW LATAN PALM

☼ ✈ ↔ 15 ft (4.5 m) ↑ 35 ft (10 m)

Native to the island of Rodrigues only. Dense white wool on leaf bases and stalks. Leaves green, not glaucous. Leaf stalks and veins bright yellow to orange. Zones 10–12.

LATHYRUS

SWEET PEA, VETCHLING, WILD PEA

This genus in the pea-flower subfamily of the legume (Fabaceae) family has far more than just the old-fashioned and popular sweet peas to offer among its 110 species of annuals and perennials. From Eurasia, North America, temperate South America, and the mountains of East Africa, many are climbers, others are low-spreading plants, and some are shrubby. The climbers support themselves with tendrils growing at the tips of the pinnate leaves, where the terminal leaflet would normally be. The typical pea-flowers occur in many colors, and

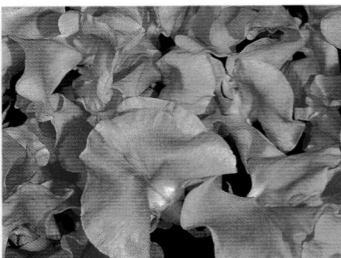

Lathyrus odoratus 'Apricot Queen'

may be borne singly or in racemes arising from the upper leaf axils. CULTIVATION: Non-climbing perennials will tolerate partial shade, but otherwise grow them in sunny well-ventilated conditions to lessen the risk of mildew and botrytis. Plant in moist well-drained soil and provide stakes or wires for climbers. Propagate annuals from seed sown in early spring, or in autumn–winter in mild climates, and perennials by division when dormant.

Lathyrus aureus

☼/◐ ❄ ↔ 40 in (100 cm) ↑ 24–36 in (60–90 cm)

From the Balkans. Bushy herbaceous perennial. Leaves with up to 12 leaflets, 1–2 in (25–50 mm) long. Racemes of golden yellow flowers, often tinted orange, ¾ in (18 mm) across, in late spring–summer. Zones 6–10.

Lathyrus cyaneus

☼/◐ ❄ ↔ 24–40 in (60–100 cm) ↑ 12 in (30 cm)

From the Caucasus region. Low-spreading perennial. Angular stems with dark green leaves; 2 to 6 paired leaflets, to 3 in (8 cm) long. Racemes of up to 15 pale-centered deep lavender blue flowers in late spring–early summer. Zones 6–9.

Lathyrus grandiflorus

EVERLASTING PEA, TWO-FLOWERED PEA

☼ ❄ ↔ 7 ft (2 m) ↑ 7 ft (2 m)

Found from Sicily to the southern Balkans. Climbing perennial. Angled stems; leaves tendril-tipped, with paired 2 in (5 cm) long leaflets. Sprays of up to 4 violet and pink flowers, 1¼ in (30 mm) across, in summer. Zones 6–10.

Lathyrus latifolius

PERENNIAL PEA

☼ ❄ ↔ 7 ft (2 m) ↑ 10 ft (3 m)

Found in central and southern Europe. Climbing perennial. Faintly angled stems; the leaves tendril-tipped, with paired 6 in (15 cm) long leaflets. Racemes of up to 15 purple, pink, or white flowers, 1¼ in (30 mm) across, are borne in summer. **'Albus'** (syn. 'Snow White'), pure white flowers; **'Pink Beauty'**, pink and red flowers; **'White Pearl'**, long-lasting white flowers. Zones 5–9.

Lathyrus laxiflorus

☼/◐ ❄ ↔ 16–24 in (40–60 cm) ↑ 12 in (30 cm)

From southeastern Europe. Low, somewhat spreading perennial. Paired lance-shaped leaflets, to 1¾ in (40 mm) long. Sprays of up to 6 white-centered violet flowers, ¾ in (18 mm) across, in summer. Zones 7–9.

Lathyrus odoratus

SWEET PEA

☼ ❄ ↔ 40 in (100 cm) ↑ 8 ft (2.4 m)

From Italy and the Mediterranean islands. Highly scented annual climber. Angled, somewhat downy stems and paired blue-green leaflets, to over 2 in (5 cm) long. The wild species has racemes of up to 3 violet and purple red flowers in summer. Garden forms are

Latania verschaffeltii

Lathyrus cyaneus

Lathyrus grandiflorus

Latania loddigesii

heavier flowering in a very wide range of colors. Sow in autumn in zones 9 and above or in spring in cooler climates. '**Alan Williams**', buff-pink and white; '**Annie Good**', pink tonings; '**Anniversary**' ★, white with pink edge; '**Bijou Mix**', only 12 in (30 cm) tall, many colors; '**Brian Clough**', orange and white; '**Charlie's Angel**', blue and lavender; '**Cream Southbourne**', pale cream; '**Eclipse**', deep lavender;

'**Evening Glow**', mid-pink and orange; '**Firebird**', orange-red; '**Jill Walton**', cream and pale pink, darker edge; '**Lilac Ripple**', white and mauve; '**Midnight**', deep purple-red; '**Noel Sutton**', deep blue; '**Sea Wolf**', lavender; '**Spencer Mixed**', old favorite, first of the large-flowered mixed color strains; '**Teresa Maureen**', lavender and cerise, purplish edge; '**Wiltshire Ripple**', brown-red and white; '**Winner**', red

Lathyrus odoratus 'Brian Clough'

Lathyrus odoratus 'Bridget Elizabeth'

Lathyrus odoratus 'Charlie's Angel'

L. odoratus 'Cream Southbourne'

Lathyrus odoratus 'Dotcom'

Lathyrus odoratus 'Eclipse'

Lathyrus odoratus 'Ethel Grace'

Lathyrus odoratus 'Firebird'

Lathyrus odoratus 'Honey Pink'

Lathyrus odoratus 'Jill Walton'

Lathyrus odoratus 'Jilly' ★

Lathyrus odoratus 'Karen Reeve'

Lathyrus odoratus 'Lilac Ripple'

Lathyrus odoratus 'Lisbeth'

Lathyrus odoratus 'Lynn Davey'

Lathyrus odoratus 'Midnight'

L. odoratus 'Mollie Rilstone'

Lathyrus odoratus 'Our Harry'

L. odoratus 'Queen Mother'

L. odoratus 'Richard and Judy'

Lathyrus odoratus 'Sally Anne'

L. odoratus 'Sarah Kennedy'

Lathyrus odoratus 'Sea Wolf'

suffused with orange. Cultivars with small, fragrant, single flowers, often known as **Heirloom** style, include: '**Blanche Ferry**', pink and white bi-color; '**Cupani**', compact, with intensely fragrant, purple and red flowers, known since 1699; '**Old Spice Mix**', very fragrant flowers in wide color range, including bicolor and striped; '**Painted Lady**', very pale pink and deep cherry red. Zones 8–11.

Lathyrus pubescens

※ ❄ ↔ 7 ft (2 m) ↑ 10 ft (3 m)

A native of Chile and Argentina. Near-evergreen climber with downy stems; the leaves tendril-tipped, with 1 to 2 pairs of leaflets to 3 in (8 cm) long. *L. pubescens* bears racemes of up to 16 lavender to purple-blue flowers, 1 in (25 mm) across, in summer. Zones 9–10.

Lathyrus sativus

DOGTOOTH PEA, INDIAN PEA

※ ❄ ↔ 40 in (100 cm) ↑ 40 in (100 cm)

Native to Europe and North Africa. Scrambling annual, grown for fodder and formerly as a pulse crop; continuous heavy consumption can eventually cause a motor neurone disease. Angled stems; the leaves with 1 to 2 pairs of narrow leaflets, to 6 in (15 cm) long. The long-stemmed flowers, pale blue, pink, or white, to 1 in (25 mm) across, are produced in summer. Zones 8–10.

Lathyrus splendens

PRIDE OF CALIFORNIA

※ ❄ ↔ 3–7 ft (0.9–2 m) ↑ 7–10 ft (2–3 m)

From the mountains of northern Baja California, Mexico. Shrubby, sometimes scrambling, evergreen perennial. Leaves tendril-tipped, with up to 10 leaflets to nearly 3 in (8 cm) long. Racemes of up to 12 violet to purple-red flowers, 1¾ in (40 mm) across. Zones 8–10.

Lathyrus vernus

SPRING VETCH

※ ❄ ↔ 24–40 in (60–100 cm) ↑ 12–24 in (30–60 cm)

From Europe. Often semi-evergreen perennial. Angular stems; leaves with 1 to 2 pairs of leaflets to 4 in (10 cm) long. Long racemes of up to 15 flowers, ¾ in (18 mm) across, initially purple-red, ageing to blue-green, in early spring. '**Alboroseus**', pink and white flowers; '**Rosenelfe**', 12 in (30 cm) tall, pale pink flowers. Zones 4–9.

LAURUS

LAUREL

There are just 2 species of evergreen trees and shrubs in this genus, which gives its name to the large and mainly tropical laurel (Lauraceae) family, one found around the Mediterranean region and the other native to the Canary Islands and the Azores. Botanists regard them as relics of the warmer evergreen "laurel forest" believed to have clothed most of Europe before the last Ice Ages. The foliage is leathery, deep green, and aromatic, and the small yellowish flowers arise along the branches in spring.
CULTIVATION: *L. nobilis* is the species commonly seen in cultivation. It is a very adaptable plant, suitable for hedging, topiary, specimen planting, or containers, and tolerates coastal conditions. In cool-temperate climates it is best grown against a warm wall. It requires a sunny site in fertile well-drained soil. Formal shapes and hedging should be trimmed in the

Lathyrus vernus

Lathyrus vernus 'Rosenelfe'

summer. Propagate from seed sown in autumn or from half-hardened cuttings taken in summer.

Laurus azorica

CANARY LAUREL

※ ❄ ↔ 20 ft (6 m) ↑ 30–60 ft (9–18 m)

Native to the Canary Islands and the Azores. Young shoots purplish brown, downy, aromatic when crushed. Leaves glossy, dark green, also aromatic. Small, fluffy, yellow flowers; black egg-shaped fruit. Zones 9–11.

Laurus nobilis

BAY LAUREL, BAY TREE, SWEET BAY, TRUE LAUREL

※ ❄ ↔ 6–15 ft (1.8–4.5 m) ↑ 10–50 ft (3–15 m)

Native to the Mediterranean region, growing in moist rocky valleys. Densely branched small tree or shrub. Leaves glossy, dark green, with slightly wavy margins. Small yellowish flowers; black egg-shaped fruit. The leaves are extremely popular as a culinary herb. '**Aurea**', yellow leaves. Zones 8–11.

LAVANDULA

LAVENDER

The 28 species of evergreen aromatic shrubs and subshrubs in this genus belong to the large mint (Lamiaceae)

Laurus nobilis

family, which includes herbs such as sage and rosemary. They occur mainly around the Mediterranean, with a few in western Asia and the Canary and Cape Verde Islands. Their natural habitat is dry and exposed rocky areas. The narrow leaves are usually grayish green, often toothed or in some species pinnately divided. The spikes of small purple flowers vary in their intensity of color and perfume. Cultivated species belong to 3 groups: the hardy **Spica** (English lavender) **Group**, with

Lathyrus odoratus 'Winner'

Lathyrus odoratus 'Spencer Mixed'

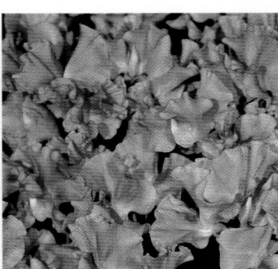
Lathyrus odoratus 'Tom Cordy'

Lathyrus odoratus 'Sylvia Moore'

L. odoratus 'Wiltshire Ripple'

Lavandula angustifolia 'Folgate'

Lavandula angustifolia 'Beechwood Blue'

Lavandula angustifolia 'Hidcote'

Lavandula angustifolia 'Imperial Gem'

L. angustifolia 'Lodden Blue'

L. angustifolia 'Martha Roderick'

L. angustifolia 'Princess Blue'

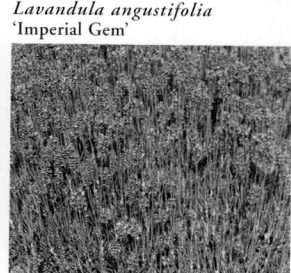

L. angustifolia 'Munstead'

L. angustifolia 'Royal Purple'

mostly basal entire leaves and long slender flower-spikes; the slightly more tender **Stoechas Group**, with flower-spikes terminating in a "top-knot" of colored bracts; and the tender **Pterostoechas Group**, with pinnately divided leaves. Some of the Spica Group lavenders are cultivated commercially for their aromatic foliage and flowerheads, which are mostly distilled to produce the lavender oil widely used in perfumes, toiletries, and air fresheners.

CULTIVATION: Lavenders are excellent for hot dry sites, containers, hedging, and positions where they can be brushed against to release their aroma. They need well-drained soil, not too fertile. Hardy species are pruned after flowering. All lavenders can be propagated from seed, or from tip cuttings in the spring or half-hardened cuttings in the autumn.

Lavandula angustifolia, Provence, France

Lavandula × allardii

HYBRID LAVENDER

☼ ❄ ↔ 3 ft (0.9 m) ↕ 3 ft (0.9 m)

Thought to be a cross between *L. dentata* and *L. latifolia*. Vigorous

Lavandula dentata

grower. The leaves are gray, relatively wide, and roundly toothed. The long narrow spikes of dark purple flowers, are carried well above the foliage, in summer. Zones 8–11.

Lavandula dentata 'Ploughman's Blue'

Lavandula angustifolia ★

syns *Lavandula officinalis*, *L. spica*, *L. vera*

ENGLISH LAVENDER

☼ ❄ ↔ 4 ft (1.2 m) ↕ 2–3 ft (0.6–0.9 m)

A Spica Group species native to the Mediterranean region. Bushy shrub, with narrow, gray, slightly downy leaves. Fragrant deep purple flower spikes are produced in early summer. *L. angustifolia* does not grow as well in hot humid areas. Cultivars include: '**Alba**', white flowers; '**Beechwood Blue**', low-growing and with short-stemmed blue flowers; '**Folgate**', mid-height, light gray-green foliage, bright blue flowers; '**Hidcote**', densely packed spikes of purple flowers; '**Imperial Gem**', narrow gray leaves, deep purple flowers; '**Lodden Blue**', to 20 in (50 cm) tall, bright silvery gray foliage, deep purple-blue flowers; '**Martha Roderick**', compact mounding habit, green-gray foliage, bright lavender

flowers; '**Munstead**' ★, dwarf variety, popular for edging; '**Princess Blue**', leaves tending green, pale lavender flowers; '**Rosea**', pink flower spikes; '**Royal Purple**', tall, narrow, gray leaves, deep purple flowers. Zones 5–10.

Lavandula dentata

TOOTHED LAVENDER

☼ ❄ ↔ 5 ft (1.5 m) ↕ 3–5 ft (0.9–1.5 m)

This Stoechas Group species is native to the Mediterranean region, Madeira and the Cape Verde Islands. The leaves are narrow, grayish green, and bluntly toothed; the stems are slightly downy. Pale purple flower spikes are borne on long stems above the foliage. *L. d.* var. *candicans* is grayer in appearance, more downy, with flowers a deeper purple. *L. d.* '**Ploughman's Blue**', lilac flower spikes on long stems, to 12 in (30 cm), good for hedging and confined to tubs. Zones 9–11.

Lavandula × *intermedia* 'Provence'

Lavandula × *intermedia*

Lavandula × intermedia

☼ ❄ ↔ 3 ft (0.9 m) ↕ 3 ft (0.9 m)
Various hybrids between *L. angustifolia* and *L. latifolia* are known by this name. Characteristics are intermediate between the 2 species, flowers paler than *L. angustifolia*. Frequently grown for cut flowers and oil production. 'Gray Hedge', attractive silvery gray foliage, purple flowers, popular as hedging plant; 'Grosso' ★, the cultivar most commonly grown for oil production, fine-leafed, long dark purple flowers; 'Provence' ★, attractive cultivar popular in the USA; 'Seal', vigorous, very free flowering, with pale purple flower spikes. Zones 7–10.

Lavandula lanata

WOOLLY LAVENDER
☼ ❄ ↔ 3 ft (0.9 m) ↕ 3 ft (0.9 m)
Native to the mountains of southern Spain. The leaves are different from other species in the Spica Group, they are wider, and covered in a whitish gray down. The spikes of purple flowers are held well above the foliage, in the summer. *L. lanata* dislikes humidity. Zones 7–10.

Lavandula latifolia

SPIKE LAVENDER
☼ ❄ ↔ 4 ft (1.2 m) ↕ 3 ft (0.9 m)
Native to the western Mediterranean regions. Rather like *L. angustifolia*, but with broader grayish green leaves and purple flower spikes carried on long stalks, which are frequently in 3 branches. Flowers later in summer than *L. angustifolia*. Zones 7–10.

Lavandula multifida

☼ ❄ ↔ 3 ft (0.9 m) ↕ 3 ft (0.9 m)
A Pterostoechas Group species, native to areas of southern Europe and northern Africa. Finely divided fern-like leaves. Soft purple flower spikes, on long, often branched stems, in summer. Lacks the true lavender fragrance. Zones 7–10.

Lavandula pinnata

CANARY ISLAND LAVENDER
☼ ❄ ↔ 3 ft (0.9 m) ↕ 3 ft (0.9 m)
Native to the Canary Islands. This Pterostoechas Group species is lightly covered in fine short hairs. Leaves green to gray, pinnate, with broad lobes. Flowerheads of soft purple spikes, usually branched into 3, in

Lavandula stoechas 'Helmsdale'

Lavandula pinnata

summer. 'Sidonie', hybrid thought to have *L. pinnata* as a parent; free flowering in warm climates, bearing deep purple flower spikes on long branching stalks for most of the year from late winter. Zones 9–11.

Lavandula stoechas

FRENCH LAVENDER, ITALIAN LAVENDER, SPANISH LAVENDER
☼ ❄ ↔ 24 in (60 cm) ↕ 24 in (60 cm)
From the Mediterranean region. Variable species. Leaves fine grayish green. Plump flower spikes of deep purple topped by prominent petal-like bracts in summer. Can become invasive. *L. s.* subsp. *pedunculata*, fatter and rounder spikes with longer bracts. *L. s.* 'Alba', dull white flower spikes; 'Avonview', fast growing, 24–32 in (60–80 cm) tall, sterile bracts long and pink, bracts of fertile heads purple with fine green mid-stripe; 'Helmsdale', compact, with burgundy-purple flowers; 'Kew Red', to 10 in (25 cm)

Lavandula stoechas 'Avonview'

Lavandula stoechas 'Regal Splendour'

tall, pink flowers; 'Major', flowering profusely with spikes of deepest intense purple; 'Marshwood', slightly bigger, to 3 ft (0.9 m), large plump spikes of purple flowers topped with very long mauve bracts; 'Otto Quast', popular American cultivar; 'Regal Splendour', deep purple flowers, lavender bracts; 'Willow Vale', unusual wavy-edged and crinkled purple bracts. Zones 8–11.

Lavandula viridis

GREEN LAVENDER
☼ ❄ ↔ 30 in (75 cm) ↕ 36 in (90 cm)
Stoechas Group species from southern areas of Portugal and Spain and on the island of Madeira. Aromatic plant. Green foliage; stems covered in fine hairs. Unusual whitish green flower spikes in summer. Zones 8–11.

LAVATERA

TREE MALLOW
There are 25 species of evergreen or deciduous annuals, biennials, perennials, and softwooded shrubs in this genus within the mallow (Malvaceae) family. Found from the Mediterranean to the northwestern Himalayas, and in parts of Asia, Australia, California, USA, and Baja California, Mexico. The leaves are usually palmately lobed and slightly downy, and most species have attractive hibiscus-like flowers with prominent staminal columns, in colors ranging from white to a rosy

Lavandula stoechas 'Kew Red'

Lavandula stoechas 'Willow Vale'

Lavatera arborea 'Variegata'

Lavatera cachemiriana

Lavatera trimestris 'Ruby Regis'

purple. *Lavatera* is closely related to *Malva*, and a recent botanical study has concluded that some of its species would be more appropriately classified under that genus. For now, these are retained in *Lavatera* but with their *Malva* names shown as synonyms.
CULTIVATION: Shrubby mallows are suitable for planting in mixed borders, where they will bloom abundantly throughout summer. They should be grown in full sun in light well-drained soil. Too rich a soil will result in an excess of foliage at the expense of flowers. Prune after flowering to prevent legginess. Mallows tend to be fairly short lived; softwood cuttings taken in spring or early summer strike readily and are the usual method of propagation for the shrubby species.

Lavatera arborea
syn. *Malva dendromorpha*
TREE MALLOW
☼ ❋ ↔ 6 ft (1.8 m) ↑ 10 ft (3 m)
From Europe and the Mediterranean region; naturalized in California, USA, and Baja California, Mexico.

Lavatera assurgentiflora

Shrubby biennial or short-lived perennial. Leaves large, lobed, soft, velvety. Purplish red flowers with darker veins in early summer. 'Variegata', leaves marbled with creamy white. Zones 8–10.

Lavatera assurgentiflora
syn. *Malva assurgentiflora*
CALIFORNIA TREE MALLOW, MALVA ROSE
☼ ❋ ↔ 6–12 ft (1.8–3.5 m)
↑ 10–20 ft (3–6 m)
From offshore islands of California, USA; naturalized on the mainland. Deciduous plant with twisted gray trunk. Leaves wide, lobed, coarsely toothed. Reddish purple flowers with darker veining in summer. Tolerates salt winds. Zones 9–11.

Lavatera cachemiriana
TREE MALLOW
☼/◐ ❋ ↔ 24 in (60 cm) ↑ 7 ft (2 m)
Semi-evergreen woody perennial. Wiry stems; mid-green ivy-shaped leaves. Silky clear pink flowers appear in midsummer–early autumn. Tolerates most soils. Zones 6–10.

Lavatera maritima
syn. *Lavatera bicolor, Malva wigandii*
SEA MALLOW
☼ ❋ ↔ 4 ft (1.2 m) ↑ 6 ft (1.8 m)
From western Mediterranean regions. Evergreen shrub. Leaves soft grayish

Lavatera maritima

green. Attractive flowers, pale pink with central area of purple veining, dark purple staminal column, in spring–autumn. Zones 8–11.

Lavatera olbia
TREE LAVATERA, TREE MALLOW
☼ ❋ ↔ 5 ft (1.5 m) ↑ 6 ft (1.8 m)
From western Mediterranean regions. True *L. olbia* is rarely cultivated; the plant sold under that name is usually *L. thuringiaca*. Evergreen shrub. Bristly stems; downy lobed leaves; reddish purple flowers. Zones 8–10.

Lavatera trimestris
ANNUAL MALLOW, REGAL MALLOW,
ROSE MALLOW, ROYAL MALLOW
☼ ❋ ↔ 18–36 in (45–90 cm)
↑ 24–48 in (60–120 cm)
From the Mediterranean region. Bushy easy-to-grow annual; does not need to be staked. Silky cup-shaped flowers. 'Ruby Regis', to 24 in (60 cm) tall, cerise pink flowers; 'Silver Cup', 24 in (60 cm) tall, pink flowers. Zones 8–10.

Lavatera, Hybrid Cultivar, 'Barnsley'

Lavatera Hybrid Cultivars
☼ ❋ ↔ 6 ft (1.8 m) ↑ 6 ft (1.8 m)
The popular perennial *Lavatera* hybrids are mainly derived from *L. thuringiaca* and *L. olbia*. They tend to be vigorous upright plants that, while sometimes short lived, always bloom reliably and sometimes with spectacular results. 'Barnsley' ★ bears masses of pale pink flowers, very easy-care; 'Bredon Springs' ★ has deep pink flowers; 'Rosea' is tall, with gray-tinted foliage and dusky pink flowers. Zones 8–10.

Lavatera, Hybrid Cultivar, 'Bredon Springs'

Lavatera, Hybrid Cultivar, 'Rosea'

Lavatera olbia

LAWSONIA

This genus, comprising a single species of evergreen tree or shrub of variable habit in the loosestrife (Lythraceae) family, is related to *Lagerstroemia*. It is native to hot dry parts of North Africa and southwest Asia, and is naturalized in tropical regions of the Americas. It has been cultivated for centuries for its leaves, which are dried and ground to powder to obtain henna, traditionally used for various medicinal purposes, and to decorate the hands and feet, especially by Hindu women. The powder stains the skin without harming it, and patterns can linger for several weeks. Henna is also widely used to dye hair and cloth.

CULTIVATION: This plant needs well-drained soil and full sun in a frost-free zone. Propagate from seed sown in spring or from softwood cuttings taken in spring. Hardwood cuttings can be taken from late autumn to winter. If cultivated in a greenhouse, grow in loam-based, moderately fertile compost with added grit and fertilize once a month. Water sparingly during its dormant period in winter.

Ledum groenlandicum

Lawsonia inermis
HENNA, MIGNONETTE TREE

☼ ✱ ↔ 7–12 ft (2–3.5 m)
↑ 10–20 ft (3–6 m)

Evergreen shrub or small tree; spiny open plant. The leaves are elliptic to lance-shaped, green, and smooth-edged, with thin tips. Large panicles of small fragrant flowers, pink, white, or red, with crumpled petals, appear in summer. This is a good ornamental shrub for warm-climate countries. Zones 10–12.

LECYTHIS

This genus of fewer than 50 species of small to large deciduous or evergreen trees and shrubs of the brazilnut (Lecythidaceae) family is found in tropical America. Its most distinctive feature is the huge fruit, which may be the size of a large melon and extremely heavy. The dried empty fruit of several species has found a remarkable use among some local people as a monkey trap. *Lecythis* species have glossy, toothed or tooth-less, leathery leaves, and the blooms of some are quite ornamental, appearing in clusters at the ends of the branches. The name is derived from the Greek word *lechtyos,* meaning oil jar, refer-ring to the shape of the fruit.

CULTIVATION: This genus needs a hot and humid tropical rainforest climate. In temperate climates it requires hot greenhouse conditions and a sandy

Ledebouria cooperi

loam-based medium. Propagate from seed or from half-hardened cuttings under mist.

Lecythis ollaria
MONKEY-POT TREE

☼ ✱ ↔ 35 ft (10 m) ↑ 80 ft (24 m)

Large evergreen tree. Leaves simple, leathery, glossy, bright green. Showy mauve flowers, Spherical or urn-shaped, hard, woody fruit, to 12 in (30 cm) in diameter, often very heavy. Seeds highly toxic. Zones 11–12.

LEDEBOURIA
AFRICAN SQUILL

This genus of about 30 species of bul-bous perennials from sub-Saharan Africa, Madagascar, and India belongs to the hyacinth (Hyacinthaceae) fami-ly. Leaves are basal, sometimes grayish, often striped or spotted red or green. The inflorescence is a simple raceme with inconspicuous bracts, borne at the branch tips. The flowers are small to very small, the 6 outer segments purple or greenish and recurved.

CULTIVATION: Grown mainly for their colored foliage, these plants are often offered by succulent specialists, as they grow well with cacti and other succu-lents. In temperate climates they grow best in a cool greenhouse in moder-ately rich compost.

Ledebouria cooperi
syns *Scilla adlamii, S. cooperi*

☼ ✽ ↔ 2–3 in (5–8 cm) ↑ 2–4 in (5–10 cm)

From South Africa. Semi-evergreen bulb. Leaves fleshy, to 10 in (25 cm) long, green, with parallel purple stripes, in summer, setting off the spikes of tiny deep purple-pink flowers in mid–late summer. Zones 9–11.

Ledebouria socialis ★
syns *Scilla socialis, S. violacea*

☼ ✽ ↔ 2–3 in (5–8 cm) ↑ 2–4 in (5–10 cm)

From South Africa. Evergreen with exposed bulb. Leaves broad, to 4 in (10 cm) long, gray with deep green blotches and purple undersides. Spikes of tiny, nodding, green bellflowers, on pink stalks, are held above the leaves. Zones 9–11.

Ledebouria socialis

Ledum palustre

LEDUM

The 3 or 4 evergreen species of this genus of the heath (Ericaceae) family are closely allied to *Rhododendron* and some botanists argue for their inclu-sion in that genus. They grow in the damp woodlands and wet swampy areas in the higher latitudes of the Northern Hemisphere. They are all bushy shrubs, producing masses of small white flowers in late spring.

CULTIVATION: Best grown in neutral to acid soil that is slightly wet, rich in humus, and has good drainage; they prefer shade or part-shade. Annual mulching with leafmold or other organic material is recommended. Propagate from seed sown in the autumn or spring, by air-layering branches in the autumn, or from half-hardened cuttings in the late summer.

Ledum groenlandicum
LABRADOR TEA

◐/☼ ❄ ↔ 3 ft (0.9 m) ↑ 3 ft (0.9 m)

From Greenland and northern parts of North America; larger in the wild. Young branches covered in rusty col-ored hairs. Leaves elliptic to oval, dark green, with rusty hairs underneath. Clusters of white flowers, borne at the branch tips, in late spring–summer. Zones 2–8.

Ledum palustre
syn. *Rhododendron tomentosum*
CRYSTAL TEA, MARSH LEDUM,
WILD ROSEMARY

◐/☼ ❄ ↔ 3 ft (0.9 m) ↑ 1–4 ft (0.3–1.2 m)

Widespread across northern and cen-tral Europe, northern Asia, and north-ern North America. Spreading or erect evergreen shrub. Young shoots covered in red-brown hairs; dark green leaves with incurved edges. Clusters of white flowers, borne at branch tips, in late spring–early summer. Zones 2–8.

LEIOPHYLLUM

There is a single species of dwarf ever-green shrub in this genus of the heath (Ericaceae) family, allied to *Ledum* and somewhat similar in appearance. Native to eastern USA, it has small

Lecythis ollaria

box-like leaves and is grown for its tiny, starry, spring flowers.

CULTIVATION: This shrub dislikes lime and should be grown in humus-rich soil in a sheltered site with morning sun or light shade. It is suitable for growing in the rock garden. Propagate from seed or half-hardened cuttings.

Leiophyllum buxifolium ★
SAND MYRTLE

☀ ❄ ↔ 22 in (55 cm) ↑ 2–12 in (5–30 cm)

Low or prostrate shrub. Leaves very small, leathery, dark green coloring bronze in autumn. Dense clusters of white or pale pink starry flowers, borne at branch tips, in late spring–early summer. Zones 5–9.

LEITNERIA
Native to southeastern USA, this genus of the quassia (Simaroubaceae) family contains only one species of small deciduous tree or suckering shrub. It grows in damp habitats and is threatened in the wild. Its branches, downy at first, become thickly barked; the leaves are alternate, simple, and clustered at the branch ends. The tiny flowers are of different sexes on different plants, borne among overlapping bracts in short catkins. The fruit is a pointed drupe with thin dry flesh.

CULTIVATION: The very lightweight wood of this shrub is traditionally used for fishing-net floats. It requires moist, humus-rich, lime-free soil. Propagate from seed or by removing suckers.

Leitneria floridana
FLORIDA CORKWOOD

☀ ❄ ↔ 15 ft (4.5 m) ↑ 15–20 ft (4.5–6 m)

Freely suckering shrub or small tree with a spreading crown. Young branches downy, turning gray and developing thicker bark with age. Leaves narrow, pointed, downy at first and remaining so on the gray undersides. Erect catkins form in spring, before the leaves begin to develop. Zones 5–10.

LENS
LENTIL

This genus comprises 4 species of annuals closely related to peas and vetches, in the pea-flower subfamily of the legume (Fabaceae) family, native to the Mediterranean region, western Asia, and Africa. The leaves are pinnate, with the terminal leaflet modified into a tendril or short bristle. The small, whitish, pea-flowers are borne in the leaf axils. The fruit is a small flattened pod with flattened disc-shaped seeds, convex on both surfaces. *Lens* is the classical Latin name of the genus, and it is from the resemblance to its seed shape that we get the English word "lens." Cultivated races of *L. ervoides* are some of the earliest known pulse crops; seeds almost 9,000 years old have been found in archeological excavations in the eastern Mediterranean. Lentils are still an important crop plant, especially in northern India and parts of Africa, and are valued by vegetarians for the high-quality protein content they contribute to their diet.

CULTIVATION: Lentils are best adapted to regions with hot dry summers and good winter or spring rainfall, or tropical plateau areas with a long dry season. Being legumes, they can thrive in sandy soils that are deficient in nitrogen, but will tolerate most open well-drained soils. Sow the seed in the early to late spring, depending on the climate; harvest in the summer as the plants wither. The seeds are separated by threshing the pods or the whole dry plant.

Leitneria floridana

Lens culinaris
syns *Ervum lens*, *Lens ervoides*, *L. esculenta*, *L. nigricans*

☀ ❄ ↔ 24 in (60 cm)
↑ 12–18 in (30–45 cm)

The various cultivated races of lentils have been grouped under the names *L. ervoides* and *L. nigricans* but are now all treated as this one species, which probably originated in the wild in Turkey. Erect to sprawling annual. Leaves pinnate, with usually 6 pairs of narrow leaflets, about ¾ in (18 mm) long. Stalked clusters of 1 to 3 flowers in spring; pods under ¾ in (18 mm) long, 1- or 2-seeded. Zones 7–11.

LEONOTIS
Comprising 15 species, this genus of softwooded annuals, perennials, and evergreen to semi-deciduous subshrubs in the mint (Lamiaceae) family, with the exception of one widely distributed tropical species, occurs wild in tropical and southern Africa. Opposite pairs of mid-green leaves are borne on upright squarish stems, and in late summer to winter whorls of narrow 2-lipped flowers are arranged densely around the stems.

CULTIVATION: These are warm-climate plants that can be grown under cover in frost-prone areas. They need moderately fertile soil in full sun and ample water in the growing season. The somewhat brittle stems can be cut back in spring. Propagate from seed or from softwood cuttings in summer.

Leonotis leonurus
syn. *Leonotis ocymifolia*
LION'S TAIL, WILD DAGGA

☀ ❄ ↔ 3 ft (0.9 m) ↑ 8 ft (2.4 m)

Most widely cultivated species of *Leonotis*. Clump-forming subshrub, semi-deciduous or evergreen depending on climate. Upright stems, with bright orange woolly flowers in the

Leonotis nepetifolia

late summer to winter. 'Alba' and 'Harrismith White', similar white-flowered cultivars. Zones 9–11.

Leonotis nepetifolia

☀ ❄ ↔ 8–12 in (20–30 cm)
↑ 3–4 ft (0.9–1.2 m)

From India and Africa; now naturalized in parts of North America. Upright annual. Serrated leaves, to 5 in (12 cm) long; curved orange trumpet-flowers in winter. Zones 8–11.

LEONTOPODIUM
A rock garden favorite, *Leontopodium* is a member of the daisy (Asteraceae) family. Its name comes from the Latin for lion's foot. The approximately 60 species that make up this genus are hardy, herbaceous, alpine perennials. Most are native to the mountain regions of east and central Asia, with only one species occurring in Europe. The woolly gray-green leaves are basal or alternate, and the flowerheads are small and white. In the wild, these tufted herbs grow in alpine meadows, on scree slopes, and among rocks.

CULTIVATION: *Leontopodium* species require a well-drained gritty or sandy soil and a position in the sun. They will not tolerate damp conditions, either in summer or winter, and generally prefer cooler temperatures. Propagate from seed.

Leonotis leonurus 'Alba'

Leonotis leonurus 'Harrismith White'

Lepidozamia hopei

Leontopodium alpinum

EDELWEISS

☀ ❄ ↔ 4–9 in (10–22 cm) ↕ 6 in (15 cm)

The only European species, growing wild in the Alps, Carpathians, and Pyrenees. Creeping short-lived perennial. Leaves silvery gray, 2–3 in (5–8 cm) long. Star-shaped white flowers with a central yellow floret surrounded by long floral bracts in early summer. Zones 4–8.

LEONURUS

There are only 3 species of perennials in this genus, which belongs to the mint (Lamiaceae) family. They are found over a wide area of Europe and temperate Asia, growing around hedges and on woodland margins, often in gravelly or alkaline soil. The opposite leaves are lobed or toothed. The 2-lipped tubular flowers are pink or white and borne on spikes in well-spaced whorls, emerging from bell-shaped calyces tipped with spines of varying harshness. *L. cardiaca* has been grown since medieval times for

medicinal purposes. Its botanical name refers to its use in treating heart disease; its common name to its use in easing the pain of childbirth and as a remedy for gynecological disorders.

CULTIVATION: Easily grown in any soil or situation. Propagate by seed or by division.

Leonurus cardiaca

MOTHERWORT

☀ ❄ ↔ 12 in (30 cm)

↕ 24–36 in (60–90 cm)

Native to continental Europe; naturalized in parts of Britain and the USA. Basal leaves palmately lobed, with 5 to 7 toothed lobes; stem leaves 3-lobed, narrower. Whorls of pinkish white flowers with spiny-tipped calyces, borne on leafy flowering stems, in summer. Zones 3–10.

LEPECHINIA

This genus comprises about 55 species of trailing to upright, slightly woody perennials in the mint (Lamiaceae) family, occurring mainly in Mexico,

Lepidozamia peroffskyana

Central America, and western South America, with 4 species native to California and 1 to Hawaii, USA. They grow in open to rocky habitats, mostly in mountain regions. They have strongly scented, usually furry, leaves, which are often large and handsome. Spikes of salvia-like flowers, mainly in shades of purple and mauve, may be produced over a very long season; in frost-free climates some species flower all year.

CULTIVATION: These plants require full sun in a well-drained fairly dry site. In frosty climates they can be overwintered in a well-lit greenhouse. Propagate by seed, which will often germinate where it falls, or by cuttings taken in summer.

Lepechinia fragrans

CHANNEL ISLAND SAGE, FRAGRANT PITCHER SAGE

☀ ❄ ↔ 3–4 ft (0.9–1.2 m)

↕ 3–4 ft (0.9–1.2 m)

From southern California's Channel Islands and nearby mainland USA, growing in chaparral on coastal hills; now rare in the wild. An evergreen shrubby perennial. Leaves large, arrow-shaped, aromatic when touched. The light pink-purple flowers in spring–summer are attractive to butterflies. Zones 7–10.

LEPIDOZAMIA

This genus of cycads in the zamia (Zamiaceae) family has only 2 living species; 2 others are known only from the fossil record. They occur in eastern Australia, growing in rainforest or

similar sheltered environments near the coast. They are large plants with mostly unbranched, stout, erect, cylindrical trunks sheathed with old frond bases. The long fronds are pinnate and decorative; new fronds are produced in flushes. Male and female plants are separate; the cylindrical male cones are green and open spirally to release their pollen, while the larger and fatter female cones start out green but turn brown with age and contain mostly red seeds. Both male and female cones are possibly the largest among all cycad genera.

CULTIVATION: For outdoor cultivation plant in part-shade or filtered light in well-drained soil. The fronds tend to fade if exposed to too much sun. Indoors they require a well-lit position. Propagate from seed, which may take 1 or 2 years to germinate.

Lepidozamia hopei

WUNU

◑/☀ ❄ ↔ 8–15 ft (2.4–4.5 m)

↕ 20–70 ft (6–21 m)

Native to rainforests of northeastern Queensland; possibly the tallest of all cycads. Palm-like, with a smooth, pale yellow-brown, straight trunk, rarely branched. Fronds arching, pinnate; leaflets very glossy, dark green, to 1 in (25 mm) wide. Male cones to 18 in (45 cm) long, female cones to 24 in (60 cm) long. Zones 10–12.

Lepidozamia peroffskyana

SCALY ZAMIA

◑ ❄ ↔ 10–15 ft (3–4.5 m)

↕ 8–20 ft (2.4–6 m)

Extending from northeastern New South Wales into southeastern Queensland. Trunk rough, with diamond pattern of old corky frond bases. Fronds deep green, glossy; leaflets to ½ in (12 mm) wide. Male cones to 30 in (75 cm) long, and female cones to 36 in (90 cm) long. Zones 10–12.

LEPTINELLA

This genus of around 30 species in the daisy (Asteraceae) family occurs in Australasia and southern South

Leontopodium alpinum

Lepechinia fragrans

Leptinella dioica

Leptodactylon californicum

America. They are mainly perennial, less commonly annual, clumping or creeping ground-cover plants. The genus is closely related to *Cotula,* under which name some species are still grown. The leaves are small, often clustered together, and may be simple or compound. The flowers are tiny, in button-like heads without the petal-like ray florets usually associated with daisies, and may be white, yellow, or even black.
CULTIVATION: Use as rock-garden plants; these little carpet plants are ideal over bulbs or between paving slabs. They prefer moist soil in sun or light shade. Usually propagated by division, but seed can also be used.

Leptinella atrata
syn. *Cotula atrata*
☼ ❋ ↔ 8 in (20 cm) ↑ 6 in (15 cm)
From Australia and South America. Mat-forming, tufted, ground-covering perennial. Delicate, gray-green, elliptical, fern-like foliage support summer spikes of black flowerheads. Zones 8–9.

Leptinella dioica
☼/◑ ❋ ↔ 40 in (100 cm) ↑ 2 in (5 cm)
From New Zealand. Creeping ground cover with fleshy, elliptical, dark green leaves in opposite pairs. Short flower spikes, only 2 in (5 cm) long, in summer. Zones 8–9.

LEPTODACTYLON
This genus, belonging to the phlox (Polemoniaceae) family, comprises 12 species of woody-based subshrubs, shrubs, or perennials native to western North America, extending from British Columbia to California. Their natural habitat is forest and scrubland. Some are of compact habit; others are straggly, usually growing to no more than 40 in (100 cm) high. The narrow leaves may be opposite or alternate and are lobed or palmately divided with rigid pointed tips. Phlox-like flowers of cream, pink, or lilac, usually in dense clusters borne at the stem tips, appear from late winter to summer.
CULTIVATION: Plant in full sun in light, fertile, very well-drained soil,

or grow in a container. Transplants can be difficult to re-establish, as these plants dislike root disturbance. Propagate from seed or cuttings.

Leptodactylon californicum
PRICKLY PHLOX
☼ ❋ ↔ 24 in (60 cm) ↑ 24 in (60 cm)
From California, USA. An upright branching shrub. Small, narrow, 5- to 9-lobed leaves with prickly young leaves in axils. Starry phlox-like flowers of pale to bright pink, covering plant, in late winter–summer. Zones 8–10.

LEPTOPTERIS
This genus of 7 species of beautiful, slow-growing, terrestrial ferns from the royal-fern (Osmundaceae) family is native to eastern Australia, New Guinea, New Zealand, and some islands of the western Pacific. Their erect rhizomes can develop with age into short fibrous trunks and carry long, arching, much divided, very thin and translucent, dark green fronds, with numerous brown globular spore-bodies crowded along the veins on the undersides.
CULTIVATION: Rather demanding in their requirements but potentially long lived in cultivation, these ferns prefer low light levels and constant high humidity in a moist humus-rich potting mix or well-drained soil. Mist frequently in warm weather. Propagate from spores or by division.

Leptopteris superba
syn. *Todea superba*
DOUBLE CRAPE FERN, PRINCE OF WALES FEATHERS
☀ ❄ ↔ 30–36 in (75–90 cm) ↑ 30–36 in (75–90 cm)
From New Zealand. Fern endemic to moist shaded forests. Erect rhizome, occasionally as much as 3 ft (0.9 m) tall; basket-like crown of elliptic tapering fronds, to 4 ft (1.2 m) long and 10 in (25 m) wide, on short stalks, lower segments smaller. Zones 9–10.

LEPTOSPERMUM
This genus in the myrtle (Myrtaceae) family is made up of about 80 species

of evergreen shrubs or small trees with small narrow leaves that are often aromatic, occasionally lemon-scented, when crushed. Mostly Australian, but 1 species is widespread in New Zealand and 2 are found in Southeast Asia. They are collectively known as tea-trees; the leaves of some species were used as a tea substitute by Captain James Cook's crew when they landed in Australia in 1770 and later by early settlers in Australia. The flowers are small and open with a wide nectar cup and 5 petals that are mostly white or shades of pink and occasionally red. Small woody capsules often persist for a long period. They are sometimes used as cut flowers.
CULTIVATION: Graceful screening plants in warm climates, they will tolerate an occasional light frost. They are best suited to well-drained soil in full sun; some species will tolerate wet conditions and nearly full shade. Light feedings with slow-release fertilizers in spring are beneficial. Prune regularly after flowering to retain bushiness. Propagate from seed or half-hardened cuttings taken in summer; cultivars must be propagated from cuttings to retain their characteristics.

Leptospermum brachyandrum
☼ ❄ ↔ 8 ft (2.4 m) ↑ 12–20 ft (3.5–6 m)
Large shrub or small, slightly weeping tree from eastern Queensland and

Leptospermum javanicum

northeastern New South Wales, Australia. Bark deciduous, peeling, shiny light brown; new bark smooth, gray or pinkish. Narrow leaves. White flowers in late spring–early summer. Grows well in moist well-drained soils, and will withstand periodic flooding. Zones 9–11.

Leptospermum grandiflorum
☼ ❄ ↔ 10 ft (3 m) ↑ 15 ft (4.5 m)
Endemic to Tasmania, Australia. Spreading shrub with small, silky, pale gray-green leaves. Masses of white flowers along branches in summer–autumn. Responds to heavy pruning; an ideal shelter or screening plant. Zones 8–9.

Leptospermum javanicum
☼ ❄ ↔ 5–10 ft (1.5–3 m) ↑ 8–25 ft (2.4–8 m)
From higher mountains of Southeast Asia, Indonesia and the Philippines. Tall shrub or small tree, often with a twisted or gnarled habit. Leaves 1¼ in (30 mm) long; new growth silky, sometimes pinkish. White flowers, borne in upper leaf axils, appear sporadically throughout the year. Zones 9–12.

Leptospermum brachyandrum

Leptopteris superba

Leptospermum juniperinum
PRICKLY TEA-TREE

☀ ✣ ↔ 4 ft (1.2 m) ↑ 6 ft (1.8 m)

From southeastern Australia. Attractive erect shrub, with slightly pendulous branches, and small, narrow, sharply pointed leaves. The small, white, fragrant flowers occur in spring–summer. Accepts relatively poor drainage, but prefers a well-drained sunny position. Zones 9–11.

Leptospermum lanigerum

Leptospermum liversidgei

Leptospermum recurvum, in the wild, Mt Kinabalu, Borneo

Leptospermum laevigatum
COAST TEA-TREE

☀ ✣ ↔ 10–15 ft (3–4.5 m) ↑ 10–20 ft (3–6 m)

Widespread in eastern coastal areas of Australia. Tall dense shrub or small tree with deciduous flaky bark. Leaves small, gray-green, with rounded tips. Conspicuous white flowers in spring. Fast growing; tolerates exposed coastal sites; can become invasive, considered a weed in South Africa. 'Reevesii', compact form with dense foliage, grown in the USA. Zones 9–11.

Leptospermum lanigerum
WOOLLY TEA-TREE

☀ ❄ ↔ 10 ft (3 m) ↑ 12 ft (3.5 m)

From southeastern Australia. Variable shrub. New growth covered in woolly hairs; silvery gray to dark green oblong leaves. Masses of white, occasionally pink-tinged flowers in spring–summer. Tolerates moist to wet soils. Zones 8–10.

Leptospermum liversidgei

☀ ✣ ↔ 7 ft (2 m) ↑ 12 ft (3.5 m)

Native to subtropical regions of coastal eastern Australia. Erect shrub. Leaves

Leptospermum novae-angliae

tiny, lemon-scented, bright green, narrow. Showy, satiny, white flowers in summer. Successful in moist well-drained soils and those subject to periodic waterlogging. Zones 9–11.

Leptospermum macrocarpum
syn. *Leptospermum lanigerum* var. *macrocarpum*

LARGE-FRUITED TEA-TREE

☀ ✣ ↔ 6 ft (1.8 m) ↑ 6 ft (1.8 m)

From the Blue Mountains near Sydney, New South Wales, Australia. Leaves are elliptic, 1 in (25 mm) long. Relatively large flowers, to 1¼ in (30 mm) across, with white, pale yellow, pink, or red circular petals and waxy green centers, often shiny with nectar, in spring–summer. Zones 9–11.

Leptospermum myrsinoides

☀ ❄ ↔ 6 ft (1.8 m) ↑ 10 ft (3 m)

Widespread in southern Australia, inhabiting sandy or swampy soils. Compact shrub. Leaves small, gray-green, incurved; new growth silky-hairy. Profuse white, sometimes pink, flowers, often with pink buds, in late spring. Zones 8–10.

Leptospermum nitidum

☀ ❄ ↔ 6 ft (1.8 m) ↑ 8 ft (2.4 m)

Endemic to wet heaths in Tasmania, Australia. Rounded shrub. Leaves are small, crowded, and glossy; the new growth is silky-hairy, and often copper-colored. Masses of small white flowers are produced in summer. These shrubs require additional water in dry periods. Zones 8–10.

Leptospermum novae-angliae
NEW ENGLAND TEA-TREE

☀ ❄ ↔ 8 ft (2.4 m) ↑ 8 ft (2.4 m)

From northern New South Wales, Australia. Dense spreading shrub. Leaves narrow, pointed. Small white flowers in spring. Useful for screening and low windbreaks. Zones 8–11.

Leptospermum myrsinoides

Leptospermum petersonii

Leptospermum petersonii
LEMON-SCENTED TEA-TREE

☀ ✣ ↔ 10 ft (3 m) ↑ 20 ft (6 m)

From the east coast of Australia. Shrub or small tree with a slightly weeping habit. This species is a popular street tree. Leaves narrow-lanceolate, lemon-scented when crushed. Small white flowers in early summer. Needs additional water during dry periods. Zones 9–11.

Leptospermum polygalifolium
syn. *Leptospermum flavescens*

TANTOON TEA-TREE, YELLOW TEA-TREE

☀/◑ ❄ ↔ 6 ft (1.8 m) ↑ 6 ft (1.8 m)

Variable tea-tree from eastern Australia. Bushy rounded shrub, or small tree to 20 ft (6 m). The leaves are narrow, and aromatic; the new growth is coppery. Masses of white flowers are produced in late spring–early summer. Adaptable species to most soils; needs additional water in dry periods. There are numerous very attractive forms and cultivars. 'Cardwell', beautiful, small, weeping shrub, to 6 ft (1.8 m) tall; 'Pacific Beauty', growing to about 3 ft (0.9 m) tall, spreading 6 ft (1.8 m) across, with pendulous branches, prolific white flowers in spring; 'Pink Cascade', having 'Pacific Beauty' as one of its parents, semi-prostrate shrub, to 24 in (60 cm) tall, with arching branches, to 5 ft (1.5 m) across, and masses of 2-toned pink flowers occurring through spring and again in autumn. Zones 8–12.

Leptospermum recurvum

☀ ✣ ↔ 5–15 ft (1.5–4.5 m) ↑ 5–60 ft (1.5–18 m)

Variable plant, endemic to Mt Kinabalu in Sabah, East Malaysia, often the dominant tree species at high altitudes. Minute leaves, turned-back margins, silky undersides. Masses of small white flowers borne in upper leaf axils, in all seasons. Zones 10–12.

Leptospermum scoparium 'Big Red'

Leptospermum scoparium
'Helene Strybing'

Leptospermum scoparium 'Kiwi'

Leptospermum scoparium 'Ray Williams'

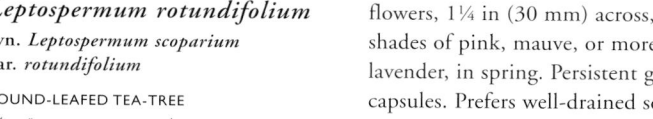

Leptospermum scoparium 'Nanum Kea'

Leptospermum scoparium 'Pink Cascade'

Leptospermum rotundifolium
syn. *Leptospermum scoparium*
var. *rotundifolium*

ROUND-LEAFED TEA-TREE

☀ ❄ ↔ 10 ft (3 m) ↑ 6 ft (1.8 m)

From southeastern Australia. Leaves dark green, almost round. Attractive

Leptospermum spectabile

Leptospermum rotundifolium

flowers, 1¼ in (30 mm) across, in shades of pink, mauve, or more rarely lavender, in spring. Persistent glossy capsules. Prefers well-drained soils. '**Julie Ann**', to about 12 in (30 cm) high, spreading habit, showy pale mauve flowers. Zones 8–10.

Leptospermum rupestre
syn. *Leptospermum scoparium*
var. *prostratum*

☀ ❄ ↔ 3 ft (0.9 m) ↑ 1–5 ft (0.3–1.5 m)

Endemic to Tasmania, Australia. Interesting shrub inhabiting rocky banks, often found scrambling up and over large boulders, closely pressed against them. Tiny oval leaves. Masses of small white flowers in summer. Ideal for alpine rock gardens. Zones 8–10.

Leptospermum scoparium
MANUKA, TEA-TREE

☀ ❄ ↔ 6 ft (1.8 m) ↑ 6 ft (1.8 m)

A native of New Zealand, Tasmania, and the southeastern corner of

Leptospermum squarrosum

mainland Australia. Small prickly leaves. Showy white flowers, to 1¼ in (30 mm) across, appear in spring–summer. Fast growing; requires pruning to shape after flowering. Many popular horticultural forms include: '**Apple Blossom**', pink-flushed white flowers; '**Autumn Glory**', deep pink single flowers, bright green foliage; '**Big Red**', covered in striking red flowers; '**Burgundy Queen**', deep red double flowers, bronze-colored foliage; '**Gaiety Girl**', dark-centered, pink, semi-double flowers, and reddish new growth; '**Helene Strybing**', pink flowers, popular in the USA; '**Kiwi**', dwarf form with single light red flowers, late spring–early summer; '**Lambethii**', large, dark-centered, single pink flowers; '**Nanum Kea**', profuse pink flowers; '**Pink Cascade**' ★, weeping branches, white flowers with pink flush; '**Pink Pearl**', pink flowers, popular in the USA; '**Ray Williams**', white flowers streaked pink; '**Red Damask**', dark green to bronze foliage, double crimson flowers; '**Ruby Glow**', deep purplish red semi-double flowers. Zones 8–10.

Leptospermum spectabile
BLOOD-RED TEA-TREE

☀ ❄ ↔ 6 ft (1.8 m) ↑ 10 ft (3 m)

Rare shrub from a small area near Sydney, New South Wales, Australia, growing along the banks of the Colo River. Narrow pointed leaves. Showy flowers, about 1 in (25 mm) across,

with smallish deep red petals around a very large receptacle glistening with nectar, in late spring. Zones 8–11.

Leptospermum squarrosum
syn. *Leptospermum persiciflorum*
PEACH-FLOWERED TEA-TREE

☀ ❄ ↔ 5 ft (1.5 m) ↑ 6 ft (1.8 m)

From southeastern Australia, growing on poor sandstone soils around Sydney. Erect open shrub. Tiny, dark green, pointed leaves. Large white to bright pink flowers, borne along older thicker branches, in autumn. Requires good drainage. Zones 8–11.

LESCHENAULTIA
syn. *Lechenaultia*

This Australian genus belonging to the Goodeniaceae family comprises about 26 species, the majority occurring in southwestern Western Australia, but with 3 in central Australia and 2 in far northern Australia, one of which also occurs in New Guinea. The genus includes perennials, subshrubs, and shrubs, with leaves that are usually small and very narrow. The flowers are the striking feature; although small and sometimes borne singly, they are profuse and in some species are very intensely colored. The flowers have 5 petals, which are fused at the base, each with a smooth central band and a broad crinkled margin; in some species they are spread in a hand-like form, in others they form more of a tube.

Leschenaultia biloba

Leschenaultia formosa, bicolored form

Leschenaultia macrantha

CULTIVATION: Perfect drainage and light gritty soils give the best results, and few species will survive, let alone thrive, where the soil stays cold and wet over winter. These plants tolerate light frosts and will withstand more cold if kept dry during winter. They prefer a position in full sun; water occasionally during the growing season. Other than a little tidying up after flowering, trimming is seldom needed. Propagate from seed or half-hardened tip cuttings of non-flowering stems.

Leschenaultia biloba
☼ ❋ ↔ 24 in (60 cm) ↑ 24 in (60 cm)
Best-known of the leschenaultias, found in the Perth region of Western Australia. Leaves sparse, rather dull gray-green. Magnificent sprays of gentian blue flowers in winter. Lighter colored and white-flowered forms are available. Zones 10–11.

Leschenaultia formosa
☼ ❋ ↔ 24 in (60 cm) ↑ 12 in (30 cm)
From southern Western Australia. Similar to *L. biloba*, but leaves slightly larger. Distinctive flowers, usually vivid red, sometimes tending toward orange, in late winter; borne singly, they smother the bush. Zones 9–11.

Leschenaultia macrantha
WREATH LESCHENAULTIA
☼ ❋ ↔ 12–24 in (30–60 cm)
↑ 2–4 in (5–10 cm)
From Western Australia. Prostrate plant forming circular mats of grayish green fleshy leaves. Wreathlike appearance in spring, when the large, cream, red-tinted flowers arise in thick clusters around the edge of the plant. Zones 9–11.

LESPEDEZA
This genus is a member of the large pea-flower subfamily of the legume (Fabaceae) family, which includes many edible plants, such as peas and beans. It contains about 40 species of prostrate annuals and perennials and deciduous shrubs, which are found in eastern and tropical Asia, Australia, and eastern USA. The leaves are tri-foliate, and the flowers are small but are usually borne in long racemes. CULTIVATION: Grow in a sunny position in deep, well-drained, fertile soil. In cooler areas these plants need the protection of a warm wall. In spring prune out the dead growth and cut back hard to rejuvenate the plant. Propagate from seed or from half-hardened cuttings.

Lespedeza bicolor
EZO-YAMA-HAGI
☼ ❋ ↔ 6 ft (1.8 m) ↑ 10 ft (3 m)
Native to Japan and eastern Asia. Semi-climbing shrub. The foliage is clover-like, vivid green above, paler beneath. Loose racemes of rosy-purple pea-flowers in late summer. Zones 5–10.

Lespedeza japonica
☼ ❋ ↔ 5–10 ft (1.5–3 m)
↑ 3–8 ft (0.9–2.4 m)
From Japan. An erect semi-evergreen or deciduous shrub, with long arching branches. Compound leaves with elliptic leaflets. Drooping racemes of pure white pea-flowers with a long-pointed calyx form in autumn. Zones 4–9.

Lespedeza thunbergii
THUNBERG BUSH CLOVER, MIYAGINO-HAGI
☼ ❋ ↔ 5–10 ft (1.5–3 m)
↑ 3–8 ft (0.9–2.4 m)
From Japan and China. An erect semi-evergreen or deciduous shrub. Long, wiry, widely spreading, interlacing branches; arching fountain-like habit. Bluish green compound leaves with 3 sharp-tipped leaflets, smooth above, finely hairy beneath. Dense drooping racemes of numerous pea-flowers with rose-purple corollas in late summer–autumn. 'Alba', white flowers; 'Albiflora', smaller leaflets, small white flowers with violet markings; 'Edo Shindori', pink and white flowers; 'Gibraltar', profuse lavender pink flowers. Zones 4–9.

LEUCADENDRON
This genus is a member of the protea (Proteaceae) family, comprising approximately 80 diverse evergreen shrubs and small trees. All are from South Africa's Western Cape province and the far west of Eastern Cape, except for 3 species, which are isolated in eastern KwaZulu-Natal. Borne on separate male and female plants in winter to spring, the flowers are in dense heads, the females commonly concealed among rather woody scales, the males in rather looser cone-like structures. The longer bracts surrounding both male and female flowerheads are often colorful, giving each head the appearance of a single "flower." They are sought after as cut flowers because of their long vase life. The leaves are simple, often leathery, and spirally arranged. Most species are insect pollinated but a few are wind pollinated. The cone-like fruits yield seed that ripens in summer. CULTIVATION: The vast majority require perfect drainage, preferring humus-rich, acid, basaltic or sandy loams low in phosphorus. They generally prefer an open, sunny, frost-free position with good air circulation. Propagate from seed sown in autumn, or cuttings, or by grafting or budding.

Leucadendron argenteum
SILVER TREE
☼ ❋ ↔ 6–20 ft (1.8–6 m)
↑ 20–30 ft (6–9 m)
Rare in the wild, occurring on the slopes of Table Mountain, South Africa. Beautiful tree; trunk with whorled branches, smooth gray bark with distinctive horizontal leaf scars. Leaves lance-shaped, to 6 in (15 cm) long, silvery, silky, with a glistening sheen. Female flowers, in silvery cone-like heads with a pinkish tinge, occur in summer. Produces silvery cone-like fruits. Zones 8–10.

Leucadendron comosum
YELLOWBUSH
☼ ❋ ↔ 5 ft (1.5 m) ↑ 6 ft (1.8 m)
From the southern mountains of Western Cape, South Africa. Evergreen

Lespedeza thunbergii 'Gibraltar'

Lespedeza bicolor

Lespedeza japonica

Leucadendron galpinii

Leucadendron discolor

shrub. Leaves varying from needle-like on male plants to linear and longer on female plants, yellow-green, darker on lower parts. Produces dark red flowerheads with light green or yellow bracts during spring. Persistent flattened fruits. Zones 8–10.

Leucadendron coniferum

☼ ❄ ↔ 4 ft (1.2 m) ↑ 6 ft (1.8 m)
Usually densely branched rounded shrub, with lance-shaped evergreen leaves. The small flower cones with yellow bracts mature in spring, reddening into seed cones. Tolerates

coastal areas and alkaline soils. The flowerheads are popular with florists. Zones 8–10.

Leucadendron discolor

☼ ❄ ↔ 6 ft (1.8 m) ↑ 6 ft (1.8 m)
Species native to the rocky sandstone soils of Table Mountain, South Africa. An erect shrub with leaves broad, oval, and gray-green. The flowerheads form in spring, the male turning bright red with yellow bracts, the female remaining light green. *L. discolor* needs well-drained soil. Excellent as cut flowers. Zones 8–10.

Leucadendron eucalyptifolium

☼ ❄ ↔ 8 ft (2.4 m) ↑ 20 ft (6 m)
Shrub with somewhat eucalyptus-like leaves, long, narrow, bright green, each with a distinctive twist. Flowerhead bracts turning bright yellow; fragrant

flowers in winter–spring. Persistent cone-like fruits. Popular with florists. Responds to pruning. Zones 8–10.

Leucadendron galpinii

☼ ❄ ↔ 4 ft (1.2 m) ↑ 10 ft (3 m)
Endemic to the coastal lowlands of Western Cape. Shrub with linear grayish leaves with a twist. Round, shiny, grayish flower cones, with an unpleasant scent, in spring. Persistent fruit. Zones 8–10.

Leucadendron nobile

KAROO CONEBUSH
☼ ❄ ↔ 5 ft (1.5 m) ↑ 6–10 ft (1.8–3 m)
From the southwestern mountains of Eastern Cape. Conifer-like appearance, with long, bright green, needle-like leaves. Ruff of bracts at base of inflorescence, the male plant carrying its florets in a long central cone, the female spike rarely over 1 in (25 mm) long. Zones 9–10.

Leucadendron eucalyptifolium, male

Leucadendron eucalyptifolium, female

Leucadendron nobile

Leucadendron comosum

Leucadendron coniferum

Leucadendron salicifolium
☀ ❄ ↔ 6 ft (1.8 m) ↑ 10 ft (3 m)

Vigorous evergreen shrub, growing from sea level to high altitudes in moist acid soils along stream banks. Leaves green, smooth, narrow, sharply pointed, with a twist. Light green-yellow bracts in winter–early spring Very popular with florists. **Zones 8–10.**

Leucadendron salicifolium

Leucadendron sessile
☀ ❄ ↔ 3 ft (0.9 m) ↑ 5 ft (1.5 m)

From mountains east of Cape Town, South Africa. Tolerates heavy clay; requires constant moisture, depends on sea mists in its native habitat. Leaves green, elliptical, smooth. Yellow flowerhead bracts, turning red with age, in winter. **Zones 8–10.**

Leucadendron sessile

Leucadendron tinctum
☀ ❄ ↔ 4 ft (1.2 m) ↑ 4 ft (1.2 m)

Common in Western Cape, South Africa. Low shrub. Leaves oblong, gray-green, rounded tips, held closely to the stems. Distinctive pink-flushed flower bracts in winter. Flower cones give off a pleasant spicy fragrance. **Zones 8–10.**

Leucadendron Hybrid Cultivars
☀ ❅ ↔ 4–8 ft (1.2–2.4 m) ↑ 4–8 ft (1.2–2.4 m)

Many hybrids have been developed, featuring large showy bracts, a compact growth habit, and interesting foliage. '**Cloudbank Jenny**' (syn. 'Cloudbank Ginny'), male *L. gandogeri* × *L. discolor* hybrid, cream bracts around orange cones; '**Duet**', most probably an *L. stelligerum* hybrid, red-edged yellow bracts around yellow cones; '**Pisa**', an *L. floridum* hybrid, silver-haired leaves, yellow bracts around silvery green cones; '**Safari Sunset**' ★, magnificent strong-growing bush, vivid red bracts, colorful young leaves; '**Silvan Red**', like 'Safari Sunset' but less robust, with slimmer bracts; '**Sundance**',

Australian hybrid, bright yellow to gold bracts; and '**Superstar**', wiry-stemmed bush, small red and yellow bracts in winter. **Zones 9–11.**

LEUCAENA
Belonging to the mimosa subfamily of the legume (Fabaceae) family, the 20-odd species of evergreen trees and shrubs in this genus range from southern Texas, USA, and Mexico to South America as far as Peru. Some are now naturalized throughout the tropics and subtropics. All species have feathery foliage and fluffy globular heads of white flowers. The leaves are bipinnate, with many small leaflets or fewer larger ones. Dark brown pods hang in drooping clusters from the branches. **CULTIVATION:** These fast-growing plants thrive in a wide range of soils; routine care is minimal. They respond to pruning or coppicing, which quickly produces regrowth. Widely planted in tropical and subtropical areas as screen or shade trees, or for fodder or green manure; in cool-temperate climates they may be grown under glass.

Leucadendron tinctum

Leucadendron, Hybrid Cultivar, 'Superstar'

Leucadendron, Hybrid Cultivar, 'Sundance'

Leucadendron, Hybrid Cultivar, 'Cloudbank Jenny'

Leucadendron, HC, 'Silvan Red'

Leucadendron, Hybrid Cultivar, 'Pisa'

Leucadendron, HC, 'Duet'

Propagate from the seed, which needs soaking in warm water for 24 hours to soften it before planting, or from half-hardened cuttings.

Leucaena leucocephala

LEAD TREE, WHITE POPINAC

☼ ⚘ ↔ 15 ft (4.5 m) ↕ 30 ft (9 m)

Vigorous, fast-growing, evergreen tree; abundantly naturalized in the tropics. Gray-green bipinnate leaves; young stems a deep copper color. Fluffy balls of creamy white flowers, on short stalks, in spring. Drooping clusters of dark brown, broad, flat pods in summer. Zones 10–12.

Leucaena retusa

GOLDENBALL, LEAD TREE, LEMONBALL, LITTLE-LEAF LEAD TREE, WAHOO TREE

☼ ❄ ↔ 15–25 ft (4.5–8 m) ↕ 12–25 ft (3.5–8 m)

From Texas, USA, and northern Mexico. Evergreen shrub or small tree. Flaky cinnamon-colored bark. Compound leaves consisting of 8 to 16 light green leaflets, each with 4 to 8 segments. Globes of bright yellow stamens, in leaf axils, in spring–autumn. Flattened brown seed pods. Zones 7–11.

LEUCANTHEMUM

Somewhat prosaically named from the Greek *leukos,* white, and *anthemon,* flower, this genus from Europe and northern Asia comprises 33 species of annual and perennial daisies (family Asteraceae), most of which do have flowers with white ray florets, usually around a central boss of golden disc florets. They have often been included in the genus *Chrysanthemum,* which botanists now define more narrowly. They form often large clumps of deep green, usually toothed, linear to spatula-shaped leaves. The flowers appear from spring to autumn, depending on the species. Garden forms include pompon-centered flowers and various colors, especially among the *L. × superbum* hybrids, many of which were developed by Luther Burbank. CULTIVATION: Grow in a sunny position in moist well-drained soil. Feeding and watering will result in

Leuchtenbergia principis

Leucanthemum × superbum

more luxuriant plants but not necessarily more flowers. Tall types may need staking. Propagate the species from seed, cultivars and hybrids by division or from basal cuttings.

Leucanthemum × superbum

syns *Chrysanthemum maximum* of gardens, *C. superbum*

SHASTA DAISY

☼/◐ ❄ ↔ 40 in (100 cm) ↕ 48 in (120 cm)

Garden hybrid of *L. maximum* and *L. lacustre,* first developed around 1900 by the Californian plant breeder Luther Burbank and named by him in tribute to snow-capped Mt Shasta in the far north of his State. Many upright flower stems emerging from dense basal clump of dark green, toothed, spatula-shaped leaves, to 8 in (20 cm) long. Flowerheads solitary, to 4 in (10 cm) across, ray florets white, disc florets golden yellow. Many cultivars. 'Aglaia' ★, white semi-double flowers; 'Becky's Shasta', 3–4 ft (0.9–1.2 m) tall, with large, single, white flowers in spring–summer; 'Cobham's Gold', creamy yellow double flowers; 'Esther Read', feathery semi-double flowers; 'Horace Read', 20 in (50 cm) tall, feathery double flowers, named for the English nurseryman who first developed double shastas; 'Marconi', very large, double, white flowers; 'Silver Princess', 12–15 in (30–38 cm) tall, single white flowers in spring–autumn; 'Snow Lady', 12–15 in (30–34 cm) tall, single white flowers in spring–autumn; 'Snowcap', 12–15 in (30–38 cm) tall, large, white, single flowers; 'Thomas Killin', 3 ft (0.9 m) tall, yellow-centered, white, semi-double flowers; 'Wirral Supreme', anemone-centered white flowers. Zones 5–10.

Leucanthemum vulgare

syn. *Chrysanthemum leucanthemum*

OX-EYE DAISY

☼/◐ ❄ ↔ 24 in (60 cm) ↕ 40 in (100 cm)

From Europe and northern Asia. Perennial forming basal clump of toothed leaves, sometimes pinnately

Leucanthemum vulgare, in the wild, Provence, France

Leucanthemum × superbum 'Aglaia'

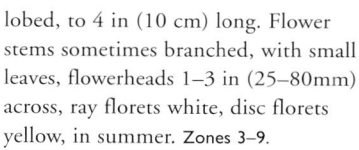

Leucanthemum × superbum 'Snowcap'

lobed, to 4 in (10 cm) long. Flower stems sometimes branched, with small leaves, flowerheads 1–3 in (25–80 mm) across, ray florets white, disc florets yellow, in summer. Zones 3–9.

LEUCHTENBERGIA

This genus of a single cactus species (family Cactaceae) is from the Chihuahuan Desert of Mexico and was named for the Duke of Leuchtenberg, the stepson of Napoleon Bonaparte. Agave-like, it has long leaf-like tubercles and long papery spines. Its large flowers open during the day and close at night, and often persist for several days. It lacks the ribs usually found in this family. Rare in its natural habitat, it is often disguised by growing in or near clumps of *Agave lechuguilla* or near yuccas. Illegal collecting of wild plants continues to reduce numbers. CULTIVATION: This solitary plant is usually raised from seed. It requires very well-drained, purely mineral soil with a distinct rest in winter and judicious watering in spring and autumn, even in the growing seasons.

Leuchtenbergia principis

AGAVE CACTUS, PRISM CACTUS

☼ ✴ ↔ 8–12 in (20–30 cm) ↕ 20–26 in (50–65 cm)

Spherical to short cylindrical form, with long tap root. Covered in thin

L. × superbum 'Thomas Killin'

3-sided tubercles. Thin, flat, yellow to gray, papery, 6 in (15 cm) spines at ends of tubercles, often twisted, amongst longest of all cactus spines. Large, fragrant, glossy yellow, funnel-shaped flowers. Green to yellow egg-shaped seed pods. Zones 9–11.

LEUCOCORYNE

Some 12 or so species of bulbs from Chile comprise this small genus in the onion (Alliaceae) family, some of which give away the relationship by their smell of garlic when crushed. The bulbs have a dark brown tunic; the leaves are narrow and usually lax, appearing in winter. These plants are grown for their umbels of showy flowers, which are usually white, blue, or purple and often scented. As they last well when cut, they are ideal for floral art.

Leucocoryne ixioides

CULTIVATION: In mild climates plant bulbs 4 in (10 cm) deep in a sunny well-drained site in sandy fertile soil. In more frost-prone climates a well-ventilated greenhouse is recommended. Propagate by seed (the plant will take some years to flower) or by small offset bulbs collected when repotting in autumn.

Leucocoryne ixioides
GLORY OF THE SUN
☼ ⚘ ↔ 3–4 in (8–10 cm)
↑ 16–18 in (40–45 cm)
Found in Chile. *L. ixioides* has narrow grassy leaves. Heads of up to 12 open, starry, bright blue flowers with a white center, ¾ in (18 mm) across, in spring, as the leaves die down. Zones 9–10.

LEUCOGENES
NEW ZEALAND EDELWEISS
Native to the high mountains of New Zealand, this small genus of 3 or 4 species of alpine mat-forming or clump-forming plants belongs to the daisy (Asteraceae) family. All grow in scree areas or rocky places. They are valued for their intensely silvery leaves and the unusual appearance of their small heads of yellow flowers, which are surrounded by woolly white bracts. These plants are often grown in containers by enthusiasts who exhibit them at alpine shows.
CULTIVATION: All species are suited to a well-drained moist rock garden with good light, but not hot sun, or for pots in an alpine house where excessive winter wet can be controlled. These plants are usually propagated by tip cuttings, or seed, if available.

Leucogenes leontopodium
syn. *Raoulia leontopodium*
NORTH ISLAND EDELWEISS
☼ ❄ ↔ 4–6 in (10–15 cm)
↑ 4–6 in (10–15 cm)
Despite the common name, found on both of New Zealand's islands. Loose mound of lance-shaped silvery leaves, to ¾ in (18 mm) long. Small yellow flowerheads with white woolly bracts. Zones 7–9.

LEUCOJUM
SNOWFLAKES
A genus of 20 species of bulbs in the amaryllis (Amaryllidaceae) family, native to Europe, the Middle East, and North Africa. Better suited than the related snowdrops (*Galanthus*) to mild and warm climates. Their overall appearance is similar, the 6 white petals of the nodding flowers at the tops of the slender stems are of equal length; snowdrops have 3 long and 3 short petals. The linear leaves, said to be poisonous to stock, appear either with or before the flowers. The name comes from the Greek *leukos*, meaning white, and *ion*, meaning violet (the latter referring to the faint fragrance).
CULTIVATION: Trouble-free, needing almost no maintenance. Propagate by division of offsets after flowering, or by sowing ripe fresh seed.

Leucojum aestivale
syn. *Leucojum aestivum*
SUMMER SNOWFLAKE
☼/☀ ❄ ↔ 12 in (30 cm)
↑ 18–22 in (45–55 cm)
Native to the damp woods of central and southern Europe. Robust, with strap-like leaves. Flowers delicate-looking, 1 to 5 per stem, white with green markings, sometimes scented; in wet-winter dry-summer climates the flowers appear in winter, in cooler wet-summer climates in summer. Requires moist conditions during the growing phase and rich soil. 'Gravetye Giant' ★, equally robust, adaptable, to 30 in (75 cm). Zones 6–9.

Leucojum autumnale
AUTUMN SNOWFLAKE
☼ ❄ ↔ 2 in (5 cm) ↑ 6–10 in (15–25 cm)
From western Europe and northwestern Africa. Thread-like leaves. Flowers are tiny, delicate-looking, scented, white bells, several per stem, sometimes lightly tinged with pink, with yellow anthers, in late summer–early autumn. Zones 6–9.

Leucojum vernum
SPRING SNOWFLAKE
☼ ❄ ↔ 12 in (30 cm)
↑ 12–30 in (30–75 cm)
From the shady hillsides and woodlands of higher parts of central Europe; widely naturalized in similar situations. Flowers are large flared bells, 1¼ in (30 mm) across, held singly on straight stems, white marked with green or yellow, in spring. Plant bulbs deeply. Zones 5–8.

LEUCOPHYLLUM
This genus belonging to the foxglove (Scrophulariaceae) family comprises about 12 species of attractive, low-spreading, evergreen shrubs, native to southwestern USA and Mexico. The foliage is pale green to gray-white, owing to the leaves being felted with short white hairs. Showy, lavender to violet, bell- to funnel-shaped flowers are borne singly in the leaf axils in summer; the fruit is capsular.
CULTIVATION: These slow-growing shrubs are often found in sandy and impoverished soils in a dry climate; they thrive in virtually any soil as long as it is well drained, and are tolerant of salt spray. Grown for their pleasing gray-white foliage and silvery stems,

Leucojum aestivale

they make undemanding specimens. They prefer a warm, sheltered, sunny spot. Although they may survive at temperatures down to 10°F (–12°C), they require higher temperatures to bloom well. In cooler areas they may be grown under glass. They withstand vigorous pruning. Propagate from seed or from half-hardened cuttings.

Leucophyllum langmaniae
MONTEREY CENIZO, RIO BRAVO SAGE
☼ ❄ ↔ 4–6 ft (1.2–1.8 m)
↑ 3–5 ft (0.9–1.5 m)
From northeastern Mexico and Texas, USA. Dense evergreen shrub. Bright green leaves, spatula shaped, wavy edges. Pale lavender to lavender-blue flowers in summer–autumn. 'Rio Bravo', heavy flowering. Zones 8–10.

LEUCOPHYTA
The sole species in this genus in the daisy (Asteraceae) family is an evergreen shrub native to the coasts of southern Australia. Rather reminiscent of lavender cotton (*Santolina chamaecyparissus),* it develops into a dense mound of wiry stems clothed in tiny, almost scale-like, silver-gray leaves. In summer and autumn small, knob-like, white to creamy yellow flowerheads lacking ray florets open from silvery buds.
CULTIVATION: Very much a coastal plant and highly resistant to salt spray, it adapts well to cultivation and can be trimmed as a low border or hedge, good for accenting darker foliage. It dislikes hot humid conditions and appreciates full sun and good air movement. The soil should be light and

Leucophyta brownii

Leucophyllum langmaniae 'Rio Bravo'

Leucopogon lanceolatus

Leucopogon setiger

Leucopogon suaveolens

well drained. While tough and drought resistant, it is short lived and eventually dies out from the center; hard pruning will not rejuvenate it. Light pinching back year round can keep it more compact and vigorous. Propagate by half-hardened tip cuttings.

Leucophyta brownii
syn. *Calocephalus brownii*
CUSHION BUSH
☼ ✤ ↔ 3 ft (0.9 m) ↕ 3 ft (0.9 m)
Intricately branched dome of bright silvery foliage. Inconspicuous yellowish flowerheads, to ½ in (12 mm) across. The Western Australian race has longer leaves, to ½ in (12 mm). Zones 9–11.

LEUCOPOGON

This genus of some 150 species of evergreen shrubs and occasional small trees of the epacris (Epacridaceae) family is found in Australia, New Zealand, the Malay Archipelago, and many western Pacific Islands. They are characterized by small, often narrow and overlapping, leaves, and tiny, white to cream, tubular to bell-shaped flowers, their often recurved petals mostly having densely furry inner faces, which open in spring to summer. Showy small drupes follow, usually in orange or red tones. Some botanists prefer to include all species in a broadly defined genus *Styphelia*, but now that name is generally restricted to a smaller group of Australian shrubs, with larger flowers.

CULTIVATION: Although some are somewhat frost tender, most *Leucopogon* species are fairly easily cultivated if grown in moist, humus-enriched, well-drained soil. Once established, they will tolerate short periods of drought. They are best grown in full sun, which keeps the growth compact, and may benefit from light trimming or occasional pinching back. Left untrimmed, they can become rangy. Propagate from the seed, which sometimes needs stratification or prolonged soaking before sowing, or from layers or half-hardened tip cuttings.

Leucopogon lanceolatus
LANCE-LEAFED BEARD HEATH
☼ ✤ ↔ 4 ft (1.2 m) ↕ 10 ft (3 m)
Found in southern Australia, including Tasmania. The leaves are narrow, lance-shaped, to 2 in (5 cm) long. Small spikes of white flowers appear at the branch tips and in leaf axils, in spring, and are followed by red drupes. Zones 9–11.

Leucopogon setiger
☼ ✤ ↔ 3 ft (0.9 m) ↕ 4 ft (1.2 m)
Occurring on sandstone ranges close to Sydney, New South Wales, Australia. Pretty shrub with bushy rounded habit. The leaves are narrow, tapering to a needle point. Pure white flowers, bell-shaped and semi-pendent, with rolled-back furry petals, 1 or 2 to each leaf axil, appear in late winter–spring. Zones 8–10.

Leucopogon suaveolens
MOUNTAIN HEATH
☼ ✤ ↔ 6 ft (1.8 m) ↕ 4–30 in (10–75 cm)
Found in subalpine and alpine areas of New Zealand. Prostrate or upright spreading shrub. Leaves are narrow, bronze-green, to ¼ in (6 mm) long, the undersurface blue-green with fine white veining. Small cream flowers in spring. White, pink, or red berries. Zones 7–9.

LEUCOSPERMUM
PINCUSHION

Unlike many plants in related genera of the protea (Proteaceae) family, leucospermums, often referred to as pincushion proteas, owe their beauty to their flowers, in roundish pincushion-like heads with long conspicuous styles. There are approximately 50 species, all evergreen shrubs, and all from a narrow coastal belt in South Africa's Western Cape province, except for a handful in eastern South Africa, one extending to Zimbabwe. The majority are compact shrubs, which flower abundantly in spring. The thick leaves are generally broadest near the tip, which usually has several rather blunt teeth.
CULTIVATION: All require well-drained soil in an open sunny situation. Some species tolerate light frosts; all prefer a dry summer with low humidity. Winter watering is desirable. Pruning is usually unnecessary apart from cutting flowers. Propagate from seed or cuttings or by grafting, which is used for many of the hybrid cultivars.

Leucospermum bolusii
BOLUS PINCUSHION, GORDON'S BAY PINCUSHION
☼ ✤ ↔ 5–6 ft (1.5–1.8 m)
↕ 5–6 ft (1.5–1.8 m)
This is an evergreen shrub with stout, erect, branching stems. The leaves are

greenish gray, sword- to oval-shaped, and notched at the tip. The yellow to apricot pincushion-like flowers, 4 in (10 cm) across, are produced in spring. Zones 8–10.

Leucospermum cordifolium ★
syn. *Leucospermum nutans*
NODDING PINCUSHION
☼ ✤ ↔ 6 ft (1.8 m) ↕ 6 ft (1.8 m)
Popular shrub with an open habit; some cultivars almost prostrate. Gray-green foliage offsetting the apricot, pink, orange, or red flowers in spring; these are valued for their long life in the garden and for floristry. Tolerant of clay soils; frost tender when young. 'Aurora', apricot-yellow flowers; 'Fire Dance', scarlet flowerheads. 'African Red', which may be a cultivar of *L. cordifolium*, bears florets with distinctive red striping and yellow styles. Zones 8–10.

Leucospermum cordifolium 'Fire Dance'

Leucospermum cordifolium 'Aurora'

Leucospermum cordifolium

Leucospermum bolusii

Leucospermum patersonii

☼ ❄ ↔ 6 ft (1.8 m) ↑ 12 ft (3.5 m)
From coastal limestone areas. Large shrub or small tree. Leaves dark green, deeply toothed, red-tipped. Bright orange flowers with scarlet styles in spring–early summer. Tolerant of alkaline soils; good drainage essential. Zones 8–10.

Leucospermum prostratum

☼ ❄ ↔ 12 ft (3.5 m) ↑ 4 in (10 cm)
Prostrate ground cover which favors very acid, poor, sandy loams. Long trailing stems produced from a subterranean rootstock. The small, rounded, sweet-smelling, bright yellow flowerheads appear in the winter, maturing to dark orange in the early summer. Zones 8–10.

Leucospermum tottum

FIREWHEEL PINCUSHION

☼ ❄ ↔ 5 ft (1.5 m) ↑ 5 ft (1.5 m)
Dense evergreen shrub. The leaves are narrow-elliptical, gray-green, and covered with fine hairs. Produces rounded scarlet flowers with creamy styles in spring–summer. Prefers well-drained gritty soils. Several hybrid cultivars are available, some extending the flowering season into mid-summer. '**Scarlet Ribbon**', a hybrid of *L. tottum* and *L. glabrum,* compact rounded habit, to 5 ft (1.5 m), frosted appearance, bearing scarlet flowers in late spring. Zones 8–10.

Leucospermum patersonii

Leucospermum 'Veldfire'

Leucospermum tottum 'Scarlet Ribbon'

Leucospermum 'Veldfire'

☼ ❄ ↔ 5 ft (1.5 m) ↑ 5 ft (1.5 m)
L. glabrum hybrid. Yellow-orange flowers, often ageing to crimson-red, with bright orange styles, in mid-spring–summer. Zones 8–10.

LEUCOTHOE

Found mainly in eastern Asia and the USA, this genus belonging to the heath (Ericaceae) family, as now understood, consists of only 6 species of evergreen and deciduous shrubs. Many more species formerly included in it are now separated as the genus *Agarista*, occurring in Central and South America, Africa, and Madagascar, with a single species from the USA. They usually have simple leathery leaves, dark green with toothed edges; some show a tendency to produce variegated foliage. The deciduous species often color well in autumn. The flowers are small, bell- or urn-shaped, and usually cream to pink. Opening in spring to early summer in racemes or panicles, they can be quite showy.
CULTIVATION: Most species prefer shade from the hottest sun and should be grown in cool, moist, humus-rich soil that is open and well drained. Other than light trimming to shape, pruning is seldom necessary. Propagation from seed is usually slow, so air-layering or half-hardened cuttings are more often used. Some species produce suckers that can be grown on.

Leucothoe racemosa

Leucothoe davisiae

Leucothoe davisiae

SIERRA LAUREL

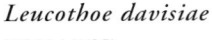 ❄ ↔ 5 ft (1.5 m)
↑ 1–6 ft (0.3–1.8 m)
From California's Sierra Nevada, USA. Evergreen, variable in size. Leaves with glossy green uppersurfaces, sparsely toothed edges. Small, white, lily-of-the-valley-like flowers, in erect terminal racemes to 4 in (10 cm) long. Zones 5–10.

Leucothoe fontanesiana

syns *Leucothoe catesbaei, L. walteri*
SWITCH IVY

 ❄ ↔ 7 ft (2 m) ↑ 6 ft (1.8 m)
From southeastern USA. Evergreen shrub with arching stems. Leaves, long-pointed to 4 in (10 cm) long, glossy uppersurfaces, toothed edges; red-tinted new growth. White lily-of-the-valley-like flowers, in short racemes, in spring. '**Rainbow**' ★ (syn. 'Girard's Rainbow'), foliage variegated with green, cream, and pink. Zones 5–10.

Leucospermum prostratum

Leucothoe fontanesiana

Leucothoe fontanesiana 'Rainbow'

Leucothoe racemosa

FETTER BUSH, SWEET BELLS

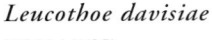 ❄ ↔ 5 ft (1.5 m) ↑ 3–8 ft (1–2.4 m)
From eastern USA. Deciduous shrub. Leaves to 2½ in (6 cm) long, with finely toothed edges; autumn foliage often developing intense yellow, orange, and cherry red tones. Short racemes of white to cream flowers in spring–summer. Zones 5–9.

LEVISTICUM

Genus in the carrot (Apiaceae) family consisting of a single species of tall upright perennial with compound triangular leaves that have a strong celery taste. Grown for its leaves, used in salads, and seeds, used for flavoring. In summer it produces the classic flat flowerheads typical of the carrot family, with tiny green-yellow blooms. The true garden celery (*Apium graveolens* var. *dulce)* is more tender and has taken its place in most kitchens.
CULTIVATION: This plant likes a position in full sun with fertile, moist but well-drained soil. Propagate by freshly sown seed or division in spring.

Levisticum officinale

LOVAGE, LOVE PARSLEY

☼/◑ ❄ ↔ 40 in (100 cm) ↑ 7 ft (2 m)
Native to the Mediterranean region. Umbelliferous perennial. Dark green, leathery, shiny leaves, similar to a carrot's but wider. Flower stalks thick and hollow, yellow flowers. Zones 3–10.

LEWISIA
BITTER ROOT

Named after the North American explorer Captain Meriwether Lewis (1774–1809) of the famed Lewis and Clark expedition of 1806–7, this is a genus of 19 species of exquisite, semi-succulent, evergreen and deciduous, alpine and subalpine perennials in the purslane (Portulacaceae) family. They are found in the Rocky Mountains from New Mexico to southern Canada and usually form basal rosettes of fleshy, linear, lance- or spatula-shaped leaves. Their starry many-petalled flowers may be solitary or clustered and are borne at the ends of short wiry stems from mid-spring through to early summer. Yellow, apricot, and pink shades predominate.
CULTIVATION: Most species have deep tap roots and prefer gritty free-draining soil that remains moist in the growing season but is otherwise dry. Plant in full- or half-sun and use gravel mulch around the crown to prevent rotting. Deciduous species generally only re-produce from seed, but evergreens can also be propagated from offsets.

Lewisia brachycalyx
☼/☀ ❅ ↔ 8 in (20 cm) ↕ 4 in (10 cm)
Found from southern Utah to New Mexico, USA. A deciduous species forming basal rosette of broad lance-shaped leaves, to 3 in (8 cm) long. Flowers are solitary, to about 2 in (5 cm) across, with up to 9 petals, white to pale pink with darker pink veins. Zones 5–9.

Lewisia columbiana
☼/☀ ❅ ↔ 8 in (20 cm) ↕ 12 in (30 cm)
Found over much of North America west of the Rockies. Evergreen species

with crowded, fleshy, narrow, basal leaves, 1–4 in (25–100 mm) long. Many-flowered heads of pink-veined white to magenta flowers, to 1 in (25 mm) across, with up to 11 petals. Zones 5–9.

Lewisia congdonii
☼/☀ ❅ ↔ 12–20 in (30–50 cm)
↕ 16–24 in (40–60 cm)
Deciduous Californian native. Basal clump of broad, strappy, rather fleshy, 2–8 in (5–20 cm) long leaves. Tall flower stem with large lax panicles of many ½–1 in (12–25 mm) wide, purple-veined, pale pink flowers with up to 7 petals. Zones 7–9.

Lewisia cotyledon
☼/☀ ❅ ↔ 8 in (20 cm)
↕ 6–12 in (15–30 cm)
From the area around the California–Oregon State line, USA. Evergreen, loose rosette of spatula-shaped leaves, to over 4 in (10 cm) long, often blue-green and/or pink-tinted, edges often wavy, rarely toothed. Forms panicle of a few to many 7- to 10-petalled flowers, to 1¾ in (40 mm) across. Flowers usually purple-pink, some-times white or yellow; cultivars come in many shades. **Sunset Group**, many shades of yellow, orange, pink, and red; **'White Splendour'**, dark green foliage, pure white flowers. Zones 5–9.

Lewisia longipetala
☼/☀ ❅ ↔ 10 in (25 cm)
↕ 6–12 in (15–30 cm)
Californian evergreen. Rosette of fleshy, often red-edged, narrow leaves, to 5 in (12 cm) long. Purple-pink flowers, to 2 in (5 cm) across, with about 9 petals. **'Little Plum'**, dark-veined mid-pink flowers with pale edges. Zones 5–9.

Leycesteria formosa

Lewisia 'Pinkie'
☼/☀ ❅ ↔ 8 in (20 cm)
↕ 6–8 in (15–20 cm)
Evergreen hybrid between *L. cotyledon* and *L. longipetala*. Resembles a com-pact *L. cotyledon* with slightly narrower leaves. Many broad-petalled apricot pink flowers with dark pink centers. Zones 5–9.

Lewisia rediviva
BITTERROOT
☼/☀ ❅ ↔ 8 in (20 cm) ↕ 4 in (10 cm)
Found over much of subalpine and alpine western North America. Decidu-ous species forming a dense basal tuft of many narrow leaves, to 2 in (5 cm) long. The flowers are solitary, to over 2 in (5 cm) across, with up to 6 petals in pink to purple shades or white. Zones 4–9.

Lewisia tweedyi
☼/☀ ❅ ↔ 8 in (20 cm) ↕ 8 in (20 cm)
From Washington State, USA, and British Columbia, Canada. Evergreen forming small clump of often purple-tinted, broad, lance-shaped leaves, to

3 in (8 cm) long. Up to 8 soft pink or yellow, 7- to 12-petalled flowers, to over 2 in (5 cm) across. Zones 5–9.

LEYCESTERIA

This genus, belonging to the wood-bine (Caprifoliaceae) family, consists of 6 species of deciduous or semi-evergreen shrubs, found in western China and the Himalayas as far west as Pakistan. They have small tubular flowers, borne over a long period, with very noticeable colored bracts. The soft berries mature so quickly that they are often carried at the same time as the flowers. In favorable climates these plants, which have a suckering habit, may become invasive weeds.
CULTIVATION: Grow in moderately fertile soil in a sunny or partially shady location, though the flower bracts and fruit color better in full sun. Less hardy species can be overwintered in a green-house in colder climates. Propagate from seed in autumn or spring or by taking softwood cuttings in summer.

Leycesteria crocothyrsos ★
☼ ❂ ↔ 6 ft (1.8 m) ↕ 6 ft (1.8 m)
From Assam in northeastern India, and northern Myanmar. Arching branches. Leaves green and tapering to a point, undersurface slightly hairy with netted veining. Racemes of yellow flowers, at branch tips, in spring–summer. Small yellowish green berries. Zones 9–11.

Leycesteria formosa
HIMALAYAN HONEYSUCKLE
☼ ❅ ↔ 6 ft (1.8 m) ↕ 6 ft (1.8 m)
Native to the Himalayas and western China. Leaves long, dark green, slightly heart-shaped at the base, smooth-edged or slightly toothed, undersur-face paler and downy. Whitish flowers with purple bracts, on pendent spikes, in summer–autumn. Fruit ripening deep red-purple to black. A weed in cool moist areas of Australia and New Zealand. Zones 7–10.

Leycesteria formosa

Lewisia columbiana

Lewisia congdonii

Lewisia longipetala 'Little Plum'

Lewisia cotyledon

Lewisia tweedyi

Lewisia cotyledon 'White Splendour'

Liatris spicata 'Callilepsis Purple'

Liatris pycnostachya

Liatris spicata 'Kobold'

Liatris spicata 'Floristan'

LEYMUS

From the northern temperate zones, with one species extending the range to Argentina, this genus comprises about 40 species of spreading and sometimes invasive, perennial, rhizomatous grasses in the family Poaceae. Most *Leymus* species were formerly classified under *Elymus*. Found in a wide range of habitats, but usually in full sun and mostly in dry soils. The foliage is stiff, often silvery blue: the summer flowers held in upright spikes on long stems. **CULTIVATION:** Most species are salt tolerant and so can be grown on sand dunes to stabilize them; this can result in weediness in non-native areas. Provide a sunny well-drained aspect and control spread. Cut down in winter and propagate by division in spring.

Leymus arenarius
syn. *Elymus arenarius*
EUROPEAN DUNE GRASS, LYME GRASS, SEA LYME GRASS
☀ ❄ ↔ 3–7 ft (0.9–2 m)
↑ 12–15 in (30–38 cm)
From Europe. Very vigorous grass with spreading rhizomes. Arching silvery

Leymus arenarius

leaves, to 24 in (60 cm) long. Upright spikes of white flowers in summer, turning cream with age. **'Findhorn'**, more compact shorter-growing selection. Zones 6–10.

LIATRIS

BLAZING STAR, GAYFEATHER, SNAKE ROOT
Native to eastern North America and growing from corms or modified flattened roots, the 35 species of perennials in this genus of the daisy (Asteraceae) family make a bold splash of color in summer; very easy to grow. They form clumps of simple linear to lance-shaped leaves, sometimes finely hairy, bearing 24–60 in (60–150 cm) tall stems, topped with long, quite un-daisy-like, bottlebrush spikes of filamentous purple-pink flowers. Native Americans used the roots medicinally, and early settlers found that the dried roots repelled clothes moths. **CULTIVATION:** While hardiness varies, most species are frost resistant. Wild plants are usually found along watercourses, though they can be grown in any sunny position in moist, humus-rich, well-drained soil. Place at back of borders to disguise the foliage clump and make use of flower stem's height. Propagate by division or from seed.

Liatris aspera
ROUGH BLAZING STAR
☀/☀ ❄ ↔ 12–20 in (30–50 cm)
↑ 40 in (100 cm)
Found across most of eastern North America. Leaves are narrow, to 6 in (15 cm) long. Spikes of up to 20 purple flowerheads in mid-summer to autumn. Zones 5–10.

Liatris pycnostachya
BUTTON SNAKE ROOT
☀/☀ ❄ ↔ 10–18 in (25–45 cm)
↑ 60 in (150 cm)
Native to southeastern USA. Strongly upright habit. Leaves narrow, sometimes downy, to 4 in (10 cm) long. Densely crowded purple-red flowerheads, in spikes to 12 in (30 cm) long, in mid-summer–autumn. **'Alexander'**, dark green foliage, purple flowerheads. Zones 3–10.

Liatris scariosa
☀/☀ ❄ ↔ 8–12 in (20–30 cm)
↑ 32 in (80 cm)
Native to southeastern USA. Compact, with more foliage and broader leaves than other species. Leaves to 6 in (15 cm) long and 2 in (5 cm) wide. Variably sparse or crowded flower spikes with purple flowerheads from mid-summer to autumn. Zones 3–9.

Liatris spicata ★
BLAZING STAR, BUTTON SNAKE ROOT, GAYFEATHER
☀/☀ ❄ ↔ 10–18 in (25–45 cm)
↑ 60 in (150 cm)
Found across most of eastern USA. Upright habit. Leaves narrow, sometimes linear, to 8 in (20 cm) long. Dense spikes, to 24 in (60 cm) long, with purple-red flowerheads in mid-summer to autumn. **'Callilepsis Purple'**, 24 in (60 cm) high, dark purple flowerheads; **'Floristan'**, 32 in (80 cm) high, deep violet flowerheads; **'Floristan White'**, 32 in (80 cm) high, white flowerheads; **'Kobold'** (syn. 'Goblin'), 20 in (50 cm) high, dense heads of purple-pink flowers. Zones 3–10.

LIBERTIA

The 9 species of perennial rhizomatous plants in this genus, a Southern Hemisphere member of the iris (Iridaceae) family, have a creeping or tufted growth habit and a prolonged flowering season. They occur in eastern Australia, New Zealand, New Guinea, and the Andes of South America. The strap-like leaves are produced in sparse to dense tufts. The flowers, usually white and recognizably iris-like in form, are borne in clusters at the top of straight stems. Often the leaves partially obscure the flowers. **CULTIVATION:** The majority of species are quite tolerant of both drought and poor soils; however, most will respond visibly to softer conditions and light feeding. In appropriate climates, with their weed-defeating habit and general vigor, some species may be used for roadside plantings. Propagate in spring by division or from seed.

Libertia caerulescens
☀/☀ ✽ ↔ 12 in (30 cm) ↑ 24 in (60 cm)
Native to Chile. A clumping perennial, with leaves narrow, strap-shaped, leathery, and blue-green. Spikes of pale blue flowers appear in the late spring. Zones 9–10.

Libertia formosa
SHOWY LIBERTIA, SNOWY MERMAID
☀ ✽ ↔ 24 in (60 cm)
↑ 18–36 in (45–90 cm)
Chilean species. Clumping perennial. Dark green leaves are narrow, strap-shaped, and leathery. Tall spikes of white or pale yellow flowers in the late spring. Zones 9–10.

Libertia formosa

Libertia grandiflora

MIKOIKOI, NEW ZEALAND IRIS, TUKAUKI

☀ ⚘ ↔ 24 in (60 cm) ↑ 30 in (75 cm)

From New Zealand. Clumping perennial. Leaves green to yellowy green, narrow, leathery. Tall spike of white flowers, in dense clusters, in spring, followed by attractive, yellow, pear-shaped seed capsules. Zones 9–11.

Libertia ixioides

MIKOIKOI, NEW ZEALAND IRIS, TUKAUKI

☀ ⚘ ↔ 24 in (60 cm) ↑ 8–12 in (20–30 cm)

From New Zealand. Clumping perennial. Leaves green to orange-brown, narrow, leathery. Spike of white flowers in late spring. Zones 9–11.

Libertia peregrinans

☀/◐ ❄ ↔ 20 in (50 cm)
↑ 15–27 in (38–70 cm)

From New Zealand. Leaves obviously veined, turning orange-brown in cold weather. White flowers with yellow anthers in spring. Needs well-drained soil. Zones 8–10.

LIBOCEDRUS

This genus of 6 species of coniferous trees in the cyprus (Cupressaceae) family is found in wet forest areas of New Caledonia, New Zealand, and southwestern South America, with 2 further species from New Guinea sometimes placed in the genus *Papuacedrus*. They are attractive cypress-like trees with bright green foliage that has distinct adult and juvenile forms. The bark peels in stringy vertical strips, and the male and female cones, borne on the same tree, are very small. The fragrant wood is ideal for making pencils because of its straight grain. CULTIVATION: The New Zealand and South American species can be grown outdoors in moderately frosty climates but the others may require greenhouse cultivation. Outdoors these conifers make very fine specimen trees that maintain their form for many years. They will grow in any reasonable deeply worked soil and should be given some shade when young. Water well in dry spells. Propagation is usually from seed, which is best sown fresh. Cuttings are difficult to strike.

Libocedrus bidwillii

PAHAUTEA

☀ ❄ ↔ 10 ft (3 m) ↑ 70 ft (21 m)

From New Zealand. Slow growing in cultivation, reaching only 6–12 ft (1.8–3.5 m) after 10 years. Slender upright form; adult branchlets dark green, compressed, the leaves scale-like; more open in the juvenile stage. Zones 8–10.

Libocedrus plumosa ★

KAWAKA

☀ ❄ ↔ 10 ft (3 m) ↑ 40 ft (12 m)

From New Zealand. Pyramidal form, maintained for many years. Slow growing in cultivation, reaching only about 8 ft (2.4 m) after 10 years. Branchlets compressed, flattened, giving a soft feathery appearance; leaves rich green, scale-like. Good container plant when young. Zones 8–11.

LIGULARIA

While some popular species formerly included in this temperate Eurasian genus of the daisy (Asteraceae) family have been reclassified, there are still some 125 species of perennials in *Ligularia*. In spring these vigorous plants soon develop into clumps of long-stalked, broad, basal leaves, usually kidney- to heart-shaped, with toothed edges. In summer and autumn flowering stems develop, ranging from broadly forking panicles of large yellow to orange daisies to tall spike-like racemes of numerous smaller heads, depending on the species. CULTIVATION: Most species are very hardy. Grow in full sun/half-sun, in deep, fertile, humus-rich soil kept moist through the year. Cut back when flowers and foliage fade. Propagate by division when dormant or from seed.

Ligularia dentata

☀/◐ ❄ ↔ 40–60 in (100–150 cm)
↑ 30–60 in (75–150 cm)

From China and Japan. A vigorous clump-forming perennial with impressive foliage. Leaves rounded to kidney-shaped, deeply toothed, with downy undersides, often red-tinted, to 16 in

Ligularia dentata

Libocedrus plumosa, in the wild, New Zealand

(40 cm) wide. Strong upright flower stems branching broadly with many gold to orange flowerheads, to 4 in (10 cm) across. 'Desdemona', purple-red leaves, orange flowers on stems to 48 in (120 cm). Zones 4–10.

Ligularia przewalskii

SHAVALSKI'S LIGULARIA

☀/◐ ❄ ↔ 40–48 in (100–120 cm)
↑ 7 ft (2 m)

Northern Chinese vigorous perennial. Leaves deeply palmately lobed and toothed, basal leaves to 12 in (30 cm) long and wide. Stems dark purple-red. Narrow spikes of many spidery golden yellow flowerheads. Zones 4–9.

Ligularia stenocephala

☀/◐ ❄ ↔ 32–40 in (80–100 cm)
↑ 60 in (150 cm)

Native to Japan, China, and Taiwan. Leaves heart-shaped to triangular, toothed, basal leaves to 12 in (30 cm) long and wide. Stems deep purple-red. Deep yellow flowerheads, to over 2 in (5 cm) across. 'The Rocket', dark black-green stems contrasting with numerous bright yellow flowerheads. Zones 5–10.

Ligularia Hybrid Cultivars

☀/◐ ❄ ↔ 32–60 in (80–150 cm)
↑ 3–7 ft (0.9–2 m)

Bred with both foliage and flowers in mind, hybrid ligularias are bold architectural plants ideally suited to moist partly shaded corners, especially near ponds and streams. 'Gregynog Gold', coarsely toothed green leaves, and pyramidal spikes of orange flowers; 'Weihenstephan', large deep golden yellow flowerheads; 'Zepter', slightly shorter than the species but with more densely crowded golden yellow flowerheads. Zones 5–9.

Ligularia przewalskii   *Ligularia stenocephala*   *L. s.* 'The Rocket'

Ligustrum ovalifolium 'Aureum'

Ligustrum sinense 'Multiflorum'

Ligustrum lucidum 'Excelsum Superbum'

Ligustrum japonicum 'Rotundifolium'

LIGUSTRUM

PRIVET

This genus of about 50 species of both deciduous and evergreen trees and shrubs is part of the olive (Oleaceae) family. Most species are found in the Himalayas and eastern Asia, with one found in Europe and North Africa. All have simple opposite leaves with smooth edges and bear panicles of scented white flowers at the branch or stem tips, followed by small blue-black drupes. In warmer climates the seed is produced in large quantities and is popular with birds, which has resulted in several species invading native vegetation and becoming weeds. *L. japonicum* and *L. ovalifolium* are weeds in the USA and New Zealand; *L. lucidum* and *L. sinense* have become pests in eastern Australia. The varieties with colored foliage can be grown with less risk but are apt to revert.
CULTIVATION: Privets are not particular about soil or exposure to the sun. Seeds can be sown as soon as they are ripe, while the colored forms are best propagated from firm tip cuttings taken in late spring or summer.

Ligustrum japonicum

JAPANESE PRIVET

☼ ❄ ↔ 8 ft (2.4 m) ↑ 10 ft (3 m)
From Japan and Korea. Compact, very dense, evergreen shrub. The leaves are camellia-like, shiny, and olive green. The large panicles of white flowers appear in late summer–early autumn. Useful as a screening or hedging plant.

'Rotundifolium', slow growing, to 6 ft (1.8 m) tall, round leaves, to 1½ in (35 mm) in diameter. Zones 5–10.

Ligustrum lucidum

BROAD-LEAFED PRIVET, GLOSSY PRIVET, WAXLEAF PRIVET

☼ ❄ ↔ 30 ft (9 m) ↑ 30 ft (9 m)
From China. Large evergreen shrub or small tree. Leaves long, pointed, shiny, deep green, to 6 in (15 cm) long. Large panicles of white flowers in the autumn. 'Excelsum Superbum' has pale green leaves edged with yellow; 'Tricolor' has narrow deep green leaves, predominantly marked with gray-green, edged with pale creamy yellow. Zones 7–11.

Ligustrum obtusifolium

☼ ❄ ↔ 10 ft (3 m) ↑ 10 ft (3 m)
From Japan. Vigorous deciduous shrub, with leaves deep green, oblong, often turning crimson in autumn. Profuse white flowers, in drooping panicles, in late summer. Round black fruit. *L. obtusifolium* var. *regelianum*, to 5 ft (1.5 m) tall, leaves slightly smaller, blunter. Zones 3–10.

Ligustrum ovalifolium

CALIFORNIA PRIVET, OVAL-LEAFED PRIVET

☼ ❄ ↔ 12 ft (3.5 m) ↑ 12 ft (3.5 m)
Cultivated for hedging. Leaves shiny, deep green, falling in very cold climates. White flowers in mid-summer. 'Argenteum', leaves with creamy white margins; 'Aureum', the golden privet, green-centered leaves with wide yellow margins, or all yellow. Zones 5–10.

Ligustrum quihoui

☼ ❄ ↔ 8 ft (2.4 m) ↑ 8 ft (2.4 m)
Chinese, profusely flowering, rounded evergreen shrub, bowed branches. Panicles of white flowers, to 2 ft (0.6 m) long, late summer–early autumn. Zones 5–10.

Ligustrum sinense

CHINESE PRIVET, SMALL-LEAFED PRIVET

☼ ❄ ↔ 12 ft (3.5 m) ↑ 12 ft (3.5 m)
Chinese, large, spreading, deciduous shrub. Leaves pale green, lance-shaped. White flowers, long compact sprays, in summer. Deep purple berries. 'Multiflorum', masses of flowers; 'Pendulum', drooping branches; 'Variegatum', gray-green leaves, white margins. Zones 7–11.

Ligustrum obtusifolium

LILIUM

LILY

Cultivated for over 5,000 years, lilies are undeniably beautiful, and there are about 100 species of these bulbs spread across the northern temperate zone. Type genus for their family, Liliaceae, they are strongly upright plants with leafy aerial stems that die back to the bulb after flowering; the bulbs are composed of many narrow, overlapping, fleshy scales with no outer covering (tunic). The leaves are short, usually linear to lanceolate. The flowers are borne at the stem tips and may be solitary or in umbels or panicles; they may be bell-, trumpet-, or cup-shaped, or have strongly recurved sepals, producing the "turk's-cap" flower shape. They come in all colors, except for blue, and are often spotted or streaked. In common with many other genera with large groups of hybrids, lilies are divided into groups of similar plants. The genus *Lilium* is split into 9 main divisions, to each of which both species and hybrids may be assigned.
CULTIVATION: Lilies flower best with sun for at least half the day. They need moist, humus-rich, fertile, well-drained soil. Do not store bulbs dry; use moist sawdust or shredded paper. Propagate from offsets, from detached bulb scales, or from leaf axil bulbils or seed.

Lilium amabile

☀/◐ ❄ ↔ 12 in (30 cm) ↑ 36 in (90 cm)
From Korea. Sparse covering of narrow leaves, to nearly 4 in (10 cm) long. Flowerheads of up to 5 turk's-cap flowers, red or dark orange with purple spotting, 3 in (8 cm) across, with unpleasant scent, in summer. Zones 5–9.

Lilium × *burbankii*

◐ ❄ ↔ 12–18 in (30–45 cm)
↑ 3–7 ft (0.9–2 m)
Garden hybrid between *L. pardalinum* and *L. parryi*. Fragrant horizontal flowers with reflexed yellow petals spotted with brown and tipped red, in summer–early autumn. Zones 5–9.

Lilium lancifolium

Lilium henrici

Lilium candidum

MADONNA LILY, WHITE LILY
☀ ❄ ↔ 12–18 in (30–45 cm)
↑ 3–7 ft (0.9–2 m)
Native to the Mediterranean region (Lebanon, Israel, Turkey, Greece); the species held by statues of the Virgin Mary. Up to 20 flowers per stem, pure white trumpets with reflexed tips and a strong fragrance, in summer–early autumn. Unlike most lilies, likes alkaline soil and a sunny aspect. Zones 6–9.

Lilium columbianum

COLUMBIA LILY, COLUMBIA TIGER LILY, OREGON LILY
☀ ❄ ↔ 12–18 in (30–45 cm)
↑ 7–8 ft (2–2.4 m)
From western North America. Lance-shaped leaves in whorls up the stems. Flowers strongly reflexed in turk's-cap fashion, yellow to orange-red spotted with maroon, 3 in (8 cm across, in summer–early autumn. Zones 5–9.

Lilium davidii

☀ ❄ ↔ 12–18 in (30–45 cm)
↑ 3–5 ft (0.9–1.5 m)
Native to western China. Slightly stoloniferous species. Scattered leaves, to 4 in (10 cm) long. Up to 20 unscented, nodding, turk's-cap flowers, to 3 in (8 cm) across, bright vermilion-red spotted with black, in summer–early autumn. Zones 5–9.

Lilium formosanum

☀ ❄ ↔ 12–18 in (30–45 cm)
↑ 3–7 ft (0.9–2 m)
From Taiwan. Tall elegant species with scattered leaves and up to 10 blooms on each stem, but usually fewer, in summer–early autumn. Flowers are trumpet-shaped, horizontal, 8 in (20 cm) long, strongly scented, white stained purple on the outside. *L. f.* var. *pricei*, dwarf form, 1 or 2 flowers per stem. Zones 5–11.

Lilium henrici

syn. *Nomocharis henrici*
◐ ❄ ↔ 12–18 in (30–45 cm)
↑ 32–36 in (80–90 cm)
From China. Rare species with leaves scattered up stems and up to 7 flowers

Lilium nepalense

Lilium amabile

per stem. Flowers pendent, almost flat, to 4 in (10 cm) across, with slightly recurved petals, almost white, lightly suffused with pink, and dark purple center. Zones 5–9.

Lilium henryi

◐ ❄ ↔ 12–18 in (30–45 cm)
↑ 7–10 ft (2–3 m)
From China. Stems, each holding up to 20 flowers, inclined to lean from the weight. Leaves relatively broad, scattered up the stems. Reflexed turk's-cap flowers, orange spotted with black. Zones 5–9.

Lilium lancifolium

syn. *Lilium tigrinum*
DEVIL LILY, KENTAN, TIGER LILY
☀ ❄ ↔ 12–18 in (30–45 cm)
↑ 3–4 ft (0.9–1.2 m)
From eastern China, Japan, and Korea. Hardy well-known lily, probably an ancient hybrid. Scattered leaves, to 8 in (20 cm) long; black bulbils produced in leaf axils. Turk's-cap flowers, to 8 in (20 cm) across, orange with bold dark purple spots, in summer–early autumn. Zones 4–10.

Lilium longiflorum

EASTER LILY
◐ ❄ ↔ 12–18 in (30–45 cm)
↑ 36–40 in (90–100 cm)
From Japan and Taiwan. Vigorous species. Scattered shiny leaves, to 7 in

Lilium × *burbankii*

(18 cm) long. Horizontally held, strongly scented, trumpet-shaped flowers, to 7 in (18 cm) long, white with green central stripes, in summer–early autumn. Zones 5–11.

Lilium martagon

MARTAGON, TURK'S CAP
◐ ❄ ↔ 12–18 in (30–45 cm)
↑ 3–8 ft (0.9–2.4 m)
Native from northwestern Europe to Mongolia. The classic lily in turk's-cap form. Leaves broad, in whorls. Up to 50 flowers per stem, usually far fewer, to 2 in (5 cm) across, dull pink with darker spots, unpleasantly scented, in summer–early autumn. *L. m.* var. *album*, pure white flowers; *L. m.* var. *cattaniae*, deep wine-red flowers without spots. Zones 4–9.

Lilium nepalense ★

◐ ❄ ↔ 12–18 in (30–45 cm)
↑ 27–40 in (70–100 cm)
Himalayan. Rare and desirable species. Scattered leaves, to 6 in (15 cm) long. Drooping, flared, trumpet-shaped flowers, 6 in (15 cm) long, usually green-white with a large purple throat, in summer–early autumn. Zones 5–9.

Lilium, Hybrid Cultivar, 1. Asiatic, 'Eros'

Lilium, Hybrid Cultivar, 1. Asiatic, 'Minstrel'

Lilium, Hybrid Cultivar, 1. Asiatic, 'Avignon'

Lilium, Hybrid Cultivar, 1. Asiatic, 'Connecticut King'

Lilium, Hybrid Cultivar, 1. Asiatic, 'Hup Holland'

Lilium, Hybrid Cultivar, 1. Asiatic, 'Her Grace'

Lilium, HC, 1. Asiatic, 'Casa Rosa'

Lilium philippinense

☀ ❄ ↔ 12–18 in (30–45 cm)
↑ 16–40 in (40–100 cm)

From the Philippines. Deep green scattered leaves, to 6 in (15 cm) long. Up to 6 highly scented trumpets per stem, to 10 in (25 cm) long, white, stained outside with green and red, in summer–early autumn. Zones 9–10.

Lilium pumilum ★

syn. *Lilium tenuifolium*
CORAL LILY

☀ ❄ ↔ 12–18 in (30–45 cm)
↑ 15–18 in (38–45 cm)

From eastern Russia, Mongolia, China, and North Korea. Narrow scattered leaves. Up to 30 scented turk's-cap flowers per stem, to 2 in (5 cm) across, bright scarlet, usually without spots, in summer–early autumn. 'Yellow Bunting', yellow flowers. Zones 5–9.

Lilium pyrenaicum

☀ ❄ ↔ 12–18 in (30–45 cm)
↑ 32–40 in (80–100 cm)

From the Pyrenees. Narrow scattered leaves. Up to 12 turk's-cap flowers per stem, to 2 in (5 cm) across, bright yellow, black spots, unpleasant smell, in summer–early autumn. Zones 3–9.

Lilium regale

REGAL LILY

☀ ❄ ↔ 12–18 in (30–45 cm)
↑ 5–7 ft (1.5–2 m)

From China. Scattered leaves, to 5 in (12 cm) long. Up to 20 flowers per stem, flared trumpets, to 6 in (15 cm) long, held horizontally, white inside with purple flushes on the outside, in summer–early autumn. Zones 5–9.

Lilium speciosum

☀ ❄ ↔ 12–18 in (30–45 cm)
↑ 3–5 ft (0.9–1.5 m)

From China, Japan, and Taiwan. Scattered leaves, to 7 in (18 cm) long. Up to 12 pendent, fragrant, turk's-cap flowers per stem, to 7 in (18 cm) across, usually pale pink, deeper pink toward center, with deep pink spots, in summer–early autumn. *L. s.* var. *album,* purple stems, white flowers; *L. s.* var. *rubrum,* purple stems, dark carmine flowers, white edges. Zones 6–9.

Lilium Hybrid Cultivars

☀/☀ ❄ ↔ 12–24 in (30–60 cm)
↑ 30 in–7 ft (75 cm–2 m)

Most garden or florists' lilies are hybrid cultivars, nearly all from generations of breeding from many wild species. The classification of *Lilium* cultivars below is that used by the *International Lily Register,* kept by the Royal Horticultural Society. Zones 5–9.

1. ASIATIC HYBRIDS

These hybrids, derived from *L. amabile, L. bulbiferum, L. cernuum, L. concolor, L. davidii, L. lancifolium, L. leichtlinii, L. maculatum, L. × hollandicum,* and *L. pumilum,* typically have one or a few large trumpet-shaped flowers and occur in a huge range of colors and patterns. Although known as Asiatic, the geographic origins of these often overlap with the Oriental hybrids, and the name should not be taken literally.

The Asiatics are subdivided by their flower form into 3 categories: 1a, upward-facing flowers; 1b, outward-facing; and 1c, pendent.

Popular Asiatic hybrids include: 'Alaska', to 48 in (120 cm) tall, white flowers; 'Avignon', to 36 in (90 cm) tall, red and orange flowers; 'Chianti', to 32 in (80 cm) tall, pink flowers; 'Connecticut King', to 36 in (90 cm) tall, yellow flowers; 'Côte d'Azur', to 27 in (70 cm) tall, pink flowers; 'Dreamland', to 36 in (90 cm) tall, yellow flowers; 'Monte Negro', to 36 in (90 cm) tall, orange to dark red flowers; 'Montreaux', to 48 in (120 cm) tall, pink flowers; 'Navona', to 36 in (90 cm) tall, white flowers with yellow-green center; 'Polyanna', over 48 in (120 cm) tall, yellow flowers; 'Vivaldi', to 42 in (105 cm) tall, pink flowers.

2. TURK'S-CAP OR MARTAGON HYBRIDS

Hybrids between *L. martagon* and *L. hansonii,* or hybrids with one of those species as a parent. They have large heads of many small to medium-sized pendulous flowers. The mixed color selection known as the **Backhouse Hybrids** are the most widely grown lilies of this style.

Lilium, Hybrid Cultivar, 2. Turk's-Cap, Backhouse Hybrid

Lilium pyrenaicum

Lilium philippinense

Lilium regale

Lilium, Hybrid Cultivar, 1. Asiatic, 'Monte Negro'

Lilium, Hybrid Cultivar, 1. Asiatic, 'Montreaux'

Lilium, Hybrid Cultivar, 1. Asiatic, 'Navona'

Lilium, Hybrid Cultivar, 1. Asiatic cultivar

Lilium, Hybrid Cultivar, 1. Asiatic, 'Vivaldi'

L., HC, 7. Oriental, 'Alliance'

L., HC, 7. Oriental, 'Ascari'

L., HC, 7. Oriental, 'Barbaresco'

L., HC, 7. Oriental, 'Black Tie'

L., HC, 7. Oriental, 'Cartouche'

L., HC, 7. Oriental, 'Compass'

L., HC, 7. Oriental, 'Esperanto'

L., HC, 7. Oriental, 'Acapulco'

L., HC, 7. Oriental, 'Candice'

L., HC, 7. Oriental, 'Imperial Day'

L., HC, 7. Oriental, 'Impressive'

L., HC, 7. Oriental, 'Expression'

L., HC, 7. Oriental cultivar

L., HC, 7. Oriental, 'Scapino'

L., HC, 7. Oriental, 'Salmon Classic'

3. *L. CANDIDUM* HYBRIDS

Hybrids of *L. candidum, L. chalcedonicum,* and a number of other related species, but not *L. martagon.* These plants are typically tall and dark-stemmed, with fragrant, often white to cream, funnel-shaped flowers.

4. AMERICAN SPECIES HYBRIDS

Hybrids between American species, such as *L. canadense, L. maritimum, L. columbianum,* and *L. grayi.* These plants should be quite variable and interesting, but as yet this group is represented by just a few plants, of which the **Bellingham Hybrids**, with brown-spotted red and orange or red and yellow flowers, are the most commonly seen.

5. *L. LONGIFLORUM* AND *L. FORMOSANUM* HYBRIDS

Hybrids between or of these 2 species usually have large, green-tinted, white, trumpet-shaped flowers.

6. TRUMPET-SHAPED AND AURELIAN LILIES

Hybrids of *L. henryi* and related species, but not including those species that make up Division 7. This group is subdivided into 4 categories based on flower shape: 6a, trumpet-shaped flowers; 6b, bowl-shaped flowers; 6c, flat flowers with recurved tips; and 6d, strongly recurved flowers.

Popular Division 6 lilies include: '**Black Dragon**', to 60 in (150 cm) tall, deep purple-red flowers with white interior; '**Pink Perfection**', to 60 in (150 cm) tall, very large, fragrant, deep magenta flowers.

7. ORIENTAL HYBRIDS

Hybrids of *L. auratum, L. speciosum, L. japonicum,* and *L. rubellum.* Includes hybrids between these species and *L. henryi* but not with Trumpet or Aurelian hybrids. Subdivided into 4 categories based on flower shape: 7a, trumpet-shaped flowers; 7b, bowl-shaped flowers; 7c, flat flowers; and 7d, strongly recurved flowers.

Popular Oriental hybrids include: '**Acapulco**', to 36 in (90 cm) tall, mauve flowers; '**Alliance**', to 48 in (120 cm) tall, pink flowers with dark mid-stripe and pale edges; '**Cartouche**', to 48 in (120 cm) tall, reddish pink flowers with dark mid-stripe and pale edges; '**Casa Blanca**', to 54 in (135 cm)

Lilium, Hybrid Cultivar, 4. American Species, Bellingham Hybrid

Lilium, Hybrid Cultivar,
7. Oriental, 'Sissi'

Lilium, Hybrid Cultivar,
7. Oriental, 'Sorbonne'

Lilium, Hybrid Cultivar,
7. Oriental, 'Star Gazer'

Lilium, Hybrid Cultivar,
7. Oriental, 'White Mountain'

Lilium, Hybrid Cultivar,
7. Oriental, 'Woodriff's Memory'

Lilium, Hybrid Cultivar, 8. Other, LA, 'Wiener Blut'

L., HC, 8. Other, 'Virginia'

L., HC, 8. Other, LA, 'California'

Lilium, Hybrid Cultivar,
8., Other, LA, 'Glossy Wings'

Lilium, Hybrid Cultivar,
8. Other, LA, 'Royal Fantasy'

Lilium, Hybrid Cultivar, 8. Other,
LA, 'Royal River'

Lilium, Hybrid Cultivar, 8. Other,
LA, 'Salmon Queen'

L., HC, 8. Other, LA, 'Royal Sunset'

tall, white flowers; **'Expression'** ★,
to 36 in (90 cm) tall, white flowers;
'Muscadet', to 27 in (70 cm) tall,
white, flushed pale pink flowers with
red spots; **'Pesaro'**, to 36 in (90 cm)
tall, deep pink flowers with pale center;
'Siberia', to 48 in (120 cm) tall, pure
white flowers; **'Sissi'**, to 36 in (90 cm)
tall, pink flowers; **'Sorbonne'**, to 48 in
(120 cm) tall, deep pink flowers with
pale edges; **'Star Gazer'**, to 36 in
(90 cm) tall, pink flowers with red
flecks and pale edges; **'Woodriff's
Memory'**, to 36 in (90 cm), purplish-
pink flowers with a yellow mid-stripe.

8. OTHER HYBRIDS
Miscellaneous hybrids not classified
elsewhere, such as: **'Virginia'**, 24–36 in
(60–90 cm), white flowers greenish
yellow at center. **LA Hybrids** appeared
in the 1990s, so named because they
combined *L. longiflorum* with Asiatic
Hybrids; they include: **'Glossy Wings'**,
to 36 in (90 cm) tall, strong salmon-
pink flowers; **'Royal Fantasy'**, to 36 in
(90 cm) tall, creamy yellow scented
flowers; **'Royal Sunset'**, to 30 in
(75 cm) tall, orange petals tipped scarlet, finely spotted; **'Wiener Blut'** ★,
to 30 in (75 cm) tall, tomato-red
flowers, major commercial cut flower.

9. SPECIES
The species as they occur in the wild,
including the many natural subspecies
and varieties. In this book the species
all have their own entries.

LIMONIUM
SEA LAVENDER, STATICE
Genus of about 150 species of mainly
summer-flowering annuals, perennials,
and small shrubs in the leadwort
(Plumbaginaceae) family, widely distributed around the world, but with
the main concentration in southern
Europe and North Africa. The name
comes from the Greek *leimon,* meadow,
referring to the fact that many species
occur in salt marshes (or salt meadows).
Most are low-growing, forming
mounds of basal leaf rosettes. The
leaves vary in size and tend to be lance-
or spatula-shaped. Flowers are minute
but showy, borne in billowing sprays
held well clear of the foliage on branching wiry stems, in white, cream, and
mauve to purple shades. The flowers
are still widely sold as "statice," and
are popular for dried flower work.
CULTIVATION: Many species are somewhat frost tender, thriving in coastal
conditions, with a preference for sheltered sunny locations and light, well-
drained, yet moist soil. If the flowers
are not cut for indoor use, they should
be removed, as allowing the plants to
set seed can shorten their life. Propagate from seed or root cuttings, or by
division, depending on the plant type.

Limonium bellidifolium
syn. *Statice caspia*
☀/◐ ❄ ↔ 12 in (30 cm) ↑ 12 in (30 cm)
From coastal areas of eastern England
to the Mediterranean and Black Sea.
Summer-flowering perennial forming
woody-based clump of rounded to
spatula-shaped leaves, to 2 in (5 cm)
long. Flowerhead made up of short
spikes of pale violet flowers. Zones 8–10.

Limonium bourgeaui
☀/◐ ❄ ↔ 12 in (30 cm) ↑ 16 in (40 cm)
From Lanzarote, one of the Canary
Islands. Perennial forming a woody-
based clump of broad pointed oval to
rhomboidal leaves, to 3 in (8 cm) long,
sometimes with small lobes at base.
Young stems and flower stems downy.
Sprays of purple and white flowers
from late spring. Zones 7–10.

Limonium brassicifolium
☀/◐ ❄ ↔ 12 in (30 cm) ↑ 16 in (40 cm)
From the Canary Islands. Perennial
with a woody rhizome producing
winged stems and 4–12 in (10–30 cm)
long, broad, pointed oval leaves. Panicles of many single-flowered spikes
with purple calyces and a white corolla.
Zones 9–11.

Limonium carthaginense
☀/◐ ❄ ↔ 12 in (30 cm) ↑ 12 in (30 cm)
From mountainous southeastern Spain;
occurs in very rocky terrain. Evergreen
perennial forming mound of small
bright green leaves, sparse lavender-
pink flowers. Tolerates zinc and other
metals in soil. Zones 7–10.

Limonium perezii
☀/◐ ❄ ↔ 20 in (50 cm) ↑ 27 in (70 cm)
From the Canary Islands. Subshrub
with broad oval leaves, to 6 in (15 cm)
long. Flower stems downy. Large heads
of flowers with deep purple calyces
and a creamy yellow to white corolla.
Zones 9–11.

Limonium platyphyllum

syn. *Limonium latifolium*

☀ ❄ ↔ 24 in (60 cm) ↕ 32 in (80 cm)

Found from southeastern to central Europe. Vigorous summer-flowering perennial. Leaves narrow, spatula-shaped to elliptical, sparsely downy, usually about 10 in (25 cm), sometimes to 24 in (60 cm) long. Rounded billowing panicles of pale violet flowers. Zones 5–10.

Limonium sinuatum

syn. *Statice sinuata*

☀/☀ ❧ ↔ 16 in (40 cm) ↕ 16 in (40 cm)

Native to the Mediterranean region. Summer-flowering perennial, often short-lived and treated as an annual. All parts downy. The leaves are pinnately lobed, lance-shaped, 1–4 in (2.5–10 cm) long. Flower stems are winged, with many short compact spikes of papery flowers. Wild species has lavender, pink, or white flowers; cultivars come in many colors. Can become invasive. 'Art Shades', pastel tones, most colors; California Series, bright tones, most colors; 'Forever Gold', deep golden yellow flowers. Zones 9–11.

LINARIA

SPURRED SNAPDRAGON, TOADFLAX

From the foxglove (Scrophulariaceae) family, this genus encompasses about 150 species of annuals and perennials found in Europe (mainly around the Mediterranean) and temperate Asia. A few North American species formerly included in *Linaria* are now placed in the genus *Nuttallanthus*. Toadflaxes are closely related to snapdragons, with similar but smaller flowers. They are

Linaria maroccana cultivar

easy to cultivate but stop flowering in hot weather. For best effect, plant in masses, as the individual plants are wispy. The name is derived from the Greek *linon*, flax, because of the similarity in foliage.

CULTIVATION: Grow in full sun or partial shade in well-drained soil. Cut perennials down to ground level in autumn. Propagate annuals and perennials from seed; perennials also by division and from cuttings. Sow seed outdoors in late autumn or early spring (even when snow is still on ground) or indoors. Seed germinates in about 2 weeks and flowering starts about 8 weeks later. Annuals also self-seed.

Linaria maroccana

ANNUAL TOADFLAX, BUNNY RABBITS, MOROCCO TOADFLAX

☀ ❧ ↔ 6–12 in (15–30 cm) ↕ 8–10 in (20–25 cm)

From Morocco; naturalized in northeastern USA. Annual. Leaves narrow, grass-like, alternate. Profuse tiny snapdragon-like flowers in white, yellow, pink, red, and dark blue to purple shades in the early summer. 'Fairy Bouquet', flowers ranging from lavender, purple, and pink to crimson;

Limonium bourgeaui

Limonium perezii

Limonium brassicifolium

Limonium sinuatum

Lindera obtusiloba

'Fantasy Blue', dwarf form, compact habit, will grow year-round in mild climates; 'Northern Lights', faintly violet-scented, jewel-like, bicolored flowers in pink, red, yellow, and purple; Soda Pop Series, magenta-rose, blue, or pink flowers. Zones 9–11.

Linaria purpurea

PURPLE TOADFLAX

☀ ❄ ↔ 6–12 in (15–30 cm) ↕ 20–36 in (50–90 cm)

From southern Europe. Narrow bushy perennial. Slender gray-green leaves. Bright blue-purple flowers with white stripes in mid-summer–early autumn. 'Canon Went', tall, with grayish foliage and soft pink flowers. Zones 5–10.

Linaria triornithophora

THREE-BIRDS-FLYING

☀ ❄ ↔ 24 in (60 cm) ↕ 36 in (90 cm)

From Spain and Portugal. Perennial. Foliage gray-green, toxic if ingested. Pale lavender and yellow spurred flowers, carried on long stems and grouped in 3s with the long spurs pointing downward, like the tails of perching birds, in late spring–late summer. Zones 7–10.

LINDERA

This genus in the laurel (Lauraceae) family consists of about 80 species of deciduous and evergreen trees and shrubs, all from East Asia except for 3 from North America. They have an open habit and aromatic alternate leaves, smooth-edged or 3-lobed. The leaves color in autumn on deciduous species. Heads of star-shaped yellow flowers, in spring, in the leaf axils, followed by clustered berry-like fruits. Leaves of the North American species have been used to make a type of tea. CULTIVATION: Suitable for a woodland or other informal garden, in a shady position when young. All species transplant well and will survive in ordinary, somewhat acidic, soil. Established trees require little or no care but may be pruned if they become ungainly. Propagate from seed sown when fresh; if the seed must be stored, do not allow it to dry. Otherwise propagate from cuttings taken in summer or by air-layering.

Lindera obtusiloba

☀ ❄ ↔ 25 ft (8 m) ↕ 30 ft (9 m)

From East Asia. Branches gray-yellow, sometimes flushed with purple. Aromatic leaves turning pale gold in the autumn. Produces tiny, yellow-green, star-shaped flowers, in umbels on the previous year's growth, in early spring, before the leaves. Fruit glossy dark red to black. Zones 6–9.

LINDHEIMERA

Monotypic genus belonging the daisy (Asteraceae) family, and containing an annual herb native to the southwest USA. Its dark green, alternate, deeply divided lower leaves are stalked; the upper leaves are opposite, oval to sword-shaped, entire and bract-like, and borne on hairy ridged stems. Loose terminal flowerheads bearing yellow to cream star-shaped ray florets and yellow disc florets appear in late spring. CULTIVATION: Plant in a sunny position in fertile well-drained soil. Propagate by division or from the seed in early spring.

Lindheimera texana

STAR DAISY, TEXAS STAR, YELLOW STAR

☼ ❄ ↔ 4–12 in (10–30 cm)
↑ 4–24 in (10–60 cm)

From Texas. Fast-growing, upright, annual herb with erect, ridged, hairy, branching stems. Leaves dark green, oval, tapered and toothed. Loose terminal flowerheads with yellow to cream ray flowers and yellow disc florets in late spring. Zones 7–10.

LINUM

FLAX

This genus, which gives its name to the family Linaceae, comprises about 180 species of tender and hardy annuals, biennials, perennials, and subshrubs, with flax, *L. usitatissum*,

Lindheimera texana

the important fiber and oilseed plant included among them. Native to temperate or subtropical regions of the world though predominantly from the Northern Hemisphere. They are delicate but easy-to-grow plants. The stems are erect and branching, and the gray-green leaves are simple and narrow. The cup-shaped to funnel-shaped 5-petalled flowers are carried in branched clusters at the stem tips, lasting only one day. Colors vary with the variety but are mostly shades of blue or yellow, less commonly red, pink, or white. However, they are produced in great numbers throughout the summer.
CULTIVATION: For the best flowering effect, grow in well-drained humus-rich soil in full sun. Provide shelter in cool climates. Annuals and perennials are easily raised from seed or from cuttings of named varieties. Plant out perennials in autumn or early spring; sow annual species in early autumn or spring. Thin seedlings as needed.

Linum doerfleri

☼ ❄ ↔ 6–12 in (15–30 cm) ↑ 3 in (8 cm)
Endemic to Crete, Greece. A compact mat-forming perennial. Leaves small, oval, pointed, dull green. Solitary, bright yellow, star-shaped flowers, borne in upper leaf axils, in spring. Good rock garden plant. Zones 8–10.

Linum 'Gemmell's Hybrid'

☼ ❄ ↔ 8 in (20 cm) ↑ 6 in (15 cm)
Short golden yellow form best grown at the front of a border or in the rock garden. Zones 6–9.

Linum grandiflorum

FLOWERING FLAX

☼ ❄ ↔ 12 in (30 cm)
↑ 15–18 in (38–45 cm)

From Algeria. Annual. Slender stems; narrow, pointed, pale green leaves.

Liparis reflexa

Single, clear rose to purple, saucer-shaped flowers, 1½ in (35 mm) across, in early–late summer. 'Bright Eyes', to 15 in (38 cm) tall, white flowers, 2 in (5 cm) across, with a carmine eye; 'Rubrum' (scarlet flax), to 12 in (30 cm) tall, brilliant crimson flowers. Zones 7–10.

Linum narbonense

☼ ❄ ↔ 12–18 in (30–45 cm)
↑ 12–24 in (30–60 cm)

From southern Europe. Perennial. Leaves gray-green, narrow. The rich blue cup-shaped flowers are 1–1¼ in (25–30 mm) across, with a white eye, appear in late spring–autumn. Usually dies back in winter but may be evergreen in mild climates. 'Heavenly Blue', more compact, with ultramarine flowers. Zones 5–9.

Linum perenne

PERENNIAL BLUE FLAX

☼ ❄ ↔ 12 in (30 cm)
↑ 12–18 in (30–45 cm)

From Europe. Vigorous but short-lived perennial. Many sky blue flowers, 1 in (25 mm) across, in early–late summer. Easy to raise from seed; self-seeds freely. Zones 4–9.

LIPARIS

The sympodial orchid genus *Liparis* (family Orchidaceae) is cosmopolitan, with about 250 species, a high percentage of which are terrestrial. In the tropics most members are epiphytes. They are mostly found in shady environments, often near creeks, where there is always high humidity. The epiphytic species often grow on the moss-covered limbs or trunks of trees

Liparis viridiflora

on the edges of rainforest. Flowers are generally in various shades of yellowish green; some species have contrasting bright orange and red labellums.
CULTIVATION: Quick-growing in cultivation if their native environment is simulated. They need to be kept moist and shaded, with circulating fresh air. Most *Liparis* species have soft leaves that will burn if exposed to full sun. Some of the creeping species do well on cork or tree-fern slabs, while many grow readily in small pots in a freely draining bark-based medium. Propagate by division.

Liparis reflexa

☼ ✿ ↔ 4–36 in (10–90 cm)
↑ 4–12 in (10–30 cm)

Australian lithophytic species with erect to arching spikes of yellowish green flowers, ½ in (12 mm) long, with narrow segments, and smelling a bit like a wet dog, in autumn and winter. Zones 10–11.

Liparis viridiflora

☼ ✿ ↔ 4–36 in (10–90 cm)
↑ 4–16 in (10–40 cm)

From Southeast Asia. Long inflorescences have over 100 yellow to green blooms, ¼ in (6 mm) long, with a most sickly fragrance, in autumn–spring. Very easy to grow under a range of conditions. Zones 10–12.

LIQUIDAMBAR

SWEET GUM

In the witchhazel (Hamamelidaceae) family, this genus comprises 4 species of tall deciduous trees found in North and Central America, East Asia, and Turkey. The meaning of the name is much as it appears, liquid amber, referring to the resin, known as storax, exuded by the winter buds. The trees

Linum doerfleri

Linum grandiflorum 'Rubrum'

Liquidambar orientalis

have an attractive conical or rounded form, and the palmately lobed leaves are similar to those of maples but arranged spirally on the twig instead of in opposite pairs. In autumn the foliage changes color dramatically to shades of orange, red, and purple. Spring flowers are greenish and inconspicuous, in small spherical heads, but the brown fruiting heads that follow are spiky and decorative. *L. styraciflua* has a number of cultivars selected for autumn color.

CULTIVATION: These are large trees requiring plenty of room to develop; their site should be chosen carefully, as they dislike being transplanted. They require a sunny situation in deep rich soil with plenty of moisture. Propagate from seed sown in autumn or softwood cuttings taken in summer, or by air-layering.

Liquidambar formosana

CHINESE LIQUIDAMBAR, FORMOSAN GUM
☀ ❄ ↔ 30 ft (9 m) ↑ 60 ft (18 m)
From mountains of east, central, and southern China, Taiwan, northern Vietnam, Laos, and South Korea. Straight-trunked tree, grayish white bark, fissures with age. Leaves broad, 3-lobed, with serrated margins, downy beneath. Inconspicuous greenish yellow flowers; spiky fruits. Zones 7–11.

Liquidambar formosana

L. styraciflua 'Golden Treasure'

Liquidambar orientalis

ORIENTAL SWEET GUM, TURKISH LIQUIDAMBAR
☀ ❄ ↔ 15 ft (4.5 m) ↑ 25 ft (8 m)
From southwestern Turkey. Broad crown; bark thick, orangey brown, cracking into small plates. Leaves 5-lobed, smaller than other species, turning orange in autumn. Zones 8–11.

Liquidambar styraciflua

LIQUIDAMBAR, SWEET GUM
☀ ❄ ↔ 35 ft (10 m) ↑ 70 ft (21 m)
Native to eastern USA, with separate occurrence in highlands of southern Mexico and Central America. Most commonly cultivated liquidambar.

Bark dark grayish brown, deeply furrowed. Leaves large, 5 to 7 tapering lobes, coloring brilliantly in shades of orange, red, and purple in autumn. Cultivars selected for their autumn colors include: 'Burgundy', deep red; 'Festival', yellow, peach, pink; 'Lane Roberts', deep reddish purple; 'Palo Alto', orange and red; 'Worplesdon', orangey yellow and purple. Other cultivars include: 'Aurea', yellow-striped leaves; 'Golden Treasure', leaves with yellow margins; 'Gumball', dwarf form and rounded shape; 'Rotundiloba' ★, which has leaves with rounded lobes; and 'Variegata', leaves splashed with yellow. Zones 5–11.

LIRIODENDRON

Genus in the magnolia (Magnoliaceae) family believed to consist of a single species native to North America until a second similar species was found in central China in 1875. Both form quite tall, fast-growing, deciduous trees with long straight trunks and unusually shaped 3-lobed leaves that turn a translucent yellow in autumn.

Liquidambar styraciflua

The greenish bell-shaped flowers have a tangerine tint at petal bases. They somewhat resemble a tulip; hence the common name, tulip tree. Capsule-like fruit follow. Hybrids between the 2 species are in cultivation.
CULTIVATION: Tulip trees grow best in fertile soil, in a cool climate in partial shade, with protection from drying winds. Some shaping of the plant in the early stages to establish a single trunk may be necessary. Propagate from seed sown in a position protected from winter frosts. Cultivars may be apical-grafted in early spring onto 1- or 2-year-old seedling understocks.

Liriodendron chinense

CHINESE TULIP TREE
☀ ❄ ↔ 35 ft (10 m) ↑ 80 ft (24 m)
Widely scattered through mountains of China, Taiwan, and northern Vietnam; still rare in cultivation in the West. Broad, columnar, fast-growing tree. Leaves deep green, smoother than those of the other species. Cup-shaped flowers, green outside, yellow-green veins inside, in spring. Zones 8–10.

Liriodendron chinense

Liriodendron tulipifera, in spring

Liriope muscari 'Monroe White'

Liriope spicata, border plant in foreground

Liriodendron tulipifera, in winter

Liriodendron tulipifera

NORTH AMERICAN TULIP TREE, TULIP TREE

☼ ❋ ↔ 40 ft (12 m) ↑ 100 ft (30 m)

Found east of Mississippi River, USA, from Gulf States up to St Lawrence River and Great Lakes. Leaves quite large. Solitary flowers, 6 petalled, yellow-green with orange-yellow blotch at base, in spring. '**Aureomarginatum**', yellow-edged leaves; '**Fastigiatum**' ★, upright columnar habit; growing only about half height of type. Zones 4–10.

LIRIOPE

LILY TURF

This small genus in the lily-of-the-valley (Convallariaceae) family, comprising 5 or 6 species of evergreen or semi-evergreen frost-hardy perennials, is closely related to *Ophiopogon*. From acid-soil woodland habitats in East Asia. Tough, mat-forming, trouble-free plants, which soon establish a dense fibrous root system and in some species develop nutrient-storing fleshy tubers.

Grass-like leaves, arching, linear, and dense. Flowers, clustered and grape-like on blunt stems, usually showy for extended late summer period, followed by black, berry-like seeds.
CULTIVATION: Grow in shade in mild climates; allow more sun in cold climates. Propagate by division or by fresh ripe seed sown in a sandy medium.

Liriope muscari

☼/◐ ❋ ↔ 18 in (45 cm) ↑ 12 in (30 cm)

Native to China, Taiwan, and Japan. Woodland plant; drought-tolerant, tough, sturdy, evergreen, spreading ground cover. Leaves narrow, grass-like, glossy deep green, mat-forming. Dense, bead-like, steely deep lavender flowers, held on blunt spikes, in late autumn. '**Christmas Tree**', large form, resplendent flowers; '**John Burch**', large flowers on tall spikes, wide leaves with a yellow-green central stripe; '**Majestic**', to 16 in (40 cm), narrow leaves, violet flowers; '**Monroe White**',

numerous white flowers, requires full shade; '**Variegata**', leaves boldly margined in yellow. Zones 4–10.

Liriope spicata

☼/◐ ❋ ↔ 18 in (45 cm) ↑ 10 in (25 cm)

From China and Vietnam. Drought-tolerant evergreen ground cover. Leaves glossy, dark, dense, mat-forming. Pale lavender flowers in late summer. '**Silver Dragon**', compact, to about 8 in (20 cm) tall, narrow dark leaves silver striped, pale purple flowers. Zones 5–10.

LITCHI

Genus in the soapberry (Sapindaceae) family of just one species, from southern China and Southeast Asia. Evergreen tree. Leaves are pinnate, with up to 8 oblong leaflets. Insignificant greenish white flowers are borne in large panicles in the upper leaf axils. Globular fruit contains a large seed enclosed in an edible juicy translucent white aril inside a thin hard skin.
CULTIVATION: Needs warm humid weather and high rainfall for vegetative growth but a cool dry spell to induce flowering, followed by warmth and humidity to ensure pollination. Hot dry winds are harmful at any time. Deep moist soil, regular watering, and protection from wind and cold provide ideal growing conditions. Remove non-fruiting flower panicles at harvest. Fruit turns bright red when ripe and is harvested immediately. Propagate by air-layering or grafting.

Litchi chinensis

LYCHEE

☼ ◖ ↔ 15 ft (4.5 m) ↑ 40 ft (12 m)

Spreading tree, with a thick canopy of dark green leaves reaching to the ground. Flowers in long panicles at branch tips, male and female flowers in the same panicle. Fruits round, about 1½ in (35 mm) in diameter, turning red when ripe. Zones 10–11.

LITHOCARPUS

Genus of about 300 oak-like evergreen trees in the beech (Fagaceae) family found on mountain slopes of East and Southeast Asia and New Guinea, with one species from western USA. Leathery leaves spirally arranged but crowded toward the ends of seasonal growths, smooth-edged or toothed. Tiny flowers are borne on stiff catkins near branch tips in spring, females close to catkin bases, males above. Seeds (acorns) mature in the second year. *Lithocarpus* differs from *Quercus* in that the male catkins are erect rather than pendulous and the acorns are crowded onto spikes.
CULTIVATION: Most enjoy cool, moist conditions. Plant in moderately fertile acid to neutral soil in full sun or part-shade. Shelter from cold drying winds in cooler climates. Propagate from seed, sown in autumn.

Lithocarpus densiflorus

TANBARK OAK

☼ ❋ ↔ 40 ft (12 m) ↑ 100 ft (30 m)

From northern California and southern Oregon, USA. Smaller in open positions. Bark thick, furrowed, red-brown. Young shoots woolly white; leaves stiff, leathery, toothed, prominently veined, with rusty hairs on the undersides, turning a leaden hue with age. Tiny whitish male flowers. Egg-shaped acorns. *L. d.* **var.** *echinoides*, to 10 ft (3 m) high, leaves smaller, less toothed, than species. Zones 7–9.

Litchi chinensis

Lithocarpus densiflorus var. *echinoides*

LITHODORA

Genus in the borage (Boraginaceae) family of 7 species of low hairy shrubs or subshrubs, native to western and southern Europe, North Africa, and Asia Minor. Plentiful, deep dark green, simple leaves are about 1 in (25 mm) long and evergreen in most conditions when grown within the zone range, though they are susceptible to frost burn. Covered with many small vibrant blue or purple flowers in late spring or early summer. Low-growing habit makes them ideal for ground covers, rockeries or at the front of borders.
CULTIVATION: Grow in well-drained acid soil in full sun to partial shade; can become leggy in too much shade. Propagate from seed in spring or from tip cuttings in mid- to late summer.

Lithodora diffusa

syn. *Lithospermum diffusum*
🌣/🌣 ❄ ↔ 24–36 in (60–90 cm)
↕ 6–12 in (15–30 cm)

From France, Spain, and Portugal. Creeping plant with green linear leaves and blue flowers in mid-spring–early summer. With age, it tends to cease producing foliage and flowers in the center. 'Grace Ward', low-creeping form, bright azure flowers; 'Heavenly Blue' ★, petals edged with brilliant white; 'Star', petals edged with clear white, giving them a starry appearance. Zones 7–9.

Lithodora oleifolia

🌣 ❄ ↔ 24–36 in (60–90 cm)
↕ 6–12 in (15–30 cm)

From the eastern Pyrenees. Olive green foliage; pale blue to purplish flowers. Lime-tolerant species. Zones 7–9.

LITHOPS

LIVING STONES

This genus of 36 species of extreme succulents from the drier parts of southern Africa belongs to the ice-plant (Aizoaceae) family. Compact plants sunk into the soil, comprising a solitary or repeatedly branched shoot. Each shoot consists for most of the year of only 2 leaves, fused into a cone with a flat or domed top marked with lines, dots, or translucent "windows,"

which camouflages the plants in their pebbly surroundings, reducing predation by animals. In areas of high light intensity, the plants of some species also have protective layers of calcium oxalate. The appearance of a single (rarely 2 or more) yellow or white flower through a fissure on top of the plant ends the season's growth; a new shoot develops in the axil of one or both leaves. The new shoots draw water from the old leaves, which remain around them as tough withered sheaths. Many species are highly variable in leaf coloration and markings; almost all species and varieties, as well as some hybrids, are in cultivation.
CULTIVATION: Can be grown in any well-drained compost of low fertility, but generally thrive best in sandy or gritty loam. Keep dry through winter; water sparingly in growing season from summer to early autumn (when they flower), starting only when the old pair of leaves has almost completely shriveled. Best grown under cover even in warm regions, in a large pot for their large root system. Can be grown with much of the plant above the soil, as opposed to their natural habitat, where only the uppersurface is exposed. Best raised from seed; can also be divided.

Lithops aucampiae

🌣 ✂ ↔ 6 in (15 cm)
↕ ½–2 in (12–50 mm)

From South Africa. Clumping species. Pairs of unequal, fleshy, reddish brown leaves, to 2 in (5 cm) wide, uppersurface flat with darker markings and dark green translucent "window." Yellow flowers, opening in sunlight, in early autumn. Numerous named varieties. *L. a.* 'Betty's Beryl', yellowish green uppersurface, olive panel, white flowers;

Lithodora diffusa 'Star'

'Storm's Snowcap', pale ginger to sandy brown face marked with darker brown, white flowers. Zones 9–11.

Lithops bromfieldii

🌣 ✂ ↔ 6–8 in (15–20 cm)
↕ ¾–1½ in (20–35 mm)

From South Africa. Variable, stone-like, clumping species. Equal pairs of fleshy, egg-shaped, brown leaves forming a body 2–4 in (5–10 cm) in diameter, uppersurface slightly convex, kidney-shaped, with dark green windows, red dots and lines, and a fissure across the center. Yellow flowers occur in the late summer to early autumn. Many varieties of this species are recognized. *L. b.* var. *insularis*, concave face, and large pitted dots in a loose network of bronze-green markings; 'Sulphurea', dull mustard uppersurface marked with gray-green. Zones 9–11.

Lithops karasmontana

🌣 ✂ ↔ 4–8 in (10–20 cm)
↕ ¾–1¼ in (2–3 cm)

From Namibia. Highly variable species. Pairs of brown to brownish yellow leaves, uppersurface convex with darker marks and brownish pits and wrinkles, elliptical to kidney-shaped face, dark brown panel with fine lines on surface, forming body 1¼–1½ in (25–35 mm) across. White flowers in late summer–early autumn. *L. k.* subsp. *bella*, gray to buff body, convex face, dull olive panel; *L. k.* var. *lericheana*, buff body, ½–¾ in (12–18 mm) across, rounded

pinkish face, olive green markings; *L. k.* var. *tischeri*, body ¾–1 in (18–25 mm) across, kidney-shaped face, dark olive to chocolate panel. Zones 9–11.

Lithops lesliei

🌣 ✂ ↔ 4–8 in (10–20 cm)
↕ 1¼–2 in (3–5 cm)

From South Africa. Egg-shaped, forming clumps 4 in (10 cm) or more wide. Pairs of thick, gray-green to buff or light velvet brown leaves forming body ¾–1¾ in (20–45 mm) across, top light reddish brown, dark brown mottling. Yellow flowers, summer–early autumn. Variable species; many subspecies and varieties have been distinguished. *L. l.* 'Albiflora', uppersurface of lobes buff marked with olive, white flowers; 'Albinica', pale gold face, panel dull olive, finely marked, white flowers; 'Storm's Albinigold', similar to *L. l.* 'Albinica', yellow flowers. Zones 9–11.

Lithops marmorata

🌣 ✂ ↔ 4–6 in (10–15 cm)
↕ ¾–1¼ in (18–30 mm)

From South Africa. Clump-forming. Unequal pairs of swollen, fleshy, pale gray-green leaves, uppersurface convex with dark gray marks, forming a body 1–1¼ in (25–30 mm) wide, narrowly kidney-shaped face, translucent dark gray or gray-green panel marked with jagged edges. White flowers, summer–early autumn. *L. m.* var. *elisae*, buff or beige body, panel markings resembling a pattern of veins. Zones 9–11.

Lithodora oleifolia

Lithops aucampiae

L. b. var. *insularis* 'Sulphurea'

Lithops karasmontana species

Lithops lesliei

Lithops marmorata

Lithops meyeri

Lithops olivacea

Lithops optica 'Rubra'

Lithops otzeniana

Lithops pseudotruncatella

Lithops meyeri

☀ ❄ ↔ 3–6 in (8–15 cm)
↑ ¾–1¼ in (18–30 mm)

From South Africa. Wrinkled pale gray body, ¾–1¼ in (18–30 mm) in diameter, with narrowly kidney-shaped face, darker translucent panel. Yellow flowers with a white center. Zones 9–11.

Lithops olivacea

☀ ❄ ↔ 4–8 in (10–20 cm)
↑ ¾–3 in (18 mm–8 cm)

Native to South Africa. Egg-shaped species forming clumps 6 in (15 cm) or more in diameter. Pairs of pale gray or beige to dark olive green leaves, uppersurface convex, kidney-shaped, with translucent olive window. The solitary yellow flowers with a white center appear in late summer–autumn. Zones 9–11.

Lithops optica

☀ ❄ ↔ 2–3 in (5–8 cm)
↑ ¾–1¼ in (18–30 mm)

From Namibia. Stone-shaped. Reddish buds, reddish-tinged white flowers. Pairs of gray-green to dove gray leaves form body like a broad bean, fissure across center, kidney-shaped to elliptic face with blue-green translucent panel. 'Rubra' (syns *L. o.* subsp. *rubra, L. rubra,*), dull ruby red body lobes, darker unmarked panel. Zones 9–11.

Lithops otzeniana

☀ ❄ ↔ 4–8 in (10–20 cm)
↑ ¾–1¼ in (18–30 mm)

From South Africa. Forming clumps 6 in (15 cm) or more across. Paired grayish olive leaves, uppersurface convex with semi-translucent windows and light border, forming stone-shaped body with central fissure. Yellow flowers with white center in late summer–early autumn. '**Aquamarine**', gray-green body with dark blue-green panel. Zones 9–11.

Lithops pseudotruncatella

☀ ❄ ↔ 3–6 in (8–15 cm)
↑ ¾–1¼ in (18–30 mm)

From Namibia. Variable egg-shaped, forming clumps to 4 in (10 cm) across. Pairs of fleshy pale gray or blue to lilac leaves, darker marks on convex uppersurfaces. Yellow flowers, summer–early autumn. *L. p.* subsp. *archerae*, kidney-shaped pale gray face, darker center, marginal red dots and dashes; *L. p.* subsp. *dendritic*, gray face with radiating fine markings; *L. p.* subsp. *groendrayensis*, pale gray body, elliptic to kidney-shaped face, blue-gray center, scattered fine red dots; *L. p.* subsp. *volkii*, pale milky gray body, unequal lobes, faint marbling or dots. *L. p.* var. *elisabethae*, gray body, dark gray markings, bright red terminal dashes. *L. p.* var. *pulmonuncula*, unequal gray leaves, dark green and red marks on uppersurfaces; *L. p.* var. *riehmerae*, milky gray body with fine, moss-like, olive patterning. Zones 9–11.

Lithops schwantesii

☀ ❄ ↔ 3–6 in (8–15 cm)
↑ ¾–1¼ in (18–30 mm)

From Namibia. Very variable egg-shaped species forming clumps to 4 in

Lithops schwantesii

(10 cm) across. Pairs of dark gray or dull buff leaves, uppersurface flat or convex, with sunken dark red or blue lines or dots, forming oblong to kidney-shaped body with olive gray panel marked with cinnamon lines. Yellow flowers in late summer–early autumn. *L. s.* subsp. *gebseri*, gray to tan body, network of reddish brown lines; *L. s.* subsp. *steineckeana*, grayish white body, semi-circular face, with grayish green dots; *L. s.* subsp. *terricolor*, buff to tan body, oblong to kidney-shaped face spotted with olive or mid-green, yellow flowers, sometimes with a white center. *L. s.* var. *marthae*, fawn to gray body, gray panel etched with ocher; *L. s.* var. *rugosa*, gray-buff to pale lilac body, network of brown lines; *L. s.* var. *urikosensis*, fawn body with a deep fissure and covered with fine burnt sienna lines. Zones 9–11.

LIVISTONA

Some 30 species of medium and tall palms in the family Arecaceae. Found naturally in tropical and subtropical Australia and Southeast Asia in a wide range of habitats, from swamps and woodlands to inland gorges, often in extensive colonies. They have large fan-shaped fronds with long stalks armed with strong prickles. Cream to yellow flowers are borne in long-branched clusters among the foliage in winter or spring. The fruits are spherical to ovoid, usually blue-black, each containing a single seed enclosed in a thin oily flesh.
CULTIVATION: These handsome fan palms make fine street trees or specimen plants for gardens. In cooler areas may be grown in deep pots in an intermediate greenhouse or conservatory.

Livistona australis, palm tree on left

Livistona decipiens

One of the easiest of the palms to grow, they prefer well-drained, neutral to acid, fertile soil but will adapt to a variety of soil types. They should be given a shady site when young. Propagate from seed in spring or summer.

Livistona australis ★

CABBAGE PALM, CABBAGE TREE PALM

☼ ◗ ↔ 15 ft (4.5 m) ↑ 80 ft (24 m)

From low, moist, coastal regions of eastern Australia. Widely cultivated fan palm with dense crown of glossy fan-shaped fronds and ringed gray to grayish brown trunk. Clusters of yellow to cream flowers in late winter. Dull purple-black globular fruit. Zones 9–11.

Livistona decipiens

RIBBON FAN PALM, WEEPING CABBAGE PALM

☼ ◗ ↔ 8 ft (2.4 m) ↑ 50 ft (15 m)

From tropical and subtropical coastal Queensland. Tall attractive fan palm with ringed brown trunk turning gray at maturity. Large glossy green fronds deeply divided into pendulous ribbon-like segments radiating in many planes; stalks strongly armed. Very small yellow flowers in spring. Fruit globular, glossy, black when ripe. Zones 10–12.

Livistona rotundifolia

Livistona humilis, in the wild, Northern Territory, Australia

Livistona humilis

SAND PALM

☼ ✻ ↔ 3–7 ft (0.9–2 m) ↑ 8–20 ft (2.4–6 m)

From far north of Australia's Northern Territory. Slender dark brown to black trunk; sparse crown of small glossy green fronds, paler beneath. Clusters of yellow flowers in summer–autumn. Glossy purple-black fruit. Larger trees impossible to transplant. Zones 11–12.

Livistona mariae

CENTRAL AUSTRALIAN CABBAGE PALM, RED-LEAFED PALM

☼ ◗ ↔ 10 ft (3 m) ↑ 50–60 ft (15–18 m)

From Palm Valley in the arid center of central Australia; rare in the wild. Pale to dark gray trunk; rounded crown of shiny, gray-green, fan-shaped fronds. Creamy to greenish yellow flowers. Dark brown-black fruit. Zones 9–11.

Livistona muelleri

CAPE YORK FAN PALM, DWARF FAN PALM

☼ ✻ ↔ 10 ft (3 m) ↑ 10–20 ft (3–6 m)

From tropical northeastern Australia and New Guinea; very slow-growing,

Livistona nitida, in the wild, Carnarvon National Park, Queensland, Australia

rarely cultivated. Trunk covered with the brown fibrous bases of old leaf stalks; stiff, circular, fan-shaped fronds, glossy dark green above, and gray-green beneath. Clusters of small yellow flowers followed by blue-black fruit. Zones 11–12.

Livistona nitida

DAWSON RIVER FAN PALM

☼ ◗ ↔ 15 ft (4.5 m) ↑ 60 ft (18 m)

From a limited area of southeastern Queensland, Australia, growing along river banks and in sandstone gorges inland from the coast; only recently distinguished from *L. australis* by its longer, more deeply divided, fronds and brilliantly glossy black fruit. Vigorous grower. Zones 9–12.

Livistona rotundifolia ★

FOOTSTOOL PALM

☼ ✻ ↔ 15 ft (4.5 m) ↑ 80 ft (24 m)

Native to eastern Indonesia, Malaysian Borneo, and the Philippines. Distinctive, large, glossy, circular fronds on the young plants give the common name. Smooth, slender, gray trunk;

moderately dense crown. Produces yellow flowers. Scarlet fruit turning black when ripe. Zones 11–12.

Livistona victoriae

VICTORIA RIVER FAN PALM

☼ ✻ ↔ 10 ft (3 m) ↑ 40 ft (12 m)

Confined in the wild to middle catchments of the Victoria and Ord Rivers in northwestern Australia; very numerous in sandstone ravines. Handsome palm with compact crown of stiff blue-gray fronds. Short panicles of cream flowers in autumn. Black fruit in winter. Zones 10–12.

LOBELIA

While the small mounding annuals often seen edging flower borders are well known, *Lobelia* is a large, enormously variable, and widespread genus of the bellflower (Campanulaceae) family, encompassing over 350 species of annuals, perennials, and shrubs, including some amazing megaherbs from the mountains of East Africa. Other than the annuals, with their massed summer display of blue, white, or pink flowers, cultivated lobelias are mainly perennials from the Americas, most of which form a basal clump of simple leaves, from which emerge upright flower stems bearing spikes of tubular 5-lobed flowers, the lower 3 lobes enlarged. *Lobelia* species were used medicinally by Native Americans; the Cherokee of the eighteenth century reputedly had an infallible lobelia-based cure for syphilis.

CULTIVATION: Requirements vary but most *Lobelia* species prefer a sunny position with moist well-drained soil. Tall types may need staking. Propagate the annuals from seed sown in spring and the perennials by division or from basal cuttings.

Livistona mariae, in the wild, Finke Gorge National Park, Northern Territory, Australia

Livistona victoriae, in the wild, Australia

Lobelia cardinalis

Lobelia × gerardii 'Tania'

Lobelia tupa

Lobelia aberdarica

Lobelia erinus

Lobelia aberdarica

☼ ❄ ↔ 10 ft (3 m) ↕ 8 ft (2.4 m)

From higher volcanic massifs of Kenya and Uganda. Tree-like, narrowly columnar. Narrow leaves, to 15 in (38 cm) long, crowded below the stunning flowerhead, an erect pyramidal panicle, to 6 ft (1.8 m) long, with many blue to white flowers. Zones 9–11.

Lobelia cardinalis

CARDINAL FLOWER

☼/❄ ❄ ↔ 12–16 in (30–40 cm) ↕ 36 in (90 cm)

North American short-lived perennial forming a clump of upright stems with often red-tinted, narrow, pointed oval to lance-shaped leaves, to 4 in (10 cm) long. Long spikes of bright red flowers, to over 1 in (25 mm) wide, from summer to autumn. Zones 3–9.

Lobelia erinus

BEDDING LOBELIA, EDGING LOBELIA

☼/❄ ❄ ↔ 12–16 in (30–40 cm) ↕ 8 in (20 cm)

South African, small, long-flowering perennial usually treated as an annual. Dense mounding habit; fine stems; small, often purple-tinted, deep green leaves, roughly oval, toothed. Masses of small pale-centered flowers, blue, mauve, purple. Seedling strains differ mainly in size and growth habit. **Cascade Series**, for hanging baskets; '**Kathleen Mallard**', mounding, with deep blue double flowers; '**Mrs.**

Clibran', mounding, with dark blue flowers; **Palace Series**, dwarf and heavy flowering, for borders and pots; '**Periwinkle Blue**', trailer, bright blue flowers; **Regatta Series**, trailer, mixed colors. Zones 9–11.

Lobelia × gerardii

☼/❄ ❄ ↔ 20–24 in (50–60 cm) ↕ 60 in (150 cm)

Garden hybrid between *L. cardinalis* and *L. siphilitica*. Vigorous perennial forming a clump of upright stems with pointed oval to elliptical leaves, to 6 in (15 cm) long, mainly crowded at base. Large heads of white-marked pink or violet to purple flowers. '**Tania**', red-tinted foliage, deep magenta flowers; '**Vedrariensis**', red-tinted foliage, purple flowers. Zones 7–10.

Lobelia laxiflora

TORCH LOBELIA

☼/❄ ❄ ↔ 4 ft (1.2 m) ↕ 3 ft (0.9 m)

From southern Arizona, USA, through the Mexican highlands to Colombia, occurring in oak and pine forests. Variable species with shrubby habit. Leaves pointed, lance-shaped. Long-stalked tubular flowers, scarlet with yellow tips, in summer. Zones 9–11.

Lobelia richardsonii

☼/❄ ✈ ↔ 24–36 in (60–90 cm) ↕ 6 in (15 cm)

Of unknown origin, possibly only a form of *L. erinus*; plants sold as

L. ricardii are possibly the same. Trailing perennial with wiry stems, small purple-tinted leaves, bright blue flowers in spring–autumn. May be grown as an annual. **Royal Jewels** seed mix, flowers in blue, mauve, and purple-red shades. Zones 10–11.

Lobelia siphilitica

BLUE CARDINAL FLOWER

☼/❄ ❄ ↔ 16 in (40 cm) ↕ 24 in (60 cm)

From eastern USA. Bushy perennial with mainly basal foliage. Leaves pointed oval to lance-shaped, toothed, to 4 in (10 cm) long. Flower stems upright, with long spikes of deep blue flowers, to 1 in (25 mm) across, in summer–autumn. Zones 5–9.

Lobelia telekii

GIANT LOBELIA

☼ ❄ ↔ 36 in (90 cm) ↕ 5–8 ft (1.5–2.4 m)

One of the giant lobelias of the East African mountains, endemic to Mt Kenya at altitudes of 10,000–14,000 ft (3,000–4,200 m), growing on rocky treeless slopes with giant senecios (*Dendrosenecio*). Unbranched, with dense basal rosette of narrow, tapering,

green leaves, 12–18 in (30–40 cm) long. After years of growth produces an erect cylindrical inflorescence, to 6 ft (1.8 m) tall, clothed in drooping bristly bracts almost concealing the numerous purple flowers. Hardly known in cultivation. Zones 8–9.

Lobelia tupa

☼ ❄ ↔ 3 ft (0.9 m) ↕ 6 ft (1.8 m)

From Chile, growing in sandy hills near the sea. Attractive leaves lightly felted, grayish green. Terminal spikes of scarlet or brick-red flowers in summer–autumn. Zones 8–10.

Lobelia Hybrid Cultivars

☼/❄ ❄ ↔ 16–20 in (40–50 cm) ↕ 48 in (120 cm)

Most involve the North American species *L. cardinalis*, *L. fulgens*, and *L. siphilitica*. Clump of upright leafy stems with dense basal clump of narrow lance-shaped leaves, to 6 in (15 cm) long, dark green, often red-tinted. Long spikes of lavender, purple, or red flowers from early summer. '**Bee's Flame**', bronze foliage, red flowers; '**Cherry Ripe**', dark green leaves, red

Lobelia laxiflora

Lobelia telekii, in the wild, Kenya

flowers; **Compliment Series**, seedling strain, with blue or red flowers; '**Fan Scarlet**', green foliage and purple-red flowers; '**Queen Victoria**' ★, deep red foliage and stems, bright red flowers; '**Russian Princess**', red-tinted foliage, purple flowers. Zones 3–10.

LOBULARIA

ALYSSUM, BEDDING ALYSSUM

Genus of 5 species of annuals and perennials in the cabbage (Brassicaceae) family from the northern temperate zones. Small mounding plants with simple linear to lance-shaped leaves, sometimes with fine silvery hairs. Tiny, often sweet-scented flowers in warmer months, in rounded heads. Garden forms in white and shades of primrose, apricot, mauve, and purple. CULTIVATION: Hardy, easily grown in sun in light free-draining soil. Water to encourage flowering, but plants often remain more compact and less likely to fall apart from center if kept dry. Propagate from seed, or the seed may be broadcast; often self-sows.

Lobularia maritima

BEDDING ALYSSUM

☀ ❄ ↔ 8–16 in (20–40 cm)
↑ 10 in (25 cm)

Widespread in northern temperate zones. Annual or short-lived perennial

Lobularia maritima, Easter Bonnet Series, 'Easter Bonnet Lavender'

Lobularia maritima, Easter Bonnet Series, 'Easter Bonnet Deep Rose'

Lobularia maritima

Lomandra banksii

forming a compact mound of narrow dull green leaves, about 1 in (25 mm) long. Tiny flowers in massed rounded heads. Species usually white- to cream-flowered; garden forms in several sizes and colors. '**Carpet of Snow**', to 4 in (10 cm) high, pure white flowers; **Easter Bonnet Series**, to 6 in (15 cm) high, compact mounding habit, in white and pink to purple shades; '**Snow Crystals**', to 8–10 in (20–25 cm) high, large white flowers. Zones 7–10.

LOLIUM

RYEGRASS

This genus comprises about 8 species of annual and perennial grasses (family Poaceae), native to temperate areas of Eurasia and northern Africa. They have smooth, erect, or shortly creeping rhizomes and narrow, flat or folded, strap-like leaves with cylindrical sheaths. They bear thin unbranched flowering spikes with 2 rows of flattened spikelets usually pressed tightly against the main axis, each spikelet bearing 5 to 9 green

Lobularia maritima, Easter Bonnet Series, mixed

Lobularia maritima 'Snow Crystals'

Lomandra longifolia, in the wild, Washpool National Park, New South Wales, Australia

florets with yellow anthers. Ryegrasses are valued for pasture and fodder, and some species are used as lawn grasses, while some can be troublesome weeds. They shed large quantities of very fine pollen; close mowing of a lawn may prevent this problem.
CULTIVATION: Adaptable to most well-drained soils in an open sunny position, though when used for lawns they can tolerate a certain amount of shade. In regions of light winter frost they are useful for lawns that remain green through winter. Propagate from seed.

Lolium multiflorum

ANNUAL RYEGRASS

☀ ❄ ↔ 10–12 in (25–30 cm)
↑ 24–36 in (60–90 cm)

Annual grass with fibrous root system. Stems are often red-tinged; leaves are bright green, smooth, tapered, sharply pointed, with the midrib prominent, and margins slightly rough. Flower-head is a spike with 5 to 38 spikelets attached edgewise. Zones 6–9.

Lolium perenne

ENGLISH RYEGRASS, PERENNIAL RYEGRASS

☀ ❄ ↔ 10–18 in (25–45 cm)
↑ 6–24 in (15–60 cm)

From temperate Eurasia and North Africa. Perennial grass distributed throughout the world as a lawn and pasture grass. '**Derby**', early-flowering turf grass; '**Loretta**', permanent and hard-wearing, light green turf grass; '**Manhattan**', dark green fine-textured lawn and playing field turf; '**Pennfine**', dense fine-textured lawn turf; '**Yorktown**', low-growing, dark green, dense, fine-textured turf grass. Zones 5–10.

LOMANDRA

MAT-RUSHES

The 50 species in this genus in the grass-tree (Xanthorrhoeaceae) family are, with a few exceptions, confined to

Australia. They are evergreen, clump-forming, rush-like perennials or sub-shrubs with tiny flowers produced in spikes or panicles usually held low down amongst the leaves. The flowers are usually creamy white to lemon yellow, and the panicles are not particularly showy. Mat-rushes are used for soil stabilization, providing a habitat for small animals such as lizards.
CULTIVATION: Once cultivated only by native plant enthusiasts, mat-rushes (mainly *L. longifolia*) are often used in Australia as roadside plantings owing to their drought tolerance. Because dead foliage builds up in the clumps, prune to the ground every so often, or set fire to in areas where this is feasible. Propagate from fresh seed or by dividing established clumps.

Lomandra banksii

CLUMPING MAT-RUSH, MAY RUSH

☀ ⚦ ↔ 2–4 ft (0.6–1.2 m)
↑ 3–5 ft (0.9–1.5 m)

From northeastern Australia, New Guinea, and New Caledonia. Unusual for its aboveground, often branched, stems with 2 rows of spreading, strap-like, tough leaves, about 12 in (30 cm) long and ½ in (12 mm) wide, the old leaf-bases often persisting. Insignificant cream flowers in summer. Zones 10–12.

Lomandra longifolia

BASKET GRASS, SPINY-HEADED MAT-RUSH

☀ ❄ ↔ 30–36 in (75–90 cm)
↑ 20–40 in (50–100 cm)

From Eastern Australia. Sedge-like perennial forming large tussocks. Leaves stiff, flat, with several points at each tip. Narrow panicle of dense clusters of small, fragrant, creamy yellow flowers with straw-colored spiny bracts, held in foliage, in the spring to early summer. Widely grown for ornament and soil stabilization. Zones 8–12.

Lomatia ferruginea

Lomatia polymorpha

Lomatium bradshawii

Lomatia ilicifolia

LOMATIA

There are 12 species in this genus of the protea (Proteaceae) family, 9 from eastern Australia and 3 from South America. All are shrubs or small trees, with a few reaching 60 ft (18 m) in rainforests. Leaves vary from smooth-edged to toothed to deeply divided. Small white, cream, yellow, or rarely pink flowers are borne on spikes in the leaf axils or at branch tips. Fruit is leathery with 2 rows of winged seeds. CULTIVATION: Some require a sheltered, moist, frost-free position, others tolerate some dryness and some frosts. Generally, well-drained acid soils give best results. Propagate from fresh seed or from cuttings taken in mid-summer from young growth that is not too soft.

Lomatia ferruginea

☼ ❅ ↔ 15 ft (4.5 m) ↑ 30 ft (9 m)

From rainforests of Argentina and Chile. Evergreen tree with divided, dark green, fern-like leaves on brown felty stems. Clusters of red and yellow flowers, in leaf axils, in summer. Cultivated in warmer parts of the UK since the mid-nineteenth century. Zones 9–10.

Lomatia ilicifolia

HOLLY-LEAFED LOMATIA

☼ ❅ ↔ 5 ft (1.5 m) ↑ 3–15 ft (1.8–4.5 m)

From New South Wales, Australia. Densely foliaged shrub able to resprout from woody rootstock after fires, notable for its scalloped-edged holly-like leaves. Prolific display of small cream flowers in summer. Zones 9–10.

Lomatia polymorpha

☼ ❅ ↔ 5 ft (1.5 m) ↑ 6–12 ft (1.8–3.5 m)

Endemic to Tasmania, Australia, from rainforests and subalpine areas. Leaves narrow, deep green to yellow-green, to 4 in (10 cm) long. Showy heads of relatively large cream flowers in late spring. Zones 8–10.

LOMATIUM

Genus of the carrot (Apiaceae) family, comprising about 75 species of carrot-like perennials from central, western, and southern North America. They have thick deep taproots or tubers, basal stalked leaves that are mostly highly dissected, and small yellow to red or purplish flowers in a dense compound umbel terminating a single leafless flowering stem. The fruit is small, dry, flattened, and aromatic, typical of the family. The roots of some species were used as food by Native Americans, either fresh or dried; the young leaves and fruit can also be eaten. CULTIVATION: These plants are rarely cultivated but should present few problems in any sunny open spot with well-drained, not too rich soil; treat like parsnips. Propagate from seed.

Lomatium bradshawii

BRADSHAW'S LOMATIUM

☼ ❅ ↔ 6–12 in (15–30 cm) ↑ 10–20 in (25–50 cm)

Confined in the wild to the Willamette Valley, western Oregon, USA; now rare. Erect perennial, large tap-root; leaves divided into fine, almost thread-like, segments. Compound umbels of small yellow flowers with green bracts, in spring. Fruit is small, with a thickened corky outer margin. Zones 7–9.

LONCHOCARPUS

This genus belonging to the pea-family subfamily of the legume (Fabaceae) family comprises some 150 species of deciduous and evergreen trees and vines. It is chiefly found in tropical America, Africa, and Australia. Some species resemble *Robinia*, although the fruit differs. They have elegant, alternate, pinnate leaves with an uneven number of leaflets and slightly scented pea-flowers in shades of white, pink, and purple. The fruit is a flat pod. Some species are commercially cultivated as a source of insecticide. CULTIVATION: Grown in tropical and subtropical regions for their elegant foliage and showy fragrant flowers, these plants are generally frost tender; mature specimens may tolerate the occasional temperature drop down to 25°F (−4°C). In temperate zones they may be grown in a large greenhouse. Although in the wild they may grow in a wide range of habitats, from swamps to dry plains, in cultivation they prefer dryish soils and full sun. Propagate from seed.

Lonchocarpus violaceus

☼ ✤ ↔ 10 ft (3 m) ↑ 25 ft (8 m)

From the West Indies. A small tree with dark green pinnate leaves; 3 to 5 pairs of leaflets. Erect racemes of fragrant flowers, corolla white outside, and pale purple or pink inside. The fruit is lance-shaped, 2 in (5 cm) long. Zones 10–12.

LONICERA

HONEYSUCKLE

Honeysuckles, belonging to the woodbine (Caprifoliaceae) family, are often regarded as somewhat untidy second-class climbers, but in the right place they are among the easiest and most rewarding plants. Occurring widely throughout the Northern Hemisphere though chiefly in temperate Eurasia, the 180-odd species in the genus encompass climbers, ground covers, and shrubs, both evergreen and deciduous, most of them very hardy. The foliage usually consists of opposite pairs of smooth-edged leaves, often somewhat leathery. The flowers, sometimes highly fragrant, vary in size; most are tubular at the base but divided at the mouth into 5 petals frequently arranged in 2 lips, an upper lip of 4 fused petals and a lower lip of a single petal. The fruit is an ornamental berry relished by birds, usually backed or partially enclosed by bract-like calyces that may color slightly. CULTIVATION: Although honeysuckles are tough adaptable plants that thrive in most conditions, they are generally best grown in rich, moist, humus-enriched, well-drained soil in full sun to partial shade. They can be raised from seed, though most are easily grown from layers or half-hardened cuttings. Cultivars and hybrids must be propagated from cuttings.

Lonicera × brownii

SCARLET TRUMPET HONEYSUCKLE

☼ ❅ ↔ 8 ft (2.4 m) ↑ 10 ft (3 m)

Garden-raised deciduous or semi-deciduous *L. sempervirens* × *L. hirsuta* hybrid, resembling *L. sempervirens*, with paired blue-green leaves. Whorls of pale orange to red unscented flowers in the late spring to early summer. 'Dropmore Scarlet', strong growing, with larger leaves, long-tubed bright red flowers in mid-summer–autumn. Zones 5–9.

Lonchocarpus violaceus

Lonicera × *brownii* 'Dropmore Scarlet'

Lonicera etrusca 'Superba'

Lonicera chaetocarpa

Lonicera caprifolium

ITALIAN HONEYSUCKLE

☀ ❄ ↔ 10 ft (3 m) ↑ 20 ft (6 m)

From Europe and western Asia. Usually seen as climber but can be grown as ground cover. Oval leaves in pairs. Whorls of very fragrant, pink-tinted creamy yellow flowers, to 2 in (5 cm) long, in spring–summer. Orange-red fruit. Zones 5–9.

Lonicera chaetocarpa

☀ ❄ ↔ 6 ft (1.8 m) ↑ 6 ft (1.8 m)

From China. Deciduous shrub. Young stems, also leaf undersides, bristly. Cream long-tubed flowers, single or in pairs, in summer. Red fruit backed by red-tinted calyces. Zones 5–9.

Lonicera etrusca

☀ ❄ ↔ 10 ft (3 m) ↑ 12 ft (3.5 m)

From the Mediterranean region. Scrambling semi-evergreen shrub or climber. Fused pairs of bright green or blue-green leaves with downy undersides. Whorls of fragrant flowers, cream with red tints, ageing to yellow, at branch tips, in summer–early autumn. '**Superba**', red young growth, many-flowered panicles opening cream, ageing to yellow-orange. Zones 7–10.

Lonicera fragrantissima

WINTER HONEYSUCKLE

☀ ❄ ↔ 8 ft (2.4 m) ↑ 6 ft (1.8 m)

From China. Shrubby, fragrant, evergreen or deciduous plant. Leaves dull green. Small, strongly scented, cream

flowers, borne in pairs in leaf axils along the arching twigs, in winter–spring. Red fruit. Zones 5–9.

Lonicera × heckrottii

☀ ❄ ↔ 6 ft (1.8 m) ↑ 15 ft (4.5 m)

Hybrid, possibly between *L. sempervirens* and *L.* × *americana*. A sprawling deciduous climber with paired oblong to elliptical leaves, purplish when young, maturing to blue-green. Whorls of yellow-throated deep pink flowers in late spring–summer. Red fruit. '**Gold Flame**', dark green leaves, purple-red flowers, which are bright yellow inside. Zones 5–9.

Lonicera involucrata

TWINBERRY

☀ ❄ ↔ 3 ft (0.9 m) ↑ 3 ft (0.9 m)

Found from Mexico through western USA to southern Canada. Deciduous shrub grown for its fruit, deep purple berries backed by large purple-red bracts. Leaves to 5 in (12 cm) long. Short-tubed, yellow to red, paired flowers in spring. Zones 4–10.

Lonicera × italica

☀/❄ ❄ ↔ 5–10 ft (1.5–3 m) ↑ 10 ft (3 m)

Evergreen vine with variegated leaves of pink, lime green, and cream. The spicy-scented, rose-purple, tubular flowers appear in mid-spring to mid-summer. Zones 5–9.

Lonicera maackii

Lonicera japonica

HALL'S HONEYSUCKLE, JAPANESE HONEYSUCKLE

☀/❄ ❄ ↔ 25 ft (8 m) ↑ 25–30 ft (8–9 m)

From Japan, Korea, and China. Vigorous, evergreen (semi-evergreen in cold climates), twining vine. Leaves oblong, dark green, slightly downy on both sides. Produces fragrant white to pale yellow flowers in early summer–late autumn, followed by black berries. Troublesome weed in southeastern USA, Australia, and New Zealand. '**Halliana**', oval bright green leaves, and very fragrant flowers changing from pure white to yellow. Zones 4–11.

Lonicera korolkowii

☀ ❄ ↔ 12 ft (3.5 m) ↑ 10 ft (3 m)

From the mountains of central Asia, Afghanistan, and Pakistan. This deciduous shrub has small leaves. Light pink flowers in appear in summer; followed by colorful red berries. '**Floribunda**' ★, ovate leaves, white flowers. Zones 5–9.

Lonicera ledebourii

☀ ❄ ↔ 8 ft (2.4 m) ↑ 6 ft (1.8 m)

From western USA. Deciduous shrub, similar to *L. involucrata*. Long narrow leaves with felty undersides. Orange-yellow flowers in summer. Heart-shaped bracts, reddening as the black berries mature. Zones 6–10.

Lonicera × *heckrottii* 'Gold Flame'

Lonicera maackii

☀ ❄ ↔ 15 ft (4.5 m) ↑ 15 ft (4.5 m)

Native to East Asia. A deciduous shrub with leaves 3 in (8 cm) long, purple-stemmed. Fragrant white flowers, ageing to yellow, are borne in spring–summer. Tiny dark red to black berries. Zones 2–9.

Lonicera nitida

syn. *Lonicera ligustrina* subsp. *yunnanensis*

BOX HONEYSUCKLE

☀ ❄ ↔ 10 ft (3 m) ↑ 12 ft (3.5 m)

From central and southwestern China. Widely grown, shrubby, evergreen honeysuckle. Leaves tiny, dark green, purple toned in winter. Small cream flowers in spring, rarely seen in some climatic zones. Purple-black berries. Dense bushy habit, responds well to pruning; used for hedging, topiary, and borders. Zones 7–10.

Lonicera nitida

Lonicera japonica

Lonicera korolkowii 'Floribunda'

Lonicera periclymenum
WOODBINE

☀ ❄ ↔ 8 ft (2.4 m) ↕ 12 ft (3.5 m)

From Eurasia. Twining, scrambling, deciduous or semi-evergreen shrub. Finely downy young leaves becoming smooth and glaucous when mature. Very fragrant pinkish red flowers with creamy yellow interiors, in whorls of 3 to 5 blooms, in summer. Red fruit. Can become invasive. '**Serotina**', narrow-leafed cultivar, red berries developing from flowers with purple exteriors. Zones 4–10.

Lonicera pileata

☀ ❄ ↔ 8 ft (2.4 m) ↕ 2 ft (0.6 m)

From China. Evergreen or semi-deciduous shrub, often prostrate, with neat mounding growth habit. Leaves to 1¼ in (30 mm) long, deep green, rhomboidal in shape. Very small cream flowers, in pairs. Light purple fruit. '**Moss Green**', low-growing, with bright green leaves. Zones 5–9.

Lonicera pileata 'Moss Green'

Lonicera × purpusii

Lonicera × purpusii

☀ ❄ ↔ 8 ft (2.4 m) ↕ 10 ft (3 m)

Hybrid between the winter-flowering *L. fragrantissima* and *L. standishii*; upright semi-deciduous shrub. Fragrant creamy white flowers, carried in clusters of 2 to 4, in winter–early spring. '**Winter Beauty**', strongly scented, with red berries. Zones 6–9.

Lonicera ruprechtiana

☀ ❄ ↔ 8 ft (2.4 m) ↕ 6–10 ft (1.8–3 m)

From northeastern Asia. Deciduous shrub; can scramble to 20 ft (6 m). Young stems downy; leaves pointed, ovate, to 4 in (10 cm) long. Pairs of ¾ in (18 mm) long white flowers, ageing to yellow, in spring–summer. Translucent red fruit. Zones 6–9.

Lonicera sempervirens
TRUMPET HONEYSUCKLE

☀/◐ ❄ ↔ 10 ft (3 m) ↕ 10–20 ft (3–6 m)

From eastern and southern USA. Deciduous twining vine with blue-green leaves; scarlet-orange trumpet-shaped blooms with yellow centers, borne on previous year's stems. '**Superba**', scarlet-orange to scarlet tubular flowers; '**Blanche Sandman**', semi-evergreen vine, rich orange-red tubular blooms in spring–summer. Zones 4–10.

Lonicera syringantha

☀ ❄ ↔ 7 ft (2 m) ↕ 10 ft (3 m)

From China and Tibet. Deciduous shrub with upright stems, graceful

Lonicera ruprechtiana

arching habit. Leaves noticeably blue tinted. Small, paired, fragrant, soft lilac flowers in spring–summer. Red berries. Zones 4–9.

Lonicera tatarica
TATARIAN HONEYSUCKLE

☀ ❄ ↔ 7 ft (2 m) ↕ 10 ft (3 m)

From central Asia and southern Russia. Deciduous shrub; parent of many hybrids and available in a wide range of cultivars. Leaves with blue-gray undersides. Flowers, in white and pink shades, in spring–summer. Pale orange to red fruit. Zones 3–9.

Lonicera × tellmanniana
REDGOLD HONEYSUCKLE, TELLMANN HONEYSUCKLE

☀/◐ ❄ ↔ 5 ft (1.5 m) ↕ 7–20 ft (2–6 m)

Deciduous, vigorous, twining climber with showy coppery gold flowers in late spring–summer. Zones 6–9.

LOPEZIA

Genus of about 20 sometimes woody annuals and perennials, from Mexico and Central America, belonging to the evening-primrose (Onagraceae) family. They have simple, usually toothed, alternate or opposite leaves and curious small flowers, usually in leafy racemes at the stem tips. Each flower has 2 narrow upper petals and 2 lower ones that are larger but narrowed into fine stalks (clawed) at the base and sometimes differently colored from the upper ones; all 4 petals may be upward-pointing and arranged in a fan-like form. The fruit is a small capsule. CULTIVATION: These plants are occasionally grown as garden annuals for their graceful intricate flowers. Plant in light well-drained soil in full sun; be careful to avoid overwatering. Propagate from seed.

Lopezia coronata
MOSQUITO FLOWER

☀ ❄ ↔ 10–20 in (25–50 cm) ↕ 8–18 in (20–45 cm)

Found on the north Mexican plateau. Bushy, erect or sprawling, annual or perennial. Leaves small, dark green, oval to sword-shaped. Small red to pink and white flowers, in leafy racemes, in spring–early summer. Zones 8–10.

LOPHOMYRTUS

This genus native to New Zealand belongs to the myrtle (Myrtaceae) family and is closely allied to *Myrtus* itself. It consists of 2 species of small evergreen trees or shrubs, which are grown primarily for their interesting foliage, though with age they also

Lonicera sempervirens

Lonicera tatarica

develop attractive dappled or streaked smooth bark. The species hybridize freely. A number of named cultivars are now placed in a group known as *L. × ralphii*.
CULTIVATION: Grow in full sun for best leaf coloration, in reasonably fertile well-drained soil. In cool-temperate climates they are best given a warm sheltered site and protection in winter. Prune for hedging or to maintain a dense shrubby form, or to a single trunk as a small tree. Species can be propagated from seed sown in spring but are usually propagated from half-hardened cuttings taken in autumn. *L. × ralphii* and its cultivars can only be propagated from cuttings.

Lophomyrtus bullata ★
RAMARAMA

☀ ◑ ↔ 8 ft (2.4 m) ↕ 8–12 ft (2.4–3.5 m)

Small tree. Leaves small, oval, with a puckered surface, greener in shade, developing bronzy purplish tones in the sun. Small fluffy cream flowers in summer. Dark reddish purple berries. Zones 9–10.

Lophomyrtus × ralphii

☀ ◑ ↔ 5 ft (1.5 m) ↕ 6 ft (1.8 m)

Hybrid with characteristics intermediate between the 2 parent species, *L. bullata* and *L. obcordata*. Leaves more rounded than those of *L. bullata* and much less puckered; flowers for a longer period over summer. '**Gloriosa**' (syn. *L. × ralphii* 'Variegata'), small,

Lopezia coronata

light green, rounded leaves variegated with cream and tinged pink; '**Indian Chief**', dark reddish brown leaves intensifying in color during the winter; '**Kathryn**', purplish red, glossy, oval leaves with a puckered surface; '**Pixie**', suitable for rock gardens, to 12 in (30 cm) tall, small bronze-green leaves, chocolate-purple when young. Zones 9–11.

LOPHOPHORA
PEYOTE

Native to Mexico and southern Texas, USA, the 2 species of small, spineless, low-growing, flattened spherical cacti with thickened tap roots that comprise this genus (family Cactaceae) are well known because of their long association with Native American religious and medicinal ceremonies. They contain the mind-altering drug mescaline, with the result that a considerable amount of pharmacological, botanic, and horticultural research has been carried out on them. The name derives from the Greek *lophos*, crest, and *phoreus*, bearer, referring to the tufts of white hair borne at the growing point and sometimes on the areoles of the plant.
CULTIVATION: These cacti are easy to grow in rich well-drained soil. They may be raised from seed, by division of mature clumps, or from cuttings dried out for a week or two. Withhold water in winter.

Lophophora diffusa
☼ ❄ ↔ 2–5 in (5–12 cm)
↕ ¾–3 in (18–80 mm)

Native to Mexico. Usually solitary but may form small clumps. Distinctly soft-stemmed, yellow-green, with flattened spherical stems and few or no ribs. Small bell-shaped flowers, yellowish white, occasionally pinkish, appear in summer. Tubular seed pods. Zones 9–11.

Lophostemon confertus

Lophophora williamsii
DEVIL'S ROOT, DUMPLING CACTUS, MESCAL BUTTON, PEYOTE, WHITE MULE
☼ ❄ ↔ 32–40 in (80–100 cm)
↕ ¾–2½ in (18–60 mm)

From Chihuahuan desert regions of Texas, USA, and northern Mexican States. Widespread variable species; its many common names reflect its narcotic effects. Often solitary but may form mats. Stems firm, gray-green; 5 to 15 well-defined ribs. Pink, pale pink, or occasionally red flowers in summer. Zones 9–11.

LOPHOSTEMON

This genus is a member of the myrtle (Myrtaceae) family, which includes such important plants as the eucalypts. Its 6 species of evergreen trees are native to Australia and New Guinea. The leaves are spirally arranged and crowded toward the end of the branchlets. The flowers, white, with 5 petals and 5 showy feather-like groups of fused stamens, are grouped in short cymes in the upper leaf axils. The fruit is a woody capsule like that of some *Eucalyptus* species, though *Lophostemon* is not closely related to *Eucalyptus*.

Loropetalum chinense

CULTIVATION: These trees are popular for street and park planting in warm climates. They should be planted in fertile free-draining soil. They will survive outdoors in regions with very light winter frosts in a warm sheltered site but in cool-temperate climates need greenhouse protection. Propagate from seed sown in spring or autumn. Variegated cultivars are propagated by budding or grafting.

Lophostemon confertus
syn. *Tristania conferta*
BRUSH BOX
☼ ❄ ↔ 30 ft (9 m) ↕ 130 ft (40 m)
Found in east-coastal Queensland and northeastern New South Wales, Australia. Densely foliaged tree with pinkish brown peeling bark. Leaves long-pointed, elliptical, dark green above, olive-green beneath. White flowers, 1 in (25 mm) across, with masses of fluffy stamens, in summer. Yields a valuable, very hard, timber. Zones 10–12.

LOROPETALUM

Botanists have yet to determine whether more species belonging to this genus exist, but currently it is treated as comprising a single species of evergreen dome-shaped shrub or small tree from the woodland regions of the Himalayas, China, and Japan. One of the witchhazel (Hamamelidaceae) family, it is grown for its distinctive flowers and its horizontal branching

Loropetalum chinense 'Plum Delight'

habit, which makes it easy to train as an espalier or bonsai. The leaves are alternate, simple, and smooth-edged, and the small flowers, borne in tight heads of 3 to 6 flowers in the leaf axils, each have 4 twisted strap-like petals. The fruit is a small nut-like capsule containing 2 seeds.
CULTIVATION: This trouble-free plant grows best in fertile, humus-enriched, well-drained soil in a position in full sun where its often widely branching habit can be fully appreciated. As it flowers on the last season's wood, prune after flowering, and only to enhance the shape. Propagate from cuttings taken in summer.

Loropetalum chinense
FRINGE FLOWER
☼ ❄ ↔ 8 ft (2.4 m) ↕ 6–15 ft (1.8–4.5 m)
Bushy shrub. Leaves small, dull green, oval. Slightly perfumed, creamy white, fringed flowerheads are borne in spring. The distinctively bronze-foliaged form *L. c.* f. *rubrum* has become popular with gardeners worldwide; sometimes sold as the cultivar '**Burgundy**', it has red new leaves and purple-pink flowers. *L. c.* '**Plum Delight**', purple-red foliage and flowers; and '**Sizzling Pink**', red spring foliage and bright pink flowers. Zones 8–11.

Lophomyrtus bullata

Lophomyrtus × *ralphii*

Lophophora williamsii

LOTUS

Genus of about 150 species of annuals, perennials, and both deciduous and evergreen subshrubs in the pea-flower subfamily of the legume (Fabaceae) family. They are found almost world-wide in open grasslands and rocky places; all but a few species are native to temperate regions of the Northern Hemisphere. The leaves are small and pinnate, often with only 4 or 5 leaflets and sometimes closely hairy, giving them a silvery appearance. The pea-flowers come in a range of colors, from white to yellow, pink, or red, and are borne singly or in clusters in the leaf axils. The most colorful are the several large-flowered species from the Canary Islands and Madeira, with yellow or red flowers adapted to polli-nation by birds. They are popular in garden borders, the trailing types are suited to hanging baskets or pots. CULTIVATION: Most species prefer well-drained soil in full sun. Propa-gate from seed or cuttings.

Lotus berthelotii

CORAL GEM, PARROT'S BEAK, PELICAN'S BEAK
☀ ✿ ↔ 3–6 ft (0.9–1.8 m) ↕ 8 in (20 cm)
From the Canary Islands. Popular, trailing, evergreen subshrub. Leaves silvery gray, with needle-like leaflets. Yellow-orange to red flowers, 1½ in (35 mm) long, in spring–summer. Zones 10–11.

Lotus formosissimus

BICOLORED LOTUS, COAST LOTUS, SEASIDE BIRD'S FOOT
☀ ✿ ↔ 18–36 in (45–90 cm)
↕ 8–20 in (20–50 cm)
From coastal California, USA, often occurring on seashores. Sprawling multi-stemmed perennial. Leaves are green and pinnate. Attractive fan-like heads of flowers, upper petal (stan-dard) broad, golden yellow, lower petals (wings and keel) white, pink, or purple, in spring. Likes moist soil. Zones 9–11.

Lotus maculatus

syn. *Heinekenia maculata*
FIRE VINE
☀ ✿ ↔ 3–6 ft (0.9–1.8 m) ↕ 8 in (20 cm)
From the Canary Islands. A trailing perennial well suited to hanging bas-kets and pots. Mid-green needle-like leaflets. Bears yellow-tipped red-orange flowers in spring–summer. '**Amazon Sunset**', long-flowering, with silvery leaves and deep red flowers; '**Gold Flash**', red-orange flowers; and '**New Gold Flash**', improved form of 'Gold Flash', abundant red-orange flowers. Zones 10–11.

LUCULIA

This genus in the madder (Rubiaceae) family comprises 5 species of decidu-ous flowering shrubs and small trees found in elevated forest regions of the

Lotus berthelotii

Lotus formosissimus

Himalayas, from northern India to western China. They are beautiful, fragrant, flowering plants, prized both for their attractive foliage and prolific clusters of pink, red, or white flowers in the form of a slender tube opening to a broad 5-lobed disc. The fruit is a capsule with 2 chambers containing flattened seeds. Although they are tech-nically deciduous, there is no long period of leaflessness, as the new foliage usually appears at about the same time as the old leaves are dropping. CULTIVATION: Tolerating only mild frosts, they prefer a moderate summer temperature and grow well in moder-ately fertile, moist, well-drained soil with plenty of humus. They need pro-tection from the wind and do not like competition from other roots. Plant in part-shade or full sun; provide ade-quate water and fertilize regularly from spring to autumn. Prune back old flowering shoots after flowering. In frost-prone areas they may be grown in a cool greenhouse. Propagate from seed in spring or from half-hardened cuttings in summer.

Luculia grandifolia

☼/☀ ✿ ↔ 7 ft (2 m) ↕ 12–20 ft (3.5–6 m)
From elevated forest regions of Bhutan. Leaves large, deep green, elliptic to ovate, prominent reddish purple veins, stalks, and margins. Large clusters of 16 to 20 very fragrant, snow white, tubular flowers in summer. Zones 9–10.

Luculia gratissima

☼/☀ ✿ ↔ 10–15 ft (3–4.5 m)
↕ 10–20 ft (3–6 m)
Native to the Himalayas. Outstanding free-flowering large shrub or small

tree. The leaves are ovate-oblong to lance-shaped, and dark green. Large trusses of fragrant, slender-tubed, rosy pink flowers, forming a wonderful rounded mass, appear in autumn to mid-winter. The fruit is egg-shaped. Zones 9–10.

LUDISIA

JEWEL ORCHID
This is a sympodial terrestrial orchid genus in the Orchidaceae family, with only one species, which is widely encountered throughout tropical Southeast Asia. It has fleshy creeping stems and small rosettes of succulent leaves. The small flowers are borne in an erect spike arising from the center of the leaf rosette. *Ludisia* is one of the few orchid genera grown primarily for their attractive foliage. CULTIVATION: Grow in shallow trays or baskets to accommodate its creep-ing habit. These plants enjoy warm humid conditions throughout the year, as they are growing almost constantly. Give them plenty of fresh air, to avoid spotting of the leaves, and a shaded position, as direct light will burn the succulent leaves and rhizomes. Propa-gate by division.

Ludisia discolor

syn. *Haemaria discolor*
☀ ✿ ↔ 4–24 in (10–60 cm)
↕ 4–16 in (10–40 cm)
Species with variable foliage color and pattern, ranging from dark green to deep purplish brown tints conspicu-ously veined in gold to coppery red. Leaf surface distinctly velvety. Upright spikes of unusual pure white flowers, arising from new growths, in autumn to winter. Zones 11–12.

LUDWIGIA

syn. *Jussiaea*
This genus of about 75 herbaceous or woody, aquatic or marginal, peren-nials belongs to the evening-primrose (Onagraceae) family. *Ludwigia* is widely distributed in bogs and marshes in warmer climates in both the Northern and Southern Hemispheres. The leaves are simple. The inconspicuous flowers

Luculia grandifolia

Luculia gratissima

Ludisia discolor

Ludwigia peruviana

may be solitary, arising from the leaf axils, or in clusters at the branch tips. They may be white or yellow, and have a long calyx tube with 4 or 5 sepals and 4 spreading petals (or sometimes no petals).

CULTIVATION: Grow adjacent to, or in, shallow water in acid soil in a protected sunny position. Propagate from cuttings or by division.

Ludwigia peruviana
COMMON PRIMROSE WILLOW, EVENING PRIMROSE, PERUVIAN PRIMROSE WILLOW

☀ ❄ ↔ 20 in–8 ft (50 cm–2.4 m)
↑ 20 in–8 ft (50 cm–2.4 m)

Occurring from southeastern USA to South America. A woody perennial shrub growing out from air-filled roots at the water's edge to form a floating mat, sometimes free-floating. Leaves finely hairy, oval, with impressed veins, deciduous in cooler climates. Solitary bright yellow flowers, clawed, with rounded petals, in late spring–autumn. Rusty red sepals remaining attached to the brown seed capsule in a star shape. Zones 7–10.

LUMA
This genus, found in Argentina and Chile, includes just 4 species of densely foliaged, round-headed, evergreen shrubs and trees. Belonging to the myrtle (Myrtaceae) family and closely allied to *Myrtus*, they have small aromatic leaves and 4-petalled white flowers with a central mass of stamens. The flowers usually open in spring and early summer, and are followed by dark berries. The bark can also be an attractive feature, as in some species it peels and is a warm cinnamon tone on the outside and white to pink on the underneath.

CULTIVATION: All species are easily cultivated in any mild climate with adequate rainfall, preferring moist well-drained soil and a position in sun or

Luma apiculata

Lupinus arboreus

light shade. Although usually neat growers, they benefit from being lightly trimmed to shape; if allowed to become old and overgrown, they can be rejuvenated with heavy pruning, which is best done over 2 or 3 seasons. Propagate from the seed or half-hardened tip cuttings.

Luma apiculata ★
syns *Myrtus apiculata, M. luma*
PALO COLORADO, TEMU

☀/❂ ❄ ↔ 20 ft (6 m) ↑ 20 ft (6 m)

Large shrub or small tree, sometimes exceeding 30 ft (9 m). Attractive, flaking, warm brown bark. Leaves deep olive green, glossy. Small white flowers, comprising over 150 stamens, in spring–summer. Small, dark purple-red fruit. Zones 9–10.

LUNARIA
This genus of 3 species of biennials and herbaceous perennials belongs to the cabbage (Brassicaceae) family. They are best raised in containers or for cut flowers, as they can be somewhat weedy and invasive. They are primarily grown for their silvery flat seed pods, which are used in dried flower arrangements. The botanical

Lunaria annua

Lupinus arboreus var. *eximius*

name is derived from the Latin *luna*, meaning moon, referring to the shape of the fruit.

CULTIVATION: Grow in full sun or partial shade in light, fertile, moist, well-drained soil. Propagate perennials from seed or by division in autumn or spring. Propagate biennials and annuals from seed in spring. These plants will readily self-seed.

Lunaria annua
HONESTY, MONEY PLANT, MONEYWORT, SILVER DOLLAR

☀/❂ ❄ ↔ 12 in (30 cm) ↑ 30 in (75 cm)

From southern Europe. Leaves bright green, alternate, heart-shaped, coarsely serrated. Rosy magenta, white, or violet-purple flowers, with 4 petals, in spring or early summer, followed by circular seed pods covered with a silvery translucent membrane.
L. a. var. *albiflora*, white flowers.
L. a. 'Variegata', variegated crimson flowers. Zones 8–10.

Lunaria rediviva
☀/❂ ❄ ↔ 24 in (60 cm)
↑ 36–42 in (90–105 cm)

Native to Europe, *L. rediviva* is a hairy-stemmed perennial that produces somewhat smaller flowers and seed pods than the annual species, but the pale mauve flowers of this species are sweetly scented. Zones 8–10.

Lunaria rediviva

LUPINUS
LUPIN, LUPINE

There are about 200 species of annuals, perennials, and evergreen shrubs in this genus in the pea-flower subfamily of the legume (Fabaceae) family from North and South America, southern Europe, and northern Africa, usually in dry habitats. Many have ornamental flowers, borne in showy terminal panicles or racemes. The leaves are palmate, with 5 to 15 leaflets, and the stems are often covered in fine soft down. Many species are grown for horticultural purposes, such as nitrogen fixing and stock fodder, and some seeds are processed for food.

CULTIVATION: Although *Lupinus* species generally tolerate poor dry conditions, they are best grown in full sun in moderately fertile well-drained soil. Propagate from seed or cuttings. The seedlings should be planted out when small, as these plants dislike root disturbance.

Lupinus albifrons
SILVER BUSH LUPINE, SILVER LUPINE

☀ ❄ ↔ 5 ft (1.5 m) ↑ 5 ft (1.5 m)

From California, USA. Rounded evergreen shrub, with stems and leaves covered in fine, silky, silvery hairs, giving the plant an attractive gray appearance. Racemes of flowers, from blue to maroon or lavender, in spring–summer. Zones 8–11.

Lupinus arboreus
TREE LUPIN, YELLOW BUSH LUPINE

☀ ❄ ↔ 4–8 ft (1.2–2.4 m)
↑ 3–7 ft (0.9–2 m)

Native to central coastal California, USA, occurring mostly on seashores. Bushy evergreen shrub. Leaves grayish green, smooth above, woolly hairs beneath. Loose racemes of flowers, usually bright yellow, occasionally blue or lavender, in spring–summer. *L. a.* var. *eximius*, hairier stems and leaves, yellow and blue flowers. Zones 8–10.

Lupinus succulentus, seed pods

Lupinus succulentus

Lupinus, Hybrid Cultivar, 'Anne Gregg'

Lupinus, Hybrid Cultivar, 'Apricot Spire'

Lupinus, Hybrid Cultivar, 'Bishop's Tipple'

Lupinus, Hybrid Cultivar, Mt Cook National Park, New Zealand

Lupinus, HC, 'Blue Moon'

Lupinus, Hybrid Cultivar, 'Candy Floss'

Lupinus, HC, 'Chelsea Pensioner'

Lupinus, HC, 'Dolly Mixture'

Lupinus, HC, 'Esmerelder'

Lupinus, HC, 'Little Eugenie'

Lupinus, HC, 'Pagoda Prince'

Lupinus chamissonis

☀ ❀ ↔ 4–10 ft (1.2–3 m) ↕ 2–7 ft (0.6–2 m)
From seashores of California, USA, often occurring on loose dunes. Often mound-forming shrub. Leaves gray to blue-green from dense hairs. Blue flowers, on 4 in (10 cm) long spikes, in mid-spring–mid-summer. Tolerates drought and salt spray. **Zones 9–10.**

Lupinus perennis

BLUEBONNETS, BLUE LUPINE, SUNDIAL LUPINE, WILD LUPINE

☀/◐ ❀ ↔ 12 in (30 cm)
↕ 12–24 in (30–60 cm)

From eastern and central USA: Maine to Florida and west to Minnesota. Perennial with spikes of bright blue-purple flowers in late spring. Hairy seed pods propel seeds several feet (about 1 m) away; mature seeds are poisonous. **Zones 4–9.**

Lupinus polyphyllus

BLUE-POD LUPINE

◐ ❀ ↔ 20–40 in (50–100 cm)
↕ 24–60 in (60–150 cm)

From mountains of western North America, from British Columbia to California, growing in moist ground. Perennial with thick rootstock, chief ancestor of Russell lupins. Leaves large, basal, long-stalked, up to 17 leaflets, to 6 in (15 cm) long. Dense tapering spikes of very showy flowers, usually blue, often in shades of red, purple, or pink, in early–mid-summer. **Zones 5–9.**

Lupinus succulentus

ARROYO LUPINE, FOOTHILL LUPINE, HOLLOWLEAF ANNUAL LUPINE

☀ ❀ ↔ 12–36 in (30–90 cm)
↕ 18–36 in (45–90 cm)

Found in California, USA, and Baja California, Mexico; widespread in disturbed habitats. Annual blooming in late winter–late spring with bright blue-purple flowers. Fragrant and drought tolerant. Excellent in wild-flower mixes. **Zones 8–11.**

Lupinus texensis

TEXAS BLUEBONNET

☀ ❀ ↔ 12 in (30 cm)
↕ 12–24 in (30–60 cm)

From Texas, USA; the State wildflower. Drought-tolerant annual blooming in early–late spring with dark blue and white flowers. Must be planted in well-drained soil. **Zones 7–10.**

Lupinus Hybrid Cultivars

☀ ❀ ↔ 2–5 ft (0.6–1.5 m)
↕ 2–4 ft (0.6–1.2 m)

Perennial lupins were first hybridized in the 1890s, but gained most popularity with the hybrids George Russell developed between 1911 and 1937. Known as the Russell lupins, these laid the foundations for later cultivars of hybrid lupins. Many of these later perennial hybrids are still informally referred to as Russell lupins, and can become invasive. **Band of Nobles Series:** rich colors of blue, purple, intense reds ('The Page'); deep pinks, creamy whites ('Noble Maiden'); and many bicolors ('The Governor', blue and white, 'The Chatelaine', soft pink and white). Other cultivars include: 'Bishop's Tipple', to 48 in (120 cm) tall, mauve and lilac flowers with ivory flecks; 'Blue Moon', to 18 in (45 cm) tall, late-blooming, tall narrow spikes of mauve-blue and white flowers; 'Candy Floss', to 24 in (60 cm) tall, delicate blush-pink and white flowers, becoming deep pink with age; 'Chandelier', 36–40 in

(90–100 cm) tall, yellow flowers in early summer; **Gallery Series**, compact plants, to 20 in (50 cm) tall, bearing 10 to 12 spikes of red, blue, or pink sweet-pea-like flowers in late spring or early summer; **'My Castle'**, 30–36 in (75–90 cm) tall, bright brick-red blooms; **'Pagoda Prince'**, 36–48 in (90–120 cm) tall, early-blooming, soft lilac to purple and white bicolor flowers; **'Red Arrow'**, to 36 in (90 cm) tall, pure red flowers flecked with yellow, ageing to mulberry; **'Terracotta'**, 36–48 in (90–120 cm) tall, early-blooming, large rusty-colored bells. Zones 3–9.

LYCASTE

These deciduous sympodial orchids in the Orchidaceae family are native to coastal and mountainous regions from Mexico to Peru. There are 45 distinct recognized species. They are cool- to warm-growing epiphytes or terrestrials with fat pseudobulbs and large, thin, pleated leaves. Many of the Central American species (particularly the yellow-flowered group, which also have highly fragrant blooms) often leave sharp spines after the previous season's leaves have fallen. Long-lasting flowers are produced singly, on erect stalks from the base of the pseudobulb, usually in spring and summer, coinciding with new growth. The sepals open fully in most species, with the petals pushed forward, often adjacent to the labellum. There are many hybrids, mostly based on the magnificent *L. skinneri*, which prefers cooler temperatures; for example, *L.* Koolena ★, *L.* Macama, and *L.* Shoalhaven.
CULTIVATION: These orchids are best grown in pots, as their roots must not dry out during the growing season, in a well-drained bark-based mix with the addition of a moisture-retaining medium such as peat moss. They are heavy feeders when in active growth, and require copious watering. Do not burn the thin leaves in summer by exposing plants to direct light. Reduce watering when the plants are dormant in winter, allowing the potting medium to dry for a few days before re-wetting. Protect from frost. Propagate by division.

Lycaste bradeorum

☀/◑ ✦ ↔ 8–24 in (20–60 cm)
↕ 4–12 in (10–30 cm)

From Central America. Very floriferous species, producing numerous single flowers from the base of the leafless pseudobulb. Fragrant 2½ in (6 cm) blooms with greenish yellow sepals and bright yellow-orange petals and labellum in summer. Zones 10–12.

Lycaste skinneri

☀ ◃ ↔ 8–24 in (20–60 cm)
↕ 4–24 in (10–60 cm)

Highly desirable and variable epiphytic species from Guatemala (where the rare white-flowered form is the national flower), Honduras, and El Salvador. Large light to deep pink blooms, 5 in (12 cm) across, in groups of up to 6, in winter–early spring. Zones 9–11.

Lycaste tricolor

◑ ✦ ↔ 8–24 in (20–60 cm)
↕ 4–16 in (10–40 cm)

From Costa Rica and Panama. Floriferous species varying in color from white to pale pink. Somewhat nodding blooms, 2½ in (6 cm) across, in the winter–spring. Zones 11–12.

Lycaste Hybrids

☀ ✦ ↔ 8–24 in (20–60 cm)
↕ 4–24 in (10–60 cm)

Many of these have hybrid vigor, are easier to grow, and bloom more readily than some of the species. **Albanensis**, primary hybrid between *L. lasioglossa* and *L. macrophylla*; **Imshootiana**, primary hybrid made over a century ago between *L. cruenta* and *L. skinneri*; **Koolena** ★, popular hybrid, both as a showbench flower and for breeding, with a high percentage of *L. skinneri* in its genetic make-up; **Leo**, with 3 different species in its background: *L. macrobulbon, L. macrophylla,* and *L. skinneri*. Zones 10–12.

Lupinus, HC, 'Polar Princess'

Lupinus, HC, 'Queen of Hearts'

Lupinus, HC, 'Red Arrow'

Lupinus, HC, 'Rosalind Woodfield'

Lupinus, HC, 'Storm'

Lupinus, HC, 'Sunset'

Lupinus, HC, 'Terracotta'

Lupinus, HC, 'Troop the Colour'

Lycaste, Hybrid, Leo

Lycaste bradeorum

Lycaste tricolor

Lycaste, Hybrid, Albanensis

Lycaste, Hybrid, Imshootiana

Lycaste, Hybrid, Koolena

LYCHNIS

CAMPION, CATCHFLY

Lychnis or lukhnis is a Greek word meaning lamp, and this genus of 20 species of biennials and perennials in the pink (Caryophyllaceae) family was given its name in the third century BC by Theophrastus, presumably because of its vivid flowerheads. It is closely allied to Silene, and recent studies have thrown some doubt on whether it can be validly distinguished from that genus. (If not, Silene is the prior name.) Found in the northern temperate zone, Lychnis species are quite variable, often forming large clumps of foliage, sometimes with silver-gray leaves. While their flowers are simple 5-petalled structures, they are brightly colored and showy, occurring in heads usually held well clear of the foliage, and maximizing the color effect.
CULTIVATION: They are mostly very hardy and easily grown in sun or part-shade in moist well-drained soil. The silvery L. coronaria prefers fairly dry conditions, but most others can be given routine watering. Deadhead frequently to encourage continuous flowering. Propagate from seed or from basal cuttings or by division, depending on the growth form.

Lychnis × arkwrightii
☼/◐ ❄ ↔ 16–24 in (40–60 cm) ↕ 12–30 in (30–75 cm)

Garden hybrids between L. × haageana forms and L. chalcedonica.

Lychnis × arkwrightii 'Vesuvius'

Lychnis coronaria 'Alba'

Sometimes short-lived perennials. Bristly bright to dark green foliage. Small heads of vivid flowers, held above the foliage, in summer. By far the best known is 'Vesuvius', to 18 in (45 cm) tall, with dark green to purplish foliage and large, striking, orange-red flowers. Zones 6–10.

Lychnis chalcedonica
MALTESE CROSS
☼/◐ ❄ ↔ 12–16 in (30–40 cm) ↕ 20 in (50 cm)

Upright, bristly, Eurasian perennial forming a clump of large, pointed, oval, basal leaves with smaller leaves up the flower stems. Heads of up to 50 small bright red flowers in summer; cultivars in other colors and forms. Zones 4–10.

Lychnis coronaria
DUSTY MILLER, ROSE CAMPION
☼/◐ ❄ ↔ 20–40 in (50–100 cm) ↕ 16–32 in (40–80 cm)

From southeastern Europe. Spreading mounding biennial or short-lived perennial. Stems and foliage with dense silver-gray hairs. Leaves lance-shaped, to about 3 in (8 cm) long, often smaller. Small heads of flowers, usually in vivid shades of pink or purple-red. 'Alba', white flowers; 'Atrosanguinea', very light foliage and deep magenta flowers; 'Oculata' ★, red-centered white flowers. Zones 4–10.

Lychnis flos-cuculi
RAGGED ROBIN
☼/◐ ❄ ↔ 16 in (40 cm) ↕ 30 in (75 cm)

Bristly Eurasian perennial. Basal leaves broad, lance- to spatula-shaped; upper leaves narrow to almost linear. Open flowerheads, with few pale purple flowers with fine petals divided in two, in summer. Zones 6–9.

Lychnis flos-jovis
☼/◐ ❄ ↔ 16 in (40 cm) ↕ 32 in (80 cm)

From Europe. Upright alpine perennial with downy white stems and foliage.

Lychnis viscaria

Leaves are lance- to spatula-shaped, broad at the base, and narrower farther up the stem. Small heads of bright red flowers with the petals divided in two, sometimes almost completely, in the summer. Zones 5–9.

Lychnis viscaria
GERMAN CATCHFLY, VISCARIA
☼/◐ ❄ ↔ 16 in (40 cm) ↕ 24 in (60 cm)

Found from Europe to Siberia. Upright perennial, with stems and leaves bristly, and sticky leaf bases. The leaves are elliptical to lance-shaped. The flower spikes are narrow, carrying small mauve to purple-red flowers, in the summer. L. v. subsp. atropurpurea, deep purple flowers. L. v. 'Flore Pleno' (syn. 'Splendens Plena') has bright magenta double flowers; 'Splendens', pale to deep pink single flowers. Zones 4–10.

LYCIUM

This genus of nightshade, belonging to the Solanaceae family, comprises some 100 species of deciduous and evergreen, often thorny shrubs that inhabit temperate, subtropical, and tropical regions around the world. The branches are often thorn-tipped. The leaves are alternate or in clusters. Small funnel-shaped or tubular flowers, white, green, or purplish, are borne in the leaf axils. The plants are primarily valued for their showy, succulent, generally bright red berries, produced in great abundance and providing a long-lasting colorful display throughout autumn into early winter. Some species have naturalized and become troublesome weeds.
CULTIVATION: Ranging from fully frost hardy to frost tender, these shrubs succeed in moderately fertile well-drained soil and prefer to be placed in a sunny location. Some species are tolerant of sea spray and are useful in coastal gardens. Lycium may be grown as a hedge or espaliered against walls. Prune in winter or early spring to maintain the plant's shape. All species propagate easily from seed in autumn. Hardwood cuttings may be taken in the winter, and softwood cuttings in the summer.

Lycium ferocissimum

Lycium ferocissimum
AFRICAN BOX-THORN
☼ ⚘ ↔ 10 ft (3 m) ↕ 15 ft (4.5 m)

From Africa. Intricately branched shrub with fleshy green leaves clustered at base of spine. Small flowers, lilac in the center, pale lilac to white toward the edge, throughout the year. Orange-red berries. Noxious weed in many areas. Zones 9–11.

LYCOPERSICON

A genus in the nightshade (Solanaceae) family containing 7 species of aromatic herbs, some of them annuals, others short-lived perennials, occurring wild in western South America and the Galapagos Islands. The distinction between Lycopersicon and the vast and diverse genus Solanum is slight, and recent botanical evidence suggests that they could be merged. The plants have erect or sprawling stems clothed in sticky hairs and deeply divided toothed leaves. Short racemes of open, yellow, star-shaped flowers with a 5-lobed calyx are borne in the leaf axils. The fruit is a fleshy berry with 2 or more chambers containing many seeds; the best-known species, which is the edible L. esculentum, comes in a myriad varieties, with fruit ranging from the size of a grape to monsters that weigh up to 4 pounds (1.8 kilograms).
CULTIVATION: In areas with a long warm growing season plant in fertile well-drained soil in an open sunny position. In cooler areas seedlings may need to be protected from late frosts. Taller plants may require staking and removal of young shoots from the leaf axils to maintain a manageable habit. Propagation is from seed, many varieties being grafted onto stronger rootstock for improved vigor.

Lycopersicon esculentum
syns Lycopersicon lycopersicum, Solanum lycopersicum

LOVE APPLE, POMODORO, TOMATO
☼ ⚘ ↔ 12–24 in (30–60 cm) ↕ 2–8 ft (0.6–2.4 m)

Native to western South America. Perennial, grown widely as an annual food crop. Stem erect or scrambling, hairy; leaves deeply cut, mid-green,

Lycopersicon esculentum

Lycopersicon esculentum
'Abraham Lincoln'

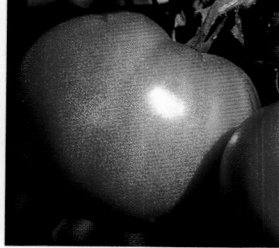

Lycopersicon esculentum
'Big Beef'

Lycopersicon, Hybrid Cultivar, 'Early Girl'

Lycopersicon esculentum
'Sherry's Sweet Italian'

L. esculentum 'Plum Dandy'

Lycopersicon esculentum 'Juliette'

L. esculentum 'Yellow Pear'

Lycopersicon, HC, 'Black Plum'

Lycopersicon, HC, 'Green Zebra'

Lycopersicon, HC, 'Joliet'

Lycopersicon, HC, 'Sungold'

with up to 9 lobes. Up to 12 yellow, open, star-shaped flowers per raceme. *L. e.* var. *cerasiforme,* the original wild Peruvian cherry tomato from which cultivars have been bred, has small red fruit, ½–¾ in (12–18 mm) in diameter. Modern cultivars may have fleshy, rounded, cylindrical or oval-shaped fruit, to 6 in (15 cm) in diameter, usually red, but sometimes yellow, orange, or blackish. '**Abraham Lincoln**', clusters of up to 9 extra large dark red fruit; '**Aranca**', vigorous, with trusses of 7 to 9 cocktail-size fruit; '**Big Beef**', large slow-maturing plant, fruit over 1 lb (450 g); '**Black Russian**', medium-sized, with dark mahogany brown fruit; '**Costoluto di Marmande**', medium to large, with ribbed red fruit; '**Gardener's Delight**' ★, clusters of 6 to 12 extra sweet bright red

cherry tomatoes; '**Gold Nugget**', small plant, with small, rich, sweet, yellow or gold, slightly elongated fruit; '**Goliath**', prolific, medium-sized, with red fruit; '**Juliette**', large plant, clusters of grape-type fruit; '**Mexico Midget**', prolific, producing cherry-sized, red, salad tomatoes; '**Moneymaker**' ★, early, heavy cropping, with medium-sized fruit; '**Mortgage Lifter**', very large red beefsteak variety, 2½–4 lb (1.1–1.8 kg); '**Plum Dandy**', compact plant, egg-shaped bright red fruit; '**Red Robin**', compact plant, red cherry-type fruit; '**Sherry's Sweet Italian**', large, thick, pointed fruit, suited to sauces and tomato paste; '**Stupice**', heavy-yielding plant, suits cooler climates; '**Sweet Cluster**', smooth, firm, glossy fruit, ripening dark red; '**Yellow Boy**' ★, medium-sized bright yellow fruit; '**Yellow Pear**', prolific, with small, yellow, sweet, juicy, pear-shaped fruit. Zones 9–12.

Lycopersicon Hybrid Cultivars

☀ ⬍ ↔ 12–24 in (30–60 cm)
↑ 2–8 ft (0.6–2.4 m)

Several species, but most notably *L. peruvianum,* hybridize with *L. esculentum,* resulting in a range of interesting colored and flavored fruit. The hybrids may have varying growth habits and climatic requirements.

'**Black Plum**', medium height, with elongated dark mahogany brown fruit, greenish at top; '**Carmello**', indeterminate habit, maturing in 70 days; '**Caspian Pink**', very large plant, with large, pink, beefsteak-type fruit; '**Early Girl**', large clusters of bright red medium-sized fruit; '**Green Zebra**', apricot-sized, mild-flavored, greenish lime fruit with darker green stripes; '**Jolly**', clusters of 9 to 14 large, dark pink, sweet, cherry-type fruit, pointed toward the top; '**Northern Exposure**', large pink to red fruit, suits cool areas with a short season; and '**Sungold**' ★, tangerine-colored, cherry-sized, very sweet fruit. Zones 9–12.

LYCOPODIELLA

This genus, which comprises about 40 species belonging to the clubmoss (Lycopodiaceae) family of so-called "fern allies," is widespread, occurring largely throughout American tropical and subtropical regions, with a few species in the temperate zones. Some authorities retain them in a broadly defined *Lycopodium.* Among the larger clubmosses and usually found in acid, rather boggy areas, they give a glimpse of how vegetation must have been before the evolution of flowering plants, when clubmosses attained tree-like proportions. The stems are often long

and creeping but have erect branches, with short, soft, needle-like foliage reminiscent of dwarf conifers. The spores are borne in small sacs at the bases of the shorter leaves arranged in cone-like bodies at the pendulous branch tips, or sometimes laterally on the stems.

CULTIVATION: These plants are difficult to transplant and do not adapt well to cultivation. Try growing them in humus-rich fertile soil that stays moist throughout the warmer months. A bright position out of the heat of direct summer sun suits *Lycopodiella* best. Propagation by spores is possible, but establishing these plants by division is difficult.

Lycopodiella cernua

syn. *Lycopodium cernuum*
NODDING CLUBMOSS, STAGHORN CLUBMOSS

◐/☀ ⬍ ↔ 3–6 ft (0.9–1.8 m)
↑ 12–30 in (30–75 cm)

Found almost worldwide in the tropics and subtropics. The long-running rhizomes are often seen hanging from cliffs or earth banks. They have erect branches resembling those of a small conifer, with tiered recurved branches and light green to golden green ferny foliage. Cream to beige spore-bearing bodies are carried at the branch tips. Zones 9–12.

Lycopodiella cernua

LYCOPODIUM

CLUBMOSS

This genus of about 40 species, found in most parts of the world, gives its name to the clubmoss (Lycopodiaceae) family. Resembling mosses in their foliage, though mostly larger and more branched, they are traditionally treated as "fern-allies" but in fact are representatives of an unrelated and far more ancient group, some of them tree-like during the Carboniferous and Permian geological periods. Clubmosses today are evergreen perennials with aerial branches arising from creeping, often underground, rhizomes, or from long scrambling stems in the case of some tropical species. The leaves are tiny, densely clothing the stems or sometimes in 2 rows. Cone-like organs containing many small spore-sacs terminate the branches. *Lycopodium* was formerly treated as a genus of about 400 species, but the majority have now been split off into the genera *Huperzia* (including all the tropical epiphytic species) and *Lycopodiella*. CULTIVATION: Quite difficult to establish and maintain, and are rarely cultivated (in contrast to the epiphytic tassel-ferns in *Huperzia,* which are widely grown). They are most likely to succeed in gritty acid soil kept permanently moist, and should be kept in a shaded position in high humidity. Propagate by division.

Lycoris aurea

Lygodium microphyllum, in the wild, New Caledonia

Lycopodium clavatum

GROUND PINE, RUNNING PINE

☀ ❄ ↔ 16–20 in (40–50 cm)
↑ 8–10 in (20–25 cm)

Widely distributed throughout temperate regions and in tropical highlands. Long trailing stems, with tiny, fine, needle-like leaves, to 4 mm long, crowded along them. Zones 2–9.

Lycopodium deuterodensum

BUSHY CLUBMOSS, TREE CLUBMOSS

☀ ❄ ↔ 8–24 in (20–60 cm)
↑ 8–24 in (20–60 cm)

From eastern Australia, the southwest Pacific, and New Zealand. Fern-like plant with aerial branches resembling those of a tiny conifer. Erect branching stems arising from long branching rhizome; spore-bodies carried at branch tips; tiny, crowded, overlapping leaves. Zones 7–10.

Lycopodium thyoides

syn. *Lycopodium complanatum* var. *validum*

☀ ❄ ↔ 18–36 in (45–90 cm)
↑ 6–18 in (15–45 cm)

From highlands of southern Mexico and Central and South America. Erect aerial stems arising from long underground rhizome, with branches of 2 types: sterile branches are spreading and repeatedly forked; fertile branches are erect and narrowly branched, with 4 to 8 long, thin, spore-bearing cones. Zones 9–10.

LYCORIS

SPIDER LILY

These cousins of the South African genus *Nerine,* often found growing at the edges of cultivated fields in Japan and China, bear a strong resemblance to nerines. A member of the amaryllis (Amaryllidaceae) family, *Lycoris* contains about 18 bulbous perennials, dormant in summer prior to flowering in late summer to early autumn. The

Lycopodium deuterodensum

spidery flowers have strongly reflexed petals and are showy and elegant, borne in an umbel at the top of a straight stem. The linear leaves emerge from the base of the bulb after the flowers and persist during winter; frost and rain can cause damage. Their name commemorates the beautiful Roman actress who was Mark Antony's mistress. CULTIVATION: These plants grow best in well-drained fertile soil, in areas with dry summers. If growing in a pot, do not transplant for several years. Withhold water from late spring through to mid-summer.

Lycoris aurea

GOLDEN SPIDER LILY, HURRICANE LILY

❂ ❄ ↔ 18 in (45 cm)
↑ 18–24 in (45–60 cm)

From limestone areas of China and Japan. Leaves fleshy, gray-green. Flowers in golden shades, recurved at tips, petal margins slightly wavy, rather crowded at top of stem. Zones 7–10.

LYGODIUM

CLIMBING FERN

A genus of some 40 species of climbing ferns in the comb-fern (Schizaeaceae) family, distributed throughout the world's tropical forests. They have creeping branching rhizomes, and unlike other ferns, the frond stems keep growing and producing pairs of leaflets from the tips. The fronds can grow to a considerable length and will wind their way up through any support. They are used for making ropes, nets, and baskets in some tropical areas. CULTIVATION: Most are too frost tender to be grown outdoors in any but tropical climates, but they are often grown in pots or hanging baskets in a humid semi-shaded greenhouse. Propagation is usually by dividing clumps before the new fronds start to grow; fronds will take root at the nodes if pinned down. Propagation from

Lycopodium thyoides

Lycopodium clavatum

freshly sown spores is possible but is usually considered extremely difficult and rarely attempted.

Lygodium microphyllum

CLIMBING MAIDENHAIR, SNAKE FERN

☀ ⚓ ↔ 12–36 in (30–90 cm)
↑ 10–17 ft (3–5 m)

Widespread from tropical Africa and Asia to northern Australia; a bad weed in Florida, USA. Long creeping rhizome, which can form large colonies. Mid-green to yellowish green leaflets, to 2½ in (6 cm) long. Zones 10–12.

LYSICHITON

SKUNK CABBAGE

The 2 species in this genus in the arum (Araceae) family grow in bogs in northeast Asia and western North America. They are herbaceous rhizomatous perennials with large paddle-shaped leaves, preceded in spring by almost stemless arum-type flowers of yellow or white. These are followed in summer by spikes of green-skinned fruit. The common name, which alludes to the musky smell of the crushed leaves is a complete overstatement. CULTIVATION: Plant in damp to wet humus-rich mud in sun or semi-shade in cool climates. They usually take several years to settle down and flower. Propagate from seed sown as soon as it is ripe. Division is possible, but given the habitat and the deeply buried rhizomes, this would be a very messy and difficult job.

Lysichiton americanus
YELLOW SKUNK CABBAGE

☀/◐ ❄ ↔ 4–5 ft (1.2–1.5 m)
↕ 3–4 ft (0.9–1.2 m)

From western North America. The larger of the 2 species, occurring in swamps and bogs. Flowers with a bright yellow spathe, rising to 16 in (40 cm), in early spring, followed by tall, bright green, paddle-shaped leaves. Zones 6–10.

LYSIMACHIA
LOOSESTRIFE

This genus of about 150 species of perennials and subshrubs belonging to the primrose (Primulaceae) family is found over much of Europe and Asia, as well as in North America and South Africa. A few species are low-spreading plants, but most are clump-forming perennials with narrow lance-shaped leaves and upright spikes of small 5-petalled flowers, often in shades of yellow, rarely white or purple-pink. The flowers appear from early summer to autumn.
CULTIVATION: Some species prefer the damp soil of pond margins or stream banks, others thrive in rockeries, but most are perfectly happy in full sun or half-sun in moist well-drained garden soil. Propagate by division or from basal cuttings or layers, depending on the growth type.

Lysimachia ciliata

☀ ❄ ↔ 20 in (50 cm) ↕ 40 in (100 cm)
From North America. Perennial with upright stems and whorls of lance-shaped leaves, to nearly 6 in (15 cm) long. The yellow flowers, solitary or paired, appear in the upper leaf axils, in summer. 'Purpurea', deep purple-red foliage. Zones 4–10.

Lysimachia clethroides
GOOSENECK LOOSESTRIFE

☀ ❄ ↔ 24 in (60 cm) ↕ 40 in (100 cm)
Native to China and Japan. Upright perennial with narrow, finely downy, lance-shaped leaves, to 5 in (12 cm)

long. Produces nodding heads of small white flowers, at the stem tips, during summer. Zones 4–9.

Lysimachia congestiflora

☀ ❄ ↔ 8–16 in (20–40 cm) ↕ 6 in (15 cm)
From temperate East Asia. Perennial forming densely foliaged mound of dark green, often red-tinted, pointed oval leaves, topped with clusters of golden yellow flowers in late spring. 'Outback Sunset', yellow-green leaves with a darker central zone. Zones 7–10.

Lysimachia ephemerum

☀ ❄ ↔ 16–24 in (40–60 cm)
↕ 40 in (100 cm)

From southwestern Europe. Upright perennial. Opposite pairs of narrow, lance-shaped, gray-green to blue-green leaves, to 6 in (15 cm) long. Terminal spikes of small white flowers, initially curved, becoming erect. Zones 7–10.

Lysimachia nummularia
CREEPING JENNY, MONEYWORT

◐/☀ ❄ ↔ 24–40 in (60–100 cm)
↕ 2–4 in (5–10 cm)

European low-spreading, sometimes mounding perennial. Leaves light-textured, wavy-edged, rounded, to 1 in (25 mm) wide. Bright yellow flowers, usually solitary, sometimes paired, in leaf axils, in summer. Can become invasive. 'Aurea', bright yellow-green to golden foliage. Zones 4–10.

Lysimachia punctata

☀ ❄ ↔ 16–24 in (40–60 cm)
↕ 40 in (100 cm)

Upright Eurasian perennial. Opposite pairs and/or whorls of downy, finely pointed, lance-shaped leaves, to 3 in (8 cm) long. Terminal heads or spikes of bright yellow flowers, to over ½ in (12 mm) across, in summer. 'Alexander', striking cream-edged foliage. Zones 5–10.

LYTHRUM

This genus of about 35 species is a member of the loosestrife (Lythraceae)

Lysichiton americanus

Lysimachia congestiflora 'Outback Sunset'

Lysimachia nummularia 'Aurea'

family. It comprises mainly herbaceous perennials but includes some annuals and small herbs. Two of the hardy herbaceous perennials have been used to produce very adaptable varieties that grow in a wide range of conditions, thriving just about anywhere except in full shade. (See note of caution for *L. salicaria*.) The flowers are small, rather star-shaped, and carried in racemes. They are attractive cut and in borders. The name *Lythrum* is derived from the Greek *lythron*, blood, referring to the color of the flowers.
CULTIVATION: Grow in ordinary garden soil in full sun/half-sun in autumn or early spring. Ideal conditions would be a damp or wet spot in part-shade.

Cut back in autumn. Propagate by dividing the roots in autumn or spring. Named varieties will not come true from seed.

Lythrum salicaria
PURPLE LOOSESTRIFE, STRIPED LOOSESTRIFE

☀/◐ ❄ ↔ 24 in (60 cm)
↕ 24–60 in (60–150 cm)

From temperate Eurasia, Africa, and Australia, but widely naturalized in North America, where it is a bad weed. Mid-green leaves. Spikes, 9–12 in (22–30 cm) long, of small red-purple flowers in early summer–early autumn. Invasive, declared illegal in some areas; both it and *L. virgatum* should be used with caution. 'Blush', large-petalled blushed pale pink flowers; 'Feuerkerze' (syn. 'Firecandle'), tall plant for back of border, intensely rosy red flowers; 'Robert', bright cerise pink flowers. Zones 3–10.

Lythrum virgatum
PURPLE LOOSESTRIFE

☀ ❄ ↔ 18 in (45 cm)
↕ 24–36 in (60–90 cm)

Native to eastern Europe and northern Asia. More slender than *L. salicaria*, with narrower leaves. 'Rose Queen', rose pink flowers; 'The Rocket', deep rose pink flowers. Zones 3–10.

Lythrum salicaria

Lythrum salicaria 'Robert'

Lysimachia p. 'Alexander'

M

Macadamia integrifolia

Maackia amurensis

Maackia amurensis subsp. buergeri

MAACKIA

This genus, in the pea-flower subfamily of the legume (Fabaceae) family, contains 8 species of deciduous trees and shrubs native to East Asia. They have attractive pinnately divided leaves made up of 7 to 13 leaflets. Small flowers, usually creamy shades, are borne on short upright racemes, standing above the foliage. *Maackia* species are hardy slow-growing plants, suitable for borders and specimen planting. Showy foliage and late-summer flowering season provide color into autumn. Plants commence flowering at a very young age.
CULTIVATION: Best grown in a fertile well-drained soil in a sunny situation, but will tolerate a wide range of soil types. They transplant quite readily. Do not over-prune. Propagate from seed sown in autumn.

Maackia amurensis
AMUR MAACKIA
☼ ❄ ↔ 30 ft (9 m) ↑ 60 ft (18 m)
Shrub or tree, native to China. Well-branched habit, peeling coppery brown bark. Pinnate leaves dark green, to 8 in (20 cm) long. Flowers white with a pale blue tint, on erect crowded racemes, in late summer. *M. a.* subsp. *buergeri* ★, downy leaves. Zones 4–10.

MACADAMIA

This genus from the protea (Proteaceae) family consists of 8 species of evergreen rainforest trees, 7 of which are native to coastal eastern Australia and one is from Sulawesi, Indonesia. In warm frost-free climates they grow into ornamental compact trees with large glossy leaves and long pendulous sprays of creamy white or pale pink blossoms. They are self-pollinating and the round hard-shelled nuts, ripening in late summer to autumn, drop when mature. Macadamia nuts have long been a food source for Aboriginal Australians and 2 species are cultivated commercially in Australia, Hawaii and California, USA, and other parts of the world.
CULTIVATION: Grow in a humus-rich well-drained soil in full sun or partial shade. Macadamias require an ample supply of water in dry periods. Propagate from seed, but trees will not bear fruit until at least 6 years old. Selected clones are commonly grafted or budded.

Macadamia integrifolia
SMOOTH-SHELLED MACADAMIA NUT
☼/◑ ❄ ↔ 20 ft (6 m) ↑ 50 ft (15 m)
World-renowned nut-bearing tree from southeastern Queensland, Australia. Glossy oblong leaves, in whorls of 3, smooth, slightly wavy edges. Creamy white to pinkish flowers are borne in long pendent racemes, in winter–spring. Edible creamy white nut in hard shell. Zones 9–11.

Macadamia tetraphylla
BOPPLE NUT, MACADAMIA NUT, QUEENSLAND NUT
☼/◑ ❄ ↔ 20 ft (6 m) ↑ 40 ft (12 m)
From subtropical rainforests of coastal eastern Australia. Whorls of dark green oblong leaves, prickly teeth. Long pendulous racemes of white or pinkish flowers, in winter–spring. Round hard nuts. Commercially grown for its sweet edible nuts. Zones 9–11.

MACHAERANTHERA

This genus of 26 annual, biennial, and perennial herbs from the daisy (Asteraceae) family is native to north-western parts of the USA. Stems rise from a sturdy taproot. They bear alternate, spiny-toothed, divided leaves, with bristly tips. Flowerheads are solitary or numerous and daisy-like with ray florets of bluish violet or purple, and yellow, red, or brown disc florets, in panicles or cymes. The fruit is a cypsela with bristles. The name comes from Greek, *machaira* meaning sword and *anthera*, anthers, referring to the branching habit of its stems.
CULTIVATION: Ideal in borders and as cut flowers. These plants prefer a position in sandy or gravelly soil in full sun. Soil should be well drained but retain moisture. Propagate from seed sown in autumn or early spring.

Machaeranthera tanacetifolia
syn. *Aster tanacetifolius*
PRAIRIE ASTER, TAHOKA DAISY, TANSYLEAF ASTER
☼ ❄ ↔ 8–15 in (20–38 cm)
↑ 12–20 in (30–50 cm)
Upright or sprawling, smooth or slightly hairy annual from western USA. Dense compact foliage, leaves deeply divided. Flowerheads with pinkish purple to bluish purple ray florets, brilliant yellow center, in late spring–early autumn. Zones 2–9.

MACKAYA

This single-species genus is a member of the acanthus (Acanthaceae) family, which also includes the well-known perennial bear's breeches, *Acanthus mollis*. Native to southern Africa, it is an evergreen shrub that grows as an understory plant in forests, often along stream banks. Leaves are very deep green with soft wavy edges and appear all year. Flowers are tubular with wide-open petals, usually mauve. They occur at the ends of branches from spring to autumn.
CULTIVATION: Grow in moist well-drained soil in full sun or partial shade in a sheltered position. Propagate from seed or from half-hardened cuttings in spring.

Mackaya bella ★
☼/◑ ❄ ↔ 4 ft (1.2 m) ↑ 8 ft (2.4 m)
South African native shrub; develops a spreading habit over time. Glossy deep green leaves, wavy edges. Tubular flowers, 5 flaring petals, pale mauve with darker veining, in loose spikes at the ends of branches, in spring–autumn. Zones 9–11.

MACLEANIA

Comprising some 40 species of evergreen shrubs, this genus from Central America and tropical South America belongs to the heath (Ericaceae) family. The plants often have swollen, partially subterranean stems, from which slender arching branches emerge. These bear simple elliptical leaves that are usually red-tinted when young. The small urn-shaped or cylindrical flowers appear in pendent racemes and are followed by inconspicuous drupes. They are superb plants for cool yet frost-free shrubberies and can be grown in large hanging baskets where their arching habit is seen to its best advantage.
CULTIVATION: Although native to the tropics and consequently intolerant of frost, many species come from moderate altitudes and have a preference for cool moist soil conditions. Grow in part-shade; feed lightly and provide plenty of humus in the soil. Sparsely foliaged or overly long stems can be cut back after flowering. Propagate from seed, cuttings, or layers.

Macleania insignis
◑ ✦ ↔ 4 ft (1.2 m) ↑ 5–6 ft (1.5–1.8 m)
Shrub found from southern Mexico to Central America. Elliptical leaves to 4 in (10 cm), on drooping branches.

Mackaya bella

M

Maclura tricuspidata

Maclura pomifera

Macropiper excelsum

Macropiper excelsum 'Variegatum'

Flowers orange to orange-red, 3 to 10 on short racemes, angled at lobes, fine throat hairs, in summer. Zones 11–12.

Macleania pentaptera
syns *Anthopterus ericae*, *Macleania sleumeriana*

↔ 3–4 ft (0.9–1.2 m) ↑ 6 ft (1.8 m)
Evergreen shrub, native to Panama, Colombia, and Ecuador, grows in cloudforest. Long trailing branches, heart-shaped leathery leaves wrap around branch. Clusters of tubular flowers on branch tips, orange in lower half, green in upper half, in summer. Zones 9–10.

MACLEAYA
PLUME POPPY

This genus from the poppy (Papaveraceae) family includes 2 species of hardy herbaceous perennials, sometimes sold under the name *Bocconia*. These bold, attractive plants can be invasive, forming dense thickets, and spread by means of underground suckers. They have scalloped, deeply lobed, heart-shaped, gray to olive green leaves, 6–8 in (15–20 cm) long. Tiny flowers are borne in large plume-like panicles, 12 in (30 cm) long. The genus is named after Alexander Macleay, a former secretary of the Linnaean Society of London.
CULTIVATION: Plant in autumn or early spring in a sheltered sunny position in deep loamy soil. Remove spent flowerheads and cut down stems in autumn. Soils with high fertility will encourage their invasive nature. Propagate from seed or by division of roots in autumn or early spring. Plants will self-seed.

Macleaya cordata
syn. *Bocconia cordata*
PLUME POPPY, TREE CELANDINE

↔ 36 in (90 cm) ↑ 8 ft (2.4 m)
Plume poppy from China and Japan. Lower stem has large deeply lobed leaves, gray-green above, gray-white beneath. Feathery plumes, to 36 in (90 cm) tall, of small, pearly white or pink flowers appear in summer. Zones 3–10.

Macleaya microcarpa
syn. *Bocconia microcarpa*

↔ 36 in (90 cm) ↑ 8 ft (2.4 m)
Plume poppy from central China. Similar to *M. cordata*. Leaves grayish green to olive with white undersides, downy. Flowers pink outside, bronze inside, in autumn. Can be very invasive. 'Coral Plume', pinker flowers; 'Kelway's Coral Plume', showy deep buff to coral flowers. Zones 3–10.

MACLURA

Notable for their spiny branches, dye-bearing flowers, and interesting fruits, this genus from the mulberry (Moraceae) family contains 12 species of evergreen or deciduous shrubs, trees, and climbers. It occurs worldwide in warm-temperate to tropical regions. There are separate male and female trees. They usually have simple, pointed, ovate leaves, sometimes with downy undersides. Male and female flowers are similar in color, yellow to green shades, female flowers occur in larger clusters. The fruits are usually spherical, maturing to yellow or orange.
CULTIVATION: Frost hardiness and drought tolerance varies. Most are easily grown in any moist well-drained soil in full sun or partial shade. Brighter positions usually result in more fruit, while shade promotes foliage; thus male trees are best planted with a little shade, while females do better in sun. Prune in winter after the fruit falls, but if winter frost damage is likely, delay pruning until spring. Propagate from seed, or from half-hardened cuttings in taken summer, or from hardwood cuttings in winter.

Maclura pomifera
OSAGE ORANGE

↔ 30 ft (9 m) ↑ 50 ft (15 m)
Deciduous tree found in drier regions of USA, from Arkansas to Texas. Lustrous leaves, 2–6 in (5–15 cm) long, bright yellow tones, in autumn. Inconspicuous green flowers, in early summer. Fruit glossy, wrinkled surface. Zones 6–10.

Maclura tricuspidata
syn. *Cudrania tricuspidata*

↔ 15 ft (4.5 m) ↑ 25 ft (8 m)
Thorny deciduous tree native to central China and Korea. Shiny green leaves. Green flowers with small spherical heads, tiny, tightly packed, in summer. Edible round red berries. Leaves are similar to mulberry and are an alternative food source for silkworms. Zones 7–10.

MACROPIPER

There are about 9 species of evergreen shrubs and small trees in this genus, which is a member of the pepper (Piperaceae) family. Found in New Zealand, New Guinea, and islands of the South Pacific, they grow in lowland forests. They have large alternately arranged leaves that are aromatic and peppery when crushed. Tiny male and female flowers are crowded on separate upright spikes, sometimes borne on separate trees. The species in cultivation are grown for their ornamental foliage and colorful candle-like fruit-bearing heads.
CULTIVATION: In cool-temperate climates these plants require greenhouse or conservatory cultivation, but in warmer regions should be given a moderately fertile well-drained soil in a lightly shaded situation. Propagate from seed or half-hardened cuttings.

Macropiper excelsum
KAWAKAWA, PEPPER TREE

↔ 7 ft (2 m) ↑ 7 ft (2 m)
Densely branched shrub from New Zealand coastal forests and scrubland. Rounded, almost heart-shaped leaves, aromatic, prominent veins. Tiny yellow flowers, year round. Bright orange berries follow, in clusters, on erect fruiting spikes. 'Variegatum', deep green leaves, light yellow markings. Zones 7–11.

Macleania pentaptera

Macleaya microcarpa

MACROZAMIA

This genus in the zamia (Zamiaceae) family contains around 38 species of cycads found in subtropical and warm-temperate Australia. Most grow in eucalypt forests or woodlands, usually in poor soil. Some are palm-like with a usually unbranched stem forming a massive trunk above ground, others have the trunk below ground. The pinnate, spirally arranged, dark green to blue-green fronds are not as prickly as many other cycads. Male and female plants are separate. The large red or orange seeds were a traditional food of Aboriginal Australians. They are poisonous if eaten raw and must be carefully processed by being soaked, pounded, and baked. Various species have poisoned stock.

CULTIVATION: Best grown in well-drained sandy soil. The larger species, such as *M. moorei* and *M. riedlei*, prefer full sun, while the smaller species do best in shaded areas. Water regularly during the growing season. Propagate from fertile seed sown as soon as hardened.

Macrozamia communis ★

BURRAWANG

☀ ❄ ↔ 7 ft (2 m) ↕ 3–6 ft (0.9–1.8 m)
Cycad, native to New South Wales, Australia. Mostly underground trunk. Fronds about 6 ft (1.8 m) long, thick dull green leaflets. Female seeds have a bright red fleshy outer layer when mature, in summer. Zones 9–11.

Magnolia acuminata

Macrozamia fawcettii ★

☀ ❄ ↔ 5 ft (1.5 m) ↕ 5 ft (1.5 m)
From New South Wales, Australia. Underground trunk to 12 in (30 cm) long. Young foliage shiny light green to bronze, becoming darker green. Narrow leaflets, 50 to 120 per frond, give distinctive twisted, untidy appearance in spring–summer. Zones 9–11.

Macrozamia lucida ★

☀ ❄ ↔ 4–6 ft (1.2–1.8 m)
↕ 4–6 ft (1.2–1.8 m)
Cycad from open-forest areas near coastal Queensland, Australia. Underground trunk to 16 in (40 cm) long. Dark green shiny leaves, finely divided, 50 to 100 narrow leaflets. Female cones ovoid to barrel-shaped, in summer. Zones 9–11.

Macrozamia miquelii

☀ ❄ ↔ 8 ft (2.4 m) ↕ 8 ft (2.4 m)
Cycad from Queensland, Australia. Broad erect trunk with crown of numerous, finely divided, dark green fronds, up to 100 leaflets. Male cones cylindrical, usually curved. Female cones cylindrical or barrel-shaped, in summer. Zones 9–11.

Macrozamia moorei ★

GIANT BURRAWANG, ZAMIA PALM

☀ ❄ ↔ 7 ft (2 m) ↕ 25 ft (8 m)
A tree-like cycad from central Queensland and northeastern New South Wales, Australia. Rounded crown of dull deep green to gray-green ridged fronds when mature. Huge broadly cylindrical- to barrel-shaped female cones, in summer. Zones 9–11.

Macrozamia riedlei

BURRAWANG, ZAMIA PALM

☀ ❄ ↔ 7 ft (2 m) ↕ 10–12 ft (3–3.5 m)
Found in the southwest corner of Western Australia. Cycad with under-

Macrozamia communis, in the wild, New South Wales, Australia

ground trunks extending to about 12 in (30 cm) above ground, or thick trunk above ground. Glossy, bright to deep green, slightly ridged to flat fronds, spineless frond stalks. Female cones in summer. Zones 9–11.

Macrozamia spiralis

☀ ❄ ↔ 3–6 ft (0.9–1.8 m)
↕ 3–6 ft (0.9–1.8 m)
Cycad native to New South Wales, Australia. Small underground trunk. Dark green fronds, erect or spreading, 40 to 120 narrow leaflets, twisted stems giving spiraling effect. Male cones cylindrical. Female cones ovoid, in summer. Zones 9–11.

MAGNOLIA

Comprising around 100 species and countless cultivars, this genus within the magnolia (Magnoliaceae) family occurs naturally throughout Asia and North America. Both evergreen and deciduous, the flowers are primitive, and many are fragrant. They are pollinated largely by beetles. The flowers are often seen to advantage on bare limbs before the foliage appears, and this simplicity contributes to their universal appeal. The fruits are often cone-like showy clusters, pink or red with colorful seeds, and are sometimes suspended on fine threads, which adds to the interest.

CULTIVATION: Although some species will tolerate lime, most do better in well-drained acid soils rich in manure and humus. Generally fast growing, their fleshy surface roots are easily damaged by cultivation. For this reason they are best left undisturbed. Wind and late frosts can also damage the large flowers. Light shade is generally ideal. Propagate by taking cuttings in summer or sowing seed in autumn. Grafting should be carried out in winter.

Macrozamia moorei

Macrozamia riedlei

Magnolia acuminata

CUCUMBER TREE

☀ ❄ ↔ 30 ft (9 m) ↕ 100 ft (30 m)
Deciduous tree from eastern North America, wide-spreading with age. Large oval leaves, undersides blue-green, usually hairy. Flowers metallic green to yellow-green with upright petals, in summer. Unripe fruits resemble cucumbers. Zones 4–9.

Magnolia amoena

☀ ❄ ↔ 40 ft (12 m) ↕ 35–40 ft (10–12 m)
Deciduous Chinese tree, similar to *M. denudata* and *M. cylindrica*. Leaves green, alternate. Fragrant white flowers, flushed with pale pink, 9 tepals, 2 in (5 cm) across, in spring. Zones 6–11.

Magnolia ashei

ASHE MAGNOLIA

☀ ❄ ↔ 20 ft (6 m) ↕ 30 ft (9 m)
Deciduous tree from moist woods in northwest Florida, USA. Large oval leaves, glaucous, finely hairy beneath, bunched at the ends of the shoots. Flowers white, fragrant, large cups, flushed purple inside, appearing with leaves, in spring. Zones 7–10.

Magnolia amoena

M

Magnolia campbellii

CAMPBELL'S MAGNOLIA, PINK TULIP TREE

☀ ❄ ↔ 30 ft (9 m) ↑ 100 ft (30 m)

Tree from Himalayan forests in southwest China to eastern Nepal. Large oval leaves, bronze when young, paler reverse. Huge slightly fragrant flowers, pale to deep pink, before the leaves, in late winter–early spring. Seedlings take 30 years to flower, grafted varieties 5 years, using the understock of *M. × soulangeana*. *M. c.* subsp. *mollicomata*, flowering younger, earlier in season, slightly larger flowers, more cold hardy; '**Lanarth**', huge cyclamen-purple flowers. *M. c.* '**Charles Raffill**', deep rose pink buds opening to rose-purple outside, white-flushed rose-purple inside; '**Darjeeling**' dark rose-purple flowers. Zones 7–9.

Magnolia cordata

YELLOW CUCUMBER TREE

☀ ❄ ↔ 15 ft (4.5 m) ↑ 25 ft (8 m)

Deciduous large shrub or small rounded tree from southeastern USA. Leaves oblong to oval, with glaucous undersides, usually appearing with flowers. Flowers pale canary yellow to lime green, in summer, repeats in early autumn. Regarded by some authorities as *M. acuminata* var. *subcordata*. Zones 6–8.

Magnolia dawsoniana

☀ ❄ ↔ 25 ft (8 m) ↑ 40 ft (12 m)

Deciduous tree or shrub from mountain forests of Sinkiang Province, China. Leaves dark green, paler reverse. Lightly fragrant flowers, white inside, tinged pink outside, fading with age, appearing before leaves, in early spring. Zones 6–9.

Magnolia delavayi

☀/◐ ❄ ↔ 30 ft (9 m) ↑ 35 ft (10 m)

From southern Yunnan Province, China. Evergreen with large dark

Magnolia denudata

Magnolia hodgsonii

green leaves, gray-green undersides. Large creamy white flowers, fragrant, short lived, opening at night, in late summer. Zones 8–10.

Magnolia denudata

JADE ORCHID, LILY TREE, YULAN

☀/◐ ❄ ↔ 30 ft (9 m) ↑ 30 ft (9 m)

Deciduous tree or shrub revered for its beauty, native to central China. Leaves alternate, green undersides. Flowers white, fragrant, chalice-shaped, a symbol of purity, emerge on bare wood before foliage appears, in summer. An exquisite magnolia, plant flowers within 3 years. Zones 6–9.

Magnolia fraseri

EAR-LEAFED MAGNOLIA, FRASER'S MAGNOLIA

☀ ❄ ↔ 30 ft (9 m) ↑ 40 ft (12 m)

Broadly spreading, open-branched, deciduous tree from southeast USA. Young bronze foliage becomes pale green. Fragrant flowers, vase-shaped becoming saucer-shaped, creamy white, green flush to outer petals, in late spring–early summer. Zones 6–9.

Magnolia grandiflora

BULL BAY, GREAT LAUREL MAGNOLIA, SOUTHERN MAGNOLIA

☀ ❄ ↔ 35 ft (10 m) ↑ 35 ft (10 m)

Evergreen tree from central Florida to North Carolina and west to Texas, USA. Leaves stiff, leathery, deep glossy green, rusty-furry undersides. Large, creamy white, saucer-shaped flowers, fragrant, in early summer. Woody fruits. '**Exmouth**', glossy green leaves, rusty-felted beneath; huge fragrant flowers at early age; '**Ferruginea**', erect form, dense habit, leaf undersides richly red-felted; '**Goliath**',

Magnolia campbellii subsp. *mollicomata*

Magnolia grandiflora

Magnolia kobus

Magnolia grandiflora

many huge globular flowers, in midsummer; '**Little Gem**', smaller leaves, slightly smaller flowers appear when young. Zones 6–9.

Magnolia hodgsonii

syn. *Talauma hodgsonii*

☀ ❄ ↔ 35–40 ft (10–12 m)
↑ 35–40 ft (10–12 m)

From the Himalayas. Tree with very large, tough, oval leaves that have a gently wavy edge. Flower buds are plum-colored, opening to pinky beige flowers, 7 in (18 cm) in diameter, with a fruity fragrance, in spring. Zones 6–10.

Magnolia hypoleuca

JAPANESE BIG-LEAFED MAGNOLIA, WHITE-BARK MAGNOLIA

☀ ❄ ↔ 30 ft (9 m) ↑ 100 ft (30 m)

Deciduous tree from the moist mountainous forests of Japan. Leaves light green, waxy, furry blue-green underside, stalks purplish. Cup-shaped

flowers, fragrant, creamy white, flushed pink on outside, in summer. Red fruit clusters. Zones 6–9.

Magnolia × kewensis

☀ ❄ ↔ 25 ft (8 m) ↑ 40 ft (12 m)

Cross between *M. kobus* and *M. salicifolia*. Deciduous large shrub or small tree; mid-green leaves, 5 in (12 cm) long. Flowers cup-shaped, fragrant, white, 5 in (12 cm) across, borne in spring before leaves. Zones 6–11.

Magnolia kobus

KOBUS MAGNOLIA

☀ ❄ ↔ 30 ft (9 m) ↑ 40 ft (12 m)

From Japan and Korea. Oval leaves dark green, smooth, paler undersides. Lightly fragrant, creamy white flowers, streaked pink at base, in early spring, before foliage. Species considered by some to be represented by forms now named *M. × loebneri* and *M. stellata*. *M. k.* var. *borealis*, more vigorous, larger leaves, sparser flowers. Zones 4–8.

Magnolia liliiflora 'Nigra', in summer

Magnolia liliiflora 'Nigra', in spring

Magnolia liliiflora 'Nigra', in winter

Magnolia liliiflora
syn. *Magnolia quinquepeta*
LILY-FLOWERED MAGNOLIA

☀ ❄ ↔ 15 ft (4.5 m) ↕ 10 ft (3 m)

Small deciduous tree or large shrub from central China; smaller than other species. Fully hardy. Oval dark green leaves, paler and downy on reverse. Purplish pink, waxy, goblet-shaped, lily-like flowers, to 3 in (8 cm) wide, appear with the foliage, in spring–summer. 'Nigra', wine-purple flowers, paler purplish inside. Zones 6–11.

Magnolia × loebneri
LOEBNER MAGNOLIA

☀ ❄ ↔ 20 ft (6 m) ↕ 30 ft (9 m)

Variable *M. kobus* and *M. stellata* hybrid. Prolifically flowering deciduous tree or shrub, grown in a wide range of soils. Leaves narrow, dark green, long oval-shaped. Flowers large, white, often pink beneath, in

spring–summer. 'Leonard Messel', spreading tree, deep rose-lilac buds in winter, pink narrow-petalled flowers, white inside; 'Merrill' ★, attractive white flowers. Zones 4–8.

Magnolia macrophylla
BIGLEAF MAGNOLIA, UMBRELLA TREE

☀ ❄ ↔ 30 ft (9 m) ↕ 50 ft (15 m)

Deciduous tree from moist forests of southeast USA. Large oval leaves, thin-textured, glaucous and downy reverse. Cup-shaped creamy yellow flowers, in early to mid-summer. Rounded pink fruit cluster. Zones 4–8.

Magnolia officinalis
MEDICINAL MAGNOLIA

☀ ❄ ↔ 25 ft (8 m) ↕ 60 ft (18 m)

Deciduous tree, possibly extinct in its native China woodlands, cultivated for medicinal uses. Oval leaves, wavy edges. Large creamy white flowers, cup-shaped, fragrant, in late spring to

Magnolia salicifolia

early summer. Fruits pinkish red, seeds scarlet. *M. o.* var. *biloba*, profuse, slightly notched leaves. Zones 6–9.

Magnolia × proctoriana

☀ ❄ ↔ 15 ft (4.5 m) ↕ 20 ft (6 m)

Hybrid between *M. salicifolia* and *M. stellata* originated in the Arnold Arboretum, Massachusetts, USA. Small tree, pyramidal habit. Small narrow leaves, pale green above. Flowers white, pink at base, fragrant, with spreading petals, in early spring. Zones 6–9.

Magnolia pyramidata
PYRAMID MAGNOLIA

☀ ❄ ↔ 25 ft (8 m) ↕ 30 ft (9 m)

Uncommon, often multi-trunked deciduous tree from the coastal plain of southeast USA. Leaves rhombic, bronze, becoming pale. Fragrant creamy flowers, in spring. Regarded by some specialists as a variety of *M. fraseri*. Zones 7–9.

Magnolia salicifolia
WILLOW-LEAFED MAGNOLIA

☀ ❄ ↔ 20 ft (6 m) ↕ 40 ft (12 m)

Shrub or deciduous tree found growing along the banks of streams in mountain oak and beech forests in Japan. Narrow, willow-like, pale green leaves, glaucous beneath; lemon-anise scent from leaves, bark, and wood when bruised. Flowers white, fragrant, before the foliage, in spring. 'Wada's Memory', fragrant white flowers. Zones 6–9.

Magnolia sargentiana

☀ ❄ ↔ 25 ft (8 m) ↕ 60 ft (18 m)

Deciduous tree from China; one of the most beautiful magnolias. Leaves deep green, glossy, undersides grayish. Flowers purplish pink to white, in

Magnolia × proctoriana

Magnolia × loebneri 'Merrill'

Magnolia macrophylla

Magnolia × loebneri 'Leonard Messel'

Magnolia × loebneri 'Leonard Messel'

Magnolia × loebneri

Magnolia sieboldii

Magnolia × soulangeana 'Picture'

Magnolia × soulangeana

Magnolia × soulangeana 'Burgundy'

spring. *M. s.* var. *robusta*, larger, more shrubby plant, earlier flowers. Sometimes regarded as a form of *M. dawsoniana*. Zones 7–9.

Magnolia sieboldii
OYAMA MAGNOLIA, SIEBOLD'S MAGNOLIA
☀ ❄ ↔ 25 ft (8 m) ↑ 20 ft (6 m)
Large, spreading, deciduous shrub from Japan, Korea, and southern China, smaller in cultivation. Leaves felty-white beneath. Spot-flowering, pure white, fragrant, nodding blooms, in late spring–late summer. Small pinkish fruits. *M. s.* subsp. *sinensis*, broadly oval leaves, felty undersides. The white, cup-shaped, pendulous flowers are strongly lemon-scented, and appear in late spring, with leaves. Large pink fruit. Zones 6–9.

Magnolia × soulangeana
SAUCER MAGNOLIA, TULIP MAGNOLIA
☀ ❄ ↔ 20 ft (6 m) ↑ 20 ft (6 m)
Deciduous low-branched tree or large shrub from a cross between *M. denudata* and *M. liliiflora*. Leaves are short, oval, dark green, and glossy. The flowers are erect, white to rose pink, with deeper color beneath, in spring–summer. Flowers appear before the foliage, even on young trees. 'Alexandrina', large erect flowers, white inside, flushed rosy purple outside, darker veins; 'Brozzonii', very large, elongated, white flowers, pink-purple veins at base; 'Burgundy', purple-pink flowers; 'Lennei',

globular flowers, very concave, thick fleshy petals magenta-purple outside, creamy white inside; 'Lennei Alba', ivory white; 'Picture', deep maroon to burgundy, fading to white at tips of petals; 'Rustica Rubra', deep rosy pink petals outside, fading to pink-white inside on smaller globular flowers. Zones 4–9.

Magnolia sprengeri
SPRENGER'S MAGNOLIA
☀ ❄ ↔ 25 ft (8 m) ↑ 40 ft (12 m)
Deciduous spreading tree from China. Leaves dark green, oval, felty undersides when young. Huge fragrant flowers, pale to deep pink, before foliage, in spring. *M. s.* var. *diva*, white flowers. Zones 7–9.

Magnolia × thompsoniana

Magnolia stellata
STAR MAGNOLIA
☀ ❄ ↔ 10 ft (3 m) ↑ 15 ft (4.5 m)
Deciduous rounded shrub from highlands of Honshu Island, Japan. Leaves dark green, oval. Clusters of fragrant ivory white flowers strap-like with curved, reflexed petals, in late winter before foliage. Regarded by some as a variety of *M. kobus* of garden origin. 'Chrysanthemiflora', double flowers, white petals, reverse flushed pink; 'Pink Star', pale pink almost white flowers; 'Rosea', petals pale pink reverse; 'Royal Star', abundant, double, snow white flowers; 'Waterlily' ★, larger, more abundant, pale pink petals. Zones 5–9.

Magnolia × thompsoniana
☀ ❄ ↔ 20 ft (6 m) ↑ 30 ft (9 m)
Large spreading deciduous shrub developed at Thompson's nursery, London, 1808. Hybrid between *M. tripetala* and *M. virginiana*. Leaves large, glossy green. Foliage is larger than *M. virginiana*, retained into early winter. Flowers large, fragrant, creamy white, in summer. Zones 6–9.

Magnolia tripetala
UMBRELLA MAGNOLIA
☀ ❄ ↔ 35 ft (10 m) ↑ 40 ft (12 m)
Broadly spreading deciduous tree from deep, moist, mountain soils in

Magnolia stellata 'Pink Star'

eastern USA. Foliage dark green above, gray-green and felty beneath. Fragrant, creamy, narrow-petalled flowers, in late spring–early summer. Fruit clusters purplish red. Zones 5–8.

Magnolia × veitchii
VEITCH'S MAGNOLIA
☀ ❄ ↔ 15 ft (4.5 m) ↑ 100 ft (30 m)
Deciduous tree of garden origin, vigorous hybrid between *M. denudata* and *M. campbellii*. Leaves bronze-purple, becoming dark green. Flowers upright, vase-shaped, fragrant, pink at base, suffusing to white, in mid-spring before the foliage. Zones 6–9.

Magnolia virginiana
SWAMP LAUREL, SWEET BAY
☀ ❄ ↔ 20 ft (6 m) ↑ 30 ft (9 m)
Adaptable tree or densely branched shrub from coastal swampy areas in USA. Evergreen or deciduous. Glossy leaves, silvery beneath. Richly lemon scented cream or white cup-shaped flowers, in late summer. Zones 6–9.

Magnolia wilsonii
WILSON'S MAGNOLIA
☀ ❄ ↔ 20 ft (6 m) ↑ 20 ft (6 m)
Spreading deciduous shrub from western China. Narrow, elliptical, dark green leaves, paler felty reverse. White flowers, fragrant, saucer-shaped, pendent, spring–early summer. Zones 6–9.

Magnolia virginiana, with developing seedpod

Magnolia stellata 'Royal Star'

Magnolia Hybrid Cultivars

☀ ❋ ↔20–30 ft (6–9 m)
↑20–40 ft (6–12 m)

Ever since the success of the first *M. × soulangeana* hybrids, breeders have focused on producing bigger, brighter magnolias. Notable are the De Vos & Kosar's Eight Little Girls, Gresham hybrids from America and those by the Jury family of New Zealand. These include: **'Ann'**, deep pink base fading to pale pink on tips; **'Apollo'**, rosy pink buds, rosy red flowers, in spring; **'Betty'**, petals deep rose; **'Charles Coates'**, scented, creamy white flowers, in spring; **'Elizabeth'**, primrose yellow, fragrant flowers, in late spring, dark green leaves; **'Freeman'**, dark green, leathery, glossy leaves, fragrant white flowers, in summer; **'Galaxy'**, soft pink flowers with creamy white interiors, upright, medium-sized to large, tulip-shaped, before foliage, in early spring; **'George Henry Kern'**, small, strappy-petalled, white to pale pink flowers with a mauve petal reverse; **'Gold Star'**, yellow flowers; **'Heaven Scent'**, one of the Gresham hybrids known as Svelte Brunettes, beautiful free-flowering, scented, narrow, deep pink, cup-shaped blooms, in early spring; **'Iolanthe'**, very large-flowered Jury hybrid; **'Jane'**, deep pink flowers with deeper vein, in early spring; **'Judy'**, small flowers, sometimes scented; **'Manchu Fan'**, velvety cream flowers; **'No. 4'**, pink flowers fading to white at tips, erect petals, turned back at tips; **'Pink Alba Superba'**, deep pink cup-shaped flowers, in spring; **'Pinkie'**, petals pink underneath, white on top; **'Randy'**, very deep pink undersides, triangular shrub or small tree; **'Ricki'**, pale pink flowers, deeper pink undersides, very erect petals; **'Rouged Alabaster'**, creamy flowers, flushed with rose pink; **'Royal Crown'**, flowers dark red to violet with white interior, outside tepals reflexed to resemble crown, in spring; **'Susan'**, pale pink flowers deepening near center, faint ribbing; **'Vulcan'**, cyclamen pink flowers; **'Yellow Lantern'**, yellow flowers. Zones 6–9.

MAHONIA

Aptly known as holly grapes, this genus from the barberry (Berberidaceae) family of some 70 species of evergreen shrubs is found in Asia and

Magnolia, Hybrid Cultivar, 'Randy'

Magnolia, Hybrid Cultivar, 'Susan'

Magnolia, Hybrid Cultivar, 'Ricki'

Magnolia, Hybrid Cultivar, 'Pinkie'

Magnolia, Hybrid Cultivar, 'Ann'

Magnolia, Hybrid Cultivar, 'Betty'

Magnolia, HC, 'Elizabeth'

Magnolia, HC, 'Freeman'

M., HC, 'George Henry Kern'

Magnolia, HC, 'Gold Star'

Magnolia, HC, 'Heaven Scent'

Magnolia, HC, 'Iolanthe'

Magnolia, Hybrid Cultivar, 'Jane'

Magnolia, Hybrid Cultivar, 'Judy'

Magnolia, Hybrid Cultivar, 'No. 4'

Magnolia, HC, 'Rouged Alabaster'

Magnolia, HC, 'Pink Alba Superba'

Magnolia, HC, 'Royal Crown'

Magnolia, HC, 'Yellow Lantern'

Mahonia aquifolium

Mahonia aquifolium 'Compacta'

Mahonia aquifolium 'Green Ripple'

North America, some species extending into Central America. Leaves are often very spiny and may be trifoliate or pinnate with relatively large leaflets; foliage may be carried alternately, or in whorls, with several changes of color during maturation. Sprays of small yellow flowers, often scented, between spring and early winter. Fruit is usually blue-black edible berries with a grape-like powdery bloom. Botanists have long debated whether *Mahonia* should be maintained as a genus distinct from *Berberis*. Most British and Continental botanists have recognised both genera, while there is a strong school in North America, where the characteristics distinguishing the two groups tend to break down, that prefers to place all species in a broadly defined *Berberis*. Some recent studies have given support to the latter classification, and *Mahonia* is recognized here only pending a more comprehensive survey.
CULTIVATION: Mahonias vary in hardiness. Most commonly grown species are temperate-zone plants tolerant of moderate to hard frosts while some tropical Asian species withstand only light frosts. Prefer moist well-drained, fertile soil and rich in humus. Protect from the hottest summer sun. Pruning seldom necessary. Propagate from cuttings, or rooted suckers that often develop at base of established plants.

Mahonia aquifolium

OREGON HOLLY GRAPE
☼ ❉ ↔ 8 ft (2.4 m) ↑ 6 ft (1.8 m)
Suckering clump-forming shrub from western North America. Pinnate leaves composed of 5 to 13 spiny

holly-like leaflets, dark green in summer, strong red tints in winter. Erect racemes of yellow to golden yellow flowers, in late winter. Purple-black fruit. 'Compacta', tiny, round, yellow flowers; 'Green Ripple', green rippled leaves. Zones 5–10.

Mahonia dictyota

syns *Berberis aquifolium* var. *dictyota*, *B. dictyota*
CALIFORNIA BARBERRY, CHALK-LEAF BERBERIS
☼ ❉ ↔ 2–4 ft (0.6–1.2 m) ↑ 6 ft (1.8 m)
Evergreen shrub from southwest USA. Leaves, 3 overlapping pairs of glossy oval leaflets, serrated, up to 4 spiny teeth on either side. Dark blue flowers, in racemes, in late spring. Zones 7–10.

Mahonia eutriphylla

☼ ❋ ↔ 3 ft (0.9 m) ↑ 5 ft (1.5 m)
Mexican shrub. Trifoliate leaves, 2 outer leaflets with 5 spines each side, smaller leaflets at stem ends. Yellow flowers, in small racemes, late spring. Glossy, blue-black fruit. Zones 9–11.

Mahonia fortunei

☼ ❉ ↔ 3 ft (0.9 m) ↑ 7 ft (2 m)
Chinese shrub, notable foliage. Leaves to 10 in (25 cm) long, dark green

Mahonia dictyota, berries

Mahonia fortunei

leaflets, 4 in (10 cm) long, pale undersides. Leaflets bronze when young, toothed rather than spiny. Short racemes of bright yellow flowers, in autumn. Zones 7–10.

Mahonia fremontii

DESERT MAHONIA
☼ ❉ ↔ 7 ft (2 m) ↑ 12 ft (3.5 m)
Drought-tolerant shrub from southwestern USA and Mexico. Open branching habit. Leaves pale green, strongly glaucous in best forms, 3 to 7 spiny toothed leaflets. Clusters of soft yellow flowers, in summer. Deep yellow to red fruit. Zones 8–11.

Mahonia 'Golden Abundance'

☼ ❉ ↔ 3 ft (0.9 m) ↑ 6–8 ft (1.8–2.4 m)
This is often listed as a cultivar of *M. aquifolium*, but is probably a hybrid. Densely foliaged, glossy holly-like leaves. Bright golden yellow flowers in large clusters, in summer. Purple-blue berries. Zones 6–9.

Mahonia gracilis

syn. *Berberis gracilista*
☼ ❉ ↔ 3–5 ft (0.9–1.5 m) ↑ 7 ft (2 m)
Sparsely branched, freely suckering, evergreen shrub from Mexico. Thin stems carry shiny, usually overlapping, light green, oval, spiny, toothed leaflets. Golden flowers in erect racemes, in late winter. Zones 7–10.

Mahonia gracilis, berries

Mahonia haematocarpa

syn. *Berberis haematocarpa*
☼ ❉ ↔ 6 ft (1.8 m) ↑ 12 ft (3.5 m)
Shrub from southwestern USA. Strong upright stems. Leaves blue-gray, leaflets with 4 spiny teeth each side. Clusters of 6 pale yellow flowers, in late spring. Deep red to purple-red fruit. Zones 8–10.

Mahonia japonica

☼ ❉ ↔ 10 ft (3 m) ↑ 6 ft (1.8 m)
Spreading shrub native to Japan, but cultivated in China and Taiwan. Long leathery leaves, with 19 spiny dark green leaflets. Fragrant bright yellow flowers, held in upright or arching racemes, in late winter. Small blue-black fruit. **Bealei Group**, upright shrub, native to western China, deep olive green leaflets, scented pale yellow flowers, appear in late winter. Zones 6–10.

Mahonia japonica Bealei Group

Mahonia haematocarpa

Mahonia fremontii

Mahonia × media 'Arthur Menzies', berries

Mahonia × media

Mahonia pinnata subsp. *insularis*

Mahonia nevinii

Mahonia lomariifolia

☀ ❄ ↔ 8 ft (2.4 m) ↕ 10 ft (3 m)

Shrub from Myanmar and western China. Upright stems, whorls of spiny leaves, bronze, maturing to dark green, 20 to 40 spiny leaflets. Erect spikes of fragrant yellow flowers, autumn–spring. Purple-blue fruit. Zones 7–10.

Mahonia × media

☀ ❄ ↔ 12 ft (3.5 m) ↕ 15 ft (4.5 m)

M. japonica and *M. lomariifolia* hybrids. Vigorous upright plants, magnificent foliage, reddens in winter. Erect racemes of yellow flowers, in summer. '**Arthur Menzies**', striking bright yellow flower spikes; '**Buckland**', fragrant flowers, long arching racemes; '**Charity**', tall, flowers in winter; '**Winter Sun**', horizontal racemes, in autumn. Zones 7–10.

Mahonia nervosa

LONGLEAF MAHONIA

☀ ❄ ↔ 36 in (90 cm) ↕ 36 in (90 cm)

Suckering shrub from northwestern North America. Leaves to 24 in (60 cm) long, 11 to 23 leathery, gray-green leaflets, yellowish undersides,

Mahonia lomariifolia

serrated edges. Crowded 8 in (20 cm) racemes of yellow flowers, in late winter. Blue-black fruit. Zones 6–9.

Mahonia nevinii ★

☀ ❄ ↔ 6 ft (1.8 m) ↕ 8 ft (2.4 m)

Shrub from California, USA. Grayish blue-green leaves, 3 to 7 narrow pointed leaflets, 6 spine-tipped teeth on each side, almost white undersides. Small, rather open racemes of light yellow flowers, in spring. Tiny dark red berries. Zones 8–10.

Mahonia pinnata

CALIFORNIAN HOLLY GRAPE

☀ ❄ ↔ 6 ft (1.8 m) ↕ 8 ft (2.4 m)

From California, USA. Shrub closely resembling *M. aquifolium*. Matt mid-green leaves, 5 to 9 leaflets, 13 spines on each side. Foliage reddens in winter, purplish undersides. Clusters of soft yellow flowers, in late winter. Blue-black berries. *M. p.* subsp. *insularis,* balls of bright yellow flowers near stems. Zones 7–10.

Mahonia pumila

☀ ❄ ↔ 36 in (90 cm) ↕ 20 in (50 cm)

Suckering shrub, native to western USA. Leaves with 5 to 7 spiny leaflets, to 6 in (15 cm) long, light purplish red on new growth, maturing to gray-green. Flowers yellow, hint of blue tone, in small racemes, in spring. Zones 7–10.

Mahonia pumila

Mahonia repens

CREEPING MAHONIA

☀ ❄ ↔ 36 in (90 cm) ↕ 18 in (45 cm)

Suckering shrub from northwest North America. Blue-green leaves, reddening in winter, to 10 in (25 cm) long, 5 leaflets, very spiny. Flowers deep yellow, fragrant, in 3 in (8 cm) racemes, in spring. Blue-black fruit. '**Denver Strain**', dark green leaves. Zones 6–9.

Mahonia trifolia

☀ ❄ ↔ 36 in (90 cm) ↕ 20 in (50 cm)

Mexican shrub. Dark foliage, often has gray tint, up to 3 leaflets, may redden in winter. Tiny racemes of golden yellow flowers, in spring. Blue-black berries. Zones 8–10.

Mahonia × wagneri

☀ ❄ ↔ 36 in (90 cm) ↕ 18 in (45 cm)

M. pinnata and *M. aquifolium* garden hybrids. Spiny, deep green to blue-green leaves. Yellow flowers appear in late spring. '**Moseri**', dark green leaves, bronze new growth, attractive blue-black fruit; '**Undulata**', bronze new growth, glossy wavy-edged leaves, deep green in summer, turning bronze in winter, masses of pale yellow flowers. Zones 7–10.

Mahonia trifolia

Mahonia repens

Mahonia repens 'Denver Strain'

Maianthemum gigas

Maianthemum racemosum

MAIANTHEMUM

This genus contains about 5 species of herbaceous perennials in the lily-of-the-valley (Convallariaceae) family. They are mostly from the northern temperate regions with some from further north. They have creeping underground rhizomes and will grow into clumps or, in some species, into substantial colonies. They are grown for their dense panicles of tiny white flowers at the ends of stems or spikes in spring. This genus is still under study, and as it stands it would seem that it should include those species that are better known as *Smilacina*.
CULTIVATION: All species grow best in humus-rich moisture-retentive soils in full sun or partial shade under deciduous shrubs and trees. Propagate by division while dormant, or by sowing seed as soon as ripe.

Maianthemum bifolium
FALSE LILY-OF-THE-VALLEY, MAY LILY
☀ ❄ ↔40–48 in (100–120 cm)
↑5–6 in (12–15 cm)
This spreading perennial is found from western Europe to Japan. It has upright unbranched stems bearing two heart-shaped leaves to 3 in (8 cm) long. A narrow spike of tiny flowers appears in spring. The taller ***M. b.* subsp. *kamtschaticum*** (syn. *M. dilatatum*), has stems to 14 in (35 cm) high, and leaves to 8 in (20 cm) long. Zones 3–10.

Maianthemum canadense
syn. *Unifolium canadense*
TWO-LEAFED SOLOMON'S SEAL
☀ ❄ ↔36–40 in (90–100 cm)
↑7–8 in (18–20 cm)
Woodland plant, native to Canada and northern parts of the USA. Leaves oval, 1 to 3 per stem, to 4 in (10 cm) long. Tiny, fragrant, white flowers, on spikes 2 in (5 cm) long, in spring. Zones 1–7.

Maianthemum gigas
syns *Smilacina gigas*, *S. paniculata*
☀ ❄ ↔27–36 in (70–90 cm)
↑6–8 in (15–20 cm)
Rhizomatous perennial herb, native to temperate regions of Northern Hemisphere. Erect stems, broad glossy leaves. Greenish white flowers on slender stalks, in terminal racemes, in spring. Greenish purple berries. Zones 7–10.

Maianthemum racemosum
syn. *Smilacina racemosa*
FALSE SOLOMON'S SEAL, FALSE SPIKENARD
☀/☀ ❄ ↔24–27 in (60–70 cm)
↑32–36 in (80–90 cm)
Clumping perennial found from North America to Mexico. Leaves are prominently veined, to 6 in (15 cm) long. Fluffy panicles of tiny creamy white flowers, in late spring. Bright red berries, sometimes spotted with dark purple. Zones 4–10.

MAIHUENIA

A genus of 2 mat-forming species, from southern South America, belonging to the cactus (Cactaceae) family. They are notable for their prostrate growth habit, their ability to withstand frequent frosts and their persistent leaves. Stems are spherical to short-cylindrical, olive green to brownish with age, with small, persistent, fleshy, green leaves and areoles bearing fine hairs. White to yellow flowers are borne singly at the ends of stems. Orange-brown seed pods are spherical to oblong with fleshy bracts.
CULTIVATION: These plants are easily grown in a reasonably rich well-drained soil. Can be propagated from

Maihueniopsis glomerata

seed or from cuttings that have been allowed to dry out for a week or two. Rest in winter.

Maihuenia poeppigii
☀ ❄ ↔40 in (100 cm) ↑4 in (10 cm)
Mat-forming cactus from Chile and Argentina. Long fleshy tap root, stems segmented, club-shaped. Numerous glossy green leaves, cylindrical pointed tip. Stiff central spine, 2 radials flattened against surface. Yellow flowers, in summer. Seed pods oval to club-shaped. Zones 9–11.

MAIHUENIOPSIS

A poorly understood genus of 18 species from Bolivia, Peru, Chile, and Argentina, belonging to the cactus (Cactaceae) family. Formerly classified as *Puna* and related to *Opuntia*. The plants normally make tightly packed mats or cushions of inconspicuously segmented stems, round or oval in cross-section. They have tuberous roots and hairy areoles. Leaves are present but soon fall off. The greenish or yellowish seed pods are fleshy, sometimes spiny, and do not split open when ripe. The genus name means that it is similar to, but not

related to, *Maihuenia;* from the Greek *opsis*, "looks like."
CULTIVATION: These plants are easily grown in rich, well-drained soil. Propagate from seed or, more usually, by division, or from stems allowed to dry out for a week or two. Rest in winter.

Maihueniopsis glomerata
syns *Opuntia glomerata*,
Tephrocactus glomeratus
☀ ❄ ↔20 in (50 cm) ↑1–2 in (2.5–5 cm)
Dwarf species from Argentina, popular with collectors. Oval tuberculate stems, 1 or 2 long, thin, flattened central spines. Pale yellow flowers, in summer. Green spineless seed pods turn yellow. Zones 9–10.

Maihueniopsis ovata
syns *Opuntia ovata*, *Tephrocactus ovatus*,
T. russellii
☀ ❄ ↔5–7 ft (1.5–2 m) ↑6 in (15 cm)
From Argentina and Chile. Very compact cushions, large tap roots. Stems initially fragile, tightly attached with age, dark green becoming pale yellowish green. Flowers intense yellow, brownish bracts, in summer. Seed pods spherical to oval, yellow, juicy, edible. Zones 9–10.

Maihueniopsis ovata

MALAXIS

This sympodial terrestrial genus from the orchid (Orchidaceae) family is of cosmopolitan distribution, with most of its more than 300 species occurring in tropical Asia. Leaves are thin, plicate, mid-green and usually deciduous. Flowers are small, ranging from green to orange or even purple. It is a poorly studied genus with many dissimilar groups likely to be transferred into other new genera. The flowers are generally of botanical interest only.
CULTIVATION: These orchids are rarely seen in cultivation. They need warm, humid conditions throughout the year, especially during the growing season. Pot the plants in a moisture-retentive medium that is also well drained. Propagate by division.

Malaxis taurina

☀ ✂ ↔ 8 in (20 cm) ↕ 4–16 in (10–40 cm)
Orchid from New Caledonia. The pseudobulb, bearing up to 4 pleated leaves, is green with a purplish tinge. Upright inflorescences produce up to 16 small green flowers, in summer. Zones 11–12.

MALCOLMIA

MAHON STOCK, MALCOLM STOCK, VIRGINIA STOCK

A genus of some 35 species of annuals and perennials from the cabbage (Brassicaceae) family, found from

Malaxis taurina

southwest Europe to Afghanistan. Mainly small mounding plants, the foliage is variably shaped but often finely hairy and with toothed edges. The purplish red, often fragrant flowers are 4-petalled, in open racemes.
CULTIVATION: Hardiness varies, though most do best in fairly mild climates. Plant in full sun with free-draining soil that can be kept moist. Avoid over-watering or over-feeding, which can result in very few flowers. Propagate common annuals from seed; perennials from basal cuttings.

Malcolmia maritima

VIRGINIA STOCK

☀ ❄ ↔ 12 in (30 cm) ↕ 14 in (35 cm)
Native of Greece and Albania. Annual with upright branching stems. Leaves hairy, 2 in (5 cm) long, elliptical, smooth-edged or toothed. Racemes of fragrant pinkish purple flowers, to 1 in (25 mm) wide, in spring–summer. Zones 8–11.

Mallotus japonicus

Mallotus philippensis

Malcolmia maritima

Malephora crocea

MALEPHORA

This genus of 15 erect or creeping, shrubby, succulent perennials from South Africa and Namibia is a member of the iceplant (Aizoaceae) family. The soft, fleshy, bluish leaves occur in pairs and are united at the base; they are triangular in cross-section. They produce solitary or a few daisy-type flowers on short stalks, growing from the leaf axils or in terminal heads; flowers generally appear from late summer to winter.
CULTIVATION: These plants are adaptable to most soils in an open sunny position. They require regular watering in summer, less in winter. Propagate from cuttings or by seed sown in spring and summer. These plants self-seed freely.

Malephora crocea

syns *Hymenocyclus crocea, Mesembryanthemum croceum, M. insititium*

CARPETWEED, COPPERY MESEMBRYANTHEMUM, ICEPLANT

☀ ❄ ↔ 8–12 in (20–30 cm) ↕ 6–8 in (15–20 cm)
Trailing succulent perennial from South Africa. Stout, fleshy, gnarled stem. Small, bluish, fleshy leaves. Flowers golden yellow inside, reddish outside, glossy petals, sparse year-round, but with spring flush. Yellow- and orange-flowered forms occur. *M. c.* var. *purpureocrocea* has brilliant red flowers. Zones 7–11.

MALLOTUS

Consisting of about 140 species, this genus of trees, shrubs, and climbers in the euphorbia (Euphorbiaceae) family is found in tropical India, Asia, Indonesia, New Guinea, Australia, Fiji, Africa, and Madagascar. Leaves are often quite large, opposite or alternate, with a shiny green upper surface and paler or hairy lower surface. A prominent pair of veins originate near the leaf base, one either side of the mid-vein, giving the appearance of 3 main veins. Small flowers are borne at ends of spikes in leaf axils or other types of inflorescence, with the male and female flowers separate. The fruits are 3-celled capsules.

Malephora crocea

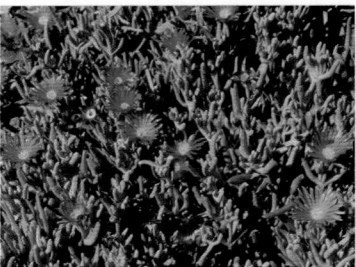
Malephora crocea

CULTIVATION: *Mallotus* is not commonly grown, except for some plantations of timber-producing species. Propagate using fresh seed, which loses its viability quite quickly, or from cuttings.

Mallotus japonicus

☀ ❄ ↔ 7 ft (2 m) ↕ 20 ft (6 m)
Deciduous shrub or small tree from secondary forests and woodlands of Japan, Taiwan, and eastern China. Leaves alternate, broadly ovate, 12 in (30 cm) long, minutely hairy. Flower spikes at ends of branches, densely hairy, to 12 in (30 cm) long, in summer. Zones 8–10.

Mallotus philippensis

RED KAMALA

☀ ❄ ↔ 15 ft (4.5 m) ↕ 40 ft (12 m)
Found from tropical Asia, south to northeastern New South Wales, Australia. Leaves oval or broadly lance-shaped, smooth-edged, dark green above, prominent veins. Brown male and female flowers appear in winter–spring. Fruits are 3-celled capsules. Zones 9–11.

MALPIGHIA

Found in tropical America and the islands of the Caribbean, this genus encompasses 45 species of evergreen shrubs and trees from the self-named family Malpighiaceae. They bear opposite pairs of sometimes hairy, rounded to lance-shaped leaves that may be smooth-edged or conspicuously toothed. Flowers very distinctive because of the long-stemmed petals held clear of the central staminal cluster. The flowers may be borne singly or in small corymbs and are followed by small brightly colored drupes.

Malus × *adstringens* 'Hopa'

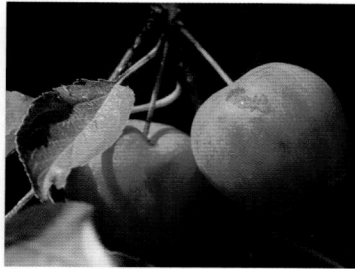

Malus × *adstringens* 'Transcendent'

Malus × *adstringens* 'Pink Beauty'

Malus × *adstringens* 'Patricia'

Malus × *adstringens* 'Radiant'

CULTIVATION: These tropical plants will not tolerate frosts or prolonged cool conditions, but are otherwise not difficult to grow, provided they are given moderately fertile well-drained soil, occasional feeding, and water during dry periods. Most species can be trimmed back quite hard and will become densely foliaged as a result. Propagate from seed or from cuttings.

Malpighia coccigera

BARBADOS HOLLY, MINIATURE HOLLY, SINGAPORE HOLLY

☀ ✣ ↔ 30 in (75 cm) ↑ 30 in (75 cm)
Small shrub native to the West Indies. Glossy deep green leaves, 1 in (25 mm) long, deeply toothed small holly leaves. Covered with pink to mauve flowers, in summer. Red drupes. Zones 11–12.

Malpighia glabra

ACEROLA, BARBADOS CHERRY

☀ ✣ ↔ 4 ft (1.2 m) ↑ 10 ft (3 m)
A shrub from southern Texas, USA, the Caribbean, Central America, and

Malpighia glabra

northern South America. It has smooth-edged glossy leaves, 4 in (10 cm) long. Pale to deep pink or red flowers, in summer. They are followed by small, round, red, edible fruit. Zones 9–12.

MALUS

APPLE, CRABAPPLE
Found in the highland regions in the tropics, and growing in harsh conditions in Siberia and northern China. The apples and crabapples comprise a large genus of around 30 species of ornamental and fruiting, small to medium-sized, deciduous trees belonging to the rose (Rosaceae) family. Nearly all have soft green leaves. The fruits are pomes; not all crabapples are edible, some being too bitter. The cultivated apple is one of the most

Malpighia coccigera

widely grown of all edible fruits and the many species and cultivars of crabapple are valued as ornamental trees.

CULTIVATION: *Malus* will grow in all cool-temperate regions. Apples and crabapples flower in spring and most cultivated varieties of apple require a cross-pollinator in order to produce fruit. While cultivated apples require careful winter pruning, crabapples, being largely ornamental, need less attention. Propagate by grafting onto a range of apple rootstocks, some of which have the effect of producing a dwarfed plant.

Malus × *adstringens*

☼ ❄ ↔ 20–40 ft (6–12 m)
↑ 25–40 ft (8–12 m)
This large spreading tree is a hybrid between *M. baccata* and *M. pumila*. Leaves softly downy beneath. Flowers pinkish, on short stalks. Fruits red, yellow, or green. Susceptible to most apple diseases, often disfigured by scab, rusts, and leaf blights. 'Hopa' has flowers in varying shades of pink; 'Patricia' has deep pink flowers with yellow stamens; 'Pink Beauty' has petals that are almost white with deep pink undersides; 'Radiant' has deep pink flowers blotched with white;

Malus × *atrosanguinea*

Malus × *arnoldiana*

'Transcendent' has deep pinkish red buds that open to reveal white flowers. Zones 4–9.

Malus × *arnoldiana*

☼ ❄ ↔ 15 ft (4.5 m) ↑ 8 ft (2.4 m)
Garden hybrid between *M. baccata* and *M. floribunda,* both Asian. Large shrub, arching stems, serrated leaves. Clusters of 4 to 6 white flowers, deep pink to red buds, in summer. Small yellow-green fruits. Zones 4–9.

Malus × *atrosanguinea*

☼ ❄ ↔ 20 ft (6 m) ↑ 20 ft (6 m)
A garden-raised hybrid of *M. halliana* × *M. sieboldii,* this is a spreading shrub or small tree. Waxy-textured serrated leaves, 2 in (5 cm) long. Small purple-red flowers, in summer. Red or red-streaked yellow fruits, less than ½ in (12 mm) wide. Zones 4–9.

Malus coronaria var. *dasycalyx* 'Charlottae'

Malus florentina

Malus baccata var. *mandshurica*

Malus baccata 'Jackii'

Malus baccata 'Spring Snow'

brilliant red fruit; '**Midwest**', very early in both leaf and flower, larger creamy white flowers. *M. b.* '**Jackii**', spreading habit, stouter branches; '**Spring Snow**', drooping white flowers. Zones 2–9.

Malus baccata
SIBERIAN CRABAPPLE

☼ ✳ ↔ 40 ft (12 m) ↑ 40 ft (12 m)

Rounded erect crabapple tree from Siberia. Buds pinkish, opening to single, white, fragrant flowers. Fruits red, sometimes yellow, on long thin stems. Resistant to most apple diseases, vital to modern hybridization programs. *M. b.* **var.** *mandshurica*, from Japan and northeastern China, lightly serrated leaves, undersides initially downy, single white flowers,

Malus coronaria
AMERICAN CRABAPPLE,
AMERICAN SWEET CRABAPPLE

☼ ✳ ↔ 30 ft (9 m) ↑ 30 ft (9 m)

Large wide-limbed crabapple tree from eastern USA. Buds dark pink, single flowers, fragrant, pale pink to pink-white, salmon pink. Green fruit unpalatable. Susceptible to scab and rust diseases. *M. c.* **var.** *angustifolia*, to 30 ft (9 m) high, short trunk, spreading branches, highly fragrant rose-colored flowers, susceptible to

disease. *M. c.* **var.** *dasycalyx*, Great Lakes crabapple, leaves paler beneath, woolly calyx; '**Charlottae**', apricot to deep pink buds, light pink semi-double to double flowers. Zones 4–9.

Malus florentina
BALKAN CRABAPPLE, ITALIAN CRABAPPLE

☼ ✳ ↔ 10 ft (3 m) ↑ 20 ft (6 m)

Small crabapple tree with erect spreading branches found in Italy and the Balkans. Dark green, serrated, ovate leaves. White flowers in clusters, in late spring. Tiny yellow fruits ripen to red. Uncommon in cultivation. Zones 6–9.

Malus floribunda
JAPANESE FLOWERING CRABAPPLE

☼ ✳ ↔ 20 ft (6 m) ↑ 12 ft (3.5 m)

Beautiful crabapple from Japan. Leaves green, serrated, tapered. Buds dark pink to red, opening to single light pink or nearly white flowers, in late spring. Fruits yellow and red,

Malus × *gloriosa*

½ in (12 mm) in diameter. May be affected by powdery mildew. Long cultivated. Zones 4–9.

Malus × gloriosa

☼ ✳ ↔ 8–10 ft (2–3 m) ↑ 10 ft (3 m)

Hybrid shrub of *M. pumila* 'Niedzwetzkyana' and *M.* × *scheideckeri*. Heavily toothed leaves, red-tinted when young. Purple-red flowers, 1½ in (35 mm) wide. Yellow fruit, ½ in (12 mm) wide, in spring. '**Oekonomierat Echtermeyer**', pendulous bronze foliage, bright pink-red flowers, red-brown fruit. Zones 4–9.

Malus halliana

☼ ✳ ↔ 10 ft (3 m) ↑ 15 ft (4.5 m)

Small tree with loose open habit, from China. Oblong leaves, dark green, often purple-tinted. Red stalks. Flowers bright rose, nodding, in late spring. Fruits purplish, ripening late. Disease resistant. *M. h.* **var.** *spontanea*, shorter, smaller whitish flowers,

Malus × *gloriosa* 'Oekonomierat Echtermeyer'

Malus floribunda, in spring

Malus floribunda, in summer

Malus floribunda, in autumn

Malus floribunda, in winter

Malus × *hartwigii* 'Katherine'

Malus halliana var. *spontanea*

greenish yellow fruits. **M. h. 'Park-manii'**, bronze-green glossy leaves, rosy buds in clusters on long red stalks, flowers double or semi-double, flesh-pink; fruit red to red-purple. Zones 4–9.

Malus × *hartwigii*

☀ ❄ ↔ 6 ft (1.8 m) ↕ 12 ft (3.5 m)

A hybrid of garden-raised *M. baccata* × *M. halliana*. This shrub or small

tree has dark brown upright stems. The smooth-edged, pointed, oval leaves are 3 in (8 cm) long. Flowers are semi-double, deep pink fading to white, 1½ in (35 mm) across, and appear in spring. They are followed by tiny red-brown fruits. **'Katherine'**, large double flowers open from pink-ish white buds, yellowish fruit flushed with red. Zones 4–9.

Malus hupehensis

HUPEH CRABAPPLE, TEA CRABAPPLE

☀ ❄ ↔ 25 ft (8 m) ↕ 15 ft (4.5 m)

Open spreading crabapple tree from China and India. Straight upright limbs. Leaves deep green, violet hue when young. Buds pink, opening to single, white, fragrant flowers, in spring. Fruits green-yellow, slight red cheek. Disease resistant. Zones 4–10.

Malus ioensis

IOWA CRABAPPLE, PRAIRIE CRABAPPLE

☀ ❄ ↔ 20 ft (6 m) ↕ 20 ft (6 m)

Beautiful crabapple native to midwest USA. Leaves dark green, deeply ser-rated, yellowish green undersides. Flowers white tinged with pink, fra-grant, in spring. Fruits shiny green. Highly susceptible to disease, several more resistant clones have been pro-duced. **'Plena'**, fully double pink flowers; **'Prairifire'** ★, dark pink buds and flowers. Zones 2–9.

Malus kansuensis

☀ ❄ ↔ 12 ft (3.5 m) ↕ 15 ft (4.5 m)

Often shrubby, sometimes tree-like species found in northwestern China. Red-brown young shoots, serrated-edged leaves with 3 to 5 lobes. Clusters of 4 to 10 white flowers, ½ in (12 mm) wide, in spring. Tiny yellow to purple-red, rough-surfaced apples. Zones 5–9.

Malus halliana

Malus × *micromalus*

☀ ❄ ↔ 15 ft (4.5 m) ↕ 15 ft (4.5 m)

This small Japanese tree is a natural hybrid between *M. baccata* and *M. spectabilis*. It has dark brown stems, and waxy serrated leaves that taper to a fine point. Pink blooms, in clusters of 3 to 5 flowers, in spring. Yellow, somewhat pointed fruits, ½ in (12 mm) wide. Zones 4–9.

Malus prunifolia

PEAR-LEAFED CRABAPPLE

☀ ❄ ↔ 25 ft (8 m) ↕ 25 ft (8 m)

Several forms occur in northeastern Asia; they vary in fruit size, shape, and color. This small tree has pinkish buds, and single white flowers, in spring, followed by yellow or red fruit. **'Fastigiata'** has profuse white flowers, in late spring. All highly sus-ceptible to disease. Zones 3–9.

Malus ioensis

Malus ioensis 'Prairifire'

Malus kansuensis

Malus hupehensis

Malus × *micromalus*

Malus prunifolia 'Fastigiata'

Malus pumila

syns *Malus* × *domestica*, *Pyrus malus*
APPLE, CRABAPPLE, ORCHARD APPLE

☼ ❄ ↔20 ft (6 m) ↑50 ft (15 m)

The origins of eating apples were uncertain, but recent intensive botanical studies have virtually solved this puzzle and also helped to establish correct botanical names. It was believed that apples were of ancient hybrid origin, so the name *M.* × *domestica* was used to distinguish them from wild species. But now DNA and other evidence has shown that only one wild species is involved, *M. pumila*, and fieldwork in Central Asia has revealed a large range of variation in wild populations, with some wild trees bearing fruit almost identical to most older named orchard cultivars. The wild range of *M. pumila* is from western China through mountain regions of Central Asia to Europe. Young leaves, flower stalks, and calyces vary in downiness. Typically it has pink buds opening to white flowers suffused with pink. Fruits over 2 in (5 cm) in diameter. It suffers from many apple diseases and pests. *M. p.* 'Niedzwetzkyana', the most significant parent of hybrid crabapples, has young leaves, buds, blossoms, fruit, bark, branches all purple-red.

Orchard apples run to many thousands of cultivars, some still popular after 200 years. Some can be eaten raw, some are better cooked, and a number are suitable only for cider. Apples often need a pollinator of a different cultivar to set good crops. 'Bramley's Seedling', late red fruit, best cooked; 'Cox's Orange Pippin', small, strong-flavored, orange to red fruit; 'Fuji' ★, white-fleshed red fruit with yellowish markings; 'Gala', good flavor, long-keeping, yellow-marked red fruit; 'Golden Delicious', white-fleshed, red-marked, golden yellow fruit; 'Honey Crisp', very juicy, yellow-marked red fruit, cold tolerant; 'James Grieve', yellow-fleshed red fruit, quite acidic; 'Red Delicious', deep red to black-red, strong-flavored, short-keeping fruit. Recent commercial varieties, such as 'Pacific Rose', are patent-protected. Zones 3–9.

Malus pumila 'Ashmead's Kernel'

Malus pumila 'Allington Pippin'

Malus pumila 'Hofstetter'

Malus pumila 'Gala'

Malus pumila 'Bramley's Seedling'

Malus pumila 'Charlotte'

Malus pumila 'Scarlet O'Hara'

M. pumila 'Cox's Orange Pippin'

Malus pumila 'Discovery'

M. pumila 'Esopus Spitzenberg'

Malus pumila 'Fuji'

Malus pumila 'George Cave'

Malus pumila 'Goldrush'

Malus pumila 'Granny Smith' ★

Malus pumila 'Honey Crisp'

Malus pumila 'Hohenzollernapfel'

Malus pumila 'Howgate Wonder'

Malus pumila 'Jonagold'

Malus pumila 'Kardinal Bea'

Malus pumila 'Starkspur Compact Mac'

Malus pumila 'Shakespeare'

Malus pumila 'Liberty'

Malus pumila 'Lobo'

Malus pumila 'Macoun'

Malus pumila 'Mutsu'

Malus pumila 'Pink Pearl'

Malus pumila 'Red Fuji'

M. pumila 'Reverend W. Wilks'

Malus pumila 'Rosemary Russett'

Malus pumila 'Scarlet Gala'

Malus pumila 'Senshu'

Malus pumila 'Spigold'

Malus pumila 'Starkspur'

Malus pumila 'Talheimer'

Malus pumila 'Tuscan'

Malus pumila 'Yellow Bellflower'

Malus pumila 'Rheinischer Krummstiel'

Malus pumila 'Winter Banana'

Malus × *purpurea* cultivar, in spring

Malus × *purpurea*

Malus × purpurea

☀ ❄ ↔ 25 ft (8 m) ↑ 20 ft (6 m)

A very early flowering crabapple, this is a hybrid of *M.* × *atrosanguinea* and *M. pumila* 'Niedzwetzkyana'. It has deep green leaves, and dark flowers that fade to pale mauve, in late spring.

'Aldenhamensis' blooms up to 3 times per season, leaves red-green to bronze-green, buds bright carmine, single and semi-double pinkish red flowers; 'Eleyi', deep red-purple foliage, purple to red flowers, subject to leaf diseases; 'Lemoinei', a popular red-flowered crabapple. Zones 4–9.

Malus × robusta

☀ ❄ ↔ 12 ft (3.5 m) ↑ 20 ft (6 m)

Conical-crowned large shrub or small tree, an *M. baccata* × *M. prunifolia* hybrid. Bright green leaves, 4 in (10 cm) long, scalloped edges. Flowers white to pink, in clusters of 3 to 8, in spring. Long-stemmed yellow to red fruits. 'Erecta', large white flowers with pink edges. Zones 3–9.

Malus × *robusta* 'Erecta'

Malus sargentii

Malus × *purpurea* cultivar, in autumn

Malus × *purpurea* 'Aldenhamensis'

Malus sargentii

SARGENT'S CRABAPPLE

☀ ❄ ↔ 15 ft (4.5 m) ↑ 6 ft (1.8 m)

This is a very small, densely branched crabapple. The leaves are broadly oval, sharp-tipped, heavy, bright green, and lobed, with serrated edges. The flowers are white, single, fragrant, and appear in spring. Tiny fruit, crimson to purple, follow the flowers. Disease resistant, blooms in alternate years. 'Rosea', deep red-pink buds, white flowers, dark red fruit. Zones 4–9.

Malus × scheideckeri

☀ ❄ ↔ 8 ft (2.4 m) ↑ 15 ft (4.5 m)

This slow-growing, small, upright tree is a hybrid of *M. floribunda* and *M. prunifolia*. It has coarsely serrated leaves. The flowers are faded rose pink, usually semi-double, in thick clusters on the branches, in late spring. The fruit is slightly ribbed, yellow-orange. Tolerates pruning. 'Exzellenz Thiel', pale pink to white flowers; 'Red Jade', drooping red fruit. Zones 4–9.

Malus × *scheideckeri* 'Exzellenz Thiel'

Malus × *purpurea* cultivar, in winter

Malus × *purpurea* 'Lemoinei'

Malus sieboldii

☀ ❄ ↔ 10 ft (3 m) ↑ 15 ft (4.5 m)

This slow-growing, small- to medium-size, rounded tree comes from Japan. Lobed or simple leaves. Buds red to

Malus × *scheideckeri*

Malus × *scheideckeri* 'Red Jade'

Malus sieboldii

Malus, Hybrid Cultivar, 'Adams'

carmine, opening to single white flowers, in spring. The fruits are very small, red. Disease resistant. ***M. s.* var. *arborescens***, larger leaves, white flowers, reddish fruit. **Zones 4–9.**

Malus spectabilis
CHINESE FLOWERING CRABAPPLE
☼ ❋ ↔ 20 ft (6 m) ↑ 25 ft (8 m)
Old, spectacular, flowering crabapple, originally from China, but now unknown in the wild. The buds are deep rose red, blush-colored flowers, attractive semi-double to double form or single form, in spring. Fruits yellowish. **'Riversii'**, largest double pink crabapple flowers. **Zones 4–9.**

Malus sylvestris
COMMON CRAB APPLE, WILD CRAB APPLE
☼ ❋ ↔ 10 ft (3 m) ↑ 30 ft (9 m)
From Europe. Small tree with dense rounded crown, dark bark. Some branches are thorny. Flowers are white or pink, followed by sour yellow-green or reddish fruits. **Zones 3–9.**

Malus transitoria
TIBETAN CRABAPPLE
☼ ❋ ↔ 30 ft (9 m) ↑ 25 ft (8 m)
Graceful specimen tree from China. Deeply lobed green leaves turn yellow in autumn. Pink buds in spring, then single white flowers. Small brownish fruits. Highly susceptible to scab. **Zones 5–10.**

Malus tschonoskii
☼ ❋ ↔ 20 ft (6 m) ↑ 40 ft (12 m)
This is one of the larger crabapples, and comes from Japan. Sturdy upright habit. Excellent autumn color; green leaves turn purple, orange, bronze, yellow, and crimson. The flowers are white with pink hue, in spring. Fruit insignificant. Susceptible to most apple diseases. **Zones 6–10.**

Malus × zumi
☼ ❋ ↔ 10 ft (3 m) ↑ 15 ft (4.5 m)
This small downy-stemmed tree has a pyramidal habit. It is a natural Japanese hybrid of *M. baccata* var. *mandshurica* and *M. sieboldii*. The leaves taper to a fine point, and have scalloped to lobed edges. Pink buds, in spring, then white flowers, 1¼ in (30in mm) wide. Small red fruits. *M. × zumi* var. *calocarpa*, spreading habit, smaller flowers, leaves smooth-edged on fruiting spurs, lobed elsewhere. **Zones 5–9.**

Malus Hybrid Cultivars
☼ ❋ ↔ 5–25 ft (1.5–8 m) ↑ 10–40 ft (3–12 m)
Numerous crabapple cultivars have been raised, many in the USA. Most are grown for floral display, some for decorative fruit, and larger fruit of some can be eaten fresh or as preserves. The parent with the most influence is *M. pumila* 'Niedzwetzkyana', originating from a single tree with red flowers and purple-red new foliage, discovered in central Asia before 1900. Some of the best are: **'Adams'**, to 20 ft (6 m)

Malus × zumi, espalier

Malus sieboldii var. *arborescens*

Malus × zumi var. *calocarpa*

high, reddish pink flowers, red fruit; **'Adirondack'**, to 12 ft (3.5 m) high, narrow upright tree, buds dark carmine, wide-spreading white flowers with traces of pink, fruits red to orange–red; **'Almey'**, deep reddish pink flowers, small fruit; **'Beverly'**,

20 ft (6 m) high, white single flowers, red fruit; **'Brandywine'**, to 20 ft (6 m) high, dome-shaped tree, buds deep rose, double fragrant flowers of rose pink, yellow-green fruits; **'Butterball'**, 25 ft (8 m) high, pinkish white flowers, orange-yellow fruit; **'Chilko'**,

single purple-pink flowers, vivid red to crimson fruits; **'Christmas Holly'** ★, 15 ft (4.5 m) high, small rounded spreading tree, buds bright red, single white flowers, fruits small, holly-like, bright red, in clusters; **'Dolgo'**, white flowers, early-ripening purple-red fruit; **'Fiesta'**, to 15 ft (4.5 m) high, weeping habit, buds carmine, single white flowers in cascades, fruits burnt coral to orange-gold; **'Golden Hornet'**, small, upright, pendulous tree, single white flowers, fruit lime-yellow;

'Gorgeous', compact dome-shaped tree, pink buds, single white flowers, fruits crimson to orange-red; **'Harvest Gold'**, upright tree, single white flowers, golden fruit, disease resistant; **'John Downie'**, pink buds, single white flowers, fruits large, orange with red cheeks, disease resistant; **'Madonna'**, 20 ft (6 m) high, compact upright tree, white buds, large, double, fragrant, white flowers, small brown-red fruits; **'Mary Potter'**, 20 ft (6 m) high, dark foliage, bright pink flowers, dark buds, deep red to purple-red fruits; **'Naragansett'**, 12 ft (3.5 m) high, broad crown, buds carmine, single white flowers, pink hue, shiny cherry red fruits, in clusters, disease resistant; **'Pink Perfection'**, sterile cultivar, pink and white double flowers; **'Profusion'**, to 20 ft (6 m) high, upright, wide, spreading tree, leaves purplish to bronze, buds deep red to purple-pink, deep rose

Malus, Hybrid Cultivar, 'Almey'

Malus, Hybrid Cultivar, 'Burgandy'

Malus, Hybrid Cultivar, 'Arrow'

Malus, Hybrid Cultivar, 'Beverly'

Malus, HC, 'Bob White'

Malus, Hybrid Cultivar, 'Anne E.'

Malus, Hybrid Cultivar, 'Callaway'

Malus, Hybrid Cultivar, 'Callaway'

Malus, Hybrid Cultivar, 'Cowichan'

Malus, HC, 'Crimson Brilliant'

Malus, Hybrid Cultivar, 'David'

Malus, Hybrid Cultivar, 'Dolgo'

M., HC, 'Girard's Weeping Dwarf'

Malus, HC, 'Goldfinch'

Malus, Hybrid Cultivar, 'Gorgeous'

Malus, HC, 'Harvest Gold'

Malus, HC, 'Henrietta Crosby'

Malus, HC, 'Indian Summer'

Malus, HC, 'Johnson's Walters'

Malus, HC, 'Mary Potter'

Malus, HC, 'Ormiston Roy'

Malus, Hybrid Cultivar, 'Makamik', in spring

Malus, Hybrid Cultivar, 'Makamik', in summer

Malus, Hybrid Cultivar, 'Makamik', in winter

Malus, Hybrid Cultivar, 'Makamik'

Malus, Hybrid Cultivar, 'Pink Perfection'

Malus, Hybrid Cultivar, 'Profusion'

Malus, Hybrid Cultivar, 'Red Jewel'

Malus, HC, 'Red Peacock'

Malus, HC, 'Red Sentinel'

Malus, HC, 'Pink Princess'

Malus, Hybrid Cultivar, 'Snowdrift'

Malus, Hybrid Cultivar, 'Snowdrift

Malus, HC, 'Strathmore'

Malus, Hybrid Cultivar, 'Turesi'

Malus, HC, 'White Angel'

Malus, Hybrid Cultivar, 'Sparkler'

Malus, Hybrid Cultivar, 'Pink Satin'

Malus, Hybrid Cultivar, 'Royal Ruby'

Malus, Hybrid Cultivar, 'Sparkler', in winter

Malus, Hybrid Cultivar, 'Sparkler', in summer

pink single flowers, fruits maroon to blood red; **'Red Sentinel'**, early white flowers, red fruits; **'Royalty'**, 15 ft (4.5 m) high, reddish foliage, purple-red flowers and fruit; **'White Angel'** (syn. 'Inglis'), white flowers, pink buds, small red fruits; **'White Cascade'**, to 15 ft (4.5 m) high, graceful weeping habit, single white flowers, green-yellow fruit, disease resistant; **'Winter Gold'**, to 20 ft (6 m) high, vase-shaped tree, carmine buds, single white flowers, fruits bright lemon yellow. Zones 4–9.

MALVA
MALLOW, MUSK MALLOW

Like the hollyhock, to which it is related, *Malva* is a member of the mallow (Malvaceae) family. These easily cultivated plants are native to Europe, North Africa, and Asia. This

Malus, Hybrid Cultivar, 'Sparkler', in spring

Malva moschata 'Alba'

Malva sylvestris 'Primley Blue'

genus contains at least 30 species of annuals, biennials, and short-lived herbaceous perennials similar to hollyhocks, but bushier and with smaller leaves. Flowers 5-petalled, single, in shades of white, pink, blue, or purple. CULTIVATION: Grow in herbaceous or annual borders. They do best in a sunny position but will tolerate partial shade in well-drained soil. Remove spent flowers to encourage a second flowering; cut down to the ground in autumn. Propagate from cuttings or seed in spring. Plants will self-seed.

Malva alcea
☼ ✽ ↔ 24 in (60 cm) ↕ 40 in (100 cm)
Southern European herbaceous perennial, naturalized in the USA. Deeply lobed light green leaves with toothed edges. Mauve-pink flowers, in midsummer to mid-autumn. Zone 3–10.

Malva moschata
MUSK MALLOW
☼ ✽ ↔ 18 in (45 cm) ↕ 40 in (100 cm)
European perennial. Narrow, finely cut, mid-green leaves; musky smell when brushed or crushed. Abundant, saucer-shaped, rose-pink flowers, in summer. 'Alba', white, bushy branching habit; 'Rosea' has profuse pink flowers. Zone 3–10.

Malva sylvestris
CHEESES, COMMON MALLOW, HIGH MALLOW
☼ ✽ ↔ 7–25 ft (2–8 m) ↕ 3 ft (0.9 m)
Biennial or perennial from Europe. Leaves green, alternate, to 4 in (10 cm) long. Flowers rose-purple with dark veins, in early summer to early autumn or until frosts. 'Primley Blue' has bluish purple flowers with dark blue veins. Zones 3–9.

MALVAVISCUS
This genus consists of 3 species of Central and South American evergreen shrubs from the mallow (Malvaceae) family. Their broad downy leaves are often lobed. They have unusually shaped flowers, borne singly in the leaf axils or in small clusters at the ends of branches. They are bright orange-red and usually held upright. The long petals stay partly furled, never really opening fully, and from their center emerges a long hibiscus-like column. Small red berries follow the flowers.
CULTIVATION: Although able to withstand the very lightest frosts, these shrubs are best grown in warm subtropical to tropical areas. They thrive in moist, humus-rich, well-drained soil and can be grown in sun or part-shade. Their branches have a tendency to die back and are often attacked by boring grubs, so some pruning, thinning, and trimming is necessary. Propagate from seed or from half-hardened cuttings.

Malvaviscus arboreus
TURK'S CAP, WAX MALLOW
☼ ✥ ↔ 10 ft (3 m)
↕ 12–15 ft (3.5–4.5 m)
Shrub from southern Texas and Florida, USA, to Peru and Brazil. Velvety ovate to heart-shaped leaves, may be 3-lobed. Long-stemmed rich red flowers, face upward or slightly bend, in summer. *M. a.* var. *drummondii*, brilliant reddish orange hibiscus-like flowers, swirled petals never fully open, in late summer–autumn. Zones 9–12.

Malvaviscus penduliflorus
syn. *Malvaviscus arboreus* var. *penduliflorus*
CARDINAL'S HAT, SLEEPING HIBISCUS
☼ ✦ ↔ 10 ft (3 m)
↕ 12–15 ft (3.5–4.5 m)
Mexican shrub, very similar to more widely grown *M. arboreus*. Less hairy leaves. Larger, pendulous rather than upright, red flowers, in late summer. Zones 11–12.

MAMMILLARIA
PINCUSHION CACTUS
A genus in the family Cactaceae containing more than 150 low-growing, solitary or clustering, hemispherical, spherical, or columnar cacti from southwestern USA, Mexico, Central America, and northern South America. They are grown for the rings of funnel-shaped flowers, in colors ranging from white through cream to pinks and reds, sometimes yellow, sometimes purplish or green, that develop near the crown. The spiny, green, spherical to cylindrical stems are covered with raised segments called areoles, containing pimple-like openings known as tubercles from which stiff spines arise. These clumping plants spread by growing offsets. The fruits are slender to spherical berry-like seed pods that grow between the tubercles.
CULTIVATION: These plants are adaptable to most well-drained soils in an open sunny position. Keep drier in winter. Propagate most species by division of offsets, or from seed in spring and summer.

Mammillaria albicoma
☼ ↔ 1¼–5 in (3–12 cm)
↕ 2–2½ in (5–6 cm)
Clustering cactus from northeastern central Mexico. Stem with hair-like bristles in axils. Up to 4 straight, darkly tipped, white central spines, white radial spines. Creamy flowers, in spring. Zones 9–11.

Mammillaria angelensis
syns *Chilita angelensis*, *Ebnerella angelensis*
☼ ✥ ↔ 1¼–1¾ in (3–4 cm)
↕ 6–10 in (15–25 cm)
Slowly offsetting columnar cactus from Mexico. Pinkish buds, cream flowers with darker mid-veins, opening late winter, occasionally late summer. Zones 9–11.

Mammillaria blossfeldiana
☼ ✥ ↔ 1¼–2 in (3–5 cm)
↕ 3–4 in (8–10 cm)
Simple or clustering cactus from central Baja California, Mexico. Dark

Mammillaria angelensis

Malvaviscus arboreus

Malvaviscus penduliflorus

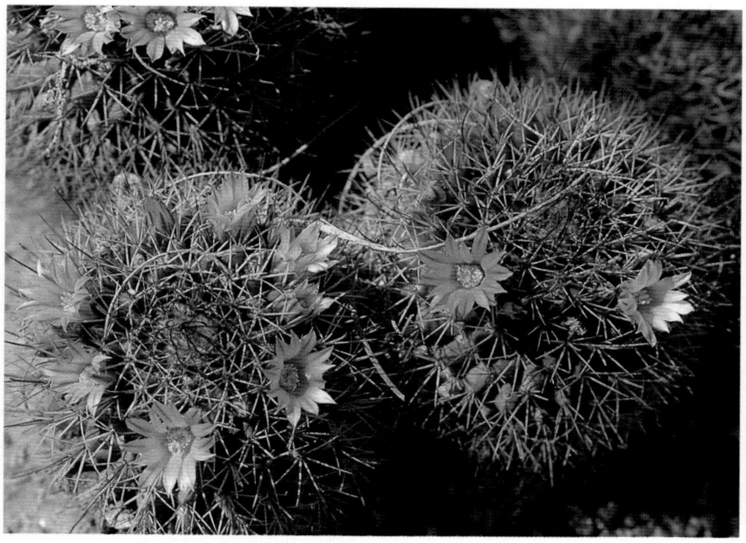

Mammillaria bocensis

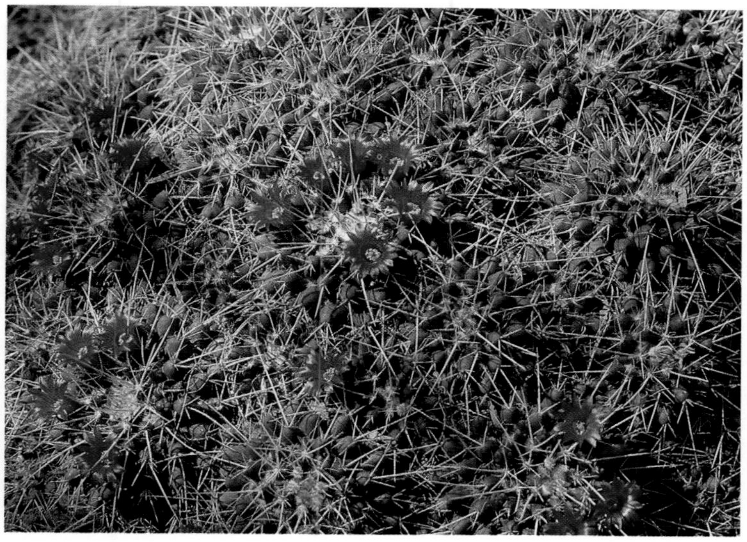

Mammillaria compressa

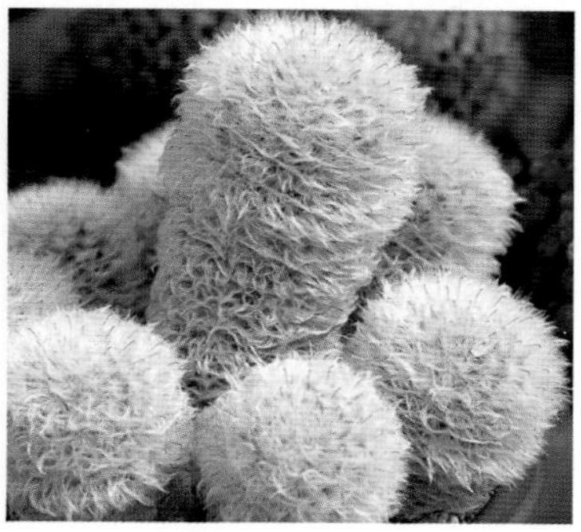

Mammillaria bocasana

green spherical to shortly cylindrical stem. Sparsely woolly axils without bristles. Central spines dark, radial spines pale yellow, dark-tipped. Flowers pinkish white, rose stripes, in summer. Zones 9–11.

Mammillaria bocasana ★

POWDER-PUFF CACTUS

↔ 12–24 in (30–60 cm)
↑ 4–8 in (10–20 cm)

A clump-forming perennial cactus from central Mexico. Spherical stem, densely covered in spines. Axils naked or with fine hairs or bristles; central spines red or brown, white radial spines. Flowers creamy white or rose pink, in spring–summer. Red seed pods. Zones 9–11.

Mammillaria bocensis

↔ 4 in (10 cm) ↑ 3–6 in (8–15 cm)

A simple or clustering cactus from northwestern Mexico. Rounded to short-cylindrical stem, usually no bristles on axils; reddish brown central spine, radial spines dark-tipped, white to red. Green or pale pink flowers, striped brown, in summer. Zones 9–11.

Mammillaria candida ★

↔ 6 in (15 cm) ↑ 4–6 in (10–15 cm)

A slow-growing, clump-forming perennial cactus from Mexico. Spherical to stout-cylindrical green stems, cylindrical tubercles. Axils with fine white bristles; central spines white. Cream to rose pink flowers, with purplish red stigmas, in spring. Zones 9–11.

Mammillaria canelensis

↔ 3–4 in (8–10 cm)
↑ 6–8 in (15–20 cm)

This cactus comes from Mexico. It has a solitary rounded stem; woolly bristly axils; 2 to 4 straight or curved, yellow to orange-brown central spines, and 22 to 25 fine white radial spines. Pink to red or yellow flowers, appear in summer. Zones 9–11.

Mammillaria carmenae

↔ 2–3 in (5–8 cm)
↑ 2–3 in (5–8 cm)

A clustering cactus from eastern central Mexico. Spherical to egg-shaped stem; no central spines, more than 100 pale radial spines. White flowers tinged pink or cream, yellow stigmas, in spring. **'Jewel'** is available in two colors, intense pink or white. Zones 9–11.

Mammillaria carnea

↔ 3½–8 in (9–20 cm)
↑ 3–3½ in (7.5–9 cm)

A clustering, sometimes simple, cactus from southern Mexico. Spherical stem; 4-angled tubercles, often red-brown toward tip, axils woolly, no bristles; usually 4 pinkish brown spines, black-tipped. Flesh pink flowers, in spring. Zones 9–11.

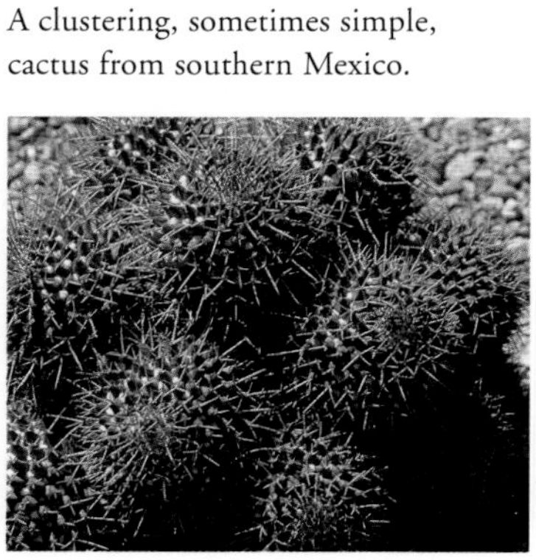

Mammillaria carnea

Mammillaria compressa ★

↔ 6 in (15 cm)
↑ 1½–2½ in (4–6 cm)

A clustering cactus from central Mexico. Flattened spherical stems; swollen angled tubercles. Woolly bristly axils. White to pale red spines, darker tips, 4 to 6 unequal. Dark purplish pink flowers, in spring. Zones 9–11.

Mammillaria crucigera

↔ 1¼–2 in (3–5 cm)
↑ 4–6 in (10–15 cm)

Simple or branching cactus from southern Mexico. Cylindrical to club-shaped stem, white wool on axils. Yellow or brown rigid central spines, waxy; white radial spines. Purple flowers and stigmas, in summer. Zones 9–11.

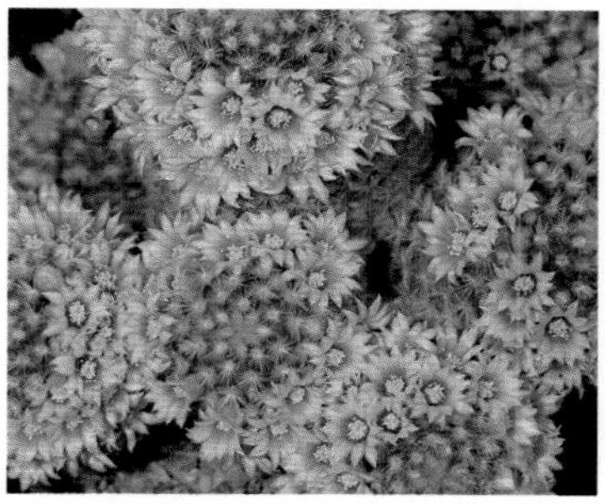

Mammillaria carmenae 'Jewel'

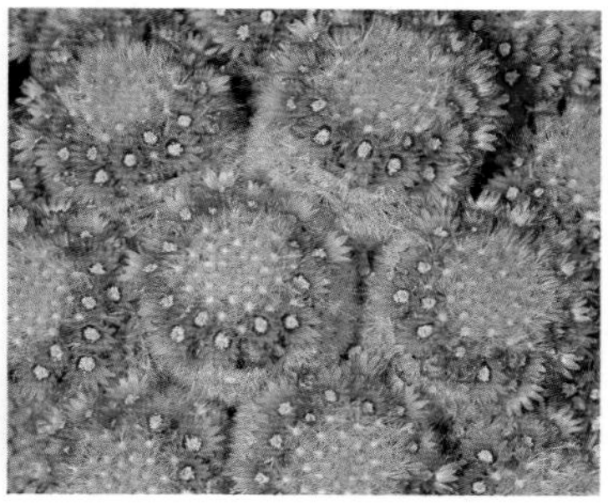

Mammillaria carmenae 'Jewel'

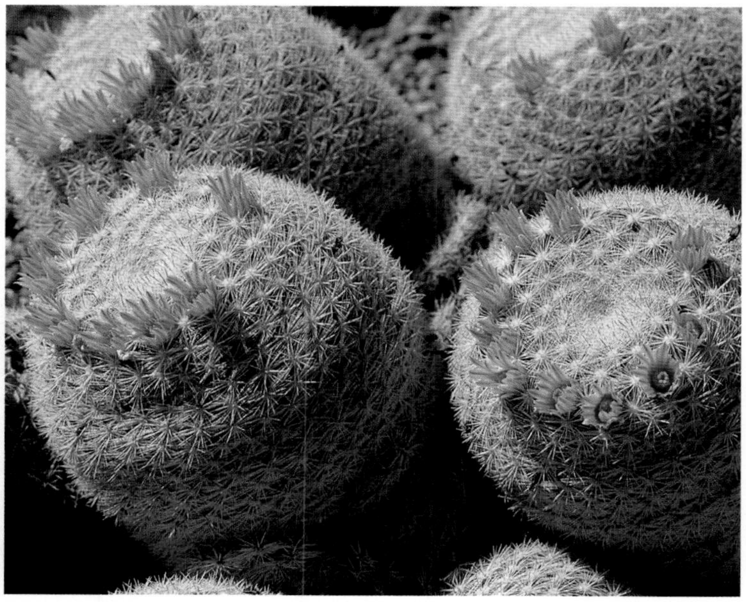

Mammillaria canelensis

Mammillaria elongata ★

LACE CACTUS

☀ ⬡ ↔ 8–12 in (20–30 cm)
↑ 4–6 in (10–15 cm)

Clump-forming perennial cactus from central Mexico. Columnar elongated stem; up to 3 pale yellow to brown central spines, 14 to 25 yellow radial spines. Pale yellow flowers, sometimes pink-tinged, in spring–summer. Offsets freely. Zones 9–11.

Mammillaria geminispina ★

☀ ⬡ ↔ 6–20 in (15–50 cm)
↑ 6–10 in (15–25 cm)

A clustering mound-forming perennial cactus from central Mexico. Spherical to cylindrical stem; woolly tubercles, short bristles. Central spines white, dark-tipped; radial spines white. Deep pink to red

Mammillaria elongata

Mammillaria haageana

Mammillaria geminispina 'Crest'

Mammillaria karwinskiana

flowers, appear in spring–autumn. 'Crest', gray-green woolly tubercles. Zones 9–11.

Mammillaria haageana

☀ ⬡ ↔ 2–4 in (5–10 cm)
↑ 4–6 in (10–15 cm)

Simple cactus from southeastern central Mexico. Small packed tubercles; woolly axils may have bristles. Central spines brown, radial spines white. Small dark purplish pink flowers, in spring. Zones 9–11.

Mammillaria hahniana ★

OLD LADY CACTUS, OLD WOMAN CACTUS

☀ ⬡ ↔ 8–12 in (20–30 cm)
↑ 6–10 in (15–25 cm)

Simple or clustering cactus from Mexico. Spherical to columnar; copious triangular to conical tubercles,

Mammillaria hertrichiana 'Superba'

long white bristles. White central spines, brown-tipped; radial spines white, hair-like. Deep purplish pink flowers, in spring. Spherical red fruits. Zones 9–11.

Mammillaria herrerae

☀ ⬡ ↔ ¾–1¼ in (18–30 mm)
↑ ¾–1¼ in (18–30 mm)

Simple or clustering cactus from Mexico. Rounded to cylindrical stem covered in small tubercles. No central spine, 60 to 100 bristly, pale, radial spines. Lavender-pink to white flowers, green stigmas, in spring. Zones 9–11.

Mammillaria hertrichiana

☀ ⬡ ↔ 6–18 in (15–45 cm)
↑ 6–18 in (15–45 cm)

Clumping cactus from Mexico with dome heads up to 5 in (12 cm) wide. Deep pink to white flowers with darker mid-stripe, in late winter. 'Superba', gray green, hairy, dome-shaped heads. Zones 9–11.

Mammillaria karwinskiana

syn. *Mammillaria multiseta*

☀ ⬡ ↔ 4–6 in (10–15 cm)
↑ 4–6 in (10–15 cm)

Simple cactus from southern Mexico, dividing by offsets. Flattened spherical to short cylindrical stem. Conical tubercles, bristly axils, reddish brown spines. Pale yellow flowers, may have red outside stripes, in spring or autumn. Zones 9–11.

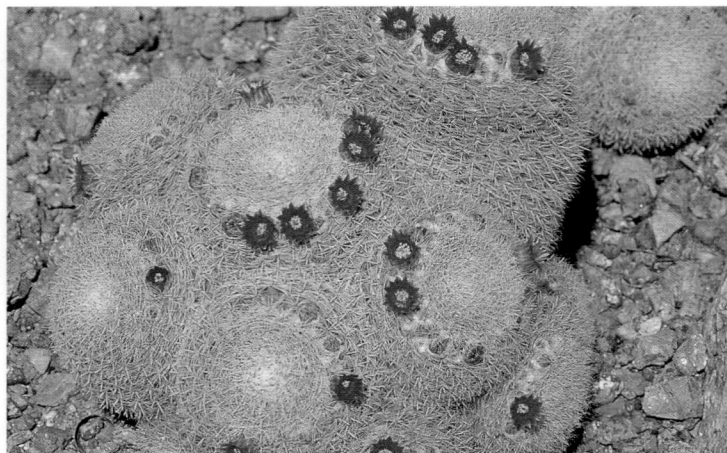

Mammillaria klissingiana

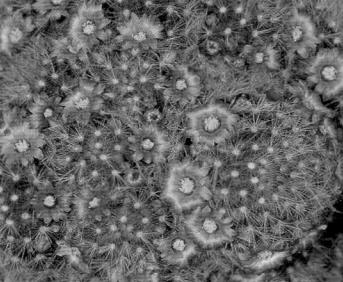

Mammillaria laui var. *rubens*

Mammillaria klissingiana

☀ ⬡ ↔ 2½–4 in (6–10 cm)
↑ 4–6 in (10–15 cm)

A simple, then clustering, cactus from central Mexico. It has spherical to club-shaped stems. The axils have white bristles; the central spines are nearly white, with darker tips, radial spines nearly white. Pink flowers, in summer. Zones 9–11.

Mammillaria laui

☀ ⬡ ↔ 1½–2 in (3.5–5 cm)
↑ 1–1½ in (2.5–3.5 cm)

A clustering cactus from east-central Mexico. It has roughly spherical stems, and cylindrical tubercles hidden by spines. There may be many or no central spines with more than 60 hair-like white radial spines. The purplish pink flowers, with white stigmas, appear in spring. *M. l.* var. *rubens*, magenta flowers, shiny, with yellow centers. Zones 9–11.

Mammillaria longimamma

syn. *Dolichothele longimamma*

☀ ✦ ↔ 3–5 in (8–12 cm)
↑ 3–5 in (8–12 cm)

A slow-growing, simple or clustering, perennial cactus from central Mexico. It has very large tubercles, oblong to cylindrical in section. The spines are pale brown, yellow, or white. The big, bright yellow flowers emerge from axils around the stems, in summer. Zones 11–12.

Mammillaria longimamma

Mammillaria magnifica ★

☼ ⚘ ↔ 2–4 in (5–10 cm)
↑ 12–16 in (30–40 cm)

Clustering cactus from south-central Mexico. Cylindrical stems; pyramidal or conical tubercles; rounded bristly axils. Clear yellow-brown hooked central spines, white or yellow radial spines. Pinkish red flowers, in spring. Zones 9–11.

Mammillaria magnimamma ★

☼ ⚘ ↔ 18–24 in (45–60 cm)
↑ 10–12 in (25–30 cm)

Perennial cactus from central Mexico. Variable, mostly clustering, and mound-forming. Pronounced, angular, dark green, pyramidal-conical tubercles; woolly axils. Curved white spines. Pale yellow to deep purplish pink flowers, in spring–late summer. Zones 9–11.

Mammillaria marksiana

☼ ⚘ ↔ 2–5 in (5–12 cm)
↑ 2½–6 in (6–15 cm)

Perennial cactus from northwestern Mexico. Simple at first, then clustering. Spherical stems with woolly apex. Golden yellow or brown spines. Yellow flowers, in summer. Zones 9–11.

Mammillaria mazatlanensis

☼ ⚘ ↔ ¾–1¾ in (18–40 mm)
↑ 4–6 in (10–15 cm)

Clustering cactus from northwestern Mexico. Slender cylindrical stems,

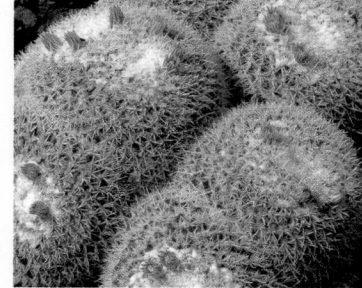

Mammillaria muehlenpfordtii

Mammillaria magnimamma

short conical tubercles, axils bare or a few small bristles. Central spines reddish brown, sometimes hooked; radial spines white. Carmine red flowers, green stigmas, in summer. Zones 9–11.

Mammillaria melanocentra

☼ ⚘ ↔ 4–6 in (10–15 cm)
↑ 3–5 in (8–12 cm)

Simple perennial cactus from northern Mexico. Flattened spherical stems, bluish green; large pyramid-shaped tubercles and axils woolly at first. Stout black central spine, unequal radial spines, black when young. Deep pink flowers, appear in spring. Zones 9–11.

Mammillaria microhelia

☼ ⚘ ↔ 12–16 in (30–40 cm)
↑ 6–8 in (15–20 cm)

Simple or clustering perennial from central Mexico. Cylindrical stem; short conical tubercles, bare axils. Deep reddish brown central spines, many yellow radial spines. Creamy white, red, or purple flowers, in spring. Zones 9–11.

Mammillaria moelleriana

☼ ⚘ ↔ 3–4 in (8–10 cm)
↑ 6–12 in (15–30 cm)

Simple cactus from western to central Mexico. Spherical to slightly cylindrical stem, egg-shaped tubercles, bare axils. Central spines browny yellow

Mammillaria marksiana

Mammillaria melanocentra

to deep reddish brown; radial spines yellow to white. Pale pink flowers, dark stripe, in spring. Zones 9–11.

Mammillaria muehlenpfordtii

☼ ⚘ ↔ 4–6 in (10–15 cm)
↑ 4–6 in (10–15 cm)

Cactus from central Mexico. Often dividing with age, flattened spherical individual heads. Conical tubercles, finely bristled axils; central spines yellow, often brown-tipped; radial spines glassy white. Pink to purplish flowers, in summer. Zones 9–11.

Mammillaria mystax

☼ ⚘ ↔ 3–4 in (8–10 cm)
↑ 4–6 in (10–15 cm)

Simple cactus, dividing later, from southern Mexico. Spherical to cylindrical stems; pyramid-shaped tubercles, bristly axils. Central spines purplish brown, later gray, distorted;

Mammillaria picta

white radial spines, brown-tipped. Dark purplish pink flowers, in spring. Zones 9–11.

Mammillaria parkinsonii ★

☼ ⚘ ↔ 3–6 in (8–15 cm)
↑ 4–6 in (10–15 cm)

Cactus from central Mexico. Simple, then dividing; pyramidal tubercles. Woolly bristly axils; central spines white or reddish brown, uppermost very short; white radial spines. Flowers creamy yellow, hint of brown or pink, in spring. Zones 9–11.

Mammillaria pennispinosa

☼ ✛ ↔ 1½–2 in (3.5–5 cm)
↑ 1½–2 in (3.5–5 cm)

Usually simple perennial cactus from northern Mexico. Nearly spherical; cylindrical tubercles; axils initially woolly; central spines brownish red with yellow bases; radial spines slender, grayish white, feathery. Flowers cream to pink, deeper mid-stripe, form ring around stem, in early spring. Zones 11–12.

Mammillaria picta

☼ ⚘ ↔ 1–2 in (2.5–5 cm)
↑ 1–2 in (2.5–5 cm)

Simple cactus from northeastern and central Mexico. Spherical to egg-shaped stems later tuberous; tubercles cylindrical, axils with fine bristles;

Mammillaria parkinsonii

Mammillaria mystax

Mammillaria prolifera

Mammillaria sonorensis

Mammillaria spinosissima

Mammillaria plumosa

hairy spines, centrals darker than radials. White flowers, tinged pale green, in spring. Zones 9–11.

Mammillaria plumosa ★

☀ ❄ ↔ 2½–16 in (6–40 cm)
↕ 4–6 in (10–15 cm)

A clustering, perennial cactus from northeastern Mexico that forms mounds. The spherical green stems are hidden by white feathery spines. There are cylindrical tubercles, woolly axils. The tiny flowers, creamy white, with a hint of brownish pink, appear in winter. Zones 9–11.

Mammillaria tayloriorum

Mammillaria sonorensis

syn. *Mammillaria craigii*

☀ ❄ ↔ 2–3 in (5–8 cm)
↕ 4–6 in (10–15 cm)

Simple cactus from northwestern Mexico. Central spines reddish brown; radial spines creamy white, tips brown. Flowers deep pink, olive green style and stigmas, in spring. Zones 9–11.

Mammillaria spinosissima ★

☀ ❄ ↔ 2½–3 in (6–8 cm)
↕ 4–6 in (10–15 cm)

Cactus from central Mexico. Simple, later clustering; cylindrical stems; oval to conical tubercles, slightly woolly axils. Central spines reddish brown or pale yellow; radial spines bristly, nearly white. Purplish pink flowers, in spring. Zones 9–11.

Mammillaria standleyi

☀ ❄ ↔ 3–5 in (8–12 cm)
↕ 3–4 in (8–10 cm)

Cactus from northwestern Mexico. Simple or erect, sometimes clustering. Flattened-spherical stems, pale bluish green, blunt tubercles. Woolly bristly axils; central spines white, reddish brown tips; radial spines white. Purple pink flowers, in spring. Zones 9–11.

Mammillaria prolifera

STRAWBERRY CACTUS

☀ ❄ ↔ 8–12 in (20–30 cm)
↕ 2½–4 in (6–10 cm)

A perennial cactus from northeastern Mexico, southwestern USA, and the West Indies. It forms dense clumps; with axils almost bare. The straight central spines are white to reddish brown; the fine radial spines are white. The creamy yellow tubular flowers, which may be pink-tinged, or brown-striped, emerge in spring–summer. The red berries taste like strawberries. Zones 9–11.

Mammillaria rhodantha

☀ ❄ ↔ 12–24 in (30–60 cm)
↕ 12–24 in (30–60 cm)

A perennial cactus from central Mexico. Usually simple, sometimes offsetting or branching; the spherical to cylindrical stems sometimes divide with age. The central spines are reddish brown; radial spines are glassy white to pale yellow. The flowers, purplish red, appear in late summer. Zones 9–11.

Mammillaria supertexta

☀ ❄ ↔ 2–3 in (5–8 cm)
↕ 4–6 in (10–15 cm)

Cactus native to southern Mexico. Simple, nearly spherical to cylindrical stems; crowded, small, conical tubercles, woolly axils; central spines white, sometimes tipped black, radial spines white. Small deep red or pink flowers, in spring. Zones 9–11.

Mammillaria tayloriorum

☀ ❄ ↔ 2½–3 in (6–8 cm)
↕ 3–6 in (8–15 cm)

A cactus from central Mexico. The spherical stems form large clusters covered with dense whitish spines. Rings of small pink flowers emerge in spring. Zones 9–11.

Mammillaria winterae

☀ ❄ ↔ 8–12 in (20–30 cm)
↕ 8–12 in (20–30 cm)

Cactus from northeastern Mexico. Simple, flattened, spherical stem; quadrangular tubercles; axils becoming densely woolly. Flowers with pale yellow outer tepals, brownish red mid-stripe, near-white inner tepals, pale sulfur yellow stripe, in summer. Zones 9–11.

Mammillaria winterae

Mammillaria standleyi

Mandevilla × amabilis 'Alice du Pont'

Mandevilla sanderi, 'Scarlet Pimpernel'

Mandevilla boliviensis

MANDEVILLA

Central and South American genus in the dogbane (Apocynaceae) family; contains some 120 species of mainly tuberous perennials, subshrubs, and twining vines. Leaves are large, deep green, elliptical to lance-shaped with prominent elongated tips. Trumpet flowers, carried singly or in racemes, often large and sometimes fragrant, throughout the warmer months. They come in white to cream and various shades of pink. More commonly cultivated are the beautiful vigorous vines. CULTIVATION: Only a few species will tolerate any frost and all prefer a mild to warm climate, dappled sunlight, and moist, humus-rich, well-drained soil. Trim if necessary. All parts exude an irritant milky latex when cut. Feeding produces lush foliage but also rampant growth. Propagate from half-hardened stems in summer, or cuttings.

Mandevilla × amabilis

☼/☀ ✦ ↔ 15 ft (4.5 m) ↑ 15 ft (4.5 m)
Vigorous climber, uncertain origins (probably *M. splendens* hybrid). Deeply veined, leathery leaves, 4–8 in (10–20 cm) long. Yellow-throated, dark-centered, pink flowers, in spring. '**Alice du Pont**', back-cross of *M. × amabilis* with *M. splendens* (syn. *M. × amoena*), lush foliage, large deep pink flowers. Zones 11–12.

Mandevilla boliviensis

WHITE DIPLADENIA
☼/☀ ✦ ↔ 10 ft (3 m) ↑ 15 ft (4.5 m)
Twining climber from Bolivia and Ecuador. Broad, glossy, elliptical

leaves, tapering to fine point, to 4 in (10 cm) long. White flowers, to 2 in (5 cm) long, with golden centers; up to 7 blooms per raceme, appear in summer. Zones 11–12.

Mandevilla laxa

CHILEAN JASMINE
☼ ✦ ↔ 17 ft (5 m) ↑ 15 ft (4.5 m)
Vigorous semi-evergreen to deciduous climber, native to Argentina. Elliptical leaves taper to fine point, dark green to bronze, downy, sometimes purplish undersides, to 3 in (8 cm) long. White flowers, 2 in (5 cm) wide, strongly scented, especially evenings, in late spring–summer. Zones 9–11.

Mandevilla sanderi

☼/☀ ✦ ↔ 17 ft (5 m) ↑ 17 ft (5 m)
Strong-growing Brazilian climber. Glossy, smooth-surfaced, leathery leaves, 3 in (8 cm) long. Deep pink yellow-throated flowers, to 2 in (5 cm) wide, up to 5 blooms per raceme, in spring. '**Scarlet Pimpernel**', very deep pink to red flowers. Zones 11–12.

MANDRAGORA

MANDRAKE
A genus of 6 species of stemless, rosette-forming, herbaceous perennials in the nightshade (Solanaceae) family. Flowers are held in clusters surrounded by the leaves, followed by fleshy rounded berries. Native to dry areas of the Mediterranean and the

Mandevilla laxa, in spring

Himalayas, they have long been thought to hold magical powers; the deep tap root, which often resembles the torso of a man, is believed to stimulate sexual desire. Many thought that uprooting a mandrake would caused madness as it would scream, so a dog was employed to remove it. The root was tied to the dog's tail. CULTIVATION: Best suited to a well-drained but moisture-retentive soil in a sunny site. Propagate from fresh seed, or from root cuttings in winter. Dislikes being transplanted.

Mandragora officinarum

DEVIL'S APPLES, LOVE APPLES, MANDRAKE
☼ ❁ ↔ 8–10 in (20–25 cm)
↑ 5–6 in (12–15 cm)
Herbaceous perennial. Rosettes of heavily wrinkled, deep green, lance-shaped leaves, to 12 in (30 cm) long. Clusters of upward-facing greenish white flowers, stained purple, in spring. Poisonous yellow berries. Zones 5–10.

MANGIFERA

Best known for the mango, *M. indica*, a fruit widely cultivated and eaten in tropical countries. This genus is from the cashew (Anacardiaceae) family and consists of around 40 to 60 species originally from the tropical

rainforests of India, Southeast Asia, and the Solomon Islands. Simple, leathery, smooth-edged leaves are reddish when young. Panicles of small bisexual and male flowers are produced on the same plant. The fruit is a large, fleshy, hanging drupe with a flat fibrous seed. Grown in tropical and warm-temperate countries for their handsome foliage and fruit. The timber of some species is used for floorboards and tea chests. The sap and plant parts may cause dermatitis. CULTIVATION: These plants do best in deep well-drained soil with regular fertilizing, and a warm frost-free climate. They must have warm dry weather to set fruit; regions with low rainfall during flowering must be selected for fruit production. Propagate from seed or by grafting.

Mandevilla laxa

Mandevilla laxa, in summer

Mangifera indica
MANGO

☀ ⚘ ↔ 25 ft (8 m) ↑ 80 ft (24 m)

From Southeast Asia, especially Myanmar and eastern India. Young leaves red, ageing to shiny dark green. Yellowish or reddish flowers, in dense panicles. Fruit irregularly egg-shaped fleshy drupe. May be "alternate-bearing," typically fruiting heavily every 2 to 4 years. '**Campeche**', deep yellow fruit with reddish pink tinge; '**Edward**', medium to large fruit, excellent flavor; '**Kensington Pride**' (syn. 'Pride of Bowen'), Australian cultivar, propagated as seedling, excellent fruit. Zones 11–12.

MANIHOT

There are about 100 species of trees, shrubs, and herbs within this genus from the euphorbia (Euphorbiaceae) family native to tropical and warm-temperate regions of Central and South America. Leaves are palmate, lobed, with lance-shaped leaflets. Color varies from gray-green to bright green. Veining is regular. They are grown for their edible roots. Both male and female organs grow on the same plant. *M. esculenta* has cyanide in its roots that has to be extracted before it can be safely eaten. With glycosides removed, they are a valuable food source, yielding cassava and tapioca. Cassoreep, a toxic juice derived from *M. esculenta*, is a base for many varied products, including glue and alcoholic drinks. The wood is made into chip and composite board.

CULTIVATION: *Manihot* species are best grown in warm, wet conditions followed by a distinct dry season. They will thrive in poor soil if well drained. Under glass the foliage needs protection from strong sunlight or it will scorch. Propagate from mature cuttings planted in a gritty loam.

Manihot esculenta
BITTER CASSAVA, MANIOC

☀ ⚘ ↔ 3 ft (0.9 m) ↑ 12 ft (3.5 m)

Shrubby tree, native to Central and South America. Brittle stems, tuberous roots. Lobed palmate leaves, 3 to 7 rounded or lance-shaped leaflets. Fruit is 6-angled, narrow wings. Tubers are an important food source. '**Variegata**', bright green leaves, yellow variegation along veins. Zones 9–11.

MANILKARA

This genus of around 70 species of evergreen trees belonging to the sapodilla (Sapotaceae) family has a wide distribution throughout the tropics. Their leaves are usually simple and large with a thin, papery texture. The flowers form in the leaf axils and may be carried singly or in clusters. They are followed by fleshy berries containing only a few seeds. Some species yield a latex that has some commercial use.

CULTIVATION: These tropical trees are somewhat variable in their climatic preferences. Some come from the seasonally dry tropics but most prefer year-round warmth, moisture, and high humidity. They thrive in well-drained humus-rich soil in part shade or full shade and can be trimmed lightly to maintain a pleasing shape. Propagate from seed or cuttings, but allow the latex that is exuded from the cut to dry before inserting the cutting into the potting mix.

Mangifera indica 'Campeche'

Mangifera indica

Manilkara zapota
SAPODILLA

☀ ⚘ ↔ 20 ft (6 m) ↑ 100 ft (30 m)

Commercially cultivated fruit tree from Mexico to Costa Rica. Simple leaves, 6 in (15 cm) long. Small white flowers, in spring. Rough-skinned, egg-shaped, golden brown fruits, to 3 in (8 cm) long. Timber known as chicozapote. Zones 9–11.

MARANTA
PRAYER PLANT

The arrowroot (Marantaceae) family has a single genus that includes around 32 species of evergreen tropical perennials from the forests of Central and South America and the West Indies. The leaves are spread flat and elliptical by day and closed "in prayer" at night; the leaves are usually attractively blotched and veined. The tiny, white, 2-lipped flowers are insignificant. These plants can be grown as attractive indoor foliage plants in all but truly tropical climates.

CULTIVATION: Grow these perennials as house plants in a light, warm, humid site or in a greenhouse out of direct sun. Potting mix should be well-drained but never wet. In tropical climates they make good ground covers under the shade of trees. Propagate by division or from basal cuttings in spring with bottom heat.

Maranta arundinacea
ARROWROOT, OBEDIENCE PLANT

☀ ⚘ ↔ 24–40 in (60–100 cm) ↑ 4–6 ft (1.2–1.8 m)

Perennial herb from the West Indies and Central America. Erect, fleshy, brittle, branching stems. Smooth, oblong to sword-shaped, pointed leaves, to 10 in (25 cm) long. Slender, open, branched heads of small white flowers, in spring. Zones 11–12.

Manihot esculenta 'Variegata'

Manilkara zapota

Maranta leuconeura

PRAYER PLANT, RABBIT TRACKS,
TEN COMMANDMENTS

☀ ☂ ↔ 10–12 in (25–30 cm)
↕ 10–12 in (25–30 cm)

Perennial herb from Brazil. Almost prostrate, spreading rhizome. Leaves broad, dark green, oval, zoned gray or maroon, veined silver, red, or purple above, grayish green or maroon below, fold upward at night. Solitary spike of white or violet flowers, spotted purple, in spring–summer. *M. l.* var. *kerchoveana* (rabbit's foot), grayish green leaves, purplish brown to dark olive blotches both sides midrib. *M. l.* 'Erythroneura' (syn. 'Erythrophylla') (herringbone plant), velvety blackish green leaves, red veins, lime green central zone; 'Tricolor', large oval leaves, strong red veining, dark green blotches on each midrib. Zones 10–11.

MARATTIA

This genus of 60 large evergreen ferns from tropical areas of the world gives its name to the family Marattiaceae. Large succulent rhizomes give rise to thick, fleshy, rounded, succulent stalks and large, coarse, frond blades with 2 or 3 leaflets and long glossy segments. Stems contain an edible starch.
CULTIVATION: These ferns require a rich moist soil in a shady position protected from frost and wind. Propagate from spores.

Margyricarpus pinnatus

Marattia salicina

Maranta leuconeura 'Tricolor'

Marattia salicina

HORSESHOE FERN, KING FERN, PARA,
POTATO FERN

☀ ☂ ↔ 10 ft (3 m) ↕ 5–6 ft (1.5–1.8 m)
Evergreen fern from tropical Australasia and Polynesia. Sturdy edible rhizome with slow-spreading swollen roots. Arching, deep green, pinnate fronds, up to 12 ft (3.5 m) long, held on dark, erect, tapering stalks, swollen at base. Zones 11–12.

MARGYRICARPUS

M. pinnatus, the sole species in this genus, part of the rose (Rosaceae) family, is a spreading evergreen shrub that mounds up to 24 in (60 cm) high. A native of the Chilean Andes, it has a densely branching habit with interwoven stems bearing bright green needle-like leaves. Flowers are small and inconspicuous, but the fruits that follow are very showy and unusual.
CULTIVATION: Hardy to light frosts, grows well in most well-drained soils in sun or part-shade but can suffer in prolonged wet conditions. It can be made shrubby by pinching back and trimming or can be left to spill over banks or retaining walls. Propagate from seed or cuttings or by layers.

Margyricarpus pinnatus

PEARL FRUIT

☀ ❄ ↔ 20 in (50 cm) ↕ 24 in (60 cm)
Spreading shrub from Chile. Leaves closely packed, whorled, pinnate, needle-like leaflets. Flowers tiny, green, in spring–summer. Bright white fruits, some purple tints. Zones 7–11.

MARKHAMIA

This genus of 12 to 15 species of evergreen trees from tropical Africa and Asia belongs in the trumpet-vine (Bignoniaceae) family. Leaves are large and pinnate, usually composed of just a few large oblong to lance-shaped leaflets. They produce showy racemes of trumpet- to bell-shaped flowers typical of the family, at branch ends.
CULTIVATION: Impressive plants in both foliage and flower. In suitably warm moist climates they are vigorous and need space to develop freely. They will not tolerate frost or even prolonged cool conditions and require even moisture through most of the year. Plant in moist, humus-enriched, well-drained soil in sun or part-shade. Propagate from seed or cuttings.

Markhamia lutea

☀/☀ ☂ ↔ 20 ft (6 m) ↕ 30 ft (9 m)
Large shrub or small tree, native to tropical Africa. Leaves 12–20 in (30–50 cm) long, 7 to 13 leaflets of variable size. Flowers yellow, red marks inside throat, in spring. Narrow pods to 18 in (45 cm) long. Small-scale local use of timber. Zones 11–12.

Markhamia obtusifolia

☀/☀ ☂ ↔ 20 ft (6 m) ↕ 30 ft (9 m)
Tropical African tree or shrub. Leaves with 5 to 11 ovate to lance-shaped

Markhamia lutea

Markhamia obtusifolia

leaflets, to 6 in (15 cm) long. Flowers 2–4 in (5–10 cm) long, yellow, red-brown throat markings, in spring. Zones 11–12.

MARRUBIUM

HOREHOUND

A genus of 40 species of woolly gray-leafed perennials from Asia, the Mediterranean, and North Africa. They are members of the mint (Lamiaceae) family and usually have rounded strong-smelling leaves. They have square stems and 2-lipped pink to mauve flowers, which can be found among the leaves. Some species have been used medicinally. They can become invasive.
CULTIVATION: These sun-loving perennials are drought-tolerant and enjoy a dry summer climate. Prune hard each winter to clean up the plant and encourage bushiness. Propagate by division or from spring-sown seed, which is inclined to germinate in an erratic fashion.

M

Marrubium incanum

syn. *Marrubium candidissimum*

☀ ❄ ↔ 24 in (60 cm) ↑ 20 in (50 cm)

Perennial from Italy and the Balkans. Densely woolly white shoots; gray-green, scalloped, rounded leaves. Dense clusters of pale mauve to nearly white flowers, in summer. Zones 6–10.

Marrubium vulgare

COMMON HOREHOUND, WHITE HOREHOUND

☀ ❄ ↔ 20 in (50 cm) ↑ 20 in (50 cm)

Native to southern Europe, northern Africa, the Canary Islands, and Asia. Leaves rounded, woolly, gray. Small, 2-lipped flowers, in summer. Poor as a garden plant, weedy outside native areas. Marginally ornamental variegated form exists. Zones 3–10.

MARSILEA

NARDOO, PEPPERWORT, WATER CLOVER

These attractive water plants come from tropical and temperate climates

Masdevallia coccinea

Masdevallia veitchiana

in Australia, Europe, Asia, and eastern USA. A genus of about 65 species of aquatic fern allies in the clover-fern (Marsileaceae) family, the plants have clover-shaped leaves that float on the water surface. Some species were dug up for their edible starchy sporocarps by Aboriginal Australians.

CULTIVATION: Can be grown in water up to 5 ft (1.5 m) deep in almost frost-free climates. May become weedy. Anchor in the mud at the bottom of a pond or grow in a container. Propagate by division during cooler months.

Marsilea drummondii

COMMON NARDOO

☀ ⚘ ↔ 7 ft (2 m) ↑ 6–12 in (15–30 cm)

Aquatic Australian plant found in all mainland states. Widely spreading rhizome, slender stems. Four-leafed clover-like leaves, pale to mid-green, to 1¾ in (40 mm) long. Zones 9–11.

Marsilea mutica ★

BANDED NARDOO, NARDOO, WATER CLOVER

☀ ⚘ ↔ 3–6 ft (0.9–1.8 m)
↑ 12–36 in (30–90 cm)

Perennial shallow-water floating fern from northern Australia and Southeast Asia. Weak, slender, spreading stems. Glossy olive green fronds, 4 wedge-shaped lobes with brown or light green zones, on stalks to 36 in (90 cm) tall. Zones 9–11.

Marrubium incanum

MASDEVALLIA

FLAG ORCHID

A genus in the orchid (Orchidaceae) family, with almost 500 different species, from Central and South America. They are generally found in the cloud forests in mountainous regions with fairly uniform conditions throughout the year. They have no pseudobulbs, produce clumps of single fleshy leaves, and store moisture in roots and foliage. Species bloom at different times; peak seasons are winter and spring. Amazing range of shapes, sizes, and bright colors, most are single-flowered; larger flowered species produce fewer blooms. Sepals often terminate with short or long tails, while petals and labellum are generally tiny. The many hybrids are more vigorous in cultivation.

CULTIVATION: They prefer small pots and sphagnum moss is the preferred medium. Keep slightly potbound, moist, shaded, and in a cool humid environment throughout the year, out of direct sunlight. Will grow in pots with a bark and perlite mix if it does not dry out. Propagate by division.

Masdevallia coccinea ★

☀ ⚘ ↔ 8 in (20 cm) ↑ 4–20 in (10–50 cm)

Spectacular summer-blooming orchid from Colombia. Large, round, 5 in (12 cm) wide flowers, on tall leafless stalks above foliage, in spring. Most variable in color—red, purple, pink, yellow, and white. Zones 9–11.

Masdevallia infracta

☀ ✦ ↔ 8 in (20 cm) ↑ 4–12 in (10–30 cm)

Intermediate-size orchid from Brazil. Up to 4 flowers, 2 in (5 cm) wide,

Masdevallia ova-avis

Marrubium vulgare

Marsilea drummondii

yellow, orange, and red-purple, in spring. Can re-bloom next season from same inflorescence. Zones 11–12.

Masdevallia ova-avis

☀ ⚘ ↔ 4–8 in (10–20 cm)
↑ 4–12 in (10–30 cm)

Multi-flowered orchid from Ecuador. Up to 8 nodding flowers, 1½ in (35 mm) wide, pinkish cream, dark maroon spots. Blooms open simultaneously, in spring. Tails on sepals bright yellow. Zones 9–11.

Masdevallia tovarensis

☀ ✦ ↔ 12 in (30 cm) ↑ 12 in (30 cm)

Delightful white-flowered orchid from Venezuela. Groups of up to 4 long-lived flowers, 3 in (8 cm) wide, in spring. Can re-bloom the following season from same inflorescence. More warmth-tolerant than other species. Zones 11–12.

Masdevallia veitchiana ★

☀ ⚘ ↔ 12 in (30 cm) ↑ 24 in (60 cm)

A majestic large-flowered orchid from Peru, known from Aztec city, Machu Picchu. Spikes of orange flowers, 5 in (12 cm) wide, with tiny bright purple tubercles, incandescent sheen in sunlight, in spring–summer. Spikes longer than leaves. Zones 9–11.

Masdevallia, Hybrid, Angelita

Masdevallia, Hybrid, Charisma

Masdevallia Hybrids

☀ ⚶ ↔ 4–12 in (10–30 cm)
↕ 4–24 in (10–60 cm)

Many hybrids have been developed to satisfy the interest in *Masdevallias*. They exhibit hybrid vigor and many will bloom several times in a year. Among the more popular cultivars are: **Angelita**, combining 3 species, *M. sanctae-inesae, M. strobelii,* and *M. veitchiana,* golden yellow centers; **Charisma**, between *M. coccinea* and the striped *M. yungasensis,* pale pink with magenta stripes; **Copperwing**, between *M. veitchiana* and the compact *M. decumana,* deep yellow with copper spotting; **Machu Picchu**, between the large-flowered *M. ayabacana* and *M. coccinea,* superb magenta; **Magdalene × Marguerite**, between 2 hybrids, deep red with the center fading slightly; **Marguerite**, between *M. infracta* and *M. veitchiana,* copper-red spotting; **Prince Charming**, between the dumpy *M. angulata* and *M. veitchiana,* with ruby red banding deepening at center; **Rose-Mary**, between *M. coccinea* and the pink-spotted *M. glandulosa,* rose pink with an orange center; and **Winter Blush**, between *M.* Angel Frost (*M. veitchiana* × *M. strobelii*) and the spotted *M. chaparensis,* golden orange with deep red markings. Zones 9–11.

Matteuccia struthiopteris

Masdevallia, Hybrid, Rose-Mary

MATRICARIA

This genus of 5 species of usually annual herbs belongs to the daisy (Asteraceae) family. Found throughout temperate areas of Europe and Asia, they have upright, branching, leafy stems with alternate, finely divided, light to bright green leaves. The foliage is often aromatic. The freely borne flowers may be single or in clusters and are either yellow and button-like or white daisies with yellow centers. *M. recutita* is used in herbal medicine for a wide range of ailments, including digestive disorders and fevers, and as a calmative. Its aroma and medicinal qualities are similar to that of chamomile but it is more bitter and generally thought to be of inferior quality.
CULTIVATION: These herbs are easily grown in a sunny position in well-drained soil. Propagate from seed, *in situ,* in late summer.

Matricaria recutita
syn. *Matricaria chamomilla*
GERMAN CHAMOMILE, SWEET FALSE CHAMOMILE, WILD CHAMOMILE

☀ ❄ ↔ 6–20 in (15–50 cm)
↕ 6–20 in (15–50 cm)

A bushy annual, native to Europe and western Asia. It has fine, pinnately divided, aromatic foliage, and small

Masdevallia, Hybrid, Marguerite

Masdevallia, Hybrid, Copperwing

Masdevallia, Hybrid, Machu Picchu

daisy-like flowers, with white ray petals that flex downward, in summer–autumn. Zones 4–10.

MATTEUCCIA

A member of the polypody (Polypodiaceae) family, this genus contains 3 species of hardy deciduous ferns and is native to North America, Europe, and Asia. Fronds are tall with alternate leaflets in soft green. These elegant plants have an arching habit and are most at home in a waterside setting. They are easy to cultivate but have invasive underground stems.
CULTIVATION: Plant from autumn to spring in a slightly shaded, constantly moist spot, in lime-free soil that contains leaf mold. For best results, plant at least 48 in (120 cm) apart. Propagate by dividing the rhizomatous roots in autumn or winter.

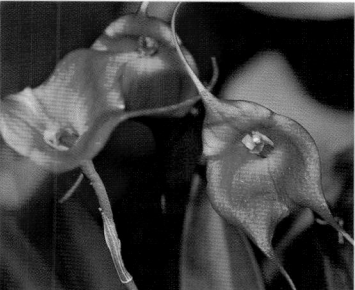
Masdevallia, Hybrid, Magdalene × Marguerite

Masdevallia, Hybrid, Prince Charming

Masdevallia, Hybrid, Winter Blush

Matteuccia struthiopteris
OSTRICH FERN, SHUTTLECOCK FERN

☀ ❄ ↔ 18–30 in (45–75 cm)
↕ 36–60 in (90–150 cm)

Fern from North America, East Asia, and Europe. Clumps of arching, leathery, pale green fronds. Dark brown spore-bearing fronds in center of clump, develop in summer–late winter and persist up to a year. Zones 6–10.

M

Matthiola incana, Cinderella Series, 'Cinderella White'

Matthiola incana, Cinderella Series, 'Cinderella Lavender'

Matthiola incana, Vintage Series, 'Vintage Lilac'

Matthiola incana, Cinderella Series, 'Cinderella Rose'

Matthiola incana, Vintage Series, 'Vintage Burgundy'

Matthiola incana, Vintage Series, 'Vintage Lavender'

MATTHIOLA

GILLYFLOWER, STOCK

The genus, a member of the cabbage (Brassicaceae) family, contains 55 mainly temperate Eurasian species of annuals, perennials, and subshrubs. They usually have simple leaves, often gray-green and sometimes toothed. Their flowers, which are 4-petalled and often evening-scented, are borne on upright, often branching stems. There are many garden strains in a wide range of flower forms and colors. Famed for their scent, stocks were once grown for medicinal purposes and a comment attributed to Italian botanist Pierandrea Mattioli, after whom the genus is named, that he grew stock only for "matters of love and lust," suggests the medicine had much to do with the scent.
CULTIVATION: Plant in full sun with moist well-drained soil. A light dressing of lime is beneficial. Taller types need shelter from strong wind or can be supported by staking. Propagate mostly from seed, which can be sown in succession for continuous spring and summer flowering.

Matthiola incana

BROMPTON STOCK

☀/☀ ❄ ↔ 12 in (30 cm) ↑ 32 in (80 cm)
Woody-based biennial from southern and western Europe. Leaves elliptical, gray-green, downy, 2 in (5 cm) long. Upright spikes, scented purple, pink, or white flowers, in summer. Long seed pods. 'Annua' (ten weeks stock), matures and flowers in one season; **Cinderella Series**, single-stemmed, most colors; **Lady Series**, biennial, branching, dense spikes, most colors, many double flowers; **Vintage Series**, 6–8 in (15–20 cm), branching, most colors, many doubles. **Zones 8–11.**

Matthiola longipetala

NIGHT-SCENTED STOCK

☀/☀ ❄ ↔ 10 in (25 cm) ↑ 20 in (50 cm)
Summer-flowering annual found from Greece and the Middle East to the Crimean region. Narrow leaves, to 3 in (8 cm) long, toothed or pinnately lobed. Creamy yellow or pink flowers, 1 in (25 mm) across, evening fragrance, in summer. Horned seed pods. *M. l.* **subsp.** *bicornis,* usually double flowers. **Zones 8–11.**

MATUCANA

This genus of 17 or more spherical to short-cylindrical South American species belongs to the cactus (Cactaceae) family. These solitary or low-clumping plants occasionally form cushions of stems up to 20 in (50 cm) high. The number of ribs varies but they are usually broad, low, and tuberculate. The spine size and coloration is extremely variable. The flowers are diurnal, asymmetrical, borne near the tip, funnelform to narrow-tubular funnelform, in bright red, orange, pink, or yellow. Named after the town of Matucana in Peru where the type species, *M. haynei,* was discovered.
CULTIVATION: Easily grown in a rich well-drained soil. Rest in winter. Propagate from seed, or from division of clumps or from cuttings that have been dried out for a week or two.

Matucana aurieflora

☀ ⚬ ↔ 5 in (12 cm) ↑ 5 in (12 cm)
Species from Peru. Solitary, shiny dark green, 11 to 17 ribs bearing low tubercles. Spines dark reddish brown, yellow tips; 8 to 14 radials in comb

shape, either side of areoles. Flowers yellow, tinged orange, in summer, broad funnelform, symmetrical. Seed pods oval, dark purple. **Zones 9–11.**

Matucana formosa ★

☀ ⚬ ↔ 6 in (15 cm) ↑ 4–6 in (10–15 cm)
A cactus from Peru. Spherical, gray-green, often offsetting at base; weakly tubercled ribs. Spines dark brown, gray with age, stiff, straight to slightly curved. Flowers bright red, slightly curved floral tube, in summer. Seed pods oval, green to red. **Zones 9–11.**

Matucana haynei

☀ ⚬ ↔ 8 in (20 cm) ↑ 12 in (30 cm)
Extremely variable species from Peru. Solitary to freely clustering. Spines white to pale brown, gray with age. Flowers red, salmon, and purple-red, mostly asymmetrical, in summer. Seed pods spherical, reddish green. *M. h.* **subsp.** *haynei,* at least 30 spines; *M. h.* **subsp.** *herzogiana,* less than 4 in (10 cm) tall, few spines; *M. h.* **subsp.** *histrix,* 4 distinct centrals, numerous radials; *M. h.* **subsp.** *myriacantha,* less than 3 in (8 cm) tall, up to 10 centrals and 25 radials. **Zones 9–11.**

Matucana haynei

Matucana aurieflora

Matucana formosa

Maytenus boaria

MAXILLARIA

This is a complex genus in the family Orchidaceae of some 600 epiphytic and lithophytic sympodial orchids from Central and South America. They exhibit an enormous range in plant habit and floral shape, size, and color. Solitary blooms emerge from the base of the pseudobulbs, and the petals are smaller than the sepals. They produce from 1 to 3 leaves at the top of the pseudobulb. For such a large genus, there have been surprisingly few artificial hybrids within *Maxillaria*, despite their obvious potential. They are related to *Lycaste*.
CULTIVATION: These orchids have varying growing requirements, but most species established in cultivation are cool- to intermediate-growing plants, enjoy bright light in a humid environment, and are easily grown in pots of a coarse bark-based mix. Many species, particularly the miniatures, also grow well on slabs of tree-fern or cork. Propagate by division.

Maxillaria biolleyi
☀ ✄ ↔ 20 in (50 cm) ↑ 36 in (90 cm)
Uncommon, tall, leafy orchid from Costa Rica, upright habit. Leaves dark green, narrow lance-shaped. Masses of white to pale pink, ¾ in (18 mm) wide flowers, from leaf axils along upper part, in spring. Zones 11–12.

Maxillaria cognauxiana
☀ ✄ ↔ 8 in (20 cm) ↑ 24 in (60 cm)
Miniature-growing, clumping, and branching orchid from Brazil. Strappy leaves, deep olive green. Very dark, glossy, long-lived, claret, 1¼ in (30 mm) wide, cup-shaped flowers, in spring–summer. Zones 11–12.

Maxillaria fractiflexa
☀ ✄ ↔ 8 in (20 cm) ↑ 4–24 in (10–60 cm)
Large-flowered orchid from Colombia. Tall mid-green leaves, strappy. Flowers

to 6 in (15 cm) wide, narrow sepals, mustard yellow to brown; twisted petals, cream, in summer. Relatively small white labellum. Zones 9–11.

Maxillaria nigrescens
☀ ✄ ↔ 4–8 in (10–20 cm) ↑ 4–24 in (10–60 cm)
An orchid native to Colombia and Venezuela. Leaves mid-green, develop spots if grown in conditions that are too warm. Thick spidery blooms, 3 in (8 cm) wide, rich reddish brown, in spring–summer. Zones 9–11.

Maxillaria porphyrostele
☀/☀ ✄ ↔ 4–8 in (10–20 cm) ↑ 4–24 in (10–60 cm)
Hardy Brazilian orchid. Round pseudobulbs, 2 strap-like leaves. Long-lasting bright yellow flowers, 2 in (5 cm) wide, that open widely, in early spring. Yellow labellum, with red-brown markings near the base. Zones 9–12.

Maxillaria variabilis ★
☀/☀ ✄ ↔ 4–8 in (10–20 cm) ↑ 4–24 in (10–60 cm)
Variable orchid species found from Mexico to Panama. Upright habit, somewhat branching in older specimens. Leaves green, long, and strap-like. The flowers vary from yellow, orange, brown, and red to a dark claret-black, in spring–summer. Zones 9–12.

Maxillaria biolleyi

MAYTENUS

This genus of the spindle-tree (Celastraceae) family, with more than 200 species, occurs in southern Europe, Africa, India, Southeast Asia, Central and South America, and Australia. Trees, shrubs, or scrambling shrubs, all are evergreen, some with rhizomes. Leaves are simple, smooth-edged or toothed. The small, usually whitish flowers can be bisexual; these may be separate males and females on the same plant or on different plants. The leathery or woody fruits are 2- to 5-celled capsules; a few species are fleshy, the seeds partly or wholly surrounded by a fleshy aril. Extracts from some species have been locally used for medicinal purposes.
CULTIVATION: Frost hardiness varies among the various species. All should be grown in a sunny position in well-drained soil. Propagate from seed or cuttings. Since the seeds have only a short viability, they must be sown while as fresh as possible.

Maytenus boaria ★
MAITEN, MAYTEN
☀ ❄ ↔ 30 ft (9 m) ↑ 70 ft (21 m)
Tree or large shrub from Chilean forests. Branches upright or pendent, glossy dark green leaves with finely toothed edges. Small, greenish, separate male and female flowers, in spring. Fruits 3- to 5-celled, orange-red, aril red. Zones 8–10.

Maxillaria variabilis

Maxillaria cognauxiana

Maytenus magellanica
☀ ❄ ↔ 12 ft (3.5 m) ↑ 20 ft (6 m)
Tree or shrub of Antarctic beech forests in southern Chile and western Argentina. Alternate pale green leaves, oval to lance-shaped, serrated margins. Small reddish flowers, in spring. Capsules of seeds with fleshy basal aril. Unknown in cultivation. Zones 8–9.

MAZUS

These 30 species of ground-covering and mat-forming perennials from the foxglove (Scrophulariaceae) family are found in Asia, Australia and New Zealand. Foliage color varies from mid- to bright greens through to brown and bronze shades. The prostrate stems hug the ground and new roots form as the plant creeps along. Often found in damp sheltered areas, they creep through and over rocks. The long, narrow, tubular flowers sit up on the mats of foliage in spring and summer. Flowers will vary from purples and blues through to pale lavender, white, and yellow. Depending on the variety, flowers may have a splash of lilac-mauve in the throat, or

Maxillaria fractiflexa

M

be marked with white and yellow.
CULTIVATION: These plants prefer
full sun, good drainage, and open
porous soils. Propagate from half-
hardened stem cuttings in summer
and autumn.

Mazus radicans

syn. *Mimulus radicans*

☼ ❋ ↔ 12 in (30 cm) ↕ 2 in (5 cm)

A New Zealand perennial species.
Round bronze-brown leaves, 1¼–2 in
(3–5 cm) long, with very tight, nearly
impenetrable, foliage mats. Flowers,
in spring–summer are white, lilac
streaked, and 1½–2 in (3.5–5 cm)
across. **Zones 7–9.**

Meconopsis cambrica var. *aurantiaca*

Meconopsis betonicifolia

Mazus reptans

☼ ❋ ↔ 20 in (50 cm) ↕ 2 in (5 cm)

The mid-green, almost glossy leaves of
this Himalayan species cover its stems.
The flowers are purple-blue, ¾ in
(18 mm) wide, with a dark center
fleck, appearing in spring–summer.
Zones 7–9.

MECONOPSIS

Mainly native to the Himalayan
region, with one notable exception.
This genus of more than 40 species
from the poppy (Papaveraceae) family,
includes annuals, biennials, and
perennials, some of which die after
flowering. The genus is known for its

Meconopsis horridula

Meconopsis betonicifolia var. *alba*

blue-flowered species, but the other
more traditional poppies of yellow,
pink, or red are often more easily
grown. They form compact mounds
of coarsely hairy lower leaves that may
be round, pinnately lobed, or deeply
toothed. The flowers, carried singly
on short stems or in heads on taller
stems, open in spring or summer.
CULTIVATION: Most species grow best
in woodland conditions in a cool-
temperate climate with reliable rainfall. Plant in a sheltered part-shaded
position with moist, deep, humus-
rich, well-drained soil. Water well in
spring and early summer. Propagate
from seed.

Meconopsis betonicifolia

BLUE POPPY

☼/◐ ❋ ↔ 8–20 in (20–50 cm)
↕ 3–6 ft (0.9 m–1.8 m)

Perennial, often short-lived, from
Himalayan China. Stems and foliage
bristly, golden brown hairs. Oblong,
often shallowly serrated leaves, to 12 in
(30 cm) long. Open heads of up to
6 bright blue flowers, to 2 in (5 cm)
long, in late spring–early summer. *M.
b.* var. *alba*, white flowers. **Zones 7–9.**

Meconopsis cambrica

WELSH POPPY

☼ ❋ ↔ 8–16 in (20–40 cm)
↕ 12–24 in (30–60 cm)

Perennial, native to western Europe.
Small clumps of ferny mid-green
leaves, to 8 in (20 cm) long. Flowers
are solitary, on hairy stems, bright
yellow, to 2 in (5 cm) wide, in late
spring–summer. Often self-sows
freely. *M. c.* var. *aurantiaca,* orange
flowers. **Zones 6–10.**

Meconopsis grandis

☼ ❋ ↔ 16–24 in (40–60 cm)
↕ 4 ft (1.2 m)

Himalayan perennial. Foliage and
stems have rusty brown hairs. Lower
leaves to 12 in (30 cm) long, elliptical, serrated to coarsely toothed.
Long-stemmed flowers, in groups of 3
or more, deep blue to purple-blue, in
late spring–early summer. **Zones 5–9.**

Mazus reptans

Meconopsis horridula

☼ ❋ ↔ 16 in (40 cm) ↕ 32 in (80 cm)

Often short-lived Himalayan perennial. Very bristly foliage and stems.
Leaves elliptical, gray-green, to 10 in
(25 cm) long. Long-stemmed flowers
in upper leaf axils, solitary or paired,
blue to light purple or white, in
summer. **Zones 6–9.**

Meconopsis napaulensis

syn. *Meconopsis wallichii*

SATIN POPPY

☼/◐ ❋ ↔ 20–32 in (50–80 cm)
↕ 6–8 ft (1.8–2.4 m)

This vigorous strongly upright perennial is found from central Nepal to
southwestern China. Stems and
foliage are covered with fine, downy,
golden brown hairs. Leaves deeply
pinnately lobed, almost to midrib.
Red or purple flowers, rarely blue
or white, on drooping heads, in
spring–summer. **Zones 8–10.**

Meconopsis punicea

☼/◐ ❋ ↔ 20–27 in (50–70 cm)
↕ 24–30 in (60–75 cm)

Perennial from Chinese Himalayas.
Broad lance-shaped leaves, to more
than 14 in (35 cm) long. Bristly
flower stems with solitary bright
flowers, to nearly 4 in (10 cm) long,
in spring–summer. **Zones 7–10.**

Meconopsis × sheldonii

☼ ❋ ↔ 16–24 in (40–60 cm)
↕ 4 ft (1.2 m)

A garden hybrid between *M. betonicifolia* and *M. grandis*, this plant
provides good color and ease of cultivation. Bristly oblong leaves, 6–10 in
(15–25 cm) long. The flower stems
are leafy, with 1¼ in (30 mm) wide
blue flowers in the upper axils, in
spring–summer. **Zones 6–9.**

Meconopsis grandis

Meconopsis napaulensis

MEDICAGO

This genus of about 56 species of annuals, perennials, and shrubs is a member of the pea-flower subfamily of the legume (Fabaceae) family and includes the important fodder crop *M. sativa* (lucerne or alfalfa). Species are found over a range of habitats in Europe, Africa, and Asia. Growth habits vary considerably but all have clover-like leaves and some species have slightly downy foliage and stems. The flowers are usually yellow and the seed pods that follow are curved or twisted and often spiny.
CULTIVATION: Shrubby species will grow in any reasonably fertile well-drained soil. They should be planted in full sun; in cooler areas they need the protection of a warm wall. They are attractive ornamentals and, with their deep rooting systems, are also useful for soil stabilization. Propagate from seed, or from softwood or half-hardened cuttings taken in summer.

Medicago sativa

ALFALFA, LUCERNE, PURPLE MEDICK
☼ ❄ ↔ 32–40 in (80–100 cm)
↕ 32–40 in (80–100 cm)

Perennial forage herb from Eurasia, naturalized worldwide. Leaves with 3 oval to narrow leaflets, toothed at tip, on short stalks. Blue to purple pea-flowers, in dense racemes, in summer–autumn. Sprouted seeds edible. Zones 4–8.

MEDINILLA

This genus of more than 150 species of evergreen shrubs and climbers, some epiphytic, is from the melastoma (Melastomataceae) family and is native to the rainforests of Africa, Southeast Asia, and the Pacific. They are grown for their ornamental value as their large leaves, conspicuous colorful bracts, and white, rose, and shell pink flowers in panicles or cymes make them showy specimens. Grown over a frame or pergola, the climbing varieties are also very attractive.
CULTIVATION: In humid tropical areas, these plants will grow under shade in fertile well-drained soil. In cooler climates, grow in a greenhouse in containers with added grit and leaf-mold in good loam soil. If grown under glass, protect from direct sun in summer. Water and feed well during growing season and mist several times daily. Water carefully in winter or cooler months to prevent wilting. Propagate from half-hardened cuttings rooted in a growing medium with added sharp sand.

Medinilla magnifica

☼ ✈ ↔ 3 ft (0.9 m) ↕ 3–6 ft (0.9–1.8 m)
Robust epiphytic species, native to the Philippines. Ribbed or winged stems. Large leathery leaves, dark green, pronounced pale veins. Long-lasting flowers, pink to red, in pendulous panicles and basal bracts, in spring–summer. Zones 11–12.

MEDIOCALCAR

CHERRY ORCHID
This is a small group of cool- to intermediate-growing creeping and scrambling sympodial orchids (family Orchidaceae) that come from the highland areas of New Guinea and parts of the Pacific Islands. There are about 20 recognized species. They have varying growth habits, but the spherical, glossy blooms that appear

Mediocalcar decoratum

from the immature new growth, either singly or in pairs, are very similar. They have been called "cherry orchids" because of these unique globular blooms. Most species flower from autumn to early spring.
CULTIVATION: The small species perform well in shallow pots of sphagnum moss, while larger plants can be grown on tree-fern rafts, as long as the substrate is kept moist. They detest hot dry conditions and must be kept moist and heavily shaded in a buoyant atmosphere. Propagate by division.

Mediocalcar bifolium

☼ ❄ ↔ 4–12 in (10–30 cm)
↕ 3–10 in (8–25 cm)

From New Guinea; upright-growing, 2-leafed, branching and clumping orchid. Small, bright red flowers, ½ in (12 mm) wide, pure white tips to segments, in winter. Zones 7–10.

Mediocalcar decoratum ★

☼ ❄ ↔ 4–24 in (10–60 cm)
↕ 2–6 in (5–15 cm)

Creeping orchid from New Guinea. Petite pseudobulbs topped with 3 or 4 small, succulent, green- to purple-stained leaves. Tiny bright orange flowers, with yellow tips to segments, appear in autumn–winter. Zones 7–10.

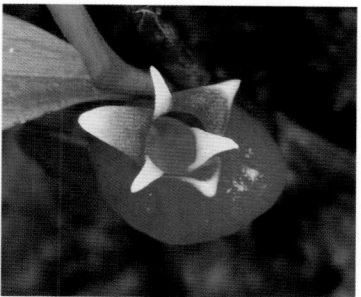
Mediocalcar bifolium

MEEHANIA

JAPANESE DEAD NETTLE
Genus of 6 creeping perennial herbs from Asia and North America from the mint (Lamiaceae) family. Sparse clusters of bell-shaped flowers with expanding lobed corolla tubes, in colors ranging from cream through to red and purple, are surrounded by leaf-like bracts or spikes. The calyx is bell-shaped.
CULTIVATION: These plants prefer a cold shady site with moist fertile soil. Propagate from seed in spring, or by division in spring or autumn.

Meehania fargesii

☼ ❄ ↔ 8–16 in (20–40 cm)
↕ 4–8 in (10–20 cm)

A creeping, finely hairy, perennial herb, from western China. The stems are sprinkled with glandular hairs. The leaves are triangular to heart-shaped, irregularly toothed. Clusters of blue, purplish red, or red flowers, streaked purple, appear in spring. Zones 7–10.

MEGASKEPASMA

The sole species in this genus from the acanthus (Acanthaceae) family is an evergreen shrub from Venezuela. It is a lushly foliaged plant with flowers that are striking in both color and shape. These appear through most of

Medinilla magnifica

Meehania fargesii

Megaskepasma erythrochlamys

the year. This plant is a must for any warm-climate garden; it is also useful as a plant for large conservatories and greenhouses.
CULTIVATION: This shrub needs warmth, moisture, and humidity to do well. Given the right climate, a humus-rich soil and regular feeding, it is the very epitome of a luxuriant tropical plant. Because its stems are soft and pliable it can be espaliered against a sheltered wall in cooler zones. Propagate from seed or half-hardened cuttings.

Megaskepasma erythrochlamys
BRAZILIAN RED CLOAK
☼ ❄ ↔ 4 ft (1.2 m) ↑ 10 ft (3 m)
Evergreen shrub from Venezuela. Heavily veined, semi-glossy, mid-green leaves. Individual flowers, white or pale pink, on upright, 12 in (30 cm) tall red spikes, almost enclosed by red bracts, showy flowerhead held above foliage, in spring–summer. Zones 10–12.

MELALEUCA
There are approximately 220 species in this genus of evergreen shrubs and trees, mostly native to Australia, from the myrtle (Myrtaceae) family. They are sometimes referred to as paperbarks for their highly ornamental, papery textured, creamy white or pale brown bark that peels off in layers. The nectar-rich bottlebrush flowers, with numerous stamens, usually united into bundles, occur in many different shades of white, yellow, orange, pink, red, and purple. Small woody seed capsules form cylindrical spikes or clusters, and often persist on the plant.
CULTIVATION: Most melaleucas are easily grown in full sun or partial shade in acidic well-drained soil. Fast-growing and adaptable plants, they can withstand pollution, some degree of coastal exposure, and moist poorly drained soil. Most species will withstand light frosts if given full sun; some species will tolerate heavy frosts. Shrubby species respond well to clipping after flowering and can be used for hedges and screens. Propagate from seed or cuttings.

Melaleuca acerosa
☼ ❄ ↔ 5 ft (1.5 m) ↑ 5 ft (1.5 m)
Rounded shrub, native to Western Australia. Gray-green needle-shaped leaves, softly pointed at tip. Perfumed yellow flowers, in dense rounded heads, in spring–early summer. Thrives in reasonably well-drained position. Zones 8–11.

Melaleuca alternifolia
TEA-TREE
☼ ❄ ↔ 10 ft (3 m) ↑ 25 ft (8 m)
Tall shrub or small tree from subtropical eastern Australia. Off-white papery bark, narrow soft green leaves. Numerous white flowers, in loose spikes, in late spring. Best in moist well-drained soils. Commercially grown for its essential oil (tea-tree oil). Zones 9–11.

Melaleuca armillaris
BRACELET HONEY MYRTLE
☼ ❄ ↔ 12 ft (3.5 m) ↑ 25 ft (8 m)
Tall shrub or small tree from south-eastern coastal Australia. Spreading canopy of narrow dark green leaves. White flowers, in small cylindrical heads, appear in late spring–summer. Zones 9–11.

Melaleuca bracteata
BLACK TEA-TREE, RIVER TEA-TREE
☼ ❄ ↔ 20 ft (6 m) ↑ 30 ft (9 m)
Variable shrub or small tree from tropical and central Australian watercourses. Soft, linear, bright green foliage. Profuse creamy white flowers, in heads at branch ends or short spikes, in spring. Shrubby forms include: '**Golden Gem**', to 6 ft (1.8 m) high, rich golden yellow leaves, colorful in early spring; '**Revolution Gold**', reddish young stems, golden foliage, bushy upright habit, to 12 ft (3.5 m) high; '**Revolution Green**', to 10 ft (3 m) high, fine bright green foliage. Zones 9–12.

Melaleuca brongniartii
☼ ❄ ↔ 3–8 ft (0.9–2.4 m) ↑ 2–5 ft (0.6–1.5 m)
A shrub endemic to New Caledonia, found growing among rocks along river banks. It has a single, contorted trunk, papery bark. Rounded crown of crowded neat rosettes of narrow,

Melaleuca armillaris

Melaleuca brongniartii

Melaleuca bracteata

Melaleuca acerosa, in the wild, Torndirrup National Park, Western Australia

Melaleuca calothamnoides

thick, sharply pointed leaves. Small dense heads of cream flowers, in summer. New shoots growing through flowerheads. Zones 10–12.

Melaleuca calothamnoides

☼ ❄ ↔ 3 ft (0.9 m) ↑ 10 ft (3 m)

Attractive multi-branched shrub from Western Australia. Crowded, narrow, linear leaves. Spikes of green, pale orange or red flowers, on short lateral shoots from old wood, in late spring. Prefers well-drained soil. Regularly prune to maintain shape. Zones 9–11.

Melaleuca capitata

☼ ❄ ↔ 6 ft (1.8 m) ↑ 6 ft (1.8 m)

Densely branched shrub from southeastern Australia, often growing in damp heath. Narrow dark green leaves, pointed tips. Flowers pale yellow, in dense heads at ends of branches, in late spring–summer. Lightly prune to encourage compact habit. Zones 8–11.

Melaleuca erubescens

Melaleuca cuticularis, in the wild, Walpole, Western Australia

Melaleuca cardiophylla

TANGLING MELALEUCA

☼ ❄ ↔ 4 ft (1.2 m) ↑ 8 ft (2.4 m)

Erect many-branched shrub from coastal Western Australia. Short stem-clasping leaves, ovate to heart-shaped. Showy creamy white flowers, in small open clusters from old wood, in spring–summer. Regularly prune to maintain compact shape. Zones 9–11.

Melaleuca cuticularis

SALTWATER PAPERBARK

☼ ❄ ↔ 10 ft (3 m) ↑ 20 ft (6 m)

Small tree from swampy areas of southern Western Australia, often submerged to lower limbs. Spreading, often twisted branches, gleaming white papery bark. Scented, creamy white flowers, in small clusters, in spring. Withstands short dry periods. Zones 9–11.

Melaleuca decussata

☼/◐ ❄ ↔ 7 ft (2 m) ↑ 12 ft (3.5 m)

Large shrub from southeastern Australia. Bluish green linear leaves arranged in pairs. Mauve flowers, in

Melaleuca elliptica

spikes, to 1 in (25 mm) long, in late spring and sporadically through summer. Popular in cultivation. Zones 8–11.

Melaleuca diosmifolia

☼ ❄ ↔ 6 ft (1.8 m) ↑ 10 ft (3 m)

Dense shrub from southern Western Australia. Crowded, spirally arranged, ovate leaves. Branches from near ground level. Yellowish green flowers, at the ends of branches, in dense oblong spikes, to 2 in (5 cm) long, in late spring–summer. Zones 9–11.

Melaleuca elliptica

☼ ❄ ↔ 7 ft (2 m) ↑ 12 ft (3.5 m)

Erect, open, or sometimes bushy shrub from southern Western Australia. Small elliptic leaves. Flowers are red, in cylindrical spikes, to 3 in (8 cm) long, in late spring–summer. Tolerates extended dry periods. Regularly prune to encourage a compact habit. Zones 8–11.

Melaleuca ericifolia

SWAMP PAPERBARK

☼ ❄ ↔ 15 ft (4.5 m) ↑ 25 ft (8 m)

Bushy shrub or small tree from coastal districts of southeastern Australia.

Melaleuca decussata

Melaleuca capitata

Gray papery bark. Dark green linear leaves. Scented creamy white flowers, in dense spikes at the ends of the branches, in late spring–summer. Forms thickets. Often in swampy areas. Zones 8–11.

Melaleuca erubescens

syn. *Melaleuca diosmatifolia*

☼ ❄ ↔ 10 ft (3 m) ↑ 6 ft (1.8 m)

Spreading bush with low-branching habit from eastern Australia. Aromatic, dark green, linear leaves, light green when young. Pale mauve flowers, in dense spikes on lateral growth, in late spring–summer. Zones 9–11.

Melaleuca ericifolia

Melaleuca fulgens
SCARLET HONEY MYRTLE

☼ ❄ ↔ 6 ft (1.8 m) ↑ 10 ft (3 m)

Erect shrub from semi-arid Western Australia. Narrow linear leaves. Spikes of red, orange, or deep pink flowers, on older stems, in spring–summer. Fairly drought tolerant. Various color forms, popular in cultivation. *M. f.* subsp. *steedmanii*, leaves obovate, flat. Zones 8–11.

Melaleuca gibbosa
SLENDER HONEY MYRTLE

☼ ❄ ↔ 6 ft (1.8 m) ↑ 6 ft (1.8 m)

Widespread in southeastern Australia; grows in moist situations. Slender wiry branches crowded with pairs of

Melaleuca lateritia

Melaleuca huegelii

tiny ovate leaves. Mauve-pink flowers, in short spikes, on lateral stems, in late spring–summer. Needs adequate moisture, prune regularly. Zones 8–11.

Melaleuca huegelii
CHENILLE HONEY MYRTLE

☼ ❉ ↔ 7 ft (2 m) ↑ 8 ft (2.4 m)

Erect or spreading shrub from coastal Western Australia. Minute spirally arranged leaves. White, slender, cylindrical flower spikes, 3 in (8 cm) long, in late spring to mid-summer. Valuable as screening or windbreak plant for salt-spray areas. Zones 9–11.

Melaleuca hypericifolia
HILLOCK BUSH

☼ ❉ ↔ 15 ft (4.5 m) ↑ 15 ft (4.5 m)

From southeastern Australia; tall, often spreading shrub. Slightly pendulous branches, oblong leaves in opposite pairs. Showy orange-red flowers, in cylindrical spikes, to 2 in (5 cm) long, in late spring to mid-summer. Tolerates exposure to salt-laden winds. Zones 9–11.

Melaleuca incana
GRAY HONEY MYRTLE

☼ ❄ ↔ 10 ft (3 m) ↑ 10 ft (3 m)

Dense weeping shrub from southwest Western Australia, grows naturally in wet situations. Gray-green linear leaves, often softly hairy, prominent

Melaleuca fulgens

oil glands. Creamy yellow flowers, in oval spikes, at branch ends, in early spring to mid-summer. Zones 8–11.

Melaleuca lateritia
ROBIN REDBREAST BUSH

☼ ❉ ↔ 3 ft (0.9 m) ↑ 6 ft (1.8 m)

Multi-stemmed shrub from Western Australia. Arching branches. Light green linear leaves, aromatic when crushed. Spikes to 3 in (8 cm) long of orange-red flowers, in spring–summer, other times sporadically. Regularly prune for compact habit. Zones 9–11.

Melaleuca leucadendra
CAJEPUT, WEEPING PAPERBARK

☼ ❉ ↔ 30 ft (9 m) ↑ 90 ft (27 m)

Spreading tree, pendulous branches and foliage, from tropical northern Australia. White to pale brown papery bark. Curved, thin-textured, lanceolate leaves. Nectar-rich, creamy white flowers, in spikes, in autumn–winter. Likes boggy situations. Zones 10–12.

Melaleuca linariifolia
FLAX-LEAFED PAPERBARK, SNOW IN SUMMER

☼ ❄ ↔ 10 ft (3 m) ↑ 20 ft (6 m)

Bushy tree of swamp and creek bed edges in eastern Australia. Creamy papery bark. Spreading crown, soft dark green foliage. Masses of creamy white flowers, in spikes, to 1½ in (35 mm) long, in early summer. 'Snowstorm' ★, prolific-flowering, to 5 ft (1.5 m) tall. Zones 8–11.

Melaleuca megacephala

☼ ❄ ↔ 12 ft (3.5 m) ↑ 10 ft (3 m)

Bushy shrub, native to Western Australia. Broadly ovate, almost rounded leaves, to 1 in (25 mm) long, deep green. Conspicuous flowers, pale yellow, in globular heads, at branch ends, in spring. Suited to warm-temperate conditions, avoid summer humidity. Zones 8–11.

Melaleuca nesophila
SHOWY HONEY MYRTLE

☼ ❉ ↔ 6 ft (1.8 m) ↑ 10 ft (3 m)

Bushy shrub from sandy parts of south coast of Western Australia. Leathery oblong leaves, to 1½ in

Melaleuca megacephala

Melaleuca linariifolia

Melaleuca nesophila

(35 mm) long. Globular heads of mauve-purple flowers. to 1¼ in (30 mm) long, at branch ends, in spring–early summer. Suits warm coastal gardens. Zones 9–11.

Melaleuca nodosa
BALL HONEY MYRTLE

☼ ❄ ↔ 8 ft (2.4 m) ↑ 12 ft (3.5 m)

Dense shrub or small tree from Australian east coast. Dark green foliage. Masses of pale yellow flowers, at ends of branches or in leaf axils, in globular heads, in late spring–summer. Requires adequate moisture during dry periods. Suits protected coastal gardens. Zones 8–11.

Melaleuca pulchella

☼ ❄ ↔ 6 ft (1.8 m) ↑ 6 ft (1.8 m)

Spreading shrub from southern coastal heathland of Western Australia. Small, crowded, oblong leaves. Unusual mauve-pink flowers, large, curved claw-like stamens, in late spring–summer. Zones 8–11.

Melaleuca quinquenervia
BROAD-LEAFED PAPERBARK

☼ ❉ ↔ 20 ft (6 m) ↑ 30–50 ft (9–15 m)

Found in the swampy areas in coastal eastern Australia, New Guinea, and New Caledonia. Thick, creamy, papery bark. Leathery lanceolate leaves. Spikes of nectar-rich creamy white flowers, at ends of branches or in leaf axils, in late spring. Suits poorly drained sites. Zones 10–12.

Melaleuca quinquenervia, in the wild, Isle of Pines, New Caledonia

M

Melaleuca radula

Melaleuca squarrosa

Melaleuca thymifolia

Melaleuca radula
GRACEFUL HONEY MYRTLE

☀ ❄ ↔ 6 ft (1.8 m) ↑ 6 ft (1.8 m)

Spreading, rather open shrub from Western Australia. Leaves narrow, linear, with raised oil glands. Pink to purple flowers, in long loose spikes, on older wood, in winter–spring. Zones 8–11.

Melaleuca rhaphiophylla
SWAMP PAPERBARK

☀ ❄ ↔ 6–10 ft (1.8–3 m) ↑ 10–20 ft (3–6 m)

Evergreen tree from Western Australia. Erect trunk, white papery bark. Drooping, alternate, cylindrical, needle-like leaves. Oblong or cylindrical terminal spikes of cream bottle-brush flowers, in spring–early summer. Fruit is a small woody capsule. Zones 9–11.

Melaleuca spathulata
☀ ❄ ↔ 36 in (90 cm) ↑ 36 in (90 cm)

Shrub from sand plains of southwest Western Australia. Small obovate leaves. Masses of mauve-purple flowers, in ball-like heads, to 1 in (25 mm) long, at ends of branches, in spring–early summer. Prune after flowering to eliminate bare branches. Zones 8–11.

Melaleuca squamea
☀ ❄ ↔ 3 ft (0.9 m) ↑ 6 ft (1.8 m)

Upright shrub from southeastern Australia. Slightly arching branches; soft, oval, pointed leaves. White, mauve, or purple flowers, in small ball-like heads, at ends of branches, in late winter–spring. Suits moist well-drained soil. Zones 8–11.

Melaleuca squarrosa
SCENTED PAPERBARK

☀ ❄ ↔ 15 ft (4.5 m) ↑ 40 ft (12 m)

Shrub or small tree from southeastern Australia. Pale brown corky or papery bark. Broad-ovate dark green leaves. Profuse creamy yellow flowers, perfumed, in cylindrical heads, at branch ends, in spring–summer. Thrives in poorly drained situations. Zones 8–11.

Melaleuca styphelioides
PRICKLY PAPERBARK

☀ ❄ ↔ 20 ft (6 m) ↑ 50 ft (15 m)

Native to eastern Australia, usually inhabits coastal swamps. Ovate slightly twisted leaves, 1 in (25 mm) long, sharply twisted point. Profuse white flowers, in loose bottlebrush-like spikes, in summer. Zones 8–11.

Melaleuca thymifolia
THYME HONEY MYRTLE

☀ ❄ ↔ 36 in (90 cm) ↑ 36 in (90 cm)

Small, spreading, aromatic shrub from damp places in eastern Australia. Slender branches, small narrow-elliptic leaves. Fringed, claw-like, mauve-purple flowers, in irregular clusters, 1½ in (35 mm) long, on older wood, throughout year. 'Cotton Candy', mauve flowers; 'White Lace', white flowers, claw-shaped. Zones 8–11.

Melaleuca uncinata
BROOM HONEY MYRTLE

☀ ❄ ↔ 10 ft (3 m) ↑ 10 ft (3 m)

Erect multi-stemmed shrub, widely distributed in dry inland of southern Australia. Gray papery bark. Needle-like leaves, 2 in (5 cm) long, with bent tips. Pale yellow flowers, in small round heads, in winter–spring. Zones 8–11.

Melaleuca thymifolia 'White Lace'

Melaleuca viridiflora
BROAD-LEAFED PAPERBARK

☀ ❄ ↔ 15 ft (4.5 m) ↑ 30 ft (9 m)

Dense tree, with spreading or weeping branches, from swampy and seasonally wet areas of tropical northern Australia. The leaves are broadly elliptic, to 8 in (20 cm) long. Usually yellowish green flowers, in dense cylindrical spikes, appear in late spring–early autumn; red forms occur. Zones 10–12.

Melaleuca wilsonii
☀ ❄ ↔ 5 ft (1.5 m) ↑ 4 ft (1.2 m)

Dense spreading shrub from southeastern Australia. Narrow pointed leaves, that give off a citrus scent when crushed. Pink or mauve flowers, clustered along older wood, in late spring. Light pruning encourages bushy growth. Zones 8–11.

MELAMPODIUM

The 37 annual or perennial herbs and subshrubs in this genus from the daisy (Asteraceae) family are native to the warmer parts of North America and Mexico. They have narrow to oval toothed or simple leaves, and carry heads of daisy-like flowers with white to pale yellow ray florets and yellow disc florets.

CULTIVATION: These plants are suited to a sunny position in moist well-drained soil. During winter reduce the amount of water given. Can be propagated from seed.

Melaleuca viridiflora

Melampodium leucanthum
BLACKFOOT DAISY

☀ ❄ ↔ 24 in (60 cm) ↑ 24 in (60 cm)

Short-lived, mound-forming, perennial shrub found from Mexico to Colorado, USA. Leaves smooth or divided into 6 lobes. Honey-scented flowerheads, white to cream ray florets, in spring–autumn. Zones 4–11.

Melampodium paludosum
BUTTER DAISY, GOLD MEDALLION FLOWER

☀ ✂ ↔ 36 in (90 cm) ↑ 24 in (60 cm)

Annual herb, from Mexico. Light green oblong leaves on purplish green stems. Solitary, yellow, daisy-like flowers, darker centers, in late spring–early autumn. May self-seed in suitable conditions. 'Showstar', golden yellow daisy-like flowers. Zones 11–12.

MELASPHAERULA
FAIRY BELLS

A genus consisting of a single species of cormous plants from southern Africa, where it grows in sheltered damp places among rocks. These delicate plants, of the iris (Iridaceae) family, have small fan-like shoots of short, very thin, light green leaves, overtopped in spring with wiry open panicles of tiny yellow flowers.

CULTIVATION: These plants like a well-drained site in full sun. Keep dry in summer and autumn. Propagate from seed, which will self-sow in the right climates. Can also be divided.

Melampodium paludosum 'Showstar'

Melampodium leucanthum

M

Melia azederach

Melianthus major

Melasphaerula ramosa
syn. *Melasphaerula graminea*

☼ ❄ ↔ 12 in (36 cm) ↕ 20 in (50 cm)
Dainty corm from southwestern Cape region of South Africa. Long, narrow, light green leaves, to 10 in (25 cm) long. Tiny corms to ½ in (12 mm), fine-branched flower stems, nodding pale yellow flowers, to ¾ in (18 mm) wide, narrow finely pointed petals, streaked brown inside, in spring. Zones 8–10.

MELASTOMA
This genus of around 70 species of tropical and subtropical shrubs from the melastoma (Melastomataceae) family is allied with the similar *Tibouchina,* and occurs primarily in East Asia. These plants have attractive

heavily veined leaves that are often bristly above, with downy undersides. The leaves are oblong to lance-shaped with smooth edges, their size varying with the species. The flowers, borne in small heads at the ends of branches, are 5-petalled, usually in pink to soft purple shades, sometimes scented; they appear from 2 small bracts and bristly calyces. Small, usually inconspicuous berries follow.
CULTIVATION: These tender warm-climate shrubs are best grown in reasonably fertile, moist, humus-rich, well-drained soil in sun or part-shade. They can be pruned after flowering, or in spring in cooler climates, to remove any winter damage. Propagation is usually from half-hardened cuttings taken in summer.

Melastoma malabathricum
INDIAN RHODODENDRON

☼ ✿ ↔ 5 ft (1.5 m) ↕ 6–8 ft (1.8–2.4 m)
A rhododendron from India and Southeast Asia, where its red berries are used medicinally. Scaly branches; 3- to 5-veined, velvety, broad, lance-shaped leaves. Up to 5 mauve to purple flowerheads, almost year-round. Zones 11–12.

MELIA
This small genus of 3 species in the mahogany (Meliaceae) family, is native to southern Asia, Australasia,

Melastoma malabathricum

and tropical Africa, and has many local geographic forms. All are deciduous trees or large shrubs with alternate, pinnate, or bipinnate leaves and showy flowers in long panicles. They are valued for their rapid growth and adaptability to a wide range of soils and climates, including dry conditions, although the best specimens are found on fertile alluvial soils.
CULTIVATION: These trees need good drainage. Severe frost will defoliate them, but is unlikely to do permanent damage. Pruning is not normally necessary, apart from the removal of competing leaders in the early stages. Propagate from seed in spring.

Melia azederach
PERSIAN LILAC, WHITE CEDAR

☼ ❄ ↔ 25 ft (8 m) ↕ 30 ft (9 m)
Fast-growing tree from southwest Asia to China and Japan and south to Australia. Variable species; a number of different races have been distinguished. Pointed mid-green leaves. Fragrant lilac flowers, in loose panicles, in summer. Clusters of persistent rounded, yellow, bead-like fruits, toxic to animals, young children, but not birds. Zones 8–12.

MELIANTHUS
This genus of 6 species of often leggy shrubs native to South Africa is a member of the honey-flower (Melianthaceae) family. *M. major* is naturalized in India. Tiny flowers borne in erect racemes produce a large quantity of nectar. Vigorous growers, they are often treated like perennials, being cut back severely to shoot again and inhibit their straggling tendencies.
CULTIVATION: Not frost hardy, they grow well in full sun or part-shade in free-draining but moisture-retentive soil. Propagate from seed in spring, softwood cuttings in spring and summer, or rooted suckers in spring.

Melianthus major
HONEY FLOWER

☼/☀ ❀ ↔ 3 ft (0.9 m) ↕ 6–10 ft (1.8–3 m)
Shrub, native to hilly grasslands of South Africa. Large, decorative,

pinnate leaves, 20 in (50 cm) long, 17 oval leaflets, toothed, gray-green. Racemes of brick red tubular flowers, in spring–mid-summer. Used in folk medicine. Can be invasive. Zones 9–11.

MELICA
MELIC
This genus of about 70 species, belongs to the grass (Poaceae) family. It is native to temperate regions, excluding Australia. These cool-season growers usually become semi-dormant in summer. The foliage is quite unremarkable and they are grown for the creamy white flowerheads that mature in spring, which is quite early in the year for an ornamental grass.
CULTIVATION: These hardy grasses need little more than a well-drained but moisture-retentive soil in full sun/half-sun. Prune down in early winter before new growth starts. Propagate from seed in summer, or by dividing large clumps.

Melica altissima
SIBERIAN MELIC, SIBERIAN MELICK

☼ ❄ ↔ 32 in (80 cm) ↕ 60 in (150 cm)
Tall grass species, native to eastern Europe and Siberia. Tall spikes of soft green strappy leaves. Fluffy, white, one-sided flowerheads, to 10 in (25 cm) long, in early summer. Can be dried for floral work. 'Atropurpurea', has mauve-pink flowerheads. Zones 5–10.

Melica altissima

Melica macra

Melicope elleryana

Melicope ternata 'Wharang'

Melica macra

☼ ❈ ↔ 24 in (60 cm) ↑ 24 in (60 cm)
Evergreen grass from Argentina.
Forms dense clumps of bright green,
sharply tipped, rough leaves. Spikes of
creamy white flowers, papery texture,
in early summer–winter. Zones 5–10.

MELICOPE

This genus in the rue (Rutaceae)
family includes about 150 species of
trees and shrubs from India, Southeast Asia, Indonesia, New Guinea,
Australia, New Zealand, and Hawaii.
They have compound leaves of 1 or
3 leaflets dotted with small oil glands,
and grow in moist habitats such as
rainforests. Flowers small, white to
pink, borne in short inflorescences in
leaf axils. Fruit has 4 or 5 segments,
each with a glossy hard-coated seed.
CULTIVATION: Prefer well-drained
moist soil and heavy pruning. Fresh
seed is the best method of propagation. However, the hard seed coat
contains germination inhibitors, so
germination is very erratic. It is possible that the recently developed
smoke germination technique may
increase reliability. Cuttings have been
successful with some species.

Melicope elleryana

PINK-FLOWERED CORKWOOD,
PINK-FLOWERED DOUGHWOOD
☼ ❈ ↔ 40 ft (12 m) ↑ 70 ft (21 m)
Small to medium-sized tree from rainforests of tropical Australia. Leaves
opposite, trifoliate, dark green leaflets.
Pinkish mauve flowers, late summer–
autumn. Fruits with 1 to 4 cells.
Zones 8–11.

Melicope ternata

WHARANGI
☼ ❈ ↔ 10 ft (3 m) ↑ 20 ft (6 m)
Heavily branched large shrub or small
tree, native to New Zealand, found in
coastal areas from northern South
Island northward. Aromatic trifoliate
leaves, glossy deep green leaflets.
Small heads of yellow-green flowers,
in summer. Handsome foliage plant.
'Wharang', wavy-edged, small, green
leaves. Zones 7–11.

MELICYTUS

This is a small genus of 12 species
of evergreen trees or shrubs from the
violet (Violaceae) family. They have
oblong or lance-shaped leaves and are
native to New Zealand and some
Pacific Islands. The small male and
female flowers are borne on separate
trees, and the female trees carry
berries in profusion.
CULTIVATION: Grow in any moderately fertile well-drained soil. In cool
climates provide the shelter of a warm
wall or grow in the greenhouse. If a
display of berries is required, both
male and female trees will need to be
planted. They may be pruned to
maintain shape if desired. Propagate
from seed sown in spring or half-
hardened cuttings taken in autumn.

Melicytus ramiflorus

MAHOE, WHITEYWOOD
☼ ❈ ↔ 7 ft (2 m) ↑ 15 ft (4.5 m)
Found on Norfolk Island, Australia,
and in Tonga, Fiji, and New Zealand.
Grayish white bark, mottled by
lichens. Pointed oval leaves, bright
green, serrated edges. Sweet-smelling
cream flowers, in spring–summer.
Clusters of purplish black berries on
female trees. Zones 8–11.

MELINIS

There are 12 species of annual and
perennial grasses in this genus, which
belongs to the family Poaceae. The
majority of species are native to tropical and southern Africa and Madagascar. One species is found in
tropical South America and the West
Indies. They grow in open grassland,
savannah woodland, and disturbed
ground. The shoots are aromatic and
the leaf blades narrow, sometimes
with fine hairs. The flowers are in
spikelets borne in open panicles.
CULTIVATION: These tropical grasses
can be invasive. Easily grown in any
soil in sun or light shade in warm and
tropical climates. Propagate annuals
from seed, and perennials from seed
or division of clumps.

Melinis minutiflora

MOLASSES GRASS
☼ ❀ ↔ 12 in (30 cm) ↑ 4–6 ft (1.2–1.8 m)
Spreading perennial grass from Africa,
often a weed. Forms loose tussocks.
Green to purple or reddish brown
leaves, sticky hairs, strong, sweet-
smelling, volatile oil. Dense, narrow,
pale pink to purple panicles, light
green or purple spikelets, in autumn.
Zones 9–12.

Melicytus ramiflorus

Melinis repens

syn. *Rhynchelytrum repens*
BLANKETGRASS, NATAL REDTOP
☼ ❀ ↔ 2 ft (0.6 m) ↑ 3–4 ft (9–1.2 m)
Native to South Africa. Naturalized
in the Pacific Islands. Perennial grass
with bluish green leaves. Flowering
panicles, to 6 in (15 cm) long,
purplish at first becoming silvery
pink with silky hairs, in summer.
Zones 9–12.

MELIOSMA

Primarily found in tropical parts of
America and Asia, with the Asian
species extending to the temperate
zones, this genus is composed of some
25 species of deciduous or evergreen
trees and shrubs from the family
Sabiaceae. Their leaves are variable
and may be simple or pinnate, small
or large. Individually their flowers are
small, but they are fragrant and carried in large pyramidal panicles, the

Melinis minutiflora

Melinis repens

reduced outer flowers of which are sterile. Tiny, sometimes brightly colored drupes follow the flowers. CULTIVATION: Cold hardiness varies with the species, though none will tolerate repeated hard frosts. They prefer a mild moist climate with moderately fertile free-draining soil and a position in full sun or half sun. If necessary they can be pruned in spring. Propagate from seed.

Meliosma dilleniifolia

☼/◐ ⬍ ↔ 20 ft (6 m) ↑ 50 ft (15 m)

Deciduous variable shrub or tree found from the Himalayas through China to Japan. Leaves mid-green, downy undersides. Upright panicles of fragrant white flowers, in summer. Small black fruits. Zones 9–11.

MELISSA
BALM

This hardy genus, which belongs to the mint (Lamiaceae) family, contains 3 species of perennial herbs that are native to Europe and central Asia. When the small heart-shaped leaves are crushed, a lemony scent is released. The flower spikes, which appear in summer, bear white or

Melissa officinalis

Melissa officinalis 'Aurea'

yellow flowers but these are relatively insignificant. The leaves can be infused to make a herbal tea or can be chopped and used in salads and soups. The name *Melissa* comes from a Greek word meaning bee, as these plants are rich in nectar and are very attractive to bees. CULTIVATION: Grow at the front of borders, along path edges, in herb gardens or containers. Plant in full sun or half-sun in moist but well-drained soil. They may die in soils that are wet in winter. Plants may self-seed. Propagate from seed or cuttings, or by division of roots in spring.

Melissa officinalis
BEE BALM, LEMON BALM

☼/◐ ✿ ↔ 18 in (45 cm) ↑ 24–36 in (60–90 cm)

Herb from Europe. Green, oval, tooth-edged leaves in opposite pairs. Insignificant white tubular flowers, in summer–early autumn. 'Aurea', green leaves, gold splotches. Zones 5–9.

MELOCACTUS
MELON CACTUS

This cactus (Cactaceae) family genus contains 31 species from tropical America, especially eastern Brazil and the Amazon Basin, Peru, Venezuela, the Caribbean, and Central America. These cacti are unbranched (unless they are damaged), the stems being spherical to columnar and strongly ribbed. The flower-bearing structure is permanently distinct, bearing wool and usually bristles. Flowers are red to pink, small and tubular, usually covered by the wool. The fruit is a red, pink, or white, juicy berry, and is usually club-shaped.

Melocactus azureus

CULTIVATION: Grow in acid cactus compost with a rather high inorganic content, in full sun with low humidity. In cool regions they need a heated greenhouse. In winter, water only enough to prevent the plants from shrivelling. The Brazilian species and *M. matanzanus*, a widely grown species from Cuba, are those in general cultivation, the others needing higher winter temperatures. Can be propagated from seed.

Melocactus azureus ★

☼ ⬍ ↔ 6–8 in (15–20 cm) ↑ 5–18 in (12–45 cm)

Cactus from limestone areas of Brazil. Spherical to cylindrical, dark green to gray-green, sometimes fine bloom, 9 or 10 triangular ribs. Spines black to reddish, becoming gray, 7 to 11 radials. Flowers pink, on thick stems with reddish bristles, brown or white wool, in summer. Seed pods white to pale pink. Zones 9–11.

Melocactus bahiensis

☼ ⬍ ↔ 4–5 in (10–12 cm) ↑ 4–8 in (10–20 cm)

Cactus from eastern Brazil. Spherical to depressed spherical, pale to dark green, 8 to 14 low ribs, variable in shape. Spines brown, reddish, or yellowish, overlaid with gray. Flowers pink, on short, thick, woolly stems, in summer. Zones 9–11.

Melocactus curvispinus
syns *Melocactus guitartii, M. maxonii, M. ruestii*

☼ ⬍ ↔ 3–12 in (8–30 cm) ↑ 2–12 in (5–30 cm)

Variable cactus found in Mexico, Central America, the Caribbean, Peru, Colombia, and Venezuela. Stems are depressed, spherical to short cylindrical, light to dark green, with a soft bloom. Erect central spines, 1 to 4, occasionally absent, 6 to 11 radials. Flowers pink to carmine to magenta, on small, thick, woolly stems with prominent reddish brown bristles, in summer. Seed pods are club-shaped. Zones 9–11.

Melocactus bahiensis

Melocactus matanzanus ★
syn. *Melocactus actinacanthus*
DWARF TURK'S CAP CACTUS

☼ ⬍ ↔ 3 in (8 cm) ↑ 3 in (8 cm)

Spherical cactus from northern Peru. Pale green stem with 8 or 9 ribs. Spines brownish white or gray. Flowers pink, open at noon, borne on thick stems, dense reddish bristles, white wool, in summer. Seed pods pink to lilac pink. Zones 9–11.

MENISPERMUM
MOONSEED

This genus contains 2 species of woody twining vines belonging to the moonseed (Menispermaceae) family and is native to northeastern America and East Asia. These plants are generally grown for their foliage. The leaves are rounded and smooth, similar to a maple leaf. The flowers are small and yellow, appearing in summer. Black fruit, similar to grapes, are produced in autumn. They are highly toxic if ingested. The dried rhizome is used in medicines. CULTIVATION: Grow these vines in a moderately fertile soil in full or partial sun. Water well in summer. Propagate from seed or cuttings of mature wood.

Menispermum canadense
COMMON MOONSEED, YELLOW PARILLA

☼/◐ ✿ ↔ 7 ft (2 m) ↑ 10–15 ft (3–4.5 m)

Vine found in North America from Quebec and Manitoba to Georgia and Arkansas. Dark green foliage, large alternate leaves, 4–10 in (10–25 cm) long. Flowers greenish yellow, followed by black fruit, in summer. Half-moon shaped seeds. Zones 4–8.

MENTHA

A genus of 25 species of fragrant and aromatic herbs in the mint (Lamiaceae) family. From Europe, Africa, and Asia, they naturalize in damp moist areas and marginal wetlands. Shallow-rooted plants, they spread easily. They have an upright branching habit and form dense bushy plants from a few inches to 5 ft (1.5 m) high. Stems can travel long distances

underground. The flowers sit on the ends of the stems in clusters or in spikes and vary from ¼ in (6 mm) to 4 in (10 cm). Foliage is aromatic. Many are used in teas and food, and for medicinal purposes; some are grown commercially for their essential oils. Species can be evergreen or deciduous, depending on conditions and varietal differences.
CULTIVATION: Mints grow in any open, fertile, moist soil, in part-shade or full sun. Propagate by dividing the rhizomes throughout the year; roots will appear in a few weeks. Seed can be sown in spring.

Mentha aquatica
WATER MINT
☀ ❄ ↔ 3–7 ft (0.9–2 m) ↑ 3 ft (0.9 m)
Marginal water herb from temperate Eurasia. Strongly scented foliage, serrated dark green leaves on purple upright stems. Small purple flowers, in summer. Zones 7–9.

Mentha × gracilis
☀ ❄ ↔ 36 in (90 cm) ↑ 12 in (30 cm)
Low-growing, ground-hugging plant from temperate Eurasia. Crinkly, dark green, rounded leaves. Tubular lilac flowers, in summer–autumn. Minty, slightly ginger taste. 'Variegata' (variegated ginger mint), leaves with yellow streaks. Zones 7–9.

Mentha longifolia
syns *Mentha incana, M. sylvestris*
HORSE MINT
☀ ❄ ↔ 3–6 ft (0.9–1.8 m) ↑ 4 ft (1.2 m)
Creeping tall-growing herb from Europe and western Asia. Hairy, gray-green, long leaves, strongly musty fragrance. Lilac to white flowers, in summer. Zones 6–9.

Mentha × piperita
PEPPERMINT
☀ ❄ ↔ 36 in (90 cm)
↑ 24–36 in (60–90 cm)
Quick-growing upright herb from Europe. Purplish stems. Long, lance-shaped, dark green leaves, serrated edge, intense minty flavor and aroma.

Mentha suaveolens

Mentha spicata 'Crispa'

Mauve-pink flowers, in summer. Sterile seeds. *M. × p.* f. *citrata* (bergamot mint), rounded toothed leaves are tinged purple, may turn bronze, lilac flowers, strong citrus aroma and flavor, use in fruit salads, can be invasive, best grown in pots; 'Chocolate' ★ (chocolate mint), leaves with dark brown tonings, delicate chocolate fragrance and taste, used in teas. *M. × p.* 'Variegata' (variegated peppermint), leaves with creamy yellow markings. Zones 3–7.

Mentha pulegium
PENNYROYAL
☀/☀ ❄ ↔ 20 in (50 cm)
↑ 8–12 in (20–30 cm)
Carpeting, spreading aromatic herb from southwest and central Europe, and the Mediterranean to Iran. Small, dark green, sometimes gray, leaves, flat on stems. Balls of tubular lilac flowers, on top of foliage, in summer–autumn. Oils deter houseflies. Zones 7–9.

Mentha requienii
syn. *Mentha corsica*
CORSICAN MINT
☀/☀ ❄ ↔ 27 in (70 cm) ↑ ¾ in (1.8 cm)
Carpeting herb from France and Italy. Tight mats of tiny leaves spread on creeping stems. Dark green foliage,

Mentha suaveolens 'Variegata'

Mentha × piperita 'Variegata'

Mentha × piperita

pales in hot sun, very aromatic when rubbed. Tiny heads of lavender-colored flowers, in summer. Zones 7–10.

Mentha spicata
SPEARMINT
☀ ❄ ↔ 3–6 ft (0.9–1.8 m) ↑ 4 ft (1.2 m)
Herb from Europe. Mid-green, narrow, pointed leaves, serrated edge. Creeping rhizomes; flowers pale mauve, pink, or white, in summer. 'Crispa' (curly spearmint), lance-shaped dark green leaves, may be red edge, survives freezing, tall-growing, pale mauve-pink flowers. Zones 3–7.

Mentha suaveolens
syn. *Mentha rotundifolia*
APPLE MINT, WOOLLY MINT
☀ ❄ ↔ 36 in (90 cm) ↑ 36 in (90 cm)
Herb from southwestern Europe. Round pale green leaves, fine hairs. Apple-like aroma. Flowers white to pink, in summer. 'Variegata' (syn. *M. rotundifolia* var. *variegata*) (pineapple mint), leaves gray-green, creamy white streaks, fruity sweet fragrance. Zones 6–9.

Mentha × villosa
BOWLES MINT
☀ ❄ ↔ 5 ft (1.5 m) ↑ 3 ft (0.9 m)
Spreading mound-forming mint. There are delicate hairs on the round

Mentha × piperita f. *citrata*

bright green leaves. Large spikes of pink tubular flowers, in summer. Zones 5–8.

MENYANTHES

This genus of perennial aquatic or marginal herbs is native to Europe and Asia and gives its name to the Menyanthaceae family, of which it is the sole member. Grown for its foliage and fragrant flowers, it has smooth, dark green, compound leaves with elliptic to oval leaflets, with slightly serrated edges. These are carried on sheathed stalks arising from a thick, rooting, creeping then rising rhizome. It carries erect racemes of 10 to 20 short-lived flowers. These are heavily fringed and bearded, 5-petalled, white, flushed with pink.
CULTIVATION: This plant prefers an open, sunny position in shallow water. Keep tidy by removing fading flower-heads and foliage. Propagate from seed or by division of overcrowded clumps in spring.

Menyanthes trifoliata
BOG BEAN, BUCK BEAN, MARSH TREFOIL

☀ ❄ ↔ 8–12 in (20–30 cm)
↑ 10–16 in (25–40 cm)

From Europe. Smooth, dark green, compound leaves; elliptic to oval leaflets, slightly serrated edges, on sheathed stalks. Erect racemes of short-lived, fringed, white flowers, flushed pink, in summer. Zones 3–9.

MERTENSIA
This genus, found in western Europe, Asia, and North America, is a member of the borage (Boraginaceae) family. It contains about 40 species of hardy herbaceous perennials, although only 4 or 5 are cultivated. Their leaves are usually lance-shaped and hairy. Most species are relatively small and produce terminal panicles of usually blue tubular or bell-shaped flowers in spring. Some species are used in wild or rock gardens.
CULTIVATION: Plant in full sun or half-sun in early spring. These plants

Menyanthes trifoliata

prefer moist, well-drained soil, rich in humus. Propagate from seed or by division after flowering.

Mertensia sibirica
SIBERIAN BLUEBELLS

☀ ❄ ↔ 12 in (30 cm)
↑ 12–18 in (30–45 cm)

Perennial from East Asia, northern China, and Siberia. Light green leaves on long stems. Deep blue-purple funnel-shaped flowers, in spring–early summer. Zones 3–7.

Mertensia simplicissima
syn. *Mertensia asiatica*
OYSTER PLANT

☀ ❄ ↔ 18 in (45 cm) ↑ 6 in (15 cm)
Perennial from Japan and Korea. Long trailing stems of fleshy silver-gray leaves. Sky blue flowers, in spring–early autumn. Needs well-drained soil. Zones 5–9.

Mertensia virginica
syn. *Mertensia pulmonaroides*
BLUEBELLS, COWSLIP, ROANOKE BELLS, VIRGINIA BLUEBELLS

☀ ❄ ↔ 12–24 in (30–60 cm)
↑ 12–24 in (30–60 cm)

Perennial from North America. Oval gray-green leaves, 8 in (20 cm) long. Blue-purple flowers, in nodding clusters, in spring. Foliage dies after blooming, so plant among other perennials. Zones 3–9.

MERYTA
This Pacific Islands genus of around 30 species of evergreen shrubs and

Mesembryanthemum crystallinum

Meryta sinclairii

small trees from the ivy (Araliaceae) family, is found as far south as northern New Zealand. It is renowned for its large lush foliage. The New Zealand species *M. sinclairii* is the most widely cultivated. Heavily veined, rather glossy, very large, elliptical leaves, some species have different juvenile and adult foliage, young leaves tending to be narrow. Sprays of insignificant greenish flowers on separate male and female plants are followed by small black fruits. Multi-stemmed, they can be trained as single-trunked trees.
CULTIVATION: Nearly all species are very frost tender but the New Zealand species will tolerate very light frosts once they become well-established. Plant in fertile, well-drained soil, rich in humus, in full sun to shade. They will not tolerate drought, and must be kept moist during the warmer months. Propagate from seed, apart from the cultivars, which must be propagated vegetatively to remain true to type.

Meryta latifolia
BROAD-LEAFED MERYTA

☀ ⚘ ↔ 4 ft (1.2 m) ↑ 15 ft (4.5 m)
Single-trunked shrub or small tree endemic to Norfolk Island, Australia. Leaves to 12 in (30 cm) long, very heavily veined, clustered at branch tips. Clusters of male and female flowers, in inflorescences at branch ends. Green fruit, blackens when ripe. Zones 11–12.

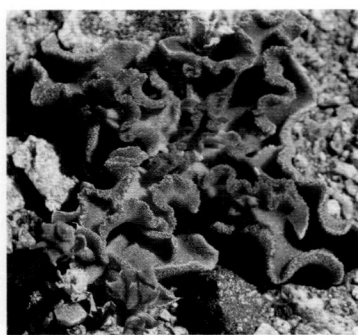

Mesembryanthemum guerichianum

Meryta latifolia

Meryta sinclairii
PUKA, PUKANUI

☀/◐ ⚘ ↔ 12 ft (3.5 m) ↑ 20 ft (6 m)
Small tree found on the Three Kings and Hen and Chicken Islands, New Zealand. Large, glossy, heavily veined, oval leaves. Separate tiny panicles of greenish male or female flowers, in late spring. Fruit like blackberry. Grow in greenhouse or conservatory. Zones 10–11.

MESEMBRYANTHEMUM
This genus contains 40 to 50 species of prostrate or creeping succulent annuals or biennials in the iceplant (Aizoaceae) family, and is native to South Africa and Namibia. All parts of the plants are covered with tiny glandular hairs. Rosettes of cylindrical or flattish, fleshy branches bearing succulent leaves of varying form grow from a central base. The glossy, daisy-like flowers are solitary or numerous, and come in a variety of shades from white to orange, red, or mauve.
CULTIVATION: These plants require a position in full sun in well-drained, very light, sandy soil. Propagate from seed in spring, or from cuttings.

Mesembryanthemum crystallinum

☀ ⚘ ↔ 12–24 in (30–60 cm)
↑ 4–8 in (10–20 cm)

Creeping annual or biennial from South Africa and Namibia. Spreading branches. Leaves thick, sometimes fleshy, oval to spatula-shaped with wavy edges. Bunches of creamy white daisy-like flowers, open only in sunlight, in summer. Can be invasive. Zones 9–11.

Mesembryanthemum guerichianum

☀ ⚘ ↔ 8–18 in (20–45 cm)
↑ 2–4 in (5–10 cm)

Highly succulent annual from South Africa and Namibia. Thick, fleshy, cylindrical stems. Opposite pairs of oval lower and basal leaves, larger than upper leaves. White or green to yellowish white and pink flowers, in summer. Zones 9–11.

Mesembryanthemum nodiflorum

☀ ❄ ↔ 36 in (90 cm) ↕ 6–8 in (15–20 cm)
An annual or biennial from South Africa, introduced widely elsewhere. Extremely succulent. Long, thick, narrow, grayish green leaves, slightly hairy underneath, covered with large glandular hairs. Reddish buds followed by white flowers, in summer. Zones 9–11.

MESPILUS

This genus within the rose (Rosaceae) family has just one species, a deciduous tree that grows in mountain woodland and scrubland throughout southeast Europe and southwest Asia. It is a good ornamental shrub or tree with large single flowers that are usually white, sometimes with a pink flush, and good autumn foliage. It is now grown less for its fruit, which is only edible after frost, when it is described as "bletted" (slightly rotted); the high malic acid content is reduced and the sugar increased in this way. Long known in cultivation, it may have been cultivated by the Assyrians and Babylonians, and brought to Great Britain by the Romans.
CULTIVATION: Grows well in any good moisture-retentive soil with shelter from strong winds. Propagate from seed in autumn, or by bud-grafting in late summer. Can also be grafted onto hawthorn to form graft hybrids.

Mespilus germanica
MEDLAR
☀ ❄ ↔ 25 ft (8 m) ↕ 20 ft (6 m)
A large shrub or small tree from Europe. Thorny branchlets in the wild, but cultivated forms are usually thornless. Leaves alternate, oblong to lance-shaped, toothed, dull green above, felty underneath, red and yellow, in autumn. Profuse apple-blossom-like flowers, in spring. Round, fleshy, brown fruit, too astringent to eat until bletted. 'Breda Giant', apple-cinnamon flavored fruit; 'Dutch', good ornamental tree; 'Large Russian', large pink tinged flowers, spreading crown, large leaves and fruit; 'Nottingham', good-flavored fruit (an acquired taste); 'Royal', medium-sized fruit; 'Stoneless', seedless cultivar, very small fruit. Zones 4–9.

MESUA

This genus of 3 species of evergreen trees in the St John's-wort (Clusiaceae) family is found in the Indo-Malaysian region, and south to Australia. They have narrow leathery leaves with conspicuous veins and small glandular dots. The flowers, borne singly or in pairs, are large, fragrant, have 4 petals and a prominent central boss of stamens. Woody brown fruits follow, with tightly compressed seeds at their center. The fruit of one species, *M. lepidota*, forms an important part of the diet of the proboscis monkey.
CULTIVATION: Easily grown in a tropical climate, *Mesua* species prefer hot humid conditions rather than the seasonally dry tropics. Soil should be moist, well-drained, and humus-rich. Regular feeding will result in lush foliage and larger flowers. Although naturally neat and bushy, young trees often require a little trimming to encourage a single-trunked tree-like habit. Propagate from seed, which is best soaked before sowing, or from half-hardened cuttings.

Mesua ferrea
IRONWOOD
☀ ✦ ↔ 20 ft (6 m) ↕ 40 ft (12 m)
National tree of Sri Lanka, found in India through Malaysia to northern parts of Australia. Bright red young foliage, ages to glossy, dark green leaves, slightly bluish undersides. Fragrant white flowers, in spring. Brown fruits. Foliage ground to paste, is used medicinally. Zones 11–12.

METASEQUOIA

A genus of a single species of conifer in the cypress (Cupressaceae) family, this plant was long thought to be extinct, known only from fossil remains found in China. In 1941 a Chinese botanist visited a village between Hubei and Sichuan and noticed a deciduous conifer known locally as *shuiskan*. It was found the tree was identical to the fossil remains. Seed was collected in 1947 and sent to the Arnold Arboretum in the USA, from where it was distributed to botanic gardens throughout the world. Finally named and described in 1948, it has become a popular ornamental tree both in and outside China. The bark is reddish brown, darkening with age. The leaves are green and flattened and turn reddish brown in autumn.
CULTIVATION: *Metasequoia* species grow rapidly, particularly in a moist but well-drained soil, and have proved hardy and relatively resistant to atmospheric pollution. It is highly regarded as an ornamental for large gardens and parks in cool temperate areas. Propagate from seed.

Mesua ferrea

Mesembryanthemum nodiflorum, Baja California, Mexico

Mespilus germanica

Metasequoia glyptostroboides

Metrosideros umbellata, in the wild, Auckland Island, New Zealand

Metrosideros carminea

Metasequoia glyptostroboides ★

DAWN REDWOOD

☀ ❄ ↔ 20 ft (6 m) ↑ 70 ft (21 m)
Vigorous, quick-growing, deciduous
conifer from China. Cinnamon-
brown bark. Flattened, linear, larch
green leaves, on short branchlets, turn
tawny pink and old gold, in autumn.
Dark brown cones, pendulous, on long
stalks. Larger in the wild. Zones 5–10.

METROSIDEROS

This genus is a member of the large
myrtle (Myrtaceae) family, which
includes *Eucalyptus* and *Psidium*

Metrosideros excelsus

(guava), and is found in South Africa,
the Pacific Islands, Australia, and New
Zealand. *Metrosideros* contains 50
species of evergreen shrubs, trees, and
woody climbers with simple, often
leathery leaves that can be aromatic.
Flowers are comprised of numerous
stamens and resemble rounded bottlebrushes, usually in shades of red,
pink, or white.

Metrosideros nervulosa

CULTIVATION: *Metrosideros* species are
best suited to warmer climates, but
will grow in any reasonably fertile well-
drained soil. *M. excelsa*, in particular,
will grow in dry soils of lower fertility
and in very exposed coastal conditions.
It can be pruned for hedging and used
as shelter. In cool climates, plants can
be grown in pots, overwintered in a
greenhouse and placed outdoors for
summer. Propagate from seed sown in
spring, or half-hardened cuttings
taken in summer.

Metrosideros carminea ★

AKAKURA

☀ ❄ ↔ 3–10 ft (0.9–3 m) ↑ 40 ft (12 m)
Rare climber from New Zealand,
climbs by clinging with aerial roots.
Small, deep green, rounded leaves.
Bright crimson flowers, in spring.
Cuttings from adult plants grow into
small spreading shrubs. 'Carousel' ★,
yellow leaf margins; 'Ferris Wheel',
compact prolific bloomer. Zones 8–11.

Metrosideros excelsus ★

NEW ZEALAND CHRISTMAS TREE,
POHUTUKAWA

☀ ❄ ↔ 25 ft (8 m) ↑ 50 ft (15 m)
Shrubby coastal tree from New Zealand. Thick, leathery, oval leaves, dark
green above, gray and felted beneath.
Red-crimson bottlebrush-like flowers,
in early summer. Young trees susceptible to frost. 'Fire Mountain',
orangey scarlet flowers. Zones 8–11.

Metrosideros polymorpha

Metrosideros kermadecensis

KERMADEC POHUTUKAWA

☀ ❄ ↔ 15 ft (4.5 m) ↑ 20 ft (6 m)
Native to Kermadec Islands, New
Zealand. Similar to *M. excelsus,* but
with smaller leaves and flowers. It
flowers spasmodically year-round.
'Variegatus', leaves variegated grayish
green, with a wide creamy yellow
margin. Zones 8–11.

Metrosideros nervulosa

LORD HOWE MOUNTAIN ROSE

☀ ❄ ↔ 5 ft (1.5 m) ↑ 25 ft (8 m)
Shrub or small tree, native to Lord
Howe Island, Australia. Slow growing
in cultivation. Thick, almost round
leaves. Clusters of deep red flowers,
in late spring–summer. Zones 9–11.

Metrosideros polymorpha

OHI'A LEHUA

☀ ⚘ ↔ 20 ft (6 m) ↑ 20–50 ft (6–15 m)
Variable species, low prostrate shrub
or tree, from Hawaiian Islands, USA.
Often first tree on new lava flows.
Bark rough, fissured. Oval to rounded
leaves, felted beneath. Bottlebrush-
like flowers, red to salmon, pink, and
yellow, in spring–summer. Zones 11–12.

Metrosideros robusta

NORTHERN RATA, RATA

☀ ❄ ↔ 25 ft (8 m) ↑ 20 ft (6 m)
Tall tree found in New Zealand's
North Island and northern South
Island. Slow growing. Begins as an

Metrosideros robusta

Metroxylon salomonense

Michelia champaca

epiphyte. Leaves thick, leathery. Red bottlebrush-like flowers, in summer. Several years to flower. Zones 8–11.

Metrosideros umbellata

SOUTHERN RATA

☀ ❄ ↔ 12 ft (3.5 m) ↑ 10–20 ft (3–6 m)

Native of New Zealand from high rainfall areas of South Island's west coast. Similar to *M. robusta*, smaller, not an epiphyte. Leathery leaves more lance-shaped. Red flowers, in summer. Very slow growing, possibly decades to flower. Zones 8–11.

METROXYLON

A palm family (Arecaceae) genus of 5 species from eastern Indonesia, New Guinea, the Solomon Islands, Samoa, Vanuatu, Fiji, and the Caroline Islands. All are large plants; some are solitary, others form clumps. They occur mostly in swampy habitats. Fronds are large and feathery, while the large branched inflorescences bear both male and bisexual flowers. Fronds are used for thatching by local peoples.
CULTIVATION: They are suitable only for tropical climates with high rainfall and reasonably high temperatures all year. Good rich soil is all that is required. Propagate from seed, which can take 12 months or more to germinate. The clumping species are also propagated from the suckers produced after the fruiting trunk has died.

Metroxylon sagu ★

SAGO PALM

☀ ⚘ ↔ 25 ft (8 m) ↑ 70 ft (21 m)

Clumping species, may have originated in New Guinea and eastern Indonesia. Large inflorescences at branch ends, above fronds, bear bisexual flowers, in spring. Fruits round, brown. After fruits fall, stem dies and suckers develop. A source of sago. Zones 11–12.

Metroxylon salomonense

☀ ⚘ ↔ 30 ft (9 m) ↑ 60 ft (18 m)

Palm occuring wild from Solomon Islands to eastern New Guinea and Vanuatu. Massive, single gray-brown trunk. Arching fronds. Giant inflorescence to 12 ft (3.5 m) high, drooping flower spikes, in summer. Scaly fruits ripen, palm dies. Zones 11–12.

MEUM

BALDMONEY, BEARWORT, SPIGNEL

This monotypic genus is in the carrot (Apiaceae) family. Its single species is a perennial herb native to temperate Europe where it grows in grassland and rough rocky areas, usually on limestone. It forms a clump of finely divided, feathery, aromatic, rich green foliage. In summer small white to pinkish flowers are borne in umbels typical of the carrot family. Both the roots and leaflets are edible, having a warm spicy taste.
CULTIVATION: Grow in a sunny position in well-drained but moisture-retentive fertile soil at the front of the border. Suitable for naturalizing in sunny wild gardens. Propagate from seed or by division.

Meum athamanticum

☀ ❄ ↔ 12–18 in (30–45 cm) ↑ 18–24 in (45–60 cm)

Perennial herb, native to Europe. Forms clumps of attractive, fresh green, feathery foliage. Umbels of small white flowers, sometimes flushed purple, in summer. Zones 6–9.

MICHELIA

This genus of about 45 species of mostly evergreen trees and shrubs in the magnolia (Magnoliaceae) family is native to tropical and subtropical regions of Asia. All have simple leaves and solitary flowers in leaf axils that are strongly perfumed, especially after nightfall. The genus was named after Pietro Antonio Michele, an early eighteenth-century Italian botanist. Oils from some species are extracted for use in perfumes, cosmetics, and medicines; some species also yield timber with commercial uses.

CULTIVATION: *Michelia* species grow best in a reasonably fertile, well-drained, and lime-free soil in a sunny position with shelter from strong winds. They are not reliably frost hardy. Pruning is seldom necessary apart from the removal of competing leaders. Propagate from seed sown as soon as hardened in a warm and humid atmosphere.

Michelia champaca

CHAMPACA

☀ ❧ ↔ 10 ft (3 m) ↑ 100 ft (30 m)

Erect evergreen tree from eastern Himalayan foothills, smaller in cultivation. Leaves bright green, shiny above, dull beneath. Cup-shaped flowers, deep yellowish cream, heavily perfumed, in mid-summer to mid-autumn. Fruits pale yellow-green, spotted brown. Zones 10–11.

Michelia doltsopa

☀ ❧ ↔ 20 ft (6 m) ↑ 30 ft (9 m)

Mostly evergreen tree, native to western China and eastern Himalayas. Pendulous dark green leaves. Cup-shaped flowers, white to deep cream, greenish hue at base, heavily perfumed, in late winter–spring. Fruits small, light green, rosy cheek. 'Silver Cloud' ★, has profuse white flowers. Zones 9–11.

Michelia figo

BANANA SHRUB, PORT-WINE MAGNOLIA

☀ ❧ ↔ 10 ft (3 m) ↑ 15 ft (4.5 m)

Medium to large shrub from southeastern China. Small, dark green, glossy leaves. Small purple-brown flowers, in spring–summer. Fragrance said to resemble bananas, pear drops, and vintage port. Zones 9–11.

Michelia maudiae

☀ ❧ ↔ 20 ft (6 m) ↑ 20–35 ft (6–10 m)

Evergreen tree from China. Large, thick, glossy leaves, to 6 in (15 cm) long. Many large, fragrant, cupped, white flowers, sometimes tinged pink, in late winter–spring. Zones 10–11.

Michelia yunnanensis

☀ ❧ ↔ 7 ft (2 m) ↑ 15 ft (4.5 m)

Slow-growing shrub or small tree native to China. Brownish velvety

Michelia yunnanensis

Michelia doltsopa

Microcachrys tetragona, in the wild, Tasmania, Australia

Microbiota decussata

covering on young leaves and buds. Leaves variably sized and shaped. Flowers yellowish white, little scent, in late winter–spring. Suitable for container. Zones 10–11.

MICRANTHOCEREUS

A genus of 9 species of columnar cacti (family Cactaceae) from central and eastern Brazil, related to the genus *Arrojadoa*. They may be shrubby to tall, columnar, upright, unbranched or branched from the base; their stems are cylindrical, ribbed, and densely spined. The thick flower-bearing stems may be continuous or discontinuous, superficial or sunken, covered with wool and bristles. The flowers are produced in clusters, in various colors; they are tubular, and may open day or night. They rarely exceed 2 in (5 cm) in length. The seed pods are small and fleshy.
CULTIVATION: Of easy culture in a rich, well-drained soil. Propagate from seed or from cuttings allowed to dry out for a week or two. Rest in winter.

Micranthocereus auriazureus
☼ ⁂ ↔ 12–20 in (30–50 cm) ↑ 4 ft (1.2 m)
Cactus from Brazil. Stems columnar, gray-blue, branching from the base; areoles large, prominent, merging, yellow, gray with age. Spines numerous, dark orange-yellow, pale yellow with age, centrals and radials similar.

Nocturnal flowers, lilac-pink to orange-pink, on very woolly indistinct stems, in summer. Zones 9–11.

Micranthocereus purpureus
syn. *Austrocephalocereus purpureus*
☼ ⁂ ↔ 5 in (12 cm) ↑ 10 ft (3 m)
Cactus from Brazil. Stems columnar, usually unbranched; areoles with white wool, almost merging. Spines brown, glassy needle-like radials. The flowers are pink to white, gray-white wool, reddish brown to black bristles, in summer. The seed pods are spherical, short cylindrical to club-shaped, red. Zones 9–11.

MICROBIOTA
RUSSIAN CYPRESS, SIBERIAN CARPET CYPRESS
This conifer genus in the cypress (Cupressaceae) family contains just one species. It is very common in the mountains of southeastern Siberia above the timber line. It is a small shrub to about 24 in (60 cm) tall, spreading to 5 ft (1.5 m) across, with the male and female cones borne on separate plants.
CULTIVATION: This shrub is quite adaptable to cultivation in milder climates in moist soil. Propagate from seed or cuttings of half-hardened shoots taken in summer.

Microbiota decussata ★
RUSSIAN CYPRESS
☼ ❄ ↔ 5 ft (1.5 m) ↑ 2 ft (0.6 m)
Small shrub from Siberia. Flattened short branches covered in tiny, scale-like, almost triangular, overlapping leaves. Male and female cones at ends of short branches, in summer. Female cones, egg-shaped. Foliage can turn bronze in cold winters. Zones 3–9.

MICROCACHRYS
This is a genus in the plum-pine (Podocarpaceae) family with a single

species. It occurs only in Tasmania, Australia, on exposed mountain tops in alpine moorlands in central, western and southwestern parts of the state, above 3,000 ft (900 m). The sole member of the genus is a shrub with very closely crowded branches and branchlets. It has tiny scale-like leaves, arranged in opposite pairs, very like a cypress *(Cupressus).* Both female and male (pollen) cones are small, the latter unusual in this family for having 20 or more tiny seeds per cone.
CULTIVATION: Creeping pine can be grown in a range of climates, but a well-drained moisture-retaining soil in full sun or only light shade gives the best results. It is frost hardy and can survive snow for short periods, but long periods of weather below freezing point can be fatal. Propagate from seed, which must be kept at about 39°F (4°C) for several weeks before sowing. Cuttings of young shoots that are not soft will strike easily.

Microcachrys tetragona
CREEPING PINE
☼ ❄ ↔ 36 in (90 cm) ↑ 12 in (30 cm)
Dwarf prostrate spreading shrub. Leaves opposite, usually overlapping, light green, quite thick. Male and female cones on separate plants; male cones, egg-shaped, very small; female cones larger, globular, turn red when ripe, in summer. Zones 8–9.

MICROLEPIA
The 45 to 50 species of this genus of deciduous, semi-evergreen, or evergreen, rock-dwelling or terrestrial ferns in the bracken (Dennstaedtiaceae) family are found in the tropics and subtropics worldwide. They have creeping underground rhizomes covered with bristles, and dense roots, with the fronds spaced along the rhizome. The fronds are erect or arching, borne on short stalks, with laminae divided, thinly textured and slightly hairy, and notched or lobed segments.
CULTIVATION: These ferns are suited to hanging baskets and containers, preferring shade or semi-shade in

Microsorum grossum

moist soil. Keep tidy by removing faded fronds. Propagate by division in spring or by spores in summer.

Microlepia speluncae
☼ ✦ ↔ 6 ft (1.8 m) ↑ 3–6 ft (1–1.8 m)
Terrestrial tropical fern from southern China. Branching, spreading rhizome. Very large triangular, papery, pinnate fronds, triangular to sword-shaped leaflets, serrated, notched or lobed, sword-shaped to triangular segments, on rough stalks, all year. Zones 11–12.

Microlepia strigosa
☼ ✦ ↔ 24 in (60 cm) ↑ 36 in (90 cm)
Evergreen fern from tropical Asia. Creeping rhizome. Broad, irregularly lance-shaped, pinnate fronds, up to 32 in (80 cm) long, with leaflets up to 8 in (20 cm) long, notched segments, on rough hairy stalks. Zones 11–12.

MICROSORUM
syn. *Microsorium*
This genus of 40 to 50 mostly epiphytic ferns from tropical and subtropical Africa, Asia, Australasia, and Polynesia belongs in the polypody (Polypodiaceae) family. Their surface-creeping or climbing rhizomes may be smooth or covered in scales and roots. Fronds arising from the rhizomes are stalked, simple or divided. The genus name is from the Greek *mikros,* "small," and *soros,* "mound," referring to scattered spore bodies of most species.
CULTIVATION: Prefer full sun to half-shade in moist, well-drained soil or fibrous mix. Propagate by division of rhizomes or from spores, from spring.

Microsorum grossum
syn. *Microsorium grossum*
☼ ✦ ↔ 24–36 in (60–90 cm)
↑ 24–36 in (60–90 cm)

Medium-sized, normally epiphytic fern from eastern Australia and

Microlepia strigosa

Microsorum punctatum

Polynesia. Widely used in the tropics as ground cover. Long-creeping rhizomes. Deeply lobed, leathery, triangular fronds, on short stalks, in summer. Spore bodies located along midribs of lobes. Zones 11–12.

Microsorum lucidum
syn. *Microsorium lucidum*

☀ ⚘ ↔ 6 ft (1.8 m) ↕ 4–6 ft (1.2–1.8 m)

Medium to large fern from India, southwestern China, and Southeast Asia. Green, fleshy, creeping rhizomes. Dark green, oblong, pinnate fronds, about 36 cm (90 cm) long, on short stalks, in summer. Zones 11–12.

Microsorum punctatum
syns *Microsorium punctatum*, *Polypodium polycarpon*

CLIMBING BIRD'S NEST FERN

☀ ⚘ ↔ 5 ft (1.5 m) ↕ 40 in 100 cm)

Epiphytic fern of tropical Africa, Asia, Australasia, and Polynesia. Dense ground-covering habit. Woody to fleshy, creeping, scaly, brownish rhizome. Long, simple, smooth, fleshy yet tough, pale to olive green, sword-shaped fronds, in summer. Dot-like spore bodies. Zones 11–12.

MILIUM
MILLET

A genus of 6 species in the grass (Poaceae) family, all clump-forming annuals and perennials with flat arching leaves and open sprays of tiny flowers in summer. Found in temperate regions of North America, Asia, and Europe, usually in woodland habitats, and are almost without exception of little ornamental value. CULTIVATION: Grow in moist humus-rich soils in half-sun. Propagate by division or from seed, which will often mildly self-seed.

Microsorum lucidum

Milium effusum
WOOD MILLET

☀ ❄ ↔ 10–12 in (25–30 cm) ↕ 10–12 in (25–30 cm)

European grass, planted in woodlands for seeds as game bird food. Arching soft green leaves, to 12 in (30 cm) long. Open sprays of minute flowers, in summer. 'Aureum' (Bowle's golden grass), grown in gardens, gold-leafed form, true from seed. Zones 5–10.

MILLETTIA

There are about 90 species in this tropical genus of trees, shrubs, and climbers from Africa and southern Asia. They are members of the pea-flower subfamily of the legume (Fabaceae) family. The leaves are alternate and compound, with a leaflet at the end of the stem, and a pronounced swelling where the leaf stalk joins the stem. Flowers, in large spikes or panicles, are pink, mauve, red, or various shades of these colors. Fruits are often large and "pea pod-like," splitting in halves to release round seeds. CULTIVATION: These plants are fast growers requiring rich moist soil and ample water in summer. Propagate from seed only, and the seed must be very fresh. Soak overnight in hot water prior to sowing.

Millettia grandis
SOUTH AFRICAN IRONWOOD

☀ ❀ ↔ 30 ft (9 m) ↕ 40 ft (12 m)

Medium-sized tree from low-altitude coastal eastern South Africa. Leaves compound, 6 to 7 pairs of oblong leaflets, undersurface with silky hairs.

× *M.* 'Mourier Bay' × *Miltonia* 'Sao Paulo'

Purple pea-flowers, on upright spikes, at ends of branches, in summer. Fruits large, woody, flat pods. Zones 9–11.

× *MILTASSIA*

This is a hardy bigeneric orchid hybrid, a combination of *Miltonia* and *Brassia,* belonging to the family Orchidaceae. These spidery sympodial hybrids, an influence from the *Brassia* parent, are more tolerant of both cool and high temperatures and flower reliably every year. They grow in a wide range of conditions and have long-lasting blooms, often fragrant, making them popular flowering pot plants. CULTIVATION: These orchids grow well in pots of a bark-based medium, with larger plants looking good in hanging baskets. In frost-free climates they can also be attached to garden trees that do not shed their bark. They are vigorous and worth cultivating, and bloom best when grown as large specimens. Most × *Miltassia* hybrids bloom in spring and summer and like bright humid conditions throughout the year. Propagate by division.

× *Miltassia* 'Charles M. Fitch'

☀/☼ ❀ ↔ 24 in (60 cm) ↕ 32 in (80 cm)

Popular easily grown hybrid between *Brassia verrucosa* and *Miltonia spectabilis*. Mid-green strappy leaves. Pale to dark pink starry blooms, darker spots over segments, in summer. Zones 9–11.

× *Miltassia* 'Mourier Bay' × *Miltonia* 'Sao Paulo'

☀/☼ ❀ ↔ 24 in (60 cm) ↕ 32 in (80 cm)

Unregistered hybrid that combines 3 *Miltonia* species and 2 *Brassia* species. Paler green strap-like leaves. Green to creamy white blooms blotched with orange marks, in summer. Zones 9–11.

Millettia grandis

× *Miltassia* 'Charles M. Fitch'

MILTONIA

This is a genus of sympodial orchids in the family Orchidaceae, containing about 10 epiphytic species, mostly from Brazil. They have showy blooms in a large variety of colors, and are vigorous plants that quickly grow into specimen size. *Miltonia* species have been hybridized with many of the related genera, including *Brassia*, to produce *Miltassia*, and with *Oncidium* to create the genus × *Miltonidium*. However, many of the hybrids labeled as *Miltonia* species in collections often refer to the closely related genus of pansy orchids, *Miltoniopsis*.

CULTIVATION: *Miltonia* species can be grown on large slabs or plaques of cork or tree-fern, or potted in squat-style pots, as they do not have a deep root system. They will take bright light and high temperatures in summer, as long as the humidity remains high. They require a cooler, dry rest period in winter. They are reliable bloomers and, for best results, feed regularly throughout the growing season. However, the plants will still perform well even with a level of neglect. Propagate by division.

Miltonia clowesii

Miltonia regnellii

Miltonia 'Sandy's Cove'

Miltonia clowesii

☀ ⚘ ↔ 8–24 in (20–60 cm)
↕ 8–27 in (20–70 cm)

A striking Brazilian orchid with tall spikes of up to 8 yellow-brown, starry, 3 in (8 cm) wide flowers, over-laid with chestnut-brown bars and blotches, in summer–autumn. Label-lum white, purple markings at base. Zones 10–12.

Miltonia flavescens

☀/☼ ⚘ ↔ 8–36 in (20–90 cm)
↕ 8–20 in (20–50 cm)

Vigorous orchid from Brazil. Prefers intermediate to warm conditions. Spikes of up to 12, pale creamy yellow, somewhat spidery blooms, 3 in (8 cm) wide, narrow segments, in summer. Zones 10–12.

Miltonia regnellii

☀ ⚘ ↔ 8–24 in (20–60 cm)
↕ 8–24 in (20–60 cm)

A striking orchid from Brazil. White flowers, with contrasting pink to mauve labellum, up to five blooms, 2½ in (6 cm) wide, on arching spike, in summer. There is also a pure white form. Zones 10–12.

× *Miltonidium* Pupukea Sunset 'H & R'

Miltonia spectabilis

☀ ⚘ ↔ 8–24 in (20–60 cm)
↕ 8–16 in (20–40 cm)

Variable orchid species from Brazil. Flowers 3 in (8 cm) wide, singly or in pairs, in spring. The common form features white petals and sepals, broad labellum, 2-tone purple; also pink and purple forms and rare albino cultivars. *M. s.* var. *moreliana*, very dark plum-purple flowers. Zones 10–12.

Miltonia 'Sandy's Cove'

☀ ⚘ ↔ 8–24 in (20–60 cm)
↕ 8–24 in (20–60 cm)

Hybrid orchid, of unusual color combination, with 5 species in its ancestry. Golden brown tepals, contrasting plum-colored labellum, in spring. Zones 10–12.

× MILTONIDIUM

This bigeneric hybrid from the orchid (Orchidaceae) family is a combination of *Miltonia* and *Oncidium*. These compact sympodial hybrids tolerate both cool and high temperatures and are reliable flowerers. Able to be grown in a wide range of conditions and with long-lasting, often fragrant blooms means they are popular flowering pot plants. Due to the diversity within the genus *Oncidium*, there are countless hybridizing possibilities for these hybrids. Most × *Miltonidium* plants produce colorful blooms in spring and summer and like bright humid conditions throughout the year.

CULTIVATION: These hybrids grow well in pots of a bark-based medium, preferring to be somewhat pot-bound. In frost-free climates they may also be attached to garden trees that do not shed their bark. They are particularly vigorous and worth cultivating, and bloom best when grown as large specimens. Propagate by division.

× Miltonidium Bartley Schwarz 'Highland'

☀/☼ ⚘ ↔ 8–24 in (20–60 cm)
↕ 8–36 in (20–90 cm)

Orchid hybrid with strong influence from *Oncidium leucochilum*. Superb

× *Miltonidium* Bartley Schwarz 'Highland'

blooms with striking strong reddish purple color and white labellum, in summer. Zones 10–12.

× Miltonidium Pupukea Sunset 'H & R'

☀/☼ ⚘ ↔ 8–24 in (20–60 cm)
↕ 8–36 in (20–90 cm)

Popular hybrid between tri-colored *Miltonia warscewiczii* and the small buttercup yellow-flowered species *Oncidium cheirophorum*. Brownish blooms, often rust-like, with red and yellow labellum. Zones 10–12.

MILTONIOPSIS

PANSY ORCHID

This genus in the family Orchidaceae is made up of 6 different sympodial orchids, mainly from Colombia and Ecuador. They were once included within *Miltonia*, but botanically, *Miltoniopsis* is closer to *Odontoglossum* than *Miltonia*. There have been many artificial hybrids created within this showy genus, known as the "pansy orchids" because of their floral shape and color markings. These plants are fragile with thin foliage. The leaves are usually bluish green and narrow. The blooms come in a variety of colors and are large and flat. Care should be taken with handling, as all parts scorch and bruise easily.

CULTIVATION: These orchids prefer a narrow temperature range; they do not want to go below 50°F (10°C) in winter or go over 79°F (26°C) in summer. The foliage prefers a shaded humid position. Blooms will readily mark if not provided with ample air movement. They are best in small pots, with sphagnum moss used exclusively as the growing medium. The hybrids are generally easier to grow than the species, due to hybrid vigor. Propagate by division.

Miltoniopsis, Hybrid, Beall's Strawberry Joy

Miltoniopsis, Hybrid, Cute 'Rodeo'

Miltoniopsis, Hybrid, Herralexandre

Miltoniopsis, Hybrid, Hudson Bay

Miltoniopsis, Hybrid, Jean Carlson

Miltoniopsis, Hybrid, Red Knight

M., Hybrid, Rouge 'California Plum'

Miltoniopsis, Hybrid, Zorro 'Yellow Delight'

Miltoniopsis phalaenopsis

☀ ⚘ ↔ 15 in (38 cm) ↕ 12 in (30 cm)
Colombian orchid, which occurs at
altitudes of 4,000–5,000 ft (1,200–
1,500 m). A clumping species with
grass-like foliage. It produces up to
5 shapely white flowers, 2½ in (6 cm)
wide, in spring. The outstanding broad
labellum, white, yellow at base, is distinguished by a waterfall pattern of
bright purple markings often passed
on to hybrids. Zones 11–12.

Miltoniopsis vexillaria

☀ ⚘ ↔ 8–24 in (20–60 cm)
↕ 8–16 in (20–40 cm)

Orchid from Colombia and Peru.
Upright to arching spikes of up to
8 flowers, to 4 in (10 cm) wide, palest
pink to deep rose, in spring. This is
a major parent among *Miltoniopsis*
hybrids. Zones 11–12.

Miltoniopsis Hybrids

☀ ⚘ ↔ 32 in (80 cm) ↕ 20 in (50 cm)
These hybrids offer a range of colors
and patterns in white, pinks, purples,

Miltoniopsis phalaenopsis

reds, yellows and often have contrasting markings on a prominent labellum.
Many of them are sweetly fragrant.
Beall's Strawberry Joy bears a rose
pink bloom with deep strawberry red
marking; **Cute 'Rodeo'**, a white-edged
bloom with a deep ruby red center;
Herralexandre, a pure white bloom
with a rich ruby center; **Hudson Bay**
produces white blooms brushed with
rose pink; **Jean Carlson** bears striking
hot pink blooms; **Red Knight** has
distinctive 2-tone pink and purple
blooms; **Robert Strauss**, creamy white
blooms with red to orange marking at
their centers; **Rouge 'California**

Miltoniopsis, Hybrid, Robert Strauss

Plum' ★, bold 2-tone plum blooms
with white edging; and **Zorro 'Yellow
Delight'**, pale yellow blooms with
orange-red marking. Zones 11–12.

MIMETES

One of the many members of the
South African protea (Proteaceae)
family, this genus is composed of
11 or 12 species of evergreen shrubs,
some of which are very endangered.
The genus name is from the Greek
mimetes, which means a mimic, and
refers to these plants' resemblance to
other species. Usually bearing simple
leaves covered with silky hairs, the
foliage near the stem tips becomes
brightly colored and conceals small
tufted flowers in the leaf axils. The
plants carry colored bracts most of the
year, though they are usually at their
most prolific in spring.
CULTIVATION: Like most plants from
the protea family, *Mimetes* species

grow best in light well-drained soil
with an airy position in full sun. They
tolerate occasional light frosts but
resent prolonged wet and cold conditions, and can suffer from root rots
and foliar fungal diseases. They can be
trimmed to shape as necessary. Cutting
the flowerheads will ensure that they
keep their color well. Propagate from
seed, as soon as it is ripe, or from half-
hardened cuttings in the late summer
or autumn.

Mimetes cucullatus ★

ROOISTOMPIE

☀ ❊ ↔ 5 ft (1.5 m) ↕ 5 ft (1.5 m)
Shrub native to Western Cape, South
Africa. The leaves, to 3 in (8 cm) long,
are yellow-green. White flowers appear
among the leaves, in summer, causing
the leaves to redden. The plant maintains its color over a long season, and
is popular with the cut-flower trade.
Zones 8–11.

Mimetes cucullatus, in the wild, Western Cape, South Africa

Mimulus, HC, 'Roter Kaiser'

Mimulus, HC, 'Highland Pink'

Mimulus, HC, 'Highland Park'

Mimulus, HC, 'Malibu Red'

Mimulus, Hybrid Cultivar, 'Puck'

Mimosa pudica

MIMOSA

Allied to *Acacia*, this genus in the mimosa subfamily of the legume (Fabaceae) family, consists of some 480 species of herbs, vines, shrubs, or trees. Most are from South and Central America, southern USA, Asia, and Africa, growing in forest to dry savannah. They have bipinnate leaves and often spiny stems. The tiny flowers are white, pink, or lilac, and have long multiple stamens and 4 or 5 petals. They are borne singly or in stalked rounded heads, or in spikes or racemes. The prickly flat seeds split open when mature. Some species are invasive.
CULTIVATION: *Mimosa* species are best suited to well-drained moderately fertile soil in a sunny position free from frost. Propagate from seed, usually pre-soaked in hot water, or cuttings taken from young growth.

Mimosa pudica
SENSITIVE PLANT

☼ ✣ ↔ 36 in (90 cm) ↕ 36 in (90 cm)
Native to tropical America, often treated as annual. Prickly branching stems. Leaves make "sleep-movements" at night. Leaflets fold together when touched, stalks droop. Light pink to lilac flowers, in summer. A weed in some areas. Zones 10–12.

MIMULUS
MONKEY FLOWER, MUSK

While it is best known for its annuals and perennials, this mostly American genus belonging to the foxglove (Scrophulariaceae) family has some 180 species and includes a few shrubs. These are vigorous upright plants with stems covered in fine hairs and sticky glands, which may also be present on the leaves. The flowers form in the leaf axils and are short tubes with widely flared throats. The annuals and perennials often have flowers with vividly contrasting color patterns, but this is less common among the shrubs.
CULTIVATION: In suitably mild climates, the shrubby *Mimulus* are easy to grow, provided they are given full sun and a well-drained soil that remains moist through summer. They are quick growing, inclined to become untidy unless routinely pinched back. They tend to be short lived. Propagate from seed or half-hardened cuttings.

Mimulus aurantiacus
BUSH MONKEY FLOWER

☼ ✣ ↔ 3 ft (0.9 m) ↕ 4 ft (1.2 m)
Upright shrub found in western USA from southern Oregon to California. Narrow, bright to dark green leaves

Mimulus cardinalis

have serrated edges. Stems and foliage have a sticky coating. Flowers are funnel-shaped, yellow, gold, and orange, in spring–summer. Zones 8–10.

Mimulus bifidus

☼ ✣ ↔ 12–40 in (30–100 cm)
↕ 12–40 in (30–100 cm)
Much-branched, sticky, hairy shrub, native to California, USA. Finely toothed spear-shaped leaves. Yellow flowers, bell-shaped corolla, up to 2½ in (6 cm) wide, in spring–summer. Zones 7–9.

Mimulus cardinalis
SCARLET MONKEY FLOWER

☼/☀ ✣ ↔ 24–27 in (60–70 cm)
↕ 32–36 in (80–90 cm)
Vigorous clumping perennial from southern North America. Roots down when a stem touches ground. Stems are sticky. Leaves to 5 in (12 cm) long. Scarlet tubular flowers, in leaf axils, in summer. Zones 6–10.

Mimulus guttatus
syn. *Mimulus langsdorfii*
COMMON LARGE MONKEY FLOWER, GAP MOUTH

☼ ✣ ↔ 36 in (90 cm) ↕ 36 in (90 cm)
Mat-forming, branching, annual or biennial herb, occurring from Alaska, USA, to Mexico. Rounded, toothed

Mimulus bifidus

or slightly divided, mid-green leaves. Hairy heads of bright yellow, tubular flowers, red to brown spots along hairy ridges, in spring–early autumn. Zones 4–8.

Mimulus lewisii
GREAT PURPLE MONKEY FLOWER

☼ ✣ ↔ 8–24 in (20–60 cm)
↕ 12–36 in (30–90 cm)
Hairy, glandular, perennial herb from Alaska to California, USA. Erect stem. Oblong to elliptic leaves, finely toothed. Magenta or white tubular flowers, on stout stalks, 2 yellow hairy creases and maroon spots in throat, in summer. Zones 3–9.

Mimulus luteus
MONKEY MUSK, YELLOW MONKEY FLOWER

☼ ✣ ↔ 24–32 in (60–80 cm)
↕ 12–16 in (30–40 cm)
Vigorous spreading perennial found from Chile, naturalized in other moist habitats. Leaves to 1¼ in (30 mm) long. Yellow tubular flowers, to 2 in (5 cm) long, in leaf axils, in spring–autumn. 'Variegatus', variegated foliage, less vigorous. Zones 7–10.

Mimulus ringens
ALLEGHENY MONKEY FLOWER

☼ ✣ ↔ 4–5 ft (1.2–1.5 m)
↕ 3–4 ft (0.9–1.2 m)
Perennial herb from North America and Europe. Smooth, 4-cornered, narrowly winged stems. Narrow green leaves. Violet-blue tubular flowers, occasionally white or pink, thin throat, on erect stalks, in summer. Zones 3–9.

Mimulus Hybrid Cultivars

☼ ✣ ↔ 12–32 in (30–80 cm)
↕ 8–36 in (20–90 cm)
Mimulus hybrids are strong and vigorous with a wide range of striking colors to choose from. Popular cultivars include: 'Highland Park', varying shades from apricot to tomato red; 'Highland Pink', strong red velvet colors with paler undersides; 'Malibu Red', larger blooms in rich red; 'Puck', clear yellow; and 'Roter Kaiser', larger trumpet-shaped blooms in rich red. Zones 3–9.

Mimulus guttatus

Mimusops zeyheri

Mimusops obovata

MIMUSOPS

This genus, containing 41 species, from the sapodilla (Sapotaceae) family, occurs in tropical Africa, Madagascar, the Mascarene Islands, the Seychelles, Indonesia, and Malaysia. They are all evergreen trees or shrubs with all parts of the plant containing a milky latex. The leaves are simple and alternate. The flowers are borne singly or in clusters of 2 to 4 blooms, in leaf axils. The relatively large fruits are fleshy or leathery, and contain several seeds that are flat with a hard coat.
CULTIVATION: Most species that have been cultivated require a rich soil in a frost-free position with water during dry periods. Propagate from seed that has been removed from the surrounding fleshy fruit and sown while fresh. Germination usually occurs within 2 to 3 weeks.

Mimusops obovata
RED MILKWOOD
☀ ⚘ ↔ 15 ft (4.5 m) ↑ 70 ft (21 m)
Evergreen tree from the dense coastal forests of eastern South Africa and southern Mozambique. Shiny dark green leaves, sweetly scented. Star-like, creamy white flowers, in clusters, in spring. Bright orange-red, fleshy, egg-shaped, edible fruits, used in jams and wine. Zones 9–11.

Mimusops zeyheri
TRANSVAAL RED MILKWOOD
☀ ⚘ ↔ 12 ft (3.5 m) ↑ 50 ft (15 m)
A large shrub to medium-sized tree, occurring from the hot regions of Angola and Zimbabwe south to northern South Africa. The leaves are thick and leathery, shiny green, paler beneath. The flowers are white, in the leaf axils, and appear in late spring–early autumn. Egg-shaped, fleshy, yellow fruit. Zones 9–11.

MINUARTIA
SANDWORT

A genus of the pink (Caryophyllaceae) family, containing about 100 annuals and perennials. Many of the latter have a mat-forming habit, often very compact. Widely distributed through temperate and arctic regions of the Northern Hemisphere. The plants have narrow leaves and clusters of 5-petalled open flowers; some of the neater ones are suited to rock gardens.
CULTIVATION: Require a moist, rich, well-drained soil in an open sunny position. Propagate from seed in spring or cuttings in late summer.

Minuartia stellata
syns *Alsine parnassica, A. stellata*
☀ ❋ ↔ 18 in (45 cm) ↑ 2 in (50 mm)
Cushion-forming plant from eastern Mediterranean grasslands. Smooth, short, pointed leaves. White flowers, about 2½ in (6 cm) wide, elongated, 5 partially opening petals, in summer. Zones 4–9.

MIRABILIS

A genus of about 50 species of annuals and tuberous-rooted perennials in the four-o'clock (Nyctaginaceae) family, native to southern North America, Central America, and South America. The leaves are in opposite pairs and are simple and smooth-edged, modified into small bracts below the flower clusters. The flowers are short lived and fragrant, and come in a wide range of bright colors.
CULTIVATION: Grow these plants in a sunny moist aspect in rich soil. In frost-prone areas, lift the tubers of perennials and store as you would dahlias. Propagate annual species from seed sown where it is to grow, or by division of tuberous perennial species.

Mirabilis jalapa
FOUR O'CLOCK FLOWER, MARVEL OF PERU
☀ ❋ ↔ 20–24 in (50–60 cm)
↑ 20–24 in (50–60 cm)
Widespread in tropical and subtropical regions of the Americas, so widely cultivated and naturalized that its exact origin is uncertain. Bushy herbaceous perennial. Tuberous roots and leaves to 4 in (10 cm) long. Short-lived, flared, trumpet-flowers, 2 in (5 cm) wide, mainly magenta, or yellow, red, or white, also striped, in summer. Zones 8–11.

MIRBELIA

This is a genus of about 25 species in the pea-flower subfamily of the legume (Fabaceae) family, from Australia. All are shrubs of various sizes with alternate, opposite or whorled leaves that are simple and smooth-edged; some species have spiny lobes. The pea-flowers are in 2 color groups: yellow-orange and shades of purple. Their small fruits are shaped like pea pods and usually contain 2 seeds. Habitats range from open forests to woodlands and heathy scrubs, usually near the coast, sometimes in the arid inland.
CULTIVATION: Grow these shrubs in sandy, acidic, well-drained soil in part-sun or shade. Propagate from seed and cuttings. There will be fruits at several stages of ripeness on any one plant, so seed can be obtained fairly readily. Pre-treatment is needed for germination: usually the hot water method, but a smoked-water treatment is likely to be as effective.

Mirbelia dilatata
HOLLY-LEAFED MIRBELIA
☀ ❋ ↔ 8 ft (2.4 m) ↑ 12 ft (3.5 m)
Large shrub from southeastern Australia. Dark green triangular leaves, 3 to 7 spiny lobes. Spikes of purplish-mauve pea-flowers, at branch ends, in spring–summer. Pods egg-shaped. Zones 8–9.

MISCANTHUS

This genus, part of the grass (Poaceae) family, contains about 20 species found from Africa to East Asia. These tufted spreading plants have showy, green, silver, white, and mottled foliage, deciduous or evergreen. They are found in moist areas with free drainage. Commonly referred to as reeds, they have upright clumps of leaves that cascade from rounded upright stems. Masses of tall flower-heads usually appear in late summer through autumn, often remaining on plants through winter. They dry well, holding their form for months, so are ideal for floral work. Autumn tonings, from orange, red, yellow, or purple.
CULTIVATION: *Miscanthus* species prefer full sun and moist open soils. Used widely in ornamental gardens as features and for screening. To propagate, divide into small clumps in autumn, or sow seed in containers in spring after frosts. Division is best, as seed is often slow to germinate.

Miscanthus floridulus
AMUR SILVERGRASS
☀ ❋ ↔ 5 ft (1.5 m) ↑ 8 ft (2.4 m)
Tall grass plant from Southeast Asia. Deciduous or evergreen. Arching mid-green leaves, silver midribs; silver flower spikes, in autumn. Zones 6–9.

Minuartia stellata

Mirbelia dilatata

Miscanthus floridulus

Miscanthus sinensis 'Gracillimus'

M. sinensis 'Morning Light'

Miscanthus sinensis 'Variegatus'

Miscanthus sinensis 'Strictus'

Miscanthus sinensis 'Yaku jima'

Miscanthus sinensis var. *condensatus*

Miscanthus transmorrisonensis

Miscanthus oligostachyus

SMALL JAPANESE SILVER GRASS

☼ ❄ ↔ 32 in (80 cm) ↕ 40 in (100 cm)
Small compact grass plant from Japan and China. Upright clumping foliage, round stems. Showy creamy white flowers, in autumn. Ideally suited to cooler climates. Zones 5–9.

Miscanthus sacchariflorus

SILVER BANNER GRASS

☼ ❄ ↔ 5 ft (1.5 m) ↕ 5 ft (1.5 m)
Deciduous creeping grass from Korea, Japan, and China. Forms dense clumps. Long green leaves hang from upright stems; orange-brown tonings in autumn. Wispy silver flowers, in autumn–winter. Zones 5–9.

Miscanthus sinensis

EULALIA, JAPANESE SILVER GRASS

☼ ❄ ↔ 4 ft (1.2 m) ↕ 15 ft (4.5 m)
Tall clump-forming grass from Japan and China. Blue-green leaves turn vivid orange–reds and yellows in autumn. Support in windy areas. Flower spikes from silver-pink to reddish purple, in autumn. *M. s.* **var.** *condensatus*, taller form, wide leaves with cream central stripe; **'Cabaret'** (Japanese silver grass), wide ribbon-like foliage, creamy white stripes, blush pink flowers, in autumn; **'Cosmopolitan'**, improved form of *M. s.* 'Variegatus', wide, more upright, non-floppy stems and leaves, flowers sit above foliage, in autumn. *M. s.* **'Gracillimus'** ★ (maiden grass), upright clumps, narrow silver leaves, bright orange foliage, in autumn, **'Kleine Silberspinne'** (silver tower Japanese spider grass), delicate silvery foliage, spider-like flowers, in autumn; **'Morning Light'** ★ (morning light Japanese silver grass), thin, narrow, green leaves, reddish bronze flowers fade to dusty cream; **'Strictus'** (porcupine grass, banded miscanthus), clump-forming, stiff, upright, gold-banded leaves and stems, copper flowers, in autumn fade to cream; **'Variegatus'** (variegated Japanese silver grass), loose, pendulous, green and white-striped foliage; **'Yaku jima'** (Yaku jima Japanese silver grass), delicate fine-textured foliage, compact plant, reddish bronze flowers; **'Zebrinus'** (zebra grass, banded miscanthus), long arching leaves, pale yellow, almost white bands, pinkish bronze flowers above foliage, in autumn. Zones 5–9.

Miscanthus transmorrisonensis

EVERGREEN MISCANTHUS, FORMOSA MAIDEN GRASS

☼ ❄ ↔ 36 in (90 cm) ↕ 40 in (100 cm)
Grass from Taiwan. Mounding ground cover. Glossy green, thin, narrow leaves, slight arching habit. Reddish bronze flowers arch over foliage, in late summer–autumn. Zones 7–10.

MITCHELLA

PARTRIDGE BERRY

There are 2 species of trailing, mat-forming, evergreen herbs in this genus belonging to the madder (Rubiaceae) family. One is native to North America and the other to Japan and Korea. They grow naturally in rather sandy soils on wooded hillsides. Dark green leaves are glossy and broadly oval. Small white or pinkish flowers are borne in pairs in summer. They are tubular with flaring lobes and velvety interiors. Although fairly inconspicuous they have a pleasant fragrance. The pea-sized scarlet berries have a noticeable dimple and are edible but have little flavor. They persist on the plant for long periods. The North American species was used by Native Americans in herbal medicine and is still used today.

CULTIVATION: Grow as ground cover in shady areas or in the rock garden in a rich soil, neutral to acid. Propagate from pieces of stem from which roots have emerged, or from seed.

Mitchella repens

☼ ❄ ↔ 24 in (60 cm) ↕ 3 in (8 cm)
Trailing prostrate perennial from North America. Roots along the stems. Small rounded leaves, whitish veins. Small pinkish white flowers, in summer. Scarlet berries. Zones 3–9.

MITELLA

BISHOP'S CAP, MITREWORT

A genus of some 20 small, clumping, evergreen perennials in the saxifrage (Saxifragaceae) family from the woods of North America and northeast Asia. Leaves are rounded and hairy, above which they produce spikes of tiny greenish flowers in summer. These plants are dainty but hardly showy.

CULTIVATION: Grow these perennials in moist humus-rich soil in a shaded site. Propagate by division or from seed, which will often self-sow.

Mitella breweri

☼ ❄ ↔ 6 in (15 cm) ↕ 4–6 in (10–15 cm)
Tiny plant from central North America. Rounded, slightly lobed leaves, to 4 in (10 cm) across. Spikes of tiny green flowers among the leaves, in summer. Zones 5–9.

MITROPHYLLUM

A genus of about 6 succulent shrubs with branching stems belonging to the iceplant (Aizoaceae) family. Native to South Africa. The narrow, fleshy, cylindrical leaves may be partly fused and paired into a tall cone, or fully fused and paired in a sheath, or paired and remote on flowering shoots. The daisy-like flowers, on short stalks, have glossy petals, from white to reddish pink. Plants have a short growing season from late summer to autumn.

CULTIVATION: Require a very well-drained soil in an open sunny position. Keep dry other than in growing season. Propagate from seed.

Mitella breweri

Mitrophyllum grande

Molinia caerulea 'Variegata'

Molinia caerulea 'Moorhexe'

Mitrophyllum grande

☼ ❄ ↔ 3–6 in (8–15 cm)
↕ 6–12 in (15–30 cm)

Succulent shrublet from South Africa. Thick, branching, columnar stems, about 4 in (10 cm) high. Solitary, glossy white, daisy-like flowers, to 2 in (5 cm) across, on stems to 12 in (30 cm) high, in summer. Zones 8–10.

MOLINIA

MOOR GRASS

There are only 2 species of these deciduous, tuft-forming perennial grasses from temperate Eurasia. Members of the grass (Poaceae) family, they grow in wetland tussock areas. The stiff upright foliage changes color in autumn, adding great contrast. Tall flower spikes sit high above the foliage from late spring to autumn. They are unusual because they are "self-cleaning." When the plants die down in winter, the foliage detaches itself from the plant, unlike most deciduous grasses that hold onto the old foliage through to the next season. This leaves the crown free of any material over the winter months giving a clean look when new growth starts in spring.
CULTIVATION: These plants prefer moist open soils and will grow in sun or shade. Propagate from seed or by division in spring. Division is the best method as it is quick and reliable. The seed may not be true to type and is very slow to germinate.

Molinia caerulea

MOOR GRASS, PURPLE MOOR GRASS

☼/☀ ❄ ↔ 16 in (40 cm) ↕ 16 in (40 cm)

Perennial grass, native to Eurasia. Clumping form with slender sword-shaped leaves, slightly arching. Purple flowers appear on spikes above the foliage, in summer. *M. c.* subsp. *arundinacea*, long, pale gray-green, arching foliage, graceful purple to brown flower spikes, fade to vivid yellow, in late summer, prefers damp, moist, boggy areas. *M. c.* 'Variegata' ★ (variegated moor grass), mid-green leaves, creamy yellow to white variegations, upright brown flowers, in summer, slow to establish. '**Moorhexe**' (witch moor grass), pale green foliage, neat clumps, purplish flowers on fine spikes. Zones 5–9.

MOLTKIA

This genus, belonging to the borage (Boraginaceae) family, is composed of 6 species of perennials, some of which become shrubby, especially in mild climates. Found from Italy through to Greece and into western Asia, they are small plants with hairy dark green foliage. Related to *Lithospermum* and once included in that now-revised genus, they usually have a more upright, less spreading growth habit and considerably larger leaves than their relatives. In summer they bear cymes of small, tubular, 5-petalled flowers in shades of mauve, blue, and sometimes yellow.
CULTIVATION: Sun-loving plants, hardy to moderate frosts and reasonably drought tolerant once established. They thrive in well-drained gritty soil, of most soil types, to which some humus has been added to aid moisture retention, and are lime tolerant. Light trimming after winter or after flowering will keep them tidy, though often they are not long lived. Grow from seed, layers, or small cuttings.

Moltkia × intermedia

☼ ❄ ↔ 16–20 in (40–50 cm)
↕ 8–10 in (20–25 cm)

Spreading herbaceous perennial, native to Europe and Asia. Narrow bristly leaves, up to 6 in (15 cm) long. Indigo blue tubular flowers, up to ¾ in (18 mm) wide, in summer. Zones 5–8.

Moltkia petraea

☼ ❄ ↔ 15 in (38 cm) ↕ 15 in (38 cm)

Found in well-drained hilly areas from the Balkans to central Greece. Fine white-bristled stems, 2 in (5 cm) tall, narrow, lance-shaped leaves. Compact flowerheads, to ½ in (12 mm) long, violet to blue flowers, in late spring. Zones 6–9.

MONANTHES

This genus in the stonecrop (Crassulaceae) family, from North Africa and the Canary Islands, contains 12 succulent herbs or shrubby annuals and perennials that grow in dense tufts. Dense terminal rosettes of smooth-edged, thick, fleshy leaves give rise to branched heads of small flowers with 6 to 8 sepals joined at the base and 6 to 8 narrow petals, appearing in summer.
CULTIVATION: Require rich, sandy, well-drained soils in a protected position in bright light but not in direct sunlight. Water in summer but allow to rest in winter. Propagate from seed in spring, from cuttings in spring or summer, or by division.

Monanthes polyphylla

☀ ⚘ ↔ 4 in (10 cm) ↕ 4–6 in (10–15 cm)

Small, low growing, dense perennial from the Canary Islands. Short, fleshy stems; bluish, fleshy, cylindrical leaves, hairy tips. Terminal clusters of 1 to 4 red flowers covered with white hairs, in spring. Zones 9–11.

MONARDA

BEE BALM, BERGAMOT, HORSEMINT

The genus *Monarda* honors Nicholas Monardes (1493–1588), a Spanish botanist, once physician to Phillip II, who wrote of plants from his long travels. His genus, a member of the mint (Lamiaceae) family, contains 16 species of annuals and perennials from North and Central America. They form large clumps, dying away completely in winter but recovering quickly in spring to form thickets of angled stems, densely clothed in lance-shaped leaves, often red-tinted and hairy, with serrated edges. In summer the top of each stem carries several whorls of tubular flowers backed by leafy bracts. The origin of the common name bee balm is obvious on any sunny day in summer, when bees continuously visit the flowers.
CULTIVATION: Very hardy and easily grown in any open sunny position with moist well-drained soil. Mildew is often a problem in late summer and good ventilation is important. Propagate by division when dormant, or from basal cuttings.

Monarda didyma ★

BEE BALM, OSWEGO TEA

☼/☀ ❄ ↔ 24–40 in (60–100 cm)
↕ 3–4 ft (0.9–1.2 m)

Perennial from Canada and the USA. Finely downy, often purple-red-tinted, serrated leaves, to 6 in (15 cm) long. Flowerheads 2 in (5 cm) wide, usually red shades, in summer. '**Cambridge Scarlet**', heavy-flowering, bright light red; '**Mahogany**', purple-red flowers, persistent red-brown bracts. Zones 4–9.

Monanthes polyphylla

Monarda didyma

Moltkia petraea

Monarda fistulosa ★
☀/☼ ❄ ↔ 24–40 in (60–100 cm)
↕ 3–4 ft (0.9–1.2 m)

Perennial found from Canada to
Mexico. Very similar to *M. didyma*.
Leaves seldom over 4 in (10 cm) long,
may be smooth-edged. Flowers lavender to pink, in summer. Zones 4–9.

Monarda punctata
☀/☼ ❄ ↔ 16–24 in (40–60 cm)
↕ 24–40 in (60–100 cm)

Annual, biennial, or short-lived
perennial of USA and northern
Mexico. Stems and foliage downy.
Leaves lance-shaped, to 4 in (10 cm)
long, sometimes serrated. Flowerheads
small, pale yellow to pink, greenish
cream or purple-tinted bracts, in
summer. Zones 6–10.

Monarda Hybrid Cultivars
☀/☼ ❄ ↔ 20–32 in (50–80 cm)
↕ 20–60 in (50–150 cm)

The 2 most commonly grown species,
M. didyma and *M. fistulosa*, hybridize
freely resulting in excellent garden
varieties such as: 'Beauty of Cobham',
50 in (130 cm) high, lavender-pink
flowers; 'Cambridge Scarlet' ★, large
ruby red flowers; 'Croftway Pink' ★,
40 in (100 cm) tall, bright mid-pink
flowers; 'Ruby Glow', 24 in (60 cm)
tall, bright red flowers, red-tinted
foliage; 'Scorpion', 40 in (100 cm)
tall, purple-pink flowerheads, purple-
red-tinted foliage; 'Vintage Wine',
27 in (70 cm) high, deep purple-red
flowers. Zones 4–9.

Monarda fistulosa

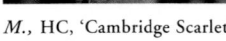

M., HC, 'Cambridge Scarlet'

Monarda, HC, 'Ruby Glow'

M., HC, 'Vintage Wine'

MONARDELLA
This genus in the mint (Lamiaceae)
family contains 19 species of annual
or perennial herbs, often with creeping stems. They are native to western
North America, where they grow on
dry rocky slopes. The small, smooth
or serrated-edged leaves smell strongly
of mint. They are often grayish green
and hairy to some degree. Round
flowerheads of small, tubular, 2-lipped
flowers are borne at stem tips in
summer and autumn. Usually red,
pink, or purple. The foliage of some
species is used by Native Americans in
herbal teas and medicines.
CULTIVATION: Grow in full sun in
a sandy well-drained soil. Perennial
species dislike cold damp soil in
winter and can be grown in a cool
greenhouse as an alternative. Propagate annuals from seed, and perennials from seed, division, or cuttings.

Monardella macrantha
☀ ❊ ↔ 8 in (20 cm) ↕ 6 in (15 cm)

Trailing subshrub native to California,
USA. Downy stems, small leaves.
Spherical heads bear small, tubular,
scarlet to yellow flowers, purple
calyces, in summer–autumn.
Zones 9–11.

Monardella odoratissima
☀ ❄ ↔ 12–24 in (30–60 cm)
↕ 4–24 in (10–60 cm)

Variable perennial with woody-based
prostrate stems from western USA.
Small, broadly oval, grayish green

Monardella odoratissima

leaves, mint odor when crushed. Pale
pink to rosy pink flowerheads, to 2 in
(5 cm) wide, in summer–autumn.
Zones 8–11.

MONOPSIS
Native to tropical, central, and southern Africa, this genus has 18 species
of small annual or perennial herbs and
is in the bellflower (Campanulaceae)
family. Leaves are serrated and small.
The solitary flowers appear on slender
stalks growing from the leaf axils.
They have horizontal calyx tubes with
spreading lobes and a lipped corolla.
CULTIVATION: Prefer moist well-
drained soil in an open sunny position. Propagate by division or from
cuttings taken throughout the year.

Monopsis lutea
GOLDEN LOBELIA
☼ ❊ ↔ 4–5 in (10–12 cm)
↕ 3–4 in (8–10 cm)

Low-growing evergreen perennial
from South Africa. Long trailing
stems, up to 3 ft (0.9 m) long.
Alternate, shiny, serrated leaves.
Yellow flowers, in summer–autumn.
Cascading habit suits hanging baskets.
Zones 9–11.

MONSTERA
FRUIT SALAD PLANT, SWISS CHEESE PLANT,
WINDOWLEAF

A genus of 22 species of epiphytic and
climbing evergreen tropical plants
from Central and South America; a
member of the arum (Araceae) family.
They are grown as handsome foliage
plants indoors or in a greenhouse in
all but tropical climates where they
are often used to grow up the trunks
of trees. The leaves often have large
holes in them, giving them a quite
bizarre look and accounting for 2 of
the common names. *M. deliciosa*, the
fruit salad plant, has edible fruit.
CULTIVATION: Grow in a humid
warm spot, completely frost-free, and
in part-shade. Make sure that the soil
is well-drained and humus-rich. Stake
or support the climbing species. Propagate from freshly sown seed with
bottom heat.

Monopsis lutea

Monstera adansonii

Monstera adansonii
☀ ≁ ↔ 3–6 ft (0.9–1.8 m)
↕ 15–25 ft (6–8 m)

Climbing species from northern
South America. Oval leaves, 36 in
(90 cm) long, irregular oblong holes
on one side or (usually) both, all year.
Zones 11–12.

Monstera deliciosa
FRUIT SALAD PLANT, MEXICAN BREADFRUIT,
SWISS CHEESE PLANT
☀ ≁ ↔ 8–20 ft (2.4–6 m)
↕ 35–50 ft (10–15 m)

Large impressive climbing plant from
southern Mexico to Panama.
Extensive aerial root system. Massive
leaves to 36 in (90 cm) long, irregular
holes, often break edges. White arum-
type flowers in suitable conditions, in
summer. Edible cone-shaped fruit, to
10 in (25 cm) long. Zones 11–12.

MONTANOA
Part of the daisy (Asteraceae) family,
this genus from tropical America
comprises about 20 species of vines
and shrubs. They are erect shrubby
perennials with short branches and
square stems. The hand-shaped leaves
are large and covered with fine hairs.
The flowers resemble dahlias, are
white with yellow centers borne in
clusters, and appear throughout
summer and into autumn. Reddish
brown seeds are borne in the old
flowerheads, which have a papery feel.

In cultivation they can be treated as giant herbaceous perennials, as some can grow to a height of 20 ft (7 m) or more in a season.

CULTIVATION: Grown for both foliage and flower display, these frost-tender plants need a warm full-sun position in fertile well-watered soil. Once the flowers have finished, the long canes can be hard pruned. Propagate from seed or from root cuttings.

Montanoa bipinnatifida
MEXICAN TREE DAISY

☼ ✤ ↔ 7 ft (2 m) ↑ 10–20 ft (3–6 m)

Evergreen shrub, sometimes becoming tree-like, from southern Mexico. Sparse deeply dissected foliage, held on fast-growing brittle canes. Masses of single white daisy flowers are seen in autumn. Provide some wind protection. Zones 11–12.

Montanoa mollissima
☼ ✤ ↔ 3 ft (0.9 m) ↑ 6 ft (1.8 m)

A shrub-like daisy from Mexico. Attractive, deeply lobed, green leaves, downy when young, age to a lustrous green. White daisy flowers, in massed bunches, in autumn. Zones 11–12.

MONTIA
MINERS' LETTUCE, WINTER PURSLANE

A genus of 15 species of annuals and perennials in the purslane (Portulacaceae) family that are usually grown as a herb and have little ornamental value. They come from as far afield as South America, Asia, tropical Africa, and temperate northern regions. Leaves are soft and fleshy. Small white or pink flowers in axillary or terminal racemes in summer. The fruit is a

Montanoa bipinnatifida

Montanoa mollissima

small capsule with shiny black seeds.

CULTIVATION: *Montia* species prefer sandy, acidic, well-drained but moist soil. Propagate from seed sown directly where it is to grow in spring for summer cropping, and in late summer to crop throughout winter.

Montia perfoliata
MINERS' LETTUCE, WINTER PURSLANE

☼ ❋ ↔ 4 in (10 cm) ↑ 12 in (130 cm)

Edible fleshy-leafed plant, foliage superficially resembling the nasturtium. Tiny white flowers, in summer. Grown as a salad green. Zones 4–10.

MORAEA

Belonging to the iris (Iridaceae) family, this genus consists of about 120 species of which only a few are commonly cultivated. They are cormous perennials, which may be deciduous or semi-deciduous, originating in sub-Saharan Africa from Ethiopia to South Africa where they are found in moist grasslands. The short-lived, iris-like, clustered flowers, often in brilliant colors, appear in succession during spring and early summer.

CULTIVATION: In garden conditions a dry dormancy period in summer is essential, as is very sharp drainage. However, when these conditions are met, the plants withstand more frost than their native habitats would suggest. They are super tough in conditions of winter wet. Propagate from seed, sowing summer-flowering species in spring and winter-growing species in autumn.

Moraea alticola
☼ ❋ ↔ 3 in (8 cm) ↑ 30 in (75 cm)

Perennial from KwaZulu-Natal, South Africa. Leaves linear, stems branched. Scented flowers, yellow with brown marks, in summer. Grows well in hot dry climates. Zones 8–10.

Moraea aristata
PEACOCK IRIS

☼ ☙ ↔ 3 in (8 cm) ↑ 15–16 in (38–40 cm)

A perennial species from Cape Town, South Africa, that is now almost extinct in the wild. Leaves hairy.

Montia perfoliata

Moraea polystachya

Moraea alticola

Moraea spathulata

Moraea ramosissima

Moraea villosa

Flowers solitary, white, hint of smoky blue, central eye with concentric crescents of blue, green, violet, and black. Long display in late spring. Zones 9–11.

Moraea polystachya
☼/◐ ☙ ↔ 3 in (8 cm) ↑ 32 in (80 cm)

Perennial from Namibia and Botswana. Leaves are linear, almost flat, stems branched. Short-lived flowers, violet, marked yellow, with white edges, are produced in a long display in early autumn–winter. Tough; in stressful conditions may lie dormant for years. Zones 9–11.

Moraea ramosissima
☼ ☙ ↔ 4 in (10 cm) ↑ 24–48 in (60–120 cm)

A perennial species from South Africa. Narrowly linear leaves, borne on much-branched stems. Yellow flowers, with darker centers, appear in spring–early summer. Zones 9–11.

Moraea spathulata
☼ ☙ ↔ 4 in (10 cm) ↑ 20–40 in (50–100 cm)

An evergreen perennial species from Swaziland, Zimbabwe, Mozambique, and Mpumalanga, South Africa. The leaves are numerous, untidy. Yellow flowers, with darker nectar guides, appear on branching stems, opening in the morning, closing in late afternoon, season variable but in summer is common. Zones 9–11.

Moraea villosa
PEACOCK IRIS

☼ ☙ ↔ 5 in (12 cm) ↑ 12–16 in (30–40 cm)

A perennial species from Western Cape, South Africa. The basal leaves are channeled. The flowers are flat, to 3 in (8 cm) wide, white to orange or blue, with large, deep blue, circular blotches at base of each of 3 petals, in late winter–early spring. Rare in the wild. Zones 9–10.

Morus alba 'Pendula', in spring

Morus alba 'Pendula', in winter

Morus indica

MORINA

A genus of 4 species of prickly-leafed evergreen perennials in the family Morinaceae; native to eastern Europe and Asia. The leaves are mainly basal, through which appear upright spikes of curved tubular flowers in whorls supported by prickly green bracts. CULTIVATION: Grow these perennials in a sunny aspect in well-drained but moist soil and protect plants from winter wet. Propagate from seed sown individually in small containers to stop disturbance, or raise from root cuttings in winter.

Morina longifolia
WHORLFLOWER

☀ ❄ ↔ 10–12 in (25–30 cm) ↑ 32–36 in (80–90 cm)

Rosette-forming perennial from the Himalayas. Spine-edged leaves, to 10 in (25 cm) long. Upright flower stem, whorls of curved tubular flowers, to 1¼ in (30 mm) across, white, turning pink with age, in spring–summer. Zones 6–9.

MORISIA

The single member of this genus belongs in the cabbage (Brassicaceae) family. It is a small, rosette-forming, perennial herb native to Corsica and Sardinia, where it grows in coastal areas on dry sandy grasslands. Small leaves are narrow with a fern-like appearance. Small, golden yellow,

4-petalled flowers on short upright stalks in spring and early summer. CULTIVATION: *Morisia* requires a poor, gritty, perfectly drained soil. Because of its small size and specific requirements, it is best suited to trough or pot culture, preferably in the cool greenhouse. It particularly dislikes rich fertilized soil and damp cold winters. Propagate from seed or by root cuttings.

Morisia monanthos
syn. *Morisia hypogaea*

☀ ❄ ↔ 6 in (15 cm) ↑ 1 in (25 mm)

Perennial herb from Corsica. Flat neat rosettes, glossy bright green leaves, coarsely serrated edges. Starry golden yellow flowers, ½ in (12 mm) wide, in spring–early summer. '**Fred Hemingway**', larger flowers. Zones 7–9.

MORUS
MULBERRY

There are about 12 species of deciduous trees and shrubs in this genus belonging to the mulberry (Moraceae) family. Most species are from Asia, a few are from North America and central Africa. The leaves are arranged alternately and are generally heart-shaped with serrated edges. Inconspicuous male and female flowers are borne on separate catkins and are followed by fruits resembling raspberries. The black mulberry (*M. nigra*) has long been cultivated for its edible

Morus nigra

fruits; leaves of the white mulberry (*M. alba*) provide food for silkworms. CULTIVATION: Mulberries will grow in any reasonably fertile well-drained soil. Pruning should be done in winter and kept to a minimum as the sap bleeds freely. Propagate from cuttings in spring or autumn, although large pieces of branch (truncheons) up to 5 ft (1.5 m) long can be planted 20 in (50 cm) into the ground.

Morus alba
WHITE MULBERRY

☀ ❄ ↔ 30 ft (9 m) ↑ 30–50 ft (9–15 m)

Long-cultivated tree native to China. Leaves broadly oval, heart-shaped base, 2- to 3-lobed, coarsely toothed; silkworm food. Greenish male and female flowers, in separate clusters, in early summer. Fruit white, becoming pale pink then red. '**Bungeana**', dense bright green foliage; '**Pendula**', weeping form; '**Venosa**', heavily veined mid-green leaves. Zones 4–10.

Morus indica
syns *Morus acidosa*, *M. australis*, *M. japonica*
MULBERRY

☀ ❄ ↔ 17 ft (5 m) ↑ 17–25 ft (5–8 m)

Deciduous tree or shrub from eastern Asia. Smooth young shoots, heart- to oval-shaped, green leaves, coarse-textured, serrated edge, deeply cut lobes. Catkins of drooping, inconspicuous, greenish flowers, in summer. Sweet, deep red, edible fruit. Zones 4–6.

Morus nigra
BLACK MULBERRY

☀ ❄ ↔ 40 ft (12 m) ↑ 50 ft (15 m)

Deciduous tree from central or southwestern Asia. Wide dense crown, relatively short trunk, gnarled with age. Broadly oval to heart-shaped leaves, serrated edges, deep green, roughened uppersurface. Greenish flowers, in spring. Edible, juicy, sweet berries ripen to purplish black. Zones 5–10.

Morus rubra
RED MULBERRY

☀ ❄ ↔ 40 ft (12 m) ↑ 50 ft (15 m)

Deciduous tree from eastern USA and southeastern Canada, rarely cultivated.

Slightly heart-shaped leaves, sometimes lobed, roughened uppersurface, very downy beneath, coarsely serrated edges. Edible fruits ripen to purple in summer. Zones 5–10.

MUEHLENBECKIA
WIRE VINE

These plants are often twining, scrambling, or forming dense mounds of tangled stems. The common name is appropriate for this genus of around 15 species of evergreen or semi-deciduous subshrubs and shrubs, which is a member of the knotweed (Polygonaceae) family. Examples are found in South America, Australia, New Zealand, and New Guinea, often in hilly country, with some extending into the alpine zone. They are well adapted to harsh windswept conditions, with reduced foliage hidden within the mass of stems. The flowers are very small and clustered in the leaf axils or at the branch tips. Small, 3-sided, nut-like fruit in a fleshy cup follow the flowers. CULTIVATION: These plants are tolerant of light to moderate frosts but are not suited to continental climates. The best features of the genus are its ground-hugging habit and resistance to wind. Plant in full sun with light well-drained soil that can be kept moist in summer. Propagate from seed in autumn, or by layers, which often form naturally, or from hardwood cuttings in winter.

Morisia monanthos 'Fred Hemingway'

Morina longifolia

Musa acuminata

Musa coccinea

Muehlenbeckia astonii

☼ ❄ ↔ 2 ft (0.6 m) ↑ 3–8 ft (0.9–2.4 m)

From New Zealand, rare in the wild. Densely interlaced branches, tiny leaves. Tiny flowers in clusters, in spring. Minute, translucent, cream fruits, black seeds. Zones 8–10.

Muehlenbeckia complexa

MAIDENHAIR VINE, MATTRESS VINE, NECKLACE VINE, WIRE VINE

☼ ❄ ↔ 10 ft (3 m) ↑ 5–15 ft (1.5–4.5 m)

Dense twining climber from New Zealand. Fine dark purple stems. Tiny, bronze-green, semi-deciduous leaves. Tiny white flowers, in spring. White fruit, one black seed. Zones 8–10.

MUKDENIA

syn. *Aceriphyllum*

A genus of only 2 species in the saxifrage (Saxifragaceae) family from the damp woods of north and northeastern China, and Korea. Clumping herbaceous perennials with attractive maple-shaped leaves and leafless stalks of tiny, white, bell flowers in spring. CULTIVATION: *Mukdenia* species require a cool moist aspect in well-drained, but never dry, humus-rich soil. Propagate from seed sown when ripe, or by division in late winter before growth starts.

Mukdenia rossii

syn. *Aceriphyllum rossii*

☀ ❄ ↔ 18 in (45 cm) ↑ 14 in (35 cm)

Clumping herbaceous perennial from South Korea and northeastern China. Maple-shaped leaves, to 6 in (15 cm)

Musa ornata

long, 5 to 9 lobes. Short panicles of white flowers, 5 mm wide, above foliage, in spring. Zones 6–9.

MURRAYA

This small genus in the rue (Rutaceae) family is a relative of *Citrus* and consists of about 4 species from Southeast Asia to Australia. They are shrubs or trees with pinnate dark green leaves, and white perfumed flowers in large panicles. Fruit are small globe- to egg-shaped berries. CULTIVATION: Most are adaptable and grow best in well-drained mulched soil with added moisture and fertilizer during the growing season. They tolerate full sun to part-shade and perform best in a warm frost-free climate. Prune to shape and to maintain a dense habit and improve flower production. Propagate from seed or cuttings.

Murraya koenigii

syn. *Bergera koenegii*

CURRY LEAF, CURRY TREE

☼ ❄ ↔ 12 ft (3.5 m) ↑ 15 ft (4.5 m)

Evergreen tree, native to Asia. Aromatic leaves, long pointed tips on leaflets, finely serrated edges. Small, white or yellowish fragrant flowers, in corymbs from branch tips, in spring. Blue-black berries. Leaves used in Indian curries; oil in soap. Zones 10–12.

Murraya paniculata

COSMETIC BARK, JASMINE ORANGE, ORANGE JESSAMINE

☼ ❄ ↔ 10 ft (3 m) ↑ 10 ft (3 m)

Attractive shrub from Southeast Asia to Australia. Globe-shaped, with many branches. Pinnate leaves pale green, maturing to dark glossy green. Orange blossom-like flowers, white, sweetly perfumed, in spring. Orange to red berries. Popular hedging or screen plant. Zones 10–12.

MUSA

BANANA

There are about 40 species in this genus of evergreen suckering perennials from Asia to Australia. They belong to the banana (Musaceae) family. Leaves are large, paddle-shaped, and smooth-edged. The flowers appear at the ends of branches on a spike that can be pendent or erect. The female or hermaphrodite flowers are near the base and the male flowers are near the tip. The fruit can be long, slim, and curved, or stubby, nearly round, sausage-shaped, or cylindrical. CULTIVATION: *Musa* species are found in light woodland and forest margins and will do best in humus-rich fertile soil in full sun, with shelter from wind to prevent new leaves from shredding. In temperate areas where frosts occur, grow in a greenhouse in loam-based compost with added leafmold. Water and feed regularly during the growing months. Propagate by division of suckers, or by seed in spring.

Murraya paniculata

Musa acuminata

syn. *Musa cavendishii*

BANANA

☼ ❄ ↔ 8 ft (2.4 m) ↑ 12–20 ft (3.5–6 m)

Suckering perennial from Southeast Asia and north Queensland, Australia. Paddle-shaped leaves, mid- to gray-green. Pendent flowers, pear-shaped, yellow, white, or cream, in summer. Edible yellow fruit. '**Dwarf Cavendish**' (syn. 'Basrai'), smaller, yellow flowers and purple bracts. Zones 9–11.

Musa coccinea

Syn. *Musa uranoscopus* of gardens

☼ ❄ ↔ 5 ft (1.5 m) ↑ 3–5 ft (0.9–1.5 m)

Native to Indochina. Glossy reddish green pseudostem; glossy oval to elliptic leaves. Erect flowerheads, shiny, fleshy, pinkish red to deep red bracts tipped yellowish green, in spring. Fruit oblong to cylindrical, reddish purple to pinkish green, ripening to orange-yellow, edible. Zones 9–11.

Musa ornata

FLOWERING BANANA

☼ ✈ ↔ 6 ft (1.8 m) ↑ 6–10 ft (1.8–3 m)

Ornamental suckering perennial, native to Myanmar and Bangladesh. Waxy green leaves, 6 ft (1.8 m) long. Inflorescences of flowers, orange to yellow, light purple bracts, in summer. Yellow or pink fruit. Zones 11–12.

M

Muehlenbeckia astonii

Mukdenia rossii

Murraya koenigii

Muscari latifolium

Muscari armeniacum 'Valerie Finnis'

Muscari aucheri

Muscari macrocarpum

Musa × paradisiaca

syn. *Musa sapientum*

BANANA, PLANTAIN

☼ ⚷ ↔ 8 ft (2.4 m) ↑ 10 ft (3 m)

An *M. acuminata* and *M. balbisiana* cross. Includes cooking and eating bananas. Leaves large, green, oblong. Fruit yellow, pale pulp, seedless, in summer. Often bags are placed over fruit to aid ripening and give protection. Zones 11–12.

Musa velutina

VELVET BANANA

☼ ⚷ ↔ 3 ft (0.9 m) ↑ 5 ft (1.5 m)

Rhizomatous plant from northeastern India. Dark green leaves, paler undersides, red midrib. Red bracts, white or yellowish flowers, in spring. Pink velvety fruit, splits when ripe. Zones 9–12.

MUSCARI

GRAPE HYACINTH

This genus, a member of the hyacinth (Hyacinthaceae) family, contains some

30 species of spring-blooming bulbous perennials. Originally from the Mediterranean basin and southwest Asia. Widely used in woodland gardens and for bedding displays. The flowers, like tiny upside-down bowls, hang in dense clusters from pole-like stems, in spring. Lower florets open before those at the top of the pile. The foliage is voluminous and can sometimes be untidy.

CULTIVATION: Feed with bone meal in spring. Divide overcrowded clumps while dormant, incorporating fresh soil if replanting in same spot. Propagate from offsets during dormancy, or by seed sown when fresh.

Muscari armeniacum

syn. *Muscari szovitsianum*

☼ ✳ ↔ 2 in (5 cm) ↑ 8 in (20 cm)

Bulbous perennial. Leaves lance-shaped, mid-green, may collapse in rough weather. Flowers in dense racemes, bright blue, pinched white mouths, faintly fragrant, in summer. Needs winter sun. 'Blue Spike', large, double, soft blue flowers; 'Cantab', vigorous, pale blue flowers, short stalks; 'Valerie Finnis' ★, pale lavender flowers, in dense showy spirals, dark semi-erect leaves, may be more closely related to *M. neglectum*. Zones 6–9.

Muscari aucheri

syn. *Muscari tubergenianum*

☼ ✳ ↔ 2 in (5 cm) ↑ 4–6 in (10–15 cm)

Bulbous perennial from Turkey. Leaves mid-green, narrowly spoon-shaped. Flowers in tight racemes,

Muscari armeniacum 'Blue Spike'

bright blue, pinched white mouths, top flowers often paler and sterile, in early summer. Requires winter sun. Zones 6–9.

Muscari azureum

syn. *Hyacinthella azurea*

☼ ✳ ↔ 2 in (5 cm) ↑ 4–6 in (10–15 cm)

Bulbous perennial from eastern Turkey. Leaves lance-shaped, gray-green. Flowers bright blue with darker stripe, bell-shaped with unconstricted mouths, in early summer. Requires winter sun. Zones 6–9.

Muscari botryoides

☼ ✳ ↔ 2 in (5 cm) ↑ 4–6 in (10–15 cm)

Bulbous perennial from central and southeastern Europe. Leaves mid-green, narrowly spoon-shaped, semi-erect. Flowers spherical, bright blue, pinched white mouths, in early summer. Requires winter sun. 'Album', slender racemes of fragrant white flowers. Zones 6–9.

Muscari latifolium

☼ ✳ ↔ 2 in (5 cm) ↑ 8 in (20 cm)

Bulbous perennial from southwest Asia. Leaves mid-green, lance-shaped. Blooms, extended urn shape, violet-black, pinched mouths, racemes topped with paler sterile flowers, in early summer. Requires winter sun. Zones 6–9.

Musa × paradisiaca

Muscari macrocarpum

☼ ✳ ↔ 4 in (10 cm) ↑ 4–6 in (10–15 cm)

Bulbous Asian perennial requiring good drainage and dry summers. Leaves erect, linear, gray-green. Flowers tubular, greenish yellow opening from brownish purple buds, strongly scented, in spring. Zones 6–9.

MUSSAENDA

This genus contains about 100 species of evergreen subshrubs, shrubs, and herbs, sometimes with twining stems, native to tropical areas of Africa and Asia. It belongs to the madder (Rubiaceae) family. They have pointed oblong leaves, opposite or in whorls of three. Small tubular flowers, in panicles or clusters throughout the year, are of secondary importance to colorful enlarged sepals that accompany them, often in startling contrast.

CULTIVATION: Plant in a tropical greenhouse in temperate climates. Require direct sunlight and should be watered well in the growing season. In warmer climates can be grown outdoors in sun or part shade, in rich well-drained soil. Propagate from seed sown in spring, or half-hardened cuttings taken in summer.

Mussaenda erythrophylla

ASHANTI BLOOD

☼ ⚷ ↔ 5 ft (1.5 m) ↑ 10 ft (3 m)

Evergreen shrub, native to tropical Africa. Erect or climbing, slightly downy, reddish stems. Flowers in dense, slightly drooping panicles, cream to pink and red, brilliant red sepals, in spring. 'Flamingo', bright pink sepals; 'Pink Dancer', salmon pink sepals. Zones 11–12.

Mussaenda glabra

☼ ⚷ ↔ 7 ft (2 m) ↑ 10 ft (3 m)

Evergreen shrub, native to tropical Asia. Erect or widespreading branches. Leaves thick and shiny. Orange to red flowers, in many-flowered clusters, accompanied by large white bracts, in spring. Zones 10–12.

Musa velutina

Myoporum bateae

Myoporum floribundum

Mussaenda Hybrid Cultivars

☼ ✲ ↔5–7 ft (1.5–2 m) ↑10 ft (3 m)
These hybrids have often been placed
under the name *M. philippica* but
may have originated from crosses
between *M. erythrophylla* and *M. fron-
dosa*. All have colorful enlarged sepals.
'Aurorae', bushy shrub to 10 ft (3 m)
high, flowers yellow, large, white, pendulous sepals; 'Queen Sirikit', salmon
pink sepals. Zones 11–12.

MUTISIA

With flowers resembling single dahlias
or large daisies, these South American
evergreen shrubs and vines are in a
genus comprising 60 species, belonging to the daisy (Asteraceae) family.
Their stems carry alternate leaves that
may be simple or pinnate, sometimes
having serrated edges, downy undersides, or a tendril at the tip. Flowers
are daisy-like, but relatively large,
nearly always more than 2 in (5 cm)
and often more than 4 in (10 cm)
wide. They are brightly colored, mostly
in red or pink shades. The flower
dries to a brown seed head.
CULTIVATION: Most species will tolerate light frosts and are not very
fussy about the soil type, provided it
is well drained. They prefer a position
in full or half-day sun and can be
trimmed after flowering. Propagation
is unfortunately difficult, which is
why *Mutisia* species are rare in cultivation. Very fresh seed offers the best
possibility for successful propagation.

Mutisia ilicifolia

☼ ✲ ↔3–6 ft (0.9–1.8 m)
↑10 ft (3 m)
Shrubby climber from Chile. Spine-
toothed leaves, 2½ in (6 cm) long,
heart-shaped base, tendril at ends.

Myoporum montanum

Flowerheads with around 8 ray florets,
soft pink, 1½ in (35 mm) wide, in
summer. Zones 8–10.

MYOPORUM

This genus in the boobialla (Myopora-
ceae) family contains around 30
species, the majority from Australia,
others from Mauritius, eastern
Malaysia, New Zealand, and Hawaii,
USA. Mostly small to medium-size
shrubs, sometimes trees, and a few
ground covers, they have simple variably shaped leaves, often leathery or
succulent, and often resinous vegetative parts. The small, somewhat bell-
shaped, white, sometimes pinkish,
flowers occur in clusters or singly
along the branches. They are followed
by mainly small, often succulent,
fruits favored by birds. Useful landscape subjects, especially for their tolerance of dry conditions, many coming
from semi-arid and temperate regions.
CULTIVATION: Most species are fairly
adaptable, requiring good drainage
and full sun or part shade. Many will
tolerate alkaline soils, medium to
heavy frosts, and lengthy dry periods.
Prune lightly to maintain shape.
Propagate from fresh seed, cuttings, or
division of layered stems for ground-
covering species.

Myoporum bateae

☼ ✲ ↔10 ft (3 m) ↑15 ft (4.5 m)
From moist stream gullies in southern
coastal New South Wales, Australia.
Branches spreading, narrow alternate

Mussaenda erythrophylla

Myoporum insulare

leaves, dark green, paler below, finely
serrated edges. Small lilac to purple
flowers, in leaf axils, in summer.
Succulent fruits. Zones 8–9.

Myoporum floribundum

WEEPING BOOBIALLA
☼ ✲ ↔8 ft (2.4 m) ↑10 ft (3 m)
Native of New South Wales and
Victoria, Australia. Graceful spreading
habit, weeping branches. Leaves
narrow, dark green, aromatic when
crushed. White, rarely mauve, perfumed flowers, in massed clusters of
false spikes, in winter–summer. Tip
prune to maintain shape. Zones 9–11.

Myoporum insulare

BOOBIALLA, COMMON BOOBIALLA
☼ ✲ ↔20 ft (6 m) ↑3–25 ft (0.9–8 m)
Shrub or small tree from New South
Wales, Victoria, South Australia, and
Western Australia. Thick fleshy leaves,
spreading branches. White flowers,

Myoporum platycarpum, in the wild,
South Australia

with purplish dots, from winter–
summer. Small edible fruits. Very
adaptable species. Zones 9–11.

Myoporum laetum

NGAIO
☼ ✲ ↔10 ft (3 m) ↑15–30 ft (4.5–9 m)
Large shrub or small tree, from New
Zealand, occurs in exposed sites.
Green fleshy leaves, lance-shaped to
oblong or obovate, sticky shoot tips.
White bell flowers, purple spotted, in
cymes, in summer. Maroon fruits.
Wind tolerant. Zones 9–11.

Myoporum montanum

WATER BUSH, WESTERN BOOBIALLA
☼ ✲ ↔10 ft (3 m) ↑25 ft (8 m)
Variable adaptable tree, throughout
inland Australia. Spreading branches,
sticky young growth, elliptic to lance-
shaped green leaves. White flowers,
spotted purple, in winter–summer.
Globe-shaped fruits. Zones 9–11.

Myoporum platycarpum

FALSE SANDALWOOD, SUGARWOOD
☼ ✲ ↔12 ft (3.5 m) ↑30 ft (9 m)
Shrub or small tree from Queensland,
Victoria, South Australia, and
Western Australia. Sticky new growth,
deeply fissured dark gray bark. Thin
lance-shaped leaves, deep green. Plentiful white flowers, sweetly scented, in
winter–summer. Zones 9–11.

M

Myoporum laetum

Mussaenda, Hybrid Cultivar, 'Queen Sirikit'

MYOSOTIDIUM

Endemic to wet, windswept Chatham Islands off east coast of New Zealand, the sole species in this genus is, in effect, the most northerly straggler of the megaherbs of the subantarctic islands further south. Genus belongs to the borage (Boraginaceae) family. It has very large, leathery, glossy leaves on stalks like small rhubarb stalks. In spring and early summer, rounded heads of tiny, 5-petalled, bright blue to purple-blue flowers appear among the leaves. An impressive plant, now rare in the wild; survives in isolated pockets away from grazing animals. CULTIVATION: Prefers cool-temperate conditions with no extremes of cold or heat. Plant in part- or full-shade with moist, humus-rich, well-drained soil. Water and feed well for lush foliage and strong flowerheads. Watch for aphids. Propagate from seed rather than by division, as established clumps are best left to naturalize.

Myosotidium hortensia

CHATHAM ISLANDS FORGET-ME-NOT

☀️/◐ ❄ ↔ 24–40 in (60–100 cm)
↕ 12–16 in (30–40 cm)

Evergreen perennial, forms clump of impressive, long-stemmed, deeply veined, dark green, heart- to kidney-

Myosotis alpestris

Myosotis alpestris 'Alba'

shaped leaves to 12 in (30 cm) long. Upright flower stems, large heads crowded with white-centered blue flowers, in early summer. Zones 8–10.

MYOSOTIS

FORGET-ME-NOT

A genus of around 50 species of annuals, biennials, and perennials of the borage (Boraginaceae) family found in Europe, Asia, North and South America. Most are small tufted plants with simple, usually lance-shaped, leaves that are sometimes grayish and often finely hairy. Their 5-petalled flowers are tiny but quite showy and are usually borne in sprays on short branching stems. Most bloom in spring and early summer and are commonly white, cream, pink, or various shades of blue and mauve. Legends about the name abound; one attributes it to a lover who, while gathering the flowers, fell into a river and cried "forget-me-not" as he drowned. CULTIVATION: Easily grown in any position, sunny or shady, that remains moist during summer. Alpine species benefit from a gritty free-draining soil but the others aren't fussy. Propagate perennials by careful division in late winter, otherwise raise from seed, which often self-sows.

Myosotis alpestris

☀️ ❄ ↔ 16 in (40 cm) ↕ 12 in (30 cm)
Long-flowering temperate Eurasian and North American perennial. Spreading mounding clump; simple, bright green, pointed oval to lance-shaped leaves, to 3 in (8 cm) long. Small sprays of bright to dark blue tiny flowers, in spring. 'Alba', white-flowered cultivar. Zones 3–9.

Myosotis scorpioides

☀️ ❄ ↔ 16–40 in (40–100 cm)
↕ 6–18 in (15–45 cm)
European perennial, spreads by rhizomes. Untidy mounding clump of

Myosotis sylvatica

bright green leaves to 4 in (10 cm) long. Tiny pale to mid-blue flowers, white, cream, or pale pink centers, in summer. Zones 3–9.

Myosotis sylvatica

BEDDING FORGET-ME-NOT

☀️ ❄ ↔ 8–16 in (20–40 cm)
↕ 6–16 in (15–40 cm)

A biennial to short-lived perennial, often treated as annual, from Europe and Asia. Bright green leaves, to 4 in (10 cm) long. Open spikes of pale-centered, ¼ in (6 mm) wide flowers, blue or pink, in summer. Cultivars and seedling strains include: '**Blue Ball**', very compact habit, deep blue flowers; '**Music**', compact, large deep blue flowers; '**Royal Blue Improved**', tall, many deep blue flowers; '**Spring Symphony Blue**', early, bright blue; **Victoria Series**, compact seedling strain, blue, pink, and white flowers. Zones 5–10.

MYRICA

With a widespread distribution centered on the northern temperate zones, this genus, from the wax-myrtle (Myricaceae) family, is composed of 35 species of evergreen or deciduous shrubs or small trees. They have simple short-stemmed leaves and small separate male and female flowers, the male flowers in short catkins and the females in rounded clusters. Egg-shaped to spherical drupes follow the flowers and are often coated with an aromatic wax. CULTIVATION: *Myrica* species vary considerably in hardiness, but provided the climate is suitable, they are not difficult to cultivate and will thrive in any well-drained soil that is not strongly alkaline or prone to prolonged drought. Plant in sun to half-day shade, water well in sun, and trim to shape if necessary. Propagate from seed, layers, or in summer to autumn from half-hardened cuttings.

Myrica cerifera

WAX MYRTLE

☀️ ❄ ↔ 15 ft (4.5 m) ↕ 30 ft (9 m)
Large evergreen shrub or small tree native to damp areas of eastern and

Myosotis sylvatica 'Music'

Myrica pensylvanica

southeastern USA; thrives in shade of other trees. Broad-based lance-shaped leaves. Flowers, small, pale yellow-brown, in summer. Tiny fruits. Grown as adaptable foliage plant. Zones 6–10.

Myrica gale

BOG MYRTLE, SWEET GALE

☀️/◐ ❄ ↔ 4 ft (1.2 m)
↕ 3–6 ft (0.9–1.8 m)

Deciduous shrub found over a wide range from Europe to Japan and in North America. Leaves, 1–2½ in (2.5–6 cm) wide, toothed. Buff-yellow fruit, in massed spikes, in summer. Grows well in damp soil. Zones 3–9.

Myrica pensylvanica

BAYBERRY, CANDLEBERRY

☀️ ❄ ↔ 4 ft (1.2 m) ↕ 6–10 ft (1.8–3 m)
Semi-evergreen to deciduous shrub, native to coastal eastern North America. Spreading suckering growth habit. Lance-shaped leaves, smooth or toothed edges. Tiny pale gray fruit, in summer. Its wax used to scent candles. Zones 2–8.

MYRIOCARPA

Found from Central America to subtropical South America, this genus of some 15 species of evergreen shrubs and trees is a member of the nettle (Urticaceae) family, though one would scarcely know it from looking at them. In common with many nettle relatives worldwide, however, they are an important food source for caterpillars and wild plants seldom have a perfect leaf. Foliage is often aromatic, rather hairy, with toothed edges, and the leaves can be up to 12 in (30 cm) long. The flowers are unisexual, borne in racemes in leaf axils, and usually white to greenish cream.

M

CULTIVATION: These tropical plants demand a warm frost-free climate with year-round moisture. They prefer humus-rich slightly acidic soil that drains freely, in sun or part-shade. They grow quickly; pinch back or trim to control growth and keep the plant compact. Propagate from seed or half-hardened cuttings.

Myriocarpa longipes

☼ ⚥ ↔ 24–36 in (60–90 cm)
↑ 24–36 in (60–90 cm)

Soft-stemmed small tree from Central America, useful in regenerating tropical forests. Large leaves, pink veins beneath, finely toothed. Cream to pale green flowers, in summer. Foliage sweetly aromatic when crushed. An important food for butterfly larvae. Zones 11–12.

MYRIOPHYLLUM

MILFOIL, WATER MILFOIL

This genus of 45 widely distributed, deciduous or evergreen, perennial, sometimes annual, submerged or terrestrial waterplants is a member of the raspwort (Haloragaceae) family. Most are from the Southern Hemisphere. Their widely spreading slender stems take root, then rise to the water surface. Leaves held above the surface are whorled or alternate, smooth or slightly serrated; the submerged leaves are whorled and finely divided. The plants bear minute flowers in reddish green terminal spikes, on short or no stalks, with 4 or no erect sepals, 2, 4 or no petals, and 4 or 8 stamens.
CULTIVATION: Plant in clear still or slowly moving water, submerged just beneath the surface. Propagate from stem cuttings, or by division in spring and summer.

Myrtus communis 'Citrifolium'

Myrtus communis

Myrtillocactus cochal

Myriophyllum aquaticum

syn. *Myriophyllum proserpinacoides*
DIAMOND MILFOIL, PARROT FEATHER

☼ ⚥ ↔ 5–15 ft (1.5–4.5 m)
↑ 3–6 ft (0.9–1.8 m)

Deciduous or evergreen perennial, partially or completely submerged waterplant, native to South America, Australia, New Zealand, and Java, Indonesia. Can be invasive. Bright yellowish green or bluish green divided leaves in whorls; reddish in cool autumn. Zones 9–11.

MYRRHIS

SWEET CICELY

Containing a single species, an aromatic herbaceous perennial from Europe, this genus is a member of the carrot (Apiaceae) family. It has delicate, ferny, bright green leaves from spring until autumn and flat heads of tiny pure white flowers in summer. It is grown for its sweet-flavored leaves and attractive appearance.
CULTIVATION: Grow in open sunny position. Propagate from seed; can self-sow copiously and become weedy.

Myrrhis odorata

GARDEN MYRRH, SWEET CICELY

☼ ❄ ↔ 4–5 ft (1.2–1.5 m)
↑ 5–7 ft (1.5–2 m)

Clumping herbaceous perennial from Europe. Fine, ferny, aniseed-flavored leaves, to 18 in (45 cm) long, hollow stems. Tiny white flowers, in flat clusters, in summer. Ridged dark brown seeds. Zones 5–10.

Myrtus communis var. *italica*

Myriocarpa longipes

MYRTILLOCACTUS

Four species of tree-like cacti from Guatemala and Mexico comprise this genus in the family Cactaceae. These densely branched cacti stand out in their natural habitat, towering over all other plants. The genus name comes from the Greek word *myrtus*, "myrtle," and refers to the tiny fruits that resemble the fruits of the true myrtle. The bell-shaped flowers are small, and highly unusual for a cactus in that up to 9 flowers may be borne at any one time from a single areole. The seed pods or fruits are small, spherical, and edible, and are widely utilized as a food, fresh or dried, throughout the range of the plants.
CULTIVATION: Easily cultivated in a rich, well-drained soil. Propagate from seed or from cuttings that have been dried out for a week or two before planting. Rest in winter.

Myrtillocactus cochal

☼ ⚥ ↔ 10–15 ft (3–4.5 m)
↑ 15–17 ft (4.5–5 m)

Cactus from Sonoran desert edges, Mexico. Densely branched, tree-like, usually short trunk, many blue-green stems with 5 to 6 ribs; with or without a central spine, black to gray, 5 to 6 black radials. Flowers pale green to white, in spring. Fruits red, spherical, edible. Zones 9–11.

Myrtillocactus geometrizans ★

BILBERRY CACTUS, GARAMBULLA CACTUS, PADRE NUESTRO

☼ ⚥ ↔ 10–15 ft (3–4.5 m) ↑ 15 ft (4.5 m)

Candelabra-shaped cactus from Mexico. Usually distinct trunk or few main lower branches; many shorter, azure blue, upper branches, club-shaped, jointed, 5 or 6 smooth to rounded ribs. Single, dagger-like, black central spine, 5 to 9 radials, brown to black. Flowers small, greenish white, in spring. Fruits resemble grapes, purplish, edible. Zones 9–11.

Myrrhis odorata cultivar

MYRTUS

Although *Myrtus* was once quite a large genus in the myrtle (Myrtaceae) family, the Southern Hemisphere species have now been classified under other genera, including *Lophomyrtus*, *Luma*, and *Ugni*, leaving only 2 species, both native to the Mediterranean region. These are small evergreen shrubs with simple, opposite, dark green leaves and small, fragrant, white flowers produced in summer.
CULTIVATION: Grow these shrubs in a moderately fertile well-drained soil in a mild climate. Normally self-shaping into a rounded bush, they will respond to light tip-pruning in late winter, which produces denser foliage and a more compact habit. They prefer a position sheltered from cold drying winds. Propagate from half-hardened cuttings taken any time between spring and early winter.

Myrtus communis

COMMON MYRTLE, TRUE MYRTLE

☼ ❄ ↔ 10 ft (3 m) ↑ 10 ft (3 m)

Shrub from the Mediterranean region, popular for topiary. Leaves dark green above, paler beneath, aromatic when crushed. Flowers solitary, in upper axils, white, reddish pink shading on reverse; numerous conspicuous stamens, in spring. Oval berries. *M. c.* var. *italica* has an upright habit. *M. c.* 'Citrifolium' has cream flowers; 'Compacta', dwarf form; 'Variegata' has leaves with a conspicuous cream margin. Zones 8–11.

M

N

Nageia minor, in the wild, Chute de la Madeleine, New Caledonia

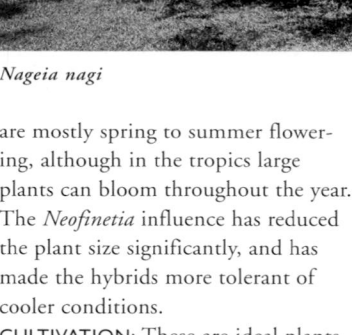

Nageia nagi

NAGEIA

This conifer genus in the plum-pine (Podocarpaceae) family consists of 6 species and occurs in the south of India, China, and Japan, in Thailand, the Malay Peninsula, the Philippines, Indonesia, and New Guinea, as well as in most of the world's tropical rainforests. They are evergreen trees with broad, lance-shaped, multi-veined leaves, unique in conifers. Male and female cones are borne on separate plants in all but one species.
CULTIVATION: Only *N. nagi* is cultivated. Plants require well-drained soil and water during dry periods. Frost tolerance is minimal. Propagate from seed or cuttings.

Nageia minor

syns *Podocarpus minor, Retrophyllum minor*

☀ ❅ ↔ 7 ft (2 m) ↑ 10 ft (3 m)
Slow-growing shrub or small tree from New Caledonia. Rough dark brown to gray bark. Tiny needle-like leaves on main shoots, larger on side shoots. Pollen cones, solitary and grouped, in late autumn. Zones 9–11.

Nageia nagi

syn. *Podocarpus nagi*
NAGI

☀ ❅ ↔ 15 ft (4.5 m) ↑ 70 ft (21 m)
Native to Japan, China, and Taiwan. Smooth dark brown bark, ageing to gray; almost horizontal branches. Leaves oval or oblong-shaped, glossy deep green, with paler undersides and numerous parallel veins. Male cones are single or clustered. Female cones occur singly, bluish green, globular, ripening in late autumn. Zones 8–10.

× NAKAMOTOARA

This is a genus of artificial monopodial hybrids between *Ascocentrum, Neofinetia,* and *Vanda,* belonging to the orchid (Orchidaceae) family. Crossing × *Ascocenda (Ascocentrum* × *Vanda)* with the miniature-growing Japanese *Neofinetia* has created most of these hybrids. These epiphytes are erect in their growth habit, with strap-like channeled leaves in 2 ranks. Larger plants may branch at the base and have numerous, very thick, cord-like roots. Inflorescences appear from the stem at the base of the leaf. They are mostly spring to summer flowering, although in the tropics large plants can bloom throughout the year. The *Neofinetia* influence has reduced the plant size significantly, and has made the hybrids more tolerant of cooler conditions.
CULTIVATION: These are ideal plants for bark-filled wooden baskets, enjoying humid, intermediate to warm conditions and high light levels, with their colorful showy blooms being long lived. Their thick roots will often venture outside the confines of the pot or basket, and this culture should be encouraged, as the roots require unimpeded air circulation and must dry out quickly after watering. Propagate by division.

× *Nakamotoara* Rainbow Gem

☀/☀ ✦ ↔ 4–12 in (10–30 cm)
↑ 4–16 in (10–40 cm)

This is a delightful hybrid between *Neofinetia falcata* and × *Ascocenda* Flambeau. The progeny have shown some variation in color. 'Pink Star', has deep green strappy leaves, with bright pink, almost glowing flowers; 'White Lady', has dark green leaves, with contrasting white flowers. Zones 11–12.

× *Nakamotoara* Rainbow Gem 'Pink Star'

× *Nakamotoara* Rainbow Gem 'White Lady'

Nanodes mathewsii

Nanodes medusae

NANDINA

HEAVENLY BAMBOO, SACRED BAMBOO

Just a single species of small evergreen shrub is contained in this genus. Despite its common name, this plant is a member of the barberry (Berberidaceae) family. It is grown for its colorful foliage and the bright red berries it bears in autumn. Plants are either male or female; some hermaphroditic cultivars are now available.
CULTIVATION: *Nandina* is easily grown in a rich soil that is moist but well drained. Leaf color is more intense when planted in full sun. For the best berry crops, make a group

planting to ensure cross-pollination. Leggy older stems can be cut back to the base in summer. Propagate from cuttings taken in summer as seed is difficult to germinate.

Nandina domestica
HEAVENLY BAMBOO

☀ ❄ ↔ 4 ft (1.2 m) ↑ 7 ft (2 m)
Native to the region from India to Japan. Erect cane-like stems. Leaves bipinnate or tripinnate, lance-shaped, soft, tinted pinkish red, becoming green and glossy with age, developing yellow, red, and purplish hues in winter. Small creamy white flowers, in summer. Showy red berries. Cultivars include: 'Filamentosa', thin green leaves, yellowish edges; 'Firepower', compact dwarf shrub, lime green leaves change to pink and cream in winter; 'Gulf Stream', compact, leaves coloring light red to scarlet; 'Harbor Dwarf', compact ground cover, can be weedy in warmer wet areas; 'Nana' (syn. 'Pygmy'), rounded dwarf shrub, leaves purple, crimson, orange, and scarlet throughout year, more intense color in winter; 'Nana Purpurea', shorter leaves than species, striking autumn color; 'Richmond', heavy crops of brilliant red berries without requiring another plant for cross-pollination; 'Woods Dwarf', low growing, red leaves in winter. Zones 7–10.

NANODES

This is a small genus of 3 distinct sympodial species (it was formerly included within the diverse genus *Epidendrum*). These orchids (family Orchidaceae) are native to parts of Central America and South America. Their fleshy leaves are 2-ranked and long lived. Their waxy flowers are produced singly, or rarely in pairs, from a small sheath at the end of the current growth.
CULTIVATION: These orchids are very popular in cultivation; however, the various species have quite different growing requirements. All must have humidity and ample air circulation. Propagate by division.

Nanodes mathewsii
syns *Epidendrum porpax, Neolehmannia porpax*

☀/◐ ✿ ↔ 4–24 in (10–60 cm)
↑ 1½–4 in (3.5–10 cm)
Found from Mexico to Peru, this is a very popular plant in cultivation. This vigorous, creeping, branching species comes in a few color forms. Produces green beetle-like flowers, with a glossy purple labellum; other forms have purple-green petals and sepals. Grows

Nandina domestica 'Gulf Stream'

well in shallow saucers or mounted on a large cork or tree-fern plaque, in intermediate to warm conditions. Zones 11–12.

Nanodes medusae

☀ ❄ ↔ 4–16 in (10–40 cm)
↑ 4–12 in (10–30 cm)
Rare species from mountainous areas in the Andes in Ecuador with clustered stems and fleshy bluish green leaves, twisted at the base. Large, waxy, green to deep maroon flowers, with a deeply fringed labellum, are produced in spring. Prefers cool, shaded, and humid conditions, in pots or baskets of sphagnum moss. Zones 8–11.

Nandina domestica 'Woods Dwarf'

Nandina domestica 'Nana Purpurea'

N

Nandina domestica 'Harbor Dwarf'

Nandina domestica

Nandina domestica

NARCISSUS

DAFFODIL, JONQUIL

Narcissus is part of the amaryllis (Amaryllidaceae) family and includes around 50 species of mainly spring-flowering bulbs found from Europe and North Africa to Japan and Australasia. They have grassy to strap-like leaves, and the flowers almost always have the typical cup- or trumpet-shaped corona backed by 6 petals. Garden forms abound in a range of colors and flower types and are classed according to flower shape and form. There are 12 divisions, listed here under *Narcissus* Hybrid Cultivars. Wild species belonging to Division 10 are listed first as individual entries. The genus name is derived from Greek mythology. When the youth Narcissus spurned the love of Echo, she sought revenge from Aphrodite, who caused him to fall in love with his reflection in a pool. Unable to pull himself away, he eventually wasted away to a flower.

CULTIVATION: Daffodils are mainly very hardy and adaptable, and will thrive in borders, pots, or naturalized in lawns. They prefer full sun/half-sun when in growth, and do well under deciduous trees. Good drainage is important. Water well until the foliage dies off. Propagate by breaking up established clumps.

Narcissus bulbocodium var. *conspicuus*

Narcissus bulbocodium

Narcissus bulbocodium

HOOP-PETTICOAT DAFFODIL

☀ ❋ ↔ 12 in (30 cm)
↑ 4–6 in (10–15 cm)

From France, Portugal, and Spain. Fine dark green leaves, more rounded than other *Narcissus*. Bright yellow to soft lemon flowers with flared trumpet, narrow much-reduced petals in same color, in early spring. *N. b.* var. *conspicuus* is a large-flowered rich yellow form. Division 10. Zones 6–10.

Narcissus cyclamineus

☀/☀ ❋ ↔ 12 in (30 cm)
↑ 6–8 in (15–20 cm)

From northwestern Portugal and Spain. Dainty little species much used in hybridizing; threatened in the wild. Dark green strappy leaves. Bright yellow flowers with long narrow trumpet, petals reflex right back, in early spring. Division 10. Zones 6–9.

Narcissus jonquilla

JONQUIL

☀/☀ ❋ ↔ 8 in (20 cm) ↑ 18 in (45 cm)

From Portugal and Spain. Narrow leaves, 2 to 4 per bulb. Thin flower stems, heads of small bright yellow flowers, seldom more than 1¼ in (30 mm) wide, with tiny cup-shaped corona, often strongly scented, in early spring. Long-lasting when cut. Division 10. Zones 4–9.

Narcissus obesus

Narcissus tazetta

Narcissus minor

☀/☀ ❋ ↔ 4 in (10 cm) ↑ 8 in (20 cm)

Native to France and northern Spain. Short, upright, gray- to blue-green leaves, often noticeably channeled, 3 to 4 per bulb. Narrow flower stem with solitary, large-cupped, bright yellow flower to 1¾ in (40 mm) wide, in early spring. Corona usually has frilled edge. Division 10. Zones 4–9.

Narcissus obesus

syn. *Narcissus bulbocodium* subsp. *obesus*

☀ ❋ ↔ 12 in (30 cm) ↑ 7–8 in (18–20 cm)

A hoop-petticoat daffodil from Portugal. The foliage sits almost flat to the ground. Large yellow trumpets to 1 in (25 mm) long, in early spring. Division 10. Zones 6–10.

Narcissus × odorus

☀ ❋ ↔ 12 in (30 cm)
↑ 14–16 in (35–40 cm)

From southern Europe. Fragrant natural hybrid between *N. jonquilla* and *N. pseudonarcissus* with bright green curved leaves. Bright yellow flowers, 1 to 2 per stem, short trumpet, spreading petals, in early spring. '**Rugulosus**', more robust form, up to 4 flowers per stem. Division 10. Zones 6–9.

Narcissus poeticus

PHEASANT'S EYE NARCISSUS,
POET'S NARCISSUS

☀ ❋ ↔ 12 in (30 cm)
↑ 12–20 in (30–50 cm)

From Italy, France, and Switzerland. Erect green leaves, somewhat glaucous. Flowers 2¾ in (7 cm) across, 1 per stem, pure white flat petals, tiny cup-shaped trumpet, yellow with red rim, green center, in late spring. Division 10. Zones 4–9.

Narcissus pseudonarcissus

LENT LILY, WILD DAFFODIL

☀ ❋ ↔ 12 in (30 cm) ↑ 8–14 in (20–35 cm)

This widespread European species is the classic Wordsworth daffodil. Thin, mid-green, erect leaves. Nodding yellow flowers to 2¾ in (7 cm) across, narrow trumpet and twisted petals, in early spring. Division 10. Zones 4–10.

Narcissus × odorus 'Rugulosus'

Narcissus rupicola

☀ ❋ ↔ 12 in (30 cm)
↑ 5–6 in (12–15 cm)

Dainty little narcissus from Spain and Portugal. Pale green leaves, very erect. Highly fragrant yellow flowers to 1¼ in (30 mm) across, with shallow-lobed cup, produced singly, in early spring. Division 10. Zones 6–9.

Narcissus tazetta

BUNCH-FLOWERED NARCISSUS, JONQUIL,
POLYANTHUS NARCISSUS

☀ ❋ ↔ 12 in (30 cm)
↑ 6–20 in (15–50 cm)

Variable species from the Mediterranean, naturalized in many places. Mid-green erect leaves, twisted. Sweetly scented flowers, up to 1¾ in (4 cm) across, in clusters of up to 20, white petals, shallow yellow cup, in late winter. *N. t.* subsp. *lacticolor* (syn. *N. canaliculatus*), dwarf form of unknown origin, white petals, orange cups. Possibly oldest known species in the genus, parent of many cultivars. Division 10. Zones 7–10.

Narcissus triandrus

ANGEL'S TEARS

☀/☀ ❋ ↔ 12 in (30 cm)
↑ 5–10 in (12–25 cm)

Dainty little species from Spain and Portugal. Leaves green, strappy, tips often curled. Flowers 2½ in (6 cm) across, cream with open cup-shaped trumpets and reflexed petals, in early spring. Division 10. Zones 4–9.

Narcissus Hybrid Cultivars

Daffodils hybridize freely and are favorites with plant breeders. The widely used Royal Horticultural Society classification system divides the many cultivars and hybrids into 12 groups or divisions based on the flower type and parentage.

DIVISION 1: TRUMPET

☀️/☀️ ❄️ ↔ 12 in (30 cm)
↕ 12–16 in (30–40 cm)

Large-cupped flowers, with one bloom per stem. The corona (cup) must be at least as long as the perianth segment, that is, the length of the petals. Division 1 hybrids include: '**Attraction**', creamy white perianth, bright yellow corona; '**Cyclope**', bright yellow flowers, broad cup; '**Dutch Master**', overall bright yellow; '**Gold Medal**', bright yellow flowers, late flowering; '**Honeybird**', green-tinged yellow perianth, white to cream corona; '**King Alfred**', typical of group, bright golden yellow blooms; '**Las Vegas**', pale cream perianth, bright yellow corona; '**Mount Hood**', white to cream flowers, tall; '**Spellbinder**' ★, soft to brighter yellow blooms with pale center; '**Standard Value**', soft golden yellow flowers, held aloft on short stems; '**Unsurpassable**', deep golden yellow blooms, tall, very early flowering; '**W. P. Milner**', elegant form, flowers open lemon yellow, paling to white with age. Zones 5–10.

Narcissus, Hybrid Cultivar, 1. Trumpet, 'King Alfred', Mt Vernon, Washington, USA

Narcissus, HC, 1. Trumpet, 'King Alfred'

Narcissus, HC, 1. Trumpet, 'Attraction'

Narcissus, HC, 1. Trumpet, 'Dutch Master'

Narcissus, HC, 1. Trumpet, 'Gold Medal'

Narcissus, HC, 1. Trumpet, 'Honeybird'

Narcissus, HC, 1. Trumpet, 'Spellbinder'

Narcissus, Hybrid Cultivar, 1. Trumpet, 'Standard Value'

Narcissus, HC, 1. Trumpet, 'W. P. Milner'

Narcissus, Hybrid Cultivar, 2. Large-Cupped, 'Fortune's Bowl'

DIVISION 2: LARGE-CUPPED

☼/◐ ❄ ↔ 12 in (30 cm)
↑ 12–16 in (30–35 cm)

The Division 2 plants are similar to the trumpet-flowered style with one flower per stem but with a smaller cup (corona) that should be shorter than the length of the perianth and at least one-third as long. Popular Division 2 members include: **'Abalone'**, white perianth, with deeper colored corona; **'Ambergate'**, deep yellow perianth, with orange corona; **'Berlin'**, yellow perianth, yellow corona with frilled bright orange edge; **'Blimey'**, primrose yellow perianth, corona of palest yellow; **'Camelot'** ★, all-over yellow; **'Ceylon'**, yellow perianth, with orange corona; **'Chilli Belle'**, white perianth, with deep pink corona; **'Coquille'**, ivory perianth, orangey pink corona, deeper colored at rim; **'Fortune's Bowl'**, yellow perianth, with rich golden corona; **'Fragrant Breeze'**, cream perianth, with yellow corona, fragrant blooms; **'Golden Aura'**, brilliant yellow perianth, with yellow corona; **'Ice Follies'**, white perianth, with pale yellow corona; **'Just So'**, creamy white perianth, with pinkish corona, deeper colored at rim; **'Modern Art'**, bright yellow perianth, with heavily ruffled orangey corona; **'Passionale'**, rich cream perianth, with ivory corona; **'Quasar'**, crisp white perianth, with deep orange-red and pink corona; **'Redhill'**, white perianth, orange-red corona; **'Saint Patrick's Day'**, all-over yellow; **'Salomé'** ★, white perianth, with yellow corona; **'Woodland'**, ivory perianth, rich cream corona, with a hint of green; **'Zampatti'**, very large flowers, cream perianth, yellow and orange-gold corona. Zones 5–10.

Narcissus, Hybrid Cultivar, 2. Large-Cupped, 'Abalone'

Narcissus, Hybrid Cultivar, 2. Large-Cupped, 'Ambergate'

Narcissus, Hybrid Cultivar, 2. Large-Cupped, 'Berlin'

Narcissus, Hybrid Cultivar, 2. Large-Cupped, 'Blimey'

Narcissus, Hybrid Cultivar, 2. Large-Cupped, 'Cabochon'

Narcissus, Hybrid Cultivar, 2. Large-Cupped, 'Charles Sturt'

Narcissus, Hybrid Cultivar, 2. Large-Cupped, 'Coquille'

Narcissus, Hybrid Cultivar, 2. Large-Cupped, 'Camelot'

Narcissus, Hybrid Cultivar, 2. Large-Cupped, 'Chilli Belle'

Narcissus, Hybrid Cultivar, 2. Large-Cupped, 'Dancing Partner'

Narcissus, HC, 2. Large-Cupped, 'Decoy'

Narcissus, HC, 2. Large-Cupped, 'Deception'

N., HC, 2. Large-Cupped, 'Flying Saucer'

N., HC, 2. Large-Cupped, 'Fragrant Breeze'

N

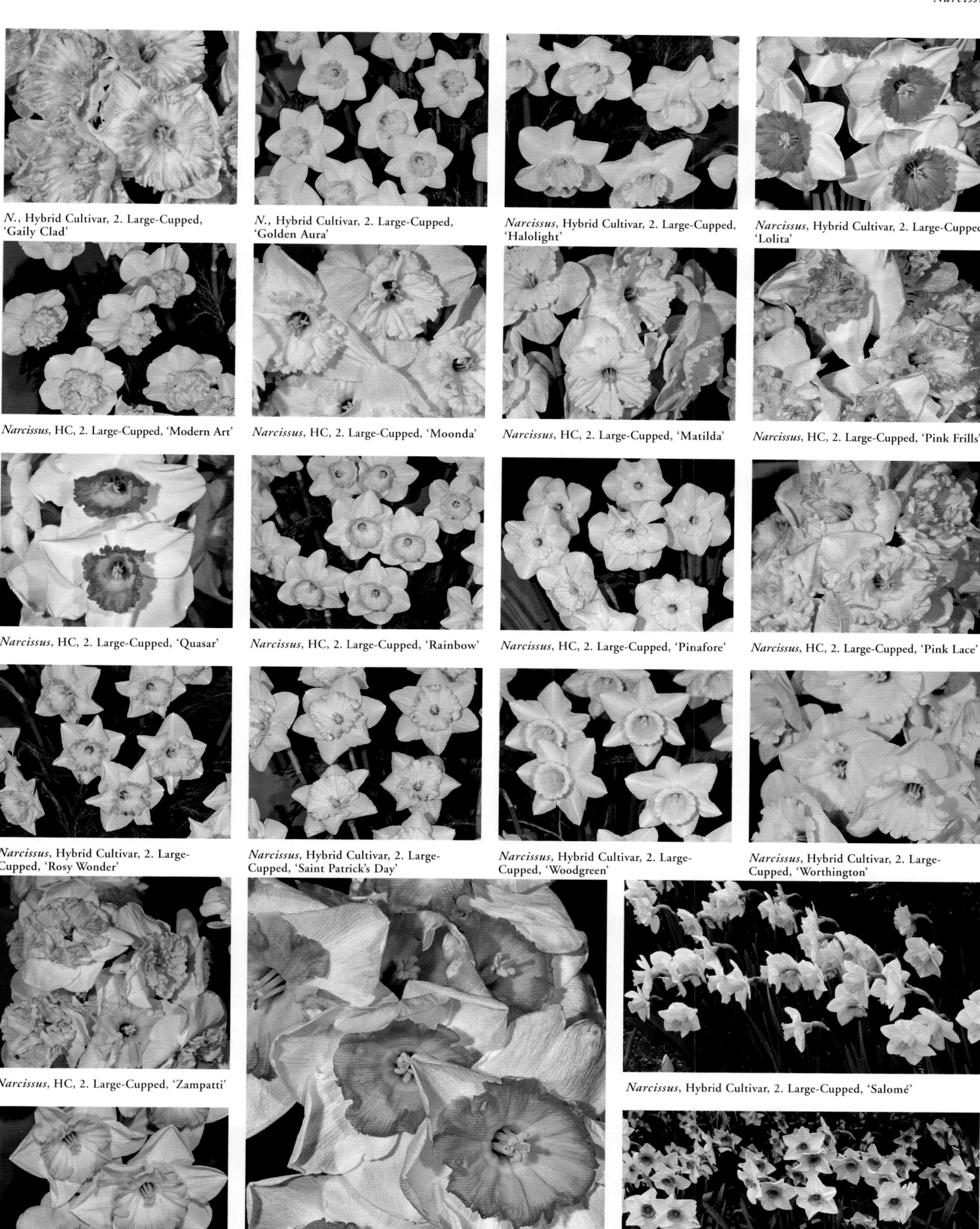

N., Hybrid Cultivar, 2. Large-Cupped, 'Gaily Clad'

N., Hybrid Cultivar, 2. Large-Cupped, 'Golden Aura'

Narcissus, Hybrid Cultivar, 2. Large-Cupped, 'Halolight'

Narcissus, Hybrid Cultivar, 2. Large-Cupped, 'Lolita'

Narcissus, HC, 2. Large-Cupped, 'Modern Art'

Narcissus, HC, 2. Large-Cupped, 'Moonda'

Narcissus, HC, 2. Large-Cupped, 'Matilda'

Narcissus, HC, 2. Large-Cupped, 'Pink Frills'

Narcissus, HC, 2. Large-Cupped, 'Quasar'

Narcissus, HC, 2. Large-Cupped, 'Rainbow'

Narcissus, HC, 2. Large-Cupped, 'Pinafore'

Narcissus, HC, 2. Large-Cupped, 'Pink Lace'

Narcissus, Hybrid Cultivar, 2. Large-Cupped, 'Rosy Wonder'

Narcissus, Hybrid Cultivar, 2. Large-Cupped, 'Saint Patrick's Day'

Narcissus, Hybrid Cultivar, 2. Large-Cupped, 'Woodgreen'

Narcissus, Hybrid Cultivar, 2. Large-Cupped, 'Worthington'

Narcissus, HC, 2. Large-Cupped, 'Zampatti'

Narcissus, Hybrid Cultivar, 2. Large-Cupped, 'Salomé'

Narcissus, HC, 2. Large-Cupped, 'Just So'

Narcissus, Hybrid Cultivar, 2. Large-Cupped, 'Synergy'

Narcissus, Hybrid Cultivar, 2. Large-Cupped, 'Redhill'

Narcissus, Hybrid Cultivar, 3. Small-Cupped, 'Barrett Browning'

Narcissus, Hybrid Cultivar, 3. Small-Cupped, 'Eminent'

Narcissus, Hybrid Cultivar, 3. Small-Cupped, 'Lough Areema'

Narcissus, Hybrid Cultivar, 3. Small-Cupped, 'Red Ember'

Narcissus, Hybrid Cultivar, 3. Small-Cupped, 'Verger'

Narcissus, HC, 3. Small-Cupped, 'Amor'

Narcissus, HC, 3. Small-Cupped, 'Enterprise'

Narcissus, HC, 3. Small-Cupped, 'John Bain'

Narcissus, HC, 3. Small-Cupped, 'Perimeter'

DIVISION 3: SMALL-CUPPED

☼/☼ ❄ ↔ 12 in (30 cm)
↕ 12–14 in (30–35 cm)

Small-cupped flowers, with one bloom per stem and a cup length of less than one-third of the perianth length. Division 3 hybrids include: 'Amor' ★, white perianth, with soft orange corona; 'Barrett Browning', white perianth, with orange corona; 'Lough Areema', white perianth, with dark-edged greenish-yellow corona; 'Red Ember', deep yellow perianth, with orange-red corona; 'Verger', white perianth, with red-edged golden corona. Zones 5–10.

DIVISION 4: DOUBLE

☼/☼ ❄ ↔ 12 in (30 cm)
↕ 10–14 in (25–35 cm)

These hybrids can have one or more flowers per stem. The corona or the perianth, or both, may be doubled. Popular doubles include: 'Bridal Crown', fully double, white and pale yellow; 'Candida', fully double, cream and pale yellow; 'Cheerfulness', fully double, creamy white, yellow center; 'Flower Drift', cream perianth, orange-red and yellow double corona; 'Gay Kybo', fully double, white perianth, yellow-orange in center; 'Madison', white double perianth, golden corona; 'Manly', fully double, white and bright yellow; 'Pink Paradise', white perianth, pink double corona; 'Sir Winston Churchill', white perianth, cream and yellow double corona; 'Tahiti', double perianth, yellow split orange corona; 'White Lion', fully double, pale yellow; 'Yellow Cheerfulness', yellow with some orange on central doubled petals. Zones 5–10.

Narcissus, Hybrid Cultivar, 4. Double, 'Gay Kybo'

Narcissus, HC, 4. Double, 'Cheerfulness'

Narcissus, HC, 4. Double, 'Gouache'

Narcissus, Hybrid Cultivar, 4. Double, 'Flower Drift'

Narcissus, Hybrid Cultivar, 4. Double, 'Candida'

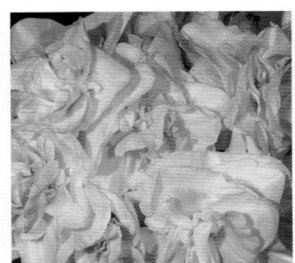

Narcissus, Hybrid Cultivar, 4. Double, 'Delnashaugh'

N., HC, 4. Double, 'Gay Song'

Narcissus, Hybrid Cultivar, 4. Double, 'Festive'

Narcissus, HC, 4. Double, 'Manly'

N., HC, 4. Double, 'Pink Paradise'

Narcissus, Hybrid Cultivar,
4. Double, 'Sir Winston Churchill'

Narcissus, Hybrid Cultivar,
4. Double, 'Siberian Pink'

Narcissus, Hybrid Cultivar,
4. Double, 'Tahiti'

Narcissus, Hybrid Cultivar,
4. Double, 'Unique'

Narcissus, Hybrid Cultivar,
4. Double, 'Yellow Cheerfulness'

Narcissus, HC, 4. Double, 'Polka'

Narcissus, HC, 4. Double, 'White Lion'

Narcissus, Hybrid Cultivar, 4. Double, 'Texas'

DIVISION 5: TRIANDRUS

☀/☼ ❄ ↔ 8 in (20 cm)
↕ 6–10 in (15–25 cm)

These plants show clear evidence of
N. triandrus parentage and usually
have two or more pendent flowers per
stem with reflexed perianth segments.
'**Hawera**', up to 5 pendulous soft-
yellow flowers; '**Lapwing**', white
perianth, yellow corona; '**Thalia**' ★,
overall white to cream. Zones 5–10.

DIVISION 6: CYCLAMINEUS

☀/☼ ❄ ↔ 8 in (20 cm)
↕ 8–12 in (20–30 cm)

Hybrids of *N. cyclamineus* parentage
with usually one flower per stem and
perianth segments strongly reflexed,

often almost to the stem. Popular
hybrids include: '**Dove Wings**', soft
yellow perianth, deep yellow corona;
'**February Gold**', all-over yellow; '**Jack
Snipe**', cream perianth, yellow corona;
'**Jetfire**', golden yellow perianth,
orange corona. Zones 5–10.

Narcissus, Hybrid Cultivar, 5. Triandrus,
'Hawera'

Narcissus, Hybrid Cultivar, 5. Triandrus, 'White Marble'

Narcissus, Hybrid Cultivar, 5. Triandrus,
'Lapwing'

Narcissus, Hybrid Cultivar, 5. Triandrus,
'Thalia'

Narcissus, Hybrid Cultivar, 6. Cyclamineus, 'February Gold'

Narcissus, Hybrid Cultivar, 6. Cyclamineus, 'Jack Snipe'

Narcissus, Hybrid Cultivar, 7. Jonquilla, 'Bell Song'

DIVISION 7: JONQUILLA

☼/◐ ❋ ↔ 12 in (30 cm)
↕ 12–18 in (30–45 cm)

Plants with *N. jonquilla* parentage evident in their small fragrant flowers, in heads of 1 to 3, sometimes more, with a starry array of perianth segments. Popular jonquils include: '**Bell Song**', cream to pale yellow perianth, pink corona; '**Quail**', overall deep golden yellow; '**Suzy**', yellow perianth, orange corona; '**Trevithian**', deep yellow perianth, darker corona. Zones 5–10.

DIVISION 8: TAZETTA

☼/◐ ❋ ↔ 18 in (45 cm)
↕ 12–18 in (30–45 cm)

Hybrids of *N. tazetta* with heads of 3 to 20 clustered, small, often highly scented flowers on sturdy stems. Popular for posies and corsages. These hybrids include: '**Avalanche**', white perianth, yellow corona; '**Geranium**', white perianth, golden orange corona; '**Golden Dawn**', yellow perianth, gold corona; '**Minnow**', soft yellow perianth, darker corona; '**Ziva**', white perianth, cream to pale yellow corona. Zones 5–10.

DIVISION 9: POETICUS

☼/◐ ❋ ↔ 10 in (25 cm)
↕ 12–16 in (30–45 cm)

Hybrids of species belonging to the *N. poeticus* group. Distinctive, usually one flower per stem, with small disc-shaped corona edged in red. Poeticus daffodils include: '**Actaea**' ★, flat white petals, tiny cup-shaped trumpet, bright yellow, edged with red; '**Cantabile**', white perianth, red-edged yellow-green corona; '**Felindre**', white perianth, red-edged, green-centered, yellow corona. Zones 5–10.

Narcissus, HC, 9. Poeticus, 'Actaea'

Narcissus, Hybrid Cultivar, 7. Jonquilla, 'Intrigue'

Narcissus, Hybrid Cultivar, 8. Tazetta, 'Chinita'

Narcissus, HC, 8. Tazetta, 'Golden Dawn'

Narcissus, HC, 8. Tazetta, 'Minnow'

Narcissus, Hybrid Cultivar, 9. Poeticus, 'Cantabile'

Narcissus, HC, 9. Poeticus, 'Felindre'

Narcissus, Hybrid Cultivar, 7. Jonquilla, 'Quail'

Narcissus, Hybrid Cultivar, 8. Tazetta, 'Falconet'

Narcissus, HC, 8. Tazetta, 'Jaune à Merveille'

Narcissus, HC, 8. Tazetta, 'Silver Chimes'

Narcissus, Hybrid Cultivar, 7. Jonquilla, 'Trevithian'

Narcissus, Hybrid Cultivar, 8. Tazetta, 'Geranium'

Narcissus, HC, 8. Tazetta, 'Laurens Koster'

Narcissus, HC, 8. Tazetta, 'Ziva'

Narcissus, Hybrid Cultivar, 8. Tazetta, 'Aspasia'

Narcissus, Hybrid Cultivar,
11. Split-Corona, 'Articol'

Narcissus, Hybrid Cultivar,
11. Split-Corona, 'Changing Colors'

Narcissus, Hybrid Cultivar,
11. Split-Corona, 'Egard'

Narcissus, Hybrid Cultivar,
11. Split-Corona, 'Mondragon'

Narcissus, Hybrid Cultivar,
11. Split-Corona, 'Palmares'

Narcissus, Hybrid Cultivar,
11. Split-Corona, 'Rosado'

Narcissus, Hybrid Cultivar,
11. Split-Corona, 'Sovereign'

Narcissus, Hybrid Cultivar,
11. Split-Corona, 'Trilune'

Narcissus, Hybrid Cultivar,
11. Split-Corona, 'Valdrome'

Narcissus, Hybrid Cultivar,
11. Split-Corona, 'Sorbet'

Nassella trichotoma

Nasturtium officinale

DIVISION 10: WILD SPECIES
See the individual species entries.

DIVISION 11: SPLIT-CORONA
☼/◐ ❄ ↔ 12 in (30 cm)
↕ 12–14 in (30–35 cm)

Unlike most daffodils with fused corona segments, split-corona forms have separate lobes, usually for more than half their length. Popular split-corona daffodils include: **'Articol'**, which has a white perianth with a pale dusky pink double corona; **'Egard'**, a white perianth with soft yellow corona; **'Palmares'**, a cream perianth with pale pink corona; and **'Sovereign'**, a white perianth with deep gold to orange corona. Zones 5–10.

DIVISION 12: MISCELLANEOUS
☼/◐ ❄ ↔ 6–12 in (15–30 cm)
↕ 6–16 in (15–40 cm)

Division 12 includes daffodil garden forms that do not fall into any other division—for example, **'Jumblie'**, up to 3 flowers per stem, bright yellow. Zones 5–10.

NASSELLA

This grass (Poaceae) family genus contains over 100 mostly perennial, occasionally annual, tussocky grasses from North and South America. Forming small clumps, they have strap-like leaves, so slender in many species that they are commonly named needlegrass. Unbranched or branched flower stalks carry small, narrow, sword-shaped membranous bracts beneath the panicles that contain a number of spikelets, each with one floret.
CULTIVATION: These grasses prefer full sun, in most well-drained soils. As a number of species have become significant weeds outside their natural habitat, care should be taken with their placement. Propagate from seed.

Nassella cernua
syn. *Stipa cernua*
NODDING NEEDLEGRASS
☼ ⚘ ↔ 6–10 in (15–25 cm)
↕ 12–40 in (30–100 cm)

Perennial found from California, USA, to northwestern Mexico. Stiff, smooth, narrow, strappy leaves. In spring–early summer, flower stalks with 5 or more nodes, often branching from upper nodes; bracts enclosing flower panicles. Zones 9–11.

Nassella tenuissima
FINE-LEAFED NASSELLA
☼ ⚘ ↔ 6–10 in (15–25 cm)
↕ 20–32 in (50–80 cm)

Perennial from southern USA and northern Mexico. Narrow, rolled, stiff leaves. Flower stalks hairy below lower nodes. Dry bracts, panicles of florets, in spring–early summer. Zones 9–11.

Nassella trichotoma
SERRATED TUSSOCK
☼ ⚘ ↔ 6–10 in (15–25 cm)
↕ 12–24 in (30–60 cm)

Perennial from South America. Stiff, narrow, rough, rolled, strappy leaves. Flower stalks with 2 to 4 hairy nodes. Sword-shaped bracts below sparse open panicles of florets, in spring. Noxious weed in Australia, New Zealand, and some parts of the USA. Zones 9–11.

NASTURTIUM
WATERCRESS
From Europe, northern Asia, northern Africa, and northern USA. Some botanists now consider this genus should be reclassified as *Rorippa*. These 6 aquatic species belonging to the cabbage (Brassicaceae) family have dark green, rounded, pinnate foliage with simple hairs. Found in marshy areas, ponds, and creeks, they freely float on water, with roots appearing from the stems.
CULTIVATION: These plants will only grow in areas where water is fresh and not stagnant. Propagate from seed in spring, or by division of rooted stems.

Nasturtium officinale
syn. *Rorippa nasturtium-aquaticum*
COMMON WATERCRESS
☼/◐ ❄ ↔ 32 in (80 cm) ↕ 8 in (20 cm)
From Europe and southwest Asia. Creeping, often floating, perennial with glossy leaves. Racemes of white flowers, in summer. Zones 6–10.

Neillia thibetica

Nectaroscordum siculum
subsp. *bulgaricum*

NAVIA

Native to the tepui summits of the Guayana Highlands of Venezuela and nearby countries, this genus, which contains over 70 brilliantly colored species, belongs to the bromeliad (Bromeliaceae) family. These small to medium-sized plants are mainly flattened, with narrow strap-like leaves forming an open rosette. The flowerhead generally nestles in the center of the leaf rosette, which often changes color at flowering. Their petals are yellow to white.
CULTIVATION: These plants are very difficult to grow, although some species from lower altitudes are acclimatizing well, and successive growing from seed may make them suitable for a wider range of climatic conditions. These bromeliads are best grown indoors or in a greenhouse or conservatory in cool-temperate areas, or outdoors with protection from direct sunlight and extremes of rain in tropical areas. Water when potting mix is dry. Extra fertilizer is not necessary. Propagate from seed or offsets.

Nectaroscordum siculum

Navia arida

☀ ✿ ↔ 12 in (30 cm) ↕ 2 in (5 cm)
Colombian species. Flat star-shaped plant. Green narrow-triangular leaves, bristly spines on edges; inner leaves turn yellow and red at flowering. Flowerhead globular, hidden in center of leaf rosette, mainly yellow, with red-tipped petals, in summer. Zones 11–12.

NECTAROSCORDUM

A member of the onion (Alliaceae) family, this genus consists of 3 species of bulbous perennials from southern Europe, western Asia, and Iran. Once included with alliums, they share the common name of ornamental onions. They also carry the unmistakable scent of stale garlic when crushed. The leaves are linear, deeply channeled, and sheathed at the base. The flowers, borne in late spring and early summer, are noted for their subtle colors and graceful nodding head carriage.
CULTIVATION: They require well-drained light soil in full sun/half-sun. Propagate from seed.

Nectaroscordum siculum

☼/☀ ❀ ↔ 4 in (10 cm) ↕ 40 in (100 cm)
Native of limestone areas in France and Italy. Slightly gangly formation. Leaves linear, basal, deeply keeled. Flowers in loose spraying umbels, bell-shaped, creamish green, flushed purple-red at base. Seed pods decorative and erect. Adaptable spreading plants, invasive in some conditions. *N. s.* subsp. *bulgaricum*, off-white flowers, flushed greenish purple. Zones 5–9.

NEILLIA

This genus, in the rose (Rosaceae) family, contains 10 species of deciduous shrubs that are closely related to *Spiraea* and are found in Asia, from the eastern Himalayas to the western side of the Malay Peninsula. They are arching shrubs with prominently veined 3-lobed leaves that color to yellow in autumn. In winter their attractive form, with a zigzag pattern of twigs, is revealed. Slender panicles or racemes of small bell-shaped flowers are borne in spring or summer.
CULTIVATION: Although not widely grown, these shrubs are easily cultivated in all but the driest soils, in full sun or part-shade. After flowering, cut out old stems at ground level to encourage new growth and retain the arching habit. Propagate from seed, from cuttings in summer, or by the removal of suckers in autumn.

Neillia sinensis ★

☼ ❀ ↔ 7 ft (2 m) ↕ 10 ft (3 m)
Native of central China. Deciduous shrub, upright habit. Smooth brown branchlets, bark exfoliates. Lobed leaves, serrated edges, purplish bronze when young. Short terminal racemes of white to pale pink bell-shaped flowers, in spring–summer. Zones 6–10.

Neillia thibetica

syn. *Neillia longiracemosa*
☼ ❀ ↔ 6 ft (1.8 m) ↕ 6 ft (1.8 m)
Native to western China. A deciduous shrub with an upright habit. Branchlets are covered in fine down. Serrated-edged leaves are prominently veined, and downy beneath. Slender racemes, to 6 in (15 cm) long, pale pink bell-shaped flowers through most of the summer. Zones 6–10.

NELUMBO

This genus of 2 species of aquatic perennials belongs to the lotus (Nelumbonaceae) family. One species is native to eastern N th America, and the other found throughout Asia and in Australia. The round leaves are borne umbrella-like on long stalks, usually above the water. Showy fragrant flowers are also borne on long stalks, often over 36 in (90 cm) tall, in shades of pink, yellow, and white. They are followed by decorative seed heads. Stalks, rootstock, and seeds are all edible, and the viability of the seeds extends to several hundred years.
CULTIVATION: In warm subtropical climates, they can be grown in outdoor ponds. In cool-temperate climates, plant in shallow water or in tubs. Plant rhizomes in baskets or beds of heavy rich soil mix. Grow in calm water in full sun. Propagate by division of rhizomes or from seed.

Nelumbo lutea

syn. *Nelumbium luteum*
AMERICAN LOTUS, WATER CHINQUAPIN, YANQUAPIN
☼ ❀ ↔ 7 ft (2 m) ↕ 7 ft (2 m)
From eastern North America. Round bluish green leaves, to 24 in (60 cm) across. Pale yellow flowers, to 10 in (25 cm) wide, in summer. Flat-topped seed heads studded with small holes resemble showerheads. Zones 4–9.

Nelumbo nucifera

syn. *Nelumbium nelumbo*
SACRED LOTUS
☼ ❀ ↔ 7 ft (2 m) ↕ 7 ft (2 m)
Found from Iran to Japan and in Australia. Bluish green wavy-edged leaves on prickly stems. Very fragrant pink or white flowers, to 12 in (30 cm)

Neillia sinensis

Nelumbo nucifera 'Sharon'

Nelumbo nucifera 'Carolina Queen'

Nelumbo nucifera

wide, in summer. Flat-topped seed heads. '**Carolina Queen**', large pink flowers, creamy at base; '**Momo Botan**', smaller with dark pink to rosy red flowers; '**Mrs Perry D. Slocum**', deep pink flowers, which age to creamy yellow; '**Sharon**', large double flowers, pink to red; and '**Speciosum**' with light pink flowers. Zones 9–11.

NEMATANTHUS

This genus of about 30 species of epiphytic climbing or trailing subshrubs, native to South America, belongs to the African violet (Gesneriaceae) family. The stems are often woody and rooting at the nodes. Leaves are opposite and pointed oval, sometimes tinged purple beneath. The tubular flowers, borne in clusters of 1 to 8, may be pouched, and are yellow, orange, pink, or purple, often with mixed colors on the lobes.
CULTIVATION: In temperate regions, grow them as house plants in bright

Nemesia denticulata

Nemesia caerulea 'Hubbird'

filtered light, in a free-draining potting mix. Water and fertilize regularly during active growth and provide medium to high humidity. In tropical areas, grow outside in a sheltered partly shady position. Propagate from leaf cuttings or seed, or by division.

Nematanthus gregarius
☀ ✿ ↔ 18–32 in (45–80 cm)
↑ 18–32 in (45–80 cm)

Pendulous semi-climbing subshrub from eastern South America. Small, shiny, somewhat fleshy leaves. Pouched flowers, to 1 in (25 mm) long, bright orange with purplish stripe on each lobe. Zones 11–12.

NEMESIA

Confined to South Africa, this genus in the foxglove (Scrophulariaceae) family includes around 65 species of annuals, perennials, and subshrubs. They form small mounds of toothed linear to lance-shaped foliage. Their flowers, which have a conspicuous lower lobe, often in a contrasting color, are borne in clusters on short stems. The annuals, mainly derived from *N. strumosa* and *N. versicolor*, are popular short-lived bedding plants in a wide range of bright colors. While less colorful, the perennials are sometimes mildly scented and are neat plants for borders, rockeries, or pots.
CULTIVATION: Grow in a sunny position in light free-draining soil kept

Nelumbo nucifera 'Momo Botan'

Nemesia caerulea

moist. Pinch back to keep compact. Sow annuals in succession for continuous bloom. Perennials will tolerate light frosts and grow from cuttings of non-flowering stems. Propagate from seed in late autumn or early spring.

Nemesia caerulea
☀/◐ ✽ ↔ 16–24 in (40–60 cm)
↑ 16–24 in (40–60 cm)

Woody-based perennial from South Africa. Bright green, narrow, lance-shaped leaves, often finely toothed. Heads of small pink to light purple-blue flowers with yellow eye, in summer. '**Hubbird**', violet flowers with yellow eye. Zones 8–10.

Nemesia denticulata
☀/◐ ✽ ↔ 16–20 in (40–50 cm) ↑ 8–12 in (20–30 cm)

South African species. Rather brittle-stemmed mounding perennial with

Nelumbo nucifera 'Mrs Perry D. Slocum'

Nemesia strumosa, Sachet Series, 'Blueberry Sachet'

small bright green leaves. Pleasantly scented mauve to dusky pink flowers, in late spring–summer. '**Confetti**', deep rose pink scented flowers. Zones 8–10.

Nemesia strumosa
☀/◐ ❅ ↔ 8–16 in (20–40 cm)
↑ 6–20 in (15–50 cm)

Fast-growing mounding annual native to South Africa. Lower leaves to 3 in (8 cm) long, bright green, toothed, with upper leaves much smaller. Produces many small flowers in crowded heads, often in warm shades of yellow-orange and apricot, sometimes purple or white, in summer. '**Blue Gem**', 8 in (20 cm) tall, bright blue flowers; '**KLM**', striking, compact, two-tone flowers, dark blue upper petals, white lower petals; **Sachet Series**, these compact heavy-flowering plants come in single colors, often fragrant. Zones 9–11.

Nemesia, Hybrid Cultivar, 'Fleurie Blue'

Nemesia, Hybrid Cultivar, 'Fragrant Cloud'

Nemesia, Hybrid Cultivar, 'Innocence'

N., Hybrid Cultivar, Maritana Series, 'Maritana Sugar Girl'

Nemesia, Hybrid Cultivar, 'Sundrops'

Nemesia, Hybrid Cultivar, 'Vanilla Sachet'

Nemesia Hybrid Cultivars

☀/☀ ✦ ↔ 8–16 in (20–40 cm)
↑ 6–16 in (15–40 cm)

Many hybrids between *N. strumosa* and *N. versicolor*, the modern seedling strains, have been bred to produce early-flowering compact plants in a wide range of colors. They are short-lived but may be sown in succession from spring–late summer. **'Fleurie Blue'**, low spreader, bright blue flowers; **'Fragrant Cloud'**, to 18 in (45 cm) tall, fragrant pale pink and white flowers; **'Innocence'**, pure white flowers, each with a small yellow throat; **Maritana Series**, low-spreading, heavy-flowering plants, wide color range including bicolors; and **'Sundrops'**, producing a mixed color selection of compact rounded plants in a range of warm tones. Zones 11–12.

NEMOPANTHUS

Native to eastern North America, this genus of one deciduous species, belongs to the holly (Aquifoliaceae) family; some botanists now consider it should be merged with the large genus *Ilex*. It is cultivated for its ornamental bright red berries and attractive autumn foliage.
CULTIVATION: Grow in moist, well-drained, humus-rich soil in sun or part-shade. Fully to marginally frost hardy. Prune to shape when young. Propagate from seed or cuttings.

Nemopanthus mucronatus

CATBERRY

☀/☀ ❄ ↔ 10 ft (3 m) ↑ 7 ft (2 m)

From the east coast of North America. Purplish young stems, with thin bluish green leaves, turning yellow in autumn. Flowers greenish yellow, 4 to 5 per whorl, in summer. Dark red berries. Prefers moist conditions. Zones 5–10.

NEMOPHILA

There are 11 species of annuals in this genus, which is a member of the waterleaf (Hydrophyllaceae) family. Native to western North America, they have small pinnate leaves on wiry stems, and form spreading mounds of ferny foliage that are smothered in small 5-petalled flowers, usually borne singly in the leaf axils, in late spring and summer. While not spectacular plants, they are graceful and often intriguingly colored, with flowers in various shades and patterns of blue and white. Although the name, coming from the Greek *nemos* (a glade) and *phileo* (to love), suggests a preference for shade, they are most at home in full sun/half-sun.
CULTIVATION: These are superb plants for narrow borders, banks, hanging baskets, and window boxes, where their semi-trailing habit is shown off to advantage. They require moist well-drained soil. Propagation is from seed, which is best sown *in situ*, as once it has germinated, the young plants resent disturbance.

Nemophila maculata

FIVE SPOT

☀ ✦ ↔ 12–20 in (30–50 cm)
↑ 8–12 in (20–30 cm)

Annual species from central California, USA. Initially upright, later spreading. Soft green pinnate leaves, up to 7 lobes. White flowers, purple blotch near petal tip, in summer. Zones 11–12.

Nemophila menziesii

☀ ✦ ↔ 12–20 in (30–50 cm)
↑ 4–6 in (10–15 cm)

Low spreading annual from California, USA. Ferny light green leaves, up to 11 lobes. The many white-centered mid-blue flowers, sometimes entirely white, appear in summer. *N. m.* subsp. *atromaria* has white flowers spotted with purple-black. *N. m.* 'Oculata' has pale blue flowers with a purple-black center; 'Pennie Black' has very dark purple-black flowers, edged with white. Zones 11–12.

NEOBUXBAUMIA

A genus of 8 very large species belonging to the cactus (Cactaceae) family. From eastern and southern Mexico, they are closely related to the enormous and well-known saguaro or *Carnegiea gigantea*, whose range extends from southern Arizona, USA, into neighboring Sonora, Mexico. *Neobuxbaumia* may be unbranched, columnar to tree-like, with some species developing a stout trunk, but all bear many ribs. A few species grow to 50 ft (15 m) tall. Spines may be stiff to flexible. The flowers are relatively small, bell-shaped to funnelform, white to pink, with outer segments covered in tubercles and small scales, naked or with just a few bristles. The seed pods are oval and spiny.
CULTIVATION: These plants are easily grown in a rich well-drained soil. Protect from frost in early growth, and keep dry from mid-autumn to early spring. Propagate from seed, or from cuttings that have been dried out for a week or two. Rest in winter.

Neobuxbaumia polylopha ★

☀ ⬧ ↔ 20 in (50 cm) ↑ 40 ft (12 m)

Native to central Mexico. Solitary, columnar, yellow-green to pale green, with 10 to 30 narrow ribs. Spines occasionally absent, flexible, brownish to yellow, graying with age. Flowers maroon, borne at random above 7 ft (2 m) up to top of stem, often in clusters. Outer segments with many tubercles and scales. Seed pods are purplish, scaly, with some wool and bristles. Zones 9–11.

NEOCALLITROPSIS

The sole species in this genus, part of the cypress (Cupressaceae) family, is an evergreen conifer found in southern New Caledonia. Only a small tree, it resembles *Araucaria* but its family is very resinous. Exploited for its fragrant timber, which is naturally rot-resistant, it is now rare in the wild.
CULTIVATION: Although most at home in a warm subtropical climate, *Neocallitropsis* will grow in frost-free warm-temperate gardens and prefers moist, humus-rich, well-drained soil in full sun or morning shade. Pruning is possible and sometimes necessary to remove damaged branches, but care

Nemophila maculata

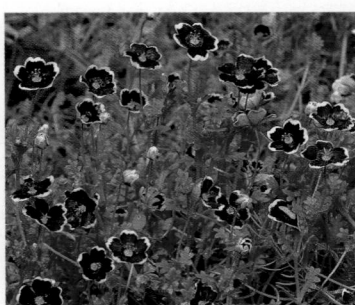

Nemophila menziesii 'Pennie Black'

Neofinetia falcata

must be taken to do any cutting when the tree is at its most dormant or the cuts may "weep" heavily. Although it responds quite well to cultivation, it is rarely seen in gardens. Propagate from seed or cuttings.

Neocallitropsis pancheri

☼/◗ ✦ ↔ 10 ft (3 m) ↑ 30 ft (9 m)

Native to New Caledonia. Tree with spreading conical crown, heavy branches densely clothed in whorls of leaves. Leaves of young trees are sickle-shaped; while adult plants have smaller linear leaves. Male and female cones small and inconspicuous. Female cones persist for longer. Seeds have minute wings. Zones 11–12.

NEOFINETIA

Belonging to the orchid (Orchidaceae) family, this small-growing monopodial genus from Japan and Korea with just one variable species is a distant relative of *Angraecum*. *N. falcata* is an erect-growing epiphyte, with small, thin, strap-like, channeled leaves, in 2 ranks. Older plants may branch at the base and usually have numerous, very thick, cord-like roots. The inflorescences are produced from the stem at the base of the leaf.
CULTIVATION: *Neofinetia* enjoys humid cool to intermediate growing conditions in bright light. Larger specimens grow well on cork plaques, while they are also suitable for culture in terracotta pots, in a well-drained gravel and bark-based mix. Propagate by division of clumps.

Neofinetia falcata

☼/◗ ⌇ ↔ 3–10 in (8–25 cm)
↑ 3–8 in (8–20 cm)

Variable species from Japan and Korea; considered a sacred plant in Japan. Small clusters of up to 8 fragrant white flowers with long 2 in (5 cm) spurs, produced on com-

pact clumping plants, in summer. Variegated-leafed forms are highly prized. Zones 9–11.

NEOLITSEA

This genus is a member of the laurel (Lauraceae) family, containing 100 species occurring in the rainforests of eastern Asia, Indonesia, New Guinea, and Australia. All species are shrubs or trees featuring simple, smooth-edged, alternate or clustered leaves, with a few prominent veins and tiny oil dots. Male and female flowers are borne on separate plants in axillary clusters. The flowers are small and relatively insignificant, and are followed by nut-like fruits.
CULTIVATION: This genus does not do well in lime-rich soil. Seedlings should be planted in a well-drained organic soil in a sheltered sunny site. Propagate from fresh seed, as seed remains viable for only a short time.

Neolitsea sericea ★

☼ ⌇ ↔ 15 ft (4.5 m) ↑ 20 ft (6 m)

Evergreen tree, occurs in woodlands throughout Korea, Japan, China, and Taiwan. Aromatic, oval-oblong, dull

green, leathery leaves, 3 prominent veins, whitish beneath, covered with dense, silky, yellow-brown hairs when young. Yellow flowers, in autumn. Egg-shaped red fruits. Zones 9–11.

NEOLLOYDIA

A genus of 14 species in the cactus (Cactaceae) family. They are small, solitary, but usually clustering cacti from Texas, USA, and northern to central Mexico. Stems are short, cylindrical, yellow-green, usually with white woolly tips, with ribs that are either poorly developed or absent. The conical tubercles are prominent. Areoles have a groove, at the base of which the flowers arise. The flowers are funnelform, in deep magenta, with naked outer segments. The spherical seed pods are greenish brown and fleshy, becoming dry with age.
CULTIVATION: These plants grow well in a rich well-drained soil. Propagate from seed, by division of clusters, or from cuttings that have been dried out for a week or two. Rest in winter.

Neolloydia conoidea

☼ ⌇ ↔ 20–32 in (50–80 cm)
↑ 2–10 in (5–25 cm)

From Texas, USA, and much of northern Mexico, as far south as Queretaro. Stems yellow-green. Spines variable throughout the large range, but usually with 1 central and 15 to 16 radials. Deep magenta flowers, in summer. Zones 9–11.

NEOMARICA

This genus of 15 species of tender rhizomatous perennials is a member of the iris (Iridaceae) family. They are native to tropical America and western Africa. The thick leaves are erect and sword-shaped, with strong veins or ribs, and are arranged in fans. Tall stems bear short-lived, flattened, iris-

like flowers, in summer. Outer petals are larger and spreading; the inner 3 petals are upright and reflexed. Some species have fragrant flowers, often marked in contrasting colors.
CULTIVATION: In suitably warm climates, grow outdoors in a sunny position in well-drained soil. In temperate areas, grow in the greenhouse in a fertile well-drained mix, in bright filtered light or full sun. Propagate by division or from seed.

Neomarica caerulea

syn. *Marica caerulea*

☼ ✦ ↔ 12 in (30 cm)
↑ 24–36 in (60–90 cm)

Rhizomatous perennial, native to Brazil. Leaves mid-green, swordshaped, erect. Flowers on tall stems, 3–4 in (8–10 cm) wide, pale blue to lilac outer petals, deep blue inner petals, veined and marked with yellow, white, and brown, in summer. Flowers rarely last more than one day but are replaced by another. Zones 11–12.

Neomarica gracilis

☼ ✦ ↔ 10 in (25 cm) ↑ 24 in (60 cm)

Native to Mexico and Brazil. Rhizomatous perennial. Strongly ribbed leaves, erect. Flowers about 2½ in (6 cm) wide, white outer petals, bluish inner petals with red and white markings, in summer. Zones 10–12.

Neomarica caerulea

Neolitsea sericea

Neocallitropsis pancheri, in the wild, Chute de la Madeleine, New Caledonia

NEOREGELIA

These highly variable members of the bromeliad (Bromeliaceae) family range from small tubular plants to large, flat, circular plants. Their leaves are generally strap-like, forming a rosette, and they can be green, silvery green, purplish, banded, spotted, striped in white, cream, or red, or marbled in a number of colors, or even tipped red. In some species the center leaves turn red or reddish blue, sometimes white. The flower stem is short, and the globular flowerhead, with up to 100 flowers, generally nestles in the center of the leaf rosette. This genus contains over 70 species covering 3 groups. The first group come from eastern Colombia and Peru and are not common in cultivation because they are quite difficult to grow. The second group come from southeastern Brazil, have 2–4 in (5–10 cm) long petals and are not common because of their rarity in the wild. The third group also come from southeastern Brazil; they are common and easy to grow, especially in tropical to warm-temperate areas. This third group provides most of the nearly 3,000 hybrids listed for this genus. CULTIVATION: Grow *Neoregelia* indoors or in a conservatory or greenhouse in cool-temperate areas, or outdoors with protection from direct sunlight and extremes of rain in warm-temperate, subtropical, and tropical areas. Water when the potting mix is dry. Try to keep the water in the leaf rosette clean. These plants do not require extra fertilizer. Propagate from offsets.

Neoregelia ampullacea
☀ ✦ ↔ 4 in (10 cm) ↑ 8 in (20 cm)
From around Rio de Janeiro, Brazil. Forms clumps by short runners. Leaves green to red, strap-like, with very small spines on edges, variable dark bands and blotches, forming a tight tube at base and halfway up, spreading outward. Flower stem short. Flowerhead globular, with up to 10 flowers, in summer. Petals blue. Zones 11–12.

Neoregelia carolinae
☀ ✦ ↔ 24 in (60 cm) ↑ 12 in (30 cm)
From Rio de Janeiro, Brazil. About 20 strap-like green leaves, with a few small spines on edges, forming spreading rosette. Flower stem short. Flowerhead globular, with up to 50 flowers opening over a long period. Center leaves turn red before flowering. Petals blue. *N. c.* f. *tricolor*, variegated form. Zones 11–12.

Neoregelia concentrica
☀ ✦ ↔ 32 in (80 cm) ↑ 12 in (30 cm)
Brazilian species. Leaves strap-like, green with varying purple blotches and broken stripes, with large black teeth on edges, forming a spreading rosette. Center leaves turn purple just before flowering, lasting for many weeks. Flower stem short. Flowerhead globular, with up to 100 flowers, in summer. Petals bluish. Zones 11–12.

Neoregelia marmorata
☀ ✦ ↔ 40 in (100 cm) ↑ 20 in (50 cm)
Brazilian species. Leaves strap-like, green with many purplish spots and splashes, underside has reverse colors, medium-sized teeth on edges, forming an open funnel-shaped rosette. Flower stem short. Flowerhead globular, with up to 40 flowers, in summer. Petals white. Zones 11–12.

Neoregelia olens
☀ ✦ ↔ 8 in (20 cm) ↑ 6 in (15 cm)
From Rio de Janeiro, Brazil. Leaves flat, but tapering to a sharp point, green to yellowish green, with red dots and splashes, especially toward tips, forming a rosette tubular at base but soon spreading wide. Lower part of center leaves turns bright red at flowering. The flower stem is short and the flowerhead globular, with about 10 flowers, in summer. Petals bluish. Also known as 'Marie' and 'Vulcan'. Zones 11–12.

Neoregelia Hybrid Cultivars
☀ ✦ ↔ 4–40 in (10–100 cm)
↑ 6–20 in (15–50 cm)
Mostly from Australia, Brazil, and USA, these are all easy to grow in warm areas. 'Amazing Grace', upright rosette in pale lime green, at flowering the whole plant blushes red in good light; 'Barbie Doll', light green leaves, red tips; 'Beef Steak', magnificent, symmetrically layered, wide-leafed rosette; 'Blushing Bride', center turns bright red on flowering; 'Bobby Dazzler', broad rich red leaves, heavy apple green spotting; 'Charm', bright wine red leaves, tiny lime green spots; impostors grown from seed have large spotting; 'Chili Verde', rich red in center at flowering; 'Chirripo', glazed centrally in rich reddish purple; 'Debbie', shy bloomer, inner leaves at first almost vertical; 'Empress', strap-like green and pink leaves; 'Fireball', shy flowering, petals blue; 'George's Prince', pale lilac leaves; 'Gespacho', wide red leaves with yellow-green markings; 'Green Apple', leaves apple green; 'Lambert's Pride', leaves with red to orange-red barring; 'Manoa Beauty', leaves with unique speckling in yellow-green; 'Medallion', inner leaves form dense crested rosette of brilliant red; 'Meyendorffii', center turns red at flowering; 'Midnight', deep burgundy central leaves, almost black; 'Ounce of Purple', dull green leaves covered in tiny purple spots; 'Painted Desert', symmetrical rosette of yellow-green leaves, developing more color in strong light; 'Passion', chartreuse-green leaves with hot lilac-pink intense areas; 'Perfection', yellow-cream central variegation; 'Red of Rio', mahogany red with small random green markings; 'Rosella', at flowering, green part of leaves turns red; 'Spots and Dots', dark red spots, blotches, and wavy lines; 'Takemura Grande', greenish plum-colored; 'Vulkan', varying darker purple blotches and broken stripes. Zones 11–12.

Neoregelia, Hybrid Cultivar, 'Manoa Beauty'

Neoregelia, HC, 'Painted Desert'

Neoregelia, HC, 'Takemura Grande'

Neoregelia Hybrid Cultivars

Neoregelia, Hybrid Cultivar, 'Empress'

Nepenthes bellii × *ventricosa*

Nepenthes albomarginata 'Penang'

× *NEOSTYLIS*

× *Neostylis* is a genus of artificial monopodial hybrids between *Neofinetia* and *Rhynchostylis,* both belonging to the orchid (Orchidaceae) family. From Brazil, these epiphytes are erect growing, with strap-like, channeled leaves, in 2 ranks. Larger plants may branch at the base, and have numerous, very thick, cord-like roots. The inflorescences appear from the stem at the base of the leaf. They are mostly spring and summer flowering, but in the tropics large plants can bloom throughout the year. The *Neofinetia* has reduced the plant size significantly, and made the hybrids more tolerant of cooler conditions.
CULTIVATION: They are ideal plants for bark-filled wooden baskets, enjoying humid intermediate to warm conditions and high light levels, with their colorful showy blooms being long lived. The thick roots will often venture outside the confines of the pot or basket, and this culture should be encouraged, as the roots require unimpeded air circulation and must dry out quickly after watering.

× *Neostylis* Lou Sneary

☼/☀ ✝ ↔ 4–12 in (10–30 cm)
↑ 4–16 in (10–40 cm)

Brazilian primary hybrid between *Neofinetia falcata* and *Rhynchostylis coelestis*. Leaves mid-green, strap-like. Flowers range from whites through pinks to pale blues, very long lasting. Pleasant scent. Zones 11–12.

NEPENTHES

MONKEY CUPS, TROPICAL PITCHER PLANTS
A remarkable genus of carnivorous plants, *Nepenthes* are found in Australia, Madagascar, and through Southeast Asia. They belong to their own pitcher-plant (Nepenthaceae) family. In all, there are over 70 species, divided into 2 main groups: highland species and lowland species. Highland species are found at altitudes greater than 3,280 ft (1,000 m), where they experience cool nights and little variation in seasonal temperatures. Lowland species experience a warmer climate where night temperatures do not drop below 59°F (15°C). Tropical pitcher plants are climbers that reach up high into the jungle canopy. They have 2 types of pitchers: rounded lower ones, and upper pitchers that are longer and narrower. The flowers of each plant are either all male or all female, and are small, with dozens carried along an upright stem. Prey is attracted by the bright colors and sweet nectar around the rim; once inside, the insect slips down the waxy sides into the digestive liquid and drowns. The prey of tropical pitcher plants is usually small insects, but small birds and even rats have been found in the pitchers. The pitchers of the larger species are often used as cooking implements.
CULTIVATION: The lowland species can be grown outside in tropical and subtropical regions, and provided the days are warm, 68°–77°F (20°–25°C), many species can withstand overnight temperatures as low as 50°F (10°C) for short periods of time. In cooler areas, *Nepenthes* are best grown in a warm greenhouse or conservatory. In the tropics, use an open soil such as bark chips, while in subtropical and temperate areas, use a mix of equal parts peat and scoria. Water overhead, never by tray. Most species prefer part-shade and high humidity. Fertilize with a light foliar feed once a month, in spring and summer. Highland species prefer a cooler night temperature, as low as 46°F (8°C). Propagate from stem cuttings; plant in sphagnum moss. Mist regularly.

Nepenthes alata

WINGED NEPENTHES
☼/☀ ✝ ↔ 20 in (50 cm) ↑ 15 ft (4.5 m)
Native to the Philippines, Malaysia, and Sumatra, occurring in both highlands and lowlands. The stem can be prostrate or climbing. Elongated green leaves, to 10 in (25 cm) long. Pitchers cylindrical, bulbous at base, green in shade, pinkish in full sun. Lower pitchers 4 in (10 cm) long, with 2 fringed wings; upper pitchers to 10 in (25 cm) long, with 2 prominent wings. There is also a spotted form. Zones 11–12.

Nepenthes albomarginata

MONKEY'S RICE POT
☼/☀ ✝ ↔ 20 in (50 cm) ↑ 7 ft (2 m)
Lowland species found in Borneo, Malaysia, and Sumatra. Slender vine, with 10 in (25 cm) long green to red leaves. Pitchers green to dark red, with white "collar" below rim. Lower pitchers cylindrical, ovate toward base. Upper pitchers cylindrical. 'Penang', usually red-spotted. Zones 9–12.

Nepenthes ampullaria

☼/☀ ✝ ↔ 20 in (50 cm) ↑ 20 ft (6 m)
Found in Borneo, Malaysia, New Guinea, Singapore, and Sumatra. Lowland climbing species, woody vine, leaves to 10 in (25 cm) long. Lower pitchers squat, about 3 in (8 cm) high, with 2 densely fringed wings, large spur behind lid. Upper pitchers are rare. A freshwater crab, *Geosesarma malayanum,* sometimes lives in pitcher. Zones 11–12.

Nepenthes bellii

☀ ✝ ↔ 10 in (25 cm) ↑ 10 ft (3 m)
Small climbing lowland species from the Philippines, often found growing with *N. merrilliana,* one of the largest species. Slender vine, lower pitchers to 3 in (8 cm) × 1 in (2.5 cm), usually green, with red lid and rim, wings heavily fringed. Rarely produces upper pitchers. *N. b.* × *ventricosa,* pitchers more red. Zones 11–12.

Nepenthes alata

Nepenthes bicalcarata

☀ ✝ ↔ 12 in (30 cm) ↑ 50 ft (15 m)
Climbing lowland species found in Borneo. Known for 2 curved thorns that hang from underside of pitcher's lid. Thick climbing stem. Lower pitchers rust-colored, squat, with 2 fringed wings. Upper pitchers slightly longer and narrower. Zones 11–12.

Nepenthes burbidgeae

PAINTED PITCHER PLANT
☀ ✝ ↔ 16 in (40 cm) ↑ 40 ft (12 m)
Beautiful climbing highland species from Borneo. Lower pitchers ivory or cream with burgundy blotches, rim with burgundy stripes. Upper pitchers funnel-shaped, pale green with purple to burgundy blotches. Zones 11–12.

N. ampullaria, in the wild, Borneo

N. burbidgeae, in the wild, Borneo

× *Neostylis* Lou Sneary

Nepenthes lowii, in the wild, Mt Kinabalu, Borneo

Nepenthes densiflora

Nepenthes gracilis, in the wild, Bako National Park, Sarawak, Borneo

Nepenthes densiflora
☀ ❄ ↔20 in (50 cm) ↑10 ft (3 m)
Highland species from Sumatra. Lower pitchers to 8 in (20 cm) × 2½ in (6 cm), bright red, with 2 lightly fringed wings. Upper pitchers yellow, red and yellow striped rim. Zones 8–12.

Nepenthes edwardsiana
☀/◑ ⚥ ↔6 ft (1.8 m) ↑12 ft (3.5 m)
From Borneo, climber in mossy forest at medium to high altitudes. Pitchers variable, to 18 in (45 cm) long x 6 in (15 cm) wide, yellow-green to reddish brown. Rim deep red, strongly ribbed. Zones 11–12.

Nepenthes edwardsiana, in the wild, Mt Kinabalu, Borneo

Nepenthes fusca
☀ ⚥ ↔14 in (35 cm) ↑35 ft (10 m)
From the highlands of Borneo. Tubular lower pitchers to 6 in (15 cm) long, with 2 fringed wings, usually purple with green blotches. Upper pitchers are similar size but funnel-shaped, green with purple blotches. Zones 11–12.

Nepenthes gracilis ★
☀ ⚥ ↔16 in (40 cm) ↑7 ft (2 m)
Common lowland species from Borneo, Malaysia, Sumatra, and Sulawesi. Lower pitchers about 2 in (5 cm) high with 2 fringed wings, cylindrical but slightly fatter at base. Upper pitchers to 6 in (15 cm) high. Pitchers usually light green but can be spotted with red markings, or totally red. Zones 11–12.

Nepenthes gracillima
☀ ⚥ ↔20 in (50 cm) ↑17 ft (5 m)
Highland species from Malaysia. The lower pitchers are cylindrical, sometimes slightly bulbous in the lower third. The upper pitchers grow to 9 in (22 cm) in length. Pitchers are usually green to purple-black. Zones 11–12.

Nepenthes hirsuta
☀ ⚥ ↔16 in (40 cm) ↑7 ft (2 m)
Species from the lowlands of Borneo. Lower pitchers to 6 in (15 cm) high, cylindrical but narrowing toward rim, green with reddish brown markings, covered with hairs. Upper pitchers to 5 in (12 cm) high. Zones 11–12.

Nepenthes khasiana ★
☀ ❄ ↔20 in (50 cm) ↑36 in (90 cm)
Climbing highland species found only in Khasi Mountains of Assam, India. Pitchers tubular, bulging slightly near base. Lower pitchers to 7 in (18 cm) high, green with red markings, with 2 fringed wings. Upper pitchers to 8 in (20 cm), with faint ribs in place of wings. Can withstand cooler day and night-time temperatures. Zones 8–12.

Nepenthes lowii
☀ ⚥ ↔26 in (65 cm) ↑25 ft (8 m)
Unusual highland species from Borneo. Lower pitchers cylindrical, with 2 prominent ribs. Upper pitchers hourglass-shaped, deep red inside, green to red outside. Lid is upright, the interior covered with bristly hairs. Zones 11–12.

Nepenthes maxima
☀ ❄ ↔30 in (75 cm) ↑10 ft (3 m)
Beautiful varied highland species found in Borneo, New Guinea, and Malaku and Sulawesi Islands, Indonesia. Three-angled climbing stem, lower pitchers to 8 in (20 cm) high with 2 prominent wings. Upper pitchers usually tubular but can be slightly funnel-shaped. Color varies from yellow-green to white with burgundy blotches, to purple with white blotches. *N. m.* × *mixta*, 6–8 in (15–20 cm) pitchers, very easy to grow. Zones 8–12.

Nepenthes maxima × mixta

Nepenthes mirabilis
☀ ❄ ↔16 in (40 cm) ↑25 ft (8 m)
The most wide-ranging species, found from southern China to Australia. Lower pitchers are tubular, slightly bulbous toward base, 2 fringed wings. Upper pitchers are cylindrical with prominent ribs. Pitchers are green to reddish brown. Often found near *N. ampullaria* and *N. gracilis,* along with hybrids of these species. Zones 8–12.

Nepenthes rafflesiana
☀ ⚥ ↔40 in (100 cm) ↑15 ft (4.5 m)
Stunning climbing lowland species found in Borneo, New Guinea, Singapore, and Sumatra. Lower pitchers broad at base and narrowing near rim, 2 very prominent wings, green with red to burgundy blotches, sometimes almost completely burgundy. Upper pitchers funnel-shaped, cream to green, with red spots. Zones 11–12.

Nepenthes rajah
☀ ⚥ ↔40 in (100 cm) ↑7 ft (2 m)
Magnificent highland species from Borneo. *N. rajah* is the "king" of *Nepenthes.* Usually a scrambling vine rather than a climber. Lower pitchers are oval-shaped, to 14 in (35 cm) high, burgundy to purple, with large mouth and even larger lid. Upper pitchers are similar except they are funnel-shaped. Small rats have been found, drowned, in the pitchers. Zones 11–12.

Nepenthes rajah, in the wild, Mt Kinabalu, Borneo

Nepenthes rafflesiana

Nepenthes ramispina

☀ ✦ ↔ 20 in (50 cm) ↑ 17 ft (5 m)

Highland species from Malaysia, previously classified as *N. gracillima*, but now considered a separate species. Beautiful slender pitchers to 8 in (20 cm) high, inside white to green, outside green to a stunning purplish black. Pitcher color is darker if given strong light. Zones 11–12.

Nepenthes reinwardtiana

☀ ✦ ↔ 16 in (40 cm) ↑ 70 ft (21 m)

Lowland climbing species from Borneo, Malaysia, and Sumatra. Lower pitchers tubular but bulging slightly in lower third, with 2 fringeless wings. Upper pitchers similar, but without wings. There are 2 forms: green and pale red. Distinctive feature is 2 highly visible pale yellow spots on inside wall of pitcher. Zones 11–12.

Nepenthes × rokko × sanguinea

☀ ✦ ↔ 26 in (65 cm) ↑ 17 ft (5 m)

Robust highland hybrid from Borneo. Lower pitchers to 8 in (20 cm) high, green with red blotches, bright red rim. Upper pitchers to 10 in (25 cm) high, funnel-shaped, green, speckled with red. Zones 11–12.

Nepenthes sanguinea ★

☀ ✦ ↔ 30 in (75 cm) ↑ 20 ft (6 m)

Highland species found in Malaysia. Lower pitchers cylindrical, bulbous near base, to 12 in (30 cm) high, with 2 fringed wings. Upper pitchers are similar but with 2 prominent ribs. Pitchers are often reddish; green forms and green forms with red blotches also occur. Zones 11–12.

Nepenthes spathulata

☀ ✦ ↔ 20 in (50 cm) ↑ 7 ft (2 m)

Beautiful highland species native to southern Sumatra. Lower pitchers are green, with a large bright red rim and 2 lightly fringed wings. Upper pitchers are more slender and totally green. *N. s. × maxima* has pitchers spotted with red. Zones 11–12.

Nepenthes tentaculata

☀ ✦ ↔ 20 in (50 cm) ↑ 7 ft (2 m)

Small, scrambling, highland species from Borneo and Sulawesi. Lower pitchers are cream to green, with burgundy blotches, narrowing toward mouth, with 2 heavily fringed wings. Upper pitchers burgundy to purple, with prominent ribs. Lid is covered with thick bristles. Zones 11–12.

Nepenthes thorelii

☀ ✦ ↔ 12 in (30 cm) ↑ 7 ft (2 m)

Lowland species native to Cambodia, Thailand, and Vietnam. Scrambling slender vine. Tubular pitchers, bulging slightly toward base, changing from green to totally red. Easily grown plant. *N. t. × alata*, pitchers grow to 8 in (20 cm) high; *N. t. × rafflesiana × mizuho*, usually has a striped rim. Zones 11–12.

Nepenthes tobaica

☀ ✦ ↔ 12 in (30 cm) ↑ 17 ft (5 m)

Small highland species from Sumatra. One of the fastest-growing *Nepenthes*. Both upper and lower pitchers are 2–4 in (5–10 cm) high. Lower pitchers have distinctly fringed wings; upper pitchers have prominent ribs. Pitchers are light green with red spots, sometimes almost entirely red, and rarely entirely green. *N. t. × lowii*, lid usually held fairly upright; *N. t. × veitchii*, red blotches, pink and green interior. Zones 11–12.

Nepenthes truncata

☀ ✦ ↔ 40 in (100 cm) ↑ 15 ft (4.5 m)

Large and spectacular lowland species native to the Philippines. The pitchers of this species are among the largest in the genus. Lower pitchers are fairly squat and cylindrical. Upper pitchers can grow to 16 in (40 cm) long. Rim is wavy, sometimes striped with green and red. The exterior is usually green, the interior patterned with red and purple. Easy to grow plant. *N. t. × veitchii* is a rare highland form whose pitchers have prominent wings. Zones 11–12.

Nepenthes tentaculata, in the wild, Mt Kinabalu, Borneo

Nepenthes ramispina, in the wild, Mt Ulu Kali, Borneo

Nepenthes spathulata × maxima

Nepenthes thorelii × alata

Nepenthes tobaica × lowii

Nepenthes sanguinea, in the wild, Borneo

Nepenthes thorelii

Nepenthes thorelii × rafflesiana × mizuho

Nepenthes truncata × veitchii

Nepenthes × ventrata

☀ ❄ ↔ 16 in (40 cm) ↑ 7 ft (2 m)

Naturally occurring hybrid of *N. ventrata* × *N. alata*; varies considerably in size and color. Pitchers usually cylindrical, bulging a little in lower third, totally green or almost bronze to red, with many variations in between. Robust easily grown plant. Zones 8–12.

Nepenthes ventricosa ★

☀ ❄ ↔ 16 in (40 cm) ↑ 7 ft (2 m)

Lovely highland species from the Philippines. Pitchers hourglass-shaped, without wings or ribs, yellow to green, often red in upper half, with red rim. *N. v.* × *mikei*, green pitchers spotted with red. Zones 8–12.

Nepenthes villosa

☀ ⚘ ↔ 20 in (50 cm) ↑ 6 ft (1.8 m)

Highland species from Mt Kinabalu, Borneo. Lower pitchers to 6 in (15 cm) × 4 in (10 cm). Upper pitchers 8 in (20 cm) × 5 in (12 cm). Both oval-shaped, densely covered in brown hairs and beautifully colored in yellow, red, and orange. Very sharply toothed rim makes this striking. Zones 11–12.

NEPETA

CATMINT, CATNIP

A member of the mint (Lamiaceae) family, this genus of around 250 mainly temperate Eurasian and North African aromatic perennials is represented in cultivation by just a few species, and one widely grown hybrid

group. Commonly grown in herbaceous borders or for edging large beds, they are valued for the hazy effect created by their gray-green foliage and mauve-blue to purple flowerheads. They are mainly low-growing sprawling plants, with small toothed leaves. In summer, the foliage disappears under upright spikes of tiny flowers. Sometimes used in herbal salads and medicines. The origin of the name is unclear but it may be named after the Etruscan city of Nepete.

CULTIVATION: Grow in full sun with light free-draining soil. Pinch back in spring to encourage compact growth and water well. Propagate from seed or cuttings of non-flowering stems.

Nepeta camphorata

☀/☀ ❄ ↔ 24 in (60 cm) ↑ 18 in (45 cm)

Very aromatic species from Greece. Somewhat sticky, toothed, pointed, oval leaves, to 1 in (25 mm) long. Foliage and stems camphor-scented when crushed. Heads of fairly widely spaced, purple-spotted, white flowers, in summer. Zones 8–10.

Nepeta cataria

CATMINT, CATNIP

☀/☀ ❄ ↔ 40 in (100 cm) ↑ 40 in (100 cm)

Bushy upright species, widely naturalized in Europe. Downy gray-green leaves. Spikes of widely spaced, mauve-spotted, white flowers, in summer. 'Citriodora', stems and foliage lemon-scented when crushed. Zones 3–10.

Nepeta cataria 'Citriodora'

Nepeta × faassenii 'Six Hills Giant'

Nepeta racemosa

Nepenthes × ventrata

Nepenthes ventricosa

Nepeta clarkei

HIMALAYAN CATMINT

☀/☀ ❄ ↔ 24 in (60 cm)
↑ 24–36 in (60–90 cm)

Himalayan native. Leaves light green to silvery, broad-based, toothed, lance-shaped, in whorls at base, in opposite pairs on flower stems. Long upright spikes of purple-blue flowers, white lower lobes, in summer. Zones 6–10.

Nepeta × faassenii ★

☀/☀ ❄ ↔ 40 in (100 cm) ↑ 24 in (60 cm)

Often sprawling hybrid of *N. racemosa* × *N. nepetella*. Leaves gray-green to silver-gray, toothed, lance-shaped to pointed oval. Spikes of long-lasting lavender to purple-blue flowers, in summer. 'Six Hills Giant', gray foliage, large sprays of lavender flowers;

Nepeta nervosa

Nepenthes villosa, in the wild, Mt Kinabalu, Borneo

Nepenthes ventricosa × mikei

'Superba', spreading habit, gray foliage, purple-blue flowers; 'Walker's Low', mounding habit, lavender-blue flowers. Zones 3–10.

Nepeta grandiflora

☀/☀ ❄ ↔ 24 in (60 cm) ↑ 24 in (60 cm)

Bushy eastern European species. Leaves toothed, downy, broad-based, pointed oval. Spikes of lavender-blue flowers, in summer. 'Bramdean', compact flowerheads; 'Dawn to Dusk', gray-green foliage, mauve flowers. Zones 3–10.

Nepeta nervosa

☀/☀ ❄ ↔ 32 in (80 cm) ↑ 20 in (50 cm)

From Kashmir. Initially upright, later sprawling. Narrow lance-shaped leaves, toothed or smooth-edged. Dense upright spikes of purple-blue flowers, in spring–summer. Yellow-flowered forms occur rarely. Zones 5–10.

Nepeta racemosa

☀/☀ ❄ ↔ 24 in (60 cm) ↑ 12 in (30 cm)

From the Caucasus and northern Iran. Stems spreading. Downy pointed oval leaves. Flowers violet-blue, also downy, in spring–summer. Rare in cultivation, plants listed under this species usually of *N.* × *faassenii* parentage. Zones 4–10.

Nepeta sibirica

☀/☀ ❄ ↔ 40 in (100 cm) ↑40 in (100 cm)
Quick-growing shrubby native of
Siberia. Leaves sparsely hairy, toothed,
dark green. Flowerheads crowded but
individual whorls widely spaced, blue
to soft purple, in spring–summer.
Zones 3–9.

Nepeta tuberosa

☀/☀ ❄ ↔ 20 in (50 cm) ↑32 in (80 cm)
Bushy rhizome-rooted species found
in coastal areas from Portugal to
Sicily. Pointed oval leaves to 3 in
(8 cm) long, finely hairy to densely
downy. Small spikes of light purple
flowers, with pink to purple-red
bracts at base, in summer. Zones 8–10.

NEPHROLEPIS

BOSTON FERN, FISHBONE FERN, SWORD FERN
Found in the wild in many tropical
areas such as Asia, Africa, Central
America, and West Indies. This genus
of about 40 species belongs to the
family Oleandraceae. They are terrestrial or epiphytic with short rhizomes
and usually wiry spreading runners.
The long tapering fronds bear varying
numbers of opposite leaflets and may
be erect, arching, or pendulous.
Colonies become established quickly
and some species are a weedy nuisance
in warm countries.
CULTIVATION: These ferns are popular
house plants in cool climates. Indoors
they need bright filtered light and a
humid atmosphere. In warm climates
they are unfussy and easily grown in

Nepeta tuberosa

part-shade or sun in a reasonably moist
soil, but they can become rampant.
Propagate by division or from spores.

Nephrolepis cordifolia

ERECT SWORD FERN, LADDER FERN
☀ ⚘ ↔ 12–48 in (30–120 cm)
↑12–48 in (30–120 cm)
Native to Asia and Australia. Erect or
arching fronds, yellowish green to dark
green. Blunt-ended, narrow, leathery
leaflets to 1½ in (35 mm) long. 'Duffii'
(Duff's sword fern), dense fronds, often
forked, crowded rounded leaflets;
'Kimberley Queen', tidier habit, tolerates more sun; 'Plumosa', leaflets
with lobed margins. Zones 11–12.

Nephrolepis exaltata

☀ ⚘ ↔ 36 in (90 cm) ↑36 in (90 cm)
Native to Polynesia, Africa, Mexico,
West Indies, and Florida, USA. Tufted
ferns with long, arching, pale lime
green fronds, wavy-edged leaflets.
'Bostoniensis' (Boston fern), broad
lance-shaped fronds, pale lime green,
fronds cascade as they mature;
'Bostoniensis Aurea' (golden Boston
fern), lime green-gold; 'Childsii',
hardy indoor plant, broad pale green
fronds that overlap each other; 'Hillii',
fast-growing, crested double fronds,
very adaptable; 'Mini Ruffle', miniature, broad triangular-shaped fronds,
definite lacy appearance. Zones 11–12.

Nephrolepis falcata

MACHO FERN, WEEPING SWORD FERN
☀ ⚘ ↔ 5 ft (1.5 m) ↑8 ft (2.4 m)
From Sri Lanka, the Maldives,
Myanmar, and southeastern Asia.
Long dark glossy green fronds, arch-
ing or weeping. Leathery leaflets

Nephrolepis cordifolia

forked toward tips. Scattered black
scales on both surfaces of frond blade.
Zones 9–11.

NERINE

GUERNSEY LILY, SPIDER LILY
This genus in the southern African
autumn-flowering amaryllis
(Amaryllidaceae) family, encompasses
around 30 species of bulbs that often
resemble small-scale versions of
Amaryllis. Their grassy to strappy
leaves may be evergreen or summer-
deciduous. Upright flower stems carry
many-flowered heads of long-tubed
funnel-shaped flowers, each with
6 widely flared, reflexed, narrow
petals. Bright pink and orange-red are
the main flower colors and white forms
are common. Named after Nereis, a sea
nymph of Greek mythology.
CULTIVATION: These plants tolerate
moderate frosts, but where the soil
freezes they are best grown in pots
that can be moved under cover. Plant
in full sun/half-sun with the bulb neck
exposed. Nerines prefer a light, gritty,
well-drained soil, but appreciate extra
humus. Keep dry when dormant.
Propagate by division, from offsets or
seed. May self-hybridize and self-sow.

Nerine bowdenii

☀ ❄ ↔ 12 in (30 cm)
↑16–18 in (40–45 cm)
Well-known South African species.
Leaves pale to dark green, glossy.

Nephrolepis exaltata

Bright pink flowers with wavy edges,
in clusters of up to 7, in autumn.
Foliage comes up in early winter when
flowering is over. 'Pink Triumph',
deep pink flowers. Zones 8–11.

Nerine flexuosa

☀/☀ ❄ ↔ 6 in (15 cm)
↑16–18 in (40–45 cm)
Almost evergreen species from South
Africa. Leaves glossy green, to 12 in
(30 cm) long. Pink flowers with wavy-
edged petals, in clusters of up to 20,
in autumn. 'Alba', commonly grown
white form, ruffled edges. Zones 8–11.

Nerine masoniorum

☀/☀ ❄ ↔ 2 in (5 cm)
↑10–12 in (25–30 cm)
Dainty little species from eastern
Cape region, South Africa. Fine,
sometimes evergreen, grassy foliage.
Soft pink flowers to ¾ in (18 mm)
across, with narrow wavy petals, in
autumn. Zones 8–11.

Nerine sarniensis

GUERNSEY LILY
☀ ❄ ↔ 6 in (15 cm) ↑16–18 in (40–45 cm)
South African species. Erect leaves,
bright green, to 12 in (30 cm) long.
Rounded heads of up to 20 brilliant
orange-red flowers with wavy-edged
petals and prominent stamens, in
autumn. *N. s.* var. *curvifolia* f.
fothergillii 'Major', larger and darker
orange-red flowers. Zones 8–10.

Nerine bowdenii

Nerine masoniorum

Nerine sarniensis

N. s. var. *curvifolia* f. *fothergillii* 'Major'

Nerium oleander 'Album'

Nerium oleander 'Docteur Golfin'

Nerium oleander 'Petite Salmon'

Nerium oleander 'Splendens'

Nerium oleander 'Splendens Giganteum Variegatum'

Nerium oleander

Nerine undulata

syn. *Nerine crispa*

☀ ✤ ↔ 6 in (15 cm) ↑16–20 in (40–45 cm)

From the eastern Cape region of South Africa. Slender bright green leaves. Flowers grow to 2 in (5 cm) across, in heads of up to 12, with wavy-edged narrow petals of mid-pink, in autumn. Zones 9–11.

NERIUM

OLEANDER

This genus of a single species from North Africa, the Middle East, northern India, and southern China belongs to the dogbane (Apocynaceae) family. It is a long-flowering evergreen shrub or small tree, with simple, smooth-edged, narrow leaves, and yellow, white, pink, and tangerine flowers. Petals are fused into a narrow tube but flaring from the end into a disc or a shallow cup, borne in terminal clusters. Tolerant of salt-laden winds and dry sandy soils; can be invasive.
CULTIVATION: Will grow in almost any type of soil except wet, but like full sun. Tolerant of light frosts if given a sheltered position. For a dense shrubby habit, remove flowering shoots and prune well-established plants in winter every 3 years. As these plants are extremely poisonous, wear protective clothing when pruning and dispose of prunings carefully (do not burn). Propagate from half-hardened cuttings taken in autumn, or seed in spring.

Nerium oleander

☀ ✤ ↔ 8 ft (2.4 m) ↑10 ft (3 m)

Evergreen shrub. Many erect shoots rising from base. Leaves dark green above, paler below. Flowers appear in late spring to early autumn, and sporadically until early winter. Many single- and double-flowered cultivars in a wide range of colors. Double cultivars have petals crimped, waved on outer edge. '**Album**', bears single white flowers; '**Casablanca**', faded pink flowers, almost white; '**Delphine**', single dark purplish red flowers; '**Docteur Golfin**', single, mauve tinged, cherry red flowers; '**Petite Pink**', dwarf cultivar, pale pink flowers; '**Petite Salmon**', dwarf cultivar, salmon flowers; '**Splendens**', deep rose pink double flowers; '**Splendens Giganteum Variegatum**', creamy yellow edge to leaves. Zones 8–11.

NEVIUSIA

Related to *Kerria*, this genus consists of a single species of deciduous shrub in the rose (Rosaceae) family. It is a threatened species in its native Alabama, USA. It increases in width by means of rooted branches. The white flowers are petal-less, with many prominent stamens.
CULTIVATION: This shrub is suitable for the border or woodland edge. It grows in moderately fertile soils and should be watered well in periods of drought. After flowering, the old and

dead wood should be cut out at the base. Propagate from seed or cuttings, or by division.

Neviusia alabamensis

ALABAMA SNOW WREATH

☀/☀ ✤ ↔ 5 ft (1.5 m) ↑5 ft (1.5 m)

From southern USA. Suckering plant, forms a wide multi-stemmed shrub. Leaves have serrated edges, downy beneath. Small flowers with a fluffy mass of white stamens, in spring. Zones 5–9.

NICANDRA

This genus of a single species is a member of the nightshade (Solanaceae) family. It is a tall-growing annual native to Peru. The pointed oval leaves grow up to 6 in (15 cm) long with irregularly lobed or toothed edges. Open bell-shaped flowers are borne in summer and autumn. The fruit that follows is enclosed in a green Chinese lantern-like calyx.
CULTIVATION: Grow in full sun in a rich well-drained soil. Propagate from seed sown *in situ* after frost danger has passed, or earlier under glass.

Nicandra physalodes

APPLE OF PERU, SHOO FLY

☀ ✤ ↔ 12–24 in (30–60 cm) ↑12–48 in (30–120 cm)

From South America. Vigorous well-branched annual. Leaves deep green, oval, indented. Flowers purple, blue, or mauve, white centers, only fully

open for a short time each day. They have a reputation for repelling flies, hence the common name. '**Splash of Cream**', foliage variegated with cream markings. Zones 8–11.

NICOTIANA

TOBACCO

Famous as the source of tobacco leaf, this genus, which is a member of the nightshade (Solanaceae) family, encompasses over 65 species, the bulk of which are annuals and perennials, most native to tropical and subtropical America, with a smaller number in Australia and the South Pacific. A few species are shrubby in habit, though they tend to be softwooded and short-lived. Their leaves are usually very large and covered with fine hairs, sticky to the touch, and may exude a fragrance when crushed. The flowers are tubular or bell-shaped, usually white or in pastel shades of green, pale yellow, pink, or soft red, and if fragrant their scent is generally released at night.

Nicandra physalodes

Neviusia alabamensis

Nidularium fulgens

Nidularium rutilans

CULTIVATION: Most tobacco species are marginally frost tolerant. They grow best in warm humid climates with ample summer rainfall, in full sun or partial shade. The soil should be well drained and reasonably fertile. Propagate from seed sown in spring, though some will grow from cuttings.

Nicotiana alata
syn. *Nicotiana affinis*
FLOWERING TOBACCO, JASMINE TOBACCO
☼/◐ ❄ ↔ 12 in (30 cm)
↕ 24–36 in (60–90 cm)
Native to South America. Sticky-stemmed perennial often grown as an annual. Large oval leaves. Narrow, tubular, greenish white flowers with flaring starry ends, in summer. They are fragrant and open at night. 'Nicky', semi-dwarf, fragrant white, lime green, or rosy pink flowers. Zones 8–10.

Nicotiana glauca
MUSTARD TREE, TREE TOBACCO
☼/◐ ❄ ↔ 6 ft (1.8 m)
↕ 6–12 ft (1.8–3.5 m)
Native of southern Bolivia and northern Argentina. Large blue-green leaves. Cream to yellow-green tubular flowers, to 2 in (5 cm) long, in late summer–autumn. Naturalized in warmer parts of USA. In Australia, there may be restrictions on growing this plant to minimize risk of virus passing to commercial tobacco crops. Zones 8–10.

Nicotiana langsdorffii
☼ ⚘ ↔ 15 in (38 cm) ↕ 5 ft (1.5 m)
From Brazil. Upright tall annual with dark green, deeply veined, ovate leaves. Masses of twiggy flower spikes, lime green tubular-shaped flowers, in summer. Zones 9–11.

Nicotiana × sanderae
☼/◐ ❄ ↔ 10 in (25 cm)
↕ 15–24 in (38–60 cm)
Garden hybrid between *N. alata* and *N. forgetiana*. Bushy hairy-leafed annual. Slightly crinkled, wavy, dark green, ovate leaves. Fragrant, flaring, tubular flowers, red, purple, and white, open all day. **Domino Series**, compact, upward-facing flowers in antique shades such as salmon pink; 'Lime Green',

bright yellow-green flowers; **Nikki Series**, prolonged flowering, red, pink, yellow, and white; **Saratoga Series**, uniform in size, mixed color range of reds, pinks, white, and lime. Zones 7–10.

Nicotiana sylvestris
☼/◐ ❄ ↔ 18–24 in (45–60 cm)
↕ 3–5 ft (0.9–1.5 m)
Native to Argentina. Vigorous annual with very large sticky leaves. Tall stems bear terminal panicles of long, white, pendulous flowers, very fragrant, in summer. Zones 8–11.

Nicotiana tabacum
TOBACCO
☼/◐ ❄ ↔ 18–24 in (45–60 cm)
↕ 3–5 ft (0.9–1.5 m)
Native to South America. Rather coarse annual or biennial, grown in the ornamental garden for its large leaves and commercially for tobacco. Small, slightly fragrant, greenish white to pinkish red, bell-shaped flowers, in summer. 'Variegata', ornamental, leaves heavily variegated with cream, flowers tinged pink. Zones 8–11.

NIDULARIUM
From southeast Brazil, this genus belongs to the bromeliad (Bromeliaceae) family. It contains 45 species and 35 hybrids. Closely related to *Neoregelia*, these medium-sized plants prefer shadier conditions. They have small-toothed strap-like leaves, mainly green, often with darker green spots, and sometimes purplish on either side, forming an open rosette with some water-holding capacity. The flower stem varies from short to just emerging above the water level in the leaf tank. The flowerhead is globular, with a main center and flat flower

Nicotiana alata 'Nicky'

clusters, and a large, stiff, flattened bract, mostly red but sometimes greenish. Each flowerhead contains many flowers. Petals are white, red, or blue but never open wide.
CULTIVATION: Grow indoors if in flower, or in a greenhouse or conservatory in cool-temperate areas, or outdoors with shade protection in warm-temperate, subtropical, and tropical areas. Water when potting mix is dry. Extra fertilizer is not necessary. Propagate from offsets.

Nidularium fulgens
☼ ⚘ ↔ 32 in (80 cm) ↕ 12 in (30 cm)
From Rio de Janeiro, Brazil. Leaves green, with scattered dark green spots, teeth up to 5 mm long on edges, forming a broad funnelform rosette. Flowerhead globular, with up to 10 flat flower clusters and a large bright red to orange bract with strong teeth and spreading widely, in spring to summer. Petals blue with white edges. Zones 11–12.

Nidularium innocentii
☼ ⚘ ↔ 36 in (90 cm) ↕ 14 in (35 cm)
Native from southeast Brazil. Leaves green, or with purplish wine underneath, small teeth on edges forming a dense funnelform rosette. Flowerhead globular, with up to 9 flat flower clusters, and a large broad bract, green with a red tip, to totally red, in spring to summer. Petals greenish. Several variegated forms. Zones 11–12.

Nidularium procerum
☼ ⚘ ↔ 40 in (100 cm) ↕ 16 in (40 cm)
From Brazil. Leaves green or reddish purple, with small teeth on edges, forming a funnelform rosette. Flowerhead globular, with up to 10 flat flower clusters and a wide stiffish bract, generally green at base, and red toward the tip, in spring–summer. Petals blue, with some white margins. Zones 11–12.

Nidularium rutilans
☼ ⚘ ↔ 32 in (80 cm) ↕ 12 in (30 cm)
From Rio de Janeiro, Brazil. Leaves green with darker green spots, small teeth on edges, forming a dense flattish rosette. Flowerhead globular, with up to 10 flat flower clusters, and a large, rounded, red bract, sometimes lilac or darker spotted, in spring to summer. Petals red. Now includes *N. regelioides*. Zones 11–12.

Nidularium Hybrid Cultivars
☼ ⚘ ↔ 20–40 in (50–100 cm)
↕ 12–20 in (30–50 cm)
Nidularium hybrids are extremely popular in gardens, due to their diverse color range and ease of care. Most prefer a subtropical garden. 'Madonna', white bracts becoming bright red at flowering, petals white; 'Miranda', variegated form of 'Madonna'; 'RaRu', apple green rosette, whitish pink flowers; 'Ruby Lee', leaves with longitudinal lines throughout on a background of either green, or green and red, or totally red. Zones 10–12.

Nicotiana × sanderae, Saratoga Series, mixed

Nicotiana sylvestris

Nicotiana tabacum

Nigella sativa

Nigella damascena

Nigella damascena 'Miss Jekyll'

NIEREMBERGIA
CUPFLOWER

There are about 23 species of annuals, perennials, and subshrubs in this genus, which is a member of the nightshade (Solanaceae) family. They are native to South America where they grow in moist sunny situations. They are slender-stemmed plants, either creeping, spreading, or erect, with small narrow leaves. The showy flowers are open and upward-facing, in shades of blue, purple, or white, often with yellow throats. They are borne for long periods from summer to autumn.
CULTIVATION: Grow in a sunny sheltered position in a gritty moisture-retentive soil. In cold climates grow in pots or as annuals. Plants flower in the first year from seed. Propagate all species from seed, and perennials also by division or from cuttings.

Nierembergia caerulea
syn. *Nierembergia hippomanica*
☼ ❄ ↔ 8 in (20 cm) ↑ 8 in (20 cm)
From Argentina. Small, upright, densely branching perennial often grown as an annual. Narrow pointed leaves. Numerous lavender flowers with yellow throats, in summer. 'Purple Robe', darker purple flowers with yellow throats. Zones 9–11.

Nierembergia repens
syn. *Nierembergia rivularis*
☼ ❄ ↔ 18 in (45 cm) ↑ 2 in (5 cm)
Native to South America. A low spreading perennial with spoon-shaped leaves. Flaring white flowers, about 1 in (25 mm) wide, tinged with yellow or pink at base, in summer. Zones 9–11.

NIGELLA
FENNEL FLOWER, LOVE-IN-A-MIST, WILD FENNEL

This genus of about 15 species of annuals, from the Mediterranean region and western Asia, is a member of the buttercup (Ranunculaceae) family. They are all easy to grow and feature fine green foliage with bushy growth. Flower colors are sky blue and mixes of white, blue, pink, purple, mauve, and rosy red. Nigellas bloom profusely and make good cut flowers. Their decorative seed pods and foliage are also used in dried floral arrangements.
CULTIVATION: Grow in full sun/half-sun in any well-drained soil and fertilize once a month with a relatively high phosphorus fertilizer. Deadhead to prolong flowering. Propagate from seed sown directly where it is to grow, since *Nigella* seedlings resent being transplanted. Plants will reseed.

Nolana humifusa

Nigella damascena
LOVE-IN-A-MIST
☼ ✈ ↔ 10 in (25 cm) ↑ 20 in (50 cm)
European species. Bright green finely cut foliage, somewhat like fennel. Fluffy flowers, in blue, pink, or white. Make successive plantings for blooms all summer. 'Miss Jekyll', semi-double, sky blue flowers. Zones 11–12.

Nigella sativa
BLACK CUMIN, BLACK SEED, NUTMEG FLOWER, ROMAN CORIANDER
☼ ❄ ↔ 9–12 in (22–30 cm)
↑ 18–24 in (45–60 cm)
From the Mediterranean. Leaves short, thin, mid-green. Delicate white or pale blue flowers, in summer. Grown for its aromatic seed, which is used as a spice in Middle Eastern cuisine. Mohammed said of it: "In it is a cure for everything except death." Zones 7–10.

NOLANA
CHILEAN BELLFLOWER

This genus of around 18 species belongs to the family Nolanaceae and is made up of perennials from South America that are grown as annuals in the Northern Hemisphere. These are heat-tolerant sprawling plants. Their leaves are spoon-shaped. The showy, tubular, blue or purple flowers have white throats and 5 lobes. The flowers open in the sun but stay closed on cloudy days. They are attractive edging plants and a pretty addition to a hanging basket. Frequently found in maritime areas in their native habitat.
CULTIVATION: Drought tolerant, they will grow in any sandy garden soil in full sun. Propagate from seed, sown directly where it is to grow, in spring.

Nierembergia repens

Nolana paradoxa

Nolana humifusa
SNOWBIRD
☼ ✈ ↔ 12 in (30 cm) ↑ 4–6 in (10–15 cm)
Quite rare species from Peru. Leaves mid-green, oval. Long trailing stems with small, bell-shaped, pale blue flowers, in summer. Zones 11–12.

Nolana paradoxa
☼ ✈ ↔ 12 in (30 cm) ↑ 4–6 in (10–15 cm)
From Chile. Trailing plant, suitable for rock gardens or hanging baskets. Mid-green oval leaves, pointed. Large blue-purple flowers, pale yellow or white throats, in summer. 'Blue Bird', blue flowers, white throat. Zones 11–12.

NOLINA

This agave (Agavaceae) family genus contains about 24 species of evergreen perennials closely related to *Yucca*, native to southern USA, Mexico, and Guatemala. Adapted to very dry climates, most have swollen bases that are conical, spherical, or bottle-shaped, with thick corky bark. The long narrow leaves are tough and fibrous. Flowers, usually only on very mature plants, are very small, creamy white, and borne densely on tall panicles. Some species included in *Nolina* are often split off into the genus *Beaucarnea*.
CULTIVATION: Most will withstand some frost. Grow outdoors in warm dry climates. In cooler regions grow in the greenhouse, in a well-drained mix. Propagate from seed or offsets.

Nierembergia caerulea 'Purple Robe'

N

Nolina parryi, in the wild, Mexico

Nomocharis aperta

Nolina bigelovii

BEARGRASS, SACAHUISTA, SAWGRASS

☀ ❄ ↔ 3–5 ft (0.9–1.5 m)
↕ 3–6 ft (0.9–1.8 m)

Native to southwestern USA and
Mexico. Slow-growing with rosettes
of stiff narrow leaves that shred into
fibers at edges. Plant eventually forms
branching trunk. Flowering panicles
grow to 10 ft (3 m) tall. Flowers
creamy white, small and numerous,
in summer. **Zones 8–11.**

Nolina microcarpa

BEARGRASS, SACAHUISTA, SAWGRASS

☀ ❄ ↔ 4 ft (1.2 m) ↕ 5 ft (1.5 m)

From southwestern USA and Mexico.
Stemless species, forming dense tufts
of arching grass-like leaves with finely
toothed margins. Flowering panicles to
7 ft (2 m) tall. Numerous, small, pale
cream flowers, in summer. **Zones 6–10.**

Nolina parryi

PARRY'S BEARGRASS

☀ ❄ ↔ 5 ft (1.5 m) ↕ 5 ft (1.5 m)

Slow-growing species, native to southwestern USA and Mexico. Eventually
forms thick stems, with terminal
rosettes of narrow leaves. Very like
N. bigelovii but leaf edges are minutely
toothed and do not shred into fibers.
Tiny white flowers on ends of long
flower stalks, in summer. **Zones 8–11.**

NOMOCHARIS

A genus of 7 species closely related to
Lilium and a member of the lily
(Liliaceae) family. They are found from
western China, through Tibet and
northern Myanmar, into northern
India. They have bulbs consisting of
loose scales and leaves scattered up the
stems. The flowers are flat to open
bowl-shaped, usually 1 to 9 per stem,
in the axils of the uppermost leaves.
They are usually spotted and in some
cases heavily so.

CULTIVATION: They need a constantly
moist, but not wet, humus-rich soil in
a sheltered, cool, humid environment.
Propagate from seed, although bulb
scales can be used at the expense of a
flowering-sized bulb. Recommended
for the collector in the right climate.

Nomocharis aperta

☀◐/☀ ❄ ↔ 10 in (25 cm)
↕ 14–32 in (35–80 cm)

From western China. Leaves are pale
green and oval. Up to 6 nodding pale
pink flowers, spotted deep purple, in
early summer. **Zones 6–9.**

NOTHOFAGUS

SOUTHERN BEECH

There are approximately 35 species in
this genus, native to temperate South
America, New Zealand, New Guinea,
New Caledonia, and southeast Australia including Tasmania. Members
of the beech (Fagaceae) family, all are
evergreen or deciduous forest trees,
with straight trunks and light lacy
foliage. In native habitats, they are
more stunted and more sparsely
foliaged at higher altitudes. Leaves are
dark green, or occasionally red, with
mostly toothed edges, and commonly
arranged in more or less a single
plane. Tiny flowers are followed by
nutlet fruits. Their timber is fine
grained and valued for cabinetwork.
CULTIVATION: A moderately rich and
well-drained acid soil is preferred with
shelter from salt-laden winds. They
require regular watering until established. Propagate from fresh seed in
autumn, from hardwood cuttings
in summer, or by layering.

Nothofagus alessandrii

RUIL

☀ ❄ ↔ 30 ft (9 m) ↕ 90 ft (27 m)

From Chile, tall deciduous tree, uncommon in the wild. Large oval leaves,
with sharp-toothed edges, and prominent veins running to each tooth. The
small fruits, clustered in groups of 7,
are a characteristic unique to this
species. **Zones 8–10.**

Nothofagus antarctica

ANTARCTIC BEECH, NIRRE

☀ ❄ ↔ 20 ft (6 m) ↕ 40 ft (12 m)

From Chile. Fast-growing deciduous
tree, elegant open habit, often with
twisted trunk and main limbs. Leaves
small, dark green, glossy, rounded to
heart-shaped, irregularly toothed margins, turn yellow in autumn. **Zones 8–9.**

Nothofagus betuloides

COIGUE DE MAGELLANES

☀ ❄ ↔ 20 ft (6 m) ↕ 50 ft (15 m)

Native to Chile and Argentina.
Densely foliaged evergreen tree. Small
oval to round leaves, closely arranged
on branchlets, glossy dark green,
bluntly toothed edges. Young shoots
sticky and furry. **Zones 8–9.**

Nothofagus cunninghamii

MYRTLE BEECH, TASMANIAN BEECH

☀ ❄ ↔ 8–30 ft (2.4–9 m)
↕ 5–100 ft (1.5–30 m)

Found in cool-temperate forests in
Tasmania and Victoria, Australia. Evergreen straight-trunked tree, variable in
habit. Dark green crown, small, shiny,
toothed leaves in fan-like fronds.
Young foliage, reddish tinge. Best
growth on basaltic soils. **Zones 8–9.**

Nothofagus dombeyi

COIGUE

☀ ❄ ↔ 25 ft (8 m) ↕ 50 ft (15 m)

Fast-growing evergreen tree from Chile
and Argentina, deciduous in very cold
climates. Spreading open habit. Leaves
oval to round, or broadly wedge-
shaped, dark glossy green above, with
unevenly toothed edges. **Zones 8–9.**

Nothofagus fusca

NEW ZEALAND RED BEECH, RED BEECH

☀ ❄ ↔ 25 ft (8 m) ↕ 100 ft (30 m)

From New Zealand, can become massive trees, smaller in cultivation. Bark
dark rusty brown to almost black, furrowed, flaking on old trees. Coarsely
serrated oval leaves, turn bright red on
young trees in winter, remain green on
older trees before falling. **Zones 8–9.**

Nothofagus gunnii

GUNN'S BEECH, TANGLEFOOT BEECH

☀ ❄ ↔ 6 ft (1.8 m) ↕ 10 ft (3 m)

Deciduous, slow-growing, sometimes
scrambling shrub from high altitudes in
Tasmania, Australia. Roundish leaves,
round-toothed edges, prominent veins.
Related to *N. pumilio*. **Zones 8–9.**

Nothofagus gunnii, in the wild,
Tasmania, Australia

Nothofagus alessandrii

Nothofagus cunninghamii

Nothofagus fusca, in the wild, Otago, New Zealand

Nothofagus menziesii, in the wild, New Zealand

Nothofagus moorei, in the wild, New South Wales, Australia

Nothofagus pumilio, in the wild, Andes, Argentina

Nothofagus solanderi var. cliffortioides, in the wild, New Zealand

Nothofagus menziesii
NEW ZEALAND SILVER BEECH

☀ ❄ ↔ 30 ft (9 m) ↑ 60 ft (18 m)

Native to New Zealand. Evergreen tree, can develop massive trunk. Distinctive, horizontally banded and flaking, gray bark. Dense dark green leaves, tiny, oval to round, coarsely serrated. New spring foliage light green. Graceful tree with spreading dome, smaller in cultivation. Zones 8–9.

Nothofagus moorei
ANTARCTIC BEECH, AUSTRALIAN BEECH

☽ ❄ ↔ 20 ft (6 m) ↑ 70 ft (21 m)

From mountain ranges in northern New South Wales and southern Queensland, Australia. Tall evergreen tree, with sturdy trunk and dense dark green crown, the trunk often leaning or crooked. Old reddish leaves are often scattered throughout the foliage. Zones 8–10.

Nothofagus obliqua
ROBLE BEECH

☀ ❄ ↔ 30 ft (9 m) ↑ 100 ft (30 m)

From Chile and Argentina. Elegant, fast-growing, deciduous tree. Reddish gray bark, becoming furrowed.

Broadly oval leaves, in opposite rows, smooth, irregularly toothed margins, dark green above, paler undersides. Useful for timber. Zones 8–10.

Nothofagus pumilio
DWARF CHILEAN BEECH, LENGA

☀ ❄ ↔ 30 ft (9 m) ↑ 70 ft (21 m)

Native to Argentina and Chile, this species becomes shrub-like in exposed sites at high altitude. Smooth oval leaves, slightly glossy, paler reverse, prominent veins to indentations of blunt-toothed edges; attractive autumn color. Fast growing, deciduous, and useful for timber. Zones 8–9.

Nothofagus solanderi
BLACK BEECH, MOUNTAIN BEECH, NEW ZEALAND BEECH

☀ ❄ ↔ 25 ft (8 m) ↑ 60 ft (18 m)

From hilly and mountainous habitats in New Zealand. Evergreen tree, distinctive black bark. Leaves shiny, bronze-green, small, oblong, paler on reverse, in fan-like sprays. Masses of small red-brown flowers, in spring. Timber valued for general construction. N. s. var. cliffortioides, oval leaves, more sharply pointed. Zones 8–9.

NUPHAR
This genus is a member of the waterlily (Nymphaeaceae) family. It contains about 25 species of aquatic perennial herbs, native to temperate regions of the Northern Hemisphere, including Spain, southern Italy, and the Mediterranean. They grow in still or slow-moving water and have large oval to round leaves that may be floating, submerged, or held above the water. Floating and emergent leaves are leathery. The rather small flowers are held above the water and have prominent yellow sepals, with smaller yellow petals.
CULTIVATION: Plant rhizomes in baskets containing a rich soil mix. Baskets can be lowered gradually to acclimatize plants to the water depth. Grow in full sun in still water, although Nuphar are more tolerant of shade and water movement than Nymphaea species. They can be invasive where conditions suit. Propagate from seed or by division.

Nuphar lutea
YELLOW WATERLILY

☀/☽ ❄ ↔ 3–8 ft (0.9–2.4 m) ↑ 3–15 in (8–38 cm)

Widespread species in northern temperate regions. Invasive plant with broadly oval or rounded, floating or emergent, leathery and shiny leaves. Produces small, globular, bright yellow flowers, in summer. Blooms emit a distinct odor. Zones 4–9.

Nuphar polysepala

Nuphar polysepala

☀/☽ ❄ ↔ 3–8 ft (0.9–2.4 m) ↑ 3–15 in (8–38 cm)

Native to North America. Broadly heart-shaped dull green leaves, usually floating. Waxy, yellowish green, globular flowers, in summer. The interiors are often tinged brownish purple. Zones 4–9.

NUXIA
This genus contains about 15 species of evergreen trees and shrubs in the family Buddlejaceae, which are found from the Arabian Peninsula to tropical Africa, South Africa, Madagascar, and the Mascarene Islands. The leaves are opposite or appear in whorls of three. They are variable and can be smooth-edged or toothed, hairy or leathery, but usually have a hairy underside. The flowers, which are mostly white, grow in terminal panicles. The fruit that follows consists of small hinged capsules with little seeds.
CULTIVATION: They are fast growing and are usually planted as decorative shade trees in frost-free areas, where they grow well in full sun or partial shade in moist soil. Propagate from half-hardened wood, as germination from seed is difficult.

Nuxia floribunda
FOREST WILD ELDER, KITE TREE

☀/☽ ❀ ↔ 10 ft (3 m) ↑ 25 ft (8 m)

Shrub or tree, native to tropical and South Africa. Variable habit. Oblong leaves, smooth-edged, scalloped, or toothed. Conspicuous, fragrant, off-white flowers, in large clusters, in autumn–spring. Zones 9–11.

NUYTSIA
This is a single-species genus in the mistletoe (Loranthaceae) family, and is one of the few members of that family to grow into a tree. Occurring

Nuxia floribunda

Nuytsia floribunda

naturally in Western Australia, its roots attach themselves to other plants where they gain nutrition. Its foliage of deep green leaves is almost totally obscured by spectacular golden yellow flowers in summer.
CULTIVATION: This parasitic species lives on the roots of other plants in its habitat, so young seedlings must be planted with seedlings or older plants of another species, preferably a grass. Some success has been achieved using couch grass as the host. Well-drained sandy soil is necessary for growth, but the tree can be quite slow growing and may take many years to flower. If damaged by frost it will resprout from the undamaged trunk or rootstock. Propagate from seed, which will germinate in about 3 to 10 weeks.

Nuytsia floribunda
WESTERN AUSTRALIAN CHRISTMAS TREE
☀ ❄ ↔ 15 ft (4.5 m) ↑ 25 ft (8 m)
From southwestern Australia. Trunk and branches rough and brittle. Leaves narrow, olive green, thick. Small, fragrant, golden flowers, in terminal clusters, in summer. Fruits, to ¾ in (18 mm) long, with 3 wings. Zones 8–10.

NYMANIA
This single-species genus, native to hot dry areas of South Africa, belongs to the mahogany (Meliaceae) family. It is a rounded shrub or small tree valued for its attractive red flowers and decorative seed pods.
CULTIVATION: Frost tender, it needs a warm climate and a fertile well-drained soil in full sun. It is occasionally grown in a greenhouse in cooler areas. Adequate water is necessary for potted specimens during the growing season. Keep just moist during winter. Propagate from seed in spring or from cuttings in summer.

Nymania capensis, seed pods

Nymania capensis
CHINESE LANTERN
☀ ✿ ↔ 5 ft (1.5 m) ↑ 10 ft (3 m)
From the Cape region of South Africa. Much-branched evergreen shrub or small tree. Crowded narrow leaves. Small, 4-petalled, pinkish red flowers, in late winter–early summer. Large, papery, inflated seed pods. Zones 11–12.

NYMPHAEA
This genus, in the self-named waterlily (Nymphaeaceae) family, is of varied distribution, growing in ponds over most of the world. It contains about 50 species of aquatic perennials split into hardy and tropical groups. The leaves are broadly oval or round, with the base cleft in 2 lobes. Their attractive flowers cover the color spectrum, are starry or globular, with pointed or rounded petals. They may be on stalks above the foliage, or sit at water level. Some are fragrant or night-opening.
CULTIVATION: Hardy water lilies are suitable for permanent pond positions in temperate climates. Tropical plants need a summer water temperature of 65–70°F (18–21°C), and a winter temperature of 50°F (10°C). Plant rhizomes in baskets in a rich soil mix, the water depth varying with plant size. Grow in full sun in still water. Overcrowded plants produce smaller flowers and the foliage lifts above the water. Propagate by dividing rhizomes.

Nymphaea alba
EUROPEAN WHITE LILY
☀ ✿ ↔ 3–10 ft (0.9–3 m)
↑ 3–15 in (8–38 cm)
Species native to temperate Eurasia and northern Africa. Rounded leaves,

12 in (30 cm) across, red when young, becoming dark green. Floating white flowers, to 8 in (20 cm) wide, open during day, in summer. Zones 5–9.

Nymphaea caerulea
syn. *Nymphaea capensis*
CAPE BLUE WATERLILY
☀ ✿ ↔ 3–12 ft (0.9–3.5 m)
↑ 3–15 in (8–38 cm)
From southern and eastern Africa. Round wavy-edged leaves, to 16 in (40 cm) wide. Fragrant blue flowers, to 8 in (20 cm) across, held well above foliage, open during day, in spring–summer. 'Colorata' (syn. *N. colorata*), smaller leaves with overlapping lobes, and smaller, mauve to blue flowers. Zones 11–12.

Nymphaea × daubenyana
☀ ✿ ↔ 3–6 ft (0.9–1.8 m)
↑ 3–15 in (8–38 cm)
Hybrid of garden origin. Bears small, fragrant, light blue flowers held well above the water. New plants arise within the axils of leaves and stalks. Day-opening, in spring–summer. Zones 11–12.

Nymphaea gigantea
AUSTRALIAN WATERLILY
☀ ✿ ↔ 3–12 ft (0.9–3.5 m)
↑ 3–15 in (8–38 cm)
Native to tropical areas of Australia and New Guinea. Large leaves, often up to 24 in (60 cm) in diameter. Day-opening flowers, to 12 in (30 cm)

wide, sky blue to purple-blue, prominent yellow stamens, from spring to summer. Zones 11–12.

Nymphaea lotus
EGYPTIAN WATERLILY, LOTUS, WHITE LILY
☀ ✿ ↔ 3–12 ft (0.9–3.5 m)
↑ 3–15 in (8–38 cm)
From Egypt and tropical southeastern Africa. Large, rounded, wavy-edged leaves to 20 in (50 cm) wide. Flowers, to 10 in (25 cm), white, fragrant, usually night-opening, closing the following noon, from spring to summer. Zones 11–12.

Nymphaea mexicana
YELLOW WATERLILY
☀ ✿ ↔ 3–12 ft (0.9–3.5 m)
↑ 3–15 in (8–38 cm)
Native to southern USA and Mexico. Vigorous plant with oval to round leaves, green blotched with purplish brown. Slightly fragrant flowers range from pale to bright yellow, in spring–summer. Zones 11–12.

Nymphaea odorata
FRAGRANT WATERLILY, POND LILY
☀ ✳ ↔ 3–8 ft (0.9–2.4 m)
↑ 3–15 in (8–38 cm)
From eastern USA. Round dull green leaves to 10 in (25 cm) wide. Fragrant white flowers open during day, in summer. 'Sulphurea Grandiflora', mottled leaves and large, starry, bright yellow flowers; 'William B. Shaw', large creamy pink flowers. Zones 3–9.

N

Nymphaea alba

Nymphaea caerulea 'Colorata'

Nymphaea × daubenyana

Nymphaea gigantea

Nymphaea stellata

Nymphaea tetragona 'Alba'

Nymphaea, Hybrid Cultivar, Tropical Day-Blooming, 'Bagdad'

Nymphaea stellata

☀ ⚘ ↔ 3–12 ft (0.9–3.5 m)
↕ 3–15 in (8–38 cm)

Native to southern and southeastern Asia. Bright green round or oval leaves, to 6 in (15 cm) wide. Flowers to 5 in (12 cm) wide, open during day, vary from blue to pink or white, in spring–summer. Zones 11–12.

Nymphaea tetragona

syn. *Nymphaea pygmaea*

PYGMY WATERLILY

☀ ❄ ↔ 12–48 in (30–120 cm)
↕ 3–15 in (8–38 cm)

Found throughout Europe, Asia, and Japan. Small, oval, dark green leaves, dull red beneath. Slightly fragrant flowers, about 2 in (5 cm) wide, white with yellow stamens, in summer. 'Alba', small leaves, purple beneath, white flowers; 'Helvola', mottled leaves, bright yellow flowers, orange stamens. Zones 3–9.

Nymphaea tuberosa

☀ ❄ ↔ 3–8 ft (0.9–2.4 m)
↕ 3–15 in (8–38 cm)

Native to the northeastern USA. Robust plant with round leaves, often to 15 in (38 cm) across. The pure white flowers, to 9 in (22 cm) wide, open during the day, in summer. Zones 3–9.

Nymphaea Hybrid Cultivars

Nymphaea hybrids are divided into hardy and tropical hybrids, with the tropical hybrids further divided into day- and night-blooming hybrids.

HARDY HYBRIDS

☀ ❄ ↔ 3–8 ft (0.9–2.4 m)
↕ 3–15 in (8–38 cm)

These hybrids are suitable for cooler climates. Day-blooming flowers are usually held close to water level and include all colors except blue shades. Some are "changeables," which alter their coloring dramatically as they age. 'Charlene Strawn', scented yellow flowers held above water; 'Charlie's Choice', changeable, apricot-yellow turning to nearly red; 'Colorado', salmon, deepening near center; 'Fire Crest', scented clear pink flowers with red stamens; 'Gladstoneana', large white flowers with gold stamens; 'Gonnère', large pure white flowers; 'James Brydon', large-cupped, bright red, scented flowers; 'Pink Sensation', rich pink flowers held above water; 'Texas Dawn', large yellow flowers; 'William Falconer', blood red flowers with yellow stamens.

The Marliacean hybrids were originated by Joseph Marliac in the mid-nineteenth century. Many of the hardy hybrids he developed are still extremely popular, such as: 'Marliacea Albida', white; 'Marliacea Carnea', soft pink with yellow stamens; 'Marliacea Chromatella', soft yellow; 'Marliacea Ignea', deep crimson. Zones 3–10.

TROPICAL DAY-BLOOMING HYBRIDS

☀ ⚘ ↔ 3–12 ft (0.9–3.5 m)
↕ 3–15 in (8–38 cm)

These hybrids need a water temperature of 70°F (21°C). Some produce flowers to 15 in (38 cm) wide. All colors, including blue shades, are covered. Flowers are usually held above the foliage. 'Evelyn Randig', hot pink flowers; 'General Pershing', deep pink fragrant flowers, to 12 in (30 cm) across; 'Margaret Randig', deep blue-purple scented flowers; 'Marion Strawn', starry, white, fragrant flowers; 'Mrs George H. Pring', scented, white, star-shaped flowers, to 10 in (25 cm) across; 'Pamela', starry sky blue flowers; 'Panama Pacific', deep plum flowers with yellow stamens; and 'Pink Platter', open soft pink flowers. Zones 11–12.

TROPICAL NIGHT-BLOOMING HYBRIDS

☀ ⚘ ↔ 3–12 ft (0.9–3.5 m)
↕ 3–15 in (8–38 cm)

These plants need a water temperature of 70°F (21°C). Flowers open about dusk and close by the following noon. They are mostly in shades of red, pink, and white. 'Emily Grant Hutchings', rich pinkish red cupped flowers, to 12 in (30 cm) wide; 'Mrs George Hitchcock', large clear pink flowers

Nymphaea, Hybrid Cultivar, Hardy, 'Anne Emmet'

Nymphaea, Hybrid Cultivar, Hardy, 'Charles de Meurville'

Nymphaea, Hybrid Cultivar, Hardy, 'Colorado'

Nymphaea, Hybrid Cultivar, Hardy, 'Conqueror'

Nymphaea, Hybrid Cultivar, Hardy, 'Ellisiana'

Nymphaea, Hybrid Cultivar, Hardy, 'Escarboucle'

Nymphaea, Hybrid Cultivar, Hardy, 'Golden Fascination'

Nymphaea, Hybrid Cultivar, Hardy, 'Laydecker Rosea Prolifera'

Nymphaea, Hybrid Cultivar, Hardy, 'Marliacea Carnea'

Nymphaea, Hybrid Cultivar, Hardy, 'Marliacea Chromatella'

N., HC, H, 'Marliacea Gloriosa'

N., HC, Hardy, 'Perry's Fire Opal'

N., HC, Hardy, 'Pink Grapefruit'

N., HC, Hardy, 'Réné Gérard'

N., HC, Hardy, 'Texas Dawn'

Nymphaea, Hybrid Cultivar, Tropical Day-Blooming, 'Key Lime'

Nymphaea, Hybrid Cultivar, Tropical Day-Blooming, 'Isamorada'

Nymphaea, HC, Tropical Day-Blooming, 'Margaret Randig'

Nymphaea, HC, Tropical Day-Blooming, 'Marion Strawn'

Nymphaea, Hybrid Cultivar, Tropical Day-Blooming, 'St Louis'

Nymphaea, HC, Tropical Day-Blooming, 'Star of Zanzibar'

Nymphaea, HC, Tropical Day-Blooming, 'Suwanee Blue Mist'

Nymphaea, Hybrid Cultivar, Tropical Day-Blooming, 'Tina'

Nymphaea, HC, Tropical Night-Blooming, 'Trudy Slocum'

Nymphaea, HC, Tropical Night-Blooming, 'Woods Blue Goddess'

Nymphoides crenata, in the wild, Bollon, Queensland, Australia

Nyssa sinensis

Nyssa sylvatica

Nyssa sylvatica 'Wisley Bonfire'

with orange stamens; **'Red Flare'**, starry, vivid red, scented flowers; **'Rosa de Noche'**, pink flowers with yellow centers; **'Sir Galahad'**, flowers of starry white with yellow stamens; **'Sturtevantii'**, pearly pink scented flowers; and **'Trudy Slocum'**, large, flat, white flowers with yellow stamens. Zones 11–12.

NYMPHOIDES

This genus of about 20 species of aquatic perennial herbs belongs to the bogbean (Menyanthaceae) family. They are of cosmopolitan distribution. The floating leaves are oval to round with heart-shaped bases. Starry, 5-petalled flowers of yellow or white are borne on stems above the water. CULTIVATION: Most species are invasive and not suitable for small ponds. Grow in full sun, in still water, planting the rhizomes in a rich soil mix. Propagate from seed or by division.

Nymphoides crenata

WAVY MARSHWORT

☼ ❁ ↔ 6 ft (1.8 m) ↑ 2–5 ft (0.6–1.5 m)
Australian species, widespread on inland plains, growing in slow-flowing or still water up to 5 ft (1.5 m) deep, can persist on drying mud. Floating leaves to 5 in (12 cm) wide with shallow wavy teeth. Flowers yellow, to

1¼ in (35 mm) across, with fringed petals, in many-flowered umbels, in spring–autumn. Zones 9–11.

Nymphoides peltata

YELLOW FLOATING HEART

☼ ❁ ↔ 3–8 ft (0.9–2.4 m) ↑ 12 in (30 cm)
Native to temperate Eurasia and naturalized in North America. Small, mottled, heart-shaped, floating leaves. Bright yellow, starry, fringed flowers, in summer. Zones 6–10.

NYSSA

This is a small genus that includes about 5 species of deciduous trees from North America and eastern and southeastern Asia. It is a member of the dogwood (Cornaceae) family. They are all noted for their spectacular foliage in autumn, which ranges in color from soft green, pale yellow, gold to orange, and brown. Most species inhabit moist land on the edges of streams, lakes, and swamps, and are rarely successful on dry soils. The leaves are simple, the flowers are

inconspicuous, and the fruits small and bluish. They are named after the water nymph of Greek mythology because of their liking for a reliable water supply.
CULTIVATION: These plants prefer well-drained, moist, fertile soil in full sun or part-shade. Little pruning is required, apart from the removal of competing leaders in the early stages. Propagate from seeds collected as soon as they are ripe in autumn. Sow immediately, before they dry out. Alternatively, they can be propagated from half-hardened cuttings in mid-summer.

Nyssa aquatica

COTTON GUM, TUPELO GUM, WATER TUPELO

☼ ❁ ↔ 15 ft (4.5 m) ↑ 50 ft (15 m)
Native to southeastern USA, rare both in the wild and in cultivation. Erect stems, dome-shaped crown. Leaves ovate-oblong, downy underneath, serrated. Flowers greenish white, in axillary clusters, in summer. Fruit deep mauve. Zones 5–10.

Nyssa sinensis

CHINESE TUPELO

☼ ❁ ↔ 30 ft (9 m) ↑ 40 ft (12 m)
Rare species from China, beautiful small tree or large shrub, open habit. Leaves narrowly ovate, to 6 in (15 cm) long, juvenile foliage red. Leaves turn to almost every shade of red and yellow, in autumn. Zones 7–10.

Nyssa sylvatica ★

BLACK GUM, BLACK TUPELO, SOUR GUM, TUPELO

☼ ❁ ↔ 30 ft (9 m) ↑ 50 ft (15 m)
Native to North America, from Canada to the Gulf of Mexico. Deciduous tree with predominantly horizontal branches. Smooth-edged leaves, shiny dark green, paler beneath; turn various shades of orange, scarlet, and purplish red in autumn. Small bluish black fruits. Thrives in wet marshy conditions. **'Sheffield Park'**, leaves start to color 2 to 3 weeks earlier than type; **'Wisley Bonfire'**, fine autumn coloring, symmetrical form. Zones 3–10.

Oberonia gracilis, in the wild, New Guinea

OBERONIA

This is a sympodial epiphytic orchid genus (family Orchidaceae) with over 300 species, found from Africa through Southeast Asia to the Pacific Islands. It is a poorly studied genus due to the very tiny blooms and similarity when not in flower. The succulent leaves, produced in 2 ranks, are generally broad, flattened, and pointed at the apex. They bloom only once off the main growth, from between the last 2 leaves, and the inflorescence is often longer than the plant. They are clump-forming and many are attractive plants even when not in bloom. The genus is named after Oberon, king of the fairies.
CULTIVATION: These botanical orchids are seen only in specialist orchid collections. They require warm, humid, shaded conditions throughout the year and are best grown on slabs of moisture-retentive tree-fern or cork, with some sphagnum moss covering the rootball. These plants rarely succeed in pots, as the roots require a lot of aeration.

Oberonia gracilis
☼ ❀ ↔ 4–8 in (10–20 cm)
↑ 4–16 in (10–40 cm)
From New Guinea. Pendent habit; strappy bright green leaves. Inflorescences produce up to 100 round, tiny, tan to brown flowers. Zones 10–12.

OBREGONIA

This single-species genus of small cacti from the limestone soils of the region around Tamaulipas, Mexico, belongs in the family Cactaceae. The genus is named after the former president of Mexico, Alvaro Obregon (1880–1928). The appealing form, rarity, and slow growth rate of this plant have all added to its attractiveness, factors which have resulted in its overcollection in its very restricted habit. It is now listed in Appendix I of CITES (Convention on International Trade in Endangered Species of Wild Flora and Fauna).
CULTIVATION: Easily grown in a well-drained mineralized soil with some added limestone. Can only be raised

from seed, as it never offsets. Benefits from some shade in the height of summer. Rest in winter.

Obregonia denegrii
☼ ❀ ↔ 1–10 in (2.5–25 cm)
↑ 2–4 in (5–10 cm)
From limestone soils in the valley of Jaumave, Tamaulipas, Mexico. Solitary, flattened, disc-like plant. It barely grows above soil level, has long, thick, turnip-like tap root. Short triangular tubercles, keeled on lower sides, arranged in spirals. Thin weak spines, at tips of tubercles, deciduous with age. Tiny, cream, funnelform flowers. Seed pods club-shaped, brownish white. Zones 9–11.

OCHAGAVIA

The 4 members of this genus in the bromeliad (Bromeliaceae) family are native to Chile. They form clumps of dense non-water-retaining rosettes. The leaves are very numerous, narrow and stiff, with many teeth on the edges. The stemless globular flowerhead, with up to 50 flowers, is sunk in the middle of the leaf rosette and surrounded with bright red bracts. The flower petals are mainly in shades of red. The innermost leaves are sometimes reddish at the base. These plants require winter temperatures down to around 32°F (0°C) in order to promote flowering.
CULTIVATION: *Ochagavia* species are recommended for pot culture in a greenhouse or conservatory in cold-temperate areas, or for outdoor culture in cool- to warm-temperate areas. Water when potting mix is dry. Do not overfertilize. Propagation is mainly from offsets.

Ochagavia carnea
☼ ❀ ↔ 32 in (80 cm) ↑ 20 in (50 cm)
Species originating from Chile. Clumping plant of dense rosettes, to 20 in (50 cm) in diameter. Leaves green, stiff, with strongly toothed edges. The flowerhead bears up to 50 pink-petalled flowers, surrounded by large fluffy pink bracts, in winter. Zones 8–10.

Ochagavia carnea

Ochagavia elegans
☼ ❀ ↔ 12 in (30 cm) ↑ 16 in (40 cm)
From the Juan Fernandez Islands of Robinson Crusoe fame. Clumping plant, with dense rosettes of stiff green leaves with toothed edges. Flowerhead with up to 40 purplish red flowers, surrounded by small red bracts, in winter. Zones 9–11.

OCHNA

There are around 80 species of deciduous and evergreen trees and shrubs included in this genus of the family Ochnaceae, all occurring in Africa and Asia. The leaves of all species are simple, alternate, and have toothed margins. The flowers are borne singly or in clusters, with 5 to 10 petals that fall soon after the flower opens. In fruit, the 5 sepals and the floral receptacle become swollen and brightly colored, with 3 or more fleshy 1-seeded fruitlets attached, usually contrasting in color when ripe.
CULTIVATION: These plants are marginally frost hardy, so they need shelter from frosts in their early years, but otherwise they can be grown in a range of well-drained soils in full sun or part-shade in tropical and subtropical climates. Propagation is from seed or cuttings.

Ochna kirkii
☼ ❀ ↔ 7 ft (2 m) ↑ 10 ft (3 m)
Little-known species, occurring in Mozambique along streamsides. Leaves are thick, leathery, oblong to elliptic, heart-shaped base, with toothed margins. Yellow flowers, borne in terminal clusters, in spring. Bright red calyx. Zones 10–11.

Ochna kirkii, fruitlet

Ochagavia elegans

Ochna natalitia

Ochna pulchra

Ochna serrulata

Ochna natalitia

YELLOW IPOMOEA

☼ ❄ ↔ 7 ft (2 m) ↕ 15 ft (4.5 m)

Shrub or small tree from KwaZulu-Natal, South Africa. Glossy elliptic leaves, bronze when young. Heads of fragrant soft to bright yellow flowers, in spring to summer. Fleshy red calyx. Black fruitlets. Zones 10–12.

Ochna pulchra

PEELING PLANE

☼ ❄ ↔ 10 ft (3 m) ↕ 25 ft (8 m)

Small tree from open woodland in southern Africa. Pale gray peeling bark. Leaves elliptic to oval, light green to yellowish green. Fragrant pale yellow or greenish yellow flowers, in spring. Reddish fleshy calyx, black kidney-shaped fruitlets. Zones 9–10.

Ochna serrulata

CARNIVAL BUSH, MICKEY MOUSE PLANT

☼ ❄ ↔ 7 ft (2 m) ↕ 12 ft (3.5 m)

Small tree from eastern South Africa. Bark smooth, brown. Leaves elliptic, glossy dark green, paler below, toothed margins. Fragrant yellow flowers, in spring–early summer. Fleshy bright red calyx, fruitlets globular, black when ripe. Serious environmental weed. Zones 9–11.

OCIMUM

BASIL

This genus encompasses 35 species of annuals and perennials from tropical and subtropical Africa and Asia that are known for their aromatic foliage. These herbs belong to the mint (Lamiaceae) family and are generally erect bushy plants, with a distinctive branching habit and narrow oval to elliptic leaves. Their foliage varies from pale to dark green through to dark red and purple. Whorls of tiny tubular flowers appear on short spikes in summer and vary from white to creamy green. The foliage is used to flavor a range of dishes. These herbs have become favorites with many, and they are often referred to as the summer herb. Basil was probably first

Ocimum basilicum 'Lemon Sweet Danny'

cultivated in India, where it is sacred and is dedicated to the gods Vishnu and Krishna.

CULTIVATION: Some basil species may be temperamental to grow. These plants need moist well-drained soil in a warm sunny position to thrive and do not tolerate frost or cold temperatures. Pinch back plants regularly to encourage bushy growth. Propagate from seed in summer for the annual species and from stem cuttings for the perennial species.

Ocimum basilicum

BASIL, SWEET BASIL

☼ ✤ ↔ 12 in (30 cm)
↕ 12–24 in (30–60 cm)

From tropical and subtropical Asia. Upright, erect, bushy annual. Oval mid-green leaves, sometimes slightly serrated around edges, often hairy on topside of leaf. Foliage is used to flavor many dishes. Whorls of creamy white flowers, on short spikes, in summer. Can be invasive, so best grown in pots. Dispose of seed carefully. *O. b.* var. *minimum* ★, (Greek bush basil) small compact leaves on very tight compact plant, short white flowers in summer, good flavor. *O. b.* 'Dark Opal' (purple leaf basil), dark red-purple, sometimes curly leaves, pale creamy green stems, pale pink flowers; '**Fino Verde Compatto**' (Italian basil), compact plant, small mid-green leaves; '**Lemon Sweet Danny**', pointed, pale green, lemon-scented foliage, weak plant; '**Mini Purple**', dwarf compact plant, dark purple

Ocimum basilicum 'Purple Ruffles'

Ocimum basilicum

Ocimum basilicum 'Dark Opal'

Ocimum basilicum var. *minimum*

O. b. 'Fino Verde Compatto'

Ocimum basilicum 'Genova'

Ocimum basilicum 'Red Rubin'

Ocimum basilicum 'Greek Mini'

Ocimum basilicum 'Holy'

Ocimum basilicum 'Minette'

Ocimum basilicum 'Napolitano'

Ocimum basilicum 'Osmin'

Ocimum basilicum 'Ruffles'

Ocimum basilicum 'Siam Queen'

Ocimum basilicum 'Sweet Dani'

Ocimum basilicum 'Valentino'

foliage, hint of green through leaves; 'Napolitano', large, crinkled, lettuce-like leaves; 'Purple Ruffles', strongly aromatic, large, purplish, glossy leaves, serrated edges; 'Red Rubin' ★, a selection from 'Dark Opal', more uniform and compact habit, foliage stays rich red-purple for longer in summer; 'Ruffles' ★, green foliage, curly and frilly leaf edges; 'Siam Queen', bushy, compact plant, long, narrow, fragrant leaves, rosy purple flowers, high foliage yields make it popular in the culinary trade, licorice flavor. Zones 10–12.

Ocimum tenuiflorum
syn. *Ocimum sanctum*
HOLY BASIL

☀ ❄ ↔ 24 in (60 cm) ↑ 36 in (90 cm)

Tall-branched deciduous shrub from India and Malaysia. Slender upright growth habit. Lightly hairy mid-green leaves, on purplish stems with visible hairs. Very spicy and pungent fragrance. Pale pink to purple flowers, yellow stamens, in summer. Zones 9–10.

× *ODONTIODA*

Belonging to the family Orchidaceae, this a cool-growing bigeneric orchid hybrid between the sympodial genera *Odontoglossum* and *Cochlioda*. The South American *Cochlioda noezliana* has given its bright red color to many of its hybrids. Sometimes the *Cochlioda* influence is barely noticeable as the hybrids have been repeatedly back-crossed onto other odontoglossums. CULTIVATION: These plants like cool, moist, humid conditions in a part-shaded position, and thrive in pots. Use sphagnum moss or a fine grade bark mixture with perlite. Keep well-watered. Propagate by division.

× *Odontioda* Hybrids

☀ ❄ ↔ 8–24 in (20–60 cm)
↑ 8–36 in (20–90 cm)

Most of these hybrids are winter and spring flowerers, with the bloom size from 2–5 in (5–12 cm). **Avranches** ★, one of the albino hybrids developed from the white-flowered forms of the species; **Durham River**, the full shape from its *Odontoglossum* parent, with intense color coming from *Cochlioda*; **Heatonensis × *Odontoglossum* Starlight**, an unregistered hybrid, with its spidery shape coming from *Odontoglossum cirrhosum*; **La Fosse**, with a most unusual color combination of maroon, white, and yellow. Zones 9–10.

× *ODONTOBRASSIA*

A cool- to warm-growing bigeneric orchid hybrid between the sympodial genera *Odontoglossum* and *Brassia* (family Orchidaceae). These spidery-bloomed hybrids, an influence from the *Brassia* parent, are more tolerant of both cool and high temperatures and are reliable flowerers every year. They grow in a wide range of conditions and have long-lasting blooms, and are popular flowering pot plants. CULTIVATION: These hybrids grow well in pots of a bark-based medium

× *Odontobrassia* Kenneth Biven 'Santa Barbara'

and they require frequent watering and fertilizing when in active growth. They may bloom at any time, but flowers are more frequently produced in the warmer months. They are suitable for bright humid conditions, out of direct sunlight, and require moisture throughout the year, with the frequency tapered off in winter months. Propagate by division.

× *Odontobrassia* Kenneth Biven 'Santa Barbara'

☀ ✈ ↔ 8–27 in (20–70 cm)
↑ 8–40 in (20–100 cm)

Dark chocolate, 5 in (12 cm) wide blooms with yellowish tips and a white labellum. A primary hybrid between *Odontoglossum cariniferum* and *Brassia arcuigera*. Zones 10–12.

× *Odontioda,* Hybrid, Ruby Eyes

× *Odontioda,* Hybrid, (Nichirei Sunrise × Ingmar)

× *Odontioda* Hybrid, Heatonensis × *Odontoglossum* Starlight

× *Odontioda,* Hybrid, Bugle Boy

× *Odontioda,* Hybrid, Avranches

× *Odontioda,* Hybrid, La Fosse

× *Odontioda,* H, Durham River

× *Odontioda,* H, Sheila Hands

× *Odontocidium*, Hybrid, Artur Elle

× *Odontocidium*, Hybrid, Bittersweet 'Sophie'

× *Odontocidium*, Hybrid, Golden Trident

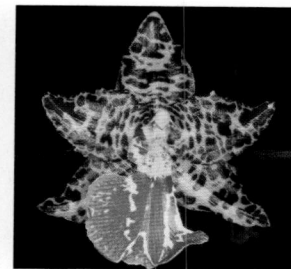

× *Odontocidium*, Hybrid, Tropic Tiger

× *Odontocidium*, Hybrid, Tigersun 'Nugget'

× *Odontocidium*, Hybrid, Dorothy Wisnom 'Golden Gate'

× *Odontocidium*, Hybrid, Mayfair 'Golden Gate'

× *Odontocidium*, Hybrid, Bittersweet 'Toffee'

× *Odontocidium*, Hybrid, Hansueli Isler

× ODONTOCIDIUM

This is a hardy bigeneric orchid hybrid, a combination of *Odontoglossum* and *Oncidium* (family Orchidaceae). More warmth tolerant than odontoglossums, these sympodial hybrids will thrive in a range of temperatures if kept in a humid environment out of direct sunlight. They have long-lasting blooms and are increasing in popularity as flowering pot plants.

CULTIVATION: These plants will grow well in pots and must be kept well watered. Use sphagnum moss or a fine grade bark mixture with perlite. Grow in part-shade. Propagate by division.

× *Odontocidium* Hybrids

☀ ◐ ↔ 8–24 in (20–60 cm)
↑ 8–36 in (20–90 cm)

These hybrids often have tall spikes of medium-sized flowers in impressive numbers. Most are winter and spring flowerers. **Bittersweet 'Sophie'** is a popular and variable hybrid; **Bittersweet 'Toffee'** is another example of this grex; **Dorothy Wisnom 'Golden Gate'** ★, one of the finest odontocidiums, with large infusions of *Odontoglossum crispum*, *Oncidium leucochilum*, and *Oncidium tigrinum* in its ancestry; **Mayfair 'Golden Gate'**, large, shapely, bright yellow to gold blooms; and **Tropic Tiger**, 7 different orchid

species in its pedigree, with green blooms overlaid with dark maroon-brown blotches, and contrasting deep red labellum. Zones 9–11.

ODONTOGLOSSUM

This family Orchidaceae genus of about 60 cool-growing orchids from mountainous regions of South America is related to *Oncidium* and *Miltoniopsis*. Most have short to long spikes of large, showy, yellow and brown blooms, often spidery. The popular ornamentals have been the species with white and pink flowers and wider segments, giving the effect of a round bloom. There are many hybrids in *Odontoglossum* and its combinations with related genera. Some of the more popular include × *Colmanara* (× *Miltonia* × *Oncidium*), × *Odontioda* (× *Cochlioda*), and × *Odontocidium* (× *Oncidium*).

CULTIVATION: Grow in pots and keep well-watered. Use sphagnum moss or a fine grade bark mixture with perlite in a 5:1 ratio. They thrive in cool growing conditions in a part-shaded position. Propagate by division.

Odontoglossum crispum

☀ ◐ ↔ 4–16 in (10–40 cm)
↑ 5–32 in (12–80 cm)

From Colombia, this is undisputably the queen of the genus. Can have over

12 large, widely opening, 3 in (8 cm) wide blooms with broad segments, often with rounded and finely serrated edges. Color varies from sparkling white to pale rose, spotted or blotched with red or purple. Zones 9–10.

Odontoglossum wyattianum

☀ ◐ ↔ 4–12 in (10–30 cm)
↑ 5–24 in (12–60 cm)

Found in mossy cloud forests at around 6,560 feet (2,000 m) in Peru and Ecuador. Up to 8 tan-brown, 3 in (8 cm) wide blooms with a contrasting, broad, 2-toned purple labellum. Closely related to *O. harryanum*. Zones 9–11.

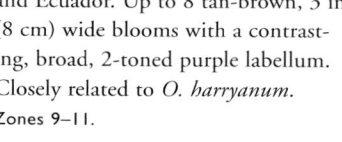

Odontoglossum wyattianum

Odontoglossum, Hybrid, Mimosa 'Oda Marcet'

Odontoglossum Hybrids

☀ ◐ ↔ 8–24 in (20–60 cm)
↑ 8–36 in (20–90 cm)

Mostly winter- and spring-flowering hybrids, with a bloom size of 1½–5 in (3.5–12 cm). (**Augres** × *nobile*), unregistered hybrid, white blooms, contrasting yellow labellum, deep pink border; (**Holiday Gold** × **Geyser Gold**), golden yellow hybrid; **Illustre**, red-brown with white markings; **La Hougue Bie**, well-defined yellow, white, and tan blotches; **Margarete Holm**, white, yellow, and maroon markings; and **Mimosa 'Oda Marcet'**, vivid plum-purple blooms with a velvety texture. Zones 9–10.

Odontoglossum, Hybrid, Illustre

O., H, (Holiday Gold × Geyser Gold)

O., Hybrid, (Augres × *nobile*)

O., Hybrid, La Hougue Bie

O., Hybrid, Margarete Holm

× *Odontonia* Susan Bogdanow

× *Odontonia* Bartley Schwarz

ODONTONEMA

Native to the tropical regions of America, this genus in the acanthus (Acanthaceae) family consists of some 25 species of evergreen perennial herbs and shrubs with opposite pairs of simple, glossy green, smooth-edged leaves. They are grown for their waxy-textured, 2-lipped or 5-lobed, tubular flowers in red, yellow, or white that are carried in upright terminal spikes or, in some species, drooping sprays. CULTIVATION: Frost tender, these warm-climate plants need rich soil and regular watering. They like well-drained soil in full sun or bright filtered light in a spot sheltered from wind. Keep them neat and bushy by pinching out the growing tips. Propagate from cuttings in summer.

Odontonema callistachyum
syn. *Odontonema strictum*
FIRESPIKE
☀ ✦ ↔ 26 in (65 cm) ↑ 6 ft (1.8 m)
Evergreen shrub, native of Central America. Upright growth habit, with glossy, wavy-edged, oblong leaves tapering to a fine point. Showy inflorescences of waxy-textured crimson flowers, borne at the branch tips, through most of year. Excellent container plant for large conservatories. Zones 10–12.

Odontonema schomburgkianum
☀ ✦ ↔ 24 in (60 cm) ↑ 6 ft (1.8 m)
Erect sparsely branched shrub from Colombia. Pale green leaves, lance-shaped to oblong, to 8 in (20 cm) long. Waxy crimson to scarlet flowers, in slender drooping racemes to 3 ft (0.9 m) long, in spring. Zones 10–12.

Odontonema tubiforme
☀/◑ ✦ ↔ 3–5 ft (0.9–1.5 m) ↑ 3–5 ft (0.9–1.5 m)
Stiff erect shrub, native to Central America. Broadly oval, shiny, deeply veined, green leaves. Narrow, bright red, tubular flowers, in dense racemes, throughout the year. Zones 10–12.

× ODONTONIA

This bigeneric orchid hybrid genus is a combination of *Odontoglossum* and *Miltonia* (family Orchidaceae). These sympodial hybrids often have spikes of up to 12 medium-sized flowers. They are more warmth tolerant than odonto-glossums and will thrive in a range of temperatures if kept in a humid environment out of direct sunlight. These orchids have long-lasting blooms and sometimes flower more than once a year. Most are spring flowerers. CULTIVATION: Grow in pots, in sphagnum moss or a fine grade bark mixture with 10 percent perlite added.

Odontonema callistachyum

Oemleria cerasiformis

They need abundant water throughout the year and prefer a part-shaded position. Propagate by division.

× *Odontonia* Bartley Schwarz ★
◑ ⚘ ↔ 8–24 in (20–60 cm) ↑ 8–36 in (20–90 cm)
Hybrid with upright inflorescences of up to 10 plum-colored blooms, 2 in (5 cm) wide, with a contrasting predominantly pure white labellum. Zones 9–11.

× *Odontonia* Susan Bogdanow
◑ ⚘ ↔ 8–24 in (20–60 cm) ↑ 8–36 in (20–90 cm)
A hybrid with large blooms, up to 3½ in (9 cm) wide, pinkish cream overlaid with darker purple to red spotting. Zones 9–11.

OEMLERIA

This single-species genus, belonging to the rose (Rosaceae) family, consists of a deciduous shrub that is closely related to *Prunus*. It is found in the moist woodlands of North America's west coast. The slender erect branches have oblong, glossy, green leaves that are gray and slightly downy beneath. White male and female flowers are borne on separate plants. CULTIVATION: Suitable for woodland plantings and shady borders. Grow in good moist soil in a shady situation.

Prune after flowering to remove old and dead shoots. Propagate from seed, cuttings, or the removal of suckers.

Oemleria cerasiformis ★
syn. *Osmaronia cerasiformis*
OREGON PLUM, OSO BERRY
☀ ❄ ↔ 12 ft (3.5 m) ↑ 8 ft (2.4 m)
Found along North America's west coast, from British Columbia, Canada, to California, USA. Suckering shrub, smooth gray stems. Spring foliage has a very fresh appearance. Dainty white flowers, in pendulous racemes, with a fragrance reminiscent of almonds, in spring. Plum-like fruits ripening to purple on female trees. Zones 6–10.

OENANTHE

This genus in the carrot (Apiaceae) family contains 30 species of perennial herbs. They are native to damp habitats of the Northern Hemisphere and southern Africa. The foliage is usually pinnately divided into small leaflets, and the tiny white flowers are borne on umbels, typical of the family. Some species are very poisonous while, conversely, *O. javanica* is cultivated as a vegetable in Asia. CULTIVATION: These plants are suitable for naturalizing in wild gardens. Grow in damp fertile soil in full sun/shade. Propagate from cuttings or seed or by division.

Odontonema schomburgkianum

Odontonema tubiforme

Oenothera 'Crown Imperial'

Oenothera 'Lemon Sunset'

Oenanthe javanica

syn. *Oenanthe japonica*

WATER CELERY, WATER DROPWORT

☼/◐ ❄ ↔ 12–16 in (30–40 cm)
↑ 12–16 in (30–40 cm)

Found from India to Japan and into southeastern Asia. Grows in very boggy ground. The divided foliage resembles celery leaves. Umbels of small white flowers in summer. Grown as a leafy vegetable crop in Asia. '**Flamingo**', variegated form with green, cream, and pink leaves. Zones 9–12.

OENOTHERA

EVENING PRIMROSE

A genus of more than 120 species of annuals, biennials, and perennials in the evening-primrose (Onagraceae) family, found in temperate zones of the Americas. Some have tap roots and tend to be upright, others have fibrous roots and a more sprawling habit. Apart from their use in homeopathic medicines, these plants are grown mainly for their short-lived but pretty summer flowers, which are cup-shaped, 4-petalled, and mainly yellow, sometimes pink, in color. The common name reflects the predominantly yellow flower color and the fact that many species open from evening or night, sometimes not lasting beyond the following morning. Elongated seed capsules follow. CULTIVATION: Mostly very hardy, these tough adaptable plants prefer full sun and light, gritty, free-draining soil. Summer watering produces stronger growth, but they will tolerate drought if necessary. Fibrous-rooted

species can be divided when dormant, otherwise propagate from seed or basal cuttings. May self-sow and naturalize.

Oenothera acaulis

☼ ❄ ↔ 16–24 in (40–60 cm) ↑ 6 in (15 cm)

Chilean biennial or perennial. Spreading clump of often red-tinted stems. Irregularly lobed pinnate leaves. White flowers, ageing to pale pink, to 3 in (8 cm) wide, in summer. Zones 5–10.

Oenothera biennis

COMMON EVENING PRIMROSE

☼ ❄ ↔ 16–20 in (40–50 cm) ↑ 5 ft (1.5 m)

Annual or biennial from eastern North America. Basal rosettes of broad lance-shaped leaves, shallowly toothed. Erect flower stems, numerous, 1 in (25 mm) wide, bright yellow flowers open from red-tinted buds, color deepening with age, in summer–autumn. Zones 4–9.

Oenothera caespitosa

FRAGRANT EVENING PRIMROSE, WHITE EVENING PRIMROSE

☼ ❄ ↔ 24 in (60 cm)
↑ 4–10 in (10–25 cm)

Low, bushy, mounding perennial from western USA. Loose rosettes of variably sized leaves, narrow lance- to spatula-shaped, shallowly toothed, wavy edges. Fragrant white flowers, to 2½ in (6 cm) wide, in summer. Zones 4–9.

Oenothera 'Crown Imperial'

☼ ❄ ↔ 12 in (30 cm)
↑ 16–20 in (40–50 cm)

Hybrid of undeclared parentage. Forms clump of bright green, lance-shaped,

basal leaves. Upright flower stems, fritillary-like heads of bright yellow flowers, to over 1¼ in (30 mm) wide, in summer. Zones 7–10.

Oenothera elata

☼ ❄ ↔ 12 in (30 cm) ↑ 40 in (100 cm)

North American perennial. Basal rosettes, gray-green, lance-shaped leaves. Upright flower stems; heads of many bright yellow flowers, to 2 in (5 cm) wide, in summer. *O. e.* subsp. *hookeri*, shorter, pale yellow flowers, widely studied due to medically promising extracts. Zones 7–10.

Oenothera fruticosa

☼ ❄ ↔ 12–16 in (30–40 cm)
↑ 20–32 in (50–80 cm)

Sometimes short-lived biennial or perennial from eastern North America. Leaves to over 4 in (10 cm) long, lance-shaped, midrib and stems usually red-tinted. Heads of golden yellow flowers, in summer. *O. f.* subsp. *glauca*, broad blue-green leaves, red-tinted when young. *O. f.* '**Fyrverkeri**' (syns 'Feuerwerkeri', 'Fireworks'), foliage tinted purple-red, bright yellow flowers. Zones 4–9.

Oenothera glazioviana

LARGE-FLOWERED EVENING PRIMROSE

☼/◐ ❄ ↔ 16–24 in (40–60 cm)
↑ 3–5 ft (0.9–1.5 m)

Erect biennial; originated in Europe, possibly natural self-perpetuating hybrid between introduced species. Basal rosettes of finely hairy, broad, lance-shaped leaves. Heads of bright yellow flowers with red sepals, in summer. Widespread, generally considered a weed. Zones 3–10.

Oenothera 'Lemon Sunset'

☼ ❄ ↔ 16–32 in (40–80 cm)
↑ 40 in (100 cm)

Erect hybrid perennial of uncertain parentage. Forms mounding clump of

small deep green leaves. Red stems; fragrant flowers, to 4 in (10 cm) wide, light yellow, ageing to deep pink or red, in summer. Zones 5–9.

Oenothera macrocarpa

MISSOURI PRIMROSE, OZARK SUNDROPS

☼ ❄ ↔ 16–32 in (40–80 cm)
↑ 8–16 in (20–40 cm)

Spreading, sometimes mounding perennial from south-central USA. Stems initially erect then sprawling; somewhat downy leaves, to 3 in (8 cm) long. Bright yellow flowers, to 4 in (10 cm) wide, in summer. Zones 5–9.

Oenothera perennis

SUNDROPS

☼ ❄ ↔ 16–32 in (40–80 cm)
↑ 8–20 in (20–50 cm)

Sprawling, often partly erect perennial from eastern North America. Wiry, sometimes branching stems. Narrow leaves, sparsely hairy, often irregularly toothed. Open heads of bright yellow flowers, in summer. Zones 5–9.

Oenothera speciosa

WHITE EVENING PRIMROSE

☼ ❄ ↔ 12–24 in (30–60 cm)
↑ 12–24 in (30–60 cm)

Perennial from southwestern USA and Mexico. Upright mounding habit; rosettes of broad lance-shaped leaves, usually irregularly toothed, sometimes lobed. Flowers open white, ageing to deep pink, in summer–early autumn. '**Alba**', white flowers; '**Rosea**', pale pink flowers; and '**Siskiyou**', pale pink to mauve flowers. Zones 5–10.

Oenothera versicolor

☼ ❄ ↔ 16 in (40 cm) ↑ 24 in (60 cm)

Native range unclear, possibly of garden origin. Upright perennial; red-tinted stems; narrow elliptic leaves taper to a fine point, toothed. Terminal heads of bright orange flowers ageing to red, in summer. Zones 6–10.

Oenothera speciosa 'Alba'

Oenothera speciosa 'Siskiyou'

Oldenburgia grandis

Olea capensis

Olea europaea

OLDENBURGIA

This small genus from the Western and Eastern Cape regions of South Africa contains about 4 species of shrubs and dwarf perennials, and belongs to the daisy (Asteraceae) family. The species usually encountered in cultivation is *O. grandis*, a bold shrub with an open domed habit, and stout branches topped with large, furry, smooth-edged, paddle-shaped leaves, to 10 in (25 cm) long, clustered toward the tips, and furry flower buds.

CULTIVATION: In frost-free climates grow *O. grandis* in well-drained to poor sandy soils in a sunny to hot aspect. In colder climates it is sometimes grown in a non-humid greenhouse in full light. With maturity, a well-grown plant makes a truly picturesque subject for a large rock garden or shrub border. Propagate from seed, which can be difficult to germinate, or from half-hardened cuttings, which are also difficult to strike.

Oldenburgia grandis
syn. *Oldenburgia arbuscula*
☼ ⬧ ↔ 7–10 ft (2–3 m) ↑ 7–10 ft (2–3 m)
Large open shrub native to South Africa. Paddle-shaped leaves, both sides white and woolly when young, later dark green above. Large white flower buds open to purple thistle-like flowers, to 4 in (10 cm) across, in summer. Zones 10–11.

OLEA
OLIVE

This genus, belonging to the olive (Oleaceae) family, includes some 20 species of evergreen shrubs and trees with a wide distribution in the warm-temperate areas of the world (excluding the Americas). With age, the branches become wonderfully gnarled and twisted. Each leaf is usually a simple narrow ellipse, deep green above and greenish white below. The flowers are massed in panicles. They are followed by the familiar fleshy drupes, each of which contains a hard pit or stone.

CULTIVATION: Olives vary in hardiness, though none are very frost tolerant, especially when young. If grown for their fruit, olives require a climate with distinct seasons. Flowering, cropping, and ripening are invariably best on trees grown in full sun with relatively mild winters and long hot summers that gradually decline into autumn. Olives are tolerant of most soils and are very drought tolerant once established; fertile well-drained soil will yield a better crop. Propagate from seed, heel cuttings, or suckers.

Olea capensis
BLACK IRONWOOD
☼ ⬧ ↔ 15 ft (4.5 m) ↑ 50 ft (15 m)
South African species. Glossy deep green leaves. White flowers, in spring. Small black fruits that while edible—

after appropriate treatment—are seldom used. Heartwood is very hard, sometimes used for producing small items such as bowls, utensils, and handles. Zones 9–11.

Olea europaea
COMMON OLIVE
☼ ❋ ↔ 20 ft (6 m) ↑ 20–30 ft (6–9 m)
In cultivation since ancient times, evergreen tree from the Mediterranean region. Gnarled branches, fissured bark with age. Leaves leathery, silver undersides. Very long lived. Fruit not edible off the tree, must be processed. *O. e.* subsp. *cuspidata* (syns *O. africana*, *O. cuspidata* and *O. e.* subsp. *africana*), to 25 ft (8 m) high, makes a good shade tree, self-seeds quite freely, can become invasive; leaves not silvery, pea-sized globular fruit. *O. e.* 'Manzanillo' ★, leathery leaves, edible black fruit; 'Mission', a vigorous cold-hardy cultivar. Zones 8–10.

OLEARIA
syn. *Pachystegia*

There are about 180 species of evergreen shrubs and small trees in this genus, of the daisy (Asteraceae) family. Most are native to Australia, with some from New Zealand, New Guinea, and Lord Howe Island. Foliage is sometimes aromatic and varies in size but is usually leathery with gray, white, or buff, tiny, soft hairs on the undersides. Daisy flowers range in color from white to pink, blue, and purple and are often borne so profusely that they smother the foliage.

CULTIVATION: Most species grow in well-drained moderately fertile soil in full sun or part-shade. In cool-temperate climates the majority are not reliably hardy below 23°F (−5°C) and need the protection of a warm wall. Prune after flowering to maintain a bushy habit. Some are suitable

for hedging and shelter planting, tolerating strong winds, including coastal conditions. Propagate from seed or from half-hardened cuttings taken in summer and autumn.

Olearia albida
DAISY BUSH, TANGURU
☼ ❋ ↔ 7 ft (2 m) ↑ 10 ft (3 m)
Vigorous species found in coastal forests of New Zealand's North Island. Erect shrub or small tree; with oblong leaves, downy white undersides. Large panicles of white daisy flowers, in summer–autumn. Zones 8–10.

Olearia avicenniifolia
AKEAKE
☼ ❋ ↔ 12 ft (3.5 m) ↑ 10 ft (3 m)
From New Zealand's South Island. Evergreen shrub, spreading habit, angular branches. Leaves broadly lance-shaped, thick, downy white below. Dense clusters of white scented daisy flowers, in autumn. Zones 8–10.

Olearia cheesemanii
☼ ❋ ↔ 7 ft (2 m) ↑ 12 ft (3.5 m)
Native to New Zealand, growing on banks of streams. Very floriferous shrub. Similar to *O. arborescens* but

Olearia albida

Olea europaea subsp. *cuspidata*

Olearia myrsinoides

Olearia paniculata

Olearia nummulariifolia

Olearia paniculata

has lance-shaped leaves. Larger panicles of white daisy flowers, in spring to summer. Zones 8–11.

Olearia frostii

☼ ❋ ↔ 36 in (90 cm) ↑ 24 in (60 cm)
Small shrub, native to alpine regions of Victoria, Australia. Young growth and small oblong leaves are woolly. Individual white or mauve daisy flowers, to 1¼ in (30 mm) wide, near branch ends, in summer. Zones 8–10.

Olearia furfuracea

☼ ❋ ↔ 7 ft (2 m) ↑ 8–15 ft (2.4–4.5 m)
Native of New Zealand's North Island. Well-branched shrub or small tree. Dark green oblong leaves, buff hairy coating beneath, wavy margins. Large clusters of small white daisy flowers, in summer. Zones 8–11.

Olearia ilicifolia

MOUNTAIN HOLLY

☼ ❋ ↔ 7 ft (2 m) ↑ 7 ft (2 m)
Spreading shrub, native to New Zealand. Lance-shaped spine-toothed

leaves, reminiscent of holly. Profuse clusters of white daisy flowers, in summer. Zones 8–10.

Olearia insignis

syn. *Pachystegia insignis*
MARLBOROUGH ROCK DAISY

☼ ❅ ↔ 3–7 ft (0.9–2 m) ↑ 3–7 ft (0.9–2 m)
Spreading shrub from New Zealand. White or brown down on stems and undersides of leathery oval leaves. Large, glistening, white daisy flowers with yellow centers open from felted drumstick-like heads, in summer. Zones 9–11.

Olearia lacunosa

☼ ❋ ↔ 8 ft (2.4 m) ↑ 5–12 ft (1.5–3.5 m)
Well-branched shrub, native to New Zealand, growing in forests and scrubland. Long, narrow, dark green leaves, wrinkled uppersurface, rusty brown hairy coating beneath. Panicles of white daisy flowers, from spring to summer. Zones 8–10.

Olearia macrodonta

☼ ❋ ↔ 7 ft (2 m) ↑ 7 ft (2 m)
New Zealand species; similar to the mountain holly *(O. ilicifolia)*. Wider grayish green leaves, toothed, musky aroma when crushed. Large rounded clusters of white daisy flowers, in summer. Zones 8–11.

Olearia furfuracea

Olearia myrsinoides

BLUSH DAISY BUSH

☼ ❋ ↔ 5 ft (1.5 m) ↑ 5 ft (1.5 m)
Low straggly shrub, native to eastern Australia, ranging from New South Wales to Tasmania. Dark green oblong leaves, with finely toothed margins and grayish undersides. Terminal panicles of scented flowers, with 2 to 4 white ray petals and a central disc of mauve or pale yellow, in summer. Zones 8–11.

Olearia nummulariifolia

☼ ❋ ↔ 5 ft (1.5 m) ↑ 5 ft (1.5 m)
Native to New Zealand, distinctive subalpine species, dense twiggy shrub. Small, closely packed, spoon-shaped

Olearia insignis

leaves, yellowish green above, buff hairy coating beneath. Small creamy white or pale yellow daisy flowers, in spring–summer, secondary to foliage. Zones 8–10.

Olearia odorata

☼ ❋ ↔ 7 ft (2 m) ↑ 12 ft (3.5 m)
Native to New Zealand. Evergreen shrub with wiry stems. Small, bright green, paddle-shaped leaves, with silver-gray undersides. Heads of ¼ in (6 mm) wide pale gray flowers, highly scented, in summer, especially noticeable on dull humid days and evenings. Zones 8–10.

Olearia paniculata

AKIRAHO

☼ ❋ ↔ 7 ft (2 m) ↑ 7–12 ft (2–3.5 m)
Shrub or small tree, native to New Zealand. Bark rough and furrowed. Oval leaves, light green above, with a white or buff hairy coating beneath and very wavy margins. Very small, fragrant, creamy white flowers, borne in clusters, in autumn. Frequently used for hedging and windbreaks. Does not tolerate wet conditions. Zones 8–11.

Olearia macrodonta

Olearia cheesemanii

Olearia phlogopappa

Olearia phlogopappa 'Blue Gem'

Olearia phlogopappa 'Comber's Mauve'

Olearia phlogopappa 'Rosea'

Olearia phlogopappa
DUSTY DAISY BUSH

☼ ❅ ↔ 7 ft (2 m) ↑ 8 ft (2.4 m)

Extremely floriferous species, native to eastern Australia from New South Wales to Tasmania. Variable species with narrow oblong leaves, deep green to bluish green above, white or gray hairy coating beneath. Terminal clusters of showy daisy flowers, white, pink, mauve, or blue, in spring. *O. p.* var. *subrepanda*, lower growing shrub of subalpine vegetation, generally under 3 ft (0.9 m) in height, leaves only ½ in (12 mm) long. Many selections for flower color have been made, with cultivar names such as **O. p.** 'Blue Gem', 'Comber's Mauve' ★, and 'Rosea'. Zones 8–10.

Olearia × scilloniensis

☼ ❅ ↔ 8 ft (2.4 m) ↑ 10 ft (3 m)

Originated in an English garden; parents believed to be *O. phlogopappa* and *O. stellulata*. Well-branched shrub. Dark green wavy-edged leaves, paler undersides. Crowded panicles of white daisy flowers, in spring. Zones 8–10.

Olearia solanderi

❅ ↔ 8 ft (2.4 m) ↑ 12 ft (3.5 m)

New Zealand coastal shrub. Angular stiff branches, slightly sticky yellowish hairy coating. Small, narrow, dark green leaves, white or yellow hairs beneath. Small creamy white daisy flowers, fragrant, borne along branches, in summer–autumn. Zones 8–11.

Olearia phlogopappa var. subrepanda

Olearia stellulata
syn. *Olearia lirata*
SNOW DAISY BUSH

☼ ❅ ↔ 10 ft (3 m) ↑ 10 ft (3 m)

Common species in the forests of eastern Australia. Pointed oval leaves, often toothed, grayish hairy coating beneath, slightly aromatic when crushed. Terminal clusters of daisy flowers, usually white, occasionally mauve or pink, in summer. Zones 8–11.

Olearia traversii
CHATHAM ISLAND AKEAKE

☼ ❅ ↔ 10 ft (3 m) ↑ 15 ft (4.5 m)

Shrub or small tree native to the Chatham Islands of New Zealand. Attractive, pale, deeply furrowed bark. Broadly oval leaves, shiny dark green above, white hairy coating beneath.

Insignificant summer flowers. Grown for attractive foliage, hedging, particularly in coastal areas. Zones 8–11.

OLINIA

There are only 8 species in this eastern and southern African genus, the sole member of the Oliniaceae family, which is related to the myrtle (Myrtaceae) family. These evergreen trees and shrubs have simple, smooth-edged, leathery leaves in opposite pairs. Flowers are pink or white, with separate narrow petals and sepals that often resemble one another. Fruits are small, reddish, berry-like drupes. They are grown more for shade and their attractive colorful fruits than for their small summer flowers.
CULTIVATION: Grow in full sun in reasonably fertile, moisture-retentive, yet well-drained soil. Plants will tolerate poorer soils provided drainage is good. Propagate from seed, although this can be slow and difficult to germinate. Cuttings do not strike readily.

Olinia emarginata
MOUNTAIN HARD PEAR, TRANSVAAL HARD PEAR

☼ ❅ ↔ 10–30 ft (3–9 m) ↑ 10–50 ft (3–15 m)

South African evergreen shrub or tree. Dense wide-spreading canopy. Dark green glossy leaves, in opposite pairs, pale green undersides. Clusters of small pink flowers, in summer. Glossy dark red fruits in autumn. Zones 8–11.

Olearia × scilloniensis

Olearia solanderi

Olinia emarginata

Oncidium cebolleta

OLNEYA

This single-species genus belongs to the pea-flower subfamily of the legume (Fabaceae) family. The sole member is a tree native to arid regions of southwestern North America. This evergreen tree is short-trunked, often with multiple stems, and a broad spreading crown. In periods of intense cold or drought, it is deciduous. In the wild, new leaves emerge shortly after the clusters of pea-flowers, following spring rains. The seeds are edible once they are roasted. The genus is named for Stephan Olney, a nineteenth century American botanist.
CULTIVATION: This small tree is best grown in full sun in very well-drained soil. Propagate from seed.

Olneya tesota
DESERT IRONWOOD
☀ ❄ ↔ 12–25 ft (3.5–8 m)
↑ 15–30 ft (4.5–9 m)

Native to southwestern USA and northern Mexico. Broad-crowned tree. Grayish green pinnately divided leaves, to 2 in (5 cm) long. Produces clusters of pink to light purple pea-flowers, in spring. Zones 8–10.

OMPHALODES
NAVELSEED, NAVELWORT

There are about 28 species of annuals, biennials, and perennials in this genus, which belongs to the borage (Boraginaceae) family. They are native to Europe, northern Africa, Asia, and Mexico, where they grow in habitats such as shady rocks and cliffs, damp woodland, or streamsides. The leaves vary from heart-shaped to lance-shaped and may be slightly hairy. The small blue or white flowers are borne in terminal clusters, in spring or early summer, and resemble forget-me-nots. The common and botanical names arise from the seed vessel's apparent resemblance to a navel.
CULTIVATION: Most species prefer a cool, somewhat shaded situation in any moist but well-drained soil high in organic matter. Low-growing species are suitable for rockeries or make excellent ground covers, while taller plants can be grown in the border. Propagate all species from seed in spring. Perennials can also be propagated by division in autumn, but care should be taken as they resent root disturbance.

Omphalodes cappadocica
NAVELWORT
☀ ❄ ↔ 12–18 in (30–45 cm) ↑ 8 in (20 cm)

Native to Turkey. Perennial, forming low clumps of heart-shaped leaves. Small, blue, forget-me-not flowers, in early to mid-summer. 'Cherry Ingram', taller vigorous form, deeper blue flowers; 'Starry Eyes', darker blue central stripe on each pale petal, creating a starry effect. Zones 6–9.

Omphalodes linifolia
VENUS' NAVELWORT
☀ ❄ ↔ 6–10 in (15–25 cm)
↑ 12–18 in (30–45 cm)

From western Europe. Annual with narrow grayish green leaves. Sprays of slightly scented white flowers, borne profusely in summer. Unlike other members of the genus, should be grown in a sunny situation. Zones 6–9.

Omphalodes verna
BLUE-EYED MARY, CREEPING FORGET-ME-NOT
☀ ❄ ↔ 24 in (60 cm) ↑ 6 in (15 cm)

Native to Europe. Low-growing perennial, suitable for ground cover. Long, creeping, rooting stems; pointed oval to heart-shaped leaves. White-centered, blue, forget-me-not flowers, in spring. Zones 6–9.

ONCIDIUM
DANCING LADY ORCHID

This large genus of sympodial orchids from tropical America contains over 650 different species and is a member of family Orchidaceae. In general, they bear yellow and brown flowers on long branching inflorescences and are most eye-catching when in full bloom. In many species, the labellum is the most prominent feature. Most members of this highly varied genus have a distinct pseudobulb with up to 4 leaves at the apex. Inflorescences generally appear from the leaf axil of recently matured growth. They bloom only once from the pseudobulb.
CULTIVATION: Most of the species are frequently grown mounted, which permits unimpeded development of the root system and allows for quick drying after watering. Some of the smaller species may be grown in pots. Cultural requirements are varied, and depend largely on the habitats and altitude of the particular species. The majority prefer intermediate growing conditions. Propagate by division.

Oncidium cebolleta
syn. *Oncidium longifolium*
☀ ✴ ↔ 4–16 in (10–40 cm)
↑ 8–48 in (20–120 cm)

Tropical species from West Indies and Central America; one of the "rat's tail" oncidiums. Long terete leaves resemble a rat's tail; reduced pseudobulb. Sprays of up to 30 golden yellow and brown blooms, to 1½ in (35 mm) across, in summer. Zones 11–12.

Oncidium crispum
☀/◗ ✴ ↔ 4–16 in (10–40 cm)
↑ 8–27 in (20–70 cm)

From Brazil. Branching inflorescence of predominantly brown, 3 in (8 cm) wide blooms, some yellow patches, in summer. Zones 10–12.

Omphalodes cappadocica

Omphalodes cappadocica 'Cherry Ingram'

Omphalodes cappadocica 'Starry Eyes'

Oncidium croesus

Oncidium sphacelatum

Oncidium croesus ★

☀ ⚘ ↔4–12 in (10–30 cm)
↑4–8 in (10–20 cm)

Native to Brazil. Miniature clump-forming species. Produces short spikes of up to 5 glossy, brown and yellow, 1¼ in (30 mm) wide flowers, in spring. Zones 10–12.

Oncidium flexuosum

☀/☀ ⚘ ↔8–36 in (20–90 cm)
↑8–60 in (20–150 cm)

Common and widespread species from South America. Climbing habit, with long rhizomes between the pseudobulbs, so needs to be mounted on a long piece of cork or tree-fern. Tall branching spikes bear masses of bright yellow, ¾ in (18 mm) wide, long-lasting flowers, in mid-summer. Zones 10–12.

Oncidium ornithorhynchum

☀ ⚘ ↔4–24 in (10–60 cm)
↑6–36 in (15–90 cm)

Native to Central America. This plant produces heavily branched pendent spikes of long-lasting pink and purple

Oncidium Sweet Sugar

flowers, 1 in (25 mm) tall, chocolate-scented, in winter. A cool-growing species. Zones 9–11.

Oncidium Sharry Baby 'Sweet Fragrance'

☀/☀ ⚘ ↔8–36 in (20–90 cm)
↑8–48 in (20–120 cm)

One of the most popular orchids used for the flowering pot plant industry. Can bloom a number of times during the year. Bears upright-branched spikes of reddish pink, brown, and white, 1½ in (35 mm) wide flowers, highly fragrant, smelling like chocolate. Zones 10–12.

Oncidium sphacelatum

☀/☀ ⚘ ↔8–36 in (20–90 cm)
↑8–60 in (20–150 cm)

Vigorous species native to Central America; adaptable throughout a range of climates in cultivation. Long, branched, and upright to arching inflorescences of typical brown and yellow, 1¼ in (30 mm) wide blooms, in spring. Very hardy and reliable species. Zones 10–12.

Oncidium Sweet Sugar

☀/☀ ⚘ ↔8–36 in (20–90 cm)
↑8–48 in (20–120 cm)

This hybrid enjoys high temperatures, as long as humidity is also high. Long branching inflorescences of bright

yellow, 2 in (5 cm) wide blooms, some tan markings on top of labellum and tepals. Zones 10–12.

Oncidium varicosum

DANCING LADY ORCHID

☀/☀ ⚘ ↔4–16 in (10–40 cm)
↑5–32 in (12–80 cm)

From Brazil. Upright branching inflorescences of up to 70 long-lasting, 2 in (5 cm) wide blooms with small petals and sepals that are yellow with brown markings. Labellum is the outstanding feature, large, flat, round lip, bright yellow, dominating the flower. This species has been dominant in the production of "varicosum-type" *Oncidium* hybrids. Zones 10–12.

ONCOBA

The 39 species of shrubs and small trees in this genus are native to tropical and southern Africa. This genus is a member of the governor's-plum (Flacourtiaceae) family. Their evergreen leaves may be leathery or thin and are alternately arranged; some species are armed with spines. The fragrant flowers are borne for long periods and may be red, white, or orange. They have spreading petals with prominent stamens.
CULTIVATION: In cool-temperate climates these are greenhouse plants, but in warm frost-free areas they can be grown outside where the spiny species can make an effective barrier hedge. Grow in full sun in a fertile well-drained soil. Propagate from seed.

Oncoba spinosa

SNUFF BOX TREE

☀ ⚘ ↔6 ft (1.8 m) ↑6–10 ft (1.8–3 m)

Spiny shrub from eastern and central Africa and southern Arabia. Narrow serrated-edged leaves. Fragrant white flowers, mass of yellow stamens, which fall as the flower ages, resemble the camellia. Round fruits with hard, shiny, brown shell. Used to make snuff boxes and rattles in Africa. Zones 9–12.

ONOCLEA

BEAD FERN, SENSITIVE FERN

This genus contains a single species of deciduous fern which belongs to the shield-fern (Dryopteridaceae) family. It is native to eastern North America and eastern Asia where it grows in damp grassy or woodland areas. Fronds are pale green, often bronze-pink on opening, and sterile and fertile fronds are different in appearance. The common name of sensitive fern arises because the leaflets of the sterile fronds fold together in cold weather. The other common name refers to the

bead-like leaflets of the fertile fronds.
CULTIVATION: Grow in damp soil in part-shade. Suitable for waterside and woodland gardens. Can be invasive where conditions suit. Propagate by division or from spores.

Onoclea sensibilis

☀/☀ ❄ ↔24 in (60 cm) ↑36 in (90 cm)

From eastern North America and eastern Asia. Spreading fern with triangular, pinnate, sterile fronds to 36 in (90 cm) long. Fertile fronds, to 24 in (60 cm) long, are narrow with bead-like leaflets, and persist over winter. Zones 4–9.

ONOPORDUM

A genus of about 40 thistles in the daisy (Asteraceae) family from the Mediterranean region and western and central Asia. They are gray-leafed plants, in some cases of impressive dimensions, with white cobwebbed foliage well armed with vicious spines. They are biennials and in their second year produce purple thistle-flowers on candelabra-like thorny and webbed stems, followed by the classic feathery seeds that are caught by the wind to be spread far and wide.
CULTIVATION: Grow in any sunny well-drained site. Propagation is from seed, best sown where it is to grow. Care must be taken in choice of site as these plants can become invasive out of their native environment. On reaching seeding stage the plants will look shabby and should be removed, leaving only a few seeds to start the next generation.

Onopordum acanthium

COTTON THISTLE, SCOTCH THISTLE

☀ ❄ ↔6–7 ft (1.8–2 m)
↑8–10 ft (2.4–3 m)

From southern Europe to central Asia. Impressive biennial starting as rosette of large, spiny, woolly leaves; in second year sends up branched, prickly, gray stem topped by purple thistle-flowers surrounded by vicious spines, in summer. A white-flowered form is sometimes grown. Zones 6–10.

Oncoba spinosa

Onopordum acaulon

Onosma alborosea

Ophiopogon planiscapus 'Nigrescens'

Onopordum acaulon

STEMLESS THISTLE

☼ ❄ ↔ 12–18 in (30–45 cm)
↑ 6 in (15 cm)

Native to Spain and northwestern Africa. Considered a weed in many places, this annual forms a low stemless rosette with white, woolly, spiny leaves. White or purple flowers open from yellow buds, sitting within center of rosette, in summer. Zones 7–10.

Onopordum nervosum

syn. *Onopordum arabicum*

COTTON THISTLE

☼ ❄ ↔ 30 in (75 cm) ↑ 8 ft (2.4 m)

Native to Spain and Portugal. Coarse robust biennial; can be a nuisance weed. Spiny stems; long, spiny, grayish leaves, prominently veined and hairy beneath. Rosy purple flowerheads, 2 in (5 cm) wide, in summer. Zones 8–10.

ONOSMA

This genus belongs to the borage (Boraginaceae) family and contains about 150 species of semi-evergreen biennial and perennial herbs that are native to the Mediterranean region and Asia. They are closely related to comfrey *(Symphytum)* and are bristly plants, often woody based. Their densely tufted leaves are usually oblong and hairy or bristly to varying degrees. The tubular to bell-shaped flowers hang in clusters and are mostly yellow, blue, or pink. CULTIVATION: These plants are best grown in full sun in well-drained soil. They have a dislike of wet summers, and their hairy leaves are prone to rotting in wet conditions. Suitable for rockeries or along banks. Propagate from seed or by division.

Onosma alborosea

☼ ❄ ↔ 6–12 in (15–30 cm)
↑ 6–12 in (15–30 cm)

Clump-forming perennial, native to southwestern Asia. Short, oblong, grayish green, hairy leaves. Clusters of small hanging bellflowers, creamy white, ageing to pinkish purple, for long periods in summer. Zones 7–9.

OPHIOPOGON

MONDO GRASS

Small genus of 4 species of evergreen perennials from Japan belonging to the lily-of-the-valley (Convallariaceae) family. They form clumps of grassy leaves and in summer bear small lily-like flowers of white to purple which are followed by blue berries. These plants are cultivated for their foliage and are popular both as ground covers and for edging. CULTIVATION: Grow in full sun or part-shade in moist but well-drained soil. All species will withstand at least short periods of frost but in cooler areas can be treated as bedding or container plants. Propagate from seed or by division.

Ophiopogon japonicus

☼/◐ ❄ ↔ 18 in (45 cm) ↑ 12 in (30 cm)

Native to Japan; popular species for ground cover. Very narrow, dark green, curving leaves form dense mats. White to pale lilac flowers, on short stems, in summer. 'Kyoto Dwarf', very tightly clumped, grows 2–4 in (5–10 cm) high; 'Nana', slightly taller, to 5–6 in (12–15 cm) high. Zones 7–10.

Ophiopogon planiscapus

☼/◐ ❄ ↔ 18 in (45 cm)
↑ 12–18 in (30–45 cm)

From Japan. Similar to *O. japonicus*; more usually seen as the cultivar 'Nigrescens' (syns 'Arabicus', 'Black Dragon', 'Ebony Knight'), commonly known as black mondo grass. Lower growing plant, purple-black foliage. Zones 6–10.

OPLOPANAX

Related to ginseng, this genus of 2 species of prickly, deciduous, semi-prostrate or erect shrubs in the ivy (Araliaceae) family is native to temperate areas of the Northern Hemisphere. The tan bark is covered with slender stiff prickles. The green leaves are deeply lobed. The flower panicles, which appear in late spring to midsummer, are white or greenish white and are followed by red flat berries, which are inedible. CULTIVATION: Grow in a very moist shaded area in acidic soil. Propagate from seed (which can take as long as 18 months to germinate), or from suckers and root cuttings. Layering is also an effective method of propagation. Pruning should be undertaken with great care.

Oplopanax horridus

DEVIL'S CLUB

☼/☀ ❄ ↔ 5 ft (1.5 m) ↑ 3–10 ft (0.9–3 m)

Found from Michigan to Oregon and southeast Alaska, USA. Deciduous shrub with spiny branches. Leaves similar to maple. White flowers, in pyramidal clusters, in late spring–early summer. Shiny red berries. Zones 4–9.

OPUNTIA

This genus in the cactus (Cactaceae) family contains more than 180 species that grow throughout the Americas, from southern Canada to the most southerly part of South America, and also the West Indies and Galapagos Islands. They range from high-altitude to temperate-region and tropical lowland species. They have stem segments that are highly variable. The flowers are cup- or funnel-shaped and appear in spring and summer, followed by prickly egg-shaped fruits. Some species have become invasive. Most species have bristles that break off and can irritate the skin. CULTIVATION: Opuntias do not like having their roots confined. Those grown outdoors do best in sandy, humus-enriched, well-drained soil that is moderately fertile. Frost-hardy species need protection from too much winter wet, and should be grown in full sun under glass, with the light filtered in hot summers. Feed regularly from spring to summer, and reduce or stop watering during winter months. Propagate in spring by sowing pre-soaked seed or by rooting stem segments.

Opuntia aciculata

syn. *Opuntia lindheimeri*

CHENILLE PRICKLY PEAR

☼ ⚘ ↔ 36–60 in (90–150 cm)
↑ 36–60 in (90–150 cm)

Shrubby species, native to southwestern USA and northwestern Mexico. Flattened oblong to round stem segments dotted with tufts of yellowish brown spines and bristles. Yellow or red flowers, from spring–summer. Zones 9–11.

Opuntia aoracantha

syns *Opuntia bispinosa, Tephrocactus aoracanthus*

☼ ⚘ ↔ 12–24 in (30–60 cm)
↑ 12–24 in (30–60 cm)

Native to Argentina. Small species often branching at ground level. Oval stem segments, to 4 in (10 cm) long, grayish blue to olive green, with red bristles and yellow spines. White to yellow or pinkish flowers, from spring–summer. Zones 9–11.

Opuntia aciculata

Opuntia aoracantha

Opuntia littoralis, in the wild, Ensenada, Baja California, Mexico

Opuntia littoralis var. *vaseyi*

Opuntia basilaris

Opuntia ficus-indica

Opuntia basilaris ★

BEAVER TAIL CACTUS

☼ ❄ ↔ 4 ft (1.2 m) ↕ 2–3 ft (0.6–0.9 m)

Perennial cactus, native to southwestern USA and northwestern Mexico. Oblong to rounded fleshy stems are bluish gray, often tinged with red, dotted with tufts of reddish bristles. Purplish red flowers, in summer. Zones 9–11.

Opuntia cochenillifera

syn. *Nopalea cochenillifera*

COCHINEAL CACTUS

☼ ❄ ↔ 8 ft (2.4 m) ↕ 12 ft (3.5 m)

Tree-like species, native to Mexico. Trunk to 8 in (20 cm) in diameter. Flat oval stem segments, often spineless, to 10 in (25 cm) long. Bright red flowers, prominent stamens, in spring–summer. Zones 9–11.

Opuntia ficus-indica

syns *Opuntia engelmannii, O. vulgaris*

INDIAN FIG, INDIAN FIG PEAR

☼ ❄ ↔ 15 ft (4.5 m) ↕ 15 ft (4.5 m)

Native to Mexico, cultivated for its fruit in warmer parts of the world, naturalized in many areas. Green or bluish green, flattened, oblong or rounded segments, areoles with 1 or 2 spines. Yellow flowers, in late spring to early summer. Purple, oval, edible fruits. Zones 9–11.

Opuntia humifusa

PRICKLY PEAR CACTUS

☼ ❄ ↔ 36 in (90 cm)

↕ 8–12 in (20–30 cm)

From eastern North America. Forms spreading clumps of fleshy dull green leaves made up of sections that are lightly spiny. Yellow frilly flowers in early summer. Dark red fruit, inedible. Zones 5–10.

Opuntia littoralis

☼ ❄ ↔ 12–48 in (30–120 cm)

↕ 12–24 in (30–60 cm)

Native to southwestern USA and northwestern Mexico. Sprawling shrub. Flattened oblong to nearly round stem segments, dotted with tufts of yellowish bristles and brown spines. Flowers yellow with red centers, in spring–summer. Red fruit. *O. l.* var. *vaseyi,* salmon flowers. Zones 9–11.

Opuntia macrocentra

Opuntia macrocentra

syn. *Opuntia violacea* var. *macrocentra*

BLACK-SPINE PRICKLY PEAR

☼ ❄ ↔ 4 ft (1.2 m) ↕ 4 ft (1.2 m)

Native to southwestern USA and northern Mexico. Sprawling shrub. Flat, nearly round, purplish gray stem segments covered with long black spines. Bright yellow flowers, red at base, in spring–summer. Zones 9–11.

Opuntia microdasys ★

☼ ❄ ↔ 18–24 in (45–60 cm)

↕ 18–24 in (45–60 cm)

From central and northern Mexico. Thicket-forming shrub. Oblong, flattened, green stem segments, to 6 in (15 cm) long, densely dotted with tufts of yellow bristles. Yellow flowers, often tinged red, in spring–summer. 'Albispina', darker green segments, white bristles. Zones 8–11.

Opuntia phaeacantha

PURPLE-FRUITED PRICKLY PEAR

☼ ❄ ↔ 48 in (120 cm)

↕ 12–36 in (30–90 cm)

Sprawling shrub found across southwestern USA and Mexico. Stem segments flattened. Clusters of fierce 2½ in (6 cm) spines stud surfaces and edges. Bright yellow flowers, often reddish within, in spring or following rain. Pear-shaped purple-red fruits. Zones 9–11.

Opuntia stenopetala

Opuntia polyacantha

PLAINS PRICKLY PEAR, STARVATION PRICKLY PEAR

☼ ❄ ↔ 48 in (120 cm) ↕ 12 in (30 cm)

Mat-forming cactus found from northern Mexico to Canada. Flattened round stem segments. Clusters of 5 to 10 blue-green spines, 2 in (5 cm) long. The flowers, yellow to yellow-green, appear in spring–summer. Dry, rather spiny, 1 in (25 mm) long fruits. Zones 3–10.

Opuntia stenopetala

syn. *Opuntia marnieriana*

TUNA COLORADA

☼ ❄ ↔ 8 ft (2.4 m) ↕ 4 ft (1.2 m)

From Mexico. Low spreading shrub. Flattened oblong grayish green stem segments, prominent reddish brown spines ageing to gray. Orangey red flowers, in spring–summer. Zones 9–11.

Opuntia stricta

PRICKLY PEAR

☼ ❄ ↔ 5 ft (1.5 m) ↕ 6 ft (1.8 m)

From southeastern USA to northern Venezuela, naturalized in various

Opuntia phaeacantha

Oreocereus celsianus

Oreocereus leucotrichus

Oreocereus doelzianus

countries. Erect or prostrate bush. Blue-green oblong to cylindrical stem segments, spines few, curved and flattened, stems sometimes spineless. Yellow flowers, in summer. Rounded purple fruit. Zones 9–12.

Opuntia strigil

☀ ⚘ ↔ 4–7 ft (1.2–2 m)
↑ 24–40 in (60–100 cm)

Native to southwestern USA and northern Mexico. Erect or sprawling shrub. Flattened oblong stem segments, dotted with tufts of reddish brown bristles and spines. Creamy white flowers, in spring–summer. Zones 9–11.

Opuntia tomentosa

VELVET PRICKLY PEAR

☀ ⚘ ↔ 10 ft (3 m) ↑ 15 ft (4.5 m)

Originally from Mexico, grows in the shape of a small tree. Flattened stem segments. May be spineless. Orange flowers with diffuse red stripes on petals, in spring to summer. Oval red fruit. Zones 9–12.

OREOCEREUS

A genus containing 9 attractive columnar cacti from the Andes at elevations above 9,840 ft (3,000 m) in southern Peru, northern Chile, southern Bolivia, and northern Argentina. These members of the cactus (Cactaceae) family are aptly named since the Greek word *oreo* means mountain. They are all low shrubby cacti with cylindrical stems, sparsely branching from the base, 7–10 ft (2–3 m) tall, rarely developing a trunk. The ribs are tubercled or deeply indented between the areoles, which often bear long white hairs and stout dense spines. Flowers are diurnal, asymmetrical, tubular to funnelform, in red to purple or orange

tones. Floral tubes are straight or somewhat curved, with scales and some hairs. Seed pods are fleshy or dry, usually bursting open from the base. All species of *Morawetzia* and some species of *Borzicactus* are now classified as *Oreocereus*.
CULTIVATION: Easily grown in a rich well-drained soil. Propagate from seed or from cuttings that have been dried out for a week or two. Rest in winter.

Oreocereus celsianus ★

syns *Borzicactus celsianus, B. fossulatus, Oreocereus maximus, O. neocelsianus*

OLD MAN OF THE ANDES

☀ ❄ ↔ 40 in (100 cm) ↑ 7 ft (2 m)

From southern Bolivia, southern Peru, and northern Argentina. Stems columnar, erect, 3–5 in (8–12 cm) in

diameter, with 10 to 25 rounded warty ribs. Stems branch from base, covered in white hairs and heavy spines. Areoles large, white with wool and hairs. Spines yellow to reddish brown, 1 to 4 centrals, 7 to 9 radials. Purplish pink flowers, near stem tips, in summer. Seed pods spherical, scaly, green, ripening to yellow. Zones 8–10.

Oreocereus doelzianus

syn. *Morawetzia doelzianus*

☀ ❄ ↔ 40 in (100 cm) ↑ 40 in (100 cm)

From central Peru. Olive green cylindrical stems, 2½–3 in (6–8 cm) in

diameter, freely branching from base, with 10 to 11 heavily warty ribs bearing heavily felted areoles. Spines yellow to reddish brown, 4 centrals, 10 to 20 radials. Terminal cephalium with long white woolly hairs and yellowish bristles. Flowers purplish red, asymmetrical, in summer. Zones 8–10.

Oreocereus leucotrichus

syns *Borzicactus hendriksenianus, B. leucotrichus, Oreocereus hendriksenianus*

☀ ❄ ↔ 40 in (100 cm) ↑ 3–7 ft (0.9–2 m)

Found from central Peru to northern Chile. Cactus with columnar trunk, clumping from base. Upright stems, 2½–5 in (6–12 cm) in diameter, bear 10 to 15 low warty ribs. Prominent areoles produce many black to white hairs. Spines stiff, in shades of yellow, orange, or dark red, with 1 to 4 centrals and 5 to 10 radials. Flowers red, asymmetrical, near stem tips, in summer. Seed pods spherical to short cylindrical, reddish yellow to yellowish green in color. Zones 8–10.

Opuntia tomentosa

Opuntia strigil

Opuntia tomentosa, Australia

Oreocereus trollii

☀ ❄ ↔ 32 in (80 cm) ↑ 20 in (50 cm)

From southern Bolivia to northern Argentina. Stems short cylindrical, 2½–3 in (6–8 cm) wide, branching from base, pale green, stout, totally covered in dense white hairs almost covering the 15 to 25 strongly warty ribs. Red, yellow, or brown spines, 3 to 5 centrals, 10 to 15 radials. Flowers violet to red, in summer. Seed pods spherical. *O. t.* var. *crassineus*, slightly longer stems. Zones 8–10.

OREOPANAX

This genus of 100-odd evergreen shrubs and trees belongs to the ivy (Araliaceae) family and is notable for the way many of its species carry two distinctly different types of foliage. Found from Mexico southward, most species have large palmate leaves, although the flowering stems often carry simpler leaves. The flowers are white to creamy green, carried in large showy heads that most commonly appear in late summer and autumn. Berry-like fruits follow and can last well into winter.

CULTIVATION: Although often tropical in origin, many species occur naturally at reasonably high altitudes and can withstand light frosts. They prefer to grow in deep, fertile, well-drained, humus-rich soil with ample summer moisture and a position shaded from the hottest summer sun. They can be

Origanum libanoticum

trimmed in spring, and often reshoot even if cut back to ground level. Some species sucker slightly. Propagate from seed or half-hardened cuttings.

Oreopanax xalapensis

BRAZIL

☀ ✿ ↔ 20 ft (6 m) ↑ 60 ft (18 m)

Found from Mexico to Panama. Evergreen tree with branching habit. Long-stemmed palmate leaves, 5 to 10 lustrous narrow leaflets to 12 in (30 cm) long. Passes through simple and trifoliate-leafed stages before adult foliage. White to creamy green flowers, most of year. Fruit deep reddish purple when ripe. Zones 10–12.

ORIGANUM

Found from the Mediterranean region to East Asia and known mainly as a genus of perennials, including some of the best-known culinary herbs, this genus belongs to the mint (Lamiaceae) family. *Origanum* also includes a few subshrubs that can become shrubby in mild climates, though they tend to be short lived. They have aromatic foliage on stems that are often noticeably 4-angled. Their flowers are borne in spikes, usually with conspicuous bracts that enclose the flowers, and may be brightly colored, often in rose shades.

CULTIVATION: Most species are very easily grown in any sunny position with light well-drained soil. They can be trimmed to shape and usually need a few damaged stems removed after winter. Hardiness varies with the species, although most will tolerate moderate frosts. Propagate the shrubby species from seed, small half-hardened cuttings, or by layering.

Origanum amanum

☀ ❄ ↔ 6 in (15 cm) ↑ 2–4 in (5–10 cm)

Native to eastern Mediterranean and Turkey. Slow-growing mat-forming

Origanum majorana

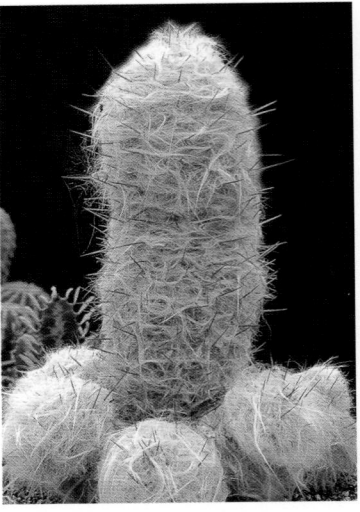

Oreocereus trollii

plant. Light green heart-shaped leaves. Tubular rosy pink flowers, on whorled spikes, from late summer–autumn. Zones 8–10.

Origanum dictamnus

DITTANY OF CRETE

☀ ❄ ↔ 8–12 in (20–30 cm) ↑ 8–12 in (20–30 cm)

Small, very pretty, Cretan evergreen shrub. Woolly white leaves, in opposite pairs. Drooping heads of pink flowers, enclosed within large pink bracts, in summer. Wonderful plant for a cool greenhouse. Zones 7–10.

Origanum × hybridum

☀ ❅ ↔ 12 in (30 cm) ↑ 8 in (20 cm)

Hybrid between *O. dictamnus* and *O. sipyleum*. Downy, grayish green, oval leaves. Pink flowers, in drooping clusters of bracts, from late summer to autumn. 'Santa Cruz', pink to purple flowers held above foliage. Zones 9–11.

Origanum laevigatum

☀ ❄ ↔ 18–24 in (45–60 cm) ↑ 12–24 in (30–60 cm)

Native to Turkey. Upright plant with suckering rootstock. Well foliaged with small oval leaves. Tubular purple flowers, on numerous airy branching stems, from spring into autumn. 'Herrenhausen', leaves and shoots flushed purple when young, pale lilac flowers. Zones 8–10.

Oreocereus trollii var. *crassineus*

Oreopanax xalapensis

Origanum libanoticum

☀ ❄ ↔ 18–24 in (45–60 cm) ↑ 24 in (60 cm)

Native to Lebanon. Upright perennial plant with small oval leaves. Produces pendent airy spikes of pink flowers, with deeper pink bracts, in summer. Zones 8–10.

Origanum majorana

syn. *Majorana hortensis*

KNOTTED MARJORAM, SWEET MARJORAM

☀ ❄ ↔ 18 in (45 cm) ↑ 24 in (60 cm)

Native to the Mediterranean region and naturalized widely throughout Europe. Grown for its grayish green leaves, which are used for flavoring many culinary dishes. Stems root readily where they touch the soil. Produces heads of small white to pink flowers, from late summer to autumn. Zones 7–10.

Origanum onites

POT MARJORAM

☀ ❄ ↔ 24 in (60 cm) ↑ 24 in (60 cm)

Shrubby, mounding culinary herb, native of the Mediterranean region. Flexible wiry stems, very aromatic bright green to sage green leaves, with a covering of very fine hairs. Produces heads of small, soft pink, thyme-like flowers, in mid-summer. 'Aureum', bright yellow foliage, more popular than the species as an ornamental. Zones 8–10.

Origanum × hybridum 'Santa Cruz'

O. vulgare 'Thumble's Variety'

Origanum vulgare var. *humile*

Origanum vulgare 'Aureum'

Origanum vulgare 'Dr Ietswaart'

Origanum vulgare 'Gold Tip'

Origanum vulgare 'Polyphant'

Origanum vulgare

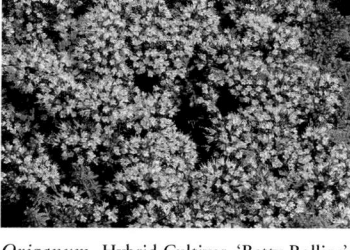

Origanum, Hybrid Cultivar, 'Betty Rollins'

Origanum, Hybrid Cultivar, 'Kent Beauty'

Origanum rotundifolium

☀ ❄ ↔ 12 in (30 cm) ↕ 12 in (30 cm)
From Turkey and the Caucasus region. Subshrub spreading from rhizomes. Small, round, bluish gray leaves. White to pink flowers, held within drooping, overlapping, green bracts with purplish pink tints, in summer–autumn. Zones 8–10.

Origanum scabrum

☀ ❄ ↔ 12–18 in (30–45 cm)
↕ 12–18 in (30–45 cm)

Native to the mountains of southern Greece. Rhizomatous perennial, small oval to heart-shaped leaves. Small pink flowers, in showy, purplish pink, overlapping bracts, in summer. Zones 8–10.

Origanum vulgare

COMMON MARJORAM, OREGANO, WILD MARJORAM

☀ ❄ ↔ 12 in (30 cm)
↕ 12–18 in (30–45 cm)

Variable species found from Europe to Asia. Popular culinary herb with very aromatic foliage and a stronger, more pungent flavor than marjoram. Dark green oval to round leaves. Produces small pink, purple, or white flowers, from summer to autumn. *O. v.* var. *humile* is a compact creeping variety with deep green leaves. *O. v.* 'Aureum' has small golden leaves; 'Dr Ietswaart' is low growing with golden leaves; 'Gold Tip' has leaves that are tipped with yellow; 'Polyphant' (syn. 'White Anniversary') has leaves edged with creamy white; 'Thumble's Variety' has large yellowish green leaves. Zones 5–9.

Origanum Hybrid Cultivars

☀ ❄ ↔ 12–24 in (30–60 cm)
↕ 4–12 in (10–30 cm)

Some hybrids are grown for their globular flowerheads with shell-like pink to red bracts, while others have less showy flowers but attractive aromatic foliage. 'Barbara Tingey', small, rounded, bluish leaves, flowers green at first, ageing to rosy pink; 'Betty Rollins', crowded dark green leaves, small pink flowers, in summer; 'Kent Beauty', small rounded leaves, small pink flowers enclosed within drooping, overlapping, pink and green bracts; 'Norton Gold', aromatic bright golden foliage in spring, later becoming greenish gold, pinkish purple flowers. Zones 6–9.

ORIXA

This single-species genus in the rue (Rutaceae) family is native to the mountainous regions of China, Korea, and Japan. It consists of a deciduous shrub with dark green alternate leaves to 5 in (12 cm) long. Male and female flowers are borne on the same plant just as the leaves emerge in spring. The 4-lobed brown fruits are about ¾ in (18 mm) in diameter. The plant is used for hedging in Japan.
CULTIVATION: Fully frost hardy, this species grows best in a well-drained fertile soil in an open sunny situation. It will tolerate dry conditions. Lightly prune in late winter or early spring to shape. Propagate from seed in spring or from cuttings in summer.

Orixa japonica ★

☀ ❄ ↔ 12 ft (3.5 m) ↕ 8 ft (2.4 m)
Wide-spreading shrub from mountain regions of China, Korea, and Japan. Attractive, dark green, aromatic leaves, turning pale yellow in autumn. Small, 4-petalled, cup-shaped, greenish flowers, in spring; female flowers borne singly, male flowers in small panicles, to 1¼ in (30 mm) long. Zones 5–9.

ORNITHOGALUM

CHINCHERINCHEE, STAR OF BETHLEHEM
This genus comprises around 80 species of bulbs in the hyacinth (Hyacinthaceae) family, native to South Africa and the Mediterranean region. They quickly form large clumps of grassy to strappy leaves, sometimes with a prominent midrib, and can be slightly invasive. In spring or summer, upright conical spikes of white to cream flowers appear, sometimes mildly scented, in whorls of 3, usually starry or cup-shaped, with 6 petals. The botanical name comes from the Greek *ornis,* "bird," and

Orixa japonica

Ornithogalum montanum

Ornithogalum arabicum

Ornithogalum dubium

gala, "milk"—when spread out a flower resembles a white bird.
CULTIVATION: Most European species tolerate moderate frosts; the South African species may need to be lifted for winter. Plant in a sunny open position in any light well-drained soil. Water well when flowering, dry off afterward. Shorter varieties are suitable for rock gardens; taller ones grow well in borders. Most species multiply rapidly; propagate by simple division or from seed. May self-sow.

Ornithogalum arabicum ★
☼/◐ ✤ ↔ 24–48 in (60–120 cm)
↑ 16–30 in (40–75 cm)

Native to the Mediterranean region. Heavily-textured leaves to 24 in (60 cm) long. Flower stem to 32 in (80 cm) long; up to 20 fragrant white or cream flowers, conspicuous black ovaries, from spring to early summer. Zones 9–10.

Ornithogalum dubium ★
☼/◐ ✽ ↔ 12–20 in (30–50 cm)
↑ 8–12 in (20–30 cm)

Native to South Africa. Hair-fringed lance-shaped leaves, to 4 in (10 cm). Crowded heads of small orange, red, yellow, or white flowers, on 12 in (30 cm) stems, from winter to spring. Zones 8–10.

Ornithogalum longibracteatum
FALSE SEA ONION, SEA ONION
☼/◐ ✤ ↔ 48 in (50–120 cm)
↑ 24–48 in (60–120 cm)

Native to Cape region of South Africa. Strappy, light green leaves, to 24 in (60 cm) long. Flower stems over 40 in (100 cm) high, flowers small, green-striped, white, largely enclosed within bracts, in early summer. Zones 9–10.

Ornithogalum montanum
☼/◐ ✽ ↔ 16–24 in (40–60 cm)
↑ 16–24 in (40–60 cm)

Eurasian native. Narrow light green leaves, to 6 in (15 cm) long. Flower stems to 24 in (60 cm) high; drooping, green-striped, white flowers, in spring–early summer. Zones 6–9.

Ornithogalum narbonense
☼/◐ ✽ ↔ 24–48 in (60–120 cm)
↑ 24–36 in (60–90 cm)

Found from the Mediterranean to northern Iran. Very narrow leaves, to 32 in (80 cm) long. Flower stems to 36 in (90 cm) tall; heads of many small flowers, white with fine green center stripe, in spring. Zones 7–10.

Ornithogalum nutans
☼/◐ ✽ ↔ 16–30 in (40–75 cm)
↑ 16–24 in (40–60 cm)

Eurasian species. Lax strappy leaves, to 16 in (40 cm) long. Nodding, translucent, green-striped, white flowers, on stems to 24 in (60 cm) tall, in spring. Zones 6–9.

Ornithogalum reverchonii
☼/◐ ✽ ↔ 16–32 in (40–80 cm)
↑ 20 in (50 cm)

Summer-dormant Mediterranean species. Lax strappy leaves, to over 12 in (30 cm) long, in autumn. Wavy-edged white flowers, on 20 in (50 cm) stems, in mid-spring. Zones 8–10.

Ornithogalum umbellatum
STAR OF BETHLEHEM
☼/◐ ✤ ↔ 20–32 in (50–80 cm)
↑ 20 in (50 cm)

Perennial from Europe and around the Mediterranean. Very narrow leaves, to 12 in (30 cm) long, with pale midvein. Broad heads of small, green-striped, white flowers, in spring. Zones 5–10.

ORONTIUM
GOLDEN CLUB

This genus in the arum (Araceae) family contains a single species of aquatic perennial. It is native to North America where it is found in streams and shallow lakes and ponds. The oblong leaves may be floating or upright. The narrow yellow spadix is borne on a long white stalk above a small green spathe, which withers and drops at flowering.
CULTIVATION: Grow in large tubs or as a marginal plant in water 4–18 in (10–45 cm) deep. Grow in full sun in a fertile soil mix. Propagate by division or from seed.

Orontium aquaticum
GOLDEN CLUB
☼ ❄ ↔ 18–24 in (45–60 cm)
↑ 12–18 in (30–45 cm)

Native to eastern USA. Aquatic perennial with leathery oblong leaves, to 12 in (30 cm) long, dark green with a metallic sheen. Erect white flowering stems, to 24 in (60 cm) long, with narrow yellow spadices, in summer. Zones 7–10.

OROYA

A genus of 2 small barrel-shaped cacti from the high Andes of Peru, belonging to the cactus (Cactaceae) family. The genus is named after the town of La Oroya, near Lima in Peru. Both species are highly variable with regard to size, color of spines and of flowers. They are usually solitary, with flattened spherical to short cylindrical trunks and a thick tap root. They have many ribs and strong spines arranged in a comb-like fashion on either side of the elongated areoles. The seed pods are club-shaped.
CULTIVATION: Easily grown in a well-drained soil. As these plants are solitary, they are usually raised from seed. Rest in winter.

Ornithogalum nutans

Ornithogalum narbonense

Ornithogalum reverchonii

Oroya peruviana

Orthosiphon aristatus

Oroya peruviana

syns *Oroya neoperuviana, O. subocculta*
☀ ❄ ↔ 4–6 in (10–15 cm)
↕ 2–8 in (5–20 cm)

From Oroya to Cuzco, central Peru, at elevations of 9,840–13,120 ft (3,000–4,000 m). Usually solitary but extremely variable throughout its range. Stems deep shiny green, with 15 to 30 ribs, distinctly warty. Areoles white, elongated. Spines yellowish to reddish brown, with 1 to 3 centrals, 15 to 25 radials, arranged in a comb-like fashion on either side of areoles. Flowers pinkish red with cream or white centers, borne in summer. Seed pods club-shaped, reddish brown. Zones 8–11.

ORPHIUM

Named after Orpheus, a character from Greek mythology, this genus contains a single species native to coastal regions of southwestern South Africa, and is a member of the gentian (Gentianaceae) family. It is a small softwooded shrub that is grown for its glistening pink to mauve saucer-shaped flowers, up to 2 in (5 cm) across, that are carried at the tips of the branches in summer.
CULTIVATION: Marginally frost hardy, this plant will grow in a sunny position in any well-drained soil, provided it is watered regularly in dry periods. Tip prune in spring to encourage a compact habit. Propagation is from cuttings in late summer.

Orphium frutescens

STICKY FLOWER
☀ ❄ ↔ 18 in (45 cm) ↕ 24 in (60 cm)
From South Africa's southwestern coast. Small evergreen shrub. Rather succulent, pale green, stem-clasping leaves, to 2 in (5 cm) long. Slightly sticky, 5-lobed, satiny flowers, in summer. Withstands moderate coastal exposure. Zones 9–11.

ORTHOPHYTUM

This bromeliad (Bromeliaceae) family genus contains 30 clump-forming species, mainly from restricted locations in the dry areas of eastern Brazil. These decorative plants may grow in the ground or on rocks, with or without stems. The non-stemmed species may have stemless flowerheads that nestle in the center of the rosette, or long-stemmed flowerheads. In species with long-stemmed flowerheads, offsets may appear in the flowerhead after the flowers have finished. The leaves may be smooth or furry, but always with strong teeth along the edges, forming an open non-water-retaining rosette. Several species are popular in cultivation, and a number of cultivars with colored foliage have been developed.
CULTIVATION: Recommended for indoor culture in a greenhouse or conservatory in cool-temperate areas, or for outdoor culture with protection from continuous direct sunlight and extremes of rain in warm-temperate, subtropical, and tropical areas. Water when potting mix is dry. Do not over-fertilize. Propagation is mainly by offsets.

Orthophytum gurkenii

☀ ❂ ↔ 10 in (25 cm) ↕ 16 in (40 cm)
From eastern Brazil. Open rosettes forming clumps. Leaves are toothed,

Orphium frutescens

purplish brown to green with irregular, creamy, wavy cross-bands. Erect flower stem, narrow cylindrical flowerhead, with up to 5 globular side-branches of 6 to 10 flowers, later producing offsets. Bracts are similar to leaves below branches. Rare in wild, popular in cultivation. Zones 9–10.

Orthophytum navioides

☀ ❂ ↔ 40 in (100 cm) ↕ 4 in (10 cm)
From eastern Brazil. Dense flattened rosettes form large clump. Small-toothed, very narrow, green leaves. Globular flowerhead nestling in the center of the rosette, up to 10 white-petalled flowers. Almost whole plant turns red at flowering. Hybridized with *Neoregelia* to produce the hardier × *Neophytum*. Zones 9–10.

Orthophytum vagans

☀ ❂ ↔ 4 in (10 cm) ↕ 12 in (30 cm)
Long-stemmed species from eastern Brazil. Forms clumps of rosettes. Leaves green with toothed edges. Globular flowerhead with white-petalled flowers, surrounded by narrow, red, spiny bracts; sometimes whole plant turns red at flowering. 'Variegata' has variegated foliage. Zones 9–10.

Orthophytum Hybrid Cultivars

☀ ❂ ↔ 4 in (10 cm) ↕ 10 in (25 cm)
Raised from species such as *O. gurkenii* and *O. navioides*, these rather few and recent hybrids have been bred for color and texture of foliage and inflorescence bracts. '**Blaze**', pointed tapered leaves in solid, bright, glossy red, closely spaced spines, central flowerhead with white petals; '**Copper Penny**', elongated stem with leaves in spiral ranks, copper to rose-copper, darker in stronger light, center of leaves becomes bright red when in bloom; '**Iron Ore**', long arching leaves, rusty orange blending to light

chocolate near tips, bicolored flowerhead with areas of green and chocolate; '**Star Lights**', leaves turn bronze-brown in good light, flecked with silver spots. Zones 9–10.

ORTHOSIPHON

This is a genus of about 40 species found in tropical regions of Africa, Australia, and parts of Polynesia, belonging to the mint (Lamiaceae) family. They are mainly softwooded shrubs with simple leaves in opposite pairs that may be smooth-edged or toothed. The elongated tubular flowers with long prominent stamens are borne in spiked whorls for long periods in spring and summer.
CULTIVATION: Frost tender, these plants prefer a protected sunny or shaded spot and a moist, moderately fertile, well-drained soil. Trim excess growth regularly, especially after flowering, to maintain density. Propagation is usually from seed or from cuttings.

Orthosiphon aristatus

CAT'S MOUSTACHE, CAT'S WHISKERS
☀ ✈ ↔ 36 in (90 cm) ↕ 36 in (90 cm)
Softwooded shrub from northeastern Australia, often found growing near streams. Dark green ovate leaves, with coarsely toothed margins. Whorls of white or pale mauve flowers with long stamens, borne in terminal racemes, in spring–summer. Zones 10–12.

Orthophytum vagans 'Variegata'

Orthophytum gurkenii

ORTHROSANTHUS
MORNING FLAG, MORNING IRIS

This genus encompasses 7 species of rhizomatous perennials and belongs to the iris (Iridaceae) family. They are native to tropical America and Australia where they grow on sandy well-drained soil. Plants form clumps of narrow grass-like foliage and bear stems of 6-petalled flowers in shades of blue. Individual flowers are short-lived but open in succession, providing a long display.
CULTIVATION: In warm climates grow in light well-drained soil in full sun or part-shade. In cool-temperate regions grow in the greenhouse in a fibrous loam. Water lightly. Propagate from seed or by division.

Orthrosanthus chimboracensis
☼/◐ ❄ ↔ 12 in (30 cm) ↑ 14–24 in (35–60 cm)

Rhizomatous perennial, native to Mexico and Peru. Clumps of long narrow leaves with minutely toothed, somewhat rough margins. Sparingly branched flowering stems, lavender-blue flowers to 1¾ in (40 mm) wide, in summer. Zones 9–11.

ORYCHOPHRAGMUS
There are 2 species of annual or biennial plants in this genus, which belongs to the cabbage (Brassicaceae) family. They have thin, lyre-shaped, pinnate, toothed leaves. The simple 4-petalled flowers are violet and borne in clusters in spring.
CULTIVATION: Can be grown in the border in fertile well-drained soil in full sun. Propagate from seed.

Orychophragmus violaceus
☼ ❄ ↔ 12 in (30 cm) ↑ 20 in (50 cm)

Native to China, where it is eaten as a leaf vegetable. Variable green leaves. Clusters of purple flowers, held above foliage, in spring. Zones 9–11.

ORYZA
This genus in the grass (Poaceae) family contains 19 species of annual and perennial grasses, including the important food crop, rice. These grasses are native to damp and swampy areas of tropical Asia and Africa. The flowering stems bear panicles of compressed flower spikelets. The ripened seed of *O. sativa* is harvested as rice, which is a staple food for more than half the world's population.
CULTIVATION: The commonly grown species *O. sativa* has many cultivars developed to suit a range of climates and soil types, and is usually grown as an annual. It requires constantly moist soil and, when cultivated as a food crop, it is usually grown in a flooded system with the water being drained away at harvest time. It is sometimes grown as a poolside ornamental or sunk in pots in pool margins, in a position in full sun.

Oryza sativa, Japonica Group

Oryza sativa, Japonica Group, 'Cigalon'

Orychophragmus violaceus

Osbeckia australiana

Oryza sativa
RICE

☼ ❄ ↔ 24–36 in (60–90 cm) ↑ 3–6 ft (0.9–1.8 m)

Native to southeastern Asia. Annual swamp grass with long tapering leaves and a drooping flowering panicle. The seeds have been harvested as rice since antiquity. Most of the many cultivars belong to the **Indica Group**, more tropical, with longer lighter green leaves, longer kernels, or the **Japonica Group**, generally grown in more northern climates, with shorter darker green leaves, shorter kernels. '**Cigalon**' is a cultivar from Japan. Zones 9–12.

OSBECKIA
This genus, a member of the melastoma (Melastomataceae) family, contains about 60 species of herbs and evergreen shrubs, most of which are found in Asia, with a small number native to Africa and Australia. They are related to *Tibouchina,* to which they bear a resemblance, as they are somewhat hairy plants with simple opposite leaves that have 3 to 7 prominent veins. The showy 5-petalled flowers are borne singly or in loose terminal heads.
CULTIVATION: In subtropical and tropical climates grow these plants in a sunny position. Water well during dry weather. In cooler climates they can be grown in the greenhouse or conservatory but need protection

Oryza sativa

Osbeckia kewensis

from the hottest sun and must be watered well. Prune after flowering to maintain a bushy habit. Propagate from half-hardened cuttings in a sandy mix in a humid environment.

Osbeckia australiana
◐ ✈ ↔ 3 ft (0.9 m) ↑ 6 ft (1.8 m)

Australian shrub. Rather soft stems clothed with long, narrow, lance-shaped leaves. Flowers usually borne singly, bright magenta pink, at branch tips, in summer. Zones 10–12.

Osbeckia kewensis
◐ ❄ ↔ 36 in (90 cm) ↑ 36 in (90 cm)

Recently recognized species, native to India. Small shrub, spreading habit. Thick, somewhat leathery, prominently veined leaves. Large showy flowers, cerise-violet with prominent yellow stamens, in summer. Zones 9–12.

Osbeckia rubicunda
☼ ❄ ↔ 24 in (60 cm) ↑ 36 in (90 cm)

Upright shrub, native to Sri Lanka. Pointed oblong leaves. Deep purple flowers, to 2 in (5 cm) across, prominent yellow stamens, carried singly or in clusters, in summer. Zones 9–12.

OSMANTHUS
This is a genus of about 15 slow-growing species of evergreen shrubs and small trees in the olive (Oleaceae) family, distributed through southern USA, Asia, and the Pacific Islands. All have simple opposite leaves, some with spiny margins, and small white or yellow flowers, often with a strong perfume suggestive of jasmine or gardenia, followed by round dark blue fruit. They are valued as ornamentals for their attractive foliage and flowers.
CULTIVATION: *Osmanthus* species require a moderately fertile well-drained soil and a position in full sun, preferably in a cool moist climate. Propagate from half-hardened cuttings taken in either summer or winter.

Osmanthus × burkwoodii ★
☼ ❄ ↔ 10 ft (3 m) ↑ 10 ft (3 m)

Hybrid between *O. delavayi* and *O. decorus;* resilient thick-set shrub.

Leaves dark glossy green, leathery, finely toothed. Flowers white, very fragrant, produced in profusion, in late spring. Zones 6–9.

Osmanthus decorus

☼ ❄ ↔ 12 ft (3.5 m) ↑ 10 ft (3 m)
Round-headed bush from western Asia. Long, slender, leathery, glossy green leaves, paler beneath. Flowers small, fragrant, pure white, in bundles, in spring. Purplish black fruits like small plums. Zones 7–9.

Osmanthus delavayi

☼ ❄ ↔ 8 ft (2.4 m) ↑ 8 ft (2.4 m)
Slow-growing shrub from western China. Strong arching branches. Leaves smooth, dark green above, paler beneath. Flowers white, highly perfumed, in terminal, occasionally axillary, clusters of 5 or 6, in late winter–spring. Purplish black fruits. Zones 7–9.

Osmanthus × fortunei

☼ ❄ ↔ 10 ft (3 m) ↑ 10 ft (3 m)
This hybrid between *O. fragrans* and *O. heterophyllus* forms a compact robust shrub. Leaves are large, prominently veined on uppersurface, edged with sharp teeth, sometimes smooth-edged on mature plants. Bears small, fragrant, white flowers, in autumn. 'San Jose', cream to orange flowers. Zones 7–11.

Osmanthus heterophyllus

Osmanthus × burkwoodii

Osmanthus fragrans

FRAGRANT OLIVE, SWEET OLIVE, SWEET OSMANTHUS

☼ ❄ ↔ 20 ft (6 m) ↑ 20 ft (6 m)
Evergreen species occurring naturally in China and Japan. Normally pruned to a 10 ft (3 m) shrub. Leaves smooth dark green above, paler underneath. Tubular flowers pure white, very fragrant, in late winter to mid-summer. The flowers have been used by the Chinese for centuries for making scented tea. *O. f.* f. *aurantiacus*, has smooth-edged leaves, orange flowers. Zones 7–11.

Osmanthus heterophyllus

HOLLY OSMANTHUS

☼ ❄ ↔ 12 ft (3.5 m) ↑ 12 ft (3.5 m)
Evergreen shrub or small tree found on the main islands of Japan as well as Taiwan. Leaves oppositely arranged, smooth, dark glossy green. Small, fragrant, pure white flowers, carried in clusters, in autumn–early winter. 'Aureomarginatus', leaves margined and splashed with broad patches of pale yellow; 'Aureus', yellow-edged

Osmanthus delavayi

leaves; 'Goshiki', cream and red-brown variegated leaves; 'Purpureus', deep purple-green leaves; 'Variegatus', leaves irregularly margined, marked with creamy white, lighter color often spreading into center. Zones 7–11.

OSMUNDA

This genus of about 10 species of tall, perennial, deciduous or evergreen, clump-forming ferns in the royal-fern (Osmundaceae) family is found in moist woods and shaded roadsides. Native to temperate and tropical areas in East Asia and North and South America, these deep-rooted ferns are attractive, rugged, and adaptable. In autumn, the green fronds turn a soft golden yellow. The fibrous dense roots may be used as a medium for growing epiphytes or orchids and are rich in nutrients. The unfurled young fronds (called croziers) are gathered in spring and are cooked as a delicacy called fiddleheads.
CULTIVATION: Grow in partial shade in damp soil or at the water's edge. Top-dress in spring with rich compost

Osmanthus heterophyllus 'Aureus'

and remove dead fronds. Propagate by division in autumn or sow spores when ripe. May take some time to recover after dividing.

Osmunda claytoniana

INTERRUPTED FERN

◗ ❄ ↔ 24–36 in (60–90 cm) ↑ 16–40 in (40–100 cm)
Native to eastern North America. Deciduous fronds grow 24–48 in (60–120 cm) long. Stems round in cross-section, sometimes with fuzzy tufts. Fertile leaflets in middle of frond wither away, leaving a space or interruption, hence the common name. Zones 3–9.

Osmanthus heterophyllus 'Aureomarginatus'

Osmanthus heterophyllus 'Variegatus'

Osmunda regalis

Osteomeles anthyllidifolia

Osmunda regalis

LOCUST FERN, ROYAL FERN

☼ ◑ ❄ ↔ 36 in (90 cm)
↑ 24–60 in (60–150 cm)

From North America, South America, Europe, and Asia. Large compound leaves, similar to the honey locust. Broadly oval to oblong, bright green fronds make a dense rounded clump. Coppery brown and bronze croziers, in spring. '**Purpurascens**', red to purplish fronds turn green in early summer; '**Cristata**', leathery green fronds, maturing to a rich golden brown. Zones 3–10.

OSTEOMELES

This genus in the rose (Rosaceae) family contains 3 species of evergreen shrubs allied to *Cotoneaster*. They are found from China to Hawaii. The leaves have many small pinnately arranged leaflets, and in summer they bear showy terminal clusters of small white flowers.

CULTIVATION: Grow in full sun in a fertile well-drained soil. In areas with consistent frosts give them the protection of a warm wall or grow in containers. Propagate from seed or half-hardened cuttings.

Osteomeles anthyllidifolia

☼ ❧ ↔ 24 in (60 cm) ↑ 24 in (60 cm)
From islands of the North Pacific, including Hawaii. Low rambling shrub, occasionally an erect shrub to 10 ft (3 m) high. Arching stems. Small, shiny, dark green leaflets, hairy underneath. Small white flowers, in loose terminal clusters, in summer. Berries ripening to pink. Zones 9–12.

Osteomeles schweriniae

☼ ❄ ↔ 10 ft (3 m) ↑ 10 ft (3 m)
Native to southwestern China. Bushy shrub with graceful arching branches. Small leaflets grayish, downy. White flowers with prominent stamens, to ¾ in (18 mm) across, appear in

Osteospermum jucundum

dense clusters, in summer. Small dark red berries ripen to bluish black color. Zones 8–10.

OSTEOSPERMUM

Mainly from southern Africa, genus in the daisy (Asteraceae) family, with some 70 species of annuals, perennials, and subshrubs. Valued for their carpeting of flowers during the warmer months, year-round in mild areas. Mainly low, spreading or mounding plants with simple, broadly toothed, elliptic to spatula-shaped leaves. Flowers are large, with showy ray florets, mainly in pinks and purples, or white. Disc florets are an unusual purple-blue that contrasts well with the golden anthers. The name comes from the Greek *osteon*, "bone," *sperma*, "seed," and refers to the hard seeds.
CULTIVATION: Most will tolerate only light frosts and do better in mild climates. Very good coastal plants. They prefer a sunny position with light well-drained soil. Overwatering can lead to straggly growth. Pinch back and deadhead to keep compact. Propagate annuals from seed and perennials from tip cuttings.

Osteospermum ecklonis

☼ ❧ ↔ 20–40 in (50–100 cm)
↑ 20–40 in (50–100 cm)

South African shrub or subshrub. Narrow, downy, lance-shaped leaves, the edges often irregularly toothed. Ray florets white with deep purple-

blue undersides, disc florets blue, appearing throughout most of the year. Zones 9–11.

Osteospermum fruticosum

☼ ❧ ↔ 20–40 in (50–100 cm)
↑ 12–24 in (30–60 cm)

Initially upright, then spreading South African perennial. Woody base; broad, irregularly toothed, lance- to spatula-shaped leaves. Ray florets white with purple-pink undersides, disc florets dusky mauve, year round. Zones 9–11.

Osteospermum jucundum

syn. *Osteospermum barberae* of gardens
☼ ❄ ↔ 20–32 in (50–80 cm)
↑ 12–20 in (30–50 cm)

Spreading, mounding, South African perennial. Narrow lance-shaped leaves, irregularly toothed. Flowerheads over 4 in (10 cm) wide, ray florets mauve-pink to purple, disc florets purple-black, late spring–autumn. *O. j.* **subsp.** *compactum*, high-altitude form, compact growth, many small flowers; '**Purple Mountain**' ★, purple-pink ray florets. *O. j.* '**Blackthorn Seedling**', purple-pink ray florets. Zones 8–10.

Osteospermum Hybrid Cultivars

☼ ❧ ↔ 16–24 in (40–60 cm)
↑ 8–12 in (20–30 cm)

Osteospermum species hybridize freely, especially in cultivation, and new forms are constantly being introduced. Most are low spreading. Among the most popular are: '**Buttermilk**',

Osteospermum sp., orange flowers, *Felicia* sp., blue flowers, in the wild, Lilliefontein, South Africa

Osteospermum, HC, 'Peach'

Osteospermum, HC, 'Pixie'

Osteospermum, HC, 'Seaside'

Osteospermum, HC, 'Stardust'

Osteospermum, HC, 'Sunny'

Osteospermum, Hybrid Cultivar, 'Sunny Gustav'

Osteospermum, Hybrid Cultivar, Nasinga Series, 'Nasinga High Side'

Osteospermum, Hybrid Cultivar, Nasinga Series, 'Nasinga Purple'

Osteospermum, Hybrid Cultivar, Nasinga Series, 'Nasinga Wild Side'

Osteospermum, Hybrid Cultivar, Symphony Series, 'Orange Symphony'

O., Hybrid Cultivars, Symphony Series, 'Orange Symphony' and 'Orange Symphony Cream'

warm buff-yellow petals, with dark reverse; '**Hopleys**', pink flowers; '**Pink Whirls**' ★, pink ray florets, crimped, dark reverse; '**Pixie**', dark green leaves, soft pink flowers; '**Silver Sparkler**', cream-variegated foliage, white flowers; '**Stardust**', deep pink flowers; '**Sunny Gustav**', large white flowers; '**Weetwood**', white flowers with blue eye; and '**Whirligig**', gray-green foliage, dusky gray-green flowers, strongly crimped ray florets. There are also seedling strains: the **Nasinga Series**, various colors, some have crimped ray florets; the **Symphony Series**, mainly bright warm colors. Zones 9–11.

OSTRYA

HOP HORNBEAM

This genus in the birch (Betulaceae) family contains about 10 species of deciduous trees related to *Betulus* and *Carpinus*. They grow throughout temperate Northern Hemisphere regions in open woodland. The alternate leaves have conspicuous veining and toothed edges, and are often hairy. The male catkins resemble the flowers of hornbeams *(Carpinus)*. The female flowers, on the same tree, develop into catkins that look like those of hops *(Humulus)*, with overlapping bracts.
CULTIVATION: These slow-growing trees are not common in cultivation. They prefer well-drained fertile soil in either sun or shade, and make good specimen trees. Propagate in spring from fresh seed, in pots protected from frosts. Seed which has dried out must be stratified to break dormancy. Graft cultivars onto *Carpinus betulus* rootstocks in the colder months.

Ostrya carpinifolia

HOP HORNBEAM

☼ ❄ ↔ 70 ft (21 m) ↑ 70 ft (21 m)

Native to southern Europe and Turkey. Shoots with a fine growth of hairs. Green leaves with pointed tips and doubly toothed edges, turning golden to pale yellow in autumn. Female flower clusters, creamy white at first, turning brown in autumn. Zones 6–9.

Ostrya virginiana ★

EASTERN HOP HORNBEAM, IRONWOOD

☼ ❄ ↔ 35 ft (10 m) ↑ 50 ft (15 m)

From the eastern part of North America. Dark brown bark. Leaves dark green above, with paler undersides, lance-shaped, double-serrated edges. Yellow male catkins produced in spring; female fruit clusters are white at first, ripening to brown. Zones 4–9.

Ostrya carpinifolia

Ostrya virginiana

OTACANTHUS

Native to Brazil, this small genus consisting of 4 species of softwooded evergreen shrubs is a member of the foxglove (Scrophulariaceae) family. Like most members of that family, they have simple smooth-edged leaves borne in opposite pairs. These frost-tender plants are grown in warm climates for their attractive spikes of snapdragon-like flowers.

CULTIVATION: These shrubs require a humus-enriched well-drained soil in a warm sheltered position in full sun or partial shade. Pinch out tips in spring to promote bushy growth. Propagate from half-hardened cuttings.

Otacanthus caeruleus

☼/◐ ✽ ↔ 20 in (50 cm) ↑ 36 in (90 cm)

Softwooded upright shrub from Brazil. Bright green leaves, lance-shaped, rough-textured. Violet-blue tubular flowers with 2 flat lobes, about 1 in (25 mm) across, most of year. 'Little Boy Blue' is an attractive cultivar. Zones 10–12.

OTATEA

This Central American genus, a member of the grass (Poaceae) family, is composed of 2 species of shrubby bamboos. They have narrow arching stems, with a dense covering of long, thin, soft green leaves crowded near the end of the stems, creating a plume-like or pompon effect. The exposed parts of the stems turn dark brown to black in their second year. Although they spread by runners, they are not invasive and are easily controlled.

CULTIVATION: Unusually for bamboos, Otatea species can be rather reluctant to grow well and often develop into rather sparse clumps. While hardy to light frosts and reasonably drought tolerant once established, they prefer warm conditions with summer moisture and do best in fertile humus-rich soil and a position in full sun or part-shade. They are excellent container plants and also grow well around ponds. Propagation is most commonly by division.

Othonna capensis

Otacanthus caeruleus 'Little Boy Blue'

Otatea acuminata

☼ ❦ ↔ 20 ft (6 m) ↑ 25 ft (8 m)

Bamboo found from Mexico to Nicaragua. Forms large clump of very narrow non-suckering stems. Stems curve gracefully, especially in the breeze. Narrow leaves, to 6 in (15 cm) long, sheaths fall, revealing distinctive white powder below leaf nodes. *O. a.* subsp. *aztecorum* (Mexican weeping bamboo) has culms 1½ in (35 mm) in diameter, mostly obscured by prolific, long, narrow leaves. Zones 10–12.

OTHONNA

This genus belonging to the daisy (Asteraceae) family contains about 150 species of perennials or small shrubs of varying habit, ranging from woody to fleshy and succulent, and erect to sprawling. Most are native to arid regions of South Africa. Leaves vary from smooth to dissected, lobed or toothed, and may be leathery or fleshy. The daisy flowers are yellow.

CULTIVATION: In cool-temperate climates grow in the greenhouse in a moderately fertile sandy soil mix. Water sparingly during the growing period. In warm climates grow outdoors in full sun in perfectly drained soil. Propagate from seed or cuttings.

Othonna arborescens

☼ ❦ ↔ 36 in (90 cm) ↑ 36 in (90 cm)

From South Africa. Succulent shrub with zigzagging stems, thick oblong leaves, to 2 in (5 cm) long. Yellow daisies, usually solitary, at stem tips, in summer. Zones 9–11.

Ottelia ovalifolia

Otatea acuminata subsp. aztecorum

Othonna capensis

LITTLE PICKLES

☼ ❦ ↔ 12–18 in (30–45 cm) ↑ 3–6 in (8–15 cm)

From South Africa. Low-growing mat-forming succulent. Thick cylindrical leaves, about 1 in (25 mm) long, resemble jellybeans. Small yellow daisies, on thin stems, borne above the foliage, in summer. Good plant for hanging basket. Zones 9–11.

Othonna euphorbioides

☼ ❦ ↔ 36 in (90 cm) ↑ 36 in (90 cm)

From South Africa. Very succulent shrub resembling some *Euphorbia* species. Upright stems with small, fleshy, tongue-shaped leaves. Yellow daisies, borne singly or in small clusters, in summer. Zones 9–11.

OTTELIA

This genus belongs to the aquatic frogbit (Hydrocharitaceae) family. It contains 21 species of annuals or perennials found in warm water areas of the tropics. The foliage, which differs between juvenile and adult leaves, is oval to round and partly or fully submerged. The 3-petalled flowers are white, pink, or shades of purple. They are showy but short-lived and are borne above spathe-like bracts.

CULTIVATION: In cool climates grow these plants in an indoor aquarium with high light levels and warm temperatures. In warm climates they can be grown in ponds in warm water in full sun. Propagate all species from seed or by division.

Ottelia ovalifolia

☼/◐ ❦ ↔ 36–48 in (90–120 cm) ↑ 12–36 in (30–90 cm)

From Australia and New Caledonia. Annual or perennial aquatic plant. Submerged leaves strap-like. Floating leaves oval, dark green to bronze. Cream to white flowers are held above spathes that are leathery and shiny when young, from summer to autumn. Zones 9–11.

OURISIA

This genus of 25 species, native to alpine regions of South America, New Zealand, and Tasmania, Australia, is a member of the foxglove family (Scrophulariaceae). These perennials and subshrubs are typically found in moist places such as along the banks of streams. They are low mat-forming plants, usually with small, leathery, oval to heart-shaped leaves of bright to dark green, sometimes hairy or shiny. The tubular flowers have 5 flaring lobes and are usually hairy within. They are borne in small racemes or clusters in summer on stems ranging in height from 4–20 in (10–50 cm). Flower color is most often white, but sometimes purple, pink, or red.

CULTIVATION: Grow these plants in dappled shade in a moisture-retentive but very free-draining soil in the rock garden or cool greenhouse. A cool moist atmosphere, with protection against drying winds, is necessary. Propagation of all species is from seed or by division.

Oxalis articulata

Ourisia macrophylla

☀ ❆ ↔ 6 in (15 cm) ↕ 12 in (30 cm)

Native to New Zealand. Perennial with somewhat variable, dark green, leathery leaves, to 6 in (15 cm) long. Tubular flowers, borne terminally in whorls, white with yellow throat, in summer. Zones 6–9.

OXALIS

A huge genus occurring worldwide of about 500 species belonging to the wood-sorrel (Oxalidaceae) family. These mainly bulbous plants also include evergreen ground-covering perennials, succulents, and shrubs. Many species have clover-shaped leaves that close at night. Flower buds are rolled like an umbrella and open to bowl- or cup-shaped 5-petalled blooms, some species opening only in full sunlight. Some of the world's worst weeds belong in *Oxalis*, but so also do many highly desirable, some-times difficult-to-keep collector's plants, so careful selection is advised. CULTIVATION: The bulbous winter-growers like almost frost-free sunny sites, dry in summer. Evergreen and woodland summer-growing species prefer shade and moist soil. Some suc-culent and shrubby forms, in all but frost-free climates, should be grown as greenhouse plants. Propagation is from seed sown fresh, by division of bulbous and perennial forms, or from cuttings of shrubby species.

Oxalis acetosella

CUCKOO BREAD, WOOD SORREL

◑/☀ ❆ ↔ 18–36 in (45–90 cm) ↕ 2–4 in (5–10 cm)

Creeping perennial ground cover from North America, Asia, and Europe. Clover-shaped leaves. White flowers, veined with purple, in summer. *O. a.* var. *subpurpurascens* has rose pink flowers with purple veins. Zones 3–10.

Oxalis adenophylla

◐/◑ ❆ ↔ 5–6 in (12–15 cm) ↕ 3–4 in (8–10 cm)

Lovely clump-forming species from the Andes in Chile and Argentina with fibrous bulbs. Suitable for rockeries. The gray-green leaves have up to

Oxalis adenophylla, dark form

22 leaflets. Pink, occasionally mauve, flowers, veined with purple, are pro-duced in the late spring. Zones 5–9.

Oxalis articulata

◐ ❆ ↔ 12–16 in (30–40 cm) ↕ 12–16 in (30–40 cm)

Semi-woody tuberous perennial from Paraguay. Leaves have 3 leaflets, to 1 in (25 mm) across. Bright mauve-pink flowers, ¾ in (18 mm) across, held well above leaves, in summer. Zones 8–10.

Oxalis bowiei

syn. *Oxalis purpurata* var. *bowiei*

◐ ❆ ↔ 6–8 in (15–20 cm) ↕ 8–10 in (20–25 cm)

Summer-growing species from South Africa. Leaves with 3 leaflets, each to 1 in (25 mm) across. Flowers are bright pink, over 1½ in (35 mm) wide, held well above leaves. Zones 8–11.

Oxalis enneaphylla

SCURVY GRASS

◐/◑ ❆ ↔ 4–6 in (10–15 cm) ↕ 2½–3 in (6–8 cm)

Native to the Falkland Islands and Patagonia. Branched, slowly spread-

Oxalis hirta

ing, scaly rhizomatous plant. Leaves have up to 20 gray-green pleated leaflets, giving them a crinkled appearance. White to pink flowers, to 1 in (25 mm) across, borne from spring to summer. '**Rosea**' has deep pink flowers. Zones 6–9.

Oxalis hirta

◐ ❆ ↔ 4–6 in (10–15 cm) ↕ 10–12 in (25–30 cm)

Bushy bulbous species from South Africa. Upright leafy stems; leaflets long and narrow; arranged in 3s but do not have classic clover appearance. Flowers may be mauve through salmon to bright pink, in autumn. Zones 8–10.

Oxalis 'Ione Hecker' ★

◐/◑ ❆ ↔ 3–4 in (8–10 cm) ↕ 2½–3 in (6–8 cm)

Small rhizomatous hybrid between two South American species, *O. enneaphylla* and *O. laciniata*. Finely divided foliage. Tiny, semi-folded, gray-green leaflets. Produces large, violet-blue, purple-veined flowers, to 1¼ in (30 mm) wide, in summer. Zones 6–9.

Oxalis, 'Ione Hecker'

Oxalis enneaphylla

Ozothamnus adnatus

Oxalis oregana

Oxalis triangularis

Oxalis oregana
RED WOOD SORREL

☀ ❄ ↔ 40 in (100 cm) ↑ 7–8 in (18–20 cm)

Creeping perennial from the woods of western North America. Leaves with 3 mid-green leaflets. Flowers pink through to lilac, sometimes white, to 1 in (25 mm) across, from spring to autumn. Zones 7–10.

Oxalis purpurea

☀ ❄ ↔ 12–24 in (30–60 cm) ↑ 3–4 in (8–10 cm)

Variable, strongly spreading bulbous perennial from South Africa. Leaves green, grayish, even purple, divided into 3 leaflets. Flowers to 2 in (5 cm) across, white, yellow, pink, mauve, or purple, in winter. Many selections available. Zones 8–10.

Oxalis rubra

☀/☀ ❄ ↔ 10–12 in (25–30 cm) ↑ 15–16 in (38–40 cm)

Tuberous summer-growing perennial from Brazil and Argentina. The leaves with 3 leaflets are green marked with brown. The flowers to ¾ in (18 mm) across, may be white, lilac, pink, or red, in summer. Zones 9–11.

Oxalis triangularis

☀ ❄ ↔ 12–20 in (30–50 cm) ↑ 8–10 in (20–25 cm)

Summer-growing South American species; branching scaly rhizome. Leaves with 3 triangular leaflets, close at night; foliage deep purple suffused with violet. Slightly nodding soft pink flowers, throughout warmer months. *O. t.* subsp. *papilionaceae* (syn. *O. regnellii*), bright green triangular leaves, pure white flowers. Zones 8–11.

Oxalis tuberosa
NEW ZEALAND YAM, OCA

☀ ❄ ↔ 6–8 in (15–20 cm) ↑ 10–12 in (25–30 cm)

Tuberous summer-growing perennial from Colombia. Knobbed red, yellow, or white tubers, edible. Stems upright, often red, with 3 leaflets per leaf. Wild form has small yellow flowers, in summer; many cultivated forms are non-flowering. Zones 7–11.

Oxalis versicolor
BARBER'S POLE OXALIS, CANDY-CANE OXALIS

☀ ❄ ↔ 8–10 in (20–25 cm) ↑ 3–4 in (8–10 cm)

Lovely winter-growing bulbous species from southern Africa. Neat clumps of

Oxydendrum arboreum

Oxalis triangularis subsp. *papilionaceae*

fine foliage with 3 narrow leaflets. Flowers pure white, deep pink edges on outsides of petals, in late winter; when closed, rolled petals give effect of barbers' poles. Zones 9–10.

Oxalis vulcanicola

☀ ❄ ↔ 12–20 in (30–50 cm) ↑ 12–20 in (30–50 cm)

Bushy small shrub from Central America. Succulent reddish stems; thick green leaves with 3 leaflets, sometimes flushed with red. Small bright yellow flowers, fine red veins, from summer to autumn. Zones 9–11.

OXYDENDRUM
The single species of deciduous shrub or small tree in this genus, is native to North America, and belongs to the same family as *Rhododendron*, the heath (Ericaceae) family. It has a slender trunk, which is sometimes multi-stemmed, with rusty red fissured bark. In autumn, small white flowers appear and the leaves color vividly before they begin to fall.

CULTIVATION: This plant is suitable for growing as a specimen or in open woodland. Grown in full sun, flowering is better and the autumn colors more intense. It needs an acid soil that is moist but well drained. Plants are slow growing and take time to become established. Propagate from seed in autumn or spring, or softwood cuttings in summer.

Oxydendrum arboreum ★
SORREL TREE, SOURWOOD

☀ ❄ ↔ 10 ft (3 m) ↑ 6–10 ft (1.8–3 m)

From woods and stream banks in eastern USA. Pointed glossy leaves, finely toothed, color vivid shades of red, purple, and yellow, in autumn. Fragrant white flowers, small urn-shaped, on slender spreading racemes at branch tips, in autumn. Zones 5–9.

OZOTHAMNUS
A member of the daisy (Asteraceae) family, this genus includes 50 species that occur in Australia, New Zealand, and New Caledonia. Most are shrubs, but a few are herbs. The compound inflorescences are composed of a large number of small daisy-like heads with a few female flowers in each head.

Oxalis vulcanicola

Ozothamnus obcordatus

Ozothamnus diosmifolius

Colors range from white to yellow to dark pink and various shades between. Most species are hairy to some degree, with several being quite woolly.
CULTIVATION: Neutral to acidic well-drained soils give best results, and most species prefer some shade rather than full sun. Extra water during long dry periods will be necessary. Most species are frost hardy, with those from high altitudes being very tolerant of long periods of snow cover. Propagate from seed, which needs to be fresh, or from cuttings. Seed from high-altitude species will need to be stratified in a refrigerator for a few weeks before being sown.

Ozothamnus adnatus
syn. *Helichrysum adnatum*
☀ ❄ ↔ 6 ft (1.8 m) ↑ 12 ft (3.5 m)
Shrub from southeastern New South Wales and eastern Victoria, Australia. Dark green linear leaves, hairy underneath, pressed close to hairy stems. Whitish flowerheads, borne in dense terminal inflorescences, from late summer to early autumn. They need light pruning to encourage flowering. Zones 8–10.

Ozothamnus coralloides
☀ ❄ ↔ 24 in (60 cm) ↑ 24 in (60 cm)
Native to New Zealand's South Island. Compact shrub with crowded branches. Small, thick, triangular leaves, shiny green on uppersurface, clothed in dense white hairs beneath; leaves overlap, closely pressed against stems. Yellow–whitish flowers, in single terminal heads, in summer. Zones 7–9.

Ozothamnus diosmifolius
syn. *Helichrysum diosmifolium*
PILL FLOWER, RICE FLOWER, WHITE DOGWOOD
☀ ❄ ↔ 7 ft (2 m) ↑ 15 ft (4.5 m)
Erect-growing shrub, commonly found from central Queensland to southeastern New South Wales, Australia. Thin dark green leaves, with hairy undersides. Tiny individual flowers, in small heads, ¼ in (6 mm) across; many hundreds of these heads form terminal clusters, in white to pink to red shades, from spring to summer. Widely grown for the cut flower trade. Zones 9–11.

Ozothamnus rosmarinifolius

Ozothamnus ledifolius
syn. *Helichrysum ledifolium*
KEROSENE BUSH
☀ ❄ ↔ 5 ft (1.5 m) ↑ 5 ft (1.5 m)
Restricted to mountains of Tasmania, Australia, at elevations above 2,500 ft (750 m). Sticky, yellow, young stems, very hairy. Narrow, hairy, aromatic leaves. Small white and yellow flower-heads, in terminal clusters, in summer. Prune after flowering to keep bushy. Zones 7–9.

Ozothamnus obcordatus
syn. *Helichrysum obcordatum*
GRAY EVERLASTING
☀ ❄ ↔ 5 ft (1.5 m) ↑ 5 ft (1.5 m)
Bushy shrub from eastern Australia, from Queensland to Tasmania. Heart-shaped leaves joined to stems by point of "heart." Tiny, shiny, green-gray leaves, hairy beneath. Dense terminal inflorescences, golden yellow flower-heads, in spring. Two subspecies: northern populations have larger leaves. Zones 8–10.

Ozothamnus rosmarinifolius
syn. *Helichrysum rosmarinifolium*
☀/☀ ❄ ↔ 6 ft (1.8 m) ↑ 10 ft (3 m)
Shrub from Tasmania, Victoria, and southern New South Wales, Australia. Stems hairy, trunk whitish. Narrow, woolly leaves, dense white hairs below. White to pink flowerheads, in spring–summer. Zones 8–10.

Ozothamnus selago
syn. *Helichrysum selago*
☀ ❄ ↔ 12 in (30 cm) ↑ 15 in (38 cm)
Found in rock crevices, in South Island, New Zealand. Tiny, thick, tri-angular leaves, pressed against stems, shiny green above, with dense white hairs below. Terminal yellow to white flowerheads, in summer. Zones 7–9.

Ozothamnus selago, in the wild, New Zealand

P

Pachira aquatica

× *Pacherocactus orcuttii*

× *PACHEROCACTUS*

A rare natural hybrid from Mexico belonging to the cactus (Cactaceae) family, discovered by the notable collector Charles Orcutt in 1886. For decades this plant was known as *Pachycereus orcuttii* but studies show that the parents are actually *Pachycereus pringlei* and *Bergerocactus emoryi*. Gordon Rowley, President of the British Cactus and Succulent Society, coined the new name for the plant in 1982.
CULTIVATION: While rarely available, it is easily grown in a rich well-drained soil. May be raised from seed, but is usually propagated from cuttings dried out for a week or two. Rest in winter.

× *Pacherocactus orcuttii*
syn. *Pachycereus orcuttii*
☼ ❀ ↔ 2½–4 in (6–10 cm) ↑ 7 ft (2 m)
Shrubby plant from Mexico. Up to 30 yellow-green branches on short trunks. Branches constricted at the end of each year's growth. Spines have 5 to 10 centrals and 20 or more radials. Flowers funnel-form, pale yellow. Calyx scaly, with numerous areoles, white wool and spines. Seed pods bear dense wool and spines. Zones 9–11.

PACHIRA

From tropical America. Genus of about 20 species of evergreen or deciduous trees in the kapok (Bombacaceae) family. They are cultivated as ornamentals for their handsome palmately lobed leaves and large flowers with a conspicuous tassel-like group of stamens fused into a tube at the base. Flowers last for a very short time and in some species are often hidden among thick foliage which is fully developed at the time of flowering. The woody fruiting capsules contain many kidney-shaped seeds embedded in a fleshy pulp.
CULTIVATION: Frost tender, these plants require a warm climate and a well-drained, moist situation in full sun. Propagate from seed or cuttings taken in autumn.

Pachira aquatica
SHAVING BRUSH TREE
☼ ✿ ↔ 10 ft (3 m) ↑ 20 ft (6 m)
Evergreen tree native to Mexico and northern South America. Large compound leaves, 5 to 9 leaflets. Large creamy white or greenish flowers, red-tipped stamens, in summer. Brown fruiting capsules, edible fruits which are roasted. Thrives in moist tropical conditions. Zones 10–12.

PACHYCEREUS

Genus of 9 species of large, tree-like cacti, family Cactaceae, all found in Mexico, with some straying into southern USA. They are upright plants, branching either at the base or further up the main stem. Shrubbier species may form clumps of unbranched stems. Stem ribbing is sharply angled, with clearly defined spine-bearing areoles along the ridges. The nocturnal flowers, usually white or in shades of pink, are tubular, around 2–3 in (5–8 cm) long, with protruding anthers.
CULTIVATION: As for all cacti, the soil should be very gritty and free draining, and the plants should receive sun for at least half the day. Some species will tolerate the occasional light frost, but in general they are warm climate plants. Moisture is appreciated in summer, but wet conditions in winter can lead to rotting. Propagate from seed or, with the unusual cultivars, by grafting.

Pachycereus marginatus ★
MEXICAN FENCE POST CACTUS
☼ ❀ ↔ 3–8 in (8–20 cm) ↑ 10–17 ft (3–5 m)
From Mexico. Stout, vertical, columnar branches are used as fences. Recognized by its 4 to 7 almost triangular ribs that bear elongated white to gray areoles. Spines yellow to gray, 1 to 3 centrals, 5 to 9 radials. Flowers funnel-form, red to pink. Seed pods spherical, with detachable spines and wool. Zones 10–12.

Pachycereus marginatus

Pachycereus pringlei
CARDON
☼ ❀ ↔ 24 in (60 cm) ↑ 35 ft (10 m)
From Mexico. Tree-like with thick trunk to 24 in (60 cm) in diameter. Branches blue-green becoming yellow-green, bearing 10 to 15 deep ribs. Spines 1 to 3 centrals, gray with black tips, 7 to 10 radials, whitish to gray. Flowering ribs develop large felted areoles bearing white funnel-form to bell-shaped flowers. Calyx scaly with masses of brown hair. Seed pod spherical, covered with dense yellowish brown felt and bristles. Zones 10–12.

Pachycereus schottii
syn. *Lophocereus schottii*
GARAMBUYO, SENITA, SINITA
☼ ❀ ↔ 2–4 in (5–10 cm)
↑ 3–10 ft (0.9–3 m)
From USA and Mexico. Tree-like to shrubby, with up to 100 yellow-green branches. Upper sections of flowering stems bear a distinctive mat of bristly gray spines, 2–40 in (5–100 cm) long. Spines 1 to 3 centrals, thin, gray, 3 to 15 radials, also gray. Flowers nocturnal,

Pachycereus pringlei, in the wild, Catavina, Baja California, Mexico

Pachycereus schottii

Pachycereus schottii 'Monstrosus'

Pachypodium densiflorum

Pachypodium horombense

Pachypodium lamerei

funnel-form, white to pink. The seed pods are spherical, red with red pulp. 'Monstrosus' ★ (syn. *Lophocereus schottii* f. *monstrosus*), completely spine-less and lacks distinct ribs. Branches are irregularly bumpy. Zones 10–12.

PACHYCORMUS

This genus of a single species in the cashew (Anacardiaceae) family, native to semi-desert regions of northwestern Mexico, is often used in the "desert garden." Valued for its massed display of tiny cup-shaped flowers, it is a slow-growing deciduous succulent, often with a very swollen trunk and stems.
CULTIVATION: Frost tender, this species requires full sun and very well-drained soil. Water adequately during the growing season and keep moist during the leafless dormant season. Propagate from seed in spring.

Pachycormus discolor

BAJA ELEPHANT TREE

☼ ✚ ↔ 3 ft (0.9 m) ↕ 12 ft (3.5 m)

Multi-branching succulent, trunk to 18 in (45 cm) thick. Bright green pinnate leaves, oval, slightly toothed leaflets. Masses of pink and cream cup-shaped flowers in terminal racemes, in summer. Zones 10–12.

PACHYPHRAGMA

This genus consists of a single species in the cabbage (Brassicaceae) family, found from northeastern Turkey to the Caucasus. It is a round-leafed perennial with spikes of small pure white flowers in spring. The foliage stays attractive throughout the growing season. *Pachyphragma* is closely allied to *Thlaspi*, possibly not distinct from it.
CULTIVATION: *Pachyphragma* makes an attractive, weed-smothering, slow-growing ground cover in lightly shaded aspects in humus-rich and moisture-retentive soils. Propagate from seed sown in autumn or from basal stem cuttings in late spring.

Pachyphragma macrophyllum

syns *Cardamine asarifolia*, *Thlaspi macrophyllum*

☼ ❋ ↔ 28–36 in (70–90 cm)
↕ 12–16 in (30–40 cm)

Herbaceous woodlands perennial with large, rounded, rich green leaves to 4 in (10 cm) across. Open spikes of pure white flowers, to ¾ in (18 mm) across, late winter–spring. Zones 7–9.

PACHYPHYTUM

Genus of 12 small Mexican succulents in the stonecrop (Crassulaceae) family. The name comes from the Greek *pachys* (thick) and *phyton* (plant), referring to the thick smooth leaves of these profusely offsetting plants. Most species grow in a distinct rosette shape, with tightly packed leaves, often with a pruinose (covered with a powdery bloom) finish to them. *Pachyphytum* is closely related to *Echeveria*, and many inter-generic hybrids are in cultivation.
CULTIVATION: Grow in a rich well-drained soil. Propagate by division of older plants, or from stem cuttings dried out for a few days, or from leaves placed on a bed of seed-raising mix. Cuttings and leaves will produce roots and new shoots within a few weeks in warmer months. May also be raised from seed. A brief rest from watering in winter is beneficial.

Pachyphytum compactum ★

☼/☀ ❋ ↔ 16 in (40 cm) ↕ 12 in (30 cm)

From Mexico. Stems branch from base, bearing rosettes of tightly packed, short, cylindrical, dark green to gray-white leaves, ¾–1¼ in (18–30 mm) long, tapering to point with keel below tip. Inflorescence, 16 in (40 cm) tall, of many green-tipped bell-shaped flowers, ⅓ in (8 mm) long. Zones 8–11.

PACHYPODIUM

The 17 species of this genus, belonging to the dogbane (Apocynaceae) family, come from Madagascar and southern Africa. They are cactus-like deciduous succulents with very spiny main stems and usually few branches. Variable in size, the largest reaching 25 ft (8 m). Leaves are smooth-edged and sprout from the upper parts of stems and branches. The 4 species from South Africa can stand cooler temperatures, but a minimum winter temperature of 50°F (10°C) is needed for most species.
CULTIVATION: They need full sun and a fertile soil with maximum drainage. If growing in containers, do not water through the dormant (winter) period. Apply a low-nitrogen fertilizer once a month during the growing season. In warm climates they grow outdoors in sharply drained, moderately fertile soil. Propagate by sowing seed in pots in a propagator or take stem tip cuttings in late spring.

Pachypodium baronii

☼ ⚘ ↔ 3 ft (0.9 m) ↕ 10 ft (3 m)

Native to northern Madagascar. Tree-like succulent, a thorny caudex and a crown of prickly branches. Elliptic gray-green leaves tapering at the tip. Brilliant red flowers, in summer, salvi-form in shape. *P. b.* var. *windsori* is shorter and its flowers have a white center. Zones 9–11.

Pachypodium densiflorum

☼ ✚ ↔ 40 in (100 cm) ↕ 20 in (50 cm)

From southern Madagascar. Tuberous succulent with thick branches. The branchlets carry paired spines to 5 in (12 mm) long. Flowers bright yellow, 1 to 10 per inflorescence. Fruits with 2 horned lobes, suffused dark red. Zones 11–12.

Pachypodium geayi

☼ ✚ ↔ 5 ft (1.5 m) ↕ 25 ft (8 m)

Candelabra-shaped succulent tree from southern Madagascar. with cigar- or bottle-shaped trunk to 32 in (80 cm) across, branching after first flowering; branchlets carry spines in 3s, to ¾ in (18 mm). Leaves to 18 in (45 cm) long, narrow, usually hairy. Flowers yellow to white inside, fragrant. Zones 11–12.

Pachypodium horombense

☼ ⚘ ↔ 27 in (70 cm) ↕ 24 in (60 cm)

From Madagascar. Succulent subshrub with trunk to 12 in (30 cm) diameter and gray-green bark. Branchlets with paired spines to ½ in (12 mm). Leaves to 3 in (8 cm long), gray on under-side. Flowers bright yellow, 4 to 11 per inflorescence. Zones 10–12.

Pachypodium lamerei ★

☼ ⚘ ↔ 6 ft (1.8 m) ↕ 20 ft (6 m)

From southern and southwestern areas of Madagascar. Tree-like succulent, thick, thorny stem, branching at top with age. Terminal clusters of glossy dark green leaves. Fragrant frangipani-like flowers, in summer. Fruit shaped like a double banana. Zones 9–11.

Pachyphragma macrophyllum

Pachycormus discolor, in the wild, Bahia de los Angeles, Baja California, Mexico

Pachypodium namaquanum

☼ ❄ ↔ 12 in (30 cm) ↑ 17 ft (5 m)

From Namibia and the Cape region of South Africa. Cactus-like, usually unbranched succulent. Tapering trunk covered in upper part with spines in 3s, to 3 in (8 cm) long. Leaves at apex of trunk, hairy, to 6 in (15 cm) long. Flowers red, sometimes yellow outside, 3 to 10 per inflorescence. Strictly protected in wild. **Zones 9–11.**

Pachypodium rosulatum

☼ ❄ ↔ 3 ft (0.9 m) ↑ 5 ft (1.5 m)

Native to Madagascar. Variable succulent, thorny stem with thick forked branches. New leaves hairy at first, becoming smooth, shiny, elliptic and frosted green in color. Slightly tubular yellow flowers, in summer. **Zones 9–11.**

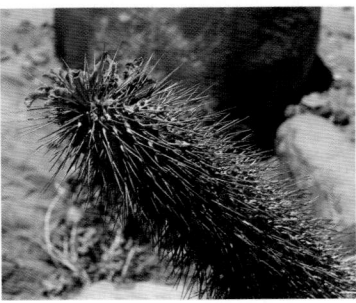

Pachypodium namaquanum, in the wild, Karoo, South Africa

Pachypodium rutenbergianum

Pachypodium rutenbergianum

☼ ❄ ↔ 15 ft (4.5 m) ↑ 40 ft (12 m)

From Madagascar. Candelabra-shaped succulent tree. Cigar- or bottle-shaped trunk to 40 in (100 cm) diameter, branchlets with paired spines to ¾ in (18 mm). Leaves to 18 in (45 cm) long, hairless. Flowers white, followed by 2-lobed brown fruit. Bark used in textile-making. **Zones 10–12.**

Pachypodium succulentum

☼ ❄ ↔ 24 in (60 cm) ↑ 7 ft (2 m)

Native to South Africa. Succulent shrub with half-subterranean tuberous trunk and branchlets with paired spines to 1 in (25 mm). The leaves are 7 in (18 cm) long. The flowers are white with pink or red lines, 1 to 9 per inflorescence, and followed by

Pachypodium rosulatum

2-lobed fruits (1 lobe sometimes not developing), pale gray, suffused dark red. **Zones 10–12.**

PACHYRHIZUS

YAM BEAN

This genus of about 6 twining, climbing herbs with long, massive, tuberous roots, within the pea-flower subfamily of the legume (Fabaceae) family, originates from tropical South America to Mexico and has naturalized in Florida, USA. Large compound leaves with 3 toothed leaflets and green, blue, purple, white, or mauve pea-flowers in dense racemes, up to 8 in (20 cm) long, appear in spring, followed by clusters of flattened pods. Some species are grown widely in Central America and parts of eastern Asia for their edible roots, the only part of the plant not poisonous.

CULTIVATION: Sow seed in sandy soil in a warm, dry, sunny area, spacing about 12 in (30 cm) apart. Remove flowers to enhance root growth and harvest before first frost. Vines may need support. Propagate from seed.

Pachyrhizus erosus

JICAMA, MEXICAN POTATO, MEXICAN TURNIP, YAM BEAN

☼ ❧ ↔ 3–6 ft (0.9–1.8 m) ↑ 10–20 ft (3–6 m)

Central American herbaceous twining climber. Edible, starchy, tuberous root to 8 ft (2.4 m) may weigh over 50 lb (23 kg). Compound leaves, 3 toothed leaflets. Flowers purple-violet to white. Green, flattened, bean-shaped pods. Root eaten raw or cooked. **Zones 10–11.**

PACHYSANDRA

Commonly known as spurge, *Pachysandra* belongs to the box (Buxaceae) family and contains 5 species of low-growing shrubby or creeping perennials native to North America and East Asia. Some are deciduous, some are semi-evergreen or evergreen, depending on the climate. They are used for ground cover in shady places and although slow to get started they are reliable once established. They spread by underground runners and have the

Pachysandra terminalis

Pachysandra terminalis

Pachysandra terminalis 'Green Spike'

advantage of being able to grow over tree roots. They have a compact growth and attractive tidy foliage, growing in whorls at the tip of the stem. The flowers are insignificant but scented and appear in the spring. The name *Pachysandra* comes from the Greek *pachys*, thick, and *andros*, man, referring to the thick stamens.

CULTIVATION: Ideal conditions for these plants include shade, in moist slightly acidic soil, with organic matter incorporated. If too much light is admitted to their growing area, the foliage will turn yellow and they will not grow well. Propagate by division or from cuttings in summer.

Pachysandra procumbens

ALLEGHENY PACHYSANDRA, ALLEGHENY SPURGE

☼ ❄ ↔ 12–18 in (30–45 cm) ↑ 6–12 in (15–30 cm)

From eastern Kentucky to Florida and Louisiana, USA. Deciduous in colder areas, semi-evergreen or evergreen elsewhere. The leaves are dull green, tinged gray; and may be mottled with brown or gray colorings. Small white or pinkish flowers. **Zones 5–9.**

Pachysandra terminalis

JAPANESE PACHYSANDRA, JAPANESE SPURGE

☼ ❄ ↔ 18 in (45 cm) ↑ 8–12 in (20–30 cm)

Native to Japan. The leaves are a shiny dark green with slightly toothed edges. The flowers are small and white. Withstands heavy shade and tree roots. 'Green Spike' is a popular cultivar; 'Variegata' has green and gray-green leaves variegated with creamy white. **Zones 5–10.**

PACHYSTACHYS

The 12 species of evergreen perennials and shrubs in this genus, a member of the acanthus (Acanthaceae) family, are native to tropical America. They are closely related to *Justicia* with similar showy, terminal flower spikes. The tubular flowers are 2-lipped and have large overlapping bracts. The opposite leaves are quite large with a rather wrinkled surface due to their prominent veining.

CULTIVATION: In cool climates these are indoor or greenhouse plants, but in warm humid areas they can be grown outside. They will require a fertile, moist but well-drained soil in a semi-shaded situation. Propagation is best done from softwood cuttings taken in summer.

Pachystachys coccinea

CARDINAL'S GUARD

☀ ✦ ↔ 2 ft (0.6 m) ↑ 7 ft (2 m)

Shrub, native to northern South America, naturalized in the West Indies. Oval leaves to 8 in (20 cm) long. Terminal spikes of bright red flowers with large green bracts, most of the year. Zones 10–12.

Pachystachys lutea

GOLDEN CANDLES

☀ ✦ ↔ 20 in (50 cm) ↑ 36 in (90 cm)

Native to Peru. Shorter narrower leaves than *P. coccinea*. Long flowering season, with terminal spikes of showy golden yellow bracts that hold white tubular flowers. Zones 10–12.

PAEONIA

PEONY

This genus of 30 or so species is a member of the peony (Paeoniaceae) family. It is named after Paeon, who was physician to the gods in Greek mythology. Most of the species are herbaceous perennials native to temperate parts of the Northern Hemisphere. There are also shrubs and subshrubs known as tree peonies, which have persistent woody stems, brilliantly colored flowers, and highly decorative foliage.

Pachystachys lutea

Paeonia anomala var. *intermedia*

Paeonia californica

CULTIVATION: Peonies are best suited to deep fertile soils of basaltic origin, heavily fed annually with organic matter; soils should not be allowed to dry out in summer. Protection from strong winds and scorching sun is essential, and some protection from early spring frost. The only pruning that is necessary is the removal of spent flowerheads and dead or misplaced shoots. Propagate from seed, which can be slow and difficult, or by division of herbaceous peonies, or by apical grafting of tree peonies, with the graft union being buried 3 in (8 cm) below soil level.

Paeonia anomala

☀ ❅ ↔ 24 in (60 cm) ↑ 20 in (50 cm)

From western Mongolia to Siberia and Russian steppes. Biternate, finely divided, dark green leaves, fine hairs on main veins, bluish green beneath; foliage orange in autumn. Single crimson flowers with slightly undulating petals in early summer. *P. a.* var. *intermedia* differs in having furry carpels. Zones 5–9.

Pachystachys lutea

Paeonia delavayi var. *lutea*

Paeonia cambessedesii

Paeonia brownii

☀ ❅ ↔ 20 in (50 cm) ↑ 18 in (45 cm)

A native to the high desert and mountain areas of the western USA. The small maroon and green flowers are never fully opened, and are borne above dark green, deeply dissected leaves in early summer. This species has adapted to extremely dry summers and becomes dormant after flowering. Zones 7–9.

Paeonia californica

☀ ❅ ↔ 20 in (50 cm)
↑ 15–30 in (38–75 cm)

From low elevations in southern and central California, USA. Smaller, less divided leaves than *P. brownii*; small purple flowers in early spring; dormant with onset of summer dryness. Needs sandy well-drained soil. Zones 7–9.

Paeonia cambessedesii

MAJORCAN PEONY

☀ ❅ ↔ 24 in (60 cm) ↑ 24 in (60 cm)

From the Balearic Islands. Leathery, ovate leaves with purple-suffused veining, wavy margins; reddish stems.

Paeonia × *chamaeleon*

Flowers single, deep rose to magenta, darker veins, in spring. Requires protection in winter. Zones 8–9.

Paeonia × *chamaeleon*

☀ ❅ ↔ 20 in (50 cm) ↑ 20 in (50 cm)

Naturally occurring hybrid between *P. mlokosewitschii* and *P. caucasica*, from mountains of Georgia. Oval leaflets are bluish green. Flowers variable in color, from pink to creamy yellow, in late spring. Zones 6–9.

Paeonia delavayi

MAROON TREE PEONY

☀/☀ ❅ ↔ 5 ft (1.5 m) ↑ 7 ft (2 m)

From western China. Deciduous suckering shrub. Dark green leaves large, deeply cut, bluish green below. Saucer-shaped flowers, dark red, deep gold anthers, in spring. Pod-like fruits with colored sepals. *P. d.* var. *lutea* (syn. *P. lutea*), lemon yellow, single flowers in mid-spring. *P. d.* var. *ludlowii* (syn. *P. l.* var. *ludlowii*), larger than *P. d.* var. *lutea*, less divided leaves, more open flowers, to 5 in (12 cm) across, profuse in early spring. Zones 6–9.

P

Paeonia lactiflora 'Carrara'

P. lactiflora 'Bowl of Beauty'

Paeonia lactiflora 'Globe of Light'

Paeonia lactiflora 'Haku-Gah'

Paeonia lactiflora 'Heirloom'

Paeonia lactiflora 'Helen'

Paeonia lactiflora 'Requiem'

Paeonia lactiflora 'Sarah Bernhardt'

Paeonia lactiflora 'White Cap'

Paeonia lactiflora cultivar

Paeonia lactiflora cultivar

Paeonia lactiflora

syn. *Paeonia albiflora*

CHINESE PEONY

☀ ❄ ↔ 24 in (60 cm) ↑ 24 in (60 cm)
Native to steppes and scrub of Siberia,
Tibet, Inner Mongolia, and China.
Erect stems, lobed, pointed leaves, good
autumn color. Two or more scented
white flowers per stem, to 4 in (10 cm)
diameter, early–mid-summer. A parent
of thousands of cultivars and hybrids.
Easy to grow in well-drained soil; tolerates winter temperatures to −22°F

(−30°C). Cultivars mostly taller, to
40 in (100 cm), include: '**A La Mode**',
scented white flowers, petals shiny,
serrated, up to 4 blooms per stem, mid-
spring; '**Angel Cheeks**', double pink
flowers; '**Barrington Belle**', deep red
outer petals, gold-edged pink or deep
red, petal-like staminodes (narrow inner petals); very free flowering; '**Bowl
of Beauty**', large, rose pink, rounded
outer petals, mass of creamy staminodes, early–mid-summer; '**Carrara**',
tall, white outer petals, mass of white
staminodes; '**Cora Stubbs**', tall, pale
lilac outer petals, cream and pale pink
petaloids; '**Dawn Pink**', large, single
pink, in late spring; '**Duchesse de
Nemours**', sweetly scented, double
cream flowers flushed pale yellow toward center; '**Globe of Light**', petals
almost white-edged, becoming bright
pink toward center, free flowering,
early summer; '**Haku-Gah**', white
flowers; '**Heirloom**' ★, fully double
pale pink; '**Helen**', old cultivar, single

pink flowers; '**Kelway's Supreme**',
scented, single or semi-double blush
pink flowers, very free flowering, late
spring–mid-summer; '**Laura Dessert**',
heavily rose-scented, double pale pink
flowers fading to white at edges of
petals, late spring; '**Miss America**', very
beautiful, large, semi-double, scented,
pure white flowers flushed creamy
yellow at center, spring; '**Moonstone**',
large flowers, blush pink fading to
white; '**Nellie Shaylor**', red flowers;
'**Peppermint**', double flowers, opening blush pink, fading to white, cream
flush at center, outer petals with crimson streak, early summer; '**Pillow Talk**',
fully double, outer petals rose pink,
pale yellow staminodes surround pink
center, late spring; '**Pink Lemonade**',
anemone- or double-flowered, pink
and yellow petals; '**Pink Princess**'
(syn. 'Pink Dawn'), rather crinkled
petals, pale pink outer edge, fading
to white at center; '**Reine Wilhelmine**',
fully double, scented, rose pink flowers,
fine carmine markings in center, very
free flowering, in the early summer;

'**Requiem**', spicy-scented, single blush
cream flowers, free flowering, late
spring; '**Sarah Bernhardt**', fully double,
scented, large, rose pink flowers fading
to blush on outer edges, early to mid-
summer; '**Sorbet**', fully double, rose
pink outer petals surrounding ring of
finely fringed cream petals enclosing
pink center, early–mid-summer; '**White
Cap**', scented, burgundy outer petals
surrounding cream, fringed inner
petals, early–mid-summer; '**White
Wings**', scented, purple-streaked buds
opening to pure white single flowers,
mid-summer. Zones 6–9.

Paeonia × lemoinei

☀/☀ ❄ ↔ 6 ft (1.8 m) ↑ 6 ft (1.8 m)
Name of a group of cultivars originating as crosses between *P. lutea* and
P. suffruticosa, inheriting the strong
yellow coloring of *P. lutea,* usually
flushed red in the center or colors
blended giving shades of orange.
'**Roman Child**' has semi-double yellow flowers with dark red blotches at
the bases of the petals. Zones 6–9.

Paeonia × *lemoinei* 'Roman Child'

Paeonia mascula subsp. *arietina*

Paeonia officinalis 'Rosea Plena'

Paeonia mascula subsp. *russii*

Paeonia mascula

MALE PEONY

☀ ❄ ↔ 24 in (60 cm)
↕ 24–36 in (60–90 cm)

Variable species from forests of southern Europe. Large, spreading clumps. Dark green ovate leaves, bluish green below. Single flowers, 5 in (12 cm) wide, usually deep rose red or pink, sometimes magenta or white, mid- to late spring. Good autumn color. Once used in medicines. *P. m.* subsp. *arietina*, from Turkey and eastern Europe, leaves biternate, narrowly elliptic, light or dark green, bluish green below, red or pink single flowers; '**Mother of Pearl**', large, pale pink, single; '**Northern Glory**', single, carmine; '**Purple Emperor**', single, magenta; '**Rosy Gem**', single, rosy pink. *P. m.* subsp. *russii*, shorter, from Mediterranean islands and central Greece; mid-green oval leaflets, purple below, purplish stems; flowers single, deep pink, in mid-spring. Zones 8–9.

Paeonia mlokosewitschii ★

CAUCASIAN PEONY, MOLLY THE WITCH

☀ ❄ ↔ 40 in (100 cm) ↕ 40 in (100 cm)

One of the most famous peonies, from sunny hillsides and oak forests of the Caucasus. Oval leaves, blue-green above, lighter below, good autumn color. Bowl-shaped flowers, clear glowing yellow, late spring. Zones 6–9.

Paeonia mollis

☀ ❄ ↔ 18 in (45 cm) ↕ 18 in (45 cm)

Dwarf peony believed to originate in Russia. Deeply cut blue-green leaves. Small red or white flowers, 3 in (8 cm) in diameter, on very short stems, in late spring. Zones 6–9.

Paeonia obovata

☀ ❄ ↔ 24 in (60 cm) ↕ 24 in (60 cm)

Found in mountain woods and scrub in Siberia, China, Japan, and Korea. The lower leaves are biternate with obovate leaflets which increase in size after flowering. The single, 2½ in (6 cm) diameter, rose purple flowers, open in mid-spring–early summer. *P. o.* var. *alba* is a white-flowered form. Zones 7–9.

Paeonia officinalis

FEMALE PEONY

☀ ❄ ↔ 24 in (60 cm)
↕ 15–24 in (38–60 cm)

Native to Europe. Most famous of all peonies, cultivated from ancient times for its medicinal properties. Lower leaves dark green, biternate, deeply cut into narrow segments. The single flowers, 5 in (12 cm) across, are magenta to deep red. '**Rosea Plena**', double, bright pink; '**Rubra**', an old cultivar, single, deep red; '**Rubra Plena**' (syn. 'Memorial Day'), very vigorous, with double flowers, deep red. Zones 8–9.

Paeonia mollis

Paeonia peregrina

RED PEONY OF CONSTANTINOPLE

☀/☀ ❄ ↔ 20 in (50 cm) ↕ 20 in (50 cm)

From the Balkans and Turkey. Shiny, dark green, biternate leaves, consisting of up to 18 segments, turning yellow in color during autumn. Very beautiful deep red, cup-shaped, single flowers up to 5 in (12 cm) across are seen in mid- to late spring. '**Fire King**', shiny petals, scarlet; '**Otto Froebel**', vermilion-red; '**Sunbeam**', orange-red. Zones 8–9.

Paeonia rhodia

☀ ❄ ↔ 15 in (38 cm) ↕ 15 in (38 cm)

Species native to the Greek island of Rhodes, where it is found growing in cypress forests and on rocky slopes. Dark green leaves, deeply dissected, consisting of up to 29 segments. The single white flowers appear in early spring. In its native habitat it dies away with the onset of dry summer weather. Zones 8–9.

Paeonia rockii

syn. *Paeonia suffruticosa* 'Joseph Rock'

ROCK'S VARIETY

☀ ❄ ↔ 3 ft (0.9 m) ↕ 7 ft (2 m)

From northern Sichuan, southern Gansu, and Qinghai Provinces, China. A sought-after tree peony which has woody stems and coarsely toothed, bipinnate, bright green leaves. It produces single white flowers, with notched petals, distinguished by a deep purple central blotch. '**Fen He**', pink flowers. Zones 7–10.

Paeonia peregrina

Paeonia rockii 'Fen He'

Paeonia tenuifolia

Paeonia veitchii

Paeonia wittmanniana

Paeonia suffruticosa

MOUTAN, TREE PEONY

☀/☀ ❋ ↔ 7 ft (2 m) ↑ 7 ft (2 m)

Found from northwestern China west to Bhutan. A freely branching upright shrub, with smooth mid-green leaves variously cut and lobed, with bluish green undersides. Large, sometimes double, white, pink, yellow, or red flowers, solitary, petals fluted, frilled on the edges, in mid-spring. Cultivar flowers in various shades of red, pink, white, and violet, with a purplish blotch near the base; some are slightly fragrant. 'Godaishu', white flowers, semi-double; 'Hiro-no-Yuki', large, semi-double, white flowers; 'Louise

Mouchelet' produces pale pink flowers; 'Mountain Treasure', white flowers, purplish blotches at petal bases; 'Shin-Shium-Ryo', yellow flowers; 'Yellow Heaven', yellow flowers; 'Zenobia', rich magenta blooms. Zones 4–9.

Paeonia tenuifolia

☀ ❋ ↔ 20–27 in (50–70 cm) ↑ 20–27 in (50–70 cm)

Dainty herbaceous species found from southeastern Europe to the Caucasus. Finely dissected feathery leaves and single, blood red, bowl-shaped flowers to 3 in (8 cm) across, with yellow stamens, in spring. 'Plena' is a full double red selection. Zones 8–9.

Paeonia veitchii

☀ ❋ ↔ 20 in (50 cm) ↑ 24 in (60 cm)

From central China, found in sub-alpine meadows and scrub. An ideal species for rock gardens. The bronze green, deeply divided leaves have good autumn color. The slightly nodding, single flowers, a deep rosy pink, are borne, 2 or more to a stem, in early summer. Zones 8–9.

Paeonia wittmanniana

☀ ❋ ↔ 32 in (80 cm) ↑ 40 in (100 cm)

This species is a native of northern Iran, Turkey, Azerbaijan, and Georgia, found in alpine valleys and on rocky hillsides. The large broadly ovate leaves are bronze when young, maturing to a dark glossy green. *P. wittmanniana* produces single bowl-shaped flowers, cream to pale yellow, which appear in the late spring. *P. w.* **var.** *nudicarpa* (syn. *P. steveniana*) is distinguished by its hairless carpels. Zones 7–9.

Paeonia wittmanniana var. *nudicarpa*

Paeonia Hybrid Cultivars

☀ ❋ ↔ 30–36 in (70–90 cm) ↑ 30–36 in (70–90 cm)

The breeding of herbaceous peonies was greatly enhanced by the introduction from China in the mid-eighteenth century of *P. lactiflora,* bringing, among other qualities, an attractive fragrance and the ability to produce double flowers. Among the best of the countless hybrid cultivars are: 'America', with large, single, scented, scarlet

Paeonia suffruticosa 'Mountain Treasure'

Paeonia suffruticosa 'Hiro-no-Yuki'

Paeonia suffruticosa 'Louise Mouchelet'

Paeonia suffruticosa 'Hakuo-jisi'

Paeonia suffruticosa

P. suffruticosa 'Shin-Shium-Ryo'

P. suffruticosa 'Yellow Heaven'

Paeonia suffruticosa 'Zenobia'

flowers; '**Avant Garde**', single, pale pink with darker veins; '**Buckeye Belle**', unusual semi-double, very dark red, rather crinkled petals; '**Burma Ruby**', a hybrid between *P. lactiflora* and *P. peregrina,* with single red flowers, an important cultivar for breeding; '**Coral Charm**', profuse, large, semi-double, coral peach, spring flowering; '**Early Windflower**', a hybrid between *P. emodi* and *P. veitchii,* with small, single, white flowers, in early spring; '**Fairy Princess**', single red flowers, in mid-spring; '**Flame**', single, orange-tinted bright red flowers, mid-spring; '**Gauguin**', large, single, long-lasting yellow flowers with red center, early spring; '**Hakuo-jisi**' (syns 'King of White Lion', 'White Tailed Lion'), a Japanese tree peony, double white flowers flushed purple toward the center; '**Honor**', single deep pink flowers; '**Paula Fay**', semi-double, bright pink, scented flowers flushed with white in the center; '**Pink Hawaiian Coral**', scented, semi-double, smallish coral pink flowers with white stripe on outer petals, spring flowering; '**Prairie Moon**', very beautiful, single to semi-double, pale yellow flowers, early spring; '**Red Charm**', a hybrid between *P. lactiflora* and *P. officinalis* 'Rubra Plena', with fully double, deep red, ruffled petals, early spring; '**Salmon Surprise**', single, salmon pink flowers; '**Sanctus**', hybrid between *P. lactiflora* and *P. officinalis,* single white flowers; '**Scarlett O'Hara**', a hybrid between *P. lactiflora* and *P. officinalis,* single bright red flowers, early spring; '**Souvenir de Maxime Cornu**' (syns 'Kinshe', 'Souvenir de Professeur Maxime Cornu'), *P. lemoinei* hybrid, with large, fully double, yellow flowers flushing to soft orange at the center with red margins; and '**Vesuvian**', smaller growing, with deep, dark red flushed purple, almost black flowers, finely divided leaves, showing good autumn color. Zones 6–9.

Paeonia, Hybrid Cultivar, 'Vesuvian'

Paeonia, Hybrid Cultivar, 'Flame'

Paeonia, Hybrid Cultivar, 'Paula Fay'

Paeonia, Hybrid Cultivar, 'Honor'

Paeonia, Hybrid Cultivar, 'Sanctus'

Paeonia, Hybrid Cultivar, 'Red Charm'

Paeonia, Hybrid Cultivar, 'Souvenir de Maxime Cornu'

Paeonia, Hybrid Cultivar, 'Burma Ruby'

Paeonia, Hybrid Cultivar, 'Buckeye Belle'

Pandanus tectorius (tree at rear), Noosa Heads, Queensland, Australia

Pandanus tectorius 'Variegatus'

PALIURUS

This genus belonging to the buckthorn (Rhamnaceae) family contains 8 species of evergreen or deciduous small trees or shrubs native to southern Europe and eastern Asia. The stems are armed with pairs of spines and the leaves are alternately arranged. Small yellowish green flowers are followed by flat round fruits with a membranous wing. CULTIVATION: Grow in a warm sunny position in fertile well-drained soil. Some species can be used for hedging. Cut out old wood in winter to prevent overcrowding. Propagate from seed or softwood cuttings taken in summer.

Paliurus spina-christi

CHRIST'S THORN

☼ ❄ ↔ 8 ft (2.4 m) ↑ 10–25 ft (3–8 m)
Found from Spain to central Asia. Slender straggling shrub or small tree. Arching stems, many thorns in pairs, 1 straight, 1 curved. Yellowish green flowers, in small clusters, in spring–summer. Flat circular fruits. Zones 8–10.

PANAX

GINSENG

In the ivy (Araliaceae) family, this once large Asian and eastern North American genus of tuberous-rooted perennials has now been reduced to just 5 species, many of its former members now being classified under *Polyscias*. Most species have a very heavy rootstock, producing upright stems with whorls of palmate leaves made up of 3 to 7 leaflets. The small white flowers, borne in clusters at the stem tips, are followed by yellow, red, or near-black drupes. The best-known species is *P. ginseng*, the roots of which are the source of the herb ginseng, which has myriad uses in Asia. CULTIVATION: *Panax* is mostly very cold hardy but requires long warm summers to perform well. Plant in humus-rich, moist, well-drained soil in a position shaded from the hottest afternoon sun and sheltered from cold drafts. Water and feed well during the growing season and propagate by division in late winter or raise from seed.

Panax ginseng

syn. *Panax* 'Schinseng'

GINSENG, NIN-SIN

☼ ❄ ↔ 8–12 in (20–30 cm)
↑ 6–8 in (15–20 cm)
Perennial herb from Korea and northeastern China. Carrot-shaped, branching, aromatic rootstock, valued in traditional medicine. Compound leaves, 5 elliptical to oval-shaped, finely serrated leaflets. Small, greenish white, summer flowers. Red berry-like fruit. Zones 4–6.

PANDANUS

The evergreen screw pines, with about 700 species in the family Pandanaceae, are found in east Africa, Madagascar, India, the Malay Peninsula, the Pacific Islands, and northern Australia, in various habitats. Most are tree-like with trunks supported by stilt roots. Stems are commonly branched with terminal clusters of long, leathery, strap-like, parallel-veined leaves. Male and female flowers borne in dense spikes on separate plants. Resembling a pineapple, the woody or fleshy fruits, many edible after cooking, can be yellow, pink, or red. Dispersed by animals or ocean currents. Leaves and roots used by local native communities for weaving baskets, mats, ropes, and fishing nets. CULTIVATION: Need full sun and moist well-drained soil in warm humid environments. Propagate from seed, soaked for 24 hours before sowing. Propagation may also be from offsets, rooted suckers, and limbs detached in storms.

Pandanus aquaticus

☼ ❄ ↔ 10 ft (3 m) ↑ 20 ft (6 m)
Found along watercourses in semi-arid or seasonally dry areas of the north of Australia. Grassy foliage clustered at branch tips. Spadices of petal-less flowers, globular multi-part fruit clusters, soft when ripe. Zones 11–12.

Pandanus odoratissimus

BREADFRUIT, HALA SCREW PINE, PANDANG

☼ ❄ ↔ 10 ft (3 m) ↑ 20 ft (6 m)
From tropical coastlines of much of the Indian and Pacific Oceans. Strongly divided stems, stilt-rooted at base, pointed leaves, sharply spined margins, pendulous tips. Female flowers, enclosed in edible yellow bracts. Fruits yellow, red, or light green. Some botanists suggest it cannot be distinguished from *P. tectorius*. Zones 11–12.

Pandanus pygmaeus

☼ ❄ ↔ 18–24 in (45–60 cm)
↑ 18–24 in (45–60 cm)
Spreading shrub from Madagascar. Stems branching from base, prop roots grow from upper parts. Long narrow leaves, bluish green beneath, edged with fine brown spines, appearing spirally arranged due to screw-like growth of stem. Simple flowers with no petals. Female plants bear cone-like fruit. Zones 10–11.

Pandanus sanderi

☼ ❄ ↔ 3–4 ft (0.9–1.2 m)
↑ 12–15 ft (3.5–4.5 m)
Perennial shrub, native to Timor. The short stems and stiff, strap-like leaves are striped with yellow or gold and have green minute spines along the margins. 'Roehrsianus' has leaves striped with yellow. Zones 10–11.

Pandanus tectorius

BEACH SCREW PINE, PANDANG

☼ ❄ ↔ 10 ft (3 m) ↑ 25 ft (8 m)
From Tahiti and the western Pacific. Spreading plant supported by strong stilt roots. Leaves have spiny margins and midribs on the undersides. Male flowers sweetly scented, orange fruits ornamental. Traditionally foliage used for weaving and thatching. 'Variegatus', yellow striped leaves. Zones 11–12.

Pandanus aquaticus, in the wild, Mataranka, Northern Territory, Australia

Pandanus odoratissimus, in the wild, Kauai, Hawaii, USA

Pandanus utilis

Pandanus utilis
COMMON SCREW PINE

☀ ⚘ ↔ 15 ft (4.5 m) ↑ 40–60 ft (12–18 m)

Many-branched Madagascan tree. Stiff, blue-green leaves arranged in spirals, red spines. Aerial roots help buttress the tree. The inflorescences carry masses of minute creamy white flowers. Rounded compound fruits of woody drupes that are edible when fully ripe. Zones 10–12.

PANDOREA

A small genus consisting of 6 species and several cultivars in the trumpet-vine (Bignoniaceae) family. This genus has been classified as *Bignonia* and *Tecoma* in the past. These woody ever-green climbers, which are grown for their flowers and foliage, are native to Australia, New Caledonia, Malaysia, and New Guinea, where they grow from sea level up to 9,840 ft (3,000 m). Leaflets are usually green and glossy, and the plant climbs by using tendrils. Flowers are 5-petalled, tubular, fra-grant, and usually white, cream, buff, or pink. An excellent choice for per-golas, archways or trellises. The genus name comes from the Greek legend of Pandora's box, referring to the box-like seed capsules.

CULTIVATION: These warm climate plants grow best in moist well-drained soil in full sun. Prune after flowering. Propagate from seed, cuttings or layers.

Pandorea jasminoides
syns *Bignonia jasminoides,*
Tecoma jasminoides

BOWER-OF-BEAUTY, BOWER PLANT

☀ ⚘ ↔ 8–15 ft (2.4–4.5 m) ↑ 17 ft (5 m)

Vigorous twining climber with glossy bright green leaflets. White flowers with hot-pink throats produced in abundance on large panicles from spring–summer. Prefers rich moist soil. '**Alba**', pure white flowering form;

Pandorea pandorana

'**Charisma**', yellow variegated form, pink flowers with a crimson throat; '**Lady Di**' (syn. 'Snow Queen'), white flowers with a creamy yellow to orange-yellow throat; '**Rosea**', pink flowers with deep pink throat; '**Rosea Superba**', pink flowers, throat spotted purple. Zones 9–11.

Pandorea pandorana
syns *Bignonia pandorana, Pandorea doratoxylon, P. oxleyii, Tecoma australis*

WONGA WONGA VINE

☀ ⚘ ↔ 10–20 ft (3–6 m) ↑ 20 ft (6 m)

Vigorous twining climber with long whippy stems. Leaflets bright green and glossy. Flowers produced in abun-dance in late winter are small, tubular and usually white, cream, buff, pinkish, or maroon, often spotted with purple. '**Golden Showers**' (syn. 'Golden Rain'), rust-colored buds open to golden yellow flowers. Zones 9–11.

PANICUM
CRAB GRASS, PANIC GRASS

A huge genus of about 470 species of grasses belonging to the family Poaceae. They can be annual or peren-nial, evergreen or deciduous, and are native to the tropics as well as North America and Europe. Only a few species of *Panicum* are considered to be ornamental, but those are admired for their light and airy looks. Some are valued as fodder crops.

Panicum virgatum 'Heavy Metal'

CULTIVATION: Species that are likely to be used in gardens all like a sunny aspect in fertile, well-drained, but moist soil. Perennial species are propa-gated by division in early spring, and annuals from seed sown in spring.

Panicum miliaceum
BROOM CORN MILLET, HOG MILLET, MILLET

☀ ❄ ↔ 8–10 in (20–25 cm) ↑ 36–40 in (90–100 cm)

An annual species from Europe and Asia. It is grown mainly for its seeds that can be fed to birds. These plants are reasonably ornamental, with up-right clumps of bright green arching leaves and sprays of soft fluffy flower-heads in summer. A form with purple leaves and flowerheads is also grown. Zones 5–9.

Panicum virgatum
SWITCH GRASS

☀ ❄ ↔ 27–32 in (70–80 cm) ↑ 36–40 in (90–100 cm)

Clumping herbaceous grass found from Canada to Central America. Bright green narrow leaves to 24 in (60 cm) long. Bears open, drooping, fluffy panicles with tiny purple-green flowers, in autumn, these turn straw-colored as they mature. '**Heavy Metal**', has more erect blue-gray leaves, pink inflorescences; '**Warrior**' is a tall form with foliage turning red-brown as it dies. Zones 5–10.

Panicum virgatum 'Warrior'

Panicum virgatum

PAPAVER
POPPY

This readily recognised and widespread group of around 50 species of annuals and perennials gives its name to the poppy (Papaveraceae) family. Today we associate poppies with war remem-brance days, though it was Homer, the ninth-century BC Greek poet, who first linked the hanging poppy bud with a dying soldier. From basal rosettes of usually finely lobed often hairy leaves emerge bristly upright flower stems, each with one nodding bud, rarely 2 or 3. The flowers most often have 4 crape-like petals around a central ovary topped with a promi-nent stigmatic disc. Red is a common color, though the range is huge.

CULTIVATION: Most are very hardy and prefer a sunny position with light, moist, and well-drained soil. Propagate perennial poppy cultivars by root cut-tings, otherwise raise from seed.

Papaver alpinum
ALPINE POPPY

☀/◑ ❄ ↔ 8–16 in (20–40 cm) ↑ 10 in (25 cm)

Variable summer-flowering perennial from mountains of southern Europe, possibly conglomerate of closely related species. Forms basal clump of finely divided, downy, gray-green to blue-green leaves. Orange, yellow, or white flowers borne singly. Zones 5–9.

Papaver alpinum

P

Papaver orientale 'Harbutt's
Choice Mixed'

Papaver orientale 'Marcus Perry'

Papaver orientale 'Mrs Perry'

Papaver orientale 'Splendissimum'

Papaver orientale, Goliath Group, 'Beauty of Livermere'

Papaver anomalum

☀/◐ ❄ ↔ 8–12 in (20–30 cm)
↕ 16 in (40 cm)

Summer-flowering perennial from
China, forming clump of blue-green
pinnate leaves to 4 in (10 cm) long.
Wiry stems with orange-brown hairs.
Solitary, narrow-petalled orange flowers
to 1½ in (35 mm) wide. Zones 7–10.

Papaver atlanticum

☀/◐ ❄ ↔ 8–12 in (20–30 cm)
↕ 18 in (45 cm)

Summer-flowering perennial from
Morocco. Broad, hairy, lance-shaped

Papaver nudicaule 'Meadhome's Strain'

Papaver nudicaule

leaves, coarsely toothed or lobed.
Flowers usually solitary but stems
sometimes forked, light orange to red.
'**Flore Pleno**' has orange double flowers
on stocky stems. Zones 6–10.

Papaver bracteatum

☀ ❄ ↔ 16–36 in (40–90 cm)
↕ 32–40 in (80–100 cm)

Summer-flowering perennial from
the Caucasus and western Asia. Forms
clump of pinnate, gray-green to light
green, basal leaves. Flowers bright red
with maroon basal blotches, on white-
haired stems. Zones 5–10.

Papaver nudicaule 'Pacino'

Papaver commutatum

☀/◐ ❄ ↔ 16 in (40 cm) ↕ 16 in (40 cm)

Summer-flowering annual native to
western Asia. Leaves, to 6 in (15 cm)
long, are sometimes shallowly lobed.
The flowers are red with black basal
blotches, 2 in (5 cm) wide. '**Lady
Bird**' is slightly taller, with bright red
flowers liberally splashed with black.
Zones 8–10.

Papaver × hybridum

ROUGH POPPY

☀/◐ ❄ ↔ 6–10 in (15–25 cm)
↕ 8–20 in (20–50 cm)

Naturally occurring hybrid. Eurasian
annual with finely divided pinnate
leaves to 4 in (10 cm) long. Bright
red flowers with a purple blotch at
the base of the petals. Zones 6–9.

Papaver nudicaule

syn. *Papaver croceum*, *P. miyabeanum*
ARCTIC POPPY, ICELAND POPPY

☀/◐ ❄ ↔ 8–12 in (20–30 cm)
↕ 12–16 in (30–40 cm)

Perennial, native to subarctic regions,
flowering in spring–summer. Often
treated as an annual. Pinnate leaves,
often light blue-green, hairy. Bears
solitary long-stemmed flowers to 3 in
(8 cm) wide, in many colors; wild
forms usually white, yellow, or orange.

Papaver commutatum

Papaver orientale 'Orangeade Maison'

P. n. var. *croceum*, orange to orange-
red flowers. *P. n.* '**Pacino**', yellow
flowers on stocky stems; mixed-color
seedling strains include: **Meadhome's
Strain**, producing a range of bright
warm colors; and **Artist Mixed** in
soft pastel tones. Zones 2–9.

Papaver orientale

ORIENTAL POPPY

☀/◐ ❄ ↔ 12–20 in (30–50 cm)
↕ 24–40 in (60–100 cm)

This is a summer-flowering western
Asian perennial. Forms a sturdy clump
of bristly, pinnate, often blue-green
leaves to 10 in (25 cm) long. The
flower stems are usually leafy on the
lower half. The flowers are solitary,
to 4 in (10 cm) wide, red, orange, or
pink, often darker blotched. There are
many cultivars of *P. orientale*. '**Black
and White**' has large white flowers
with a black center; '**Cedric Morris**' ★,
very hairy leaves and dark-blotched
soft pink flowers; the **Goliath Group**
are sturdy plants, and have very large
flowers in bright colors with dark centers, such as '**Beauty of Livermere**',
deep red with small black blotches;
'**Mrs Perry**', large salmon pink flowers
with dark blotches; and '**Princess
Victoria Louise**', ruffled apricot pink
flowers with dark blotches. Zones 3–10.

Papaver rhaeticum

☼/◐ ❋ ↔ 6 in (15 cm) ↑ 4 in (10 cm)

Summer-flowering alpine perennial native to the Pyrenees. Small compact plant forming basal tuft of downy, pinnate leaves to 3 in (8 cm) long. Solitary, 1½ in (35 mm) wide, yellow or orange flowers. Zones 5–9.

Papaver rhoeas

CORN POPPY, FIELD POPPY, FLANDERS POPPY

☼/◐ ❋ ↔ 12–16 in (30–40 cm)
↑ 36–48 in (90–120 cm)

Vigorous, hardy, summer-flowering annual from Old World temperate zones. Pinnate leaves to 6 in (15 cm) long. Bristly flower stems, solitary bright red flowers to 3 in (8 cm) wide, sometimes with black basal blotch. Mixed color strains include: 'Mother of Pearl', unusual pastel mauves, pink, red, gray tones, often subtly blended; Shirley Mixed, single or double flowers in range of colors. Zones 5–9.

Papaver rupifragum

☼/◐ ❋ ↔ 8–12 in (20–30 cm)
↑ 18 in (45 cm)

Perennial, native to Spain. Tufted clump of finely divided, downy, pinnate leaves 4 in (10 cm) long. Solitary flowers to 3 in (8 cm) wide, dusky shade of red-brown, late spring–summer. Zones 7–10.

Papaver somniferum

OPIUM POPPY

☼ ❋ ↔ 12–24 in (30–60 cm)
↑ 3–4 ft (0.9–1.2 m)

Vigorous summer-flowering annual from southeastern Europe and western Asia. Leaves light blue-green, heavy textured, deeply cut with jagged teeth. Strong, leafy flower stems. Flowers 4 in (10 cm) wide, white, mauve, or purple, sometimes with a dark basal blotch. The conspicuous seed pods are the source of opium. *P. s.* var. *paeoniflorum*, deep blue-green leaves, peony-like maroon-black double flowers. *P. s.* 'Hen & Chickens', lavender flowers, large seed pod surrounded by small pods; 'White Cloud', tall, white double flowers. Zones 7–10.

Papaver rhaeticum

Paphiopedilum bellatulum

PAPHIOPEDILUM

SLIPPER ORCHID

The slipper orchids from the family Orchidaceae have long been highly prized in horticulture, with their distinctive modified labellum or "pouch." They are cultivated throughout the world, and countless hybrids have been produced from the 80 or so different species. The range extends from India eastward across southern China to the Philippines and throughout Southeast Asia and Malaysia to New Guinea and the Solomon Islands. New species continue to be discovered, particularly in remote rainforest areas of Borneo and China. There is a huge amount of diversity within the genus: some are terrestrial, growing through the leaf litter on the forest floor; others are lithophytes that show a preference for limestone cliffs; while a number are epiphytes, happy to live in the major forks of rainforest trees. Most species produce a single flower, but some may have up to a dozen or more open at one time, and then there are others that flower sequentially. They are generally found in quite bright situations, but not receiving direct sunlight. These flowers, which come in a wide range of colors and form, often last for well over a month in pristine condition. Most have plain green strap leaves, others have distinctive mottled foliage, which makes them attractive plants even when they are not in flower. Slipper orchids generally grow in quite moist and humid environments. They do not have pseudobulbs but store water in their fleshy leaves and thick, hairy root system. This genus was

Papaver rupifragum

Paphiopedilum species

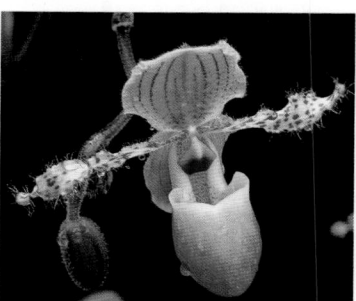

Paphiopedilum glaucophyllum

named for the temple to Aphrodite (Venus) at Paphos, on the island of Cyprus, and the Greek *pedilon* meaning a slipper. The French call slipper orchids *sabots de Venus*.

CULTIVATION: They are best grown in pots, in a well-drained, bark-based medium. Select a pot size that fits the roots snugly, as they will not tolerate stagnant conditions around the root system. Pot the plant so that it is only slightly buried, as often the roots will push it out of the mix, and any exposed new roots can become dry and not develop further. Keep plants shaded and moist during the warmer months, and mist foliage frequently. Many of the multi-flowered species need a drier rest in winter, in combination with a significant drop in day and night-time temperature. There are cool-, intermediate-, and warm-growing species. Cultural requirements depend on the origin, habitat, and altitude of the particular species. Propagate by division.

Paphiopedilum barbatum

☼ ✿ ↔ 6–16 in (15–40 cm)
↑ 6–12 in (15–30 cm)

From Peninsular Malaysia. Tessellated foliage and a single, 3 in (8 cm) bloom, white and green overlaid with distinct purple stripes and suffusions, that appears in spring to summer. This species is closely related to *P. callosum*. Zones 10–12.

Paphiopedilum barbatum

Paphiopedilum bellatulum

☼ ✿ ↔ 8–12 in (20–30 cm)
↑ 2½–6 in (6–15 cm)

Native to Thailand and Myanmar. This summer-blooming species produces large white flowers with sizeable dark maroon spots. The very short flower stem lets the single 3 in (8 cm) wide bloom rest on the waxy tessellated leaves. Zones 10–12.

Paphiopedilum exul

☼/◐ ✿ ↔ 8–16 in (20–40 cm)
↑ 4–12 in (10–30 cm)

Small, summer-flowering, tropical species from Thailand. Stiff plain green leaves and a single, 2½ in (6 cm) wide, green and white bloom with bold maroon spotting on the base of the dorsal sepal. Closely related to *P. insigne*. Zones 11–12.

Paphiopedilum glaucophyllum

☼ ✿ ↔ 8–20 in (20–50 cm)
↑ 4–24 in (10–60 cm)

From Java. Long spikes of sequentially flowering, yellowish green, pink, and white, 3 in (8 cm) wide flowers, with plain bluish green foliage. Can bloom throughout the year. Zones 10–12.

P

Paphiopedilum gratrixianum

Paphiopedilum hainanense

Paphiopedilum haynaldianum

Paphiopedilum insigne

Paphiopedilum gratrixianum

☀ ⁑ ↔ 8–16 in (20–40 cm)
↕ 4–16 in (10–40 cm)

From Vietnam and Laos. Single, 3 in (8 cm) wide bloom, predominantly glossy brown with some maroon spotting and white edges to the dorsal sepal; winter-flowering. Zones 9–12.

Paphiopedilum hainanense

☀ ✄ ↔ 8–12 in (20–30 cm)
↕ 6–20 in (15–50 cm)

A native of Hainan Island, China, this species has tessellated foliage and produces a single 3 in (8 cm) wide bloom, predominantly green and pale purple, in late winter–spring. Some

botanists consider this species to be within the range for the related *P. appletonianum*. Zones 10–12.

Paphiopedilum haynaldianum

☀ ✄ ↔ 12–24 in (30–60 cm)
↕ 4–32 in (10–80 cm)

A native of the Philippines. Multi-flowered spring- and summer-blooming species. Plain green leathery leaves. Up to 5, 5 in (12 cm) wide flowers are produced at the same time and are green, white, and mauve marked with dark red blotches. Zones 10–12.

Paphiopedilum henryanum

☀ ✄ ↔ 8–12 in (20–30 cm)
↕ 4–16 in (10–40 cm)

Stunning and distinctive spring-flowering species from China and

Paphiopedilum mastersianum

Paphiopedilum henryanum

Vietnam. Plain green leaves and a single, 2½ in (6 cm) wide, colorful bloom. The dorsal sepal is green with bold maroon spots, the petals are brownish purple, the labellum is a bright dark pink. Zones 10–12.

Paphiopedilum hirsutissimum

☀ ⁑ ↔ 8–16 in (20–40 cm)
↕ 4–16 in (10–40 cm)

From India to Indochina. Winter- to spring-flowering species with hairy flower stems. Green, brown, and purple, 6 in (15 cm) wide flowers also densely covered in hairs. Zones 9–11.

Paphiopedilum insigne ★

☀ ⁑ ↔ 8–12 in (20–30 cm)
↕ 4–16 in (10–40 cm)

From Nepal and northern India. Commonly grown, variable, winter-flowering species with glossy, brownish yellow, 5 in (12 cm) wide flowers, heavily spotted in red-brown. A cool-growing species that readily grows into a specimen. Zones 9–11.

Paphiopedilum lowii

☀ ✄ ↔ 12–24 in (30–60 cm)
↕ 8–40 in (20–100 cm)

From Peninsular Malaysia, Borneo, and Indonesia. Variable multi-flowered species, similar to *P. haynaldianum*, but lacking spotting on the dorsal sepal. The 6 in (15 cm) wide flowers are green, white, and deep purple, produced on stems of up to 6 blooms in spring–summer. Zones 10–12.

Paphiopedilum niveum

Paphiopedilum mastersianum

☀ ✄ ↔ 8–12 in (20–30 cm)
↕ 4–20 in (10–50 cm)

From Ambon, Indonesia. Tessellated-leafed species, single bloom in summer. Flower 4 in (10 cm) wide, very glossy, mainly tan, and olive green dorsal sepal with a pure white border. Zones 11–12.

Paphiopedilum moquettianum

☀ ✄ ↔ 8–24 in (20–60 cm)
↕ 4–27 in (10–70 cm)

From Java. Long spikes of sequential, green, pink, and yellow, 3 in (8 cm) wide flowers; plain green leaves. It can bloom throughout year. Closely related to *P. glaucophyllum*. Zones 10–12.

Paphiopedilum niveum

☀ ✄ ↔ 4–8 in (10–20 cm)
↕ 4–12 in (10–30 cm)

From Thailand. In the wild, summer-blooming on limestone cliffs near sea level. Wide-segmented, 3 in (8 cm) wide flowers, white with maroon peppering. Tessellated leaves. Zones 11–12.

Paphiopedilum moquettianum

Paphiopedilum hirsutissimum

Paphiopedilum villosum

Paphiopedilum philippinense

☀ ✚ ↔ 8–16 in (20–40 cm)
↕ 8–24 in (20–60 cm)

From Philippines and north Borneo. Multi-flowered green-leafed, up to 5, 4 in (10 cm) wide, summer blooms,

Paphiopedilum philippinense

Paphiopedilum spicerianum

white dorsal sepal with maroon stripes, reddish brown, elongated, often twisted petals, mustard labellum. Zones 10–12.

Paphiopedilum primulinum

☀ ✚ ↔ 8–16 in (20–40 cm)
↕ 4–24 in (10–60 cm)

From Sumatra. Blooms throughout year. Long spikes of sequential, bright canary yellow, 3 in (8 cm) wide flowers, green tinged dorsal sepal. Zones 10–12.

Paphiopedilum rothschildianum

☀ ✚ ↔ 8–32 in (20–80 cm)
↕ 8–36 in (20–90 cm)

From Sabah (north Borneo). Regal spring- to summer-blooming species

Paphiopedilum rothschildianum

that produces up to 5 dark-striped flowers on an upright spike; each flower to 12 in (30 cm) across the extended petals. *P. rothschildianum* is the most impressive and majestic species in the genus and endemic to Mt Kinabalu where it often occurs in large clumps. Zones 10–12.

Paphiopedilum spicerianum

☀ ⚘ ↔ 8–12 in (20–30 cm)
↕ 4–16 in (10–40 cm)

This species is native to India and blooms in autumn. *P. spicerianum* produces flowers with olive green undulating petals, a bronze pouch, and a broad dorsal sepal that is white with a green base and has a narrow, central, purple stripe. These blooms are 3 in (8 cm) across. Zones 9–11.

Paphiopedilum primulinum

Paphiopedilum victoria-regina

Paphiopedilum victoria-regina

☀ ✚ ↔ 8–24 in (20–60 cm)
↕ 4–27 in (10–70 cm)

From Sumatra. Long spikes of up to 20 sequentially produced, green, maroon, and pink flowers, 3 in (8 cm) wide. Can bloom throughout the year. Previously well-known in cultivation as *P. chamberlainianum*. Zones 10–12.

Paphiopedilum villosum

☀ ⚘ ↔ 8–12 in (20–30 cm)
↕ 4–16 in (10–40 cm)

From India to Indochina. Commonly grown. Flowers glossy, 5 in (12 cm) wide, with bronze overlay. Dorsal sepal green with very dark brown markings at base. Petals 2-tone; top half reddish brown, bottom half yellowish green. Blooms in winter–spring. Zones 9–11.

Paphiopedilum Hybrids

☀ ❄ ↔ 4–8 in (10–20 cm)
↑ 4–24 in (10–60 cm)

While there are hundreds of possible combinations, there have been 3 basic styles of hybrids, popular with orchid enthusiasts for over a century. The "Maudiae"-type hybrids (*P.* Maudiae, an antique hybrid between *P. callosum* and *P. lawrenceanum*) have tessellated 2-tone foliage and single blooms with prominent stripes on the broad, white, dorsal sepal. Of these, the "albino" hybrids have green stripes on the dorsal, with green petals and pouch; the "coloratum" hybrids are the same, but with purple stripes, while the "vinicolors" have deep beetroot-colored flowers and almost black stripes. Multifloral hybrids have grown in popularity, and often feature larger flowered, spectacular species, such as *P. rothschildianum*, *P. philippinense*, *P. stonei,* and, since

its rediscovery, *P. sanderianum*. The third group are the "complex hybrids;" these are the large, round, single-flowered plants often seen at orchid shows. Ironically, despite being developed for over a century, there is only a handful of species in their pedigree. They are mostly multiple generation hybrids, with high ratios of *P. insigne*, *P. spicerianum*, and *P. villosum*, with minor influences of *P. bellatulum*, *P. charlesworthii*, *P. druryi*, *P. exul*, and *P. niveum*. Obviously, many of today's desirable species were unknown when most of this breeding was undertaken. Here is a selection of slipper orchid hybrids, most of which are hybrids that are crosses between 2 different species. **Booth's Sand Lady**, a multi-flowered hybrid; **Delophyllum**, a hybrid between *P. delenatii* and *P. glaucophyllum*; **Gael**, an albino "Maudiae-type" hybrid; **Gold Dollar**,

Paphiopedilum, Hybrid, Pathfinder Norm

Paphiopedilum, Hybrid, Madame Martinet

P., Hybrid, Booth's Sand Lady

Paphiopedilum, Hybrid, Darling

P., Hybrid, Delophyllum

P., Hybrid, Faire-Maud

Paphiopedilum, Hybrid, Morganiae

Paphiopedilum, Hybrid, Gael

P., Hybrid, Gold Dollar

Paphiopedilum, Hybrid, Honey

Paphiopedilum, Hybrid, Juno

P., Hybrid, Lebaudyanum

Paphiopedilum, Hybrid, Mitylene

Paphiopedilum, Hybrid, Onyx

Paphiopedilum, Hybrid, Oriental Enchantment

Paphiopedilum, Hybrid, Pinocchio 'Yellow'

Paphiopedilum, Hybrid, Pinocchio

P., Hybrid, Red Fusion

Paphiopedilum, Hybrid, Rolfei

Paphiopedilum, Hybrid, Yospur

Paphiopedilum, Hybrid, Saint Swithin

Paphiopedilum, Hybrid, Sioux

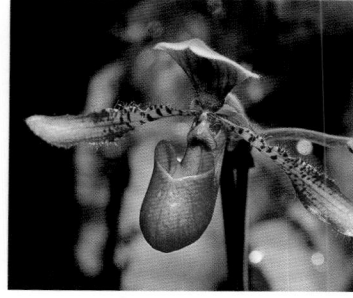

Paphiopedilum, Hybrid, Song of Love

a hybrid of the yellow-flowered species *P. armeniacum* and *P. primulinum*; **Honey**, a hybrid of *P. philippinense* and *P. primulinum*; **Lebaudyanum**, a hybrid of the multi-flowered species *P. haynaldianum* and *P. philippinense*; **Madame Martinet**, a hybrid between *P. delenatii* and *P. callosum;* **Mitylene**, an albino "Maudiae-type" hybrid; **Onyx**, an albino "Maudiae-type"; **Oriental Enchantment**, an albino "Maudiae-type" hybrid with white blooms striped with bright green; **Pathfinder Norm**, a "complex" or "exhibition" style *Paphiopedilum* hybrid; **Pinocchio**, a hybrid between *P. primulinum* and *P. glaucophyllum*; **Red Fusion**, a vinicolor "Maudiae-type" hybrid with deep claret colored blooms; **Rolfei**, a hybrid between *P. bellatulum* and *P. rothschildianum*;

Saint Swithin, a hybrid between *P. philippinense* and *P. rothschildianum* with large flowers; **Sioux**, a "complex" or "exhibition" style *Paphiopedilum* hybrid; and **Yospur** with round white blooms overlaid with some fine pepper spotting of purple. Zones 9–11.

PARADISEA

PARADISE LILY, ST BRUNO'S LILY

A genus of 2 species in the asphodel (Asphodelaceae) family, native to the woods and alpine pastures of Europe. Perennials with a short underground rhizome, strappy basal leaves, and stems of fragrant white trumpet flowers in summer. Excellent cut flowers.
CULTIVATION: Prefer moist but well-drained humus-rich soil in full sun or partial shade. Propagate from seed sown fresh or divide when dormant.

Paradisea liliastrum

☼/◐ ❄ ↔ 10–12 in (25–30 cm)
↕ 16–24 in (40–60 cm)

Clump-forming perennial with narrow, gray-green, grass-like foliage to 10 in (25 cm) long through which emerge upright spikes of slightly drooping, fragrant, white trumpets to 2½ in (6 cm) long. '**Major**' has larger trumpets. Zones 7–9.

PARAHEBE

Revised in recent years, this genus of some 30 species belonging to the fox-glove (Scrophulariaceae) family grows largely in New Zealand with a few species in Australia and New Guinea. Low, spreading plants best regarded as subshrubs, sometimes developing a few woody branches with age. The leaves, on pliable wiry stems, are

small, dark green, and elliptical, often with toothed edges. Racemes of small, rounded flowers, usually white, pink, or mauve with contrasting veining, appear in late spring and summer.
CULTIVATION: Ideal for rock gardens, tubs, or among dwarf shrubs, para-hebes are easily cultivated in moist, well-drained soil and a reasonably sunny aspect. Tolerate moderate frosts but will not withstand drought without becoming sparsely foliaged and untidy. If necessary, trim back after flowering. Propagate from seed, layers (which often form naturally) or by taking small tip cuttings in summer and autumn.

Parahebe × *bidwillii*

☼ ❄ ↔ 6 in (15 cm) ↕ 4 in (10 cm)
Native to New Zealand. Cross between *P. decora* and *P. lyallii*. Mat-forming subshrub with tiny, round, dark green, leathery leaves and small, saucer-shaped, white flowers stained crimson in summer. Zones 6–11.

Parahebe catarractae

☼ ❄ ↔ 24 in (60 cm) ↕ 12 in (30 cm)
New Zealand native, larger species, most widely cultivated. Serrated, lance-shaped leaves, purple-red-tinted stems that often take root as they spread. Flowers white with purple veining. Pale blue, pink, and mauve-flowered forms, such as '**Falling Skies**', are quite common. Zones 8–10.

Parahebe lyallii

☼ ❄ ↔ 18 in (45 cm) ↕ 8 in (20 cm)
White to pale pink-flowered species from New Zealand develops a dense, mound of fine stems. Leaves have toothed edges, less than ½ in (12 mm) long. Flowers in sprays, held well clear of the foliage, in summer. Zones 8–10.

Paradisea liliastrum

Parahebe catarractae 'Falling Skies'

Parahebe catarractae

P

Paris polyphylla

Paraserianthes lophantha

Pardoglossom cheirifolium

PARAQUILEGIA

This genus belonging to the buttercup (Ranunculaceae) family contains 4 to 6 species, all native to the Himalayas and central and northern Asia, and found growing in alpine meadows and rock crevices. They are small, tufting plants like a miniature *Aquilegia* and distinguished from *Semiaquilegia* by the absence of staminodes.
CULTIVATION: Need a moist, well-drained soil and are usually grown in a cool greenhouse or scree garden as they require a cool summer and dry winter. Propagate from seed. All are very rare (and difficult) in cultivation.

Paraquilegia anemonoides
syns *Isopyrum grandiflorum*, *Paraquilegia grandiflora*
☀ ❄ ↔ 6 in (15 cm) ↑ 7 in (18 cm)
Choice collector's plant. Fragile species. Bluish green lobed leaves forming neat mound. Nodding, cup-shaped, spurless flowers on fine stems held above foliage. Two forms, one from the western Himalayas with small white flowers, the other from the eastern Himalayas with larger lilac flowers. Zones 5–9.

PARASERIANTHES
A member of the mimosa subfamily of the legume (Fabaceae) family, this

genus of 4 species occurs from Indonesia to tropical Australia and the Solomon Islands. All species have previously been included in the genus *Albizia*. *P. moluccana* holds the record for the world's fastest growing tree—just over 35 ft (10 m) in 13 months. These shrubs or trees are found in lowland rainforests and in moist areas of other types of vegetation.
CULTIVATION: Propagate from seed, which germinates readily without pretreatment, unlike most members of this subfamily. Fast growing in well-drained acid soils in full sun.

Paraserianthes lophantha
CAPE LEEUWIN WATTLE
☀ ❋ ↔ 10 ft (3 m) ↑ 25 ft (8 m)
From Indonesia, and naturalized in Australia. Fast-growing small tree, leaves bipinnate, many small leaflets. Small creamy flowers, inconspicuous petals, long prominent stamens, in spring. Long, flat, brownish pods contain many black seeds. Can become invasive, and is considered a weed in South Africa and parts of Australia. Zones 9–10.

PARDOGLOSSOM
Belonging to the borage (Boraginaceae) family, this genus is made up of around

6 biennials and perennials, formerly included in *Solenanthus* and *Cynoglossum*. They are found in northern temperate zones, mainly Eurasia, and are notable for their very hairy stems and foliage, which are often silver-gray. The flowers are small but their blue, purple, or pink coloration contrasts well with the foliage, white less so. Not the fanciest plants but very easy to cultivate and they naturalize well.
CULTIVATION: Mostly hardy in temperate zones where winters are not severe, these plants thrive in a sunny spot with light, gritty, well-drained soil and some added humus for moisture retention. The perennial species will grow from divisions or basal cuttings, like the biennials, but are most often raised from spring-sown seed.

Pardoglossom cheirifolium
syn. *Cynoglossum cheirifolium*
☀/❋ ❄ ↔ 12–16 in (30–40 cm)
↑ 12–16 in (30–40 cm)
Summer-flowering, southern European biennial. Upright stems, narrow, silvery white, spatula to lance-shaped leaves to over 2 in (5 cm) long. Heads of up to 12, ½ in (6 mm) wide, purple-red flowers at stem tips, age to purple-blue. Zones 7–10.

PARIETARIA
PELLITORY, STICKY WEED
A small genus of widely distributed herbaceous plants and small bushes from the nettle (Urticaceae) family, originating in warm and tropical regions. The leaves are alternate and slender lanceolate to ovate; the flowers are borne in axillary clusters and, on the same plant, may be male, female or bisexual. The fruits are covered in small, hooked, clinging hairs. *P. officinalis* was formerly grown for medicinal purposes. Some species may become weedy when they are outside their native habitat.

CULTIVATION: They prefer partial shade or partial to full sun, in soil which should be kept wet. Propagate from seed or by cuttings.

Parietaria judaica
syn. *Parietaria diffusa*
SPREADING PELLITORY
☀ ❋ ↔ 14–20 in (35–50 cm)
↑ 14–20 in (35–50 cm)
Perennial from the Mediterranean area, with sprawling, brittle, reddish stems. Oval-shaped leaves, with hairs on the veins on the underside. Inconspicuous green flowers cluster in the leaf axils in summer. Zones 5–8.

PARIS
A genus of more than 20 species of rhizomatous perennials in the wakerobin (Trilliaceae) family, found in woodlands from Europe across to eastern Asia. Erect stems from extremely slow-growing rhizomes. A whorl of leaves surrounds the unusual flowers at the top. These appear in summer, with spidery or lance-shaped petals, often in shades of green.
CULTIVATION: Grow in a cool aspect with moist not wet humus-rich soil. Propagate from seed, which can take 2 years or more to germinate, or by division of old clumps when dormant.

Paris polyphylla
syn. *Daiswa polyphylla*
☀/◐ ❋ ↔ 8–12 in (20–30 cm)
↑ 36–40 in (90–100 cm)
Slow-growing perennial found from the Himalayas to Myanmar and Thailand. Upright stems topped with up to 12 lance-shaped leaves to 7 in (18 cm) long. Flowers consist of up to 8 narrow green sepals, thread-like yellow petals, and a purple ovary. If cross-pollinated, the plant produces large green pods that contain red seeds. *P. p.* var. *yunnanensis alba* has white filament-like petals. Zones 6–9.

Parietaria judaica

Parodia alacriportana subsp. *buenekeri*

Paris quadrifolia

HERB PARIS

☀/◐ ❄ ↔ 10–12 in (25–30 cm)
↑ 8–16 in (20–40 cm)

Slow-growing herbaceous perennial from Europe and East Asia. Upright stems topped with 4 leaves to 6 in (15 cm) long. The flowers consist of 4 mid-green sepals and narrow white petals followed by blue-black seed capsules. Zones 6–9.

PARKIA

Genus of 30 species of tropical trees occurring in Asia, Africa, Madagascar, and the Americas, from the mimosa subfamily of the legume (Fabaceae) family. Small red or reddish brown, yellow, or white flowers, in dense heads, are either erect or pendulous, and last only one night. Asian species have pendulous flowerheads and American species are erect, reflecting the habits of their pollinating bats: the Asian bats land head up, the American bats head down! Leaves are bipinnate with many small leaflets. Fruits flat, elongated, or cylindrical, with flattish seeds embedded in a mealy pulp.

CULTIVATION: Propagation is from fresh seed that requires hot water soaking or scarification before sowing. Plants are fast growing and not very tolerant of frosts, being suitable only for the tropics and the warmer subtropics in well-drained organic soils that receive adequate rainfall or supplementary watering in drier times.

Parkia speciosa

PETAI

☀ ✦ ↔ 25–50 ft (8–15 m) ↑ 150 ft (45 m)

Large tree from lowland rainforests of the Malay Peninsula. Leaves bipinnate, 10 to 20 pairs of opposite leaflets. Densely crowded heads of creamy white flowers, in summer. Large green pods, ripen black. Used as food. Young seeds, leaves, and flower stalks are eaten raw. Zones 11–12.

PARKINSONIA

syn. *Cercidium*

A member of the pea-flower subfamily of the legume (Fabaceae) family, this genus of 12 evergreen or deciduous trees and shrubs is found in warmer arid regions of North America. It has narrow leaves and racemes of yellow pea-flowers. The fruit is a flattish pod containing numerous seeds.

CULTIVATION: *Parkinsonia* species prefer rich, moist, well-drained soils in a protected position. Propagate from seed which should be scarified for successful germination.

Parkinsonia aculeata

JERUSALEM THORN, PALO VERDE

☀/◐ ⬧ ↔ 20 ft (6 m) ↑ 30 ft (9 m)

Found on ephemeral watercourses of southwest USA and Mexico, naturalized in many countries. Spiny shrub or tree, drooping branches, pinnate leaves in pairs, with 25 pairs of leaflets. Clusters of yellow flowers in spring. Long narrow seed pods. Zones 9–11.

Parkinsonia florida

PALO VERDE

☀ ⬧ ↔ 25 ft (8 m) ↑ 25 ft (8 m)

Deciduous tree, native to southwestern USA. Pendulous foliage. Leafless for most of the year, foliage appears in spring, soon falls. Yellow flowers, to ¾ in (18 mm) across, in spring. Seed pods to 3 in (8 cm) long. Zones 9–11.

Parkinsonia praecox

PALO BREA

☀ ⬧ ↔ 20–30 ft (6–9 m) ↑ 20–30 ft (6–9 m)

Thorny deciduous tree from southwest USA. Blue-green pinnate leaves, rounded leaflets. Loose sprays of funnel-shaped yellow flowers form in spring. Lovely small shade tree for arid areas. Zones 9–10.

PARMENTIERA

From Mexico and Central America, this is a small genus of fewer than 10 species of evergreen shrubs or trees, often with spines. They belong to the trumpet-vine (Bignoniaceae) family. The bell-shaped or funnel-like, white or greenish flowers are produced singly or in small clusters emerging from the trunk or older branches. The opposite compound leaves are made up of 3 leaflets, and the linear or narrow

Parkinsonia aculeata

cylindrical fleshy fruit bears a similarity to candles. At least 1 species, *P. aculeata,* has sweet edible fruit.

CULTIVATION: Frost tender, they are occasionally cultivated in tropical and subtropical gardens where they prefer fertile, moist but well-drained soil in full sun. Propagate from seed or half-hardened cuttings in summer.

Parmentiera aculeata

syn. *Parmentiera edulis*

GUAJILOTE

☀ ✦ ↔ 10 ft (3 m) ↑ 30 ft (9 m)

Thorny Central American tree, broad crown, leaflets 2 in (5 cm) long. Greenish yellow funnel-shaped flowers, to 2½ in (6 cm) long. Yellowish green cucumber-shaped fruits, eaten fresh, cooked or pickled. Zones 10–12.

Parmentiera cereifera

CANDLE TREE

☀ ✦ ↔ 10 ft (3 m) ↑ 20 ft (6 m)

Native to Panama, small tree, branches from near ground level. Elliptic to almost diamond-shaped leaflets 2 in (5 cm) long. Waxy, greenish white, tubular flowers, to 3 in (8 cm) long. The greenish yellow fruits resemble candles. Zones 10–12.

PARODIA

This genus of about 50 succulent perennials in the cactus (Cactaceae) family is native to South America, from southern Brazil to northwestern Argentina. They may be simple or clustering, and range in form from small and spherical to columnar cacti up to 3 ft (0.9 m) tall. The stems are usually small, green, spherical, or cylindrical, with tubercles arranged in ribs that often spiral around them. The yellow to red many-petalled flowers are short and funnel-shaped with hairy, bristly tubes and narrow scales, borne on areoles with hairs and bristles around the top of the stem, from spring to autumn.

CULTIVATION: Prefer full sun or part-shade in a very well-drained soil, with regular watering in summer, but less in winter. Propagation is from seed in spring or summer, from cuttings in summer or by division of the offsets.

Parodia alacriportana

☀ ⬧ ↔ 2½–3 in (6–8 cm)
↑ 3–5 in (8–12 cm)

From southern Brazil. Simple or clustering. Spherical to elongated stem, 1 to 31 vertical ribs with tubercles. Bristly, white, brown, or orange spines, ageing to gray, in tuft at top of stem. Central spines 4 to 6, 1 often hooked, 14 to 20 radial spines. Golden yellow flowers in spring. *P. a.* subsp. *buenekeri* (syn. *P. buenekeri*) has fewer central spines. Zones 9–11.

Parmentiera cereifera

Parmentiera aculeata

Parkia speciosa

Parodia buiningii

syn. *Notocactus buiningii*

☀ ✂ ↔ 4–5 in (10–12 cm)
↕ 2½–3 in (6–8 cm)

From Southern Brazil and northern Uruguay. Pale green, spherical, sometimes flat stem with about 16 straight, thinly pointed ribs and blade-like tubercles; 3 or 4 straight, stiff, pale yellow central spines with dark brown base; 2 or 3 smaller radial spines. Yellow flowers in summer. Zones 9–11.

Parodia chrysacanthion

syns *Echinocactus chrysacanthion*, *Malacocarpus chrysacanthion*

GOLDEN POWDER PUFF

☀ ✂ ↔ 3–4 in (3–10 cm)
↕ 1¼–1¾ in (3–4 cm)

Slow-growing, simple, globular to columnar species from northern Argentina. Flattened-spherical to spherical stem, woolly tufted top,

Parodia comarapana

Parodia concinna

Parodia buiningii

with erect spines. Tubercles spirally arranged; 30 to 40 straight, golden yellow or paler spines. Yellow flowers, late winter–late spring. Zones 9–11.

Parodia comarapana

☀ ✂ ↔ 3 in (8 cm) ↕ 2–3 in (5–8 cm)

From central Bolivia. Simple or clustering. Stem has 12 to 21 straight or spiraling ribs patterned with tubercles and 4 to 8 straight, white to pale yellow brown-tipped central spines, 18 to 35 thin yellow radials. Yellow to orange flowers, in spring–summer. Zones 9–11.

Parodia concinna

syn. *Notocactus tabularis*

☀ ✂ ↔ 3–4 in (8–10 cm)
↕ 1¼–4 in (3–10 cm)

From southern Brazil and Uruguay. Usually simple. Flattened spherical stem elongates with maturity; 15 to 32 low ribs. Brown, reddish brown, or partly white to pale yellow spines, bristly, curved or twisted; 4 to 6 central spines, perhaps more, 9 to 25 shorter radial spines held close to stem. Yellow flowers in spring. Zones 9–11.

Parodia erinacea

syns *Notocactus acuatus*, *N. erinaceus*, *N. tetracanthus*, *Wigginsia erinacea*

☀ ✂ ↔ 2½–12 in (6–30 cm)
↕ 2½–12 in (6–30 cm)

From southern Brazil, Uruguay, and northern Argentina. Simple with

Parodia haselbergii

spherical or shortly cylindrical stem, very woolly top in older plants, 12 to 30 pointed ribs. Nearly white, gray, or brown, straight to curved spines; young plants less woolly, more spiny. Glossy yellow flowers in summer. Zones 9–10.

Parodia haselbergii ★

syns *Brasilicactus haselbergii*, *Notocactus haselbergii*

☀ ✂ ↔ 1¾–6 in (4–15 cm)
↕ 1¾–6 in (4–15 cm)

From southern Brazil. Simple with a spherical stem with depressed top, becoming distorted with age; 30 to 60 or more ribs with small tubercles, 25 to 60 straight, white or slightly yellow spines covering stem. Brilliant orange-red, occasionally orange-yellow, flowers appear in winter–spring. *P. h.* var. *stellatus* has yellowish spines. Zones 9–11.

Parodia horstii

syns *Notocactus horstii*, *N. muegelianus*, *N. purpureus*

☀ ✂ ↔ 4–6 in (10–15 cm)
↕ 8–12 in (20–30 cm)

From southern Brazil. Simple or slowly clustering. The spherical to elongated green stem becomes corky from the base with age; 12 to 19 well-defined ribs with low tubercles, 1 to 6 needle-shaped, yellow to brown, straight, curved or twisted central spines, and 10 to 15 fine, white to pale brown radial spines. Yellowish orange, red, or purple flowers, appear in summer–autumn, and occasionally in the spring. Zones 9–11.

Parodia horstii

Parodia magnifica

Parodia microsperma

Parodia leninghausii ★

syns *Eriocactus leninghausii*, *Notocactus leninghausii*

GOLDEN BALL CACTUS

☀ ✂ ↔ 3–4 in (8–10 cm)
↕ 3–24 in (8–60 cm)

From southern Brazil. Simple or clustering. Branching and becoming columnar with age. Cylindrical stem with slanted top, 30 to 35 straight ribs; 3 or 4 straight or curved, yellow or pale brown central spines, 15 to 20 or more radial spines. Lemon yellow flowers in summer, only at maturity. Zones 9–11.

Parodia magnifica ★

syns *Eriocactus magnificus*, *Notocactus magnificus*

☀ ✂ ↔ 3–6 in (8–15 cm)
↕ 3–12 in (8–30 cm)

From southern Brazil. Simple, occasionally clustering. Blue-green spherical to elongated stem, 11 to 15 straight pointed ribs; golden yellow spines. Sulfur yellow flowers, in late spring–summer. Zones 9–11.

Parodia mammulosa

syn. *Notocactus mammulosus*

☀ ✂ ↔ 2–5 in (5–12 cm)
↕ 2–10 in (5–25 cm)

From southern Brazil and Uruguay. Solitary with very dark, spherical to elongated stem with 13 to 21 well-defined vertical ribs, large pointed tubercles; 2 to 4 stiff, straight, stout, white, gray, or pale brown central spines, one strongly flattened; 6 to 25 off-white to pale brown radial spines. Yellow flowers. Zones 9–10.

Parodia microsperma

syns *Hickenia microsperma*, *Microspermia microsperma*, *Parodia webberiana*

☀ ✂ ↔ 2–4 in (5–10 cm)
↕ 2–8 in (5–20 cm)

Native to northern Argentina and southern Bolivia. Usually solitary, rarely offsetting. Flattened spherical stem, sometimes elongated, around 15 to 21 ribs with spiraling tubercles; 3 or 4 red, brown, or darker central pines, the lowermost hooked; 7 to 20 bristly, white radial spines. Yellow

to red flowers, spring–summer.
P. m. **var.** *rigidispina* has stouter
spines. Zones 9–11.

Parodia nivosa

syns *Parodia faustiana, P. uhligiana*
☀ ‡ ↔ 2–3 in (5–8 cm) ↕ 3–6 in (8–15 cm)
From northern Argentina. Solitary
with spherical to cylindrical stem,
tubercles in spiral pattern; 4 straight,
bristly, white central spines, about
18 finer white radial spines. Bright
red flowers in spring. Zones 9–11.

Parodia ottonis

syns *Notocactus acutus, N. ottonis*
☀ ‡ ↔ 1¼–6 in (3–15 cm)
↕ 1¼–6 in (3–15 cm)

Species from southern Brazil, Uruguay,
northeastern Argentina, and southern
Paraguay. Ball-shaped, solitary, later
clustering. More or less spherical, variably colored stem, tapered at base;
6 to 15 rounded or pointed ribs. Hair-
like, straight, curved, or twisted spines,
1 to 6 brown or yellow central spines,
4 to 15 off-white, yellow, or brown
radial spines. Yellow, sometimes reddish
orange, summer flowers. Zones 9–11.

Parodia rutilans

☀ ‡ ↔ 1½–2 in (3.5–5 cm)
↕ 1½–4 in (3.5–10 cm)

From northern Uruguay. Simple, dark
green spherical to elongated stem, 18
to 24 vertical or spiraled ribs; 2 stiff,
straight, reddish brown central spines,
14 to 16 whitish, needle-like, radial
spines, darker tips. Soft pink summer
flowers, yellow centers. Zones 9–11.

Parodia saint-pieana

☀ ‡ ↔ 2–2½ in (5–6 cm)
↕ 2–2½ in (5–6 cm)

Clustering spherical cactus native to
northern Argentina. Bright yellow
flowers. Zones 9–11.

Parodia schumanniana

syns *Eriocactus ampliocostatus, E. grossei,
Notocactus schumannianus*
☀ ‡ ↔ 10–12 in (25–30 cm)
↕ 1–6 ft (0.3–1.8 m)

Large, usually simple cactus from
southern Paraguay and northern

Parodia saint-pieana

Parrotia persica, in winter

Argentina. Green, globular to columnar
stem, 21 to 48 straight, pointed ribs,
fewer in young plants. Bristly, straight
or slightly curved, golden yellow,
brown, or reddish brown spines, ageing to gray; 3 to 4 central spines, about
4 radial spines. Produces lemon to
yellow flowers in summer. *P. s.* **subsp.**
claviceps (syn. P. claviceps) is not as
tall. Zones 9–11.

Parodia scopa ★

syns *Notocactus scopa, N. soldtianus*
SILVER BALL CACTUS
☀ ‡ ↔ 2½–4 in (6–10 cm)
↕ 2–20 in (5–50 cm)

From southern Brazil, Uruguay, and
northern Argentina. Simple or clumping, columnar. Dark green spherical
to cylindrical stem, mostly obscured
by spines; 25 to 40 low ribs with fine
tubercles, 3 to 4 brown, red, or white
central spines, 35 to 40 or more fine
white or pale yellow radial spines.
Bright yellow flowers in summer, in
ring around top of stem. Zones 9–11.

PARROTIA

This genus of a single species in the
witchhazel (Hamamelidaceae) family
is native to northern Iran and Russia,
where it is found in the forests south
and southwest of the Caspian Sea. It
was named after Dr F. W. Parrot, a
German plant collector who travelled
through the Middle East in the early
nineteenth century. It is grown mainly
for its beautiful leaf color, especially

Parodia schumanniana subsp. *claviceps*

Parrotia persica, in autumn

Parrotia persica, in spring

Parrotia persica, in summer

in spring and autumn. It is a useful
small tree for street planting and a very
suitable species for parks and gardens
in cool climates, where the foliage
colors brilliantly.
CULTIVATION: Any moderately fertile
soil with free drainage is suitable, including chalk soils; exposure to full
sun is desirable. Propagation is usually
from seed, which should be collected
just before being expelled from the
capsules, and sown immediately, taking
up to 18 months to germinate. Softwood cuttings taken in summer are
sometimes used.

Parrotia persica

IRON TREE, PERSIAN IRONWOOD, PERSIAN
PARROTIA, PERSIAN WITCH HAZEL
☀ ❋ ↔ 20 ft (6 m) ↕ 25–40 ft (8–12 m)
Small deciduous tree, short trunk with
flaking bark. Leaves simple, alternate,
leathery, shallowly toothed, and pale
lettuce-green. Spectacular range of
crimson, scarlet, orange, and yellow
tones, in autumn. Flowers, bright red
stamens, green calyx, enclosed in a
bract of dark brown hairy scales, in
late winter–spring. 'Pendula' ★, with
drooping branches, slowly develops into a dome-shaped mound. Zones 5–9.

PARROTIOPSIS

This genus belonging to the witch-hazel (Hamamelidaceae) family consists of a single deciduous small tree reaching 20 ft (6 m) high. Native to the Himalayas, it has hairy young shoots and toothed, ovate to rounded leaves 3 in (8 cm) long. The large flowerheads, about 2 in (5 cm) in diameter, are made up of densely packed yellow stamens surrounded by large, white, petal-like bracts. The fruit is an egg-shaped 2-beaked capsule. CULTIVATION: Moderately frost hardy, this is a beautiful species which requires a sunny, protected site and grows best in fertile, moist but well-drained soil. Propagation is from cuttings in the summer or from seed during autumn.

Parrotiopsis jacquemontiana

☼ ❄ ↔ 15 ft (4.5 m) ↑ 20 ft (6 m)
Slightly toothed ovate leaves turn shades of yellow in autumn. Produces attractive, creamy white and yellow flowerheads over a long period, in spring–early summer. Zones 5–9.

Passiflora alata

Passiflora caerulea

PARTHENOCISSUS

BOSTON IVY, VIRGINIA CREEPER

A genus of 10 species of deciduous tendril-producing climbers in the grape (Vitaceae) family from East Asia and North America. Grown for their attractive foliage and, in most species, their self-clinging habit, which makes them ideal to clothe walls. The leaves are either maple-shaped or divided into leaflets, and usually turn brilliant colors before they shed. The flowers are tiny and green, and, like the small black berries, have no ornamental value. CULTIVATION: They will grow in any moderately fertile soil in sun or part shade. Propagate from cuttings at almost any time or by removing rooted layers. Can also be raised from seed.

Parthenocissus henryana

CHINESE VIRGINIA CREEPER, SILVER VEIN CREEPER

☼/☀ ❄ ↔ 20 ft (6 m) ↑ 30–35 ft (9–10 m)
Lightly self-clinging species from China with 5 leaflets, to 5 in (12 cm) long, green above with a slightly purple reverse and white veins when grown in shade, the veins fading in sunlight. In autumn, the leaves turn brilliant red with white veins. Zones 7–10.

Parthenocissus inserta

☼ ❄ ↔ 30 ft (9 m) ↑ 30–35 ft (9–10 m)
North American species with leaves divided into 5 leaflets to 5 in (12 cm) long that color intensely before shedding. Differs from the true Virginia creeper, *P. quinquefolia*, in having tendrils without suction cups and slightly thicker foliage. Zones 3–10.

Parthenocissus tricuspidata 'Veitchii'

Parthenocissus quinquefolia

syn. *Vitis quinquefolia*

VIRGINIA CREEPER

☼/☀ ❄ ↔ 30 ft (9 m) ↑ 40–50 ft (12–15 m)
Fast-growing self-clinging climber with suction cups on the tendrils and 5 leaflets to 5 in (12 cm) long, turning brilliant scarlet before shedding. *P. q.* var. *engelmannii* has smaller leaves. Zones 3–10.

Parthenocissus tricuspidata

BOSTON IVY, JAPANESE CREEPER

☼ ❄ ↔ 20 ft (6 m) ↑ 50–70 ft (15–21 m)
Strongly self-clinging species from China, Japan, and Korea with maple-shaped leaves to 8 in (20 cm) long, usually with 3 lobes although juvenile plants usually have leaves divided into 3 leaflets. Leaves sit almost like slates, one overlapping the other to the very top of any support, turning brilliant colors before shedding. 'Veitchii' ★, slightly smaller leaves that turn dark plum before shedding. Zones 4–10.

PASSIFLORA

PASSIONFLOWER, PASSIONFRUIT

Type genus for its family, Passifloraceae, the 500-odd species of passionflowers are mainly evergreen tendril-climbing vines from tropical America, though there are a few shrubby species and the range does extend to Asia and the Pacific Islands. Grown mainly for their flowers and fruit, the great vigor of passionflowers makes them superb plants for covering unsightly objects. The flowers have an unusual structure, with a tubular calyx, 5 conspicuous sepals, usually 5 petals, a corona of anthers, and 3 styles on an extended central tube. The common name comes from the association by Jesuit missionaries of the flower structure with the crucifixion of Christ. The genus name is simply a transliteration to Latin. CULTIVATION: Most are frost tender and prefer a warm climate in full or half-sun with deep, moist, humus-rich, well-drained soil. Feed and water well. Trim to shape and remove any frosted foliage in spring. Propagate from seed or cuttings, or by layering.

Parthenocissus quinquefolia

Passiflora alata

☼/☀ ✿ ↔ 8–20 ft (2.4–6 m) ↑ 20 ft (6 m)
Vigorous climber from Amazonian Brazil and Peru. Winged stems with simple pointed oval leaves, sometimes with finely toothed edges, to 6 in (15 cm) long. Flowers, scented, to 5 in (12 cm) wide, deep red petals, purple and white banded filaments, in summer. Ovoid to pear-shaped yellow fruit to 4 in (10 cm) long. Zones 10–12.

Passiflora belotii

syn. *Passiflora × alato-caerulea*

☼/☀ ✿ ↔ 6–15 ft (1.8–4.5 m) ↑ 15 ft (4.5 m)

Summer- to autumn-flowering garden hybrid between *P. alata* and *P. caerulea*. Shallowly winged stems and smooth-edged 3-lobed leaves. Flowers, to 4 in (10 cm) wide, mauve-blue and white petals and many radiating purple and white banded filaments around a yellow-green center. Zones 9–11.

Passiflora caerulea

BLUE PASSIONFLOWER

☼/☀ ❄ ↔ 6–15 ft (1.8–4.5 m) ↑ 30 ft (9 m)

Summer- to autumn-flowering species from Brazil and Argentina. Tolerant of repeated frosts, though partly deciduous in cold. Broadly palmate leaves with 3 to 9 lobes, often with toothed edges. Flowers to over 4 in wide, petals mostly creamy white, many radial purple and white banded filaments around a greenish center. 'Constance Elliott', creamy white flowers. Zones 7–10.

Passiflora × caeruleo-racemosa

☼/☀ ✿ ↔ 6–15 ft (1.8–4.5 m) ↑ 20 ft (6 m)

Summer-flowering hybrid of *P. caerulea* and *P. racemosa*. Dark green palmate leaves, 5 deep lobes. Deep purple-pink flowers with darker filaments. Best known form is mauve-pink **'Eynsford Gem'** with white filaments. Zones 9–11.

Passiflora citrina

☼/◐ ✢ ↔ 15 ft (4.5 m) ↑15 ft (4.5 m)

Relatively recently discovered native of Honduras and Guatemala. Simple, downy, deeply veined, dark green, elliptical to bilobed leaves to 4 in (10 cm) long. Flowers yellow-green to bright yellow, 1½ in (35 mm) wide, throughout the year. Zones 10–12.

Passiflora coccinea

RED GRANADILLA, RED PASSIONFLOWER

☼/◐ ✢ ↔ 12–30 ft (3.5–9 m)
↑12 ft (3.5 m)

Vigorous summer-flowering climber from tropical South America. Deep green, heavily textured, toothed ellip-tical leaves to 6 in (15 cm) long. Long-tubed flowers to 5 in (12 cm) wide, bright red with dark filaments around a pale pink to white center. Fruit yellow to orange, sometimes mottled, to 2 in (5 cm) long. Zones 10–12.

Passiflora edulis

GRANADILLA, PASSIONFRUIT, PURPLE GRANADILLA

☼/◐ ✢ ↔ 8–15 ft (2.4–4.5 m)
↑15 ft (4.5 m)

Strong summer-flowering climber from Brazil. Glossy, 3-lobed leaves to 4 in (10 cm) long. White flowers with white and purple banded filament. Ovoid edible fruit to around 3 in (8 cm) long, becoming purple-black and wrinkled when ripe. *P. e. f. flavicarpa* has golden yellow fruit, hybrids between these 2 forms include: **'Lacey'** and **'Purple Gold'** ★, which have large, light purple fruit; **'Fredrick'** has red fruit. *P. e.* **'Edgehill'**, large purple-black fruit; **'Kahuna'**, pale purple fruit; **'Red Rover'**, large red fruit. Zones 10–12.

Passiflora foetida

LOVE-IN-A-MIST, RUNNING POP

☼/◐ ✢ ↔ 3–6 ft (0.9–1.8 m)
↑6–10 ft (1.8–3 m)

Summer- to autumn-flowering climber from tropical South America and the

Passiflora citrina

Passiflora racemosa

Passiflora violacea

Caribbean. Light-textured dark green leaves, 3- to 5-lobed, to around 3 in (8 cm) long and similarly sized mauve-pink flowers with long, pale filaments. Bristly yellow to red fruits follow. Invasive weed in some tropical areas. Zones 10–12.

Passiflora incarnata

MAY APPLE, MAY POPS, WILD PASSIONFLOWER

☼/◐ ❋ ↔ 6–15 ft (1.8–4.5 m)
↑6 ft (1.8 m)

Vigorous climber from eastern USA. Evergreen in mild areas, dies back to ground in cold conditions, but regrows up to 15 ft (4.5 m) in summer. Leaves 3-lobed, to 6 in (15 cm) long and wide, with toothed edges and blue-green undersides. Lavender and white flowers to 3 in (8 cm) wide followed by ovoid, 2 in (5 cm) long fruit. Zones 6–10.

Passiflora manicata

RED PASSIONFLOWER

☼/◐ ❅ ↔ 8–15 ft (2.4–4.5 m)
↑10 ft (3 m)

Native to Colombia and Peru. Leaves toothed, 3-lobed, around 3 in (8 cm)

Passiflora foetida, in bud

long and slightly wider, downy under-sides. Flowers with pale green sepals, bright red petals, mauve-blue and white banded filaments. Green ovoid fruit to 2 in (5 cm) long. Zones 9–11.

Passiflora mollissima

BANANA PASSIONFRUIT, CURUBA

☼/◐ ❅ ↔ 8–15 ft (2.4–4.5 m)
↑15 ft (4.5 m)

Very vigorous summer- to autumn-flowering climber from northern South America. Leaves to 4 in (10 cm) long, 3-lobed, downy, usually with serrated edges. Long-tubed bright mid-pink flowers, filaments reduced to small protuberances. Edible, yellow, ovoid fruit to 3 in (8 cm) long. Zones 9–11.

Passiflora quadrangularis

GIANT GRANADILLA

☼/◐ ✢ ↔ 10–20 ft (3–6 m) ↑50 ft (15 m)

Very vigorous climber from tropical South America. Pointed oval leaves, deep green, leathery, to 8 in (20 cm) long. Flowers dusky gray-pink, with many twisted blue, white, purple-red banded filaments, to 5 in (12 cm) wide. Edible, bright yellow, ovoid fruit to 12 in (30 cm) long. Zones 10–12.

Passiflora racemosa

RED PASSIONFLOWER

☼/◐ ✢ ↔ 6–15 ft (1.8–4.5 m)
↑15 ft (4.5 m)

Brazilian species with pointed oval to 3-lobed leaves to 4 in (10 cm) long and wide. Large pendulous racemes of bright red, rarely white, flowers to nearly 4 in (10 cm) wide, short white filaments. Zones 10–12.

Passiflora incarnata

Passiflora reflexiflora

Passiflora reflexiflora

☼/◐ ✢ ↔ 4–8 ft (1.2–2.4 m)
↑6–10 ft (1.8–3 m)

Very distinctive Ecuadorian native. Leaves 3-lobed with 1 long central lobe and 2 small lobes held at right angles to the midrib. Long-tubed magenta flowers, with petals becoming strongly reflexed, and much reduced filaments. Zones 10–12.

Passiflora violacea

☼/◐ ✢ ↔ 3–6 ft (0.9–1.8 m)
↑10 ft (3 m)

Found from central Bolivia to northern Argentina. Autumn-flowering, with 3-lobed leaves to 5 in (12 cm) long. Flowers to 4 in (10 cm) wide, deep violet-pink, radiating white filaments. Zones 10–12.

Passiflora vitifolia

☼/◐ ✢ ↔ 6–15 ft (1.8–4.5 m)
↑15 ft (4.5 m)

Spring- to summer-flowering species from Central and northern South America. Grape-like, glossy, 3-lobed, toothed leaves to 6 in (15 cm) long

P

Paullinia cupana, Turrialba, Costa Rica

and wide, often red-tinted. Flowers to 4 in (10 cm) wide, with strongly reflexed, narrow, bright red petals and short white filaments. These are followed by small yellow to red fruits. Zones 10–12.

Passiflora Hybrid Cultivars

☼/☀ ❄ ↔ 6–15 ft (1.8–4.5 m)
↑ 6–12 ft (1.8–3.5 m)

There are many hybrid passionflowers, often based on *P. caerulea* to increase their hardiness, though some frost-tender hybrids have been raised specifically for tropical gardens. 'Amethyst' has 3-lobed leaves to 4 in (10 cm) wide, and blue flowers with purple-blue filaments and center; 'Bluebird', blue flowers; 'Coral Sea', coral-pink flowers; 'Debby', 3-lobed leaves, white flowers, many purple and white banded filaments; 'Incense', 5-lobed leaves, fragrant deep purple flowers with many fine, frilly filaments; 'New Incense', ('Incense' back-crossed with *P. cincinnata*) preferable to the older hybrid due to its greater vigor and disease resistance; 'Sunburst', large pointed oval leaves, and camphor-scented golden orange flowers. Zones 8–12.

PASTINACA
PARSNIP

A genus of 14 biennial or perennial herbs from Eurasia, from the carrot (Apiaceae) family, one of which, *P. sativa,* is grown for its edible roots. They have simple or divided leaves, with segments sometimes deeply lobed, and compound umbels of 3 to 30 small, yellow or red, daisy-like flowers with no sepals but yellow, oval-shaped petals curving inward. Fruit is flattened and elliptical with ridged edges. CULTIVATION: Plant parsnips in full sun in deep, rich soil. Sow seeds in spring in rows 16–18 in (40–45 cm) apart. Dig roots in autumn and store, or leave in the ground until spring. Propagation is from seed.

Pastinaca sativa
PARSNIP

☼ ❄ ↔ 18–24 in (45–60 cm)
↑ 3–5 ft (0.9–1.5 m)

Strong-smelling, finely hairy biennial from Europe and western Asia. Angled or cylindrical, hollow or solid, grooved stems. Thick, white, edible rootstock. Base leaves usually simple, remainder divided, with 5 to 11 oval-shaped, curling, serrated lobes. Umbels of greenish yellow daisy-like flowers, in summer. Zones 4–8.

PATRINIA

Genus of 15 perennial herbs in the valerian (Valerianaceae) family from temperate Asia and northern Europe, inhabiting damp rocky crevices in mountain areas. They have erect stems and divided or deeply lobed leaves, the basal leaves entire. Panicles up to 4 in (10 cm) across, of small yellow or white flowers with very short (4–6 mm) corolla tubes, with 5 spreading lobes, appear from early to late summer. The fruit is an achene. The dried roots of *P. scabiosifolia* are valued in traditional Chinese medicine as a diuretic. CULTIVATION: These plants may be useful for damp, shady spots. They prefer full shade to partial shade in poor soil that is kept consistently moist. Propagate from seed in spring, or by division in spring and autumn.

Patrinia scabiosifolia
SCABIOUS PATRINIA, VALERIAN

☼/☀ ❄ ↔ 18–24 in (45–60 cm)
↑ 3–6 ft (0.9–1.8 m)

Perennial herb from temperate East Asia. Sparsely leafed stems grow from a central mound. Divided, deeply toothed, oblong to oval-shaped foliage and open, terminal panicles of yellow flowers over long period in summer. Zones 5–8.

Patrinia triloba
syn. *Patrinia palmata*

☼ ❄ ↔ 12–18 in (30–45 cm)
↑ 12–24 in (30–60 cm)

From Japan. Hairy at nodes and on flower stalks. Heart-shaped palmate leaves, upper leaves coarsely toothed.

Loose 3-branched panicles of fragrant, golden yellow, cup-shaped flowers, on reddish stems, in late spring–early summer. Zones 5–8.

PAULLINIA
BRAZILIAN COCOA, GUARANA BREAD, UABANO, UARANZEIRO

This genus consists of 180 climbing shrubs, members of the soapberry (Sapindaceae) family, mostly from tropical regions from southern USA and Mexico to Argentina and Brazil. Plants have alternate, compound leaves and racemes of irregular flowers that grow from the leaf axils. The fruit is a fleshy capsule. The genus was named after the eighteenth-century German medical botanist C. F. Paullini. The seeds contain caffeine and those of *P. sorbilis* are often used alone or mixed with those of *P. cupana* by the Guaranis (a tribe of South American Indians) to make the traditional stimulant and aphrodisiac guarana, as well as for soft-drink flavoring. CULTIVATION: They prefer a protected position in half-sun or shade, with rich, moist, well-drained soil and high humidity. Propagate from cuttings in early spring, or by layering or grafting.

Paullinia cupana
FRUITS OF YOUTH, GUARANA

☼/☀ ⚘ ↔ 10–20 ft (3–6 m)
↑ 6–10 ft (1.8–3 m)

Climbing shrub from the rainforests of Venezuela and Brazil. Divided leaves with 5 leaflets and small yellow flowers. Fruit are chestnut-like, yellowish to red, ¾–1 in (18–25 mm) in diameter, with 2 or 3 black and white seeds that resemble eyes. Zones 11–12.

Passiflora, Hybrid Cultivar, 'Debby'

Passiflora, Hybrid Cultivar, 'New Incense'

Passiflora, Hybrid Cultivar, 'Coral Sea'

Passiflora, Hybrid Cultivar, 'Bluebird'

PAULOWNIA

This is a genus of about 6 species in the foxglove (Scrophulariaceae) family, native to East Asia. All are deciduous trees with handsome leaves that in some species are very large in the juvenile stage, and bear large panicles of flowers in spring. Paulownias have been cultivated in China for more than 3,000 years, both for their strong light timber, and for their attractive flowers; the bark, wood, leaves, flowers and fruit all have medicinal uses. They are characterized by their extremely rapid growth rate.

CULTIVATION: Paulownias do best in a moderately fertile and free-draining soil with adequate summer water. Protection from wind is important, especially in the early stages when the large leaves are easily damaged. Although quite hardy, dormant flower buds can be damaged by late frosts. The young trees are sometimes pruned back to 2 or 3 basal buds in order to encourage the vigorous growth of a single trunk. Propagation is from the seed, or from root cuttings.

Paulownia fortunei
POWTON, WHITE-FLOWERED PAULOWNIA

☀ ❄ ↔ 40 ft (12 m) ↑ 60 ft (18 m)

Found mainly in the Yangtze delta area of China. Tall tree, straight-trunked, with a rounded crown. The flowers open before the leaves appear, in upright terminal panicles, 4 in (10 cm) long, white to cream, mauve or soft violet. Zones 6–10.

Paulownia × taiwaniana
syn. *Paulownia australis*

☀ ❄ ↔ 20 ft (6 m) ↑ 12–25 ft (3.5–8 m)

Deciduous tree from Taiwan. Naturally occurring hybrid of *P. kawakamii* and *P. fortunei*. Spreading branches form a

Paulownia tomentosa

rounded crown of oval to heart-shaped, sticky, finely hairy leaves with pointed tips. Dense, upright, conical heads, to 32 in (80 cm) high, of flowers with purple, tubular to bell-shaped corolla, 2–3 in (5–8 cm) long, in spring, followed by oval capsules, in late summer to autumn. Zones 7–10.

Paulownia tomentosa
EMPRESS TREE, HAIRY PAULOWNIA, PRINCESS TREE

☀ ❄ ↔ 30 ft (9 m) ↑ 50 ft (15 m)

Native to northern and central China, Korea, and Japan. Medium-sized tree, broad spreading crown. Pinkish lilac flowers in upright terminal panicles, 50 to 60 flowers in each panicle. Heart-shaped leaves are downy, pale green maturing darker green, and turning yellow-brown, in autumn. '**Lilacina**', lilac-purple flowers, hairy on the outside, pale lemon yellow on the inside; '**Sapphire Dragon**', prominent clusters of creamy buff flowers. Zones 5–10.

Paulownia tomentosa 'Sapphire Dragon'

PAVETTA

Genus of around 400 species of evergreen shrubs and small trees in the madder (Rubiaceae) family. Widespread in the tropics and subtropics, particularly in Africa and Asia. Opposite or sometimes whorled leaves are variable in size and shape with tiny black spots. Flowers, often scented, in terminal corymbs arising from fused bracts; each tubular flower has 4 or 5 spreading lobes, a long protruding style and is often twisted in bud. Fruit is a fleshy black berry, about the size of a pea.

CULTIVATION: Most species are frost sensitive but some do well in large containers and can be used as greenhouse plants in cold areas. They prefer full sun and good drainage in humus-rich soil. Most benefit from supplementary watering during extended dry periods. Prune when young to promote bushy growth. Propagate from fresh seed or from half-hardened cuttings.

Pavetta lanceolata
FOREST BRIDE'S-BUSH

☀ ✦ ↔ 7 ft (2 m) ↑ 5 ft (1.5 m)

South African shrub. Clusters of very strongly sweet-scented white flowers,

Paulownia tomentosa 'Lilacina'

waxy petals, in summer. Dense clusters of black berries in autumn. Good, low, compact hedge. '**Bride's Bush**' is a popular cultivar. Zones 10–11.

PAVONIA

Found in the tropics and subtropics, especially in the Americas, this genus of the mallow (Malvaceae) family is composed of around 150 species of perennials, subshrubs and shrubs. Easy-care plants with pretty flowers, they are popular in tropical gardens and grown as house or greenhouse plants elsewhere. Their leaves, which have serrated or toothed edges, may be simple or lobed. The flowers most often

Pavetta lanceolata

Pavetta lanceolata 'Bride's Bush'

occur singly in the leaf axils but may be in terminal clusters or panicles; they vary in color and have an unusual form with petals that fold back to reveal a hibiscus-like central column of stamens. Dry 2-part seed capsules follow. CULTIVATION: All species are sensitive to frost and most cannot tolerate prolonged cool conditions. They respond well to container cultivation. Plant in moist, well-drained soil in sun or partial shade and provide some protection from strong winds as the foliage is easily damaged. Propagate from seed or half-hardened tip cuttings.

Pavonia × *gledhillii*

☼ ✦ ↔ 3 ft (0.9 m) ↑ 5 ft (1.5 m)

A hybrid between the Brazilian species *P. makoyana* and *P. multiflora*. This upright shrub has deep green, lance-shaped leaves, with serrated edges. Flowers, deep pink, gray-blue central column, in leaf axils, branch tips, much of the year. 'Rosea', dark pink flowers. Zones 10–12.

Pavonia hastata

☼ ⚘ ↔ 24 in (60 cm) ↑ 36 in (90 cm)

Native to tropical South America, naturalized in southeast USA. Subshrub or shrub reshoots if cut to the ground by frost. The lance-shaped leaves have toothed edges. The flowers, usually red, may be white with red basal spotting. Zones 9–12.

Pavonia hastata

Pedilanthus tithymaloides 'Variegatus'

Pavonia multiflora

☼ ✦ ↔ 4 ft (1.2) ↑ 6 ft (1.8 m)

Brazilian shrub. Leaves to 10 in (25 cm) long, smooth or toothed edges. Bright red 3 in (8 cm) wide flowers with blue anthers. Regular tip pinching encourages heavier flowering. Compact growth habit. Zones 11–12.

PAXISTIMA

Genus in the spindle-tree (Celastraceae) family consisting of 2 North American species of low-growing, ornamental, evergreen shrubs. They have 4-angled corky stems and opposite leathery leaves, sometimes finely toothed. The tiny, 4-petalled, greenish white or red-tinted white flowers are produced singly or in axillary clusters in spring and summer, and are followed by tiny, 2-valved capsules. CULTIVATION: They are fully frost hardy and will thrive in humus-rich, moist but well-drained soil in full sun or part-shade. Cut back occasionally to encourage a neat compact habit. Propagate from seed, layers, or half-hardened cuttings in late summer.

Paxistima canbyi

CLIFF GREEN, MOUNTAIN-LOVER, PACHISTIMA

☼ ❄ ↔ 36 in (90 cm) ↑ 15 in (38 cm)

Spreading self-layering shrub. Small, glossy, linear, evergreen leaves, deep green, curled back margins. Small clusters greenish white flowers, in spring–summer. Neat ground cover plant for the rock garden. Zones 3–8.

PECLUMA

This is a genus of about 25 species of ferns in the polypody (Polypodiaceae) family from tropical America, formerly included in *Polypodium* itself. They are mainly epiphytic on mossy tree trunks, less often on rocks or on the forest floor. Rhizomes are shortly creeping, clinging by aerial roots, unbranched. Fronds are narrow, of the

Pavonia × *gledhillii*

"fishbone" type, divided into many narrow segments that broaden at the base, those on one side of the midrib alternating with those on the other. Spore-bodies are small and circular, brown, numerous on frond undersides, and arranged in 2 regular rows along each segment. CULTIVATION: They require a very sheltered, humid environment in filtered light and are inclined to be slow-growing. Outside the tropics or warmer subtropics they will need the protection of a greenhouse. Best planted on a slab of fern fiber or bark, or in a basket in orchid compost. Propagate from spores.

Pecluma pectinata

syn. *Polypodium pectinatum*

☼/◐ ✦ ↔ 12–36 in (30–90 cm) ↑ 12–36 in (30–90 cm)

Widespread in Central America and northern South America in mountain rainforests, creeping on tree trunks or rocks. Fronds long and narrow. Usually remains small when cultivated outside the tropics. Zones 11–12.

PEDILANTHUS

In the euphorbia (Euphorbiaceae) family, this genus of around 14 species of clump-forming succulent shrubs or small trees is native to the drier regions of Central and South America, the West Indies, and southern USA. They are closely related to *Euphorbia* and similarly contain a milky sap that may be poisonous if ingested. They have light green or variegated fleshy leaves with a thickened midrib and bear greenish white flowers enclosed by colorful bracts that are shaped like a bird's head. CULTIVATION: They prefer a warm climate and partial shade in a very well-drained soil. Most species will withstand extended dry periods. Propagate from cuttings or from seed.

Pedilanthus tithymaloides ★

DEVIL'S BACKBONE

◐ ⚘ ↔ 2 ft (0.6 m) ↑ 6 ft (1.8 m)

Species originally from the West Indies and southern USA. Evergreen

Pavonia × *gledhillii* 'Rosea"

or deciduous succulent shrub. Has fleshy erect stems zigzagging at each node, mid-green boat-shaped leaves, and small, reddish green, tubular flowers with red bracts, in summer. 'Variegatus', commonly grown form, green leaves variegated white and red. Zones 9–11.

PEDIOCACTUS

In the family Cactaceae, this is a genus of 8 rare, dwarf, globular to short cylindrical, mostly endangered cacti from the USA. The genus name is derived from the Greek *pedion* (plains), referring to the Great Plains of America. Solitary to clustering. The spines vary considerably in number, color, and direction, and are usually so dense that they obscure the dark green plant bodies. Central spines are pale gray or white, spreading, straight or curved, needle-like, bristly or corky. Radials are reddish to whitish, straight or curved, occasionally comb-shaped. Flowers are bell-shaped, yellow to purple to white. Seed pods are spherical, greenish to brown. CULTIVATION: Most species are a challenge to grow outside their native habitat and need a well-drained mineralized soil, careful watering, and a large diurnal and annual temperature range. Propagation is from seed; some species needing freezing temperatures to assist germination. Rest in winter and in the heat of summer.

Pediocactus simpsonii

☼ ❄ ↔ 1¼–6 in (3–15 cm) ↑ 1–6 in (2.5–15 cm)

Widespread, variable, solitary to clustering species, with up to 50 heads on oval to depressed spherical stems. Spines dense, straight and spreading, with 4 to 10 reddish to blackish brown centrals, 15 to 35 white radials. Flowers are white, pink, magenta, or yellow. Seed pods are spherical, greenish to brown. Zones 7–11.

PELARGONIUM
STORKSBILL

Most of the 250 species of annuals, perennials, and subshrubs in this genus of the geranium (Geraniaceae) family come from South Africa, a few from the rest of Africa, Australia, and the Middle East. Foliage is variable but often light green, rounded or hand-shaped, with conspicuous lobes, fine hairs and darker blotches. Some have succulent leaves. Flowers are simple 5-petalled structures, often massed and/or brightly colored, making a spectacular show. The name is from the Greek *pelargos,* stork, which refers to the shape of the seed pod.
CULTIVATION: Tolerant of light frosts only, many pelargoniums are treated as annuals in areas with cold winters. Plant most species in full sun in light well-drained soil. Drought tolerant once established. Ideal in coastal conditions. Propagate annuals and species from seed; perennials and shrubs from cuttings.

Pelargonium abrotanifolium
SOUTHERNWOOD GERANIUM
☼ ⬦ ↔ 24 in (60 cm) ↑ 20 in (50 cm)
Bushy South African subshrub. Finely divided, aromatic, gray-green leaves to 1 in (25 mm) wide. Flowers a little over ½ in (12 mm) wide, in clusters of up to 5, white or pink, in spring–summer. Zones 9–11.

Pelargonium australe
☼ ⬦ ↔ 20 in (50 cm) ↑ 12 in (30 cm)
Spring- to summer-flowering perennial from southeastern Australia including Tasmania. Rather straggling habit with downy, rounded, 5- to 7-lobed leaves to 4 in (10 cm) across. Clusters of 5 to 10 dark-veined pale pink or white flowers to slightly over ½ in (12 mm) wide. Zones 9–10.

Pelargonium betulinum
BIRCH-LEAF GERANIUM
☼ ⬦ ↔ 16–32 in (40–80 cm) ↑ 12–24 in (30–60 cm)
Sprawling, woody-based, late spring-flowering South African subshrub.

Pelargonium crithmifolium

Leaves blue-green, toothed, and sometimes red-tinted, to around 1¼ in (30 mm) wide. Dark-veined pink or purple, rarely white, flowers to 1 in (25 mm) wide in groups of 3 or 4, narrow lower petals. Zones 9–11.

Pelargonium bowkeri
☼ ⬦ ↔ 20–40 in (50–100 cm) ↑ 12–16 in (30–40 cm)
South African winter-dormant tuberous species with tuber sometimes partly exposed. The first basal leaves are simple, rounded, and toothed; later leaves are plume-like with very finely divided foliage reminiscent of asparagus fern. The flowers are flesh pink, with 2 "normal" upper petals and lower petals finely divided into numerous filaments, appearing in spring before the foliage. Zones 9–10.

Pelargonium cordifolium ★
☼/◐ ⬦ ↔ 40 in (100 cm) ↑ 40 in (100 cm)
South African spring- to summer-flowering subshrub with hairy stems and foliage. Leaves to over 2 in (5 cm) wide, 3- to 5-lobed, toothed, with pale undersides. Produces a head of up to 8 purple, 1¼ in (30 mm) wide flowers, the upper petals broad, the lower petals linear. Zones 9–11.

Pelargonium cortusifolium
☼ ✛ ↔ 12–16 in (30–40 cm) ↑ 8–20 in (20–50 cm)
Namibian species, dormant in periods of cold and drought. Gray-green leaves with a covering of fine silvery hairs, roughly heart-shaped, shallowly lobed and up to 1½ in (35 mm) wide. Heads of up to 11 small, long-stemmed, purple-pink flowers are borne in the summer. Zones 10–11.

Pelargonium crispum
LEMON-SCENTED GERANIUM
☼ ⬦ ↔ 36 in (90 cm) ↑ 30 in (75 cm)
South African aromatic shrub. Small, 3-lobed leaves, crinkled edges. Pink flowers, dark markings, ¾ in (18 mm) wide. Foliage has a strong lemon scent when crushed. *P. crispum* is the parent of a number of cultivars with small

Pelargonium fruticosum

Pelargonium species, in the wild, Tanqwa Karoo, South Africa

fragrant leaves. 'Major', larger leaves; 'Minor', upright habit with tiny leaves; 'Peach Cream', pink flowers, subtle scent of peaches; 'Variegatum', cream-edged foliage. Zones 9–11.

Pelargonium crithmifolium
SAMPHIRE-LEAFED GERANIUM
☼ ✛ ↔ 12–20 in (30–50 cm) ↑ 20 in (50 cm)
Summer- to autumn-flowering South African and Namibian species with thick succulent stems and fleshy, gray-green, pinnate leaves to 6 in (15 cm) long. Heads of up to 8 starry white to pale pink flowers with reddish basal blotch, to over ½ in (12 mm) wide. Zones 10–11.

Pelargonium echinatum
CACTUS GERANIUM, SWEETHEART GERANIUM
☼ ✛ ↔ 20 in (50 cm) ↑ 20 in (50 cm)
A summer-dormant, tuberous, spring-flowering subshrub, native to western South Africa. The erect succulent stems have spiny leaf bases and a basal clump of short-lived pointed oval leaves to over 2 in (5 cm) long, with downy undersides. *P. echinatum* produces heads of up to 8 starry white or purple flowers with dark purple basal blotches. Zones 10–11.

Pelargonium endlicherianum
☼ ⬦ ↔ 8–16 in (20–40 cm) ↑ 10–14 in (25–35 cm)
Rhizome-rooted, summer-flowering, Turkish perennial with leaves that are mostly basal, hairy, rounded, to over 2 in (5 cm) wide, with 5 shallow lobes. Produces heads of 5 to 15 fragrant light magenta flowers with large upper petals and very small or absent lower petals. Zones 9–10.

Pelargonium ferulaceum
☼ ✛ ↔ 12–24 in (30–60 cm) ↑ 12–20 in (30–50 cm)
Summer- to autumn-flowering evergreen tuberous South African subshrub with thickened succulent stems and light green pinnate leaves to 4 in (10 cm) long. Heads of small white flowers with red markings. Zones 10–11.

Pelargonium fruticosum
☼ ⬦ ↔ 16–20 in (40–50 cm) ↑ 12–16 in (30–40 cm)
Low-spreading and mounding spring- to autumn-flowering South African perennial, with downy bright green leaves divided into short linear segments. Starry, red-stemmed, white to pink flowers, sometimes with red basal markings. Zones 9–11.

Pelargonium fulgidum

☼ ⟡ ↔ 20–32 in (50–80 cm) ↑ 27 in (70 cm)

This woody based spring- to early summer-flowering scrambling sub-shrub is a native of South Africa. It has succulent stems and pinnate silver-haired leaves to around 4 in (10 cm) long, and produces heads of bright red flowers to over ¾ in (18 mm) wide. Zones 9–11.

Pelargonium graveolens

ROSE-SCENTED GERANIUM

☼ ⟡ ↔ 26 in (65 cm) ↑ 4 ft (1.2 m)

This shrub, native to South Africa, is possibly a hybrid. Erect stems. The rounded, deeply divided leaves release a strong scent of rosewater when they are crushed. The foliage and young stems are covered with fine hairs. The clusters of small, purple-veined pink flowers, appear in summer. 'Lady Plymouth' produces compact growth with cream-edged strongly scented foliage, which is often used in floral decorations. Zones 9–11.

Pelargonium incrassatum

☼ ⟡ ↔ 12 in (30 cm) ↑ 12 in (30 cm)

Summer-dormant, tuberous, spring-flowering perennial, found in the Western Cape region of South Africa. This species has basal rosettes of long-stemmed, silver-haired, pinnate leaves to a little more than 2 in (5 cm) long. The plants form sturdy stems carrying heads of 10 to 20, rarely up to 40, deep mauve-pink flowers to ¾ in (18 mm) across, with much-reduced lower petals. Zones 9–11.

Pelargonium fulgidum

Pelargonium triste

Pelargonium peltatum 'Barbe Bleu'

Pelargonium odoratissimum

APPLE GERANIUM

☼/◑ ⟡ ↔ 24 in (60 cm) ↑ 12 in (30 cm)

Low-spreading, spring- to summer-flowering perennial, native to South Africa. P. odoratissimum has fragrant leaves, apple-scented, rounded, pale green, and toothed, to around 1½ in (35 mm) wide. The branching flower stems carry heads of up to 10, ½ in (12 mm) wide, red-marked white flowers. Zones 9–11.

Pelargonium peltatum

IVY-LEAFED GERANIUM

☼ ⟡ ↔ 8 ft (2.4 m) ↑ 8 ft (2.4 m)

Sprawling, scrambling, climbing, continuous-flowering, woody-stemmed South African perennial. The succulent rounded leaves, with 5 triangular lobes, are often zonally marked. Short-stemmed heads of up to 9 flowers. There are many cultivars in a wide range of flower and foliage colors and forms. 'Barbe Bleu' produces deep purple double flowers ageing to deep red; 'Crocketta' has light veined leaves and white flowers with red markings; 'Evka' has white-edged foliage with bright red flowers; and 'Mutzel' has gray-green and white variegated leaves, and flowers of bright red. Zones 9–11.

Pelargonium quercetorum

☼ ⟡ ↔ 12 in (30 cm) ↑ 16 in (40 cm)

This summer- to autumn-flowering perennial is a native of Turkey and northern Iraq. The plant forms a small basal clump of rounded, 5- to 9-lobed, mid-green leaves to slightly more

Pelargonium peltatum 'Crocketta'

P. peltatum 'Mini Cascade Lavender'

than 2 in (5 cm) wide. Wiry upright flower stems carry deep pink flowers. Zones 9–10.

Pelargonium quercifolium

ALMOND GERANIUM, OAK-LEAF GERANIUM

☼ ⟡ ↔ 24–32 in (60–80 cm) ↑ 3–5 ft (0.9–1.5 m)

Upright spring- to summer-flowering South African subshrub. Hairy, aromatic, deeply lobed foliage, often with toothed edges, olive green, dark central zone. Small heads of ½ in (12 mm) wide purple-pink flowers. Zones 9–11.

Pelargonium rodneyanum

MAGENTA STORKSBILL

☼ ⟡ ↔ 12–20 in (30–50 cm) ↑ 8–12 in (20–30 cm)

Spreading, summer-dormant, spring-flowering, tuberous perennial from Australia. It forms rosettes of dark green, elongated, heart-shaped leaves to 4 in (10 cm) long, with notched edges. The short wiry stems support heads of up to 25 small bright pink flowers. Zones 9–11.

Pelargonium sidoides

☼ ⟡ ↔ 12–20 in (30–50 cm) ↑ 12–20 in (30–50 cm)

Tuberous South African perennial. Rosettes of long-stemmed, velvety, lobed, heart-shaped leaves to around 2 in (5 cm) wide. Flowers year-round; sprawling wiry stems carry open sprays of dark purple-red flowers. Zones 9–11.

Pelargonium suburbanum

☼ ⟡ ↔ 12–24 in (30–60 cm) ↑ 6–8 in (15–20 cm)

Winter- to summer-flowering, sprawling South African subshrub with small,

Pelargonium peltatum 'Evka'

Pelargonium peltatum 'Mini Cascade Red'

deeply lobed, light green leaves and large, magenta, rarely white, flowers held just above the foliage on short stems. Upper petals large, lower petals small and narrow. Zones 9–11.

Pelargonium tomentosum

☼ ⟡ ↔ 40 in (100 cm) ↑ 20 in (50 cm)

Spring- to summer-flowering South African perennial developing into a low, spreading clump of velvety, peppermint-scented, 3- to 5-lobed, rounded leaves to a little under 3 in (8 cm) wide. Erect flower stems with heads of up to 15 white flowers to over ½ in (12 mm) wide. Upper petals purple-marked, lower petals long and narrow. Zones 9–11.

Pelargonium triste

☼ ⟡ ↔ 24–40 in (60–100 cm) ↑ 20 in (50 cm)

Tuberous spring-flowering perennial native to South Africa's Cape region and the first species to enter cultivation. Finely divided, hairy, carrot-leaf-like foliage. Heads of 5 to 20 aromatic, mustard yellow, ½ in (12 mm) wide flowers with purple-brown markings. Zones 9–11.

Pelargonium Hybrid Cultivars

☼ ⟡ ↔ 8–40 in (20–100 cm) ↑ 6–30 in (15–75 cm)

Pelargonium species interbreed freely; the first hybrids appeared soon after the plants entered cultivation. The parentage of these early crosses is long-lost, but their legacy lives on in a range of hybrid groups of mostly compact plants with large showy flowers.

Angel Hybrids: Similar to Regal Hybrids but are usually only 12 in

(30 cm) tall or less and do not produce double flowers. **'Black Night'**, 16 in (40 cm) tall, pale center, upper and lower petals dark purple-red with thin pale pink margin; **'Captain Starlight'**, 10 in (25 cm) tall, upper petals purple-red, lower petals pink-flushed white; **'Quantock Marjorie'**, 12 in (30 cm) tall, upper petals purple-red, lower petals very pale pink; **'Quantock Matty'**, 16 in (40 cm) tall, upper petals deep purple, lower petals pink-flushed white; **'Quantock Rita'**, 10 in (25 cm) tall, upper petals maroon, lower petals pink-flushed white; **'Quantock Star'**, 12 in (30 cm) tall, upper and lower petals dark red with broad pale pink margin; **'Spanish Angel'**, 12 in (30 cm) tall, upper petals purple-red edged with mauve, lower petals mauve with maroon blotch and veins; **'Tip Top Duet'**, 12 in (30 cm) tall, upper petals maroon, lower petals lavender.

Pelargonium, HC, Angel, 'Black Night'

P., HC, Angel, 'Cottenham Harmony'

Pelargonium, Hybrid Cultivar, Angel, 'Captain Starlight'

Pelargonium, Hybrid Cultivar, Angel, 'The Culm'

P., HC, Angel, 'Molly'

Pelargonium, Hybrid Cultivar, Angel, 'Cottenham Charm'

P., HC, Angel, 'Oldbury Duet'

Pelargonium, Hybrid Cultivar, Angel, 'Quantock Marjorie'

Pelargonium, Hybrid Cultivar, Angel, 'Quantock Matty'

Pelargonium, Hybrid Cultivar, Angel, 'Quantock Rita'

Pelargonium, Hybrid Cultivar, Angel, 'Quantock Star'

Pelargonium, Hybrid Cultivar, Angel, 'Suffolk Emerald'

Pelargonium, Hybrid Cultivar, Angel, 'Suffolk Garnet'

Pelargonium, Hybrid Cultivar, Angel, 'Tip Top Duet'

Pelargonium, Hybrid Cultivar, Dwarf, 'Brackenwood'

Pelargonium, Hybrid Cultivar, Dwarf, 'Brenda'

Pelargonium, Hybrid Cultivar, Dwarf, 'Orion'

Pelargonium, Hybrid Cultivar, Dwarf, 'Redondo'

Pelargonium, Hybrid Cultivar, Dwarf, 'Sandown'

Pelargonium, Hybrid Cultivar, Dwarf, 'Brookside Flamenco'

P., HC, Dwarf, 'Beryl Read'

P., HC, Dwarf, 'Little Alice'

Dwarf Hybrids: Resembling Zonal Hybrids in their foliage and stature, but with Regal-like flowers, these small plants often have fully double blooms, which is the main point of difference from the Angel Hybrids. Flower display tends to be damaged by rain and they are best used in pots and window boxes. '**Beryl Read**', 6 in (15 cm) tall, pink flowers, darker blotch; '**Brackenwood**', 8 in (20 cm) tall, salmon pink double flowers;

'**Brenda**', mid-pink flowers, red blotch; '**Brookside Flamenco**', 6 in (15 cm) tall, vivid pink double flowers; '**Hope Valley**', 8 in (20 cm) tall, golden yellow leaves, pink double flowers; '**Little Alice**', 6 in (15 cm) tall, deep green leaves, dark salmon pink flowers; '**Orion**', 8 in (20 cm) tall, orange-red double flowers; '**Redondo**', 8 in (20 cm) tall, large red double flowers.

Regal Hybrids: These, also known as Martha Washington Hybrids, are around 20 in (50 cm) tall, though plant size ranges from dwarfs under 12 in (30 cm) tall through to shrubs of 4 ft (1.2 m) or more. Flowers large and reminiscent of evergreen azaleas; may be single or double and occur in a huge range of colors and patterns. '**Askham Fringed Aztec**', frilly white flowers with red veining; '**Australian Mystery**', cut-edged upper petals, magenta with lighter veining, lower petals white with magenta veining and blotch; '**Bert Pearce**', large, frilly, pink flowers with red veining; '**Bosham**', pink with dark purple-red upper blotch and magenta veining; '**Cherry Orchard**', bright red with lighter center and dark red upper veining; '**Doris Hancock**', bright light purple-pink; '**Eileen Postle**', many-flowered heads of bright mid-pink with purple-red upper blotch; '**Harbour**

Lights**', bright pink with pink-edged, dark-blotched, light red upper petals; '**Joan Morf**', white flushed mid-pink with red upper blotch; '**Kimono**', lavender-pink with white throat, deep magenta veining; '**Lara Susan**', single, pale pink-edged purple-red upper petals, near white lower petals with small purple-red blotch; '**Lavender Sensation**', lavender-pink with purple-red upper blotch; '**Lord Bute**', simple single flowers, unusual colors, dark maroon with narrow bright pink margin; '**Rembrandt**' ★, purple edged with mauve-pink; '**Rimfire**', black-red with red to pink margin; '**Rosmaroy**', bright pink, pale red upper blotch, lower spotting; '**Springfield Black**', dark purple-red with lighter center; '**Super Spot on Bonanza**', white flecked and sectored bright orange-red; '**Virginia Louise**', pale pink, blotched deeper pink.

P., HC, Regal, 'Aldwyck'

P., HC, Regal, 'Anne Hoystead'

P., Hybrid Cultivar, Regal, 'Askham Fringed Aztec'

P., HC, Regal, 'Australian Mystery'

P., HC, Regal, 'Bert Pearce'

P., HC, Regal, 'Bosham'

P., HC, Regal, 'Brown's Butterfly'

P., HC, Regal, 'Burgundy'

P., HC, Regal cultivar

Pelargonium, Hybrid Cultivar, Regal, 'Eileen Postle'

Pelargonium, Hybrid Cultivar, Regal, 'Fareham'

Pelargonium, Hybrid Cultivar, Regal, 'Fringed Aztec'

Pelargonium, Hybrid Cultivar, Regal, 'Funchal'

Pelargonium, Hybrid Cultivar, Regal, 'Harbour Lights'

P., HC, Regal, 'Hazel Cherry'

P., HC, Regal, 'Doris Hancock'

P., HC, Regal, 'Delhi'

P., HC, Regal, 'Imperial'

P., HC, Regal, 'Joan Morf'

P., HC, Regal, 'Jupiter'

Pelargonium, HC, Regal, 'Kimono'

P., HC, Regal, 'Kyoto'

P., HC, Regal, 'Lara Susan'

P., HC, Regal, 'Lavender Sensation'

P., HC, Regal, 'Lord Bute'

P., HC, Regal, 'Minstrel Boy'

P., HC, Regal, 'Primavera'

P., HC, Regal, 'Rembrandt'

Pelargonium, HC, Regal, 'Rosmaroy'

Pelargonium, Hybrid Cultivar, Regal, 'Springfield Black'

Pelargonium, Hybrid Cultivar, Regal, 'Super Spot on Bonanza'

Pelargonium, Hybrid Cultivar, Regal, 'White Phyllis Richardson'

Pelargonium, Hybrid Cultivar, Regal, 'Rimfire'

P., HC, Regal, 'Taspo'

P., HC, Regal, 'Virginia Louise'

P., HC, Regal, 'Spring Song'

Pelargonium, Hybrid Cultivar, Scented-leafed, 'Ardwick Cinnamon'

Pelargonium, Hybrid Cultivar, Scented-leafed, 'Atomic Snowflake'

P., Hybrid Cultivar, Scented-leafed, 'Bodey's Peppermint'

Pelargonium, Hybrid Cultivar, Scented-leafed, 'Camphor Rose'

Pelargonium, Hybrid Cultivar, Scented-leafed, 'Copthorne'

Pelargonium, Hybrid Cultivar, Scented-leafed, 'Fragrans'

P., Hybrid Cultivar, Scented-leafed, 'Fragrans Variegatum'

P., Hybrid Cultivar, Scented-leafed, 'Fringed Apple'

P., Hybrid Cultivar, Scented-leafed, 'Graveolens'

Pelargonium, Hybrid Cultivar, Scented-leafed, 'Joy Lucille'

Pelargonium, Hybrid Cultivar, Scented-leafed, 'Brunswick'

Pelargonium, Hybrid Cultivar, Scented-leafed, 'Gemstone'

Pelargonium, Hybrid Cultivar, Scented-leafed, 'Lara Starshine'

P., HC, Scented-leafed, 'Lara Ballerina'

P., HC, Scented-leafed, 'Lilian Pottinger'

Scented-leafed Hybrids: Grown mainly for the aroma of their foliage, though their flowers can be very showy. '**Camphor Rose**', minty camphor scent, small lavender flowers; '**Lara Ballerina**', sharp citrus scent, white to pale pink flowers flushed with purple-red; '**Lara Starshine**', mild citrus scent, many small, deep pinkish red flowers.

Unique Hybrids: These are woody-based perennials and most of them have *P. fulgidum* parentage, which shows in the large pinnate leaves. Foliage is aromatic; flowers are large. '**Bolero**', vivid pink flowers with darker center, single; '**Mystery**', red flowers with darker blotch; '**Scarlet Unique**', rich red flowers, aromatic velvety leaves; '**Shrubland Pet**', (syn. 'Shrubland Rose'), dwarf form, rose-red petals, deeper colored toward petal edges.

Pelargonium, Hybrid Cultivar, Scented-leafed, 'Olga Shipstone'

Pelargonium, Hybrid Cultivar, Scented-leafed, 'Pink Capricorn'

Pelargonium, Hybrid Cultivar, Scented-leafed, 'Rose'

Pelargonium, Hybrid Cultivar, Scented-leafed, 'Shottesham Pet'

Pelargonium, Hybrid Cultivar, Scented-leafed, 'Village Hill Oak'

Pelargonium, Hybrid Cultivar, Scented-leafed, 'Orsett'

Pelargonium, Hybrid Cultivar, Scented-leafed, 'Sweet Mimosa'

P., Hybrid Cultivar, Unique, 'Bolero'

P., Hybrid Cultivar, Unique, 'Mystery'

P., Hybrid Cultivar, Unique, 'Scarlet Unique'

P., Hybrid Cultivar, Unique, 'Shrubland Pet'

Zonal Hybrids: These are mainly of *P. inquinans* × *P. zonale* parentage with many now classified as *P.* × *hortorum*. They have a low bushy habit with succulent stems and light green, rounded to kidney-shaped, shallowly lobed leaves with dark zonal markings, to 4 in (10 cm) across. The heads of brightly colored flowers, to nearly 1 in (25 mm) wide, are held above the foliage on upright stems throughout the warmer months, year-round in frost-free areas. Many cultivars and seedling strains, including: **'Dolly Vardon'**, tricolored leaves red and green with creamy white edges, red single flowers; **'Milden'**, dwarf habit, white single flowers with red splashes; **'Pink Champagne'**, dwarf habit with green and gold foliage, bright pink double flowers; **'Retah's Crystal'**, variegated leaves, large soft pink flowers. Stellar

P., Hybrid Cultivar, Zonal, 'Milden'

P., Hybrid Cultivar, Zonal, 'Retah's Crystal'

Pelargonium, Hybrid Cultivar, Zonal, 'Pink Champagne'

P., Hybrid Cultivar, Zonal, 'Belchandons'

P., HC, Zonal, Diabolo/'Fiscrid'

Pelargonium, Hybrid Cultivar, Zonal, 'Osna 2'

Pelargonium, Hybrid Cultivar, Zonal, 'Antik Orange'

Pelargonium, Hybrid Cultivar, Zonal, 'Antik Pink'

Pelargonium, Hybrid Cultivar, Zonal, 'Antik Salmon'

Pelargonium, Hybrid Cultivar, Zonal, 'Bird Dancer'

Pelargonium, Hybrid Cultivar, Zonal, 'Cathay'

Pelargonium, Hybrid Cultivar, Zonal, 'Colin Tilley'

Pelargonium, Hybrid Cultivar, Zonal, 'Grandad Mac'

Pelargonium, Hybrid Cultivar, Zonal, 'Jana 2'

Pelargonium, Hybrid Cultivar, Zonal, 'Laura Parmer'

Pelargonium, Hybrid Cultivar, Zonal, 'Melocherry'

forms have narrow, pointed petals and more sharply lobed foliage. These include: **'Annsbrook Gemini'**, leaves with dark red-brown central zone, bright pink double flowers with red flecks; **'Bird Dancer'**, very dark foliage, spidery salmon pink single flowers; **'Grandad Mac'**, dark foliage and orange-pink double flowers; **'Laura Parmer'**, dwarf habit, dark foliage, mid-pink single flowers; **'Mrs Pat'**, golden brown leaves, with a dark central zone, and salmon pink single flowers; **'Pagoda'**, strongly marked foliage and pale pink double flowers; **'Red Cactus'**, green foliage and starry bright red flowers with long petals; **'Vancouver Centennial'**, red leaves with light green edges and small, bright magenta, single flowers. Zones 9–11.

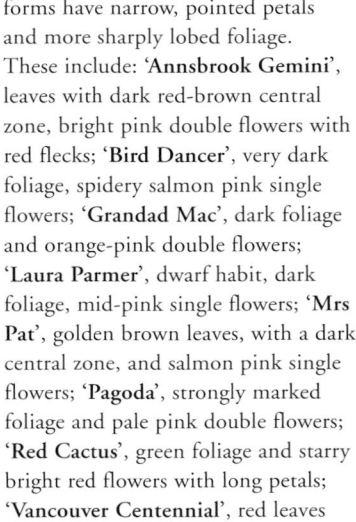

Pelargonium, Hybrid Cultivar, Zonal, 'Gemini'

P., HC, Zonal, 'Meloda'

P., HC, Zonal, 'Melody'

P., HC, Zonal, 'Mrs Pat'

P., HC, Zonal, 'Pagoda'

P

Pelargonium, HC, Zonal, 'Rocky Mountain Scarlet'

Pelargonium, Hybrid Cultivar, Zonal, 'Stella Mini'

Pelargonium, HC, Zonal, 'Vancouver Centennial'

P., HC, Zonal, 'Perlenkette Orange'

P., HC, Zonal, 'Perlenkette Sabine'

P., HC, Zonal, 'Perlenkette Scarlet'

P., HC, Zonal, 'Sassa'

P., Hybrid Cultivar, Zonal, 'Robe'

P., Hybrid Cultivar, Zonal, 'Rose Crystal'

P., Hybrid Cultivar, Zonal, 'Shocking Pink'

P., Hybrid Cultivar, Zonal, 'Wispy'

Pelargonium, Hybrid Cultivar, Zonal, 'Red Cactus'

Pelargonium, Hybrid Cultivar, Zonal, 'Skies of Italy'

PELECYPHORA

Belonging to the family Cactaceae, this genus contains 2 rare, dwarf, Mexican cacti, both listed in Appendix I of CITES. They have long been popular with collectors for their small size and the shape of their areoles and tubercles. The genus name comes from the Greek *pelekys*, hatchet, and *phoreus*, bearer, referring to the shape of the tubercles on *P. aselliformis*. Solitary or clumping, low to the ground, with long tap roots, the plant bodies are green to yellow-green with no distinct ribs, just tubercles spiraly arranged. Spines are whitish and very small. Flowers are funnel-form, magenta, borne at the tip. Seed pods are greenish brown and spherical.

CULTIVATION: Both species need a well-drained mineralized soil. Do not overwater. Propagate from seed. Rest these plants in winter and again in the heat of summer.

Pelecyphora aselliformis

HATCHET CACTUS, WOODLOUSE CACTUS

☀ ❄ ↔ ¾–2 in (18–50 mm)
↕ ¾–1¾ in (18–40 mm)

Exquisite miniature cactus with tubercles shaped like tiny hatchets or woodlice, greatly endangered by over-collecting and habitat destruction. Spines, 40 to 60, arranged like microscopic combs along edges of elongated tubercles. Flowers ¾–1 in (18–25 mm) in diameter. Zones 8–11.

Pelecyphora aselliformis

Pellaea falcata

Pelecyphora strobiliformis

PINECONE CACTUS

☀ ❄ ↔ 1¾–2½ in (40–60 mm)
↕ ¾–1¾ in (18–40 mm)

Diminutive rarities shaped like tiny pinecones, with keeled triangular tubercles, ¼–½ in (6–12 mm) long, closely flattened against the plant body. Spines, 7 to 14, more or less comb-shaped, flexible, 5 mm long. Magenta flowers. Zones 8–11.

PELLAEA

CLIFF BRAKE

This genus of 80 small to medium-sized, rock-loving ferns from the maidenhair-fern (Adiantaceae) family is found mostly in tropical to warm-temperate regions and has creeping or short rhizomes. Divided fronds are carried on dark or black stems, with small broad leaflets, with spore-bodies carried in bands along the frond margins. The genus is named from the Greek *pellos*, dusky, referring to the bluish gray leaves of some species.

CULTIVATION: Cliff brakes prefer a rich, well-drained, slightly alkaline soil, in a partially or fully shaded protected position with high humidity. Propagate from spores or by division.

Pellaea falcata

syn. *Platyloma falcatum*

AUSTRALIAN CLIFF BRAKE, SICKLE FERN

☀ ❄ ↔ 6–9 in (15–22 cm)
↕ 6–9 in (15–22 cm)

Small, variable, terrestrial fern found naturally from temperate to subtropical areas from India to Australia and New Zealand. It has stout, creeping rhizomes and wiry, dark brown stems, 2–6 in (5–15 cm) long, covered with dark brown scales when young. Fishbone-like, shiny, leathery fronds, to 18 in (45 cm) long, with sword-shaped leaflets, to 2 in (5 cm) long, dull dark green above and brownish underneath. Zones 7–8.

Peltophorum africanum

Pellaea rotundifolia

ROUNDLEAF FERN

☀ ❄ ↔ 15–18 in (38–45 cm)
↕ 12–18 in (30–45 cm)

Fern from New Zealand and Australia with creeping stout rhizomes. Narrowly oblong, dull dark green fronds, 6–12 in (15–30 cm) long, with narrowly oblong to nearly circular, minutely serrated leaflets carried on stems to 6 in (15 cm) tall, which are covered with rust-colored scales. Zones 10–12.

PELTANDRA

ARROW ARUM

The 3 aquatic, rhizomatous, perennial herbs in this arum (Araceae) family genus inhabit the bogs and marshes of eastern North America and are grown for their decorative foliage. They have simple, arrowhead-shaped leaves on long, sheathed stalks, and tiny, unisexual flowers borne on spikes, carried on stalks the same length or longer than the leaf stalks, and enclosed by undulating spathes with overlapping margins. The fruit is a berry.

CULTIVATION: Arrow arums thrive in full or half-sun in damp, acidic soil adjacent to water, or in water up to 12 in (30 cm) deep. Propagate by division in spring or from seed, which should be stratified prior to sowing.

Peltandra virginica

GREEN ARROW ARUM, TUCKAHOE

☀ ❄ ↔ 12–36 in (30–90 cm)
↕ 12–36 in (30–90 cm)

From swamps and marshes of eastern and southeastern USA. Large, glossy, dark green leaves, 12–36 in (30–90 cm) long, in spring, clustered on succulent stalks, 18–36 in (45–90 cm) long. Narrowly opening yellowish green spathe, up to 8 in (20 cm) long, edged with white or yellow, enclosing an erect, whitish green flower spike, followed by green berries in late summer–autumn. Zones 5–7.

PELTOPHORUM

Consisting of 8 species of evergreen or deciduous trees from the cassia subfamily of the legume (Fabaceae) family, this genus occurs in the tropical

Peltophorum pterocarpum, Thailand

savannah and coastal forests of Africa, Asia, the Americas, and northern Australia. Some species have been harvested for timber, others widely planted as ornamentals. The glossy green leaves are bipinnate, up to 18 in (45 cm) long, the ultimate leaflets being in 15 pairs, each about ½ in (12 mm) long. Prominent terminal panicles up to 24 in (60 cm) long bear many fragrant yellow flowers, with crinkly edges to the petals. Brown fruit pods contain several seeds.

CULTIVATION: Like most legumes, propagation is from seed which requires pre-treatment such as soaking in boiling water or scarification of the seed coat. These plants are only suitable for the tropics. Young plants require some shelter when first planted, but when established, full sun and well-drained moist soils are necessary.

Peltophorum africanum

☀ ✈ ↔ 20 ft (6 m) ↕ 40 ft (12 m)

Common semi-deciduous species of tropical Africa, south to northern South Africa, and Namibia. Leaves bipinnate, 7 pairs of leaflets, 20 pairs of ultimate leaflets. Bright yellow flower, in summer. Dark brown, flat, leathery seed pods. Zones 11–12.

Peltophorum pterocarpum

YELLOW FLAME TREE

☀ ✈ ↔ 30 ft (9 m) ↕ 50 ft (15 m)

Found in tropical India, Southeast Asia, Malay Archipelago, New Guinea, and Australia's "Top End." Medium-sized tree, with spreading branches. Leaves consist of bipinnate leaflets, 10 to 20 pairs. Terminal panicles of numerous fragrant yellow flowers, in summer. Flat, brown, leathery pods. Zones 11–12.

PENIOCEREUS

From southwestern USA, northern Mexico, and Central America, this genus of 18 species of shrubby,

prostrate or climbing plants with thickened or tuberous roots belongs to the family Cactaceae, and includes species formerly placed in *Cullmannia*, *Neoevansia*, *Nyctocereus*, and *Wilcoxia*. Made up of thin often weedy-looking stems to 15 ft (4.5 m) high, the branches of some species have downy or velvety skin. Stems are always ribbed but rarely have tubercles. Spines are often conspicuous, usually even in shape and size, occasionally flattened against the stem. Large often white flowers with spiny pericarpels open by day or night, mostly borne laterally, occasionally terminally. Seed pods are spherical to pear-shaped, red, with deciduous spines.
CULTIVATION: Grow in a rich well-drained soil. Propagate from seed or cuttings dried out for a week or two. Rest in winter to avoid rotting underground stems.

Peniocereus greggii
ARIZONA QUEEN OF THE NIGHT,
SWEET POTATO CACTUS
☀/☀ ❄ ↔ 20 in (50 cm) ↑ 10 ft (3 m)
From southwestern USA and Mexico. Shrubby plant with a stem ½–¾ in (12–18 mm) in diameter, branching only occasionally. Large, white, nocturnal flowers, 6–8 in (15–20 cm) long, borne on stems arising from large tuberous roots to 24 in (60 cm) in diameter. Seed pods red and oval. Zones 8–11.

PENNISETUM
A genus of about 80 clump- or mat-forming, rhizomatous or stoloniferous, annual or perennial grasses from the family Poaceae, native to tropical, subtropical, and warm-temperate regions of Eurasia, Africa, Arabia and Australasia. They have round, hollow, prostrate to erect and tufted stems with solid swollen nodes, and alternate, narrow, strap-like, flat leaves rising

Pennisetum villosum

Pennisetum setaceum 'Burgundy Giant'

from a central base as well as from the stems. The cylindrical or rounded, feathery, spike-like flowerheads grow at the ends of stems or from leaf axils, and contain clusters of up to 4 sword-shaped to oblong spikelets, minute bisexual flowers with 3 stamens and 2 stigmas, appearing in late summer and autumn. Fruit is an achene-like grain. Some species are cultivated for ornamental and foodcrop value. The genus is named from the Latin *penna*, feather, and *seta*, bristle, referring to the plant's feathery bristles.
CULTIVATION: They prefer moist, well-drained soil with either full sun or light shade. Propagate species from seed and hybrids by division in spring.

Pennisetum alopecuroides ★
syn. *Pennisetum japonicum*
CHINESE PENNISETUM, FOUNTAIN GRASS,
SWAMP FOX-TAIL GRASS
☀/☀ ❄ ↔ 18–24 in (45–60 cm)
↑ 4–5 ft (1.2–1.5 m)
Clump-forming, upright, perennial grass, found from eastern Asia to northwestern Australia. Solitary, terminal, yellowish green to dark purple, cylindrical to narrowly oblong flowerheads, to 8 in (20 cm), with spikelets with purplish anthers and long bristles. Leaves to 24 in (60 cm) long, rough to the touch. 'Cassian', to 4 ft (1.2 m) tall, light brown, foxtail-shaped flowerheads contrast with foliage, which turns gold with reddish tints in autumn; 'Hameln', clump-forming to 20 in (50 cm) high, with buff-colored flowerheads, golden leaves in autumn; 'Little Bunny', very compact form, to 18 in (45 cm) tall, with heads of whitish green flowers; 'Moudry', dark

Pennisetum flaccidum

Pennisetum setaceum 'Atrosanguineum'

Pennisetum setaceum

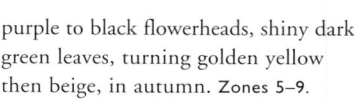

purple to black flowerheads, shiny dark green leaves, turning golden yellow then beige, in autumn. Zones 5–9.

Pennisetum flaccidum
FLACCID GRASS, KIKUYU GRASS
☀ ❄ ↔ 18–24 in (45–60 cm)
↑ 3–5 ft (0.9–1.5 m)
Tall-growing, spreading, perennial grass, native to much of Asia. Arching, slender, hairy, purple plumes, ageing to brown, on purple stems. Narrow grayish green leaves; many pencil-like, purple flowers, over a very long season, turning buff with age. Zones 7–9.

Pennisetum orientale
ORIENTAL FOUNTAIN GRASS, TALL TAILS
☀ ❄ ↔ 3–4 ft (0.9–1.2 m)
↑ 5–6 ft (1.5–1.8 m)
Rhizomatous perennial grass, native from central and southwestern Asia to northwestern India, which forms upright, arching clumps of slightly rough, green leaves to 4 in (10 cm) long. Loose, hairy flowerheads, to 6 in (15 cm) long, with 2 to 5 pinkish spikelets. Zones 8–10.

Pennisetum setaceum
FOUNTAIN GRASS
☀ ⚘ ↔ 24–36 in (60–90 cm)
↑ 3–5 ft (0.9–1.5 m)
A clumping, perennial grass native to tropical Africa, southwestern Asia,

Pennisetum setaceum cultivar

and Arabia, annual in cooler climates. It has an erect slender stem and very narrow, rough, rigid leaves, 8–26 in (20–65 cm) long. The feathery, erect or inclined flowerheads, to 12 in (30 cm) long, are tinged with pink to purple, and contain 1 to 3 purplish spikelets in summer. 'Atrosanguineum' has burgundy foliage and its soft reddish purple, nodding flower plumes appear in summer; 'Burgundy Giant' has broad burgundy leaves, to 1 in (25 mm) wide, and whitish pink flowers on stalks to 4 ft (1.2 m) long, bright green in summer, and turning golden brown in autumn. Zones 9–10.

Pennisetum villosum ★
syn. *Pennisetum longistylum*
FEATHERTOP
☀ ❄ ↔ 18–24 in (45–60 cm)
↑ 2–4 ft (0.6–1.2 m)
A slowly spreading perennial grass, grown as an annual in cooler climates, and a native of northeastern tropical Africa. It forms loosely clumped, spreading mats. Sheathed leaves with bluish green blades, 2–16 in (5–40 cm) long. Solitary, compact, plumed, cylindrical to almost spherical flower spikes are 2–5 in (5–12 cm) long, with long, feathery bristles, and tinged with tawny brown to purple spikelets. This species self-seeds prolifically and can be invasive. Zones 8–10.

Penstemon eatonii

Penstemon azureus

PENSTEMON

This genus of around 250 species of perennials and subshrubs in the foxglove (Scrophulariaceae) family is found from Alaska to Guatemala, with one straggler in cool-temperate Asia. Some are mat-forming, some shrubby, but most form clumps of simple linear to lance-shaped leaves in opposite pairs. Their flowers, borne mainly in summer on upright terminal spikes reminiscent of foxgloves *(Digitalis)*, are tubular to bell-shaped, with 2 upper lobes and 3 larger lower lobes. Native Americans used parts of several species in herbal medicines, primarily for pain relief and to control bleeding.

CULTIVATION: Because some species and garden forms are frost tender, considerable work has recently been put into producing hardy hybrids. Gardeners in cold winter areas should look for these. Plant in full or half-sun with moist well-drained soil. Alpine and southwestern species often prefer gritty soil but others like added humus. Propagate by division or from cuttings of non-flowering stems. The species may be raised from seed.

Penstemon alamosensis
ALAMO BEARDTONGUE
☀/◗ ❄ ↔ 12 in (30 cm) ↑ 27 in (70 cm)
Summer-flowering perennial from the mountains around New Mexico/Texas border, USA. Pointed, silvery to blue-gray, lance-shaped leaves to about 3 in (8 cm) long. Wiry stems with narrow heads of downy, bright red, ½–1 in (12–25 mm) long flowers. Zones 8–10.

Penstemon ambiguus
☀/◗ ❄ ↔ 16–20 in (40–50 cm)
↑ 24 in (60 cm)
Shrubby summer- to autumn-flowering perennial from alpine areas of western and southwestern USA and nearby parts of Mexico. Very narrow, finely toothed leaves to 2 in (5 cm) long. Open panicles of ½–1 in (12–25 mm) long flesh pink flowers, ageing to white. Zones 3–9.

Penstemon angustifolius
☀/◗ ❄ ↔ 12–16 in (30–40 cm)
↑ 12 in (30 cm)
Summer-flowering perennial found in central USA from South Dakota to Colorado. Forms a tufted mound of fleshy, narrowly lance-shaped leaves to 3 in (8 cm) long. The wiry flower stems have small heads of ½–¾ in (12–18 mm) long pink flowers, ageing to mid-blue. Zones 3–9.

Penstemon azureus
☀/◗ ❄ ↔ 8–12 in (20–30 cm)
↑ 12–20 in (30–50 cm)
From California, USA, this species is a late summer-flowering perennial with narrowly lance-shaped blue-green leaves to over 2 in (5 cm) long. Thin stems support small heads of narrow purple-blue or bright blue flowers to 1¼ in (30 mm) long. Zones 8–10.

Penstemon barbatus
BEARDLIP, CORAL PENSTEMON
☀/◗ ❄ ↔ 12–20 in (30–50 cm)
↑ 40 in (100 cm)
Sturdy, strong-stemmed, summer-flowering perennial from Colorado, Arizona, and New Mexico, USA. Narrow lance-shaped leaves to around 3 in (8 cm) long and heads of pink to red flowers to 1½ in (35 mm) long, with extended upper lobes. 'Coccineus', bright red flowers; 'Elfin Pink' is 14 in (35 cm) tall with bright pink flowers; 'Rose Elf', 14 in (35 cm) tall, deep pink flowers; 'Schooley's Yellow', 24 in (60 cm) tall with bright yellow flowers. Zones 3–9.

Penstemon campanulatus
☀/◗ ❄ ↔ 8–12 in (20–30 cm)
↑ 12–24 in (30–60 cm)
Late spring- to early summer-flowering perennial from the mountains of Mexico and Guatemala. The leaves are narrow, toothed, and lance-shaped, to nearly 3 in (8 cm) long. Inflorescences of funnel- to bell-shaped, deep pink to purple flowers to 1 in (25 mm) long. Zones 9–10.

Penstemon cardwellii
☀/◗ ❄ ↔ 20 in (50 cm) ↑ 8 in (20 cm)
Found in the low coastal ranges of Washington and Oregon, USA. Summer-flowering perennial forms low clump of short upright stems with 1 in (25 mm) long, blue-green, spatula-shaped leaves. The flowers are bright purple, and large in comparison to the plant size, nearly 1½ in (35 mm) long. Zones 8–10.

Penstemon centranthifolius
SCARLET BUGLER
☀/◗ ❄ ↔ 12–20 in (30–50 cm)
↑ 4 ft (1.2 m)
This late spring- to early summer-flowering perennial, a native of Baja California, Mexico, and California, USA, has erect stems with blue-green, lance- to spatula-shaped leaves to 4 in (10 cm) long. Inflorescences of narrow, tubular, bright red flowers around 1¼ in (30 mm) long. Zones 9–11.

Penstemon davidsonii
☀/◗ ❄ ↔ 20–24 in (50–60 cm)
↑ 4 in (10 cm)
Low, spreading, summer-flowering perennial from western USA. Forms a mat of fine stems with ½ in (12 mm) long elliptical leaves, studded with short inflorescences of bright pink flowers around 1 in (25 mm) long. Zones 6–9.

Penstemon digitalis
FOXGLOVE BEARDTONGUE
☀/◗ ❄ ↔ 12–24 in (30–60 cm)
↑ 5 ft (1.5 m)
Summer-flowering perennial from central USA. Strongly upright stems clothed in glossy, purple-tinted, blue-green leaves, 4–6 in (10–15 cm) long. The top 4–12 in (10–30 cm) of stems is composed of panicles of purple-pink flushed white flowers to around 1¼ in (30 mm) long. 'Husker Red' has deep purple-red foliage, especially on new growth. Zones 3–9.

Penstemon eatonii
EATON'S FIRECRACKER
☀/◗ ❄ ↔ 8–16 in (20–40 cm)
↑ 24 in (60 cm)
Late summer-flowering perennial from western USA. Forms a clump of fairly short, upright stems but with large lance-shaped basal leaves to over 6 in (15 cm) long, the upper leaves are much smaller. Small-branched heads of 1 in (25 mm) long bright red flowers. Zones 4–9.

Penstemon fruticosus
SHRUBBY PENSTEMON
☀/◗ ❄ ↔ 20 in (50 cm) ↑ 16 in (40 cm)
Spring- to summer-flowering perennial from western USA. Forms a bushy clump of mostly erect stems with lance-shaped leaves to 2 in (5 cm) long, sometimes finely toothed. Heads of lavender to purple flowers around ¾ in (18 mm) long. Zones 4–9.

Penstemon grandiflorus
LARGE BEARDTONGUE
☀/◗ ❄ ↔ 12–20 in (30–50 cm)
↑ 40 in (100 cm)
Found in central USA from North Dakota to Texas. Summer-flowering perennial with 1–4 in (2.5–10 cm) long, leathery, rounded, blue-green leaves. Inflorescences are up to 12 in (30 cm) long, with 1½ in (35 mm) long, lavender to pale blue flowers. 'Prairie Snow', 24 in (60 cm) tall, is a heavy-blooming white-flowered cultivar. Zones 3–9.

Penstemon digitalis 'Husker Red'

Penstemon parryi

Penstemon procerus var. *tolmiei*

Penstemon strictus

Penstemon pinifolius

Penstemon heterophyllus
FOOTHILLS PENSTEMON

☼/◐ ❄ ↔ 8–12 in (20–30 cm)
↑ 12–20 in (30–50 cm)

This is a shrubby summer-flowering Californian perennial. Narrow, dark green to blue-green leaves to 2 in (5 cm) long. Fairly short heads of lavender-pink to bright blue flowers around 1¼ in (30 mm) long. '**Blue Bedder**' ★ has compact, bright blue flowers; '**Heavenly Blue**', dark mauve-blue to blue flowers. Zones 8–10.

Penstemon hirsutus

☼/◐ ❄ ↔ 8–12 in (20–30 cm)
↑ 16–32 in (40–80 cm)

Clump-forming, late summer-flowering perennial from eastern North America. The stems are erect, with toothed, lance-shaped leaves, 2–4 in (5–10 cm) long with downy uppersurfaces. The flowers are slightly pendulous, around 1 in (25 mm) long, purple with white-edged lobes. '**Pygmaeus**' is a 6 in (15 cm) tall cultivar with purple flowers. Zones 3–9.

Penstemon isophyllus

☼/◐ ❄ ↔ 40 in (100 cm) ↑ 27 in (70 cm)

Spring-flowering Mexican perennial with purple-tinted stems initially spreading, then upright. The leaves are leathery and lance-shaped with slightly rolled edges, to 1½ in (35 mm) long. The inflorescence to 12 in (30 cm) long, bears 5-lobed, white-haired, red flowers to 1½ in (35 mm) long. Zones 9–11.

Penstemon laevis
SOUTHWESTERN BEARDTONGUE

☼/◐ ❄ ↔ 16 in (40 cm) ↑ 20 in (50 cm)

Summer-flowering perennial native to western North America. Lance-shaped 2–3 in (5–8 cm) long leaves and spikes of rather widely spaced, bulbous, large-lobed mauve flowers to over 1 in (25 mm) long. Zones 5–9.

Penstemon newberryi
MOUNTAIN PRIDE

☼/◐ ❄ ↔ 20–32 in (50–80 cm)
↑ 6–12 in (15–30 cm)

From California and Nevada, USA. Spreading, mat-forming, summer-flowering perennial. Finely toothed, pointed oval leaves about 1 in (25 mm) long. Short upright stems with heads of narrow, tubular, pinkish red flowers to 1¼ in (30 mm) long. Zones 8–10.

Penstemon palmeri
SCENTED PENSTEMON

☼/◐ ❄ ↔ 16–24 in (40–60 cm)
↑ 32–55 in (80–140 cm)

Erect summer-flowering perennial from western USA. Pointed oval leaves to 6 in (15 cm) long, teeth tipped with small spines. Large, showy, scented heads of bulbous white flowers marked and flushed deep pink to red, to over 1¼ in (30 mm) long. Zones 5–9.

Penstemon parryi

☼/◐ ❄ ↔ 16–24 in (40–60 cm)
↑ 12–24 in (30–60 cm)

Erect, short-stemmed, spring-flowering perennial from southern Arizona, USA. Broad, blue-green, lance- to spatula-shaped leaves to 3 in (8 cm) long. Short-branched racemes of funnel-shaped, ¾ in (18 mm) long, magenta flowers. Zones 8–10.

Penstemon pinifolius

☼/◐ ❄ ↔ 16–24 in (40–60 cm)
↑ 16 in (40 cm)

Woody-based summer-flowering perennial native to Arizona and New Mexico, USA, and nearby parts of Mexico. Very narrow filament-like leaves with heads of bright red, 1 in (25 mm) long flowers. '**Mersea Yellow**' is an 8 in (20 cm) tall cultivar with bright yellow flowers. Zones 8–10.

Penstemon procerus
SMALL-FLOWERED PENSTEMON

☼/◐ ❄ ↔ 12–16 in (30–40 cm)
↑ 6–16 in (15–40 cm)

Clump-forming summer-flowering perennial from northwestern North America. The stems are slender with broad, dark green, lance-shaped leaves to over 2 in (5 cm) long. The short-branched inflorescences of ½ in (12 mm) long carry white-centered lavender-blue and purple-pink flowers. *P. p.* var. *tolmiei* is just 4 in (10 cm) tall, with bright lavender-blue flowers. Zones 3–9.

Penstemon spectabilis

☼/◐ ❄ ↔ 16–20 in (40–50 cm)
↑ 32–48 in (80–120 cm)

Strongly erect, early summer-flowering perennial native to California, USA, and northern parts of Baja California, Mexico. The coarsely toothed, green to blue-green, pointed oval to lance-shaped leaves to 4 in (10 cm) long, often partly or entirely encircle the stems. It produces short-branched heads of narrow, white-centered light purple flowers to over 1¼ in (30 mm) long. Zones 7–10.

Penstemon strictus
STIFF BEARDTONGUE

☼/◐ ❄ ↔ 12–16 in (30–40 cm)
↑ 32 in (80 cm)

Clumping summer-flowering perennial from the mountains of southwestern USA. Long-stemmed spatula-shaped basal leaves to over 3 in (8 cm) long, upper leaves linear to lance-shaped. Narrow heads of large-lobed, 1¼ in (30 mm) long violet to purple-blue flowers. Zones 3–9.

Penstemon newberryi

Penstemon laevis

Penstemon heterophyllus

Penstemon superbus

☀/◐ ◑ ↔ 20–32 in (50–80 cm)
↑ 5–6 ft (1.5–1.8 m)

Vigorous, erect, summer-flowering Mexican perennial with blue-green, leathery, pointed oval leaves to 6 in (15 cm) long, sometimes partly or entirely encircling the stems. Short-branched heads of whorls of many large-lobed bright red flowers to 1½ in (35 mm) long. **Zones 9–11.**

Penstemon venustus

LOVELY PENSTEMON

☀/◐ ❋ ↔ 16–32 in (40–80 cm)
↑ 16–32 in (40–80 cm)

Late spring- to early summer-flowering subshrub found from Washington and Oregon to Idaho, USA. The leaves are finely toothed and lance-shaped, to over 4 in (10 cm) long, and it produces panicles of 1¼ in (30 mm) long, violet to purple flowers with hair-fringed lobes. **Zones 5–9.**

Penstemon virens

☀/◐ ❋ ↔ 16–32 in (40–80 cm)
↑ 8–16 in (20–40 cm)

Mat-forming summer-flowering perennial species from Colorado, USA. Finely toothed or smooth-edged leaves to 4 in (10 cm) long; 3–6 in (8–15 cm) long inflorescences of large-lobed, ½ in (12 mm) long violet-blue and purple flowers. **Zones 4–9.**

Penstemon watsonii

☀/◐ ❋ ↔ 12–16 in (30–40 cm)
↑ 12–24 in (30–60 cm)

Clump-forming, summer-flowering perennial from the mountains of Colorado, Utah, and Nevada, USA. Leaves pointed oval to lance-shaped, 1–2 in (25–50 mm) long, and sometimes finely toothed. Inflorescence with small branches, the flowers violet with occasional white markings, funnel-shaped and slightly over ½ in (12 mm) long. **Zones 3–9.**

Penstemon Hybrid Cultivars

☀/◐ ❋ ↔ 8–16 in (20–40 cm)
↑ 24–48 in (60–120 cm)

Formerly listed under *P.* × *gloxinioides*, these hybrids have a complex parentage largely lost in the mists of time, though it is likely that *P. hartwegii* and *P. cobaea* were major influences. Modern hybrids are bred with large flowers, compact habit, bright colors, and frost tolerance as the main objectives and have proved to be among the most reliable performers in the perennial border. 'Alice Hindley', 4 ft (1.2 m) tall, white-centered mauve flowers; 'Andenken an Friedrich Hahn' (syn. 'Garnet'), 32 in (80 cm) tall flowers, paler at first, becoming purple-red; 'Apple Blossom', 32 in (80 cm) tall, small pink-tipped white flowers; 'Burgundy', 4 ft (1.2 m) tall, deep purple-red; 'Chester Scarlet' ★,

Penstemon virens

Penstemon watsonii

Penstemon venustus

Penstemon, Hybrid Cultivar, 'Countess of Dalkeith'

Penstemon, Hybrid Cultivar, 'Jean Grace'

Penstemon, Hybrid Cultivar, 'Maurice Gibbs'

Penstemon, Hybrid Cultivar, 'Purple Passion'

Penstemon, Hybrid Cultivar, 'Raven'

Penstemon, Hybrid Cultivar, 'Rich Ruby'

Penstemon, Hybrid Cultivar, 'Shoenholzeri'

Penstemon, Hybrid Cultivar, 'Stapleford Gem'

Penstemon, HC, 'George Home'

Penstemon, HC, 'Swan Lake'

P., HC, 'Andenken an Friedrich Hahn'

Penstemon, HC, 'Hidcote'

Penstemon, HC, 'Peace'

32 in (80 cm) tall, bright red with darker throat stripes; '**Countess of Dalkeith**', 36 in (90 cm) tall, white-throated deep purple flowers; '**Hewell Pink Bedder**', 32 in (80 cm) tall, gray-green foliage, reddish pink flowers; '**Hidcote Pink**', 36 in (90 cm) tall, gray-green foliage, deep pink flowers with darker throat markings; '**Maurice Gibbs**', 36 in (90 cm) tall, purple-red with white throat; '**Myddleton Gem**', 30 in (75 cm) tall, vivid pinkish red with white throat; '**Osprey**', 36 in (90 cm) tall, large-lobed pink flowers with white throat; '**Peace**', 24 in (60 cm), narrow pink and white flowers; '**Pennington Gem**', 36 in (90 cm), deep pink with red-marked white throat; '**Raven**', 36 in (90 cm), purple-red with white throat; '**Rich Ruby**', 36 in (90 cm) tall, purple-red with darker throat; '**Schoenholzeri**' (syn. '**Firebird**'), 36 in (90 cm) tall, deep red; '**Stapleford Gem**', 36 in (90 cm), violet and light purple tones; '**White Bedder**', 27 in (70 cm) tall, 1930s seedling strain with compact habit and white flowers, sometimes pink in bud. Zones 6–10.

PENTACHONDRA

This is a genus belonging to the epacris (Epacridaceae) family of 3 to 5 species of small spreading or prostrate shrubs native to subalpine and alpine regions of Australia and New Zealand. The alternately arranged leaves are usually crowded on the stems, and the numerous, small, tubular flowers have flaring petal lobes. They are followed by red berries that split open when ripe.
CULTIVATION: *Pentachondra* species are slow growing and need moist but free-draining, gritty, acidic soil. They are best planted in the rock garden. Propagation is easiest from rooted pieces as seeds are difficult to germinate and cuttings are slow to establish.

Pentachondra pumila
☼ ❄ ↔ 36 in (90 cm) ↕ 6 in (15 cm)
Mat-forming shrub from Australia and New Zealand. Small densely packed leaves often tinged red. Tiny white, starry flowers, hairy inside, in spring–summer. Red berries take up to a year to ripen, present with the flowers. Zones 8–10.

PENTAS

Mainly biennials and perennials, the 30 to 40-odd species in this genus of the madder (Rubiaceae) family from tropical parts of Arabia, Africa, and Madagascar also include a few shrubs. They have 3–8 in (8–20 cm) long ovate to lance-shaped leaves and small flowers in showy terminal heads. Flowers occur in all shades of pink, white, purple, mauve, and red. Removing the spent flowers extends the flowering season. Dry seed heads follow the flowers.
CULTIVATION: All are tender and will not tolerate frosts or prolonged cold conditions. Cultivated outdoors in the tropics and subtropics, they are treated as house or greenhouse plants elsewhere. They are not drought tolerant and need plenty of moisture while actively growing and flowering. Plant in a moist, fertile, humus-rich, well-drained soil and keep stem tips pinched back to ensure a compact habit. Propagate from seed or half-hardened cuttings, which strike quickly.

Peperomia caperata

Pentas lanceolata
STAR CLUSTER
☼ ✤ ↔ 3 ft (0.9 m) ↕ 6 ft (1.8 m)
Found from Yemen to tropical east Africa, smaller in cultivation. Velvety leaves dark green. Large heads of flowers, white through shades of pink to magenta to lavender-blue, in summer. '**New Look Red**' ★ has scarlet flowers; '**New Look Rose**', deep pink flowers. The **Butterfly Series** includes '**Butterfly Blush**', '**Butterfly Cherry Red**', and '**Butterfly Light Lavender**'. Zones 10–12.

PEPEROMIA

RADIATOR PLANT
Genus of about 1,000 largely succulent herbs from the pepper (Piperaceae) family, mainly originating from South America, with 17 species from Africa, and valued for their ornamental foliage. Fleshy leaves, usually on long stalks, and dense, erect, slender spikes of minute, bisexual flowers, normally whitish cream, mostly in late summer.
CULTIVATION: In warm climates they can be grown as ground covers or as epiphytes on tree trunks. Otherwise, grow in pots or hanging baskets in light, well-drained compost; a soil-less mixture is best for epiphytic species. Avoid over-watering; protect from slugs and snails. Propagate by division or from stem, tip, or leaf cuttings.

Pentachondra pumila

Peperomia argyreia
syn. *Peperomia sandersii*
WATERMELON BEGONIA, WATERMELON PEPPER
◐/☼ ❋ ↔ 6–9 in (15–22 cm)
↕ 6–12 in (15–30 cm)
Evergreen succulent perennial from northern South America to Brazil. Thick, wrinkled, broadly heart-shaped, dark green, concave leaves, pointed at tip, rounded at base, silvery gray above, with dark green stripes resembling watermelon rind, on erect red stalks. White flower spikes are covered with tiny yellowish white flowers. '**Emerald Ripple**', corrugated, deep green leaves, greenish white flower spikes on pinkish stalks; '**Little Fantasy**', dwarf form; '**Silver Ripple**', tight clusters of showy, deeply corrugated or ribbed heart-shaped leaves, 2–3 in (5–8 cm) across, with variable colors from green to red and even variegated, often highlighted with frosted ridges; '**Tricolor**' (syn. '**Variegata**'), small leaves with broad white borders. Zones 9–12.

Peperomia caperata
◐/☼ ❋ ↔ 6–10 in (15–25 cm)
↕ 6–10 in (15–25 cm)
From Brazil. Bushy perennial with heart-shaped, dark green, deeply veined leaves on pinkish stems. White flowers. Zones 10–12.

Pentas lanceolata 'New Look Red'

Pentas lanceolata 'Butterfly Blush'

Pentas lanceolata 'New Look Rose'

P. lanceolata 'Butterfly Light Lavender'

Pentas lanceolata 'Butterfly Cherry Red'

Pereskia grandifolia, Jardín Botánico Lankester, Costa Rica

Peperomia clusiifolia

☀️/☀️ ⚡ ↔6–10 in (15–25 cm)
↑6–10 in (15–25 cm)

Erect semi-succulent perennial, native to the West Indies and parts of northern South America. Oval to elliptical, glandular leaves, 3 in (8 cm) long, pointed or rounded tips, taper toward base. They are mid-green or tinged with purple, with margins flushed with maroon, and a reddish main vein, on dark red stalks. 'Variegata', light green leaves, variegated with cream toward the edges and red margins. Zones 9–11.

Peperomia fraseri

FLOWERING PEPPER

☀️ ⚡ ↔12–16 in (30–40 cm)
↑12–16 in (30–40 cm)

Erect perennial from Colombia and Ecuador. The broadly oval to almost circular leaves, to 1½ in (35 mm) long, are pointed at the tips, heart-shaped at the base, and tinged with purple on the veins, pale green underneath with bright red to pink veins, carried on dull red to pink, minutely hairy stalks. This species produces

spikes, to 1½ in (35 mm) long, of white, fragrant, mignonette-like flowers. Zones 9–11.

Peperomia griseoargentea

IVY-LEAF PEPPER, PLATINUM PEPPER, SILVER-LEAF PEPPER

☀️ ⚡ ↔6–8 in (15–20 cm)
↑6–8 in (15–20 cm)

An erect perennial herb from Brazil. Heart-shaped, leathery leaves, 1½ in (35 mm) long, with pointed tips and rounded base, are grayish green above and paler beneath, with deeply impressed veins, on pale green to pink stalks. Zones 9–11.

Peperomia fraseri

Peperomia orba

Peperomia obtusifolia

AMERICAN RUBBER PLANT, BABY RUBBER PLANT, PEPPER-FACE

☀️ ✈ ↔6–8 in (15–20 cm)
↑6–8 in (15–20 cm)

Erect or sprawling perennial. From Mexico to northern South America and the West Indies. Stems to 6 in (15 cm) long, take root at the nodes. Alternate, thick, elliptical to oval leaves, to 4 in (10 cm) long, rounded tips and wedge-shaped at base, on winged stalks. 'Golden Gate', yellow-blotched leaves; 'Variegata', more pointed variegated pale green leaves, marked with cream or yellow toward margins; 'White Cloud', bluish green leaves with yellow markings. Zones 10–12.

Peperomia orba

☀️ ⚡ ↔4–6 in (10–15 cm)
↑4–6 in (10–15 cm)

Bushy, erect perennial. Leathery and hairy, oval or elliptical, dull green leaves with lighter central stripe, with pointed tips and rounded at the base. Spikes of tiny green flowers. Zones 9–11.

PERESKIA

This genus is an unusual member of the cactus (Cactaceae) family, as its

16 species of trees, shrubs, and woody climbers have leaves. From southern Mexico and areas of Central and South America. The stems and leaves are not noticeably succulent but spines are numerous. Some species have tuberous roots. The clustered or solitary flowers are red, pink, or white.
CULTIVATION: These rather tender plants require greenhouse cultivation in cool climates. In warm climates they can be grown outdoors in a light well-drained soil. They dislike humidity and should be kept dry in winter. Propagation is from seed or cuttings.

Pereskia aculeata ★

BARBADOS GOOSEBERRY, LEMON VINE

☀️ ⚡ ↔6–15 ft (1.8–4.5 m)
↑25–30 ft (8–9 m)

Woody climber from tropical America with a thick, cane-like main stem. Sword-shaped, elliptical or oval leaves, 3–5 in (8–12 cm) long, with 2 or 3 spines emerging from the leaf tips. Panicles of numerous scented, white, yellow, or pinkish flowers, 1–2 in (25–50 mm) in diameter, in autumn. *P. a.* var. *rubescens* (syn. *P. rubescens*), leaves variegated with red. Zones 9–12.

Pereskia grandifolia

☀️ ⚡ ↔3 ft (0.9 m) ↑7–15 ft (2–4.5 m)
Native to Brazil. Shrub or small tree. Thin broadly lance-shaped leaves, brownish black spines. Flowers pink to purplish pink in clusters, from spring–autumn. Zones 9–11.

PERICALLIS

CINERARIA

This genus of 14 species of perennials and shrubs in the daisy (Asteraceae)

Peperomia obtusifolia

Peperomia obtusifolia 'Variegata'

Peperomia obtusifolia 'Golden Gate'

Peperomia obtusifolia 'White Cloud'

family, mostly Canary Island natives, is known mainly for its fancy-flowered hybrids. With soft, bristly or hairy leaves, some of the species carry their flowers singly but the cultivated plants produce large heads of daisies. Pink to purple is the predominant flower color in the wild, but the hybrids occur in a wide range of shades. The name is from Greek *peri,* around, and *kallos,* beauty, referring to the circle of showy ray florets.

CULTIVATION: Cinerarias prefer temperate climates; in cool areas treat as summer annuals or winter-flowering indoor plants. They like shade in summer but need more light in winter. Plant in humus-rich, cool, moist, well-drained soil. Usually propagated by seed, but the shrubby types will grow from cuttings.

Pericallis × *hybrida*
CINERARIA

☀/◐ ☽ ↔ 16–40 in (40–100 cm)
↑ 16–32 in (40–80 cm)

Perennial hybrids mainly between *P. lanata* and *P. cruenta* parents, ranging from small mounding plants to taller, more open, shrubby forms. The preferred compact types have downy, angular heart-shaped leaves with toothed edges, sometimes purplish undersides; flowerheads clustered, often densely, in many colors. Zones 9–11.

Perovskia atriplicifolia, HC, 'Blue Spire'

Perovskia atriplicifolia

Pericallis × *hybrida*

Pericallis lanata
☀ ☽ ↔ 40 in (100 cm) ↑ 40 in (100 cm)
Subshrub with densely downy to woolly stems and foliage. Leaves roughly pointed oval to heart-shaped, up to 7 clearly defined lobes, irregularly toothed. Flowerheads solitary or in small clusters, fragrant, ray florets violet, disc florets purple. Zones 9–11.

PERILLA
A genus of 6 annual herbs belonging to the mint (Lamiaceae) family, found naturally in Asia from India to Japan. Tight, dense spikes of flowers with a 5-toothed, bell-shaped calyx, and a 5-lobed corolla tube which is shorter than the calyx. Opposite pairs of leaves are often variegated or colored, with those of some species used in Oriental cuisine. Fruit is a 1-seeded nutlet.
CULTIVATION: Space plants about 12 in (30 cm) apart, in rich but well-drained soil and full sun to light shade. Sow seeds outdoors in warm soil; the seeds require light to sprout. Deadhead to prevent invasive self-sowing.

Perilla frutescens
BEEFSTEAK PLANT, CHINESE BASIL, WILD SESAME

☀/◐ ❄ ↔ 18–24 in (45–60 cm)
↑ 24–40 in (60–100 cm)

An erect, finely hairy, annual herb that resembles basil. Native species of the Himalayas and eastern Asia. Forms spikes, up to 4 in (10 cm) long, of

Perovskia atriplicifolia, HC, 'Longan'

Perilla frutescens var. *crispa*

small, white, pink, or reddish flowers with a corolla to 4 mm across, in the late summer to autumn. The leaves, which are green or purple or sometimes speckled with purple, are often wrinkled, and are broadly oval, heavily serrated, pointed, and 1½–5 in (3.5–12 cm) long, with a scent resembling cinnamon. *P. f.* var. *crispa* (syn. *P. f.* var. *nankinensis*) is an attractive plant, with extra-crinkled bronze or dark purplish brown leaves. Zones 8–11.

PEROVSKIA
A genus of 7 species belonging to the mint (Lamiaceae) family. They are deciduous subshrubs or perennials from central Asia and the Himalayas. They are grown for their finely divided grayish foliage and large sprays of small blue flowers that are produced in late summer and autumn.
CULTIVATION: These hardy plants require little more than a sunny well-drained position and a heavy pruning each winter. Propagate from softwood or semi-hardwood cuttings.

Perovskia atriplicifolia
RUSSIAN SAGE

☀ ❄ ↔ 18–36 in (45–90 cm)
↑ 30–60 in (75–150 cm)

Clump-forming deciduous perennial, from Iran, Afghanistan, and western Pakistan. Upright stems. Sword-shaped, grayish green, coarsely toothed, lobed leaves, 2–2½ in (5–6 cm) long, pungent when crushed. Narrow spikes, 12 in (30 cm) or longer, of tubular, tiny, blue to lavender flowers in late summer–autumn. Zones 5–9.

Perovskia Hybrid Cultivars
☀ ❄ ↔ 18–36 in (45–90 cm)
↑ 24–48 in (60–120 cm)

Thought to be hybrids of *P. atriplicifolia* and *P. abrotanoides*: 'Blue Haze', leaves hardly lobed; 'Blue Mist', light blue flowers, blooms earlier in the season; 'Blue Spire' ★, darker, violet flowers in large panicles and deeply cut leaves; 'Filigren', finely dissected, almost fern-like leaves; 'Little Spire', sturdy, compact form; 'Longan', upright habit and compact. Zones 5–9.

P

PERSEA

Belonging to the laurel (Lauraceae) family, this genus of around 200 species of evergreen shrubs or trees comes chiefly from subtropical and tropical America and Southeast Asia. *Persea* species have prominently veined alternate leaves, and bear panicles of small greenish flowers in the leaf axils. The fruits contain a single large stone, and may be large or small, pear-shaped or rounded; the yellowish green flesh is smooth and rich. The best-known species is the avocado (*P. americana*), which has been cultivated for centuries for its high-energy fruit. CULTIVATION: They are best suited to a sheltered but sunny position in a well-drained soil rich in humus. Water moderately during the growing season. Little pruning is necessary once the plants are established, but unwanted lower branches should be removed in the first few years. Propagation is from seed or from cuttings. Plants may take up to 7 years to bear fruit; grafted plants are recommended for varieties grown for their fruits.

Persea americana

ALLIGATOR PEAR, AVOCADO

☼ ❄ ↔ 30 ft (9 m)   ↑ 60 ft (18 m)

Native to Central America and the West Indies. Fast-growing evergreen tree; grafted trees are smaller. Leathery elliptical leaves, panicles of yellowish green flowers. Large dark green fruits, pear-shaped or rounded. '**Haas**', thick-skinned variety. Zones 9–11.

Persea borbonia

RED BAY PERSEA

☼ ❄ ↔ 25 ft (8 m)   ↑ 40 ft (12 m)

Native to the swamps of southern North America; often cultivated as an ornamental shade tree. Lance-shaped glaucous leaves with panicles of small flowers, and dark blue fruits to ½ in (12 mm) in diameter. Zones 9–11.

Persea lingue

☼ ❄ ↔ 50 ft (15 m)   ↑ 100 ft (30 m)

Attractive forest tree from Chile. Forms a dense, luxuriant, rounded crown. Glossy green, prominently veined, elliptical leaves, small reddish flowers, small, blackish purple, oval fruits. The high-quality timber is prized for parquetry, doors, window frames, and staircases. Zones 5–9.

PERSICARIA

KNOTWEED

A large and somewhat confused genus of between 50 and 80 species in the knotweed (Polygonaceae) family, found around the world. Many species were once listed in the genera *Polygonum, Bistorta, Tovara, Antenoron,* or *Aconogonon,* and are still often so listed. Some are annuals, but most cultivated species are creeping perennials

Persea americana, Persea americana 'Haas' (inset)

or occasionally subshrubs. Some can be quite weedy under ideal growing conditions. Many are grown for their attractive foliage, and some are cultivated for their upright or drooping spikes of small flowers, which are usually pink turning to red as they age. CULTIVATION: Most like a moist to very moist soil, in full sun to partial shade. Propagate by division or from softwood cuttings in spring.

Persicaria affinis

syns *Bistorta affinis, Polygonum affine*

☼ ❄ ↔ 20–24 in (50–60 cm)

↑ 8–10 in (20–25 cm)

Evergreen creeping perennial from the Himalayas. Upright stems clothed with leaves to 6 in (15 cm) long that turn bronze in frost-prone areas in winter. Produces tight upright spikes of tiny pink flowers in late summer, turning brown in winter. '**Darjeeling Red**', larger leaves, flowers that open pink and turn red; '**Superba**', vigorous form, producing large spikes of tiny pink flowers that turn red and then brown. Zones 3–10.

Persicaria amplexicaulis

syns *Bistorta amplexicaulis, Polygonum amplexicaule*

KNOTWEED, MOUNTAIN FLEECE

☼ ❄ ↔ 3–4 ft (0.9–1.2 m)

↑ 3–4 ft (0.9–1.2 m)

Upright perennial, native to the Himalayas. Forms large, dense, bushy, slowly spreading clumps from woody rootstock. Stem-clasping, dark green, oval to sword-shaped, pointed leaves, 3–10 in (8–25 cm) long, heart-shaped at base and downy underneath, on long stalks. Dense, bottlebrush-like, erect flower spikes, 3–6 in (8–15 cm) long, of tiny rose red to purple or white flowers over a very long period from early summer–early autumn. '**Firetail**', low-growing form with bright crimson flowers. Zones 4–7.

Persicaria bistorta

syn. *Polygonum bistorta*

BISTORT, EASTER LEDGES, SNAKEWEED

☼ ❄ ↔ 6–30 in (15–75 cm)

↑ 6–30 in (15–75 cm)

Perennial from northern Europe and northern and western Asia. Stout rootstocks and wavy, triangular, oval or oblong leaves, 4–8 in (10–20 cm) long, with rounded tips and flattened bases, borne on winged stalks. Dense cylindrical spikes of white or rose pink flowers in summer. Eaten as a blood-purifying vegetable in parts of Britain, and in the Lake District as a traditional Easter dish known as "Yarby," or herb pudding. '**Superba**' ★ (syn. '**Superbum**'), dense spikes of soft pinkish red flowers. Zones 3–7.

Persicaria bistortoides

syn. *Polygonum bistortoides*

AMERICAN BISTORT, SMART WEED

☼ ❄ ↔ 8–20 in (20–50 cm)

↑ 8–20 in (20–50 cm)

Perennial herb from moist to wet sub-alpine meadows in northwest USA. Sword-shaped to elliptical leaves, 4–10 in (10–25 cm) long, arising from central base on winged stalks. Leafless flower stems also arise from the central base. White to pinkish white, small, 5-petalled flowers in spike-like, dense, terminal racemes in summer. Zones 3–5.

Persicaria campanulata

syn. *Polygonum campanulatum*

LESSER KNOTWEED

☼ ❄ ↔ 3–5 ft (0.9–1.5 m)

↑ 2–4 ft (0.6–1.2 m)

Creeping deciduous perennial, native to the Himalayas. Stems are branched and slightly hairy. Leaves, which are borne on short stalks, are pinkish brown in color, oval or sword-shaped, 1½–5 in (3.5–12 cm) long, with the upper sides grooved in a herringbone pattern and undersides felted with

Persicaria bistorta 'Superba'

Persicaria campanulata

Persicaria bistorta

white hair. Bears nodding, loosely branched, spike-like heads of fragrant, pinkish red or white flowers, from summer–early autumn. *P. c.* **var.** *lichiangense*, grayish white leaves, white flowers. '**Album**', more open spreading habit, white flowers; '**Rosenrot**' (syn. 'Roseum'), upright habit, dark rose flowers; '**Southcombe White**', white flowers. Zones 5–9.

Persicaria capitata

syn. *Polygonum capitatum*

KNOTWEED

☼ ❋ ↔ 6–12 in (15–30 cm)
↕ 3–6 in (8–15 cm)

Spreading perennial, native to the Himalayas. Dense, trailing, stalked heads of pink to red flowers from summer–autumn. Silvery grayish green heart-shaped or oval leaves, 1–2 in (25–50 mm) long, with intricate, purplish maroon, V-shaped bands, on hairy, glandular, rooting and creeping stems, to 12 in (30 cm) long. Best treated as an annual in cooler climates; can become invasive in warmer regions. '**Magic Carpet**', fast-growing, compact, creeping form, to 4 in (10 cm) high. Zones 5–9.

Persicaria microcephala

☼/◐ ❋ ↔ 5–7 ft (1.5–2 m)
↕ 40–48 in (100–120 cm)

Spreading, open-habited, herbaceous species from China. Green spearhead-shaped leaves to 7 in (18 cm) long, marked with bronze and pewter. Open heads of tiny white flowers at the tips in summer–autumn. '**Red Dragon**', spectacular form with burgundy red leaves marked with pewter and chocolate brown. Zones 5–10.

Persicaria odorata

syn. *Polygonum odoratum*

VIETNAMESE CORIANDER, VIETNAMESE MINT

☼ ⚘ ↔ 6–18 in (15–45 cm)
↕ 6–18 in (15–45 cm)

Spreading, colony-forming, tropical perennial, grown as an annual in cooler climates, with erect jointed stems that fall and take root. Pink flowers in summer–autumn. Used fresh as both a medicinal herb and

Persicaria virginiana

as a strongly flavored and aromatic culinary herb that resembles coriander. Zones 8–10.

Persicaria orientalis

syn. *Polygonum orientale*

KISS-ME-OVER-THE-GARDEN-GATE, ORIENTAL PERSICARY, PRINCE'S FEATHER

☼ ❋ ↔ 15–18 in (38–45 cm)
↕ 36–60 in (90–150 cm)

Sturdy annual, native to eastern and southeastern Asia and northern Australia, naturalized in North America. Lush, oval, bronze-green leaves, 4–8 in (10–20 cm) long, with soft fine hairs, on stout branching stems. Dense, drooping, many-branched spikes of bead-like, rose-purple, pink, or white flowers, in late summer–early autumn, lasting until frost. Self-seeds. Zones 8–10.

Persicaria tenuicaulis

syns *Bistorta tenuicaulis*, *Polygonum tenuicaule*

☼ ❋ ↔ 8–16 in (20–40 cm)
↕ 4–10 in (10–25 cm)

Slow-growing, mat-forming, deciduous or semi-evergreen perennial from Japan. Short dense spikes of tiny, bell-shaped, fragrant, white flowers in late spring–summer. Triangular, oval or elliptical, light or dark green leaves, 1¼–3 in (3–8 cm) long, on narrowly ridged stalks growing from a central, thick, trailing rootstock. Zones 4–6.

Persicaria vacciniifolia

syn. *Polygonum vacciniifolium*

☼ ❋ ↔ 20–36 in (50–90 cm)
↕ 6–7 in (15–18 cm)

Trailing, slightly woody, deciduous ground cover from the Himalayas.

Persicaria virginiana 'Painter's Palette'

Persicaria odorata

P. microcephala 'Red Dragon'

Leaves to 1 in (25 mm) long, often turning attractive colors before shedding. Produces small spikes to 3 in (8 cm) long of tiny pink flowers in late summer. Zones 7–10.

Persicaria virginiana

syn. *Polygonum virginianum*

☼/◐ ❋ ↔ 32–60 in (80–150 cm)
↕ 24–48 in (60–120 cm)

Large perennial with a mounding habit, found from the Himalayas to Japan, and also in northeastern USA. Leaves pointed oval in shape, growing to 6 in (15 cm) long, tapering to a fine tip, downy to bristly, with dark markings. Narrow spikes of minute, pink-tinted, greenish white flowers, in late summer. '**Painter's Palette**', intricately variegated foliage combining cream with yellow, green and red-brown patches. Zones 5–9.

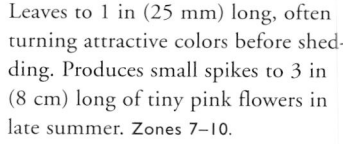
Persicaria tenuicaulis

Persicaria vivipara

syns *Bistorta vivipara*, *Polygonum viviparum*

ALPINE BISTORT, SERPENT GRASS

☼ ❋ ↔ 2–12 in (5–30 cm)
↕ 2–12 in (5–30 cm)

This tufting perennial species is widely distributed throughout the Northern Hemisphere from temperate regions to the Arctic Circle. The erect stems emerge from a thick bulb-like rootstock. The leaves are narrow, dark green, and sword-shaped, 1–4 in (2.5–10 cm) long; the leaf margins are rolled, and the lower leaves have long stalks. The plants bear slender terminal spikes, 1–4 in (25 mm–10 cm) long, of white or pale pink flowers with burnt red tips, the lower flowers replaced by purplish brown bulbils, in summer. Zones 2–4.

Persicaria vivipara, in winter

Persicaria vivipara, in spring

Persicaria vivipara, in summer

Persoonia chamaepitys

Persoonia mollis

PERSOONIA

This is an Australian genus of about 90 species of evergreen shrubs, or sometimes small trees, in the protea (Proteaceae) family, named for the eighteenth-century German botanist and mycologist Christian Hendrik Persoon. They have very attractive bright green leaves with smooth edges, and masses of almost stalkless, small, tubular, yellow flowers that have 4 rolled-back segments when they open. The flowers are followed by succulent yellow or green fruits, sometimes produced in large heavy clusters. They are commonly called geebungs, a version of the Dharuk Aboriginal word *jibbong*, referring to the edible fruits of some species.
CULTIVATION: They are best suited to full sun or semi-shade, light acidic soil, and very good drainage. They respond well to pruning or regular clipping. Propagation is from heat-treated seed or from young tip cuttings (which are notoriously difficult to strike).

Persoonia chamaepitys
☀ ❄ ↔ 36 in (90 cm) ↕ 8 in (20 cm)
From southeastern Australia. Prostrate trailing shrub, hairy branchlets. Bright green needle-like leaves, and fragrant bright yellow flowers in short clusters towards the ends of the branches, in late spring–summer. Attractive rock garden or container plant. Zones 9–11.

Persoonia linearis
NARROW-LEAF GEEBUNG
☀ ❄ ↔ 10 ft (3 m) ↕ 15 ft (4.5 m)
Erect open shrub widely distributed in southeastern Australia. Narrow softly pointed leaves. Short-stalked yellow flowers on branch ends, in summer. Zones 9–11.

Persoonia mollis
GEEBUNG
☀ ❄ ↔ 10 ft (3 m) ↕ 10 ft (3 m)
From eastern Australia. Soft, hairy, light green foliage, silky copper colored new growth. Small golden yellow flowers in the leaf axils, in summer. Prefers sandy soil. Zones 9–11.

Persoonia oxycoccoides
☀ ❄ ↔ 18 in (45 cm) ↕ 36 in (90 cm)
Prostrate or low spreading shrub from eastern Australia. Small ovate leaves with recurved margins. Showy yellow flowers singly on slender, sometimes nodding stalks, in summer. Zones 8–10.

Persoonia pinifolia
PINELEAF GEEBUNG
☀ ❄ ↔ 10 ft (3 m) ↕ 10–15 ft (3–4.5 m)
From eastern Australia. Erect shrub with slightly drooping branchlets and soft pine-like foliage. Profuse golden-yellow flowers in leaf axils at branch tips, in late summer–autumn. Small, pale green, succulent fruits. Zones 9–11.

PESCATOREA

This is a genus of about 15 sympodial epiphytes in the family Orchidaceae, occurring in Central and South America from Costa Rica to Colombia. They have a fan-shaped growth habit with quite thin narrow leaves, and the single blooms are produced from leaf axils towards the base of the plant. They are increasing in popularity as seedlings of a number of the species have become available.

Persoonia linearis

CULTIVATION: *Pescatorea* species require humid, shaded, intermediate conditions throughout the year, with no rest period. Direct sunlight will invariably burn the soft leaves. They need to be kept moist, as they have no pseudobulbs for water storage. Constant, fresh, moving air around the thin foliage is essential. The large, colorful, fragrant, long-lived blooms are extremely attractive, and appear singly from the leaf axils, in spring and summer. Propagate by division.

Pescatorea cerina
☀ ✈ ↔ 8–16 in (20–40 cm) ↕ 4–16 in (10–40 cm)
From Panama and Costa Rica. Bears highly fragrant creamy white to pale lemon yellow blooms, 3 in (8 cm) long, with broad segments. Labellum yellow with fine, dark red, longitudinal stripes. Zones 10–12.

Pescatorea lehmannii
☀ ✈ ↔ 8–16 in (20–40 cm) ↕ 4–20 in (10–50 cm)
From Colombia and Ecuador. Bears white flowers, 4 in (10 cm) long, longitudinally striped with maroon on the petals and sepals; some clones appear to be almost solid purple. Labellum is dark purple, and is covered with cream-colored bristle-like hairs. Zones 10–12.

PETASITES
BUTTERBUR, SWEET COLTSFOOT
A genus of about 15 species of herbaceous perennials from Europe, Asia, and North America in the daisy (Asteraceae) family. All have kidney-shaped leaves on upright stems and clusters or spikes of smallish flowers that are sometimes sweetly scented before the foliage emerges in spring. Some species are found in damp mountain meadows, but most are from swamps or damp soil in woods. They provide good ground cover in damp sites and make attractive poolside plants, but some can be quite invasive. In Japan, one species is used to make a condiment.
CULTIVATION: Grow in a humus-rich moist to wet soil in a sheltered site with morning sun or shade. Propagate by division while dormant.

Petasites albus
WHITE BUTTERBUR
☀/❂ ❄ ↔ 3–7 ft (0.9–2 m) ↕ 12–16 in (30–40 cm)
From northern and central Europe and western Asia. Leaves to 16 in (40 cm) across. Yellow-white flowers, to ½ in (12 mm) across, in upright sprays, in late winter. Zones 5–10.

Petasites frigidus
☀/❂ ❄ ↔ 36–40 in (90–100 cm) ↕ 6–10 in (15–25 cm)
Northern European species. Heart-shaped leaves are serrated around the edges and may be slightly lobed. The flowers grow in open spikes and are yellow-white or reddish. Zones 5–10.

Petasites albus

Pescatorea cerina

Pescatorea lehmannii

Petrea arborea

Petasites hybridus
BUTTERBUR

☼ ❄ ↔ 24–36 in (60–90 cm)
↑ 24–36 in (60–90 cm)

Perennial shrub found throughout Europe, and also in parts of Asia and North America, growing in marshy ground in damp forests and near rivers and streams. Used to treat many ailments, including plague and fever. Erect stems grow from stout rhizomes, appearing before the large, downy, palm-shaped, coarsely toothed leaves. Flowers take 2 forms, with heads containing both pistillate and daisy-like disc flowers with white to pale yellow, sometimes pink or purplish, corollas. Fruits are cylindrical, with bristles and 5 to 10 ribs. Zones 4–6.

Petasites japonicus

☼/☀ ❄ ↔ 10–17 ft (3–5 m)
↑ 40–48 in (100–120 cm)

From China, Japan, and Korea. Huge kidney-shaped leaves grow to 32 in (80 cm) across, on a stem 40 in (100 cm) tall, or more. *P. j.* var. *giganteus,* even larger-leafed form; 'Nishiki-buki', which is sometimes called 'Variegata', streaks of variegated yellow. Zones 5–10.

PETREA
BLUE BIRD VINE

This genus of 30 evergreen, woody-stemmed, twining climbers, shrubs, or small trees, belonging to the vervain (Verbenaceae) family, is native to tropical America and the West Indies. They have simple, opposite, leathery leaves and long racemes of blue, purple, violet, or white flowers, growing from leaf axils or at the ends of branches. The narrow, bell-shaped corolla tubes have 5 flared and rounded lobes and 4 stamens. The fruit is a drupe.
CULTIVATION: Plant in full sun in fertile well-drained soil, and water regularly—less when not in growth. Plants may require support. Thin out

crowded spring growth and protect against sucking insects. Propagate in sumer from semi-ripe tip cuttings, or from seed.

Petrea arborea
BLUE PETREA, TREE PETREA

☼ ✤ ↔ 10–12 ft (3–3.5 m)
↑ 20–25 ft (6–8 m)

Evergreen shrub or small tree with a climbing habit; native to northern South America and the West Indies. Slender gray branches covered with pores. Pairs of thinly textured, elliptical, grayish green leaves, to 6 in (15 cm) long, without stalks or on short stalks. Blue flowerheads, erect or nodding, finely hairy, 2–6 in (5–15 cm) long. 'Broadway', white flowers. Zones 10–12.

Petrea volubilis
PURPLE WREATH, QUEEN'S WREATH, SANDPAPER VINE

☼ ✤ ↔ 10–20 ft (3–6 m)
↑ 20–60 ft (6–18 m)

Evergreen woody vine or subshrub with intertwining pale brown to ash gray branches covered with pores. Native to Central America and the West Indies. Rough-textured leaves, about 8 in (20 cm) long, are dark green, oblong or elliptical, lighter green underneath. Erect or drooping cylindrical flowerheads, 3–12 in (8–30 cm) long. Flowers have a lilac calyx with lobes longer than the tube, and an indigo to amethyst corolla with a densely hairy tube. Dead flowers fall to the ground, rotating like helicopter blades. 'Albiflora', white flowers. Zones 10–12.

PETROPHILE

This genus of some 50 species in the protea (Proteaceae) family is endemic to Australia, the majority being found in the southwestern corner of Western Australia. They are highly decorative small to medium-sized shrubs with a

wide variety of foliage, a tidy growth habit, prominent flowers, and woody fruiting cones that look like miniature pine cones. Some species produce colorful flushes of reddish new growth. Flowers, foliage, and cones all make attractive indoor decorations.
CULTIVATION: Most species tolerate occasional light frosts. Grow in full sun in a light, well-drained, acidic soil. Tip pruning from an early age will form a shapely shrub. Propagate from stem cuttings or seed.

Petrophile linearis

☼ ❄ ↔ 36 in (90 cm) ↑ 30 in (75 cm)
From Western Australia. Small shrub, spreading or erect habit. Flat, rather thick, curved leaves. Heads of woolly grayish pink to mauve flowers in leaf axils or ends of branches, appearing in late winter–spring. Prefers areas with winter rainfall; withstands long dry periods. Zones 9–11.

Petrophile sessilis

☼ ❄ ↔ 4 ft (1.2 m) ↑ 10 ft (3 m)
From eastern Australia. Erect sparsely branched shrub. Cylindrical leaves divided into stiff prickly segments. Creamy yellow flowers in ovoid heads, in spring–early summer, sporadically at other times. Decorative fruiting cone. Zones 9–11.

PETRORHAGIA

A genus of 25 to 30 erect, annual or perennial herbs belonging to the pink (Caryophyllaceae) family, native to temperate Eurasia, especially the eastern Mediterranean to southern Asia. They grow from tap roots, and their leaves are sheathed at the base with narrow sword-shaped blades that have 3 prominent veins. They bear terminal heads of few to several flowers with bracts and 5 fused, smooth, or minutely hairy sepals, and a prominent

cylindrical corolla tube with 5 rounded, sometimes lobed, petals. Fruits are egg-shaped capsules with 4 chambers containing many blackish brown to black seeds. Some species grow in rock fissures, and this is reflected in the genus name, from two Greek words: *petros* (rock); *rhagas,* (chink).
CULTIVATION: Grow in rock gardens and banks, in full sun or part-shade, in well-drained sandy soil. Propagate from seed in spring or autumn (they self-seed readily in appropriate conditions), or by division in spring.

Petrorhagia saxifraga
syns *Kohlrauschia saxifraga,* *Tunica saxifraga*

COAT FLOWER, SAXIFRAGE PINK

☼ ❄ ↔ 12–24 in (30–60 cm)
↑ 4–16 in (10–40 cm)

Mat-forming perennial from Turkey and southern and central Europe. Erect tuft-forming stems and narrow, ridged, smooth-edged, pointed leaves. Delicate loosely flowered cymes of cup-shaped flowers with short-clawed pale pink or white petals and darker veins, in summer. 'Alba', white flowers; 'Alba Plena', double white flowers; 'Lady Mary', to 3 in (8 cm) tall, soft pink double flowers; 'Pleniflora Rosea', low-growing form, pink double flowers; 'Rosea', light pink flowers; 'Rosette', compact form, pink double flowers. Zones 4–6.

Petasites hybridus

Petrophile sessilis

PETROSELINUM

PARSLEY, ROCK PARSLEY, ROCK SELINEN

A genus of 3 annual or biennial tap-rooted herbs, these are members of the carrot (Apiaceae) family, and are native to temperate Eurasia. They have erect or spreading, branching stems and divided foliage. The compound leaf blades are broadly oblong, triangular, or oval, with toothed or lobed leaflets, often ornately curled. In late summer to autumn compound umbels of small greenish yellow or reddish flowers appear, followed by flat, ribbed, oval seeds. *P. crispum* is a widely cultivated culinary herb, which can become weedy; the leaves, roots, and seeds also have many medicinal purposes. The genus was named by Dioscorides, a herbalist of ancient Greece, from the words *petros* (rock) and *selinon* (celery).
CULTIVATION: Sow seeds after last frosts in early spring to autumn in moist well-drained garden soils in an open, sunny position, about 6–8 in (15–20 cm) apart in rows 12 in (30 cm) apart. Cut back frequently to maintain vigor. Plants last 2 years and will need to be replanted but may also self-seed. Otherwise, propagate from seeds soaked in warm water before planting to promote germination.

Petroselinum crispum

Petroselinum crispum

syns *Petroselinum hortense, P. sativum*
CURLY PARSLEY, PARSLEY

☼ ❊ ↔ 9–36 in (22–90 cm)
↑ 12–36 in (30–90 cm)

Biennial herb, native to Europe and western Asia. Erect or spreading stems. Grown widely for the culinary and medicinal value of its foliage. Dark to bright green, aromatic, edible leaves are mostly triangular, deeply divided, with toothed or deeply cut oval segments, sometimes flat, often curling. Terminal umbels of many

small greenish yellow flowers appear, mostly above the leaves. There are many cultivars and varieties of garden parsley, with a wide variety of growth habits, leaf forms, and flavor strength. '**Afro**', tall upright form, tightly curled dark green leaves; '**Champion Moss Curled**', curled, finely cut, deep green leaves; '**Clivi**', neat dwarf form; '**Darky**', very cold-tolerant form, tightly curled very dark green leaves; '**Forest Green**', strong-flavored variety; '**Italian Plain Leaf**', plain, flat, deeply cut, dark green leaves; '**Krausa**', triple-curled leaves; '**New Dark Green**', very compact hardy form, emerald green leaves; '**Paramount**', hardy vigorous form, dense, very dark green, closely curled leaves; *P. c.* var. *neapolitanum* (Italian parsley), flat uncurled leaves; *P. c.* var. *tuberosum* (Hamburg parsley, turnip-rooted parsley), thick, fleshy, edible root. Zones 7–9.

PETUNIA

Known mainly for the showy annual and perennial hybrids classified as *Petunia* × *hybrida*, this tropical South American genus from the nightshade (Solanaceae) family includes some 35 species of annuals, perennials, and shrubs. The genus is closely allied to tobacco (*Nicotiana*), and its name is derived from Tupian Indian *petun*, "tobacco." Most are low spreading

Petroselinum crispum 'Krausa'

plants with soft, downy, rounded leaves and large funnel-shaped flowers with 5 fused lobes. Cultivated varieties occur in virtually every color, but lack the fragrance of some of the species.
CULTIVATION: Plant in full sun in moist, humus-rich, well-drained soil. Flowers are vulnerable to water spray and wet weather, although modern types are sturdier. Most are raised from seed; the more reliably perennial forms all grow well from cuttings.

Petunia axillaris

LARGE WHITE PETUNIA

☼/☀ ✦ ↔ 16–24 in (40–60 cm)
↑ 12–20 in (30–50 cm)

Annual from Argentina, Uruguay, and southern Brazil. Sticky, short-haired, thin leaves with rounded tips. Conical white or creamy yellow flowers, night-scented, to 2 in (5 cm) long and wide, in summer. Zones 10–12.

Petunia × hybrida

☼/☀ ❖ ↔ 8–40 in (20–100 cm)
↑ 4–16 in (10–40 cm)

Garden hybrids, mostly between *P. axillaris* and *P. integrifolia*.

Petroselinum crispum 'Forest Green'

Generally low, spreading, short-lived perennials treated as annuals and raised from seed; they are often sold as mixed color strains. '**Colorwave**' is a distinct cultivar propagated vegetatively. *Petunia* × *hybrida* forms are sometimes grouped in classes such as Grandiflora (large flowers), Milliflora (small flowers, compact habit), and Multiflora (many flowers, spreading habit). Popular forms include: **Carpet Series**, mounding bushes in many colors; **Celebrity Series**, compact, heavy-flowering, several color mixes; **Daddy Series**, shades of pink and purple, large flowers, veins in contrasting colors; **Fantasy Series**, very

Petunia × *hybrida*, Celebrity Series, 'Celebrity Blue Ice'

Petunia × *hybrida* 'Summer Sun'

P

Petunia × *hybrida,* Fantasy Series, 'Fantasy Pink Morn'

Petunia × *hybrida,* Marco Polo Series, 'Marco Polo Adventurer'

Petunia × *hybrida,* Lemon Series, 'Lemon Candy'

Petunia × *hybrida,* Passionata Series cultivar

Petunia × *hybrida,* Supercascade Series, 'Supercascade Blue'

Petunia × *hybrida,* Fantasy Series, 'Fantasy Blue'

Petunia × *hybrida,* Storm Series, 'Storm Lavender'

Petunia × *hybrida,* Surfinia Series, 'Surfinia Pink'

Petunia × *hybrida,* Wave Series, 'Misty Lilac Wave'

Petunia × *hybrida,* Wave Series, 'Purple Wave' ★

Petunia × *hybrida,* Celebrity Series, 'Celebrity Burgundy'

Petunia × *hybrida,* Mirage Series, 'Mirage Red'

Petunia × *hybrida,* Surfinia Series, Surfinia Blue Vein/'Sunsolos'

compact, many small flowers, good container plant; **Giant Victorious Series,** all-double flowers, huge color range including bicolors and picotées; **Marco Polo Series,** double-flowered, mainly pinks, mauves, and purples; **Mirage Series,** large single flowers, often light colors, striking contrasting dark veins; **Supercascade Series,** compact but with trailing habit, wide color range; **Surfinia Series,** mainly purples, pinks, and blues; **Wave Series,** mounding bushes, large flowers. Zones 9–10.

Petunia integrifolia

☼/◐ ❄ ↔ 16–24 in (40–60 cm)
↑ 12–20 in (30–50 cm)

Annual or short-lived perennial from Argentina. Sticky, downy, elliptical leaves, leaf stalks roughly equal in length; long-tubed violet flowers with purple-pink interior, to nearly 2 in (5 cm) wide, summer. Zones 8–10.

PHACELIA

SCORPION WEED

This genus of about 150 glandular, hairy, annual, biennial, or perennial herbs is a member of the waterleaf (Hydrophyllaceae) family, and originates from North and South America. The plants grow from thick tap roots. They have alternate leaves, divided or smooth-edged, and they bear dense terminal heads of white to purple flowers, which have a narrow 5-lobed calyx and an open to spreading bell-shaped corolla with lobed petals. The fruits are oblong or spherical capsules containing one to many brownish seeds with a pitted or furrowed appearance. The genus name comes from the Greek *phakelos* (cluster)—a reference to the dense flowerheads. The bristly hairs of this plant may cause severe dermatitis, and some species can become invasive and weedy.
CULTIVATION: Propagate both annuals and biennials in spring, sowing seed where plants are to grow in full sun in fertile well-drained soil. Tall species may need to be supported. Perennial species can also be propagated by division.

Petunia × *hybrida,* Wave Series, 'Pink Wave'

Petunia integrifolia

Phaius tankervilleae, in the wild, New Guinea

Phacelia ixodes

Phacelia campanularia

syn. *Phacelia minor* var. *campanularia*

CALIFORNIA BLUEBELL, DESERT BLUEBELL,
WILD CANTERBURY BELL

☼ ❄ ↔ 6–24 in (15–60 cm)
↑ 6–24 in (15–60 cm)

Annual herb from sandy or gravelly
dry or desert regions of southern
California, USA. Simple, short-haired,
erect stems; stiffly hairy, elliptical to
oval, toothed leaves. Loose clusters of
dark blue bell-shaped flowers with
tubular to broadly bell-shaped corollas
to 1½ in (35 mm) across, spotted with
white, in early spring. Hairy glandular
calyx lobes; oval, fine-haired, beaked
fruits containing 40 to 80 pitted seeds.
Zones 7–10.

Phacelia ixodes

☼ ❄ ↔ 8–24 in (20–60 cm)
↑ 8–24 in (20–60 cm)

Densely glandular and hairy annual
from California, USA, and Baja
California, Mexico. Erect sparsely
branched stem, and lobed or compound, oval, toothed leaves. Bears
flowers with oval calyx lobes and
white to rose-colored bell-shaped
corolla, in spring. The oblong fruits
contain 10 to 18 brownish pitted
seeds. Zones 6–9.

Phacelia tanacetifolia

FIDDLENECK

☼ ❄ ↔ 4–24 in (10–60 cm)
↑ 6–60 in (15–150 cm)

Moderately fast-growing annual from
California, USA, to Mexico, Central
America. The plant is covered with
bristly hairs and has an erect, sparsely
branched stem and compound, oval
to oblong, toothed or lobed leaves.
The flowers have a wide, bell-shaped
corolla colored blue, lilac, or mauve,
and appear in spring. The egg-shaped
fruits contain1 or 2 wrinkled pitted
seeds. Zones 7–10.

Phacelia campanularia

PHAEDRANASSA

QUEEN LILY

This genus of 7 bulbous herbaceous
perennials belonging to the amaryllis
(Amaryllidaceae) family is native to
dry and barren zones of the South
American Andes from Peru to the
southern parts of Colombia. They are
dormant in winter, and produce
narrow to broadly oblong leaves on
stalks after the flowers bloom. Their
drooping umbels consist of narrow
tubular or funnel-shaped to cylindrical
flowers with narrow, spreading lobes.
CULTIVATION: They prefer full sun
or part-shade and rich well-drained
soil. Water sparingly in winter, and
apply fertilizer high in potash during
summer. Propagate from seed, or by
division of offsets in spring.

Phaedranassa dubia ★

☼ ❄ ↔ 12–18 in (30–45 cm)
↑ 12–18 in (30–45 cm)

From the Peruvian Andes. Unusual
stalked leaves, heads of waxy, tubular,
purplish pink to reddish flowers, 2 in
(5 cm) long or more, tipped with
green, from spring–summer, on stalks
up to 18 in (45 cm) tall. Zones 6–8.

PHAIUS

SWAMP ORCHID

This is a group of some 50 distinct,
evergreen, terrestrial species in the
family Orchidaceae, found in Africa,
Madagascar, and India, and throughout Southeast Asia, south to Australia
and the Pacific Islands. They have
clustered pseudobulbs, with large,
pleated, broad but thin leaves. They
produce tall spikes of showy colorful
flowers in spring and summer.
CULTIVATION: Generally, they enjoy
intermediate to warm conditions, and
bright light, and need to be kept moist.
If grown in pots, these should be deep
with a well-drained medium incorporating pine bark, sand, and peat moss.
The pots can be sat in a saucer of
water, about 2 in (5 cm) deep, during
summer. They need less water during
winter, when the plants are semi-
dormant. Propagate by division.

Phaius tankervilleae

☼/❂ ❄ ➹ ↔ 8–36 in (20–90 cm)
↑ 12–48 in (30–120 cm)

From Southeast Asia, Australia, and
the Pacific Islands. The most commonly seen species in cultivation, it
has become naturalized in some tropical countries. Up to 20 blooms, 5 in
(12 cm) long, tan-brown on the inside
with a white trumpet-like labellum
that has some purple markings.
Zones 10–12.

PHALAENOPSIS

MOTH ORCHID

These members of the family Orchidaceae are popular with florists and
are often used for weddings. The 60
or so species are found throughout
the tropical rainforests of Asia, and
south to New Guinea and northern
Australia. They are epiphytes, and the
monopodial plants consist of only a
few leathery often deep green leaves.
There are also some species with
attractive tessellated foliage.
CULTIVATION: *Phalaenopsis* species
and hybrids need warm, humid, damp
conditions, and will grow and bloom
in quite deep shade. These orchids are

Phacelia tanacetifolia

Phaedranassa dubia

Phalaenopsis schilleriana

Phalaenopsis amabilis

mostly grown in pots in a bark-based medium, but a number of species perform well on long slabs of tree-fern or cork when grown in the greenhouse. They are marketed as flowering pot plants, and are one of the most majestic flowers in horticulture; even better, they are the best orchids to grow indoors as they are compact in habit, will grow in a range of light conditions, and prefer a temperature range that is also pleasant for humans. Cut off the flower spike only after it has died and turned brown. As long as the stem remains green, there is the potential for more flowers to be produced along dormant eyes of the peduncle—the part of the flowering stem between the plant and the first flower. Most *Phalaenopsis* species and their hybrids can bloom throughout the year, but peak flowering occurs in spring and summer.

Phalaenopsis amabilis ★

☀ ✛ ↔ 8–20 in (20–50 cm)
↕ 12–36 in (30–90 cm)

From Indonesia, Borneo, and the Philippines. Bears long arching sprays of large, flat, pure white flowers, 3 in (8 cm) wide. *P. rosenstromii* is a closely related white-flowered species from northeastern Australia and New Guinea. Zones 11–12.

Phalaenopsis aphrodite subsp. *formosana*

☀ ✛ ↔ 8–16 in (20–40 cm)
↕ 12–36 in (30–90 cm)

Endemic to a restricted area of Taiwan and some of its offshore islands. The similar *P. aphrodite* is found only in the Philippines. The shapely cream to white blooms, 2½ in (6 cm) wide, are smaller than those of *P. amabilis*, with a different labellum structure and shorter, broader leaves. Zones 11–12.

Phalaenopsis equestris

☀ ✛ ↔ 5–12 in (12–30 cm)
↕ 4–12 in (10–30 cm)

From the Philippines and Taiwan. A popular miniature-flowered species that produces branched sprays of numerous pink to rose-purple blooms, 1¼ in (30 mm) wide. Zones 11–12.

Phalaenopsis aphrodite subsp. *formosana*

Phalaenopsis equestris

Phalaenopsis lueddemanniana

☀ ✛ ↔ 6–16 in (15–40 cm)
↕ 4–16 in (10–40 cm)

Highly variable species from the Philippines. Greenish white flowers, 1½ in (35 mm) wide, with concentric purple barring that may give the blooms an overall pink appearance. The old inflorescences often produce plantlets, which can be removed when roots have formed. Zones 11–12.

Phalaenopsis parishii

☀ ✛ ↔ 5–8 in (12–20 cm)
↕ 4–8 in (10–20 cm)

From India to Thailand. Compact-growing miniature-flowered species that can become deciduous during dry winters. Short sprays of white blooms, ¾ in (18 mm) wide, with a contrasting bright wine-colored labellum. Zones 11–12.

Phalaenopsis pulcherrima

syn. *Doritis pulcherrima*

☀/☀ ✛ ↔ 5–12 in (12–30 cm)
↕ 4–36 in (10–90 cm)

Terrestrial or lithophytic species from Southeast Asia. Upright inflorescences that in summer carry as many as 20 blooms, 1 in (25 mm) wide, varying from light pink to dark purple. There are also rare white, lilac, and unusual splash-petaled cultivars. Zones 11–12.

Phalaenopsis schilleriana

☀ ✛ ↔ 8–20 in (20–50 cm)
↕ 12–36 in (30–90 cm)

From the Philippines. Pale pink to lilac to deep rose species, with numerous large flowers, 4 in (10 cm) wide, on a branched inflorescence. This species also has showy foliage mottled in green and silver. Zones 11–12.

Phalaenopsis lueddemanniana

Phalaenopsis parishii

P

Phalaenopsis Hybrids

☀ ☂ ↔ 5–24 in (12–60 cm)
↑ 8–36 in (20–90 cm)

Many *Phalaenopsis* hybrids have been produced, and this is almost certainly the most important commercial genus of orchids grown. Tens of thousands of plants are sold in flower annually throughout the world to cater for the growing flowering pot plant trade. White *Phalaenopsis* hybrids, mostly derived from *P. amabilis*, are still one of the most popular flowers, and are often used in wedding bouquets, including **Cottonwood**, **Oregon Delight**, **Snow City**, and **Taisuco Adian**. Previously there were similar hybrids known under the generic name of *Doritaenopsis*, but these are all now classified as *Phalaenopsis*. There is some variation in color, apart from the classic white and pink standard hybrids. Bi-colored hybrids include: **Brother Pico Sweetheart**, **City Girl**, **Livingston's Gem**, **Luchia Lip**, and **Quevedo**. Hybrids in pink and purple include: **Brother Juno**, **Brother Pico Vallezac**, **Cosmic Star**, **Ho's Amaglad**, **Hwafeng Redqueen**, **Little Kiss**, **Night Shine**, **Queen Beer**, **Sogo Firework**, **Sogo Yukidian**, **Sonoma Spots**, **Taisuco Pixie**, and **Timothy Christopher** × *pulcherrima*. Candy stripe hybrids include: **Brother Pico Pink**, **Brother Showpiece**, **Formosa Mini**, **Hsinying Facia**, **Minho Stripes**,

Phalaenopsis, Hybrid, Antique Gold

Phalaenopsis, Hybrid, Brother Pico Vallezac

Phalaenopsis, Hybrid, Coral Harbor

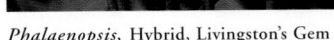

Phalaenopsis, Hybrid, Livingston's Gem

P., Hybrid, Brother Cefiro

Phalaenopsis, Hybrid, Artemis

P., H, Brother Golden Potential

P., Hybrid, Brother Juno

P., Hybrid, Brother Little Spottie

Phalaenopsis, Hybrid, Brother Golden Wish

P., Hybrid, Brother Pico Pink

P., H, Brother Pico Sweetheart

P., Hybrid, Brother Showpiece

Phalaenopsis, Hybrid, Chancellor

Phalaenopsis, Hybrid, City Girl

P., Hybrid, Cosmic Star

P., Hybrid, Cottonwood

P., Hybrid, Formosa Mini

Phalaenopsis, Hybrid, Hakugin

P., Hybrid, Hsinying Facia

P., Hybrid, Hwafeng Redqueen

Phalaenopsis, Hybrid, Little Kiss

Phalaenopsis, Hybrid, Luchia Lip

P., Hybrid, Minho Stripes

P., Hybrid, Night Shine

P., Hybrid, Oregon Delight

Phalaenopsis, Hybrid, Queen Beer

Phalaenopsis, Hybrid, Quevedo

P., Hybrid, Sand Stone

Phalaenopsis, Hybrid, Snow City

P., Hybrid, Sogo Firework

P., Hybrid, Sogo Yukidian

P., Hybrid, Sonoma Spots

P., Hybrid, Striped Eagle

Phalaenopsis, Hybrid, Taida Sunset

Phalaenopsis, Hybrid, Taisuco Adian

Phalaenopsis, Hybrid, Taisuco Firebird

Phalaenopsis., Hybrid, Taisuco Pixie

Phalaenopsis, Hybrid, (Timothy Christopher × *pulcherrima*)

Phalaenopsis, Hybrid, Ho's Amaglad

Phalaenopsis, Hybrid, Pumpkin Patch

Phalaenopsis, Hybrid, Quilted Beauty

Quilted Beauty, and **Striped Eagle**. Hybrids in yellow-bronze shades include: **Antique Gold**, **Brother Cefiro**, **Brother Golden Potential**, **Brother Golden Wish**, **Coral Harbor**, **Hakugin**, **Pumpkin Patch**, **Sand Stone**, and **Taida Sunset**. More recently, new hybrids have been bred from some of the smaller, often rather unusual or brightly colored species, which have provided new shapes, sizes, and color combinations. Zones 11–12.

PHALARIS
CANARY GRASS, GARDENER'S GARTERS, RIBBON GRASS

A genus of around 15 species of both clumping annual and running perennial plants in the grass (Poaceae) family. They come from a wide range of habitats in North America, Asia, southern Africa, and Europe. It is

Phalaris arundinacea 'Picta'

Phaseolus coccineus 'Painted Lady'

Phaseolus coccineus 'Painted Lady'

Phalaris canariensis

only the perennial species, and even then only in their variegated forms, that are usually grown in gardens. *P. canariensis,* an annual species long cultivated for birdseed, is now considered a major weed in many places. CULTIVATION: *Phalaris* species are easily grown in any well-drained to moist soil in a sunny to part-shaded site, and can become weedy. Propagate annual species from seed, and perennial species by division.

Phalaris arundinacea

GARDENER'S GARTERS, REED CANARY GRASS, RIBBON GRASS

☼/◐ ❄ ↔ 7–10 ft (2–3 m)
↑ 4–5 ft (1.2–1.5 m)

Hardy perennial from Europe, Asia, southern Africa, and North America. Soft arching leaves to 14 in (35 cm) long grow on upright stems topped with soft fluffy flowerheads that are pale green at first and turn buff with maturity. Usually grown in only one of its variegated forms, such as 'Picta', which has leaves boldly striped with white. Zones 4–11.

Phalaris canariensis

CANARY GRASS

☼ ❄ ↔ 9–18 in (22–45 cm)
↑ 18–72 in (45–180 cm)

Clumping or rhizomatous annual grass, native to the Mediterranean region, now naturalized in parts of North America. It is grown for its shiny straw-colored seeds, about 4 mm long, which are widely used for birdseed. It has green leaves, to 6 in (15 cm) long, with open membranous sheaths. Hairy flower spikes, egg-shaped to oblong, to 1½ in (35 mm) long, appear from summer to autumn on stems that are generally erect. Zones 6–8.

PHASEOLUS

BEAN

This is a genus of about 20 annual or perennial, usually climbing herbs belonging to the pea-flower subfamily of the legume (Fabaceae) family. They are native to the Americas, with many species grown widely as food crops. Most have divided leaves, usually with 3 smooth-edged or lobed leaflets and sickle-shaped buds, which grow from the leaf axils and open as loose racemes of pea-flowers with persistent bracts. Fruits are narrow oblong pods, often flattened. The fruits contain several oval or flattened seeds.

CULTIVATION: Perennial species are often grown as annuals then sown and harvested during frost-free months. Grow in humus-rich well-drained soil in full sun, providing support for stems of climbing varieties. Water freely during growth and propagate from seed in autumn or spring.

Phaseolus acutifolius

DESERT BEAN, PAVI, TEXAS BEAN, WILD TEPARY BEAN

☼ ❄ ↔ 12–24 in (30–60 cm)
↑ 18–40 in (45–100 cm)

Drought-tolerant twining or sprawling annual herb, native to southwestern USA and Mexico. Compound leaves with 3 to 5 narrow, pointed, oval or sword-shaped leaflets up to 2½ in (6 cm) long, and few white, yellow, or pale purple flowers on very short stalks. Oblong seed pods are short, slightly hairy, and green, drying to a light straw color. Seeds, usually 2 to 10 per pod, are normally flat and buff colored, and resemble a small butterbean. The cultivated varieties are bush types, best suited for use as dried rather than fresh beans. *P. a.* var. *latifolius* (Tepary bean), bushy or twining plant, larger leaflets and narrower fruits than the species; 'Golden', very prolific form, yellow

seeds; 'Mitla Black', black seeds, ideal for soups, crops twice a year; 'Sonoran Brown', early-maturing form, tolerates drought and heat, brown seeds. Zones 8–10.

Phaseolus coccineus

DUTCH CASE-KNIFE BEAN, SCARLET RUNNER BEAN

☼ ❄ ↔ 24 in (60 cm) ↑ 4–6 ft (1.2–1.8 m)

Tall, twining, perennial vine, native to tropical Americas. Grown as an annual. Compound leaves with broad oval to heart-shaped leaflets, to 5 in (12 cm) long. Long racemes of many bright scarlet flowers appear in spring. Pods, to 12 in (30 cm) long, contain black seeds, to 1 in (25 mm) long, mottled with red. *P. c.* var. *albonanus*, bushy form, white seeds. *P. c.* var. *rubronanus*, erect form, red flowers. *P. c.* 'Albus', white seeds and flowers; 'Painted Lady' ★, red and white flowers. Zones 8–10.

Phaseolus lunatus

syn. *Phaseolus limensis*

LIMA BEAN

☼ ❄ ↔ 9–12 in (22–30 cm)
↑ 24–36 in (60–90 cm)

Twining or erect perennial, native to tropical South America. Grown widely as an annual food crop. Long stalks bear compound leaves with oval to triangular leaflets, to 4 in (10 cm) long, and flowerheads, to 8 in (20 cm) long, of yellowish green, white, or lilac. Pods, to 4 in (10 cm) long, containing 2 to 4 small, reddish brown, kidney-shaped seeds, appear from winter–spring. *P. l.* var. *lunonanus*, non-climbing bushy form; *P. l.* var. *salicis*, narrow spear-shaped leaves; *P. l.* 'Kate May Giant' and 'King of the Garden', good cropping forms. Zones 8–10.

Phaseolus lunatus 'Kate May Giant'

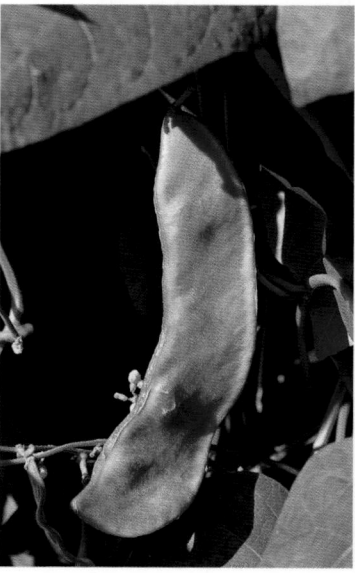

Phaseolus lunatus 'King of the Garden'

Phellodendron amurense

Phaseolus vulgaris

FRENCH BEAN, HARICOT, KIDNEY BEAN, STRING BEAN

☀ ✣ ↔ 6–9 in (15–22 cm)
↕ 3–10 ft (0.9–3 m)

Erect or twining annual from tropical Americas. Widely grown in cooler areas, but needs some protection. Compound leaves with oval or rounded leaflets, to 4 in (10 cm) long, and racemes of up to 6 white, pink, or purple flowers, with corollas up to ¾ in (18 mm) across, in spring. Fruits are flat or nearly cylindrical pods, to 20 in (50 cm) long, containing elongated or spherical red, brown, black, white, or mottled seeds, harvested in summer. *P. v.* var. *humilis*, low-growing, non-climbing. *P. v.* 'Ferrari', 'Goldmarie' ★, 'Purple Speckled', popular cultivars. Zones 8–11.

PHEBALIUM

Primarily Australian, this genus of around 40 species of evergreen shrubs and small trees in the rue (Rutaceae) family includes several species that are most often grown as hedges or windbreaks. Their leaves, usually narrow, are variable in shape and are aromatic. The flowers are small and white to creamy yellow with clustered stamens, and sometimes scented. They develop in the leaf axils and most often open in spring to early summer. Insignificant seed capsules follow.
CULTIVATION: Hardiness varies with the species, though none will tolerate repeated severe frosts or drought. However, once established, most will withstand dry conditions quite well. They prefer moist, well-drained, rather gritty soil, and are best grown in full sun or partial shade. Regular trimming and pinching will keep the growth compact. Propagation is usually from cuttings, either hardwood outdoors or half-hardened under mist. They may also be raised from seed.

Phebalium nudum

MAIREHAU

☀ ❧ ↔ 3 ft (0.9 m) ↕ 3–7 ft (0.9–2 m)
Native to northern areas of New Zealand. Bushy shrub with narrow leathery leaves that are aromatic when crushed. Small, white, fragrant, star-life flowers appear in clusters, in spring–summer. Zones 9–11.

Phebalium squamulosum

SCALY PHEBALIUM

☀ ❧ ↔ 3–12 ft (0.9–3.5 m)
↕ 3–10 ft (0.9–3 m)

Small to medium-sized shrub from eastern Australia. Bright green foliage, noticeable scaly glands on pale undersides, strongly aromatic. Cream to bright yellow flowers appear in spring. Zones 9–11.

PHELLODENDRON

This is a genus of 10 species of deciduous trees from temperate East Asia. Somewhat surprisingly, the genus is classified as a member of the rue (Rutaceae) family. Notable for their aromatic foliage and corky bark, these species have large pinnate leaves composed of broad, often glossy leaflets. Their flowers are small and yellow-green in color and are carried in panicles, followed by small, black, fleshy fruits. The autumn foliage, however, is often bright yellow and can be quite spectacular in some years.
CULTIVATION: Most species in this genus need a climate with seasons that are well differentiated, and a cool winter is important to ensure proper dormancy. On the other hand, they handle hot summers and harsh sun with ease, though the foliage is easily damaged by strong winds. They seem to thrive in any well-drained soil with a position in full sun. Plants may be propagated from seed, from cuttings, by layering, or by grafting.

Phellodendron amurense ★

AMUR CORK TREE

☀ ❋ ↔ 40 ft (12 m) ↕ 50 ft (15 m)
Found in northern China. Corky pale gray bark. Strongly aromatic leaves composed of 9 to 13 broad leaflets, dark glossy green upper sides, blue-green undersides, turning yellow in autumn. Flower panicles, in early summer. Clusters of fruit held erect above the foliage. Zones 3–9.

Phaseolus vulgaris 'Ferrari'

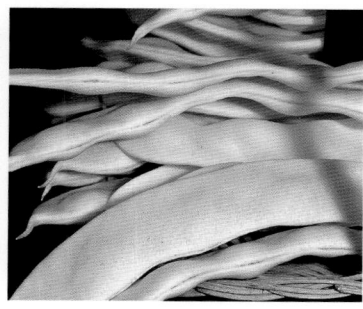

Phaseolus vulgaris 'Goldmarie'

Phaseolus vulgaris 'Purple Speckled'

Phebalium nudum

Phebalium squamulosum, in the wild, Pilliga State Forest, New South Wales, Australia

Phellodendron lavallei

Phellodendron chinense

Phellodendron sachalinense

Phellodendron chinense

☼ ❄ ↔ 35 ft (10 m) ↑ 30 ft (9 m)
From central China. Thin gray-brown bark, young stems rusty felted coating. Yellow-green leaves, lighter hairy coating on undersides. Zones 5–9.

Phellodendron lavallei

☼ ❄ ↔ 35 ft (10 m) ↑ 30 ft (9 m)
Native of central Japan. Thick corky bark, young shoots with a rusty coating. Leaves to 15 in (38 cm) long, with 5 to 13 light green pointed leaflets, undersides covered in fine hairs. Flowers from early summer. Zones 6–9.

Phellodendron sachalinense

☼ ❄ ↔ 35 ft (10 m) ↑ 25 ft (8 m)
Found in Korea, Sakhalin (an island between Russia and Japan), and western China. Bark thin, shallowly channeled, deep brown. Spreading crown of matt mid-green leaves, 8–12 in (20–30 cm) long. Colors well in autumn. Good shade tree. Zones 3–9.

PHILADELPHUS

MOCK ORANGE

Occurring within the hydrangea (Hydrangeaceae) family, this genus from temperate regions of Central and North America, southeast Europe, the Himalayas, and Asia includes 60 or so species of mainly deciduous shrubs. They usually have peeling bark. They are frequently grown for ornamental purposes, but are also cultivated for their scented double or single flowers, as specimen shrubs in woodland, or in a shrub border.
CULTIVATION: They grow well in full sun or partial shade, or in deciduous open woodland in moderately fertile well-drained soil, but flower better in full sun. If grown in pots, a loam-based compost is best, and regular feeding and watering are necessary throughout the growing season. Propagate from softwood cuttings taken in summer or hardwood cuttings taken in autumn and winter.

Philadelphus coronarius

SWEET MOCK ORANGE, SYRINGA

☼ ❄ ↔ 8 ft (2.4 m) ↑ 10 ft (3 m)
Native to southern Europe and western Asia. Deciduous upright shrub, peeling bark. Egg-shaped leaves have irregular shallow toothing, with down on the main veins. Very fragrant almost white flowers appear in early summer, on short terminal racemes. 'Aureus' ★, compact growth, golden leaves turn lime green with age, fragrant flowers, best in part-shade; 'Bowles' Variety', leaves with white margins; 'Variegatus', leaves have wide white margins. Zones 5–9.

Philadelphus delavayi

☼ ❄ ↔ 8 ft (2.4 m) ↑ 10 ft (3 m)
Native to western China and northern Myanmar. Deciduous upright shrub. Leaves narrow, egg-shaped, toothed, with a pointed tip, larger on non-flowering shoots, dense flattened hair on undersides. Saucer-shaped flowers, white and fragrant, 9 per raceme, in early summer. Zones 6–9.

Philadelphus incanus

☼ ❄ ↔ 6 ft (1.8 m) ↑ 12 ft (3.5 m)
Erect shrub native to the Hubei and Shaanxi Provinces in China. Branches hairy when young, peeling with age. Leaves oval to elliptical, larger on non-flowering shoots. White blooms in racemes of up to 11 individual flowers, in late summer. Zones 5–9.

Philadelphus inodorus

☼ ❄ ↔ 4 ft (1.2 m) ↑ 10 ft (3 m)
Native to eastern USA. Arching shrub, bark peels, second year. Leaves variable in size, shape, and amount of hair on either side, faintly toothed or smooth-edged. Several white flowers, in cymes, in summer. Zones 5–9.

Philadelphus lewisii

INDIAN ARROWWOOD, LEWIS MOCK ORANGE, LEWIS SYRINGA

☼ ❄ ↔ 10 ft (3 m) ↑ 10 ft (3 m)
State flower of Idaho, USA. Arching shrub native to the west of North America. Leaves bright green, egg-shaped, margins occasionally finely toothed. Racemes carrying 5 to 11 mildly scented flowers appear in early summer. Zones 5–9.

Philadelphus mexicanus

MEXICAN MOCK ORANGE

☼ ❄ ↔ 8 ft (2.4 m) ↑ 15 ft (4.5 m)
Native to Guatemala and Mexico. Evergreen climbing shrub. Pendulous branches, long bristles on current growth, egg-shaped leaves may have toothed margins. Bears rose-scented lemony white flowers, often solitary, in summer. Zones 9–10.

Philadelphus microphyllus

☼ ❄ ↔ 3 ft (0.9 m) ↑ 3 ft (0.9 m)
Native to southwestern USA. Erect deciduous shrub. Bark peels second year, new growth is felty. Small, mid-green, shiny, smooth-edged leaves. Cross-shaped, scented, white flowers, in early–mid-summer. Zones 6–9.

Philadelphus pubescens

MOCK ORANGE, SYRINGA

☼ ❄ ↔ 7 ft (2 m) ↑ 15 ft (4.5 m)
Native to southeastern USA. Egg-shaped pointed leaves are bristly and hairy on the undersides. White flowers carried in racemes of 5 to 11 blooms appear in early summer. Zones 6–9.

Philadelphus coronarius

Philadelphus coronarius 'Aureus'

Philadelphus inodorus

Philadelphus mexicanus

Philadelphus subcanus var. *magdalenae*

Philadelphus, Hybrid Cultivar, 'Rosace'

Philadelphus, HC, 'Schneesturm'

Philadelphus, HC, 'Manteau d'Hermine'

Philadelphus subcanus

☼ ❁ ↔ 8 ft (2.4 m) ↑ 20 ft (6 m)

Shrub native to southwestern China. Upright habit, peeling bark on mature branches only. Leaves are fine-toothed on flowering shoots, deeply toothed on non-flowering wood. Racemes of white, fragrant flowers, slightly cup-shaped, in early summer. *P. s.* var. *magdalenae,* shorter, with smaller leaves and flowers. Zones 6–9.

Philadelphus Hybrid Cultivars

☼ ❁ ↔ 6 ft (1.8 m) ↑ 5 ft (1.5 m)

Most early hybrid cultivars were created by the French plant breeder Pierre Lemoine, and were crosses of *P. coronarius* and *P. microphyllus*, often grouped as *P.* × *lemoinei.* The influence of *P. inodorus* and *P. insignis* prompted the new hybrid names *P.* × *cymosus* and *P.* × *polyanthus,* respectively. Crosses between earlier hybrids and *P. coulteri* were grouped under *P.* × *purpureo-maculatus.* Finally, a group emerged in which *P. pubescens* showed its influence, under the name *P.* × *virginalis.* 'Ava-lanche', an early Lemoine hybrid, up-right growth to 6 ft (1.8 m), scented white flowers; 'Beauclerk', a later English hybrid, height and spread of 8 ft (2.4 m), large, fragrant, single, cup-shaped, white flowers, pink-tinged centers, early–mid-summer; 'Belle Etoile', *P.* × *purpureo-maculatus* hybrid, purple-red central splash on flowers, sweet pineapple-like fragrance; 'Boule d'Argent', *P.* × *polyanthus* hybrid, compact slightly arching shrub to 5 ft (1.5 m) tall and spread, double or semi-double flowers, in summer; 'Bouquet Blanc', *P.* × *cymosus* hybrid, profuse semi-double flowers; 'Buckley's Quill', to 6 ft (1.8 m), upright shrub, fragrant double flowers in early–mid-summer, up to 30 long quill-like petals per flower; 'Dame Blanche', Lemoine hybrid, cream colored semi-double flowers; 'Fimbriatus', Lemoine hybrid, compact fine-cut petal edges; 'Glacier', *P.* × *virginalis* hybrid, compact shrub to 5 ft (1.5 m) in height and spread, fragrant double white flowers, mid-summer; 'Innocence', Lemoine hybrid, to 10 ft (3 m), yellow foliage, fragrant, white, single or semi-double flowers, summer; 'Manteau d'Her-mine', Lemoine hybrid, to 30 in (75 cm) high, creamy double flowers, summer. Other *P.* × *virginalis* types include: 'Minnesota Snowflake', double white flowers; 'Natchez', single flowers; 'Rosace', *P.* × *cymosus* hybrid, semi-double flowers; 'Schneesturm', *P.* × *virginalis* hybrid, pure white double flowers; 'Sybille', *P.* × *purpureo-maculatus* hybrid, to 4 ft (1.2 m), purple patches in the center of single white flowers; 'Virginal' (the original member of the *P.* × *virginalis* group), fragrant double white flowers carried in loose heads. Zones 5–9.

PHILLYREA

This is a small genus of 4 species of evergreen shrubs or small trees in the olive (Oleaceae) family. They are found in Madeira, the Mediterranean region, and southwest Asia, and are allied to the olive genus *Osmanthus.* Smaller-leafed species mature into elegant masses of feathery foliage. CULTIVATION: They like all soil types, but prefer those that are moist and well drained; they tolerate dry condi-tions. They are useful for hedging, as they cope well with frequent trim-ming. Propagate from cuttings.

Phillyrea angustifolia

☼ ❀ ↔ 10 ft (3 m) ↑ 10 ft (3 m)

Native to southern Europe and North Africa. Compact rounded shrub. Leaves narrow, smooth, lanceolate, dark green. Clusters of small creamy white flowers appear in leaf axils, in early summer. Useful shrub for coastal regions. Zones 7–10.

Phillyrea latifolia

MOCK PRIVET

☼ ❀ ↔ 25 ft (8 m) ↑ 25 ft (8 m)

From southern Europe and Turkey. Profuse small glossy dark green leaves. Dull white flowers, late spring. Tiny blue-black berries. Zones 7–10.

PHILODENDRON

This genus in the arum (Araceae) family consists of around 500 species, most from tropical America and the West Indies. They are mainly epiphytic climbing or twining vines with aerial roots, but the genus also includes some evergreen shrubs and small trees. The large glossy leaves may be smooth-edged, variously lobed, or deeply divided in a feather-like pattern. The flowers are insignificant and without petals; they are held on a flower spike. Plant parts are poisonous, and contact with the sap may cause skin irritation. Suitable species can make attractive landscape plants in warm climates to create a tropical atmosphere. Many are used as indoor plants. CULTIVATION: Philodendrons do best in the tropics and subtropics, requir-ing a moist, well-drained, humus-rich soil with generous watering in the growth phase. Many species are toler-ant of low light and should be grown in dappled shade. Propagate from seed, from cuttings, or by layering.

Phillyrea angustifolia

Phillyrea latifolia

Philodendron bipinnatifidum
syn. *Philodendron selloum*
TREE PHILODENDRON

☀/◑ ❄ ↔ 10 ft (3 m) ↑ 10 ft (3 m)

Native to southeastern Brazil, this is a large tree-like shrub with stout aerial roots. Its shiny deep green leaves are quite spectacular, growing to 3 ft (0.9 m) long, and are deeply divided, lobed, broadly ovate, and somewhat arrow-shaped at their bases; the leaf stalks are as long as the leaves. The flowers are white or greenish in color. Zones 10–12.

Philodendron bipinnatifidum

Philodendron domesticum
syn. *Philodendron hastatum*
ELEPHANT EAR PHILODENDRON, EMERALD DUKE PHILODENDRON

◑ ❄ ↔ 2–3 ft (0.6–0.9 m)
↑ 6–10 ft (1.8–3 m)

Slow-growing, evergreen, woody-based climber from northern South America. Lustrous, coarse-textured, bright green leaves, arrowhead- to heart-shaped, 12–24 in (30–60 cm) long, waxy coating, prominent lobes at base, on thick stalks. Spathes of white or green flowers. Zones 10–12.

Philodendron erubescens
BLUSHING PHILODENDRON, RED-LEAF PHILODENDRON

◑/☀ ❄ ↔ 3–8 ft (0.9–2.4 m)
↑ 6–10 ft (1.8–3 m)

Erect, scrambling, woody-based climber from Colombia. Lustrous dark green leaves with a coppery finish, oval to triangular, to 10 in (25 cm) long, carried on long red stalks. Spathes of dark purple flowers, to 6 in (15 cm) long. Zones 10–12.

Philodendron radiatum

Philodendron hederaceum
syn. *Philodendron scandens*

◑ ❄ ↔ 2–6 ft (0.6–1.8 m)
↑ 10–15 ft (3–4.5 m)

Evergreen tree-climbing vine, native to the West Indies, and much of northern South and Central America. Reddish green young leaves and oval to heart-shaped, leathery, dark green mature leaves, to 4–16 in (10–40 cm) long, often purplish or violet underneath, on long thick stalks, with 5 to 6 pairs of prominent raised veins. Solitary erect or drooping flower spikes, on tall pale green stalks, sometimes tinged with red-purple, usually with green spathes and a tube that is reddish to purple inside. Greenish white berries follow. Zones 10–12.

Philodendron radiatum
syn. *Philodendron dubium*

◑ ❄ ↔ 7 ft (2 m) ↑ 6–8 ft (1.8–2.4 m)

Epiphytic or sprawling vine, rarely terrestrial, native from Mexico to Colombia. The thick stem is translucent or orange colored, and contains a sticky watery sap. The stem features conspicuous leaf scars and internodes with swollen nodes. The leaves are leathery, dark green, sheathed, triangular to oval in shape, deeply divided and lobed, 12–40 in (30–100 cm) long. It bears creamy white spikes of

P. aureum var. *areolatum* 'Mandaianum'

Philodendron. radiatum, in the wild, Costa Rica

minute flowers, 1 to 4 to each leaf axil, surrounded by a yellowish green, erect, semi-glossy spathe dotted with purple outside and pink to dull red or brownish on the inside, on tall stalks. The berries are oblong, white, sticky, and slightly translucent. Zones 10–12.

PHLEBODIUM

This genus of 4 evergreen or semi-evergreen ferns belongs to the polypody (Polypodiaceae) family. Native to the tropical Americas and the West Indies, they have thick, fleshy, creeping rhizomes sheathed with rust-colored to gold scales, and smooth, oval, divided fronds, leathery or papery in texture, on jointed stems. The genus name is from the Greek *phlebodes,* meaning full of veins, and refers to the many veins on the fronds.
CULTIVATION: *Phlebodium* species like a rich, well-drained, moist soil in half-sun to shade, with regular watering and protection from frost. They are suited to cultivation in pots or hanging baskets, and are propagated from spores or by division.

Phlebodium aureum
syn. *Polypodium aureum*
HARE'S FOOT FERN, RABBIT'S FOOT FERN

☀ ✦ ↔ 24–36 in (60–90 cm)
↑ 24–36 in (60–90 cm)

Widespread and variable evergreen epiphytic fern, found on palm trunks or tree limbs in tropical and subtropical regions of Mexico and the West Indies. Thick creeping rhizomes covered with golden yellow hairs. Deeply divided fronds, oval to triangular, to 40 in (100 cm) long. Large narrow or strap-shaped leaflets vary in color from grayish green and silvery green to an intense powdery-looking blue-green, often with undulating margins.

Philodendron hederaceum, in the wild, Costa Rica

They turn purplish in cold weather. There are several cultivars with highly crested or wavy-margined fronds that are a metallic gray-blue, including: *P. a.* **var.** *areolatum*, erect, smooth, leathery fronds; '**Mandaianum**', leaflets curved and wavy; '**Mayi**', ruffled and fringed leaflets. Zones 10–12.

PHLEUM
MARSH REED

This genus is made up of about 15 annual or perennial grasses in the family Poaceae. They are native to the temperate regions of both hemispheres. They have erect stems and flat leaves with rough margins, the leaves growing from a central base as well as from the stems. The flowerheads are cylindrical to almost spherical panicles of compressed spikes, appearing in spring and summer. The genus takes its name from the Greek word *phleos* (marsh reed). CULTIVATION: *Phleum* species prefer sandy well-drained soil in an open, sunny position. Propagate from seed.

Phleum pratense
HERDS GRASS, TIMOTHY GRASS
☼ ❄ ↔ 2–5 ft (0.6–1.5 m)
↑ 2–5 ft (0.6–1.5 m)

Native to Europe, northwestern Africa, and northern Asia; naturalized

Phleum pratense, Saint Mary Lake Glacier National Park, Montana, USA

Phlomis fruticosa 'Yellow'

Phlomis fruticosa

in North America. Widely cultivated for pasture and hay. Rough spreading leaves, yellowish green, 1½–12 in (3.5–30 cm) long, growing from a central clump, with solitary to loosely clumped, erect, smooth, flowering stems with swollen bases. Cylindrical flowerheads, tinged with green to purple, fading to buff, spikelets with rough bristly ridges, in late spring–early summer. Zones 5–8.

PHLOMIS

This is a genus of about 100 low-growing shrubs, subshrubs and herbs in the nettle (Urticaceae) family. These species are widely distributed through Europe and Asia, from the Mediterranean regions to China. Most have felted leaves and tubular flowers, which are borne in whorls along the stems. The flowers have 2 lips at their tips, the upper lip being hooded over the lower one; they may be yellow, cream, pink, mauve, or purple in color. CULTIVATION: Most *Phlomis* species are quite frost hardy, and are best planted in exposed sunny positions where the felted leaves can dry out quickly after rain. They are drought tolerant, to the point at which they generally resent receiving too much water in summer. Propagation is from seed, or else from tip cuttings from non-flowering shoots.

Phlomis cashmeriana
☼ ❄ ↔ 36 in (90 cm) ↑ 36 in (90 cm)
A robust plant with very woolly stems, native to Kashmir and the western Himalayas. The narrow oval leaves are downy, with white undersides. The pale lilac flowers, held in crowded whorls, appear in summer. Zones 8–11.

Phlomis chrysophylla
☼ ❄ ↔ 3 ft (0.9 m) ↑ 4 ft (1.2 m)
Small evergreen subshrub, native to Lebanon. Erect branching stems and broad oval leaves, which are covered in golden down when young and fade to a yellowish gray as they mature. The bright golden yellow flowers are borne in whorls in the leaf axils, in summer. Zones 7–10.

Phlomis 'Edward Bowles'
☼ ❄ ↔ 36 in (90 cm) ↑ 36 in (90 cm)
Robust hybrid subshrub. Pointed oval leaves, growing to 6 in (15 cm) long, have wrinkled surfaces. Whorls of sulfur yellow flowers appear in summer. Zones 7–11.

Phlomis fruticosa
JERUSALEM SAGE
☼ ❄ ↔ 30 in (75 cm) ↑ 30 in (75 cm)
From the Mediterranean region. Leaves green and felty; bright yellow flowers, in summer. Tolerates coastal conditions. Prune vigorously, to half its size, in autumn. '**Yellow**', rich yellow flowers. Zones 7–10.

Phlomis 'Edward Bowles'

P

Phlomis lycia

Phlomis russeliana

Phlomis purpurea

Phlomis lanata

(5–10 cm) long. The yellow flowers are borne in whorls of 4 to 10 in summer. Zones 8–11.

Phlomis lycia
☼ ❄ ↔ 3 ft (0.9 m) ↕ 3–5 ft (0.9–1.5 m)
From Turkey. Small shrub, with leaves that are shallowly toothed and gray-felted. Yellow flowers appear in whorls of 6 to 12 blooms, 1 or 2 whorls per flower spike. The young stems of the flowers spikes are downy. Zones 9–10.

Phlomis purpurea
☼ ❄ ↔ 24 in (60 cm) ↕ 24 in (60 cm)
From Spain and Portugal. Woolly-stemmed plant with narrow, wrinkled, leathery, grayish green leaves that have very hairy undersides. Downy purple to pink flowers are borne in whorls in summer. Zones 8–11.

Phlomis russeliana
☼ ❄ ↔ 24 in (60 cm) ↕ 36 in (90 cm)
Native to just a small area of western Syria, but common in cultivation. It is a small shrub with long-stemmed heart-shaped leaves that are covered with fine hairs, especially on the undersides. It bears spikes of pale yellow hooded flowers in summer. It does not thrive in prolonged wet conditions. Zones 7–9.

Phlomis italica
☼ ❄ ↔ 12 in (30 cm) ↕ 12 in (30 cm)
Subshrub from the Balearic Islands, Spain. The leaves are narrow and oblong, and have white hairs. The flowers, which are borne in well-spaced whorls of 6 in summer–autumn, have grayish white calyces and are pink or pale lilac in color. Zones 8–11.

Phlomis lanata ★
☼ ❄ ↔ 20 in (50 cm) ↕ 20 in (50 cm)
Native to Crete, Greece. Small shrub with golden hairy stems. The small oblong leaves and flower calyces are very woolly. The orange-yellow flowers are carried in whorls of 2 to 10 blooms, in summer. Zones 8–11.

Phlomis lychnitis
LAMPWICK PLANT
☼ ❄ ↔ 27 in (70 cm) ↕ 27 in (70 cm)
Subshrub native to southwest Europe. All its parts are white-haired. The narrow oblong leaves are 2–4 in

Phlomis samia
☼ ❄ ↔ 24–36 in (60–90 cm) ↕ 24–36 in (60–90 cm)
From northern Africa, Greece, and the Balkans. Clump-forming perennial with hairy, pointed oval leaves to 8 in (20 cm) long. Pale creamy pink flowers are borne in whorls of 10 to 20 blooms. Zones 7–10.

Phlomis tuberosa
☼ ❄ ↔ 36 in (90 cm) ↕ 36 in (90 cm)
Tuberous-rooted deciduous perennial, from central Europe to central Asia. Lightly hairy, pointed oval leaves to 10 in (25 cm) long. Whorls of purple to pink flowers, more crowded near the stem ends, in summer. Zones 6–10.

Phlomis viscosa
☼ ❄ ↔ 3–4 ft (0.9–1.2 m) ↕ 3–4 ft (0.9–1.2 m)
Native to southwestern Asia and Turkey. Well-branched shrub, sometimes confused with the perennial *P. russelliana,* which is often misnamed *P. viscosa.* Hairy leaves to 6 in (15 cm) long, and whorls of 12 to 20 yellow flowers in summer. Zones 8–11.

PHLOX
This North American genus of 67 annuals and perennials belongs in the

Phlomis italica

phlox (Polemoniaceae) family. All types have similar terminal heads of small bell-shaped flowers with long widely flaring tubes, but growth habits differ markedly. Annual species tend to be small mounding bushes; the ground-hugging rock phlox has tiny leaves; trailing forms have long stems and suit hanging baskets; and border phlox species are upright and bushy, often with plenty of foliage. *Phlox* is Greek for "flame"—a very appropriate epithet for the annual, rock, and border types, with their vivid bursts of incandescent color.
CULTIVATION: All phlox species prefer well-drained soil that can be kept moist; annual and rock phlox need full sun; border and trailing forms will take part shade. Border phlox need good ventilation to prevent late-season mildew. Propagate by seed, by division, or from cuttings.

Phlox adsurgens
WOODLAND PHLOX
☼/◐ ❄ ↔ 12–20 in (30–50 cm) ↕ 4–6 in (10–15 cm)
From western USA, a spreading perennial, stem tips sometimes partly erect. Oval leaves, ½–1 in (12–25 mm) long. Open flowerheads of pink to purple blooms, to 1 in (25 mm) wide, in late spring–summer. Zones 6–10.

Phlox bifida
SAND PHLOX
☼/◐ ❄ ↔ 12–16 in (30–40 cm) ↕ 4–8 in (10–20 cm)
Tufted perennial from central USA. Rather sparse hairy leaves, elliptical to near-linear. Drooping downy inflorescences of honey-scented, starry, white to lavender flowers with notched petals, spring–summer. Zones 6–10.

Phlomis viscosa

Phlox paniculata

Phlox paniculata 'Prospero'

Phlox paniculata 'Eva Cullum'

Phlox paniculata 'Tenor'

Phlox carolina

THICKLEAF PHLOX

☼/◗ ❋ ↔ 16–24 in (40–60 cm)
↑ 4 ft (1.2 m)

Upright clump-forming perennial from eastern USA. Leaves leathery, glossy, narrow, lance-shaped, sometimes linear. In spring–early summer, large showy heads of pink or purple flowers, to 1 in (25 mm) wide. 'Bill Baker', 18 in (45 cm) tall, compact, large pink to mauve flowers. Zones 5–10.

Phlox divaricata

BLUE PHLOX, WILD SWEET WILLIAM

☼/◗ ❋ ↔ 24–40 in (60–100 cm)
↑ 12–18 in (30–45 cm)

Spreading low-clump-forming perennial from central North America. Wiry stems, pointed oval to narrow-lance-shaped leaves. In spring, small heads of lavender-pink, mauve, or white flowers to 1½ in (40 mm) wide. *P. d.* subsp. *laphamii* is best known for the cultivar 'Chattahoochee' ★, 6 in (15 cm) tall, lavender flowers with red eye. Zones 4–9.

Phlox douglasii

☼/◗ ❋ ↔ 12–20 in (30–50 cm)
↑ 2–6 in (5–15 cm)

Perennial from northwestern USA; usually mat-forming, but sometimes stem tips ascend slightly. Fine downy stems with very narrow hair-fringed leaves. Flowers in showy, tightly clustered heads, mainly in deep pink, red, mauve, and purple, in spring–early summer. 'Boothman's Variety', 3 in (8 cm) tall, dark-centered lavender flowers; 'Crackerjack', neat compact habit, magenta flowers; 'Kelly's Eye', pale pink flowers, purple-red center;

'Red Admiral', mounding to 4 in (10 cm) high, crimson flowers; 'Rosea', silvery pink flowers. Zones 5–10.

Phlox drummondii

☼/◗ ❋ ↔ 8–16 in (20–40cm)
↑ 6–16 in (15–40 cm)

Annual native to Texas, USA, now widely established as a wildflower. Upright, sometimes sprawling stems with pointed oval to narrow lance-shaped leaves. Showy heads of small flowers, bright lavender to purple-red, often with notched petals, in summer. Mixed color seedling strains include **Beauty Series**, many colors, including yellow; **Brilliancy Series**, wide color range; **Buttons and Bows Series**, mainly bright colors, often with contrasting eye; **Phlox of Sheep Series**, primrose-centered pastel shades, including yellow, orange-red, and apricot; **Tapestry Series**, wide range of pastel shades with contrasting eye color, fragrant. Zones 6–10.

Phlox maculata

MEADOW PHLOX, WILD SWEET WILLIAM

☼/◗ ❋ ↔ 16 in (40 cm) ↑ 27 in (70 cm)

Erect rhizome-rooted perennial native to eastern USA. Thick, lustrous, dark

Phlox drummondii

green leaves, usually pointed oval in shape, sometimes linear. Densely packed heads of pink, violet, or white flowers, often with purplish centers, appear in summer. 'Alpha', fragrant lavender pink flowers; 'Omega', fragrant white flowers with deep violet centers. Zones 5–10.

Phlox nana

SANTA FE PHLOX

☼/◗ ❋ ↔ 12–20 in (30–50 cm)
↑ 6–10 in (15–25 cm)

Small, bushy, mounding perennial from southwestern USA. The leaves are very narrow and lance-shaped. The long-tubed flowers are solitary or in small clusters, to ¾ in (18 mm) wide, in shades of pink and purple, blooming in late spring–summer. 'Mary Maslin', distinctive red flowers with yellow centers. Zones 8–10.

Phlox nivalis

TRAILING PHLOX

☼/◗ ❋ ↔ 12–24 in (30–60 cm)
↑ 4–12 in (10–30 cm)

Subshrub from southeastern USA. Usually has a spreading habit, but is sometimes partly erect. The leaves are lance-shaped. The downy flowerheads appear in spring and consist of 3 to 6 blooms. The flowers may be pink or white, and often have notched petals. Zones 6–10.

Phlox douglasii 'Crackerjack'

Phlox paniculata

BORDER PHLOX, SUMMER PHLOX

☼/◗ ❋ ↔ 16–40 in (40–100 cm)
↑ 24–48 in (60–120 cm)

Vigorous eastern USA perennial that forms thick clumps of upright stems with pointed oval to lance-shaped leaves, often toothed, sometimes downy. Large rounded flowerheads, usually pink, lavender, and purple, in summer. 'Brigadier', dark foliage, apricot pink flowers; 'Europa', honey-scented white flowers, scarlet eye; 'Eva Cullum', dark pink flowers, deep pink center; 'Eventide', mauve-blue flowers; 'Fujiyama' ★, white flowers; 'Le Mahdi', purple-blue flowers; 'Mother of Pearl', pale silvery pink flowers; 'Prospero', lavender to light purple flowers; 'Starfire', deep red flowers; 'Tenor', scarlet flowers; 'White Admiral', pure white; 'Windsor', white flowers suffused with lavender blue. Zones 4–10.

Phlox divaricata subsp. *laphamii* 'Chattahoochee'

Phlox douglasii 'Rosea'

Phlox carolina 'Bill Baker'

Phlox pilosa
PRAIRIE PHLOX

☼/◐ ❀ ↔ 12–20 in (30–50 cm)
↕ 24 in (60 cm)

Clump-forming perennial from Texas, USA. Leaves linear to lance-shaped. Large heads of pink to purple or white blooms, in spring. Zones 5–10.

Phlox × procumbens

☼/◐ ❀ ↔ 12–32 in (30–80 cm)
↕ 4–8 in (10–20 cm)

Garden hybrid of *P. stolonifera* and *P. subulata*. Spreading, sometimes partly erect clump of broad lance-shaped leaves. Many lax heads of purple-pink flowers to ¾ in (18 mm) wide, from mid-spring. Zones 4–9.

Phlox stolonifera

☼/◐ ❀ ↔ 20–40 in (50–100 cm)
↕ 6–10 in (15–25 cm)

Mounding perennial native to southeastern USA. Spreads by underground runners. Broad, pointed, oval leaves. Lax heads of about 6 violet to purple flowers, 1 in (25 mm) wide, in spring. 'Blue Ridge', glossy foliage, bright mid-blue flowers. Zones 4–9.

Phoenix canariensis

Phlox × procumbens

Phlox subulata
MOSS PHLOX, MOUNTAIN PHLOX

☼/◐ ❀ ↔ 12–20 in (30–50 cm)
↕ 2–4 in (5–10 cm)

Prostrate mat-forming perennial from eastern USA. Small, narrow, pointed leaves. Only a few blooms per head, but densely clustered; flowers usually pink to lavender or white, often with notched petals, in spring–early summer. 'Bonita', glossy leaves, bright pink flowers; 'Emerald Blue', compact habit, bright green foliage, mid-blue flowers; 'Emerald Pink', compact habit, bright green foliage, vivid pink flowers; 'Late Red', purple-red flowers; 'McDaniel's Cushion', bright pink flowers; 'Scarlet Flame', very compact, deep purple-red flowers. Zones 3–9.

PHOENIX

This genus in the palm (Arecaceae) family consists of around 17 species,

Phoenix rupicola

mostly from tropical and subtropical Africa, Madagascar, the Grecian island of Crete, the Canary Islands, and Asia. They are solitary or clustered feather-leafed palms. Male and female plants are separate. They have long pinnate leaves, lower leaflets on each frond reduced to stiff sharp spines. Panicles of small, 3-petalled, often yellow flowers are followed by yellow, orange, green, brown, or red to black fruits with 1 seed. They are widely grown as landscape specimens, street plantings, or container plants. Some produce dates and palm sugar.
CULTIVATION: Most species are fairly adaptable and tolerant of poorer drier soils in full sun as long as drainage is good, but better results are achieved from increased watering and more productive soils. Propagate from seed, or from suckers from suckering varieties. Remove old fronds carefully.

Phoenix canariensis ★
CANARY ISLAND DATE PALM

☼ ❧ ↔ 30 ft (9 m) ↕ 70 ft (21 m)

From the Canary Islands. Spreading crown, and thick trunk covered in old frond base scars. Large, arching, green fronds to 20 ft (6 m), sharply spined at the base. Cream to yellow flowers in drooping panicles, many orange fruits. Can be massive and set lots of seed; dispose of seeds carefully. Zones 9–11.

Phlox subulata 'G. F. Wilson'

Phlox subulata 'Late Red'

Phlox subulata 'Emerald Blue'

Phoenix dactylifera
DATE PALM, EDIBLE DATE

☼ ❧ ↔ 30 ft (9 m) ↕ 70 ft (21 m)

Commercial date palm cultivated for at least 5,000 years. Graceful spreading crown, gray-green fronds, lower leaflets reduced to spines. The sweet edible fruits are produced only in hot dry climates. Excellent coastal plant. Commercially developed varieties have superior fruits. Zones 9–12.

Phoenix loureiroi
DWARF DATE

☼ ❧ ↔ 12 ft (3.5 m) ↕ 6–15 ft (1.8–4.5 m)

Small mostly clump-forming palm from India to southern China. Stiff dark green fronds, leaflets arranged in several planes along midribs. Panicles of cream flowers. Oblong fruits ripen to dark purple. Zones 10–12.

Phoenix roebelenii ★
DWARF DATE PALM

☼ ❧ ↔ 8 ft (2.4 m) ↕ 10 ft (3 m)

Popular, elegant, small palm from Laos. Solitary rough trunk clothed with the remains of old frond stalks. Attractive, arching, deep green fronds, leaflets silvery beneath, lower leaflets reduced to sharp spines. Panicles of cream flowers, small, egg-shaped, black, edible fruits. Zones 10–12.

Phoenix rupicola
CLIFF DATE PALM

☼ ❧ ↔ 15 ft (4.5 m) ↕ 25 ft (8 m)

Native to India. Small to medium palm, slender solitary trunk. Arching fronds to 10 ft (3 m). Bright green leaflets, which are held in one plane. Panicles of yellow flowers, shiny yellow to reddish fruits. Zones 10–12.

Phoenix dactylifera, in the wild, Grand Erg, Algeria

Phoenix loureiroi

PHORMIUM

FLAX LILY, NEW ZEALAND FLAX

Phormium is a genus of only 2 species of large evergreen perennials in the family Phormiaceae, and is restricted to New Zealand. The leaves are long and fibrous, and in summer the plants produce large candelabras of upright curved flowers, dripping nectar that is highly attractive to birds. Glossy decorative seed pods follow. The foliage was traditionally used to make rope, and the dried seed heads are often used for decoration.
CULTIVATION: Give these plants a sunny spot in moisture-retentive soil; in frosty climates, cover them in winter. Propagate from seed, or by division of the colored leaf or dwarf clones in early spring.

Phormium cookianum

syn. **Phormium colensoi**

NEW ZEALAND MOUNTAIN FLAX

☼ ❄ ↔ 7–8 ft (2–2.4 m)
↑ 7–7½ ft (2–2.2 m)

Arching leaves to 5 ft (1.5 m) long, and yellow-green flowers with thick petals, followed by glossy brown seed pods that are curled and pendulous. *P. c.* **subsp.** *hookeri* '**Cream Delight**'

Phormium tenax 'Purpureum'

Phormium tenax (in foreground), in the wild, New Zealand

has narrow creamy yellow bands toward the edges of the leaves and broader bands further in; '**Tricolor**' is an old clone whose leaves have irregular bands of creamy yellow and fine red edges. Zones 8–11.

Phormium tenax

NEW ZEALAND FLAX, NEW ZEALAND HEMP

☼ ❄ ↔ 7–10 ft (2–3 m)
↑ 10–15 ft (3–4.5 m)

Large impressive species with upright leaves to 10 ft (3 m) long, usually gray-green in the wild forms of the species. Flowers are upright, waxy, red-brown trumpets, followed by upright black seed heads. '**Purpureum**', dark green leaves. Zones 8–10.

Phormium Hybrid Cultivars

☼ ❄ ↔ 1–6 ft (0.3–1.8 m)
↑ 1–6 ft (0.3–1.8 m)

The 2 *Phormium* species hybridize readily, both in the wild and in cultivation. There are a large number of cultivars available, in dwarf to tall sizes, with weeping or erect foliage, and in a range of colors and variegations. Cream and green striped cultivars include: '**Duet**', to 3 ft (0.9 m); '**Tricolor**', to 4 ft (1.2 m); and '**Yellow Wave**', to 3 ft (0.9 m). Variegated cultivars in tones of pink, red, and bronze include: '**Rainbow Maiden**' (syn. '**Maori Maiden**') and '**Sundowner**', both erect forms, and '**Evening Glow**' and '**Pink Panther**', both weeping forms. Cultivars with dark purple to black foliage include: '**Bronze Baby**' and '**Tom Thumb**', dwarf forms, and '**Black Prince**' and '**Dark Delight**', taller weeping forms. Zones 8–11.

PHOTINIA

This genus in the rose (Rosaceae) family consists of around 60 species of evergreen and deciduous shrubs and trees, most from the Himalayas

to Japan and Sumatra, Indonesia. The leaves are often strikingly colored when young, especially in spring. The flowers are small, mostly white, with 5 petals, and grow in dense, flattish, clustering panicles along the shoots or at their tips. The fruits are small pomes, usually red. The evergreen species are cultivated for their strikingly colored foliage and are popular plants for hedging; the deciduous species are more reliable than the evergreens in flowering, and in autumn their foliage can be attractively colored.
CULTIVATION: Most *Photinia* species are fairly adaptable, with good drainage being a key requirement. For best results, plant in a well-drained fertile soil in a sunny position. Prune to promote dense growth, particularly when used as hedging plants. Propagate from seed or cuttings.

Photinia beauverdiana

☼ ❄ ↔ 20 ft (6 m) ↑ 30 ft (9 m)

Deciduous spreading tree native to western China. Narrow obovate to lance-shaped dark green leaves, small-toothed margins, turn orange-red, in autumn. New growth purple-brown.

Photinia davidiana

Phormium cookianum, in the wild, Te Mata Peak, Hawkes Bay, New Zealand

Photinia beauverdiana

Clustering panicles of small white flowers, in late spring. Egg-shaped orange-red fruits. Zones 6–9.

Photinia davidiana

syn. **Stransvaesia davidiana**

☼ ❄ ↔ 20 ft (6 m) ↑ 25 ft (8 m)

From western China. Large evergreen shrub or small tree. Leaves leathery, elliptical to inversely lance-shaped, dark green; older leaves may color red in autumn. Clustering panicles of small white flowers, in summer. Small, red, hanging, persistent fruits. Zones 7–10.

Photinia × fraseri

FRASER PHOTINIA

☼ ❄ ↔ 15 ft (4.5 m) ↑ 15 ft (4.5 m)

Hybrid between *P. glabra* and *P. serratifolia*, developed at Fraser Nurseries in Alabama, USA. Large shrub, many stems, leathery dark green leaves, finely serrated margins, new leaves bronze to bright red. Small white flowers in panicles, in spring. '**Red Robin**' ★, compact cultivar from

Photinia villosa

Photinia × fraseri 'Red Robin'

Photinia prionophylla, fruit

Photinia × fraseri

New Zealand with shiny red new growth; **'Robusta'**, widely grown for its flushes of brilliant red new growth, which are encouraged by repeated trimming. Zones 8–10.

Photinia glabra

JAPANESE PHOTINIA

☀ ❄ ↔ 12 ft (3.5 m) ↑ 15 ft (4.5 m)

From Japan. Small tree with narrow-domed crown, bright red new leaves that mature to green. Small white flowers in clustering panicles bloom in summer. The small, fleshy, red drupes ripen to black and persist throughout winter. **'Rubens'**, popular for hedging in cool climates. Zones 7–10.

Photinia prionophylla

☀ ☌ ↔ 5 ft (1.5 m) ↑ 6–8 ft (1.8–2.4 m)

Chinese evergreen shrub with upright stiffly branched habit. Leaves 1–3 in (25–80 mm) long, leathery, and dark green, with sharply serrated edges and pale undersides. Upright clusters of white to cream flowers, 3 in (8 cm) wide, in summer. Zones 9–10.

Photinia prunifolia

☀ ❄ ↔ 12 ft (3.5 m) ↑ 15 ft (4.5 m)

From Vietnam; resembles *P. glabra*, but has numerous small black dots on the undersides of the leaves. Flowers are somewhat larger than those of *P. glabra*. Zones 7–10.

Photinia serratifolia

syn. *Photinia serrulata*

CHINESE HAWTHORN

☀ ❄ ↔ 25 ft (8 m) ↑ 30 ft (9 m)

Native of China. Small tree, leathery oblong leaves, saw-toothed margins. Young copper-red foliage ages to dark green. Small white flowers in clustering panicles, in spring. Many red berries. Zones 7–10.

Photinia villosa

syn. *Pourthiaea villosa*

ORIENTAL PHOTINIA

☀ ❄ ↔ 15 ft (4.5 m) ↑ 15 ft (4.5 m)

Native to China, Korea, and Japan. Deciduous tree or large shrub, often vase-shaped. Downy young shoots. Elliptical to obovate dark green leaves, sharply serrated, bronze when young, yellow, orange, and red in autumn. Panicles of small white flowers, in spring. Red fruits. Zones 4–9.

PHRAGMIPEDIUM

SOUTH AMERICAN SLIPPER ORCHID

This is a genus from Central and South America, consisting of about 20 species in the family Orchidaceae. The sympodial plants have plain green leaves and multiple flowers, generally blooming sequentially; some particularly robust species have branching spikes of blooms. They are well known to orchid growers; their popularity rose dramatically in the early 1980s with the discovery of the bright red species *P. besseae*, which has been used to create a number of attractive orange and red hybrids. Most flower during the warmer months, but very productive plants can bloom throughout the year.

CULTIVATION: They have similar requirements to those recommended for the related *Paphiopedilum*, but require stronger light levels and frequent watering. They grow well in a bark-based medium with the addition of washed pea-sized river gravel and perlite. Some growers use pure sphagnum moss. Much success has been achieved by placing the plants (which prefer deep plastic pots) in shallow saucers of water, to a depth of 2 in (5 cm). Propagate by division.

Phragmipedium besseae

☀ ✈ ↔ 8–16 in (20–40 cm)

↑ 8–20 in (20–50 cm)

From Colombia, Ecuador, and Peru. Broadly segmented orange to bright red flowers, 2½ in (6 cm) across. There is also a rare yellow-flowered form. Zones 10–12.

Phragmipedium caudatum

☀ ✈ ↔ 12–24 in (30–60 cm)

↑ 8–36 in (20–90 cm)

From Central America and western South America. The largest flowered member of the genus, bearing up to 4 yellow-green to brown blooms, with long pendulous sepals that can be 24 in (60 cm) long and only ½ in (12 mm) wide. Zones 11–12.

Phragmipedium longifolium

☀ ✈ ↔ 12–24 in (30–60 cm)

↑ 8–36 in (20–90 cm)

From Costa Rica to Ecuador. Variable species that has predominantly green blooms, 6 in (15 cm) across, with red-brown markings on the narrow out-stretched petals. Zones 11–12.

Phragmipedium Hybrids

☀ ✈ ↔ 8–24 in (20–60 cm)

↑ 8–36 in (20–90 cm)

There has been an upsurge of interest in hybrids in this genus. Two styles come to the fore: the long-sepalled types from *P. caudatum* and *P. longifolium*, and the pink and red types from *P. schlimii* and *P. besseae* respectively. The following hybrids all have the red *P. besseae* in their ancestry, and can have up to 6 blooms 2–4 in (5–10 cm) across: **Don Wimber ★**, between *P. Eric Young* and *P. besseae*; **Eric Young**, between *P. besseae* and *P. longifolium*; **Sergeant Eric**, between *P. Eric Young* and the greenish brown Brazilian species *P. sargentianum*. Zones 10–12.

PHRAGMITES

REED

The 3 or 4 members of this genus in the family Poaceae are widely distributed in swamps and wet areas in tropical and temperate climates. They are perennial grasses with thick rhizomes or runners, and grow in dense stands. They have broad or narrow, flat or folded, generally deciduous leaves

Phragmipedium longifolium

Phragmipedium, Hybrid, Don Wimber

Phragmipedium, Hybrid, Sergeant Eric

Phragmipedium, Hybrid, Eric Young

Phygelius × rectus 'African Queen'

Phygelius × rectus 'Moonraker'

Phygelius × rectus 'Salmon Leap'

Phygelius aequalis

P. aequalis 'Trewidden Pink'

with open sheaths, and bear large, soft, hairy or feathery terminal panicles of spikelets of 1 to 10 florets, on tall, erect, robust stems. Named from the Greek *phragma* (fence or screen), referring to plants growing in hedges. CULTIVATION: They prefer a position in full sun in damp soil near ponds or slowly moving water. Propagate from seed or by division.

Phragmites australis

syn. *Phragmites communis*

CARRIZO, COMMON REED, FEATHER GRASS

☀ ❉ ↔ 27–40 in (70–100 cm)
↑ 6–10 ft (1.8–3 m)

Widely distributed perennial grass, growing from thick rhizomes along moist shores or in water several feet deep. Stiff erect stems to 15 ft (4.5 m) tall. Narrow, arching, flat, strap-like leaves with blades, 8–24 in (20–60 cm) long, tapering to a long tip, with rough margins and smooth sheaths. Flowerheads feathery, erect or drooping, oblong to egg-shaped, tinged with brown to purple, 18–30 in (45–75 cm) long, with spikelets on stems to 10 ft (3 m) tall, appearing in summer–autumn. **'Rubra'** has reddish flowerheads; **'Variegatus'**, leaves striped with bright yellow fading to white. Zones 4–6.

Phragmites australis 'Variegatus'

PHUOPSIS

This genus in the madder (Rubiaceae) family contains one mat-forming finely hairy perennial, native to the Caucasus region of Asia. It has whorls of narrow sword-shaped leaves and clusters of tiny pink flowers with 5 lobes. CULTIVATION: Suited to rock gardens and banks, *Phuopsis* prefers full sun or part-shade in moist well-drained soil. Propagate by division in spring, from semi-ripe cuttings in summer, or from seed in autumn; it may self-seed in the right conditions.

Phuopsis stylosa

syn. *Crucianella stylosa*

CROSSWORT

☀ ❉ ↔ 8–12 in (20–30 cm)
↑ 8–12 in (20–30 cm)

Low-growing herb forming a mat of wiry ground-hugging stems. Whorls of small, coarse, pale green or grayish leaves, terminating in rounded heads of tiny pink flowers in late spring–early summer. **'Purpurea'** (syn. 'Rubra'), purplish red flowers. Zones 7–8.

PHYGELIUS

This genus of evergreen subshrubs from South Africa is in the foxglove (Scrophulariaceae) family. It consists of only 2 species, which have been crossed to produce numerous hybrids. They are often grown as herbaceous perennials where winters fall below freezing. The soft green leaves grow on erect stems and hold pendent, fuchsia-like, tubular flowers in warm tones throughout late summer. When

Phragmites australis

Phygelius aequalis 'Yellow Trumpet'

grown as a perennial, the suckering or running rootstock can form attractive clumps 3 ft (0.9 m) in diameter. CULTIVATION: Given fertile, moist, humus-enriched soil, these plants will thrive in a morning sun position in warmer climates, but need the protection of a wall or a similar warm spot to minimize frost damage in cold climates. They are fleshy-leafed plants that dislike dry conditions, so they should be well watered throughout summer. Propagation is from cuttings taken in summer.

Phygelius aequalis

☀ ❉ ↔ 3 ft (0.9 m) ↑ 3 ft (0.9 m)

A suckering shrub, or herbaceous perennial in colder climates. Upright stems, soft bright green foliage, dusky pink tubular flowers. **'Trewidden Pink'**, soft flesh pink flowers; **'Yellow**

Trumpet'**, dense bushy habit with leaves and flowers larger than those of its parent. Zones 8–10.

Phygelius capensis ★

CAPE FIGWORT, CAPE FUCHSIA

☀ ❉ ↔ 22 in (50 cm) ↑ 6 ft (1.8 m)

Well-clothed suckering shrub. Soft green leaves, lance-shaped. Masses of orange tubular flowers with distinctive recurved lobes. Zones 8–10.

Phygelius × rectus

☀ ❉ ↔ 4 ft (1.2 m) ↑ 4 ft (1.2 m)

A cross of garden origin between *P. aequalis* and *P. capensis*. Compact suckering shrub. Dark green leaves, upright stems. Masses of pendent tubular flowers. **'African Queen'**, pale red flowers; **'Moonraker'**, creamy yellow flowers; **'Salmon Leap'**, deeply lobed orange blooms. Zones 8–10.

PHYLA
FROGFRUIT

A genus of 15 perennial herbs, creeping or mat-forming, in the vervain (Verbenaceae) family, and native to warm-temperate to subtropical Central and South America. Sprawling or erect branches arise from a stem with runners. The hairy leaves are opposite or clustered. Solitary or paired flowerheads grow from the leaf axils, with many small flowers with oval to wedge-shaped bracts, a compressed membranous calyx with 2 to 4 teeth, and a straight or slightly curved corolla tube with 2 or 4 lobes. Fruits are pairs of nutlets with 2 compartments.
CULTIVATION: Most are salt-tolerant and make good ground covers, grown in full sun or part-shade, in moist but well-drained soil. Propagate by division in spring or autumn.

Phyla nodiflora
CAPEWEED, MATGRASS, TURKEY TANGLE
☼ ❄ ↔ 3–6 ft (0.9–1.8 m)
↕ 1¼–6 in (3–15 cm)
Vigorous salt-tolerant perennial herb. Leaves oblong to spatula-shaped, green or grayish green, to 3 in (8 cm) long, margins serrated toward the tips, on stems covered with fine furry hairs. Flowerheads, to 1 in (25 mm) long, of slightly hairy blooms with green or

Phyla nodiflora

Phylica buxifolia, Harold Porter National Botanic Garden, South Africa

violet bracteoles and white, reddish, or lilac corollas with a yellow eye, in spring–summer. Zones 9–10.

PHYLICA

Primarily native to South Africa, this genus in the buckthorn (Rhamnaceae) family has around 150 species of evergreen shrubs. A few are cultivated for their flowerheads, long lasting when cut. Leaves are dark green with lighter undersides, usually with a coating of silky silvery hairs. The true flowers are often petal-less or with fine filamentous petals, and are usually nearly enclosed by large feathery bracts or surrounded by white woolly hairs.
CULTIVATION: Plant in light, gritty, well-drained, slightly acidic soil and full sun. They tolerate high humidity, but their foliage suffers in prolonged rain. Coastal conditions suit them. Added humus and water will give lusher foliage, but a looser habit and fewer flowers. Prune by removing spent flowers and general tidying. Propagate from seed or half-hardened cuttings from non-flowering stems.

Phylica buxifolia
BOX HARD-LEAF
☼ ❄ ↔ 10 ft (3 m) ↕ 10 ft (3 m)
Only in rocky mountains near Cape Town, South Africa. Branches broad,

× *Phylliopsis*, Hybrid Cultivar, 'Sugar Plum'

twigs and new growth covered in light brown down, leaves box-like. Small dense heads of tiny white flowers, in spring. May be short-lived. Zones 9–10.

Phylica plumosa
syn. *Phylica pubescens*
FLANNEL FLOWER
☼ ❄ ↔ 3 ft (0.9 m) ↕ 3–6 ft (0.9–1.8 m)
South African shrub. Hairy buff bracts enclose tiny white flowers. Plant densely covered with fine hairs, deep green foliage shows through. Flowerheads mature in early winter. Long lasting cut flower. Zones 9–11.

PHYLLANTHUS

A genus of about 600 species of evergreen or deciduous herbs, shrubs, and trees in the euphorbia (Euphorbiaceae) family, native to the tropics and subtropics. Smooth-edged leaves, short-stalked or stalkless, often with pinnate veining, grow alternately or spiraly. Small petal-less flowers grow singly or in clusters in the leaf axils in spring–summer, followed by small fruits with 2 seeds. The fruits of some species are edible.
CULTIVATION: They need a warm climate, full sun, humus-enriched well-drained soil, and plenty of water in dry weather. They do well in coastal conditions. Propagate from seed or from firm tip cuttings.

Phylica plumosa

Phyllocladus glaucus

Phyllanthus acidus
OTAHEITE GOOSEBERRY, STAR GOOSEBERRY
☼ ✿ ↔ 10 ft (3 m) ↕ 30 ft (9 m)
Native of southern Asia. Fast-growing tree with 2-ranked, ovate leaves, 3 in (8 cm) long. Tiny red flowers along leaf-like branches, spring. Pale greenish yellow edible fruits, used in preserves and pickles in India. Zones 11–12.

× PHYLLIOPSIS

This hybrid genus of small evergreen shrubs, of garden origin, results from crosses between *Phyllodoce* and *Kalmiopsis*, members of the heath (Ericaceae) family. Plants have shiny brown bark, small, lustrous, dark green, oblong to oval leaves with rounded tips, and elongated racemes, on short red stalks, of flowers with 5 slightly hairy sepals and a reddish purple, bell-shaped, 5-lobed corolla, in spring.
CULTIVATION: × *Phylliopsis* plants prefer part-shade and peaty acidic soil. Trim back after flowering to maintain compact habit, and propagate from half-hardened cuttings in late summer.

× Phylliopsis Hybrid Cultivars
☼ ❄ ❄ ↔ 8–12 in (20–30 cm) ↕ 12 in (30 cm)
Small shrubs suitable for containers or rock gardens. 'Coppelia', large pinkish lilac flowers, cup-shaped,; 'Pinocchio', compact form; 'Sugar Plum', candy pink blooms. Zones 3–9.

Phyllanthus acidus, fruit

PHYLLOCLADUS

CELERY PINE

A genus of 5 or 6 coniferous trees or shrubs in the family Phyllocladaceae, from the Philippines and the Malay Peninsula to New Zealand and Tasmania, Australia. Its "leaves" are flattened extended stems called phylloclades and resembling celery leaves, hence its common name. Male and female cones may be on the same or different trees. CULTIVATION: Grow in moist well-drained soil in sun or partial shade, watering during dry spells. Propagate from seed or from half-hardened cuttings taken in autumn; the cuttings can be difficult to strike.

Phyllocladus glaucus

TOA TOA

☼/◐ ✤ ↔ 10–15 ft (3–4.5 m) ↑ 35–50 ft (10–15 m)

This New Zealand species has whorls of large, gray-green, compound phylloclades and thick branches radiating in whorls up the trunk. The fruiting body looks like a pine cone. Rare, even in the wild. Zones 10–11.

Phyllocladus hypophyllus

☼ ✤ ↔ 20 ft (6 m) ↑ 100 ft (30 m)
From the Philippines, Indonesia, and New Guinea. Spirally arranged phylloclades dark to yellowish green, roughly oval, shallow-toothed or lobed edges. Catkin-like male cones, yellow, ripening to red or pink. Zones 10–11.

Phyllocladus trichomanoides

NEW ZEALAND CELERY-TOP PINE, TANEKAHA

◐ ✤ ↔ 20 ft (6 m) ↑ 70 ft (21 m)
New Zealand native, faster growing than other species, smaller in cultivation. Conical in shape, symmetrical whorled branches, attractive, gray-brown, mottled bark. Bright green leathery phylloclades resemble small celery leaves. Zones 9–11.

Phyllostachys aureosulcata

PHYLLODOCE

A genus of 5 small, evergreen, heath-like shrubs in the heath (Ericaceae) family, from the Arctic and the alpine regions of the Northern Hemisphere, western North America, and Japan. Leaves are crowded, alternate, linear, with finely toothed margins. Terminal racemes or umbels of open, bell-shaped, nodding flowers appear in spring and early summer. They make ideal rock garden plants for regions with cool summers. CULTIVATION: Frost hardy, they grow best in moist, acidic, peaty soil in part shade. Do not allow to dry out in summer; mulch to keep roots cool. Trim after flowering to maintain compact habit. Propagate from seed or by layering in spring, or from cuttings in late summer.

Phyllodoce aleutica

☼ ✳ ↔ 10 in (25 cm) ↑ 10 in (25 cm)
From eastern Asia to Alaska. Small mat-forming shrub, mid-green leaves, yellowish hairs and white lines beneath. Pale yellow-green urn-shaped flowers in small, drooping, terminal clusters, in late spring–early summer. Zones 2–8.

Phyllodoce caerulea

☼ ✳ ↔ 12 in (30 cm) ↑ 8 in (20 cm)
From alpine regions of Asia, Europe, and USA. Small upright or spreading shrub, fine heath-like leaves about ½ in (12 mm) long. Single or umbel-like clusters of bell-shaped purple flowers, in late spring–summer. Zones 2–8.

Phyllodoce × intermedia

☼ ✳ ↔ 15 in (38 cm) ↑ 10 in (25 cm)
Natural hybrid, a cross between *P. empetriformis* and *P. aleutica* var. *glanduliflora*, from the west coast of North America. Low-spreading shrub, glossy, dark green, minutely toothed leaves. Small clusters of urn-shaped rose pink flowers, in mid-spring. 'Drummondii', low growing, purple flowers. Zones 3–9.

PHYLLOSTACHYS

This is the largest and best known genus of running bamboos (family Poaceae), consisting of 50 or more

Phyllocladus hypophyllus

Phyllodoce × intermedia 'Drummondii'

species ranging from the eastern Himalayas to Japan, most native to China. They are medium to tall, with widely spaced culms arising from deep long-running rhizomes, so that they spread rapidly when conditions suit. The culm internodes are flattened or shallowly grooved on one side, and each lower node bears just 2 lateral branches, though there may be a third smaller branch. Foliage is not very distinctive, and flowers are rare and inconspicuous. The genus includes species for edible shoots, as well as many used in Asia for building, furniture, fishing-rods, umbrella handles, and similar items. CULTIVATION: Although ornamental, they spead aggressively. Some are very frost hardy, and when grown near their cold limit they remain fairly compact, though vigorous spreaders in warmer climates. Their spread can be contained by inserting concrete, steel, or plastic barriers in the soil to a depth of about 24 in (60 cm), or by cutting a deep bench on the downhill edge of a stand. Smaller species can be grown in tubs or planter boxes; water generously. They are not choosy about soil, as long as they have ample moisture in summer. They are readily propagated from excavated lengths of rhizome, each with several culm bases, planted in spring and kept well watered.

Phyllostachys aurea

FISHPOLE BAMBOO, GOLDEN BAMBOO

☼/◐ ✳ ↔ 20–40 ft (6–12 m) ↑ 25 ft (8 m)

From south-eastern China. Culms smooth olive-green to quite yellowish, depending on exposure to sun, the stronger ones 1–1½ in (25–40 mm) thick but usually mixed with many smaller ones, making dense bushy stands; bases of culms with crowded, often crooked nodes. Versatile species, tolerating dry air, suitable for screens or even for indoor use where light is adequate; can be kept trimmed to a small size. 'Holochrysa', whole culm bright yellow, turning a transient red in first season (in full sun); 'Flavescens Inversa', dark green culms, contrasting bright yellow groove; 'Koi', golden culms, prominent green groove. Zones 7–11.

Phyllostachys aureosulcata

CROOKSTEM BAMBOO, YELLOW GROOVE BAMBOO

☼/◐ ✳ ↔ 25–50 ft (8–15 m) ↑ 25 ft (8 m)

Vigorous spreader from north-eastern China. Matt green culms with broad yellow groove in the cultivated form. Slightly rough to the touch, sometimes slightly zigzagging between lower nodes. Straight and upright in warm climates, inclined to bend over in cooler areas. Wind tolerant, ideal for roof tops and containers. 'Aureocaulis', young culms sulfurous yellow, flushed crimson where facing sun, older culms dark yellow; 'Harbin', like 'Aureocaulis' but with narrow green stripes on internode, excellent when planted with 'Harbin Inversa', its opposite, green internode with narrow yellow stripes; 'Spectabilis', bright golden-yellow culms with green groove. Zones 6–11.

Phyllostachys nigra

Phyllostachys nigra

Phyllostachys flexuosa

Phyllostachys bambusoides
JAPANESE TIMBER BAMBOO

☀ ❄ ↔ 20–60 ft (6–18 m)
↕ 40–70 ft (12–21 m)

One of the largest timber bamboos, valued for construction due to its thick, straight, strong culms, up to 6 in (15 cm) in diameter. Native to China, but long cultivated in Japan. Slower to mature and later shooting than *P. vivax*, which it resembles. Ornamental cultivars, mostly 25 ft (8 m) or smaller, include: '**Allgold**', rich golden culms; '**Castillon**', like '**Allgold**' but with green groove and stronger apricot-variegated foliage; '**Castillon Inversa**', reverse of '**Castillon**' with randomly variegated foliage; '**Kawadana**', green culm subtly striped white and finely white-striped foliage, requires dappled sun; '**Richard Haubrich**', apricot-striped foliage; '**Marliac**', corrugated internodes. Zones 7–11.

Phyllostachys dulcis
SWEETSHOOT BAMBOO

☀ ❄ ↔ 30–60 ft (9–18 m)
↕ 25–40 ft (8–12 m)

Vigorous bamboo of uncertain wild origin. Spreads strongly even in cooler regions. Fresh green culms arch up to the light, growing to 3 in (8 cm) in diameter; internodes often compact with prominent nodes on leaning face, giving skeletal effect. New shoots very sweet, hence the common name. Zones 7–10.

Phyllostachys edulis
syns *Phyllostachys heterocycla*, *P. pubescens*

MAO ZHU, MOSO, MOUSOU CHIKU

☀ ❄ ↔ 30–100 ft (9–30 m)
↕ 40–75 ft (12–22 m)

Believed native to Japan, but long cultivated in China. Most important bamboo for edible shoots, canned in large quantity; also valued as a timber bamboo. Culms up to 7 in (18 cm) in diameter though 3–4 in (8–10 cm) is more usual, clothed in dense hairs when young, pale matt green ageing to deep yellowish; long branches and fine leaves give a plume-like appearance. '**Bicolor**', golden culms with green groove; '**Gold Stripe**', only 20 ft (6 m) tall, culms and foliage striped golden; '**Heterocycla**', smaller-growing with some lower nodes crooked due to slanted nodes; '**Spring Beauty**', small, delicate, fine-white-striped variegation prominent in spring; '**White Stripe**', like '**Gold Stripe**' but striped white. Zones 6–10.

Phyllostachys flexuosa
ZIG-ZAG BAMBOO

☀ ❄ ↔ 10–20 ft (3–6 m)
↕ 8–15 ft (2.4–4.5 m)

Gracefully arching, dark green, aerial stems, fast growing. Leaves dark green, becoming golden in the sun. Aerial stems become almost black with age; may show white powdering at the nodes. Zones 6–10.

Phyllostachys nigra ★
BLACK BAMBOO

☀ ❄ ↔ 20–50 ft (6–15 m)
↕ 25–50 ft (8–15 m)

From China, but long cultivated in Japan. Original wild plants are not as black as the commonly grown form. New culms are green but soon develop brown stippling that transforms them to black; this happens more rapidly in full sun. Probably the most popular bamboo species; its color is unique among running bamboos. '**Bory**', like '**Henon**' but developing brown cloud-like markings; '**Henon**', larger culms, blue-gray in shade or golden green in sun; '**Megurochiku**', like '**Henon**' but groove matures to dark brown. Zones 7–10.

Phyllostachys vivax
ELEGANT BAMBOO, VIVAX BAMBOO

☀ ❄ ↔ 20–60 ft (6–18 m)
↕ 30–60 ft (9–18 m)

From eastern China. Similar to *P. bambusoides*, but more cold hardy and faster to establish. Culms to 4 in (10 cm) in diameter but thin-walled, susceptible to wind damage, and yielding poor-quality timber. '**Aureocaulis**', glossy pale yellow culms with random green stripes; '**Huangwenzhu**', green culms with yellow groove; '**Huanwenzhu Inversa**', reverse of '**Huanwenzhu**', yellow culm with green groove. Zones 6–10.

PHYMOSIA

This is a small subtropical genus belonging to the mallow (Malvaceae) family. It consists of 8 species of decorative evergreen shrubs or small trees from Mexico, Guatemala, and the West Indies. Their leaves are broad and palmately lobed with toothed or serrated margins. They are cultivated for their pretty clusters of bell-shaped flowers with 5 overlapping petals in shades of red, pink, or mauve.

CULTIVATION: In warm frost-free climates, grow in partial shade in a very well-drained soil. They need ample watering, especially during the growing season. Tip prune when young to promote bushy growth. In cool-temperate climates, grow in a temperate or warm greenhouse. Propagate from cuttings or seed.

Phymosia umbellata

☀ ☘ ↔ 7 ft (2 m) ↕ 20 ft (6 m)

Native of Mexico. Tall shrub or small tree; resembles hibiscus. Large, shallowly toothed, lobed leaves grow to 8 in (20 cm) long. Red flowers, about 1½ in (35 mm) long, in small clusters. Zones 10–12.

PHYSALIS
GROUND CHERRY, HUSK TOMATO

This genus in the nightshade (Solanaceae) family consists of about 80 erect, bushy, or sprawling annual and rhizomatous perennial herbs. It is widely distributed, especially in the Americas, but also in temperate Eurasia and Australia. Alternate simple or divided leaves, sometimes roughly opposite and often in groups of 2 or 3, grow from erect or straggling stems, sometimes woody at the base. Nodding, mostly solitary flowers, on short stalks or none, grow from the leaf axils, with widely bell-shaped to open, blue, yellowish, or white corollas. The bell-shaped calyx has 5 lobes and enlarges into a papery husk enclosing the spherical, 2-celled, greenish, yellowish, orange, or purple fruits, which contain many spherical to kidney-shaped seeds. The husks split open as fruits ripen in late summer to autumn. Unripe berries may be toxic to humans and livestock, although those of some species are edible and are used in preserves, pickles, and Mexican salsa dishes. Named from the Greek *physa* (bladder), referring to the enlarged calyx.

CULTIVATION: Sow seed in autumn or early spring and plant out seedlings of annual species in a warm, sunny, exposed or part-shaded position, in fertile well-drained soil. Perennials can be propagated by division of rhizomes or from tip cuttings in spring.

Physalis alkekengi
ALKEKENGI, BLADDER CHERRY, CHINESE LANTERN, WINTER CHERRY

☀ ❄ ↔ 12–24 in (30–60 cm)
↕ 12–24 in (30–60 cm)

Perennial growing from long, creeping, underground rhizomes. Native to central and southern Europe, and from western Asia to Japan. Erect, leafy, finely glandular, hairy stems. Mid-green triangular to oval leaves, to 5 in (12 cm) long. Inconspicuous drooping flowers, calyx expanding to 2 in (5 cm) across as it encloses the fruit, yellow to cream corolla, red to scarlet berries, in late summer. '**Gigantea**' (syn. '**Monstrosa**'), larger growing, larger fruits. Zones 4–6.

Phymosia umbellata

Physalis ixocarpa 'Indian Strain'

P. philadelphica 'Purple de Milpa'

Physalis ixocarpa

MEXICAN GROUNDCHERRY, STRAWBERRY TOMATO, TOMATILLO

☼ ❋ ↔ 3–4 ft (0.9–1.2 m)
↑ 3–4 ft (0.9–1.2 m)

Annual herb from Mexico and southern USA, grown as a culinary seasoning; possibly not distinct from *P. philadelphica*. Simple or toothed sword-shaped to oval leaves, to 3 in (8 cm) long. Flowers bowl-shaped to bell-shaped, yellow corollas, 5 brown or purple central spots, twisting blue or yellow anthers. Sticky yellow to purple berry almost fills the purple-veined yellow calyx when mature. 'Indian Strain', attractive cultivar. Zones 8–10.

Physalis peruviana

syn. *Physalis edulis*

CAPE GOOSEBERRY, GOLDEN BERRY, TEPAREE

☼ ❋ ↔ 2–3 ft (0.6–0.9 m)
↑ 2–6 ft (0.6–1.8 m)

Herbaceous spreading perennial, from Peru and Chile. Widely introduced elsewhere. Branches ribbed, spreading, often purplish; leaves nearly opposite, randomly toothed, velvety, pointed, mid-green, heart-shaped to oval, 2½–6 in (6–15 cm) long; flowers inconspicuous, bell-shaped, yellow, with 5 dark purple-brown markings, in summer. Purple-green hairy calyx becomes a straw-colored husk enclosing glossy, smooth-skinned, orange-yellow fruit; juicy pulp contains many tiny yellowish seeds. Fruits eaten fresh or stewed, canned, used in jams, sauces, and preserves; worn as jewelry in Peru; used as a diuretic and anti-asthmatic in Colombia, and as a poultice or enema in South Africa. Zones 8–10.

Physalis philadelphica

syn. *Physalis subglabrata*

JAMBERRY, PURPLE GROUND CHERRY, TOMATILLO

☼ ❋ ↔ 18–24 in (45–60 cm)
↑ 24–40 in (60–100 cm)

From Mexico. Cultivated widely as a food crop. Smooth-edged, toothed, oval to broadly sword-shaped leaves, 1½–4 in (3.5–10 cm) long; flowers with a green calyx, yellow-veined, enlarging to 2 in (5 cm) to enclose the yellow to purple edible berry; open yellow corollas marked with purplish brown. 'Purple de Milpa', small, purple, acidic fruits. Zones 7–10.

PHYSOCARPUS

NINEBARK

From North America and temperate northeastern Asia, the 10 deciduous shrubs in this genus in the rose (Rosaceae) family have showy flowerheads, foliage that is attractive in spring, and sometimes in autumn, and flaking bark. Most have conspicuously veined lobed foliage like that of raspberry or blackberry. Flowers are white or pale pink, small, massed in flat corymbs. Inflated fruits with 3 to 5 lobes ripen in late summer.

CULTIVATION: They are best grown in full sun in fertile well-drained soil that remains moist through summer. They are not fussy, but dislike lime; foliage exposed to drought becomes desiccated and brown. The plants form thickets of stems; thin these and cut back the remaining growth after flowering. Propagate from seed or half-hardened cuttings.

Physocarpus amurensis

☼ ❋ ↔ 7 ft (2 m) ↑ 10 ft (3 m)

From Korea and China. Leaves, 3 to 5 pointed lobes, serrated edges, deep green above, almost white, below, fine hairs. Flowers white, pinkish streaks, in corymbs to 2 in (5 cm) wide, in late spring–early summer. Zones 5–9.

Physocarpus capitatus

☼ ❋ ↔ 8 ft (2.4 m) ↑ 10 ft (3 m)

Upright shrub native to western parts of North America. Leaves, felted

Physocarpus amurensis

coating beneath, to 3 in (8 cm) long, deeply lobed. Fine display of large rounded corymbs of tiny cream flowers, in spring–early summer. Zones 6–10.

Physocarpus monogynus

MOUNTAIN NINEBARK

☼ ❋ ↔ 4 ft (1.2 m) ↑ 4 ft (1.2 m)

From central USA. Spreading bush, forming a thicket of arching stems. Toothed, rounded leaves to 2 in (5 cm) long, 3 to 5 lobes. Flat heads of small white flowers, around 2 in (5 cm) wide, in spring–summer. Zones 5–9.

Physocarpus opulifolius

COMMON NINEBARK, NINEBARK

☼ ❋ ↔ 15 ft (4.5 m) ↑ 10 ft (3 m)

From central and eastern North America, most widely grown species in the genus. Leaves usually 3-lobed, light green, with toothed margins. Corymbs of flowers, commonly white,

Physocarpus capitatus

Physocarpus opulifolius

but may be pink-tinged or entirely pink, in late spring–early summer. *P. o.* var. *intermedius* (syn. *P. intermedius*), compact form around 5 ft (1.5 m) tall, slightly smaller leaves, more densely packed heads of flowers; *P. o.* 'Dart's Gold' ★, low-growing golden yellow foliage, pink-tinted white flowers; 'Diabolo', burgundy foliage; 'Luteus', golden new growth, ageing to deep green, then bronze; 'Nanus', dense covering of small deep green leaves. Zones 2–9.

Physocarpus opulifolius 'Nanus'

Physocarpus opulifolius var. *intermedius*

Physocarpus opulifolius 'Diabolo'

Physocarpus opulifolius 'Dart's Gold'

PHYSOSTEGIA

FALSE DRAGON HEAD, OBEDIENT PLANT

A member of the mint (Lamiaceae) family, this North American genus has 2 species of upright perennials, one widely cultivated. They normally form a clump of unbranched stems bearing simple, dark green, toothed, narrow, elliptical to lance-shaped leaves. In summer to autumn flowerheads of many 5-lobed tubular to bell-shaped blooms, mainly pink and purple, develop at most stem tips. It is often known as "obedient plant" because the flowers stay in place when twisted. CULTIVATION: They are hardy, and are easily grown in full or half-sun in moist well-drained soil. They spread by rhizomes that can become invasive, but provided the clumps are broken up occasionally this causes few problems. Propagate by division.

Physostegia virginiana

OBEDIENT PLANT

☼/◐ ❄ ↔ 12–20 in (30–50 cm)
↑ 32–48 in (80–120 cm)

Vigorous perennial from eastern USA, forming clumps of upright stems with narrow, toothed, lance-shaped leaves. Narrow conical flower spikes to 8 in (20 cm) long, with downy, tubular, purple-pink flowers to 1¼ in (30 mm) long, in summer–autumn. 'Alba', white flowers; 'Rose Queen', pink flowers; 'Rosea', large light pink flowers; 'Summer Snow', white flowers; 'Variegata', white-edged gray-green leaves; 'Vivid', bright purple-red flowers. Zones 5–10.

PHYTEUMA

HORNED RAMPION

This genus of about 40 perennial herbs are members of the bellflower (Campanulaceae) family, and native to Europe and Asia. Alternate simple leaves grow from the base of the stem, and terminal spikes or heads of flowers with bracts and curved horn-like flower buds open as narrow spreading corollas with 5 lobes. Fruits are capsules. CULTIVATION: Horned rampions are suited to rock garden culture in any good soil. Propagate from seed in autumn or by division in spring.

Phyteuma spicatum

SPIKED RAMPION

☼ ❄ ↔ 32–48 in (80–120 cm)
↑ 32–48 in (80–120 cm)

Erect perennial herb, native to southern Europe. Oval to heart-shaped serrated leaves. Dense, rounded to cylindrical flowerheads, with narrow bracts and curved, white, cream, or deep blue corollas, in summer. *P. s.* subsp. *spicatum*, white to pale yellowish green flowers, yellow to yellowish brown style; *P. s.* subsp. *coeruleum*, bluish flowers with yellowish brown to blue stigmas. Zones 6–8.

PHYTOLACCA

From temperate, warm-temperate, and subtropical regions, this genus in the pokeweed (Phytolaccaceae) family comprises 35 species of perennials, subshrubs, and deciduous or evergreen shrubs and trees, usually upright, with simple, often large leaves that can develop vivid colors in autumn. Their flowers lack petals and are most often cream to beige, massed in racemes, and followed by conspicuous berries that in many species are poisonous. CULTIVATION: Apart from variable frost hardiness and an intolerance of drought, most species are easily grown in moist, moderately fertile, well-drained soil in sun or partial shade. Prune at any time, but winter is often best as it will not affect the flower and fruit production or the autumn color. Propagate from seed, from rooted basal shoots, or from cuttings taken during the growing season.

Phytolacca americana

POKE, POKEBERRY, POKEWEED

☼ ❄ ↔ 3 ft (0.9 m) ↑ 12 ft (3.5 m)

From North and Central America. Can be herbaceous in severe winters. Young stems purple-red, leaves take on purple-red and pink tones in autumn. Racemes of tiny cream to pink flowers. Clusters of berries that turn red and purple-black as they ripen. Zones 4–10.

Phytolacca dioica

BELLA SOMBRA TREE, OMBU

☼ ❄ ↔ 30 ft (9 m) ↑ 50 ft (15 m)

Native to South America. Wide-spreading evergreen tree with buttressed multi-stemmed trunk. Leaves leathery, 4 in (10 cm) long, with a purple midrib. Bears racemes of tiny white flowers, and golden berries ripening to black. Zones 10–11.

Phytolacca americana

Physostegia virginiana 'Rose Queen'

Phytolacca dioica

Physostegia virginiana 'Alba'

Physostegia virginiana 'Rosea'

P. virginiana 'Summer Snow'

P. virginiana 'Variegata'

Phyteuma spicatum

Picea abies

Picea abies 'Humilis'

Picea abies 'Pendula'

Picea abies 'Cranstonii'

Picea abies 'Cranstonii'

Picea abies 'Clanbrassiliana'

Picea abies 'Little Gem'

Picea abies 'Nidiformis'

Picea abies 'Procumbens'

Picea abies 'Pumila'

Picea abies 'Reflexa'

Picea abies 'Tabuliformis'

Picea species, in the wild, Denali Highway, Alaska, USA

PICEA

SPRUCE

About 45 species and many cultivars make up this genus of resinous evergreen conifers in the pine (Pinaceae) family, from cool latitudes or high altitudes in the Northern Hemisphere. Most are large symmetrical trees, favoring deep, rich, acidic, well-drained soils in mountainous areas. The foliage is green, blue, silver, or gray, and consists of needle-like leaves on short, persistent, peg-like shoots. The large cones are pendulous at maturity.

CULTIVATION: Some are slow growing, but all are wind-firm, and taller species make good windbreaks in large gardens and parks. They tolerate a range of soils and climates, but dislike mild areas or polluted atmospheres. Smaller cultivars are suitable bonsai subjects. Propagation is from seed or, for cultivars, firm cuttings or grafting.

Picea abies

COMMON SPRUCE, NORWAY SPRUCE

☀ ❄ ↔ 20 ft (6 m) ↑ 200 ft (60 m)

Native to southern Scandinavia and parts of Europe. Columnar habit, slow-growing, smaller in cultivation. Thick reddish brown bark, spreading branches, 4-sided dark green leaves. Light brown cones, erect at first, becoming pendulous, to 8 in (20 cm) long. There are many ornamental cultivars, some of which are: '**Clanbrassiliana**', very slow-growing dwarf selection, 5 ft (1.5 m) tall with a spread of 8 ft (2.4 m), dark green foliage; '**Cranstonii**', sparse irregularly branched form; '**Cupressina**', broadly conical habit, 60 ft (18 m); '**Echiniformis**', slow-growing dwarf form, long prickly foliage; '**Gregoryana**', rounded dwarf form to 30 in (75 cm) in diameter; '**Humilis**', slow-growing compact dwarf form to less than 18 in (45 cm) tall, small deep green leaves; '**Little Gem**', very slow-growing, flat-topped, dwarf shrub; '**Maxwellii**', short thick branches to 12 in (30 cm) long, bright green foliage, good for rock gardens and borders; '**Nidiformis**' (bird's nest spruce), outward-spreading branches forming a nest-shaped central depression, bright green young shoots in spring, grows to 5 ft (1.5 m) in diameter; '**Pendula**', drooping branches; '**Procumbens**', slow-growing, flat-topped, spreading bush with densely layered branches to 3 ft (1 m) across. Others include: '**Pumila**', '**Pyramidalis**', '**Gracilis**,' and '**Repens**'. '**Reflexa**' is mat-forming to 12 ft (3.5 m) wide, young shoots point upwards at first, then relax into a typically pendulous habit; '**Tabuliformis**' has horizontal prostrate branches. Zones 2–9.

Picea alcoquiana

Picea alcoquiana

Picea alcoquiana

syn. *Picea bicolor*

ALCOCK'S SPRUCE

☀ ❄ ↔ 20 ft (6 m) ↑ 80 ft (24 m)

Evergreen conifer from Japan. Broadly pyramidal habit. Branches horizontal, stiff needle-like leaves have prominent white bands. Cylindrical cones purplish pink when young, maturing to brown. Prefers moist soil and a clean atmosphere. Zones 8–10.

P

Picea glauca 'Densata'

P. glauca var. albertiana 'Conica'

Picea glauca 'Rainbow's End'

Picea glauca. var. albertiana 'Alberta Globe'

Picea glauca 'Echiniformis'

Picea engelmannii, in the wild, near Aspen, Colorado, USA

Picea glauca

Picea glauca

Picea asperata

DRAGON SPRUCE

☼ ❄ ↔ 20 ft (6 m) ↑ 100 ft (30 m)

Evergreen conifer, native to western China. Bark grayish red, peeling in flakes. Young shiny yellow shoots age to blue-green. Stiff prickly leaves around the shoots. Gray pendulous cones age to red-brown. Zones 4–8.

Picea brachytyla

SARGENT SPRUCE

☼ ❄ ↔ 20 ft (6 m) ↑ 70 ft (21 m)

From the Himalayas. Evergreen conifer, conical habit, more rounded in open situations. Branches horizontally spreading with upturned tips. Flat, short, yellow-green, crowded leaves,

glaucous bands, beneath. Pendulous cylindrical cones purplish, becoming dull brown at maturity. Zones 8–10.

Picea breweriana

BREWER'S SPRUCE, WEEPING SPRUCE

☼ ❄ ↔ 15 ft (4.5 m) ↑ 120 ft (36 m)

From North America. Horizontal whorled branches from which hang "streamers" of blunt-tipped, flattened, blue-green leaves. Often slender under crowded conditions. Prefers freedom from competition. Zones 2–8.

Picea engelmannii

ENGELMANN SPRUCE

☼ ❄ ↔ 15 ft (4.5 m) ↑ 150 ft (45 m)

North American evergreen, dense columnar-pyramidal habit. Leaves sharp-pointed, 4-angled, gray-blue. Cylindrical pendulous cones green flushed with purple. Zones 1–8.

Picea glauca

DWARF ALBERTA SPRUCE, WHITE SPRUCE

☼ ❄ ↔ 12–20 ft (3.5–6 m) ↑ 80 ft (24 m)

Slow-growing evergreen conifer from Canada, grown commercially for

paper making. Bright green shoots in spring; 4-angled, aromatic, needle-like leaves, on drooping branchlets. Small narrow cones. *P. g.* var. *albertiana* 'Alberta Globe', mound-forming conifer, to 12 ft (3.5 m); 'Conica' ★, slow-growing to a perfect conical form, fine blue-green foliage, deepening with age to gray-green, widely regarded as one of the best dwarf conifers, reaching only 6 ft (1.8 m) in height. *P. g.* 'Alberta Blue', blue-green foliage; 'Densata', slow-growing form, blue-green needle-like leaves; 'Echiniformis' and 'Nana', dwarf forms; 'Rainbow's End', conical form, attractive yellow young growth. Zones 1–8.

Picea jezoensis

YEZO SPRUCE

☼ ❄ ↔ 25 ft (8 m) ↑ 120 ft (36 m)

From Japan and northeast Asia. Branches with upturned tips sweep to ground level. Gray bark fissured with age, shed in plates. Flat dark green leaves, glaucous beneath. Small cylindrical cones crimson when young, maturing to rich brown. Zones 8–10.

Picea koyamae

Picea koyamae

☼ ❄ ↔ 20 ft (6 m) ↑ 80 ft (24 m)

From temperate to cool-temperate East Asia. Forest-forming spruce, flaking gray bark. Densely packed graygreen to blue-green leaves. Cones around 3 in (8 cm) long, green maturing to brown. Zones 5–9.

Picea likiangensis

LIJIANG SPRUCE

☼ ❄ ↔ 20 ft (6 m) ↑ 100 ft (30 m)

From Sichuan Province, China. Variable evergreen conifer, sturdy straight trunk with thick deeply furrowed bark. Overlapping sharply pointed leaves; shorter and more spreading leaves in 2 rows lower down. Young cones generally violet-purple. Zones 7–10.

Picea asperata

Picea mariana
AMERICAN BLACK SPRUCE

☀ ❄ ↔ 10 ft (3 m) ↑ 60 ft (18 m)

From the USA. Pyramidal evergreen conifer. Whorled branches, narrow, blue-green, blunt-tipped leaves. Many small persistent purple-brown cones. Distinctive densely hairy shoots. '**Doumetii**', broader-leafed than the species; '**Nana**', more rounded dwarf form. Zones 1–8.

Picea meyeri
MEYER SPRUCE

☀ ❄ ↔ 4–17 ft (1.2–5 m)
↑ 10–40 ft (3–12 m)

Evergreen from northwestern China. Purplish gray bark, falling in thick chunks. Upswept branches, blue or bluish green leaves, to 1¼ in (30 mm) long, pale brown cones with rounded striped scales. Zones 4–7.

Picea obovata
SIBERIAN SPRUCE

☀ ❄ ↔ 20 ft (6 m) ↑ 200 ft (60 m)

Resembles *P. abies*. Leaves 4-sided, dark green, bluntly pointed, whitish lines on each side. Pendulous, cylindrical, shiny, brown cones; pinkish catkins, in spring. Young shoots covered with fine red-brown hairs. Zones 1–8.

Picea omorika
DWARF SERBIAN SPRUCE, SERBIAN SPRUCE

☀ ❄ ↔ 20 ft (6 m) ↑ 100 ft (30 m)

From Bosnia and Serbia. Elegant evergreen, narrow pyramidal form. Fast-growing, drooping branches upturned at the ends. Flattened, blunt-tipped, needle-like, bright green leaves, grayish beneath. '**Nana**', dwarf form, rounded to conical. Zones 4–8.

Picea orientalis
CAUCASIAN SPRUCE

☀ ❄ ↔ 20 ft (6 m) ↑ 100 ft (30 m)

From sheltered sites in the Caucasus and Turkey. Upright, pyramidal, slow-growing, evergreen conifer. Pendulous branches to ground level. Short glossy green leaves. Short, pendulous, purplish cones. Brick red flower catkins, in spring. '**Aureospicata**', upward-curving branches; '**Connecticut Turnpike**', shorter denser cultivar. Zones 3–8.

Picea pungens
COLORADO BLUE SPRUCE

☀ ❄ ↔ 20 ft (6 m) ↑ 100 ft (30 m)

Evergreen pyramidal conifer from the western coast of the USA. Gray bark. Horizontal branches bear stiff, sharp, needle-like, blue-green leaves. '**Compacta**', silvery green foliage; '**Glauca**', steel blue-foliaged form, slower growing than species, drought hardy; '**Glauca Compacta**', silvery blue-foliage. Other blue-foliaged cultivars—for example, '**Globosa**', '**Hoopsii**', '**Koster**', and '**Moerheimii**'—make a striking contrast against green lawns. They are usually propagated by grafting, but seedlings of the blue-foliaged cultivars are also sometimes available. Zones 2–8.

Picea mariana 'Nana'

Picea orientalis 'Connecticut Turnpike'

Picea orientalis

Picea pungens

Picea pungens 'Moerheimii'

Picea pungens 'Thuem'

Picea pungens 'Compacta'

Picea pungens 'Glauca'

Picea omorika 'Nana'

Picea omorika

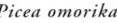

Picea purpurea
PURPLE-CONED SPRUCE
☼ ❄ ↔ 20 ft (6 m) ↑ 100 ft (30 m)
Commonly considered a form of
P. likiangensis, but leaves are shorter
and more crowded leaves. Densely
hairy shoots. Cones small, violet-
purple when young. Zones 7–10.

Picea rubens
AMERICAN RED SPRUCE
☼ ❄ ↔ 20 ft (6 m) ↑ 70 ft (21 m)
From North America, often at high
altitudes. Evergreen pyramidal conifer.
Slender branches, scaly red-brown
bark. Grass green leaves, twisted and
crowded, on the uppersides of shoots.
Short cylindrical cones purplish green,
glossy brown at maturity. Zones 4–8.

Picea sitchensis
ALASKA SPRUCE, SITKA SPRUCE
☼ ❄ ↔ 25 ft (8 m) ↑ 100 ft (30 m)
From the west coast of North America.
Broadly conical evergreen conifer,
widely planted for timber. Narrow
stiff leaves, green above, silvery beneath, tips sharply pointed. Favored
Christmas tree. Zones 4–8.

Picea smithiana
syn. *Picea morinda*
WEST HIMALAYAN SPRUCE
☼ ❄ ↔ 20 ft (6 m) ↑ 75 ft (23 m)
Elegant, pyramidal, evergreen conifer
from northern India. Horizontal
branches, cascading foliage. Needle-
like, finely pointed, dark green leaves
surround the branches. Pendulous,
shiny, brown-purple cones. Highly
ornamental. Zones 6–8.

Picea spinulosa
EAST HIMALAYAN SPRUCE, SIKKIM SPRUCE
☼ ❄ ↔ 25 ft (8 m) ↑ 200 ft (60 m)
From the Himalayas. Evergreen
conifer, scaly plated bark. Pendulous
branches, crowded, irregular, overlapping, flattened leaves with sharp tips,
upper-surface dark green, 2 whitish
bands on underside. Cones green,
cylindrical, glossy brown when
mature. Zones 4–8.

Picea wilsonii
WILSON'S SPRUCE
☼ ❄ ↔ 15 ft (4.5 m) ↑ 40 ft (12 m)
Evergreen conifer from China.
Horizontal branch spread, narrow,
dark, glossy, dense, sharp-pointed
leaves. Young shoots smooth, whitish,
shiny, becoming brown and furrowed
with age. Small pale brown cones fall
when mature. Zones 6–10.

PICRASMA
This genus of 8 species of deciduous
trees in the quassia (Simaroubaceae)
family occurs from China throughout
Southeast Asia to the tropical Americas
and the West Indies . They have alternate pinnate leaves crowded at the
branch ends, and bear loose panicles
of tiny bowl-shaped flowers in the leaf
axils. Small berry-like fruits.
CULTIVATION: Plant in full sun or
partial shade in well-drained soil with
protection from cold drying winds.
An open position is best to obtain
the full effect of the bright autumn
foliage colors. Propagate from seed.

Picrasma quassioides
syn. *Picrasma ailanthoides*
☼ ❄ ↔ 25 ft (8 m) ↑ 25 ft (8 m)
Northern Asian species. Erect, wide-
crowned, deciduous tree. Pinnate
leaves, opposite sharp-toothed leaflets,
turning yellow to deep orange in late
autumn. Small pale green flowers in
loose clusters, in summer. Zones 3–9.

PIERIS
This genus belonging to the heath
(Ericaceae) family comes mainly from

Picrasma quassioides

subtropical and temperate regions
of the Himalayas. Widely cultivated
and extensively hybridized, the best
known of the 7 species are common
garden plants and popular evergreen
shrubs for gardens in temperate climates, but the genus also includes a
vine and some shrubby species from
the eastern regions of the USA and
from the West Indies. Typically, the
leaves are simple pointed ellipses,
often with serrated edges, and the
flowers are bell-shaped, downward-
facing, and carried in panicles. They
usually open in spring, and are sometimes scented.
CULTIVATION: Like most members of
the erica family, *Pieris* species prefer
cool, moist, well-drained soil with
ample humus. A position in full sun
yields more flowers; light shade results
in lusher foliage. Heavy pruning is
seldom required as the the plants are
naturally tidy; light trimming and
pinching back is all that is necessary.
Propagate from half-hardened cuttings
or by layering.

Pieris floribunda
FETTER BUSH
☼ ❄ ↔ 7 ft (2 m) ↑ 6 ft (1.8m)
From southeastern USA. Pointed
serrated-edged leaves to 3 in (8 cm)
long. Flowers white, ¼ in (6 mm)
long, carried in showy panicles, in
spring. Flowerheads differ from those
of the Asian species, being stiffer and
held more erect. Zones 5–9.

Pieris 'Forest Flame'
☼ ❄ ↔ 6 ft (1.8 m) ↑ 12 ft (3.5 m)
Hybrid between *P. formosa* 'Wakehurst' and *P. japonica*. Strongly upright shrub, can be kept compact by
pruning. Panicles of white flowers,
in spring. Young foliage bright red,
changing to pink, then cream, then
pale green, then dark green. Zones 6–9.

Picea sitchensis, in the wild, near Paxsom, Alaska, USA

Pieris 'Forest Flame'

Picea purpurea

Picea spinulosa

Picea smithiana

Pieris japonica

Pieris japonica 'Bert Chandler'

Pieris japonica 'Firecrest'

Pieris japonica 'Karenoma'

Pieris japonica 'Little Heath'

Pieris japonica 'Mountain Fire'

Pieris japonica 'Purity'

Pieris japonica 'Robinswood'

Pieris japonica 'Scherzo'

Pieris japonica 'Scarlett O'Hara'

Pieris formosa var. *forrestii*

Pieris japonica 'Valley Fire'

Pieris japonica 'Valley Valentine'

Pieris japonica 'Variegata'

Pieris formosa var. *forrestii* (at rear), in spring

Pieris formosa

☼ ❄ ↔ 7 ft (2 m) ↑ 10 ft (3 m)
Native to the Himalayan region. Leaves are slightly glossy with finely serrated edges. Flower panicles mainly erect but with a tendency to droop,

Pieris japonica 'Whitecaps'

flowers white or sometimes pink-tinted. *P. f.* var. *forrestii*, vivid red new growth, fragrant white flowers in drooping panicles; *P. f.* 'Wakehurst', leaves ageing from red to pink to green. Zones 6–10.

Pieris japonica

syn. *Pieris taiwanensis*

JAPANESE PIERIS, LILY-OF-THE-VALLEY BUSH

☼ ❄ ↔ 8 ft (2.4 m) ↑ 8–10 ft (2.4–3 m)
This species now includes *P. taiwanensis*, found in Japan, Taiwan, and eastern China. Leaves, pink to bronze when young, ageing to dark green. Floral racemes erect or drooping, flowers usually white, in spring. 'Bert Chandler', light pink new growth turning yellow, then green; 'Christmas Cheer', early white and pink flowers; 'Karenoma', red-brown new growth; 'Little Heath', dwarf form, white-edged leaves; 'Mountain Fire' ★, reddish new leaves; 'Purity', white flowers; 'Robinswood', green leaves, yellowish green edges, bright red new growth; 'Valley Valentine', purple-red flowers, crimson buds; 'Variegata', cream and green foliage, young leaves pink-tinted; 'Whitecaps', white flowers. Zones 6–10.

Pieris phillyreifolia

☼ ❄ ↔ 3 ft (0.9 m) ↑ 3 ft (0.9 m)
Unusual species from eastern USA. In the wild behaves like a liana vine. In cultivation train as a small shrub. Leaves small, covered in fine hairs. Racemes of small white flowers in leaf axils, from winter–spring. Zones 7–10.

PILEA

This genus of about 600 creeping, sprawling, or erect annual or perennial herbs, sometimes with a woody base, is a member of the nettle (Urticaceae) family, and is native to tropical regions worldwide except in Australia. Leaves are usually opposite, often unequal, smooth-edged or serrated, covered with carbon deposits (cystoliths) that give the appearance of opalescent spots. From the leaf axils appear solitary flowerheads or loose panicles of minute whitish green flowers that become pinkish brown. The fruits are achenes. Their name comes from the Latin *pileus* (cap), a reference to the shape of the flowers. CULTIVATION: They require abundant moisture during active growth, in any moist, well-drained soil, out of direct sunlight and drafts. Pinch out terminal buds to encourage compact bushy growth. Propagate perennial species from stem cuttings or by division in spring or summer, and annual species from seed in spring or autumn.

Pilea involucrata
FRIENDSHIP PLANT, PANAMICA
☀ ✶ ↔ 6–12 in (15–30 cm)
↑ 4–18 in (10–45 cm)

Evergreen, bushy, hairy, trailing to erect herb, from tropical regions of Central and South America. Branches 8–12 in (20–30 cm) long. Hairy, oval, toothed leaves, to 2½ in (6 cm) long, marked with bronze, red, or silver. Tiny pink or red flowers in summer. 'Moon Valley', quilted, scalloped, oval leaves, tinged with bronze, broad silver central band, edges dotted with silver; 'Norfolk', compact, dense habit, leaves broad, oval, black to dark green, raised silver bands. Zones 10–12.

Pilea peperomioides
☀ ✶ ↔ 6–20 in (15–50 cm)
↑ 6–20 in (15–50 cm)

Erect herb native to the West Indies. Smooth elongated stems. Succulent,

Pilosella aurantiaca

Pimelea ferruginea 'Bonne Petite'

elliptical to nearly circular, pale green, prominently veined leaves, to 3½ in (9 cm) long and wide, on stalks to 2½ in (6 cm) long, resembling those of *Peperomia* species. Insignificant flowers in summer. Zones 10–12.

PILEOSTEGIA
This is a genus of 4 climbing or prostrate evergreen shrubs, members of the hydrangea (Hydrangeaceae) family. They are native to Asia, and grow with the support of aerial roots. They have glossy dark green leaves, and bear large crowded heads of flowers with conspicuous stamens in late summer to early autumn. CULTIVATION: They prefer moist, heavy, loamy soils, in full sun or part-shade, with protection from wind. Propagate from cuttings.

Pileostegia viburnoides
☀/☀ ✶ ↔ 10 ft (3 m) ↑ 20–30 ft (6–9 m)
Woody self-clinging climber from India, Taiwan, and China. Leathery, pitted, narrowly oblong to sword-shaped, dull dark green leaves to 18 in (45 cm) long. White or cream flowers grow in crowded panicles to 6 in (15 cm) across. Zones 7–9.

PILOSELLA
This genus is made up of 18 rhizomatous and hairy perennial herbs, members of the daisy (Asteraceae) family and native to temperate Eurasia and northwestern Africa. Rosettes of few to numerous stems with swollen runners grow from a central base, bearing oval or lobed leaves with smooth or slightly toothed margins. Single or multiple umbrella-shaped flowerheads appear in summer. CULTIVATION: *Pilosella* species prefer well-drained fertile soil in full sun, and a long season of hot weather. Space plants 6 in (15 cm) apart so they can

Pimelea ligustrina

support each other. Propagate from seed germinated in late winter or early spring; transplant in late spring.

Pilosella aurantiaca
☀ ✳ ↔ 16–20 in (40–50 cm)
↑ 20–27 in (50–70 cm)
Perennial herb native to Europe. Pale green, oval to elliptical, hairy leaves, to 8 in (20 cm) long. Bears 2 to 25 flowerheads, to 1 in (25 mm) across, of orange to orange-red florets, at the ends of stalks to 26 in (65 cm) tall, covered with long dark hairs, in summer. Can be invasive. Zones 3–5.

PILOSOCEREUS
This is a genus of around 45 species of shrubby or tree-like cacti in the family Cactaceae, found from Florida, USA, through Central America and the Caribbean, to tropical South America. They have a stocky ribbed trunk that with age becomes deeply furrowed, studded with often woolly areoles. Spines are clustered, some 3 in (8 cm) long. Flowers open at night, developing from exceptionally hairy areoles. They are tubular to bell-shaped, usually white or in pastel shades, and last only a day. The fruits are fleshy and green to purple. CULTIVATION: These large cacti grow well in sun or partial shade. Drought tolerant, they appreciate regular moisture during the growing and flowering seasons, and light well-drained soil with a little extra humus. Some tolerate light frosts, but most grow best in mild frost-free areas. The large tree-like species may be pruned. Propagate from seed or from cuttings of young stems. Allow the cut end to dry before inserting in soil.

Pilosocereus leucocephalus
syns *Cephalocereus maxonii, C. palmeri, C. sartorianus*
OLD MAN CACTUS, OLD MAN OF MEXICO
☀ ✳ ↔ 7–10 ft (2–3 m) ↑ 7–17 ft (2–5 m)
From Mexico, Guatemala, and Honduras. Tree-like plant, branching from below. Stems upright, green to bluish, with 7 to 12 ribs. Spines brownish, becoming gray with age, 1 central and

Pimelea linifolia

8 to 12 radials. Flower-bearing areoles on the upper parts of stems produce white wool. Flowers funnel-shaped to bell-shaped, pink to white. Seed pods green to purple. Zones 8–11.

PIMELEA
This genus consists of about 100 species in the daphne (Thymelaeaceae) family. Evergreen shrubs or subshrubs of Australasian origin, they are valued for their spectacular spring flowering. Some species, known as rice flowers, are highly valued as cut flowers. Plant size can be variable. Flower color is also variable within a species, ranging from white to deep pink; some species produce yellow or purple flowers. Terminal starry flowers with open reflexed tubes appear in showy heads, sometimes surrounded by prominent colored bracts. Fruits are small, dry, or fleshy, and contain a single seed. CULTIVATION: They prefer well-drained acidic soils enriched with organic matter, and full sun or partial shade. They are tolerant of wind and salt-laden air, but dislike heavy frost. They respond well to regular light pruning. Life expectancy is usually short. Propagate from tip cuttings taken from late spring to summer, or from seed when it can be obtained. Germination may be slow.

Pimelea ferruginea
ROSY RICE FLOWER
☀ ✳ ↔ 3 ft (0.9 m) ↑ 3 ft (0.9 m)
Commonly seen species from Western Australia. Tolerant of salt spray. Oval leaves, shiny green, pointed, arranged along the stems. Clusters of pink, open, tubular flowers appear on the branch tips in spring, and intermittently at other times. 'Bonne Petite', profuse clusters of pink flowers. Zones 8–10.

P

Pimelea ligustrina
TALL RICE FLOWER

☼ ❄ ↔ 4 ft (1.2 m) ↕ 5 ft (1.5 m)

From alpine areas of southern Australia. Bushy evergreen shrub. Smooth light green leaves. White flowers on branch tips, silky-edged green bracts, orange anthers, in pincushion-like flowerheads, in spring. Attracts moths and butterflies. Zones 8–10.

Pimelea linifolia
SLENDER RICE FLOWER

☼/◐ ❄ ↔ 2 ft (0.6 m) ↕ 3 ft (0.9 m)

Evergreen shrub from southern Australia. Leaves small, soft, narrow, oval. White flowers, hairy orange anthers, broad floral bracts, held in roundish heads, in early spring, intermittently at other times. Zones 8–10.

Pimelea nivea
WHITE COTTON BUSH

☼ ❄ ↔ 3 ft (0.9 m) ↕ 6 ft (1.8 m)

Sometimes straggly evergreen shrub from Tasmania, Australia. White or occasionally pink, star-shaped flowers, in large heads, in summer. White hairs cover plant, except upper surfaces of the small round to oval glossy dark green leaves. Zones 8–9.

Pimelea physodes
QUALUP BELLS

☼ ⬩ ↔ 2 ft (0.6 m) ↕ 3 ft (0.9 m)

From Western Australia. Small hanging flowers surrounded by large red bracts. Popular cut flower. Thrives in the harsh silica soils of the Stirling Ranges. Difficult to cultivate outside its natural range. Zones 9–10.

Pimelea prostrata
NEW ZEALAND DAPHNE

☼ ❄ ↔ 36 in (90 cm) ↕ 6 in (15 cm)

From New Zealand. Evergreen, prostrate shrub, dense foliage. Leaves tiny,

Pimelea nivea

blue-gray, along the wiry stems in 4 rows. Small white flowers, in summer. Fruits small white berries. Excellent embankment and spillover plant. Zones 8–10.

PIMPINELLA

This genus of about 150 annual or perennial herbs with branching stems, members of the carrot (Apiaceae) family, is native to temperate Eurasia and North Africa. The leaves may be simple, or they may be divided with up to 3 leaflets. Compound umbels of small white or yellow flowers appear in summer, and are followed by oval fruits. One species, *P. anisum* (anise), is widely cultivated for its medicinal and flavoring value.

CULTIVATION: They will grow in light and dry to marshy, wet, alkaline soils, in an open, sunny position. Propagate from seed.

Pimpinella anisum
ANISE, ANISEED

☼ ❄ ↔ 16–20 in (40–50 cm) ↕ 20–24 in (50–60 cm)

Annual, aromatic, finely hairy herb, native to eastern, central, and southern Europe, to the eastern parts of the Mediterranean, and to Syria and Egypt. Grown for the distinctive flavor of its seeds. On its stems it bears rounded or oval leaves, finely cut into 3 narrow leaflets, and simple, broader, oval, toothed or slightly lobed leaves grow closer to the

Pinellia cordata

Pimelea physodes

ground. In mid-summer, thin stems are topped with umbrella-shaped clusters of 7 to 15 daisy-like yellow or white flowers, heavy enough to make the stems flop. Zones 4–8.

PINANGA

This large genus in the palm (Arecaceae) family contains 120 species, occurring as understory plants in moist shady forests in China, Southeast Asia, and New Guinea. Height varies; some species have multiple trunks. Leaf shape varies within the genus from undivided to pinnate, with few to many leaflets. Separate male and female flowers are borne on the same inflorescence, on stalks often brightly colored, usually reddish and swollen. The fruits are also often brightly colored.

CULTIVATION: All species require a shady position with plenty of water and high humidity. Most make good indoor plants, provided the level of humidity is not too low. In the garden many adapt to a neutral well-drained soil. Fresh seed of most species germinates readily; clumping species can be divided into two or more new plants.

Pinanga kuhlii ★

☼ ⬩ ↔ 10 ft (3 m) ↕ 25 ft (8 m)

Native to Java and Sumatra, Indonesia, cultivated widely. Several smooth stems. Leaves all along the trunk (not just at the top), divided into 6 to 8 pairs of broad leaflets. Inflorescences bearing cream to pink flowers. Dark reddish egg-shaped fruits. Zones 11–12.

Pimelea prostrata

PINELLIA

A genus of 6 species in the arum (Araceae) family that come from wooded regions of China, Korea, and Japan. They are summer-growing tuberous perennials that have handsome leaves and strange usually green flowers consisting of a slightly hooded spathe with a long curving spadix.

CULTIVATION: Grow *Pinellia* species in a semi-shaded aspect in moisture-retentive soil. Propagate from seed sown as soon as it is ripe, or by division of tubers when dormant. Some species produce tiny bulbils where the stem and leaf meet.

Pinellia cordata

◐ ❄ ↔ 4–6 in (10–15 cm) ↕ 4–6 in (10–15 cm)

Chinese species. Deep green spearhead-shaped leaves marked with white, and with purple undersides. It produces a single bulbil where the stem joins the leaf. Flowers are held at same level as the leaf and are green throughout. Zones 6–10.

Pinanga kuhlii

Pinus aristata, in the wild, Mount Washington, Great Basin National Park, Nevada, USA

Pinus albicaulis

PINGUICULA
BUTTERWORTS, PINGS

A varied genus of more than 75 carnivorous plants belonging to the bladderwort (Lentibulariaceae) family, found in a variety of damp tropical and temperate habitats in North America, Asia, and Europe. In South America they favor drier conditions, sometimes as epiphytes. Most are perennials, with fibrous roots, very pale to bright green leaves forming a rosette, and beautiful flowers held singly on leafless stems. Some species form a tight winter resting-bud (hibernacula). Tiny glandular hairs covering the leaves produce a greasy mucilage. Once an insect is trapped by this, a second type of gland

Pinus albicaulis 'Nana'

produces digestive enzymes to break it down. The leaves were traditionally used to curdle milk and heal sores on the udders of cattle.
CULTIVATION: Tropical species prefer an equal mix of sand, peat, and perlite, and filtered sun; keep moist in spring and summer, and just damp in winter, when succulent non-carnivorous leaves form. Feed each week in spring and summer with a weak foliar fertilizer. In temperate areas grow in a warm greenhouse or on a sunny windowsill. Propagate from leaf cuttings of winter leaves. Temperate species prefer an equal mix of peat and sand or vermiculite, and filtered light. If grown in pots water by tray in spring and summer; keep plants with hibernacula fairly dry in winter. Propagate from leaf cuttings. Re-pot in winter.

Pinguicula emarginata
☼/◐ ❄ ↔ 4 in (10 cm) ↕ 1½ in (35 mm)
Lovely species from Mexico, found in damp sandy soil. Oval-shaped green

Pinus armandii

leaves 2 in (5 cm) long. Pretty ¾ in (18 mm) flowers, white to violet, with violet to purple veins. *P. e.* × *P. vulgaris*, purple or violet flowers spotted with white. Zones 8–11.

Pinguicula moranensis ★
syn. *Pinguicola caudata*
☼ ❄ ↔ 10 in (25 cm) ↕ 2 in (5 cm)
Native to Mexico, growing in damp, mossy soil in filtered light. Oval green leaves to 5 in (12 cm) long, slightly curved edges, sometimes tinged pink. Flowers to 2 in (5 cm) wide, lavender or pink, sometimes pink and white or all white. Zones 8–11.

Pinguicula vulgaris ★
COMMON BUTTERWORT
☼/◐ ❄ ↔ 5 in (12 cm) ↕ 2 in (5 cm)
From rocky mountainous areas of Europe and North America, in open grass or bogs. Leaves yellow to green, curved inwards along edge. Violet-like flowers held singly on 6 in (15 cm) stems. Often found growing near carnivorous *Darlingtonia californica* and *Drosera intermedia*. Zones 2–7.

PINUS
PINE

This very variable genus of conifers in the pine (Pinaceae) family has around 110 species, found throughout Europe, Asia, northern Africa, North and Central America, and the West Indies.

They grow in a range of climates and conditions, from tropical equatorial forests to the extreme cold at the edge of the Arctic Circle. Predominantly large trees, only a couple of species are shrubs. The leaves are needle-like, and may be quite small to as long as 18 in (45 cm). They are generally found in bundles of 3 or 5, with never more than 8 in a group. The seed cones vary in shape, color, and dimension. The genus includes some of the world's most important timber species.
CULTIVATION: Most can easily withstand cold and extended dry periods, and also tolerate a range of soils, although they must have full sun. Some species are popular for bonsai. Propagation of the species is from seed; the cultivars are grafted.

Pinus albicaulis
WHITEBARK PINE
☼ ❄ ↔ 20 ft (6 m) ↕ 30 ft (9 m)
Native to the mountains of southwestern Canada and northeastern USA. Evergreen tree, larger in the wild. Bark smooth and white, turns gray and separates with age. Spreading ascending branches, short yellow-green needles. Small persistent cones. Dwarf cultivars include 'Flick', 'Nana', 'Noble's Dwarf'. Zones 4–8.

Pinus aristata
ROCKY MOUNTAIN BRISTLECONE PINE
☼ ❄ ↔ 15 ft (4.5 m) ↕ 15 ft (4.5 m)
Small tree from mountainous and subalpine western USA. Slow growing, irregularly shaped, dense crown of short, resin-flecked, 2 in (5 cm) long leaves. Cones have a brittle prickle. Some specimens have been dated at around 2,500 years old. Zones 4–7.

Pinus armandii
CHINESE WHITE PINE, DAVID'S PINE
☼ ❄ ↔ 20 ft (6 m) ↕ 60 ft (18 m)
Large tree from central and western China, southern Japan, and the island of Taiwan. Wide-spreading horizontal branches. Green leaves to 6 in (15 cm) long. Ovoid, pendulous, yellow-brown cones. Zones 5–7.

Pinguicula moranensis

Pinguicula emarginata × *P. vulgaris*

Pinus bungeana

Pinus brutia

Pinus bungeana

Pinus canariensis

Pinus attenuata

KNOBCONE PINE

☼ ❋ ↔ 20 ft (6 m) ↑ 50 ft (15 m)

Naturally occurring in rocky mountainous soils in Oregon and California, USA. Medium tree, narrow pointed crown, horizontal to ascending branches. Groups of 3 yellow-green leaves. The large woody cones can remain unopened on the tree for decades. Zones 7–10.

Pinus ayacahuite

MEXICAN WHITE PINE

☼ ❋ ↔ 20 ft (6 m) ↑ 90 ft (27 m)

Central American tree. Conical or oval in habit, older trees more irregularly shaped. Green leaves, bluish cast, 3 in (8 cm) long. Very resinous cylindrical cones, to 12 in (30 cm) long fall in autumn. Zones 8–11.

Pinus balfouriana

FOXTAIL PINE

☼ ❋ ↔ 20 ft (6 m) ↑ 50 ft (15 m)

From mountains of California; very uncommon in the wild. Narrowly conical, stiff 1 in (25 mm) needles, crowded in groups of 5, slightly upcurved. Pendulous, symmetrical, brown cones, 2 years to mature. Zones 7–9.

Pinus banksiana

JACK PINE

☼ ❋ ↔ 20 ft (6 m) ↑ 60 ft (18 m)

Native to southern Canada and northeastern USA. Straight tree,

irregular in outline, short twisted leaves growing in pairs. Light brown cones slightly curved. The species is grown and harvested for pulpwood, telephone poles, and railway ties, and is planted for land rehabilitation and for commercial trade in Christmas trees. Zones 2–8.

Pinus brutia

syn. *Pinus halepensis* var. *brutia*

TURKISH PINE

☼ ❋ ↔ 20 ft (6 m) ↑ 60 ft (18 m)

Open-crowned tree from the eastern Mediterranean with irregular branching. Leaves bright green, 6 in (15 cm) long, fairly stiff. The small cones are horizontal or erect, ripening to a shiny red-brown. Zones 8–10.

Pinus cembroides 'Pina Nevada Gold'

Pinus bungeana

LACEBARK PINE

☼ ❋ ↔ 20 ft (6 m) ↑ 60 ft (18 m)

Multi-trunked tree from northwestern China. Rare in cultivation. Stiff leaves give off the smell of turpentine when crushed. Cones small and egg-shaped. Gray-green peeling bark, splotched white and brown. Zones 5–9.

Pinus canariensis

CANARY ISLAND PINE

☼ ❋ ↔ 25 ft (8 m) ↑ 130 ft (40 m)

From the Canary Islands. Straight solid main trunk, dense oval crown of 6–12 in (15–30 cm) needles that tend to droop. Attractive dark reddish brown bark, shiny, brown cones. Naturalized in Australia and South Africa. Zones 8–11.

Pinus cembra

AROLLA PINE, SWISS STONE PINE

☼ ❋ ↔ 15 ft (4.5 m) ↑ 30 ft (9 m)

From central Europe. Narrowly conical to almost columnar in shape, branching from ground level up. Densely foliaged with stiff 3 in (8 cm) needles, dark green and twisted. Small cones on very old trees. '**Chlorocarpa**', popular cultivar. Zones 4–7.

Pinus cembroides

MEXICAN NUT PINE, PINYON

☼ ❋ ↔ 15 ft (4.5 m) ↑ 25 ft (8 m)

Small tree from Mexico and southern USA. Rounded crown, short gray-

Pinus densiflora

Pinus densiflora 'Pendula'

green leaves. Pale yellow to glossy brown, symmetrical, oval cones. An important food source; the edible nuts are high in protein. '**Pina Nevada Gold**', attractive cultivar. Zones 7–8.

Pinus contorta

LODGEPOLE PINE, SHORE PINE

☼ ❋ ↔ 25 ft (8 m) ↑ 75 ft (23 m)

Tall tree native to western North America, from Alaska to Mexico. Variable in habit, generally tall, straight, conical. Dense, stiff, dark green needles, small, asymmetrical, orange-brown cones. Zones 5–9.

Pinus coulteri

BIG-CONE PINE, COULTER PINE

☼ ❋ ↔ 30 ft (9 m) ↑ 100 ft (30 m)

From the dry mountain slopes of California, USA. Fast-growing imposing conifer. Long, stiff, glaucous green needles in bundles of 3. Huge, spiny, brown cones. Tolerates all soils as well as wind and drought. Zones 8–10.

Pinus densiflora

JAPANESE RED PINE

☼ ❋ ↔ 20 ft (6 m) ↑ 70 ft (21 m)

Tree from Japan, Korea, and China. Open irregular crown. Green leaves, 5 in (12 cm) long, growing in tufts at ends of branches. Bark reddish brown, cones dull brown. '**Pendula**' ★, vigorous, semi-prostrate; '**Umbraculifera**', very slow-growing, shaped like an umbrella. Zones 4–9.

Pinus contorta, in the wild, Yellowstone River at Hayden Valley, Wyoming, USA

Pinus durangensis
DURANGO PINE

☀ ❄ ↔ 25 ft (8 m) ↑ 130 ft (40 m)

Mexican species. Conical to rounded crown. This is the only pine to hold its needles in bundles of 6. Needles gray-green, to 8 in (20 cm) long. Red-brown cones, oval to conical, with a sharp prickle. Zones 8–11.

Pinus edulis
NUT PINE, ROCKY MOUNTAIN PINYON

☀ ❄ ↔ 20 ft (6 m) ↑ 25 ft (8 m)

Found on dry mountain slopes in southwestern USA and Mexico. Small tree with a rounded crown. Short, stiff, blue-green leaves. Small, symmetrical cone, edible nuts. Zones 5–9.

Pinus elliottii
SLASH PINE

☀ ❄ ↔ 25 ft (8 m) ↑ 100 ft (30 m)

From southeastern USA. Straight central leader, often free of lower branches to a considerable height. Leaves 8 in (20 cm) long. Cones caramel colored, bark sheds in thin flakes. This species is an important timber tree, valued for its strong heavy wood. Zones 7–11.

Pinus engelmannii
APACHE PINE, ENGELMANN PINE

☀ ❄ ↔ 20 ft (6 m) ↑ 100 ft (30 m)

Tall tree from Mexico and southwestern USA, often found in dry mountain ranges. Open rounded crown, leaves to 15 in (38 cm) long. Asymmetrical cones, occuring in groups of 4 or pairs. Zones 8–10.

Pinus flexilis
LIMBER PINE

☀ ❄ ↔ 20 ft (6 m) ↑ 40 ft (12 m)

Small to medium tree from western North America. Dense conical shape when young, broadening out with age. Short dark green needles, yellow-brown cones. Some specimens have been dated at over 1,600 years old. Zones 4–7.

Pinus glabra
SPRUCE PINE

☀ ❄ ↔ 20 ft (6 m) ↑ 100 ft (30 m)

Found in southeastern USA, particularly on the coastal plain. Dark gray bark, almost smooth at first but roughening with age. Narrow open crown, medium-sized leaves. Small reddish brown cones often remain on the tree for several years. Tolerates shade. Zones 9–11.

Pinus halepensis
ALEPPO PINE

☀ ❄ ↔ 20 ft (6 m) ↑ 60 ft (18 m)

Mediterranean tree with low branches and a flattened top. Leaves are 4 in (10 cm) long, often curved and twisted. Medium-sized cones persist for many years. Naturalized in parts of Australia, South Africa, and New Zealand. Zones 8–11.

Pinus hartwegii
syn. *Pinus montezumae* var. *hartwegii*

☀ ❄ ↔ 25 ft (8 m) ↑ 100 ft (30 m)

Tall tree with a dome-shaped crown, from Mexico, Guatemala, and El Salvador. Leaves 6 in (15 cm) long, dark green. Cones variable in shape, very dark brown to purple-black when mature. Zones 8–11.

Pinus heldreichii
BOSNIAN PINE

☀ ❄ ↔ 20 ft (6 m) ↑ 60 ft (18 m)

Found on the western Balkan Peninsula southward to Greece. Sometimes shrubby tree. Irregular outline, open habit. Leaves stiff and sharp. Cones in clusters of 2, 3, or 4, opening when ripe. *P. h.* var. *leucodermis*, used as an ornamental; 'Compact Gem', dwarf cultivar, dark green needles; *P. h.* 'Smidtii', compact dwarf, bright green needles. Zones 6–9.

Pinus hwangshanensis

☀ ❄ ↔ 20 ft (6 m) ↑ 80 ft (24 m)

Eastern Chinese tree, very similar to *P. thunbergii*. Paired bright green needles, 2–3 in (5–8 cm) long. Cones up to 2 in (5 cm) long. Zones 7–10.

Pinus jeffreyi
JEFFREY PINE

☀ ❄ ↔ 25 ft (8 m) ↑ 200 ft (60 m)

Occurs in western regions of North America from Oregon, USA, to Baja California, Mexico. Straight-trunked tree, irregular outline. Large red-brown cones, 8 in (20 cm) long needles. New growth and bark aromatic. Important timber tree. Zones 6–9.

Pinus koraiensis
KOREAN PINE

☀ ❄ ↔ 20 ft (6 m) ↑ 90 ft (27 m)

From southeastern China, northern Korea, and central Japan. Narrow conical outline when young, rounded with age; smaller in cultivation. Rough bluish needles, 4 in (10 cm) long. Not widely cultivated. Zones 3–9.

Pinus lambertiana
SUGAR PINE

☀ ❄ ↔ 20 ft (6 m) ↑ 150 ft (45 m)

Occurs from central Oregon, USA, to northern Baja California, Mexico. Extremely tall tree; has been known to reach a height of 216 ft (65 m). Narrow irregular crown. Needles stiff, sharp, bluish. Pendulous cones, 20 in (50 cm) long, on long stalks. Valuable timber species. Zones 7–9.

Pinus leiophylla
SMOOTH-LEAF PINE

☀ ❄ ↔ 15 ft (4.5 m) ↑ 50 ft (18 m)

From southeastern Arizona, southwestern New Mexico, USA, and Mexico. Small to medium tree, irregular narrow crown. Gray-green needles. Small, symmetrical, egg-shaped cones, in pairs on short stems. Will sprout from a cut stump. Zones 7–10.

Pinus edulis, Checkerboard Mesa, Utah, USA

Pinus engelmannii

Pinus hartwegii

Pinus jeffreyi, in the wild, Baja California, Mexico

Pinus flexilis, in the wild, Yellowstone National Park, Wyoming, USA

P. halepensis, in the wild, Majorca, Spain

Pinus hwangshanensis

P

Pinus mugo

Pinus mugo 'Paul's Dwarf'

Pinus mugo var. *pumilio*

Pinus mugo 'Green Candles'

Pinus longaeva

ANCIENT PINE, GREAT BASIN
BRISTLECONE PINE

☀ ❄ ↔ 15 ft (4.5 m) ↑ 60 ft (18 m)

From the dry subalpine peaks of western USA. Small stiff leaves, medium-sized cones. Often asymmetrical, due to harsh growing conditions, or occasionally partially dead. Zones 5–8.

Pinus lumholtzii

LUMHOLTZ PINE

☀ ❄ ↔ 20 ft (6 m) ↑ 70 ft (21 m)

Occurs in the mountains of western and northwestern Mexico. Open crown of horizontal branches. Very long bright green leaves, reaching 12 in (30 cm), hanging straight down. Symmetrical, oval, pendulous, brown cones, to 2 in (5 cm). Zones 8–10.

Pinus merkusii

SUMATRAN PINE

☀ ❄ ↔ 20 ft (6 m) ↑ 150 ft (45 m)

Only species found south of the equator, in Sumatra, Indonesia, and also in the Philippines. Conical to rounded crown, stiff needles 8 in (20 cm) long. Cones single or in pairs. Tapped to produce turpentine. Zones 9–12.

Pinus monophylla

SINGLE-LEAF PINYON

☀ ❄ ↔ 15 ft (4.5 m) ↑ 30 ft (9 m)

Occurs naturally in semi-arid country in Nevada, Arizona, and California, USA, and Baja California, Mexico. Multi-stemmed, leaves gray-green, 2 in (5 cm) long, stiff, curved, occur singly. Small cones hold edible nuts. 'Glauca', bluish foliage. Zones 6–9.

Pinus montezumae

MONTEZUMA PINE, ROUGH-BARKED
MEXICAN PINE

☀ ❄ ↔ 25 ft (8 m) ↑ 100 ft (30 m)

Large tree from southern Mexico and Guatemala. Dense conical outline when young, lower branches spreading, sagging with age. Arching or pendulous leaves. Cones oval to conical, light brown, with a small deciduous prickle. Zones 9–11.

Pinus monticola

WESTERN WHITE PINE

☀ ❄ ↔ 20 ft (6 m) ↑ 100 ft (30 m)

Growing in northwestern North America, from Canada to California and eastward to Montana, USA. Large tree, narrow crown, solid straight main trunk. Foliage dense, leaves to 4 in (10 cm) long. Narrow cylindrical cones. Valuable timber. Zones 4–9.

Pinus mugo

DWARF MOUNTAIN PINE, MUGO PINE,
SWISS MOUNTAIN PINE

☀ ❄ ↔ 12 ft (3.5 m) ↑ 25 ft (8 m)

From the mountains of central Europe. Small tree, often shrub-like, windswept habit. Long, bright green, needle leaves growing in pairs. Cones small, dark brown. Favorite for bonsai cultivation, containers, and rock gardens. Many forms tolerant of a wide range of soils. *P. m.* var. *pumilio,* low-growing form, can be invasive in cool high-rainfall areas. *P. m.* 'Green Candles', dense shrub; 'Honeycomb', very compact rounded form, yellowish foliage; 'Paul's Dwarf', 'Slowmound', tiny needle-like leaves; 'Tannenbaum',

very erect symmetrical form with a pointed leader; 'Teeny', attractive dwarf form. Zones 2–8.

Pinus muricata

BISHOP PINE

☀ ❄ ↔ 20 ft (6 m) ↑ 30 ft (9 m)

Occurs in western USA, and Baja California and Isla Cedros, Mexico; fairly rare in the wild. Small tree, open rounded crown, flat-topped with age. Needles green, bluish in the northern populations. Glossy red-brown cones stay on the tree for decades. Zones 8–10.

Pinus nigra

AUSTRIAN PINE, BLACK PINE, CORSICAN PINE

☀ ❄ ↔ 25 ft (8 m) ↑ 120 ft (36 m)

Variable species, naturally occurring in southern Europe. Straight central trunk, silvery gray. Stiff needles 6 in (15 cm) long, cones light brown, glossy. Important timber tree, naturalized in New Zealand and parts of the USA. 'Hornibrookiana', dwarf cultivar forming a compact mound. Zones 4–9.

Pinus oaxacana

☀ ❄ ↔ 20 ft (6 m) ↑ 80–100 ft (24–30 m)

Found in mountainous regions from southeastern Mexico to Honduras. Beautiful pine with long, drooping,

soft green needles in groups of 5, to 12 in (30 cm) long. Dark brown ovoid cones. Zones 9–11.

Pinus occidentalis

☀ ❄ ↔ 25 ft (8 m) ↑ 100 ft (30 m)

Tall tree from Haiti and the Dominican Republic. Often clear of branches for two thirds of its height. Dense tufts of rigid leaves at ends of branches. Cones oval, symmetrical, scales have a short prickle. Zones 9–12.

Pinus oocarpa

OCOTE PINE

☀ ❄ ↔ 20 ft (6 m) ↑ 70 ft (21 m)

From Central America, Mexico, Guatemala, Honduras, and Nicaragua. Dense, rounded crown of stiff, rough needles. Yellowish oval to round cones release seeds after extended dry period, remaining on the tree. Zones 9–11.

P

Pinus nigra

Pinus montezumae

Pinus oaxacana

Pinus leiophylla

Pinus palustris

Pinus parviflora

Pinus peuce 'Compacta'

Pinus pinaster

Pinus pumila

Pinus ponderosa, in the wild, Yosemite National Park, California, USA

Pinus palustris
LONG-LEAF PINE, PITCH PINE

☀ ❄ ↔ 15 ft (4.5 m) ↑ 100 ft (30 m)

From southeastern USA. Open crown, straight trunk. Long leaves to 18 in (45 cm), clustered at branch tips. Brown cones have short thorns. Seedlings look like a tuft of grass before trunk develops. Zones 7–10.

Pinus parviflora
JAPANESE WHITE PINE

☀ ❄ ↔ 20 ft (6 m) ↑ 80 ft (24 m)

From Japan. Dense rounded crown, half the species height in cultivation. Stiff, curved, blue-green leaves. Redbrown oval to cylindrical cones. Slow growing, favorite bonsai species. 'Adcock's Dwarf', small, grows slowly to 30 in (75 cm). Zones 4–9.

Pinus patula
MEXICAN PINE, WEEPING PINE

☀ ❄ ↔ 30 ft (9 m) ↑ 50 ft (15 m)

From the mountains of Mexico. Broadly conical stout-trunked conifer, horizontal branches, fine weeping foliage. Long pale green needles in groups of 3. Clusters of 2 to 5 brown, conical, curved cones. Zones 7–10.

Pinus peuce
MACEDONIAN PINE

☀ ❄ ↔ 25 ft (8 m) ↑ 120 ft (36 m)

From the Balkan Peninsula. Large tree, slender conical crown, branches to ground level. Bark on young trees silvery gray. Grayish-green very thin leaves, narrow pendulous cones, to 8 in (20 cm). 'Compacta', compact dense foliage. Zones 5–9.

Pinus pinaster
CLUSTER PINE, MARITIME PINE

☀ ❄ ↔ 30 ft (9 m) ↑ 100 ft (30 m)

From the Mediterranean; world's main source of resin. Long, stiff, shiny, gray-green needles, in pairs. Ornamental bark, deep red-brown fissures between gray plates. Orange-brown cones. Enjoys coastal situations. Zones 7–10.

Pinus pinea
ROMAN PINE, STONE PINE, UMBRELLA PINE

☀ ❄ ↔ 20 ft (6 m) ↑ 80 ft (24 m)

From southern Europe and Turkey. Flat-topped conifer, fissured reddish gray bark, leaning trunk. Needles bright green, in pairs. Rounded cones, resinous, shiny, brown. Edible seeds known as "pine nuts." Zones 8–10.

Pinus ponderosa
PONDEROSA PINE, WESTERN YELLOW PINE

☀ ❄ ↔ 20 ft (6 m) ↑ 130 ft (40 m)

From western North America. Solid straight trunk, fissured pale yellow bark. Prickly brown cones to 6 in (15 cm). Stiff pointed leaves to 10 in (25 cm). Used for timber. Zones 3–9.

Pinus pumila
DWARF SIBERIAN PINE, JAPANESE STONE PINE

☀ ❄ ↔ 10 ft (3 m) ↑ 10 ft (3 m)

Occurs in extremely cold regions of northeastern Asia. Dwarf, often creeping shrub. Glossy, dense, twisted needles. Oval cones 2 in (5 cm) long, dark when young, maturing to yellow-brown. Many cultivars. Zones 5–9.

Pinus radiata
syn. *Pinus insignis*
MONTEREY PINE, RADIATA PINE

☀ ❄ ↔ 25 ft (8 m) ↑ 100 ft (30 m)

From coastal central California, USA, and Guadalupe and Cedros Islands off Mexico. Tall tree, straight trunk, irregular, open crown. Leaves 6 in (15 cm) long. Cones asymmetrically conical, 5 in (12 cm) long. Very important timber tree. Zones 8–10.

Pinus resinosa
RED PINE

☀ ❄ ↔ 20 ft (6 m) ↑ 100 ft (30 m)

From northeastern USA and southeastern Canada. Reddish brown bark. Sharp, pointed, 5 in (12 cm) leaves. Symmetrical oval to conical cone 2 in (5 cm) long. Trunk straight, crown narrow oval. Timber tree. Zones 2–8.

Pinus rigida
NORTHERN PITCH PINE

☀ ❄ ↔ 20 ft (6 m) ↑ 100 ft (30 m)

From northeastern USA and southeastern Canada. Smaller than the species in cultivation. Multiple trunks, irregular outline, flattened top. Stiff spread-out leaves, Cones curved, light brown, 3 in (8 cm) long, in clusters. Sprouts from the trunk and base after fire. Zones 4–8.

Pinus roxburghii
CHIR PINE, HIMALAYAN LONG-LEAF PINE

☀ ❄ ↔ 15 ft (4.5 m) ↑ 100 ft (30 m)

Broad-crowned tree from Himalayan foothills. Mottled gray and light brown bark. Sharp-pointed pendulous leaves. Cones 8 in (20 cm) long, light brown. In Nepal, the resin is used for medicinal purposes. Zones 6–11.

Pinus sabiniana
DIGGER PINE, GRAY PINE

☀ ❄ ↔ 20 ft (6 m) ↑ 70 ft (21 m)

Drought-tolerant, native to California, USA, with open irregular crown. Forked trunk, often free of branches for quite some height. Drooping gray-green leaves. Heavily spiked cones bear edible seeds. Zones 8–11.

Pinus serotina
POND PINE

☀ ❄ ↔ 35 ft (10 m) ↑ 70 ft (21 m)

From swamps and poor marshy soils of southeastern USA, from Alabama to New Jersey. Open crown of straight leaves, 8 in (20 cm) long. Cones light brown, symmetrical, almost round, with small spines. Young trees sprout from cut stumps. Zones 3–9.

Pinus strobus
EASTERN WHITE PINE, WHITE PINE

☀ ❄ ↔ 20 ft (6 m) ↑ 165 ft (50 m)

From southeastern Canada and northeastern USA. Tall tree, straight trunk, irregular crown of horizontal branches. Leaves blue-green and pendulous; symmetrical cones. Useful timber tree. 'Banzai Nana', bright green foliage; 'Fastigiata', upcurved branches; 'Horsford', compact habit, rich green foliage; 'Nana', dwarf form; 'Pendula',

Pinus rigida, in the wild, Cape Cod, USA

Pinus resinosa, in the wild, Minnesota, USA

P

Pinus strobus 'Fastigiata'

Pinus strobus 'Pendula'

Pinus strobus 'Prostrata'

Pinus strobus, in the wild, Algonquin National Park, Ontario, Canada

weeping branches; '**Prostrata**', low spreading habit; '**Radiata**', dwarf form, light green foliage. Zones 3–9.

Pinus sylvestris

SCOTCH PINE, SCOTS PINE

☼ ❄ ↔ 20 ft (6 m) ↑ 100 ft (30 m)

Across Europe and northern Asia. Round-crowned tree, straight trunk, smaller in cultivation. Pairs of bluish green leaves. Gray-green symmetrical cones 2½ in (6 cm) long. Valuable for timber and as Christmas trees. *P. s.* var. *lapponica*, smaller leaves and cones; *P. s.* var. *mongolica*, leaves up to 4 in (10 cm) long; *P. s.* '**Argentea**' (syn. 'Edwin Hillier'), silver-blue foliage; '**Fastigiata**', narrow erect habit, to 25 ft (8 m) tall; '**Moseri**', dwarf form, yellowish needles; '**Saxatilis**', low growing, dark green leaves; '**Troopsii**', appealing foliage; '**Watereri**', bluish leaves, slow growing, eventually

Pinus sylvestris 'Saxatilis'

Pinus sylvestris, in the wild, Scotland

Pinus strobus 'Pendula'

reaching 12–15 ft (3.5–4.5 m) tall, can be invasive in cool high-rainfall areas. Zones 2–9.

Pinus tabuliformis

CHINESE RED PINE

☼ ❄ ↔ 20 ft (6 m) ↑ 80 ft (24 m)

From temperate montane areas, central and northern China. Broad-crowned, flat-topped with age, needles crowded at branch tips. Buff, oval, symmetrical cones, small prickle. Zones 5–10.

Pinus taeda

LOBLOLLY PINE

☼ ❄ ↔ 25 ft (8 m) ↑ 100 ft (30 m)

Leading timber tree, southeastern USA. Dense oval crown, straight trunk, lower half often free of branches. Twisted bright green leaves, oval to conical cones 4 in (10 cm) long. Zones 7–11.

Pinus thunbergii

JAPANESE BLACK PINE

☼ ❄ ↔ 20 ft (6 m) ↑ 130 ft (40 m)

Tall tree from Japan and South Korea. Irregular outline, single main trunk

Pinus sylvestris var. *lapponica*

Pinus tabuliformis

Pinus strobus 'Horsford'

often curved. Dense dark green leaves, small oval cones. Popular for bonsai and Japanese-style gardens. Cultivars include '**Majestic Beauty**' and the attractive '**Tsukasa**', both compact and hardy. Zones 5–9.

Pinus virginiana

SCRUB PINE, VIRGINIA PINE

☼ ❄ ↔ 20 ft (6 m) ↑ 50 ft (15 m)

From eastern USA. Leaves in pairs, red-brown, oval to conical, symmetrical cones. Variable species in the wild, often open-crowned and contorted. Dense, conical, young trees are grown in plantations for sale as Christmas trees. Zones 4–9.

Pinus wallichiana

BHUTAN PINE, BLUE PINE, HIMALAYAN PINE

☼ ❄ ↔ 20 ft (6 m) ↑ 150 ft (45 m)

Very tall tree with a conical crown, naturally occurring in the Himalayas. Blue-green leaves reach 8 in (20 cm) long, frequently arching or drooping. Cones very long, thin and cylindrical, hanging from the tips of the branches. Zones 6–9.

Pinus strobus 'Banzai Nana'

Pinus wallichiana

Pinus taeda

Pinus yunnanensis

YUNNAN PINE

☼ ❄ ↔ 30 ft (9 m) ↑ 50 ft (15 m)

From temperate montane areas of southwestern China. Conical outline becomes flat with age. Leaves pendulous, thin, to 12 in (30 cm). Cones pale brown to red-brown, oval to egg-shaped, in groups of 3. Zones 8–10.

P

Piper nigrum

Piper aduncum

Piptanthus nepalensis

PIPER

Belonging to the pepper (Piperaceae) family, this large genus of about 2,000 species of shrubs, trees and, more usually, woody-stemmed climbers is widely distributed in tropical regions. Smooth-edged, alternate, prominently veined leaves are often aromatic. Tiny flowers, borne in a dense axillary spike or raceme, are followed by small, single-seeded fruit. *P. nigrum* is the source of black and white pepper used throughout the world as a seasoning. CULTIVATION: All species are frost tender. In temperate climates, they make decorative indoor plants, climbing species needing some support structure. Indoors they are best suited to humid conditions and good light. Outdoor plants require a protected position in moist, fertile, well-drained soil in full sun or partial shade. Propagate from seed, half-hardened cuttings or by division.

Piper aduncum

COW'S FOOT, FALSE KAVA, FALSE MATICO, JOINTWOOD, SPIKED PEPPER

☼ ✿ ↔ 8–17 ft (2.4–5 m)
↑ 17–25 ft (5–8 m)

This multi-branched shrub or small tree is native to Central America and northern South America. The trunk grows to 4 in (10 cm) or more in diameter. It has erect branches with smooth gray bark, and cord-like flexible flower spikes growing from stems. The leaves, which are opposite, alternate, and elliptical, grow to 10 in (25 cm) long, with tapered, pointed tips. The fruit is a berry containing small black seeds. All parts have a peppery taste and odor. The plant is used medicinally in a variety of ways: as an aromatic stimulant; to prevent gonorrhea, leukorrhea, hemorrhoids, hemorrhages, and dyspepsia; and for the relief of ulcers. Zones 10–12.

Piper betle

BETEL, BETLE PEPPER, PAN

☼ ✿ ↔ 4–8 ft (1.2–2.4 m)
↑ 10–17 ft (3–5 m)

Slender evergreen climber, native from India to Malaysia. Twining, rounded stems bearing adventitious roots. Smooth, oval to heart-shaped leaves, to 6 in (15 cm) long, pointed at tips, rounded at base. Large spikes of green flowers, followed by berry fruit embedded in a fleshy red mass. Across southern Asia, leaves are used to wrap the nut of the betel palm, *Areca catechu*, and then chewed as a stimulant. They are also brewed as a tea and medicinal tonic. Zones 10–12.

Piper nigrum

BLACK OR WHITE PEPPER, COMMON PEPPER, MADAGASCAR PEPPER, PEPPER PLANT

☼ ✿ ↔ 12 ft (3.5 m)   ↑ 10–25 ft (3–8 m)

Climbing perennial vine, native to India and Myanmar. Round, woody, smooth, branching stems. Smooth, broadly tapered, oval to heart-shaped leaves, to 3 in (8 cm) long, rounded at base, with pointed tips. Spikes of small, creamish green flowers, followed by fruit, which is a drupe, dark red when mature, the source of commercial black or white pepper. Zones 10–12.

PIPTANTHUS

The 2 species in this genus are shrubs or small trees native to western Asia. They belong to the pea-flower subfamily of the legume (Fabaceae) family and are *Laburnum*-like, with trifoliate leaves and racemes of yellow pea-flowers during spring and early summer. Stems are hollow and tend to be rather bare of foliage at the base. Flowers followed by small seed pods. CULTIVATION: Nominally evergreen, but tolerant of moderate frosts, these plants will shed much of their foliage in lengthy cold periods. They are easily grown in any well-drained soil that remains moist over summer and prefer a position in sun or partial shade. Light pruning after flowering will keep them densely foliaged; avoid cutting back to bare wood as they can be slow to reshoot. If a complete rejuvenation is required, spread it over 2 or 3 seasons. Propagate from seed or half-hardened tip cuttings.

Piptanthus nepalensis

syn. *Piptanthus laburnifolius*

☼ ❄ ↔ 6 ft (1.8 m)   ↑ 8 ft (2.4 m)

Found in the Himalayas. Leaflets to 6 in (15 cm) long. Young leaves covered with fine down. Flowers bright yellow, in summer, sporadically after the main flowering. Zones 8–10.

PIPTURUS

Consisting of 30 species, this genus in the nettle (Urticaceae) family occurs as shrubs and small trees, with 1 or 2 as semi-climbers, in the tropics from Réunion and Mauritius, to Indonesia, Malaysia, Australia, and Polynesia. In some places, the local people use the bark to make cloth and twine. The leaves are alternate with 5 or 6 veins prominent on the uppersurface. The flowers are small and insignificant, with the male and female flowers borne on separate plants. The fruits are also small and are in clusters in the leaf axils. CULTIVATION: These plants prefer a warm climate. Propagation is from fresh seed or cuttings.

Pipturus argenteus

NATIVE MULBERRY

☼ ✿ ↔ 12 ft (3.5 m)   ↑ 15 ft (4.5 m)

From northeastern Queensland to northern New South Wales, Australia. Silvery hairy new growth. Leaves, broadly lance-shaped, long point, toothed margins. Small flowers in clusters, in summer (wet season). Succulent edible white fruits, in winter (dry season). Zones 9–11.

PISONIA

A genus of trees, shrubs, and climbers, this member of the four-o-clock (Nyctaginaceae) family occurs widely in tropical regions of the world, with the bulk of the species occurring in the Americas. *P. grandis,* found on most of the island groups in the Indian and Pacific Oceans, forms dense thickets on coral cays. The leaves are smooth-edged, opposite or alternate or whorled, the flowers are unisexual or bisexual in axillary or terminal inflorescences. The fruits are various shapes, but all are sticky and trap insects and small animals. Various bird species disperse the fruits that stick to their feathers. CULTIVATION: Propagate from very fresh seed. Cuttings are also successful. There are a few leaf color variants in cultivation and these must be propagated in this manner to remain true.

Pipturus argenteus

Pistacia chinensis

Pistacia lentiscus

Pistia stratiotes

Pisonia grandis

BIRDLIME TREE

☼ ☀ ↔ 20 ft (6 m) ↑ 80 ft (24 m)

A softwood tree with brittle spreading branches, this species originates from the islands of the Indian and Pacific Oceans. Leaves elliptical, light green. Tiny greenish white flowers, terminal inflorescences, in summer–autumn. Fruits have rows of sticky hairs. Rarely cultivated. Zones 11–12.

Pisonia umbellifera

BIRDLIME TREE

☼ ❄ ↔ 15 ft (4.5 m) ↑ 80 ft (24 m)

Widespread species from the islands of Réunion and Mauritius to Asia, Australia, and New Zealand. The leaves are elliptical, dark green and shiny, crowded toward the ends of the branches. Small, scented, whitish flowers, produced in axillary or terminal clusters, in winter–spring. Elongated sticky fruits. 'Variegata', yellow and green leaves. Zones 9–10.

PISTACIA

This small genus in the cashew (Anacardiaceae) family consists of around 9 species from the Mediterranean region, eastern and southeastern Asia, Central America, and southern USA. They are mainly deciduous trees with compound, mostly pinnate leaves terminated by a pair of leaflets, and panicles of small-petalled flowers. The flowers are followed by peppercorn-like fruits produced on the female plants; male plants are separate. Some species are important for their oils and edible seeds, while others make fine ornamental trees with colorful autumn foliage. Most species originated in dry, warm-temperate regions. CULTIVATION: Most species are fairly adaptable and grow best in a well-drained moderately fertile soil in full sun. Propagate from seed, cuttings, budding, or grafting.

Pistacia chinensis

CHINESE PISTACHIO

☼ ❄ ↔ 15 ft (4.5 m)
↑ 25–50 ft (8–15 m)

Deciduous tree from China and Taiwan. Mostly pinnate leaves, 10 to 12 leathery dark green leaflets, turn shades of orange, red and yellow, in autumn. Panicles of inconspicuous reddish flowers, in summer. Small bluish fruit. Popular street and shade tree. Zones 7–9.

Pistacia lentiscus

LENTISCO, MASTIC TREE

☼ ❄ ↔ 12 ft (3.5 m) ↑ 12 ft (3.5 m)

Native of the Mediterranean region. Aromatic tree or shrub. Pinnate leaves of 2 to 7 pairs of glossy, leathery, dark green leaflets, terminated by a pair of leaflets. Panicles of small flowers appear in spring. Small black fruit. Zones 9–11.

Pistacia mexicana

COPALL

☼ ❄ ↔ 15 ft (4.5 m) ↑ 20 ft (6 m)

Found in Mexico and Guatemala. Angular branches, pinnate leaves of 16 to 36 thin leaflets, terminal leaflet smaller. Panicles of small flowers, male flowers, bracts covered with downy hairs. Small, red to black fruit. Zones 10–11.

Pistacia terebinthus

CYPRUS TURPENTINE, TEREBINTH TREE

☼ ❄ ↔ 15 ft (4.5 m) ↑ 25 ft (8 m)

Deciduous, large shrub or tree, native to the Canary Islands, Portugal to Turkey, and North Africa. Leaves pinnate, 12 semi-glossy, aromatic, green leaflets. Panicles of flowers, in spring–early summer. Reddish purple fruit. Zones 9–10.

Pistacia texana

AMERICAN PISTACHIO, LENTISCO

☼ ❄ ↔ 15 ft (4.5 m) ↑ 30 ft (9 m)

Native of southern USA and Mexico. Tree branches from low down the trunk. Pinnate leaves, 10 to 22 leaflets, terminal leaflet smaller. Female trees produce fleshy, dark brown fruit. Zones 10–11.

PISTIA

SHELL FLOWER, WATER LETTUCE

This genus, with just 1 aquatic evergreen herb, belongs to the arum (Araceae) family. It was found on Lake Victoria, on Africa's Nile River, and is now widely distributed through the tropics. It has spreading, feathery roots and floating rosettes of broadly wedge-shaped, ribbed, bluish green leaves in lettuce-like arrangements. Named from the Greek, *pistos*, water. CULTIVATION: Water lettuce are best grown in aquariums and ponds in warmer climates, in a protected, sunny position, out of direct sunlight in the middle of the day. Propagate by dividing plantlets in summer.

Pistia stratiotes

☼ ❄ ↔ 4–6 in (10–15 cm)
↑ 4–6 in (10–15 cm)

Aquatic herb with rosettes of oval to hairy, round, bright green leaves to 8 in (20 cm) long, covered with fine, water-repellent hairs. Small flowers without petals are enclosed by a leaf-like spathe. Zones 9–11.

Pisonia grandis

Pisonia umbellifera 'Variegata'

PISUM

This is a genus of 2 bushy or climbing annual herbs from the pea-flower subfamily of the legume (Fabaceae) family. They are native to the Mediterranean region. Divided leaves have 4 to 6 opposite leaflets with leafy, rounded stipules and the main axis ending as a tendril. Single, or groups of 2 or 3, butterfly-like flowers grow from the leaf axils. Fruit is a flattened, oblong pod, containing few to several seeds. One species, *P. sativum*, has been known as a garden vegetable since prehistoric times. The word *pisum* is Latin for pea.
CULTIVATION: A cool-season plant, in warmer climates plant from autumn into winter, and from summer to autumn in cooler climates, avoiding flowering and fruiting when frosts are likely. Peas prefer full sun in a rich, fertile, well-drained soil. Sow seed where plants are to grow. Pods are ready to harvest within 3 to 5 months of planting. Climbing plants will require support.

Pisum sativum ★

FIELD PEA, GARDEN PEA, SUGAR PEA

☀ ❄ ↔ 2 ft (0.6 m) ↑ 5–6 ft (1.5–1.8 m)
Annual, native to southern Europe. Compound leaves with 3 nearly circular to oblong leaflets, to 3 in (8 cm) long, with smooth-edged or toothed

margins. Groups of 1 to 3 flowers, to 1½ in (35 mm) across, white with dark reddish purple markings, and elongated pods, to 6 in (15 cm) long, containing 3 to 10 seeds. *P. s.* var. *arvense*, stipules spotted with red, with angled and blotched seeds; *P. s.* var. *macrocarpa*, broad, flat, edible pod. Zones 7–9.

PITCAIRNIA

There are more than 350 species in this, one of the more primitive genera in the bromeliad (Bromeliaceae) family, found throughout more humid areas in the American tropics, with a single species native to Guinea, in West Africa. The few species in cultivation are very popular. Species vary greatly in size, most growing in the ground but sometimes on rocks, rarely on trees. Leaves are generally narrow and grass-like, sometimes wider, the edges sometimes toothed, forming an open erect rosette. Some species have both grass-like and short, very prickly leaves. Conspicuous red, sometimes yellow, white or even violet flowerheads, held on long slender stems above leaves. Fruit, a dry capsule.
CULTIVATION: Recommended for greenhouse or conservatory cultivation in cool temperate areas, and outdoors with protection from direct continuous sunlight in warmer areas. Water when potting mix is almost dry. Extra feeding is not necessary. Propagation is by seed or offsets.

Pitcairnia atro-rubens

☀ ✷ ↔ 8 in (20 cm) ↑ 32 in (80 cm)
From Mexico to Colombia. Erect, open, rosettes of strap-like green leaves with few small teeth; forming clumps. Flower stem erect, cylindrical flowerhead of erect bright red bracts spiraling to top, and erect, long, whitish petals. Zones 10–12.

Pitcairnia halophila, in the wild, Parque Nacional Manuel Antonio, Quepos, Costa Rica

Pitcairnia halophila

☀ ✷ ↔ 6 in (15 cm) ↑ 27 in (70 cm)
From Costa Rica, growing just above high-tide line. Erect open rosettes in clumps. Leaves green, variable–long, thin, smooth-edged or very short with many teeth. Flower stems slender, cylindrical flowerhead to 12 in (30 cm). Yellow flowers. Zones 10–12.

Pitcairnia heterophylla

☀ ✷ ↔ 5 in (12 cm) ↑ 8 in (20 cm)
From Mexico to Venezuela and Peru. Small plant with large bulb, forming clumps. Leaves very thin, brown, very spiny. From center of leaf rosette, depending on maturity of bulb, emerges short flower stem or second set of leaves, narrow, green, smooth-edged, to 27 in (70 cm) long. Globular flowerhead and up to 10 flowers, reddish, with petals of red, orange, or white. Zones 10–12.

PITHECELLOBIUM

This genus in the mimosa subfamily of the legume (Fabaceae) family contains about 20 species of thorny shrubs or trees native to subtropical and tropical America. They have bipinnately divided leaves and bear panicles of pea-flowers with numerous showy stamens.
CULTIVATION: Grown for their attractive foliage and nectar-rich flowers, these plants must be kept in the greenhouse in temperate zones. In warm areas they can be grown outside in any reasonable garden soil. Propagation is from seed or greenwood cuttings.

Pithecellobium flexicaule

TEXAS EBONY

☀ ✷ ↔ 20 ft (6 m) ↑ 15–30 ft (4.5–9 m)
From northern Mexico and southeastern USA. Very drought-tolerant, evergreen tree with whippy branches armed spines, clothed with dark green leaves, 3 to 6 pairs leaflets. Sprays of fragrant, creamy yellow, acacia-like flowers, in summer. Seed pods 6 in (15 cm) long. Zones 9–11.

Pithecellobium mexicanum

MEXICAN EBONY

☀ ✷ ↔ 30 ft (9 m) ↑ 20–50 ft (6–15 m)
Small, rounded, deciduous tree or shrub from northwestern Mexico. Stems and trunks have gray bark, armed with many small, curved thorns, and branchlets with weeping habit. Pairs of compound, grayish green leaves grow from nodules on twigs. Flowers are loose, light yellow puffballs, in spring. Fruits are green pods, 3 in (8 cm) long, maturing to brown. Zones 10–11.

Pittosporum crassifolium

PITTOSPORUM

This genus consists of about 200 species of evergreen trees and shrubs in the family Pittosporaceae. They are found in Africa, southern and eastern Asia, Australia, New Zealand, and the Hawaiian Islands, USA. The foliage is usually glossy with leaves arranged alternately or in whorls. The small flowers, 5-petalled, may be cup-shaped or reflexed, single or in clusters, some have a sweet fragrance. Capsules contain seeds with a sticky coating. Some species are useful for shelter and hedging, borders or containers. Can be clipped for formal situations and to keep the foliage dense.
CULTIVATION: Most species will grow in sun or part-shade in any well-drained soil. In cool-temperate climates they may require the protection of a sunny wall, or they can be grown in the conservatory or greenhouse. Propagation is from seed, which germinates erratically, or from half-hardened cuttings taken in summer or autumn. Cultivars are propagated from cuttings only.

Pittosporum bicolor

BANYALLA

☀ ✷ ↔ 10 ft (3 m) ↑ 8–40 ft (2.4–12 m)
Native to Tasmania and southeastern Australia. Erect bushy shrub or small tree. Lance-shaped to narrowly oval leaves, leathery, dark green, felted undersides. Small, scented flowers, yellow with dark red markings, in spring. Grayish capsules. Zones 9–11.

Pittosporum colensoi

☀ ❄ ↔ 8 ft (2.4 m) ↑ 35 ft (10 m)
New Zealand native, similar to *P. tenuifolium*. Stout, dark branches. Oblong leaves leathery, glossy dark green, flat edges. Small dark red flowers with reflexed petals, in early summer. Zones 9–11.

Pittosporum crassifolium

KARO

☀ ✷ ↔ 8 ft (2.4 m) ↑ 10–20 ft (3–6 m)
Robust New Zealand species, withstands coastal conditions. Dark green

Pittosporum dallii

Pittosporum tenuifolium

Pittosporum tenuifolium 'Tom Thumb'

leaves, thick and leathery, white hairy coating beneath. Flowers, small, dark red, and noticeably fragrant in the evening. Down-covered fruits, shiny black seeds. Zones 9–11.

Pittosporum dallii
☀ ↭ ↔ 10 ft (3 m)
↑ 10–17 ft (3–5 m)

Native to New Zealand, this rare species is from the northwest of the South Island. Slow-growing shrub or small tree. Leathery dark green leaves, serrated edges. Clusters of small, white, sweetly scented flowers, in summer. Zones 9–11.

Pittosporum napaulense

Pittosporum eugenioides

Pittosporum eugenioides
LEMONWOOD, TARATA
☀ ↭ ↔ 12 ft (3.5 m) ↑ 40 ft (12 m)

From New Zealand, smaller in cultivation. Glossy, light green, oval leaves, distinct pale midrib and wavy edges, release a lemony aroma when crushed. Small creamy yellow flowers, honey-scented, in spring–summer. Popular hedging and specimen planting. 'Variegatum' has irregularly marked creamy edges to its leaves. Zones 9–11.

Pittosporum 'Garnettii'
☀ ↭ ↔ 7 ft (2 m) ↑ 7–10 ft (2–3 m)

Hybrid between *P. tenuifolium* and *P. ralphii*. Attractive, oval leaves, creamy white variegations flushed pink. Solitary dark purple flowers borne along branches, in spring. Zones 9–11.

Pittosporum napaulense
☀ ↭ ↔ 7 ft (2 m) ↑ 20 ft (6 m)

Found in northern India, Nepal, and Bhutan. Shrub or small tree sometimes has a scrambling habit. Leaves, leathery, pointed, oval, in clusters near the branch tips. Panicles of small, fragrant, yellow flowers, in late spring–summer. Zones 9–11.

Pittosporum 'Garnettii'

Pittosporum tobira

Pittosporum obcordatum
☀ ↭ ↔ 3 ft (0.9 m) ↑ 12 ft (3.5 m)

A rare plant, native to New Zealand with a divaricating, branching habit. It makes an interesting specimen tree. The dense, tangled, grayish brown branches bear tiny rounded leaves that clothe the plant from ground level. Very small, light yellow flowers appear along the branches, in summer. Zones 9–11.

Pittosporum ralphii
☀ ↭ ↔ 8 ft (2.4 m) ↑ 20 ft (6 m)

This New Zealand species is very similar to *P. crassifolium* but it is not as tolerant of coastal winds. Its oblong leaves are thinner, longer, and less densely felted. Small dark red flowers, in spring–early summer. Capsules smaller, less woody. 'Variegatum', grayish green leaves with broad, irregularly marked, creamy white edges. Zones 9–11.

Pittosporum revolutum
YELLOW PITTOSPORUM
☀ ↭ ↔ 7 ft (2 m)
↑ 7–10 ft (2–3 m)

Native to forests of eastern and southeastern Australia. Young shoots have a dense, rusty brown, hairy coating. Pointed oval leaves, slightly rolled edges, glossy, dark green above, fine brown hairs beneath. Fragrant yellow flowers, in spring. Zones 9–11.

Pittosporum tobira 'Nanum'

Pittosporum tenuifolium
KOHUHU
☀ ↭ ↔ 15 ft (4.5 m) ↑ 15–20 ft (4.5–6 m)

Variable species native to New Zealand, usually a large shrub. Thin, slightly leathery, oblong leaves, wavy edges. Small flowers, reflexed petals, dark red, almost black, in spring, strong honey fragrance. Capsules turn black on maturity. 'Deborah', grayish green leaves with creamy margins flushed with pink; 'Elia Keightley' (syn. 'Sunburst'), rounded leaves with central yellow variegations; 'Irene Paterson', slower-growing form with almost white leaves speckled with pale green; 'James Stirling', blackish red branchlets, silvery green leaves; 'Limelight', two-toned leaves of lime and dark green; 'Marjorie Channon', popular cultivar in the USA; 'Tom Thumb', dwarf variety with foliage that ages to dark purple; 'Variegatum', cream-edged green leaves; 'Warnham Gold', light green leaves that change to creamy yellow and gold. Zones 9–11.

Pittosporum tobira
JAPANESE PITTOSPORUM, TOBIRA
☀ ↭ ↔ 7 ft (2 m) ↑ 20 ft (6 m)

Erect bushy shrub that is native to China and Japan. Leathery oblong leaves, dark glossy green, have rolled edges. Orange-scented flowers, flaring petals creamy white, lemony yellow

Pittosporum umbellatum

Pittosporum undulatum

with age, in spring–early summer. 'Nanum', bright green leaves; 'Variegatum' tolerates coastal conditions, the leaves have an irregularly marked white margin; 'Wheeler's Dwarf' is a compact miniature to about 24 in (60 cm) high. Zones 9–11.

Pittosporum umbellatum

This bushy tree is found in eastern areas of New Zealand's North Island. The leaves are leathery, oval, glossy, dark green, arising on blackish branchlets. The very fragrant flowers are pinkish red, and are borne in showy, crowded, terminal clusters, appearing in spring. Zones 9–11.

Pittosporum undulatum

SWEET PITTOSPORUM, VICTORIAN BOX

↔ 20 ft (6 m) ↕ 15–40 ft (4.5–12 m)
Native to eastern Australia. Vigorous species. Shiny, dark green, pointed, oval leaves, wavy edges. Creamy white flowers, sweetly scented, in terminal clusters, in spring. Orangey brown capsules. Has become a weed outside its natural forest habitat. Zones 9–11.

PITYROGRAMMA

GOLD AND SILVER FERNS

This genus of about 40 semi-evergreen or evergreen, terrestrial ferns from the maidenhair-fern (Adiantaceae) family, is found in tropical regions of Africa and the Americas. It has short-creeping or climbing rhizomes. Tufted, linear to triangular, divided fronds, with a silver or gold powdery appearance underneath, are borne on dark, glossy, wiry stems. The genus is named from the Greek *pityron*, chaff or bran, and *gramma*, writing, an allusion to the powder on the fronds.

CULTIVATION: These plants grow well in hanging baskets, in part-shade in well-drained humus-rich soil. Propagate from spores in summer.

Pityrogramma calomelanos

syn. *Gymnogramma calomelanos*

SILVER FERN

↔ 32 in (80 cm) ↕ 32 in (80 cm)
Densely clumping, evergreen fern, native to tropical America and now growing widely throughout the tropics. Divided, oval to triangular, papery fronds, to 24 in (60 cm) long. Silvery white powdery appearance underneath, tall dark purple stems. Deeply lobed, pointed leaflets, to 7 in (18 cm) long, with narrowly triangular, lobed segments. Zones 10–11.

Pityrogramma triangularis

syn. *Gymnogramma triangularis*

CALIFORNIAN GOLD FERN, GOLDBACK FERN, GOLDENBACK FERN

↔ 4–20 in (10–50 cm)
↕ 4–20 in (10–50 cm)
Small semi-evergreen fern, inhabiting rocky slopes and crevices in North America, from California to Alaska. Divided, broadly triangular to pentagonal, dark to mid-green fronds, to 7 in (18 cm) long, with narrow leaflets and rounded segments, on stiff, very dark brown stems, about twice the length of the frond, with a white, yellow, or orange powdery appearance underneath. Fronds curl up in drought, rejuvenating when rain comes. Zones 10–11.

PLAGIANTHUS

RIBBONWOOD

The 2 species in this genus in the mallow (Malvaceae) family are natives of New Zealand. One is unusual among that country's flora because it is deciduous; the other because it is divaricating (keeping its foliage largely within a mass of densely interwoven stems), which is quite common among New Zealand plants but less often seen elsewhere. They are known as ribbonwoods because their downy gray bark peels away in ribbon-like strips. Their leaves are very simple and sometimes much reduced. They flower in summer, producing small blooms on conspicuous inflorescences, as separate male and female flowers.

Plantago coronopus

CULTIVATION: Apart from being unable to withstand the severe frosts of inland areas, ribbonwoods are tough adaptable plants that will tolerate most soil conditions and exposure to strong winds. They can be pruned heavily. Propagate from seed or half-hardened cuttings.

Plagianthus regius

syn. *Plagianthus betulinus*

RIBBONWOOD

↔ 10 ft (3 m) ↕ 50 ft (15 m)
This has a divaricating habit when young. Its leaves are lance-shaped, soft olive green, with coarsely toothed edges. The tree flowers heavily; the individual blooms are small but the massed inflorescences of greenish white flowers are conspicuous. Zones 8–10.

PLANTAGO

PLANTAIN

A genus of at least 200 species, most of which are rosette-forming perennials in the plantain (Plantaginaceae) family. Those that are best known to gardeners tend to be persistent lawn weeds. Even so, some are attractive foliage plants, including alpine species, and in a genus that specializes in tiny inconspicuous green flowers in tight spikes, some even have rather interesting blooms.

CULTIVATION: Grow ornamental species in moist fertile soil in full sun. Propagate from seed, which, not surprisingly, often self-sows.

Plantago coronopus

BUCK'S-HORN PLANTAIN, CUT-LEAFED PLANTAIN

↔ 12 in (30 cm) ↕ 12 in (30 cm)
European species with some weed potential and minimal ornamental

Plagianthus regius

Platanus × hispanica

value. Green leaves are deeply cut and sit almost flat to the ground, above which it produces spikes of tiny green flowers. Zones 6–10.

Plantago nivalis
☼ ❄ ↔ 3 in (8 cm) ↕ ¾–1 in (18–25 mm)
A tiny alpine species from Spain with narrow silky silvered leaves to ½ in (12 mm) long, above which, in summer, it produces tiny heads of brown-green flowers. Zones 6–10.

PLATANUS
PLANE TREE
This genus in the plane (Platanaceae) family consists of about 8 species from the northern temperate zone, including Eurasia, North America, and Mexico. These deciduous trees have inconspicuous spring flowers; globe-shaped fruits on hanging stalks; large, alternate, palmately lobed, simple leaves; and ornamental, flaking, mottled bark. They are useful large shade trees and are widely planted as street trees. Many species are highly tolerant of compacted soils and air pollution and will grow well in both temperate and cool climates.
CULTIVATION: Most species are adaptable, as can be seen by the many cases of street trees in less than optimal conditions, but they perform best on deep, productive, alluvial soils with a consistent water source, such as a permanent stream, in full sun. Pruning is not essential, though it is desirable in the early years if a single trunk is to be established. Propagate from seed, cuttings, or by layering.

Platanus × hispanica
syns *Platanus × acerifolia, P. × hybrida*
LONDON PLANE
☼ ❄ ↔ 60 ft (18 m) ↕ 100 ft (30 m)
Believed to be a hybrid between *P. occidentalis* and *P. orientalis,* it has a rounded pyramidal form. Gray to light brown bark, variable bright green leaves, usually 5-lobed. Fruits small. Tolerates heat, drought and pollution. 'Pyramidalis', upright cultivar with coarse bark, leaves 3-lobed, often slightly toothed. Zones 4–9.

Platanus occidentalis
AMERICAN PLANE, BUTTON-BALL, BUTTONWOOD, SYCAMORE
☼ ❄ ↔ 70 ft (21 m) ↕ 150 ft (45 m)
Native to USA and Canada. Very tall deciduous tree, broad open crown, spreading branches. Attractive flaking bark, 3 to 5 bright green shallow-lobed leaves. Single hanging nutlets, sometimes in pairs. Timber used for furniture and pulp. Zones 4–9.

Platanus orientalis
ORIENTAL PLANE
☼ ❄ ↔ 90 ft (21 m) ↕ 100 ft (30 m)
Large, spreading, deciduous tree from southeastern Europe to western Asia. Huge trunk with mottled, brown, gray and greenish white bark. Dark green leaves, palmately lobed. Inconspicuous flowers, in early spring. Clusters of 2 to 6 globe-shaped fruit. *P. o.* var. *insularis*, bright green leaves, toothed lobes; hairy fruits. Zones 5–9.

Platanus racemosa
ALISO, CALIFORNIA PLANE, CALIFORNIA SYCAMORE, WESTERN SYCAMORE
☼ ❄ ↔ 75 ft (23 m) ↕ 100 ft (30 m)
Large, strong-growing, deciduous tree, from southern California, USA, and Mexico. Dark green leaves, 3 to 5 deep lobes, downy undersides. Clusters of 2 to 7 bristly hanging fruits turn brown when mature. Zones 7–10.

PLATYCARYA
This genus from China, Korea, Japan, and Vietnam belongs to the walnut (Juglandaceae) family. It contains 2 or

Platanus occidentalis

3 species of deciduous large shrubs or small trees featuring elegant pinnate leaves that color yellow in autumn. Flowers of both sexes are borne separately on the same plant in late spring and early summer; the males are produced in branched, pendent, yellowish green catkins, and the female inflorescence is a solitary catkin that becomes cone-like as the fruits ripen.
CULTIVATION: Fully frost hardy, members of this genus prefer moist, rich, well-drained soil in a protected sunny or partially shaded position. Propagate from seed or by layering.

Platycarya strobilacea
◐ ❄ ↔ 35 ft (10 m) ↕ 50 ft (15 m)
Deciduous tree from China. Pinnate leaves to 12 in (30 cm) long, 7 to 15 pairs of toothed leaflets. Tiny yellowish green summer flowers. Cone-like autumn fruits persist through winter. Bark yields a black dye. Zones 5–9.

Platanus orientalis var. *insularis*

Platycarya strobilacea

Platanus racemosa

Platycladus orientalis 'Aurea Nana'

Platycladus orientalis

PLATYCERIUM
syn. *Alcicornium*

ANTELOPE EARS, ELKHORN FERN,
STAGHORN FERN

This genus consists of about 18 evergreen, epiphytic ferns, members of the
polypody (Polypodiaceae) family,
widely spread throughout tropical
areas. A short rhizome, concealed by
the fronds, normally clasps the tree
supporting the plant. Broad, flat,
overlapping sterile fronds to 6 ft
(1.8 m) long, without stems, become
brown and papery with age. Erect or
drooping, repeatedly forked fertile
fronds grow on stems from the base
of the sterile fronds, with spore-bodies
underneath. The genus is named from
the Greek *platys*, broad, and *keras*, a
horn, referring to the branching habit
of the fertile fronds.
CULTIVATION: These ferns normally
grown on tree trunks or fastened to
pieces of wood. They prefer warm,
humid conditions in part-shade, in
fibrous, peaty, well-drained compost.
Propagate by division of suckers in
spring or summer or from spores in
summer or early autumn.

Platycerium bifurcatum

COMMON STAGHORN FERN,
ELKHORN FERN

☀ ❄ ↔ 27–40 in (70–100 cm)
↑ 27–40 in (70–100 cm)
Native to Southeast Asia, Polynesia,
and northern Australia. Grayish green
sterile fronds, erect, rounded, wavy
and shallowly lobed, papery, stemless,
to 24 in (60 cm) long. The fertile
fronds are drooping, divided, to 36 in
(90 cm) long, with strap-like segments. *P. b.* var. *majus* is larger,
greener, and has a more leathery form.
Zones 8–10.

Platycladus orientalis 'Balaton'

Platycerium veitchii

SILVER ELKHORN FERN

☀ ❄ ↔ 32 in (80 cm) ↑ 60 in (150 cm)
From northeastern Australia. Stemless,
elliptical, brownish sterile fronds, to
18 in (45 cm) long, close together and
forked into 2 strap-like lobes. Erect,
spreading fertile fronds, to 27 in
(70 cm), divide into up to 3 twisted,
triangular to linear lobes. Both frond
types have a silvery appearance from
fine white hairs beneath. Zones 9–11.

PLATYCLADUS
At times put in the genus *Thuja*, this
genus, in the cypress (Cupressaceae)
family, is now considered distinct. It
contains only 1 species, an evergreen
coniferous tree featuring flattened
spray-like branchlets of lightly aromatic foliage. Native to Korea, China,
and northeastern Iran, it is rarely seen
outside eastern Asia in its typical form,
but rather as one of its numerous cultivars. These generally have a more
rounded low-branching habit and are
highly ornamental and dependable.
Many are suitable for hedging. Dwarf
varieties are excellent in rock gardens
or containers and as a low border.
CULTIVATION: Grow this fully hardy
genus in a moist well-drained soil in a
sunny position protected from strong
winds. Prune lightly in spring. Propagate from seed or cuttings.

Platycladus orientalis
syn. *Thuja orientalis*

CHINESE ARBOR-VITAE

☀ ❄ ↔ 15 ft (4.5 m) ↑ 40 ft (12 m)
Small conical tree, upward-curving
branches. Small, mid-green, scale-
like leaves in flattened vertical sprays.
Fleshy, ovoid, female cones, ripen to
a waxy silvery sheen. 'Aurea Nana' ★,
dense oval shape to 3 ft (0.9 m) high,
creamy yellow foliage darkens to a rich
green, in autumn–winter; 'Balaton',
soft light green foliage; 'Elegantissima',
compact conical bush to 15 ft (4.5 m)
tall, golden yellow foliage develops
bronze tones, winter; 'Meldensis',
dwarf rounded bush to 3 ft (0.9 m),
with soft blue-green foliage, purplish
toning, winter; 'Rosedalis', to 5 ft
(1.5 m) tall, fine soft foliage, changes
from bright yellow in spring to sea
green in summer, has purplish tones
in winter. Zones 6–11.

PLATYCODON

BALLOON FLOWER, CHINESE BELLFLOWER

The sole species in this genus in the
bellflower (Campanulaceae) family is
a vigorous herbaceous perennial found
in Japan and nearby parts of China.
It forms a clump of bold, lance-
shaped leaves with toothed edges. The
flowers open from enlarged, balloon-
like buds and are cup- to bell-shaped,
white, pink, or blue, with 5 broad
lobes. Double-flowered and dwarf
forms are common. *Platycodon* root,
used in traditional Chinese medicine,
is being studied for its mutagenic
effects on tumors.
CULTIVATION: A perennial species
suitable for a distinctly seasonal
temperate climate. Plant in sun or
part-shade in moist, humus-rich,
well-drained soil. Slow to establish,
but long lived and very hardy. May
be raised from seed; cultivars are
propagated by division.

Platycerium veitchii

Plectranthus argentatus

Platycodon grandiflorus
BALLOON FLOWER, CHINESE BELLFLOWER
☀/◑ ❄ ↔ 24 in (60 cm) ↑ 27 in (70 cm)
Broad lance-shaped, toothed leaves held whorled around sturdy, usually upright, sometimes sprawling stems. Bell-shaped blue, purple, white, or pink flowers open from inflated buds in summer. '**Apoyama**', low growing, large deep lavender flowers; '**Fuji Blue**' ★, erect habit, flowers large, blue; '**Fuji White**', pure white flowers; '**Perlmutterschale**' (syn. 'Mother of Pearl'), large pale pink flowers; '**Sentimental Blue**', dwarf habit, large mauve-blue flowers. Zones 4–9.

PLATYLOBIUM
An Australian genus of 4 species in the pea-flower subfamily of the legume (Fabaceae) family, from southern Queensland in higher rainfall zones through New South Wales to Victoria, Tasmania, and South Australia. Their habitats are the well-drained acid soils, in open woodlands, forests, heaths, and scrubs. All are small shrubs, prostrate or straggling, with a lignotuber that allows them to regenerate after fires. Leaves are simple or lobed, opposite (alternate in 1 species). The pea-flowers are yellow to orange with markings of other colors on various parts of the flower. Flowers are followed by broad flat pods with several seeds. CULTIVATION: Propagation is from seed with a long viability requiring pre-treatment such as scarification or hot water before sowing. Young plants grow well in well-drained soils with adequate water in full sun or part-shade positions. Cuttings have been successful with some species.

Platylobium obtusangulum
COMMON FLAT PEA
☀ ❄ ↔ 36 in (90 cm) ↑ 36 in (90 cm)
Occurring in southeastern South Australia, southern Victoria, northern and eastern Tasmania. Small shrub, many thin stems. Leaves roughly arrow-shaped, 3 pointed lobes. Pea-flowers yellow-orange blotched with brown, red and pink, in spring–summer. Brown hairy pods. Zones 8–9.

PLATYSTEMON
CALIFORNIAN POPPY, CREAMCUPS
This monotypic genus belongs to the poppy (Papaveraceae) family and contains a rather variable annual herb native to the western USA where it grows in open grassy areas, often emerging after fires. It may be erect or spreading and has narrow oblong leaves to 3 in (8 cm) long. The attractive open flowers are 6-petalled with prominent stamens. They may be cream, yellow or two-toned, with the cream petals having yellow basal spots or tips. They are borne singly on short hairy stems in summer.
CULTIVATION: Grow at the front of the border in a sunny position in well-drained soil. Propagate from seed sown in the position they are to flower and when germinated thin to about 4 in (10 cm) spacing.

Platystemon californicus
☀ ❄ ↔ 4 in (10 cm) ↑ 12 in (30 cm)
From California and Arizona, USA. Annual with hairy grayish green leaves. Pale yellow or cream 6-petalled flowers are individually short-lived but profuse in summer. Zones 8–10.

PLECTRANTHUS
Over 200 species of annuals, perennials, and shrubs make up this large genus of herbaceous, semi-succulent or succulent plants in the mint (Lamiaceae) family. They come from Africa, Asia, Australia, and the Pacific Islands. Most are grown for their attractive evergreen foliage and ease of growing, either in the garden, in pots, or as hanging basket specimens in greenhouses, where necessary. Although individual tubular flowers are usually insignificant, the massed flower display provided by the spikes is captivating.
CULTIVATION: Many of these undemanding plants can be grown as ground covers in lightly shaded areas in warmer climates or as easy-care specimens for pot or basket. Others of shrub-like proportions can be grown in a warm sheltered position. Any fertile soil or potting mix will suit. Provide ample water during growing season. They are quite rapid growers; the succulent stems are easily pruned and can be used for propagating.

Platylobium obtusangulum

Plectranthus ambiguus
LARGE-FLOWERED PLECTRANTHUS
◑ ❈ ↔ 16 in (40 cm) ↑ 27 in (70 cm)
Low-growing, evergreen perennial suits ground cover, container, or basket growth, with stems that root freely as they touch the ground. Fragrant, green, hairy foliage. Erect heads of small, unusually narrow, mauve to dark purple flowers, in spring. Zones 9–10.

Plectranthus argentatus
☀ ❈ ↔ 36 in (90 cm) ↑ 36 in (90 cm)
Spreading shrub from Australia. Silvery gray, softly felted, slightly hairy leaves, one of the few silver-leafed plants to endure damp shade. Lilac flowers held in the branch tips. Regularly tip prune to keep bushy. Zones 10–11.

Plectranthus ambiguus

Platycodon grandiflorus 'Apoyama'

Platycodon grandiflorus 'Fuji Blue'

Platycodon grandiflorus

Plectranthus australis
CREEPING CHARLIE, SWEDISH BEGONIA, SWEDISH IVY

☼ ❧ ↔ 40 in (100 cm) ↑ 40 in (100 cm)

Evergreen, trailing perennial with erect, slender, suckering stems, square in section. Rounded, glossy, waxy, dark green leaves, about 1 in (25 mm) long, with scalloped margins. Whorls of tubular, pale mauve to white flowers in terminal racemes appear irregularly throughout the year. '**Variegata**' has leaves marked with white. Zones 9–10.

Plectranthus ciliatus

☼ ❧ ↔ 4 in (10 cm) ↑ 2–4 in (5–10 cm)

Straggling herb or shrub, native to eastern South Africa. Trailing stems covered in purple hairs, spreads by runners. Opposite pairs of shining, hairy leaves, to 5 in (12 cm) long, purple underneath, dotted with glands, especially on veins. Raceme-like flowerheads, to 12 in (30 cm) long, sometimes with short branches near base. Tiny flowers with white corolla tube and a 2-lobed upper lip, purple dots inside the lower lip, winter–autumn. Fruit dark brown nutlets. Zones 9–11.

Plectranthus ecklonii

☼ ❧ ↔ 3 ft (0.9 m) ↑ 5 ft (1.5 m)

Native to South Africa. Bushy shrub, mid-green tapering leaves with prominent veining. Pale lilac flowers in tightly packed upright clusters, in autumn. Zones 9–11.

Plectranthus oertendahlii

Plectranthus forsteri

☼ ❧ ↔ 10 ft (3 m) ↑ 3–8 ft (0.9–2.4 m)

Sprawling, aromatic perennial herb from eastern Australia and nearby Pacific Islands. Hairy straggling stem, to 40 in (100 cm) long. Serrated, oval, hairy leaves, and whorled racemes of 6 to 10 small, pale to mid-blue or mauve flowers. '**Marginatus**' (syn. 'Variegatus'), small white flowers and leaves variegated with cream. Zones 8–10.

Plectranthus madagascariensis
MADAGASCAR SPUR FLOWER

☼ ❧ ↔ 18 in (45 cm) ↑ 4–6 in (10–15 cm)

Sprawling, evergreen, perennial ground cover from Mozambique, Madagascar, and South Africa. Hairy stem, to 40 in (100 cm) long, roots freely where it touches the ground. Slightly succulent, oval to nearly round, toothed, green or variegated, fragrant leaves, to 2 in (5 cm) long. Solitary or branching heads to 5 in (12 cm) long, of white, mauve, or purple flowers, often dotted with red glands. '**Variegated Mintleaf**' (syn. *P. coleoides* 'Variegatus'), fragrant, variegated foliage. Zones 10–11.

Plectranthus oertendahlii

☼ ❧ ↗ ↔ 36 in (90 cm) ↑ 8–12 in (20–30 cm)

Evergreen semi-succulent, freely branching perennial herb from South Africa. Sprawling, rooting, glandular, long, hairy stem. Simple or branching racemes of 3-flowered cymes of white or pale mauve, tubular flowers, irregularly during the year. Semi-succulent, oval to nearly circular, purple, hairy, scalloped leaves, to 1½ in (35 mm) long, white veins above, reddish green beneath. Zones 10–11.

Plectranthus verticillatus
SWEDISH IVY

☼ ❧ ↔ 12 in (30 cm) ↑ 12 in (30 cm)

Succulent, sprawling, perennial herb from Southeast Asia, Swaziland, and Mozambique. Oval to rounded, toothed leaves, to 1½ in (35 mm) long, on smooth or slightly hairy stems, to more than 40 in (100 cm) long. Heads, singly or in pairs of cymes, of 1 to 3 white to pale mauve flowers, speckled with purple, without stalks. Zones 9–11.

PLEIOBLASTUS

A genus, in the grass (Poaceae) family, of about 20 species of mainly small-growing running bamboos from Japan and China. Leaves lance-shaped. Over the years many attractive variegated clones have been selected, many of which are still grown as species because they haven't been properly classified.
CULTIVATION: Prefers well-drained but moist rich soil in full or half-sun. Variegated clones need sun to keep their color. Most are best pruned to ground level each spring. Propagate by division in spring.

Pleioblastus pygmaeus
syn. *Arundinaria pygmaeus*
DWARF FERN-LEAFED BAMBOO, KE-OROSHIMA-CHIKU, PYGMY BAMBOO

☼/☼ ❉ ↔ 60 in (150 cm) ↑ 16 in (40 cm)

A dwarf suckering species long cultivated in Japan but of uncertain origin. Leaves to 1¾ in (40 mm) long, midgreen and usually slightly downy. *P. p.* var. *distichus* is taller, to 40 in (100 cm), with leaves to 2½ in (6 cm) long. Zones 6–10.

Pleione formosana

Pleione formosana 'Clare'

Pleioblastus variegatus
syns *Arundinaria fortunei, A. variegata*
CHIGO-ZASA, DWARF WHITE-STRIPED BAMBOO

☼ ❉ ↔ 40–60 in (100–150 cm) ↑ 28–40 in (70–100 cm)

An upright form from Japan with upright leaves to 6 in (15 cm) long, boldly striped with white. Long cultivated in Japan and obviously a selection of an as yet unidentified green-leafed species. Zones 5–10.

PLEIONE

This is a small genus of about 20 mostly semi-alpine, bulbous orchids (family Orchidaceae), related to *Coelogyne*. Pleiones grow in a wide variety of mountain habitats, at high altitudes, from Nepal to China. They grow as terrestrials or epiphytes on mossy limbs or fallen rotting logs and produce showy *Cattleya*-like blooms, singly or in pairs, in early spring.
CULTIVATION: Pleiones are easy to cultivate in cool climates and perform at their best if repotted annually, in a rich, well-drained, terrestrial mix. The pseudobulbs are best planted (not buried), as groups, in squat pots, saucers, or trays, as they have a shallow root system. Healthy plants will produce 2 new growths, which develop into new plants, as the older pseudobulbs will shrivel and die. Keep the potting mix moist from spring to early autumn while the plants are actively growing. They need to be kept cool and dry during the winter months. Propagate by division of the dormant pseudobulbs in late winter.

Pleione formosana

☼ ❉ ↔ 16 in (40 cm) ↑ 16 in (40 cm)

From China and Taiwan, hardiest species in the genus. The 4 in (10 cm) flowers come in numerous shades of pink, with many named cultivars, and there are also pure white forms, such as '**Clare**'. The fringed labellum has a white and yellow base, with small, red-brown blotches. Some botanists consider *P. bulbocodioides* to be the same species. Zones 8–10.

Plectranthus ciliatus

Plectranthus ecklonii

Pleione Hybrids

☼ ❄ ↔ 8–16 in (20–40 cm)
↕ 8–16 in (20–40 cm)

There have been numerous hybrids created, using *P. formosana* as a foundation with other pink- and purple-flowered species, as well as incorporating some of the more difficult-to-grow, yellow-flowered species from China. **Shantung** is a hybrid between *P. formosana* and *P. Confusa* (*P. albiflora* × *P. forrestii*), flowers vary from peach and cream tones through to pale pink to lilac, due to the influence of the yellow-flowered *P. forrestii*; **Soufrière** has pale pink flowers with a white-fringed labellum that has brownish red and yellow markings; **Tolima**, a purple-flowered hybrid between *P. formosana* and *P. speciosa*; **Tongariro**, a purple-flowered hybrid between *P. Versailles* and *P. speciosa*; and **Versailles** is a vigorous pink to purple-flowered hybrid between *P. formosana* and *P. limprichtii*. Zones 8–10.

PLEIOSPILOS

A genus of 4 succulent species, often referred to as "split rock plants," in the iceplant (Aizoaceae) family, from the Little Karoo region of southern Africa. The genus name comes from the Greek *pleio* (full) and *spilos* (dots), referring to the dark green spots on the skin of these plants. They are small, compact and occasionally solitary, but usually clustering with 1 to 4 pairs of leaves per branch. Leaves are often purplish brown, thick, rock-like, fused at their bases and somewhat rounded. Flowers are large, yellow to reddish orange, occasionally white, borne on short stems. The seed pods have 9 to 15 compartments that open when wet.

Pleurophyllum criniferum

CULTIVATION: Grow in rich well-drained soil. Propagate from seed or stem cuttings dried out for a week or two, or by division of older clumps. Rest in winter.

Pleiospilos bolusii

☼ ❄ ↔ 6 in (15 cm) ↕ 2½ in (6 cm)

From South Africa's eastern and western Cape region. Solitary to 3-branched, with hood-shaped leaves, flat on uppersurface, deeply keeled below. Flowers flat funnelform, yellow, about 2 in (5 cm) long. Seed pods flattened, spherical, with 12 compartments. Zones 8–11.

Pleiospilos nelii ★

☼ ❄ ↔ 1¾–2½ in (4–6 cm)
↕ 2–2½ in (5–6 cm)

From South Africa's eastern and western Cape region. Easily distinguished by its hemispherical leaves, ¾–1¼ in (18–30 mm) long, flat on upper surface, without a keel on lower side.

Pleurophyllum speciosum

Flowers flat funnelform, salmon pink to yellow, rarely white. Seed pods flattened, spherical, with 11 compartments. Zones 8–11.

PLEUROPHYLLUM

The 3 species of perennial herbs in this genus, in the daisy (Asteraceae) family, are native to the subantarctic island groups south of New Zealand. They are striking plants often described as "mega-herbs" due to the large size they attain, despite their inhospitable habitat, the islands being cool, very windy, and wet. Their leaves may be as much as 40 in (100 cm) long and their flowering stems up to 7 ft (2 m) tall. The daisy flowers are usually in purple shades or white. In 2 of the species the ray florets are inconspicuous. They flower for a short period in summer.

CULTIVATION: These plants have evolved to grow in rich, acidic soil with cool temperatures and low light levels. It is difficult to meet these needs and maintain them in cultivation and so they are rarely seen. Propagate from seed.

Pleurophyllum criniferum

☼/◐ ❄ ↔ 3–4 ft (0.9–1.2 m)
↕ 3–7 ft (0.9–2 m)

Native to Auckland Islands and Campbell Islands. Tapering oval leaves to 40 in (100 cm) long. Upper surface lightly ribbed, lower surface downy white. Tall stalks bear heads of purplish brown daisies with inconspicuous rays. Zones 7–9.

Pleurophyllum speciosum

☼/◐ ❄ ↔ 24 in (60 cm) ↕ 36 in (90 cm)

Native to Auckland Islands and Campbell Islands. Broadly oval leaves, to 24 in (60 cm), are thick, bright green and deeply ribbed. Flowering stalks carry large heads of white to pink daisies with purple centers. Zones 7–9.

Pleione, Hybrid, Britannia

Pleione, Hybrid, El Pico

Pleione, Hybrid, Tongariro

Pleione, Hybrid, Alishan

Pleione, Hybrid, Shantung

Pleione, Hybrid, Tolima

Pleione, Hybrid, Soufrière

Pleione, Hybrid, Zeus Weinstein

Pleione, Hybrid, Versailles

PLEUROTHALLIS

This is a large genus of over 1,000 species of sympodial orchids (family Orchidaceae) from the American tropics. They are generally epiphytes of the mountainous rainforests, but there are many species that grow in open situations, on rocks or as terrestrials, generally in thick mosses. A single leaf is produced, often on a thin, flattened "stem," called a ramicaul, as they lack pseudobulbs. The flowers are produced from a spathe or sheath at the base of the leaf, either singly or on an inflorescence. There is an amazing range in color, shape, and size within the blooms of the various species. Plants range from miniatures to species that can grow over 3 ft (0.9 m) tall. Most are cool-growing, but there are also examples from lowland regions that require warm conditions in cultivation. They are mainly of interest to species orchid enthusiasts, who enjoy the challenge of growing these more unusual botanical subjects in their collections.

CULTIVATION: Members of this genus have similar cultural requirements to the related *Masdevallia*, but will generally tolerate a wider range of temperatures and stronger light intensities. They like to be somewhat pot-bound and prefer small pots. Keep them moist, shaded, and generally in a humid environment throughout the year, but avoid direct sunlight. Most species may be grown in sphagnum moss or in a fine bark mix, with some of the creeping species suitable for mounting on tree-fern. Propagate by root division.

Pleurothallis grobyi

☀ ✣ ↔ 2½–12 in (6–30 cm)
↑ 1½–6 in (3.5–15 cm)

From Central America, the West Indies, Brazil, and Peru. A common and variable species, having small, lax spikes of tiny green to yellow-orange flowers, striped maroon; these often do not open fully. Attractive compact foliage. Zones 9–11.

Pleurothallis schiedei

☀ ✣ ↔ 1½–6 in (3.5–15 cm)
↑ 1½–6 in (3.5–15 cm)

Found in Mexico and Guatemala. This somewhat bizarre miniature species has short, fine spikes of up to 5 tiny flowers. They range from greenish yellow through orange-brown to deep maroon, with darker spotting over the sepals. The unusual feature is the white filaments that dangle from the edges of the sepals, which move in the slightest breeze. Zones 9–11.

Pleurothallis tuerckheimii

☀ ✤ ↔ 4–20 in (10–50 cm)
↑ 8–20 in (20–50 cm)

Robust Central American species producing long inflorescences of up to 20 reddish brown blooms, about 1 in (25 mm) tall, in summer. Zones 10–11.

Plumbago auriculata

PLUMBAGO

LEADWORT

There are about 15 species of annuals, perennials, and shrubs in this genus, which is a member of the leadwort (Plumbaginaceae) family. They are widely distributed throughout the tropics and subtropics. They have simple light to mid-green leaves and can become rather sparsely foliaged and twiggy if not trimmed. Their main attraction is their flowers, which appear throughout the warmer months. Carried on short racemes, they are very narrow tubes tipped with 5 relatively large lobes. The flowers come in white or various shades of pink and blue.

CULTIVATION: The taller shrubby species can be trained as climbers if grown against a wall. The shorter forms do well in containers. Plumbagos are not fussy about soil, as long as it is moist and well drained. Prune them in late winter to thin out the summer's congested growth and remove any frost-damaged wood. Plant in full sun; propagate from seed, half-hardened cuttings, or by layers.

Plumbago auriculata

syn. *Plumbago capensis*

CAPE LEADWORT, PLUMBAGO

☀ ✣ ↔ 7 ft (2 m) ↑ 15 ft (4.5 m)

Native to South Africa. Tough vigorous shrub with long arching stems. Profuse pale blue flowers are produced throughout the warmer months. 'Alba' has white flowers; 'Escapade Blue' has light blue flowers; 'Royal Cape' ★ has darker blue flowers. Zones 9–11.

Plumbago auriculata 'Escapade Blue'

Plumbago indica

☀ ✤ ↔ 3 ft (0.9 m) ↑ 5 ft (1.5 m)

Sprawling shrub or subshrub from Southeast Asia, popular in subtropical and tropical gardens. Long spikes of deep pink, pale red or purple-red flowers, warmer months, intermittently at other times. Zones 10–12.

PLUMERIA

This small genus in the dogbane (Apocynaceae) family contains about 8 species from tropical America. Mostly deciduous or semi-evergreen shrubs and small trees, they have simple smooth-edged leaves arranged alternately or spirally toward the ends of fleshy branches with a poisonous milky sap. Grown for their fragrant flowers: 5 petals, arranged in a propeller-like form and joined at the base into a narrow tube; they are produced in clusters on the ends of branches.

CULTIVATION: Easily cultivated in a warm humid climate in a sunny position protected from strong cold winds. In cooler climates they require a warm frost-free position in a well-drained moderately fertile soil. Propagate from stem cuttings, which can be branch size; these are most successful if taken in late winter when the plant is dormant. Allow the cut end to seal before inserting it into the growing medium.

Plumeria cubensis

☀ ✤ ↔ 10 ft (3 m) ↑ 25 ft (8 m)

Small evergreen tree native to the Caribbean Islands. Dark green oblong leaves to 6 in (15 cm) long. White waxy flowers, rounded spreading petals, 3 in (8 cm) across, yellow center, intensely fragrant. Zones 10–12.

Plumeria obtusa

PAGODA TREE, WHITE FRANGIPANI

☀ ✤ ↔ 12 ft (3.5 m) ↑ 25 ft (8 m)

Native to the Bahamas and Greater Antilles. Evergreen in tropical climates. Leaves have rounded or blunt tips. Fragrant flowers, white with a yellow center, petals radiate like spokes of a wheel. 'Singapore White' ★, particularly attractive white-flowered cultivar. Zones 10–12.

Plumeria obtusa 'Singapore White'

Plumeria obtusa

Plumeria rubra 'Bridal White'

Plumeria rubra 'Celandine'

Plumeria rubra 'Dark Red'

Plumeria rubra 'Rosy Dawn'

Plumeria rubra 'Starlight'

Poa chaixii

Poa cita

Plumeria rubra var. *acutifolia*

Plumeria rubra ★

FRANGIPANI

☀ ✿ ↔15 ft (4.5 m) ↑25 ft (8 m)

From Central America, Mexico, and Venezuela. Popular deciduous tree, spreading branches creating a broad rounded shape. Leaves large, dark green, shiny. Strongly fragrant funnel-shaped flowers, variable in color, in summer–autumn. *P. r.* var. *acutifolia*, widely cultivated, panicles of yellow-centered white flowers with wide petals. *P. r.* 'Bridal White', compact shrub with 3 in (8 cm) wide, mildly scented, white to creamy white flowers with a small yellow center and long deep green leaves with red edges; 'Celandine', golden yellow flowers; 'Dark Red', striking rich red flowers; 'Rosy Dawn', yellow flowers tinged with pink; 'Starlight', large flowers, up to 4 in (10 cm) wide, white suffused into an apricot to yellow center. Zones 10–12.

POA

BLUE GRASS, MEADOWGRASS, SPEAR GRASS

This is a genus of about 500 mostly perennial and some annual species with slender to robust stems, members

Podalyria calyptrata

of the grass (Poaceae) family and native to cool-temperate regions. Sheathed, narrow, strap-like leaves with flat, folded, or curled blades, and usually smooth with raised, rough veins. Flowerheads, on erect stems, 1–4 ft (0.3–1.2 m) tall, are open or compact panicles of normally 2 to 6 spikelets, often tufted with long, cobweb-like hairs with branches drooping or held close to the stem. The genus is named from *poa*, Greek for grass.

CULTIVATION: These grasses are adaptable to most soils and prefer an open sunny position. Propagate from seed or by division.

Poa annua

ANNUAL BLUEGRASS, ANNUAL MEADOW GRASS, DWARF MEADOW GRASS

☀ ❄ ↔6–12 in (15–30 cm) ↑9–12 in (22–30 cm)

Annual or biennial grass, native to Europe and North America. Smooth, creeping or erect stems, to 12 in (30 cm) high. Soft, flat, bright or yellowish green leaves, to 4 in (10 cm) long. Flower panicles, loose, spreading, pyramid-shaped, 2–4 in (5–10 cm) long, with hairy spikelets only in the top half, appear in winter and spring, or continuously when moisture permits. Zones 6–8.

Poa chaixii

BROAD-LEAFED MEADOW GRASS, FOREST BLUEGRASS

☀ ❄ ↔12–24 in (30–60 cm) ↑36–48 in (90–120 cm)

Perennial grass, native to temperate Eurasia and southwestern Asia. Bright green, flat or folded leaf blades, to 2 in (5 cm) long, and open, egg-shaped to

oblong panicles of cream-colored flowers, to 10 in (25 cm) long, in spring–summer. Zones 3–5.

Poa cita ★

SILVER TUSSOCK

☀ ❄ ↔9–12 in (22–30 cm) ↑12–40 in (30–100 cm)

Perennial grass from New Zealand. Forms dense clumps of tightly folded, leathery, sharply tipped, brownish or silvery green leaves smooth above and fringed with hairs along the margins, with a creamy brown, shiny sheath with rough margins. Feathery pale green flowerheads, which do not stand above the leaves, consist of an open, slender, rough panicle with twisted branches. Zones 7–9.

Poa pratensis

JUNE GRASS, KENTUCKY BLUEGRASS, MEADOW GRASS

☀ ❄ ↔12–24 in (30–60 cm) ↑24–36 in (60–90 cm)

This loosely tufted perennial grass is a native of North Africa and central Europe. It grows from long, stout rhizomes, and is widely planted as a lawn or pasture grass. The loose, spreading, pyramid-shaped panicles have spreading branchlets of cream-colored flower spikelets, to 8 in (20 cm) long, in spring–early summer. The spikelets often fall to one side. The leaves are flattened or

folded, smooth or rough, to 6 in (15 cm) or more long, with open sheaths. Zones 3–6.

PODALYRIA

Containing some 25 species of evergreen shrubs and trees, this South African genus is in the pea-flower subfamily of the legume (Fabaceae) family. It is notable for its downy foliage and young growth and for the attractive pea-flowers, which are usually in shades of pink and mauve. The leaves are simple smooth-edged ellipses made attractive by their covering of fine hairs, which gives them a silvery or pale golden sheen. The flowers, carried singly or in pairs in the leaf axils, open from similarly downy buds and are lightly scented.

CULTIVATION: These plants prefer a light, well-drained soil and a position in full sun. They are drought tolerant once established and thrive in coastal conditions. A light pruning after flowering will keep them compact. Propagation is from seed, half-hardened cuttings or by layering.

Podalyria calyptrata

SWEET PEA BUSH

☀ ❀ ↔12 ft (3.5 m) ↑12 ft (3.5 m)

Large shrub or small tree. Dark green leaves, silvery sheen from the coating of short fine hairs. Pale pink to lavender flowers, 1¼ in (30 mm) wide, in spring–early summer. Zones 9–10.

P

Podocarpus macrophyllus

Podocarpus henkelii

Podocarpus grayae

Podocarpus elongatus

Podocarpus latifolius

PODOCARPUS

Widely distributed in warm-temperate areas of the Southern Hemisphere to tropical zones of eastern Asia and Japan, this genus in the plum-pine (Podocarpaceae) family consists of around 100 species of evergreen trees and shrubs. They have simple, usually spirally or alternately attached leaves that are mostly flat and narrow. The male and female plants are usually separate. The female flowers turn into round drupe-like fruits, often on a fleshy red or purple receptacle. Most species are useful landscape subjects and can be utilized as specimen trees, shrub borders or hedging plants in streets, parks, golf courses, or larger gardens in mild areas; some species are valued as timber trees.

CULTIVATION: Most *Podocarpus* species prefer a well-drained soil in a sunny position protected from cold strong winds. Once established, they will tolerate extended dry periods. Propagate from seed, preferably fresh, or from cuttings.

Podocarpus elatus

BROWN PINE, PLUM PINE

↔ 20 ft (6 m) ↑ 50 ft (15 m)

Native to Queensland and New South Wales, Australia. Tall shrub or tree. Deep green leathery leaves, oblong to linear. Single greenish fruit. Especially suited for bonsai and hedging. Zones 9–12.

Podocarpus elongatus

BREEDE RIVER YELLOWWOOD, CAPE YELLOWWOOD

↔ 20 ft (6 m) ↑ 40 ft (12 m)

From South Africa. Shrub or tree with rounded appearance. Grayish green to dark gray thin bark. Green leaves tinged blue above, scattered pores above and below. Fruits produced on swollen, scarlet stalks. Zones 9–12.

Podocarpus grayae

↔ 12 ft (3.5 m) ↑ 20 ft (6 m)

Tall shrub occurs in the rainforests of Cape York Peninsula, Queensland, Australia. Leaves alternate, narrow, dark green, pendent. Male cones in groups, female cones borne singly, in early summer. Single seed on a red fleshy stalk. Zones 9–11.

Podocarpus hallii

HALL'S TOTARA

↔ 25 ft (8 m) ↑ 70 ft (21 m)

From the South Island and Stewart Island of New Zealand. Thin papery bark, peels in large thin sheets. Linear to ovate green leaves, spirally arranged on mature trees. Nut-like seed on a fleshy, often red stalk. Zones 8–11.

Podocarpus henkelii

FALCATE YELLOWWOOD

↔ 20 ft (6 m) ↑ 100 ft (30 m)

Densely branching tree, native to southeastern Africa. Gray to khaki bark, drooping, shiny, dark green foliage. Mature leaves wide in the middle, tapering both ends. Waxy olive green seeds on small, blue-green, thickened stalks. Zones 9–12.

Podocarpus latifolius

YELLOWWOOD

↔ 15 ft (4.5 m) ↑ 90 ft (27 m)

Large, evergreen shrub or tree native to Africa, from Sudan south to Kwa-Zulu-Natal, South Africa. Smooth, dark gray bark, peeling in long strips; leaves rigid, dark green, narrowly elliptical, 1¼–4 in (3–10 cm) long, tinged with blue above. Male and female cones resemble small pine cones, female cone developing into a small, fleshy, berry-like fruit, red tinged with purple. National tree of South Africa. Zones 10–11.

Podocarpus nivalis

Podocarpus lawrencei

MOUNTAIN PLUM PINE

↔ 4 ft (1.2 m) ↑ 12 ft (3.5 m)

Very variable species, dwarf to tall shrub. Deep green, linear leaves, bluish tinge above, paler below. Seed greenish on an enlarged, pinkish red, fleshy stalk. Low-growing variants can be used as ground covers. Zones 7–10.

Podocarpus macrophyllus

KUSAMAKI, LOHAN PINE

↔ 20 ft (6 m) ↑ 60 ft (18 m)

Native to China and Japan. Outer branches droop. Dark green, leathery, linear to lance-shaped leaves, bluish green below. Fruits on succulent purplish red stalk. **'Maki'**, more compact, smaller leaves. Zones 7–11.

Podocarpus nivalis

ALPINE TOTARA

↔ 6 ft (1.8 m) ↑ 10 ft (3 m)

From New Zealand. Ground-trailing, sometimes low shrub. Linear to oblong leaves, thickened at midrib and leaf edges. Seeds nut-like on enlarged, red, fleshy stalks. Ground-hugging variants suitable as ground covers. Zones 7–10.

Podocarpus salignus

WILLOW PODOCARP

↔ 25 ft (8 m) ↑ 70 ft (21 m)

From Chile. Elegant tree with willow-like leaves. Pyramidal habit, slightly pendulous branches, bluish green leaves. Brown-red fibrous bark peels off in strips. Green seeds on a fleshy, red to violet, enlarged stalk. Zones 8–9.

Podocarpus salignus

P

Podocarpus totara

Podocarpus totara

TOTARA

☼ 〰 ↔ 25 ft (8 m) ↑ 80 ft (24 m)

Long-lived New Zealand tree. Dense rounded crown, giant trunk, timber highly prized, resistant to marine borers. Linear, leathery, dark green leaves. Single seeds on the ends of reddish fleshy stalks. 'Aureus' grows to 10 ft (3 m) tall, with a narrow conical form and yellow foliage. Zones 9–11.

PODOPHYLLUM

MAY APPLE

This genus of 7 perennial herbs from the barberry (Berberidaceae) family, native from eastern North America to eastern Asia and the Himalayas, grows from stout rhizomes. Large, palm-shaped, lobed leaves, on long stalks, and groups of single or several, over-lapping, ruff- or parasol-like flowers with 6 to 9 petals, rise on erect stems, to 16 in (40 cm) tall. The fruit is a large, fleshy, egg-shaped berry. Native Americans made an extract from the rhizomes of *P. peltatum*, to treat intestinal worms and for use as a laxative.
CULTIVATION: Most may apples prefer a shady position, often in wet or marshy ground. Propagate by division or from seed.

Podophyllum difforme

◐ ❊ ↔ 20 in (50 cm) ↑ 8 in (20 cm)

Western Chinese species. Leaves have 5 to 8 lobes with a marbled cyclamen-like pattern and cream and purple-brown central markings, maturing to light green. Up to 5 flowers per cluster, dark purple-red or less commonly pink, followed by plum-like fruits. Zones 7–10.

Podophyllum hexandrum

HIMALAYAN MAY APPLE

☼ ❊ ↔ 16 in (40 cm) ↑ 16 in (40 cm)

Native to western China and the Himalayas. Leaves to 10 in (25 cm)

Podophyllum difforme

across, with 3 to 5 lobes, each tipped with a further 3 lobes, and often flushed with reddish bronze. Solitary, erect terminal flowers appear before the leaves mature, with 6 white to rose pink petals, in spring, followed by red fruit. Zones 4–6.

Podophyllum peltatum

AMERICAN MANDRAKE, DEVIL'S APPLE, HOG APPLE, INDIAN APPLE, MAY APPLE

☼ ❊ ↔ 24 in (60 cm) ↑ 24 in (60 cm)

From the woodlands of eastern USA south to Texas. A single, round, simple, forked stem and only 2 leaves, to 12 in (30 cm) across, with 3 to 9 lobes, finely hairy underneath. Flowering stem with 2 to 3 leaves or leafless, with solitary, nodding, fragrant flowers with white or rose pink petals, with toothed points, in spring. Fruit is a single berry, greenish yellow, occasionally red, with pulpy flesh; it ripens in late summer, the only part of the plant not poisonous. Zones 4–6.

PODRANEA

This genus is made up of 2 evergreen, twining, climbing shrubs, members of the trumpet-vine (Bignoniaceae) family and natives of South Africa, grown for their foxglove-like flowers. They have divided leaves and terminal, pyramid-shaped flowerheads. The fruit is a long capsule or pod containing winged seed. *Podranea* is an anagram of the closely related *Pandorea*.
CULTIVATION: Grow in full sun in any fertile, well-drained soil. Plants may need support. Propagate by striking half-hardened cuttings in summer or from seed sown in spring.

Polemonium boreale

Podranea ricasoliana

syns *Pandorea brycei*, *P. ricasoliana*, *Tecoma ricasoliana*

PINK TRUMPET VINE

☼ ✈ ↔ 20 ft (6 m) ↑ 12–20 ft (3.5–6 m)

A fast-growing, climbing shrub with slender, twining stems and compound leaves with 5 to 11 smooth-edged, green leaflets. Loose clusters of pale pink, fragrant, funnel-shaped flowers, to 2½ in (6 cm) across, striped with red, appear from spring to autumn. Zones 10–11.

POLEMONIUM

JACOB'S LADDER, SKY PILOT

A genus of 25 erect or spreading or rhizomatous annual or sometimes short-lived perennial herbs from the phlox (Polemoniaceae) family, native from temperate to Arctic regions of the Americas, Europe, and Asia. Plants have pinnate leaves with simple or divided leaflets, with or without stalks. Heads of 5-lobed, tubular, bell- or funnel-shaped flowers, in blue, purplish, white, or yellow, grow from the leaf axils or at the ends of sprawling or erect stems. Egg-shaped to spherical fruit contain 3 to 10 brown or black seeds per compartment.
CULTIVATION: They grow well in sun or part-shade in rich, well-drained, moist, loamy soil. Propagate by division in autumn or early spring, or from seed sown in autumn or winter.

Polemonium boreale

syns *Polemonium macranthum*, *P. nudipedum*, *P. richardsonii*

ARCTIC POLEMONIUM, NORTHERN JACOB'S LADDER

☼ ❊ ↔ 3–12 in (8–30 cm) ↑ 3–12 in (8–30 cm)

Erect, hairy or glandular perennial, growing naturally in crevices and rocky slopes in central Asia. Erect stems and leaves mostly from a central base, with 13 to 23 oval leaflets.

Terminal heads of bell-shaped flowers, blue, violet, or white, about ½ in (12 mm) across, in summer. Zones 3–8.

Polemonium caeruleum

CHARITY, GREEK VALERIAN, JACOB'S LADDER

☼ ❊ ↔ 12–20 in (30–50 cm) ↑ 12–36 in (30–90 cm)

Hairy and glandular perennial, a native of northern and central Europe and northern Asia. Leaves to 16 in (40 cm) long and with 11 to 27 sword-shaped to oblong leaflets, growing from a central base. Loose heads of flowers with blue, occasionally white, widely bell-shaped corollas, with oval lobes, appear in late spring–summer. *P. c.* subsp. *caeruleum*, heads of many blue flowers, with stamens protruding beyond the corolla. *P. c.* 'Brise d'Anjou' ★, stunning variegated form. Zones 2–4.

Polemonium carneum

☼ ❊ ↔ 4–24 in (10–60 cm) ↑ 4–24 in (10–60 cm)

Clump-forming, minutely hairy, erect perennial, native to western USA from California to Oregon. Erect or sprawling, hollow, angular stems and leaves with 5 to 21 elliptical to oval, green leaflets. Loose clusters of 3 to 7 flowers with bell-shaped, lilac, pink, or yellow corollas, ½–1 in (12–25 mm) long, on short stalks, in early summer, followed by fruit. Zones 4–6.

Podranea ricasoliana

Polemonium caeruleum 'Brise d'Anjou'

Polemonium pulcherrimum

SHOWY POLEMONIUM, WESTERN SKY PILOT

☼/☀ ❄ ↔ 20–24 in (50–60 cm)
↕ 20–24 in (50–60 cm)

Vigorous, erect, clumping, deciduous perennial, growing naturally from slender, branching rhizomes on moist to dry, often rocky slopes in north-western North America. There are 4 to 10 sprawling or erect stems, covered with soft hairs. Leaves grow from a central base, with 9 to 37 bright green, oval leaflets covered in fine hairs. Dense, glandular clusters of flowers with a bell-shaped, blue, violet, or white corolla, surrounded by 2 leaf-like bracts, yellow inside, on stalks to 1 in (25 mm) long, in late spring–summer. Zones 4–7.

Polemonium reptans

ABSCESS ROOT, CREEPING JACOB'S LADDER, GREEK VALERIAN

☼ ❄ ↔ 12–27 in (30–70 cm)
↕ 8–27 in (20–70 cm)

Erect or spreading perennial, native to eastern USA. Fleshy roots and many

Polyalthia longifolia

Polygala calcarea 'Lillet'

erect, smooth, hollow, branching, herbaceous, greenish stems, sometimes with a reddish tinge, growing from a small crown. Leaves to 8 in (20 cm) or more long, with 7 to 19 elliptical to oval, dull green leaflets, silvery green underneath. Loose panicles, with bracts of drooping flowers with a densely glandular, bell-shaped calyx and a smooth, lilac to light blue, funnel-shaped corolla, in spring–early summer. Roots traditionally used by Native Americans for a variety of ailments from bronchitis to snakebite. 'Blue Pearl' grows to 10 in (25 cm) high, with blue flowers. Zones 4–7.

Polemonium viscosum

SKUNK POLEMONIUM, SKY PILOT, STICKY POLEMONIUM

☼/☀ ❄ ↔ 16 in (40 cm) ↕ 16 in (40 cm)

Perennial, native to northwestern North America. Erect, angular, hollow stems, and densely glandular leaves, to 8 in (20 cm) long, with many tiny, lobed leaflets, mostly growing from a central base. Dense heads of drooping, blue to violet flowers, with tubular or funnel-shaped corollas, in late spring–summer. Zones 3–5.

POLIANTHES

This Mexican genus in the agave (Agavaceae) family comprises 13 species of strongly rhizomatous perennials forming clumps of linear to lance-shaped, sometimes strappy basal leaves, from which emerge upright flower stems bearing several pairs of very fragrant, waxy flowers backed by leafy bracts. The flowers of the commonly grown *P. tuberosa*, cultivated for the perfume and florist trades, last well when cut. Introduced to Europe in the sixteenth century, *P. tuberosa* was cultivated by local tribespeople and is not known in the wild.

Polemonium reptans

CULTIVATION: These plants are best grown in a mild climate. Summer-flowering outdoors, but can be forced into bloom at any time indoors. Plant in a sunny, sheltered position in fertile, moist, humus-rich, well-drained soil. Although perennial, they flower only once. Propagate by removing the strongest side-shoots before discarding spent crowns, or from seed.

Polianthes tuberosa

TUBEROSE

☼/☀ ≵ ↔ 20 in (50 cm) ↕ 48 in (120 cm)

Mexican perennial forming basal clump of narrow, strap-like green to gray-green leaves. Erect flower stems carry racemes of fragrant, funnel-shaped, waxy, white flowers to 2 in (5 cm) long, with 6 widely flared lobes, summer–autumn. 'The Pearl', strongly scented, white, double flowers. Zones 9–10.

POLYALTHIA

This genus of around 100 species of shrubs or trees belongs to the custard-apple (Annonaceae) family. It is widespread in tropical regions, particularly in Southeast Asia, with a few species occurring in Australia. They have large glossy leaves that have very fine oil dots and are aromatic when crushed. Their open star-like flowers have 6 to 8 petals and are borne singly or in clusters on older leafless wood. These are followed by decorative clusters of succulent berry-like fruit.
CULTIVATION: All species demand warm, frost-free conditions. They prefer moist, humus-rich, well-drained soil in full sun or part-shade. Water liberally during dry periods. Propagate from fresh seed or cuttings.

Polyalthia longifolia

INDIAN WILLOW

☼ ⚘ ↔ 3–10 ft (0.9–3 m) ↕ 50 ft (15 m)

Occurring naturally in Sri Lanka. Low-branching column-like tree, widely planted as a street and park tree in tropical Asia. Pendulous, bright green, elliptic leaves. Small greenish yellow flowers in axillary clusters, in summer. Zones 11–12.

Polemonium reptans 'Blue Pearl'

Polianthes tuberosa

POLYGALA

Covering over 500 species of almost every growth form, except tall trees, this genus, a member of the milkwort (Polygalaceae) family, is very widespread. The foliage ranges from small and linear to large and oval but is usually simple with smooth edges. The flowers have a pea-flower-like structure with distinct wings and a keel, which usually has a feathery tuft unique to polygalas. The flowers, carried in clusters or racemes, come in a range of colors, with purple and pink dominant, and are followed by small seed pods.
CULTIVATION: While frost hardiness varies, most prefer a light well-drained soil with a position in sun or partial shade. The European and American alpine species are ideal subjects for pots or troughs. The shrubby species can be trimmed or pruned to shape, spring usually being the best time as it ensures the speediest recovery. Propagate from seed, layers, or cuttings.

Polygala calcarea

☼ ❄ ↔ 4–6 in (10–15 cm)
↕ 1–1¼ in (2.5–3 cm)

Evergreen, occasionally upright, perennial shrub from western Europe including southern England. Stems, with runners, terminate in rosettes of small, wedge- to egg-shaped leaves, with smaller, narrow leaves on stems. Erect flowering stems, to 8 in (20 cm) tall, with loose racemes of 6 to 20 flowers, normally pale or dark blue, sometimes white, in late spring–early summer. 'Lillet', bright blue flowers. Zones 5–7.

Polygala chamaebuxus

☼ ❋ ↔15 in (38 cm) ↕2–6 in (5–15 cm)

Tiny spreading shrublet from the mountains of central Europe. Long, elliptical, leathery, glossy leaves. White-winged, yellow-keeled, pea-flowers. Popular for troughs, alpine houses, and well-drained rock gardens. *P. c.* **var.** *grandiflora* has purple-winged flowers. Zones 6–9.

Polygala × *dalmaisiana*

☼ ❄ ↔3 ft (0.9 m) ↕3–10 ft (0.9–3 m)

Evergreen shrub, garden hybrid between *P. oppositifolia* and *P. myrtifolia*; neat, compact if trimmed occasionally. Mid-green, 1 in (25 mm) long leaves. Magenta to pale purple flowers, most of the year. Zones 9–11.

Polygala myrtifolia

☼ ❄ ↔3–6 ft (0.9–1.8 m) ↕6 ft (1.8 m)

South African evergreen shrub. Elliptic to oblong, mid-green leaves, often develop purplish tints, in winter. Small clusters of pale-tufted purple-pink flowers most of the year. Trim to keep compact. Zones 9–11.

Polygala virgata

CAPE PURPLE BROOM

☼ ❄ ↔5 ft (1.5 m) ↕3–6 ft (0.9–1.8 m)

South African deciduous or semi-evergreen shrub (can grow into a small tree). Simple leaves; flowers purple-pink in racemes to 6 in (15 cm) long. Small seed pods. Can become weedy, suits coastal conditions. Zones 9–11.

POLYGONATUM

SOLOMON'S SEAL

The approximately 50 species of this member of the lily-of-the-valley

Polygala × *dalmaisiana*

Polygala myrtifolia

Polylepis tomentella, in the wild, Peru

(Convallariaceae) family are found in the temperate zones of the Northern Hemisphere. Most of these easy-to-grow herbaceous perennials are fully hardy. The taller species have graceful arching stems, attractive leaves, and carry the delicate flowers in small pendulous clusters from the upper leaf axils. Small blue-black berries often follow the flowers. There is one dwarf variety that is perfect for rock gardens. The plant spreads by slow-growing underground rhizomes. Plant in a woodland garden with hostas, hellebores, wild ginger, ferns, or astilbe.

CULTIVATION: Plant in a shady or partly shady position in a rich, moist, peaty soil. Propagate from seed or divide the rhizomes in spring or autumn. Cut the stems down to soil level in late autumn. Mulch annually with leaf mold.

Polygonatum cirrhifolium

☼ ❋ ↔24 in (60 cm) ↕7 ft (2 m)

From China. Whorls of long thin leaves, curling slightly at tips. Narrow, tubular, pink to purple flowers with tips sometimes differently colored, in late spring–early summer; red berries in autumn. Zones 6–8.

Polygala virgata

Polygonatum cirrhifolium

Polylepis species

Polygonatum hookeri

☼ ❋ ↔12 in (30 cm) ↕2–4 in (5–10 cm)

From China's western Szechuan province and Tibet. Dwarf species for rock garden. Mid-green ovate leaves; upturned, star-shaped, lilac-pink flowers appear with the leaves, in mid-spring. Zones 6–8.

Polygonatum × *hybridum*

syn. *Polygonatum multiflorum* of gardens

❋/☼ ❋ ↔12–24 in (30–60 cm) ↕36 in (90 cm)

White, green-tipped, bell-shaped flowers hang from arching stems in late spring–early summer. Oval green leaves turn a buttery yellow color in autumn. Easy to grow in almost any soil. Protect the roots from the sun. Zones 3–9.

Polygonatum odoratum

syn. *Polygonatum officinale*

ANGULAR SOLOMON'S SEAL

☼ ❋ ↔24 in (60 cm) ↕36 in (90 cm)

From Europe, northern Iran, Siberia, and Japan. Grows in woods, in limestone. Flowers mid-spring–early summer. 'Flore Pleno' ★, attractive double flowers; 'Variegatum', leaf margins and tips edged white. Zones 3–9.

POLYLEPIS

This genus of around 20 species from Andean South America belongs to the rose (Rosaceae) family. It includes several species that make up what is regarded as the world's highest altitude forest, a forest with a few species that occur at over 13,000 ft (4,000 m). They are especially useful in their native environment for their erosion protection abilities and are vitally important to several bird species. Height range is 3–20 ft (0.9–6 m). They have flaky bark, small gray-green leaves and small flowers with no petals that are followed by dry seed capsules.

Polylepis tomentella, in the wild, Bolivia

CULTIVATION: Rarely cultivated, they prefer cool humid conditions with ample rainfall, as might be expected for plants that spend much of their lives in the clouds. Plant in cool, moist, gritty soil with extra humus for moisture retention; in lowland gardens they would probably need shade from the hottest sun and shelter from drying winds. Propagate from seed.

Polylepis tomentella

QUEÑOA

❋ ❋ ↔15 ft (4.5 m) ↕20 ft (6 m)

Attractive species from low forests on the Andes slopes at altitudes over 12,000 ft (3,600 m). Low branching thick gnarled limbs, red-brown papery bark. Dense, dull green foliage coated in woolly hairs. Endangered by collection for firewood. Zones 7–9.

POLYPODIUM

POLYPODY

A genus of about 75 deciduous, semi-evergreen or evergreen, epiphytic, rock-dwelling, or terrestrial ferns in the polypody (Polypodiaceae) family, from temperate regions of the Northern

Polypodium californicum

Polypodium scouleri

Polypodium triseriale

Hemisphere. They have stemmed, simple or divided fronds, with yellow spore-bodies on the backs of veins, and grow from creeping scaly rhizomes. The fronds dry up and fall in summer, but new fronds appear with autumn rain. The genus name comes from the Greek words *polys*, many, and *pous*, foot, referring to the much-branching rhizomes.
CULTIVATION: Polypody prefer a fibrous, well-drained soil but cope with heavy clay or gravel kept moist, particularly in winter, in part-shade. Propagate from spores in late summer, or by division of clumps or rhizomes in spring.

Polypodium californicum
CALIFORNIA POLYPODY
☀ ❄ ↔ 20 in (50 cm) ↑ 40 in (100 cm)
Summer-deciduous, creeping, perennial fern naturally inhabiting moist rock crevices in California, USA. Arching, deeply divided, oblong to triangular, green fronds, to 12 in (30 cm) long and 6 in (15 cm) wide, on straw-colored stems to 8 in (20 cm) high. Zones 7–10.

Polypodium cambricum
syn. *Polypodium australe*
SOUTHERN POLYPODY, WELSH POLYPODY
☀ ❄ ↔ 8–20 in (20–50 cm)
↑ 8–20 in (20–50 cm)
Perennial fern, native to Europe. Broad, soft, divided, triangular to

oblong fronds, 5–20 in (12–50 cm) long, on brown stems to 8 in (20 cm) tall. 'Cambricum', feathery fronds with lacerated segments, 12–16 in (30–40 cm) long; 'Grandiceps Fox', with crests on leaflets and large frond tip; 'Whilharris', tall, leathery, narrow fronds, 12–16 in (30–40 cm) long, with deeply lacerated leaflets. Zones 4–6.

Polypodium glycyrrhiza
syn. *Polypodium vulgare* var. *occidentale*
LICORICE FERN
☀ ❄ ↔ 12–24 in (30–60 cm)
↑ 12–24 in (30–60 cm)
Epiphytic, colonizing, summer-deciduous fern grows on wet mossy logs and rocks on the western coast of North America, from Alaska to California. Named for its perennial licorice-flavored rhizomes, which Native Americans used medicinally and for food flavoring. Rhizomes are shallow, branching, yellowish green, roundish, up to ¼ in (6 mm) thick. Thinly textured, sword-shaped to elliptical, light green fronds, to 14 in (35 cm) long, with 10 to 20 offset pairs of notched pointed segments, on straw-colored stems. Zones 6–9.

Polypodium scouleri
COAST POLYPODY, LEATHERY POLYPODY
☀ ❄ ↔ 36 in (90 cm) ↑ 15 in (38 cm)
Evergreen fern, native to the west coast of North America, from British

Columbia to California. Rigid, thickly textured, glossy, leathery, oval to triangular, deep green fronds, to 16 in (40 cm) long, with up to 14 pairs of narrow, spreading segments with smooth-edged or notched margins, on smooth stems to 4 in (10 cm) high. Zones 8–10.

Polypodium triseriale
ANGLE-VEIN FERN
☀ ❄ ↔ 16–24 in (40–60 cm)
↑ 16–24 in (40–60 cm)
Fern from the West Indies, Central America, and northern South America. Herbaceous or leathery, divided fronds, to 24 in (60 cm) long. Spreading, narrow, strap-shaped leaflets on lustrous, straw-colored to reddish brown stems to 14 in (35 cm) long. Zones 9–10.

Polypodium vulgare
ADDER'S FERN, COMMON POLYPODY, GOLDEN MAIDENHAIR, WALL FERN
☀ ❄ ↔ 10–12 in (25–30 cm)
↑ 10–12 in (25–30 cm)
Evergreen fern, widely distributed through North America, Europe, Africa, and East Asia, suited to rock gardens. It grows from creeping, brownish, scarred rhizomes covered with copper-brown scales. Arching or erect, smooth, thinly textured, sword-shaped to oval, leathery, herringbone-like fronds, to 12 in (30 cm) long, with closely set, horizontal or spreading segments carried on straw-colored stems. Zones 3–5.

POLYSCIAS
This genus of around 150 species of evergreen shrubs to large trees is part of the ivy (Araliaceae) family. It is found in tropical and subtropical regions of Africa, Southeast Asia, Australia, and the Pacific Islands. They have alternate compound leaves that are pinnate to tripinnate and tend to be spirally arranged toward

the ends of the branches. Very small greenish white or purplish flowers are produced in terminal racemes, which are often prominent and profuse. The fruit is a rounded or slightly compressed berry that turns purplish black when ripe. Some species are cultivated for their attractive foliage and are suitable for use as indoor potted plants.
CULTIVATION: Most species are only suited to warm-temperate to tropical climates and prefer well-drained, acidic soils in a sunny to partially shaded position. Provide supplementary watering during extended dry periods. Propagate from fresh seed, cuttings in summer, or by division of root suckers.

Polyscias elegans
CELERY WOOD
☀ ❄ ↔ 15 ft (4.5 m) ↑ 100 ft (30 m)
Native to eastern Australia and New Guinea. Straight-trunked tree. Bipinnate leaves, glossy, dark green leaflets, celery-like fragrance. Masses of tiny purplish flowers, in terminal panicles, in autumn–winter. Purplish black fruit. Zones 9–12.

Polyscias filicifolia
FERN-LEAF ARALIA
☀ ✈ ↔ 4 ft (1.2 m) ↑ 15 ft (4.5 m)
Native to the Pacific Islands. Erect shrub, slightly arching branches when young. Deeply dissected leaves divided into many small, bright green, toothed leaflets, prominent purple veining. Tiny star-shaped flowers, in summer. Regularly tip prune to keep compact. Zones 11–12.

Polyscias guilfoylei
GERANIUM ARALIA
☀ ✈ ↔ 8 ft (2.4 m) ↑ 20 ft (6 m)
Native to eastern Malay Peninsula, northern Australia, and Polynesia. Sparsely branched shrub. Pinnate leaves, broadly ovate to almost diamond-shaped leaflets, toothed,

Polyscias elegans, in center

Polyscias sambucifolia

Polystachya johnstonii

white margins. Yellowish green flowers, umbels forming large panicles, in summer. Tiny, purplish black fruit. Zones 11–12.

Polyscias sambucifolia
ELDERBERRY PANAX

☀ ❊ ↔ 8 ft (2.4 m) ↑ 15 ft (4.5 m)

Multi-branched shrub from eastern Australia. Leaves variable; pinnate or bipinnate, 10 pairs deeply lobed or smooth-edged leaflets. Insignificant cream or light green flowers, in large sprays, in late spring–summer. Fruits ripen steely blue to mauve. Zones 9–12.

POLYSTACHYA

This is a large genus of sympodial orchids (family Orchidaceae) from Africa, with a few outlying species in other tropical countries. They are mostly miniature clumping species with small pseudobulbs. Interesting, non-resupinate, botanical flowers are produced on upright inflorescences, from between the leaves of the immature new growth. The labellum is uppermost in the bloom. They are found in a range of colors, with yellows and oranges dominating. CULTIVATION: Most of their active growth takes place during the warmer months, with the plants entering a dormant phase during winter. Reduce watering during this time. They enjoy similar conditions to those recommended for intermediate-growing dendrobiums. Propagate by division.

Polystachya bella

☀ ✦ ↔ 4–12 in (10–30 cm) ↑ 4–12 in (10–30 cm)

From Kenya, this is a warm-growing species. In summer bears flowering inflorescences, which sometimes branch, of bright orange-yellow, 1 in (25 mm) blooms. These darken with age. Zones 11–12.

Polystachya johnstonii

☀ ✦ ↔ 2–6 in (5–15 cm) ↑ 2–4 in (4–10 cm)

From Malawi. Small growing and variable spring-flowering species.

Greenish blooms, ¾ in (18 mm) long, with purple suffusions and a contrasting pink labellum. Zones 11–12.

POLYSTICHUM

HOLLY FERN, SWORD FERN

A genus of more than 175 evergreen, semi-evergreen, or deciduous terrestrial ferns, widely distributed throughout the world. Members of the shield-fern (Dryopteridaceae) family, they grow from stout, woody, densely scaly, erect or sprawling rhizomes. Tufted, thin to leathery fronds are divided into up to 3 narrow, toothed leaflets with a tapered base, with rounded spore-bodies underneath, carried on straw-like, densely scaly stems. The genus is named from the Greek *polys*, many, and *stichos*, a row or file, a reference to the regular rows of spore. CULTIVATION: These ferns prefer part-shade and moist, well-drained, soil with plenty of organic matter. Propagate by division in spring or from spores sown in summer.

Polystichum acrostichoides

CHRISTMAS FERN, DAGGER FERN

☀ ❊ ↔ 18–24 in (45–60 cm) ↑ 18–24 in (45–60 cm)

Evergreen fern from wooded slopes of North America. One of its common names reflects the resemblance of its leaf segments to Christmas stockings. Compact, sometimes branched rhizome covered with brownish orange scales, has long fibrous roots. Narrowly sword-shaped fronds, 8–30 in (20–75 cm) long, with 20 to 35 finely toothed, dark green leaflets per side,

Polystichum braunii

with hair-like scales underneath and a densely scaly midrib. Native Americans used the rhizomes to make a tea to treat chills, fevers, pneumonia, and to induce vomiting. Zones 3–9.

Polystichum aculeatum

HARD SHIELD FERN, PRICKLY SHIELD FERN

☀ ❊ ↔ 18–24 in (45–60 cm) ↑ 18–24 in (45–60 cm)

Variable evergreen or semi-evergreen fern from Europe has rigid, sword-shaped, leathery fronds, 12–36 in (30–90 cm) long, with up to 50 toothed leaflets per side. Fronds are yellowish green in spring, maturing to dark glossy green, carried on short brown stems. *P. a.* var. *densum*, densely massed fronds. *P. a.* 'Pulcherrimum', sharply edged, delicate, dark green fronds. Zones 4–8.

Polystichum andersoni

ALASKAN HOLLY FERN, ANDERSON'S HOLLY FERN, ANDERSON'S SWORD FERN

☀ ❊ ↔ 24–30 in (60–75 cm) ↑ 24–30 in (60–75 cm)

Evergreen fern, native to northwestern North America. Fronds, sword-shaped to elliptical, 16–36 in (40–90 cm) long, with numerous, narrowly triangular, deeply toothed leaflets. Zones 4–8.

Polystichum braunii

syn. *Aspidium braunii*

BRAUN'S SWORD FERN, EASTERN HOLLY FERN, SHIELD FERN

☀ ❊ ↔ 24–36 in (60–90 cm) ↑ 24–36 in (60–90 cm)

Semi-evergreen fern from moist woodlands of North America and temperate Eurasia. Arching, dark green, glossy, soft, oblong to sword-shaped, twice-cut fronds, with 30 to 40 leaflets per side, with oval to triangular, finely toothed and slightly hairy segments, on thick stems. The stalks, midribs, and undersides of

fronds are covered in light brown scales, with few small spore-bodies underneath. Zones 4–8.

Polystichum californicum

syn. *Aspidium californicum*

CALIFORNIAN SHIELD FERN

☀ ❊ ↔ 20–30 in (50–75 cm) ↑ 20–30 in (50–75 cm)

Fern from woods, streambanks and rocky open slopes of western North America, from California to British Columbia. A naturally occurring hybrid between *P. munitum* and *P. dudleyi*. Sword-shaped fronds, 8–30 in (20–75 cm) long, numerous leaflets, on brown stems. Zones 7–9.

Polystichum dudleyi

☀ ❊ ↔ 20–30 in (50–75 cm) ↑ 20–30 in (50–75 cm)

Fern from moist forests of California, USA. Oblong, narrowly oval or sword-shaped fronds, 10–30 in (25–75 cm) long, with serrated leaflets. Zones 7–9.

Polystichum falcinellum

☀ ❊ ↔ 18–24 in (45–60 cm) ↑ 18–24 in (45–60 cm)

Evergreen fern from eastern North America and the North Atlantic island of Madeira. Stems covered with glossy brown scales. Sword-shaped, leathery fronds are 12–60 in (30–150 cm) long, with numerous toothed leaflets. Zones 5–8.

Polystichum falcinellum

Polystichum aculeatum

P

Polystichum munitum

syn. *Aspidium munitum*
GIANT HOLLY FERN, WESTERN SWORD FERN
☀ ❀ ↔ 36–48 in (90–120 cm)
↕ 36–48 in (90–120 cm)

Evergreen fern, native to the wooded hillsides of western North and Central America from California, USA, to Mexico, with rigid, erect or arching, linear or sword-shaped, leathery, dark green fronds, forming a crown from an erect or sprawling rhizome. Fronds, 20–48 in (50–120 cm) long, have up to 40 spiny-toothed leaflets on each side, with large, circular, orange spore-bodies underneath. Zones 4–6.

Polystichum polyblepharon

HOLLY FERN, TASSEL FERN
☀ ❀ ↔ 48 in (120 cm) ↕ 48 in (120 cm)
Evergreen or semi-evergreen fern from South Korea and Japan. Narrowly

Polystichum setiferum, Rotundatum Group cultivar

P. setiferum 'Divisilobum Densum'

Polystichum setiferum

oblong to oval, deep green, slightly lustrous fronds, which unfurl in a normal manner. They are clothed with white scales, then flip backward in a lax droop or tassel habit. They are 12–32 in (30–80 cm) long, have leaflets with oblong to oval, overlapping leaflets. The fronds are densely scaly on the underside, and are carried on stout brown stems. Zones 5–9.

Polystichum setiferum

SOFT SHIELD FERN
☀ ❀ ↔ 18–24 in (45–60 cm)
↕ 18–24 in (45–60 cm)

Evergreen or semi-evergreen fern, native to southern, western, and central Europe. Soft, sword-shaped, mid-green fronds, 12–48 in (30–120 cm) long, with up to 40 leaflets per side, carried on stems that are covered with pale orange to brown scales. Bulbils form on frond midribs. 'Cristatum', crested, dark green, frilly fronds; 'Divisilobum' ★, large light green fronds are very frilly; 'Divisilobum Densum', delicate-looking fern; Divisilobum Group 'Herrenhausen', leathery, dark green fronds with pointed leaflets; Plumosodivisilobum Group, compact soft fronds; 'Plumosum Densum', slightly smaller version with frilly lace-like fronds; 'Pulcherrimum Bevis', elongated crested tips on ends of fronds;

P. setiferum, Divisilobum Group, 'Herrenhausen'

Polystichum polyblepharon

Rotundatum Group 'Rotundatum', fronds with rounded leaflets; 'Wakeleyanum', narrow fronds, with leaflets forming cross-pattern across midrib. Zones 5–7.

Polystichum × setigerum

syn. *Polystichum alaskense*
ALASKAN HOLLY FERN
☀ ❀ ↔ 18–24 in (45–60 cm)
↕ 18–24 in (45–60 cm)

Evergreen fern, naturally occurring hybrid of *P. braunii* and *P. munitum*, native to western North America from Alaska to British Columbia. Pointed, diamond-shaped fronds, 10–36 in (25–90 cm) long, deeply lobed, sword-shaped leaflets, carried on pale brown stems. Zones 3–6.

Polystichum tsussimense

syn. *Aspidium tsus-simense*
KOREAN ROCK FERN, TSU-SHIMA HOLLY FERN
☀ ❀ ↔ 12–16 in (30–40 cm)
↕ 6–18 in (15–45 cm)

Clump-forming, evergreen or semi-evergreen fern, native to northeastern Asia, with thin, gently tapering,

Polystichum setiferum 'Divisilobum'

broadly sword-shaped to oval, dull green fronds, with distinctive black veining, 8–16 in (20–40 cm) long. Oval, finely toothed leaflets are carried on pale green to straw-colored stems covered with black to brown scales. Zones 6–9.

Polystichum vestitum

PRICKLY SHIELD FERN, PUNIU
☀ ❀ ↔ 12–36 in (30–90 cm)
↕ 12–36 in (30–90 cm)

Coarse, prickly, dark green fern from the South Atlantic region, New Zealand, and Tasmania, Australia. Oblong to sword-shaped fronds, 12–30 in (30–75 cm) long, with oblong to sword-shaped leaflets on stout stems that are covered with dark scales. Zones 7–8.

POMADERRIS

This is a genus of 55 species of small trees and shrubs occurring in Asia, Australia, and New Zealand and placed in the buckthorn (Rhamnaceae) family. They are all shrubs or small trees with alternate simple leaves; the hairy undersurface imparts a silvery sheen. Small white or yellow flowers are borne in terminal inflorescences, followed by a small dry fruit that breaks into 3 when mature. Their habitats are varied, covering a variety of soils, usually acid, in heaths, scrubs, woodlands, and forests at altitudes from sea level to alpine regions, in reasonably high rainfall zones.
CULTIVATION: Most of the species prefer well-drained acid soil in a partly shaded position. They are best propagated from seed and cuttings. The seed must be very fresh and needs pre-treatment, either by scarification or a short period of immersion in hot water. The lateral shoots that are a few months old, but not yet woody, seem to give the best results as cuttings.

Pomaderris eriocephala

Pomaderris apetala

☀ ❀ ↔ 20 ft (6 m) ↕ 50 ft (15 m)

From Victoria and Tasmania, Australia, and New Zealand. Shrub or small tree, 2 subspecies: tall, moist, forest dweller *P. a.* subsp. *apetala*; smaller, shrubby, coastal form *P. a.* subsp. *maritima*. Young shoots and small branches covered with grayish hairs. Oval leaves, dark green, margins toothed, grayish hairs beneath. Creamy flowers, in compound heads, in summer. Zones 8–9.

Pomaderris elliptica

☀ ❀ ↔ 8 ft (2.4 m) ↕ 15 ft (4.5 m)

From Victoria and Tasmania, Australia. Has 2 subspecies: *P. e.* subsp. *elliptica* more widespread, occurs in moist forests; *P. e.* subsp. *diemenica,* more restricted, in less forested communities. Both similar in habit, differing in size of flower parts and hair. Extremely hairy young growth on the medium-sized shrub, very light hairiness on leaf undersurface. Small yellow flowers with tiny petals, in spring. Zones 8–9.

Pomaderris eriocephala

☀ ❀ ↔ 10 ft (3 m) ↕ 10 ft (3 m)

From northeastern New South Wales to eastern Victoria, Australia. Young shoots and small branches covered in rusty hairs. Dark green leaves oval-shaped, pale hairs above, rusty hairs beneath. Small creamy colored flowers in tight globular heads, in spring. Zones 8–9.

Pomaderris lanigera

WOOLLY POMADERRIS

☀ ❀ ↔ 10 ft (3 m) ↕ 10 ft (3 m)

From eastern Australia, from central Queensland to Victoria, inhabiting dry sites. Plant covered with rusty reddish hairs, oval to elliptical leaves, green and hairy on both surfaces. Small yellow flowers, in terminal clusters, in late winter–spring. Zones 8–10.

Pomaderris lanigera

PONCIRUS

syn. *Aegle*

This single species in the rue (Rutaceae) family is a deciduous shrub or small tree native to China and Korea, where it grows in open woodland. Poncirus shares features with the presumed ancestral stock of *Citrus* and produces fertile hybrids with most *Citrus* species, so recent botanical opinion is that it might well be included in Citrus. It is often used as a hardy rootstock for oranges and other *Citrus* cultivars. It is a dense fast-growing shrub suitable for hedging.

CULTIVATION: Does best in full sun, despite growing in woodland in the wild. Needs fertile, free-draining soil and protection from cold drying winds. Sow seed in a position protected from frost in autumn, or take half-hardened cuttings in summer.

Poncirus trifoliata

JAPANESE BITTER ORANGE,
TRIFOLIATE ORANGE

☀ ❀ ↔ 15 ft (4.5 m) ↕ 15 ft (4.5 m)

Native to north China and Korea. Deciduous, densely shrubby, dark green trifoliate leaves turn yellow in autumn. Solitary, fragrant, white flowers, on second-year wood, in late spring–early summer. Fruit green, turning orange when ripe. It is grown for its interesting winter form, showing deep green branches with stout thorns. Zones 5–11.

PONGAMIA

A small genus of 2 or 3 species of evergreen shrubs or trees, native to Australia and parts of tropical Asia.

Poncirus trifoliata

Closely allied to *Millettia*, they belong to the pea-flower subfamily of the legume (Fabaceae) family and have typical pea-flowers, borne on racemes. Leaves alternate, pinnately divided. *P. pinnata* is often used in street plantings, parks, and as a shade tree in subtropical and tropical climates.

CULTIVATION: Require excellent drainage and a sunny situation in a deep, moderately fertile soil. In temperate zones plants can be grown in the greenhouse. Propagation is from seed.

Pongamia pinnata

INDIAN BEECH, PONGAM, PONGAMIA

☀ ⚘ ↔ 20 ft (6 m) ↕ 20–60 ft (6–18 m)

Native to northern Australia and tropical Asia. Attractive tree, rich in nitrogen. Foliage bright green, glossy. Night-fragrant flowers pinky mauve or cream, in spring or summer. All parts of plant are toxic. Zones 10–12.

PONTEDERIA

PICKEREL WEED, WAMPEE

A genus of 5 perennial, aquatic or marginal herbs, members of the pickerel-weed (Pontederiaceae) family, from the east of North and South America and the Caribbean. Erect or prostrate stems grow from a branching, often submerged rhizome, with smooth-edged, sword-shaped, dark green leaves on long stalks. Spikes of small tubular flowers, usually blue with 3 lobes, the largest lobe spotted with yellow. The genus is named for eighteenth-century Italian botanist, Guilio Pontedera.

CULTIVATION: Plant in full sun in ponds and bog gardens, in water 8–12 in (20–30 cm) deep. Propagate in spring by division or from seed.

Pontederia cordata

PICKEREL RUSH, PICKEREL WEED, WAMPEE

☀ ❀ ↔ 27 in (70 cm) ↕ 48 in (120 cm)

Deciduous, perennial, marginal water plant found mostly on the east of

North America and the Caribbean. Dense cylindrical spikes, 1–6 in (25 mm–15 cm) long, of blue to white flowers, to ¾ in (18 mm) in diameter, carried on erect stalks, to 14 in (35 cm) tall. Zones 2–5.

POPULUS

ASPEN, POPLAR

About 35 species of poplars or aspens in this genus, deciduous trees that range over much of the temperate Northern Hemisphere. They are in the willow (Salicaceae) family. Many poplars have deltoid-shaped leaves, but foliage shapes, sizes, and textures vary widely. Tiny flowers on pendulous catkins appear before foliage. Small capsules follow, often filled with cotton-like down. Male and female catkins are usually on separate trees.

CULTIVATION: Poplars prefer full sun in deep, moist, well-drained soil. Short-lived, seldom exceeding 60 years before becoming rotten. They have vigorous invasive root systems and can sucker heavily, which often makes them a problem near drains and paving. Prune to shape; propagate from winter hardwood cuttings.

Pontederia cordata

Populus species, in the wild, Zion National Park, Utah, USA

Populus × canescens, in summer

Populus alba

Populus × canadensis 'Aurea'

Populus × canescens, in autumn

Populus × canescens, in winter

Populus × canescens, in spring

Populus alba

BOLLEANA POPLAR, SILVER POPLAR,
WHITE POPLAR

☼ ❅ ↔ 40 ft (12 m) ↑ 80 ft (24 m)

Vigorous tree from Europe and North
Africa to central Asia. Can become
a weed. Young stems and leaves are
covered with downy white hairs,
uppersurface becoming deep green
with age. Leaves broad-based, egg-
shaped, with coarsely toothed edges.
Cultivars include the chalky white
'**Nivea**'; the weeping '**Pendula**'; and
the upright '**Raket**' (syn. 'Rocket').
Zones 3–10.

Populus balsamifera

BALSAM POPLAR, TACAMAHAC

☼ ❅ ↔ 25 ft (8 m) ↑ 80 ft (24 m)

Northern North American and Russian
species, notable for the fragrant resin
that coats its young twigs, buds and
new foliage, giving bronze coloration.
This wears away to glossy mid-green
color below. Leaves roughly egg-
shaped. Zones 3–8.

Populus × canadensis

CANADIAN POPLAR, CAROLINA POPLAR,
HYBRID POPLAR

☼ ❅ ↔ 35 ft (10 m) ↑ 80 ft (24 m)

Hybrid between *P. deltoides* and
P. nigra. Leaves egg-shaped to triangular, sparsely toothed edges, leaf stalks
red. '**Aurea**', new growth golden;
'**Eugenei**', tall columnar habit, new
growth bronze; '**Robusta**', dense foliage, strongly upright columnar habit;
'**Serotina**', male form with conical
habit coming into leaf late. Zones 4–9.

Populus × canescens

GRAY POPLAR, TOWER POPLAR

☼ ❅ ↔ 40 ft (12 m) ↑ 100 ft (30 m)

Natural hybrid between *P. alba* and
P. tremula. Rounded crown of large
triangular to oval leaves, toothed at
edges, felted beneath. Yellow-gray
bark, scarred and fissured. Zones 4–9.

Populus deltoides

COTTONWOOD, EASTERN COTTONWOOD

☼ ❅ ↔ 60 ft (18 m) ↑ 100 ft (30 m)

From eastern half of North America.
Leaves, deltoid, coarse-toothed edges.
Buds, new shoots, and leaves covered
in balsam-scented resin. Zones 2–10.

Populus fremontii

ALAMILLO, FREMONT COTTONWOOD,
WESTERN COTTONWOOD

☼ ❅ ↔ 40 ft (12 m) ↑ 100 ft (30 m)

Western North American tree. Stocky
trunk, rounded head of yellow-green,
broad-based, deltoid leaves, tapering
to a point, toothed. Female trees shed
masses of seed "cotton." Zones 7–10.

Populus × generosa

☼ ❅ ↔ 30 ft (9 m) ↑ 100 ft (30 m)

Natural hybrid between *P. deltoides*
and *P. trichocarpa*, found in the western USA. Young twigs, leaf buds, and
new foliage covered in a yellow-brown
resin. Leaves roughly deltoid, finely
toothed edges. Zones 6–10.

Populus grandidentata

BIGTOOTH ASPEN

☼ ❅ ↔ 30 ft (9 m) ↑ 60 ft (18 m)

From eastern North America. Leaves
on shorter older twigs very sharply
toothed, on younger longer shoots,
more ovoid, with wavy rather than
toothed edges. Short branches that
form a narrow rounded crown.
Zones 3–9.

Populus heterophylla

BLACK COTTONWOOD, SWAMP POPLAR

☼ ❅ ↔ 25 ft (8 m) ↑ 50–80 ft (15–24 m)

From eastern USA. Short branches
forming a narrow rounded head, buds
and young foliage coated in resin.

Leaves egg-shaped, toothed. Female
trees shed copious quantities of down-
covered seeds. Zones 4–9.

Populus lasiocarpa

CHINESE NECKLACE POPLAR

☼ ❅ ↔ 35 ft (10 m) ↑ 50–80 ft (15–24 m)

From southwestern China. Rounded
crown, young stems initially have a
woolly coating. Glossy gray-green
leaves, very large, from 6–12 in
(15–30 cm) long, egg- to heart-
shaped, downy undersides. Zones 5–10.

Populus lasiocarpa

Populus fremontii, in the wild, Grand Canyon, Arizona, USA

Populus nigra 'Italica', in winter

Populus nigra 'Italica', in spring

Populus nigra 'Italica', in summer

Populus nigra 'Italica', in autumn

Populus tremuloides

Populus nigra

Populus maximowiczii
syn. *Populus koreana*
DORONOKI, JAPANESE POPLAR

☼ ❄ ↔ 30 ft (9 m) ↑ 100 ft (30m)

Native of Japan, Korea, and nearby parts of China. Deeply fissured gray bark. The twisted tips of its sharply pointed, elliptical leaves are somewhat wrinkled. The young twigs are red and hairy. Foliage is very dark green on upper surfaces, lighter undersides. Zones 4–9.

Populus nigra
BLACK POPLAR, THEVES POPLAR

☼ ❄ ↔ 60 ft (18 m) ↑ 100 ft (30 m)

Native to Europe, North Africa, and western Asia. Round-headed, with a thick trunk, deeply fissured, knotted and gnarled, gray bark. Triangular to diamond-shaped leaves, develop brilliant yellow tones, in autumn. 'Italica', broadly columnar up to 100 ft (30 m) high, orange young twigs, more intense autumn color;

'**Lombardy Gold**' has bright golden yellow foliage from summer through autumn. Zones 2–10.

Populus simonii
☼ ❄ ↔ 25 ft (8 m) ↑ 80–100 ft (24–30 m)

From northwestern China. Narrow crown, pendulous branch tips. Young twigs and leaf stalks red. Leaves, fresh green, can exceed 4 in (10 cm). '**Pendula**', weeping branches. Zones 2–9.

Populus tremula
ASPEN, EUROPEAN ASPEN, QUAKING ASPEN, SWEDISH ASPEN

☼ ❄ ↔ 35 ft (10 m) ↑ 50 ft (15 m)

From northwestern Europe south to North Africa and east to Siberia. Dark deeply fissured bark. Leaves gray-green, tremble in slightest breeze, finely hairy, lighter undersides, yellow, orange, and red in autumn. Zones 2–9.

Populus tremuloides ★
AMERICAN ASPEN, QUAKING ASPEN, TREMBLING ASPEN

☼ ❄ ↔ 30 ft (9 m) ↑ 50 ft (15 m)

North American tree, foliage moves in the slightest breeze. Slender, upright,

with yellow-gray bark. Leaves broad, glossy, dark green, serrated edges, glaucous undersides, turn yellow in autumn. Zones 1–9.

Populus trichocarpa
BLACK COTTONWOOD

☼ ❄ ↔ 35 ft (10 m)
↑ 80–120 ft (24–36 m)

Tree that is native to western North America, with furrowed dark gray bark, brittle branches. Leaves leathery, shallowly toothed, dark glossy green above, pale brown to nearly white, beneath, turning yellow, in autumn. Female trees shed copious amounts of "cotton." '**Fritz Pauley**', a male cultivar. Zones 7–10.

Populus yunnanensis
YUNNAN POPLAR

☼ ❄ ↔ 40 ft (12 m) ↑ 50–80 ft (15–24 m)

Tree from southwestern China, sometimes grown for quick shelter. Bright green, lance-shaped to triangular leaves with red veins and leaf stalks. Young leaves and twigs also red-tinted, bare trees colorful in winter. Resistant to poplar rust. Zones 5–10.

Populus trichocarpa, in the wild, Glacier National Park, Montana, USA

P

PORTEA

There are 8 species, all from the eastern states of Brazil, in this genus belonging to the bromeliad (Bromeliaceae) family. Several species with spectacular flowerheads are popular in plantings in botanic gardens. They are medium to large plants, with green strap-like leaves, toothed on the edges, forming an open rosette. The flowerhead is branched, sometimes reaching 5 ft (1.5 m) tall, each flower borne on a slender stem. The flower petals are generally blue-violet but sometimes red.
CULTIVATION: Recommended for greenhouse or conservatory cultivation in cool temperate areas, or outdoors with protection from direct continuous sunlight and extremes of rain in warm temperate, subtropical and tropical areas. Water when potting mix is dry. Extra feeding is not necessary. Propagation is mainly from offsets.

Portea petropolitana

☀ ❄ ↔ 3 ft (0.9 m) ↑ 7 ft (2 m)
From central eastern Brazil. Open rosette of long, green, toothed-edged, strap-like leaves. Flower stem to 32 in (80 cm), many-branched, pyramidal flowerhead to 4 ft (1.2 m) high, each branch bearing open cluster of red-stemmed violet flowers, long red bract below each branch. *P. p.* var. *extensa* with longer branches is stunning in flower. Zones 9–10.

PORTULACA

PURSLANE

This genus of some 40 species occurring in the warmer parts of the world belongs to the purslane (Portulacaceae) family. They are mostly succulent herbs, usually with tuberous roots. Leaves are flat or cylindrical, opposite or spirally arranged, usually with hairs in their axils, though these are absent in Australian species (subgenus *Portulacella*). Flowers are solitary or in heads, surrounded by a whorl of bracts formed by the upper leaves, the Australian species with distinct stalks. There are 2 sepals and usually 5 pink, purple, or yellow petals, which open in direct sun and close in shade. There are 8 to many stamens. The fruit is a small conical capsule, opening when the top falls off to release the many small seeds. The various species are often very difficult to distinguish. Some are grown as ornamentals, some for eating.
CULTIVATION: They are easily grown from seed in well-drained soils in sunny but sheltered positions.

Portulaca grandiflora

syn. *Portulaca pilosa* subsp. *grandiflora*
ELEVEN-O'CLOCK, GARDEN PORTULACA, MOSS ROSE, ROSE MOSS, SUN PLANT

☀ ❄ ↔ 6–12 in (15–30 cm)
↑ 6–12 in (15–30 cm)

Slow-growing annual, native to Brazil, Argentina, and Uruguay. Partially prostrate or climbing stem, to 12 in (30 cm) long, reddish twigs and alternate, thick, fleshy, lance-shaped, cylindrical, pale green leaves. Single or double flowers of rose, red, purple, lavender, yellow, or white, often striped, open only in sunlight. 'Sundance', semi-double flowers remain open most of the day. Other popular cultivars include: '**Double Mix**', '**Margarita Rosita**', the **Sundial Series**, and '**Tutti Frutti Mix**'. Zones 8–10.

Portulaca oleracea

syn. *Portulaca retusa*
COMMON PURSLANE, PUSSLEY

☀ ❄ ↔ 20 in (50 cm) ↑ 40 in (100 cm)
Soft, prostrate, fleshy annual, probably from India but now widely

Portea petropolitana

naturalized. Several or many, spreading to erect reddish brown stems forming mats of simple, flat, alternate or opposite, succulent, spatula- to egg-shaped leaves. Bright yellow flowers, with 2 sepals and 4 to 6 petals, grow singly or in clusters of 2 to 5 from leaf axils or stem tips, from spring–autumn. Capsules contain many dark brown to black, kidney-shaped seeds. Zones 7–10.

PORTULACARIA

In a single-species genus of its own, this ornamental, evergreen, multibranched, succulent belongs to the purslane (Portulacaceae) family and is native to South Africa. The branches

Portulaca grandiflora, Sundial Series, 'Sundial Tangerine'

Portulaca grandiflora, Sundial Series, 'Sundial Fuchsia'

Portulaca grandiflora 'Tutti Frutti Mix'

Portulaca grandiflora 'Margarita Rosita'

P. g., Sundial Series, 'Sundial Gold'

P. g., Sundial Series, 'Sundial Peach'

Portulaca grandiflora 'Double Mix'

are often held horizontally and develop twists to create a plant that has great character even when young. The leaves are less than 1 in (25 mm) long and rounded, with a smooth, glossy green surface. Clusters of pale pink flowers open from late spring and are followed by 3-lobed pink fruit (rarely seen in cultivation).
CULTIVATION: Suitable for mild almost frost-free gardens, especially near the coast, this succulent shrub is an ideal plant for arid areas, well-drained raised beds or for growing in large containers. It prefers light gritty soil and a position in full sun or light partial shade. Thinning the branches to emphasize the plant's tree-like character can be very effective, otherwise light trimming is all that is required to keep it tidy. Propagate from seed or cuttings in summer.

Portulacaria afra
CHINESE JADE PLANT, ELEPHANT BUSH, ELEPHANT'S FOOD, SPEKBOOM
☀/☀ ⚘ ↔ 5 ft (1.5 m) ↑ 10 ft (3 m)
An attractive shrub with bright green glossy foliage that contrasts well with the dark purple-brown of the branches. It produces an abundance of small pink flowers. Zones 9–11.

POSOQUERIA
This is a genus of some 12 species of evergreen shrubs or trees belonging to the madder (Rubiaceae) family. They come from tropical America and the West Indies, are frost-tender, and are grown for their attractive and very fragrant, white or red, exceptionally long, tubular flowers. These are often borne in profusion and continue to open throughout spring. The flowers each have 5 spreading petal lobes and are borne in large crowded clusters at branch tips. Large glossy leaves are smooth-edged and arranged in opposite pairs. Fruit is a plum-sized, fleshy, yellow berry containing several seeds.
CULTIVATION: They require a humus-enriched well-drained soil in a warm sheltered position in full sun or partial shade. Propagate from half-hardened cuttings taken in late summer.

Potentilla cinerea

Posoqueria latifolia
BRAZILIAN OAK
☀ ⚘ ↔ 15 ft (4.5 m) ↑ 6–20 ft (1.8–6 m)
From Mexico to South America and the West Indies. Bushy, evergreen, shrub or small tree. Glossy, green leaves, prominent veins. Pure white, heavily perfumed, tubular flowers, in dense terminal clusters, in spring. Edible yellow fruits. Zones 10–12.

POTAMOGETON
PONDWEED
A genus of about 90 aquatic perennials from the pondweed (Potamogetonaceae) family, widely distributed, mostly in temperate regions of the Northern Hemisphere. They have submerged or floating, simple, elliptical, flat, green, leathery, alternate leaves growing from cylindrical or flattened upright stems, rooting at the lower nodes and usually growing from a bottom-rooting, simple or branched rhizome. Fleshy, cylindrical spikes of inconspicuous flowers grow on stalks above or below the water. Plants also produce small, bulb-like, winter buds and stalkless, egg-shaped, floating fruit. The genus is named from the Greek *potamos*, river, and *geiton*, neighbor, for its aquatic habit.
CULTIVATION: They suit aquariums and pond cultivation, in full sun. Propagate from stem cuttings in spring and summer, by division, or by planting out bulb-like winter buds.

Potamogeton perfoliatus
CLASPING LEAF PONDWEED, PERFOLIATE PONDWEED, REDHEAD GRASS
☀ ❄ ↔ 15 ft (4.5 m) ↑ 2 in (5 cm)
Freshwater pondweed, native to Europe and northern North America. Branching, densely crowded stem. Deep green, glossy, stalkless, oval to heart-shaped, submerged leaves, up to 4 in (10 cm) long, with a heart-shaped base. Spikes of small green flowers, in summer. Zones 3–6.

POTENTILLA
This is a large genus of some 500 species in the rose (Rosaceae) family from the Northern Hemisphere. While most are herbaceous perennials, the shrubby species are exceptionally useful as small ornamentals, being very hardy, thriving in most soils, in sun and in partial shade. The flowers are like small single roses, and are produced over a long period, from spring throughout summer and in some species well into autumn.
CULTIVATION: Prefer a fertile well-drained soil. Cultivars with orange, red, or pink flowers tend to fade in

Posoqueria latifolia

Portulacaria afra

Potamogeton perfoliatus

very strong sunshine and should be given a position where they receive some shade in the hottest part of the day. Propagation is usually from seed in autumn or cuttings in summer.

Potentilla alba
WHITE CINQUEFOIL
☀ ❄ ↔ 10 in (25 cm) ↑ 10 in (25 cm)
Vigorous, low-growing, spreading, mat-forming, perennial herb from central, southern, and eastern Europe. Sprays of 5 white, single flowers, to 1 in (25 mm) in diameter, appear in spring–summer. Dark green lower leaves are palm-shaped with 5 oblong leaflets, to 2½ in (6 cm) long, with toothed tips; stem leaves smaller, simple or divided into leaflets, silvery silky at first. Zones 3–5.

Potentilla atrosanguinea
syns *Potentilla argyrophylla* var. *atrosanguinea*, *P. leucochroa*
RED CINQUEFOIL
☀ ❄ ↔ 36 in (90 cm) ↑ 36 in (90 cm)
Clump-forming perennial herb from grassland and thickets of the Himalayas and western China. Branching stems with few branches. Forms a mound of semi-evergreen leaves with 3 elliptical to oval, toothed, silky leaflets, each up to 3 in (8 cm) long, with white hairs underneath, carried on long stems. Loose clusters of deep red to reddish purple, orange, or yellow flowers, to

1½ in (35 mm) across, usually with dark "eyes," on slender stalks, in late summer–early autumn. Zones 3–7.

Potentilla aurea
syns *Potentilla chrysocraspeda*, *P. halleri*, *P. ternata*
☀ ❄ ↔ 12 in (30 cm) ↑ 12 in (30 cm)
Rounded, mat-forming, perennial herb with woody base, native to grassland and thickets of the European Alps and the Pyrenees. Hand-shaped leaves with 5 oblong leaflets with silver hairs along the margins and veins, toothed at tips, and growing from a central base; smaller leaves on stems. Loose clusters of few golden yellow flowers, with deeper orange centers, in spring–summer. Zones 3–5.

Potentilla cinerea
syns *Potentilla arenaria*, *P. subacaulis*, *P. tommasiniana*
☀ ❄ ↔ 4 in (10 cm) ↑ 2–4 in (5–10 cm)
Dwarf, clump-forming perennial herb from dry, stony grasslands of temperate central, eastern, and southern Europe. Sprawling stems densely covered with fine gray hairs and rooting where they touch the ground. Compound leaves have 3 to 5 narrow, toothed, grayish green leaflets, to 1 in (25 mm) long. Heads of up to 6 pale yellow flowers, to 1 in (25 mm) in diameter, in summer. Zones 3–5.

P

P. fruticosa 'Abbotswood Silver'

Potentilla fruticosa 'Beesii'

Potentilla fruticosa 'Ochraleuca'

Potentilla fruticosa 'Daydawn'

P. fruticosa 'Abbotswood' ★

P. fruticosa 'Dart's Golddigger'

Potentilla fruticosa 'Elizabeth'

Potentilla fruticosa 'Goldstar'

P. fruticosa 'Hopleys Orange'

Potentilla fruticosa 'Little Joker'

P. fruticosa 'Longacre Variety'

Potentilla fruticosa 'Primrose Beauty'

Potentilla fruticosa Princess/'Blink'

Potentilla fruticosa 'Red Ace'

Potentilla fruticosa 'Snowflake'

Potentilla fruticosa 'Parvifolia'

Potentilla fruticosa var. *dahurica*

Potentilla glandulosa

Potentilla megalantha

Potentilla fruticosa

CINQUEFOIL, POTENTILLA,
SHRUBBY CINQUEFOIL

☼ ❊ ↔ 5 ft (1.5 m) ↕ 5 ft (1.5 m)

Distributed widely through Northern Hemisphere. Dense shrub with striking yellow flowers, summer–autumn. Small palmately arranged leaves with 5 to 7 narrow leaflets. **P. f. var. *dahurica*** up to 20 in (50 cm), white, sometimes yellow, disc-shaped flowers. **P. f. 'Daydawn'**, yellow flowers tinged with pink; **'Katherine Dykes'**, lemon yellow flowers; **'Ochraleuca'**, lemony white flowers; **'Primrose Beauty'**, rich cream flowers; **'Tangerine' ★**, orange flowers. Zones 3–9.

Potentilla glandulosa

syn. *Drymocallis glandulosa*

STICKY CINQUEFOIL

❊ ❊ ↔ 24 in (60 cm) ↕ 24 in (60 cm)

This tufted perennial herb is a native of western North America. It grows from a loosely branched, woody base with erect, spreading, glandular stems. The round to egg-shaped leaves are divided, with 5 to 7 downy, toothed leaflets; they grow from a central base. The open, leafy cymes of attractive light yellow or crimson flowers, ½–¾ in (12–18 mm) wide, appear in spring–summer. The flowers are followed by golden to reddish brown fruit, which can be smooth or ridged. Zones 6–10.

Potentilla megalantha

syns *Potentilla fragiformis*

☼ ❊ ↔ 8–12 in (20–30 cm)
↕ 8–12 in (20–30 cm)

This clump-forming, softly hairy, tufted perennial herb is native to Japan and the Siberian and North American tundra. It produces solitary, rich bright yellow, saucer-shaped flowers, in summer–autumn. The soft, palm-shaped, thick basal leaves grow to 3 in (8 cm) wide, and have

× *Potinara,* Hybrid,
Afternoon Delight 'Magnificent'

× *Potinara,* Hybrid,
Atomic Fireball

× *Potinara,* Hybrid,
Little Toshi 'Gold Country'

× *Potinara,* Hybrid,
Netrasiri Starbright

× *Potinara,* Hybrid,
Super Nova

3 broad, oval leaflets, with scalloped margins; leaves are finely hairy underneath. Zones 5–9.

Potentilla nepalensis
CINQUEFOIL
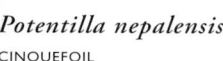 ↔ 12–24 in (30–60 cm)
↕ 12–24 in (30–60 cm)

Easily grown, freely flowering, clump-forming, perennial herb, originating in grassland and thickets of the western Himalayas. Numerous, slender, erect, leafy, branching, purple stems. Oval, coarsely toothed, palm-shaped, strawberry-like leaves with 5 leaflets, 1¼–3 in (3–8 cm) long on tall stalks, grow from a central base. Long, branching panicles of pink, purplish red, or crimson flowers, with 5 petals, in summer. 'Miss Willmott' ★ (syn. 'Willmottiae'), freely flowering dwarf form with pink flowers with a darker pink center and veining. Zones 5–8.

Potentilla neumanniana
syns *Potentilla crantzii,*
P. tabernaemontani, P. verna
SPRING CINQUEFOIL
↔ 6–12 in (15–30 cm)
↕ 3–4 in (8–10 cm)

Prostrate, mat-forming, evergreen, perennial herb with a sprawling, woody stem, from temperate northern, western, and central Europe.

Potentilla nepalensis 'Miss Willmott'

Potentilla neumanniana 'Nana'

Spreads rapidly by runners to form dense ground cover. Spicily scented, strawberry-like, shiny, hand-shaped, deep green leaves, usually with 5 leaflets, occasionally 3, up to 1½ in (35 mm) long, with toothed tips. Small clusters of up to 12 buttery yellow, 5-petalled flowers, in spring, on stalks growing from the leaf axils. 'Nana' (syn. *P. verna* 'Nana') grows to 3 in (8 cm) high with vivid green leaves and gold flowers. Zones 5–8.

Potentilla nitida
↔ 5–16 in (12–40 cm)
↕ 2–4 in (5–10 cm)

Dense, tufted, silvery gray, downy, carpet-forming, perennial herb, native to rocky areas in the European Alps. Compound leaves with 3 silvery, silky, oval to nearly sword-shaped leaflets, to ½ in (12 mm) long, with 3-toothed tips. White or deep pink flowers, 1 in (25 mm) or more across, singly or in pairs at ends of branches, in summer. 'Rubra', abundant, pink to rose-pink flowers. Zones 3–5.

Potentilla recta
SULPHUR CINQUEFOIL
↔ 20–30 in (50–75 cm)
↕ 20–30 in (50–75 cm)

Tufted, perennial, hairy herb, native to the European Alps, growing from

Potentilla nitida 'Rubra'

Potentilla × *tonguei*

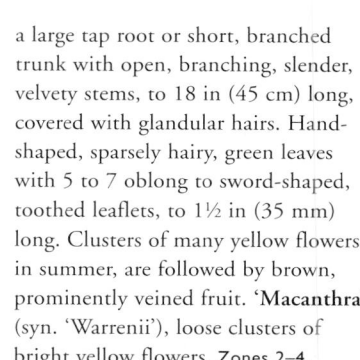
× *Potinara,* Hybrid, Burana Beauty

a large tap root or short, branched trunk with open, branching, slender, velvety stems, to 18 in (45 cm) long, covered with glandular hairs. Hand-shaped, sparsely hairy, green leaves with 5 to 7 oblong to sword-shaped, toothed leaflets, to 1½ in (35 mm) long. Clusters of many yellow flowers, in summer, are followed by brown, prominently veined fruit. 'Macantha' (syn. 'Warrenii'), loose clusters of bright yellow flowers. Zones 2–4.

Potentilla × *tonguei*
↔ 12–20 in (30–50 cm)
↕ 6–10 in (15–25 cm)

This perennial herb is a hybrid of garden origin, a cross between *P. anglica* and either *P. nepalensis* or *P. nevadensis*. Sprawling, non-rooting stems and compound leaves, with 3 to 5 narrowly oval, coarsely toothed leaflets. Flowers with an apricot corolla and carmine red eye, in summer. Zones 3–5.

× *POTINARA*

× *Potinara* (family Orchidaceae) has 4 different orchid genera in its genetic make-up, being a combination of the sympodial genera *Brassavola, Cattleya, Laelia,* and *Sophronitis*. They are like sophrolaeliocattleyas, but differ in having an extra infusion of *Brassavola*. Generally, the flowers are also slightly larger than those of the parents.
CULTIVATION: These hybrids require part-shade to strong light, but will

burn in direct sunlight. They grow best in pots incorporating a course bark-based medium to ensure unimpeded drainage. Healthy plants will develop an extensive system of thick white roots, which are long lived and branch freely. Plants require additional warmth on winter evenings, but will withstand cooler winter temperatures for short periods if kept dry while dormant. Flowers are long lasting and the whole plant can be enjoyed indoors when in bloom. Propagate by division after flowering.

× *Potinara* Hybrids
↔ 8–24 in (20–60 cm)
↕ 8–24 in (20–60 cm)

There is a huge color range in these attractive hybrids with bright yellow and reds predominating. Many can bloom more than once a year; however most flower in spring. **Afternoon Delight 'Magnificent'**, rich orange blooms; **Atomic Fireball** has solid red blooms, 4 in (10 cm) across; **Burana Beauty** ★, a distinctive 2-tone yellow and red splash-petalled hybrid, with the labellum markings also expressed in the petals; **Little Toshi 'Gold Country'** has pure yellow, 3 in (8 cm) blooms with a contrasting deep red labellum; **Netrasiri Starbright** varies from pale orange to red; **Super Nova** has a very round, well-shaped, 3½ in (9 cm) flower with golden yellow segments with red markings on the labellum. Zones 10–12.

POUTERIA

A genus of evergreen trees belonging to the sapodilla (Sapotaceae) family. They are distributed through tropical and subtropical areas of Asia, Australasia, and South America. Trees have a milky sap and alternately arranged, papery or leathery, ornamental leaves. The small tubular flowers are green or white to yellow, borne along branches, and followed by often edible fruits. Fruits, seeds, and timber have been much used by indigenous peoples, the range of uses reflected in the many common names of some species.
CULTIVATION: Attractive specimen trees. Species with edible fruits require greenhouse cultivation outside warm subtropical areas and are unlikely to produce fruit. They grow in a range of soils but must have good drainage, and light feeding. Propagate from fresh seed; some fruit species grafted.

Pouteria cainito
syns *Lucuma caimito, Pouteria caimito*
ABIU
☀ ✛ ↔ 15 ft (4.5 m) ↑ 35 ft (10 m)
Native to northern South America. Oblong leaves to 4–8 in (10–20 cm)

Pouteria caimito

Pouteria sapota

long. Flowers greenish white. Oval, smooth, pale yellow edible fruit, sweet pulp usually eaten fresh, or used in ices and ice creams. Zones 10–11.

Pouteria campechiana
syns *Lucuma campechiana, L. nervosa*
CANISTEL, EGGFRUIT, SAPOTE BORRACHO
☀ ✛ ↔ 25 ft (8 m) ↑ 60 ft (18 m)
Found in Central America from Mexico to Panama. Papery leaves arranged in spirals. Small greenish white flowers. Yellow to greenish brown fruit to 3 in (8 cm) long. Orangey yellow pulp, edible and sweet. Zones 10–11.

Pouteria sapota
syns *Calocarpum mammosum, C. sapota, Pouteria mammosa*
MAMEY SAPOTE, MARMALADE PLUM, SAPOTE
☀ ✛ ↔ 20 ft (6 m) ↑ 40 ft (12 m)
Native of Central America and northern South America. Broad oblong leaves and small whitish flowers clustered toward branch tips. The flowers are followed by large ovoid fruits, sweet edible pulp in shades of orangey pink, that take 1 to 2 years to ripen. 'Magana' has fruit that weighs up to 6 lb (2.75 kg). Zones 10–11.

PRATIA

This genus is made up of about 20 evergreen, mostly prostrate, matforming perennial herbs from the bellflower (Campanulaceae) family. They are native to Australia, New

Pratia angulata

Pratia pedunculata 'County Park'

Zealand, Africa, and South America, and have slender, creeping and rooting stems. Suitable for use in rock gardens. Small narrow leaves are usually less than ½ in (12 mm) long. Masses of small, solitary, star-shaped flowers are followed by red to bluish black berries. Named after a nineteenth-century French naval officer, Prat-Bernon.
CULTIVATION: *Pratia* species prefer shade to half-sun in moist, well-drained soil. Propagate by division or from seed sown in spring or autumn, or cuttings taken in late summer.

Pratia angulata
syn. *Lobelia angulata*
☀ ❄ ↔ 36 in (90 cm)
↑ ¼–2 in (6–50 mm)
Carpet-forming perennial herb, native to New Zealand. Reddish stems, to 12 in (30 cm) long. Coarsely toothed, alternate, bronze or dark green leaves are succulent and almost circular. Almost stalkless, white flowers to ½ in (12 mm) across, with purple veins on 5 unevenly spaced petals, in summer. Fruit is a large, spherical, purplish red to bluish black berry, in autumn. Zones 7–9.

Pratia pedunculata
☀ ❄ ↔ 2–5 ft (0.6–1.5 m)
↑ ¼–½ in (6–12 mm)
A vigorous spreading, mat-forming, perennial herb, native to southern Australia, with small, oval to circular leaves with few teeth. Small pale blue flowers, to 8 mm across, on stalks longer than the leaves, appear from spring to early summer. Can become invasive. 'County Park' has blue flowers. Zones 7–9.

Pratia physaloides
syn. *Colensoa physaloides*
KORU
☀ ❄ ↔ 3 ft (0.9 m) ↑ 3–5 ft (0.9–1.5 m)
Native to New Zealand. Soft shrubby plant, sometimes allocated its own genus, *Colensoa*. Dark green, prominently veined, serrated-edged leaves. Deep blue tubular flowers in spring. These are followed by dark blue berries. Zones 8–11.

Primula alpicola var. *luna*

PRIMULA
COWSLIP, POLYANTHUS, PRIMROSE
A widespread, mainly Northern Hemisphere perennial genus that gives its name to the family Primulaceae. The name is from *primavera*, Italian for "spring," and it is as spring-flowering woodland plants that primroses are best known. Most primulas form basal rosettes of heavily veined leaves from which emerge the flower stems, sometimes with just a single bloom, but often with a large terminal head or several well-shaped whorls of flowers. Various species, especially cowslip (*P. veris*), have been used medicinally and are known to be astringent and mildly sedative.
CULTIVATION: Most prefer dappled shade in woodland gardens and moist, humus-rich, well-drained soil. So-called bog primroses like damper conditions and often naturalize along streams. Propagate from seed or dividing thriving clumps when dormant.

Primula alpicola
◐/☀ ❄ ↔ 10–16 in (25–40 cm)
↑ 16–36 in (40–90 cm)
From the Himalayas. Genuine bog primroses, prefer wet peaty soil. Toothed elliptical leaves. Flowers white, yellow, mauve, purple, to 1 in (25 mm) wide, atop stems with powdery white coating, in late spring–early summer. *P. a.* var. *luna* has pale yellow flowers. Zones 6–9.

Primula amoena
syn. *Primula elatior* subsp. *meyeri*
◐/☀ ❄ ↔ 12 in (30 cm) ↑ 8 in (20 cm)
Native to the Caucasus. Leaves elliptical to spatula-shaped, often red-tinted, with downy undersides; heads of up to 10 lavender to purple, ½–1 in (13–25 mm) wide flowers, in early spring. Zones 5–9.

P

Primula auricula 'Alicia'

Primula auricula 'Beatrice'

Primula auricula 'Bradford City'

Primula auricula 'Butterwick'

Primula auricula 'Coffee'

Primula auricula 'Dales Red'

Primula auricula 'Haffner'

Primula auricula 'Jane'

P. auricula 'Jeannie Telford'

Primula auricula 'Lavender Lady'

Primula auricula 'Rowena'

Primula auricula 'Sea Mist'

Primula auricula 'Sirius'

P. auricula 'Spring Meadows'

Primula auricula 'Trouble'

Primula auricula 'Hawkwood'

Primula auricula 'Lucy Locket'

Primula auricula 'Gwen Baker'

Primula auricula 'Pegasus'

Primula auricula

☽/☀ ❄ ↔ 6–16 in (15–40 cm)
↕ 4–8 in (10–20 cm)

Spring-flowering, native to mountains of southern Europe. Foliage and stems with dusty coating, clump-forming.

Primula auriculata

Leaves fleshy, light green, rounded to broad lance-shaped, usually toothed; heads of few to many flat, ½–1 in (12–25 mm) wide flowers on 6 in (15 cm) high stems, in the wild most often yellow or purple-red with yellow center, some with a white band. Large number of cultivars: '**Alicia**', dark purple-red with broad lighter margin; '**Beatrice**', purple with mauve border and cream center; '**Butterwick**', red-brown, golden yellow center; '**C. W. Needham**', dark purple-blue, yellow-green center; '**Dales Red**', red with heavy powdery white coating and white band, yellow center; '**Hawkwood**', red with white edge and band, yellow center; '**Jeannie Telford**', purple-red with mauve edge, cream center; '**Lavender Lady**', light purple, white center; '**Lucy Locket**', buff yellow, cream center; '**Rowena**', maroon with lavender edges, yellow center and

white band; '**Sirius**', coffee-colored with purplish red markings, yellow center; '**Spring Meadows**', cream with yellow-green center, light green edges; and '**Trouble**', pinkish beige double flowers. Zones 3–9.

Primula auriculata

☽/☀ ❄ ↔ 8–24 in (20–60 cm)
↕ 8–24 in (20–60 cm)

From mountains of Turkey and southern Caucasus. Rosettes of toothed, lance-shaped leaves develop quickly in spring from overwintering buds. Erect stems bear drumstick-style heads of up to 20 yellow-green-centered purple-pink flowers in spring. Zones 5–9.

Primula baileyana

☽/☀ ❄ ↔ 12 in (30 cm) ↕ 6 in (15 cm)

Dainty spring-flowering Himalayan species. Small, rounded, toothed leaves, powdery white undersides and

Primula auricula 'Vivace'

stems. Heads of 3 to 5 white-centered light purple flowers to nearly 1 in (25 mm) wide. Zones 7–9.

Primula beesiana

☀/☀ ❄ ↔ 20 in (50 cm) ↕ 32 in (80 cm)

Native to Himalayan area of western China. Narrow, toothed leaves that lengthen as seed heads ripen. Candelabra-style flowerheads with up to 8 whorls. Flowers deep pink, yellow-centered, in summer. Zones 5–9.

P

Primula denticulata

Primula boveana

Primula capitata

Primula bulleyana

Primula × chunglenta

Primula boveana

☀️/◑ ❄️ ↔ 8 in (20 cm) ↕ 8 in (20 cm)

From the mountains of Egypt. Light green, spatula-shaped leaves, coarsely toothed edges, white-powdered undersides and flower stems. Flowers bright yellow with conspicuous calyces, in small head backed by leafy bracts, in spring. Zones 6–9.

Primula bulleyana

☀️/◑ ❄️ ↔ 12–27 in (30–70 cm) ↕ 24 in (60 cm)

From southwestern China. Leaves toothed and tapering to narrow base. Flower stems with up to 7 whorls of golden yellow to orange flowers, in late spring–early summer. Zones 6–9.

Primula Candelabra Hybrids

☀️/◑ ❄️ ↔ 12–20 in (30–50 cm) ↕ 24–36 in (60–90 cm)

Mainly hybrids between *P. bulleyana* and *P. beesiana;* they are often listed as *P. × bulleesiana*. Foliage resembles the parents. Tall, erect stems with several whorls of flowers, may be sterile. Wide range of colors as named cultivars, such as 'Inverewe' ★, bright orange-red flowers, sterile; or mixed color seedling strains, such as **Sunset Shades**. Zones 6–9.

Primula capitata

☀️/◑ ❄️ ↔ 12–18 in (30–45 cm) ↕ 10–15 in (25–38 cm)

From the Himalayas. Stems and undersides of foliage powdery white. Leaves coarsely toothed. Sturdy, erect flower stems, somewhat flattened heads of many small, violet to purple flowers, in late spring–early summer. Zones 5–9.

Primula × chunglenta

☀️/◑ ❄️ ↔ 12–20 in (30–50 cm) ↕ 24 in (60 cm)

Garden hybrid between *P. chungensis* and *P. pulverulenta*, raised in 1929. Spatula-shaped leaves. Candelabra-style flower stems with whorls of pinkish red flowers from late spring. Zones 6–9.

Primula denticulata

DRUMSTICK PRIMULA

☀️/◑ ❄️ ↔ 10–18 in (25–45 cm) ↕ 8–12 in (20–30 cm)

From mountains of Afghanistan to Myanmar. Overwinters as a conical bud, producing rounded heads of mauve to purple-red flowers in spring, rarely white, with or before new leaves. Flower stems, undersides of toothed leaves downy white. Zones 5–9.

Primula elatior

OXLIP

☀️/◑ ❄️ ↔ 6–16 in (15–40 cm) ↕ 6–12 in (15–30 cm)

Eurasian perennial forming clump of long-stemmed, toothed, rounded to elliptical leaves, undersides sometimes downy. Rather wiry flower stems with heads of pale yellow flowers, in spring–early summer. Zones 5–9.

Primula farinosa

☀️/◑ ❄️ ↔ 12 in (30 cm) ↕ 8 in (20 cm)

Found from Scotland to northwestern Pacific. Spatula-shaped, wavy-edged bright green leaves. Short flower stems with heads of usually a few, sometimes many, bright pink, starry flowers with notched petals, in spring. Zones 4–9.

Primula flaccida

☀️/◑ ❄️ ↔ 16 in (40 cm) ↕ 16 in (40 cm)

This is a summer-flowering Chinese species. It has toothed leaves with powdery undersides; the stems, and conical flowerheads are also powdery. Downward-facing funnel-shaped violet to purple flowers to 1 in (25 mm) wide. Zones 6–9.

Primula florindae

☀️/◑ ❄️ ↔ 8–16 in (20–40 cm) ↕ 36 in (90 cm)

Tibetan species. Long-stemmed, broad pointed oval, toothed leaves. Tall sturdy flower stems, open heads of up to 40 scented yellow flowers, in late spring–early summer. Several probably hybrid groups such as **Kaillour Group** produce flowers in oranges, reds, and several yellow tones. Zones 6–9.

Primula forrestii

☀️/◑ ❄️ ↔ 12–18 in (30–45 cm) ↕ 16–24 in (40–60 cm)

This form is native to China. It has woody, sometimes branch-like rhizomes. The long-lived rosettes of coarsely toothed, long-stemmed, elliptical leaves have red-hairs above, and are powdery white below. Flower stems with up to 25 golden yellow flowers are backed by leafy bracts, in summer. Zones 6–9.

Primula frondosa

☀️/◑ ❄️ ↔ 6–10 in (15–25 cm) ↕ 6 in (15 cm)

Small Balkan species. Stems and foliage heavily white powder-coated. Leaves spatula-shaped, coarsely toothed, to 4 in (10 cm) long. Flower stems to 5 in (12 cm) long, with ½ in (12 mm) wide mauve-pink flowers, in spring. Zones 5–9.

Primula, Candelabra Hybrid

Primula florindae, Kaillour Group

Primula elatior

Primula forrestii

Primula kisoana

Primula kisoana 'Alba'

Primula marginata 'Linda Pope'

Primula palinuri

Long-stemmed, downy, rounded leaves, lobed and coarsely toothed. Numerous flower stems with heads of up to 20 lavender flowers. Cultivars in shades of pink, lavender, purple, and white. Zones 8–10.

Primula marginata
☼/☀ ❄ ↔ 4–10 in (10–25 cm)
↑ 5 in (12 cm)

From the Cottian Alps on the border between France and Italy. Coarsely toothed, leathery, spatula-shaped leaves with powdery edges. Short stems with heads of up to 20 funnel-shaped flowers, lavender to purple-blue, in spring. '**Linda Pope**' (probably a hybrid with *P. allionii*), very powdery foliage, white-centered mauve flowers. Zones 7–9.

Primula obconica
GERMAN PRIMROSE, POISON PRIMROSE
☼/☀ ❅ ↔ 8–16 in (20–40 cm)
↑ 8 in (20 cm)

Perennial from southern China. Broad elliptical leaves with fine downy hairs, frequently causing contact dermatitis.

Open heads of up to 15 lavender to purple flowers, notched petals, in winter. Mixed-color seed strains include '**Libre Mixed**', large flowers in apricots, pinks, mauves, purples, and white. Zones 9–10.

Primula palinuri
☼/☀ ❄ ↔ 6–12 in (15–30 cm)
↑ 6–8 in (15–20 cm)

Surprisingly hardy southern Italian native. Finely hairy, variably toothed, 2–8 in (5–20 cm) long spatula-shaped leaves. Powdery heads of up to 25 yellow flowers, 1 in (25 mm) wide, in spring. Zones 5–9.

Primula latifolia

Primula halleri
☼/☀ ❄ ↔ 4–6 in (10–15 cm)
↑ 8 in (20 cm)

From mountains of southern Europe. Makes several rosettes of bright green, sometimes yellow-powdered leaves. Wiry flower stems with several long-tubed magenta flowers, in spring. Zones 5–9.

Primula japonica
☼/☀ ❄ ↔ 12–24 in (30–60 cm)
↑ 18 in (45 cm)

A clump-forming plant native to Japan. It has broad, coarsely toothed, spatula-shaped leaves to 10 in (25 cm) long. The flower stems bear up to 6 whorls of white, pink, magenta to red flowers, to ¾ in (18 mm) wide, in late spring–early summer. '**Postford White**', white flowers with pink eye; '**Valley Red**', bright pinkish red flowers. Zones 5–9.

Primula juliae
☼/☀ ❄ ↔ 6–10 in (15–25 cm)
↑ 2 in (5 cm)

From the Caucasus. The flowers sometimes appear before the foliage. Rounded, toothed leaves with red-tinted leaf stems. Flowers among foliage, solitary, mauve to purple-red with conspicuous yellow eye, in spring. Zones 5–9.

Primula × kewensis
☼/☀ ❅ ↔ 12–18 in (30–45 cm)
↑ 12 in (30 cm)

Hybrid, probably between *P. floribunda* and *P. verticillata*. Faintly powdery, toothed, spatula-shaped leaves. Flower

stems bear closely spaced whorls of fragrant yellow flowers to ¾ in (18 mm) wide, in spring. Zones 9–10.

Primula kisoana
☼/☀ ❄ ↔ 8–18 in (20–45 cm)
↑ 8 in (20 cm)

From Japan. Downy, rounded, lobed and coarsely toothed leaves to 6 in (15 cm) long, often considerably smaller. Flower stems carry heads of up to 6 deep pink to mauve flowers, 1 in (25 mm) wide, in spring. '**Alba**' is white-flowered form. Zones 6–10.

Primula latifolia
☼/☀ ❄ ↔ 15 in (38 cm) ↑ 8 in (20 cm)
From the European Alps. Leaves, deep green, spatula-shaped, fleshy, finely hairy with teeth mainly near the tips; flower stems bear heads of up to 20 fragrant violet flowers, in late spring–early summer. Zones 5–9.

Primula malacoides
☀/☼ ❄ ↔ 16 in (40 cm) ↑ 12 in (30 cm)
From China. Winter-flowering, usually short lived and treated as annual.

Primula juliae

Primula japonica 'Valley Red'

Primula japonica cultivar

Primula japonica

P

Primula polyneura

☼/☀ ❊ ↔ 6–18 in (15–45 cm)
↕ 8–10 in (20–25 cm)

Western Chinese species spreading by runners. Large, rounded, lobed, deeply toothed, bright green leaves. Few or many pink to purple-red flowers per stem, petals notched, in late spring–early summer. Zones 5–9.

Primula prolifera

☼/☀ ❊ ↔ 16–20 in (40–50 cm)
↕ 27–36 in (70–90 cm)

From subtropical Asian mountains south-eastward from Assam. Leaves grow to more than 12 in (30 cm) long, toothed. Tall flower stems, up to 6 whorls of fragrant, bright yellow flowers. Zones 7–10.

Primula, Pruhonicensis Hybrid, 'Ken Dearman'

Primula Pruhonicensis Hybrids

POLYANTHUS

☼/☀ ❊ ↔ 6–16 in (15–40 cm)
↕ 4–12 in (10–30 cm)

Complex group of garden and natural hybrids involving combinations of *P. elatior, P. juliae, P. veris,* and *P. vulgaris,* ranging from very small, long-lived rock-garden types, such as 'Wanda' (purple-red flowers) to the large showy hybrid polyanthus (usually mixed color seedling selections, such as the **Crescendo, Kaleidoscope, Pacific Giants,** and **Rainbow Series**), which are often treated as annuals. There are also named single-flowered hybrids; rosebud-double-flowered types ("double primroses"); hose-in-hose, appearing to have two blooms sleeved one within the other, and "gold-" or "silver-laced" forms with light-edged brownish black flowers. Popular single-flowered forms include: '**Dorothy**', pale yellow flowers; '**Guinevere**' (syn. 'Garryard Guinevere'), bronze-green leaves, white flowers with red stems and sepals; '**Iris Mainwaring**', lavender blue suffused with pink; '**Old Port**', deep purple-red; '**Schneekissen**', dark green foliage, pure white flowers; and '**Velvet Moon**',

Primula polyneura

Primula pulverulenta

very dark foliage, deep velvet red flowers. Double primroses include: '**April Rose**', deep red flowers; **Bon Accord Series**, a range mainly named by color, such as '**Bon Accord Purple**'; '**Ken Dearman**', apricot-pink suffused with yellow, deep pink buds; '**Quaker's Bonnet**', lavender pink flowers; and '**Sunshine Susie**', bright yellow to gold flowers. Zones 7–9.

Primula × *pubescens*

☼/☀ ❊ ↔ 10 in (25 cm) ↕ 6 in (15 cm)
Hybrid between *P. auricula* and *P. hirsuta*. Leaves often powdery, toothed, usually quite rounded, to 4 in (10 cm) long. Flowers to over 1 in (25 mm) wide, in small, short-stemmed heads, most shades, except darker blue tones. '**Boothman's Variety**' (syn. 'Carmen'), white-centered deep crimson flowers; '**Harlow Carr**', large cream flowers; '**Wharfedale Buttercup**', sulfur yellow. Zones 5–9.

Primula pulverulenta

☼/☀ ❊ ↔ 20 in (50 cm) ↕ 36 in (90 cm)
Native to China. Coarsely toothed leaves to 12 in (30 cm) long. The tall

Primula prolifera

flower stems, candelabra-like, have several whorls of purple-red flowers with dark red centers; flowers are up to 1 in (25 mm) wide and appear in late spring–summer. **Bartley Strain**, typically dark-centered pink-flowered form, is also available in variations. Zones 6–9.

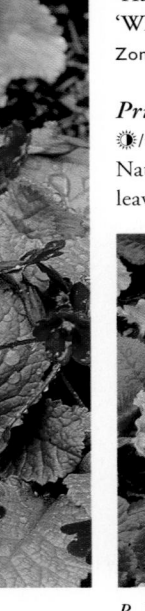

Primula, Pruhonicensis Hybrid, 'Old Port'

P., Pruhonicensis Hybrid, 'Iris Mainwaring'

P., Pruhonicensis Hybrid, 'Dorothy'

Primula, PH, 'Quaker's Bonnet'

P., Pruhonicensis Hybrid, 'Wanda'

Primula, PH, 'Schneekissen'

Primula, PH, 'Sunshine Susie'

Primula, PH, 'Velvet Moon'

Primula rosea

Primula rosea 'Grandiflora'

Primula verticillata

Primula rosea

☼/☀ ❋ ↔6–15 in (15–38 cm)
↑4–6 in (10–15 cm)

From the northwest Himalayas. The glowing deep pink flowers appear before the foliage, or before it is fully expanded. The leaves are toothed, developing slowly, and are often flushed bronze when immature. Heads of up to 12 flowers, with the petal tips notched, appear in spring. '**Grandiflora**' has large flowers on stems to more than 6 in (15 cm) tall. Zones 6–9.

Primula veris subsp. *macrocalyx*

Primula veris subsp. *columnae*

Primula scotica

☼/☀ ❋ ↔4–6 in (10–15 cm)
↑1¼–4 in (3–10 cm)

Native to northern Scotland. The leaves are spatula-shaped, and grow up to 2 in (5 cm) long. They can be toothed or smooth-edged, with the undersides heavily powdery, other parts sparsely so. Heads of small, yellow-centered, purple-pink flowers over an extended period. Zones 4–8.

Primula sieboldii

☼/☀ ❋ ↔12–24 in (30–60 cm)
↑12 in (30 cm)

Native to Japan and nearby parts of temperate mainland Asia. The leaves are very coarsely toothed with an indented heart-shaped base. The flowers are white, pink, or purple, and are borne in small heads to just above foliage height, in late spring–summer. '**Blush Pink**' ★ has bright pink flowers with hint of apricot; '**Cloth of Mist**' has pale lavender flowers; '**Mikado**' has dark purple-pink flowers. Zones 5–9.

Primula veris

Primula sieboldii 'Cloth of Mist'

Primula sieboldii cultivar

Primula sieboldii 'Blush Pink'

Primula sieboldii 'Mikado'

Primula sikkimensis

☼/☀ ❋ ↔10–24 in (25–60 cm)
↑12–36 in (30–90 cm)

Native to Nepal and the Chinese western Himalayas. Dark green, serrated to toothed leaves. Partly pendulous flowers, white to yellow and funnel-shaped, borne in heads atop sturdy erect stems, in late spring–early summer. Zones 6–9.

Primula sinensis

POISON PRIMROSE

☼/☀ ❋ ↔10–16 in (25–40 cm)
↑6 in (15 cm)

Native to China. Leaves are rounded, downy, long-stemmed, conspicuously lobed and toothed, can cause contact dermatitis. Short stems with usually one flowerhead, sometimes whorls. The flowers are usually in pink shades with yellow centers, in winter–spring. Zones 8–10.

Primula veris

COWSLIP

☼/☀ ❋ ↔16 in (40 cm) ↑12 in (30 cm)

Eurasian species. Leaves smooth-edged to coarsely toothed, 2–8 in (5–20 cm) long, undersides sometimes downy. Downy flower stems, heads of up to 16 fragrant yellow flowers, in late spring–early summer. *P. v.* subsp. *columnae,* pointed oval leaves with downy white undersides; *P. v.* subsp. *macrocalyx,* large hairy calyces, larger flowers, rounded leaves. Zones 5–9.

Primula verticillata

ABYSSINIAN PRIMROSE

☼/☀ ✴ ↔20 in (50 cm) ↑24 in (60 cm)

From mountains of northeastern Africa and Arabian Peninsula. Leaves toothed, lance-shaped, with powdery white undersides. Leafy whorls of fragrant, long-tubed, bright yellow flowers on stems in spring. Zones 9–10.

Prinsepia uniflora

Prinsepia sinensis

Primula vialii

☼/☀ ❄ ↔ 6–16 in (15–40 cm)
↕ 8–16 in (20–40 cm)

Western Chinese species. Narrow, downy, toothed leaves, 4–12 in (10–30 cm) long. Strong flower stems with cylindrical heads of small purple-pink flowers topped with a conical cap of overlapping red buds, in summer. Zones 7–10.

Primula vulgaris

ENGLISH PRIMROSE, PRIMROSE

☀/☼ ❄ ↔ 6–16 in (15–40 cm)
↕ 4–6 in (10–15 cm)

European species. Leaves toothed, sometimes coarsely, undersides often faintly downy. Fragrant pale yellow flowers, 1¼ in (30 mm) wide, emerge at ground level on thin stems, in spring. Extensively hybridized. *P. v.* subsp. *sibthorpii,* very compact, light mauve-pink flowers. *P. v.* 'April Rose', crimson flowers; '**Blaue Auslese**' (syn. 'Blue Selection'), lavender blue flowers. Zones 6–9.

PRINSEPIA

Native to northern China, Taiwan, and the Himalayas, and belonging to the rose (Rosaceae) family, this is a genus of about 4 species of deciduous thorny shrubs grown for their ornamental glossy leaves, attractive arching branches, and fragrant, yellow or white, blossom-like flowers. The crowded bright green leaves are smooth-edged or sparsely toothed and are arranged alternately along the stems. The pendent, cherry-like, edible fruit is at first yellow, later ripening to deep red or purple. CULTIVATION: Frost hardy, *Prinsepia* species grow best in a well-drained moderately fertile and moist soil in full sun or partial shade. They must have room to spread, so position them where their thorny branches will not be a nuisance. Propagate from seed or from cuttings.

Prinsepia sinensis ★

CHERRY PRINSEPIA

☼ ❄ ↔ 6 ft (1.8 m) ↕ 6 ft (1.8 m)

Spreading, rather open shrub from northeastern China. Bright green lance-shaped leaves to 3 in (8 cm) long. Fragrant flowers, bright yellow, 5-petalled, along entire stem length, in spring. Edible red cherry-like fruit. Zones 5–9.

Prinsepia uniflora

☼ ❄ ↔ 6 ft (1.8 m) ↕ 5 ft (1.2 m)

Native to northwestern China. Arching shrub, sharp spines, narrow, dark green, oblong leaves to 2½ in (6 cm) long. Fragrant white flowers, in early spring–summer, appear along the stem. Red to purplish black cherry-like fruit. Zones 5–9.

Prinsepia utilis

☼ ❄ ↔ 8 ft (2.4 m) ↕ 10 ft (3 m)

Very thorny shrub from western China. Thorns up to 2 in (5 cm) long. Lance-shaped leaves around 4 in (10 cm) long. Creamy white, fragrant flowers, appear in autumn. The purple oblong fruit ripens the following year. Zones 5–9.

PRITCHARDIA

This is a genus of around 25 species of tropical fan palms, in the family Arecaceae, native to the Pacific Islands. They are grown for their impressive, large, flat fronds that are divided only about halfway to the midrib and have a neat pleated appearance. These palms, which may reach up to 70 ft (21 m) in height, have a smooth, slender, columnar trunk with grooved rings. They produce small, cream to orange, bell-shaped flowers in spikes or panicles at the base of the crown, usually in summer. These are followed by small dark brown to black fruits. CULTIVATION: Frost tender, *Pritchardia* species require a warm humid climate and prefer humus-enriched well-drained soil in full sun with some protection from the midday sun when young. Propagate from seed.

Pritchardia gaudichaudii

☼ ✈ ↔ 6–10 ft (1.8–3 m)
↕ 20–30 ft (6–9 m)

A colony-forming palm from the Hawaiian Islands, suits coastal conditions. Large, stiff, pleated fronds, bright green, to 3 ft (0.9 m) across, covered with white wool when young. Spherical, shiny fruit. Zones 11–12.

Pritchardia hillebrandii

LELO PALM, LOULOU

☼ ✈ ↔ 12–20 ft (3.5–6 m)
↕ 15–25 ft (4.5–8 m)

Solitary, unarmed fan palm from the Hawaiian Islands with fan-shaped, bluish green fronds with stiff leaflets with a waxy coating, carried on bluish green stems that are densely woolly underneath. Shiny, bluish black, spherical fruit. Zones 10–12.

Primula vialii

Primula vulgaris

Primula vulgaris 'April Rose'

Prosopis glandulosa var. *torreyana*

Pritchardia pacifica ★

FIJI FAN PALM

☼ ⚘ ↔ 15 ft (4.5 m) ↑ 30 ft (9 m)

Probably originally native to Tonga. Fan palm with very wide, lush, long-stemmed, pleated fronds, dense foliage head, rain-shedding skirt. Insignificant heads of yellow flowers. Fruit blackens when ripe. Zones 11–12.

Pritchardia thurstonii

☼ ⚘ ↔ 12 ft (3.5 m) ↑ 25 ft (8 m)

Occurring in large colonies on one of the Fijian island groups. Slender palm, fan-shaped pleated leaves. Inflorescences to 8 ft (2.4 m) long hang below the leaves, yellow flowers. Dark red globular fruits. Zones 11–12.

PROSOPIS

Native to tropical Africa and Asia and to warmer arid parts of North and South America, this genus of some 40 species of shrubs and trees is closely related to *Acacia* and belongs to the mimosa subfamily of the legume (Fabaceae) family. They have spiny branches and bipinnate leaves with numerous pairs of tiny olive green leaflets. Fragrant, nectar-rich, greenish white to dull yellow flowers are borne in axillary spike-like catkins. The elongated, pale yellow, bean-like pods are a valuable source of food. The pods and young shoots are also valued as livestock feed in hot climates with very little rainfall. The aromatic timber gives off a slightly sweet smoke and is used for barbecues and smoking foods. CULTIVATION: These fast-growing, tough plants are easily grown in a warm dry climate. They prefer deep well-drained soil in full sun. Although most species tolerate only light frosts, they are extremely drought-resistant and provide welcome shade in arid regions. Propagate from seed or half-hardened cuttings.

Prosopis glandulosa

HONEY MESQUITE

☼ ❄ ↔ 25 ft (8 m) ↑ 30 ft (9 m)

From southern USA and northern Mexico. Large deciduous shrub or small tree. Spiny stems, bipinnate leaves. Fluffy yellow flowers, nectar-rich, in racemes, in spring–summer. Pale yellow linear pods. A prohibited plant in some countries. *P. g.* **var.** *torreyana* (syn. *P. juliflora* var. *torreyana*), smaller with shorter leaves. Zones 8–11.

Prosopis pubescens

syns *Strombocarpa odorata, S. pubescens*

CREOSOTE BUSH SCRUB, SCREWBEAN, SCREWBEAN MESQUITE, TORNILLO

☼ ❄ ↔ 17 ft (5 m) ↑ 17–30 ft (5–9 m)

Deciduous shrub or tree from southwestern USA and northwestern Mexico, often with a twisted trunk; branches covered with narrow spines. Compact crown of feathery light green leaves with 5 to 9 pairs of narrow, elliptical to oblong, hairy leaflets to ½ in (12 mm) long. Spike-like racemes, to 3 in (8 cm) tall, of small, slightly hairy cream or yellow flowers with fused petals from spring–autumn. Unusual, tightly coiled, yellow seed pods covered with minute hairs, containing oval or egg-shaped seeds that are used for food and as a coffee substitute. Zones 6–10.

Prosopis velutina

syn. *P. glandulosa* subsp. *velutina*

VELVET MESQUITE

☼ ❄ ↔ 15–40 ft (4.5–12 m) ↑ 15–40 ft (4.5–12 m)

Large shrub or medium-sized tree from southwestern USA and north-western Mexico. Smooth dark brown bark; spine-covered velvety branches. Narrow, dull green, compound leaves with 2 to 3 leaflets, each with 15 to 20 pairs of minor leaflets with finely hairy surfaces. Clusters of small pale yellow to yellow-green flowers, appear in late spring–early summer, sometimes again in autumn. Slender brown pods ripen in mid- to late summer. Zones 8–11.

Pritchardia thurstonii

PROSTANTHERA

This Australian genus of around 100 species of evergreen shrubs belongs to the mint (Lamiaceae) family, noted for its Mediterranean culinary herbs, such as mint, sage, basil, and rosemary. Most have highly aromatic opposite leaves on squarish stems and produce masses of spring and summer flowers, usually in shades of blue, mauve, or purple, sometimes white or red, and rarely yellow. The tubular flowers are irregular, usually 2-lipped and 3-lobed, often in clusters encircling the upper part of the stem. These plants are short lived in garden situations, but prostantheras are extremely fast growing and flower well, even when quite small. CULTIVATION: They require a warm climate, excellent drainage and thrive in a sheltered position. As many species prefer some shade, they can be planted beneath the light overhead cover of trees with open foliage. Tip prune from an early age and immediately after flowering to ensure compact bushy growth and a pleasing shape. Propagate from half-hardened tip cuttings taken in summer.

Prostanthera aspalathoides

SCARLET MINT BUSH

☼ ⚘ ↔ 24 in (60 cm) ↑ 36 in (90 cm)

Compact glandular shrub from drier areas of southeastern Australia. Strong scent; leaves small, linear to cylindrical; single flowers, deep pink, scarlet, or yellow, in spring. Zones 9–11.

Prostanthera calycina

RED MINT BUSH

☼/☀ ⚘ ↔ 12 in (30 cm) ↑ 24 in (60 cm)

This small shrub is native to South Australia. It has aromatic, bright green leaves, ovate to almost rounded. The large orange to red flowers, emerging from the leaf axils, appear in spring. Zones 9–10.

Prostanthera aspalathoides

Pritchardia hillebrandii

Prostanthera cuneata
ALPINE MINT BUSH
☼/◐ ❄ ↔ 5 ft (1.5 m) ↑ 3 ft (0.9 m)
From southeastern Australia. Dense, very aromatic shrub. Thick oval leaves along stems, dotted with oil glands. Large white or pale mauve flowers with purple blotches at the throat cover the plant in summer. Zones 8–9.

Prostanthera howelliae
☼ ⚘ ↔ 5 ft (1.5 m) ↑ 3 ft (0.9 m)
Low, spreading shrub from eastern Australia. Aromatic, glandular, dark green leaves, narrow-ovate to ½ in

Prostanthera lasianthos

(12 mm) long. Small, profuse, mauve or violet, axillary flowers with dark dots in throat, in spring. Zones 9–11.

Prostanthera incana
☼ ⚘ ↔ 6 ft (1.8 m) ↑ 6 ft (1.8 m)
Erect, moderately dense, hairy shrub from near-coastal districts of southeastern Australia. Velvety ovate leaves, shallowly toothed, slightly aromatic when crushed. Violet to lilac flowers in short racemes, in spring–summer. Zones 9–11.

Prostanthera incisa
CUT-LEAFED MINT BUSH
☼ ⚘ ↔ 7 ft (2 m) ↑ 8 ft (2.4 m)
From coastal districts of eastern Australia. Strongly aromatic erect open shrub. Oval toothed leaves, masses of mauve flowers in short axillary clusters, in spring. Zones 9–11.

Prostanthera cuneata

Prostanthera ovalifolia

Prostanthera lasianthos ★
VICTORIAN CHRISTMAS BUSH
☼ ❄ ↔ 12 ft (3.5 m) ↑ 15 ft (4.5 m)
Tall shrub or small tree of southeastern Australia. Toothed lance-shaped leaves to 5 in (12 cm) long. Showy sprays of white to pale mauve flowers marked with purple and orange spots in the throat, in summer. Zones 8–10.

Prostanthera magnifica
MAGNIFICENT MINT BUSH,
SPLENDID MINT BUSH
☼ ⚘ ↔ 5 ft (1.2 m) ↑ 6 ft (1.8 m)
From semi-arid regions of Western Australia. Highly decorative, erect shrub. Leathery, elliptic leaves to 1¼ in (30 mm) long. Showy pale mauve or pink flowers in leafy spike-like clusters, late winter–early summer. Zones 9–11.

Prostanthera nivea
SNOWY MINT BUSH
☼/◐ ⚘ ↔ 7 ft (2 m) ↑ 12 ft (3.5 m)
Erect, bushy shrub, native to eastern Australia. Softly hairy branches, narrow-ovate leaves to 1½ in (35 mm)

Prostanthera ovalifolia 'Variegata'

long. Abundant, white to pale mauve flowers with yellow-spotted throats, in spring. Zones 9–11.

Prostanthera ovalifolia
PURPLE MINT BUSH
☼ ⚘ ↔ 6 ft (1.8 m) ↑ 6 ft (1.8 m)
Shrub from eastern Australia. Aromatic oval leaves, 1½ in (35 mm) long. Mass of purple or mauve flowers, darker spotted throats, in spring. 'Variegata', leaves with yellow edges. Zones 9–11.

Prostanthera 'Poorinda Ballerina'
☼ ⚘ ↔ 5 ft (1.5 m) ↑ 5 ft (1.5 m)
Upright hybrid, aromatic leaves narrow, up to 2 in (5 cm) long, deep

Prostanthera incisa

Prostanthera magnifica

Prostanthera 'Poorinda Ballerina'

green, leathery, with olive tints. White flowers that have mauve spotting, in spring–early summer. Zones 9–10.

Prostanthera rotundifolia

☀ ◖ ↔ 8 ft (2.4 m) ↑ 10 ft (3 m)
Tall aromatic shrub from eastern Australia. Variable ovate to almost circular leaves, smooth edges, a rounded tip. Abundant lilac to purple (sometimes pinkish) flowers, axillary or terminal sprays, in spring. Zones 9–11.

Prostanthera walteri

BLOTCHY MINT BUSH
☀ ❄ ↔ 4 ft (1.2 m) ↑ 3 ft (0.9 m)
Sprawling shrub from alpine and subalpine regions of southeastern Australia. Wiry rigid stems, ovate leaves to 1¼ in (30 mm) long. Single bluish green flowers streaked with purple in leaf axils, in summer. Zones 8–9.

PROTEA

Named after the sea-god of classical mythology, Proteus, who could change his form at will, proteas belong to the family Proteaceae. The 100 or so evergreen trees and shrubs in *Protea* are all indigenous to Africa. They have bisexual flowers in cone-like heads with colored leaf-like bracts at the base, and are greatly valued for floristry because of their beauty and long vase life. Most flower between autumn and late spring.
CULTIVATION: Undemanding once established, they are fairly specific in requirements—an open sunny situation and very free-draining, gravelly, sandy or basaltic loam, generally acid, and a climate with most rainfall in winter. They will not tolerate fertilizers rich in phosphorus. Regular flower removal encourages less straggly growth. Propagation is from seed, cuttings, or grafting. Hybrid cultivars are usually grown from cuttings. Light frosts are tolerated once established. Summer mulching is desirable but cultivation of the soil surface is resented. Good air circulation discourages fungal diseases.

Protea aristata

CHRISTMAS PROTEA, PINE SUGAR BUSH
☀ ❄ ↔ 5 ft (1.5 m) ↑ 5 ft (1.5 m)
Rounded shrub from mountain slopes of Cape region of South Africa. Pine-like leaves, flat, linear with a recurved, black, pointed tip. Cup-shaped, silky, flowerheads, pink-red with dark crimson bracts, in summer. Zones 8–10.

Protea aurea

☀ ❄ ↔ 10 ft (3 m) ↑ 10 ft (3 m)
Evergreen, sprawling shrub. Foliage soft silvery when young, becoming leathery with age, leaves are oval-shaped. Flowers cream, pink or red, in autumn–winter, spot flowering at other times. Zones 8–10.

Protea caffra

☀ ❄ ↔ 10 ft (3 m) ↑ 15 ft (4.5 m)
Evergreen shrub or gnarled tree from South Africa with linear-elliptical, gray-green leaves. Flattened goblet-shaped flowerheads, with pink, cream or red bracts, in spring–early summer. Zones 8–10.

Protea compacta

PRINCE PROTEA, RIVER PROTEA
☀ ❄ ↔ 7 ft (2 m) ↑ 8 ft (2.4 m)
Found on the south coast of South Africa's Cape region. Erect, straggly

Protea aristata

Protea cynaroides

Protea aurea

Protea eximia, in the wild, Little Karoo region, southern Africa

shrub, with leathery blue-green leaves, orange-fringed along their margins. Long, pointed buds, flowers rose pink, reddish bracts fringed silky white, in autumn–winter. Popular cut flower. Zones 8–10.

Protea convexa

☀ ❄ ↔ 3–7 ft (0.9–2 m) ↑ 10 in (25 cm)
Uncommon evergreen shrub. In arid situations, leafy mat of horizontal branches, large, blue-gray, "cabbage-like" leaves, waxy bloom. Branches appear almost varnished from exuded resin. Pink, bowl-shaped flowerheads, greenish pink bracts, in spring. Zones 8–10.

Protea cynaroides ★

GIANT PROTEA, KING PROTEA
☀ ❄ ↔ 7 ft (2 m) ↑ 7 ft (2 m)
Floral emblem of South Africa. Evergreen shrub, responds well to pruning. Bluntly oval leathery leaves and numerous, wide, bowl-shaped flowers with silky white hairs and

Protea caffra

pointed pink bracts, from mid-winter–early summer. Sought-after by florists worldwide. Zones 8–10.

Protea eximia

syn. *Protea latifolia*
DUCHESS PROTEA, RAY-FLOWERED PROTEA
☀ ❄ ↔ 10 ft (3 m) ↑ 10 ft (3 m)
Evergreen upright shrub from South Africa's Cape region. Gray-green broadly oval to heart-shaped leaves.

Protea magnifica

Protea lacticolor

Large pink to dark crimson flowers, with dark crimson centers, at any time, but with a winter flush. Zones 8–10.

Protea gaguedi
SUGARBUSH

☀ ❄ ↔ 8 ft (2.4 m) ↑ 10 ft (3 m)

A semi-deciduous protea, which often occurs at reasonably high altitudes. It is found naturally through much of central Africa. A dense clump of foliage, it has mildly scented, silvery white flowers, flushed with pink. Zones 9–10.

Protea grandiceps
PEACH PROTEA, PRINCESS PROTEA, RED SUGARBUSH

☀ ❄ ↔ 5 ft (1.5 m) ↑ 5 ft (1.5 m)

Evergreen protea that is native to South Africa's Cape region, considered to be one of the most beautiful of the proteas. Leathery, oval, gray-green leaves. Large light peach-pink bracts, fringed with reddish purple, white stamens, in late winter–early summer. Zones 8–10.

Protea holosericea

☀ ❄ ↔ 5 ft (1.2 m) ↑ 7 ft (2 m)

An evergreen shrub from the Cape region of South Africa, with large, distinctive, cream flowers with black-fringed bracts. Regular pruning retains a nice shape. Excellent cut flowers. Zones 8–10.

Protea lacticolor

☀ ❄ ↔ 7 ft (2 m) ↑ 7–15 ft (2–4.5 m)

An evergreen shrub or slender tree that is native to the Cape region of South Africa. Blue-green foliage is stiff and thick. Narrow spring buds

Protea longifolia

open to cream flowers, with shell pink bracts, in autumn to early winter. Zones 8–10.

Protea lepidocarpodendron
BLACK PROTEA

☀ ❄ ↔ 5 ft (1.5 m) ↑ 10 ft (3 m)

An erect evergreen shrub from South Africa's Cape region. Dark purple-black flowers, white-fringed bracts, in late autumn–early summer, peaking in winter. Popular cut flowers. May be hidden by foliage on plant. Zones 8–10.

Protea longifolia
SIR LOWRY'S PASS PROTEA

☀ ❄ ↔ 5 ft (1.5 m) ↑ 7 ft (2 m)

South African evergreen with long slender leaves. Striking flowers fluffy white with a peaked black center surrounded by pointed cream to pink bracts, all year, except summer, peak in winter. Zones 8–10.

Protea magnifica
BEARDED PROTEA, QUEEN PROTEA

☀ ❄ ↔ 5 ft (1.5 m) ↑ 5 ft (1.5 m)

From South Africa's Cape region. Variable evergreen shrub. Flowers vary from cream to pink or red with a fringe of white or black at the center, bracts also fringed with white. Regular pruning establishes a pleasing shape. Zones 8–10.

Protea mundii

☀ ❄ ↔ 8 ft (2.4 m) ↑ 15–30 ft (4.5–9 m)

Native to South Africa's Cape region. An evergreen shrub or slender tree. Mostly pink flowering, narrow buds appearing in late summer–mid-winter, peaking in autumn. The foliage is an attractive blue-green color. Regular pruning establishes a sturdy plant. Zones 8–10.

Protea nana
MOUNTAIN ROSE

☀ ❄ ↔ 3 ft (0.9 m) ↑ 3 ft (0.9 m)

This upright evergreen shrub originates from the Cape region of South Africa. The foliage is needle-like and the flowers are small, cup-shaped, deep claret color, and appear in early winter–late spring. This species is susceptible to soil-borne fungal diseases. Zones 8–10.

Protea nana

Protea gaguedi, in the wild, Iosiolo Lookout, Maralal Mountain, Kenya

Protea neriifolia

Protea neriifolia 'White Brow'

Protea neriifolia

BLUE SUGARBUSH, OLEANDER-LEAFED
PROTEA, PINK MINK

☀ ❄ ↔ 7 ft (2 m) ↑ 7 ft (2 m)

From the south coast of South Africa's
Cape region. Erect evergreen shrub.
Foliage resembles that of oleander.
Long fluffy flowerheads vary from
cream and pink to crimson, black

feathery "beards" to the bracts, in
autumn–spring. '**White Brow**', light
crimson flowers. Zones 8–10.

Protea nitida

☀ ❄ ↔ 12 ft (3.5 m) ↑ 15 ft (4.5 m)

From sandy, gravelly, and rocky
mountain slopes in South Africa.
Evergreen tree, gnarled habit, old
plants can be much taller. Leaves
oblong, light green or blue-green.
Saucer-like flowerheads, white or
pinkish, intermittently throughout
the year. Zones 8–10.

Protea obtusifolia

☀ ❄ ↔ 8 ft (2.4 m) ↑ 8 ft (2.4 m)

Evergreen shrub from South Africa's
Cape region. Goblet-shaped bloom,
dark red, cream or white with waxy,
shiny bracts, in autumn-winter.
Tolerates coastal winds. Zones 8–10.

Protea pudens

GROUND ROSE

☀ ❄ ↔ 3 ft (0.9 m) ↑ 6 in (15 cm)

Trailing ground cover from South
Africa's Cape region. Leaves linear,
narrow. Stems tipped with bell-
shaped, hairy, white flowerheads enclosed in burnished red bracts, in
winter–early spring. Zones 8–10.

Protea repens

HONEY PROTEA, SUGARBUSH

☀ ❄ ↔ 7 ft (2 m) ↑ 8 ft (2.4 m)

From slopes of coastal mountains in
Western Cape, South Africa. Open,
erect shrub. Nectar-rich flowers,
greenish white to pale pink or claret
red, with white or yellowish pink-
tipped bracts, waxy appearance, in
early autumn–winter. Zones 8–10.

Protea roupelliae

☀ ❄ ↔ 15 ft (4.5 m) ↑ 20 ft (6 m)

Native to eastern South Africa. Evergreen upright tree. Oblong leaves variable color, smooth green to silky and
silvery. Pink, goblet-shaped flowerheads
in late summer–autumn. Zones 8–10.

Protea rubropilosa

☀ ❄ ↔ 12 ft (3.5 m) ↑ 25 ft (8 m)

From northern South Africa. Evergreen tree thrives on high winter

rainfall and frequent mists. White
flowerheads, enclosed by dark, velvety,
red bracts, short, red hairs on outer
surfaces, in spring. Fruits persistent,
retaining seed for a year. Zones 8–10.

Protea scolymocephala

GREEN BUTTON PROTEA, GREEN PROTEA,
MINI PROTEA

☀ ❄ ↔ 3 ft (0.9 m) ↑ 3 ft (0.9 m)

From the western mountain ranges of
South Africa's Cape region. Small ever-
green shrub, irregular spiky growth.
Tiny flowers, around 1½ in (35 mm)

Protea scolymocephala

Protea repens

Protea roupelliae

Protea, Hybrid Cultivar, 'Pink Ice'

Protea speciosa

Protea, Hybrid Cultivar, 'Pink Mink'

Protea, Hybrid Cultivar, 'Silvertips'

Protea, Hybrid Cultivar, 'Satin Mink'

wide, yellowy greenish or red with pink-tipped bracts, in early winter–spring. Zones 8–10.

Protea speciosa
BROWN-BEARDED SUGARBUSH

☼ ❄ ↔ 3 ft (0.9 m) ↑ 3 ft (0.9 m)
Found in South Africa's Western Cape province. This multi-stemmed shrub is from a group commonly known as bearded sugarbushes. The flowerheads are pink, or sometimes cream, and they appear in summer–autumn. The gray-green leaves are usually oblong. This is now classed as an endangered species. Zones 9–10.

Protea stokoei

☼ ❄ ↔ 3 ft (0.9 m) ↑ 5 ft (1.5 m)
A compact, slow-growing, evergreen shrub from South Africa's Cape region. It has large, leathery leaves, with defined, red borders. Large, pink flowers, pale brown, feathery-tipped bracts, in winter–spring. Difficult to grow under cultivation, requiring humus-rich, acidic soil with very free drainage. Zones 8–10.

Protea venusta

☼ ❄ ↔ 8 ft (2.4 m) ↑ 30 in (75 cm)
Low-growing, evergreen, hardy shrub, at elevations up to 6,000 ft (1,800 m), sometimes covered in snow. Oval blue-green leaves. Held face-upward, small white flowerheads surrounded by pink-tipped, rounded bracts, in summer–autumn. Zones 8–10.

Protea Hybrid Cultivars

☼ ❄ ↔ 10 ft (3 m) ↑ 5–8 ft (1.5–2.4 m)
Proteas are popular with florists, whose preferences have influenced hybrid cultivar selection. Most widely used parent species is *P. neriifolia*. 'Clark's Red', to about 7 ft (2 m), oval glaucous leaves, popular cut flowers, slender crimson buds, bright red flowers, mid-summer; 'Frosted Fire', bright rosy red flowers, waxy white-fringed bracts, late autumn–late winter; 'Pink Ice' ★, one of the world's most popular cut flowers, bright pink flowers with silvery white fringed bracts, giving a frosted appearance; 'Pink Mink', deep pinkish red bracts, tipped black; 'Satin Mink', pink bracts, tipped black; 'Silvertips', deep reddish bracts with profuse silvery white wool toward their tips. Zones 8–10.

PRUMNOPITYS
Previously in genus *Podocarpus* and belonging to the podocarp (Podocarpaceae) family, this genus comprises about 8 evergreen trees with a tall, elegant habit. Under cultivation they often become shrub-like. Mainly from South America, Southeast Asia, New Zealand, New Caledonia, and eastern Australia, a number are valued for their timber. Leaves are a rich green; fleshy fruits are red, yellow, or blue-black.

CULTIVATION: Under cultivation, all species tolerate full sun to full shade and free drainage. They are excellent hedge plants and equally good indoor plants. Propagation is from seed or heeled cuttings taken in late summer or early autumn.

Prumnopitys amara
syn. *Sundacarpis amara*

☼ ❄ ↔ 50 ft (15 m) ↑ 150 ft (45 m)
From Queensland, Australia, New Guinea, Indonesia, the Philippines and nearby islands. Straight-trunked evergreen tree. Juvenile leaves narrow, long tapering "drip-tip." Mature leaves, glossy rich green above, paler beneath. Fruits, reddish, then dark purple. Zones 8–10.

Prumnopitys andina
syn. *Podocarpus andinus*
PLUM-FRUITED YEW

☼ ❄ ↔ 20 ft (6 m) ↑ 60 ft (18 m)
From high altitudes in the Andes of southern Chile. Evergreen tree, dark

Prumnopitys andina

Prumnopitys ferruginea

brown bark, shrubby, with sweeping branches in cultivation. Leaves, yew-like, spiraly arranged, bright green above, paler undersides. Fruits round, fleshy, yellowish. Zones 8–10.

Prumnopitys ferruginea
syn. *Podocarpus ferrugineus*
MIRO
☀ ❄ ↔ 15 ft (4.5 m) ↑ 80 ft (24 m)
Native to the South Island of New Zealand. Evergreen tree, dark green foliage, black-brown bark with distinct indentations. Valued for timber. Bright red succulent fruits with a waxy bloom, eaten by birds, poisonous to people. Zones 8–10.

Prumnopitys ladei
syn. *Podocarpus ladei*
BLACK PINE
☀ ❄ ↔ 15 ft (4.5 m) ↑ 20 ft (6 m)
Slow-growing tree from a limited mountain area in northeastern Queensland, Australia. Smooth red-brown bark is shed in papery flakes. Fern-like leaves, mid-green, short, narrow, with blunt tip, almost waxy texture. Purple, solitary, round, fruits. Zones 8–10.

PRUNELLA
syn. *Brunella*
HEAL ALL, SELF-HEAL
These 7 semi-evergreen, spreading, sprawling then climbing perennial

Prunella grandiflora 'Pink Loveliness'

Prumnopitys ladei

herbs belong to the mint (Lamiaceae) family and are native to temperate Eurasia, North Africa, and North America. The plants' creeping, grooved, and slightly hairy stems sometimes take root at lower nodes. Opposite leaves with generally smooth-edged blades grow on stalks from the base of the plant or from the stems. Heads of densely whorled spikelets of 4 to 6 bluish violet or purplish red, tubular to bell-shaped flowers, with an erect, hooded, 2-lipped corolla with 3 lobes, are borne on stubby stalks surrounded by leaf-like bracts. Fruit, egg-shaped nutlet.
CULTIVATION: They grow well in sun or shade in dry to moist, well-drained soil, and are suited to rock gardens and shaded areas. Propagate from seed or by division in spring.

Prunella grandiflora
BIGFLOWER, LARGE SELF-HEAL, SELF-HEAL
☀ ❄ ↔ 12–24 in (30–60 cm) ↑ 12–24 in (30–60 cm)
European mat-forming herb with woody branching stems covered with tiny, oval to sword-shaped leaves with scalloped margins. Showy heads of off-white, pale blue, or purple flowers, with deep violet lips, appear in summer. '**Loveliness**' ★, has pale lilac flowers; '**Pink Loveliness**', has pink flowers. Zones 4–9.

Prunella laciniata
☀ ❄ ↔ 9–12 in (22–30 cm) ↑ 9–12 in (22–30 cm)
From southwestern and central Europe. Lobed or divided leaves,

Prunella grandiflora 'Loveliness'

to 3 in (8 cm) long, densely covered with fine hairs. Spikes of ¾ in (18 mm) wide yellowish white, sometimes rose pink or purple, flowers in spring–summer. Zones 6–9.

Prunella vulgaris
syn. *Prunella incisa*
HEAL ALL, SELF-HEAL
☀ ❄ ↔ 16–24 in (40–60 cm) ↑ 16–24 in (40–60 cm)
Native to Europe. Leaves, to 2–4 in (5–10 cm) long, oval, with hairy margins. Terminal spikes of flowers, dark blue or purplish red, may be white, with slightly hairy upper lip, and with a dark green to purplish calyx, from late spring–early autumn. *P. v.* **var. lanceolata** (syn. *P. v.* var. *atropurpurea*) has purplish leaves. Zones 3–5.

PRUNUS
CHERRY, CHERRY PLUM
This widely grown genus, a member of the rose (Rosaceae) family, is naturally widespread throughout the northern temperate regions of the world and mountain parts of Africa. Best known for the edible stone fruits (cherries, plums, apricots, peaches, and nectarines) and their ornamental flowering cousins, the genus includes a range of shrubs and trees, mostly deciduous. Flowers are 5-petalled,

Prunella laciniata

single or in clusters, in colors ranging from white through to dark pink, followed by fleshy single-seeded fruit. The leaves are usually simple pointed ellipses, often with serrated edges; sometimes brilliant autumn colors.
CULTIVATION: Although hardiness varies with the species, most need some winter chilling to flower and fruit properly. Wind protection is important. Most species prefer cool, moist, well-drained soil that is both fertile and rich in humus. Correct pruning techniques are important for the fruiting varieties. Propagate the species from seed, the fruiting forms by grafting, and the ornamentals by grafts or, in some cases, from cuttings.

Prunus africana
AFRICAN CHERRY, RED STINKWOOD
☀ ❄ ↔ 25–35 ft (8–10 m) ↑ 100 ft (30 m)
Found in mountainous habitats over much of Africa. Evergreen tree with white flowers, small red fruit. Bark harvested commercially to produce an anti-prostatitis drug known as pygeum. Now endangered species due to overharvesting. Zones 9–11.

Prunella vulgaris var. *lanceolata*

Prunus africana

Prunus americana

AMERICAN PLUM, AMERICAN RED PLUM,
GOOSE PLUM, HOG PLUM, WILD PLUM

☼ ❄ ↔12 ft (3.5 m) ↑25 ft (8 m)

Eastern and central North American
tree with spiny branches, peeling dark
brown bark. Leaves to 4 in (10 cm)
long, white flowers. Small, yellow-
fleshed, red to plum-blue fruit.
Zones 3–9.

Prunus × *amygdalo-persica*

FLOWERING ALMOND

☼ ❄ ↔20 ft (6 m) ↑20 ft (6 m)

Hybrid between *P. dulcis* and
P. persica. Highly ornamental flowers;
inedible green fruits. 'Pollardii',
regarded as the typical form, large
bright pink flowers, in late winter
before the foliage expands. Zones 4–9.

Prunus armeniaca

APRICOT

☼ ❄ ↔15 ft (4.5 m) ↑25 ft (8 m)

Flat-topped tree, red-brown bark,
leaves large, heavily serrated. Needs
winter chilling, summer heat to

Prunus americana

Prunus armeniaca var. *ansu*

produce fruit. Flowers white or pale
pink, on bare wood, prone to damage
from late frosts. Golden orange fruit.
P. a. var. *ansu*, cultivated race from
Japan, Korea, and coastal regions of
China and Siberia, broader leaves,
fruit's stone is rougher. Zones 5–10.

Prunus avium

GEAN, MAZZARD, SWEET CHERRY,
WILD CHERRY

☼ ❄ ↔20 ft (6 m) ↑50 ft (15 m)

The main parent of edible cherries. A
deciduous Eurasian tree with serrated-
edged leaves. Flowers white, massed in
small clusters, open before the new
leaves. Purple-red fruit. 'Asplenifolia',
deeply cut leaves; 'Cavalier', an eating
cherry, with medium-sized to large
fruit, black, very sweet, produced
early to mid-season; 'Plena' (syn.

Prunus avium 'Cavalier'

Prunus campanulata

Prunus × *blireana*

'Multiplex'), peeling bark, orange-
red autumn foliage, white double
flowers. Zones 3–9.

Prunus × *blireana*

DOUBLE PINK FLOWERING PLUM

☼ ❄ ↔15 ft (4.5 m) ↑15 ft (4.5 m)

A cross between a *P. cerasifera* cultivar and a double-flowered form of

P. mume. Small, deciduous tree,
drooping branch tips, bronze new
growth. Large, bright pink, double
flowers, are abundant. 'Moseri',
slightly taller, small-flowered cultivar
with red-tinted foliage. Zones 5–10.

Prunus campanulata

TAIWAN CHERRY

☼ ❄ ↔25 ft (8 m) ↑30 ft (9 m)

Deciduous tree from Taiwan and
southern Japan. Leaves large, doubly
serrated, color in autumn. Flowers,
deep cerise, pendulous in clusters,
open before the foliage. Small purple-
black fruits. Flowers in winter in mild
climates. Zones 7–10.

Prunus caroliniana

CAROLINA LAUREL-CHERRY, WILD ORANGE

☼ ❄ ↔20 ft (6 m) ↑40 ft (12 m)

Found in southern USA. Evergreen
tree, glossy, elliptical, smooth-edged
leaves, cream flowers, densely massed
in racemes, in spring. Small, shiny,
black fruit. Used for hedging and util-
ity plantings. Zones 7–11.

Prunus cerasifera

CHERRY PLUM, FLOWERING PLUM,
MYROBALAN

☼ ❄ ↔30 ft (9 m) ↑30 ft (9 m)

Eurasian species found in many cultivated varieties. Deciduous, large shrub
or a small tree. Leaves, bronze tinted,
fairly small, veins on their undersides,

Prunus cerasifera

Prunus cerasifera 'Pissardii'

Prunus cerasifera subsp. *divaricata*

hairy. White flowers, small yellow to red fruit. *P. c.* subsp. *divaricata*, lax habit, bears smaller, yellow flowers. *P. c.* '**Hessei**', shrubby, with light green foliage, and snow white flowers; '**Lindsayae**', reddish young foliage maturing to green, pale pink flowers; '**Newport**', shrubby in habit, with bronze foliage, small, white to pale pink flowers; '**Nigra**' has deep purple-black foliage; '**Pendula**' has weeping growth habit; '**Pissardii**' has red to

purple leaves, white flowers opening from pink buds, plum-red fruit; '**Thundercloud**', a tall cultivar with deep bronze foliage, pink flowers. Zones 4–10.

Prunus cerasus
SOUR CHERRY

☼ ❄ ↔ 15 ft (4.5 m) ↑ 20 ft (6 m)

Found from southeastern Europe to India. Large deciduous shrub or small tree. Small, deep green, glossy leaves,

finely serrated edges. Long-stemmed umbels of small white flowers, in spring. Fruit resembles sweet cherries. Zones 3–9.

Prunus × *cistena*
PURPLE-LEAFED SAND CHERRY, RED-LEAF PLUM

☼ ❄ ↔ 6 ft (1.8 m) ↑ 8 ft (2.4 m)

Hybrid between *P. cerasifera* 'Atropurpurea' and *P. pumila*. Slow-growing shrub with lustrous, bronze-tinted leaves with serrated edges. White flowers develop into small, dark purple-red fruits. Zones 3–9.

Prunus cyclamina
CYCLAMEN CHERRY

☼ ❄ ↔ 20 ft (6 m) ↑ 30 ft (9 m)

From central China. Leaves, coarsely serrated, heavily veined, 3 in (8 cm) long, tapering abruptly to a point. Flowers, in clusters of 4, long-stemmed, deep rose pink, fringed edges, in spring. Small red fruits. Zones 6–9.

Prunus davidiana
DAVID'S PEACH

☼ ❄ ↔ 30 ft (9 m) ↑ 30 ft (9 m)

Deciduous Chinese tree. Young branches upright, whippy, dark green

Prunus cerasifera 'Lindsayae'

leaves, very small, tapering point, sharp teeth. White or pale pink flowers, in late winter–spring. Yellow furry edible fruit. Zones 4–9.

Prunus × *domestica*
EUROPEAN PLUM, PLUM

☼ ❄ ↔ 15 ft (4.5 m) ↑ 30 ft (9 m)

The common plum has been grown since ancient times, a hybrid, probably between *P. spinosa* and *P. cerasifera* subsp. *divaricata*. Leaves to 4 in (10 cm) long, flowers white, soft-fleshed yellow or red-skinned fruit. '**Angelina Burdett**' (syn. 'Angelina'), early fruiting, light red skin, yellow flesh; '**Bühlerfrühwetsch**', purple-skinned cultivar from Germany; '**Coe's Golden Drop**', mid-season, yellow skin, yellow flesh; '**Greengage**', mid-season, greenish yellow skin, yellow flesh, largely self-fertile; '**Hauszwetsch**' and '**Mount Royal**', purple-skinned; '**President**', mid- to late season, large, purplish blue skin, yellow flesh. Zones 5–9.

Prunus cyclamina

Prunus × *cistena*

Prunus × *domestica* 'Bühlerfrühwetsch'

Prunus × *domestica* 'Hauszwetsch'

Prunus × *domestica* 'Mount Royal'

Prunus dulcis

Prunus japonica

P

Prunus dulcis
ALMOND

☀ ❄ ↔ 15 ft (4.5 m) ↑ 20–30 ft (6–9 m)

Species native to eastern Mediterranean and North Africa. Deciduous tree with 5 in (12 cm) long narrow leaves with finely serrated edges. Large white to deep pink flowers, followed by edible kernels. '**Alba Plena**' has white double flowers;

'**Macrocarpa**' has large pale pink flowers; '**Roseoplena**' has pink double flowers. Zones 7–10.

Prunus fasciculata
DESERT ALMOND

☀ ❄ ↔ 7 ft (2 m) ↑ 6–10 ft (1.8–3 m)

This species is a deciduous shrub from arid regions of southwestern USA. Densely branched from the central trunk. Small leaves, clusters of tiny white flowers, in spring. Felted, brown fruit, ½ in (12 mm) wide. Zones 7–10.

Prunus fruticosa
GROUND CHERRY, STEPPE CHERRY

☀ ❄ ↔ 8 ft (2.4 m) ↑ 4 ft (1.2 m)

A suckering deciduous shrub found from central Europe to Siberia, with glossy, deep green leaves to 2 in (5 cm) long. Flowers are white, frilly-

edges, in umbels of 3 to 4 blooms, in spring. Dark red, cherry-like, edible fruits. Zones 4–9.

Prunus glandulosa
DWARF FLOWERING ALMOND

☀ ❄ ↔ 5 ft (1.5 m) ↑ 5 ft (1.5 m)

Lovely deciduous shrub from China and Japan. Densely branched, rather narrow leaves, finely serrated edges. Smothered in deep pink to red flowers, in spring. Dark red fruits. Prune to near ground level after flowering to encourage strong growth, with heavy flowering next season. '**Alba Plena**' has white double flowers; '**Sinensis**' has large leaves, pink double flowers. Zones 4–9.

Prunus grayana
JAPANESE BIRD CHERRY

☀ ❄ ↔ 20 ft (6 m) ↑ 30 ft (9 m)

Deciduous tree from Japan with 3 in (8 cm) long, short-stemmed, bristle-edged leaves. Flowers white, fairly small, clustered in showy racemes. Small black fruits. Zones 6–10.

Prunus hortulana
HORTULAN PLUM

☀ ❄ ↔ 15 ft (4.5 m) ↑ 20–30 ft (6–9 m)

Deciduous tree from central USA. Leaves yellow-green with a slight gloss, fine hairs, serrated edges. Dark brown branches with peeling bark. Flowers white, in umbels of 2 to 5 blooms. Edible red or yellow fruit. Zones 6–9.

Prunus ilicifolia
HOLLY-LEAFED CHERRY, ISLAY

☀ ❄ ↔ 20 ft (6 m) ↑ 25 ft (8 m)

A densely branched evergreen shrub or small tree that is native to California. Leathery, glossy, green, holly-like leaves with spiny edges. Small creamy white flowers massed in racemes. Red, sometimes yellow fruit. Zones 9–11.

Prunus incisa
FUJI CHERRY

☀ ❄ ↔ 15 ft (4.5 m) ↑ 15–20 ft (4.5–6 m)

Small deciduous tree from Japan. White to pale pink flowers with deeply incised petals, in spring, on bare wood. Leaves, heavily serrated edges, develop fiery yellow, orange, and red tones, in autumn. Fruit small, purple-black in color. Zones 6–9.

Prunus japonica
ORIENTAL BUSH CHERRY

☀ ❄ ↔ 3–6 ft (0.9–1.8 m) ↑ 5 ft (1.5 m)

Thin-branched, deciduous shrub from central China to Korea and Japan. Heavily serrated foliage. Clusters of small, white to pale pink flowers, in spring. Small, cherry-like, red fruits. Zones 4–9.

Prunus laurocerasus
CHERRY LAUREL, LAUREL CHERRY

☀ ❄ ↔ 30 ft (9 m) ↑ 20 ft (6 m)

A popular hedging plant. This evergreen Eurasian shrub or small tree has lustrous deep green leaves, and racemes of tiny creamy white flowers, in spring. The flowers are followed by small black fruits. Cut back hard in late spring or early summer. '**Etna**', finely toothed shiny leaves; '**Zabeliana**', low-growing, reaching up to 3 ft (0.9 m) high with a greater spread, narrow pale green leaves. Zones 7–10.

Prunus laurocerasus '**Etna**'

Prunus grayana

Prunus laurocerasus

Prunus lusitanica

Prunus mume 'Geisha'

Prunus lusitanica

PORTUGAL LAUREL, PORTUGUESE LAUREL

☼ ❄ ↔ 30 ft (9 m) ↑ 20 ft (6 m)

Superficially similar to *P. laurocerasus*, this plant is native to the Iberian Peninsula. Evergreen with large, glossy, deep green leaves. Flowers later than *P. laurocerasus*, racemes of cream flowers. Fruit deep purple to near-black shade. *P. l.* subsp. *azorica*, the Azores cherry laurel, shrubby, rarely exceeding 12 ft (3.5 m) tall, smaller leaves, shorter racemes. Zones 7–10.

Prunus maackii ★

AMUR CHOKE CHERRY,
MANCHURIAN CHERRY

☼ ❄ ↔ 25 ft (8 m) ↑ 50 ft (15 m)

From Korea and nearby parts of China, smaller in cultivation. Small cream flowers in racemes, in spring. Purple-tinted leaves, peeling papery bark, light orange-red shade. Small black fruit. Zones 2–9.

Prunus mandshurica

MANCHURIAN APRICOT

☼ ❄ ↔ 25 ft (8 m) ↑ 15–20 ft (4.5–6 m)

From northeastern China and Korea. Small, spreading, rounded tree. Beautiful, single, pinkish flowers, in spring, before leaves emerge. Green leaves turn yellow to reddish in autumn; yellow rounded fruit in autumn. Zones 3–9.

Prunus maritima

BEACH PLUM, SAND PLUM

☼ ❄ ↔ 7 ft (2 m) ↑ 6 ft (1.8 m)

From eastern USA. Deciduous shrub, dark green leaves, pale undersides, dark bark. White flowers, in pairs or small clusters, spring. Fruit purple, red or yellow, edible. 'Eastham', large fruit; 'Hancock', early-ripening. Zones 3–9.

Prunus maximowiczii

MIYAMA CHERRY

☼ ❄ ↔ 20 ft (6 m) ↑ 20 ft (6 m)

Deciduous tree from Japan, Korea, parts of China. Small heavily serrated leaves. Creamy white flowers, upright racemes, in spring. Zones 4–9.

Prunus mume

JAPANESE APRICOT, MEI

☼ ❄ ↔ 25 ft (8 m) ↑ 20–30 ft (6–9 m)

Early flowering deciduous tree from southern Japan. Rounded crown of

Prunus maackii

Prunus maximowiczii

leaves to 4 in (10 cm) long. Flowers, more than 1 in (25 mm) wide, soft fragrance, dusky rose pink. Yellow fruit. 'Benishidori' has small, deep pink, fragrant, double flowers; 'Dawn' has large, light pink, double flowers, blooming late; 'Geisha' has dusky pink, semi-double, fragrant flowers, blooming very early; 'Pendula' is

a small weeping plant with single pale pink flowers, appearing early in spring. Zones 6–10.

Prunus munsoniana

WILD GOOSE PLUM

☼ ❄ ↔ 20 ft (6 m) ↑ 25 ft (8 m)

Native of central USA. Deciduous tree, young stems red. Lustrous, deep green leaves, finely serrated edges. Small clusters of white flowers, in spring. Bright red fruit, edible but bitter. Zones 6–9.

Prunus padus

BIRD CHERRY, EUROPEAN BIRD CHERRY,
MAYDAY TREE

☼ ❄ ↔ 25 ft (8 m) ↑ 30–50 ft (9–15 m)

Found from Europe to Japan, this deciduous tree (which is often shorter in cultivation) has drooping branch tips. Racemes of numerous white flowers, in spring, and tiny black fruits. 'Aucubifolia', with yellow-speckled leaves; 'Colorata', pink flowers with purple-tinted young branches, new leaves and fruit; 'Pendula', with strongly drooping

Prunus padus

P

Prunus pumila var. *depressa*

Prunus persica, Peach Group, 'Jerseyglo'

branches; '**Plena**' has semi-double flowers; '**Stricta**' has strongly erect racemes. Zones 3–9.

Prunus pensylvanica
PIN CHERRY, RED CHERRY

☀ ❄ ↔ 30 ft (9 m) ↑ 30 ft (9 m)

North American tree. Deciduous, leaves to 4 in (10 cm) long, conspicuously toothed. White flowers, about ½ in (12 mm) wide, in clusters of up to 8 blooms, in spring. Tiny red fruits. Zones 2–9.

Prunus persica
syn. *Amygdalus persica*
PEACH

☀ ❄ ↔ 6–20 ft (1.8–6 m)
↑ 8–20 ft (2.4–6 m)

Believed native to China. Deciduous tree. Leaves 4–6 in (10–15 cm) long; white or pink flowers.

Peach Group: Cultivars subdivided as freestone or clingstone; yellow or white fleshed; early-, mid-, or late-season ripening. '**Cresthaven**' and '**Jerseyglo**', late-season, yellow, free-

Prunus persica, Peach Group, 'Cresthaven'

stone peaches; '**Texstar**' early to mid-season, semi-freestone, yellow peach.

Nectarine Group: '**Anderhone**', large, very sweet, late-season fruit.

Ornamental Group: Cultivars grown for flowers, mostly double, white or pink to red, some flecked different colors. '**Klara Meyer**', compact, deep pink double flowers. Zones 5-10.

Prunus pseudocerasus
JAPANESE CHERRY TREE

☀ ❄ ↔ 15 ft (4.5 m) ↑ 25 ft (8 m)

From China. Flowers about 1 in (25 mm) across, white, and fragrant. Red fruit is edible. Zones 6–8.

Prunus pumila
SAND CHERRY

☀ ❄ ↔ 30 in (75 cm) ↑ 30 in (75 cm)

A hardy small shrub from northeastern USA, it sometimes has a prostrate growth habit. Leaves, 1½ in (35 mm) long, serrated near the tips, gray-green above, blue-tinted below. Clusters of white flowers, appear in spring. Small dark red edible fruits. *P. p.* var. *depressa*, prostrate habit, narrow leaves, bluish white undersides. Zones 2–9.

Prunus rufa
HIMALAYAN CHERRY

☀ ❄ ↔ 15 ft (4.5 m) ↑ 20 ft (6 m)

Found in the Himalayan lowlands. Deciduous tree, rusty felt-like coating on young shoots. Flowers, white or pink-tinted, backed by red calyces, in spring. Tiny red fruit. Zones 8–10.

Prunus salicifolia
CAPULIN, MEXICAN BIRD CHERRY

☀ ❄ ↔ 20 ft (6 m) ↑ 30 ft (9 m)

Found in mountains from Mexico to Peru. Deciduous tree, hardy. Serrated leaves, 3 in (8 cm) long, flowers small, white, in loosely packed racemes. Fruit cherry-like, red, sweet. Zones 6–10.

Prunus persica

Prunus persica, Peach Group, 'Texstar'

Prunus salicina
JAPANESE PLUM

☼ ❄ ↔ 25 ft (8 m) ↑ 30 ft (9 m)

Deciduous tree from Japan and China. New shoots red, lush dark green foliage, bluntly toothed edges. Flowers in pairs or small clusters, white, in spring. Yellow to red fruit, 2–3 in (5–8 cm) wide, edible, sometimes rather bitter. '**Methley**' grows to 25 ft (8 m) tall and wide, large, purple-skinned, yellow-fleshed fruit; '**Red Heart**', small tree, heavy cropping from a young age, large red fruit that preserves well. Zones 6–10.

Prunus sargentii
SARGENT CHERRY

☼ ❄ ↔ 35 ft (10 m) ↑ 50 ft (15 m)

Native to Japan, smaller in cultivation. Red-toothed leaves, 4 in (10 cm) long. Clusters of large, frilly, dusky pink flowers. Small red cherries. Zones 4–9.

Prunus, Sato-zakura Group
JAPANESE FLOWERING CHERRY

☼ ❄ ↔ 30 ft (9 m) ↑ 20–40 ft (6–12 m)

Large group, composed mainly of hybrids, probably derived from

Prunus salicina, Languedoc-Roussillon, France

Prunus sargentii

Prunus salicina 'Methley'

Prunus salicina 'Red Heart'

Prunus, Sato-zakura Group, 'Alborosea'

Prunus, Sato-zakura Group, 'Kanzan', in autumn

Prunus, Sato-zakura Group, 'Kiku-shidare'

Prunus, Sato-zakura Group, 'Okumiyako'

Prunus, Sato-zakura Group, 'Kanzan', in winter

P., Sato-zakura Group, 'Kanzan', in summer

Prunus, Sato-zakura Group, 'Kanzan', in spring

Prunus serotina

P. serrulata, ornamentals grown for early–mid-spring flower display. '**Albo-rosea**', white to pink double flowers; '**Kanzan**' (syn. 'Sekiyama'), strongly upright growth when young, clusters of bright pink double flowers, vivid autumn foliage; '**Kiku-shidare**' (syn. 'Cheal's Weeping Cherry'), pendulous growth, pink double flowers; '**Okumi-yako**' (syn. 'Shimidsu-sakura'), flat-topped tree with large, white, double flowers from pink buds; '**Shirotae**' (syn. 'Mt Fuji'), massed, large, single to semi-double, white flowers, golden autumn foliage; '**Ukon**', pale green, semi-double flowers. Zones 5–9.

Prunus scopulorum

☼ ❄ ↔ 12 ft (3.5 m) ↑ 40 ft (12 m)
Chinese tree; strongly upright growth habit. Clusters of very fragrant, pink-tinted, white flowers, in spring. Small red fruit. Zones 6–9.

Prunus serotina

BLACK CHERRY, CAPULIN, RUM CHERRY
☼ ❄ ↔ 30 ft (9 m) ↑ 100 ft (30 m)
Deciduous North American tree. Glossy, mid-green, finely serrated leaves, lighter beneath, over 3 in (8 cm) long. White flowers, in short pendulous racemes, in spring. Small near-black fruit. Zones 3–9.

Prunus, Sato-zakura Group, 'Shirotae'

Prunus triloba 'Multiplex'

Prunus triloba 'Multiplex'

Prunus serrulata

JAPANESE FLOWERING CHERRY,
ORIENTAL CHERRY

☼ ❄ ↔ 15 ft (4.5 m) ↑ 12 ft (3.5 m)
Small deciduous tree from China.
Leaves somewhat over 4 in (10 cm)
long. White flowers, to 1¼ in

(30 mm) wide, in spring. Small black
fruit. '**Pink Cloud**', pink flowers.
Zones 5–9.

Prunus spinosa

BLACKTHORN, SLOE

☼ ❄ ↔ 15 ft (4.5 m) ↑ 20 ft (6 m)
Deciduous shrub or small tree found
in Eurasia and North Africa, covered
in sharp spines. Small white flowers,
prune-like black fruit. This plant has
been recorded in hedgerows from
ancient times. Zones 4–10.

Prunus subcordata

OREGON PLUM, PACIFIC PLUM

☼ ❄ ↔ 10 ft (3 m) ↑ 15 ft (4.5 m)
Deciduous shrub native of western
North America, can reach 25 ft (8 m)

Prunus tomentosa

high. Small, serrated-edged leaves,
furrowed, gray-brown bark, flakes off
in scales. Flowers white, ¾ in (18 mm)
wide, in small clusters, in spring.
Purple-red or yellow fruit. Zones 7–10.

Prunus × subhirtella

SPRING CHERRY

☼ ❄ ↔ 25 ft (8 m) ↑ 50 ft (15 m)
Broad, deciduous tree from Japan,
smaller in cultivation. Leaves serrated
to 3 in (8 cm) long. Flowers before
foliage, small, white or pink. Tiny
purple-black fruit. '**Autumnalis**',
flowers early; '**Pendula**', long-lived,
weeping; '**Pendula Rosea**', weeping,
pink flowers; '**Stellata**', clusters of
starry, single, pink flowers. Zones 5–9.

Prunus tenella

DWARF RUSSIAN ALMOND

☼ ❄ ↔ 5 ft (1.5 m) ↑ 5 ft (1.5 m)
Deciduous Eurasian shrub sometimes
confused with a flowering quince

(*Chaenomeles*). Leaves larger, dull
yellow fruit smaller. Deep pinkish red
flowers. Zones 2–9.

Prunus tomentosa

DOWNY CHERRY, MANCHU CHERRY,
NANKING CHERRY

☼ ❄ ↔ 8 ft (2.4 m) ↑ 8 ft (2.4 m)
Shrub from the Himalayas with
downy young stems. Puckered deep
green leaves slightly over 2 in (5 cm)
long, fluffy undersides. White to pale
pink flowers, 1 in (25 mm) wide, carried singly or in pairs. Downy red
fruit. Zones 2–8.

Prunus triloba

DWARF FLOWERING ALMOND,
FLOWERING PLUM, ROSE TREE OF CHINA

☼ ❄ ↔ 12 ft (3.5 m) ↑ 12 ft (3.5 m)
From China. Pale pink flowers, semi
or fully double, open before or with
leaf buds. Leaves 2½ in (6 cm) long,

Prunus serrulata

Prunus serrulata 'Pink Cloud'

Prunus × subhirtella 'Pendula Rosea'

Prunus × subhirtella 'Pendula'

often 3-lobed. Red fruit with downy skin is rather unreliable, but can make a good show in some years. '**Multiplex**', soft pink flowers. Zones 5–9.

Prunus virginiana

COMMON CHOKE CHERRY, CHOKE CHERRY

☼ ❄ ↔ 12 ft (3.5 m) ↑ 12 ft (3.5 m)

Large deciduous shrub or small tree from North America. Leaves 3 in (8 cm) long. Racemes of small white flowers, in spring. Zones 2–9.

Prunus × yedoensis

TOKYO CHERRY, YOSHINO CHERRY

☼ ❄ ↔ 30 ft (9 m) ↑ 40 ft (12 m)

Hybrid between *P.* × *subhirtella* and *P. speciosa*. Upright tree with spreading crown. Deep green, serrated leaves, turn vivid orange and red, in autumn. Racemes of scented white flowers, in spring. Tiny black fruit. '**Shidare-yoshino**' ★ has weeping branches and profuse snow white flowers. Zones 5–9.

Pseudocydonia sinensis

PSEUDERANTHEMUM

From tropical regions, this genus of the acanthus (Acanthaceae) family contains about 60 species of small, evergreen perennials, shrubs or subshrubs. They are grown mostly for their attractive, often prominently veined leaves and dainty white flowers flecked or flushed with red or mauve. CULTIVATION: Suited to warm-climate gardens, the frost-tender members of this genus need well-drained soil enriched with organic matter in a protected, partially shaded position. Outside the tropics they are best grown as greenhouse or conservatory plants. They prefer bright, filtered light and regular water and fertilizer during the growing season. Tip prune from an early age to encourage a bushy habit or, if the plants become leggy, cut back hard in spring. Propagate from half-hardened cuttings or by division.

Pseuderanthemum atropurpureum

◐ ↔ 3 ft (0.9 m) ↑ 4 ft (1.2 m)

Erect, evergreen shrub from Polynesia. Showy, deep purple, ovate, pointed leaves, marked with pink or green along the veins. Tubular white flowers with purple markings in the centers in dense terminal spikes, in summer. Zones 11–12.

Pseuderanthemum reticulatum

◐ ↔ 3 ft (0.9 m) ↑ 3 ft (0.9 m)

An evergreen, bushy shrub from Vanuatu. Golden stems, bright green ovate leaves, wavy margins, network of creamy yellow lines. White tubular flowers, cerise markings in the throat, in large terminal panicles, in summer. '**Andersonii**', yellow blotches on foliage. Zones 11–12.

PSEUDOCYDONIA

There is only the one species of deciduous shrub or small tree in this genus, which is closely related to the flowering quince (*Chaenomeles*). A member of the rose (Rosaceae) family, the genus is very close to the true quince genus, *Cydonia*, and some botanists now think they should be combined. Native to China, it has oval serrated-edged leaves that emerge in spring, at around the same time as the flowers. The large oval to pear-shaped fruits, 6 in (15 cm) in size, are yellow and can be used in the same

Prunus × *yedoensis* 'Shidare-yoshino'

Pseuderanthemum reticulatum 'Andersonii'

ways as the culinary quince. They seldom develop fully in cool climates. CULTIVATION: In cool-temperate climates this plant should be given the protection of a warm wall. It is tolerant of dry and poor conditions but is best grown in a reasonably fertile soil that is well drained. After flowering, prune to remove any overcrowded branches. Propagation is from seed sown in autumn.

Pseudocydonia sinensis

syns *Chaenomeles sinensis*, *Cydonia sinensis*

CHINESE QUINCE

☼ ❄ ↔ 20 ft (6 m) ↑ 20 ft (6 m)

Dappled bark exfoliates in large plates, young shoots downy. Leaves glossy above, dense brown fur beneath, colors to shades of red and yellow, in autumn. Pale pink blossoms, in spring. Fruits ripen to deep yellow, in autumn. Zones 6–10.

PSEUDOGYNOXYS

This is a genus of 13 perennial shrubs or climbers, native to tropical South America and members of the daisy (Asteraceae) family. They have alternate leaves and solitary or many radiate heads or clusters of pale to deep orange or red, daisy-like flowers. CULTIVATION: *Pseudogynoxys* species prefer a sunny position in moist, moderately fertile, well-drained soil. Water sparingly when not actively growing. Propagate from seed.

Pseudogynoxys chenopodioides

Pseudogynoxys chenopodioides

syn. *Senecio confuses*

MEXICAN FLAMEVINE, ORANGEGLOW VINE

☼ ⚘ ↔ 10 ft (3 m) ↑ 12–17 ft (3.5–5 m)

Moderately bushy, evergreen, twining climber from Mexico to Honduras and Colombia, cultivated for its brightly colored orange flowers, attractive to butterflies, bees and hummingbirds. Smooth, thick, alternate, narrowly oval, toothed, light green leaves, up to 3 in (8 cm) long. Few radiate heads of fragrant bright orange flowers fading to red, mainly in summer, at branch ends or growing from the leaf axils. Zones 9–11.

PSEUDOLARIX

The sole species in this genus, part of the pine (Pinaceae) family, is a larch-like deciduous conifer from eastern China, with leaves larger and strappier than true larches. Young foliage is bright green but changes to fiery hues of yellow, orange, and red-brown before falling with the first hard frosts. CULTIVATION: Although hardy to quite severe frosts, young plants may be damaged by very early or late freezes. Plant in deep, fertile, humus-rich, well-drained soil with sun or morning shade. Trees that are too shaded will develop poor autumn color. Naturally upright and conical, this tree needs little pruning, other than to lightly shape or tidy. Propagation is usually from seed.

Pseudolarix amabilis

GOLDEN LARCH

☼ ❄ ↔ 25 ft (8 m) ↑ 100 ft (30 m)

Upright conifer has deeply fissured, warm red-brown bark. Leaves to 2 in (5 cm) long, in whorls on short side-shoots. Female cones, purplish, to 3 in (8 cm) long, persist on the tree after shedding their seed. 'Nana' ★,

Pseudopanax crassifolius

Pseudopanax lessonii 'Gold Splash'

3 ft (0.9 m) tall with a spreading habit, one of several dwarf cultivars. Zones 6–9.

PSEUDOPANAX

syns *Neopanax, Nothopanax*

There are about 20 species of evergreen shrubs or small trees in this genus of the ivy (Araliaceae) family. Most are native to New Zealand and the rest are found in Chile and Tasmania, Australia. They have ornamental and interesting foliage, which in several species undergoes a distinct metamorphosis from juvenile to mature stages. The leaves are simple or palmate and may have toothed edges. Tiny, greenish, male or female flowers are borne in large clusters, sometimes on separate trees, and the small fruits that follow are often black. CULTIVATION: Cultivated for their attractive foliage and, in species such as *P. crassifolius*, for their striking form, members of this genus will grow in any fertile well-drained soil in sun or part-shade. Most will tolerate at least light frost, but should be given a warm sheltered site in cool areas or

Pseudopanax ferox

Pseudolarix amabilis

grown in a greenhouse or conservatory. Propagate from seed or from half-hardened cuttings taken in autumn.

Pseudopanax arboreus

FIVE-FINGER

☼ ⚘ ↔ 15 ft (4.5 m) ↑ 10–20 ft (3–6 m)

Common throughout its native New Zealand. Rounded tree. Leathery palmate leaves, 5 to 7 leaflets, deep shiny green with serrated edges. Tiny flowers, in winter. Small purplish berries on the female trees. Zones 9–11.

Pseudopanax crassifolius

HOROEKA, LANCEWOOD

☼ ⚘ ↔ 7 ft (2 m) ↑ 12–50 ft (3.5–15 m)

Juvenile form, single stem, drooping, leathery, shallowly toothed leaves, just ¾ in (18 mm) wide, dark green to bronze, orangey midrib. After 10 years develops into a round-headed tree, stem thickens, branches form, leaves become shorter. Zones 9–11.

Pseudopanax ferox

TOOTHED LANCEWOOD

☼ ⚘ ↔ 7 ft (2 m) ↑ 15 ft (4.5 m)

Native to New Zealand. Very like *P. crassifolius*, with distinct juvenile and adult stages. Grown for its

dramatic juvenile form. Narrow leathery leaves to 20 in (50 cm) long; large coarse toothed edges. Dark green with bronze tones, orangey-red midrib. Zones 9–11.

Pseudopanax laetus

☼ ⚘ ↔ 10 ft (3 m) ↑ 5–15 ft (1.5–4.5 m)

A small bushy tree native to New Zealand's North Island. Similar to *P. arboreus*, leaves much bigger, to 12 in (30 cm) long. More leathery, margins have a purplish line. Small purplish berries. Zones 10–11.

Pseudopanax lessonii

HOUPARA

☼ ⚘ ↔ 7 ft (2 m) ↑ 12 ft (3.5 m)

Attractive foliage shrub native to New Zealand's North Island. Thick, glossy, dark green leaves, 3 to 5 broadly oval leaflets, shallowly toothed near the tips. 'Cyril Watson', slow-growing, very bushy, displays 2 leaf forms on the same plant, 3 to 5 short, broad lobes, coarsely toothed, or simple with shallowly toothed margins, very thick, leathery, glossy fresh green; 'Gold Splash', dark green leaves with bright yellow splashed along the veins and midribs. Zones 9–11.

Pseudophoenix lediniana

Pseudophoenix sargentii

Pseudorhipsalis lankesteri (red-spotted strap-like stems), Jardín Botánico Lankester, near Cartago, Costa Rica

PSEUDOPHOENIX
CHERRY PALM

These 4 solitary palms are members of the family Arecaceae, and are native to the West Indies. They often have swollen trunks, a prominent, swollen crownshaft, and sparse crown of few feathery fronds. Separate male and female flowers appear in the same head, followed by the fruit, which is a 2- or 3-lobed drupe. The genus is named from the Greek *pseudo*, false, and *phoenix*, a date palm.
CULTIVATION: Cherry palms will adapt to most well-drained soils, in a sunny position, and will tolerate some neglect. Propagate from seed, which remains viable for up to 2 years.

Pseudophoenix lediniana
PAL, TI PALMIS MARON

☀ � ↔ 17 ft (5 m) ↕ 50–75 ft (15–23 m)
An attractive palm from Haiti, with a columnar, prominently ringed trunk,

which is slightly swollen near the middle. The fronds are glossy, dark green, finely divided. The flowers appear in broad, much branched clusters, which are followed by red fruit. Zones 10–11.

Pseudophoenix sargentii
BUCCANEER PALM, FLORIDA CHERRY PALM, SARGENT'S PALM

☀ ✓ ↔ 8–12 ft (2.4–3.5 m)
↕ 10–25 ft (3–8 m)
This slow-growing palm has a slender, tapering trunk and a sparse crown of long arching fronds. It has regularly arranged, stiff, dark green leaflets that are gray or silvery underneath. Clusters of yellow flowers are followed by dense, erect, branching bunches of cherry red to orange-scarlet, pear-shaped fruit. *P. s.* subsp. *saonae* produces heavier, larger fruit and has hanging rather than erect flowerheads. Zones 10–11.

Pseudophoenix vinifera
BUCCANEER PALM, CACHEO, KATIE, WINE PALM

☀ ✓ ↔ 10–17 ft (3–5 m)
↕ 30–75 ft (9–23 m)
Evergreen palm grows a stout bulging trunk up to 75 ft (23 m) tall, narrows just below the crown of arching feathery fronds with dark green leaflets. Clusters of flowers hang straight down close to the trunk, followed by huge clusters of large, bright red fruit, covered with a thin layer of wax at maturity. Zones 10–11.

PSEUDORHIPSALIS
A genus of 6 epiphytic shrub-like members of the family Cactaceae from Central America and the Caribbean, with one species widely spread into South America. The genus continues to challenge taxonomists, some of whom feel it is related to *Rhipsalis*, hence the botanical name. The spineless stem segments are rounded at first but later become flattened and leaf-like, with notches on the margins. Flowers are short, funnelform or salverform, diurnal, white or pale yellow, up to 1½ in (35 mm) long. Seed pods are spherical to oval, white often tinged with purple, to ½ in (12 mm) long.
CULTIVATION: Grow in a rich well-drained soil. Propagate from stem cuttings, dried out for a week or two, or from seed. Rest in winter.

Pseudorhipsalis lankesteri

☀/◐ ✓ ↔ 8–20 in (20–50 cm)
↕ 40 in (100 cm)
From Costa Rica. Pendent primary stems to 26 in (65 cm) long, rounded, becoming flattened and leaf-shaped, with secondary stems in 3 ranks below, also rounded, becoming flattened and lance-shaped at end.

Flowers borne singly, saucer-shaped, cream. Seed pods magenta to pink. Zones 10–12.

Pseudorhipsalis ramulosa

☀/◐ ✓ ↔ 24 in (60 cm) ↕ 7 ft (2 m)
From Central and South America. Shrubby plant, branching from base. Primary stems rounded at base, flattened, leaf-like. Secondary stems arising in 4 to 5 rows, rounded at first, becoming flattened at end, often branching again, lance-shaped to straight, reddish becoming green. Flowers borne singly, saucer-shaped, pink or greenish cream. Seed pods oval, white to pinkish. Zones 10–12.

PSEUDOSASA
A genus of 6 species of bamboo in the grass (Poaceae) family, from China, Japan, and Korea. They can be clump-forming or running and vary from dwarf to quite tall species. Some can be invasive and need to be controlled. The stems are woody and erect and the foliage is usually lance-shaped and normally without hairs.

Pseudophoenix vinifera

Pseudowintera colorata

CULTIVATION: They will grow well in any moist fertile soil in full sun or half-sun. Propagate by division in early spring.

Pseudosasa japonica

ARROW BAMBOO, METAKE

☼/☀ ❄ ↔ 15 ft (4.5 m)
↑ 17–20 ft (5–6 m)

Strong running species with upright stems that start green and turn beige, forming branchlets in the second year. Leaves to 14 in (35 cm) long, with a yellowish midrib and a grayish reverse. Zones 6–10.

PSEUDOTSUGA

DOUGLAS FIR

There are 6 to 8 species of coniferous trees within this genus in the pine (Pinaceae) family. All are evergreen forest trees from western North America, Mexico, Taiwan, Japan, and China. They are major timber trees used for power poles, railway sleepers, plywood, and wood pulp and are also a source of Oregon balsam. Some trees reach 300 ft (90 m) in height in their native habitat, but this is rare in cultivation. The foliage and cones are frequently used as Christmas decorations, as the foliage sheds its needles less readily than other species. The linear leaves grow radially on the shoots. The female cones have 3-pronged bract scales protruding from between the cone scales; the cylindrical male cones are smaller.

CULTIVATION: These hardy trees prefer colder climates and will grow in any well-drained soil in full sun. Propagate the species from seed in spring, or graft cultivars in late winter.

Pseudotsuga menziesii

syns *Pseudotsuga douglasii, P. taxifolia*
DOUGLAS FIR

☼ ❄ ↔ 15–30 ft (4.5–9 m)
↑ 80–150 ft (24–45 m)

Native to North America, from British Columbia to California. Fast growing, long lived. Bark has corky plates, deep fissures developing with age. Narrow leaves, dark blue-green above, 2 white bands beneath, juvenile foliage apple-green in spring. Female cones, produced on mature trees. *P. m.* var. *glauca*, glaucous blue leaves, smaller cones; *P. m.* 'Densa' and 'Fletcheri' are dwarf forms. Zones 4–9.

Pseudotsuga sinensis

CHINESE DOUGLAS FIR

☼ ❄ ↔ 10–25 ft (3–8 m) ↑ 120 ft (36 m)

From southern central China, much smaller in cultivation. Leaves glossy green above, gray beneath, turned-in margins. Ovoid to conical cones, pale purple to purplish brown. Zones 7–9.

Pseudotsuga wilsoniana

TAIWAN DOUGLAS FIR

☼ ❄ ↔ 10–25 ft (3–8 m) ↑ 120 ft (36 m)

Native to Taiwan, tree scarcely more than a shrub in cultivation. Narrow

Pseudotsuga menziesii 'Densa'

leaves ¾–1 in (18–25 mm) long. Cones the same as *P. sinensis*. Zones 8–9.

PSEUDOWINTERA

This New Zealand genus in the family Winteraceae contains 3 species of evergreen trees and shrubs grown for their attractive foliage. Leathery leaves, alternately arranged, unusually colored. Leaves are aromatic when crushed and pungent to taste, giving rise to the common name of pepper tree. Insignificant cream flowers are followed by large black berries.

CULTIVATION: Best suited to mild climates, members of this genus should be grown in a rich moist but well-drained soil in sun or light shade. In cool climates they can be grown in the greenhouse or conservatory. The foliage of the most commonly cultivated species, *P. colorata*, will color more intensely in full sun. They are

quite slow-growing plants and will remain tidy for many years. Propagate from seed or from half-hardened cuttings taken in autumn.

Pseudowintera colorata

HOROPITO, PEPPER TREE

☼/☀ ⧗ ↔ 5 ft (1.5 m) ↑ 7 ft (2 m)

Colorful shrub, fresh shoots bright red, yellowish green leaves mottled and speckled with various shades of red, undersides bluish gray. Leaves have a particularly pungent taste. Zones 9–11.

Pseudowintera traversii

☼ ⧗ ↔ 36 in (90 cm) ↑ 36 in (90 cm)

Native to New Zealand's South Island. Slow-growing, densely branched shrub. Closely packed oblong leaves are yellowish green above and bluish green beneath. Foliage not as aromatic as other species. Zones 9–11.

Pseudotsuga menziesii, in the wild, Canyon National Park, Utah, USA

Pseudotsuga menziesii 'Fletcheri'

PSIDIUM

This tropical American genus, in the myrtle (Myrtaceae) family, contains about 100 species of evergreen shrubs or trees widely grown for their decorative edible fruits. They branch freely, almost to the ground. and have thick opposite leaves with prominent veins. White 5-petalled flowers with numerous stamens are rather like large eucalyptus blossoms. Fruit is a rounded or pear-shaped berry ripening to red or yellow. It can be eaten fresh, or used for making juice, jellies, or preserves. CULTIVATION: Members of this genus need a warm to hot climate, moist but well-drained soil with protection from strong winds, and regular watering during summer. They are pruned to tree form, and after fruiting to retain a compact shape. Propagate from seed or cuttings, or by layering or grafting.

Psidium cattleianum

CHERRY GUAVA, STRAWBERRY GUAVA

☼ ⚘ ↔ 8 ft (2.4 m) ↑ 20 ft (6 m)

Red-barked, dense, evergreen shrub. Elliptic, shiny, green leaves. Flowers

Psychopsis krameriana

Psidium guajava

white, solitary about 1 in (25 mm) across. Small round fruit, dark red flesh, extremely rich in vitamin C, often made into jams and jellies. Zones 9–11.

Psidium guajava

GUAVA

☼ ⚘ ↔ 15 ft (4.5 m) ↑ 30 ft (9 m)

Widely grown tropical fruit tree. Dark brown scaly bark, light to mid-green oval leaves with prominent veins, downy undersides. Large white flowers, in spring. Edible pear-shaped fruit, pink strongly aromatic flesh used for making jams and jellies. Zones 10–12.

PSORALEA

Found mainly in the Americas and South Africa, this genus of perennials and evergreen shrubs, in the pea-flower subfamily of the legume (Fabaceae) family, is made up of about 150 species. Their leaves, which are often narrow, sometimes scale-like, and may be single, trifoliate, or pinnate, are often downy or hairy. Clusters of white, blue, purple to pink, or sometimes yellow pea-flowers appear at various times and are followed by insignificant brown seed pods. CULTIVATION: Cold hardiness varies with the species, though few will tolerate anything but the lightest of frosts. Often rather untidy, open-growing plants, they can be kept compact if pruned after flowering. They prefer light but reasonably moist soil that is well drained; they will flower best if grown in full sun. Propagate from seed or from half-hardened cuttings.

Psoralea pinnata

Psoralea esculenta

syn. *Pediomelum esculentum*

INDIAN BREADROOT, POMME BLANCHE, POMME DE PRAIRIE

☼ ❋ ↔ 12–20 in (30–50 cm) ↑ 12–20 in (30–50 cm)

Perennial from North America. Tuberous, edible roots, hairy stems. Compound leaves, to 2 in (5 cm) long, 5 oblong to sword-shaped light green leaflets, edged white, hairy underneath. Dense spikes, to 4 in (10 cm) long, of white, yellow, or blue pea-flowers, in spring–early summer. In autumn, stem breaks off and blows across the prairie like tumbleweed. Some botanists suggest this species should be classified as *Pediomelum esculentum*. Zones 2–4.

Psoralea pinnata

AFRICAN SCURF-PEA, BLUE PEA BUSH

☼ ⚘ ↔ 7 ft (2 m) ↑ 6–10 ft (1.8–3 m)

Most widely cultivated *Psoralea* species, South African shrub. Leaves with 5 to 11 narrow deep green leaflets, often covered in fine hairs. Clusters of violet to bright blue flowers with white wings, in late spring–summer. Zones 9–11.

PSYCHOPSIS

This is a small orchid genus (family Orchidaceae) of about 4 impressive and distinctive species from the West Indies and tropical parts of South America. They were formerly treated with the genus *Oncidium*. They have round, flattened pseudobulbs and a single, leathery, tessellated broad and upright leaf. They have large flowers, somewhat resembling butterflies, that are produced singly on a long, often flattened inflorescence. Flowers will be produced from the apex of the same spike for many months. They have a very narrow, and predominantly brown dorsal sepal and petals, broader lateral sepals that are yellow

Psoralea pinnata

and brown banded. The labellum is wide, flat, and brown, centered with a large pale yellow blotch. Their peak blooming season is summer. CULTIVATION: They are best grown in small terracotta or plastic pots in a coarse bark-based mix, or on cork or tree-fern slabs kept either vertical or horizontal. Larger specimens can be grown in small wooden baskets. Plants need to dry out between waterings and must have unimpeded drainage. They enjoy bright to strong light and are best suited to greenhouse culture in all but tropical climates. They require humid and warm conditions throughout the year, disliking temperatures that drop below 54°F (12°C). Propagate by division.

Psychopsis krameriana

☼/◐ ⚘ ↔ 5–24 in (12–60 cm) ↑ 8–36 in (20–90 cm)

From tropical parts of Central and South America. Large flowers, up to 5 in (12 cm) tall, produced singly on a tall cylindrical inflorescence. The blooms are brown and yellow. Zones 11–12.

Psychopsis Mendenhall

☼/◐ ✦ ↔ 5–24 in (12–60 cm)
↕ 8–36 in (20–90 cm)

This vigorous hybrid is a backcross of *P.* Butterfly (*P. papilio* × *P. sanderae*) onto *P. papilio*. The yellow and brown blooms can be up to 8 in (20 cm) tall. Zones 11–12.

Psychopsis papilio

BUTTERFLY ORCHID

☼/◐ ✦ ↔ 5–24 in (12–60 cm)
↕ 8–36 in (20–90 cm)

Large flowers, to 6 in (15 cm) tall, produced singly on a tall, flattened inflorescence. The blooms are brown and yellow. *P. krameriana* is a closely related species. Zones 11–12.

PSYCHOTRIA

With between 800 and 1,500 species, this genus of the madder (Rubiaceae) family is one of the largest genera of flowering plants. All are trees or shrubs, with a few species adapting to an epiphytic habit. They are widely distributed in all tropical continents and into the subtropics in Africa, Australia, and South America. A major characteristic of the genus is the presence of opposite simple leaves with an associated pair of stipules at the leaf bases. The flowers are small, with tubular petals, and are borne in terminal or axillary heads. They are followed by fleshy fruits that are globular or egg-shaped. Many species contain alkaloids and other chemicals. One New Caledonian species has the highest known concentration of nickel—4.7 percent dry weight—accumulated in its leaves.
CULTIVATION: Since only a few species have been grown in cultivation, little is known of the methods

of propagation of the vast majority. Seeds and cuttings have been successful with the few.

Psychotria capensis

WILD COFFEE

◐ ✦ ↔ 8 ft (2.4 m) ↕ 25 ft (8 m)

Shrub or small tree native to the east coast of South Africa. Leaves oval-shaped to elliptical, leathery, glossy green. Small creamy yellow flowers, in terminal heads, in spring–summer. Egg-shaped fruit. Zones 9–10.

PSYLLIOSTACHYS

STATICE

This genus of 6 annuals and perennials from the leadwort (Plumbaginaceae) family, originated from Syria to Iran and central Asia and around the Black Sea. Often grown for cut and dried flowers. Divided or smooth-edged leaves usually grow from a central base. Flowerheads are slender-stalked panicles of spikelets of 2 to 4 flowers with a tubular, 5-lobed calyx and small, funnel-shaped corolla with 5 lobes.
CULTIVATION: Statice is suitable for coastal areas, and is grown in full sun in fertile well-drained soil. Propagate annuals from seed sown under glass in early spring; perennial species can be grown from softwood cuttings taken in spring.

Psylliostachys spicata

syn. *Limonium spicatum*

☼ ✳ ↔ 4–8 in (10–20 cm)
↕ 4–16 in (10–40 cm)

Annual, native to the Crimea, the Caucasus, and Iran. Glossy green, oblong to sword-shaped leaves, 2–6 in (5–15 cm) long, with finely hairy midribs. Flowers on terminal spikelets on stalks, or lateral spikelets, shorter

Ptelea trifoliata

and without stalks. Flowers, in spring, have ribbed, glandular, hairy calyx and a tiny rose pink corolla. Zones 7–9.

Psylliostachys suworowii

syn. *Limonium suworowii*

☼ ✳ ↔ 4–8 in (10–20 cm)
↕ 4–16 in (10–40 cm)

Slow-growing, erect, branching annual from central Asia, Iran, and northern Afghanistan. Glossy green, oblong to sword-shaped leaves, 2–6 in (5–15 cm) long. Terminal spikelets, to 3½ in (9 cm) long, on stalks finely hairy toward flowerhead; lateral spikelets are shorter and without stalks. Flowers have ribbed, glandular, hairy calyx and a tiny rose pink to purple corolla, in spring. Zones 7–9.

PTELEA

Despite looking rather more like lilacs than oranges, and bearing sycamore-like seeds, the 11 deciduous shrubs or small trees in this North and Central American genus are *Citrus* relatives, and belong to the rue (Rutaceae) family. This is only apparent in the aromatic oil glands of the foliage, which is usually trifoliate, with a dominant central leaflet flanked by a smaller one on each side. The leaves often become bright yellow in autumn. The small white to pale green flowers are scented and clustered together in conspicuous cymes. They appear first in spring or early summer, then sporadically later. Small, 2-seeded, winged fruit, a little like hop seeds, follow.
CULTIVATION: Species from southern USA and northern Mexico are a little tender. Otherwise, most are adaptable and easily grown in any well-drained soil in sun or partial shade. In areas with hot summers, some shade from the afternoon sun is advisable. Propagate from seed, layers, or grafts.

Psychotria capensis

Ptelea angustifolia

WESTERN HOP TREE

☼ ✳ ↔ 12 ft (3.5 m) ↕ 12 ft (3.5 m)

Found in northern Mexico and southern USA. Shrub has fine hairs on its young foliage and new stems. Mature leaves usually smooth, blue-green undersides. Flowers open in early summer. Fruit rounded, with much-reduced wings. Zones 8–10.

Ptelea trifoliata

COMMON HOP TREE

☼ ✳ ↔ 12 ft (3.5 m) ↕ 25 ft (8 m)

From eastern and central USA. Leaves mid-green, 3 leaflets, semi-glossy, paler undersides, slightly notched edges. Pale green flowers, in early summer. Fruit to 1 in (25 mm) wide. 'Aurea', yellow-green foliage; 'Glauca', blue-green foliage. Zones 5–10.

PTERIDIUM

BRACKEN, BRAKE

This genus of the bracken (Dennstaedtiaceae) family occurs worldwide, except for arctic and arid regions. Botanists disagree about the number of species: some argue that all bracken plants fall within such a narrow range of variation that only one species (*P. aquilinum*) can be recognized, though divided into varieties; others recognize a number of species, most

Psychopsis Mendenhall

Pteridium esculentum, in the wild, Col de Prony, New Caledonia

with large geographical ranges that do not overlap. Fronds tough, triangular, much-divided, arising from deeply buried, long-running, repeatedly branched rhizomes; one plant can form a patch 50 ft (15 m) or more across. Spores are borne in continuous bands along curled-under margins of frond segments, but reproduction from spores seems rare as plants spread so effectively by rhizomes. Fronds are frost-killed in autumn and new ones emerge in spring. Bracken is often seen as a weed because of its aggressive spread and difficulty of removal. Farmers dislike it because it smothers pastures and is toxic to livestock, but it is part of a healthy natural ecosystem and provides shelter to birds and other wildlife. Some hunter-gatherer societies eat the starchy rhizomes.
CULTIVATION: Deliberate cultivation is rarely attempted; management of bracken is usually the requirement. It is resistant to many herbicides. The most successful removal method from grassed areas is continual cutting; this eventually depletes its food reserves.

Pteridium aquilinum

↔ 30–60 ft (9–18 m)
↑ 2–8 ft (0.6–2.4 m)

Common bracken of Europe, Asia, Africa, and temperate North America. Fronds hairy beneath to varying degrees, more so when young, bipinnate with primary divisions regularly spaced and evenly tapering, the secondary divisions deeply and fairly regularly lobed. *P. a.* var. ***latiusculum*** is the race from eastern North America, while *P. a.* var. ***pubescens*** is widespread in western North America. Zones 3–10.

Pteridium esculentum

syn. *Pteridium aquilinum* var. *esculentum*

↔ 60 ft (18 m) ↑ 10 ft (3 m)

Common bracken of Australia, New Zealand, and some South Pacific islands. Fronds somewhat irregularly divided with thick but narrow segments, hairless except when young. Zones 8–11.

Pteridium revolutum

syn. *Pteridium aquilinum* var. *wightianum*

↔ 30–60 ft (9–18 m)
↑ 2–5 ft (0.6–1.5 m)

Ranges from tropical Asia to northeastern Australia, mostly in elevated areas. Fronds very regularly divided with long, fishbone-like, secondary divisions with dense coating of hairs below, hairy along midveins above. Zones 9–11.

PTERIS

BRAKE, DISH FERN, TABLE FERN

This is a genus of about 300 semi-evergreen or evergreen terrestrial ferns, native to tropical and subtropical regions and part of the brake (Pteridaceae) family. The plants have erect or creeping, scaly or hairy rhizomes and deciduous, arching, divided fronds on slender, erect, grooved stems. Spore-bodies are carried in hair-like structures along the frond margins. *Pteris* is Greek for fern, referring to the feathery fronds.
CULTIVATION: Brakes can grow in sun or shade, depending on the species, in moist peaty soil. Propagate by division in spring or from spores sown in summer.

Pteris argyraea

SILVER BRAKE

↔ 20–40 in (50–100 cm)
↑ 3–6 ft (0.9–1.8 m)

Evergreen fern native to the tropics. Erect or short-creeping rhizome, covered with papery brown scales. Green fronds with a broad, silvery white center line and narrow, oblong leaflets, 6–12 in (15–30 cm) long. Zones 10–12.

Pteris biaurita

↔ 20–60 in (50–150 cm)
↑ 27–60 in (70–150 cm)

Evergreen fern from the tropics with upright stems that hold the triangular apple green fronds. Very similar to *P. argyraea* but the leaflets do not have white markings. Zones 10–11.

Pteris cretica

CRETAN BRAKE, RIBBON FERN

↔ 12–20 in (30–50 cm)
↑ 12–20 in (30–50 cm)

This evergreen or semi-evergreen fern is native to tropical regions of the Old World. It grows from slender, erect or short-creeping rhizomes. The fronds are oval or rounded, to 12 in (30 cm) long, with 1 to 5 pairs of simple or finger-like, forked, narrow, olive green leaflets, 4–8 in (10–20 cm) long, on slender, straw-colored stems. **'Albolineata'** ★ has wider leaflets with a broad white stripe; **'Mayi'** is up to 12 in (30 cm) high and has crested frond tips; and **'Wilsonii'** has crested bright green fronds that give the plant a fan-like appearance. Zones 10–12.

Pteris dentata

TOOTHED BRAKE

↔ 20–40 in (50–100 cm)
↑ 20–40 in (50–100 cm)

Native of tropical and subtropical Africa. Develops clusters of triangular to oval, bright green fronds, 20–40 in (50–100 cm) long, divided into many toothed lobes that fold inward along the midrib. Zones 10–12.

Pteris ensiformis

syn. *Pteris crenata*

SWORD BRAKE

↔ 8–12 in (20–30 cm)
↑ 8–12 in (20–30 cm)

This slender fern is found from the Himalayas to Japan, the Philippines, Polynesia, and tropical Australia. It has dark green fronds, 6–12 in (15–30 cm) long, with slightly compound terminal leaflets and 4 to 5 pairs of lateral leaflets cut into 2- to 6-toothed oval lobes, grayish white around the midribs. **'Arguta'**, to 20 in (50 cm) tall, has dark green fronds with central silvery white markings. Zones 10–12.

Pteris tremula

AUSTRALIAN BRACKEN OR BRAKE, SHAKING BRAKE, TENDER BRAKE

↔ 24–40 in (60–100 cm)
↑ 24–40 in (60–100 cm)

An evergreen fern, native to New Zealand, Australia, and Fiji. Forms dense clumps of bracken-like fronds from a stout, brown, scaly, tuft-forming, short-creeping rhizome. Oval, bright green to yellowish green fronds, 12–36 in (30–90 cm) long, with narrow, wavy-toothed leaflets. Zones 8–10.

Pteris tricolor

PAINTED BRAKE

↔ 3 ft (0.9 m) ↑ 5 ft (1.5 m)

Evergreen fern with broad, very glossy, triangular fronds divided into long, finger-like leaflets. Foliage emerges brilliant red, ages to copper or bronze, finally becoming dark green. Stems are a dark mahogany color. Zones 10–11.

Pterocarya fraxinifolia

Pterocarpus indicus

PTEROCARPUS

This genus, in the pea-flower subfamily of the legume (Fabaceae) family, contains some 20 species of tropical trees or climbers highly regarded for their ornamental timber. Widely grown as attractive shade and shelter trees in tropical and subtropical regions, they have wide graceful crowns and large pinnate leaves, and are usually deciduous in dry season. Racemes of scented yellow to orange pea-flowers are borne just before, or with, new leaves. Flat rounded pods follow, their edges often extended into parchment-like wings. CULTIVATION: These plants need a warm frost-free climate. Plant in a moist well-drained soil in full sun. Propagate from seeds or cuttings.

Pteris umbrosa
JUNGLE BRAKE
☀ ⌖ ↔ 27–40 in (70–100 cm)
↑ 27–40 in (70–100 cm)

Evergreen fern forms dense clumps in sheltered positions in its native Australia, from a stout, creeping, brown, scaly rhizome. Erect dark green fronds, 12–20 in (30–50 cm) long, with narrow, finely toothed leaflets, 6 to 9 lateral leaflets per side. Zones 10–11.

Pteris vittata
☀ ⌖ ↔ 12–20 in (30–50 cm)
↑ 12–20 in (30–50 cm)

An evergreen fern that inhabits moist rocky sites in tropical and temperate regions of Europe, Africa, Asia, and Australasia. It grows from a stout, short-creeping rhizome and is well-suited to being grown in containers. The fronds are mid- to dull green, thickly textured, elongated, oblong, 8–40 in (20–100 cm) long, and have narrow leaflets that can be either smooth or covered with brown scales. Zones 9–11.

Pterocarpus indicus
BURMESE ROSEWOOD
☀ ⌖ ↔ 35 ft (10 m) ↑ 80 ft (24 m)

Widespread in tropical Asia, ranging from India to the Philippines. Broadly spreading tree, pinnate leaves, leaflets to 4 in (10 cm) long. Showy sprays of yellow scented flowers, in spring. Wood is rose-scented. Zones 11–12.

PTEROCARYA

There are 10 deciduous trees in this genus, which belongs to the walnut (Juglandaceae) family, and these are found from the Caucasus to the temperate areas of East Asia and Southeast Asia. They are commonly known as wingnuts because of their fruits, which have a wing either side of a small hard shell that contains a single seed. The effect is something like the winged fruit of a sycamore, though the trees are more closely related to walnuts. The leaves are pinnate and can be quite large, sometimes with more than 20 leaflets up to 4 in (10 cm) long. The foliage seldom shows much autumn color. In spring, long bract-studded catkins of tiny green flowers open, developing into strings of winged nutlets that become brown as they ripen. CULTIVATION: Most species are tolerant of quite severe frosts and will thrive in any reasonably fertile, moist, well-drained soil with a position in full sun. Propagate from seed, suckers, or cuttings.

Pterocarya fraxinifolia
CAUCASIAN WINGNUT
☀ ❈ ↔ 60 ft (18 m) ↑ 80 ft (24 m)

Found from the Caucasus to northern Iraq. Dark deeply furrowed bark, leaves to 15 in (38 cm) long, with up to 11 to 21 leaflets. Catkins yellow-green shade. Zones 7–9.

Pterocarya × rehderiana
☀ ❈ ↔ 60 ft (18 m)
↑ 50–100 ft (15–30 m)

Raised in 1908 at New York's Arnold Arboretum. A hybrid between *P. fraxinifolia* and *P. stenoptera*, vigorous, quick-growing. Leaves 10 in (25 cm) long, with up to 21 leaflets. Long pendulous catkins, in spring. Zones 6–9.

Pterocarya rhoifolia
JAPANESE WINGNUT
☀ ❈ ↔ 60 ft (18 m)
↑ 70–100 ft (21–30 m)

Japanese tree. Leaves with up to 21 leaflets, 4 in (10 cm) long. Young stems and leaflets have fine downy hairs that wear off with time. Zones 6–9.

Pterocarya stenoptera
☀ ❈ ↔ 40 ft (12 m) ↑ 70 ft (21 m)

Chinese species notable for leaves to 15 in (38 cm) long with up to 23 leaflets; new foliage is downy. A fine tan down covers young twigs. Catkins often longer than the leaves. *P. s.* var. *brevifolia* has fewer leaflets, making a shorter leaf. Zones 7–9.

PTEROCELTIS

This single-species genus, belonging to the elm (Ulmaceae) family, is native to north and central China. Valued for its graceful arching habit, bright green foliage and winged green fruit, it is a slow-growing deciduous tree with hard and durable timber similar to teak and oak.

Pterocarya × rehderiana

Pterocarya stenoptera var. *brevifolia*

Pterocarya stenoptera

CULTIVATION: Fully frost hardy, it grows best in a fertile, moist but well-drained soil in a protected sunny position. Propagate from seed or cuttings or by grafting.

Pteroceltis tatarinowii

☼ ❄ ↔ 30 ft (9 m) ↑ 30 ft (9 m)

Broadly spreading crown, pale gray peeling bark. Bright green oval to lance-shaped leaves, finely serrated edges. Inconspicuous small, green, male and female flowers, in spring. Round winged fruits to 1 in (25 mm) wide. Zones 5–9.

PTEROCEPHALUS

These 25 or more compact annual or perennial herbs and small shrubs are members of the teasel (Dipsacaceae) family and native from the Mediterranean to eastern Asia. They are grown for their bristly flowers and feathery seed heads, and are suited to rock gardens. Flattened, disc-shaped flowerheads appear in summer, on long stalks, and are surrounded by narrow bracts; the outermost flowers have 2 lips and are larger than those in the center.

CULTIVATION: Plant in a sunny position in well-drained soil. Avoid areas that are wet in winter. Propagate from softwood or semi-ripe cuttings in summer, from fresh seed sown in autumn, or by division in spring. This plant self-seeds readily.

Pterocephalus dumetorum

syn. *Pterocephalus canus*

☼ ❄ ↔ 3–4 in (8–10 cm) ↑ 3–4 in (8–10 cm)

Native to dry rock crevices in Iran and Anatolia, Turkey. Leaves oblong to elliptical, smooth-edged, finely hairy. Flower-heads of yellow flowers are at least 1 in (25 mm) across, and appear in summer. Zones 4–6.

Pterocephalus perennis

syns *Pterocephalus bellidifolius, P. involucratus, P. parnassi*

☼ ❄ ↔ 4–8 in (10–20 cm) ↑ 2–4 in (5–10 cm)

Semi-evergreen, cushion-forming, tufted perennial growing in grassland and rocks in subalpine to alpine Greece and Albania. Simple, elliptical, finely hairy, grayish green, crinkled, oval to oblong leaves, to 1½ in (35 mm) long. Large tight heads of tubular purplish pink flowers appear in summer, followed by feathery seed heads. Zones 4–6.

Pterocephalus perennis

Pterospermum acerifolium

PTEROSPERMUM

This genus, in the cacao (Sterculiaceae) family, contains about 25 species of trees and shrubs native to tropical Asia. They are grown for shade and for their attractive leaves and perfumed flowers, which open at night. The 5-valved fruit is a large woody capsule, covered with brown hairs, which splits to release numerous winged seeds. The timber is similar to teak and oak.

CULTIVATION: Frost tender, they require a warm climate and prefer full sun and moist but friable soil. Propagation is from seed, by layering, or from half-hardened cuttings.

Pterospermum acerifolium

MAPLE-LEAF BAYUR

☼ ⚘ ↔ 30 ft (9 m) ↑ 120 ft (36 m)

Native to India and Indonesia. Semi-deciduous tree, smaller in cultivation. Bright green, almost rounded leaves, to 12 in (30 cm) long, downy whitish undersides. Dark brown felty flower buds split open at night revealing creamy trumpet-shaped flowers. Zones 10–12.

PTEROSTYLIS

GREENHOOD ORCHID

This is a large genus of temperate, deciduous terrestrial orchids (family Orchidaceae), known as "greenhoods," with the majority of the species occurring in Australia. There are also representatives from New Zealand, New Caledonia, and New Guinea. Most of the species have green blooms with reddish brown suffusions and transparent "light windows" to deceive pollinators that would normally avoid a restricted darker area. The dorsal sepals and petals overlap to form a hood. The

Pterostylis curta

labellum is sensitive, mobile, and capable of rapid movement, and an important attractant for potential pollinators. Most species have a rosette of leaves, with the single bloom produced on a slender stem, originating from the crown of the foliage.

CULTIVATION: The colony-forming species are relatively easy to cultivate, flower, and multiply. They require moist, humid, and cool conditions when in growth, from autumn to spring. *Pterostylis* are best grown in a well-drained terrestrial mix, containing a high proportion of peat moss and coarse sand. They go dormant in summer, at which time they should be kept dry, and revert to round, white tubers about ½ in (12 mm) in diameter. Repot annually, repositioning the dormant tubers 2 in (5 cm) below the soil surface.

Pterostylis curta

☽ ❄ ↔ 1½–3 in (3.5–8 cm) ↑ 1½–12 in (3.5–30 cm)

Australian species. Dark green and yellowish green, 1½ in (35 mm) wide flowers, with a light brown labellum that has a distinctive slight twist. It blooms in early spring. Zones 8–11.

PTEROSTYRAX

The 3 species of deciduous shrubs or trees in this genus, belonging to the storax (Styracaceae) family, are native to eastern Asia. Leaves alternately arranged, serrated edges; numerous long open panicles of small flowers.

CULTIVATION: These are quick-growing plants that should be given a deep, rich, acid soil in a sheltered position in sun or semi-shade. Plants can be pruned after flowering to retain their shape. Propagate from seed or half-hardened cuttings.

Pterostyrax corymbosa

☀ ❄ ↔ 20 ft (6 m) ↑ 40 ft (12 m)

Native of Japan. Spreading shrub or tree. Dark green leaves, bristly toothed margins. Small, fragrant, white, bell-shaped flowers, in panicles, in spring. Zones 6–10.

Pterostyrax hispida ★

EPAULETTE TREE

☀ ❄ ↔ 20 ft (6 m) ↑ 25 ft (8 m)

Native to Japan and China. Large leaves with finely serrated edges. Panicles of fragrant creamy white flowers to 8 in (20 cm) long, in summer. Small green and bristly fruit. Zones 6–10.

PTILOTUS

MULLA MULLA

This genus of about 100 annual or perennial herbs and shrubs from the amaranth (Amaranthaceae) family is native to arid inland areas of Australasia. They bear dense shaggy spikes of flowers with membranous bracts; the outer part is a tube of 5 segments. CULTIVATION: Prefer an open sunny position in well-drained, composted, relatively dry, sandy soil. Propagate from cuttings or from seed sown in spring; germination can be difficult.

Ptilotus exaltatus

PINK MULLA MULLA, TALL PUSSY-TAILS

☀ ❄ ↔ 40 in (100 cm) ↑ 40 in (100 cm)

Erect, sturdy, bushy annual or perennial, native to mainland Australia.

Pterostyrax hispida

Pterostyrax corymbosa

Thick, undulating, oblong to sword-shaped, bluish green leaves with pointed tips, tinged with red, to 3 in (8 cm) long. Feathery, conical to cylindrical spikes, to 6 in (15 cm) long, of lilac to pink flowers, sometimes white, from winter–summer. Suited to container growth. Zones 7–9.

Ptilotus manglesii

PINK MULLA MULLA

☀ ❄ ↔ 9–12 in (22–30 cm) ↑ 9–12 in (22–30 cm)

Sprawling or climbing, perennial or annual native to Western Australia. Rosettes of oval to narrow, rounded or pointed leaves; lower leaves to 3 in (8 cm) long. Trailing stems with fluffy, circular or oval spikes, to 4 in (10 cm) long, of pink to violet-purple flowers, in summer. Zones 7–9.

Ptilotus obovatus

☀ ❄ ↔ 12–24 in (30–60 cm) ↑ 12–24 in (30–60 cm)

Spreading, bushy, perennial or sub-shrub from arid areas of mainland Australia. Compact crown of hairy, rounded, silvery gray leaves, and erect, feathery spikes of pink and gray flowers in spring. Zones 7–9.

PTYCHOSPERMA

These 30 solitary or clump-forming, feathery palms belong to the family Arecaceae and are native to Australia, New Guinea, the Solomon Islands, and Micronesia. They have slender, smooth, ringed trunks and distinct crownshafts. Gracefully curved, divided fronds have slender pointed leaflets, jagged or smooth-edged at the tips. Flowers are spirally arranged in groups of 3. The fruit is small, egg-shaped or elliptical, and sometimes beaked, containing a single furrowed seed. The genus is named from the Greek *ptychos*, wrinkled, and *sperma*, seed.

Ptilotus exaltatus, in the wild, Great Victoria Desert, southern Australia

Ptilotus obovatus

CULTIVATION: These palms need warmth and humidity, in a shaded position when young, in moist, well-drained and composted soil. Propagate from seed, which takes 6 to 12 weeks to germinate.

Ptychosperma elegans ★

ALEXANDER PALM, SEAFORTHIA PALM, SOLITAIRE PALM

☀ ✦ ↔ 10–12 ft (3–3.5 m) ↑ 12–50 ft (3.5–15 m)

This fast-growing palm is found in northeastern Australia. It has a gray, solitary trunk, and a woolly green crownshaft. There are relatively few, arching, bright green leaves, to 8 ft (2.4 m) long, and these have regularly arranged leaflets to 24 in (60 cm) long, toothed or notched at tips. They are carried on long stems emerging from under the crownshaft. The large branching clusters of fragrant greenish white flowers are followed by large clusters of decorative, bright red, spherical to oval, berry-like fruit. Zones 10–11.

Ptychosperma macarthurii

Ptychosperma macarthurii ★

syns *Actinophlaeus macarthurii*, *Kentia macarthurii*

MACARTHUR PALM

☀ ✦ ↔ 6–12 ft (1.8–3.5 m) ↑ 15–25 ft (4.5–8 m)

Densely clumping evergreen palm, native to New Guinea and northeastern Australia, common in tropical gardens. Gray trunk; green woolly crownshaft. Small crown of dark green, arched fronds, to 6 ft (1.8 m) long, with regularly arranged, broad leaflets with toothed tips. Branching sprays of yellowish flowers, appear on stems emerging from below the crownshaft, growing into long pendulous clusters of bright red fruits. Zones 10–11.

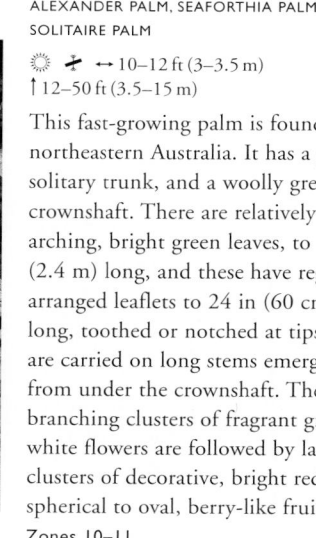

P

Pueraria lobata, Mississippi, USA

Pulmonaria mollis

PUERARIA

This genus, comprising about 20 herbaceous or woody, twining climbers, members of the pea-flower subfamily of the legume (Fabaceae) family, are native to Southeast Asia and Japan. The compound leaves have 3 leaflets, and long flowerheads with butterfly-like flowers grow from the leaf axils or cluster as racemes at the ends of branches. These are followed by narrow flattened pods. The roots of some species are used for medicinal extracts. The genus is named after nineteenth-century Swiss botanist Marc Nicolas Puerari.

CULTIVATION: *Pueraria* species prefer a position in full sun in moist well-drained soil. Propagate from seed or cuttings, or by division of roots. They can be invasive.

Pueraria lobata

syn. *Pueraria montana* var. *lobata*
JAPANESE ARROWROOT, KUDZU VINE,
THE VINE THAT ATE THE SOUTH

☀ ❄ ↔ 30–100 ft (9–30 m)
↕ 30–60 ft (9–18 m)

This fast-growing, semi-woody vine is native to China and Japan. It has fleshy tuberous roots, and very hairy stems. The alternate, finely hairy leaves have 2 to 3 oval to diamond-shaped leaflets. Erect racemes of flowers, 10 in (25 cm) long, grow from the leaf axils in autumn. They have many purple flowers, to ¾ in (18 mm) across, with a distinct yellow patch on the largest petal. Fruit is a several-seeded, brown, finely hairy, flat legume. Zones 5–11.

PULMONARIA

LUNGWORT

Starting into growth at the first sign of spring, this genus of 14 Eurasian perennials of the borage (Boraginaceae) family overcomes its rather unappealing name by being indispensable for woodland, perennial border, and rock-garden cultivation. Their simple, long-stemmed, lance-shaped leaves are sometimes white spotted and can grow to a considerable size. The first flowers, while welcome, are sparse but, as spring warms further, the plants carry larger heads of small 5-petalled blooms. Blue is the usual color, though white and pink forms are common. "Wort" is a word often attached to plants that are used for medicinal purposes.

CULTIVATION: Lungworts are very hardy and need a temperate climate with distinct seasons. They can be grown in full sun, but are best cultivated in moist, humus-rich, well-drained soil, in a partly shaded position. Propagate by division, or from basal cuttings or seed.

Pulmonaria angustifolia

Pulmonaria angustifolia

BLUE COWSLIP, BLUE LUNGWORT

◑/☀ ❄ ↔ 16–40 in (40–100 cm)
↕ 8–16 in (20–40 cm)

European species. Often in flower well before foliage is fully expanded. Forms a spreading mat of unspotted, pointed oval leaves to 12 in (30 cm) long. Heads of bright blue flowers in spring. *P. a.* subsp. *azurea* has intense

Pulmonaria angustifolia 'Beth's Pink'

Pulmonaria longifolia 'Bertram Anderson'

gentian blue flowers, no purple tones. *P. a.* 'Beth's Pink', has broad spotted leaves, mauve-pink flowers. Zones 3–9.

Pulmonaria longifolia

◑/☀ ❄ ↔ 48 in (120 cm) ↕ 16 in (40 cm)
European species. Forms clump of narrow, often white-spotted, dark green leaves to 20 in (50 cm) long. Heads of tightly clustered mauve to purple-blue flowers in late winter–late spring. *P. l.* subsp. *cevennensis* is smaller, with foliage blotched silver-white and violet-blue flowers. *P. l.* 'Bertram Anderson', especially narrow, heavily white-spotted leaves, purplish blue flowers. Zones 6–9.

Pulmonaria mollis

◑/☀ ❄ ↔ 40 in (100 cm) ↕ 16 in (40 cm)
European species. Leaves downy, usually unspotted, to 20 in (50 cm) long. Flowers violet to purple-blue; early spring–summer. Several pink- or white-flowered cultivars. Zones 6–9.

P. longifolia subsp. *cevennensis*

Pulmonaria rubra 'Bowles' Red'

Pulmonaria rubra 'David Ward'

Pulmonaria officinalis 'Blue Mist'

Pulmonaria officinalis

JERUSALEM SAGE

☀/☀ ❄ ↔ 16–24 in (40–60 cm)
↑ 12 in (30 cm)

European perennial, usually flowering well into spring when foliage is well expanded. Leaves pointed elliptical, white-spotted, to around 6 in (15 cm) long; mauve through blue to purple-red flowers in tightly clustered heads. '**Blue Mist**' and '**White Wings**', popular cultivars. Zones 6–9.

Pulmonaria rubra

☀/☀ ❄ ↔ 20–40 in (50–100 cm)
↑ 12–18 in (30–45 cm)

Native to Europe. Leaves often spotted white or silver-gray. Small heads of light red flowers, sometimes mauve tinted, on flower stems that tend to be erect, in spring–early summer. '**Bowles' Red**', white-spotted leaves, red-pink flowers; and '**David Ward**', creamy white-edged leaves, red-pink flowers. Zones 6–9.

Pulmonaria saccharata

JERUSALEM SAGE

☀/☀ ❄ ↔ 16–32 in (40–80 cm)
↑ 12–16 in (30–40 cm)

A native of northern Italy, this plant flowers after the foliage is well developed. Spring leaves are small, lance-shaped, spotted, while the summer leaves are larger. The flowers are white, or shades of mauve to purple or purple-red. '**Argentea**', silver-mottled leaves, mauve-blue flowers (it has given rise to other cultivars, which are together known as the **Argentea Group**); '**Dora Bielefeld**', white- or lighter green-spotted leaves, mauve-pink flowers; '**Janet Fisk**', silver-spotted and marbled leaves, purple flowers opening from red buds; '**Leopard**', white-spotted leaves, purplish pink flowers; '**Mrs Moon**', white-spotted leaves, red-tinted mauve flowers; and '**Sissinghurst White**', large white-spotted leaves, and white flowers, produced early in the season. Zones 3–9.

Pulmonaria officinalis 'White Wings'

Pulmonaria vallarsae cultivar

Pulmonaria vallarsae

☀/☀ ❄ ↔ 20–40 in (50–100 cm)
↑ 12–18 in (30–45 cm)

Northern Italian species. Forms clump of finely hairy, often white-spotted or variegated leaves. First flowers appear with new growth, red-tinted buds opening to purple flowers, in early spring–early summer. Zones 6–9.

Pulmonaria Hybrid Cultivars

☀/☀ ❄ ↔ 16–40 in (40–100 cm)
↑ 8–16 in (20–40 cm)

Lungworts hybridize freely, in the wild and in cultivation, and there are many widely grown hybrids, often of indeterminate parentage. Modern forms tend to have showy variegated foliage and short flower stems. '**Benediction**', silver-flecked leaves,

Pulmonaria, Hybrid Cultivar, 'Benediction'

mauve-blue flowers; '**Blue Pearl**', small rounded leaves, light blue flowers; '**High Contrast**', silver-gray leaves with irregular green edges, flowers deep pink ageing to purple-blue; '**Lewis Palmer**', white-spotted leaves, purple-blue flowers; '**Margery Fish**' ★, silver-mottled foliage, pink

Pulmonaria saccharata

Pulmonaria saccharata 'Dora Bielefeld'

Pulmonaria saccharata 'Janet Fisk'

Pulmonaria saccharata 'Leopard'

Pulmonaria saccharata 'Mrs Moon'

Pulmonaria, Hybrid Cultivar, 'High Contrast'

Pulmonaria, Hybrid Cultivar, 'Lewis Palmer'

Pulmonaria, Hybrid Cultivar, 'Margery Fish'

Pulmonaria, Hybrid Cultivar, 'Mary Mottram'

Pulmonaria, Hybrid Cultivar, 'Reginald Kaye'

Pulmonaria, Hybrid Cultivar, 'Silver Mist'

Pulmonaria, HC, 'Roy Davidson'

Pulmonaria, HC, 'Silver Streamers'

Pulmonaria, HC, 'Smoky Blue'

Pulmonaria, HC, 'Trevi Fountain'

flowers ageing to blue; **'Purple Haze'**, white-spotted leaves, purple flowers; **'Roy Davidson'**, long silver-spotted leaves, light blue flowers; **'Silver Streamers'**, large silver-gray leaves with ruffled edges, pink flowers darkening with age; **'Smoky Blue'**, dark green white-spotted leaves, purplish blue flowers; **'Trevi Fountain'**, silver-spotted leaves, open sprays of deep blue flowers. Zones 6–9.

PULSATILLA
PASQUE FLOWER
These beautiful Eurasian and North American relatives of the anemones, in the buttercup (Ranunculaceae) family, race into growth in early spring. Clumps of ferny leaves, silvery in most species from a dense covering of fine hairs. Long-stemmed, very graceful, cup- or bell-shaped flowers in a wide color range. Carried singly, they have 5 to 8 petals and a prominent boss of golden stamens. *Pasque* is an old French word for Easter, when the plants usually flower. The significance of the proper name, taken from Latin *pulso,* "to strike," is obscure, possibly referring to the drooping buds turning upward as they open.
CULTIVATION: Pasque flowers need a seasonal temperate climate. They grow well in woodland conditions but are at their best in rock gardens with sun or part-shade, in gritty, humus-rich, well-drained yet moist soil. Propagate by division when dormant, or raise from seed.

Pulsatilla albana
☼/◐ ❋ ↔ 8 in (20 cm) ↑ 8 in (20 cm)
From alpine meadows of the Caucasus and northeastern Turkey. Green, fine-cut pinnate foliage. Hairy stems and buds opening to distinctive, nodding, bell-shaped, yellow flowers. Zones 5–9.

Pulsatilla alpina ★
ALPINE PASQUE FLOWER
☼/◐ ❋ ↔ 16 in (40 cm) ↑ 18 in (45 cm)
From the mountains of central Europe to western Russia. Small, ferny, often bronze-tinted, dark green

Pulsatilla caucasica

leaves and wide-open, bright yellow flowers to more than 2 in (5 cm) in diameter. Zones 5–9.

Pulsatilla caucasica
☼/◐ ❋ ↔ 16 in (40 cm) ↑ 12 in (30 cm)
From the Caucasus and northeastern Turkey. Fine feathery foliage and bright yellow flowers to 2 in (5 cm) wide. Plant hair-covered but not noticeably silvery. Zones 5–9.

Pulsatilla halleri
☼/◐ ❋ ↔ 12 in (30 cm) ↑ 10 in (25 cm)
From mountains of central and southeastern Europe. Densely covered with silky silvery hairs. Flowers often well advanced before finely divided feathery foliage appears. Flowers erect, usually upward-facing, violet to lavender blue. Zones 5–9.

Pulsatilla koreana

Pulsatilla koreana
☼/◐ ❋ ↔ 16 in (40 cm) ↑ 12 in (30 cm)
Subalpine species from Japan, Korea, nearby parts of China, and Siberia. Densely hairy overall, with very finely divided leaves. Deep purple flowers are produced late in the season. Zones 4–9.

Pulsatilla montana
☼/◐ ❋ ↔ 8–15 in (20–38 cm) ↑ 8–18 in (20–45 cm)
Found from Switzerland to Bulgaria. Downy, very finely divided leaves. Flowers, to 1½ in (40 mm) wide,

Pulsatilla montana

Pulsatilla patens

Pulsatilla pratensis subsp. *bohemica*

Pulsatilla vulgaris

bell-shaped, pendent, violet to purple-blue, on short stems that elongate as the seed heads mature. Zones 6–9.

Pulsatilla patens
EASTERN PASQUE FLOWER
☼/◑ ❈ ↔8–12 in (20–30 cm)
↕6–10 in (15–25 cm)

From northern Europe to Siberia and Alaska, USA. Leaves lightly hairy, heavy textured, less finely divided than most silvery species. Flowers quite late, purple shades, sometimes with yellow tint, rarely white, stems silky. Zones 4–9.

Pulsatilla pratensis
☼/◑ ❈ ↔16 in (40 cm)   ↕12 in (30 cm)
Found through most of Europe. Entirely covered with dense, silky, silvery hairs. Foliage very finely divided. Pendent, narrow bell-shaped flowers, to 1½ in (40 mm) wide, mauve to

Pultenaea cunninghamii

deep purple. *P. p.* subsp. *bohemica* has small, very dark purple flowers. Zones 5–9.

Pulsatilla vulgaris
PASQUE FLOWER
☼/◑ ❈ ↔8–16 in (20–40 cm)
↕8–15 in (20–38 cm)

From Britain through Europe to Ukraine. Entirely covered in fine, silky, silvery hairs. Foliage very finely divided, feathery. Many flower stems with usually upward-facing, open bell-shaped, 2–3 in (5–8 cm) wide, mauve to purple flowers. 'Alba', white flowers; 'Rubra', red flowers. 'Papageno' (syn. *P. v.* subsp. *grandis* 'Papageno') is a mixed color strain in many shades, including apricot and purple-black. Zones 5–9.

PULTENAEA
All 100 species of this genus in the pea-flower subfamily of the legume (Fabaceae) family are endemic to Australia, found in all eastern states, with a few species in South Australia and Western Australia. Habits vary from small prostrate shrubs to tall erect shrubs, with a diversity of leaf shapes, and occurring in a diversity of habitats. The pea-flowers are yellow, or yellow with some reddish blotches. The fruits are rounded pods containing several seeds.

Pulsatilla vulgaris 'Alba'

CULTIVATION: Propagation is from pre-treating seed, such as soaking in hot water or by scarification. Cultivated species require excellent drainage in acid to neutral soil, part-shade or full sun; they seem to benefit from the application of mulch.

Pultenaea cunninghamii
☼ ❈ ↔4 ft (1.2 m)   ↕3 ft (0.9 m)
Small shrub with drooping foliage occurring in the eastern mainland states of Australia. Leaves gray-green, almost circular, in whorls of 3, main vein ending in a sharp spine. Flowers yellow-orange with reddish blotches, in late spring–summer. Zones 8–9.

Pulsatilla vulgaris 'Papageno'

Pulsatilla vulgaris 'Rubra'

Pultenaea elliptica
☼/◑ ❈ ↔4 ft (1.2 m)   ↕5 ft (1.5 m)
Evergreen shrub native to New South Wales, Australia, especially common around Sydney. Erect stems with tiny elliptical deep green to blue-green leaves, sometimes adpressed to the stems, often covered with fine silvery hairs. In summer, terminal heads of small golden pea-flowers, often suffused with orange-red. Zones 9–11.

Pultenaea pedunculata
MATTED PEA BUSH
☼ ❧ ↔4 ft (1.2 m)   ↕4 in (10 cm)
Found in southeastern Australia, including Tasmania. Trailing ground cover, densely matted stems, whorls of small elliptical leaves. Yellow to orange pea-flowers, in spring. Cultivars include the bright yellow-flowered 'Pyalong Gold' and the deep pink and cream-flowered 'Pyalong Pink'. Zones 9–10.

Pultenaea elliptica, in the wild, Brisbane Water National Park, New South Wales, Australia

Pultenaea pedunculata

Pultenaea scabra

☼ ❄ ↔4 ft (1.2 m) ↑7 ft (2 m)

From southeastern Australia, from northern New South Wales to Victoria and South Australia. Shrub with densely hairy branches. Leaves generally wedge-shaped, dark green, paler below. Clusters of 3 to 4 yellow and red flowers, in spring. Zones 8–9.

Pultenaea stipularis

☼ ᠅ ↔3 ft (0.9 m) ↑3 ft (0.9 m)

From the sandstone heaths of Sydney, Australia. Long, narrow, pine-like leaves. Dense terminal heads of yellow flowers, in spring. When destroyed by fire, regenerates from seed stored in soil from previous years. Zones 9–11.

Pultenaea villosa

☼ ᠅ ↔7 ft (2 m) ↑4 ft (1.2 m)

Found from southern New South Wales to southern Queensland, Australia. Spreading shrub, pendulous branches. Leaves about ¼ in (6 mm) long, hairy, narrow, oblong. Yellow flowers, in spring. Prostrate form also occurs. Zones 9–10.

PUNICA

This genus in the pomegranate (Punicaceae) family contains only 2 species, both small, deciduous, fruiting trees native to the Mediterranean region, North Africa, Iran, and Afghanistan.

Puschkinia scilloides

They have simple lance-shaped leaves, scarlet flowers, and reddish yellow apple-shaped fruits. They are quite hardy, tolerating quite low temperatures as well as sustained high temperatures with low humidity, but need hot dry summers for fruit to ripen.
CULTIVATION: They respond to a well-aerated coarsely textured soil, preferably enriched with organic matter. Light pruning of the current year's growth in late winter helps retain a dense leafy habit. Propagate from seed sown in spring, or from soft-tip or half-hardened cuttings between spring and autumn.

Punica granatum

COMMON POMEGRANATE

☼ ᠅ ↔15 ft (4.5 m) ↑25 ft (8 m)

Small tree, broad domed crown, lateral shoots thorny. Leaves opposite, broadly lance-shaped, reddish in spring, then bright green, turning yellow in autumn. Flowers with 5 to 8 bright scarlet petals, many stamens, from late spring–late summer. The orange-red fruit has jelly-like crimson pulp. '**Nana**', dwarf form, 3 ft (0.9 m) or less in height; '**Nana Plena**', double-flowered non-fruiting form of 'Nana'; '**Nochi Shibari**', popular North American cultivar; '**Wonderful**', double-flowered form with fruit said to taste of wine. Zones 9–11.

PURSHIA

This genus, in the rose (Rosaceae) family, consists of 2 species of shrubs or small trees native to western North America. They have gray-green leaves with 3 to 5 lobes and slightly toothed or rolled-under edges. Small, white to light yellow, 5-petalled, tubular flowers are produced at the ends of the previous season's growth. They come from regions that are warm but dry, or with a pronounced dry season.

Pultenaea scabra

CULTIVATION: They are moderately frost hardy, but resent winter-wet soil. Grow in a warm, sheltered position with excellent drainage. Propagate from seed or by layering.

Purshia tridentata

ANTELOPE BUSH

☼ ᠅ ↔6 ft (1.8 m) ↑10 ft (3 m)

From southern USA. Erect shrub, wide-spreading branchlets. Glossy, green, wedge-shaped leaves to 1 in (25 mm) long, white, bristly underside. Creamy yellow flowers, about ½ in (12 mm) across, in spring–summer. Zones 9–11.

PUSCHKINIA

From Turkey, this single-species genus in the hyacinth (Hyacinthaceae) family is related to *Scilla*. Strap-shaped leaves from tubular base. Flowers striped, pale, in clusters on slender stems.
CULTIVATION: Plant the bulbs under deciduous shrubs in part-shade in soil that gives good drainage. Plant them in autumn, 3 in (8 cm) deep and the same distance apart. They shouldn't be disturbed for several years. When flowering lessens, dig the bulbs up after the foliage has ripened. Small bulbs require a cool spot where they will not become too hot and dry in summer. Bulbs can be detached for propagation.

Pultenaea stipularis

Pultenaea villosa, **prostrate form**

Puschkinia scilloides ★

STRIPED SQUILL

☼/◑ ❄ ↔3 in (8 cm)
↑2–4 in (5–10 cm)

Two green leaves at base, from which a stalk emerges in early spring bearing fragrant, white to pale blue, bell-shaped flowers with a darker blue stripe in the center of each of 6 petals. *P. s.* **var.** *libanotica*, slightly smaller flowers. Zones 4–6.

PUYA

More than 200 species, mainly from the Andes of South America, make up this ground-dwelling genus in the bromeliad (Bromeliaceae) family, most of them preferring colder conditions than other bromeliads. Many species are large plants forming trunks, and are not often seen in private gardens; they are popular in botanic gardens in subtropical areas. One species reaches a height of 35 ft (10 m) in flower, but the smallest species reaches only 3 in (8 cm). They form rosettes of green, narrow-triangular leaves, generally with large spines along the edges. The flowerheads may be cylindrical or pyramidal and branched, and the flowers are generally large and showy.
CULTIVATION: Recommended for greenhouse, conservatory or outdoor cultivation in cool temperate areas; some species will adapt to warmer areas if kept on the dry side. Water when potting mix is dry. Extra feeding may speed up their slow-growing habit. Propagation is generally by seed. Most produce offsets but these are generally very difficult to root.

Puschkinia scilloides **var.** *libanotica*

Punica granatum (bonsai)

Puya berteroniana

☀ ❄ ↔ 7 ft (2 m) ↑ 15 ft (4.5 m)

From central Chile. Forming a trunk with age. Leaves green, narrow-triangular, strongly toothed edges, forming a dense rosette. Flower stem stout, to 10 ft (3 m). Flowerhead to 40 in (100 cm) long and 20 in (50 cm) wide, up to 100 side branches, each carrying about 15 large blue-green flowers. Upper part of branches without flowers. Zones 7–9.

Puya chilensis

☀ ❄ ↔ 7 ft (2 m) ↑ 15 ft (4.5 m)

From central Chile. Forming trunk with age. Leaves green, narrow-triangular, strongly toothed edges, forming a dense rosette. Flower stem to 12 ft (3.5 m) high, erect, stout. Flowerhead over 40 in (100 cm) long, up to 100 side branches each with up to 12 large yellow flowers. Upper part of branches without flowers. Zones 7–9.

Puya venusta

☀ ❄ ↔ 20 in (50 cm) ↑ 40 in (100 cm)

From coastal Chile. Clump-forming, branching plant. Leaves gray-green, narrow-triangular, toothed-edged, forming dense rosette. Flower stem stout, bright red. Flowerheads reddish, like pine cones, end of some branches, flowers deep violet. Zones 8–9.

PYCNANTHEMUM

syn. *Koellia*

AMERICAN MOUNTAIN MINT

This genus of 21 smooth or hairy, perennial herbs in of the mint (Lamiaceae) family, is native to eastern North America, and has erect, simple or branched stems and opposite, smooth-edged, mint-scented leaves on short stalks. Simple or branching flowerheads of compact clusters, on stalks, usually with a pair of leaf-like bracts and a corolla tube expanding

to form 2 lips, appear from summer to autumn, followed by smooth or finely hairy fruit. Genus is named from the Greek *pyknos*, dense, and *anthos*, flower, referring to the densely crowded flowers. It is sometimes used for flavoring teas.
CULTIVATION: Mountain mints prefer open, sunny positions and are adaptable to most soil conditions. Propagation is from seed or cuttings.

Pycnanthemum virginianum

syn. *Pycnanthemum lanceolatum*

WILD HYSSOP

☀ ❄ ↔ 40 in (100 cm) ↑ 40 in (100 cm)

Upright, stiff, many-branched herb with short, leafy branches; narrow to sword-shaped, serrated, tapering leaves to 2½ in (6 cm) long. Flat-topped heads of fragrant, pink and white flowers, in mid- to late summer. All plant parts emit a strong, mint-like aroma when crushed. Zones 3–7.

PYCNOSTACHYS

Native to tropical and southern Africa, these 40 or so species of perennials and soft-wooded shrubs are grown for their dense terminal spikes of 2-lipped deep blue flowers. Members of the mint (Lamiaceae) family, they have squarish stems and opposite or whorled leaves that are often aromatic when bruised.
CULTIVATION: These plants need a warm, frost-free climate and are best suited to fertile, moist but well-drained soil in full sun. In cool areas they are grown in the greenhouse or conservatory, with a plentiful supply of water during the growing season. Propagate from seed or cuttings.

Pycnostachys reticulata

☀ ❄ ↔ 18 in (45 cm) ↑ 40 in (100 cm)

Perennial from South Africa and Madagascar with profuse clusters of

Pyracantha coccinea

Pyracantha angustifolia

Pycnostachys urticifolia

Pycnostachys reticulata

white and purple flowers like a witch's hat, in late summer and autumn, carried on long stems. Zones 9–12.

Pycnostachys urticifolia

☀ ⚘ ↔ 4 ft (1.2 m) ↑ 8 ft (2.4 m)

Soft-wooded shrub with erect branching stems. Oval leaves, 5 in (12 cm) long, toothed edges. Tubular deep blue to purple flowers in dense terminal spikes, to 4 in (10 cm) long, summer–autumn. Zones 9–12.

PYRACANTHA

FIRETHORN

This small genus in the rose (Rosaceae) family consists of 9 species of mostly spiny shrubs, from eastern Asia and southeast Europe. They have simple leaves that are often toothed on the margins, and whitish flowers in corymbs are produced at the ends of branches. The flowers are followed by masses of red, orange, or yellow fruit, which persist into winter. Most species perform best in cool, moist climates, where they are useful landscape subjects for the shrubbery or used as espalier specimens or for hedging. *Pyracantha* species can naturalize in favorable areas.
CULTIVATION: Most are fairly adaptable shrubs tolerating exposed sites in full sun. They perform best in a fertile well-drained soil. Pruning is not essential but may be helpful to control size; hedges can be pruned from early

to mid-summer. Watch for fireblight, scab and wilt problems. Propagate from seed or cuttings.

Pyracantha angustifolia

NARROW-LEAFED FIRETHORN,
ORANGE FIRETHORN

☀ ❄ ↔ 12 ft (3.5 m) ↑ 12 ft (3.5 m)

Native to southwest China. Spiny bushy shrub, horizontal branches, dark green shiny leaves, gray and furry beneath. Dense corymbs of small white flowers, in mid-summer. Yellow to deep orange berries. Zones 7–10.

Pyracantha coccinea

EUROPEAN FIRETHORN, SCARLET FIRETHORN

☀ ❄ ↔ 15 ft (4.5 m) ↑ 15 ft (4.5 m)

From southern Europe, Turkey, and the Caucasus. Dense shrub. Shiny, dark green, ovate to lance-shaped, toothed leaves, new growth finely downy. Small white flowers. Attractive scarlet berries on downy stalks. 'Lalandei' ★, strong growth habit,

Puya berteroniana

Puya venusta

Pyracantha, Hybrid Cultivar, 'Watereri'

Pyracantha, Hybrid Cultivar, 'Mohave'

Pyracantha crenulata

reaching up to 20 ft (6 m) tall, with glossy bright orange-red fruits. Zones 5–9.

Pyracantha crenulata
HIMALAYAN FIRETHORN

☼ ❄ ↔ 12 ft (3.5 m) ↑ 15 ft (4.5 m)

From the southern slopes of the Himalayas. Spiny shrub or small tree. Rusty, downy, new shoots. Glossy dark green leaves, finely notched margins. Corymbs of up to 30 small white flowers. Dark red berries. Zones 7–10.

Pyracantha koidzumii
TAIWAN FIRETHORN

☼ ❄ ↔ 12 ft (3.5 m) ↑ 12–15 ft (3.5–4.5 m)

Native to Taiwan. Many-branched species with reddish, downy, young stems becoming smooth and purplish with age. Leaves dark green, glossy above, paler below. Small white

Pyracantha, Hybrid Cultivar, 'Shawnee'

flowers in corymbs, in summer. Fruit is a berry, in variable colors, sometimes orange-scarlet. Zones 7–10.

Pyracantha rogersiana
ROGERS FIRETHORN

☼ ❄ ↔ 12 ft (3.5 m) ↑ 12 ft (3.5 m)

From China. Shrub develops a broad bun shape with age. Mid-green glossy leaves to 1½ in (35 mm) long. Small white flowers in corymbs, mostly from 2-year-old branches, in spring. Yellow to orange-red berries. 'Flava' has yellow berries. Zones 8–10.

Pyracantha Hybrid Cultivars

☼ ❄ ↔ 6–10 ft (1.8–3 m) ↑ 5–10 ft (1.5–3 m)

Spreading shrubs which make good hedges and suit shrub borders. '**Golden Charmer**', vigorous arching shrub with long branches, finely toothed glossy green leaves, rounded orange-yellow fruits; '**Golden Dome**', mound of arching branches, white summer flowers, small deep yellow fruits; '**Harlequin**', variegated form, attractive pink-flushed leaves, cream margins; '**Mohave**', dense medium-sized shrub, dark green leaves, masses of persistent bright orange-red fruits; '**Orange Charmer**' can be trimmed as a free-standing shrub from 3–8 ft (0.9–2.4 m) tall, long-lasting orange-red berries; '**Orange Glow**', dense,

Pyracantha rogersiana

vigorous shrub, bright orange-red fruits persist into winter; '**Shawnee**', spiny shrub, dense-branched, widely spreading at base, masses of white flowers, yellow to light orange fruits; '**Sparkler**', variegated form, slightly tender, leaves strikingly mottled, white, becoming pink-tinged in autumn; '**Watereri**', compact yet vigorous shrub, covered in summer with white flowers, bright red fruits. Zones 5–9.

PYROSTEGIA

These 4 evergreen, woody-stemmed, tendril climbers belong to the trumpet-vine (Bignoniaceae) family. Native to the tropical Americas, they are grown for their showy flowers. They have angled branches and compound leaves with 2, sometimes 3, oval leaflets, with or without a terminal tendril, and clusters, at the ends of branches, of flowers with curved, tubular corollas with protruding stamens. The genus is named from the Greek *pyr*, fire, and *stege*, a roof, referring to the flower shape and crimson-orange color.

CULTIVATION: They grow best in full sun in fertile, well-drained soil. Require support. Propagate from half-hardened cuttings taken in summer.

Pyrostegia venusta
syn. *Pyrostegia ignea*

FLAME VINE, GOLDEN SHOWER, ORANGE TRUMPET CREEPER, TANGO POI

☼ ✦ ↔ 20 ft (6 m) ↑ 20–30 ft (6–9 m)

Fast-growing, vigorously branching climber, native to Brazil, Paraguay, Bolivia, and northeastern Argentina.

Pyrostegia venusta

Smooth, papery or leathery leaflets, to 4 in (10 cm) long, blunt tips. Terminal clusters of orange flowers appear in autumn–spring. Zones 8–10.

PYRROSIA
FELT FERN

This genus of about 100 epiphytic, rock-dwelling or terrestrial ferns from the polypody (Polypodiaceae) family has creeping, branched rhizomes, and is found in tropical regions of Asia, Africa, and Australia. Their usually simple and smooth-edged fronds are fleshy, leathery, finely hairy and scaly but becoming smooth, felty underneath. Fronds grow with or without stems, and sometimes the fertile fronds are longer than the sterile fronds.

CULTIVATION: Felt ferns prefer a rich, peaty soil in a moist, protected, shady environment. Propagate by division or from spores.

Pyrrosia confluens
ROBBER FERN

☼ ❄ ↔ 10–14 in (25–35 cm) ↑ 10–14 in (25–35 cm)

From tropical Australia, with a long-creeping, much-branching rhizome. Sterile fronds are narrowly oval. Fertile fronds are narrowly elliptical, 2–7 in (5–18 cm) long, with a prominent midvein. Fronds grow on stems to 2 in (5 cm) long. Zones 8–10.

Pyrrosia lingua
JAPANESE FELT FERN, TONGUE FERN

☼ ✦ ↔ 6 in (15 cm) ↑ 3–6 in (8–15 cm)

Native to China, Taiwan, and Japan. Grows from long-creeping rhizome. Sword-shaped to oval fronds, to 12 in (30 cm) long, have narrow, pointed tips and are wedge-shaped at base, carried on stems to 2 in (5 cm) long. '**Shisha**' (syn. 'Cristata'), fronds with forked tips, giving a crested appearance. Zones 10–12.

Pyrrosia confluens

Pyrus calleryana 'Bradford'

Pyrrosia serpens

Pyrrosia serpens

☼ ✈ ↔ 8–12 in (20–30 cm)
↕ 8–12 in (20–30 cm)

From Australasia, growing from a long-creeping rhizome. Oval sterile fronds, to 6 in (15 cm) long, and narrowly oblong fertile fronds, to 10 in (25 cm) long, are carried on stems to 2 in (5 cm) long. Zones 10–12.

PYRUS
PEAR

Widely distributed through Europe and Asia, this genus of about 20 species is related to the apple *(Malus)* and is part of the rose (Rosaceae) family. It comprises deciduous trees of small to medium size, some thorny, with simple leaves that sometimes color to yellow and red in autumn. The flowers are mostly white, and are followed by fruits, edible in some species, that vary in size and shape. The ornamental species are deep-rooted, tolerant of drought and reasonably tolerant of atmospheric pollution. Fruiting forms require a cross-pollinator to set fruit.
CULTIVATION: Pears will grow in most moderately fertile soils and are at their best in cool-temperate climates. Pruning of the ornamental species is seldom necessary, apart from forming a well-shaped tree in the early stages. They can be propagated from seed sown very fresh, but clonal forms are propagated by grafting to keep them true to type.

Pyrus calleryana 'Bradford'

Pyrus amygdaliformis
ALMOND-LEAFED PEAR

☼ ❋ ↔ 12 ft (3.5 m) ↕ 20 ft (6 m)

From coastal areas north and east of the Mediterranean. Large shrub or small tree, occasionally with spiny branches. Leaves narrow, shallowly toothed or smooth-edged, silvery at first, ageing to sage green. Fruits small, rounded, yellow-brown. *P. a.* var. *cuneifolia* has narrower wedge-shaped leaves. Zones 5–9.

Pyrus betulifolia
BIRCH-LEAF

☼ ❋ ↔ 15 ft (4.5 m) ↕ 30 ft (9 m)

Small slender tree from northern China. Ovate or rounded leaves, slender tip, strongly toothed; grayish green when young, becoming green and glossy on the uppersurface. Small dark brown fruit. Zones 5–9.

Pyrus × bretschneideri

☼ ❋ ↔ 25 ft (8 m) ↕ 50 ft (50 m)

From northern China. Deciduous tree, broad, pyramidal shape. Narrow-oval, shiny, dark green leaves, to 4 in (10 cm) wide, serrated edges. Profuse, scented, white flowers, in spring. Clusters of small, yellowish brown fruits with white flesh. Zones 3–9.

Pyrus calleryana
CALLERY PEAR

☼ ❋ ↔ 40 ft (12 m) ↕ 40 ft (12 m)

From southeastern China, Korea, Japan, and Taiwan. Ornamental tree, branches thorny. Glossy green leaves turn red, in late autumn. Flowers, white, unpleasant scent. Small pitted brown fruit on slender stalks. '**Bradford**', non-thorny selected form, dark red autumn color, flowers heavily in spring; '**Chanticleer**'/**Glen's Form** ★, rich scarlet autumn color, similar but much narrower in form. Zones 5–9.

Pyrus amygdaliformis var. *cuneifolia*

Pyrus betulifolia

Pyrus calleryana

Pyrus communis 'Beurré d'Anjou'

Pyrus communis 'Beurré Hardy'

Pyrus communis 'Thorn'

Pyrus communis 'Conference'

Pyrus communis

Pyrus communis 'Cascade'

Pyrus communis 'Williams' Bon Chrétien'

Pyrus communis 'Doyenné du Comice'

Pyrus communis
CALLERY PEAR, COMMON PEAR,
GARDEN PEAR

☀ ❄ ↔ 20 ft (6 m) ↕ 50 ft (15 m)
Medium-sized tree with rounded or
oval, glossy, green leaves. Thorny
branches covered in white blossoms,
in spring. Large, edible, sweet-tasting
fruit. Has been in cultivation for centuries. Over 1,000 named cultivars
have been raised. '**Beurré d'Anjou**',
very old French cultivar, a late bearer,
smooth green fruit, slight red cheek
or all red, flesh is sweet and juicy;
'**Cascade**', heavy bearer, almost
globular fruit, bright red, some yellow
showing through, white flesh is sweet
and juicy; '**Clapp's Favourite Liebling**',
small fruit, very juicy delicious flavor;
'**Conference**', large pear, with a
long neck, brown skin, yellow-green
showing through, sweet juicy flesh
faintly pink-tinged; '**Doyenné du
Comice**' ★ (syn. 'Comice'), old
French pear, with many variants,
fruit smooth-skinned, ripening to
pale green, sweet creamy flesh, very
juicy and aromatic; '**Gellerts Butter-
bine**', greenish yellow fruit, bronze-
orange cheek; '**Red Bartlett**', bright
red fruit; '**Williams' Bon Chrétien**'
(syn. 'Bartlett'), bright green with a
slight red cheek, ripening yellowish,
very juicy and deliciously flavored.
Zones 2–9.

Pyrus kawakamii
EVERGREEN PEAR

☀ ❄ ↔ 30 ft (9 m) ↕ 30 ft (9 m)
From Japan. Evergreen shrub or small
tree, thorny branches. Attractive,
glossy, green, oval leaves around 4 in
(10 cm) long. White flowers in small
clusters, in late winter. Tiny, rounded
fruit. Zones 8–10.

Pyrus salicifolia

Pyrus pyrifolia 'Hosui'

Pyrus pyrifolia 'Shinko'

Pyrus nivalis

SNOW PEAR

☼ ❄ ↔ 20 ft (6 m) ↑ 30 ft (9 m)

Native to southern Europe. Small tree, thornless ascending branches. White flowers in racemes as the young leaves open in spring. Smooth-edged oval or egg-shaped leaves. Small rounded fruits yellowish green. Suitable tree for small gardens. Zones 5–9.

Pyrus pashia

HIMALAYAN PEAR

☼ ❄ ↔ 25 ft (8 m) ↑ 40 ft (12 m)

From the Himalayas and western China. Small round-headed tree. Finely toothed leaves, sometimes 3-lobed. Flowers pink-flushed in the bud, opening white with red anthers. Fruits rounded, brown with paler speckles. Zones 5–9.

Pyrus pyraster

WILD PEAR

☼ ❄ ↔ 25 ft (9 m) ↑ 30 ft (9 m)

Native to central and southwestern Europe. Spreading tree, with thorny branches and twigs. Thin oval leaves to 2 in (5 cm) long. Small, scented, white flowers, in spring. Clusters of small, slightly pear-shaped fruit, brown-speckled when ripe. Zones 4–9.

Pyrus pyrifolia

CHINA PEAR, SAND PEAR

☼ ❄ ↔ 30 ft (9 m) ↑ 50 ft (15 m)

Native to China and Japan. Leaves oblong, serrated, in shades of orange and bronze, in autumn. Small white flowers appear just before or with emerging leaves. Small, hard, brown fruit. '**Chojuro**', squat, russet brown, densely dotted fruit; '**Hosui**', yellow-brown fruit; '**Nijisseiki**' ★, green-yellow fruit; '**Shinko**', medium-sized fruit of regular globular form, the skin bronze, flesh crisp, aromatic and sweet, but coarse-textured. Zones 4–9.

Pyrus salicifolia

SILVER PEAR, WILLOW-LEAFED PEAR

☼ ❄ ↔ 15 ft (4.5 m) ↑ 25 ft (8 m)

From the Caucasus. Small graceful tree with slender drooping branches. Narrow willow-like leaves, silvery when young, turn grayish green and shiny uppersurface as they age. Flowers creamy white. Small brown pear-shaped fruit. '**Pendula**' is smaller with fully pendulous branches; '**Silver Cascade**', silvery gray foliage. Zones 4–9.

Pyrus ussuriensis

MONGOLIAN PEAR, USSURIAN PEAR

☼ ❄ ↔ 20 ft (6 m) ↑ 50 ft (15 m)

From northeastern China, Korea, and northern Japan. Sometimes used in street plantings. Yellowish green leaves ovate or rounded, bristle-toothed, turn crimson-bronze, in autumn. Broad corymb of white flowers, in early spring. Fruits greenish brown ripen in autumn–winter. Zones 4–9.

Pyrus salicifolia 'Silver Cascade'

Pyrus salicifolia 'Pendula'

Pyrus ussuriensis

Quercus species, in the wild, Zion National Park, Utah, USA

Quercus acutissima

Quercus alba

QUERCUS

OAK

This large genus of some 600 species, both evergreen and deciduous, is a member of the beech (Fagaceae) family. Most are trees, a few are shrubs, widely distributed throughout the Northern Hemisphere. Many are large and impressive trees that live to a great age; their timber has long been valued for ship-building, fine furniture, and paneling. Fruits (acorns) are partly enclosed in a cup. All have simple leaves, often finely and deeply lobed, turning to spectacular tones of red or yellow-brown in autumn. Male and female flowers are carried on separate catkins on the same tree, usually in early spring.

CULTIVATION: Oaks grow well in deep alluvial valley soils; only a few of the Mediterranean species are tolerant of poor dry soil. Most enjoy cool moist conditions. Some early pruning may be needed to help establish a single straight trunk. Seeds, sown as soon as ripe in summer or autumn, germinate readily; cultivars and sterile hybrids are usually grafted in late winter or early spring.

Quercus bicolor

Quercus acutissima

JAPANESE CHESTNUT OAK, JAPANESE OAK

☼ ❆ ↔ 40 ft (12 m) ↑ 80 ft (24 m)

Native of Japan, Korea, China, and the Himalayas. Deciduous tree. Dark gray bark, roughly ridged and fissured. Narrow, oblong, chestnut-like leaves, polished green, edged with bristle-tipped teeth, persisting until winter. Oval acorns half-enclosed in cups. Zones 5–10.

Quercus agrifolia

CALIFORNIA LIVE OAK, COAST LIVE OAK

☼ ❆ ↔ 35 ft (10 m) ↑ 40 ft (12 m)

From California and Mexico. Evergreen tree or large shrub, branched almost to the ground. Smooth black bark, roughens with age. Leaves oval or rounded, hard-textured, edged with spine-tipped teeth, smooth undersides. Acorns half-enclosed in cups. Zones 8–10.

Quercus alba

AMERICAN WHITE OAK, STAVE OAK, WHITE OAK

☼ ❆ ↔ 100 ft (30 m) ↑ 100 ft (30 m)

Large deciduous tree from southeastern Canada and eastern USA. Straight, often massive trunk, spreading branches, broad canopy of foliage. Bark dark gray. Oval leaves deeply and irregularly lobed, soft green when young, turning purple-crimson in autumn. Acorns held in shallow scaly cups. Zones 3–9.

Quercus bicolor

SWAMP WHITE OAK

☼ ❆ ↔ 40 ft (12 m) ↑ 80 ft (24 m)

Found growing naturally in southeastern Canada and eastern USA. Matures into a well-developed trunk, with ascending branches. Bark is pale gray with thick ridges that are blackish gray. Leaves are egg-shaped, shallowly lobed, shiny green, grayish and felted on the undersides. Acorns in clusters. Zones 4–10.

Quercus brantii

☼ ❆ ↔ 20 ft (6 m) ↑ 30 ft (9 m)

Found from eastern Turkey through to southwestern Iran. A small, semi-evergreen or deciduous oak which is drought-tolerant. Leaves 2–4 in (5–10 cm) long, with short pointed teeth and downy undersides. Clusters of relatively large acorns appear in the second year. Zones 7–10.

Quercus canariensis

ALGERIAN OAK, CANARY OAK, MIRBECK'S OAK

☼ ❆ ↔ 40 ft (12 m) ↑ 80 ft (24 m)

A semi-deciduous fast-growing tree from North Africa, southern Portugal, and Spain. Leaves large, egg-shaped or oval, shallowly lobed, dark shiny green on uppersurfaces, paler on undersides. Acorns are hemispheric. Succeeds in heavy clay or shallow chalky soil. Zones 7–10.

Quercus agrifolia

Quercus brantii

Quercus canariensis

Quercus crassifolia

Quercus chrysolepis

CANYON LIVE OAK, MAUL OAK

☀ ❄ ↔ 30 ft (9 m) ↑ 70 ft (21 m)

From southwestern USA and Mexico. Variable, slow-growing, evergreen tree or large shrub, with a generous spreading crown. Bark rather thick, smooth, gray-brown tinged with red. Leaves oval or ovate, spine-toothed, downy. Acorns almost stalkless. Zones 7–10.

Quercus coccinea

SCARLET OAK

☀ ❄ ↔ 40 ft (12 m) ↑ 70 ft (21 m)

From eastern and central USA. Deciduous tree with wide-spreading branches. Leaves oblong or elliptic, shiny dark green above, paler beneath, a few leaves turn bright deep red, later whole crown colors, in autumn. Acorns in shallow cups. '**Splendens**', larger leaves, more reliable autumn color. Zones 2–9.

Quercus crassifolia

☀ ❄ ↔ 35–50 ft (10–15 m) ↑ 50–70 ft (15–21 m)

Deciduous tree from central Mexico. Leaves initially unlobed and velvety,

Quercus × deamii

becoming leathery at maturity, margins slightly recurved. Acorns ripen in first year; cup covering at least one-third. Zones 8–10.

Quercus × deamii

☀ ❄ ↔ 40 ft (12 m) ↑ 60–120 ft (18–36 m)

A natural hybrid which occurs around Indiana, USA, where its parent species, the burr oak *(Quercus macrocarpa)* and the yellow chestnut oak *(Quercus muehlenbergii)*, coexist. Deciduous tree; the 4 in (10 cm) long leaves, 7 to 9 lobes per side, have hairy undersides. Acorns on stalks. Zones 4–9.

Quercus dentata

DAIMYO OAK

☀ ❄ ↔ 30 ft (9 m) ↑ 50 ft (15 m)

A deciduous tree from Japan, Korea, and China. Horizontal branches arise from a short and sinuous bole. The leaves are like those of a giant form of *Quercus robur*, up to 15 in (38 cm) long and 8 in (20 cm) wide; most of the leaves turn brown and remain on the tree during winter. The scaly cups are half-enclosed in egg-shaped acorns. Zones 7–9.

Quercus coccinea

Quercus douglasii

BLUE OAK

☀ ❄ ↔ 20 ft (6 m) ↑ 70 ft (21 m)

Native of California. Deciduous large shrub to medium-sized tree, rounded crown. Bark thin, gray, scaly. Leaves bluish with lobed margins. Small cone-shaped acorns in a hairy shallow cup. Zones 8–10.

Quercus ellipsoidalis

NORTHERN PIN OAK

☀ ❄ ↔ 40 ft (12 m) ↑ 70 ft (21 m)

From central and southern USA. A deciduous tree with a spreading habit. Leaves deeply lobed, turn a deep crimson-purple in autumn. Closely resembles *Q. palustris*, but has ellipsoidal acorns. Zones 5–10.

Quercus ellipsoidalis

Quercus cerris 'Laciniata'

Quercus castaneifolia

CHESTNUT-LEAFED OAK

☀ ❄ ↔ 60 ft (18 m) ↑ 100 ft (30 m)

Found in the Caucasus, Iran, and Algeria. A deciduous tree which develops a broadly domed crown. Leaves oblong or narrowly oval, tapered at both ends, with coarse teeth, shiny dark green on the uppersurfaces, grayish downy on the undersides. Acorns dark brown. '**Green Spire**', broadly columnar form with a compact habit. Zones 6–10.

Quercus cerris

TURKEY OAK

☀ ❄ ↔ 75 ft (23 m) ↑ 100 ft (30 m)

Large, fast-growing, deciduous tree from southern Europe and the Middle East. Slender crown when young, becoming broad-domed. Bark dull gray, roughly fissured. Leaves oval or oblong, shallowly lobed, and coarsely toothed. Stalkless acorns are enclosed in mossy cups. '**Argenteovariegata**' (syn. 'Variegata') features leaves with a conspicuous creamy white margin; '**Laciniata**' has leaves with narrow spreading lobes. Zones 7–10.

Quercus gambelii (golden foliage), in the wild, Aspen, Colorado, USA

Quercus falcata var. *pagodifolia*

Quercus ilex

Quercus imbricaria

Quercus falcata

SOUTHERN RED OAK, SPANISH OAK

☼ ❄ ↔ 35 ft (10 m) ↑ 80 ft (24 m)
Deciduous tree from southern USA.
Bark thick, nearly black, deeply furrowed. Leaves egg-shaped to ovate,
shallowly 3-lobed or deeply 5- to 7-
lobed, dark green above, pale gray-
green, woolly beneath. Acorns nearly
stalkless. **Q. f. var. pagodifolia**, bark
smoother, becoming scaly with age,
larger leaves. Zones 8–10.

Quercus frainetto

FARNETTO, HUNGARIAN OAK

☼ ❄ ↔ 60 ft (18 m) ↑ 100 ft (30 m)
Native to southern Italy, the Balkans,
and Hungary. Large, fast-growing,
deciduous tree, broad-domed, wide-
spreading. Bark pale gray, closely fissured. Leaves egg-shaped and deeply
lobed. Acorns are egg-shaped, half-
enclosed in cups. **'Hungarian Crown'**,
erect habit. Zones 7–10.

Quercus gambelii

GAMBEL OAK, ROCKY MOUNTAIN WHITE OAK

☼ ❄ ↔ 25 ft (8 m) ↑ 30 ft (9 m)
Deciduous tree from central west USA.
Shrubby in very harsh winters, spreads
by underground runners, forming
small clumps. Leaves with 3 to 6 deep
lobes on each side, fine hairs beneath.
Acorns ovoid. Zones 4–9.

Quercus garryana

OREGON OAK, OREGON WHITE OAK

☼ ❄ ↔ 15 ft (4.5 m) ↑ 15 ft (4.5 m)
Deciduous tree from western USA.
Short stout trunk, large branches,
spreading crown. Leaves oval, deeply
cut, shiny dark green above, paler and
slightly hairy beneath. Acorns stalkless
or nearly so. Zones 5–9.

Quercus glandulifera

☼ ❄ ↔ 25 ft (8 m) ↑ 35 ft (10 m)
From China, Korea, and Japan. Slow-
growing deciduous tree with rounded
crown. Leaves variable, oblong-obovate
to ovate-lanceolate, edged with gland-
tipped teeth, bright apple green above,
grayish white beneath. Acorns solitary
or in small clusters. Zones 7–9.

Quercus glauca

syn. *Quercus myrsinifolia*

☼ ❄ ↔ 15 ft (4.5 m) ↑ 50 ft (15 m)
From Japan, Taiwan, China, and the
Himalayas. Evergreen tree or shrub,
stout leafy branches. Bark tough,
fissured. Leaves elliptic to obovate-
oblong, toothed; bronze when young,
becoming glossy green above, glaucous
below. Ovoid acorns in cups. Zones 7–9.

Quercus × heterophylla

BARTRAM'S OAK

☼ ❄ ↔ 40 ft (12 m) ↑ 80 ft (24 m)
Hybrid between *Q. phellos* and *Q.
rubra*. Deciduous tree, open crown,
spreading branches. Bark smooth,
dark gray with fine fissures. Leaves
oblong or oval, smooth-edged or
strongly toothed. Acorns in shallow
cups. Zones 5–9.

Quercus × hispanica

SPANISH OAK

☼ ❄ ↔ 25 ft (8 m) ↑ 100 ft (30 m)
Natural cross between *Quercus suber*
and *Q. cerris*. Variable tree, sometimes
nearly evergreen. Bark has thick fissures. Dark green lobed leaves. Acorns
oblong to egg-shaped. Lime tolerant.
Often seen in the form **'Lucombeana'**,
raised in the UK around 1762, a tall
tree resembling *Q. cerris*, with pale
gray shallowly fissured bark and long
leaves. Zones 6–9.

Quercus ilex

HOLLY OAK, HOLM OAK

☼/☀ ❄ ↔ 60 ft (18 m) ↑ 70 ft (21 m)
Found naturally in southern Europe
and North Africa. A large evergreen
tree with a broad-domed crown,
branching close to the ground. Bark is
brownish or black. Leaves are leathery,
glossy, smooth-edged or toothed, dark
green on the uppersurfaces, grayish
and downy on the undersides. The
pointed acorns are held in cups that
have many rows of small fluted scales.
Zones 6–10.

Quercus imbricaria

SHINGLE OAK

☼ ❄ ↔ 40 ft (12 m) ↑ 70 ft (21 m)
Native to eastern USA. A deciduous
tree with a broad-domed crown. Bark
is wrinkled and warty, gray, becoming
purplish pink as the tree matures.
Leaves are oblong or narrowly oval,
smooth-edged, shiny dark green on
the uppersurfaces with autumn tints.
Acorns on short stalks. This species
was used by early settlers for roof
shingles. Zones 8–10.

Quercus glandulifera

Quercus frainetto 'Hungarian Crown'

Quercus macrocarpa

Quercus macranthera

Quercus infectoria

☼ ❄ ↔ 10 ft (3 m) ↑ 10 ft (3 m)

A native of Greece and Turkey. Semi-evergreen shrub or small tree. Bark scaly, deeply fissured, gray. Glaucous spine-toothed leaves, smooth or nearly smooth. Acorns held in shallow scaly cups. Zones 7–10.

Quercus kelloggii

CALIFORNIAN BLACK OAK

☼ ❄ ↔ 40 ft (12 m) ↑ 60–90 ft (18–27 m)

From California and Oregon, USA. Medium-sized to large deciduous tree with a large, open, globe-like crown. Bark is thick, divided by deep furrows into wide ridges. Leaves are deeply lobed, bristle-toothed, shiny yellow-green above, paler, usually hairy beneath. Acorns are carried on short stalks. Zones 7–10.

Quercus laurifolia

LAUREL OAK

☼ ❄ ↔ 60 ft (18 m) ↑ 60 ft (18 m)

From eastern USA. A medium-sized, semi-evergreen tree, dense rounded habit. Bark thick, nearly black, deeply furrowed. Leaves are glossy green,

oblong or egg-shaped, smooth-edged, occasionally shallowly lobed. Acorns are stalkless or nearly so. Zones 7–10.

Quercus × leana

☼ ❄ ↔ 35 ft (10 m) ↑ 60 ft (18 m)

Deciduous tree, a natural hybrid between *Quercus imbricaria* and *Q. velutina*. Resembles *Q. imbricaria*, differs only in its 3-lobed leaves and slightly larger acorns. Zones 5–9.

Quercus libani

LEBANON OAK

☼ ❄ ↔ 25 ft (8 m) ↑ 25 ft (8 m)

Native of Lebanon and Syria. Elegant, small, deciduous tree with slender branches. Bark dark gray-blackish. Long oblong-lanceolate leaves persist until late in year, glossy green above, edged with bristle-tipped teeth. Acorns on a short broad stalk. Zones 7–10.

Quercus lyrata

OVERCUP OAK

☼ ❄ ↔ 30 ft (9 m) ↑ 60 ft (18 m)

Deciduous tree from southeastern USA with an open crown and large crooked branches. Leaves oblong to egg-shaped, deeply and irregularly

lobed, dark green above, paler, smooth or white-hairy beneath. Acorns are stalkless or nearly so. Zones 8–10.

Quercus macranthera

CAUCASIAN OAK, PERSIAN OAK

☼ ❄ ↔ 40 ft (12 m) ↑ 90 ft (27 m)

Native to the Caucasus region and northern Iran. Fast-growing tree, becomes deciduous with age. Bark purplish gray. Leaves large, broadly ovate, strongly lobed. Twigs, winter buds, and leaf undersurfaces clothed with pale gray velvety down. Acorns held in scaly cups. Zones 6–10.

Quercus macrocarpa

BURR OAK, MOSSYCUP OAK

☼ ❄ ↔ 40 ft (12 m) ↑ 120 ft (36 m)

Found in northeastern and central North America from Nova Scotia, Canada, to Texas, USA. Large decidu-ous tree, massive trunk, spreading branches. Bark coarsely ridged, scaly, gray-brown. Leaves egg-shaped, con-spicuously lobed. Young shoots and leaf undersurfaces covered in pale down. Acorns large, cup with long recurved scales. Zones 4–9.

Quercus marilandica

BLACKJACK OAK

☼ ❄ ↔ 35 ft (10 m) ↑ 20–50 ft (6–15 m)

Found over much of southeastern USA, deciduous tree from woodlands. Dark heavily textured bark. Broad glossy leaves, lobes near tip, rusty

hairs beneath. Egg-shaped acorns, solitary or paired, half-enclosed by scaly cups. Zones 5–9.

Quercus mongolica

MONGOLIAN OAK

☼ ❄ ↔ 40 ft (12 m) ↑ 100 ft (30 m)

From Japan, Korea, northeastern China, Mongolia, and eastern Siberia. Deciduous tree with thick smooth branches. Leaves short, oval to oblong, strongly lobed, in clusters at branch ends. Egg-shaped acorns. Zones 4–9.

Quercus muehlenbergii

CHINQUAPIN OAK, YELLOW CHESTNUT OAK, YELLOW OAK

☼ ❄ ↔ 40 ft (12 m) ↑ 100 ft (30 m)

Deciduous tree found in central and southern USA. Grayish bark fissured vertically. Leaves oblong to lanceolate, coarsely toothed, yellow-green above, pale and downy beneath; turn to rich reds and crimsons in autumn. Acorns half-enclosed in a scaly cup. Zones 5–9.

Quercus marilandica

Quercus infectoria

Quercus × leana

Quercus lyrata

Quercus kelloggii

Quercus nigra, in the wild, Shenandoah National Park, Virginia, USA

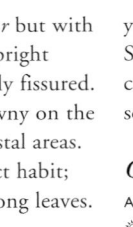

Quercus palustris

Quercus nigra
WATER OAK

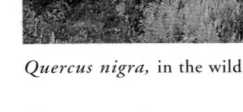 ↔ 40 ft (12 m) ↑ 50 ft (15 m)

A native of southern USA. A broad-domed, deciduous tree. Bark is dark gray and develops scaly ridges. Leaves appear on slender stalks and are egg-shaped, variously lobed, glossy deep green, persisting until winter. Acorns enclosed in shallow cups. Zones 6–10.

Quercus palustris
PIN OAK, SWAMP OAK

 ↔ 60 ft (18 m) ↑ 100 ft (30 m)

Native of southeastern Canada and eastern USA. Large, dense, deciduous tree, slender branches droop at their extremities. Bark silver-gray becoming purplish gray with age. Leaves deeply lobed, shiny green; turn scarlet in autumn, persist until winter. Acorns held in shallow hairy cups. Zones 3–10.

Quercus petraea
syn. *Quercus sessilis*
DURMAST OAK, SESSILE OAK

 ↔ 75 ft (23 m) ↑ 150 ft (45 m)

Found naturally in central and south-eastern Europe. Spreading deciduous tree, similar to *Quercus robur* but with stalkless acorns and more upright branches. Bark is gray, deeply fissured. Leaves are large, usually downy on the undersides. Suitable for coastal areas. 'Columna', an erect compact habit; 'Longifolia', exceptionally long leaves. Zones 5–9.

Quercus phellos
WILLOW OAK, WILLOW-LEAFED OAK

↔ 40 ft (12 m) ↑ 100 ft (30 m)

A large deciduous tree with slender branches, native to eastern USA. Bark smooth, gray, becoming fissured with age. Leaves narrow, willow-like, glossy green on the uppersurfaces, turning yellow and orange tones in autumn. Small acorns are enclosed in shallow cups. This species requires lime-free soil. Zones 5–9.

Quercus pontica
ARMENIAN OAK, PONTINE OAK

↔ 15 ft (4.5 m) ↑ 20 ft (6 m)

A shrub or a small tree that is native to Armenia and the Caucasus region. The leaves are large, oval to egg-shaped, strongly ribbed and toothed, with a yellow stalk and midrib; the whole leaf turns warm rich red tones in the autumn months. The ovoid acorns are enclosed in shallow gray cups. Zones 6–10.

Quercus prinus
BASKET OAK, SWAMP CHESTNUT OAK

↔ 60 ft (18 m) ↑ 100 ft (30 m)

From southeastern Canada and eastern USA. Deciduous tree, often forks just above the ground into large spreading branches. Bark dark red-brown to black, deeply fissured. Egg-shaped to oblong leaves, yellow-green, lustrous above, paler, finely hairy beneath; turn rich yellow in autumn. Acorns half-enclosed in hairy cups. Zones 3–9.

Quercus pontica

Quercus pubescens

Quercus petraea 'Longifolia'

Quercus robur

Quercus robur subsp. *pedunculiflora*

Quercus robur f. *fastigiata*

Quercus pubescens

DOWNY OAK

☼ ❄ ↔ 35 ft (10 m) ↑ 60 ft (18 m)

Southern European deciduous tree, occasionally shrubby. Hairy twigs. Dark gray bark deeply and finely cracked into small plates. Oval to egg-shaped leaves with wavy edges, deeply lobed, downy. Egg-shaped acorns. Zones 8–10.

Quercus robur

COMMON OAK, ENGLISH OAK, PEDUNCULATE OAK

☼ ❄ ↔ 70 ft (21 m) ↑ 100 ft (30 m)

Native of Europe, western Asia, and North Africa. A large and long-lived, deciduous tree. Bark pale gray, closely fissured into short, narrow, vertical plates. Leaves shallowly lobed. Long-nosed acorns in shallow cups. May be invasive in cooler climates. *Q. r.* subsp. *pedunculiflora,* native to Greece, Turkey, and the Caucasus region, leaves with fewer lobes, bluish undersides. *Q. r.* f. *fastigiata,* columnar habit. *Q. r.* 'Concordia', the golden oak, leaves suffused with golden yellow; 'Pendula', drooping branches. Zones 3–10.

Quercus rubra

syn. *Quercus borealis*

NORTHERN RED OAK, RED OAK

☼ ❄ ↔ 70 ft (21 m) ↑ 100 ft (30 m)

Deciduous tree from eastern Canada to Texas, USA. Broad head, horizontal branches. Bark smooth, silvery gray, can become brown-gray with age. Leaves large, oval to egg-shaped, lobed, turn red then red-brown to yellow and brown on old trees before falling. Dark red-brown acorns, on short stalks, in shallow scaly cups. 'Schrefeldii', more deeply lobed leaves, lobes overlapping. Zones 3–9.

Quercus rugosa

NETLEAF OAK

☼ ❄ ↔ 30 ft (9 m) ↑ 30 ft (9 m)

Evergreen tree found from southern North America to the mountains of Central America. Flaking, somewhat corky bark. Heavily veined, rounded, shallowly lobed leaves, uppersurfaces dark green, undersides very pale. Small acorns. Zones 8–11.

Quercus × runcinata

BOTTOM OAK

☼ ❄ ↔ 30 ft (9 m) ↑ 50–80 ft (15–24 m)

Deciduous tree from eastern USA, a natural hybrid between *Quercus imbricaria* and *Q. rubra.* Leaves long-stemmed, with 3 or 4 irregular sickle-shaped lobes, thin covering of rusty hairs beneath. Small-cupped egg-shaped acorns. Zones 5–9.

Quercus sadleriana

DEER OAK

☼ ❄ ↔ 7 ft (2 m) ↑ 7 ft (2 m)

Rare species found in the Siskiyou Mountains in California, USA. It is a small, slowly branching shrub with conspicuously scaly buds, prominently veined serrated leaves. Acorns ripen in first year. Zones 8–10.

Quercus shumardii

SHUMARD OAK

☼ ❄ ↔ 40 ft (12 m) ↑ 100 ft (30 m)

Native of the prairie states of central USA. Large deciduous tree, wide-spreading crown. Bark thick, furrowed. Leaves 5- to 7-lobed, toothed, dark green above, paler below; turn red or golden brown in autumn. Acorns in a thick shallow cup. *Q. s.* var. *schneckii,* smoother bark, less deeply lobed leaves. Zones 5–9.

Quercus suber

CORK OAK

☼ ❄ ↔ 70 ft (21 m) ↑ 70 ft (21 m)

A native of southwestern Europe and North Africa. Short-stemmed, wide-spreading, evergreen tree. Thick rugged bark provides the cork of commerce. Leaves leathery, broadly toothed, shiny green above, grayish green and felted beneath. Egg-shaped acorns held in scaly cups. Zones 8–10.

Quercus × *runcinata*

Quercus shumardii var. *schneckii*

Quercus rubra

Quercus suber

Quercus texana

syn. *Quercus buckleyi*
SPANISH OAK

☼ ❄ ↔ 50–70 ft (15–21 m)
↑ 50–70 ft (15–21 m)

From Texas and Oklahoma, USA. Broad deciduous tree, often branching close to the ground. Leaves with 2 or 3 pairs of lobes, up to 5 in (12 cm) long, mature to yellow-green. Acorns ripen in second year; only the base held in cup. Zones 7–10.

Quercus texana

Quercus tomentella

Quercus × turneri

Quercus tomentella

ISLAND OAK

☼ ❄ ↔ 25 ft (8 m) ↑ 30 ft (9 m)

Found on the Channel Islands off the California coast, USA. Evergreen tree, open spreading crown. Leaves broadly lance-shaped, toothed edges, downy when young. Acorns large for size of tree. Zones 8–11.

Quercus × turneri

☼ ❄ ↔ 50 ft (15 m) ↑ 50 ft (15 m)

One of the few hybrids between evergreen and deciduous species, *Q. ilex* and *Q. robur.* Tree is semi-evergreen to evergreen, with a spreading crown. Leathery lobed leaves. Acorns half-enclosed in cups. '**Pseudoturneri**', narrow leaves and lobes. Zones 7–10.

Quercus velutina

BLACK OAK, YELLOW BARK OAK

❄ ↔ 75 ft (23 m) ↑ 100 ft (30 m)

Large deciduous tree found in central and southern USA. Bark is dark gray, smooth, deeply fissured with age. Leaves large, deeply lobed, glossy dark green above, downy below. Acorns are half-enclosed in scaly cups. Zones 3–9.

Quercus virginiana

LIVE OAK

☼ ❄ ↔ 35 ft (10 m) ↑ 70 ft (21 m)

From southeastern USA, Mexico, and Cuba. Wide-spreading evergreen. Bark charcoal gray, fissured. Twigs downy, leaves elliptic or oblong, leathery, smooth-edged, glossy dark green above, grayish to whitish hairs below. Acorns singly or in clusters. Used for ship-building and posts. Zones 7–11.

Quercus wislizeni

INTERIOR LIVE OAK

☼ ❄ ↔ 35 ft (10 m) ↑ 80 ft (24 m)

From Mexico and California, USA. Large evergreen shrub or rounded

Quercus wislizeni

tree. Bark thick, nearly black, deeply furrowed with scaly ridges. Leaves holly-like, oblong to ovate, slender spiny teeth. Acorns mature in the first autumn. Zones 8–10.

QUESNELIA

The 16 species in this genus in the bromeliad (Bromeliaceae) family are indigenous to southeastern Brazil and fall into two main groups: one which contains plants which form large clumps and have a flowerhead in the form of an elongated cone with startlingly bright, red, erect bracts; the other made up of plants that are not clump-forming and mostly having an open flowerhead reminiscent of *Billbergia* but with the petals uniform rather than opening at an angle. Leaves are green and strap-like, with some teeth on the edges, forming an open rosette. Petals may be red, blue, or yellow.

CULTIVATION: These plants are recommended for indoor culture in the greenhouse or conservatory in cool-temperate areas, or outdoors with protection from direct continuous sunlight and extremes of rain in warmer areas. Water when soil is dry. Extra feeding is generally not necessary. Propagation is mainly by offsets.

Quesnelia liboniana

☀ ⊞ ↔ 4 in (10 cm) ↑ 32 in (80 cm)

From Brazil's Rio de Janeiro area. Forming offsets on small rhizomes, leaves few, green, strap-like, few teeth on edges, forming a tube that soon flares out. Flower stem is slender;

Quercus virginiana, in the wild, Cape Hatteras, North Carolina, USA

Quercus virginiana (with *Tillandsia usneoides* in trees), Fontainebleau State Park, Louisiana, USA

flowerhead is a short cylinder, with about 8 well-separated red flowers emerging at all angles. Petals are blue. Zones 9–11.

Quesnelia marmorata

☀ ✷ ↔ 4 in (10 cm) ↑ 24 in (60 cm)

From central eastern Brazil. Leaves are few, stiff, strap-like, with dark green or brown irregular cross-bands and toothed edges, forming a tight tube that flares at the top. Flowerhead just emerging from leaf tube, pyramidal, spreading branches on all sides getting smaller towards the top. Large red bracts below branches tend to droop. Flowers mainly violet, petals blue. Zones 10–12.

QUILLAJA

There are about 3 species in this genus of evergreen shrubs or trees from South America, which belongs to the rose (Rosaceae) family. They have shiny, bright green, thick and leathery leaves and white hairy flowers which appear in clusters of 3 to 5 blooms in spring. The fruit comprises 5 leathery follicles that open out into a star shape. The bark of some species is used as soap and for medicinal purposes.

CULTIVATION: These plants need a warm climate and a moist fertile soil that is well drained. Grow in a protected partially shaded position. Propagate from seed or cuttings.

Quillaja saponaria

SOAPBARK TREE

☀ ❄ ↔ 15–25 ft (4.5–8 m) ↑ 50–60 ft (15–18 m)

Evergreen tree, native to Peru and Chile. Shiny, short-stalked, oval leaves. Purple-centered white flowers in spring. Thick dark bark contains a glucoside called saponin which lathers in water, used as a soap substitute in its native lands. Zones 8–10.

Quisqualis indica

QUISQUALIS

This Combretaceae family genus contains 16 species from tropical Africa and Southeast Asia. They are evergreen woody climbers or trailing plants grown in their steamy homelands for their tubular flowers that flare into 5 lobes and are used to cover walls or grow over arches. The leaves are simple and are usually in opposite pairs.

CULTIVATION: In tropical climates provide a well-drained but moist soil that isn't too fertile as this encourages growth at the expense of flowers. In temperate to cold climates they require a heated greenhouse with a minimum temperature of 56°F (13°C). They prefer full light but must be sheltered from the hot midday sun. Propagation is usually from softwood cuttings or by layering.

Quisqualis indica

RANGOON CREEPER

☀/◑ ✷ ↔ 25 ft (8 m) ↑ 35 ft (10 m)

Ranging from mainland Southeast Asia to New Guinea. Rampant evergreen climber, usually shrubby to begin with. Leaves to 7 in (18 cm) long, smooth-edged with prominent veins. Perfumed, very narrow, tubular flowers initially white, ageing from pink to bright red over 3 days, in summer–autumn. Zones 10–12.

RADERMACHERA

This genus in the trumpet-vine family (Bignoniaceae) is made up of around 15 species, mostly trees or shrubs, from tropical Southeast Asia. The compound leaves may be bipinnate or tripinnate. The tubular to trumpet-shaped flowers, often fragrant, in shades of orange, green-yellow to yellow, pink, and white, are borne in loose panicles, mostly at the ends of branches. The capsular fruits contain flat seeds that are winged at each end.

Quillaja saponaria

Rafflesia arnoldii (unopened), in the wild, Mt Kinabalu, Borneo

Rafflesia arnoldii, in the wild, Borneo

They are grown in warm frost-free areas; in cooler areas some species are grown as container plants. Some species are used for timber in their native regions.

CULTIVATION: Most species are fairly adaptable, but give the best results in a well-drained fertile soil in full sun to semi-shade. Protection from strong winds is necessary, and moderate irrigation is required during the growing period. Prune after flowering to maintain a bushy habit. Propagate from seed or cuttings or by aerial layering.

Radermachera sinica

ASIAN BELL

☀ ✷ ↔ 15 ft (4.5 m) ↑ 30 ft (9 m)

Shrub or small tree from Southeast Asia. Dark green, glossy, bipinnate leaves, 8 ovate to lance-shaped leaflets. Scented deep yellow or white flowers, open at night, in spring–summer. Popular indoor foliage plant in cooler climates. Zones 10–12.

RAFFLESIA

A genus of remarkable parasitic plants renowned for their enormous flowers. There are about 15 species including *R. arnoldii*, which has the largest flower in the plant kingdom, a foul-smelling bloom that can measure up to 40 in (100 cm) in diameter! *Rafflesia*, which gives its name to the

Radermachera sinica

family Rafflesiaceae, is from Malaysia, Borneo, Sumatra, and the Philippines. The plants make their homes in cissus vines *(Tetrastigma)* growing along the jungle floor, feeding through filaments penetrating their hosts. The only visible part is the flower. Named for Sir Thomas Stamford Raffles, the founder of the British colony of Singapore. Many species are endangered; some are thought already extinct.

CULTIVATION: Cultivation of *Rafflesia* has never been attempted with success due to their specialized, totally parasitic growth habit.

Rafflesia arnoldii

☀ ✷ ↔ 40 in (100 cm) ↑ 24 in (60 cm)

Largest and heaviest flower in the world, up to 15 lb (7 kg), found in the rainforests of Sumatra and Borneo. Five dark red fleshy petals, mottled with pink to white spots, surround a disc with a central hole. From the appearance of the bud to flower's opening can take 10 months; once open the flower lasts for only a few days. Fruit, 6 in (15 cm) wide, contains thousands of little seeds; dispersal method is unknown. Zones 11–12.

Ranunculus acris 'Flore Pleno'

Ramonda myconi 'Rosea'

RAMONDA

This small genus containing 3 species belongs in the African violet family (Gesneriaceae). They are evergreen, rosette-forming, alpine plants of great beauty, found from the mountains of northeastern Spain to the Balkans. The leaves are a rich green and heavily veined; the flowers, which are held well above them in late spring and early summer, are 4- or 5-petalled, more or less flat-faced, and range in color from white through shades of pink and lavender to violet-blue. CULTIVATION: These plants are for cool to cold climates only and due to their dislike of winter wet are usually grown in a cool greenhouse or on their sides in a drystone wall. Propagation is quite difficult from seed. They are usually propagated by division or, better still, from leaf cuttings taken in late summer.

Ramonda myconi
syn. *Ramonda pyrenaica*
☼ ❄ ↔ 7–8 in (18–20 cm)
↑ 4–5 in (10–12 cm)

Charming rosette-forming perennial from northeastern Spain. Crinkled

Ramonda myconi

hairy leaves. Clusters of violet-blue flowers, to 1 in (25 mm) across, with yellow anthers, held above the leaves, in late spring–early summer. 'Rosea', pink flowered form; a white form is also grown. Zones 6–9.

Ramonda nathaliae
☼ ❄ ↔ 4–5 in (10–12 cm)
↑ 4–5 in (10–12 cm)

From western Greece, Macedonia, and Bosnia and Herzegovina; similar to *R. myconi*. Rosettes of crinkled leaves; mauve-blue, sometimes white, flowers, to 1½ in (35 mm) across, in late spring–early summer. Zones 6–9.

RANUNCULUS
BUTTERCUP

The type genus for the buttercup (Ranunculaceae) family, this widespread group encompasses some 400 species of annuals, biennials, and perennials, many of which are cultivated, others are admired in the wild, and some are despised as invasive weeds. The foliage varies markedly, though pinnate, glossy, leathery, kidney-shaped leaves predominate. The flowers too are often glossy and commonly have 5 petals. Most species produce yellow flowers but cultivated forms occur in many different colors. *Ranunculus* is Latin for little frog, a name given by the Roman Pliny due to the wet conditions in which wild buttercups are often found growing.

Ranunculus amplexicaulis

CULTIVATION: Buttercups are very hardy and will grow in a wide range of conditions, but generally prefer to have their roots kept cool and moist. Many species have strong rhizomes that can be invasive, so take care to plant where they can be controlled. Bedding ranunculus "corms" can be lifted and stored dry. Propagate by division or from seed. Mildew can be a problem in autumn.

Ranunculus aconitifolius
☼/☀ ❄ ↔ 40 in (100 cm)
↑ 24 in (60 cm)

Found in damp subalpine meadows of western and central European mountains. Forms a large clump of dark green, 3- to 5-lobed palmate leaves. White flowers, ¾ in (18 mm) wide, backed by purple-red-tinted sepals, in spring. 'Flore Pleno', a fully double-flowered form cultivated since the sixteenth century, also known as fair maids of France or fair maids of Kent. Zones 6–9.

Ranunculus acris
MEADOW BUTTERCUP
☼/☀ ❄ ↔ 24–48 in (60–120 cm)
↑ 24–40 in (60–100 cm)

A widely naturalized perennial from temperate Eurasia. The toothed leaves are 3- to 7-lobed. Small clusters of bright golden yellow flowers, to 1 in (25 mm) wide, in spring. Can be

R. asiaticus, **Bloomingdale Series**, cultivar

invasive and is considered a weed in many areas. 'Flore Pleno', a double-flowered form that is also known as bachelor's buttons. Zones 5–10.

Ranunculus amplexicaulis
☼/☀ ❄ ↔ 12–20 in (30–50 cm)
↑ 8–12 in (20–30 cm)

Perennial species from the Pyrenees and northern Spain. Blue-green, pointed oval to lance-shaped leaves. Small clusters of white, sometimes pink-tinted, flowers, to 1 in (25 mm) wide, in spring. Zones 6–10.

Ranunculus anemoneus
ANEMONE BUTTERCUP
☼/☀ ❄ ↔ 12–16 in (30–40 cm)
↑ 8–14 in (20–35 cm)

Alpine perennial from Mt Kosciuszko, New South Wales, Australia, with a low spreading habit. Basal leaves are 3- to 5-lobed and toothed. White flowers are solitary or paired, around 2 in (5 cm) wide, with up to 30 petals, in late spring. Zones 7–9.

Ranunculus aquatilis
WATER CROWSFOOT, WHITE WATER BUTTERCUP
☼/☀ ❄ ↔ 40 in (100 cm)
↑ 24 in (60 cm)

An aquatic annual or perennial from temperate Eurasia. Submerged and floating leaves and emergent flower stems. Submerged leaves are feathery, finely divided and widely spaced on wiry stems; floating leaves rounded and lobed. Flowers are white or pink, usually solitary, to ¾ in (18 mm) wide, in spring–summer. Zones 5–9.

Ranunculus asiaticus
☼/☼ ❄ ↔ 8–12 in (20–30 cm)
↑ 18 in (45 cm)

Rhizome-rooted southern Eurasian perennial. Finely divided, ferny, basal leaves; hairy upright flower stems. Large, often double flowers, in late

Ranunculus asiaticus

R. a., Bloomingdale Series, cultivar

R. a., Bloomingdale Series, cultivar

R. a., Bloomingdale Series, cultivar

R. a., Bloomingdale Series, cultivar

R. a., Bloomingdale, cultivar

R. asiaticus, Bloomingdale Series, cultivar

Ranunculus asiaticus, Tecolote Hybrid

Ranunculus asiaticus, Tecolote Hybrid

spring–summer, mainly in yellow to red shades in the wild, but cultivated forms are available in many colors. Often sold as mixed color strains, such as **Bloomingdale Series**, 8 in (20 cm) tall, fully double flowers and compact habit, wide color range excluding mauve to purple shades; and **Tecolote Hybrids**, 18 in (45 cm) tall, very large double flowers, all colors except blue. Zones 8–10.

Ranunculus auricomus

GOLDILOCKS BUTTERCUP

☀/◐ ❄ ↔ 12 in (30 cm) ↕ 12 in (30 cm)

Perennial from Europe and western Russia. Palmate, 5- to 7-lobed leaves with narrow toothed segments. The flowers are usually solitary, bright golden yellow, around ¾ in (18 mm) wide, backed by a ruff of leaves, in spring. Zones 4–9.

Ranunculus bulbosus

☀/◐ ❄ ↔ 20–40 in (50–100 cm)

↕ 12–20 in (30–50 cm)

Widely naturalized perennial from temperate Eurasia and North Africa. Pointed oval leaves divided into 3 large toothed and lobed segments. Shiny bright yellow flowers, to 1¼ in (30 mm) wide, from late spring to summer. Vigorous, somewhat invasive rootstock. Zones 7–10.

Ranunculus calandrinioides

☀/◐ ❄ ↔ 12 in (30 cm) ↕ 6 in (15 cm)

Perennial species from Morocco, with wavy-edged, lance-shaped, blue-green, long-stemmed leaves to 2 in (5 cm) long. Flowers solitary or in small groups, white to pale pink, 2 in (5 cm) wide, in winter–spring. Zones 7–10.

Ranunculus constantinopolitanus

☀/◐ ❄ ↔ 12–32 in (30–80 cm)

↕ 16–30 in (40–75 cm)

Perennial from southeastern Europe to the Middle East. Heart-shaped leaves are divided into 3 lobed, toothed segments. Glowing golden yellow flowers are clustered on erect stems, in spring to early summer. **'Flore Pleno'** (syns 'Plenus', 'Speciosus Plenus'), fully double flowers. Zones 6–9.

Ranunculus ficaria

COMMON BUTTERCUP, LESSER CELANDINE, PILEWORT

☀/◐ ❄ ↔ 8–24 in (20–60 cm)

↕ 2–8 in (5–20 cm)

Very widely naturalized perennial from temperate Eurasia and North Africa. Forms a carpet of long-stemmed, lustrous dark green, heart-shaped leaves, to 1½ in (35 mm) long. The flowers are usually solitary, 1 in (25 mm) wide, glowing golden yellow, and borne in spring. Mildly invasive. *R. f.* var. *albus,* dark-blotched leaves, light yellow flowers ageing to white; *R. f.* var. *aurantiacus* (syn. *R. f.* 'Cupreus'), dark-blotched and silver-mottled

Ranunculus auricomus

foliage, orange flowers. *R. f.* **'Brazen Hussy'** ★, dark bronze-green foliage and deep golden flowers; **'Flore Pleno'**, double flowers. Zones 5–9.

Ranunculus flammula

LESSER SPEARWORT

☀/◐ ❄ ↔ 32–60 in (80–150 cm)

↕ 4–12 in (10–30 cm)

This semi-aquatic perennial is indigenous to temperate Eurasia, and is

Ranunculus ficaria

Ranunculus ficaria 'Brazen Hussy'

found growing naturally in shallow streams, pond margins, or permanently wet soil. The creeping stems strike root as they spread, and have narrow to broad, approximately 1½ in (35 mm) long, lance-shaped leaves. The flowers are ½–1 in (12–25 mm) wide, a bright yellow, and are produced throughout the summer months, carried either singly or in small clusters. Zones 5–9.

Ranunculus flammula

Ranunculus glacialis

◐/☀ ❋ ↔ 8–16 in (20–40 cm)
↕ 4–10 in (10–25 cm)

A perennial found from Iceland and Greenland to the mountains of southern Europe. Dark green, rather fleshy leaves, 3 deeply divided lobes. Flowers in groups of up to 3, around 1 in (25 mm) wide, opening white to pink, becoming red after pollination, from spring to summer. Zones 4–9.

Ranunculus gramineus

☀/◐ ❋ ↔ 6–12 in (15–30 cm)
↕ 8–20 in (20–50 cm)

Perennial from southern Europe and North Africa. Forms clumps. Gray-green to blue-green leaves, to 12 in

Ranunculus gramineus

(30 cm) long. Lemon yellow flowers, ¾ in (18 mm) wide, solitary or in groups of up to 3, in spring–summer. Zones 7–10.

Ranunculus graniticola

GRANITE BUTTERCUP

◐/☀ ❋ ↔ 8–12 in (20–30 cm)
↕ 8–12 in (20–30 cm)

Native to subalpine areas of Victoria and New South Wales, Australia. Perennial with rosettes of small, deep green, lobed leaves. Bright yellow flowers, to over 1¼ in (30 mm) wide, on erect stems, from mid-spring in lowland areas, early summer at higher altitudes. Zones 7–9.

Ranunculus lingua

GREATER SPEARWORT

☀/◐ ❋ ↔ 3–7 ft (0.9–2 m)
↕ 8–12 in (20–30 cm)

Semi-aquatic perennial found in shallow streams or continually damp areas from Europe to Siberia. Long spreading stems, striking roots as they grow; long-stemmed pointed oval leaves, to 8 in (20 cm) long. Clusters of bright yellow flowers, 2 in (5 cm) wide, in summer. Zones 4–9.

Ranunculus graniticola, in the wild, Kosciuszko National Park, New South Wales, Australia

Ranunculus sprunerianus

Ranunculus lyallii

MOUNT COOK BUTTERCUP, MOUNT COOK LILY

◐/☀ ❋ ↔ 24–48 in (60–120 cm)
↕ 24–48 in (60–120 cm)

A perennial from damp subalpine areas of New Zealand's South Island. Leathery, dark green, kidney-shaped leaves, to 16 in (40 cm) wide. Tall branching stems with panicles of pure white flowers, to 3 in (8 cm) wide, in late spring–early summer. Zones 7–9.

Ranunculus parnassifolius

◐/☀ ❋ ↔ 8–12 in (20–30 cm)
↕ 2–4 in (5–10 cm)

Perennial native to southern Europe. Leathery, dark green, pointed oval, sometimes downy leaves, to 2 in (5 cm) long. Solitary white or light pink flowers, to 1 in (25 mm) wide, in spring–summer. Zones 5–9.

Ranunculus penicillatus

☀/◐ ❋ ↔ 24–48 in (60–120 cm)
↕ 8–12 in (20–30 cm)

Aquatic perennial found in shallow fast-flowing streams from northwestern Europe to the Crimea. Submerged leaves very fine and feathery, floating leaves elliptic, to 2 in (5 cm) long, often absent. Flowers emergent, cream to pale yellow, 1–2 in (25–50 mm) wide, in summer. Zones 6–9.

Ranunculus repens

CREEPING BUTTERCUP

◐/☀ ❋ ↔ 12–32 in (30–80 cm)
↕ 6–20 in (15–50 cm)

European perennial. Leaves with 3 coarsely toothed lobes. Flowers deep yellow, around 1 in (25 mm) wide, usually solitary, in spring–summer. Widely naturalized, invasive and considered a moderately pernicious weed in some areas. 'Pleniflorus' (syn. *R. r.* 'Flore Pleno'), fully double flowers. Zones 3–9.

Ranunculus sprunerianus

◐/☀ ❋ ↔ 8–16 in (20–40 cm)
↕ 8–18 in (20–45 cm)

A tuberous perennial found in the Balkans and western Asia. Downy, 3- to 5-lobed, toothed, heart-shaped

Ranunculus velutinus

Ranunculus lyallii, in the wild, Mt Cook National Park, New Zealand

leaves. Clusters of bright yellow flowers, 1 in (25 mm) wide, are borne in spring. Zones 4–9.

Ranunculus velutinus

VELVETY BUTTERCUP

◐/☀ ❋ ↔ 16–32 in (40–80 cm)
↕ 16–24 in (40–60 cm)

European perennial. Downy triangular to heart-shaped leaves, 3 to 5 toothed lobes. Branching stems; small heads of glowing golden yellow flowers, ¾ in (18 mm) wide, in spring–early summer. Zones 6–9.

RAOULIA

SCABWEED

Found in screes or open rocky places from sea level to alpine areas throughout New Zealand, these 20 to 30 species of tiny-leafed, cushion- or mat-forming, evergreen perennials or subshrubs belong to the daisy family (Asteraceae). Their leaves are green or silvery in appearance, caused by minute silky hairs. Flowers are tiny, disc-like and pale white, cream, or yellow. The largest cushion-forming species are known as vegetable sheep because from a distance these plants look like sheep sitting down!
CULTIVATION: *Raoulia* species will do well in pots, troughs, or rock gardens. Grow in moist well-drained soil in full sun. Propagate from seed or sections of the mat (rooted stems).

Raoulia australis
syn. *Raoulia lutescens*
COMMON MAT DAISY, GOLDEN SCABWEED
☼ ❄ ↔12 in (30 cm) ↕½ in (12 mm)
From New Zealand's South Island.
A mat-forming perennial that layers
itself as it creeps. Tiny leaves, gray or
silver. Yellow flowers, 5 mm wide, in
summer. Zones 7–9.

Raoulia bryoides
VEGETABLE SHEEP
☼/☀ ❄ ↔20–48 in (50–120 cm)
↕12–20 in (30–50 cm)
From New Zealand. A silvery alpine
species. Forms solid hummocks of
densely packed minute leaves in
woolly rosettes. Flowers are tiny tufts
at the center of rosettes, and appear in
summer. Zones 7–9.

Raoulia eximia
TUTAHUNA, VEGETABLE SHEEP
☼ ❄ ↔20 in (50 cm) ↕12 in (30 cm)
From New Zealand's South Island.
Dense cushion-like perennial, eventually forming large mounds. Yellowish
white flowers in summer. Zones 7–9.

Raoulia hookeri
MAT DAISY, SCABWEED
☼/☀ ❄ ↔24 in (60 cm)
↕¾–1¼ in (18–30 mm)
Found on New Zealand's South Island
and southern regions of the North
Island. Dense mat-forming plant.
Tiny silvery leaves. Flowers creamy
white, in summer. Grows from sea
level to 5,900 ft (1,800 m). Zones 7–9.

Raoulia parkii
☼/☀ ❄ ↔24 in (60 cm)
↕¾–1¼ in (18–30 mm)
From the South Island, New Zealand.
Mat-forming species. Overlapping
leaves with a yellowish powdery coating. Tiny yellow flowers, in summer.
Subalpine in scree areas. Zones 7–9.

Raoulia rubra
☼/☀ ❄ ↔12–24 in (30–60 cm)
↕¾–1¼ in (18–30 mm)
This species comes from mountain
regions of the far southwestern corner

Raoulia hookeri

Raoulia rubra, in the wild, Nelson,
New Zealand

of the North Island and the northeastern tip of the South Island, New
Zealand. Stems produce a compact
rosette of gray-green leaves, about
10–15 mm long. Red flower produced
in the center of a 3 mm wide rosette,
in summer. Subalpine in scree areas.
Zones 7–9.

Raoulia subsericea
TURF MAT DAISY
☼/☀ ❄ ↔12–16 in (30–40 cm)
↕¾–1¼ in (18–30 mm)
From the South Island, New Zealand.
Wide spreading grayish leaves form
rosette-like tufts at tips of branchlets.
Scented, white, daisy-like flowers,
½ in (12 mm) wide, appear in
summer. Zones 7–9.

RAPHANUS
RADISH
These 8 annual, biennial, or perennial
herbs are members of the cabbage
family (Brassicaceae) and natives of
Europe and temperate Asia, with a
tall, branching habit, often with stems
and leaves covered with bristly hairs,
and often with swollen, sometimes
edible, tap roots. Leaves are divided or
lobed, with the terminal lobe rounded
and toothed side lobes; the lower
leaves appear on stalks, upper and
stem leaves are nearly or completely
stalkless. Long racemes, of white or
yellow flowers with erect sepals and
long-clawed petals veined with purple
are borne at the ends of leafy stems.

Raoulia subsericea

Raoulia bryoides, in the wild, New Zealand

Fruit is a jointed, narrow, grooved,
long-beaked pod or silique, commonly constricted between the seeds.
Roots, seeds, and sometimes the
flowers are edible, and rich in potassium and iron. Radish can become an
invasive weed. Genus named from the
Greek, *raphanis*, appearing rapidly,
referring to fast seed germination.
CULTIVATION: Sow spring radish seed
in spring and early autumn. Winter
radishes require a longer time to
mature and should be sown in late
summer or beyond. Adaptable to
most soils in an open sunny position.
Harvest seed pods when half-grown.

Raphanus sativus
RADISH
☼ ❄ ↔12–24 in (30–60 cm)
↕2–5 ft (0.6–1.5 m)
Annual or biennial herb, probably of
garden origin, from southern Asia.
Red, white, or yellow edible tap root.
Rough, alternate, divided leaves,
larger terminal segment. Branching
clusters of white to pale purple
flowers strongly veined, in summer. *R.
s.* var. *longipinnatus* (daikon, Japanese
or Chinese radish), deeply divided
leaves, up to 24 in (60 cm) long, long
durable root, widely grown. Cultivars
include: *R. s.* **Caudatus Group** (syn.
R. caudatus) (potting radish, rat-tail
radish), vigorous plants, up to 5 ft
(1.5 m) tall, with a non-tuberous
root, grown for their thick seed pods,
8–12 in (20–30 cm) long, used in
pickles; 'Cherriette', uniform, bright
red, crisp, spherical roots; 'Cherry
Belle' ★, bright cherry red spherical
roots; 'Icicle' ★, compact, heat-
tolerant variety with pure white, crisp,

Raphanus sativus var. *longipinnatus*

sweet-tasting, carrot-shaped roots, to
6 in (15 cm) long; 'Scarlet White-
Tipped', bright scarlet red spherical
roots, white crisp flesh. Zones 6–9.

RAPHIA
Raphia is a genus of about 30 species
of tall tropical palms, often with large
sturdy trunks. This genus is a member
of the family Arecaceae. Some species
have short underground stems and
appear to be stemless. Erect or,
more usually, arching pinnate fronds
radiate in terminal heads or tufts. *R.
farinifera* has the world's largest
fronds, to 70 ft (21 m) or more long,
and these are the source of raffia.
Large panicles of 3-petalled flowers
are borne either between the fronds
or just beneath the base of the crown
and are followed by 1-seeded ovoid
fruit covered with scales.
CULTIVATION: These palms are not
frost hardy but will grow in most fertile soils where organic matter and
moisture are sufficient, even tolerating
boggy conditions. They prefer partial
shade, especially when young. Cut off
old fronds close to the stem when
they have become dead and dry.
Propagate from seed in spring.

R

Ratibida columnifera, in the wild, Creel, Chihuahua, Mexico

Rauvolfia serpentina

Raphia australis

KOSI PALM, SOUTHERN RAPHIA

☀ ✝ ↔ 15–30 ft (4.5–9 m)
↑ 25–30 ft (8–9 m)

Fast-growing, spectacular, solitary palm with erect roots that absorb oxygen. Forms loose groups in fresh-water swamps of Mozambique and northeastern South Africa. Stiffly upright, bluish green leaves, up to 60 ft (18 m) long; leaflets with spiny edges, bright orange to red stalks and midribs. In 25 to 35 years one huge terminal head is produced, up to 10 ft (3 m) long, of brownish flowers, followed by shiny brown, scaly, oval-

shaped fruit, about 2 in (5 cm) long, then the plant dies. Leaves are used for construction and for raffia fiber. Zones 10–12.

RATIBIDA

CONEFLOWER

This genus in the daisy (Asteraceae) family contains 5 biennial or perennial species that are found throughout North America, from Ontario, Canada, through to New York, Minnesota, South Dakota, Nebraska, south to Georgia and Texas, USA. These plants are stiff and erect, with deeply cut leaves covered with rigid hairs. Flower-heads are similar to those of *Rudbeckia* species but have fewer ray florets and a round or cylindrical central disc, unlike the flat disc of the *Rudbeckia* flowerheads. The crushed seed heads have an aromatic anise scent. The genus was named by wanderer-botanist Constantine Rafinesque-Schmaltz (1773–1840), who often assigned unexplained names to plants.
CULTIVATION: Use in casual settings, in native flower gardens, or cottage

Rauvolfia caffra

gardens. Grow in full sun in a very well-drained soil. Propagate from seed, which will self-sow.

Ratibida columnifera

LONG-HEAD CONEFLOWER, MEXICAN HAT, PRAIRIE CONEFLOWER

☀ ❋ ↔ 18 in (45 cm) ↑ 24 in (60 cm)
Perennial found from North America to Mexico. Hairy gray-green leaves. Flowers bright yellow or brown-purple, in drooping rays, in summer to autumn. Floral disc is cylindrical or columnar, and brown. Zones 4–9.

Ratibida pinnata

GRAY-HEAD CONEFLOWER, PRAIRIE CONE-FLOWER, YELLOW CONEFLOWER

☀ ❋ ↔ 12–18 in (30–45 cm)
↑ 48 in (120 cm)

A perennial from eastern North America. Leaves lance-shaped, blue-green and toothed. Yellow ray flowers, rounded brown disc, from mid-summer to early autumn. Zones 3–8.

RAUVOLFIA

This genus contains over 60 species of small trees and shrubs from the tropics of Africa, Asia, and the Americas, and belongs to the dogbane family (Apocynaceae). They all have a milky sap, large glossy leaves arranged opposite or in distinct whorls of 3 to 5, and small waxy flowers. These are held terminally in stalked clusters, are either white or greenish and are followed by 1 or 2 rounded drupes. Some plants are deciduous in a dry habitat. Parts of some species, including the bark, sap, and roots, have been used medicinally.
CULTIVATION: They prefer a moist well-drained soil in full sun. Give them shelter from wind, and water regularly during the growing season. Propagate from seed or cuttings.

Rauvolfia caffra

QUININE TREE

☀ ❁ ↔ 10–15 ft (3–4.5 m)
↑ 15–20 ft (4.5–6 m)

Fast-growing, easily cultivated tree, native to South Africa. Leaves to about 12 in (30 cm) long; striking, prominent, white midrib. Abundant, showy, dense heads of scented white flowers, in winter–spring. Although some plant parts are poisonous, the bark and roots are used medicinally. Zones 9–11.

Rauvolfia serpentina

INDIAN SNAKEROOT

☀ ✝ ↔ 15 in (38 cm) ↑ 24 in (60 cm)
Occurs naturally from eastern India to Thailand, the Malay Peninsula, and Indonesia. Shrub with simple smooth-edged leaves. Dense terminal heads of small white or pinkish flowers. Fruits purple-black drupes. Most important species of *Rauvolfia* medicinally, the source of the drug alkaloid reserpine. Zones 11–12.

RAVENALA

This genus belonging to the banana (Musaceae) family consists of a single species from Madagascar, a clump-forming tree with trunks resembling those of palm trees. The top third of the stem is clothed in old leaf bases. The new leaves resemble those of the banana; when wind-blown they become split and frayed. The spathes are boat-shaped and enclose small flowers, which are followed by edible seeds. Originally from rainforest areas, this species is grown as an ornamental in many tropical and subtropical regions of the world, being admired for its striking form, foliage, and spathes. The common name traveler's tree comes from the ability of the flower bracts and leaf sheaths to hold

Raphia australis

R

Ravenala madagascariensis

water, which is believed to provide travelers with an emergency supply. CULTIVATION: Grow in moist, fertile, well-drained soil in a sunny position with protection from frosts and high winds. Propagate from seed or from rooted suckers.

Ravenala madagascariensis

TRAVELER'S PALM, TRAVELER'S TREE

☼ ⚘ ↔ 7–15 ft (2–4.5 m) ↕ 30 ft (9 m)

From Madagascar. Palm-like tree with many trunks, and a fan-shaped crown. Bright green paddle-shaped leaves, in 2 opposite rows, long leaf stalks. Clusters of white flowers, in summer. Fruit capsules contain edible seeds. Zones 11–12.

REBUTIA

syns *Aylostera, Weingartia*

These 40 evergreen, low-growing, simple or clustering cacti from the family Cactaceae are native to the mountains of Bolivia and northwestern Argentina. The small stems, 4 in (10 cm) in diameter or less, are lightly ribbed or with a warty surface, and have weak spines, with the radial and central spines often similar. Funnel-shaped flowers, which emerge from the lower part of the stem, are mostly yellow to red or white, with a sometimes bristly or scaly, slender, curved corolla, opening in daylight. The genus is named after P. Rebut, a nineteenth-century French cactus dealer. CULTIVATION: *Rebutia* species prefer a gritty, well-drained, slightly acidic soil in an open sunny position. Propagate from seed less than 12 months old or by dividing offsets.

Rebutia aureiflora

syn. *Mediolobivia aureiflora*

☼ ⚘ ↔ 3–8 in (8–20 cm) ↕ 2 in (5 cm)

A clustering globular cactus from northwestern Argentina. Warty stems, often tinged with red, 3 to 4 central spines, smaller radial spines. Broadly funnel-shaped yellow flowers, usually with a white throat and a paler tube, are borne in summer. *R. a.* var. *rubelliflora*, over 10 radial spines, 1 darker central spine, and deep orange flowers. Zones 9–12.

Rebutia fiebrigii ★

syns *Aylostera fiebrigii, Rebutia muscula*

☼ ⚘ ↔ ¾–3 in (18–80 mm) ↕ 1¼–2 in (3–5 cm)

Variable clumping cactus, native to Bolivia and northwestern Argentina. Stems to 2 in (5 cm) tall, depressed at the top, with a warty surface; brown-tipped central spines, white bristly radial spines. Funnel-shaped orange to red flowers, with a slender upcurved tube, are produced in summer. Zones 9–12.

Rebutia flavistyla

☼/◑ ⚘ ↔ 2–6 in (5–15 cm) ↕ 2–4 in (5–10 cm)

Bolivian species. Usually solitary globular stem studded with tubercles bearing very fine white spines. Long-tubed vivid orange flowers, to 3 in (8 cm) wide, from spring. Zones 10–12.

Rebutia heliosa ★

☼ ⚘ ↔ ½–4 in (12–100 mm) ↕ ¾–2 in (18–50 mm)

Clustering cactus, simple initially, a native of Bolivia. Gray-green stem, spiralled with very small tubercles, and with white spines. Dark pink to orange-pink funnel-shaped flowers, inner petals with light purple mid-stripe, in summer. Zones 9–12.

Rebutia marsoneri

syn. *Rebutia krainziana*

☼ ⚘ ↔ 1¾–8 in (4–20 cm) ↕ 1¼–4 in (3–10 cm)

Clumping cactus, native to northern Argentina. Pale green stem, warty surface, nest-shaped clusters of reddish brown spines. Funnel-shaped yellow to orange-yellow or red flowers, in summer. Zones 9–12.

Rebutia neocumingii

syn. *Weingartia neocumingii*

☼ ⚘ ↔ 3–4 in (8–10 cm) ↕ 4–8 in (10–20 cm)

Usually solitary cactus, a native of Bolivia. Stems grow up to 4 in (10 cm) wide, and 8 in (20 cm) tall, with 16 to 18 spiraling ribs of tubercles; 2 to 8 central spines, 5 to 24 radial spines, yellowish with brown tips. Flowers are day-blooming, funnel-shaped, yellow to orange in color, with a yellow throat, to 1 in (25 mm) long, borne near the tip of the stem in summer. Zones 9–10.

Rebutia perplexa

☼ ⚘ ↔ 1–3 in (25–80 mm) ↕ ½–1 in (12–25 mm)

This normally clumping cactus is indigenous to Bolivia. Stems with flattened spherical heads. Tall, funnel-shaped, lilac-pink flowers, up to 1½ in (35 mm) across. Zones 9–12.

Rebutia spegazziniana

syns *Aylostera spegazziniana, Rebutia tarvitaensis*

☼ ⚘ ↔ 2–6 in (5–15 cm) ↕ 2–3 in (5–8 cm)

Spherical cactus from northwestern Argentina. Stems light to dark green, ribs with warty surface. Funnel-shaped, dark red flowers, summer. Zones 9–12.

Rebutia spinosissima

syns *Aylostera spinosissima, Rebutia hoffmannii*

☼ ⚘ ↔ 1¼–8 in (3–20 cm) ↕ 1¼–2½ in (3–6 cm)

Clustering cactus from northern Argentina. Forms flat clumps of light green stems, slightly depressed at top; many bristly white spines, brown-tipped central spines. Funnel-shaped apricot to orange flowers open from pink buds at base of stem, in spring. Small spherical fruit. Zones 9–12.

Rebutia perplexa

Rebutia marsoneri

Rebutia neocumingi

Rebutia fiebrigii

Rebutia spinosissima

Rebutia flavistyla

REEVESIA

This is a small genus of 3 or 4 species of evergreen trees and shrubs in the cacao (Sterculiaceae) family, native to the Himalayas and Southeast Asia, and closely allied to *Sterculia*. Leaves are spirally arranged, simple with smooth margins. Small white flowers are numerous, borne in crowded panicles terminating the branchlets. Fruit is a capsule of up to 5 compartments, each containing 1 to 2 seeds. *Reevesia* species are suitable only for mild climates.

CULTIVATION: These plants require a deep, preferably lime-free soil and a position in sun or part-shade. Propagate from seed or cuttings.

Reevesia thyrsoidea

☼ ❄ ↔ 15 ft (4.5 m) ↑ 40 ft (12 m)
Native to southeastern China. Tall evergreen shrub or small tree. Oval to lance-shaped leaves, glossy green, to 10 in (25 cm) long. Closely packed clusters of cream to white fragrant flowers, about 2–3 in (5–8 cm) across, in summer. Zones 7–10.

REHDERODENDRON

This is a small genus of 9 species of deciduous shrubs and small trees in the storax (Styracaceae) family, native to the woods of China and

Reevesia thyrsoidea, fruit

Rehderodendron macrocarpum

Rehmannia elata

northern parts of Vietnam. Only *R. macrocarpum* is in cultivation, being valued for its masses of delightfully fragrant, drooping, white bells in spring. The flowers are followed by large winged seeds and richly colored leaves in autumn.

CULTIVATION: These plants grow well in deep humus-rich soil that doesn't dry out, in a sheltered site in amongst other trees or facing into the morning sun. Propagation is from seed, which can be quite slow to germinate, or from half-hardened cuttings in summer with bottom heat.

Rehderodendron macrocarpum

☼ ❄ ↔ 15–17 ft (4.5–5 m)
↑ 25–35 ft (8–10 m)
From mountains of western China. Small tree with flat layers of branches. Leaves up to 6 in (15 cm) long, color well before they shed. White, scented, bell-shaped flowers, to 2½ in (6 cm) across, held in drooping clusters, in spring. Ridged seed pods. Zones 8–10.

REHMANNIA

CHINESE FOXGLOVE

This genus of up to 9 species of herbaceous perennials in the foxglove (Scrophulariaceae) family is native to the woods and hills of China. They are grown for their large exotic-

Rehmannia angulata 'Beverley Bells'

looking flowers which are produced over a prolonged period. These blooms are usually a magenta-pink with patterns of brown and yellow in the throat. The foliage is heavily serrated and hairy to sticky.

CULTIVATION: Grow these perennials in moisture-retentive but not wet, humus-rich soil in a spot that receives lots of light but not the very hottest sun. Propagate from seed, or from stem cuttings early in the growth cycle, or more usually by division.

Rehmannia angulata

☼ ❄ ↔ 12–16 in (30–40 cm)
↑ 8–12 in (20–30 cm)
From central China; similar to *R. glutinosa*. Stemless leaves. Trumpet-flowers, 2½ in (6 cm) long, magenta, in spring–early summer. Very rarely grown in true form; the name is often incorrectly used for *R. elata* in horticulture. 'Beverley Bells', pink flowers. Zones 8–10.

Rehmannia elata

syn. *Rehmannia angulata* of gardens
CHINESE FOXGLOVE
☼ ❄ ↔ 20–32 in (50–80 cm)
↑ 40–60 in (100–150 cm)
Vigorous suckering perennial from China. Lobed hairy leaves, to 10 in (25 cm) long, in basal foliage. Slightly drooping trumpet-flowers, to 4 in (10 cm) long, heavily spotted in throat, in late spring–summer. Zones 8–10.

Rehmannia glutinosa

☼ ❄ ↔ 12–16 in (30–40 cm)
↑ 8–12 in (20–30 cm)
A native of northern China. Strongly suckering habit. Scalloped basal

Reineckea carnea

Rehmannia angulata

leaves, to 4 in (10 cm) long. Trumpet-flowers, 2 in (5 cm) long, classic magenta color, darker markings inside trumpet, yellow-brown lips, in spring. Zones 8–10.

REINECKEA

This genus, which is a member of the lily-of-the-valley (Convallariaceae) family, contains 1 species of grassy-leafed rhizomatous perennial native to China and Japan. Its prostrate stems form clumps of narrow glossy foliage. Flowering stems, to 6 in (15 cm) tall, bear small fragrant flowers in varying shades of pink.

CULTIVATION: This perennial will do well in half-sun, in a rich moisture-retentive but well-drained soil. Where summers are cool, flowering may be limited. Propagate from seed or by division.

Reineckea carnea

☼ ❄ ↔ 6 in (15 cm) ↑ 8 in (20 cm)
Clump-forming perennial, native to China and Japan. Narrow arching leaves. Individual pink flowers, ¼ in (6 mm) wide, spreading starry petals, in late spring. Small scarlet berries. Zones 7–10.

REINWARDTIA

This small genus of subshrubs with softwooded stems in the flax family (Linaceae) is named after Professor Kaspar Reinwardt, one-time director of the Leiden Botanic Gardens in the Netherlands. They are evergreen only in warm climates, with simple alternate leaves and slender, yellow, tubular flowers with 5 spreading petals.

CULTIVATION: They are best grown in a light fibrous soil with free drainage, in a warm position sheltered from wind. Pruning should be severe, almost to half-height, in late winter in order to encourage suckering from the base; this should be followed by a good mulching and deep watering. Propagate from soft-tip cuttings, which may be taken from the young growths in early spring.

Reinwardtia indica
YELLOW FLAX BUSH
☼ ❀ ↔ 24 in (60 cm) ↑ 36 in (90 cm)
From northern India, mostly in the foothills of the Himalayas. Soft erect stems sucker to form a large clump. Smooth soft-textured leaves, elliptic to oval, bright green above, duller underneath. Bright butter yellow flowers, in late autumn–spring. Zones 9–11.

× RENANTANDA
This is an artificial monopodial Orchidaceae family genus between *Renanthera* and *Vanda*. These epiphytic orchids are erect-growing, with strap-like channeled leaves in 2 ranks. Larger plants may branch at the base and have numerous, very thick, cord-like roots. The inflorescences appear from the stem at the base of the leaf. The hybrids are not as tall as many of the *Renanthera* species, as the *Vanda* influence has reduced the plant size while increasing the floral size and imparting wider petals to the bloom.
CULTIVATION: These vandaceous epiphytes require warm to hot conditions with bright light, and are suited to tropical gardens and greenhouses in climates away from the tropics. They are best grown in pots using a coarse grade of pine bark as the potting medium. The thick roots will often venture outside the confines of the pot or basket, and this culture should be encouraged, as the roots require unimpeded air circulation and must dry out quickly after watering. In the tropics they bloom throughout the

Renanthera, Hybrid, Tan Keong Choon

year, with a peak during the summer months. Propagate from cuttings with at least 3 roots attached.

× Renantanda Tuanku Bainun
☼ ✈ ↔ 8–32 in (20–80 cm) ↑ 8–48 in (20–120 cm)
This hybrid between *Vanda* Keeree's Delight and *Renanthera storiei* bears shapely red blooms, 3 in (8 cm) tall, with darker tessellation throughout the flower. Zones 11–12.

RENANTHERA
FIRE ORCHID
This is a robust monopodial genus in the family Orchidaceae, with some 15 species found throughout Malaysia, Indonesia, the Philippines, and New Guinea. Here these orchids grow in hot, humid, lowland conditions. Most species bear very bright long-lasting flowers on branched inflorescences. There have been a number of hybrids made both within the genus and with related genera, particularly to exploit the bright red colors and improve the overall shape of the bloom.
CULTIVATION: These tall-growing vandaceous epiphytes require warm to hot conditions with strong light, and are suited to tropical gardens and large greenhouses in climates away from the tropics. Because of their rambling habit they can be difficult

× *Renantanda* Tuanku Bainun

Renanthera, Hybrid, Tom Thumb

to confine to pots, and are best grown in wooden baskets or on large slabs of cork. In the tropics they bloom throughout the year, with a peak during summer. In this habitat they can be tied to the trunks of trees and grown in full sun. They will not withstand temperatures below 54°F (12°C). Propagate from cuttings with at least 3 roots attached.

Renanthera coccinea
☼ ✈ ↔ 8–32 in (20–80 cm) ↑ 8–48 in (20–120 cm)
Widespread and variable species from Southeast Asia. Numerous 2 in (5 cm) wide blooms range from dark orange to deep red, with darker spotting peppered over the flower. Zones 11–12.

Renanthera Hybrids
☼ ✈ ↔ 8–36 in (20–90 cm) ↑ 1–8 ft (0.3–2.4 m)
These vandaceous hybrids bloom in the warmer months of the year, or throughout the year in the tropics. They are generally hardier than the species. **Monaseng**, bright orange blooms, heavily overlaid with red, it has *Renanthera imschootiana*, *R. monachica,* and *R. storiei* in its pedigree; **Tan Keong Choon**, a striking red hybrid bred from *R. matutina*, *R. philippinensis*, and *R. storiei*; **Tom Thumb**, a red-flowered primary hybrid between *R. monachica* and *R. imschootiana*. Zones 11–12.

Renanthera, Hybrid, Monaseng

RENEALMIA
Genus of about 70 aromatic perennial herbs, growing from rhizomes. Native to tropical Central and South America and Africa, the genus is a member of the ginger (Zingiberaceae) family. Clumps of strap-like leaves with a ginger fragrance grow in 2 ranks, forming a reed-like stem. Flowers have bracts and are carried in panicles or cymes at the ends of leafy stems or on their own stalks. Corollas may be fused at the base or an upright tube, with a 3-lobed lip. Fruit is a capsule.
CULTIVATION: Plant them in frost-free spots in full sun or part-shade in moist soil, and give them regular watering. Can be grown as a container plant in cooler climates. Propagate from seed or by division of rhizomes.

Renealmia alpinia
syns *Amomum alpinia, Renealmia exaltata*
MASUSA
☼ ❀ ↔ 3–6 ft (0.9–1.8 m) ↑ 5–7 ft (1.5–2 m)
Widespread through tropical America. A robust perennial, growing from a creeping rhizome. Leaves about 36 in (90 cm) long. Flowers surrounded with white, pink, or red bracts. Young red capsular fruits mature to blackish violet, and contain brownish seeds surrounded by orange-yellow fibers and a fatty substance known as arrilles, used as a yellow food coloring and for flavoring rice. Zones 10–12.

Reinwardtia indica

Renealmia alpinia

R

Retama monosperma

Restrepia guttulata

RESEDA

MIGNONETTE

This genus of some 50 to 60 species of annuals and perennials gives its name to the mignonette (Resedaceae) family. Although mainly from the Mediterranean area, some species come from India, Asia, and East Africa. They have small leaves that can be smooth-edged or lobed to toothed, and bear tiny flowers in upright spikes that are rarely showy, usually green or white, and in some species sweetly fragrant. All are good bee-attractant plants. *R. odorata* is cultivated for an essential oil used in the perfume industry; *R. luteola* produces a yellow dye used since Neolithic times, and popular in Roman times for dying wedding garments. CULTIVATION: These plants will all grow well in a sunny site in fertile, well-drained, and preferably alkaline soil. Propagate from seed planted in position and thin out as seedlings get larger.

Reseda lutea

YELLOW MIGNONETTE

☼ ❁ ↔ 20–27 in (50–70 cm)
↑ 20–27 in (50–70 cm)

Annual herb from the Mediterranean to Iran. Plants have deep roots, and many erect and very fast-growing stems. Leaves with simple blades or 1 to 3 deep lobes, with or without stalks. Flowers with 4 to 8 white-edged sepals, 4 to 8 yellow petals, each with 2 to 3 lobes, in summer. Fruit is an erect 3-parted capsule containing smooth seed. Zones 7–9.

Reseda luteola

☼ ❁ ↔ 8–12 in (20–30 cm)
↑ 36–48 in (90–120 cm)

An upright annual or short-lived perennial from Europe and central Asia. Leaves smooth-edged, to 1 in (25 mm) long. Sometimes branched, upright, 24 in (60 cm) tall flower spikes, tiny, yellow-green, unscented flowers, in summer. Zones 6–10.

Reseda odorata

BASTARD ROCKET, MIGNONETTE, SWEET RESEDA

☼ ❁ ↔ 7–8 in (18–20 cm)
↑ 12–24 in (30–60 cm)

A well-known annual from the Mediterranean region. Smooth-edged leaves, occasionally 3-lobed. Loose clusters of highly scented, tiny, greenish white flowers, tuft of soft orange stamens, in early summer. Zones 6–10.

RESTREPIA

COCKROACH ORCHID

This is an increasingly popular genus of miniature sympodial orchids in the family Orchidaceae. They are single-leafed and single-flowered epiphytes from Central and South America that are easily recognized, even out of flower. Related to *Pleurothallis* and *Masdevallia*, they have comparatively large flowers, to 3 in (8 cm) tall, which are fairly uniform in shape, in a range of bright and subtle colors. The lateral sepals are invariably fused together to form a structure known as a synsepal, which is the most prominent feature of a *Restrepia* flower. It is the length and color pattern of the synsepal that are important features for identification. The common name refers to the flowers' resemblance to some types of cockroach.
CULTIVATION: They are tolerant of a wide temperature range, as long as they are kept moist, in a humid environment, with ample air circulation. They enjoy being copiously watered throughout the year. Sphagnum moss is the preferred medium for potted plants, while larger specimens can be grown on slabs or plaques of cork or tree-fern. They benefit from bright light, but will not take direct sun. When the lighting levels are correct, the leaves will often take on a slight purplish tone. *Restrepia* are one of the few genera of orchids that can be propagated from leaf-cuttings as well as by division.

Restrepia guttulata

☀ ❁ ↔ 3–8 in (8–20 cm)
↑ 3–6 in (8–15 cm)

This species occurs from Venezuela to Peru. It has 2 in (5 cm) wide blooms that range in color from orange to red and pink to deep purple, while its synsepal is strikingly peppered with bold dark reddish purple blotches. Zones 9–11.

RETAMA

Once included among other broom genera such as *Genista*, the 4 shrubby brooms that make up this genus, which is a member of the pea-flower subfamily of the legume (Fabaceae) family, are found in the Mediterranean region and the Canary Islands. While they are usually leafless when mature, as the chlorophyll-bearing green stems perform the functions of foliage, young plants often carry small linear leaves which sometimes also appear on adult plants in spring. Often rather untidy and wiry-stemmed, these shrubs are at their best in spring when smothered with flowers. These may be white or yellow, sometimes with purplish markings, and are often scented. The flowers are followed by conspicuous, somewhat inflated, sometimes downy seed pods.
CULTIVATION: Best grown in full sun, and drought tolerant once established, these tough shrubs prefer a reasonably fertile, light, well-drained soil. They can be trimmed after flowering, but could never be called neat. Propagate from seed, which should be soaked before sowing, or from summer cuttings.

Retama monosperma

syn. *Genista monosperma*

SILVER BROOM

☼ ❁ ↔ 10 ft (3 m) ↑ 10 ft (3 m)

A native of Spain and northern Africa. An upright, near-leafless plant with slender arching branches, silvery and downy when young, becoming grayish green as the plant matures. Short racemes of small, white, fragrant pea-flowers, backed by purplish calyces, in spring. Zones 9–11.

RHAMNUS

There are more than 125 species within this genus in the buckthorn (Rhamnaceae) family. Mostly prickly evergreen or deciduous shrubs or trees, they are found throughout the Northern Hemisphere, as well as Brazil, eastern Africa, and South Africa, in woodland and heathland areas. The simple dark green leaves can be smooth-edged or toothed. The flowers are insignificant; some are fragrant. Green, blue-green, and yellow dyes are made from some species, while others are used medicinally, or wood is used commercially for turning. Cultivated for ornamental foliage and decorative berries.

Reseda lutea

Reseda odorata

Rhamnus saxatilis

Rhamnus imeretina

CULTIVATION: Depending on the species, these shrubs or trees prefer moist to very dry conditions in full sun or part-shade, in moderately fertile soil. Some species tolerate alkaline soil and coastal sites. Propagate by sowing seed in autumn, as soon as it is ripe, giving protection from winter frosts; or from softwood cuttings of deciduous species in early summer. Half-hardened cuttings can be taken from evergreen species in summer and layering can be done in autumn or spring.

Rhamnus alaternus
ITALIAN BUCKTHORN

☀ ❄ ↔ 12 ft (3.5 m) ↑ 15 ft (4.5 m)

An evergreen shrub, native to the Mediterranean and Caucasus regions. Leathery leaves are dark green and shiny. Small yellow-green flowers, in late spring–early summer. Fruit ripens to black, in late summer. Tolerates dry soil conditions, pollution, and salt-laden air. '**Argenteovariegata**' (syn. 'Variegata'), slightly less hardy than the species, leaves with marbled grayish green center and prominent white leaf edges. Zones 7–10.

Rhamnus californica
COFFEEBERRY

☀ ❄ ↔ 10 ft (3 m) ↑ 12 ft (3.5 m)

Evergreen to semi-evergreen upright shrub from western USA. Red new growth, shiny green leaves. Clusters of pale greenish yellow flowers, in late spring–early summer. Round red berries, ripen to black. Zones 7–10.

Rhamnus cathartica
BUCKTHORN, COMMON BUCKTHORN

☀ ❄ ↔ 15 ft (4.5 m) ↑ 20 ft (6 m)

From temperate Asia, Europe, and Africa. A deciduous thorny thicket-forming shrub, rarely a small tree. Green leaves elliptic to oval, finely toothed edges, turn yellow in autumn. Yellow-green flowers in late spring to early summer. Red fruit ripens to black. Zones 3–9.

Rhamnus crocea
REDBERRY

☀ ❄ ↔ 7 ft (2 m) ↑ 6 ft (1.8 m)

Native to Mexico and southwestern USA. Evergreen spreading shrub with thorny twigs. Leaves are glossy, egg-shaped to elliptic, with slightly toothed edges. Small flower clusters are followed by red fruit. Zones 8–10.

Rhamnus dahurica
DAHURSK BUCKTHORN

☀ ❄ ↔ 10 ft (3 m) ↑ 20 ft (6 m)

Found in temperate East Asia, including Japan. Large deciduous shrub or

Rhamnus californica

small tree. Heavy spiny twigs with leathery, 2–4 in (5–10 cm) long, gray-green leaves. Flowers greenish cream, in late spring. Drupes red. Zones 5–9.

Rhamnus frangula
ALDER BUCKTHORN

☀ ❄ ↔ 15 ft (4.5 m) ↑ 15 ft (4.5 m)

Deciduous shrub from North Africa, Europe, and parts of Russia. Shiny, dark green, oval leaves, paler beneath, turn red in autumn. Axillary clusters of small, greenish, hermaphroditic flowers, in spring to summer. Fruit ripens from red to black. Zones 3–9.

Rhamnus imeretina

☀ ❄ ↔ 15 ft (4.5 m) ↑ 10 ft (3 m)

Native to the Black Sea region. A deciduous spreading shrub. Oval to oblong leaves, prominent veins, dull green above, felty lighter undersides, turn dark brownish purple in autumn. Axillary clusters of unisexual greenish flowers, in summer. Fruit ripens to black. Zones 6–9.

Rhamnus prinoides
SOUTH AFRICAN DOGWOOD

☀ ❄ ↔ 15 ft (4.5 m) ↑ 25 ft (8 m)

From the mountains of eastern South Africa and tropical Africa. Tall, bushy, evergreen shrub or small tree. Leaves leathery, glossy deep green above, paler olive green beneath. Cream flowers, in spring–early summer. Red berries ripen to blackish. Zones 9–11.

Rhamnus crocea

Rhamnus saxatilis

☀ ❄ ↔ 8 ft (2.4 m) ↑ 6–8 ft (1.8–2.4 m)

From southern and central Europe. Deciduous shrub, very twiggy, sideshoots often tipped with spines. Toothed lance-shaped leaves, seldom over 2 in (5 cm) long. Flowers cream to pale green, in spring. Drupes red, ripening to black. Zones 6–9.

RHAPHIOLEPIS

There are up to 10 species of evergreen shrubs in this genus of the rose (Rosaceae) family, allied to *Photinia*. Originating in East and Southeast Asia, these plants do not bear spines or thorns; they have leathery deep green leaves and clusters of white or pink flowers in spring, often blooming again in autumn. Flowers are followed by blue-black berries highly attractive to some birds, which can distribute the seeds.
CULTIVATION: Considered tough low-maintenance plants that are suitable for seaside planting, these shrubs can withstand quite hard pruning, which makes them ideal for hedges. Plant them in full sun in reasonable soil topped up with an organic mulch into which branches can be layered to produce further plants. The soil should be forked over as little as possible as the plants resent root disturbance. In addition to layering, the plants can be propagated from cuttings or seed.

Rhamnus prinoides

Rhamnus dahurica

R

Rhaphiolepis × delacourii

HYBRID INDIAN HAWTHORN

☼ ❄ ↔ 8 ft (2.4 m) ↕ 6 ft (1.8 m)

This name is applied to a number of plants intermediate in character between *R. indica* and *R. umbellata*. The first were deliberate crosses made by a M. Delacour at Cannes shortly before 1900. Cultivars from these crosses include: '**Spring Song**', light pink flowers held for a long time; '**Spring Time**', a low spreading plant with pink-flushed new growth, clear pink semi-double flowers; and '**White Enchantress**', a dwarf form with small white flowers. Zones 8–11.

Rhaphiolepis indica

INDIAN HAWTHORN

☼ ❄ ↔ 8 ft (2.4 m) ↕ 8 ft (2.4 m)

From southern China. Leathery leaves serrated, narrow, pointed, dark green above, olive green beneath. Pinkish brown new growths. Pink-tinted white flowers in clusters, at ends of branches, in spring. Invasive in warm-temperate climates. '**Ballerina**', pink flowers, reddish autumn foliage; Springtime/ '**Monme**', small pink flowers, bronzy new growth. Zones 8–11.

Rhaphiolepis umbellata

☼ ❄ ↔ 7 ft (2 m) ↕ 6 ft (1.8 m)

Dense mound-like shrub from coastal areas of southern Japan and Korea. Broad, thick, grayish green leaves, rounded tip, recurved edges. Bunches

Rhaphiolepis indica

of white perfumed flowers, in spring to early summer, spasmodically into winter in warmer areas. Blue-black berries. '**Minor**' ★, dwarf form with smaller leaves and flowers. Zones 8–11.

RHAPIS

This genus in the family Arecaceae consists of 12 species of small multi-stemmed palms found in higher rainfall areas of subtropical and tropical regions of southern China and across Southeast Asia. They have a clumping habit, with bamboo-like stems and fan-shaped fronds that are deeply divided into finger-like segments. Rhapis palms are mostly dioecious, so both male and female plants are needed for seed production. Small, bowl-shaped, creamy yellow flowers are produced in panicles. The fruit is berry-like. Highly valued in horticulture, most species are long-lived landscape specimens in the garden; they are also used as a screen, or as tub or indoor plant.
CULTIVATION: Most members of the genus are fairly adaptable, tolerating full sun to semi-shade and bright positions indoors. In full sun, some bleaching of the leaves may occur. Grow in fertile well-drained soil protected from strong winds and frost. Humid conditions favor growth. Propagate from seed, which can be slow, or by division.

Rhapis excelsa

LADY PALM, RHAPIS PALM

☼ ❄ ↔ 8 ft (2.4 m) ↕ 15 ft (4.5 m)

Native to southern China, one of the most popular species in the genus. Multi-stemmed fan palm. Slender stems covered in brown interwoven fibers. Light green fronds, 5 to 8 stiff segments with blunt tips. Bowl-shaped cream flowers, in summer. Excellent tub plant. '**Variegata**', leaves with a white stripe. Zones 10–12.

Rhapis excelsa

Rhapis humilis

SLENDER LADY PALM

☼ ❄ ↔ 10 ft (3 m) ↕ 12 ft (3.5 m)

A native of southern China. Forms a spreading clump; numerous slender stems covered in interwoven brown fibers. Thin dark green fronds divided into many drooping segments with pointed tips. Propagate by division. Excellent indoor plant. Zones 10–12.

RHEUM

RHUBARB

This genus of 50 robust perennials includes several ornamental foliage plants as well as the popular edible rhubarb. *Rheum* belongs to the knotweed (Polygonaceae) family and species are native to a wide area of Asia. Their large leaves, which are often wavy-edged or palmate, are borne on stout stems and form basal clumps. The small greenish white or red tinged flowers are wind-pollinated and borne in large panicles on strong upright stems.
CULTIVATION: Ornamental species of *Rheum* make excellent feature plants with their architectural foliage and stately flowering spikes. They will do best when grown in sun or part-shade

Rhapis humilis

in a rich, deep, moisture-retentive but well-drained soil. Propagate from seed or by division. Edible rhubarb should be planted at a 30–36 in (75–90 cm) spacing in a deeply cultivated soil with plenty of compost added. The plants require plenty of moisture but should be well-drained. Rhubarb cultivars are propagated by division of the crown.

Rheum australe

syn. *Rheum emodi*

HIMALAYAN RHUBARB, RED-VEINED PIE PLANT

☼/☀ ❄ ↔ 5 ft (1.5 m) ↕ 5 ft (1.5 m)

From the Himalayas. Leaves rounded or broadly oblong, prominently veined, and with wavy margins. Stout

Rhaphiolepis × delacourii

Rhaphiolepis × delacourii 'Spring Song'

Rhinerrhiza divitiflora

red-tinged flowering stalks, dense clusters of small white to red flowers, in summer. Zones 6–9.

Rheum × *hybridum*

RHUBARB

☼ ❄ ↔ 3–6 ft (0.9–1.8 m) ↕ 3 ft (0.9 m)

Hybrid of unclear origin grown for culinary use in Europe since the 1700s. Stout edible stems, large, wavy-edged, triangular leaves. Cultivars differ in flavor, degree of stem color, and productive season. **'Cherry'**, thick red stems; **'MacDonald'**, brilliant red stems; and **'Victoria'**, thick green stems shaded red near base. Zones 6–10.

Rheum palmatum

☼/☼ ❄ ↔ 5 ft (1.5 m)
↕ 5–8 ft (1.5–2.4 m)

Majestic plant native to northwestern China. Deeply lobed and toothed leaves, to 40 in (100 cm) wide, purplish red when young. Fluffy panicles of small pink flowers, on tall stems, in summer. *R. p.* var. *tanguticum*, even more robust with very deeply lobed leaves. *R. p.* **'Atrosanguineum'**, cerise flowers, leaves open vivid red; and **'Bowles' Crimson'**, leaves crimson beneath. Zones 6–9.

RHINERRHIZA

This is a genus of only 2 epiphytic orchid species, from the Orchidaceae family and related to *Sarcochilus*, from eastern Australia and lowland parts of New Guinea. The monopodial plants

are relatively large, with durable leathery leaves and a strong root system. They produce long pendent inflorescences of up to 60 flowers that only last for 2 days.

CULTIVATION: These orchids resent having their roots covered, so are best mounted on narrow but long sections of cork or tree-fern, to accommodate the extensive root system. They must be kept in a part-shaded position in a humid environment, with plenty of free circulating air. This is not an easy genus to maintain in cultivation.

Rhinerrhiza divitiflora

RASPY ROOT ORCHID

☼ ⚘ ↔ 3–12 in (8–30 cm)
↕ 3–16 in (8–40 cm)

A distinctive Australian species with flat roots with rough surface. Spidery, yellowish orange, 2½ in (6 cm) wide blooms, covered with fine red spots. Comparatively tiny labellum, white with yellow and red markings. Spring-flowering. Zones 10–11.

RHIPSALIS

This genus is made up of 35 species of epiphytic cacti (family Cactaceae) from tropical America, especially the Caribbean and Brazil. They usually grow as pendulous shrubs with hundreds of intertwining branches, hence the genus name, from the Greek *rhips*, "basketwork." Stems of most species are rounded in cross-section; others are angled, ribbed, winged, even flat.

Rheum palmatum

Most species are spineless, new stems usually arising singly or in clusters at the ends of older stems. Flowers are small, saucer-shaped, mostly white; seed pods are small and spherical.

CULTIVATION: Easily grown in a humus-rich well-drained soil with regular liquid feeding; very sensitive to alkaline soil. Propagate from stem cuttings dried out for a week or two; also grown from seed. Need more water than most terrestrial cacti, but keep dry for 6 to 8 weeks in autumn to induce winter flowering. Often grown in hanging baskets.

Rhipsalis cereuscula

☼/☼ ✿ ↔ 12 in (30 cm) ↕ 24 in (60 cm)

From northeastern and eastern South America. Shrubby, much-branched, pendent cactus with cylindrical stems, 4–12 in (10–30 cm) long, from which shorter stems, 4 -or 5-angled, arise in clusters; areoles with 2 to 4 short bristles. Small white flowers at ends of stems, in spring. Zones 9–12.

Rhipsalis paradoxa ★

☼/☼ ✿ ↔ 3 ft (0.9 m)
↕ 5–15 ft (1.5–4.5 m)

From southern Brazil. Large, freely branching, pendent, producing large clusters of new stems at tips of old ones. Stems short, pale green, 3- or 4-angled; angles discontinuous, in zigzag

links, pairs or whorls of 3 to 8; areoles spineless, woolly. Single white flowers near stem tips, summer. Seed pods white tinged pink. Zones 9–12.

RHIZANTHELLA

UNDERGROUND ORCHID

This is a bizarre saprophytic orchid genus that grows and blooms entirely underground, with the ripe seed capsules barely reaching the soil surface. Part of the family Orchidaceae, there are 2 known species, one occurring in eastern Australia (*Rhizanthella slateri*), the other (*R. gardneri*) endemic to Western Australia. They are generally only found by accident. The heads of small succulent blooms resemble fungi, and it is thought that ants or fungus gnats that co-exist in the leaf litter may pollinate the flowers. They are known to flower in spring and summer.

CULTIVATION: This orchid is rarely seen and its cultivation has never been attempted except in a laboratory.

Rhizanthella slateri

☼ ⚘ ↔ 3–12 in (8–30 cm)
↕ 3–8 in (8–20 cm)

Branched rhizome; mature plants produce a rounded inflorescence of numerous crowded blooms, protected by triangular bracts. Each tiny bloom is fleshy, cream to purplish, from spring–summer. Zones 10–11.

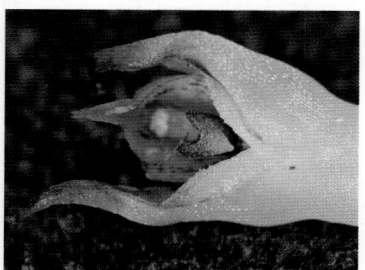

Rhizanthella slateri, individual flower

Rhizanthella slateri, flowerhead

Rhizophora mangle, in the wild, the Everglades, Florida, USA

Rhodanthe floribunda

Rhodanthe manglesii

Rhodanthe chlorocephala

RHIZOPHORA

MANGROVE

This genus gives its name to the family Rhizophoraceae, and contains fewer than 10 species of mangroves found along tropical coastlines around the world. They are trees with the trunk supported by dramatically arching aerial roots that allow them to grow on soft mud in the intertidal zone. Leaves are simple and smooth-edged, arranged in opposite pairs. Flowers, borne in leaf axils, are fleshy and star-like. Fruits each contain a single seed that begins growing while still on the tree, elongating into a long cylinder, which falls and floats in water, continuing to grow when it becomes stranded on mud banks. CULTIVATION: Mangroves thrive in open sunny positions in marshy coastal areas surrounded by brackish or salt water. Propagate from seed.

Rhizophora mangle

AMERICAN MANGROVE, RED MANGROVE
☀ ✈ ↔ 8–30 ft (2.4–9 m)
↕ 15–40 ft (4.5–12 m)

Evergreen tree, native to muddy tidal shores and shoals of southern USA and the West Indies. Thick, round, bushy canopy; dense, tangling, aerial roots that form stilts or trunks. Reddish brown bark. Simple, thick, opposite, shiny, dark green, elliptic, leathery leaves. White to pale yellow 4-petalled flowers, in small clusters, in spring–autumn. Dark rusty brown, egg-shaped berries release floating seedlings, undamaged by salt water, to wash up on sand or mud flats, establishing new populations. Zones 11–12.

RHODANTHE

STRAWFLOWER

This genus in the daisy (Asteraceae) family, one of several in the complex *Helichrysum* group, was extensively revised in the early 1990s and is now considered to be exclusively Australian. The 40 species in the genus are annuals, perennials, and small shrubs with simple, narrow, light green to silver-gray leaves. They are rather sprawling plants grown for their long-lasting show of flowers, which are made colorful by dry, papery, petal-like structures known as phyllaries. Some species have long-stemmed flowerheads that last well when cut. Some are ephemeral plants native to desert regions, remaining in the ground as seeds for many years ready to burst into a carpet of bloom with the arrival of rain. CULTIVATION: Hardiness varies but most are surprisingly tough and are ideal for dry banks or rockeries. Plant in full sun with light, gritty, very free-draining soil. Tolerant of poor soil. Propagate from seed or cuttings. Some will self-layer.

Rhodanthe anthemoides

syn. *Helipterum anthemoides*
☀◐ ❋ ↔ 12–20 in (30–50 cm)
↕ 4–8 in (10–20 cm)

Wiry-stemmed evergreen perennial or subshrub from southeastern Australia. Narrow, pointed, gray-green leaves, less than ½ in (12 mm) long. Clusters of 1 in (25 mm) wide, papery, white, daisy-like flowerheads, from spring to summer. 'Paper Baby', compact habit, red buds open to white flowers; and 'Paper Star', an especially heavy flowerer with a compact habit, superb rockery plant. Zones 8–10.

Rhodanthe chlorocephala

syn. *Helipterum roseum*
☀ ✤ ↔ 8–12 in (20–30 cm)
↕ 12–24 in (30–60 cm)

Annual from southwestern Australia; usually erect or rounded. The narrow gray-green leaves are around 1 in (25 mm) long. Flowerheads 1–2 in (25–50 mm) wide, white to pink ray florets around a conspicuous soft yellow disc, from late spring to early summer; winter-flowering in mild areas. *R. c.* subsp. *rosea*, flowerheads with bright pink ray florets; *R. c.* subsp. *splendida*, white flowerheads, to 2½ in (6 cm) wide, with many ray florets. Zones 9–11.

Rhodanthe floribunda

syn. *Helipterum floribundum*
☀ ✤ ↔ 2–12 in (5–30 cm)
↕ 3–12 in (8–30 cm)

Annual found over much of drier inland Australia. Compact bushy habit with tiny gray-green leaves.

After rain it can form a carpet of white flowerheads, to over 2 in (5 cm) wide. Zones 9–11.

Rhodanthe manglesii

syn. *Helipterum manglesii*
SWAN RIVER EVERLASTING
☀ ❋ ↔ 6–12 in (15–30 cm)
↕ 12–18 in (30–45 cm)

Western Australian annual. Erect stems; pointed oval to narrow heart-shaped, gray-green to blue-green leaves, to 2 in (5 cm). Many white to pink flowerheads, 1¼ in (30 mm) wide, in spring or after rain. 'Sutton's Rose', an attractive cultivar. Zones 8–11.

RHODANTHEMUM

A mainly alpine Eurasian and North African genus of some 15 to 20 species that was established with the revision of *Chrysanthemum* in the 1980s and 90s, and belongs to the daisy (Asteraceae) family. These shrubby perennials have ferny, usually silver-gray foliage, sometimes in whorls or loose rosettes, and develop into dense mounds. In spring and early summer they are covered in wiry-stemmed flowerheads with white ray florets, often pink-tinted, around a yellow disc. In mild areas flowers occur less heavily throughout the year. CULTIVATION: Although generally frost tolerant, few species will withstand prolonged cold, damp winter conditions. They are best grown in an alpine house or dry winter climate. Plant in full sun or half-sun in gritty free-draining soil with a little added humus. Water in summer and feed very lightly. Propagate from seed or from small basal cuttings of non-flowering shoots.

Rhodanthemum catananche

syns *Chrysanthemum catananche*, *Pyrethropsis canatanche*
☀ ❋ ↔ 6–10 in (15–25 cm)
↕ 4–6 in (10–15 cm)

Compact cushion-forming perennial from Morocco. Persistent, silky, greenish gray leaves, finely divided into linear segments. Coppery yellow flowers, in spring. Zones 8–10.

Rhodanthemum catananche

Rhodanthemum hosmariense

Rhodiola kirilowii, fruit

Rhodanthemum gayanum

syns *Chrysanthemum gayanum,*
Pyrethropsis gayana

☀ ❄ ↔ 24–40 in (60–100 cm)
↥ 8–12 in (20–30 cm)

A low-growing perennial subshrub, native to Algeria and Morocco. Forms a dense spreading cushion of lacy, finely divided, dark green, glossy foliage. Abundant, bright pink, daisy-like flowers with yellow to burgundy centers, in winter–spring. Zones 8–10.

Rhodanthemum hosmariense

syns *Chrysanthemum hosmariense,*
Pyrethropsis hosmariensis

MOROCCAN DAISY

☀ ❄ ↔ 12–16 in (30–40 cm)
↥ 4–8 in (10–20 cm)

Spreading, drought-resistant, bushy perennial herb from Morocco's Atlas Mountains. Forms a compact cushion of finely cut silvery gray leaves. Scaly, decorative floral buttons in winter open to white daisy-like flowers with yellow centers, from spring to autumn, with scattered blooms throughout the year. Zones 8–10.

RHODIOLA

A genus of about 50 perennial herbs from the stonecrop (Crassulaceae) family, native to the Himalayas, northwestern China, central Asia, North America, and Europe. They feature a single rosette of stems with stalkless, smooth-edged to toothed, alternate, fleshy leaves growing from thick, fleshy, branching, woody rhizomes. with brown, scaly, radical leaves. Stems bear dense spreading terminal heads of solitary to numerous 4- or 5-petalled flowers with 4 or 5 fleshy sepals, fused at the base, with 8 or 10 stamens and dark purple anthers. The erect fruit contains many brown seeds. The genus was named from the Greek, *rhodon*, a rose, referring to the rose-scented roots. Tibetans consider the root of *Rhodiola*, particularly *R. sacra* and *R. crenulata*, to be a superior, life-prolonging, wisdom-enhancing, sacred herb.

CULTIVATION: They prefer a position in full sun, and are adaptable to most

well-drained soils. Propagate from seed in spring or from softwood cuttings taken from non-flowering branches.

Rhodiola kirilowii

syn. *Sedum kirilowii*

☀ ❄ ↔ 12–36 in (30–90 cm)
↥ 12–36 in (30–90 cm)

Perennial herb from central Asia, northern China, and Mongolia, growing from a thick, branching rhizome with scaly radical leaves. Crowded, small, narrow to sword-shaped leaves, sharply toothed near the tip. Stout erect flowering stem; heads of many flowers, up to ¼ in (6 mm) across, with reddish green sepals and 5 yellowish green or brownish red oval petals, in early summer. Ancient herb, helps to maintain homeostasis in the body by fighting stress and fatigue on a cellular level. Zones 5–7.

Rhodiola rosea

syn. *Sedum roseum*

GOLDEN ROOT, ROSE-ROOT

☀ ❄ ↔ 2–30 in (5–75 cm)
↥ 2–30 in (5–75 cm)

Perennial herb of extremely variable habit, native to dry sandy ground at high altitudes in arctic areas of Europe and Asia. Thick branching rhizome, fragrant when cut. Smooth, oblong, sometimes red-tinged leaves, to 1¾ in (40 mm) long, with rounded base and pointed tip, smooth-edged or irregularly toothed. Rarely more than 1 to 3 flowering stems with heads of 25 to 70 greenish yellow flowers, up to ¼ in (6 mm) in diameter, in early summer. Zones 1–8.

RHODOCHITON

Native to Mexico, this single-species genus is a member of the foxglove (Scrophulariaceae) family. It is a slender, climbing, short-lived, perennial vine with purplish stems, heart-shaped dusky green leaves, and purple-brown flowers. Treat it as an annual in colder climates. The flowers bloom from mid-summer to late autumn. The name *Rhodochiton* is derived from the Greek *rhodon* (red) and *chiton* (tunic or cloak).

CULTIVATION: *Rhodochiton* does best in warm bright locations in rich well-drained soil. Easily raised from seed but can also be propagated from cuttings from vigorous plants.

Rhodochiton atrosanguineus

syn. *Rhodochiton volubilis*

PURPLE BELL VINE

☀ ❀ ↔ 18 in (45 cm) ↥ 15 ft (4.5 m)

From Mexico. Tender perennial vine treated as an annual. Small flowers hang down on a slender stem. A deep purple-red tubular flower emerges from the 4-pointed fuchsia-red calyx in mid-summer. Zones 9–10.

RHODODENDRON

AZALEA, RHODODENDRON

This very diverse genus of 800 or more species of mostly evergreen and some deciduous shrubs is widely distributed across the Northern Hemisphere, with the majority growing in temperate to cool regions. Particular concentrations occur in western China, the Himalayas and northeastern Myanmar, while the so-called "tropical" Vireya rhododendrons grow mostly at higher altitudes throughout tropical southeastern Asia, as far south as the northern tip of Australia, with more than 200 species occurring on the island of New Guinea alone. Deciduous azalea species are scattered across cooler Northern Hemisphere climates, notably in Europe, China, Japan, and North America. Rhododendrons vary in form from tiny, ground-hugging, prostrate and miniature plants adapted to exposed conditions to small trees, often understory species in the forests of mountainous areas. Many species grow at high altitudes of 3,000 ft (900 m) or more and some can grow as epiphytes in the branches of trees or on rock faces. As members of the

heath (Ericaceae) family, they are closely related to heathers (*Erica* and *Calluna* species), *Pieris* and strawberry trees (*Arbutus* species) and have similar growing requirements. Some rhododendrons have solitary flowers but most bear terminal racemes, known as "trusses," of up to 24 or more spectacular blooms, in a wide palette of colors including whites, pinks, reds, yellows, and mauves, excluding only shades of pure blue. Flowers may be a single color but are often multi-colored, with spots, stripes, edging, or a single blotch of a different color or shade in the throat of the flower. With the exception of some Vireya species and hybrids, fragrant rhododendrons are always white or very pale pink. Blooms vary in size and shape but are generally campanulate (bell-shaped), with a broad tube ending in flared lobes, and usually single. Flowers with double petals do occur, particularly among the evergreen azaleas, which may also be "hose-in-hose," when the calyx is enlarged and the same color as the petals.

Most rhododendrons flower from early spring (early season) to early summer (late season), although some bear spot flowers briefly in autumn, and Vireya rhododendrons can flower at various times during the year, often in winter. Deciduous azaleas flower in

Rhodochiton atrosanguineus

R

Rhodiola rosea

Rhododendron arboreum

spring on bare branches, usually just before new leaf growth starts to emerge. The fruit is a many-seeded capsule, normally woody but sometimes soft, and sometimes bearing wings or tail-like appendages designed to aid transportation.

The genus is divided into 2 botanically distinct groups known as lepidotes and elepidotes, and these groups are subdivided further into the various rhododendron types. Plants from one group may not breed with plants from the other, thus limiting the options for hybridizers. The leaves, and sometimes the flowers and other parts, of lepidote rhododendrons are covered with scales, which is thought to aid transpiration. This group includes many of the cool-climate evergreen plants, including the Vireya rhododendrons. The rest of the genus, the elepidote rhododendrons, with no scales on leaf or flower parts, includes the remaining cool-climate evergreen plants and the evergreen and deciduous azaleas, which are normally rather more compact plants with 5 stamens rather than the more usual ten. Azaleas were originally classified as a separate genus but are now regarded as botanically part of the *Rhododendron* genus. Vireya rhododendrons can be grown in just about any climate as long as protection from frost is provided. Many are well suited to growing in hanging baskets and containers. The nectar of some species and some flower parts are poisonous and care should be taken when handling the flowers.
CULTIVATION: Establishing an ideal growing environment before planting is the key to success with rhododendrons. Many of the problems likely to afflict them in the home garden can be minimized by maintaining soil

quality and ensuring adequate ventilation. All prefer acidic soils between pH 4.5 and 6, that is high in organic matter and freely draining. A cool root run is essential and is best achieved by applying a deep mulch of organic material that also helps to reduce moisture loss and control weed growth, while minimizing disturbance of the delicate roots. Many rhododendrons, particularly those with larger leaves, prefer a shaded or semi-shaded aspect. They are ideally suited to planting under deciduous trees, allowing winter sun and summer shade. While most prefer some protection from wind, sun, and frost, many others are tolerant of these conditions and some are well suited to exposed rock gardens.

Evergreen rhododendrons may be propagated by taking tip cuttings of new growth in spring, while deciduous azaleas are best grown from hardwood cuttings taken in winter. Plants may be grown from seed but germination and development is slow, and plants grown from the seed of hybrids are unlikely to be the same as their parents. Layering enables new plants to be created from low-hanging branches pinned to the ground and covered in a moist organic medium such as sphagnum moss. Plants which are difficult to propagate and establish by other means can be grafted onto the roots of stronger plants with more vigorous root systems. Regular pruning of rhododendrons is not necessary other than as required to control size, maintain shape, and to remove any damaged or diseased material, while some species and hybrids actually resent unnecessary pruning. Cultivated rhododendrons are normally more compact and attain only about

half the height of similar plants growing in the wild. The growing habit of all species and hybrids varies widely according to the amount of shade the plant receives.

Rhododendron aberconwayi

☀ ❄ ↔ 4 ft (1.2 m) ↕ 6 ft (1.8 m)
From western China. Freely flowering, upright, evergreen shrub. Thick, smooth, glossy, dark green, elliptic leaves. Delicate, saucer-shaped, pale rose flowers, to 1½ in (35 mm) long, crimson or purple spots, in trusses of 5 to 12 blooms, in late spring–early summer. Zones 7–9.

Rhododendron adenogynum

☀/◐ ❄ ↔ 5–10 ft (1.5–3 m)
↕ 7–15 ft (2–4.5 m)
Large shrub or small tree, native to southwestern China. Narrow elliptic leaves, to over 4 in (10 cm) long, dense yellowish brown to olive hairy coating on undersides. Trusses of up to 12 white to soft pink funnel-shaped flowers, to over 2 in (5 cm) long, sometimes red-spotted, in mid-spring. Zones 6–10.

Rhododendron alabamense

ALABAMA AZALEA
☀ ❄ ↔ 5 ft (1.5 m) ↕ 5 ft (1.5 m)
Deciduous azalea from southern USA; rarely grown. Masses of dazzling white, lemon-scented, funnel-shaped flowers, distinctive yellow blotch, with new spring growth of hairy pale gray-green leaves. Zones 7–9.

Rhododendron albrechtii

☀ ❄ ↔ 4 ft (1.2 m) ↕ 7 ft (2 m)
Deciduous azalea, native to central and northern Japan. Compact shrub. Whorls of 5 finely toothed leaves, gray hairy coating underneath. Openly bell-shaped, reddish purple flowers, in trusses of 3 to 5 blooms, in mid- to late spring. Zones 5–8.

Rhododendron alutaceum

☀/◐ ❄ ↔ 5–12 ft (1.5–3.5 m)
↕ 7–15 ft (2–4.5 m)
Large bushy shrub found in southwestern China. Broad, leathery, lance-

shaped leaves, 2–6 in (5–15 cm) long, dense tan to red-brown hairs on the undersides. Trusses of up to 12 white to pale pink, funnel-shaped, red-spotted flowers, to 1½ in (35 mm) long, in early spring. Zones 7–10.

Rhododendron anagalliflorum

☀ ✺ ↔ 24–48 in (60–120 cm)
↕ 8 in (20 cm)
A tiny Vireya species from New Guinea, with a prostrate creeping habit. Whorls of tiny delicate leaves are covered with a textured mass of scales. Solitary, miniature, bell-shaped, red or pinkish flowers. Ideal subject for containers or hanging baskets. Zones 10–11.

Rhododendron anthopogon

☀ ❄ ↔ 36 in (90 cm) ↕ 36 in (90 cm)
Evergreen species from the Himalayas and western China. Compact rounded shrub; leaves aromatic when crushed. Pale pink to reddish tubular flowers, in compact trusses, are produced in spring. Zones 7–9.

Rhododendron arborescens

☀ ❄ ↔ 8 ft (2.4 m) ↕ 10 ft (3 m)
Deciduous azalea, native of woodlands of the Appalachian region of eastern USA. Fragrant flowers white or pink, funnel-shaped, open with or after bright green obovate leaves. Zones 4–8.

Rhododendron arboreum

☀ ❄ ↔ 15 ft (4.5 m) ↕ 60 ft (18 m)
Slow-growing tree species; a common plant of the Himalayan rhododendron forests, also in southern India, western China, and Thailand. The tough

Rhododendron alutaceum

Rhododendron adenogynum

Rhododendron albrechtii

R. arboreum subsp. *cinnamomeum* var. *album*

Rhododendron arboreum subsp. *delavayi*

broad green leaves are brown and spongy, with a hairy coating beneath. Flowers are fleshy, narrowly bell-shaped, 2 in (5 cm) wide, white or pink to blood red, in trusses of 15 to 20 blooms, in spring. *R. a.* subsp. *cinnamomeum*, leaves with reddish brown hairs beneath; *R. a.* subsp. *cinnamomeum* var. *album*, white flowers with tiny blood red spots on inner surface of petals. *R. a.* subsp. *delavayi*, red-flowered form from China, Myanmar, and Thailand. Zones 7–9.

Rhododendron arizelum

☀ ❄ ↔ 6–25 ft (1.8–8 m) ↑ 6–25 ft (1.8–8 m)

Variable evergreen shrub or small tree from northeastern Myanmar, northeastern India, and western China. Bell-shaped flowers pale or deep yellow, cream, or deep rose pink, in

trusses of 12 to 25 blooms, mid- to late season. Oval-shaped leaves, velvety coating underneath. Zones 8–9.

Rhododendron atlanticum ★

COAST AZALEA

☀ ❄ ↔ 36 in (90 cm) ↑ 36 in (90 cm)

Compact deciduous azalea occurs on the USA east coast. Highly fragrant, white, funnel-shaped flowers, a distinctly cylindrical tube, flushed with purple or pink, open with or just before the bright bluish green foliage. 'Seaboard', white flowers with a pink corolla tube. Zones 6–9.

Rhododendron augustinii

☀ ❄ ↔ 2–10 ft (0.6–3 m) ↑ 3–20 ft (0.9–6 m)

Compact, freely flowering, variable, evergreen shrub from China. Elliptic leaves, hairy beneath. Flowers mauve-

blue to purple, greenish spots; funnel-shaped, in trusses of 2 to 6 blooms, mid- to late season. Zones 6–9.

Rhododendron auriculatum

☀ ❄ ↔ 15 ft (4.5 m) ↑ 30 ft (9 m)

Evergreen shrub or tree from western China. Large oblong-oblanceolate leaves, whitish brown hairs underneath. Fragrant, funnel-shaped, white flowers, in loose trusses of 7 to 15 blooms, in mid-spring. Zones 6–9.

Rhododendron austrinum

FLORIDA AZALEA

☀ ❄ ↔ 10 ft (3 m) ↑ 10 ft (3 m)

A rarely grown, freely flowering, deciduous azalea from southeastern USA. Fragrant, funnel-shaped, creamy yellow to golden yellow, orange or red flowers, with distinctive long protruding stamens, bloom before or as the downy leaf shoots open. Zones 6–9.

Rhododendron barbatum

☀ ❄ ↔ 20 ft (6 m) ↑ 20 ft (6 m)

Evergreen species from the Himalayas. Smooth, peeling, mahogany-colored

bark. Long stiff bristles on young shoots; dark green, glossy, elliptic to oblong leaves, to 8 in (20 cm) long, pale mat green undersides. Brilliant scarlet or blood red, or occasionally pure white, fleshy flowers, up to 3 in (8 cm) long, in very compact rounded trusses of 10 to 20 blooms, in early spring. Zones 7–9.

Rhododendron brachycarpum

☀ ❄ ↔ 8 ft (2.4 m) ↑ 10 ft (3 m)

An evergreen species from Japan and Korea. Young shoots hairy, bright green leaves, smooth uppersurface, compacted, gray to fawn, hairy coating underneath. White to pale pink funnel-shaped flowers spotted with green, in early summer. Zones 6–9.

Rhododendron brookeanum

☀ ✈ ↔ 4 ft (1.2 m) ↑ 6 ft (1.8 m)

Vireya species from Borneo. Leaves large and attractive. Rich golden yellow, orange, or red, funnel-shaped, often lemon-scented flowers, white or cream center, in loose trusses of 5 to 14 blooms, in winter. Zones 10–11.

Rhododendron barbatum

Rhododendron augustinii

Rhododendron arizelum

Rhododendron brookeanum

Rhododendron atlanticum

Rhododendron austrinum

R

Rhododendron bureavii

☀ ❄ ↔ 10 ft (3 m) ↕ 20 ft (6 m)

Evergreen shrub from southwestern China. The elliptic foliage is covered with pink to rusty red hairs. Bell-shaped white flowers, to 2 in (5 cm) wide, sometimes flushed with pink, occasionally spotted with purple, are produced in late spring. 'Ardrishaig' bears pale pink flowers that are flushed with darker pink, with red spotting. Zones 6–9.

Rhododendron burmanicum

☀ ☂ ↔ 5 ft (1.5 m) ↕ 8 ft (2.4 m)

Compact, abundantly flowering, evergreen shrub from the slopes of Mt Victoria in Myanmar. White, creamy yellow, or greenish yellow, funnel-shaped flowers, in trusses of 4 to 6 blooms, in late spring. Flowers and dark green foliage densely covered with scales. Zones 9–10.

Rhododendron calendulaceum ★

FLAME AZALEA

☀ ❄ ↔ 10 ft (3 m) ↕ 10 ft (3 m)

Originating in southeastern USA, this attractive deciduous azalea is a densely

branched shrub, The slightly fragrant, funnel-shaped, orange, red, or yellow flowers, to 2 in (5 cm) wide, open with the leaves, in late spring. Zones 5–8.

Rhododendron callimorphum

☀ ❄ ↔ 8 ft (2.4 m) ↕ 10 ft (3 m)

An evergreen shrub from southwestern China, with broad, almost circular, leaves. Bell-shaped, white, pink, or rose flowers, to 2 in (5 cm) in length, sometimes with purple spots, are held in trusses of 5 to 8 blooms, in late spring. Zones 7–9.

Rhododendron calophytum

☀ ❄ ↔ 20 ft (6 m) ↕ 15 ft (4.5 m)

Native of China, evergreen small tree, shorter in cultivation. Long, dark green, smooth leaves curl and droop in colder weather. White or pink bell-shaped flowers, with purple basal blotch, early to mid-season. Zones 6–9.

Rhododendron calostrotum

☀ ❄ ↔ 36 in (90 cm) ↕ 27 in (70 cm)

A prostrate mat-forming, evergreen species that is distributed across the

Rhododendron campanulatum

Himalayas, western China, as well as northern Myanmar and India. Shiny dark green leaves are almost circular. The magenta, rose-crimson, or sometimes pink and purple flowers, are carried in trusses of 1 to 5 blooms, in late spring. *R. c.* **subsp.** *keleticum* produces abundant purplish crimson flowers, about 1½ in (35 mm) across, widely funnel-shaped, densely spotted with crimson, in trusses of 2 or 3, late in the season, and has leaves with brown or fawn scales on the undersides. *R. c.* 'Gigha' is a compact, freely flowering cultivar that bears rosy crimson blooms. Zones 6–9.

Rhododendron campylogynum

Rhododendron campanulatum

☀ ❄ ↔ 15 ft (4.5 m) ↕ 15 ft (4.5 m)

From the Himalayas, a shrub or small tree which varies widely in form and height. Smooth leaves, undersides densely covered with brown woolly hairs. Bell-shaped flowers, lavender-blue or white to pale mauve, with purple spots, in trusses of 6 to 12 blooms, in spring. Zones 5–8.

Rhododendron campylogynum

☀ ❄ ↔ 30 in (75 cm) ↕ 18 in (45 cm)

Ideal for rock gardens, creeping evergreen shrub from eastern India and northeastern Myanmar. Dark green leaves, distinctive white or silvery hairy undersides. Nodding creamy white or bright pink flowers, in delicate trusses of 1 to 3 blooms, in late spring to summer. Zones 7–9.

Rhododendron camtschaticum

☀ ❄ ↔ 30 in (75 cm) ↕ 10 in (25 cm)

Deciduous rhododendron found from Alaska across the Bering Strait down to northern Japan. Leaves are 1–2 in (25–50 mm) long. Flowers on new spring growth, small, hairy, purple-pink, in late spring. It has an unusual flowering habit for a rhododendron. Zones 5–9.

Rhododendron canadense

RHODORA

☀ ❄ ↔ 36 in (90 cm) ↕ 36 in (90 cm)

Native of woodlands in eastern North America. Dull bluish green elliptic to oblong leaves, hairy coating beneath. Broadly bell-shaped flowers, 5-lobed, rose-purple, occasionally white, in late spring. Zones 3–8.

Rhododendron canescens

FLORIDA PINXTER AZALEA, PIEDMONT AZALEA, SWEET AZALEA

☀ ❄ ↔ 8 ft (2.4 m) ↕ 15 ft (4.5 m)

Deciduous azalea native to eastern USA, from North Carolina southward and west to Oklahoma. Oblong to lance-shaped leaves. Scented pink flowers, funnel-shaped, before or with leaves, in spring. White- or magenta-flowered forms occur. Zones 6–10.

Rhododendron burmanicum

R. calostrotum subsp. *keleticum*

Rhododendron carneum

Rhododendron calophytum

Rhododendron carneum

☀ ❄ ↔ 6 ft (1.8 m) ↑ 6 ft (1.8 m)

Found in the mountains of Myanmar. The lustrous, dark green, 6–8 in (15–20 cm) long leaves are bluish and scaly on the undersides. Trusses of 4 to 5 fragrant, tubular, pinkish blooms, in early spring. Zones 8–10.

Rhododendron catawbiense ★

CATAWBA RHODODENDRON, MOUNTAIN ROSEBAY

☀ ❄ ↔ 10 ft (3 m) ↑ 10 ft (3 m)

From eastern USA; robust evergreen similar in form to *R. ponticum*. Glossy dark green leaves, broadly elliptic to obovate. Funnel-shaped faintly spotted flowers, lilac-purple, in compact showy trusses of 15 to 20 blooms, in late spring–early summer. Important parent of many frost-hardy hybrids. '**Album**', heat-tolerant form, mid-green leaves, large white flowers opening from lilac buds; '**English Roseum**', also heat tolerant, bright pink flowers tinged with lilac. Zones 4–8.

Rhododendron cephalanthum

☀ ❄ ↔ 4 ft (1.2 m) ↑ 4 ft (1.2 m)

Variable evergreen shrub from western China and upper Myanmar. Young shoots densely bristly, aromatic, oblong leaves, smooth above, scaly underneath. Trusses of about 8 white or pink tubular flowers, up to ¾ in (18 mm) long, in spring. Zones 7–9.

Rhododendron dauricum

Rhododendron ciliatum

Rhododendron ciliatum

☀ ❄ ↔ 6 ft (1.8 m) ↑ 6 ft (1.8 m)

Evergreen species from the Himalayas. Young shoots and uppersurfaces of elliptic leaves distinctively bristly. Bell- to funnel-shaped flowers, white or white flushed with pink, in trusses of 2 to 4 blooms, in spring. Zones 7–9.

Rhododendron ciliicalyx

☀ ❄ ↔ 7 ft (2 m) ↑ 7 ft (2 m)

Evergreen species, native of western China. Dense narrow foliage, covered with fine hairs. Fragrant flowers in trusses of 2 to 4 large, funnel-shaped, white flowers, yellow basal blotch, in late spring. Zones 7–9.

Rhododendron cinnabarinum

☀ ❄ ↔ 7 ft (2 m) ↑ 10 ft (3 m)

Evergreen species from the Himalayas and northern Myanmar. Roundish, glaucous, green leaves. Waxy, red to deep orange, narrowly bell-shaped flowers, trusses of 3 to 9 blooms, mid-to late season. '**Mount Everest**', apricot flowers, yellowish inside. Zones 6–9.

Rhododendron concinnum

☀ ❄ ↔ 6–10 ft (1.8–3 m) ↑ 6–20 ft (1.8–6 m)

Vigorous evergreen shrub or small tree from western China. Smooth dark green leaves, scaly above, gray-brown scales underneath. Purple or reddish purple, funnel-shaped flowers, scaly

Rhododendron cinnabarinum 'Mount Everest'

Rhododendron ciliicalyx

Rhododendron cephalanthum

on the outside, in trusses of 2 to 8, in mid- to late spring. **Pseudoyanthinum Group**, ruby red flowers. Zones 7–9.

Rhododendron cumberlandense

syn. *Rhododendron bakeri*

CUMBERLAND AZALEA

☀ ❄ ↔ 3–8 ft (0.9–2.4 m) ↑ 3–8 ft (0.9–2.4 m)

From Kentucky, Virginia, Tennessee, Georgia, and Alabama, USA. Compact deciduous shrub ranging from dwarf to medium height. Branches rather horizontal. Funnel-shaped flowers in red, yellow, or orange shades appear in early to mid-summer. Zones 5–7.

Rhododendron dauricum

☀ ❄ ↔ 8 ft (2.4 m) ↑ 8 ft (2.4 m)

From northern latitudes across Asia, from eastern Siberia to Japan. Evergreen straggly shrub, scaly young shoots, densely scaly dark green leaves, hairy beneath. Widely funnel-shaped flowers, pink or violet-pink, singly or in pairs, early season. Zones 5–8.

Rhododendron davidsonianum

☀ ❄ ↔ 7 ft (2 m) ↑ 7 ft (2 m)

An upright, open-growing shrub from western China. The lance-shaped

Rhododendron concinnum

leaves have deep scaly undersides. Flowers are carried in trusses of 2 to 6 blooms, funnel-shaped, usually white or white suffused with pink, may be pink or lavender, flecked with red or green, and appear in mid- to late spring. Zones 7–10.

Rhododendron decorum

☀ ❄ ↔ 8 ft (2.4 m) ↑ 20 ft (6 m)

Native of western China, northeastern Myanmar, and Laos. Evergreen shrub or small tree, with large smooth leaves, to 8 in (20 cm) long. Scented, white to pale pink, funnel-shaped flowers, carried in trusses of 8 to 12 blooms, late in the season. *R. d.* subsp. *diaprepes* has larger leaves and flowers. Zones 7–9.

Rhododendron davidsonianum

Rhododendron elliottii

Rhododendron falconeri

Rhododendron degronianum

☀ ❄ ↔ 7 ft (2 m) ↑ 8 ft (2.4 m)

Evergreen species from central and southern Japan. Shiny, dark green, deeply veined leaves, fawn-colored felt-like hairs underneath. Pink, rose, reddish, or white, bell-shaped flowers, carried in trusses of 6 to 15 blooms, mid- to late season. Although a slow grower, the low-growing, spreading form *R. d.* subsp. *yakushimanum* (syn. *R. yakushimanum*) is sought-after and used extensively in developing compact hybrids; from the island of Yakushima, it has glossy dark green leaves with distinctive recurved margins, and produces compact trusses of 8 to 12 rose-colored buds and pink flowers. Zones 7–9.

Rhododendron durionifolium

☀/☀ ✦ ↔ 4–7 ft (1.2–2 m)
↑ 5–10 ft (1.5–3 m)

A Vireya species, native to Borneo, which is mostly epiphytic in the wild. Pointed elliptic leaves, to 6 in (15 cm) long, with a heavy covering of waxy scales. It bears loose trusses of up to

Rhododendron facetum

35 orange to red tubular flowers, up to 1¼ in (30 mm) long, mainly in late summer. Zones 10–11.

Rhododendron edgeworthii

☀ ❄ ↔ 6 ft (1.8 m) ↑ 6 ft (1.8 m)

Evergreen species from the Himalayas, upper Myanmar, and southwestern China. Deeply textured, wrinkled leaves, brown hairy coating, scales beneath. Fragrant, white, funnel-shaped flowers, occasionally flushed with pink, in trusses of 2 to 3 flowers, mid-season. Zones 9–10.

Rhododendron elliottii

☀ ❄ ↔ 8 ft (2.4 m) ↑ 10 ft (3 m)

Evergreen shrub or small tree from northeastern India. Bright red flowers, very late, fleshy, narrowly bell-shaped, in trusses of 9 to 15 blooms. Young glandular shoots covered with hairs, dark green glossy leaves. Zones 9–10.

R. degronianum subsp. *yakushimanum*

Rhododendron facetum

☀ ❄ ↔ 8 ft (2.4 m) ↑ 30 ft (9 m)

Closely related to *R. elliottii*; freely flowering evergreen shrub or tree from western China and northeastern Myanmar. Mat green leaves. Flowers deep pink to scarlet, narrowly bell-shaped, in trusses of 8 to 15 blooms, very late in season. Zones 8–9.

Rhododendron falconeri

☀ ❄ ↔ 30 ft (9 m) ↑ 40 ft (12 m)

A native of the Himalayas, and one of the finest rhododendrons. An evergreen plant with brown flaking bark. Large, wrinkled, dark mat green leaves are white with a reddish hairy coating underneath. Fragrant, creamy white to pink or pale cream, bell-shaped flowers, held in large trusses of 12 to 25 blooms, mid- to late season. *R. f.* subsp. *eximium* has a more persistent hairy coating under the leaves, and is regarded by some as a separate species, *R. eximium*. Zones 9–10.

Rhododendron fastigiatum

☀ ❄ ↔ 36 in (90 cm) ↑ 36 in (90 cm)

Prostrate or cushion-forming, alpine, evergreen shrub, from the western Chinese province of Yunnan. Scaly, glaucous, gray leaves. Bright, widely funnel-shaped, lavender or bluish purple flowers, bloom in trusses of 2 to 5, mid- to late season. **'Blue Steel'**, bluish green leaves. Zones 6–9.

Rhododendron ferrugineum

ALPINE ROSE

☀ ❄ ↔ 5 ft (1.5 m) ↑ 6 ft (1.8 m)

Native of the European Alps and the Pyrenees. Small, rounded, evergreen shrub. Bristly, dark green, elliptic leaves, edges rolled under, undersides densely covered with reddish brown scales. Crimson-purple to deep pink flowers, very late in the season. Other forms include: **'Album'**, white flowers; **'Coccineum'**, crimson flowers; and **'Glenarn'**, deep rose pink flowers. Zones 4–8.

Rhododendron flammeum

FLAME AZALEA

☀ ✦ ↔ 3 ft (0.9 m) ↑ 6 ft (1.8 m)

Freely flowering deciduous azalea from eastern states of USA, from Georgia to South Carolina. Compact shrub, slender branches. Scarlet flowers open with leaves, late spring to early summer. Rare in cultivation. Zones 10–11.

Rhododendron fastigiatum 'Blue Steel'

Rhododendron durionifolium, in the wild, Mt Kinabalu, Borneo

Rhododendron forrestii subsp. *papillatum* 'Scarlet Runner'

R. forrestii, Repens Group, 'May Day'

Rhododendron fortunei subsp. *discolor*, Houlstonii Group, cultivar

Rhododendron fletcherianum

☀/◑ ❄ ↔ 3–5 ft (0.9–1.5 m)
↕ 3–5 ft (0.9–1.5 m)

This neat rounded shrub is native to southwestern China and Tibet. The bristly, deep green to olive green, pointed oval leaves, up to 2 in (5 cm) long and often with a wavy edge, turn an attractive bronze color in winter. The small bright yellow flowers are produced in clusters, from early spring. Zones 7–10.

Rhododendron floribundum

☀ ❄ ↔ 10 ft (3 m) ↕ 20 ft (6 m)

Evergreen shrub or small tree from western China. Smooth leaves, off-white woolly hairs underneath. Bell-shaped flowers, purplish lavender, in trusses of 8 to 12 blooms, in mid-spring. 'Swinhoe', rose-purple flowers with a deep red blotch. Zones 8–9.

Rhododendron formosum

☀/◑ ❄ ↔ 3–5 ft (0.9–1.5 m)
↕ 5–7 ft (1.5–2 m)

A densely foliaged shrub, native to Taiwan. The pointed narrowly elliptic leaves, to 3 in (8 cm) long, have scaly undersides. Trusses of 10 to 20 widely flared, dark-spotted white to pale pink funnel-shaped flowers, up to 2 in (5 cm) long, are often late-flowering. *R. f.* var. *formosum* is a compact form with bristly young growth and leaf edges; **Iteaphyllum Group** has very narrow leaves and white to soft pink flowers. Zones 8–10.

Rhododendron forrestii

☀ ❄ ↔ 48 in (120 cm) ↕ 4 in (10 cm)

Native to western China and northeastern Myanmar. Creeping, prostrate, evergreen shrub. Leaves leathery, dark green, purple-red beneath. Bright scarlet tubular-campanulate flowers, singly or in pairs, mid- to late season. Used in breeding programs. *R. f.* subsp. *papillatum* has narrow leaves,

Rhododendron fulvum

light brown beneath; 'Scarlet Runner' bears scarlet flowers. *R. f.* **Repens Group** is a dwarf form with a creeping habit, leaves extensively veined, and red flowers; '**May Day**' produces scarlet flowers. Zones 8–9.

Rhododendron fortunei

☀ ❄ ↔ 8 ft (2.4 m) ↕ 15 ft (4.5 m)

A species that is widespread in its native eastern China. An evergreen, broadly upright, sometimes spreading shrub or tree. Rough grayish brown bark, reddish, bluish, or purplish leaf stalks. Fragrant, pale pink, rose, lilac to white, bell-shaped flowers, held in trusses of 6 to 12 blooms, late in the season. *R. f.* subsp. *discolor*, abundant pink flowers, late season; *R. f.* **Houlstonii Group**, soft pink to light purple flowers, mid-season. Zones 6–9.

Rhododendron fulvum

☀ ❄ ↔ 5–12 ft (1.5–3.5 m) ↕ 25 ft (8 m)

Evergreen rounded shrub or small tree, smaller in cultivation, from western China and northeastern Myanmar. Brownish hairs cover young growth and dark green leaves. White, pink, or mauve bell-shaped flowers, dark crimson basal blotch, trusses of 3 to 15 blooms, early to mid-season. Zones 7–9.

Rhododendron glaucophyllum

☀ ❄ ↔ 4 ft (1.2 m) ↕ 4 ft (1.2 m)

Evergreen shrub from the Himalayas and western China. Glossy leaves, dark brownish green, undersides glaucous, whitish, covered with scales. Bell-shaped flowers pink, or white flushed with pink or sometimes reddish purple, in trusses of 4 to 10 blooms, mid- to late season. Zones 8–9.

Rhododendron glaucophyllum

Rhododendron fletcherianum

R. formosum var. *f.*, Iteaphyllum Group, cv

Rhododendron fortunei

R

Rhododendron glischrum

☀ ❄ ↔ 10 ft (3 m) ↑ 25 ft (8 m)

Evergreen shrub or tree, native of western China and upper Myanmar. Rough greenish gray bark. Sticky leaf buds and flower buds. Dark or yellowish green leaves, bristly underneath. Trusses of 10 to 15 plum-rose, pink, or white, bell-shaped flowers, crimson blotch, early in the season. Zones 7–9.

Rhododendron griersonianum

☀ ❄ ↔ 8 ft (2.4 m) ↑ 8 ft (2.4 m)

Evergreen species from western China and northeastern Myanmar. Rough brown bark. Smooth leaves, heavy hair beneath. Deep red buds, bright geranium-scarlet, deep pink, or crimson flowers, in trusses of 5 to 12 blooms, late season. Zones 8–9.

Rhododendron glischrum

R. haematodes subsp. *chaetomallum*

Rhododendron griffithianum

☀ ❄ ↔ 10 ft (3 m) ↑ 60 ft (18 m)

Himalayan evergreen tree species with an open habit. Flaking peeling bark and smooth oblong leaves. Fragrant flowers, white, shades of pale pink, even yellowish, carried in trusses of 3 to 6 blooms, in mid- to late season. Zones 8–9.

Rhododendron haematodes

☀ ❄ ↔ 5 ft (1.5 m) ↑ 5 ft (1.5 m)

Evergreen shrub from western China and northeastern Myanmar. Young shoots densely bristly; mature leaves matted with fawn to reddish brown hairs underneath. Fleshy, tubular-campanulate, scarlet to deep crimson flowers, from late spring to early summer. *R. h.* subsp. *chaetomallum* has bristly young shoots and leaf stems. Zones 7–9.

Rhododendron hanceanum

☀ ❄ ↔ 24 in (60 cm)
↑ 12–18 in (30–45 cm)

A small western Chinese shrub. Scaly, dark green, lance-shaped leaves with pale undersides. Slightly scented, small, cream to pale yellow blooms, held in many-flowered, 1 in (25 mm) long trusses, in spring. Makes a neat addition to a rockery or alpine garden. Zones 7–10.

Rhododendron hippophaeoides

☀ ❄ ↔ 5 ft (1.5 m) ↑ 5 ft (1.5 m)

Compact evergreen shrub from western China, well suited to the rock garden. Pale gray-green oblong leaves, with creamy yellow scales on the undersides. Delicate, funnel-shaped, lavender-blue or purplish blue flowers, in trusses of 3 to 8 blooms, mid- to late season. Zones 6–9.

Rhododendron hodgsonii

☀ ❄ ↔ 15 ft (4.5 m) ↑ 30 ft (9 m)

Evergreen shrub or small tree from the Himalayas and western China, smaller in cultivation. Flaking bark. Leaves smooth, dense silvery to cinnamon brown hairs beneath. Fleshy tubular-campanulate flowers, pink to magenta or purple, in trusses of 15 to 20 blooms, in spring. Zones 9–10.

Rhododendron horlickianum

☀/❄ ❄ ↔ 4–8 ft (1.2–2.4 m)
↑ 5–10 ft (1.5–3 m)

From northern Myanmar, an upright shrub with lance-shaped, dark green, 3–6 in (8–15 cm) long leaves, waxy blue-green bloom beneath. Cream flowers, to 3 in (8 cm) long, with faint pink banding, in groups of 2 or 3 blooms, in early spring. Zones 8–10.

Rhododendron hyperythrum

Rhododendron hyperythrum

☀ ❄ ↔ 6 ft (1.8 m) ↑ 8 ft (2.4 m)

Evergreen species from Taiwan. Smooth young shoots, dark green elliptic leaves. White or pink funnel-shaped flowers, sometimes with red spots, mid- to late season. Zones 8–9.

Rhododendron impeditum

☀ ❄ ↔ 12 in (30 cm) ↑ 12 in (30 cm)

Compact, ground-covering evergreen, western China. Dense, shiny, dark green, scaly foliage. Violet to purple funnel-shaped flowers, small trusses of 1 to 3 blooms, mid-season. Zones 4–8.

Rhododendron indicum

INDIAN AZALEA, JAPANESE EVERGREEN AZALEA

☀ ❄ ↔ 24 in (60 cm) ↑ 36 in (90 cm)

Originating in southern Japan, this variable evergreen species is densely

Rhododendron impeditum

Rhododendron horlickianum

Rhododendron hippophaeoides

Rhododendron kiusianum, white form

Rhododendron kiusianum, deep pink form

R. kiusianum 'Mountain Gem'

Rhododendron javanicum

branched and has a low, sometimes prostrate, habit. It features a mass of shiny dark green foliage. Red broadly funnel-shaped flowers, singly or in pairs, are produced in spring. '**Balsaminiflorum**' is a dwarf form with salmon red double flowers; '**Macranthum**' is a compact shrub with orange-red flowers. Zones 6–9.

Rhododendron intricatum

☀ ❄ ↔ 5 ft (1.5 m) ↑ 5 ft (1.5 m)
From western China. A fast-growing, delicately branched, evergreen shrub. Small, mat, smooth, grayish green leaves are densely scaly below. Tiny flowers, pale lavender to dark purplish blue, with very short stamens, held in compact trusses of 2 to 10 blooms, in mid- to late season. Zones 5–8.

Rhododendron johnstoneanum

Rhododendron keiskei

Rhododendron jasminiflorum

☀ ✈ ↔ 22 in (55 cm) ↑ 22 in (55 cm)
A Vireya species found naturally in the Malay Peninsula, the Philippines, and Sumatra. The leaves have scaly undersides. Trusses of 6 to 12 tubular flowers, white, sometimes flushed with pink, appear in winter. Used extensively in hybridizing. Spreading habit makes it ideal for hanging baskets. Zones 10–11.

Rhododendron javanicum

☀ ✈ ↔ 4 ft (1.2 m) ↑ 10 ft (3 m)
Vireya species from Sumatra and Java, spreading shrub or small tree, often used in hybridizing. Shiny leaves in whorls, densely scaly. Trusses of 4 to 20 funnel-shaped flowers, normally orange, with distinctive purple stamens, in winter. Zones 10–11.

Rhododendron johnstoneanum

☀ ❄ ↔ 8 ft (2.4 m) ↑ 15 ft (4.5 m)
A native of northern India with smooth, peeling, reddish brown bark. Hairy-edged leaves are scaly on the undersides. Funnel-shaped flowers,

slightly fragrant, creamy white, often flushed pink or purple, in trusses of up to 5 blooms, in spring. '**Demi-John**', white flowers flushed with yellow-green; '**Double Diamond**', pale yellow double flowers; '**Rubeotinctum**', white and pink stripes on each petal. Zones 7–9.

Rhododendron kaempferi

KAEMPFER AZALEA
☀ ❄ ↔ 4 ft (1.2 m) ↑ 4 ft (1.2 m)
A native of Japan, this species is deciduous in cool climates. A densely branched shrub, with reddish brown bristles on the young shoots. Salmon or brick red, funnel-shaped flowers, in trusses of 2 to 4 blooms, are produced in late spring. Zones 5–8.

Rhododendron keiskei

☀ ❄ ↔ 36 in (90 cm) ↑ 24 in (60 cm)
This variable evergreen species from Japan forms a low-growing, creeping, twiggy mat, more erect in shade. Bronze young shoots, dark or olive green hairy leaves, lower surfaces pale green. Creamy to pale yellow funnel-shaped flowers, carried in

Rhododendron intricatum

Rhododendron jasminiflorum

Rhododendron kaempferi

trusses of 2 to 6 blooms, in spring. '**Ebino**', a freely flowering dwarf form with pale yellow flowers. Zones 5–8.

Rhododendron kiusianum

KYUSHU AZALEA
☀ ❄ ↔ 36 in (90 cm) ↑ 36 in (90 cm)
A parent of the Kurume Group of azaleas, this evergreen species from Kyushu, Japan is deciduous at higher altitudes. it is a much-branched, often prostrate shrub with small hairy leaves. The funnel-shaped flowers, in trusses of 2 to 3 blooms, rose-purple, purple, red, pink, or sometimes white, are produced in late spring. '**Mountain Gem**', bears rose-purple flowers. Zones 6–9.

R

Rhododendron konori

☀ ⚘ ↔ 6 ft (1.8 m) ↑ 12 ft (3.5 m)

Vireya species from New Guinea. Large leaves with a mat green, bluish tinge, reddish brown hairy coating underneath. Fragrant, delicate, orchid-like, pure white or pinkish flowers carried in trusses of 5 to 8 blooms, in winter. Zones 10–11.

Rhododendron lacteum

☀ ❄ ↔ 12 ft (3.5 m) ↑ 12 ft (3.5 m)

Evergreen shrub or small tree found naturally in western China. Leaves have hairy undersides. Large, bell-shaped, cream flowers, sometimes flushed with pink, up to 2 in (5 cm) long, in large compact trusses of 15 to 30 blooms, in spring. Prefers a well-sheltered position. Zones 7–9.

Rhododendron laetum

☀ ⚘ ↔ 4 ft (1.2 m) ↑ 10 ft (3 m)

Native of northwestern New Guinea, Vireya species more compact in cultivation. Broad elliptic leaves. Large funnel-shaped flowers of pure golden

Rhododendron laetum

Rhododendron luteiflorum

yellow, ageing to red, orange, or salmon, held in open trusses of 6 to 8 blooms, autumn to spring. Zones 10–11.

Rhododendron lepidostylum

☀ ❄ ↔ 5 ft (1.5 m) ↑ 3 ft (0.9 m)

From western China. Evergreen low spreading shrub. Bluish green young foliage, leathery leaves, edges rolled downward, bristles and golden scales underneath. Flowers solitary or in 2s or 3s, funnel-shaped, clear yellow, in late spring. Zones 6–9.

Rhododendron leucaspis

☀ ❄ ↔ 4 ft (1.2 m) ↑ 4 ft (1.2 m)

Shrub from western China. Compact, rounded, evergreen. Hairy elliptic leaves. Flowers bell-shaped, milky white, often tinged pink, singly, in 2s, or threes. Very early flowers, protect from late winter frosts. Zones 7–9.

Rhododendron lindleyi

☀ ⚘ ↔ 6 ft (1.8 m) ↑ 8 ft (2.4 m)

Evergreen shrub found as an epiphyte among rocks in the Himalayas region.

Rhododendron lindleyi

Elliptic leaves. Large, scented, tubular, funnel-shaped flowers, 3 in (8 cm) long, white or white tinged with pink, with a yellow blotch, in trusses of 3 to 6 blooms, from late spring to early summer. Zones 9–10.

Rhododendron lochiae

AUSTRALIAN RHODODENDRON

☀ ⚘ ↔ 24 in (60 cm) ↑ 36 in (90 cm)

Slow-growing, compact, bushy Vireya species from the northeastern tip of Australia. Scaly young shoots, dark green broadly obovate leaves, scaly underneath. Bright scarlet, funnel-shaped flowers, in loose trusses of 2 to 7 blooms, in winter. Well suited to hanging baskets. Zones 10–11.

Rhododendron loranthiflorum

☀ ⚘ ↔ 3 ft (0.9 m) ↑ 6 ft (1.8 m)

Vireya species from the islands around New Guinea, with distinctive, rust-colored, scaly young leaf shoots. The fragrant, creamy white, tubular

Rhododendron lochiae

Rhododendron loranthiflorum

flowers, carried in trusses of 4 to 5 blooms, are produced in autumn–spring. Zones 10–11.

Rhododendron lowii

☀ ⚘ ↔ 8 ft (2.4 m) ↑ 25 ft (8 m)

Variable Vireya species, shrub or small tree, found only on Mt Kinabalu in Malaysia. Trusses of 7 to 15 fragrant flowers, funnel-shaped, clear pale to deep yellow, flushed variably with apricot. Zones 10–11.

Rhododendron luteiflorum

syn. *Rhododendron glaucophyllum* var. *luteiflorum*

☀/☀ ❄ ↔ 18–32 in (45–80 cm) ↑ 12–36 in (60–90 cm)

This alpine species from northern Myanmar has aromatic, pointed oval to lance-shaped, olive green leaves, around 1 in (25 mm) long. Nodding, yellow-green to yellow, 1 in (25 mm) long flowers, in trusses of 3 to 6 blooms, in mid-spring. Zones 6–9.

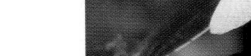

Rhododendron lacteum

Rhododendron maddenii

Rhododendron lutescens
☀ ❋ ↔ 15 ft (4.5 m) ↑ 20 ft (6 m)
From western China, straggly habit, gray or brown flaking bark. Bright bronze-red young foliage in spring, show of color in autumn. In late winter to early spring, small, delicate, pale yellow, funnel-shaped flowers with long elegant stamens are held in trusses of 1 to 3 blooms. Zones 7–9.

Rhododendron luteum
PONTIC AZALEA
☀ ❋ ↔ 8 ft (2.4 m) ↑ 12 ft (3.5 m)
Widely grown deciduous azalea from eastern Europe, used extensively in breeding programs. Foliage colors red, orange, and purple in autumn.

Tubular, funnel-shaped, clear yellow flowers, in trusses of 7 to 12 blooms, before the leaves in spring. Zones 5–9.

Rhododendron macabeanum
☀ ❋ ↔ 20 ft (6 m) ↑ 50 ft (15 m)
Evergreen from northeastern India. Shiny mature leaves, white or fawn hairy coating beneath. Bell-shaped, pale or greenish lemon yellow flowers, deep red or purple blotch, in trusses of 12 to 20 blooms, in spring. Zones 8–9.

Rhododendron macgregoriae
☀ ✛ ↔ 7 ft (2 m) ↑ 15 ft (4.5 m)
Shrub or small tree, most widespread of New Guinea's Vireya rhododendrons. Leaves with scaly undersides.

Rhododendron makinoi

Flowers light yellow to dark orange or red, narrow corolla tube, in trusses of 8 to 15 flowers, winter. Zones 10–11.

Rhododendron macrophyllum
☀ ❋ ↔ 12 ft (3.5 m) ↑ 12 ft (3.5 m)
Robust evergreen shrub from western North America. Dark green leaves, paler undersides, smooth-edged. Bell-shaped flowers, white to pink with yellow spots, in trusses of 9 to 20 blooms, late season. Zones 6–9.

Rhododendron maddenii
☀ ✦ ↔ 8 ft (2.4 m) ↑ 25 ft (8 m)
From the Himalayas, southwestern China, Myanmar, and Vietnam. Leaves smooth, thick, brownish, hairy below, heavy scaling. Large funnel-shaped flowers, white, often flushed pink or purple, yellow basal blotch, trusses of 1 to 11 blooms, late spring. Zones 9–10.

Rhododendron makinoi
☀ ❋ ↔ 7 ft (2 m) ↑ 8 ft (2.4 m)
An evergreen shrub from Japan. Long, narrow, dark green mature leaves,

Rhododendron lutescens

smooth on the uppersurfaces, brown woolly coating on undersides. Trusses of 5 to 8 funnel-shaped flowers, pink or rose, with or without red spots, in late spring. Zones 8–9.

Rhododendron mallotum
☀ ❋ ↔ 12 ft (3.5 m) ↑ 20 ft (6 m)
Evergreen shrub or small tree from western China and northeastern Myanmar. Young leaf shoots and thick, stiff, leathery leaves have a gray or brown hairy coating. Trusses of up to 20 tubular bell-shaped, red or crimson flowers, early spring. Zones 7–9.

Rhododendron macabeanum

Rhododendron luteum

Rhododendron macgregoriae

Rhododendron molle subsp. *japonicum*

Rhododendron morii

Rhododendron maximum

GREAT LAUREL RHODODENDRON, ROSEBAY RHODODENDRON

☀ ❄ ↔ 7 ft (2 m) ↕ 6 ft (1.8 m)

Compact, spreading, evergreen shrub from eastern North America. Smooth leaves, fine hairy coating underneath. Bell-shaped flowers white to pinkish purple with yellow-green spots, in late spring–early summer. 'Summertime', white flowers, tips of petals flushed reddish purple. Zones 3–8.

Rhododendron megeratum

☀ ❄ ↔ 15 in (38 cm) ↕ 15–30 in (38–75 cm)

Found growing naturally in northeastern India, northeastern Myanmar, and western China. A very early-flowering, evergreen, prostrate species. The small almost circular leaves have a whitish

---

Rhododendron maximum (left and center), in the wild, Grotto Falls, Great Smoky Mountains National Park, Tennessee, USA

hairy coating on the undersides. It produces broad, bell-shaped, creamy white to yellow flowers. Zones 9–10.

Rhododendron minus

☀ ❄ ↔ 3–5 ft (0.9–1.5 m) ↕ 3–5 ft (0.9–1.5 m)

Small evergreen from North America. Pointed elliptic leaves, densely scaly below. Flowers usually scaly, white to pink or mauve, in trusses of 6 to 12 blooms, in mid-spring. **Carolinianum Group**, dark green leaves, dense scales below; pink or pale rose-purple flowers, in summer. Zones 4–9.

Rhododendron molle

DECIDUOUS AZALEA

☀ ❄ ↔ 4 ft (1.2 m) ↕ 4 ft (1.2 m)

This small deciduous azalea is native to eastern China. The funnel-shaped

Rhododendron minus

flowers are a golden yellow or orange color with a large greenish blotch, in trusses of 6 to 12 blooms; they open with or before the mid-green leaves, in mid-spring. *R. m.* subsp. *japonicum*, from Japan, yellow or orange flowers, one parent of the Mollis group of hybrids. Zones 7–9.

Rhododendron morii

☀ ❄ ↔ 8 ft (2.4 m) ↕ 25 ft (8 m)

An evergreen shrub or small tree from Taiwan. The young leaf shoots have a blackish hairy coating and mature to dark green shiny leaves. White, sometimes tinged pink, bell-shaped flowers in trusses of 12 to 15 blooms, are borne in mid- to late spring. Needs sun in cool climates. Zones 7–9.

Rhododendron moupinense

☀ ❄ ↔ 4 ft (1.2 m) ↕ 4 ft (1.2 m)

An evergreen shrub native to western China. Oval shiny leaves, dense scales, bristly edges, pale green underneath. White funnel-shaped flowers, singly

or paired, sometimes flushed with pink, dark red spots inside, in early spring. Zones 7–9.

Rhododendron mucronulatum

KOREAN RHODODENDRON

☀ ❄ ↔ 3 ft (0.9 m) ↕ 6 ft (1.8 m)

Straggly deciduous shrub from eastern Russia, northern and central China,

Rhododendron moupinense

Rhododendron megeratum

central USA. Small oblong leaves, hairy undersides. Clusters of 5 to 9 funnel-shaped flowers, in pink shades, with a dark blotch, open with the leaves, in late spring. Zones 4–9.

Rhododendron protistum

☀ ❄ ↔ 15 ft (4.5 m) ↑ 100 ft (30 m)

Evergreen species from western China and northern Myanmar; usually a tall shrub in cultivation. Young shoots, dense, yellowish gray, hairy coating; dark green leaves. Large trusses of 20 to 30 bell-shaped creamy white flowers, flushed with rose, in late winter to early spring. Protect in cooler areas. Zones 9–10.

Rhododendron prunifolium

☀ ❄ ↔ 4 ft (1.2 m) ↑ 6 ft (1.8 m)

Deciduous azalea, allied to *R. calendulaceum*, native to a limited area of Alabama and Georgia, USA. Smooth leaves, often edged with tiny hairs. Heads of rich scarlet flowers, about 1½ in (35 mm) wide, in late spring. Zones 6–9.

Rhododendron quinquefolium

FIVE-LEAF AZALEA

☀ ❄ ↔ 4–8 ft (1.2–2.4 m) ↑ 8–25 ft (2.4–8 m)

Deciduous azalea from central Japan. Oval-shaped leaves, in whorls of 4 to 5, at ends of branches. Pure white

Rhododendron prunifolium

Rhododendron protistum

Rhododendron rubiginosum

flowers with green spots appear in late spring. 'Five Arrows', white flowers spotted with olive green. Zones 6–8.

Rhododendron racemosum

☀ ❄ ↔ 5 ft (1.5 m) ↑ 5 ft (1.5 m)

Widely variable evergreen shrub from western China with smooth leathery leaves. Funnel-shaped flowers, white to pale pink, held in trusses of up to 6 blooms, are produced in spring. 'Forrest', dwarf form, pink flowers; 'Glendoick', taller, with deep pink flowers; 'Rock Rose', bright purplish pink flowers. Zones 5–8.

Rhododendron reticulatum

☀ ❄ ↔ 4 ft (1.2 m) ↑ 4 ft (1.2 m)

A freely flowering, hardy, evergreen azalea from Japan. Leaves are hairy initially, becoming smooth. Reddish purple to magenta bell-shaped flowers, to 2 in (5 cm) wide, carried singly or in pairs, appear in mid- to late spring. Zones 6–9.

Rhododendron rex

☀ ❄ ↔ 12 ft (3.5 m) ↑ 15 ft (4.5 m)

From western China, evergreen shrub, larger in the wild. Young shoots are covered with a dense, white or fawn, hairy coating. Dark green leaves. In spring, large rose, pale pink, or white flowers, in magnificent trusses of 20 to 30 blooms. Zones 7–9.

Rhododendron quinquefolium

Rhododendron racemosum

Rhododendron rupicola var. *chryseum*

R. scabrifolium var. *spiciferum*

Rhododendron rubiginosum

☀ ❄ ↔ 20 ft (6 m) ↑ 30 ft (9 m)

Evergreen species from western China and northeastern Myanmar, freely flowering from a young age. Smooth aromatic leaves. Bell-shaped flowers, in pink, rose, or lilac shades, in trusses of 4 to 8 blooms, in spring. Zones 7–9.

Rhododendron rupicola

☀ ❄ ↔ 22 in (55 cm) ↑ 24 in (60 cm)

Evergreen species from western China and northeastern Myanmar. Low mat or cushion of small, densely scaly, mat green leaves. Deep plum-purple to deep magenta-red funnel-shaped flowers, in trusses of 2 to 8 blooms, in spring. Good for rock gardens. *R. r.* var. *chryseum*, creamy yellow flowers. Zones 5–9.

Rhododendron russatum

☀ ❄ ↔ 6–48 in (15–120 cm) ↑ 6–60 in (15–150 cm)

Native to western China and northeastern Myanmar. Prostrate or upright evergreen shrub. Dark green leaves,

dense covering of reddish brown scales underneath. Intense deep bluish purple flowers, funnel-shaped, in trusses of 3 to 6, occasionally up to 14 blooms, in spring. Zones 5–9.

Rhododendron saluenense

☀ ❄ ↔ 18–60 in (45–150 cm) ↑ 18–60 in (45–150 cm)

Native to northeastern Myanmar and western China. A robust, prostrate, variable, evergreen shrub. Shiny, dark green, aromatic leaves. Funnel-shaped flowers, deep pinkish purple, in trusses of 2 to 5 blooms, in spring. Zones 6–9.

Rhododendron scabrifolium

☀ ❄ ↔ 6 ft (1.8 m) ↑ 8 ft (2.4 m)

An evergreen species from western China which prefers a well-sheltered position. Bristly new growth, opens into narrow leaves. Trusses of 2 to 3 tubular funnel-shaped flowers, white, pink, or deep rose, early spring. *R. s.* var. *spiciferum*, profuse pink flowers, prominent stamens. Zones 8–9.

Rhododendron scopulorum

Rhododendron schlippenbachii

Rhododendron schlippenbachii

ROYAL AZALEA

☀ ❄ ↔ 15 ft (4.5 m) ↑ 15 ft (4.5 m)

This prevalent deciduous azalea from Korea and eastern Russia has light green foliage, in whorls at the ends of the branches, which turns bronze in autumn. The widely funnel-shaped star-like flowers, pale pink or white, open with or shortly after the leaves, in late spring. Zones 4–8.

Rhododendron scopulorum

☀ ❀ ↔ 8 ft (2.4 m) ↑ 15 ft (4.5 m)

This native of southwestern China is smaller in cultivation than in the wild. Dark green grooved leaves, pale green and scaly underneath. Fragrant, white or apple blossom pink, widely funnel-shaped flowers, in trusses of 2 to 7 blooms, crinkled margins, yellowish blotch, scaly, mid- to late season. Zones 9–10.

Rhododendron serpyllifolium

THYME-LEAF AZALEA

☀ ❄ ↔ 24 in (60 cm) ↑ 24 in (60 cm)

A low-growing, normally evergreen azalea of central and southern Japan. Tiny leaves; deciduous in severe climates. Solitary, pink, funnel-shaped flowers, early in the season, require overhead protection from late frosts. Zones 6–9.

Rhododendron sinogrande

☀ ❄ ↔ 30 ft (9 m) ↑ 50 ft (15 m)

An evergreen understory tree from western China and northern Myanmar, the largest of any rhododendron. Long, dark green, heavily wrinkled leaves; silvery white, pale brown, or tan coating underneath. Creamy white or yellow flowers, held in trusses of 15 to 30 blooms, appear in mid-spring. Zones 8–9.

Rhododendron smirnowii

Rhododendron smirnowii

TURKISH RHODODENDRON

☀ ❄ ↔ 15 ft (4.5 m) ↑ 12 ft (3.5 m)

Robust evergreen species from northeastern Turkey and adjacent Georgia. Dense, white, woolly hairs cover ovaries, young leaf growth, and undersides of mature leaves. Funnel-shaped flowers, pink with yellow spots, in trusses of 10 to 12 flowers, late season. Zones 4–8.

Rhododendron souliei

☀ ❄ ↔ 12 ft (3.5 m) ↑ 12 ft (3.5 m)

Evergreen rhododendrons from western China. Pale purple-pink saucer-shaped flowers, in trusses of 5 to 9 blooms, late season. Prefers a sheltered spot; difficult to propagate from cuttings. Zones 6–9.

Rhododendron spinuliferum

☀ ❄ ↔ 8 ft (2.4 m) ↑ 10 ft (3 m)

An evergreen shrub, native to western China, with attractive, smooth, dark purple-brown bark. Juvenile leaves hairy, mature leaves smooth. Narrow, tubular flowers, crimson, brick red, or

Rhododendron sinogrande

orange, in trusses of 1 to 5 blooms, filament and style project beyond corolla tube, in mid-spring. Zones 8–9.

Rhododendron stamineum

☀ ❀ ↔ 10 ft (3 m) ↑ 10 ft (3 m)

Evergreen shrub or small tree from western China, larger in the wild. Smooth leaves. Trusses of 1 to 3 funnel-shaped blooms, white with a yellow blotch, stamens longer than the small tubular corolla, mid- to late spring. Sheltered position. Zones 9–10.

Rhododendron stenopetalum

☀/❀ ❄ ↔ 3–5 ft (0.9–1.5 m) ↑ 3–6 ft (0.9–1.8 m)

A Japanese evergreen azalea, with pointed elliptic leaves, 1 in (25 mm) long, hairy. Deep pink to purple-red flowers, to 1½ in (35 mm) wide. 'Linearifolium' (syn. *R. linearifolium*), the spider azalea, very narrow strappy leaves and petals. Zones 8–10.

Rhododendron spinuliferum

Rhododendron stenopetalum 'Linearifolium'

Rhododendron strigillosum

Rhododendron vaseyi

Rhododendron strigillosum

☀ ❄ ↔ 10 ft (3 m) ↑ 12 ft (3.5 m)

A native of western China. Evergreen bushy shrub or small tree. Bristly young leaf shoots, bright green leaves. Brilliant crimson narrowly bell-shaped flowers, in trusses of 8 to 12 blooms, early season. Zones 8–9.

Rhododendron sutchuenense

☀ ❄ ↔ 20 ft (6 m) ↑ 30 ft (9 m)

From western China. Large, umbrella-shaped, evergreen shrub, smaller in cultivation. Smooth dark green leaves. Widely bell-shaped flowers, pale pink to pale mauve, in open trusses of 10 blooms, in late winter to early spring. Best in a semi-shaded woodland environment. Zones 6–9.

Rhododendron tephropeplum

☀ ❄ ↔ 3–8 ft (0.9–2.4 m)
↑ 3–8 ft (0.9–2.4 m)

From the Himalayas and northeastern India and Myanmar. Compact evergreen shrub; scaly brown bark. Dark green shiny leaves, scaly underneath. Trusses of 3 to 9 dark or pale rose, pink, or crimson-purple flowers, in spring. Spreading forms suited to rock gardens. Zones 8–9.

Rhododendron thomsonii

☀ ❄ ↔ 2–20 ft (0.6–6 m)
↑ 2–20 ft (0.6–6 m)

Variable evergreen species found in the Himalayas, clinging to steep, rocky, exposed sites. Reddish brown, fawn, or pinkish bark. Thick, leathery, rounded leaves. Bell-shaped flowers, rich blood red or deep crimson, darker spots, in trusses of 6 to 13 blooms, in spring. Zones 6–9.

Rhododendron trichanthum

syn. *Rhododendron villosum*

☀ ❄ ↔ 8 ft (2.4 m) ↑ 8 ft (2.4 m)

Evergreen rhododendron from western China, 20 ft (6 m) high in the

wild. Leaf shoots densely covered with bristles. Purple funnel-shaped flowers, in trusses of 3 to 5 blooms, late in the season. Sheltered position. Zones 7–9.

Rhododendron trichostomum

☀ ❄ ↔ 3 ft (0.9 m) ↑ 5 ft (1.5 m)

Highly variable evergreen shrub from western China; normally a compact, often tiny, twiggy, intricately branched, miniature bush. Aromatic, narrow, stiff, leathery, dark green leaves. Tiny flowers white, pink, or deep rose, in spherical trusses of 8 to 20 blooms, in late spring. Zones 7–9.

Rhododendron tuba

☀ ❄ ↔ 4 ft (1.2 m) ↑ 6 ft (1.8 m)

Vireya rhododendron from eastern New Guinea, higher in the wild, to 15 ft (4.5 m). Glossy, rounded, bluish green to olive green leaves. White to pale pink, curved, tubular, fragrant flowers, 5 to 7 blooms. Zones 9–11.

Rhododendron ungernii

☀ ❄ ↔ 10 ft (3 m) ↑ 3–20 ft (0.9–6 m)

Native to northeastern Turkey and Georgia. Evergreen shrub or small tree, flaking brown bark. Large dark green leaves; dense, woolly, white coating covers undersides and young shoots. White funnel-campanulate flowers, in trusses of 12 to 30 blooms, in summer. Prefers protected position. Zones 5–9.

Rhododendron uniflorum

☀ ❄ ↔ 4 ft (1.2 m) ↑ 4 ft (1.2 m)

Dwarf evergreen species, rarely found in its native habitat of western China. Leaves have smooth uppersurfaces and scaly undersides. Broadly funnel-shaped purple flowers, singly or in pairs, are seen in spring. This is a fairly fast-growing rock-garden plant. Zones 8–9.

Rhododendron vaseyi

PINK-SHELL AZALEA

☀ ❄ ↔ 15 ft (4.5 m) ↑ 15 ft (4.5 m)

This deciduous azalea from eastern North America has shiny dark green leaves. Trusses of 4 to 8 funnel-shaped flowers, rose pink, pale pink, or white, with orange-red or red spots, open before the leaves in late spring. Zones 4–8.

Rhododendron thomsonii

Rhododendron tuba

Rhododendron tephropeplum

Rhododendron sutchuenense

Rhododendron veitchianum

Rhododendron veitchianum, Cubittii Group, cultivar

Rhododendron weyrichii

Rhododendron williamsianum

Rhododendron veitchianum

◐ ❂ ↔ 8 ft (2.4 m) ↑ 8 ft (2.4 m)
Spreading evergreen shrub from Laos, Myanmar, Thailand, and Vietnam, often grows epiphytically. Smooth, peeling, reddish brown bark. Dark green leaves, paler below. Large, highly fragrant, pure white, funnel-shaped flowers, yellow blotch, trusses of up to 5 blooms, late spring to early summer. **Cubittii Group**, bristle-edged leaves, fragrant pink flowers. Zones 9–10.

Rhododendron vernicosum

◐ ❉ ↔ 12 ft (3.5 m) ↑ 12 ft (3.5 m)
Freely flowering, evergreen shrub or tree from western China with smooth leaves. Trusses of 6 to 12 rose, lavender-rose, or white flowers, funnel-campanulate, mid- to late spring. Zones 7–9.

Rhododendron viscosum

SWAMP AZALEA, SWAMP HONEYSUCKLE
◐ ❉ ↔ 8 ft (2.4 m) ↑ 8 ft (2.4 m)
This compact deciduous azalea is native to eastern and central North

America. New leaf growth is yellowish or grayish brown. Dark green leaves have paler undersides. Funnel-shaped white flowers, spicy fragrance, held in trusses of 4 to 9 blooms, in late spring to early summer, after new leaves appear. Zones 4–9.

Rhododendron wardii

◐ ❉ ↔ 15 ft (4.5 m) ↑ 25 ft (8 m)
This evergreen shrub from western China has grayish brown bark. The leathery, dark green, rounded leaves are pale green and glaucous underneath. Saucer-shaped pale yellow or bright yellow flowers, in loose trusses of 5 to 14 blooms, are produced in late spring. Zones 7–9.

Rhododendron weyrichii

◐ ❉ ↔ 3 ft (0.9 m) ↑ 4 ft (1.2 m)
Evergreen azalea from southern Japan and southern Korea. Shrub or small tree, larger in the wild. Long rounded leaves, covered with reddish brown hairs when young. Pink funnel-shaped flowers, in trusses of 2 to 4 blooms, in spring. Zones 5–9.

Rhododendron williamsianum

◐ ❉ ↔ 4 ft (1.2 m) ↑ 5 ft (1.5 m)
Evergreen shrub, native to western China. Bristly young shoots, rounded

leaves, reddish glands underneath. The bell-shaped flowers, pale pink with darker spots, appear in 2s or 3s, in spring. Zones 7–9.

Rhododendron wiltonii

◐ ❉ ↔ 15 ft (4.5 m) ↑ 15 ft (4.5 m)
This evergreen species from western China has olive green shiny leaves that have a dense, cinnamon-colored, hairy coating on the undersides. Bell-shaped flowers, white to pink, held in trusses of 6 to 10 blooms, appear in spring. Zones 6–9.

Rhododendron yedoense

KOREAN AZALEA, YODOGAWA AZALEA
◐ ❉ ↔ 36 in (90 cm) ↑ 36 in (90 cm)
Deciduous or semi-deciduous azalea species from Korea. Compact densely branched shrub, foliage turning rich orange and crimson in autumn. The fragrant, double, funnel-shaped, lilac-purple flowers, held in trusses of 2 to 4 blooms, are produced in late spring. Originally named from this double-flowered cultivated form, wild plants

were subsequently named *R. y.* var. *poukhanense* ★, and feature single pale to deep pink flowers. Zones 5–8.

Rhododendron yunnanense

◐ ❉ ↔ 10 ft (3 m) ↑ 12 ft (3.5 m)
This evergreen shrub from northeastern Myanmar and western China is deciduous in cooler conditions. It has narrow leaves and scaly branchlets. Abundant, white, pale pink, rose pink, rose-lavender, or lavender, funnel-shaped flowers, densely spotted with red, green, or yellow, in trusses of 3 to 5 blooms, are borne in late spring. Zones 7–9.

Rhododendron zoelleri

◐ ✦ ↔ 3 ft (0.9 m) ↑ 6 ft (1.8 m)
A Vireya rhododendron from New Guinea and the nearby Moluccas, with elliptic leaves. Large, brilliant, almost iridescent flowers of pinkish orange to yellow, carried in open trusses of up to 8 funnel-shaped blooms, are borne from autumn to spring. Zones 10–11.

Rhododendron yedoense var. *poukhanense*

R

Rhododendron Hybrid Cultivars

Rhododendron hybrids are cultivated as ornamental plants, valued for their masses of colorful flowers and year-round foliage in great diversity of form; some are also sought-after for their attractive textured bark and rich fragrance. The new leaf shoots of evergreen rhododendrons often form attractive perpendicular "candle-sticks," while mature leaves vary enormously in size. The foliage of deciduous azaleas progresses through the growing season from bright green shoots in spring to bronze in summer, followed by rich reds to yellows in autumn before falling.

HARDY SMALL HYBRIDS

☀ ❄ ↔ 12–40 in (30–100 cm)
↕ 12–40 in (30–100 cm)

The hardy small hybrids are a variable group, ranging from those derived from tiny alpine species and best suited to rockery cultivation to dense mounding bushes with large leaves and upright flower trusses. '**Blue Crown**' has deep lilac-blue or violet flowers with a lighter center blotched with magenta, held in trusses of 20 blooms, mid- to late season; '**Blue Tit**', small leaves, abundant grayish blue flowers; '**Bric-à-Brac**', small, rounded, downy leaves, small white flowers with faint pink markings on upper lobes, contrasting chocolate-colored anthers; '**Carmen**', a dwarf form, less than 12 in (30 cm) high, deep red bell-shaped flowers, in trusses of 2 to 5 blooms, in early to mid-season; '**Chevalier Félix de Sauvage**' features medium-sized coral rose flowers with a dark blotch in the center, in trusses of 12 blooms, early to mid-season; '**Chikor**', soft yellow flowers, delicate foliage which turns to red in winter; '**Chrysomanicum**', bright buttercup yellow flowers, in trusses of 8 blooms, very early in the season; '**Cilpenense**', shiny deep forest green foliage, blush pink bell-shaped flowers with a deeper pink shading, early in the season; '**Creeping Jenny**' (syn. 'Jenny'), bright red funnel-campanulate flowers, held in large loose trusses of 5 to 6 blooms, early to mid-season; '**Curlew**', abundant soft yellow flowers with green-brown markings; '**Dora Amateis**' bears pure white fragrant flowers, lightly spotted with green, held in trusses of 3 to 6 blooms, in early to mid-season; '**Elizabeth**' has bright red funnel-campanulate flowers, in loose trusses of 6 to 8 blooms, early to mid-season; '**Ginny Gee**' bears dark pink flowers shading to shell pink, with white stripes, carried in trusses of 4 to 5 blooms, in early to mid-season; '**Jingle Bells**' produces orange flowers with a red throat that fade to yellow, mid-season; '**Lemon Mist**', small, bright greenish yellow, funnel-shaped flowers in trusses of 2 to 3 blooms, early to mid-season; '**May Day**', cerise or light scarlet funnel-shaped flowers in loose trusses of 8 blooms, in early to mid-season; '**Prostigiatum**', dwarf shrub, tiny grayish green leaves, rich deep

Rhododendrum, Hybrid Cultivar, Hardy Small, 'Carmen'

Rhododendron, Hybrid Cultivar, Hardy Small, 'April Glow'

R., Hybrid Cultivar, Hardy Small, 'Chevalier Félix de Sauvage'

R., HC, Hardy Small, 'Bach Choir'

Rhododendron, Hybrid Cultivar, Hardy Small, 'Blue Tit'

R., HC, Hardy Small, 'Bluebird'

R., HC, Hardy Small, 'Bluette'

Rhododendron, Hybrid Cultivar, Hardy Small, 'Balta'

R

purple flowers, in trusses of 2 to
3 blooms, in mid- to late season;
'**Ptarmigan**', delicate foliage, densely
scaly underneath, broadly funnel-
shaped white flowers, in terminal
clusters of several trusses of 2 to 3
blooms, in early to mid-season;
'**Ramapo**', pinkish violet flowers, early
to mid-season, almost circular leaves
with distinctive deep metallic hue in
winter; '**Ruby Hart**', dark blackish red
flowers, in loose trusses of 7 blooms,
early to mid-season; '**Scarlet Wonder**',
bright cardinal red bell-shaped flowers
with wavy edges, in trusses of 5 to 7
blooms, mid-season; '**Snow Lady**',
dark green hairy leaves, white flowers
with dark anthers, early to mid-
season. Zones 6–9.

Rhododendron, Hybrid Cultivar, Hardy Small, 'Chikor'

R., HC, Hardy Small, 'Baden-Baden'

R., HC, Hardy Small, 'Cowslip'

R., HC, Hardy Small, 'Dora Amateis'

R., HC, Hardy Small, 'Elisabeth Hobbie'

R., HC, Hardy Small, 'Golden Wit'

Rhododendron, Hybrid Cultivar, Hardy Small, 'Chelsea Seventy'

R., HC, Hardy Small, 'Chrysomanicum'

R., HC, Hardy Small, 'Elizabeth'

R., HC, Hardy Small, 'Jaipur'

R., HC, Hardy Small, 'Jingle Bells'

Rhododendron, Hybrid Cultivar, Hardy Small, 'Honey'

Rhododendron, Hybrid Cultivar, Hardy Small, 'Lampion'

Rhododendron, Hybrid Cultivar, Hardy Small, 'Odee Wright'

R., HC, Hardy Small, 'May Day'

R., HC, Hardy Small, 'Molly Anne'

R., HC, Hardy Small, 'Mrs T. H. Lowinsky'

R., HC, Hardy Small, 'Olga'

R., HC, Hardy Small, 'Praecox'

R., HC, Hardy Small, 'Ruby Hart'

R., HC, Hardy Small, 'Thunderstorm'

R., HC, Hardy Small, 'Vintage Rose'

HARDY MEDIUM HYBRIDS

☼ ❋ ↔ 2–6 ft (0.6–1.8 m)
↕ 3–6 ft (0.9–1.8 m)

The medium-sized hybrids are the plants best suited to general cultivation and this size range is where most hybridizers have placed the emphasis of their development programs. Consequently this group encompasses hundreds of beautiful plants that bloom in the full color range over the entire flowering season. **'Admiral Piet Hein'**, rosy lilac fragrant flowers, mid-season; **'Alison Johnstone'**, bluish gray waxy foliage, cream flowers initially, changing to a delicate light apricot-pink, in trusses of 9 blooms, early to mid-season; **'Anah Kruschke'**, conical trusses of lavender to purple-red flowers, late spring; **'Arthur Bedford'** (syn. 'A. Bedford'), red-stemmed glossy green leaves, flowers light mauve with darker

Rhododendron, Hybrid Cultivar, Hardy Medium, 'Anah Kruschke'

Rhododendron, Hybrid Cultivar, Hardy Medium, 'Angel'

R., Hybrid Cultivar, Hardy Medium, 'Belle of Lockington'

Rhododendron, Hybrid Cultivar, Hardy Medium, 'Blue Diamond'

Rhododendron, Hybrid Cultivar, Hardy Medium, 'Blue Ensign'

Rhododendron, Hybrid Cultivar, Hardy Medium, 'Boule de Neige'

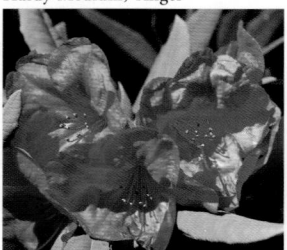

R., HC, HM, 'C. P. Raffill'

R., HC, HM, 'Champagne'

R., HC, HM, 'Colonel Coen'

R., HC, HM, 'Donvale Cheer'

R., HC, HM, 'Donvale Pearl'

R., HC, HM, 'Donvale Ruffles'

R., HC, HM, 'Elsie Watson'

R., HC, Hardy Medium, 'Fabia'

R., HC, HM, 'Fire Walk'

R., HC, HM, 'Florence Mann'

R., HC, Hardy Medium, 'Blue Peter'

R., HC, Hardy Medium, 'Britannia'

R., HC, Hardy Medium, 'Cynthia'

R., HC, Hardy Medium, 'Desert Sun'

lobes, marked with deep rose to almost black, in domed trusses of 16 funnel-shaped blooms; '**Arthur J. Ivens**', rose pink bell-shaped flowers; '**Award**', fragrant white flowers with light yellow flare, margins shaded with pink, in ball-shaped trusses of 14 blooms, mid-season; '**Blue Diamond**', deep lilac-blue flowers, early to mid-season; '**Blue Peter**', light lavender-blue flowers, large blackish purple blotch, frilly edges to petals, in tight conical trusses, mid- to late season; '**Bow Bells**', cup-shaped light pink flowers, in loose trusses of 4 to 7 blooms, early to

mid-season; '**C. I. S.**', twisted leaf tips, orange-yellow flowers, bright orange-red throat, in trusses of about 11 blooms, mid-season; '**Canary**', deeply veined leaves, bright lemon yellow flowers, in tight trusses, early to mid-season; '**C. P. Raffill**', deep orange-red to red flowers, in large rounded trusses, late in season; '**Creamy Chiffon**', salmon-orange buds, creamy yellow double flowers, in mid- to late season; '**Crossbill**', small, tubular flowers, yellow flushed with apricot, early in season; '**Fabia**', scarlet flowers, shading to orange in the tube, in drooping trusses of bell-shaped blooms, mid-season; '**Fireman Jeff**', bright blood red flowers, bright red calyx, in compact trusses of 10 blooms, mid-season; '**Flora Markeeta**', coral pink buds open to ivory white flowers, flushed with coral, fringed with bright pink, in rounded trusses of 10 blooms, early

to mid-season; '**Florence Mann**', one of the best "blue" rhododendrons in milder climates with deep lavender-blue or lavender-violet flowers, early to mid-season; '**Furnivall's Daughter**', bright pink flowers with a cherry blotch, in conical trusses of 15 blooms, mid-season; '**Golden Star**', mimosa yellow flowers, with 7 wavy lobes, in ball-shaped trusses of up to 13 blooms, in mid- to late season; '**Goldflimmer**', striking variegated foliage, mauve flowers, late in season; '**Helene Schiffner**', pure white flowers with faint yellow to brown markings, in upright, dome-shaped trusses; '**Hotei**', canary yellow bell-shaped flowers with a darker throat, in round trusses of 12 blooms, mid-season; '**Humming Bird**', deep pink to red bell-shaped flowers, in loose trusses of 4 to 5 blooms, early to mid-season; '**Lady Clementine Mitford**' (syn.

'Lady C. Mitford') has glossy green foliage covered with silver hairs when young, soft peach-pink flowers, darker at the edges, slight yellow eye, mid- to late season; '**Letty Edwards**', pale pink buds opening to pale primrose yellow flowers, in rounded trusses of 9 to 11 blooms, mid-season; '**Markeeta's Prize**', leathery dark green leaves, scarlet-red flowers, in trusses of 12 blooms, mid-season; '**Matador**', dark orange-red tubular flowers, in trusses of 8 blooms, early to mid-season; '**Midnight**', dark green glossy foliage, very deep magenta-mauve flowers, blackish throat, heavily spotted with dark red on upper lobe, in rounded trusses of 16 blooms, mid- to late season; '**Moonstone**', creamy yellow, pink, or cream, bell-shaped flowers, flushed with pink, in loose trusses of 3 to 5 blooms, early to mid-season; '**Mrs A. T. de la Mare**, large, white,

Rhododendron, Hybrid Cultivar, Hardy Medium, 'Midnight'

Rhododendron, Hybrid Cultivar, Hardy Medium, 'Mrs E. C. Stirling'

R., HC, HM, 'Furnivall's Daughter'

R., HC, HM, 'Haida Gold'

R., HC, Hardy Medium, 'Holden'

R., HC, HM, 'Holmslee Missi'

R., HC, Hardy Medium, 'Jancio'

R., HC, Hardy Medium, 'Latona'

R., HC, HM, 'Lord Roberts'

R., HC, Hardy Medium, 'Max Sye'

R., HC, HM, 'Moonshine Bright'

R., HC, HM, 'Moonstone'

R., HC, HM, 'Mrs Betty Robertson'

R., HC, HM, 'Naomi Astarte'

R., HC, HM, 'Naomi Pink Beauty'

R., HC, Hardy Medium, 'PJM'

R., HC, Hardy Medium, 'Paris'

R., HC, HM, 'President Roosevelt'

Rhododendron, Hybrid Cultivar, Hardy Medium, 'Nova Zembla' upright flowers with a faint green blotch, in large dome-shaped trusses of 12 to 14 blooms, mid-season; **'Mrs Betty Robertson'** (syn. 'Mrs Betty Robinson'), soft creamy yellow flowers with red speckled upper petal, in upright dome-shaped trusses, mid-

R., HC, Hardy Medium, 'Ross Maud'

season; **'Mrs E. C. Stirling'**, slightly ruffled, pink, medium-sized blooms, mid- to late season; **'Mrs Furnivall'**, widely funnel-shaped light rose pink flowers, paler at the center, with conspicuous deep sienna blotch, in large trusses, mid- to late season; **'PJM'**, small, rounded, aromatic leaves, green in summer, turning mahogany in winter, bright lavender-pink flowers, early in season; **'President Roosevelt'**, strongly variegated leaves, frilled flowers white flushed red with bold red edging, in medium-sized conical trusses early to mid-season; **'Purple Splendor'**, very dark purple flowers, with a blackish blotch, in dome-shaped to spherical trusses, mid- to late season; **'Purpureum Elegans'**, bluish purple

flowers marked green or brown, in dense rounded trusses, mid- to late season; **'Roman Pottery'**, pale orange flowers with copper lobes, in loose drooping trusses, mid-season; **'Russautinii'**, masses of lavender-blue flowers with a darker eye, in trusses of 2 to 5 blooms, early to mid-season; **'Sappho'**, narrow olive green leaves, medium-sized, white, widely funnel-shaped flowers with a striking deep maroon-black blotch, in large conical trusses, mid- to late season; **'Seta'**, very narrow, bell-shaped flowers of white with bold margins of rose pink, early in the season, over a long period; **'Tally Ho'**, clear orange-red flowers, in compact trusses, late in the season; **'The Hon. Jean Marie de Montague'**

(syn. 'Jean Mary Montague'), thick emerald green leaves, large bright scarlet flowers, in dome-shaped trusses of 10 to 14 blooms, in mid-season; **'Unique'**, strong pink buds open to subtle apricot-pink flowers on medium-sized trusses, early- to mid-season; **'Vanessa Pastel'**, pointed mossy green leaves, brick red flowers, changing to apricot then to deep cream, with a bronze-yellow throat, in trusses, mid- to late season, a pinker variety is also available; **'Winsome'**, reddish winter buds open to rosy cerise flowers, in mid-season; **'Yellow Hammer'**, small, light green, and scaly leaves, very deep yellow tubular flowers, in trusses of 3 blooms, early to mid-season. Zones 6–9.

Rhododendron, Hybrid Cultivar, Hardy Medium, 'The Hon. Jean Marie de Montague'

Rhododendron, Hybrid Cultivar, Hardy Medium, 'Saki'

R., HC, HM, 'Winning Post'

R., HC, HM, 'Starry Night'

R., HC, HM, 'St Breward'

R., HC, Hardy Medium, 'Unique'

R., HC, HM, 'Wilgen's Surprise'

R., HC, HM, 'Purple Splendor'

R., HC, Hardy Medium, 'Seta'

R., HC, Hardy Medium, 'Suomi'

R., HC, Hardy Medium, 'Van'

R., HC, HM, 'Wheatley'

HARDY TALL HYBRIDS

☀ ❄ ↔ 5–17 ft (1.5–5 m)
↕ 6–35 ft (1.8–10 m)

Many of the taller hybrids will eventually become tree-like, though they take many years to reach such proportions. While they undoubtedly demand more space, few sights are more spectacular than a large rhododendron in full bloom. 'Alice' takes some years before producing large conical flower trusses of pale rose or frosty pink flowers, mid-season; 'Anna Rose Whitney', large mid-green leaves, upright trusses of deep pink flowers; 'Auguste van Geert', large reddish purple flowers, in generous trusses, early in the season; 'Beauty of Littleworth', pure white flowers, spotted with dark purple markings, in very large trusses of 16 to 19 blooms, mid-season; 'Bernstein', old gold flowers with vivid coral-red flare; 'Betty Wormald', pastel pink flowers, paler center and light purple spotting, in huge dome-shaped trusses, late season; 'Bibiani', deep bright blood red flowers, in dense rounded trusses of 14 blooms, early in the season; 'Boddaertianum' (syn. 'Croix d'Anvers'), lavender-pink buds opening as white flowers, dark purple blotch, crimson ray, in compact rounded trusses of 18 to 22 blooms, mid-season; 'Brigitte',

purple flowers, reddening toward the center, green blotch; 'Broughtonii', rosy crimson flowers, darker spots, in large pyramid-shaped trusses of 20 blooms, mid-season; 'Caractacus', purplish red flowers, lighter shading toward center; 'Carita', rich green leaves, pink buds open to primrose yellow flowers; 'Cornubia', blood red flowers, in large conical trusses, early season; 'Crest' (syn. 'Hawk Crest'), bright primrose yellow flowers, slightly darkening around throat, in large dome-shaped trusses, mid-season; 'Cunningham's White', white flowers, yellowish green at center; 'David', deep red bell-shaped flowers, white anthers and frilly margins, in loose trusses, early to mid-season; 'Everestianum', rosy lilac flowers, spotted in throat, frilled edges, in compact rounded trusses of about 15 blooms, mid- to late season; 'Fastuosum Flore Pleno', deep green foliage, medium-sized, semi-double, mauve flowers, in loose trusses, mid- to late season; 'Fire Bird', glowing salmon red flowers, bright yellow anthers, in large trusses, mid- to late season; 'Fusilier', bright orange-red flowers, in medium-sized trusses, mid- to late season; 'Gill's Crimson', bright blood red long-lasting flowers, in tight rounded trusses, early to mid-season; 'Gladys', cream or bright

Rhododendron, Hybrid Cultivar, Hardy Tall, 'Alice'

R., HC, Hardy Tall, 'Auguste van Geert'

R., HC, Hardy Tall, 'Betty Wormald'

Rhododendron, HC, Hardy Tall, 'Bibiani'

R., HC, Hardy Tall, 'Broughtonii'

Rhododendron, Hybrid Cultivar, Hardy Tall, 'Corinne Boulter'

R., HC, Hardy Tall, 'Catawbiense Boursault'

R., HC, Hardy Tall, 'Colehurst'

R., HC, Hardy Tall, 'Dame Nellie Melba'

R., HC, Hardy Tall, 'Ethel Stocker'

R., HC, Hardy Tall, 'Lem's Cameo'

R., HC, Hardy Tall, 'Loderi King George'

R., HC, Hardy Tall, 'Mother of Pearl'

R., HC, Hardy Tall, 'Mrs Charles E. Pearson'

Rhododendron, Hybrid Cultivar, Hardy Tall, 'Fastuosum Flore Pleno'

R., HC, Hardy Tall, 'Mrs G. W. Leak'

R., HC, Hardy Tall, 'Saint Tudy'

R., HC, Hardy Tall, 'Scintillation'

R., Hybrid Cultivar, Hardy Tall, 'Susan'

R., HC, Hardy Tall, 'Trewithen Orange'

R., HC, Hardy Tall, 'Trude Webster'

R., Hybrid Cultivar, Hardy Tall, 'Vesuvius'

R., Hybrid Cultivar, Hardy Tall, 'Virgo'

R., HC, Hardy Tall, 'Margaret Mack'

primrose yellow flowers, with crimson markings, small rounded trusses of 10 blooms, early to mid-season; '**Gomer Waterer**', pure white flowers open from slightly rose pink-tinged buds, mid- to late season; '**Lady Chamberlain**', slender willowy branches, bluish green new foliage, fleshy, tubular, trumpet-shaped flowers, bright orange to salmon pink, in drooping trusses of 3 to 6 blooms, mid- to late season; '**Lem's Cameo**', widely bell-shaped, apricot-cream and pink flowers, with a small, scarlet, dorsal blotch, in large dome-shaped trusses of about 20 blooms, mid-season; '**Loder's White**', slightly fragrant flowers, white, edged with pale lilac, tinge of yellow in throat, in large conical trusses, mid-season; '**Mrs Charles E. Pearson**', lush deep green foliage, pale pinkish mauve flowers edged with lavender, heavy chestnut spotting, in very large coni-cal trusses, mid- to late season; '**Mrs G. W. Leak**', startling bright pink flowers, deep reddish carmine blotch, crimson markings, in large, compact, conical trusses, early to mid-season; '**Red Admiral**', glowing red bell-shaped flowers, early in season; '**Scintillation**', pastel pink flowers, yellowish brown flare in the throat, in large trusses of about 15 blooms, mid-season; '**Sir Charles Lemon**', pure white flowers faintly spotted in the throat, in large rounded trusses, early to mid-season; '**Souvenir de Doctor S. Endtz**', rose pink buds open to rich pink widely funnel-shaped flowers, marked with a crimson ray, in domed trusses of 15 to 17 blooms, mid-season; '**Susan**', bluish mauve flowers, fading to nearly white, dark margins, purple spots, rounded trusses of about 12 blooms, mid-season; '**Taurus**', long-lasting deep green leaves, large trusses of bright red flowers, with faint black spotting; '**Trewithen Orange**', sea-green foliage, tubular deep orange-brown flowers, in loose pendulous trusses, mid-season; '**Trude Webster**', slightly twisted glossy leaves, clear pink flowers, spotting on upper lobe, mid-season. Zones 6–9.

TENDER HYBRIDS

☼/◑ ᛆ ↔ 3–10 ft (0.9–3 m)
↕ 3–17 ft (0.9–5 m)

Many of the lowland southern Asian rhododendrons are intolerant of heavy or repeated frosts. However, they are beautiful plants that in addition to the color and size of their flowers often also offer heavy fragrance and lush foliage. In mild areas, plants derived from species such as *Rhododendron nuttallii* and *R. maddenii* are among spring's best-remembered highlights. '**Countess of Haddington**' (syn. 'Eureka Maid'), pink buds open to fragrant white flowers which are flushed with rose, in loose trusses of funnel-shaped flowers, mid- to late season; '**Eldorado**', dark yellowish green leaves, primrose yellow flowers, in loose clusters of 3 to 4 medium-sized funnel-shaped blooms, mid-season; '**Else Frye**', fragrant flowers, white, flushed pink with yellow centers, in clusters of 3 to 6 blooms, early to mid-spring; '**Forsterianum**', densely foliaged, loose clusters of funnel-shaped white blooms with a yellow flare, fragrant; '**Fragrantissimum**', large, heavily perfumed, white, trumpet-shaped flowers, tinged with pink, with a creamy yellow center, in loose

Rhododendron, Hybrid Cultivar, Tender, 'Countess of Haddington'

trusses, early to mid-season; '**Harry Tagg**', fragrant, white, frilly, long-lasting flowers with a greenish yellow stain, in trusses of 3 to 4 blooms, early to mid-season; '**Pink Gin**', blue-green foliage, abundant flowers of a soft peach-pink to purplish; '**Princess Alice**' (syn. 'Caerhays Princess Alice'), fragrant white flowers, flushed with pink, a small yellow eye, in loose trusses, in early to mid-season; '**Saffron Queen**', masses of sulfur yellow flowers, dark spotting, in small trusses of 8 to 9 blooms, early to mid-season; '**Suave**', fragrant, blush pink to white, bell-shaped flowers, fading to white, early to mid-season; '**Tyermannii**', dark glossy green foliage, rich brownish bark on the main trunk, fragrant pure

R., Hybrid Cultivar, Vireya, 'Coral Flare'

R., Hybrid Cultivar, Tender, 'Suave'

white flowers, yellow stain in throat; '**Wedding Gown**', yellowish white funnel-shaped flowers in trusses of 5 to 7 blooms. Zones 9–10.

VIREYA HYBRIDS

◑/☼ ⚘ ↔ 12–60 in (30–150 cm)
↕ 18–72 in (45–180 cm)

Extending the range of the genus *Rhododendron* into the southern hemisphere, these tropical Southeast Asian species enjoyed great popularity in Victorian times and are now back in vogue, with many new hybrids appearing recently. Part of their appeal lies in their vivid coloration, with fragrance and non-seasonal flowering completing the package. '**Alisa Nicole**', cerise pink bell-shaped

R., Hybrid Cultivar, Tender, 'Princess Alice'

flowers; '**Aravir**', beautifully fragrant, soft, white, tubular flowers, in domed trusses of 7 to 10 blooms; '**Bold Janus**', very large, lightly perfumed flowers of apricot edged with pink; '**Coral Flare**', large coral pink flowers in trusses of 3 to 7 blooms, throughout the year; '**Craig Faragher**', damask pink or mauve tubular flowers, lobes of pale cyclamen pink, in trusses of 6 to 8 blooms; '**Cristo Rey**', brilliant orange flowers with yellow center; '**Dresden Doll**', waxy, heavily veined, lime green leaves, deep salmon pink flowers with cream throat; '**Esprit de Joie**', large, fragrant, soft rose pink flowers with creamy throat, in trusses of 4 to 6 blooms; '**Great Scent-sation**', large, highly fragrant, bell-shaped, carmine pink flowers; '**Hari's Choice**', generous vivid crimson flowers in very full trusses; '**Iced Primrose**', beautifully fragrant, very large, creamy primrose flowers, with a faint hint of pastel green in throat; '**Liberty Bar**', red flowers, in trusses of 10 to 15 blooms, flowering throughout year; '**Little One**', tiny mandarin-pink flowers, in trusses of 2 to 3 blooms, appear for up to 3 months; '**Littlest Angel**', petite, waxy,

Rhododendron, Hybrid Cultivar, Vireya, 'Cristo Rey'

R., Hybrid Cultivar, Vireya, 'D. B. Stanton'

R

and deep red flowers in trusses of 4 blooms; '**Nancy Miller Adler**', very glossy foliage, soft blush pink flowers; '**Ne Plus Ultra**', waxy foliage, bright red, tubular, funnel-shaped flowers, in trusses of 8 to 14 blooms; '**Niugini Firebird**', medium-sized trumpet flowers, bright red with glowing orange throat; '**Popcorn**', trusses of 10 to 14 pale cream flowers with white lobes; '**Princess Alexandra**', open trusses of tubular, medium-sized, slightly flared flowers of white, sometimes with a blush of pale pink; '**Scarlet Beauty**', bright scarlet-orange flowers, deep yellow throat, mid-red lobes; '**Simbu Sunset**', large, bicolored, funnel-shaped flowers, brilliant orange with buttercup yellow center, in trusses of 4 to 6 blooms; '**Sir George Holford**', orange-yellow flowers, in trusses of

8 to 10 blooms; '**Souvenir de J. H. Mangles**', very full trusses of soft coral red flowers; '**Sweet Amanda**', large, fragrant, tubular, pale yellow flowers in trusses of 5 to 8 blooms; '**Sweet Wendy**', abundant, perfumed, light orange flowers; '**Triumphans**' has glowing scarlet-crimson flowers, in trusses of 8 to 14 blooms, from winter to early spring; '**Tropic Fanfare**',

R., Hybrid Cultivar, Vireya, 'George Bugden'

Rhododendron, Hybrid Cultivar, Vireya, 'Souvenir de J. H. Mangles'

Rhododendron, Hybrid Cultivar, Vireya, 'Our Marcia'

R., Hybrid Cultivar, Vireya, 'Pink Delight'

R., Hybrid Cultivar, Vireya, 'Liberty Bar'

Rhododendron, Hybrid Cultivar, Vireya, 'Scarlet Beauty'

R., Hybrid Cultivar, Vireya, 'Pink Veitch'

R., Hybrid Cultivar, Vireya, 'Sunny'

R., HC, Vireya, 'Princess Alexandra'

R., Hybrid Cultivar, Vireya, 'Wattlebird'

R., HC, Yak, 'Dusty Miller'

R., HC, Yak, 'Harkwood Pemiere'

R., Hybrid Cultivar, Yak, 'Marion'

R., HC, Yak, 'Morgenrot'

R., HC, Yak, 'Yellow Pippin'

R., HC, Yak, 'General Practitioner'

R., Hybrid Cultivar, Yak, 'Golden Torch'

R., Hybrid Cultivar, Yak, 'Grumpy'

R., Hybrid Cultivar, Yak, 'Hydon Dawn'

R., Hybrid Cultivar, Yak, 'Jane Redford'

R., Hybrid Cultivar, Yak, 'Patricia's Day'

R., Hybrid Cultivar, Yak, 'Percy Wiseman'

R., Hybrid Cultivar, Yak, 'Pink Cherub'

Rhododendron, Hybrid Cultivar, Yak, 'Fantastica'

R., Hybrid Cultivar, Yak, 'Stanley Rivlin'

R., Hybrid Cultivar, Yak, 'Tequila Sunrise'

R., Hybrid Cultivar, Yak, 'Renoir'

trusses of 8 to 10 bright pink waxy flowers; **'Tropic Tango'**, delicate flowers of soft tangerine; **'Wattlebird'** (syn. 'Wattle Bird'), loose trusses of 7 to 9 large, open, flared, bell-shaped flowers, bright clear golden yellow. Zones 10–12.

YAK HYBRIDS

☀ ❄ ↔ 2–5 ft (0.6–1.5 m)
↕ 1–6 ft (0.3–1.8 m)

"Yaks" are hybrids in which the dominant parent is *Rhododendron degronianum* subsp. *yakushimanum*. They are low growing and very hardy, with attractive foliage and abundant flowers, usually in combinations of pink and white. **'Bashful'**, camellia pink flowers, deeper shades of rose, reddish brown blotch, early in season; **'Doc'**, rose pink flowers with deeper rims and spots on the upper lobes, in rounded trusses of 9 blooms, in mid-

season; **'Dopey'** has glossy, red, bell-shaped flowers, paler toward edges, dark brown spots on the upper lobes, in spherical trusses of 16 blooms, in mid-season; **'Golden Torch'** has soft yellow flowers, in compact trusses of 13 to 15 blooms, in mid- to late season; **'Grumpy'**, orange buds open as creamy flowers tinged with pink, in rounded trusses of 11 blooms, in mid-season; **'Hoppy'**, white flowers with greenish speckling appear in ball-

shaped trusses of 18 blooms, in mid-season; **'Hydon Dawn'**, flowers with pink frilled petals, fading to the edges, with reddish brown spots, in large, compact, and rounded trusses of 14 to 18 blooms, in mid-season; **'Percy Wiseman'** has pink funnel-shaped flowers fading to white, with a pale yellow center and orange spots, in trusses of 14 blooms, mid-season; **'Peste's Blue Ice'**, deep purplish pink flowers, fading to very pale purple,

lightly spotted with green, in trusses of 21 blooms, in mid-season; **'Polaris'** has abundant pinkish purple flowers, with lighter shading at the center; **'Renoir'**, deeply bell-shaped rose pink flowers with a white throat and crimson spots, in rounded trusses of 11 blooms, in mid-season; **'Surrey Heath'**, rose pink flowers with a lighter center bloom, in mid-season; **'Titian Beauty'** bears turkey red flowers, in mid-season. Zones 7–9.

R

Rhododendron, Hybrid Cultivar, Deciduous Azalea, Ghent, 'Pucella'

R., HC, DA, Ghent, 'Coccineum Speciosum'

R., HC, Deciduous Azalea, Ghent, 'Daviesii'

R., HC, DA, Ghent, 'Gloria Mundi'

DECIDUOUS AZALEA HYBRIDS

Deciduous azaleas are multi-stemmed from the ground, never forming a central trunk. The leaves have a thin texture, and the large, often sticky, winter buds contain both the flowers and the spring foliage flush. Flowers of deciduous azaleas are trumpet-shaped, flaring from a narrow tube, and are predominantly in shades of cream to salmon, yellow, orange, and scarlet. Deciduous azaleas bloom in spring with or before the new leaves; if they are to flower well, they require a climate with fairly cold winters.

GHENT HYBRIDS

☀ ❄ ↔ 3–6 ft (0.9–1.8 m)
↕ 5–8 ft (1.5–2.4 m)

These very hardy hybrids were bred in the early 1800s in the Belgian city of Ghent, starting with the American species *Rhododendron calendulaceum* and *R. periclymenoides*. Large bushes

R., HC, DA, Ilam and Melford, 'Ilam Ming'

flower in late spring to early summer, with large trusses of relatively small flowers, up to 2 in (5 cm) in diameter, often fragrant, with long tubes, mostly single, but occasionally double. There are numerous cultivars: 'Altaclarense', white flowers with an orange blotch; 'Coccineum Speciosum', bright orange-red flowers, attractive autumn foliage; 'Corneille', double cream flowers, petals pink tinged on reverse, colorful autumn foliage; 'Daviesii', fragrant white flowers with a yellow flare; 'Gloria Mundi', orange and yellow flowers; 'Nancy Waterer', large golden yellow flowers, pleasantly scented; 'Narcissiflorum', double yellow flowers, shaded darker at the center and on petal reverse; 'Phoebe', double deep yellow flowers; 'Pucella', pink flowers with a bright orange blotch; 'Vulcan', deep red flowers with an orange blotch. Zones 5–9.

ILAM AND MELFORD HYBRIDS

☀/☀ ❄ ↔ 4–7 ft (1.2–2 m)
↕ 4–10 ft (1.2–3 m)

Bred in New Zealand, the Ilam and Melford hybrids were created by crossing Knap Hill and Exbury hybrids with *Rhododendron calendulaceum*, *R. viscosum*, and *R. molle* to create larger fragrant flowers. 'Dark Red Ilam', dark red flowers; 'Dr Yates', pink to red flowers, frilled petals; 'Gallipoli', apricot flowers with orange markings; 'Ilam Ming', orange flowers with yellow flare; 'Yellow Beauty', golden yellow flowers with a faintly spotted orange blotch. Zones 5–9.

KNAP HILL AND EXBURY HYBRIDS

☀/☀ ❄ ↔ 4–7 ft (1.2–2 m)
↕ 4–10 ft (1.2–3 m)

These hybrids were developed from the late 1800s onwards by the Waterer family at Knap Hill in Surrey, England. They are large bushy shrubs up to

Rhododendron, Hybrid Cultivar, Deciduous Azalea, Ilam and Melford, 'Yellow Beauty'

Rhododendron, Hybrid Cultivar, Deciduous Azalea, Ilam and Melford, 'Dr Yates'

Rhododendron, Hybrid Cultivar, Deciduous Azalea, Knap Hill and Exbury, 'Berryrose'

R., HC, DA, Knap Hill and Exbury, 'Balzac'

R., HC, DA, Knap Hill and Exbury, 'Annabella'

Rhododendron, Hybrid Cultivar, Deciduous Azalea, Knap Hill and Exbury, 'Cecile'

Rhododendron, Hybrid Cultivar, Deciduous Azalea, Knap Hill and Exbury, 'Homebush'

Rhododendron, Hybrid Cultivar, Deciduous Azalea, Knap Hill and Exbury, 'Daybreak'

R., Hybrid Cultivar, Deciduous Azalea, Knap Hill and Exbury, 'Fireglow'

R., Hybrid Cultivar, Deciduous Azalea, Knap Hill and Exbury, 'Golden Sunset'

R., HC, DA, Knap Hill and Exbury, 'Gog'

R., HC, DA, Knap Hill and Exbury, 'Ginger'

Rhododendron, Hybrid Cultivar, Deciduous Azalea, Knap Hill and Exbury, 'Eisenhower'

R

10 ft (3 m) tall and 7 ft (2 m) wide. The leaves of most turn bronze then brilliant red or yellow before falling in autumn. Large, open, sometimes fragrant, richly colored flowers, up to 4 in (10 cm) wide, are borne in very large trusses of up to 30 blooms. Numerous cultivars: '**Aurora**', strong yellowish pink flowers with an orange blotch; '**Balzac**', fragrant reddish orange flowers; '**Berryrose**', fragrant orange-red flowers with a vivid yellow blotch; '**Brazil**', slightly frilled bright tangerine-red flowers; '**Buzzard**', fragrant pale yellow flowers tinged with pink; '**Cannon's Double**', a low-growing cultivar with creamy yellow flowers; '**Crinoline**', ruffled white flowers flushed with pink; '**Firefly**', vivid purplish red flowers with a subtle orange flare; '**Gibraltar**', bright orange-red flowers; '**Golden Eagle**', reddish orange flowers; '**Homebush**', semi-double crimson-pink flowers; '**Hotspur Red**', deep orange flowers, almost red; '**Klondyke**', deep golden orange flowers with an orange-yellow blotch; '**Krakatoa**', orange-red flowers; '**Lady Jane**', fragrant vivid yellow flowers flushed with reddish orange, with wavy-edged petals; '**Orange Supreme**', orange flowers flushed with deep orange and a mid-orange blotch; '**Satan**', brilliant red flowers; '**Silver Slipper**', snow white flowers, flushed with pink, with a yellow flare; '**Tunis**', dark red flowers with a reddish orange blotch; '**Wryneck**', vivid yellow flowers, edged with pink. Zones 5–9.

Rhododendron, Hybrid Cultivar, Deciduous Azalea, Knap Hill and Exbury, 'Klondyke'

Rhododendron, Hybrid Cultivar, Deciduous Azalea, Knap Hill and Exbury, 'Strawberry Ice'

R., Hybrid Cultivar, Deciduous Azalea, Knap Hill and Exbury, 'Hotspur Red'

R., Hybrid Cultivar, Deciduous Azalea, Knap Hill and Exbury, 'Kathleen'

R., Hybrid Cultivar, Deciduous Azalea, Knap Hill and Exbury, 'Lady Roseberry'

R., Hybrid Cultivar, Deciduous Azalea, Knap Hill and Exbury, 'Knighthood'

Rhododendron, Hybrid Cultivar, Deciduous Azalea, Knap Hill and Exbury, 'Golden Eagle'

Rhododendron, Hybrid Cultivar, Deciduous Azalea, Knap Hill and Exbury, 'Pink Delight'

R

R., Hybrid Cultivar, Deciduous Azalea, Knap Hill and Exbury, 'Scarlet Pimpernel'

R., Hybrid Cultivar, Deciduous Azalea, Knap Hill and Exbury, 'Sun Chariot'

Rhododendron, Hybrid Cultivar, Deciduous Azalea, Knap Hill and Exbury, 'Westminster'

R., HC, DA, Knap Hill and Exbury, 'Persil'

R., HC, DA, Knap Hill and Exbury, 'Toucan'

MOLLIS HYBRIDS

☼/◐ ❄ ↔ 5–7 ft (1.5–2 m)
↕ 5–8 ft (1.5–2.4 m)

Created from crosses between *Rhododendron molle*, *R. molle* subsp. *japonicum*, and the earlier Ghent hybrids, the numerous Mollis azaleas were developed in the Netherlands and Belgium from the 1860s and 1870s. Large hardy shrubs, to 8 ft (2.4 m) in height, with single flowers, 2 in (5 cm) wide, sometimes fragrant, appearing from mid-spring in strong colors including creams, yellows, oranges,

R., Hybrid Cultivar, Deciduous Azalea, Knap Hill and Exbury, 'Wallowa Red'

and reds. Difficult to propagate from cuttings, so often sold as variable seedlings, best selected for purchase when in flower. '**Anthony Koster**', yellow flowers; '**Apple Blossom**', light pink flowers; '**Babeuff**', glowing salmon-orange flowers; '**Carat**', reddish orange flowers, orange blotch; '**Christopher Wren**', large flowers of brilliant yellow with a strong orange blotch; '**Dr M. Oosthoek**', vivid reddish orange flowers, lighter blotch; '**Esmeralda**', red buds open to orange flowers; '**Hortulanus H. Witte**',

orange-yellow flowers with an orange blotch; '**Hugo Koster**', orange flowers; '**J.C. van Tol**', flowers apricot-pink; '**Koningin Emma**', orange flowers; '**Koster's Brilliant Red**', reddish orange flowers; '**Koster's Yellow**', orange-yellow flowers with an orange blotch; '**Saturnus**', bright orange-red flowers, petals red-tingd on reverse; '**Spek's Brilliant**', large trusses of bright orange-red flowers; '**Spek's Orange**', deep orange buds open to orange-red flowers; '**Winston Churchill**', orange-red flowers. Zones 6–9.

R., HC, DA, Mollis, 'Hortulanus H. Witte'

R., HC, Deciduous Azalea, Mollis, 'Babeuff'

R., HC, Deciduous Azalea, Mollis, 'Saturnus'

R., HC, DA, Mollis, 'Koningin Emma'

R

Rhododendrom, Hybrid Cultivar, Deciduous Azalea, Mollis, 'Christopher Wren'

Rhododendrom, Hybrid Cultivar, Deciduous Azalea, Mollis, 'Apple Blossom'

R., HC, DA, Occidentale, 'Bridesmaid'

R., HC, DA, Occidentale, 'Exquisitum'

Rhododendron, Hybrid Cultivar, Deciduous Azalea, Occidentale, 'Coccinto Speciosa'

R., HC, DA, Occidentale, 'Magnifica'

Rhododendron, Hybrid Cultivar, Deciduous Azalea, Occidentale, 'Delicatissimum'

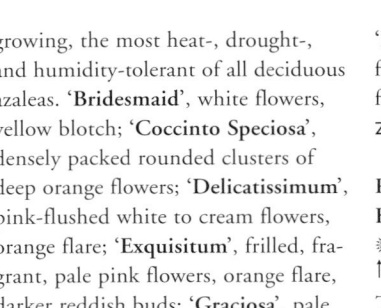

Rhododendron, Hybrid Cultivar, Deciduous Azalea, Rustica Flore Pleno, 'Norma'

OCCIDENTALE HYBRIDS

☀/◐ ❄ ↔ 6–10 ft (1.8–3 m)
↑ 6–10 ft (1.8–3 m)

Developed in England in early twentieth century from *R. occidentale* and Mollis hybrids. Usually a broad spreading shrub to about 8 ft (2.4 m) tall. White or pale pink fragrant flowers, to 3 in (8 cm) wide, open after leaves in mid-spring. Most characterized by deep yellow blotch on flowers. Slow-growing, the most heat-, drought-, and humidity-tolerant of all deciduous azaleas. 'Bridesmaid', white flowers, yellow blotch; 'Coccinto Speciosa', densely packed rounded clusters of deep orange flowers; 'Delicatissimum', pink-flushed white to cream flowers, orange flare; 'Exquisitum', frilled, fragrant, pale pink flowers, orange flare, darker reddish buds; 'Graciosa', pale orange-yellow flowers, flushed pink; 'Magnifica', white to yellow flowers flushed pink, yellow flare; 'Superba', frilled pink flowers, apricot blotch. Zones 7–10.

RUSTICA FLORE PLENO HYBRIDS

☀/◐ ❄ ↔ 4–6 ft (1.2–1.8 m)
↑ 6–8 ft (1.8–2.4 m)

The double-flowering Ghent and Mollis hybrids were crossed in Belgium in the late nineteenth century to produce the Rustica Flore Pleno hybrids, which have double flowers. 'Byron', white flowers flushed pink; 'Freya', pale pink flowers flushed salmon pink; 'Norma', red buds opening to bright rose pink flowers; 'Phideas', pink buds opening to cream flowers flushed pink; 'Ribera', rose pink flowers with a yellow throat. Zones 5–9.

Rhododendron, Hybrid Cultivar, Deciduous Azalea, Other, 'Arpège'

Rhododendron, Hybrid Cultivar, Deciduous Azalea, Other, 'Jolie Madame'

Rhododendron, Hybrid Cultivar, Deciduous Azalea, Other, 'Orchid Lights'

Rhododendron, Hybrid Cultivar, Deciduous Azalea, Other, 'Rosata'

R., HC, DA, Other, 'Soir de Paris'

OTHER DECIDUOUS AZALEA HYBRIDS

☼/☀ ❅ ↔ 5–8 ft (1.5–2.4 m)
↑ 5–8 ft (1.5–2.4 m)

The American-bred Lights Group, probably the most widely grown of the many American-raised deciduous azalea groups, are very hardy, with abundant small flowers, and include: 'Apricot Surprise', vigorous, with golden yellow flowers from orange-pink buds; 'Golden Lights', golden yellow flowers; 'Northern Lights', fragrant pale to deep pink flowers; and 'White Lights', white flowers with yellow markings. Other deciduous azalea hybrids include: 'Antilope', fragrant moderate pink flowers with darker median lines and a faint yellow blotch; 'Arpège', fragrant vivid yellow flowers, tube flushed yellowish pink; 'Rosata', broad upright shrub, fragrant pink flowers with darker ribs; and 'Soir de Paris', fragrant light pink flowers with an orange blotch and darker lines. Zones 5–9.

EVERGREEN AZALEA HYBRIDS

Like deciduous azaleas, the evergreen azalea hybrids are multi-stemmed plants. The leaves are of 2 types: spring leaves that surround the flower-heads and are crowded at the ends of the previous year's shoots; and summer growth flush that produces longer leaves, more widely spaced on the branchlet. Flowers are widely funnel-shaped, in shades from white to pink, red, and purple, often bicolored. Most of these azaleas flower well in warmer temperate climates where winter frost is mild or even absent.

Rhododendron, Hybrid Cultivar, Deciduous Azalea, Other, 'Rêve d'Amour'

R., HC, Deciduous Azalea, Other, 'Antilope'

Rhododendron, Hybrid Cultivar, Deciduous Azalea, Other, 'Windsor Peach Glo'

INDICA HYBRIDS

☼/☀ ❄ ↔ 1–12 ft (0.3–3.5 m)
↑ 1–10 ft (0.3–3 m)

The most widely grown azaleas in temperate climates, the Indica hybrids were first developed as Christmas-flowering container plants intended for a short life indoors. The breeders developed the plants for flower qualities over landscaping attributes, so in general they are not very hardy. They were developed from *Rhododendron simsii*, originally in Belgium, but breeding continues today worldwide. They are reasonably fast-growing medium-sized shrubs. Flowers are normally large and single, but there are also numbers of double, semi-double, and hose-in-hose types, in strong colors. Zones 8–11.

BELGIAN INDICA HYBRIDS

☼/☀ ❄ ↔ 3–6 ft (0.9–1.8 m)
↑ 2–5 ft (0.6–1.5 m)

One of the first evergreen azaleas to arrive in Europe from Asia was the tender species *R. simsii*. Its willingness to be forced into bloom in winter quickly endeared it to the Belgian flower growers, who from the mid-nineteenth century developed hundreds of hybrids. Although damaged by repeated frosts, these spectacular, compact, heavy-flowering plants are among the most widely grown azaleas. 'Advent Bells' (syns 'Adventglocke', 'Chimes'), strong purple-red, semi-double, cup-shaped flowers; 'Albert Elizabeth', pale pink flowers, darker pink edges, olive green spotting in throat; 'Comtesse de Kerchove', soft pink, medium-sized, double flowers edged with white; 'Elsa Karga', glowing red double flowers; 'Eri Schaume', coral pink double flowers edged with white; 'Gretel', compact growth, white, medium-sized, double flowers edged with deep cerise; 'Haeren's Saumona' (syn. 'California Sunset'), moderate red flowers with edges fading to pink; 'Helmut Vogel', long-flowering shrub, vivid purplish red semi-double or double flowers; 'James Belton', white to pale pink flowers, darker pink stamens; 'Kelly's Cerise', purplish red semi-double to double flowers; 'Leopold Astrid', large, frilled, double, white flowers bordered with rose red; 'Only One Earth', ruffled, semi-double, hose-in-hose flowers, bright red to deep purplish pink; 'Orchidiflora', semi-double pink flowers; 'Osta', very large, single, blush pink to white flowers with red throat, also comes in a red-flowering form; 'Red Wings', long-flowering, ruffled hose-in-hose deep red blooms, compact sun-tolerant shrub. Zones 8–11.

R., HC, EA, Indica, Belgian, 'Advent Bells'

Rhododendron, Hybrid Cultivar, Evergreen Azalea, Indica, Belgian, 'Albert Elizabeth'

Rhododendron, Hybrid Cultivar, Evergreen Azalea, Indica, Belgian, 'Anniversary Joy'

Rhododendron, Hybrid Cultivar, Evergreen Azalea, Indica, Belgian, 'Agnes Neale'

R., HC, EA, Indica, Belgian, 'Alaska'

R., HC, EA, Indica, Belgian, 'Alba Magna'

R., HC, EA, Indica, Belgian, 'Apex Flame'

R., HC, EA, Indica, Belgian, 'Bonnie McKee'

R., HC, EA, Indica, Belgian, 'Auntie Mame'

Rhododendron, Hybrid Cultivar, Evergreen Azalea, Indica, Belgian, 'Cha Cha'

Rhododendron, Hybrid Cultivar, Evergreen Azalea, Indica, Belgian, 'Cameo'

Rhododendron, Hybrid Cultivar, Evergreen Azalea, Indica, Belgian, 'Armand Haerens'

Rhododendron, Hybrid Cultivar, Evergreen Azalea, Indica, Belgian, 'Phil Sherringham'

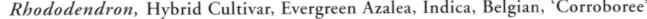

Rhododendron, Hybrid Cultivar, Evergreen Azalea, Indica, Belgian, 'Corroboree'

R., HC, EA, Indica, Belgian, 'Niobe'

Rhododendron, Hybrid Cultivar, Evergreen Azalea, Indica, Belgian, 'Only One Earth'

Rhododendron, Hybrid Cultivar, Evergreen Azalea, Indica, Belgian, 'Mrs Gerda Kint'

Rhododendron, Hybrid Cultivar, Evergreen Azalea, Indica, Belgian, 'Pink Dream'

Rhododendron, Hybrid Cultivar, Evergreen Azalea, Indica, Belgian, 'Pink Ice'

Rhododendron, Hybrid Cultivar, Evergreen Azalea, Indica, Belgian, 'Princess Caroline'

R., HC, EA, Indica, Belgian, 'Red Wings'

R., HC, EA, Indica, Belgian, 'Saidee Kirk'

R., HC, EA, Indica, Belgian, 'South Seas'

R., HC, Evergreen Azalea, Indica, Belgian, 'Silver Anniversary'

R., HC, EA, Indica, Belgian, 'Road Runner'

Rhododendron, Hybrid Cultivar, Evergreen Azalea, Indica, Belgian, 'Pink Phryne'

Rhododendron, Hybrid Cultivar, Evergreen Azalea, Indica, Belgian, 'Southern Aurora'

R., HC, EA, Indica, Belgian, 'White Schaume'

Rhododendron, Hybrid Cultivar, Evergreen Azalea, Indica, Belgian, 'Violet Ray'

R., HC, EA, Indica, Belgian, 'The Professor'

R., HC, EA, Indica, Belgian, 'The Teacher'

R., HC, EA, Indica, Belgian, 'Violacea'

Rhododendron, Hybrid Cultivar, Evergreen Azalea, Indica, Belgian, 'White Mrs Kint'

Rhododendron, Hybrid Cultivar, Evergreen Azalea, Indica, Belgian, 'Eureka', white form

Rhododendron, Hybrid Cultivar, Evergreen Azalea, Indica, Belgian, 'Eureka', red form

R., Hybrid Cultivar, Evergreen Azalea, Indica, Belgian, 'Wonder Girl'

R., Hybrid Cultivar, Evergreen Azalea, Indica, Belgian, 'Doctor Bergmann'

R., Hybrid Cultivar, Evergreen Azalea, Indica, Belgian, 'Doctor Arnold'

Rhododendron, Hybrid Cultivar, Evergreen Azalea, Indica, Belgian, 'Eri Schaume'

Rhododendron, Hybrid Cultivar, Evergreen Azalea, Indica, Belgian, 'Eureka'

Rhododendron, Hybrid Cultivar, Evergreen Azalea, Indica, Belgian, 'Eugene Mazel'

Rhododendron, Hybrid Cultivar, Evergreen Azalea, Indica, Belgian, 'Fiery Boy'

Rhododendron, Hybrid Cultivar, Evergreen Azalea, Indica, Belgian, 'Hexe'

Rhododendron, Hybrid Cultivar, Evergreen Azalea, Indica, Belgian, 'Firefly'

R., HC, EA, Indica, Belgian, 'Festival Queen'

R., HC, EA, Indica, Belgian, 'Glamor Girl'

R., HC, EA, Indica, Belgian, 'Goyet'

Rhododendron, Hybrid Cultivar, Evergreen Azalea, Indica, Belgian, 'Kalimna Pearl'

Rhododendron, Hybrid Cultivar, Evergreen Azalea, Indica, Belgian, 'James Belton'

Rhododendron, Hybrid Cultivar, Evergreen Azalea, Indica, Belgian, 'Lucille K.'

Rhododendron, Hybrid Cultivar, Evergreen Azalea, Indica, Belgian, 'Mauve Schreyderi'

R., HC, EA, Indica, Belgian, 'Madonna'

R., HC, EA, Indica, Belgian, 'Little Girl'

R., HC, EA, Indica, Belgian, 'Leopold Astrid'

R., HC, EA, Indica, Belgian, 'Karl Glaser'

Rhododendron, Hybrid Cultivar, Evergreen Azalea, Indica, Belgian, 'Mission Bells'

Rhododendron, Hybrid Cultivar, Evergreen Azalea, Indica, Belgian, 'M. J. Rose'

Rhododendron, Hybrid Cultivar, Evergreen Azalea, Indica, Belgian, 'Madame Van Heka'

R

Rhododendron, Hybrid Cultivar, Evergreen Azalea, Indica, Kerrigan, 'Gay Paree'

Rhododendron, Hybrid Cultivar, Evergreen Azalea, Indica, Kerrigan, 'Super Red'

Rhododendron, Hybrid Cultivar, Evergreen Azalea, Indica, Kerrigan, 'Bride's Bouquet'

Rhododendron, Hybrid Cultivar, Evergreen Azalea, Indica, Kerrigan, 'Ripples'

KERRIGAN INDICA HYBRIDS

☀ ❄ ↔ 12–40 in (30–100 cm)
↕ 12–40 in (30–100 cm)

Bred in the USA from the 1950s onward principally as greenhouse plants, these compact early-flowering plants are effectively just another form of the Belgian Indica hybrids. The majority of these hybrids can be fairly frost tender when they are young, but they produce extremely showy flowers and can easily be forced into bloom for indoor winter flowering. Popular Kerrigan hybrids include: **'Bride's Bouquet'**, 27 in (70 cm) tall, white rosebud double flowers; **'Gay Paree'**, 24 in (60 cm) tall, white with deep pink edge, semi-double flowers; **'Ripples'**, 24 in (60 cm) tall, deep purple-pink ruffled petals, double flowers; and **'Super Red'**, 32 in (80 cm) tall, bright red, very full double flowers. Zones 8–10.

RUTHERFORD INDICA HYBRIDS

☀/☀ ▩ ↔ 4–8 ft (1.2–2.4 m)
↕ 3–8 ft (0.9–2.4 m)

The Rutherford hybrids were bred in the 1920s in the USA as short-lived greenhouse plants for the florist trade. Many are hose-in-hose and have ruffled or frilled petals, in colors which include reddish orange, pinks, purples, and white. Larger than the Belgian hybrids, they usually reach 3–8 ft (0.9–2.4 m) in height. **'Constance'**, vigorous bushy growth habit to 3 ft (0.9 m) high, purplish pink single to hose-in-hose flowers, darker markings; **'Dorothy Gish'**, orange-salmon, semi-double, hose-in-hose flowers; **'Fire-light'**, bright red flowers; **'Gloria USA'**, semi-double hose-in-hose flowers, salmon pink or white, red throat, white petal margins; **'Louise J. Bobbink'**, usually purplish red, occasionally light pink, semi-double, hose-in-hose flowers, lighter throat, edged white; **'Purity'**, snow white flowers; **'Rose King'**, deep rose pink semi-double flowers; **'Rose Queen'**, deep purplish pink, semi-double, hose-in-hose flowers, white throat, darker blotch; **'White Gish'**, compact, to 3 ft (0.9 m) high, white, semi-double, hose-in-hose flowers, greenish yellow markings; **'White Prince'**, white, semi-double, hose-in-hose flowers, red throat, sometimes flushed pink. Zones 9–11.

R., HC, EA, Indica, Rutherford, 'Dorothy Gish'

Rhododendron, Hybrid Cultivar, Evergreen Azalea, Indica, Rutherford, 'Constance'

R., HC, EA, Indica, Rutherford, 'Rose King'

R., HC, EA, Indica, Rutherford, 'Rose Queen'

R., HC, EA, Indica, Rutherford, 'White Prince'

R., HC, EA, Indica, Rutherford, 'Firelight'

Rhododendron, Hybrid Cultivar, Evergreen Azalea, Indica, Rutherford, 'White Gish'

Rhododendron, Hybrid Cultivar, Evergreen Azalea, Indica, Rutherford, 'Louise J. Bobbink'

Rhododendron, Hybrid Cultivar, Evergreen Azalea, Indica, Rutherford, 'Purity'

R

SOUTHERN INDICA HYBRIDS

☼/◐ ✳ ↔ 6–12 ft (1.8–3.5 m) ↑ 5–10 ft (1.5–3 m)

Bred in the USA, the Southern Indica azaleas refined the characteristics of the earlier Indica hybrids to produce vigorous sun-tolerant plants which are hardier than the Belgian hybrids. They are early flowering, usually with single flowers, 2 in (5 cm) wide, in shades of pink, red, and dark purple; the flowers are sometimes striped. There are no hose-in-hose forms in this group. '**Alphonse Anderson**', pale pink flowers with darker blotch; '**Brilliantina**' (syn. 'Brilliant'), deep pink flowers with purple-red blotch; '**Concinna**', deep rose-violet flowers; '**Desirée**', deep pink flowers, bright green leaves; '**Duc de Rohan**', salmon flowers with a rose throat; '**Exquisite**', fragrant lilac-pink flowers; '**Fielder's White**', white flowers, greenish tinge in throat; '**Formosa**', deep purple-red flowers with darker blotch; '**Glory of Sunninghill**', large, single, orange-red flowers; '**Mucronatum**', profuse clusters of large, fragrant, widely funnel-shaped, white or occasionally pink flowers; '**Pink Lace**', light pink single flowers with a rose throat, white-edged petals; '**Pride of Dorking**', brilliant carmine or deep pink flowers, bronze-red and orange forms also available; '**Redwing**', cerise flowers; '**Snow Prince**', rounded bush, abundant flowers, predominantly white; '**Splendens**', salmon pink flowers; '**White Lace**', plain white flowers. Zones 8–11.

Rhododendron, Hybrid Cultivar, Evergreen Azalea, Indica, Southern, 'Alphonse Anderson'

Rhododendron, Hybrid Cultivar, Evergreen Azalea, Indica, Southern, 'Dancer'

Rhododendron, Hybrid Cultivar, Evergreen Azalea, Indica, Southern, 'Amethystinum'

Rhododendron, Hybrid Cultivar, Evergreen Azalea, Indica, Southern, 'Duc de Rohan'

Rhododendron, Hybrid Cultivar, Evergreen Azalea, Indica, Southern, 'Evelyn Hyde'

Rhododendron, Hybrid Cultivar, Evergreen Azalea, Indica, Southern, 'Snow Prince'

Rhododendron, Hybrid Cultivar, Evergreen Azalea, Indica, Southern, 'Exquisite'

Rhododendron, Hybrid Cultivar, Evergreen Azalea, Indica, Southern, 'Fielder's White'

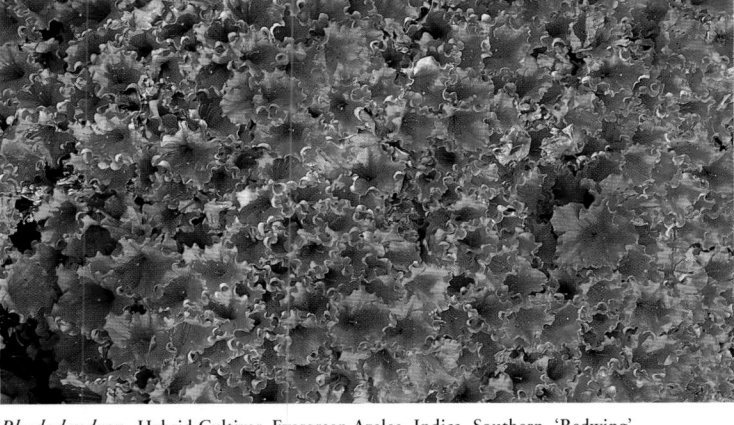

Rhododendron, Hybrid Cultivar, Evergreen Azalea, Indica, Southern, 'Redwing'

R., HC, EA, Indica, Southern, 'Flag of Truce'

R., HC, EA, Indica, Southern, 'Mardi Gras'

Rhododendron, Hybrid Cultivar, Evergreen Azalea, Indica, Southern, 'Rosemary Hyde'

Rhododendron, Hybrid Cultivar, Evergreen Azalea, Indica, Southern, 'Pink Lace'

R., HC, EA, Indica, Southern, 'Mucronatum'

R., HC, EA, Indica, Southern, 'Splendens'

Rhododendron, Hybrid Cultivar, Evergreen Azalea, Indica, Southern, 'Desirée'

R

R., HC, EA, Kaempferi, 'Beethoven'

Rhododendron, Hybrid Cultivar, Evergreen Azalea, Kaempferi, 'Double Beauty'

R., HC, EA, Kaempferi, 'Beattie'

KAEMPFERI OR MALVATICA HYBRIDS

☼/◑ ❄ ↔ 3–7 ft (0.9–2 m)
↑ 2–8 ft (0.6–2.4 m)

The late spring- or early summer-flowering Kaempferi or Malvatica hybrids were developed in the Netherlands in the 1920s by crossing the hardy *Rhododendron kaempferi* with *R.* 'Malvaticum', a garden plant of unknown origin. The large flowers are mostly single, but occasionally double or hose-in-hose, and tend to fade in full sunlight. Kaempferi hybrids typically grow to around 4 ft (1.2 m) in height with a spread of around 5 ft (1.5 m). Cultivars include: '**Blue Danube**' with strong purplish pink flowers, deep purplish red midribs, and deep red blotches; '**Cleopatra**', upright shrub, deep pink flowers; '**Double Beauty**', pink hose-in-hose flowers, mid-season; '**Fedora**', deep purplish pink flowers; '**John Cairns**', orange-red flowers; '**Othello**', red flowers; '**Orange King**', reddish orange flowers; '**Sunrise**', reddish orange flowers. Zones 6–10.

Rhododendron, Hybrid Cultivar, Evergreen Azalea, Kaempferi, 'Blue Danube'

Rhododendron, Hybrid Cultivar, Evergreen Azalea, Kaempferi, 'Cleopatra'

Rhododendron, Hybrid Cultivar, Evergreen Azalea, Kaempferi, 'Christina'

Rhododendron, Hybrid Cultivar, Evergreen Azalea, Kaempferi, 'Johanna'

Rhododendron, Hybrid Cultivar, Evergreen Azalea, Kaempferi, 'Sir William Lawrence'

Rhododendron, Hybrid Cultivar, Evergreen Azalea, Kaempferi, 'Othello'

R., Hybrid Cultivar, Evergreen Azalea, Kaempferi, 'Jeanette'

GABLE HYBRIDS

☼/☼ ❄ ↔ 3–7 ft (0.9–2 m)
↑ 4–8 ft (1.2–2.4 m)

Bred in the USA from various species and hybrids to produce a fully frost-hardy group, many of these hybrids have showy double flowers. '**Herbert**', frilled, hose-in-hose, vivid reddish purple flowers, darker blotch; '**James Gable**', with red hose-in-hose flowers, darker blotch; '**Louisa Gable**', double flowers, salmon pink; '**Rosebud**', double soft pink flowers; '**Stewart-sonian**', bright red flowers, rich red winter foliage. Zones 6–10.

VUYK HYBRIDS

☼/☼ ❄ ↔ 3–7 ft (0.9–2 m)
↑ 2–8 ft (0.6–2.4 m)

The Vuyk hybrids were developed in the 1920s from original Kaempferi hybrids and are very similar to them but more compact. While some Mollis azalea parentage was initially suggested, this now seems unlikely. '**Palestrina**', snow white flowers, light green throat; '**Vuyk's Rosyred**', deep pink-red flowers; '**Vuyk's Scarlet**', vivid red flowers. Zones 6–10.

Rhododendron, Hybrid Cultivar, Evergreen Azalea, Kaempferi, 'Sunrise'

Rhododendron, Hybrid Cultivar, Evergreen Azalea, Kaempferi, Gable, 'Stewartsonian'

Rhododendron, Hybrid Cultivar, Evergreen Azalea, Kaempferi, Vuyk, 'Palestrina'

R., HC, EA, Kaempferi, 'Girard's Rose'

R., HC, Evergreen Azalea, Kaempferi, 'Pippa'

Rhododendron, Hybrid Cultivar, Evergreen Azalea, Kaempferi, Vuyk, 'Vuyk's Scarlet'

R

KURUME HYBRIDS

☼/◐ ❄ ↔ 2–4 ft (0.6–1.2 m)
↑ 2–4 ft (0.6–1.2 m)

The Kurume hybrids were introduced to the West by the noted plant-hunter Ernest H. Wilson, working on behalf of the Veitch Nursery in England. His selection, known as Wilson's Fifty, was drawn from plants which had been cultivated for several centuries in Japan, and were believed to be crosses between *Rhododendron kaempferi*, *R. kiusianum*, and *R. × obtusum*. Large, normally single flowers, in shades of pink or white, appear early to mid-season in a wide range of strong colors, including pinks, reds, and purples. They are occasionally striped or "freckled," and sometimes hose-in-hose, flowering abundantly. The plants are hardy, slow growing, usually up to about 3 ft (0.9 m) high, occasionally up to about 5 ft (1.5 m), and with age they can spread to be much larger than this. They are best planted in fully exposed positions. **'Anniversary'**, a shrub with compact growth to 2 ft (0.6 m) high, light to pale purplish pink hose-in-hose flowers; **'Emily Knights'**, bright red flowers, crinkled star-shaped petals; **'Fairy Queen'** (syn. 'Aioi'), small, semi-double, hose-in-hose, almond-blossom pink flowers; **'Hatsu Giri'**, vivid reddish purple flowers, pink spotting in the throat; **'Hinomayo'**, strong purplish pink flowers; **'Iroha Yama'**, white flowers, pale lavender at edges; **'Kasane Kagaribi'** (syn. 'Rositi'), shrub with low, dense, spreading growth, yellowish to salmon pink flowers; **'Kumo-no-Ito'** (syn. 'Suga no Ito'), strong pink hose-in-hose flowers, darker center; **'Kure-no-yuki'**, white hose-in-hose flowers; **'Mother's Day'**, dense low-growing bush that produces abundant cherry red colored flowers; **'Osaraku'** (syn. 'Penelope'), small single flowers, soft lavender or light purple; **'Seikai'** (syn. 'Madonna'), white, semi-double, hose-in-hose flowers; **'Seraphim'** (syn. 'Tancho'), small, single, hose-in-hose flowers, blush pink edged with rose; **'Sherwood Red'**, orange-red single flowers; **'Shin Utena'** (syn. 'Santoi'), white flowers flushed with strong yellowish pink; **'Show Girl'**, small hose-in-hose flowers, a bright salmon-orange; **'Takasago'** (syn. 'Cherryblossom'), white hose-in-hose flowers, flushed with deep red or pale pink and with dark spots; **'Vida Brown'**, pink-red hose-in-hose flowers; **'Waka Kayede'** (syn. 'Red Robin'), a sun-tolerant shrub that produces strong red flowers; **'Ward's Ruby'**, featuring blood red flowers, is less hardy than other Kurume azaleas. Zones 7–10.

Rhododendron, Hybrid Cultivar, Evergreen Azalea, Kurume, 'Blaauw's Pink'

R., HC, EA, Kurume, 'Colyer'

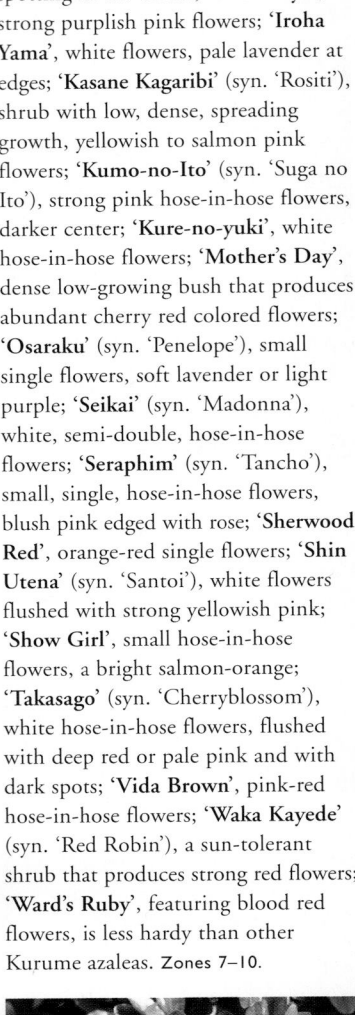

R., HC, EA, Kurume, 'Azuma Kagami'

R., HC, EA, Kurume, 'Christmas Cheer'

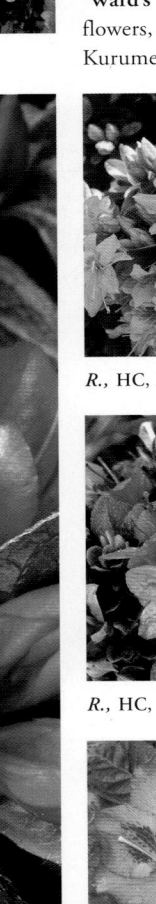

R., HC, EA, Kurume, 'Elizabeth Belton'

Rhododendron, Hybrid Cultivar, Evergreen Azalea, Kurume, 'Addy Wery'

Rhododendron, Hybrid Cultivar, Evergreen Azalea, Kurume, 'Hana-asobi'

Rhododendron, Hybrid Cultivar, Evergreen Azalea, Kurume, 'H. O. Carre'

R., HC, EA, Kurume, 'Happy Birthday'

R., HC, EA, Kurume, 'Haru-no-Sato'

R., HC, EA, Kurume, 'Esmeralda'

Rhododendron, Hybrid Cultivar, Evergreen Azalea, Kurume, 'Flora'

Rhododendron, Hybrid Cultivar, Evergreen Azalea, Kurume, 'Emily Knights'

Rhododendron, Hybrid Cultivar, Evergreen Azalea, Kurume, 'Favorite'

Rhododendron, Hybrid Cultivar, Evergreen Azalea, Kurume, 'Hatsu Giri'

Rhododendron, Hybrid Cultivar, Evergreen Azalea, Kurume, 'Hino-crimson'

R., HC, EA, Kurume, 'Helene'

R., HC, EA, Kurume, 'Iwato-kagami'

R., HC, EA, Kurume, 'Kasane Kagaribi'

Rhododendron, Hybrid Cultivar, Evergreen Azalea, Kurume, 'Hinode-giri'

Rhododendron, Hybrid Cultivar, Evergreen Azalea, Kurume, 'Ima Shojo'

Rhododendron, Hybrid Cultivar, Evergreen Azalea, Kurume, 'Hinomayo'

Rhododendron, Hybrid Cultivar, Evergreen Azalea, Kurume, 'Katsura-no-Hana'

Rhododendron, Hybrid Cultivar, Evergreen Azalea, Kurume, 'Kumo-no-Ito'

Rhododendron, Hybrid Cultivar, Evergreen Azalea, Kurume, 'Kumo-no-Uye'

R., HC, Evergreen Azalea, Kurume, 'Kirin'

R., HC, EA, Kurume, 'Kiritsubo'

Rhododendron, Hybrid Cultivar, Evergreen Azalea, Kurume, 'Little Red Riding Hood'

Rhododendron, Hybrid Cultivar, Evergreen Azalea, Kurume, 'Kermesinum'

Rhododendron, Hybrid Cultivar, Evergreen Azalea, Kurume, 'Kimigayo'

Rhododendron, Hybrid Cultivar, Evergreen Azalea, Kurume, 'Mizu-no-Yamabuki'

Rhododendron, Hybrid Cultivar, Evergreen Azalea, Kurume, 'Mother's Day'

Rhododendron, Hybrid Cultivar, Evergreen Azalea, Kurume, 'Orange Beauty'

R., HC, EA, Kurume, 'Sakura-Tsukasa'

R., HC, Evergreen Azaleas, Kurume, 'Seikai'

R., HC, Evergreen Azalea, Kurume, 'Omoine'   *R.,* HC, EA, Kurume, 'Purple Glitters'

Rhododendron, Hybrid Cultivar, Evergreen Azalea, Kurume, 'Orion'

Rhododendron, Hybrid Cultivar, Evergreen Azalea, Kurume, 'Oino Mezame'

Rhododendron, Hybrid Cultivar, Evergreen Azalea, Kurume, 'Scarlet Gem'

R., HC, EA, Kurume, 'Shin Sekai'

R., HC, EA, Kurume, 'Tsuta Momiji'

Rhododendron, Hybrid Cultivar, Evergreen Azalea, Kurume, 'Snow'

Rhododendron, Hybrid Cultivar, Evergreen Azalea, Kurume, 'Shin Utena'

Rhododendron, Hybrid Cultivar, Evergreen Azalea, Kurume, 'Waka Kayede'

R., HC, EA, Kurume, 'White Pearl'

R., HC, EA, Kurume, 'Tamafuyo'

Rhododendron, Hybrid Cultivar, Evergreen Azalea, Kurume, 'Violetta'

Rhododendron, Hybrid Cultivar, Evergreen Azalea, Kurume, 'Takasago'

Rhododendron, Hybrid Cultivar, Evergreen Azalea, Kurume, 'Ward's Ruby'

R., HC, EA, Satsuki, 'Hitoya-no-Haru'

R., HC, EA, Satsuki, 'Nani-Wagata'

R., HC, EA, Satsuki, 'White Shiko'

R., HC, EA, Satsuki, 'Shinnyo-no-Hikari'

Rhododendron, Hybrid Cultivar, Evergreen Azalea, Satsuki, 'Banzai'

SATSUKI HYBRIDS

☀/☼ ❄ ↔ 24–48 in (60–120 cm)
↕ 12–36 in (30–90 cm)

Introduced to the West in the early 1900s, these late-flowering low-growing plants have been cultivated for centuries in Japan, and most likely originate from crosses between *R. indicum* and *R. eriocarpum* or *R. simsii*. In Japan they are valued for their landscaping qualities and were also traditionally used for bonsai and container cultivation. They are normally small spreading bushes up to 3 ft (0.9 m) in height. The Gumpo series of dwarf plants is useful in rockeries. 'Banzai', white flowers flushed with pink; 'Gumpo', large white flowers, petals wavy-edged; 'Gumpo Lavender', large, single, lavender flowers; 'Gumpo Pink', ruffled, single, pink flowers edged with white;

'Gumpo Salmon', ruffled salmon pink flowers; 'Gumpo Stripe', white flowers with mauve-red stripes and flecks; 'Gumpo White' frilly white flowers; 'Gyoten', single flowers, up to 3 in (8 cm) across, pale pink with white edges, yellowish blotch and often with random red or white stripes; 'Hitoya-no-Haru', large lilac-pink flowers, olive green spotting in throat; 'Kunpu', pale pink, wavy-edged, single flowers, 2½ in (6 cm) across; 'Mansaku', salmon pink flowers, rounded wavy petals; 'Nani-Wagata', abundant white flowers; 'Osakazuki', smallish, deep pink, single blooms, darker blotch in throat; 'Otome', white and pink flowers; 'Shin-Kyo', light salmon pink flowers, 'Shinnyo-no-Hikari', white flowers, green throat; 'White Shiko', white flowers with green blaze. Zones 7–11.

INTERGROUP HYBRIDS

☀/☼ ❄ ↔ 3–6 ft (0.9–1.8 m)
↕ 2–6 ft (0.6–1.8 m)

These hybrids include crosses between the various other groups of azalea hybrids, as well as plants bred from later species introductions, and plants which do not neatly fall into any particular category. *R.* × *pulchrum* (syn. *R.* 'Phoeniceum') was introduced into the West from China as *Azalea indica* in the early nineteenth century, but in fact is a hybrid between *R. indicum* and *R.* 'Mucronatum', and known only as a garden plant in China and Japan, where it has been cultivated for centuries. Its very large single flowers are purplish red or violet-rose on a very tough shrub which grows to about 6 ft (1.8 m) high. 'Chippewa', dwarf spreading plant, pink flowers; 'Dew Drop' (syn. 'Nuccio's Dew Drop'), blush pink to white single to semi-double flowers, flushed with green, pink spots in throat; 'Dogwood' and 'Dogwood Red', sun-tolerant plants, red flowers edged with white or pure red, greenish throat; 'Dogwood Variegated', bright salmon pink flowers streaked white; 'Easter Delight', abundant, clear purple, tubular flowers, tolerates full sun; 'Fascination', large,

Rhododendron, Hybrid Cultivar, Evergreen Azalea, Intergroup, 'Content'

R., HC, EA, Intergroup, 'Chippewa'

Rhododendron, Hybrid Cultivar, Evergreen Azalea, Intergroup, 'Anna Kehr'

Rhododendron, Hybrid Cultivar, Evergreen Azalea, Intergroup, 'Fairy Bells'

Rhododendron, Hybrid Cultivar, Evergreen Azalea, Intergroup, 'Jeanne Weeks'

Rhododendron, Hybrid Cultivar, Evergreen Azalea, Intergroup, 'Dogwood'

Rhododendron, Hybrid Cultivar, Evergreen Azalea, Intergroup, 'Margaret Rowell'

Rhododendron, Hybrid Cultivar, Evergreen Azalea, Intergroup, 'Nuccio's Pink Bubbles'

R., HC, EA, Intergroup, 'Happy Days'

R., HC, EA, Intergroup, 'Hotline'

Rhododendron, Hybrid Cultivar, Evergreen Azalea, Intergroup, 'Nuccio's Dream Clouds'

Rhododendron, Hybrid Cultivar, Evergreen Azalea, Intergroup, 'Hydie'

Rhododendron, Hybrid Cultivar, Evergreen Azalea, Intergroup, 'Lemur'

R

R., Hybrid Cultivar, Evergreen Azalea, Intergroup, Glenn Dale, 'Alight'

single, pink flowers, red edging on petals; '**Gloria Still**', compact bush to 2 ft (0.6 m) high, variegated light pink and white flowers in large trusses; '**Jeanne Weeks**', buds resemble rosebuds, open as strong purplish pink hose-in-hose flowers; '**Orange Delight**' (syn. 'Mrs John Ward'), shrub with low dense growth to 30 in (75 cm) high, very large bright reddish orange flowers; '**Summerland Chiffon**', light pink double flowers; '**Summerland**

R., Hybrid Cultivar, Evergreen Azalea, Intergroup, 'Port Knap'

R., HC, EA, Intergroup, 'Tokay'

R., Hybrid Cultivar, Evergreen Azalea, Intergroup, Glenn Dale, 'Bonanza'

Mist', ruffled, semi-double, white flowers; '**Swashbuckler**', reddish flowers, red blotch, stamens, and pistil; '**Sweetheart Supreme**', shrub with spreading habit, deep or salmon pink, frilled, semi-double, hose-in-hose flowers, darker blotch; '**Teena Maree**', semi-double hose-in-hose flowers, salmon or yellowish pink; '**Tokay**', best when fully mature, purplish pink flowers, lighter blotch. Zones 6–10.

GLENN DALE HYBRIDS
☼/◐ ❄ ↔ 5–10 ft (1.5–3 m)
↕ 4–8 ft (1.2–2.4 m)

The Glenn Dale hybrids are also included in the Intergroup category. Bred in the USA from the 1930s, they combine the large flowers of the Southern Indica hybrid azaleas with cold hardiness and a later flowering season, from spring to summer. They range in form from low-growing dwarf plants to open bushes that

R., HC, EA, Intergroup, 'Squirrel'

Rhododendron, Hybrid Cultivar, Evergreen Azalea, Intergroup, Glenn Dale, 'Aphrodite'

R., Hybrid Cultivar, Evergreen Azalea, Intergroup, Glenn Dale, 'Corydon'

R., Hybrid Cultivar, Evergreen Azalea, Intergroup, Glenn Dale, 'Gaiety'

R., Hybrid Cultivar, Evergreen Azalea, Intergroup, Glenn Dale, 'Glamour'

are 8 ft (2.4 m) or more in height. Large spectacular flowers can be of a solid color, striped or speckled, semi-double or double in form, and they often have frilled petals. '**Alight**', strong purple-pink flowers, lighter center, mid-season; '**Aphrodite**', light purplish pink flowers with a darker blotch, mid-season; '**Bonanza**', vivid purplish red flowers, darker blotch, mid-season; '**Chanticleer**', purple flowers; '**Corydon**', early-flowering shrub, strong purplish pink flowers, a few darker blotches, and overlapping lobes; '**Dimity**', white single flowers with purplish red flecks; '**Firedance**', large, double, glowing rose red flowers; '**Gaiety**', light purplish pink

flowers, darker blotch, early to mid-season; '**Greeting**', flowers coral red; '**Louise Dowdle**', bright purple-pink flowers; '**Martha Hitchcock**', white flowers edged with lilac; '**Revery**', medium, single, rose pink flowers;

Rhododendron, Hybrid Cultivar, Evergreen Azalea, Intergroup, 'Swashbuckler'

Rhododendron, Hybrid Cultivar, Evergreen Azalea, Intergroup, 'Sunburst'

Rhododendron, Hybrid Cultivar, Evergreen Azalea, Intergroup, Glenn Dale, 'Jubilant'

Rhododendron, Hybrid Cultivar, Evergreen Azalea, Intergroup, Glenn Dale, 'Illusions'

R., Hybrid Cultivar, Evergreen Azalea, Intergroup, Glenn Dale, 'Illusions'

R., Hybrid Cultivar, Evergreen Azalea, Intergroup, Glenn Dale, 'Picotee'

Rhododendron, Hybrid Cultivar, Evergreen Azalea, Azaleodendron, 'Ria Hardijzer'

Rhododendron, Hybrid Cultivar, Evergreen Azalea, Intergroup, Glenn Dale, 'Moonbeam'

Rhododendron, Hybrid Cultivar, Evergreen Azalea, Intergroup, Glenn Dale, 'Paradise'

'**Romance**', double hose-in-hose flowers, rich purplish pink; '**Saffrano**', white flowers flushed with yellowish green on upper lobe, mid-season; '**Tanager**', vivid purplish red flowers, darker blotch. Zones 7–10.

AZALEODENDRON HYBRIDS

☀/◐ ❄ ↔ 2–7 ft (0.6–2 m) ↕ 2–8 ft (0.6–2.4 m)

A group of hybrids that lies between deciduous azaleas and other (ever-green) rhododendrons, these plants are usually semi-evergreen, flowering in summer, and may sometimes have fragrant flowers. '**Broughtonii Aureum**', yellow flowers; '**Dot**' and '**Galloper Light**', both with salmon pink flowers; '**Glory of Littleworth**', cream flowers, flushed with orange; '**Govenianum**', deep mauve flowers, fragrant; '**Hardijzer Beauty**', purplish pink flowers; '**Martine**', soft pink flowers; '**Ria Hardijzer**', deep pink-red flowers. Zones 8–10.

R., HC, EA, Azaleodendron, 'Hardijzer Beauty'

R., HC, EA, Azaleodendron, 'Maritine'

Rhodohypoxis baurii var. *confecta*

Rhodohypoxis baurii

Rhodohypoxis baurii 'Tetra Red'

RHODOHYPOXIS

A genus of about 6 low-growing, clump-forming, free-flowering, cormous perennials which belongs to the star-flower (Hypoxidaceae) family. Coming from the damp-summer climates of southern Africa, they rarely thrive in wet-winter dry-summer climates without some assistance. The leaves are generally grassy in character. The starry flowers, borne on slender stems about the height of the leaves, have 6 petals of equal length, arranged alternately in 2 ranks.

Rhodohypoxis milloides

CULTIVATION: In suitable climates, conditions, and lime-free soils, they can bloom fairly constantly from late spring until early autumn. They are suitable for planting in peaty pockets and troughs where a dry winter dormancy period can be assured.

Rhodohypoxis baurii

RED STAR, ROSY POSY

☀ ❄ ↔ 2½–4 in (6–10 cm) ↑ 2½–4 in (6–10 cm)

Perennial from South Africa. Leaves are dull gray-green, grass-like, tuft-forming, lance-shaped, very hairy. Flowers held on short stems, upturned 6-petalled stars, almost flat, white through pink and red, throughout summer. *R. b.* var. *confecta*, white flowers reddening with age, a parent of many cultivars and hybrids. *R. b.* 'Tetra Red' ★, large dark pink-red flowers. Zones 8–9.

Rhodohypoxis milloides

☀ ❄ ↔ 8 in (20 cm) ↑ 4–6 in (10–15 cm)

From KwaZulu-Natal, South Africa. Vigorous clump-forming species, spreading from numerous runners. Leaves light green, linear, folded, sparsely hairy, erect. Deep crimson, cerise, pink, or white flowers. Tolerates wetter winters than *R. baurii*. Zones 8–9.

Rhodohypoxis Hybrid Cultivars

☀ ❄ ↔ 3–6 in (8–15 cm) ↑ 2½–4 in (6–10 cm)

There is often some confusion between the numerous named hybrid cultivars, but they include the fairly distinctive 'Albrighton', deep cherry-pink flowers; 'Appleblossom', pale pink flowers; 'E. A. Bowles', light candy pink petals; 'Fred Broome', sugar pink petals, cream at base; 'Great Scott', magenta petals; 'Harlequin', pink flowers, flushed white; 'Monty', bright cerise-pink flowers; 'Pinkeen', narrow rich pink petals; 'Stella', large lavender-pink blooms; 'Susan B. Bottfield', light pink petals. Zones 8–9.

RHODOLEIA

There is some doubt about the number of species in this genus, in the witch-hazel (Hamamelidaceae) family. Some authorities consider that there is just a

Rhodohypoxis, Hybrid Cultivar, 'Douglas'

Rhodohypoxis, HC, 'E. A. Bowles'

Rhodohypoxis, Hybrid Cultivar, 'Extra Red'

Rhodohypoxis, HC, 'Fred Broome'

Rhodohypoxis, HC, 'Great Scott'

Rhodohypoxis, HC, 'Lily Jean'

Rhodohypoxis, HC, 'Monty'

Rhodohypoxis, HC, 'Pinkeen'

Rhodohypoxis, HC, 'Stella'

R., HC, 'Susan B. Bottfield'

Rhodohypoxis, Hybrid Cultivar, 'Albrighton'

Rhodotypos scandens

single variable species in several countries, from southern China to eastern Indonesia, others have recognized up to 7 species. Most, if not all, of the plants in cultivation, seem to have originated from material collected in Hong Kong. The range of variability within the species is not evident and the "other" species are not at all well known. All the forms are very similar; they are small evergreen trees with thick dark green leaves that are paler on the underside, and pendent bunches of reddish flowers surrounded by reddish bracts during spring. CULTIVATION: These plants are not frost tolerant and should be grown in a well-drained, acid, sandy soil to which plenty of organic matter has been added. Conditions should be the same as for azaleas and camellias. Propagation is from seed or cuttings.

Rhodoleia championii

☼ ✦ ↔ 12 in (3.5 m) ↑ 20 ft (6 m)
Variable species, occurs from southern China to Indonesia. Forms a small tree. Thick oval leaves, whitish undersides. Stems and leaf stalks yellowish red. Pendent bunches of pinkish red flowers, in late winter–early spring. Zones 10–11.

RHODOTHAMNUS

This monotypic genus is a member of the heath (Ericaceae) family. The sole species, which is found in the eastern European Alps, grows on dry stony slopes. It is a dwarf evergreen shrub with small leathery leaves and attractive rose pink flowers that have reddish purple stamens.
CULTIVATION: This cold-hardy shrub requires a well-drained, humus-rich, acid soil with a cool root run. It will grow in sun or part-shade outdoors and can also be grown in an alpine house. Propagation is from seed, layering, or half-hardened cuttings taken in summer.

Rhodothamnus chamaecistus

☼ ✲ ↔ 12 in (30 cm) ↑ 16 in (40 cm)
Dwarf shrub with neat well-branched habit. Small tapering leaves, leathery, dark green, outlined with fine white hairs. Saucer-shaped rose pink flowers, to 1 in (25 mm) wide, in late spring–early summer. Zones 6–9.

RHODOTYPOS

The sole species in this genus is a deciduous shrub native to China and Japan. A member of the rose (Rosaceae) family, it is cultivated mainly for its spring flowers and, to a lesser extent, for the black berries that ripen over summer and last well into winter. The serrated foliage is a fresh green throughout the warmer months and sometimes develops slight red or yellow colors in autumn.
CULTIVATION: *Rhodotypos scandens* is frost hardy and easily cultivated in most temperate areas in sun or partial shade. It prefers a well-drained humus-rich soil and ample summer moisture, which will also result in a better fruit crop. It is best to prune this plant in winter after the last berries have fallen. Propagate from

stratified seed, layers, or hardwood cuttings in winter, or half-hardened cuttings in summer.

Rhodotypos scandens ★

☼ ✲ ↔ 6 ft (1.8 m) ↑ 8 ft (2.4 m)
Deciduous shrub from China and Japan. Several upright or slightly arching stems, 1–2 in (25–50 mm) wide. Rose-like, 4-petalled, white flowers at branch tips, in spring. Calyces remain after flowers fall, partially enclosing developing fruit. Zones 5–9.

RHOPALOSTYLIS

This genus, in the family Arecaceae, contains just 2 species of palm tree. One is native to Norfolk Island, east of Australia, and the other, the world's most southerly growing palm, is found in New Zealand. They have pinnately divided fronds arising from the top of a solitary unarmed stem, which bears the scars of fallen leaves. Large heads of tiny flowers hang from below the prominent crownshaft. The red berries that follow are very showy.
CULTIVATION: These palms are slow-growing and slow to flower. Forest-dwellers by nature, they should be given a shady and sheltered site to prevent damage to the fronds. They require a deep moist soil. In cool-temperate climates they make very good container plants for the greenhouse or conservatory. Propagate from seed, which can be slow to germinate.

Rhopalostylis baueri

NORFOLK PALM
☼ ✦ ↔ 15 ft (4.5 m) ↑ 20 ft (6 m)
Native to Norfolk Island. Arching deep green fronds, to 10 ft (3 m) long; ringed trunk. Flowerheads to 24 in (60 cm) long, tiny white flowers, in late spring–summer. Large sprays of red berries. Zones 10–11.

Rhopalostylis sapida ★

NIKAU PALM
☼ ✦ ↔ 10 ft (3 m) ↑ 20–35 ft (6–10 m)
From New Zealand. Wider and lighter green fronds than those of *R. baueri*, arise almost erectly above bulbous crownshaft. Hanging flower-heads of tiny purplish pink flowers, in late spring–summer. Bright red fruits. Tree is 30 years old before flowering. Zones 9–11.

RHUS

SUMAC
There are about 200 species of deciduous or evergreen trees, shrubs and climbers in this genus within the cashew (Anacardiaceae) family. Widely distributed throughout the temperate and subtropical regions of the world, they are used to produce laquer, dyes, tannin, wax, and drinks. *Rhus* species are mainly grown in the garden for their good autumn color, interesting foliage, and fruit, which can persist on the tree into winter and often drop off only when the new leaves appear.

Rhopalostylis baueri

Rhodoleia championii

Rhopalostylis sapida, in the wild, New Zealand

CULTIVATION: *Rhus* species grow in full sun in moderately fertile, moist but free-draining soil with shelter from the wind. Propagate from root cuttings in winter, half-hardened stem cuttings in late summer or divided root suckers taken when the plant is dormant. Seed can be sown in autumn. Feed and water well during growing season; do not feed in winter and water sparingly.

Rhus aromatica

FRAGRANT SUMAC, LEMON SUMACH, POLECAT BUSH

☀ ❄ ↔ 5 ft (1.5 m) ↑ 3–5 ft (0.9–1.5 m)
Native to eastern North America. Suckering deciduous shrub. Palmate

Rhus lucida

leaves, oval toothed leaflets, aromatic. Small yellow flowers on panicles, in spring. Round red fruit. '**Gro-Low**' ★, to 2 ft (0.6 m) high, fragrant deep yellow flowers. Zones 3–9.

Rhus chinensis

CHINESE GALL, NUTGALL

☀ ❄ ↔ 15 ft (4.5 m) ↑ 20 ft (6 m)
Erect deciduous tree, native to Japan and China. Leaves compound, mid-green, 3 to 7 oblong leaflets, scalloped edges, turn red in autumn. White conical clusters of flowers, in late summer–early autumn. Rounded scarlet fruit. Zones 8–11.

Rhus copallina

DWARF SUMAC, MOUNTAIN SUMACH, SHINING SUMAC

☀ ❄ ↔ 5 ft (1.5 m) ↑ 5 ft (1.5 m)
From eastern North America. Erect deciduous shrub. Dark green pinnate leaves, 15 lance-shaped leaflets, winged stalks. Yellowish green flowers on up-right panicles, in summer. Rounded red fruit. Foliage turns red in autumn. *R. c.* var. *latifolia* (prairie flame sumac), compact male form, reddish orange autumn foliage. Zones 5–9.

Rhus glabra 'Laciniata'

Rhus copallina var. *latifolia*

Rhus glabra

SCARLET SUMAC, SMOOTH SUMAC, VINEGAR TREE

☀ ❄ ↔ 8 ft (2.4 m) ↑ 8 ft (2.4 m)
Bushy deciduous shrub, native to North America and Mexico. Bronze-colored stems, whitish bloom, pinnate leaves, deep blue-green leaflets, turn rich red in autumn. Dense upright panicles of greenish red flowers, in summer. Rounded, crimson, hairy fruits. '**Laciniata**', finely cut leaves. Zones 2–9.

Rhus lancea

KAREE, WILLOW RHUS

☀ ⚘ ↔ 25 ft (8 m) ↑ 25 ft (8 m)
Evergreen tree that is native to South Africa. Leaves dark green above, paler beneath, with 3 lance-shaped leaflets, sometimes with

Rhus pendulina

toothed edges. Tiny yellow-green flowers appear in late summer. Fruit is glossy brown . Zones 9–11.

Rhus lucida

☀ ⚘ ↔ 12 ft (3.5 m) ↑ 12 ft (3.5 m)
From coastal regions of South Africa. Evergreen tree or shrub. Leaves have 3 shiny dark green leaflets. Off-white flowers in small heads, from leaf axils or ends of branches, in spring. Small, glossy, brown fruits. Zones 9–11.

Rhus microphylla

CORREOSA, DESERT SUMAC, SCRUB SUMAC

☀ ❄ ↔ 4–6 ft (1.5–1.8 m)
↑ 6–10 ft (1.8–3 m)
From southern USA and northern Mexico. Rounded deciduous shrub. Compound leaves with up to 9 leaflets; usually evergreen but can shed leaves in cold or dry conditions. Tight spikes of tiny white flowers, in spring. Tiny orange-red fruit. Zones 8–11.

Rhus pendulina

syn. *Rhus viminalis*

☀ ⚘ ↔ 15 ft (4.5 m) ↑ 15 ft (4.5 m)
Evergreen South African tree or shrub, willow-like in habit. Trifoliate leaves, lance-shaped leaflets. Light green flowers, in summer. Small oblong fruit. Zones 9–11.

Rhus lancea

Rhus potaninii

☀ ❋ ↔ 20 ft (6 m) ↑ 30 ft (9 m)

Native to central and western China. Deciduous tree, rounded in shape. Dark green pinnate leaves, up to 11 oblong leaflets, turn red in autumn. Drooping panicles of cream flowers, in summer. Round, downy, red fruit. Zones 5–9.

Rhus trilobata

syn. *Rhus aromatica* subsp. *trilobata*

SKUNKBUSH SUMAC, THREE-LOBE SUMAC

☀ ❋ ↔ 10 ft (3 m) ↑ 8 ft (2.4 m)

Deciduous shrub from western and central USA and northern and central Mexico. Hairy new growth. Leaves with 3 toothed leaflets. Clusters of light green flowers, in spring. Round red fruit. Zones 5–9.

Rhus typhina

STAGHORN SUMAC, STAG'S HORN SUMAC

☀ ❋ ↔ 15 ft (4.5 m) ↑ 15 ft (4.5 m)

Deciduous tree or shrub from eastern North America. Can reach 30 ft (9 m) high in the wild. Pinnate leaves, up to 31 dark green leaflets, turn flame red in autumn. Green-yellow flowers, in summer. Felty red fruit. 'Dissecta', finely divided leaves. Zones 3–9.

Rhus verniciflua

syn. *Toxicodendron vernicifluum*

CHINESE LACQUER TREE, VARNISH TREE

☀ ❋ ↔ 6–10 ft (1.8–3 m)
↑ 20–30 ft (6–9 m)

Small deciduous tree, native of China and Japan. Straight upright trunk. Divided leaves, on short stalks, 11 to 15 oval leaflets, up to 5 in (12 cm) long. Small, yellowish green, insignificant flowers, in summer. Yellowish drupes. Highly poisonous sticky sap is used as for making lacquer. Zones 4–8.

RHYNCHOSTELE

This is a genus consisting of some 16 species of sympodial orchids from Central America and the northern

Rhus typhina

part of South America. Belonging to the family Orchidaceae, they are related to *Odontoglossum*, and were previously included within that genus. They have egg-shaped, somewhat flattened pseudobulbs topped with up to 3 thin textured leaves. Most of the species in this genus have showy colorful flowers on short or long stems.

CULTIVATION: These orchids grow well potted in a fine grade bark mixture with the addition of 20% perlite. Sphagnum moss is also a popular potting medium. They are suitable for humid intermediate growing conditions, and require abundant water throughout the year and a part-shaded position. They are more tolerant of warm conditions than *Odontoglossum*. Propagate by division.

Rhynchostele bictoniensis

☀ ✈ ↔ 8–16 in (20–40 cm)
↑ 8–24 in (20–60 cm)

Found from Mexico to Panama. Upright inflorescences of up to 14 blooms, 2 in (5 cm) across, petals and sepals vary from yellowish green to brown, with darker spotting and barring over segments and broad white labellum, in winter–spring. Zones 10–11.

Rhynchostele cordata

☀ ✈ ↔ 8–16 in (20–40 cm)
↑ 8–16 in (20–40 cm)

Found from Mexico to Venezuela. Starry blooms, 3 in (8 cm) wide, mustard colored with dark brown blotches, appear in summer–autumn. Zones 11–12.

Rhynchostele bictoniensis

Rhus typhina 'Dissecta'

Rhynchostele Stanfordiense

Rhynchostele Stanfordiense

☀ ✈ ↔ 8–16 in (20–40 cm)
↑ 8–27 in (20–70 cm)

This is a primary hybrid between *R. bictoniensis* and *R. uro-skinneri*. Upright inflorescences of blotched and barred brown, 2 in (5 cm) wide flowers, pink labellum. Zones 10–11.

RHYNCHOSTYLIS

These tropical, lowland, vandaceous species are known as foxtail orchids because of their densely flowered inflorescences. These epiphytes are erect growing, with strap-like channeled leaves in 2 ranks. Larger plants may branch at the base, and have numerous, very thick, cord-like roots. The inflorescences appear from the stem at the base of the leaf. *Rhynchostylis* is a small genus of monopodial plants with only 4 or 5 members,

CULTIVATION: These thick-leafed epiphytes grow in brightly lit situations, and require year-round warm conditions. They are best grown in wooden baskets, with the thick, fleshy roots attaching to the timber and being allowed to ramble, as the roots require unimpeded air circulation and must dry out quickly after watering.

Rhynchostylis gigantea

☀/☼ ✈ ↔ 8–20 in (20–50 cm)
↑ 8–24 in (20–60 cm)

From Thailand and Indochina; most popular species in cultivation. Blooms 1¼ in (30 mm) wide, come in a range of colors, from white with pink spotting and blotching through various shades of purple to red; there are also bicolored and pure white strains. Zones 11–12.

Rhynchostele cordata

Rhynchostylis retusa

☀/☼ ✈ ↔ 8–20 in (20–50 cm)
↑ 8–30 in (20–75 cm)

Widespread species from Southeast Asia with long pendulous inflorescences of up to 60 flowers, ¾ in (18 mm) wide, white with pink markings. Also a rare pure white form. Zones 11–12.

RIBES

CURRANT

Mainly from the northern temperate regions, with some species native to South America, this genus of around 150 species of shrubs is in the gooseberry (Grossulariaceae) family. Some are ornamental; others are grown for their fruit. They are usually deciduous, with twiggy or wiry stems. Usually with 3 to 5 lobes, leaves often have scalloped or toothed edges and bristly hairs. Flowers are small, sometimes in racemes, followed by often bristly, many-seeded, frequently edible berries. Some species are important commercial or home garden crops.

CULTIVATION: Some are not self-fertile and must be planted in groups to ensure good fruiting. Apart from this, and the need for some winter chilling, most are easily grown, requiring little more than a well-drained soil, moisture in summer, and some shade from the very hottest summer sun. Rust or mildew can cause problems with some species, but disease-resistant cultivars are often available. Propagate from seed or cuttings, or by layering.

Ribes alpinum
ALPINE CURRANT, MOUNTAIN CURRANT

☼ ❀ ↔ 3 ft (0.9 m) ↑ 3–6 ft (0.9–1.8 m)
Deciduous shrub found over much of Europe and extending to North Africa and Russia. Smooth purple-red stems, leaves usually 3-lobed. Erect racemes of tiny yellow-green flowers, in spring. Bitter red fruit. 'Aureum', yellow-green young growth; 'Green Mound', non-fruiting low-growing form; 'Pumilum', low and spreading with small leaves; 'Schmidt', slower growing, smaller than the species. Zones 2–9.

Ribes aureum
GOLDEN CURRANT, GOLDEN FLOWERING CURRANT

☼ ❀ ↔ 6 ft (1.8 m) ↑ 6 ft (1.8 m)
From western USA and northwestern Mexico. Upright deciduous bush. Leaves 3-lobed, coarsely toothed. Pendent racemes of strongly scented yellow flowers, in spring. Fruit purple-black. *R. a.* var. *gracillimum*, unscented red-tinted flowers, yellow fruit. Zones 2–9.

Ribes alpinum 'Green Mound'

Ribes fasciculatum var. *chinense*

Ribes cereum
SQUAW CURRANT

☼ ❀ ↔ 3 ft (0.9 m) ↑ 3–6 ft (0.9–1.8 m)
Smooth-stemmed deciduous shrub from western USA. Rounded to kidney-shaped leaves, 3 to 5 lobes, downy, shallowly toothed edges. Short pendent racemes of flowers, white, pale green, or light yellow, in spring. Shiny red fruit. Zones 5–9.

Ribes × culverwellii

❀ ↔ 5 ft (1.5 m) ↑ 5 ft (1.5 m)
Garden hybrid between *R. nigrum* and *R. uva-crispa*. Gooseberry-like, hairy leaves, 3 to 5 lobes. Clusters of downy, seedless, black-red fruit, very sweet when ripe. Zones 6–9.

Ribes fasciculatum
CLUSTERED REDCURRANT

☼ ❀ ↔ 4 ft (1.2 m) ↑ 5 ft (1.5 m)
Deciduous shrub from temperate East Asia. Leaves rounded, downy, 3 to 5 lobes, toothed edges. Yellow flowers, in spring; female flowers scented. Smooth red fruit, yellow flesh. Plants of both sexes required for cropping. *R. f.* var. *chinense*, larger, with leaves up to 4 in (10 cm) long. Zones 5–9.

Ribes gayanum
CHILEAN BLACKCURRANT

☼ ❀ ↔ 3 ft (0.9 m) ↑ 5 ft (1.5 m)
Evergreen shrub from the Chilean Andes. Leaves covered in woolly down, 3 to 5 coarsely toothed lobes. Short upright racemes of yellow flowers, pleasant honey scent, in early summer. Edible black fruit has a downy coating. Zones 8–10.

Ribes indecorum
WHITE-FLOWERED CURRANT

☼ ❀ ↔ 3–7 ft (0.9–2 m) ↑ 7–8 ft (2–2.4 m)
Deciduous shrub from California, USA. Downy shoots and lobed leaves

Ribes aureum

Ribes laurifolium

similar to *R. sanguineum*. White flowers in drooping spikes, in early spring. Downy fruit. Zones 8–10.

Ribes inerme
WHITE-STEMMED GOOSEBERRY

☼ ❀ ↔ 5 ft (1.5 m) ↑ 3–6 ft (0.9–1.8 m)
Deciduous shrub that is native to USA. Small leaves with 3 to 5 rounded lobes, edged with blunt teeth. Small clusters of greenish flowers with pink or white petals, in late spring. Fruit purple-red, edible. Some thorns. Zones 6–9.

Ribes laurifolium

☼ ❀ ↔ 6 ft (1.8 m) ↑ 5 ft (1.5 m)
Evergreen shrub from western China. Coarsely toothed leaves, up to 4 in (10 cm) long. Yellow-green flowers droop gracefully, in late winter. Downy red-black fruit. Zones 8–11.

Ribes magellanicum

☼ ❀ ↔ 6 ft (1.8 m) ↑ 6–8 ft (1.8–2.4 m)
Deciduous shrub found in southern parts of Argentina and Chile. Leaves with 3 to 5 lobes. Drooping racemes of creamy yellow flowers, age to a soft gold tone, in spring. Fruit red-black. Zones 8–10.

Ribes alpinum 'Pumilum'

Ribes malvaceum

Ribes nigrum 'Ben Connan'

Ribes malvaceum
CHAPARRAL CURRANT

☼ ❀ ↔ 6 ft (1.8 m) ↑ 6 ft (1.8 m)
Deciduous shrub that is native to California, USA, similar to the far better known *R. sanguineum*. Hairy stems, downy dull green leaves, felting beneath. Pink flowers on pendulous racemes, in mid-winter to spring. Zones 7–10.

Ribes nigrum
BLACKCURRANT

☼ ❀ ↔ 6 ft (1.8 m) ↑ 7 ft (2 m)
Deciduous shrub, native to Eurasia. Upright multi-stemmed habit. Stems downy when young, leaves with 3 to 5 lobes, downy beneath. Downy pendent racemes of red-centered yellow-green flowers, in spring. Fruiting and foliage cultivars include: 'Ben Connan', attractive award-winning cultivar; 'Ben Lomond', late large fruit; 'Black Beauty', popular American cultivar; 'Boskoop Giant', vigorous form, large fruit; 'Coloratum', variegated foliage; 'Jet', large dark fruit. Zones 5–9.

Ribes odoratum
BUFFALO CURRANT, CLOVE CURRANT, GOLDEN CURRANT

☼ ❀ ↔ 6 ft (1.8 m) ↑ 6 ft (1.8 m)
From central USA. Spice-scented leaves, 3 to 5 lobes, toothed edges. Pendent racemes of sweetly scented

yellow flowers, in spring–early summer. Edible black fruit. '**Xanthocarpum**', orange-yellow berries. Zones 5–9.

Ribes oxyacanthoides

MOUNTAIN GOOSEBERRY, NORTHERN GOOSEBERRY

☼ ❋ ↔ 27 in (70 cm)
↑ 18–32 in (45–80 cm)

Deciduous shrub found in northern USA and Canada. Slender bristly stems with thorns. Glossy, dark green, heart-shaped leaves, 5 deep lobes. Paired or single, greenish white to light mauve flowers, in spring. Edible purple-red berries. Zones 2–8.

Ribes rubrum

syn. *Ribes spicatum*
NORDIC CURRANT

☼/◐ ❋ ↔ 32–60 in (80–150 cm)
↑ 5–7 ft (1.5–2 m)

Smooth-stemmed shrub found from Scandinavia to eastern China. Leaves are 3- to 5-lobed, to 4 in (10 cm) in diameter, with undersides sometimes downy. Upright to pendulous racemes

Ribes uva-crispa

Ribes viburnifolium

Ribes oxyacanthoides

Ribes sanguineum var. *glutinosum* 'Joyce Rose'

Ribes sanguineum 'King Edward VII'

of small red-flushed green flowers appear in early summer. Translucent red fruit. '**Macrocarpum**', large-fruited; '**Red Lake**', vigorous pest- and disease-resistant cultivar; '**White Grape**', pale yellow to cream fruit. Zones 3–9.

Ribes sanguineum

FLOWERING CURRANT, WINTER CURRANT

☼ ❋ ↔ 10 ft (3 m) ↑ 10 ft (3 m)

Deciduous shrub from western USA. Branches warm red-brown. Leaves dark green, 3 to 5 lobes, downy beneath. Pendent racemes of soft pink to red flowers, in spring, before the leaves appear. Fruit deep blue-black with a white bloom. *R. s.* var. *glutinosum*, pink flowers, leaves less downy than the species; '**Joyce Rose**', rich pink flowers. Popular cultivars include: *R. s.* '**Brocklebankii**', clear pink scented flowers; '**Claremont**', developed recently by the University of British Columbia in Canada, almost white flowers, ageing to deep pink; '**Elk River Red**' ★, blooms bright rose

Ribes rubrum

Ribes speciosum

Ribes sanguineum, in winter

Ribes sanguineum, in spring

red, very early in season, can become weedy; '**Inverness White**', greenish white flowers in long sprays; '**King Edward VII**', compact, with deep pink flowers; '**Plenum**', red double flowers; '**Pulborough Scarlet**', red flowers; '**Spring Showers**', pink flowers, bright green foliage; and '**Tydeman's White**', white flowers. Zones 6–10.

Ribes speciosum

FUCHSIA-FLOWERED CURRANT

☼ ❋ ↔ 10 ft (3 m) ↑ 12 ft (3.5 m)

From California, USA. Evergreen bushy upright shrub. Thorny stems, small smooth leaves, 3 to 5 lobes, toothed edges. Flowers bright red, pendulous, with long red stamens, singly, pairs, or groups of 3, in summer. Fruit bristly and red. Zones 7–10.

Ribes uva-crispa

GOOSEBERRY

☼ ❋ ↔ 36 in (90 cm) ↑ 36 in (90 cm)

Found through Europe to North Africa and the Caucasus region. Thorny many-branched bush. Leaves small, heart-shaped, 3 to 5 lobes, downy undersides. Green flowers. Bristly green fruit. Makes excellent tarts, pies,

Ribes sanguineum, in summer

and jams. Fruit of some cultivars ripen to yellow or red. Cultivars include: '**Crown Bob**', '**Leveller**' ★, and '**Roaring Lion**'. Zones 5–9.

Ribes viburnifolium

☼ ❋ ↔ 5 ft (1.5 m) ↑ 5 ft (1.5 m)

Native to California, USA. Smooth-stemmed evergreen shrub. Stems droop and take root. Leaves strongly aromatic, with a turpentine scent. Small erect racemes of pink flowers, in spring. Red fruit. Zones 8–10.

R

Richea scoparia, in the wild, Cradle Mountain–Lake St Clair National Park, Tasmania, Australia

Richea dracophylla

Ricinocarpos pinifolius

RICHEA

In the heath (Ericaceae) family, this Australian genus contains 11 species, 9 of them occurring in Tasmania and 2 on the mainland. They grow in alpine and subalpine habitats, including cool-temperate rainforests, usually in acid, often boggy, organically rich soils. They vary from small shrubs to 50 ft (15 m) tall trees. All have stiff tapering leaves that clasp the stems, with veins giving them a palm-like appearance. White or pink flowers, in dense terminal spikes, are followed by capsular fruits with many seeds.
CULTIVATION: *Richea* species prefer an acid to neutral, moist, well-drained soil. All are frost hardy to some degree. They are not easy to grow; seeds are not readily obtained and do not germinate easily, and cuttings are variable in performance. Potting or transplanting can easily damage the fine root system.

Richea dracophylla

☀ ❄ ↔ 7 ft (2 m) ↑ 15 ft (4.5 m)
From mountain regions and rainforests of Tasmania, Australia. Erect plant with few branches. Leaves taper to a

long sharp point. White flowers in dense spikes, in spring–early summer. Small 5-celled fruits. Zones 8–9.

Richea pandanifolia

PANDANI, TREE HEATH
☀ ❄ ↔ 7 ft (2 m) ↑ 50 ft (15 m)
Usually a tree with bare trunk or old leaves still attached, from the wet mountain forests of central and southwestern Tasmania, Australia. Stiff leaves taper to a long point, coarsely toothed margins. Flowers are reddish pink, in branched heads in the leaf axils, in summer. Zones 8–9.

Richea scoparia

KEROSENE BUSH
☀ ❄ ↔ 24 in (60 cm) ↑ 36 in (90 cm)
Native to mountainous regions of Tasmania, Australia. Dense rounded shrub. Tough, triangular, sharp-pointed leaves, to 3 in (8 cm) long. White, red, pink, orange, or yellow flowers, in terminal spikes, in summer. Zones 8–9.

RICINOCARPOS

This genus, a member of the euphorbia (Euphorbiaceae) family, contains 16 species, one from New Caledonia, the

others from eastern and southern Australia. All are woody shrubs that grow to 10 ft (3 m) tall, often less. Male and female flowers are separate, but in groups of a few males and 1 female. Male flowers have 5 white or pink petals with a bunch of united stamens in the center. Female flowers have smaller petals with a 3-celled ovary in the center. Fruits are relatively large, over ½ in (12 mm) in diameter.
CULTIVATION: All species grow in acid sandy soils in various habitats. Frost hardiness varies, with western Australian species the most tolerant. Propagation has been achieved using seeds and cuttings. Treating seeds with smoke or water may improve the rate of germination.

Ricinocarpos pinifolius

WEDDING BUSH
☀ ❄ ↔ 36 in (90 cm) ↑ 36 in (90 cm)
Evergreen shrub occurring in all eastern Australian States. Narrow leaves,

margins rolled under. White flowers, 1 in (25 mm) wide, in spring. Prefers extremely free-draining and acidic soil. Zones 9–11.

RICINUS

This single-species genus, a member of the euphorbia (Euphorbiaceae) family, comes from northeast Africa but has naturalized throughout the tropical regions. It is considered a prized annual in many cold-climate gardens, and is grown for its deeply lobed, and often colored, leaves.
CULTIVATION: *Ricinus communis* requires fertile soil with ample organic matter added to ensure moisture retention and free drainage. This plant's brittle stems need to be protected from winds and frost. When grown from seed care must be taken as the seed coats, and other parts of the plant, are extremely toxic.

Ricinus communis

CASTOR BEAN PLANT, CASTOR OIL PLANT
☀ ❄ ↔ 3 ft (0.9 m) ↑ 5 ft (1.5 m)
Fast-growing plant from northeast Africa; can grow to 40 ft (12 m) high in the wild. Somewhat brittle stems; distinctive, lobed, green leaves. Smaller growing cultivars include: '**Cambodgensis**', purple-black stems, dark purple leaves; '**Red Spire**', red stems, bronze-green foliage; '**Zanzibarensis**', taller, with large white-veined green leaves. Zones 9–12.

Ricinus communis

Richea pandanifolia, in the wild, central highlands, Tasmania, Australia

RIMACOLA

This is a monotypic orchid genus (family Orchidaceae) found only in sandstone areas near Sydney, New South Wales, Australia. It grows in sandstone rock crevices that always have water flowing through them so the plants never dry out. It produces several arching to pendulous leaves, and, while it lacks a pseudobulb, stores water and nutrients in its fleshy, brittle, and extensive root system. Flowering is in late spring and summer.
CULTIVATION: Unfortunately this species has proved to be impossible to maintain in cultivation due to its highly specialized habitat.

Rimacola elliptica

☼ ☽ ↔ 4–12 in (10–30 cm)
↕ 2½–12 in (6–30 cm)

Distinctive Australian species. Inflorescences with up to a dozen green,

1 in (25 mm) wide blooms with purple brown markings on a mainly white labellum. Zones 9–10.

ROBINIA

The 20 or so species of deciduous trees and shrubs in this genus, in the pea-flower subfamily of the legume (Fabaceae) family, are found mainly in eastern USA. They bear pendulous racemes of white, cream, pink, or lavender pea-flowers, followed by flat seed pods. Leaves are pinnate, often quite large; some species have vivid yellow autumn colors. Stems may have fierce thorns.
CULTIVATION: These tough adaptable plants grow quickly and tolerate most soils provided they are well drained. They are, however, rather brittle, with branches that are prone to break or tear in strong winds. It is best to prune when young to establish a

strongly branched structure. Some species sucker freely and the suckers can be used for propagation, otherwise they are propagated from stratified seed or cuttings. Special growth forms are usually grafted.

Robinia fertilis

BRISTLY LOCUST
☼ ❋ ↔ 4 ft (1.2 m) ↕ 8 ft (2.4 m)

From North Carolina to Georgia, USA. Deciduous small shrub, thicket-forming, often used for erosion control. Branches bristly. Compound leaf with many small blue-green leaflets. Spring flowers rose-colored, somewhat like sweet peas, though unscented. Zones 4–10.

Robinia hartwegii

☼ ❋ ↔ 10 ft (3 m) ↕ 25 ft (8 m)

Large shrub or tree, native to southeastern USA. Leaves to 1½ in (35 mm)

long, 11 to 23 leaflets, with silky undersides. Racemes of white, lavender or magenta flowers, in summer. Zones 6–10.

Robinia hispida

ROSE ACACIA
☼ ❋ ↔ 10 ft (3 m) ↕ 10 ft (3 m)

Large shrub from southeastern USA, dense and bushy, suckering. Branches covered in red bristles. Leaves with 7 to 15 leaflets, dark green above, gray-green below, bristles at tips. Flowers magenta to purple, in small racemes, in late spring. Zones 5–9.

Robinia pseudoacacia

BLACK LOCUST, FALSE ACACIA
☼ ❋ ↔ 35 ft (10 m) ↕ 50 ft (15 m)

Most widely grown robinia, parent of many cultivars, native to eastern and central parts of the USA. Thorny stems, red-tinted when young. Leaves with 19 bright green leaflets. White to cream flowers, in racemes, in summer. 'Appalachia', narrowly erect form; 'Aurea', greenish yellow spring foliage; 'Bessoniana', thornless rounded form; 'Coluteoides', very rounded, compact, with closely crowded leaflets; 'Frisia', bright golden foliage, thornless, few flowers; 'Inermis', thornless form, upright habit; 'Tortuosa', twisted branches; 'Umbraculifera', rounded form, dense foliage. Zones 3–10.

Rimacola elliptica

Robinia hispida

Robinia pseudoacacia 'Twisted Beauty'

Robinia pseudoacacia

R. pseudoacacia 'Appalachia'

Robinia pseudoacacia 'Aurea'

Robinia pseudoacacia 'Bessoniana'

R. pseudoacacia 'Coluteoides'

Robinia pseudoacacia 'Frisia'

R. p. 'Monophylla Fastigiata'

R. pseudoacacia 'Robusta Vigneii'

Robinia pseudoacacia 'Tortuosa'

R

Robinia × slavinii

☼ ❄ ↔ 10 ft (3 m) ↕ 15 ft (4.5 m)

Shrubby hybrid between *R. kelseyi* and *R. pseudoacacia*. Foliage deep green and pinnate; rose pink racemes in spring. '**Hillieri**', tree-like growth habit, pink flowers with distinct mauve tint. Zones 5–9.

Robinia viscosa

CLAMMY LOCUST

☼ ❄ ↔ 20 ft (6 m) ↕ 30 ft (9 m)

Deciduous tree, native to southeastern USA. Sticky, dark brown, young stems with thorns. Leaves composed of 13 to 25 dark green leaflets, gray hairs beneath. Flowers pink with yellow markings, in tightly packed racemes, in late spring. Zones 3–10.

ROBIQUETIA

Belonging to the family Orchidaceae, this is a genus consisting of about 40 different epiphytic orchid species, distributed from India and Sri Lanka through Southeast Asia to northern Australia and some islands in the Pacific Ocean. They are monopodial epiphytes, with leathery leaves

Robinia × slavinii

Robinia viscosa

Rodgersia podophylla

produced in 2 ranks. They are generally tropical species of the lowlands and produce large numbers of relatively small but colorful fleshy flowers. Flowering occurs during the warmer months of the year, with some species blooming throughout the year in tropical regions.
CULTIVATION: *Robiquetia* species are best grown on cork or tree-fern slabs (either vertical or horizontal), as few of them like their roots covered. Keep them moist throughout the year. Larger specimens can be grown in small baskets. They enjoy part-shade and are best suited to greenhouse culture in all but tropical climates. They require warm conditions throughout the year, disliking temperatures below 50°F (10°C).

Robiquetia cerina

☼ ⚥ ↔ 5–14 in (12–35 cm) ↕ 4–20 in (10–50 cm)

Showy species from the Philippines. Thick bluish green leaves. Short, densely packed inflorescences of hot pink to purple, 8 mm wide blooms that do not open fully. Zones 11–12.

Robiquetia wassellii

☼ ⚥ ↔ 5–10 in (12–25 cm) ↕ 4–16 in (10–40 cm)

Australian species with pendulous inflorescences of numerous bottle green flowers, about ½ in (12 mm) long. Zones 11–12.

RODGERSIA

While at first glance they may be difficult to reconcile with their small alpine relatives, the 6 large perennials of this genus are members of the saxifrage (Saxifragaceae) family. Found among the woodlands and streamsides of temperate Asia, they have a preference for damp conditions. They have large pinnate leaves with toothed edges and are grown primarily as foliage plants. Their astilbe-like plumes of tiny flowers are also attractive, if quite short lived. Foliage develops quickly in spring and the flowers, which are white, cream, or pink, open at about the time the leaves reach their maximum size. Named for American Rear Admiral John Rodgers (1812–82) who from 1852–56 led a botanical expedition in the western Pacific.
CULTIVATION: Plant in part- or full shade in cool, moist, humus-rich soil. Although preferring constant moisture, rodgersias are not happy in stagnant boggy conditions and often do better alongside moving water rather than ponds. Propagate from seed or divide when dormant.

Rodgersia aesculifolia

☼ ❄ ↔ 3–7 ft (0.9–2 m) ↕ 5–7 ft (1.5–2 m)

Perennial from China. Large palmate leaves, to over 16 in (40 cm) long, reminiscent, as the Latin name suggests, of horse chestnut (*Aesculus*) foliage. White flowers, in dense panicles, to 24 in (60 cm) long, in summer. Zones 5–9.

Rodgersia pinnata

☼ ❄ ↔ 3–7 ft (0.9–2 m) ↕ 32–48 in (80–120 cm)

Perennial, native to southwestern China. Leaves partly pinnate, with

Rodgersia pinnata 'Rosea'

Robiquetia cerina

5 to 9 dark green, deeply veined leaflets, to 8 in (20 cm) long. Deep pink to red, rarely white flowers, in long-stemmed panicles held well clear of foliage, in summer. '**Rosea**', deep pink flowers; '**Superba**' ★, bronze- to purple-tinted foliage, large panicles of pink flowers. Zones 6–9.

Rodgersia podophylla

☼ ❄ ↔ 3–7 ft (0.9–2 m) ↕ 32–48 in (80–120 cm)

Perennial, native to Japan and Korea. Broad palmate leaves, usually 5-lobed, to over 12 in (30 cm) long and wide, with lobes at tips. Foliage reddens in autumn, sometimes brilliantly. White flowers, in heads to 12 in (30 cm) long, in summer. Zones 6–9.

Rodgersia sambucifolia

☼ ❄ ↔ 24–48 in (60–120 cm) ↕ 24–36 in (60–90 cm)

Perennial from China. Pinnate leaves, to over 12 in (30 cm) long, with up to 11 deeply veined, finely hairy, dark green leaflets. Flat-topped, often rather open panicles of white to light pink flowers, in summer. Zones 6–9.

RODRIGUEZIA

Belonging to the family Orchidaceae, this is a genus of some 40 different species of sympodial orchids from tropical America. They often grow in cloud forests as twig epiphytes, rarely growing on the trunks or main branches of trees. The small pseudobulbs are flattened with 1 or 2 leaves at the apex. Flowering is in autumn and winter, with inflorescences produced from the leaf axil at the base of the recently matured pseudobulb. Related to *Oncidium*, many of the species have showy colorful blooms.
CULTIVATION: These epiphytic orchids are best mounted on sections

of cork or tree-fern, to accommodate the extensive and wiry root system. They must be kept in a part-shaded to bright spot in a humid environment, with plenty of free circulating air. Propagate by division of large clumps.

Rodriguezia decora

☀ ✤ ↔ 4–24 in (10–60 cm)
↕ 4–16 in (10–40 cm)

From Brazil. This species has a long rhizome between the pseudobulbs and hence needs a long mount in cultivation. Spikes of up to a dozen pale pink to purple-brown, 1 in (25 mm) wide blooms, flared creamy pink labellum. Zones 10–12.

ROELLA

This genus, a member of the bellflower (Campanulaceae) family, consists of about 30 species, all from the Cape region of South Africa. They are perennials or small evergreen shrubs, mostly with slender branchlets clothed in small leaves and attractive bell-shaped flowers borne singly or in short spikes at the branch tips.
CULTIVATION: At least 1 species was introduced to greenhouse cultivation in Europe by the late eighteenth century, part of the fad for Cape plants that continued to the mid-nineteenth century. Their requirements are similar to those of the Cape ericas, namely a gritty acid soil with perfect drainage, and a constant supply of moisture. Propagate from seed or tip cuttings.

Roella ciliata

☀ ✤ ↔ 24 in (60 cm)   ↕ 36 in (90 cm)
Native of South Africa's Western Cape. Slender erect shrub. Small pointed leaves, bristle-haired edges. Large bell-shaped flowers with violet-blue petals, much darker blue zone in throat, at end of branches, in late spring–early summer. Zones 9–10.

ROLDANA

This genus of bushy daisies from Central America includes some 50-odd species and is a member of the daisy (Asteraceae) family. While many

are annuals or perennials, the genus also includes a few shrubs. The leaves are usually large and rounded to hand-shaped with shallow lobes, dark green on top and often considerably lighter on the undersides. The leaves and young stems are covered with fine hairs that can sometimes be dense enough to become felted. The flowers, which are most commonly bright yellow, are carried in corymbs and occur throughout the year if the climate is mild enough.
CULTIVATION: Many species are frost tender, though the hardiest of them will withstand light frosts and relatively cool winters. They prefer moist, well-drained, fertile soil and flower best if grown in full sun. The foliage, however, is often more luxuriant with a little shade. Propagate from seed or cuttings in general, but in some cases by division.

Roldana petasitis

syn. *Senecio petasitis*
☀ ✤ ↔ 6–10 ft (1.8–3 m)
↕ 6–10 ft (1.8–3 m)

From Central America. Grown as a perennial or an annual. Leaves with 7 or more pointed lobes, densely felted beneath. Yellow daisy flowers in flat-topped corymbs or in spikes, in winter. Zones 9–11.

ROMNEYA

This is a genus of only 2 species in the poppy (Papaveraceae) family, native to western North America and Mexico, both with glaucous stems and deeply cut leaves. The flowers are large, 6-petalled, white and poppy-like, with a central mass of golden yellow stamens. Romneyas are sometimes difficult to establish but once settled they spread quickly by underground stems, so should be allowed plenty of space.
CULTIVATION: These plants thrive in a warm sunny position and are quite frost hardy. They prefer a fertile and well-drained soil and resent being transplanted. Propagation is from seed or from cuttings.

Roldana petasitis

Romneya coulteri

CALIFORNIA TREE POPPY
☀ ❆ ↔ 7 ft (2 m)   ↕ 8 ft (2.4 m)
From southern California, USA. Small to medium-sized shrubby perennial. Persistent stems. Leaves silvery gray, finely cut. Flowers solitary, buds smooth, slightly conical, opening to large white flowers, crumpled crape-like petals, in late summer to mid-autumn. '**Butterfly**', smaller flowers, pure white ruffled petals; '**White Cloud**', large white flowers, silvery gray leaves. Zones 7–10.

ROMULEA

This is a genus of some 80 or so species of small, crocus-like, cormous plants in the iris (Iridaceae) family, found from Europe through to South Africa, where they grow to their most flamboyant and are found in the largest numbers. They have narrow to thread-like basal leaves from among which arise open funnel-shaped flowers on fine stems, singly or, in some species several to a stem, opening in succession. In most species the flowers do not open till about midday, closing again at dark, and do not open at all on dull or wet days.
CULTIVATION: The hardiest species can be grown in a sunny well-drained rock garden in areas that get little to no frosts; otherwise they must be container-grown in an alpine house and kept dry in summer. Propagation is by seed sown in autumn and by dividing the clumps of corms when dormant.

Romulea ramiflora

☀ ❆ ↔ 6–10 in (15–25 cm)
↕ 10–12 in (25–30 cm)
Dainty species from Mediterranean region. Erect or curved leaves. Pale

Romulea ramiflora

lilac flowers, yellow or white throat, to 1 in (25 mm) across, in spring; produces 1 to 4 flowers per corm. Zones 8–10.

RONDELETIA

This small genus of evergreen shrubs and small trees in the madder (Rubiaceae) family, from Central America, is named for Professor Guillaume Rondelet, a sixteenth-century French naturalist. These shrubs and trees have opposite leaves and terminal or axillary inflorescences of red, yellow, pink, or white tubular flowers that are rich in nectar.
CULTIVATION: *Rondeletia* species need a warm position in full sun, and may be damaged by frost. A light friable soil that drains freely is ideal. Pruning should be moderately severe after flowering, with flowering shoots cut back to within several nodes of the previous season's growth. Propagation is from half-hardened leafy tip cuttings, 2–4 in (5–10 cm) long, which can be taken during spring.

Roella ciliata

Romneya coulteri

Rondeletia odorata

Rondeletia amoena

☀ ❋ ↔ 8 ft (2.4 m) ↑ 10 ft (3 m)

Species native to Mexico and Central America. Evergreen shrub, many erect stems rising from base. Dense foliage, leaves pale bronze-green, ageing to dark glossy green above, hairy below. Small salmon pink flowers, in terminal cymes, faint perfume, in spring. Zones 10–12.

Rondeletia odorata

FRAGRANT RONDELETIA

☀ ✿ ↔ 3 ft (0.9 m) ↑ 5 ft (1.5 m)

From Panama. Small evergreen shrub; upright, vase-shaped. Leaves elliptic-ovate, dark velvety green above, reddish green below. Flowers in a terminal cluster, orange-scarlet to crimson, bright yellow throat, sweetly fragrant, in late summer–autumn. Zones 11–12.

ROSA

ROSE

The genus *Rosa* is one of the most widely grown and best loved of all plant genera around the world. It belongs to the large rose (Rosaceae) family, which includes a wide range of favorite fruiting plants such as apples, plums, and strawberries as well as ornamentals. Since ancient times roses have been valued for their beauty and fragrance as well as for their medicinal, culinary, and cosmetic properties. There are between 100 to 150 species of rose, which range in habit from erect and arching shrubs to scramblers and climbers. The majority of species are deciduous and most have prickles or bristles. They are found in temperate and subtropical zones of the Northern Hemisphere; none are native to the Southern Hemisphere. The pinnate leaves are usually comprised of 5 to 9, but sometimes more, serrated-edged leaflets. Flowers range from single, usually 5-petalled, blooms to those with many closely packed petals. They are borne singly or in clusters. Many are intensely fragrant. The majority of species and old garden roses flower only once but most of the modern cultivars are repeat-blooming. Rose fruits (hips or heps) are very rich in vitamin C. They are usually orangey red, but can be dark, and can be very decorative. They may be small and in clusters or single large fruits. Roses have been bred for many centuries and are divided into a number of recognized groups. The old garden roses were originally bred from a handful of species and include groups such as Gallica and Alba. In the late eighteenth century the repeat-flowering China rose (*R. chinensis*) arrived in Europe and subsequent cross-breeding extended the number of Old Rose groups further. The Tea Roses, also repeat-flowering, followed in the nineteenth century, and fifty years later a Frenchman bred the first Large-flowered Rose, heralding the start of modern rose breeding. Large-flowered, Polyantha, Cluster-flowered, and Shrub Roses proliferated in the twentieth century. While most of the species and Old Roses are in shades of pink, red, purple, or white, modern rose-breeding programs have seen the color range increase to include shades of yellow and orange.

CULTIVATION: Roses can be grown in separate beds or mixed borders, in formal and informal settings, as ground covers, climbing up arches and pergolas, scrambling up trees, as hedging, and in containers. Such is the popularity of roses that numerous books are devoted to their cultivation. Roses generally require a site that is sunny for most of the day, as shade inhibits flowering. They should not be overcrowded and there should be good air movement around the plants, factors that help reduce the risk of disease. Roses will grow in most well-drained medium-loamy soils in which compost or organic manure has been incorporated. When planting, the point at which the plant is grafted should be about 1 in (25 mm) below the soil. Granular or liquid rose fertilizer can be applied once or twice a year from spring. Plants should be watered well in dry periods and a mulch will help to conserve moisture in summer. Roses that flower more than once should be deadheaded to encourage further blooms. Roses should be pruned to maintain strong healthy growth, a good shape, and to let light into the plant. A number of pruning regimes are promoted for different rose groups, but recent research has shown that a simple "tidying up" of dead wood and pruning for size may be just as effective. Most pruning is done when the plants are dormant in winter. Fungal diseases such as rust, black spot, and mildew can be a problem, particularly in humid areas. Insect pests can also be troublesome, the most common being aphids. Others include spider mites, thrips, leafhoppers, froghoppers, and scale. Fungicidal and insecticidal sprays, both chemical and organic, are available to combat these problems. Roses planted in a position previously occupied by another rose can suffer rose sickness—to prevent this a generous amount of the old soil should be removed and replaced with a fresh supply. Most roses are very hardy and indeed benefit from a period of winter cold, but some of the old Tea Roses are a little tender and are better suited to warm-temperate climates. In warm areas roses often grow much larger than their cool-climate counterparts and can be more prone to problems caused by mild winters not killing off pests and diseases. Propagation in commercial quantities is usually from budding, but the gardener can take hardwood cuttings in autumn or softwood cuttings in summer. While hybrid plants will not come true from seed, the species can be propagated in this way. Seeds will need to be stratified before planting.

Rosa acicularis

☀ ❋ ↔ 4 ft (1.2 m) ↑ 6 ft (1.8 m)

Widespread species, found throughout northern areas of Europe, Asia, and America. Lax shrub, densely packed bristles of varying lengths, grayish green foliage. Mildly fragrant, single, deep pink flowers, in summer. Hips are bright red, pear-shaped. Zones 2–9.

Rosa amblyotis

☀ ❋ ↔ 4 ft (1.2 m) ↑ 6 ft (1.8 m)

Upright shrub, native to northeastern Asia. Leaves grayish green. Mildly fragrant, single, purplish pink flowers, in summer. Globular or pear-shaped red hips. Zones 5–9.

Rosa amblyotis

Rosa acicularis

Rosa banksiae normalis

Rosa banksiae lutea

Rosa banksiae banksiae

Rosa arkansana

PRAIRIE ROSE

☀ ❄ ↔ 20 in (50 cm)
↑ 24–48 in (60–120 cm)

Native to central USA. Small sucker-ing shrub. Erect branches very bristly, leaves shiny green. Single, mildly fragrant blooms, from pink to red, in summer. Round, small, red hips. Zones 4–9.

Rosa banksiae

BANKSIA ROSE

☀ ❄ ↔ 30 ft (9 m) ↑ 30 ft (9 m)

Near-evergreen in mild climates, once-flowering climbing rose from western and central China, seldom cultivated. Leaves with 3 to 5 leaflets. Massed sprays of small white flowers, in spring–early summer. *R. b. banksiae*, double white scented flowers; *R. b. lutea* ★, yellow double flowers; *R. b. normalis*, thornless form, fragrant ivory white flowers. Zones 7–10.

Rosa arkansana

mid-pink flowers appear in summer. Ovoid to pear-shaped hips, red in color. Zones 3–9.

Rosa bracteata

MACARTNEY ROSE

☀ ❄ ↔ 8 ft (2.4 m) ↑ 8 ft (2.4 m)

Evergreen species that is native to China but has become naturalized in southern USA. It forms a shrub or small climber in colder areas. Stems with hooked thorns; leaves dark green. Single white flowers with prominent yellow stamens, in summer to autumn. Hips round, orangey red. Zones 7–10.

Rosa californica

☀ ❄ ↔ 6 ft (1.8 m) ↑ 7 ft (2 m)

Species common west of the Sierra Nevadas in the USA south to Baja

Rosa beggeriana

☀ ❄ ↔ 8 ft (2.4 m) ↑ 8 ft (2.4 m)

Deciduous shrub, native to central Asia. Grayish green leaves. Small white flowers, in clusters of 8 or more at the end of new shoots, from mid-summer. Small, round, reddish hips. Zones 4–9.

Rosa blanda

HUDSON BAY ROSE, MEADOW ROSE, SMOOTH ROSE

☀ ❄ ↔ 3 ft (0.9 m) ↑ 3–7 ft (0.9–2 m)

An erect brown-stemmed shrub that is found in eastern and central North America. It is similar to *R. canina*. Few prickles near the base, and dull green leaves. Mildly fragrant, single,

California, Mexico. Stems bear stout prickles; leaves are mid-green. Single, slightly fragrant, pink flowers, in clusters, appear in summer. Round hips are orangey red. *R. c. plena* has grayish green leaves; semi-double, more strongly scented than the species, and the flowers are deeper pink. Zones 5–10.

Rosa canina

COMMON BRIAR, DOG ROSE

☀ ❄ ↔ 10 ft (3 m) ↑ 10 ft (3 m)

This is a vigorous suckering shrub that is common in its native UK and continental Europe. It has prickly stems, and leaves with 5 to 7 leaflets. Scented flowers, single, pale or blush pink, occasionally white, appear in summer. Hips are orangey red in color. Zones 3–10.

Rosa bracteata

Rosa californica plena

Rosa canina (snow-covered hips), Veneto, Italy

Rosa chinensis cultivar

Rosa chinensis spontanea

Rosa cinnamomea plena

Rosa dumalis

Rosa chinensis

CHINA ROSE

☼ ✽ ↔ 8 ft (2.4 m)   ↑ 20 ft (6 m)

From China. Variable species, from dwarf shrub to semi-climber. Lustrous leaves, 3 to 5 leaflets. Flower color varies from red and pink to white, single or semi-double, in summer. Hips greenish brown to scarlet. This species brought repeat-flowering into modern rose breeding. *R. c. spontanea*, vigorous climbing form. Zones 7–10.

Rosa cinnamomea plena

syn. *Rosa majalis*

CINNAMON ROSE, MAY ROSE

☼ ✽ ↔ 5 ft (1.5 m)   ↑ 6 ft (1.8 m)

Deciduous shrub from northeastern Europe. Slender purplish stems, downy grayish green leaves. Single to double flowers, mid- to purplish pink, in early summer. Elongated hips, dark red. Zones 6–10.

Rosa corymbifera

☼ ✽ ↔ 10 ft (3 m)   ↑ 10 ft (3 m)

Vigorous shrub, native to Europe, southwestern Asia, and northern Africa. Rounded downy leaflets. Clusters of single, creamy white to pale pink flowers, in summer. Orangey red hips. Zones 6–10.

Rosa davidii

☼ ✽ ↔ 8 ft (2.4 m)   ↑ 10 ft (3 m)

Deciduous shrub, native of western and central China. Arching stems, red-tinged prickles, wrinkled leaves. Single flowers in small to large clusters, in summer, soft pink, mildly fragrant. Flagon-shaped orangey red hips. Zones 6–10.

Rosa davurica

☼ ✽ ↔ 4 ft (1.2 m)   ↑ 3–5 ft (0.9–1.5 m)

Found in northeastern Asia and northern China. Deciduous shrub, small leaves, straight prickles. Groups of 1 to 3 pink flowers, in summer. Small, oval, red hips. Zones 5–9.

Rosa eglanteria

Rosa dumalis

☼ ✽ ↔ 3–7 ft (0.9–2 m)   ↑ 3–7 ft (0.9–2 m)

Found in Europe, Turkey, and southwestern Asia. Deciduous shrub. Stems and uppersurfaces of leaves often covered in a white bloom. Single pale pink flowers, in summer. Red hips. Zones 4–9.

Rosa ecae

☼ ✽ ↔ 4 ft (1.2 m)   ↑ 4 ft (1.2 m)

Native to Afghanistan and Pakistan, much-branched suckering shrub. Very prickly stems. Small, fern-like, aromatic leaves. Buttercup-sized, deep yellow flowers, in spring. Shiny reddish brown hips. Zones 7–10.

Rosa eglanteria

syn. *Rosa rubiginosa*

BRIAR ROSE, EGLANTINE, SWEET BRIAR

☼ ✽ ↔ 10 ft (3 m)   ↑ 10 ft (3 m)

Deciduous shrub from Europe and western Asia. Arching prickly stems, apple-scented leaves. Small, single, pink, fragrant flowers, in summer. Ovoid orangey red hips. Best in the wild garden or as a hedgerow plant. Zones 4–10.

Rosa elegantula

syn. *Rosa farreri*

THREEPENNY-BIT ROSE

☼ ✽ ↔ 8 ft (2.4 m)   ↑ 3–7 ft (0.9–2 m)

Dense suckering shrub, native of northwestern China. Stems thickly covered in red bristles. Fern-like foliage, grayish green, turns purple and crimson shades in autumn. Small single flowers, white to rose pink, in summer. Zones 6–10.

Rosa fedtschenkoana

☼ ✽ ↔ 3–8 ft (0.9–2.4 m)   ↑ 3–8 ft (0.9–2.4 m)

Species native to mountain areas of central Asia. Vigorous suckering shrub. Prickles tinged pink, leaves grayish green. Single white flowers, prominent yellow stamens, mildly fragrant, in summer–autumn. Pear-shaped hips, bristly, orangey red. Zones 4–10.

Rosa foetida

AUSTRIAN BRIAR, AUSTRIAN YELLOW

☼ ✽ ↔ 6 ft (1.8 m)   ↑ 3–10 ft (0.9–3 m)

An erect shrub that is native to Asia, with large blackish thorns, bright green leaves. Single flowers, deep

Rosa foetida

Rosa fedtschenkoana

Rosa davurica

Rosa foetida bicolor

Rosa foetida persiana

yellow with prominent stamens, which give off an unpleasant aroma, in summer. Round red hips. *R. f. bicolor* (Austrian copper rose) has coppery orange flowers; *R. f. persiana* (Persian yellow rose) has double yellow flowers. Zones 4–10.

Rosa foliolosa

☼ ❄ ↔ 36 in (90 cm)
↕ 18–36 in (45–90 cm)

Small suckering shrub, native of southeastern USA, with relatively thornless, narrow leaflets. Single bright pink flowers, slightly scented, appear in summer. Small round hips, bright red. Tolerant of wet soils. Zones 6–10.

Rosa gallica

FRENCH ROSE, RED ROSE

☼ ❄ ↔ 4 ft (1.2 m) ↕ 4 ft (1.2 m)

Ancient rose native to southern, central, and eastern Europe. Low suckering shrub. Lightly bristled, leathery dark green leaves. Mildly fragrant flowers, usually single, soft to deep pink, prominent light yellow stamens. Small ovoid hips, brick red. Species not as well known as its 2 forms: *R. g. officinalis* ★ (apothecary's rose or Provins rose), slightly smaller, with quite large, semi-double, heavily perfumed, crimson flowers, can become weedy. *R. g. versicolor* (syn. 'Rosa

Mundi'), sport of *R. g. officinalis*, identical except for its striped white, pink, and crimson flowers. Zones 5–10.

Rosa gigantea

☼ ❄ ↔ 20–40 ft (6–12 m)
↕ 30–60 ft (9–18 m)

Near-evergreen climbing rose native to northeastern India, upper Myanmar, and western China. It is capable of growing to an enormous size. Thorny stems, glossy deep green leaves. Flowers are cream, white, or sometimes pink, in early summer. Large red hips. Zones 8–11.

Rosa glauca

syn. *Rosa rubrifolia*
REDLEAF ROSE

☼ ❄ ↔ 6 ft (1.8 m) ↕ 6 ft (1.8 m)

Deciduous shrub, native to Europe. Arching stems dark purplish red when

Rosa gallica versicolor

young, leaves bluish gray. Flowers starry-petalled, deep pink fading to white near center, in summer. Ovoid hips, purplish red. Zones 3–10.

Rosa gymnocarpa

WOOD ROSE

☼ ❄ ↔ 7 ft (2 m) ↕ 3–10 ft (0.9–3 m)

North American native. Slender plant with moderately thorny stems, small rounded leaflets. Small, single, pale pink flowers appear in summer. Pear-shaped hips are red and shiny. Zones 6–10.

Rosa helenae

☼ ❄ ↔ 15 ft (4.5 m) ↕ 20 ft (6 m)

Rambling rose from central China. Young branches with purplish hue, stems well armed with strong curved prickles. Light green leaves, long narrow leaflets, pale undersides. Small, white, single, fragrant flowers, in corymbs, in summer. Large orange to red hips. Zones 5–10.

Rosa hemisphaerica

SULFUR ROSE

☼ ❄ ↔ 7 ft (2 m) ↕ 7 ft (2 m)

From southwestern Asia. Well-branched shrub. Stiffly upright stems bear scattered thorns, leaves grayish green. Double flowers cupped, deep sulfur yellow, in summer. Round dark red hips. Zones 6–10.

Rosa holodonta

syn. *Rosa moyesii rosea*

☼/☀ ❄ ↔ 7 ft (2 m) ↕ 10 ft (3 m)

Large western Chinese bush; many erect stems with bristles and pale thorns to over 1¼ in (30 mm) long. Leaves with 7 to 13 leaflets, to 2 in (5 cm) long, deep green above, blue-green below, toothed. Flowers pink to red, to 2 in (5 cm) wide, single or in pairs, rarely to 4 in a cluster, in summer. Bottle-shaped bright red fruit, to 2 in (5 cm) long. Zones 5–9.

Rosa hugonis

syn. *Rosa xanthina* f. *hugonis*

☼ ❄ ↔ 6 ft (1.8 m) ↕ 7 ft (2 m)

Chinese species; very similar to *R. xanthina*. Differs from *R. xanthina* in having broader leaflets and primrose yellow flowers to well over 2 in (5 cm) wide. Zones 5–10.

Rosa holodonta

Rosa hugonis

Rosa glauca

Rosa gallica

Rosa inodora

syn. *Rosa elliptica*

☼ ❋ ↔ 10 ft (3 m) ↕ 8 ft (2.4 m)

Native to southern Europe. Coarse vigorous shrub, suited to wild gardens. Foliage scented like the sweet briar. Single flowers, soft pink to blush white, in summer. Bright red oval hips. Zones 6–9.

Rosa laevigata

CHEROKEE ROSE

☼ ❋ ↔ 20 ft (6 m) ↕ 30 ft (9 m)

From warm-temperate and subtropical East Asia; shrubby if cut back hard. Evergreen foliage, leathery, glossy, deep green leaflets, toothed edges. Flowers large, single, white to cream blooms, fragrant, in summer. Bristly orange-red hips. Zones 7–10.

Rosa laxa

☼/◐ ❋ ↔ 5–10 ft (1.5–3 m) ↕ 7–8 ft (2–2.4 m)

Shrub found in Siberia and northwestern China. Arching cane-like stems, bristly, with a few large recurved thorns. Compound leaves, with up

Rosa minutifolia

to 9 leaflets, to nearly 2 in (5 cm) long, toothed, with undersides that are sometimes sparsely hairy. Clusters of 1 to 6 white to pale pink flowers, to nearly 2 in (5 cm) wide, in summer. Fruit is red, ½ in (12 mm) long. Zones 5–9.

Rosa macrophylla

☼ ❋ ↔ 10 ft (3 m) ↕ 10 ft (3 m)

Native to the Himalayan region. Dark red stems almost thornless, leaves purplish green. Cerise-pink, single flowers, in summer. Orangey red bristly hips. Zones 7–10.

Rosa laxa

Rosa marretii

Rosa moschata

Rosa marginata

syn. *Rosa jundzillii*

☼ ❋ ↔ 8 ft (2.4 m) ↕ 3–8 ft (0.9–2.4 m)

Suckering shrub native to eastern Europe. Moderately thorny, with thorns few in number, slender and scattered. Dark green leaves, sometimes downy on undersides. Slightly fragrant, single, pale to bright pink flowers, in summer. Red hips, round or ovoid. Zones 5–10.

Rosa marretii

☼ ❋ ↔ 4 ft (1.2 m) ↕ 6 ft (1.8 m)

Upright shrub, native to the Middle East. Purplish stems, mid-green leaves. Flowers mid- to pale pink, in small clusters, in summer. Hips round and red. Zones 6–9.

Rosa moyesii

Rosa moyesii fargesii

Rosa moschata nepalensis

Rosa minutifolia

☼/◐ ✴ ↔ 4 ft (1.2 m) ↕ 4 ft (1.2 m)

Near-evergreen small bush from California, USA, and Baja California, Mexico. Hairy, with dense covering of fine red-brown spines. Pinnate leaves, under 1 in (25 mm) long, leaflets under ¼ in (6 mm) long. Purple-pink or white single flowers, around ¾ in (18 mm) wide, in summer. Zones 9–11.

Rosa moschata

MUSK ROSE

☼ ❋ ↔ 10 ft (3 m) ↕ 10–35 ft (3–10 m)

Ancient species from southern Europe and Middle East. Arching or semi-climbing habit. Few thorns, shiny grayish green leaves. Single creamy flowers, fading to white, in loose clusters, in summer. Small, downy, ovoid, orange-red hips. *R. m. nepalensis* (Himalayan musk rose), fragrant white flowers. Zones 6–10.

Rosa moyesii

☼ ❋ ↔ 10 ft (3 m) ↕ 10 ft (3 m)

Deciduous shrub from western China. Stout erect stems, scattered thorns, dark green leaves. Single deep red flowers, in summer. Pendulous, flagon-shaped, orange-red hips. *R. m. fargesii*, reddish pink flowers. Zones 5–10.

Rosa inodora

Rosa pomifera

Rosa pendulina

Rosa mulliganii

☀ ❄ ↔ 7–10 ft (2–3 m)
↑ 10–15 ft (3–4.5 m)

Vigorous shrub, native to China.
Purplish gray young shoots and leaves.
Single white flowers, scented, in small
clusters, in summer. Showy, small,
round, red hips. Zones 4–9.

Rosa multiflora

JAPANESE ROSE

☀ ❄ ↔ 10 ft (3 m) ↑ 10–15 ft (3–4.5 m)
Robust shrub from eastern Asia and
Japan, used in hybridization and as a
rootstock for grafting. Prickly stems,
leaves with 7 to 9 leaflets. Clusters of
small, single, creamy white flowers,
in summer. Small, rounded, red hips.
R. m. carnea, fully double flowers of

Rosa mulliganii

Rosa × *pteragonis*

white to pale pink. *R. m. cathayensis*,
found in China, single rosy pink
flowers. Zones 5–10.

Rosa nitida

☀ ❄ ↔ 4 ft (1.2 m) ↑ 3 ft (0.9 m)
Suckering shrub, native to eastern
North America. Slender prickly stems,
small fern-like leaves, turning crimson
in autumn. Small, single, fragrant,
deep pink flowers, in summer. Dark
scarlet hips. Suitable for a ground
cover. Zones 3–10.

Rosa nutkana

☀ ❄ ↔ 7 ft (2 m) ↑ 6–10 ft (1.8–3 m)
Vigorous rose, native to western
North America. Almost thornless purplish brown stems, dark grayish green
leaves. Fragrant single flowers, medium
pink, in summer. Small, round, red
hips. *R. n. hispida*, fragrant pink
flowers. Zones 4–10.

Rosa palustris

SWAMP ROSE

☀ ❄ ↔ 6 ft (1.8 m) ↑ 4–7 ft (1.2–2 m)
Deciduous shrub from eastern North
America, grows in wet boggy con-
ditions. Erect suckering habit, reddish
stems, mid- to dark green leaves.
Single deep pink flowers, in summer.
Small red hips. Zones 4–10.

Rosa pendulina

☀ ❄ ↔ 5 ft (1.5 m) ↑ 2–7 ft (0.6–2 m)
From the mountains of central and
southern Europe. Deciduous shrub.
Arching reddish purple stems, almost
thornless. Leaves dark green. Deep
pink or purplish pink single flowers,

Rosa nitida

Rosa nutkana

Rosa primula

with prominent yellow stamens, in
summer. Red elongated hips, often
pendulous. Zones 5–10.

Rosa pisocarpa

CLUSTER ROSE

☀ ❄ ↔ 4 ft (1.2 m) ↑ 3–7 ft (0.9–2 m)
Deciduous shrub from western North
America. Arching stems, small leaves,
bristly at base. Small single flowers in
clusters, rosy pink, in summer. Small,
bright red, shiny hips. Zones 6–10.

Rosa pomifera

syn. *Rosa villosa*

APPLE ROSE

☀ ❄ ↔ 4 ft (1.2 m) ↑ 6 ft (1.8 m)
From central and southern Europe and
Turkey. Deciduous shrub. Branches
stiff, straight, scattered thorns, downy
gray-green leaves. Single deep pink,
fragrant, flowers, in summer. Large,
round, red, bristly hips. Zones 5–10.

Rosa primula

AFGHAN YELLOW ROSE, INCENSE ROSE

☀ ❄ ↔ 5 ft (1.5 m) ↑ 5–10 ft (1.5–3 m)
Species native to central Asia and
China. Deciduous shrub with erect

Rosa pisocarpa

branching habit and thorny brown
stems. The aromatic fern-like foliage
is this species' distinctive feature.
Perfumed single flowers of primrose
yellow with prominent stamens, in
spring. Smooth, rounded, reddish
maroon hips. Has been confused with
R. ecae in cultivation. Zones 5–10.

Rosa × *pteragonis*

☀ ❄ ↔ 5 ft (1.5 m) ↑ 6 ft (1.8 m)
Hybrid of *R. xanthina* and *R. sericea*,
dark red prickles similar to *R. sericea*.
Single white flowers, pale yellow
centers, prominent golden stamens,
in spring. Zones 5–9.

R

Rosa rugosa

Rosa rugosa alba

Rosa rugosa rubra

Rosa roxburghii

BURR ROSE, CHESTNUT ROSE

☼ ❄ ↔ 7 ft (2 m) ↑ 7 ft (2 m)

Deciduous shrub, native to western China. Branches angular, bark becomes flaky and peels with age. Leaves with 15 small light green leaflets. Single pink flowers, fragrant, in summer. Yellowish green hips covered in short prickles. *R. r. plena*, form usually seen in cultivation, fully double rosy pink flowers. Zones 5–10.

Rosa rubus

BLACKBERRY ROSE

☼ ❄ ↔ 10 ft (3 m) ↑ 8–15 ft (2.4–4.5 m)

Vigorous rose from western and central China. Spreading or semi-climbing habit. Thorny greenish

Rosa setigera

purple stems, leaves glossy, often tinged purple when young. Tight clusters of small, single, white flowers, in summer. Small dark red hips. Zones 8–10.

Rosa rugosa

BEACH ROSE, JAPANESE ROSE, RAMANAS ROSE

☼ ❄ ↔ 5–8 ft (1.5–2.4 m) ↑ 5–8 ft (1.5–2.4 m)

Vigorous deciduous shrub, native to Japan and eastern Asia. Stout prickly stems. Dark green leaves, wrinkled surface. Scented single flowers, light to deep pink, in summer–autumn. Round rich red hips. *R. r. alba*, large white flowers opening from pink buds, large tomato red hips; *R. r. rubra*, single deep pink-purple flowers. Zones 2–10.

Rosa sericea omeiensis

Rosa sherardii

Rosa sempervirens

EVERGREEN ROSE

☼ ❄ ↔ 20–35 ft (6–10 m) ↑ 1–6 ft (0.3–1.8 m)

Semi-evergreen shrub, native to southern Europe. Trailing or scrambling stems. Mid- to dark green foliage. Fragrant, white, single flowers, in clusters, from early summer. Small orangey red hips. Zones 7–10.

Rosa sericea

MALTESE CROSS ROSE

☼ ❄ ↔ 8 ft (2.4 m) ↑ 10 ft (3 m)

From western China and Himalayas. Vigorous. Stout erect branches, large hooked thorns, foliage fern-like. Single, white, 4-petalled flowers, in spring. Pear-shaped bright red hips. *R. s. omeiensis* (syn. *R. omeiensis*), large wedge-shaped thorns, up to 1½ in (35 mm) long at base. Zones 6–10.

Rosa setigera

syn. *Rosa rubifolia*

PRAIRIE ROSE

☼ ❄ ↔ 10 ft (3 m) ↑ 7–15 ft (2–4.5 m)

Trailing shrubby species from North America. Long arching stems, scattered thorns, deep green leaves. Clusters of single deep pink flowers, ageing to white, in summer. Round hips, bristly, red to greenish brown. Zones 4–10.

Rosa setipoda

☼ ❄ ↔ 5 ft (1.5 m) ↑ 8 ft (2.4 m)

Deciduous shrub from western China. Shrubby branching habit, stout stems, thick well-spaced thorns. Foliage aromatic when crushed. Large clusters of single flowers, pale pink, prominent yellow stamens, in summer. Bristly, flagon-shaped, deep red hips. Zones 6–10.

Rosa sherardii

☼ ❄ ↔ 6 ft (1.8 m) ↑ 7 ft (2 m)

Densely branched deciduous shrub native to northern and central Europe. Bluish green hairy leaves. Clusters of single deep pink flowers, slightly fragrant, appear in spring. Hips are urn-shaped and bright red. Zones 5–9.

Rosa soulieana

☼ ❄ ↔ 6 ft (1.8 m) ↑ 10 ft (3 m)

Vigorous shrub that is native to western China, with slender arching or semi-climbing branches. Small oval leaflets are grayish green in color. Dense clusters of small, single, white

Rosa sempervirens

Rosa roxburghii

Rosa spinosissima

Rosa stellata mirifica

Rosa willmottiae

flowers, opening from creamy buds, in summer. Small, ovoid, orange hips. Zones 7–10.

Rosa spinosissima
syn. *Rosa pimpinellifolia*
BURNET ROSE, SCOTCH BRIAR
☼ ❋ ↔ 4 ft (1.2 m) ↑ 3–7 ft (0.9–2 m)
Small suckering rose found over a wide area of Europe and Asia. Well branched, prickly stems, coarse fern-like leaves. Single creamy white flowers, in spring. Small, round, black, shiny hips. *R. s. altaica*, beautiful pure white flowers, prominent yellow stamens. Zones 4–10.

Rosa stellata
DESERT ROSE
☼ ❋ ↔ 36 in (90 cm) ↑ 36 in (90 cm)
Deciduous shrub from hot south-western areas of the USA. Forms a dense spiny thicket. Light green wedge-shaped leaflets, small, slightly

hairy. Single rich pink flowers, in mid-summer. Flower buds and red hips covered with soft spines. *R. s. mirifica*, flowers range from pink to purplish red. Zones 6–10.

Rosa sweginzowii
☼ ❋ ↔ 15 ft (4.5 m) ↑ 12 ft (3.5 m)
Native of northern and western China. Upright bush, spreading habit. Large thorns, bristly reddish stems. Light to mid-green leaves, heavily toothed, rounded leaflets. Small clusters of deep pink flowers, in mid-summer. Bottle-shaped orange-red hips. Zones 6–10.

Rosa virginiana
VIRGINIA ROSE
☼ ❋ ↔ 5 ft (1.5 m) ↑ 5 ft (1.5 m)
Erect, sometimes suckering shrub native to eastern North America. Leaves shiny green, coloring well in autumn. Flowers single deep pink

Rosa sweginzowii

Rosa virginiana

Rosa webbiana

blooms, with prominent yellow stamens, in mid-summer. Round red hips. Zones 3–10.

Rosa webbiana
☼/◐ ❋ ↔ 7 ft (2 m) ↑ 7 ft (2 m)
Shrub from Himalayas and eastern Asia. Arching or trailing shoots. Small grayish blue leaves. Small scented flowers, pale pink, in autumn. Orangey red pear-shaped hips. Zones 4–9.

Rosa wichurana
syn. *Rosa luciae* var. *wichurana*
MEMORIAL ROSE
☼ ❋ ↔ 20 ft (6 m) ↑ 6 ft (1.8 m)
Dense spreading shrub or short climber from eastern Asia. Trailing stems bear stout thorns, glossy green foliage almost evergreen. Clusters of single, fragrant, white flowers, in summer. Small, dark red, oval hips. Species much used in breeding programs. Regarded by some as doubtfully distinct from *R. luciae*. Zones 5–10.

Rosa willmottiae
MISS WILLMOTT'S ROSE
☼ ❋ ↔ 5 ft (1.5 m) ↑ 6 ft (1.8 m)
Species native to China; its names commemorates a well-known British rosarian. Deciduous shrub. Arching habit, grayish green fern-like foliage. Single light purplish pink flowers, prominent yellow stamens, appear in summer. Small, ovoid, orangey red hips. Zones 6–10.

Rosa woodsii
WESTERN WILD ROSE
☼ ❋ ↔ 5 ft (1.5 m) ↑ 3–7 ft (0.9–2 m)
Native to North America. Stiffly branching shrub. Stems purplish brown when young, very prickly. Foliage colors well in autumn. Mid-pink single flowers, in small clusters, in summer. Bright red hips. *R. w. ultramontana*, from northwestern USA and adjacent areas of Canada, smaller flowers than the typical variety. Zones 4–10.

Rosa woodsii ultramontana

Rosa woodsii

R

MODERN ROSES

The term "Modern Roses" is somewhat misleading as a number of them were being developed in the latter half of the 1800s, at the same time as some of the Old Rose groups. Modern Roses are best characterized by their mainly repeat-flowering qualities, their floriferousness and the yellow and orange shades that have been introduced. The crossing of Large-flowered Roses (Hybrid Teas) and Polyanthas resulted in the Cluster-flowered (Floribunda) Roses; others have followed, most recently the Ground Cover Roses and David Austin's English Roses. A breeding program initiated by the Canadian Department of Agriculture in the early 1900s has produced some very hardy roses, some tolerant to Zone 1, notably the Explorer Series, named after explorers of Canada. The Modern Roses are divided into major categories based on habit—Bush, Shrub, Climbing, Miniature, and Ground Cover.

BUSH ROSES

The Bush Roses usually have a tidy habit, the biggest growing no more than 5 ft (1.5 m) tall. They have a long flowering season and are suitable for growing as bedding plants and in borders. The complex crossing and re-crossing of the various groups can make classification difficult, with some Large-flowered Roses bearing flowers in quite large clusters and taller-growing Cluster-flowered Roses being more shrub-like.

CLUSTER-FLOWERED (FLORIBUNDA) ROSES
☀ ❄ ↔ 3–6 ft (0.9–1.8 m)
↕ 4–7 ft (1.2–2 m)

These Bush Roses resulted from the crossing of the small cluster-flowered Polyantha Roses (described on page 1257) and the Large-flowered Roses. The individual blooms, while usually smaller than those of the Large-flowered Roses, are borne in large crowded clusters, and the flowers are usually flatter when fully open. The majority are double or semi-double. **'Amber Queen'**, quite large, cup-shaped, clear amber-yellow flowers; **'Apricot Nectar'**, cupped golden-apricot flowers, well-scented; **'Betty Boop'** ★ (syn. 'Centenary of Federation'), highly fragrant single

Rosa, Modern Rose, Cluster-Flowered, 'Bad Füssing'

Rosa, Modern Rose, Cluster-Flowered, 'Aberdeen Celebration'

Rosa, Modern Rose, C-F, 'Allgold'

Rosa, MR, C-F, 'Amber Queen'

Rosa, MR, C-F, 'Angel Face'

Rosa, MR, C-F, 'Anna Livia'

Rosa, MR, C-F, 'Anna Louisa'

Rosa, MR, C-F, 'Anne Harkness'

Rosa, MR, C-F, 'Apricot Nectar'

Rosa, MR, C-F, 'Atlantic Star'

Rosa, Modern Rose, C-F, 'Atlantis'

Rosa, MR, C-F, 'Australian Gold'

Rosa, Modern Rose, C-F, 'Bazaar'

Rosa, MR, C-F, 'Bendigold'

Rosa, Modern Rose, C-F, 'Bengali'

Rosa, MR, C-F, 'Betty Boop'

Rosa, Modern Rose, Cluster-Flowered, 'Betty Prior'

Rosa, Modern Rose, Cluster-Flowered, 'Black Beauty 99'

Rosa, Modern Rose, Cluster-Flowered, 'Bonfire Night'

Rosa, Modern Rose, Cluster-Flowered, 'Betty Harkness'

Rosa, MR, C-F, 'Bridal Pink'

R., MR, C-F, 'Bright Smile'

R., MR, C-F, 'Brilliant Pink Iceberg'

Rosa, MR, C-F, 'Brownie'

R., MR, C-F, 'Buisman's Triumph'

Rosa, MR, C-F, 'Butterfly Wings'

Rosa, MR, C-F, 'Cairngorm'

Rosa, MR, C-F, 'Camille Pissarro'

Rosa, Modern Rose, Cluster-Flowered, 'Cathedral'

Rosa, Modern Rose, Cluster-Flowered, 'Catherine McAuley'

Rosa, Modern Rose, Cluster-Flowered, 'Centenaire de Lourdes'

Rosa, MR, Cluster-Flowered, 'Centenaire de Lourdes Rouge'

Rosa, Modern Rose, Cluster-Flowered, 'Chateau de Bagnols'

blooms of creamy white to yellow, shading to red toward petal edges; '**Brass Band**' ★, lightly scented blooms in dark and light apricot shades; '**Chinatown**', long-stemmed fragrant blooms of rich bright yellow with pink highlights at petal edges; '**City of Belfast**', large clusters of scarlet-red blooms; '**City of London**', very fragrant, cupped, double flowers of soft pink fading to blush; '**Dearest**', very fragrant, large, salmon pink flowers open to reveal prominent yellow stamens; '**Dicky**' (syn. 'Anisley Dickson'), lightly scented, orange-pink, double flowers; '**Elizabeth of Glamis**' (syn. 'Irish Beauty'), named for the UK's Queen Elizabeth the Queen Mother, very fragrant well-shaped flowers of clear salmon pink; '**Fragrant Delight**', strong perfume, large flowers in soft salmon-orange shades; '**Frensham**', vigorous rose,

deep red semi-double flowers; '**Gavnø**' (syn. 'Buck's Fizz'), high-centered blooms of soft orange; '**Glad Tidings**', velvety dark red blooms; '**Gold Badge**' ★, large, rich yellow, double flowers; '**Hannah Gordon**' (syn. 'Raspberry Ice'), creamy white petals suffused with deep pink at edges; '**Iceberg**' ★ (syns 'Fée des Neiges', 'Schneewittchen'), large clusters of pure white flowers; '**Lilac Charm**', almost-single rose, large petals of pale lilac, prominent red stamens; '**Lilli Marleen**', large, velvety, deep red flowers; '**Livin' Easy**' ★ (syn. 'Fellowship'), fiery orange-red blooms; '**Ma Perkins**', large cupped flowers in shades of clear pink and salmon; '**Margaret Merril**', very fragrant, large, white flowers with a hint of pink at center; '**Mariandel**' ★, vivid red semi-double flowers with a mild fragrance; '**Matangi**', one of a number

of so-called "hand-painted" roses that appear to be brushed with secondary colors, bright orangey vermilion with a silvery white central eye and petal reverse; '**Matilda**' (syn. 'Seduction'), large, white, double flowers, petals delicately edged with pink; '**Picasso**', "hand-painted" rose, flowers brushed with deep pink, carmine, and silvery white; '**Prima**' (syn. 'Many Happy Returns'), semi-double flowers of palest pink; '**Queen Elizabeth**', long pointed buds open to large, high-centered, clear pink blooms; '**Radox Bouquet**' (syn. 'Rosika'), very fragrant cupped blooms of soft rose pink; '**Rosemary Rose**', camellia-like flowers of deep pinkish red, in large clusters with distinctive maroon foliage; '**Sexy Rexy**' ★, large clusters of soft salmon pink camellia-like flowers; '**Sheila's Perfume**' ★, very fragrant yellow

Rosa, MR, C-F, 'Charleston'

flowers edged with red; '**Southampton**' (syn. 'Susan Ann'), apricot flowers flushed with orange and red; '**Sunsprite**' (syns 'Friesia', 'Korresia'), rounded buds open to very fragrant double flowers of bright yellow; '**Sweet Dream**' ★, double blooms of soft apricot-orange; '**Trumpeter**', flowers of brilliant scarlet-orange. Zones 4–10.

Rosa, Modern Rose, Cluster-Flowered, 'Coppélia'

R., MR, C-F, 'Cherish'

R., MR, C-F, 'Chuckles'

R., MR, C-F, 'City of Belfast'

Rosa, Modern Rose, Cluster-Flowered, 'Cyclamen'

Rosa, Modern Rose, Cluster-Flowered, 'Chinatown'

R., MR, C-F, 'City of Leeds'

R., MR, C-F, 'City of London'

R., MR, C-F, 'Class Act'

R., MR, C-F, 'Cocorico'

R., MR, C-F, 'Confetti'

Rosa, Modern Rose, Cluster-Flowered, 'Copper Pot'

R., MR, C-F, 'Constance Finn'

R., MR, C-F, 'Coronation Gold'

R., MR, C-F, 'Côte Jardins'

R., MR, C-F, 'Courvoisier'

R., MR, C-F, 'Crimson Wave'

R., MR, C-F, 'Dainty Maid'

R., MR, C-F, 'Dale Farm'

R., MR, C-F, 'Diadem'

R., MR, C-F, 'Dicky'

R., MR, C-F, 'Edith Holden'

R., MR, C-F, 'Elizabeth of Glamis'

R., MR, C-F, 'Escapade'

R., MR, C-F, 'Ethel Austin'

R., MR, C-F, 'Europeana'

R., MR, C-F, 'Eurostar'

R., MR, C-F, 'Eyepaint'

R., MR, C-F, 'Fame!'

R., MR, C-F, 'Fashion'

R., MR, C-F, 'First Edition'

R., MR, C-F, 'Flirt'

R., MR, C-F, 'Fragrant Delight'

R., MR, C-F, 'François Rabelais'

R., MR, C-F, 'Fredensborg'

R., MR, C-F, 'Frederiksborg'

Rosa, Modern Rose, Cluster-Flowered, 'Eurorose'

Rosa, Modern Rose, Cluster-Flowered, 'Fancy'

Rosa, Modern Rose, Cluster-Flowered, 'Florange'

R., MR, C-F, 'Frensham'

R., MR, C-F, 'Gavnø'

R., MR, C-F, 'Gene Boerner'

R., MR, C-F, 'Gentle'

R., MR, C-F, 'Glenfiddich'

R., MR, C-F, 'Gold Badge'

R., MR, C-F, 'Golden Gloves'

R., MR, C-F, 'Golden Slippers'

R., MR, C-F, 'Grace Abounding'

Rosa, Modern Rose, Cluster-Flowered, 'Gay Princess'

Rosa, Modern Rose, Cluster-Flowered, 'Ginger Meggs'

Rosa, Modern Rose, Cluster-Flowered, 'Gordon's College'

Rosa, Modern Rose, Cluster-Flowered, 'Frenzy'

Rosa, Modern Rose, Cluster-Flowered, 'High Summer'

Rosa, Modern Rose, Cluster-Flowered, 'Intrigue'

R., MR, C-F, 'Greetings'

R., MR, C-F, 'Gruss an Aachen'

R., MR, C-F, 'Gruss an Bayern'

R., MR, C-F, 'Guggleilmo Marconi'

R., MR, C-F, 'Guitare'

R., MR, C-F, 'Guy de Maupassant'

R., MR, C-F, 'H. C. Andersen'

R., MR, C-F, 'Harold Macmillan'

R., MR, C-F, 'Harper Adams'

R., MR, C-F, 'Harry Edland'

R., MR, C-F, 'Hillary, First Lady'

R., MR, C-F, 'Hospitality'

R., MR, C-F, 'Iceberg'

R., MR, C-F, 'Illumination'

R., MR, C-F, 'Imp'

R., MR, C-F, 'International Herald Tribune'

R., MR, C-F, 'Invincible'

R., MR, C-F, 'Jack Frost'

R., MR, C-F, 'Jasper'

R., MR, C-F, 'Jubilee Celebration'

Rosa, Modern Rose, Cluster-Flowered, 'Hannah Gordon'

R

Rosa, Modern Rose, Cluster-Flowered, 'Lilli Marleen'

Rosa, Modern Rose, Cluster-Flowered, 'La Sévillana'

R., MR, C-F, 'Julie Delbard'

R., MR, C-F, 'Kalinka'

R., MR, C-F, 'Kanegem'

Rosa, Modern Rose, Cluster-Flowered, 'Lively Lady'

R., MR, C-F, 'Karl Weinhausen'

R., MR, C-F, 'Kerry Gold'

R., MR, C-F, 'Kiskadee'

R., MR, C-F, 'Krönborg'

R., MR, C-F, 'Lilian Baylis'

R., MR, C-F, 'Lady of the Dawn'

R., MR, C-F, 'Laminuette'

R., MR, C-F, 'Léonardo de Vinci'

Rosa, Modern Rose, Cluster-Flowered, 'Kerryman'

R., MR, C-F, 'Little Darling'

R., MR, C-F, 'Little Wallace'

R., MR, C-F, 'Livin' Easy'

R., MR, C-F, 'Madam President'    *R.,* MR, C-F, 'Magenta'

R., MR, C-F, 'Mariandel'    *R.,* MR, C-F, 'Marie Curie'

R., MR, C-F, 'Marie-Louise Velge'    *R.,* MR, C-F, 'Marmalade Skies'

Rosa, Modern Rose, Cluster-Flowered, 'Mme Dimitriu'

Rosa, Modern Rose, Cluster-Flowered, 'Mme Fernandel'

Rosa, Modern Rose, Cluster-Flowered, 'Margaret Merril'

Rosa, Modern Rose, Cluster-Flowered, 'Love Potion'

Rosa, Modern Rose, Cluster-Flowered, 'Mary Cave'

R., MR, C-F, 'Michelangelo'

R., MR, C-F, 'Matilda'

R., MR, C-F, 'Matador'

R., MR, C-F, 'Matthias Meilland'

R., MR, C-F, 'Mazurka'

R., MR, C-F, 'Memento'

R., MR, C-F, 'Messara'

R., MR, C-F, 'Mio Mac'

R., MR, C-F, 'Mrs Iris Clow'

R., MR, C-F, 'Mr E. E. Greenwell'

R., MR, C-F, 'Model of Perfection'

R., MR, C-F, 'Molly McGredy'

R., MR, C-F, 'Moulin Rouge'

Rosa, Modern Rose, Cluster-Flowered, 'Melrose'

R., MR, C-F, 'Mountbatten'

R., MR, C-F, 'My Girl'

R., MR, C-F, 'Mr J. C. B.'

R., MR, C-F, 'Nearly Wild'

R., MR, C-F, 'Niccolo Paganini'

R., MR, C-F, 'Nina Weibull'

Rosa, Modern Rose, Cluster-Flowered, 'Old John'

R., MR, C-F, 'Nouvelle Europa'

R., MR, C-F, 'Octavia Hill'

R., MR, C-F, 'Olive'

Rosa, Modern Rose, Cluster-Flowered, 'Passionate Kisses'

Rosa, Modern Rose, Cluster-Flowered, 'Pink Iceberg'

R., MR, C-F, 'Orange Silk'

R., MR, C-F, 'Orangeade'

R., MR, C-F, 'Parfum Liffreen'

Rosa, Modern Rose, Cluster-Flowered, 'Party Trick'

R., MR, C-F, 'Pat James'

R., MR, C-F, 'Patricia'

R., MR, C-F, 'Peacekeeper'

R., MR, C-F, 'Pernille Poulsen'

R., MR, C-F, 'Peter Cottrell'

Rosa, Modern Rose, Cluster-Flowered, 'Piccolo'

R., MR, C-F, 'Picasso'

R., MR, C-F, 'Pillar Box'

R., MR, C-F, 'Pink Abundance'

R., MR, C-F, 'Pink Puff'

R., MR, C-F, 'Playboy'

R., MR, C-F, 'Playgirl'

Rosa, Modern Rose, Cluster-Flowered, 'Remembrance'

Rosa, Modern Rose, Cluster-Flowered, 'Regensberg'

R., MR, C-F, 'Pretty Lady'

R., MR, C-F, 'Pleasure'

R., MR, C-F, 'Poppy Flash'

R., MR, C-F, 'Prestige de Bellegarde'

R., MR, C-F, 'Pride of Maldon'

R., MR, C-F, 'Queen Elizabeth'

R., MR, C-F, 'Radox Bouquet'

R., MR, C-F, 'Red Glory'

R., MR, C-F, 'Redgold'

R., MR, C-F, 'Régine Crespin'

R., MR, C-F, 'Remembrance'

Rosa, Modern Rose, Cluster-Flowered, 'Princess Michael of Kent'

R., MR, C-F, 'Riberhus'

R., MR, C-F, 'Ripples'

R., MR, C-F, 'Rödhätte'

R., MR, C-F, 'Rumba'

R., MR, C-F, 'Rustica'

R., MR, C-F, 'Samba'

R., MR, C-F, 'Santa Maria'

R., MR, C-F, 'Satchmo'

R., MR, C-F, 'Scarlet Queen Elizabeth'

R., MR, C-F, 'Scented Air'

R., MR, C-F, 'Sea Pearl'

R., MR, C-F, 'Sheila's Perfume'

R., MR, C-F, 'Shepherd's Delight'

R., MR, C-F, 'Shocking Blue'

R., MR, C-F, 'Simplicity'

R., MR, C-F, 'Singin' in the Rain'

R., MR, C-F, 'Sir Alec Rose'

R., MR, C-F, 'Snowline'

R., MR, C-F, 'Southampton'

R., MR, C-F, 'Starlet'

R., MR, C-F, 'Stroller'

R., MR, C-F, 'Sue Lawley'

R., MR, C-F, 'Sun Flare'

Rosa, Modern Rose, Cluster-Flowered, 'Sir Lancelot'

Rosa, MR, Cluster-Flowered, 'Stargazer'

Rosa, MR, Cluster-Flowered, 'Sexy Rexy'

Rosa, MR, Cluster-Flowered, 'Showbiz'

Rosa, MR, C-F, 'Royal Occasion'

Rosa, MR, Cluster-Flowered, 'Tom Tom'

Rosa, MR, Cluster-Flowered, 'Ville du Roeulx'

Rosa, MR, Cluster-Flowered, 'Wee Cracker'

R., MR, C-F, 'Sundra'

R., MR, C-F, 'Sunset Boulevard'

R., MR, C-F, 'Sunsprite'

R., MR, C-F, 'Superior'

R., MR, C-F, 'Tall Story'

R., MR, C-F, 'The Sun'

R., MR, C-F, 'Titian'

R., MR, C-F, 'Tombola'

R., MR, C-F, 'Travemünde'

R., MR, C-F, 'Tourbillon'

R., MR, C-F, 'Trumpeter'

R., MR, C-F, 'Uwe Seeler'

R., MR, C-F, 'Vesper'

R., MR, C-F, 'Victoria Gold'

R., MR, C-F, 'Victorian Spice'

R., MR, C-F, 'Violet Carson'

R., MR, C-F, 'Vivacious'

R., MR, C-F, 'Walko'

R., MR, C-F, 'Wandering Minstrel'

R., MR, C-F, 'Wapiti'

R., MR, C-F, 'Warrior'

R., MR, C-F, 'White Bouquet'

R., MR, C-F, 'Wishing'

R., MR, C-F, 'Woburn Abbey'

R., MR, C-F, 'Yellow Cushion'

Rosa, Modern Rose, Large-Flowered, 'Ambossfunken'

Rosa, MR, L-F, 'Adair Roche'

Rosa, MR, L-F, 'Adolph Horstmann'

Rosa, MR, L-F, 'Adriana'

Rosa, MR, L-F, 'Abbaye de Cluny'

LARGE-FLOWERED (HYBRID TEA) ROSES

☀ ❄ ↔ 3–6 ft (0.9–1.8 m)
↑ 5–8 ft (1.5–2.4 m)

This group has become the most popular of all roses and thousands have been bred. They are generally sturdy plants, growing to about 3 ft (0.9 m) in height, with an upright bushy habit and mid- to dark green, often glossy leaves. The very large flowers are usually double or semi-double and borne singly or in clusters. They have elegant long-pointed buds and when open retain the high center, to varying degrees, as the outer petals reflex. The Large-flowered Rose usually

acknowledged as the first is 'La France', bred in 1867. Only a very small selection of the vast numbers available is included here. '**Abbeyfield Rose**', rich deep pink double flowers; '**Alec's Red**', plump black-red buds open to double well-perfumed flowers; '**Alexander**', lightly scented, double, vermilion blooms; '**Brandy**', large, sweetly perfumed, apricot flowers; '**Carina**', fragrant double blooms of rosy pink; '**Congratulations**', high-centered clear rose pink flowers on long stems; '**Dainty Bess**', large single flowers of silvery rose pink, prominent golden-brown stamens; '**Deep Secret**' (syn. 'Mildred Scheel'), very dark, deep crimson-red flowers, velvety-textured, very fragrant; '**Double Delight**', very fragrant creamy pink flowers, darkening to cherry red at edges; '**Elina**' ★ (syn. 'Peaudouce'), lemony yellow flowers fading to cream at edges; '**Fragrant Cloud**' (syns 'Duftwolke', 'Nuage Parfumé'), highly perfumed coral red flowers; '**Indian Summer**', fragrant double blooms in orange shades; '**Ingrid Bergman**' ★, named for the actress, has deep red velvety blooms, long lasting, good for picking; '**Irish Gold**' (syn. 'Grandpa Dickson'), very prickly plant, elegant

lemony yellow flowers; '**Just Joey**' ★, large coppery orange flowers that pale to soft pink at edge of petals; '**La France**', high-centered, well-perfumed, silvery pink flowers; '**Lady Rose**', high-centered bright salmon and orange flowers emerge from long pointed buds; '**Love**', high-centered scarlet flowers, silvery white reverse on petals; '**Lovely Lady**', fragrant, double, rosy pink flowers emerge from long buds; '**Loving Memory**' (syns 'Burgund 81', 'Red Cedar'), high-centered bright crimson blooms on long stems; '**Mme Butterfly**', very fragrant soft pink flowers emerge from long buds; '**Mrs Oakley Fisher**', single

Rosa, MR, L-F, 'Alexander'

Rosa, MR, L-F, 'Adventure'

Rosa, Modern Rose, Large-Flowered, 'Adagio'

Rosa, MR, L-F, 'Admiral Rodney'

Rosa, MR, L-F, 'Alec's Red'

R

Rosa, Modern Rose, Large-Flowered, 'American Heritage'

Rosa, Modern Rose, Large-Flowered, 'Annapurna'

Rosa, Modern Rose, Large-Flowered, 'Anne Marie Trechslin'

Rosa, Modern Rose, Large-Flowered, 'Antigone'

Rosa, Modern Rose, Large-Flowered 'Antigua'

Rosa, MR, L-F, 'Apéritif'

Rosa, MR, L-F, 'Ambassador'

Rosa, MR, L-F, 'Alpine Sunset'

Rosa, MR, L-F, 'Apollo'

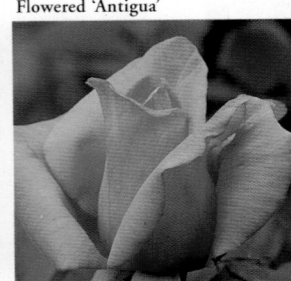

Rosa, MR, L-F, 'Appreciation'

Rosa, MR, L-F, 'Apricot Delight'

Rosa, MR, L-F, 'Apricot Silk'

Rosa, MR, L-F, 'Arianna'

Rosa, MR, L-F, 'Athena'

Rosa, MR, L-F, 'Auguste Renoir'

Rosa, Modern Rose, Large-Flowered, 'ARC Angel'

Rosa, Modern Rose, Large-Flowered, 'Apogée'

deep buff-yellow flowers, prominent amber stamens; '**Moonstone**' ★, lightly scented, large, white flowers, highlighted with shades of soft pink; '**National Trust**', large, high-centered, bright red flowers; '**New Zealand**' ★ (syn. 'Aotearoa New Zealand'), soft pink fragrant flowers open from long pointed buds; '**Olympiad**' ★, brilliant red, velvety, double flowers, delicately scented; '**Pascali**', considered one of the best whites, long, nearly thornless stems topped with ivory white flowers;

'**Paul Shirville**' (syn. 'Heart Throb'), perfumed, high-centered, pink flowers with a hint of salmon; '**Peace**', probably the most famous and popular Large-flowered Rose of all, large pale yellow flowers suffused with creamy pink; '**Perfume Delight**', cupped deep pink flowers, very fragrant; '**Pot o' Gold**', bright yellow blooms touched with gold, very fragrant; '**Precious Platinum**' (syns 'Opa Pötschke', 'Red Star'), bright red high-centered flowers with a velvety sheen; '**Pristine**', long

pointed buds open to reveal large, shapely, white flowers flushed with pale pink; '**Remember Me**', coppery orange flowers; '**Royal William**', large, rich red, velvety blooms; '**Savoy Hotel**', fully double soft pink flowers, deeper colored on petal reverse, lightly scented; '**Shot Silk**', globular silky-petalled blooms of salmon pink with a yellow base; '**Silver Jubilee**', silvery pink and apricot flowers with a deeper colored reverse; '**Sunblest**' (syn. 'Landora'), rich yellow flowers

emerge from slim buds; '**Sutter's Gold**', deep yellow flowers flushed with orange and pink; '**Touch of Class**' (syn. 'Maréchale LeClerc'), long-stemmed high-centered flowers in shades of cream, coral, and salmon pink; '**Valencia**' ★, fragrant, apricot-yellow, double blooms; '**White Lightnin**', vigorous plant, well-scented pure white flowers; '**White Wings**', long pointed buds open to large, single white flowers, prominent chocolate brown stamens. Zones 4–10.

Rosa, Modern Rose, Large-Flowered, 'Avon'

Rosa, Modern Rose, Large-Flowered, 'Aztec'

Rosa, Modern Rose, Large-Flowered, 'Bacchus'

Rosa, Modern Rose, Large-Flowered, 'Ballet'

Rosa, MR, Large-Flowered, 'Baronne Edmond de Rothschild'

Rosa, MR, L-F, 'Belle Blonde'

Rosa, MR, L-F, 'Bewitched'

Rosa, MR, L-F, 'Bill Temple'

Rosa, MR, L-F, 'Bing Crosby'

Rosa, MR, L-F, 'Bingo'

Rosa, MR, L-F, 'Blessings'

Rosa, MR, L-F, 'Blessings'

Rosa, MR, L-F, 'Blue Moon'

Rosa, MR, L-F, 'Blue Nile'

Rosa, MR, L-F, 'Blue River'

Rosa, MR, L-F, 'Bobby Charlton'

Rosa, MR, L-F, 'Bonsoir'

Rosa, MR, L-F, 'Bob Hope'

Rosa, Modern Rose, Large-Flowered, 'Belle Epoque'

Rosa, Modern Rose, Large-Flowered, 'Blue Diamond'

Rosa, Modern Rose, Large-Flowered, 'Bettina'

Rosa, MR, L-F, 'Britannia'

Rosa, MR, L-F, 'Candelabra'

Rosa, MR, L-F, 'Caprice de Meilland'

Rosa, MR, L-F, 'Cannes Festival'

Rosa, Modern Rose, Large-Flowered, 'Chimène'

Rosa, MR, L-F, 'Bride's Dream'

Rosa, MR, L-F, 'Broceliande'

R., MR, L-F, 'Bronze Masterpiece'

Rosa, MR, L-F, 'Cabaret'

Rosa, MR, L-F, 'Candia'

Rosa, MR, L-F, 'Candlelight'

Rosa, MR, L-F, 'Candy Stripe'

Rosa, MR, L-F, 'Captain Christy'

Rosa, MR, L-F, 'Cara Mia'

Rosa, MR, L-F, 'Caribbean'

Rosa, MR, L-F, 'Carina'

Rosa, MR, L-F, 'Carla'

Rosa, MR, L-F, 'Casque d'Or'

Rosa, MR, L-F, 'Century Two'

Rosa, MR, L-F, 'Champs-Elysées'

Rosa, MR, L-F, 'Charity'

Rosa, MR, L-F, 'Charles de Gaulle'

Rosa, MR, L-F, 'Cherry Brandy'

Rosa, MR, L-F, 'Chicago Peace'

Rosa, MR, L-F, 'Chivalry'

R

Rosa, Modern Rose, Large-Flowered, 'Colour Wonder'

Rosa, Modern Rose, Large-Flowered, 'Cocktail '80'

R., MR, L-F, 'Christopher Columbus'

Rosa, MR, L-F, 'Chrysler Imperial'

Rosa, MR, L-F, 'Claude Monet'

Rosa, MR, L-F, 'Colorama'

Rosa, MR, L-F, 'Columbia'

Rosa, MR, L-F, 'Columbus Queen'

Rosa, MR, L-F, 'Comanche'

Rosa, MR, L-F, 'Comtesse Vandal'

Rosa, Modern Rose, Large-Flowered, 'Dawn Chorus'

Rosa, MR, L-F, 'Congratulations'

Rosa, MR, L-F, 'Crimson Bouquet'

Rosa, MR, L-F, 'Crimson Glory'

Rosa, MR, L-F, 'Dame de Coeur'

Rosa, MR, L-F, 'Deep Secret'

Rosa, MR, L-F, 'Diamond Jubilee'

R

Rosa, MR, L-F, 'Diana Allen'

Rosa, MR, L-F, 'Dinah'

Rosa, MR, L-F, 'Diorama'

Rosa, MR, L-F, 'Dioressence'

Rosa, MR, L-F, 'Dream Pink'

Rosa, MR, L-F, 'Double Delight'

Rosa, MR, L-F, 'Duchesse de Savoie'

Rosa, MR, L-F, 'Diane'

Rosa, MR, L-F, 'Duke of Windsor'

Rosa, MR, L-F, 'Eiffel Tower'

Rosa, MR, L-F, 'El Capitan'

Rosa, Modern Rose, Large-Flowered, 'Duet'

Rosa, Modern Rose, Large-Flowered, 'Doris Tysterman'

Rosa, MR, L-F, 'Electron'

Rosa, MR, L-F, 'Elina'

Rosa, MR, L-F, 'English Sonnet'

Rosa, Modern Rose, Large-Flowered, 'Dr A. J. Verhage'

Rosa, Modern Rose, Large-Flowered, 'Elle'

Rosa, Modern Rose, Large-Flowered, 'Flamingo'

Rosa, Modern Rose, Large-Flowered, 'Fragrant Cloud'

Rosa, MR, L-F, 'Esther Geldenhuys'

Rosa, MR, L-F, 'Fairy Dancers'

Rosa, MR, L-F, 'Fantasia'

Rosa, Modern Rose, Large-Flowered, 'Ernest H. Morse'

Rosa, MR, L-F, 'Fascination'

Rosa, MR, L-F, 'Felicity Kendal'

Rosa, MR, L-F, 'Ferry Porsche'

Rosa, MR, L-F, 'Fêtes Galantes'

Rosa, MR, L-F, 'First Federal Gold'

Rosa, MR, L-F, 'Flora Danica'

Rosa, MR, L-F, 'Folklore'

Rosa, MR, L-F, 'Forever Yours'

Rosa, Modern Rose, Large-Flowered, 'Evening Star'

Rosa, MR, L-F, 'Fortuna'

Rosa, MR, L-F, 'Fountain'

Rosa, MR, L-F, 'Fragrant Dream'

Rosa, Modern Rose, Large-Flowered, 'Frances Phoebe'

Rosa, MR, L-F, 'Fred Howard'

Rosa, MR, L-F, 'Fragrant Gold'

Rosa, MR, L-F, 'Garden Party'

Rosa, MR, L-F, 'Gemini'

Rosa, MR, L-F, 'Gift of Life'

Rosa, MR, L-F, 'Givenchy'

Rosa, Modern Rose, Large-Flowered, 'Fulton Mackay'

Rosa, Modern Rose, Large-Flowered, 'Friendship'

Rosa, Modern Rose, Large-Flowered, 'Freedom'

Rosa, Modern Rose, Large-Flowered, 'Golden Girl'

Rosa, MR, L-F, 'Harriny'

Rosa, MR, L-F, 'Harry Wheatcroft'

Rosa, MR, L-F, 'Glowing Peace'

Rosa, MR, L-F, 'Gold Medal'

Rosa, MR, L-F, 'Golden Choice'

R., MR, L-F, 'Golden Masterpiece'

Rosa, MR, L-F, 'Glenara'

Rosa, MR, L-F, 'Golden Bettina'

Rosa, MR, L-F, 'Granada'

Rosa, MR, L-F, 'Grand Amore'

Rosa, MR, L-F, 'Grand Siècle'

Rosa, MR, L-F, 'Grand'mere Jenny'

Rosa, MR, L-F, 'Guy Laroche'

Rosa, MR, L-F, 'Hacienda'

Rosa, MR, L-F, 'Hallé'

Rosa, MR, L-F, 'Headline'

Rosa, MR, L-F, 'Hector Berlioz'

Rosa, MR, L-F, 'Helen Hayes'

Rosa, MR, L-F, 'Helmut Schmidt'

Rosa, MR, L-F, 'Henri Matisse'

Rosa, MR, L-F, 'Heroïca'

R., MR, L-F, 'Heureux Anniversaire'

Rosa, MR, L-F, 'Hilda Heinemann'

Rosa, MR, L-F, 'Holsteinperle'

Rosa, MR, L-F, 'Honey Favorite'

Rosa, MR, L-F, 'Honore de Balzac'

Rosa, MR, L-F, 'Honor'

Rosa, Modern Rose, Large-Flowered, 'Indian Summer'

Rosa, MR, L-F, 'Imperial'

Rosa, MR, L-F, 'Ingrid Bergman'

Rosa, MR, L-F, 'Interview'

Rosa, MR, L-F, 'Irish Gold'

Rosa, MR, L-F, 'Isabelle de France'

Rosa, MR, L-F, 'Isobel Derby'

Rosa, MR, L-F, 'Ita Buttrose'

Rosa, MR, L-F, 'It's a Winner'

Rosa, MR, L-F, 'Jacaranda'

Rosa, MR, L-F, 'Jamaica'

Rosa, MR, L-F, 'Jardins de Bagatelle'

Rosa, Modern Rose, Large-Flowered, 'Ilona'

Rosa, Modern Rose, Large-Flowered, 'Jason'

Rosa, Modern Rose, Large-Flowered, 'Isobel Harkness'

Rosa, Modern Rose, Large-Flowered, 'Kabuki'

Rosa, Modern Rose, Large-Flowered, 'John S. Armstrong'

Rosa, Modern Rose, Large-Flowered, 'Just Joey'

Rosa, MR, L-F, 'Jean Gaujard'

Rosa, MR, L-F, 'Jessika'

Rosa, MR, L-F, 'Joe Roscoe'

Rosa, MR, L-F, 'John Waterer'

Rosa, MR, L-F, 'Josephine Baker'

Rosa, Modern Rose, Large-Flowered, 'John F. Kennedy'

Rosa, MR, L-F, 'Joyfulness'

Rosa, MR, L-F, 'Josysigal'

Rosa, MR, L-F, 'Julia's Rose'

Rosa, MR, L-F, 'Julie'

Rosa, MR, L-F, 'Julie Y'

Rosa, MR, L-F, 'Julien Potin'

Rosa, Modern Rose, Large-Flowered, 'Limelight'

Rosa, MR, L-F, 'Lady Seton'

Rosa, MR, L-F, 'Lagerfeld'

Rosa, MR, L-F, 'Kordes' Perfecta'

Rosa, MR, L-F, 'Legacy Jubilee'

Rosa, MR, L-F, 'Kardinal'

Rosa, MR, L-F, 'Katherine Kordes'

Rosa, MR, L-F, 'Kathryn McGredy'

Rosa, MR, L-F, 'Keepsake'

Rosa, MR, L-F, 'Kentucky Derby'

Rosa, MR, L-F, 'Kleopatra'

Rosa, MR, L-F, 'Konrad Henkel'

Rosa, MR, L-F, 'La Marseillaise'

Rosa, MR, L-F, 'La Stupenda'

Rosa, MR, L-F, 'Lady Elgin'

Rosa, MR, L-F, 'Lady Rose'

Rosa, MR, L-F, 'Lady Trent'

Rosa, MR, L-F, 'Lady X'

Rosa, MR, L-F, 'Lanvin'

Rosa, MR, L-F, 'LeAnn Rimes'

Rosa, MR, L-F, 'Lemon Sherbet'

Rosa, MR, L-F, 'Lemon Spice'

Rosa, MR, L-F, 'Leonidas'

Rosa, MR, L-F, 'Léonor de March'

Rosa, MR, L-F, 'Lily de Gerlache'

Rosa, MR, L-F, 'Lord Gold'

Rosa, MR, L-F, 'Lotte Günthart'

Rosa, MR, L-F, 'Louise Gardner'

Rosa, MR, L-F, 'Madelon'

Rosa, Modern Rose, Large-Flowered, 'Lolita'

Rosa, MR, L-F, 'Mamy Laperrière'   *Rosa,* MR, L-F, 'Manou Meilland'   *R.,* MR, L-F, 'Marigold Harkness'   *Rosa,* Modern Rose, Large-Flowered, 'Lovely Lady'

Rosa, Modern Rose, Large-Flowered, 'Love'

Rosa, Modern Rose, Large-Flowered, 'Loving Memory'   *Rosa,* Modern Rose, Large-Flowered, 'Majorette'

R

Rosa, Modern Rose, Large-Flowered, 'Mary Jean'

Rosa, MR, L-F, 'Marjorie Atherton'

Rosa, MR, L-F, 'Matilda'

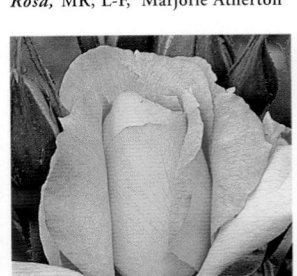

Rosa, MR, L-F, 'McGredy's Sunset'

Rosa, MR, L-F, 'Medallion'

Rosa, MR, L-F, 'Mercedes'

Rosa, MR, L-F, 'Mexicana'

Rosa, Modern Rose, Large-Flowered, 'Mascotte '77'

Rosa, Modern Rose, Large-Flowered, 'Mary Pope'

Rosa, Modern Rose, Large-Flowered, 'Megan Louise'

Rosa, Modern Rose, Large-Flowered, 'Mrs Fred Danks'

Rosa, Modern Rose, Large-Flowered, 'National Trust'

Rosa, Modern Rose, Large-Flowered, 'Norris Pratt'

Rosa, MR, L-F, 'Minnie Watson'

Rosa, MR, L-F, 'Mirato'

Rosa, MR, L-F, 'Miriana'

Rosa, MR, Large-Flowered, 'Miss All-American Beauty'

Rosa, Modern Rose, Large-Flowered, 'Mischief'

Rosa, Modern Rose, Large-Flowered, 'Mister Lincoln'

Rosa, Modern Rose, Large-Flowered, 'Misty'

Rosa, Modern Rose, Large-Flowered, 'Mitsouko'

Rosa, Modern Rose, Large-Flowered, 'Michèle Meilland'

Rosa, MR, L-F, 'Mount Shasta'

Rosa, MR, L-F, 'My Joy'

Rosa, MR, L-F, 'New Zealand'

Rosa, MR, L-F, 'New Day'

Rosa, MR, L-F, 'New Year'

Rosa, MR, L-F, 'New Yorker'

Rosa, Modern Rose, Large-Flowered, 'Oklahoma'

Rosa, Modern Rose, Large-Flowered, 'Olave Baden-Powell'

Rosa, Modern Rose, Large-Flowered, 'Oldtimer'

Rosa, Modern Rose, Large-Flowered, 'Olé'

Rosa, Modern Rose, Large-Flowered, 'Olivia'

Rosa, MR, L-F, 'Olympic Torch'

Rosa, MR, L-F, 'Ondella'

Rosa, MR, L-F, 'Opening Night'

Rosa, MR, L-F, 'Ophelia'

Rosa, MR, L-F, 'Oriana'

Rosa, MR, L-F, 'Osiria'

Rosa, MR, L-F, 'Otohime'

Rosa, MR, L-F, 'Paddy Stephens'

Rosa, MR, L-F, 'Painted Moon'

Rosa, MR, L-F, 'Papa Meilland'

Rosa, MR, L-F, 'Paradise'

Rosa, MR, L-F, 'Paris-Match'

Rosa, MR, L-F, 'Pariser Charme'

Rosa, MR, L-F, 'Parmelia'

Rosa, MR, L-F, 'Paul Ricard'

Rosa, MR, L-F, 'Paul Gaugin'

Rosa, MR, L-F, 'Peace'

Rosa, Modern Rose, Large-Flowered, 'Paul Shirville'

Rosa, MR, L-F, 'Parfum de Franche-Comte'

Rosa, MR, L-F, 'Opaline'

R

Rosa, Modern Rose, Large-Flowered, 'Pierre B'

Rosa, Modern Rose, Large-Flowered, 'Pink Panther'

Rosa, Modern Rose, Large-Flowered, 'Peggy Rockerfeller'

Rosa, MR, L-F, 'Peer Gynt'

Rosa, MR, L-F, 'Peach Surprise'

Rosa, MR, L-F, 'Penthouse'

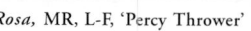

Rosa, MR, L-F, 'Percy Thrower'

Rosa, MR, L-F, 'Piccadilly'

Rosa, Modern Rose, Large-Flowered, 'Peter Frankenfeld'

Rosa, MR, L-F, 'Perfect Moment'

Rosa, MR, L-F, 'Pharoah'

Rosa, MR, L-F, 'Philippe Noiret'

Rosa, MR, L-F, 'Pink Parfait'

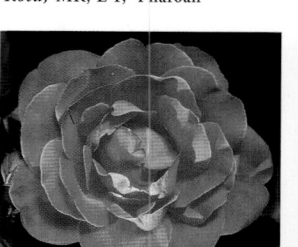

Rosa, MR, L-F, 'Pink Peace'

Rosa, MR, L-F, 'Pink Silk'

Rosa, Modern Rose, Large-Flowered, 'Privé'

Rosa, Modern Rose, Large-Flowered, 'Pristine'

Rosa, MR, L-F, 'Polarstern'

Rosa, MR, L-F, 'Polynesian Sunset'

Rosa, MR, L-F, 'Pot o' Gold'

Rosa, Modern Rose, Large-Flowered, 'Prima Ballerina'

R

Rosa, Modern Rose, Large-Flowered, 'Portrait'

Rosa, MR, Large-Flowered, 'Professeur Jean Barnard'

Rosa, MR, Large-Flowered, 'President Herbert Hoover'

Rosa, MR, Large-Flowered, 'Président Leopold Senghor'

R., MR, L-F, 'Princesse de Monaco'

Rosa, Modern Rose, Large-Flowered, 'Pretoria'

Rosa, MR, L-F, 'Preziosa'

Rosa, MR, L-F, 'Precious Platinum'

Rosa, MR, L-F, 'Princess Royal'

Rosa, MR, L-F, 'Prominent'

Rosa, MR, L-F, 'Rachel Crawshay'

Rosa, MR, L-F, 'Rainy Day'

Rosa, MR, L-F, 'Rebell 96'

Rosa, MR, L-F, 'Reconciliation'

Rosa, MR, L-F, 'Red Chief'

Rosa, MR, L-F, 'Red Devil'

Rosa, MR, L-F, 'Red Planet'

Rosa, Modern Rose, Large-Flowered, 'Red Lion'

Rosa, MR, L-F, 'Red Success'

Rosa, MR, L-F, 'Regatta'

Rosa, MR, L-F, 'Remember Me'

Rosa, Modern Rose, Large-Flowered, 'Queen Wilhelmina'

Rosa, Modern Rose, Large-Flowered, 'Proud Land'

Rosa, Modern Rose, Large-Flowered, 'Sheer Elegance'

Rosa, MR, L-F, 'Renaissance'

Rosa, MR, L-F, 'Royal Dane'

Rosa, MR, L-F, 'Résurrection'

Rosa, Modern Rose, Large-Flowered, 'Roxane'

Rosa, Modern Rose, Large-Flowered, 'Savoy Hotel'

Rosa, Modern Rose, Large-Flowered, 'Révolution Française'

Rosa, Modern Rose, Large-Flowered, 'Romantica '76'

Rosa, Modern Rose, Large-Flowered, 'Rose Gaujard'

Rosa, Modern Rose, Large-Flowered, 'Rosemary Harkness'

Rosa, Modern Rose, Large-Flowered, 'Rosie O'Donnell'

Rosa, MR, L-F, 'Roundelay'

Rosa, MR, L-F, 'Royal Highness'

Rosa, MR, L-F, 'San Antonio'

Rosa, MR, L-F, 'San Diego'

Rosa, MR, L-F, 'Sarah Arnot'

Rosa, MR, L-F, 'Saturnia'

Rosa, MR, L-F, 'Scarlet Knight'

Rosa, MR, L-F, 'Secret'

Rosa, MR, L-F, 'Shannon'

Rosa, MR, L-F, 'Sharon Louise'

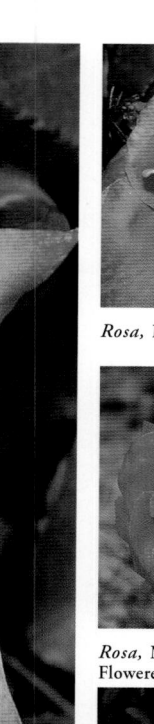

Rosa, MR, L-F, 'Silver Jubilee'

Rosa, MR, L-F, 'Silver Star'

Rosa, Modern Rose, Large-Flowered, 'Sir Harry Pilkington'

Rosa, Modern Rose, Large-Flowered, 'Snowfire'

Rosa, Modern Rose, Large-Flowered, 'Shiralee'

Rosa, MR, L-F, 'Solitaire'

Rosa, MR, L-F, 'Song of Paris'

Rosa, Modern Rose, Large-Flowered, 'Silva'

Rosa, Modern Rose, Large-Flowered, 'Sonia'

Rosa, Modern Rose, Large-Flowered, 'Showtime'

Rosa, Modern Rose, Large-Flowered, 'Soraya'

Rosa, Modern Rose, Large-Flowered, 'Spiced Coffee'

Rosa, Modern Rose, Large-Flowered, 'Starion'

Rosa, Modern Rose, Large-Flowered, 'Stella'

Rosa, Modern Rose, Large-Flowered, 'Stephens' Big Purple'

Rosa, Modern Rose, Large-Flowered, 'Summer Sunshine'

Rosa, Modern Rose, Large-Flowered, 'Sundowner'

Rosa, Modern Rose, Large-Flowered, 'Sunlit'

Rosa, Modern Rose, Large-Flowered, 'Sunset Celebration'

Rosa, Modern Rose, Large-Flowered, 'Sweet Home'

Rosa, MR, L-F, 'Sweet Love'

Rosa, MR, L-F, 'Sweetie Pie'

Rosa, MR, L-F, 'Tanagra'

Rosa, MR, L-F, 'Tarantella'

Rosa, MR, L-F, 'Tatjana'

Rosa, MR, L-F, 'Tendresse'

Rosa, MR, L-F, 'Tequila Sunrise'

Rosa, MR, L-F, 'The Lady'

Rosa, Modern Rose, Large-Flowered, 'Sunset Song'

Rosa, Modern Rose, Large-Flowered, 'Sterling'

Rosa, Modern Rose, Large-Flowered, 'Sutter's Gold'

R

Rosa, Modern Rose, Large-Flowered, 'Thelma Barlow'

Rosa, Modern Rose, Large-Flowered, 'Tournament of Roses'

Rosa, Modern Rose, Large-Flowered, 'Terracotta'

Rosa, MR, L-F, 'Terracotta'

Rosa, MR, L-F, 'Tiffany'

Rosa, MR, L-F, 'Tino Rossi'

Rosa, MR, L-F, 'Tradition'

Rosa, Modern Rose, Large-Flowered, 'Valencia'

Rosa, Modern Rose, Large-Flowered, 'Tropical Sunset'

Rosa, MR, L-F, 'Tropicana'

Rosa, MR, L-F, 'Tynwald'

Rosa, MR, L-F, 'Typhoon'

Rosa, MR, L-F, 'Tzigane'

Rosa, MR, L-F, 'Uncle Joe'

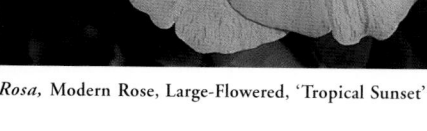

Rosa, MR, L-F, 'Uncle Walter'

Rosa, MR, L-F, 'Velvet Fragrance'

Rosa, MR, L-F, 'Violaine'

Rosa, MR, L-F, 'Victor Borge'

Rosa, MR, L-F, 'Violon d'Ingres'

Rosa, MR, L-F, 'Whisky Mac'

Rosa, MR, L-F, 'White Butterfly'

Rosa, Modern Rose, Large-Flowered, 'Worthwhile'

Rosa, Modern Rose, Large-Flowered, 'Village de Taradeau'

Rosa, Modern Rose, Large-Flowered, 'Wiener Charme'

Rosa, MR, L-F, 'White Knight'

Rosa, MR, L-F, 'White Masterpiece'

Rosa, MR, L-F, 'Young at Heart'

Rosa, MR, L-F, 'White Christmas'

Rosa, MR, L-F, 'Wilfred Pickles'

Rosa, MR, L-F, 'Winefred Clark'

Rosa, MR, L-F, 'World's Fair Salute'

Rosa, MR, L-F, 'Yankee Doodle'

Rosa, MR, L-F, 'Yellow Pages'

Rosa, MR, L-F, 'Youth of the World'

Rosa, Modern Rose, Patio, 'Anna Ford'

Rosa, Modern Rose, Patio, 'Queen Mother'

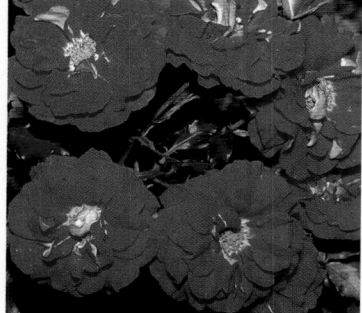

Rosa, Modern Rose, Patio, 'Festival'

PATIO (DWARF CLUSTER-FLOWERED) ROSES

☼ ❄ ↔ 18–36 in (45–90 cm)
↑ 18–30 in (45-75 cm)

The roses in this more recent group are the result of much cross-breeding between Polyanthas, Miniatures, and Cluster-flowered Roses, and classification of them can be difficult. They are usually bushier and slightly taller than the Miniatures, around 2 ft (0.6 m) tall, and most resemble the Cluster-flowered Roses with all parts proportionately smaller. They are suitable for beds and borders as well as for patios and growing in containers. Some popular examples of this group are: 'Anna Ford', which bears long

pointed buds opening to cup-shaped deep orange flowers with a yellow eye; 'Boys' Brigade', single crimson flowers with paler eye; 'Brass Ring' (syn. 'Peek-a-Boo'), deep peachy orange buds opening to peach and pale apricot, fading to pink at edges; 'Dainty Dinah', soft coral red flowers on a spreading plant; 'Festival', carrying clusters of striking deep red flowers, semi-double; 'Queen Mother' ★, delicate pink semi-double flowers; and 'Rexy's Baby', an offspring of the Cluster-flowered Rose 'Sexy Rexy', which produces pale pink flowers deepening to salmon pink at the center. Zones 4–11.

Rosa, MR, Polyantha, 'Gloire du Midi'

POLYANTHA ROSES

☼ ❄ ↔ 24–36 in (60–90 cm)
↑ 24–36 in (60–90 cm)

Introduced in 1875, only a few of these small roses are still available, usually growing to about 2 ft (0.6 m) tall. They are very hardy, withstanding the winter cold of northern Europe, and very free flowering, with small pompon-like flowers covering the plants for months. 'Baby Faurax', small, amethyst-violet, pompon flowers; 'Cameo', semi-double blooms in shades of salmon and coral pink; 'Gloire du Midi', orange-red blooms; 'Mlle Cécile Brünner', profuse shell pink flowers open from long pointed buds; 'Mevrouw Nathalie

Nypels', pink semi-double flowers, sweet fragrance; 'Nypels Perfection', semi-double blooms in shades of pink; 'Pinkie', cupped, semi-double, very fragrant rosy pink flowers; 'The Fairy', large crowded clusters of small, very double, clear pink flowers smother the plant constantly throughout summer; 'White Cécile Brünner', slightly fragrant, double, white flowers with yellow centers; 'White Pet' (syn. 'Little White Pet'), sometimes classed as a Cluster-flowered Rose, small, pompon-like, white flowers, with a pink tint in the bud; 'Yesterday', purple-pink double blooms emerge from dark buds. Zones 3–10.

Rosa, MR, Polyantha, 'White Cécile Brünner'

Rosa, MR, Polyantha, 'Nypels Perfection'

Rosa, Modern Rose, Polyantha, 'Excellenz von Schubert'

Rosa, MR, Polyantha, 'Mevrouw Nathalie Nypels'

Rosa, MR, Polyantha, 'Climbing Mlle Cécile Brünner' ★

R., MR, Polyantha, 'Jean Mermoz'

Rosa, MR, P, 'Mrs R. M. Finch'

R., MR, Polyantha, 'Phyllis Bide'

Rosa, MR, Polyantha, 'The Fairy'

Rosa, MR, Polyantha, 'White Pet'

SHRUB ROSES

Shrub Roses, usually bigger and more vigorous than Bush Roses, range from 4–10 ft (1.2–3 m) in height. Flower formation varies considerably and some cultivars flower only once in the season. Suitable for specimen or shrubberies and mixed borders, and some can be trained as small climbers or pillar roses.

HYBRID RUGOSA ROSES

☼ ❄ ↔5–10 ft (1.5–3 m) ↑2–7 ft (0.6–2 m)

The Hybrid Rugosa Roses are a distinctive group with stout bristly branches and rather coarse wrinkled leaves that often color to a buttery yellow in autumn. These roses are tough and healthy plants, ranging from 2–7 ft (0.6–2 m) in height. Many of them have very fragrant flowers; blooms range in formation from single to double, in shades of pink and crimson, with a few white and yellow. As a group they span the eras of Old and Modern Roses, with plants being bred from the late 1800s to the present day. **'Agnes'**, a dense bush, bearing very fragrant, creamy yellow, double flowers; **'Blanc Double de Coubert'**, vigorous plant with heavily perfumed semi-double flowers of purest white; **'Dr Eckener'**, very large, heavily perfumed, semi-double flowers in soft shades of pale yellow and coppery rose, fading to pale pink; **'Fimbriata'** (syns 'Diantheflora', 'Phoebe's Frilled Pink'), small, white, double flowers, frilled petal edges resembling *Dianthus*; **'Fru Dagmar Hartopp'**, large, single, silvery pink flowers, sometimes darker; **'Hansa'**, fragrant, double, pink-purple flowers; **'Henry Hudson'** (one of the Explorer Series), hardy to Zone 1, fragrant white flowers, tinged with pink; **'Martin Frobisher'** (Explorer Series), hardy to Zone 1, fragrant soft pink flowers; **'Roseraie de l'Haÿ'**, dense and vigorous bush, with large, semi-double, extremely fragrant flowers of rich crimson-purple; **'Scabrosa'**, modern introduction with large, single, cerise flowers; **'Souvenir de Philémon Cochet'**, fully double flowers, white with pale pink center; **'Thérèse Bugnet'**, large fragrant flowers, up to 4 in (10 cm) in diameter, opening reddish pink, maturing to light pink; and **'Vanguard'**, large, double, apricot-pink to salmon flowers, which are highly aromatic. Zones 3–10.

Rosa, Modern Rose, Hybrid Rugosa, 'Robusta'

Rosa, MR, Hybrid Rugosa, 'Belle Poitevine'

Rosa, MR, Hybrid Rugosa, 'Blanc Double de Coubert'

Rosa, MR, Hybrid Rugosa, 'Delicata'

Rosa, MR, Hybrid Rugosa, 'Dr Eckener'

Rosa, MR, Hybrid Rugosa, 'F. J. Grootendorst'

Rosa, MR, HR, 'Fimbriata'

R., MR, HR, 'Fru Dagmar Hartopp'

Rosa, MR, HR, 'Hansa'

R., MR, HR, 'Bernadette Chirac'

Rosa, MR, HR, 'Agnes'

Rosa, MR, Hybrid Rugosa, 'Rose à Parfum de l'Haÿ'

Rosa, MR, Hybrid Rugosa, 'Roseraie de l'Haÿ'

Rosa, MR, Hybrid Rugosa, 'Sarah Van Fleet'

Rosa, MR, Hybrid Rugosa, 'Scabrosa'

Rosa, MR, Hybrid Rugosa, 'Souvenir de Philémon Cochet'

Rosa, MR, HR, 'Schneezwerg'

Rosa, MR, HR, 'Thérèse Bugnet'

Rosa, MR, HR, 'Topaz Jewel'

Rosa, MR, HR, 'Vanguard'

Rosa, MR, HR, 'Yankee Lady'

MODERN SHRUB ROSES

☀ ❋ ↔ 4–8 ft (1.2–2.4 m)
↕ 4–8 ft (1.2–2.4 m)

These roses are a miscellany of plants bred from a variety of different parents and they do not have a definitive characteristic. They vary in size and growth habit and the flowers range through all colors and from single to double. 'Adelaide Hoodless', hardy to Zone 1, semi-double clear red flowers in clusters of up to 35 blooms; 'Anna Zinkeisen', double flowers of ivory white, lemon tones at base; 'Berlin', semi-double flowers of rich red, paling at center, prominent yellow stamens; 'Bonica' ★ (syn. 'Bonica 82'), long arching stems of double light pink flowers, rather frilled petals; 'Canary Bird', fragrant, single, canary yellow flowers, prominent stamens; 'Cantabrigiensis' (syn. *R. × cantabrigiensis*), large pale primrose flowers; 'Cerise Bouquet', semi-double deep pink-red flowers; 'Champlain' (from the Explorer Series), slightly fragrant, dark red, velvety flowers, hardy to Zone 2; 'Eddie's Jewel', repeat-flowering form; 'Flower Carpet' ★, semi-double rich pink flowers with a light scent; 'Fred Loads', large, almost-single, bright salmon pink flowers on large trusses; 'Fritz Nobis', once-flowering shrub, large double flowers of light pink to soft salmon; 'Geranium' ★, more compact habit, good display of larger hips; 'Golden Wings', single pale primrose yellow flowers, prominent gold stamens; 'Goldstern', large golden yellow blooms emerge from elegant, long, pointed buds; 'J. P. Connell', hardy to Zone 2, clusters of 3 to 8 lemon yellow flowers fade to cream; 'Lavender Dream', clusters of flattish lilac-pink flowers, may be slightly fragrant; 'Nevada', almost-single white flowers, up to 4 in (10 cm) across, prominent yellow stamens; 'Phantom', slightly fragrant saucer-shaped flowers, rich deep red petals, bright yellow stamens; 'St John's Rose' (syn. *R. sancta*), dark green leaves, single flowers, mildly fragrant, clear delicate pink; it is commonly known as the holy rose, and its flowers have been found in Egyptian tombs; 'Sally Holmes' ★, large, creamy white, single flowers open from soft apricot-pink buds; and 'Westerland', fragrant, apricot, double blooms.

Rosa, Modern Rose, Modern Shrub, 'Carefree Delight'

Rosa, MR, Modern Shrub, 'Bonica'

R., MR, Modern Shrub, 'Carefree Wonder'

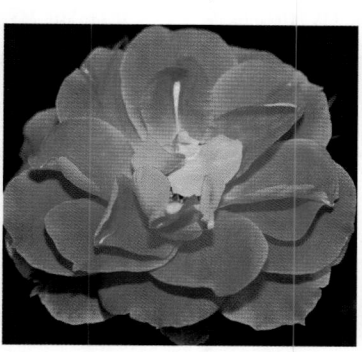

Rosa, MR, MS, 'Canterbury Wonder'

Rosa, MR, MS, 'Chartreuse de Parme'

Rosa, MR, Modern Shrub, 'Candy Rose'

Rosa, MR, Modern Shrub, 'Cantabrigiensis'

Rosa, MR, Modern Shrub, 'Angelina'

Rosa, MR, Modern Shrub, 'Armada'

Rosa, MR, Modern Shrub, 'Cardinal Hume'

R., MR, Modern Shrub, 'Chessum's Choice'

Rosa, MR, MS, 'Anna Zinkeisen'

Rosa, MR, MS, 'Baby Blanket'

Rosa, MR, MS, 'Bloomin' Easy'

Rosa, MR, MS, 'Carefree Sunshine'

R., MR, MS, 'Comtesse de Ségur'

Rosa, MR, MS, 'Concerto'

Rosa, MR, MS, 'Coral Gables'

Rosa, MR, MS, 'Country Dancer'

Rosa, MR, MS, 'Déborah'

Rosa, MR, MS, 'Décor Arlequin'

Rosa, MR, MS, 'Dortmund'

Rosa, MR, MS, 'Elveshorn'

Rosa, MR, MS, 'Feuerwerk'

Rosa, MR, MS, 'Fleurette'

Rosa, MR, MS, 'Fritz Nobis'

Rosa, MR, MS, 'George Vancouver'

Rosa, MR, MS, 'Geranium'

Rosa, MR, MS, 'Golden Wings'

Rosa, MR, MS, 'Gypsy Dancer'

Rosa, MR, MS, 'Happenstance'

Rosa, Modern Rose, Modern Shrub, 'Déclic'

Rosa, MR, MS, 'Hawkeye Belle'

Rosa, MR, MS, 'Hertfordshire'

Rosa, MR, MS, 'Highdownensis'

Rosa, MR, MS, 'Hot Fire'

Rosa, MR, MS, 'Flower Carpet'

R., MR, MS, 'Fuchsia Meidiland'

Rosa, Modern Rose, Modern Shrub, 'Morgenrot'

Rosa, Modern Rose, Modern Shrub, 'Linderhof'

Rosa, Modern Rose, Modern Shrub, 'Marguerite Hilling'

Rosa, MR, MS, 'Huntington's Hero'

Rosa, MR, MS, 'Knock Out'

Rosa, MR, MS, 'Lavender Dream'

Rosa, MR, MS, 'Lichtkönigin Lucia'

Rosa, MR, MS, 'Pimpernelle'

Rosa, Modern Rose, Modern Shrub, 'Lyric'

Rosa, Modern Rose, Modern Shrub, 'Parkdirektor Riggers'

Rosa, Modern Rose, Modern Shrub, 'Mistress Quickly'

Rosa, Modern Rose, Modern Shrub, 'Marjorie Fair'

Rosa, Modern Rose, Modern Shrub, 'Miss Dior'

Rosa, MR, MS, 'Maigold'

Rosa, MR, MS, 'Nevada'

Rosa, MR, MS, 'Pearl Drift'

Rosa, MR, MS, 'Phantom'

Rosa, MR, MS, 'Pink Chimo'

R., MR, MS, 'Raymond Chenault'

Rosa, MR, MS, 'Red Simplicity'

Rosa, MR, MS, 'Robusta'

Rosa, MR, MS, 'Rush'

Rosa, MR, MS, 'St John's Rose'

Rosa, MR, MS, 'Sally Holmes'

Rosa, Modern Rose, Modern Shrub, 'Pink Meidiland'

Rosa, Modern Rose, Modern Shrub, 'Surrey'

Rosa, MR, MS, 'Scharlachglut'

Rosa, MR, MS, 'Sonnenschirm'

Rosa, MR, MS, 'Sparrieshoop'

Rosa, MR, MS, 'Sunny June'

Rosa, MR, MS, 'Sympathie'

Rosa, MR, MS, 'Yellow Butterfly'

Rosa, Modern Rose, Modern Shrub, 'Raubritter'

Rosa, Modern Rose, Modern Shrub, English, 'A Shropshire Lad'

Rosa, Modern Rose, Modern Shrub, English, 'Cottage Rose'

Rosa, Modern Rose, Modern Shrub, English, 'Charlotte'

Rosa, MR, MS, English, 'Anne Boleyn'

Rosa, MR, MS, English, 'Barbara Austin'

Rosa, MR, MS, English, 'Benjamin Britten'

Rosa, MR, MS, English, 'Blythe Spirit'

Rosa, MR, MS, English, 'Brother Cadfael'

Rosa, MR, MS, English, 'Buttercup'

Rosa, MR, MS, English, 'Comtes de Champagne'

Rosa, MR, MS, English, 'Cordelia'

Rosa, MR, MS, English, 'Charles Rennie Mackintosh'

Rosa, MR, MS, English, 'Corvedale'

Rosa, MR, MS, English, 'Ambridge Rose'

Rosa, MR, MS, English, 'Crocus Rose'

Rosa, MR, MS, English, 'Crown Princess Margareta'

Rosa, MR, MS, English, 'Cymbaline'

Rosa, MR, MS, English, 'Dapple Dawn'

Rosa, MR, MS, English, 'Alnwick Castle'

English Roses: These roses are also classed as Modern Shrub Roses. In the early 1960s Englishman David Austin began a breeding program that crossed Old and Modern Roses. English Roses, as they are now known, have become very popular, combining as they do the flower forms and fragrance of Old Roses with the growth habits, repeat-flowering ability, and wider color range of Modern Roses. They range from 3–7 ft (0.9–2 m) in height. Most are well perfumed. A large number are now available, including: 'Abraham Darby' ★, large, orange-pink, fully double flowers; 'Charles Rennie Mackintosh', fragrant blooms open rose pink, age to lilac-pink; 'Constance Spry', the first of the group, lax plant, large, cupped, soft pink flowers, myrrh-like fragrance also found in some other English Roses, in late spring–summer; 'Gertrude Jekyll', very fragrant, rich pink, very double flowers; 'Golden Celebration' ★, highly fragrant, deep yellow, double flowers throughout summer–autumn; 'Graham Thomas', long-stemmed, rich yellow, double flowers, sweetly scented; 'Jude the Obscure', strongly scented yellow blooms; 'Mary Rose', rich rose pink flowers; 'Winchester Cathedral', fragrant white blooms; and 'Windrush', large semi-double flowers, pure soft lemon, prominent yellow stamens, very sweetly perfumed.

Rosa, Modern Rose, Modern Shrub, English, 'Dr Herbert Gray'

Rosa, Modern Rose, Modern Shrub, English, 'English Elegance'

Rosa, MR, MS, English, 'Eglantyne'

Rosa, MR, MS, English, 'Emily'

Rosa, MR, MS, English, 'England's Rose'

Rosa, MR, MS, English, 'English Garden'

Rosa, MR, MS, English, 'Graham Thomas'

Rosa, MR, MS, English, 'Happy Child'

Rosa, Modern Rose, Modern Shrub, English, 'Ellen'

Rosa, Modern Rose, Modern Shrub, English, 'Geoff Hamilton'

Rosa, MR, MS, English, 'Gertrude Jekyll'

Rosa, MR, MS, English, 'Golden Celebration'

Rosa, MR, MS, English, 'Heavenly Rosalind'

Rosa, MR, MS, English, 'Evelyn'

Rosa, MR, MS, English, 'Falstaff'

Rosa, MR, MS, English, 'Grace'

Rosa, MR, MS, English, 'Heritage'

Rosa, MR, MS, English, 'Hero'

Rosa, MR, MS, English, 'James Galway'

Rosa, MR, MS, English, 'Jaquenetta'

Rosa, MR, MS, English, 'Jayne Austin'

Rosa, MR, MS, English, 'John Clare'

Rosa, MR, MS, English, 'Jude the Obscure'

Rosa, MR, MS, English, 'Kathryn Morley'

Rosa, MR, MS, English, 'Leander'

Rosa, MR, MS, English, 'Leonard Dudley Braithwaite'

Rosa, MR, MS, English, 'Lilian Austin'

Rosa, MR, MS, English, 'Mary Magdalene'

Rosa, MR, MS, English, 'Mary Rose'

Rosa, MR, MS, English, 'Miss Alice'

Rosa, MR, MS, English, 'Mrs Doreen Pike'

Rosa, Modern Rose, Modern Shrub, English, 'Marinette'

Rosa, Modern Rose, Modern Shrub, English, 'Lucetta'

Rosa, Modern Rose, Modern Shrub, English, 'Molineux'

Rosa, Modern Rose, Modern Shrub, English, 'Sophy's Rose'

Rosa, MR, MS, English, 'Pat Austin'

Rosa, MR, MS, English, 'Redouté'

Rosa, MR, MS, English, 'Portmeiron'

Rosa, MR, MS, English, 'Prospero'

Rosa, MR, MS, English, 'Proud Titania'

Rosa, MR, MS, English, 'Queen Nefertiti'

Rosa, MR, MS, English, 'Mortimer Sackler'

Rosa, MR, MS, English, 'Noble Antony'

Rosa, MR, MS, English, 'Othello'

Rosa, MR, MS, English, 'Pegasus'

Rosa, MR, MS, English, 'Scepter'd Isle'

Rosa, MR, MS, English, 'Sharifa Asma'

Rosa, MR, MS, English, 'Sir Edward Elgar'

Rosa, MR, MS, English, 'Sir Walter Raleigh'

Rosa, MR, MS, English, 'Teasing Georgia'

Rosa, MR, MS, English, 'Tess of the d'Urbervilles'

R., MR, MS, English, 'Red Coat'

R., MR, MS, English, 'St Cecilia'

R., MR, MS, English, 'St Swithun'

R., MR, MS, English, 'Scintillation'

R., MR, MS, English, 'Sweet Juliet'

Rosa, MR, MS, English, 'The Alexandra Rose'

Rosa, MR, MS, English, 'The Countryman'

Rosa, MR, MS, English, 'The Mayflower'

Rosa, MR, MS, English, 'William Shakespeare 2000'

Rosa, MR, MS, English, 'The Dark Lady'

Rosa, MR, MS, English, 'The Pilgrim'

Rosa, MR, MS, English, 'The Prince'

Rosa, MR, MS, English, 'The Herbalist'

Rosa, MR, MS, English, 'Trevor Griffiths'

Rosa, MR, MS, English, 'Winchester Cathedral'

Rosa, MR, MS, English, 'Windflower'

Rosa, MR, MS, English, 'Windrush'

Rosa, MR, MS, English, 'Wise Portia'

Rosa, MR, MS, English, 'Yellow Button'

Rosa, Modern Rose, Modern Shrub, English, 'William Morris'

Rosa, Modern Rose, Modern Shrub, English, 'Tradescant'

Hybrid Musk Roses: Although under the mantle of Modern Shrub Roses, this group is often thought of as "Old." The first Hybrid Musk Rose was introduced in 1913 by Rev. Joseph Pemberton and most of this group were bred by him. The name Hybrid Musk relates to the fragrance, which is inherited very indirectly from the musk rose (*R. moschata*). They have a shrubby habit, often with dark green leaves and purplish stems, and a long flowering season when they bear clusters of single to double flowers. Their popularity is undiminished and most are still available today. Growing 4–8 ft (1.2–2.4 m) tall, they make very good specimen or shrubbery plants. **'Belinda'** ★, mid-pink flowers, often highlighted with white at petal base; **'Buff Beauty'**, double apricot blooms age to buff-yellow; **'Cornelia'**, small, double, very pale pink flowers with orange base, musk-like fragrance; **'Danaë'**, double blooms open rich yellow, age to white; **'Erfurt'**, fragrant semi-double blooms of pink, shaded yellow toward petal base; **'Moonlight'**, one of the first Hybrid Musk Roses to be introduced, clusters of almost-single creamy white flowers, prominent yellow stamens; **'Mozart'**, a large white eye accents the rich pink single flowers; **'Paul's Himalayan Musk Rambler'** ★, small double flowers of soft lilac-pink; **'Penelope'**, semi-double blooms of palest pink that age to white; and **'Prosperity'**, large clusters of double white flowers on long arching stems. Zones 4–10.

Rosa, MR, MS, Hybrid Musk, 'Erfurt'

Rosa, MR, MS, Hybrid Musk, 'Danaë'

Rosa, Modern Rose, Modern Shrub, Hybrid Musk, 'Cornelia'

Rosa, Modern Rose, Cluster-Flowered Climbing, 'Sparkling Scarlet'

CLIMBING ROSES

Modern climbing roses are usually long-flowering and not quite as rampant as the early introductions. They encompass a huge range of colors and frequently have double flowers. Non-rambling climbers are most often produced from Bush Rose sports and some popular Bush Roses, such as 'Iceberg', also occur in climbing forms.

CLUSTER-FLOWERED CLIMBING ROSES

☼/☀ ❄ ↔8–15 ft (2.4–4.5 m)
↕10–20 ft (3–6 m)

Frequently the most satisfying of the climbers because their smaller flowers are more weather resistant while being just as showy as the larger-flowered forms. Also, their whippy stems are less inclined to break under the weight of blooms and are more easily trained. **'Climbing Diablotin'**, small, rich red, semi-double flowers; **'Climbing Iceberg'**, lightly scented, white, double blooms; **'John Cabot'** (Explorer Series), hardy to Zone 1, fragrant red-pink flowers; **'Santa Catalina'**, slightly scented semi-double flowers of palest pink; **'Sparkling Scarlet'**, semi-double blooms of vivid scarlet, fruity fragrance; **'William Baffin'** (Explorer Series),

Rosa, Modern Rose, Cluster-Flowered Climbing, 'Climbing Diablotin'

hardy to Zone 1, slightly fragrant mid-red flowers in clusters of as many as 30 blooms. Zones 5–9.

LARGE-FLOWERED CLIMBING ROSES

☼/☀ ❄ ↔7–17 ft (2–5 m)
↕7–17 ft (2–5 m)

Large-flowered climbers have the same fancy double and large single flowers as their bushy cousins. They tend to have heavier, less pliable stems than other climbers and need support to prevent weather damage and to ensure long-lasting displays. **'Albertine'**, fragrant, pink to salmon, double flowers; **'Compassion'** ★, fragrant, apricot-pink, double flowers; **'Dublin Bay'** ★, fragrant, rich red, double flowers; **'Golden Showers'**, large double flowers of bright light yellow, paling with age; **'New Dawn'** ★, large, fragrant, double blooms of palest pink; **'Pierre de Ronsard'** ★, lightly scented, large, double blooms of ivory suffused with pink. Zones 5–9.

Rosa, MR, Large-Flowered Climbing, 'Alpin'

Rosa, MR, L-FC, 'Altissimo'

Rosa, Modern Rose, L-FC, 'Albertine'

Rosa, Modern Rose, L-FC, 'Anne Dakin'

Rosa, Modern Rose, Large-Flowered Climbing, 'Arielle Dombasle'

Rosa, Modern Rose, Large-Flowered Climbing, 'Chaplin's Pink Climber'

Rosa, Modern Rose, Large-Flowered Climbing, 'Climbing Mme Abel Chatenay'

Rosa, MR, L-FC, 'Aschermittwoch'   *Rosa,* MR, L-FC, 'Bantry Bay'   *Rosa,* MR, L-FC, 'Black Boy'

Rosa, MR, Large-Flowered Climbing, 'Blossomtime'

Rosa, MR, Large-Flowered Climbing, 'Campanile'

Rosa, MR, Large-Flowered Climbing, 'César'

R., MR, Large-Flowered Climbing, 'Climbing Christopher Stone'

R., MR, Large-Flowered Climbing, 'Climbing Editor McFarland'

R., MR, Large-Flowered Climbing, 'Climbing Ena Harkness'

R., MR, Large-Flowered Climbing, 'Climbing Etoile de Hollande'

R., MR, Large-Flowered Climbing, 'Climbing Forty-Niner'

Rosa, Modern Rose, Large-Flowered Climbing, 'Climbing Fragrant Cloud'

R., MR, L-FC, 'Climbing Hadley'   *R.,* MR, L-FC, 'Climbing Sonia'   *R.,* MR, L-FC, 'Climbing Tiffany'

R

Rosa, Modern Rose, Large-Flowered Climbing, 'Danny Boy'

Rosa, Modern Rose, Large-Flowered Climbing, 'Climbing Talisman'

Rosa, MR, Large-Flowered Climbing, 'Climbing Mardi Gras'

R., MR, Large-Flowered Climbing, 'Climbing Mme Butterfly'

Rosa, MR, Large-Flowered Climbing, 'Climbing Mary Hart'

Rosa, Modern Rose, Large-Flowered Climbing, 'Climbing Queen Elizabeth'

Rosa, MR, Large-Flowered Climbing, 'Climbing New Yorker'

Rosa, MR, L-FC, 'Climbing Peter Frankenfeld'

Rosa, MR, Large-Flowered Climbing, 'Climbing Pink Peace'

Rosa, MR, Large-Flowered Climbing, 'Climbing Tropicana'

Rosa, MR, Large-Flowered Climbing, 'Compassion'

Rosa, MR, Large-Flowered Climbing, 'Condesa de Sástago'

Rosa, MR, Large-Flowered Climbing, 'Countess of Stradbroke'

Rosa, Modern Rose, Large-Flowered Climbing, 'Climbing Shot Silk'

Rosa, MR, L-FC, 'Cortège'

R., MR, L-FC, 'Crimson Descant'

R., MR, L-FC, 'Dreaming Spires'

Rosa, MR, L-FC, 'Dizzy Heights'

Rosa, MR, L-FC, 'Golden Future'

Rosa, MR, L-FC, 'Guinée'

Rosa, MR, L-FC, 'Handel'

Rosa, MR, L-FC, 'Highfield'

Rosa, Modern Rose, Large-Flowered Climbing, 'Morning Jewel'

R., MR, L-FC, 'Mme Louis Lens'

Rosa, MR, L-FC, 'Malaga'

Rosa, MR, L-FC, 'Mary Wallace'

Rosa, MR, L-FC, 'Michka'

Rosa, MR, L-FC, 'Lady Waterlow'

Rosa, Modern Rose, Large-Flowered Climbing, 'Nancy Hayward'

Rosa, Modern Rose, Large-Flowered Climbing, 'Grand Hotel'

Rosa, Modern Rose, Large-Flowered Climbing, 'Mme Grégoire Staechelin'

Rosa, MR, L-FC, 'New Dawn'

Rosa, MR, L-FC, 'Parade'

Rosa, MR, L-FC, 'Paul Noël'

Rosa, Modern Rose, Large-Flowered Climbing, 'Dublin Bay'

Rosa, Modern Rose, Large-Flowered Climbing, 'Etude'

Rosa, Modern Rose, Large-Flowered Climbing, 'Exploit'

Rosa, MR, Large-Flowered Climbing, 'Paul's Scarlet Climber'

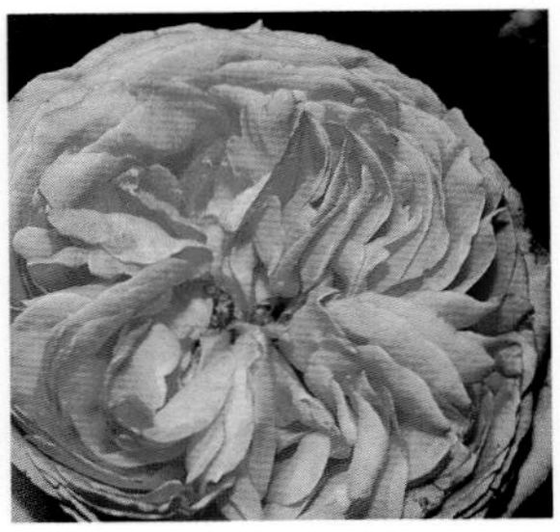

Rosa, MR, Large-Flowered Climbing, 'Pierre de Ronsard'

Rosa, MR, L-FC, 'Pink Perpétué'

Rosa, MR, L-FC, 'Polka'

Rosa, MR, L-FC, 'Princeps'

Rosa, Modern Rose, Large-Flowered Climbing, 'Penny Lane'

Rosa, MR, Large-Flowered Climbing, 'Reine Marie-Henriette'

Rosa, MR, Large-Flowered Climbing, 'Rosarium Uetersen'

Rosa, MR, Large-Flowered Climbing, 'Royal Gold'

Rosa, Modern Rose, Large-Flowered Climbing, 'Pink Cloud'

Rosa, Modern Rose, Large-Flowered Climbing, 'Rosy Mantle'

Rosa, MR, L-FC, 'Schoolgirl'

Rosa, MR, L-FC, 'White Cockade'

Rosa, MR, L-FC, 'Zenith'

Rosa, Modern Rose, Large-Flowered Climbing, 'Easlea's Golden Rambler'

R

R., Modern Rose, Rambler, 'Trier'

R., MR, Rambler, 'Albéric Barbier'

Rosa, MR, Rambler, 'Excelsa'

Rosa, MR, Rambler, 'May Queen'

R., Modern Rose, Rambler, 'Thalia'

RAMBLER ROSES

☀/☀ ❄ ↔ 10–25 ft (3–8 m)
↕ 10–25 ft (3–8 m)

Often very thorny plants, Rambler Roses, which are principally of *R. wichurana* and *R. multiflora* parentage, differ from other Climbing Roses in not only elongating their stems, but also producing many vigorous new basal shoots each year. This results in a clump of cane-like stems. Pruning is mainly cutting out the older and less productive stems. Ramblers are usually once-flowering. '**Albéric Barbier**', lightly scented, ivory, double blooms, color deepening toward center; '**Bobbie James**', highly perfumed, semi-double, cupped blooms in ivory white, accented with prominent bright yellow stamens; '**Bonfire**', pink-red double blooms; '**Excelsa**', white-centered crimson double blooms; '**François Juranville**', salmon pink double flowers, tinged yellow near center, fruity fragrance; '**May Queen**', double blooms of rose pink, fruity fragrance; '**Rambling Rector**', highly fragrant, white, semi-double blooms; '**Sander's White Rambler**', small, white, double flowers, fruity fragrance; '**Seagull**', fragrant, snow white, double flowers, lustrous golden yellow stamens; '**Super Elfin**', orange-red blooms; '**Thalia**', small, pure white, double blooms; '**Trier**', semi-double blooms of ivory, deepening to pale golden yellow toward center; '**Veilchenblau**', semi-double blooms of violet-pink with white markings, fruity fragrance. Zones 5–9.

MINIATURE ROSES

Among the more recent large groups to be developed, Miniature Roses of the style we know today first appeared in the late 1930s. Their tiny flowers are perfect replicas in miniature of those of the large bushes. What they lack in scent, they more than make up for in intricate beauty.

CLIMBING MINIATURE ROSES

☀/☀ ❄ ↔ 3–7 ft (0.9–2 m)
↕ 3–12 ft (0.9–3.5 m)

There are a few small climbers, but Climbing Miniatures are frequently only miniature in their flowers, and produce a tremendous display. The dividing line between Polyanthas and Climbing Miniatures can be difficult to discern. '**Nozomi**', taller plant, small, single, starry flowers of pearly pink; '**Warm Welcome**' ★, small scented blooms of orange-red. Zones 4–11.

MINIATURE ROSES

☀ ❄ ↔ 12–18 in (30–45 cm)
↕ 8–24 in (20–60 cm)

True Miniature Roses grow only 8–24 in (20–60 cm) high and are perfect miniature replicas of the Bush Roses, with tiny leaves and dainty buds and flowers. They are useful for edging borders and make very good container plants. Some roses classed as Miniatures are somewhat taller, but bear small flowers and leaves. '**Air France**' (syns 'American Independence', 'Rosy Meillandina'), double flowers of clear rose pink; '**Autumn Splendour**' ★, light fruity fragrance, large, double, yellow-orange flowers, deeper coloring at petal edges intensifies with age; '**Baby Darling**', double apricot flowers; '**Baby Love**' ★, small, single, buttercup yellow flowers, prominent stamens; '**Cachet**' ★, large, unscented, white blooms; '**Cider Cup**', rich apricot double blooms, lightly scented; '**Cinderella**', pearly white flowers lightly flushed with pink; '**Claret Cup**', clusters of small, fragrant, crimson blooms; '**Fairy Tale**', small, delicately

Rosa, Modern Rose, Miniature, 'Arctic Sunrise'

Rosa, Modern Rose, Miniature, 'Beauty Secret'

Rosa, Modern Rose, Miniature, 'Fire Princess'

Rosa, Modern Rose, Miniature, 'Freegold'

Rosa, Modern Rose, Miniature, 'Magic Carrousel'

Rosa, Modern Rose, Miniature, 'Persian Princess'

Rosa, Modern Rose, Miniature, 'Little Sunset'

Rosa, MR, Miniature, 'Gizmo'

Rosa, MR, Miniature, 'Green Ice'

Rosa, MR, Miniature, 'Claret Cup'

Rosa, MR, Miniature, 'Fairy Tale'

Rosa, MR, Miniature, 'Hot Tamale'

R

Rosa, Modern Rose, Miniature, 'Sun Sprinkles'

Rosa, MR, Miniature, 'Rosmarin'

Rosa, MR, Miniature, 'Tapis Jaune'

Rosa, MR, Miniature, 'Pride 'n' Joy'

Rosa, MR, Miniature, 'Stacey Sue'

Rosa, MR, Miniature, 'Scarlet Moss'

Rosa, MR, Miniature, 'Starina'

perfumed, pink flowers, mature to pale pink; '**Gentle Touch**', small, soft pink, double flowers, lightly scented; '**Gourmet Popcorn**' ★, lightly scented, semi-double, snow white flowers; '**Holy Toledo**', double flowers of apricot-orange; '**Hot Tamale**', striking pink-orange flowers, either singly or in clusters; '**Hula Girl**', long pointed buds open to deep salmon pink flowers; '**Irresistible**' ★, fragrant double blooms, almost pure white, becoming pink-tinged toward center; '**Little Red Devil**', well-perfumed, double, deep red flowers; '**Loving Touch**', long pointed buds open to fragrant high-centered flowers in apricot tones; '**Magic Carrousel**' ★, double flowers, creamy white, petals red-edged; '**My Valentine**', high-centered deep red flowers; '**Party Girl**' ★, fragrant, soft apricot-yellow, double blooms; '**Pride 'n' Joy**', profuse orange blooms,

fruit-like perfume; '**Red Ace**' (syns 'Amanda', 'Amruda'), velvety deep red blooms; '**Rosina**' (syns 'Josephine Wheatcroft', 'Yellow Sweetheart'), semi-double blooms of clear yellow; '**Rosmarin**', slightly fragrant double flowers range in color from pale pink to pale red, depending on air temperature; '**Snow Carpet**', small, very double, white flowers; '**Sweet Magic**', orange semi-double blooms; '**Tapis Jaune**', profuse, double, yellow, small flowers. Zones 4–11.

GROUND COVER ROSES

☀ ❄ ↔ 5–12 ft (1.5–3.5 m)
↑ 12–24 in (30–60 cm)

Some sprawling Shrub Roses are classed as Ground Cover Roses. With their lax spreading habit they are useful for growing on banks and cascading over low walls, as well as for covering large areas of ground. More recent

breeding has led to the introduction of a number of plants that are very long flowering and have a densely foliaged habit. '**Bassino**', single cupped flowers of brilliant scarlet; '**Diamant**', rich orange-red double blooms; '**Eyeopener**', single bright red flowers with white eye; '**Pink Bells**', lightly scented double flowers of rich pink; '**Pretty in Pink**', scented pink blooms; '**Rosy Cushion**', soft pink almost-single blooms, taller plant; '**Sommermärchen**', lightly scented rich pink flowers. Zones 4–10.

OLD (HERITAGE) ROSES

Under the umbrella term "Old Roses" fall a number of groups containing roses that, through deliberate breeding, have similar characteristics to each other. Some of the oldest groups, such as Gallica, contain roses that have been cultivated for centuries, while other groups, like Bourbon, are the product

of nineteenth-century breeding. The term "Old Rose" is a misnomer as some Old groups contain plants bred more recently, and the term is often used in reference to shrubs such as the Hybrid Musks (included here under Modern Roses), which are of twentieth-century origin. Many people consider that it is a rose's attributes rather than its date of introduction that earn it the title of "Old." Some of the Old Rose groups, such as the Teas, include a number of climbing plants and there are also Old groups of climbers and ramblers, like the Noisettes.

OLD NON-CLIMBING ROSES

For as long as roses have been cultivated gardeners have been improving on the wild species. Old Non-climbing Roses, which include such groups as the China Roses, Damask Roses, and Gallica Roses, may be once-flowering

Rosa, MR, Ground Cover, 'Bassino'

Rosa, MR, GC, 'Rosy Cushion'

Rosa, MR, Ground Cover, 'Hampshire'

Rosa, MR, GC, 'Pretty in Pink'

Rosa, MR, Ground Cover, 'Pink Bells'

Rosa, MR, GC, 'Diamant'

Rosa, MR, Ground Cover, 'Satina'

Rosa, MR, GC, 'Twilight'

Rosa, MR, Ground Cover, 'Sommermärchen'

Rosa, MR, GC, 'Worcestershire'

Rosa, Old Rose, Alba, 'Alba Maxima'

Rosa, Old Rose, Alba, 'Celestial'

Rosa, OR, Alba, 'Königin von Dänemark'

Rosa, Old Rose, Alba, 'Maiden's Blush'

and limited in color range but they more than make up for those failings with delicate tones, unusually shaped flowers, and fragrance that combine to conjure up a bygone era.

ALBA ROSES

☀ ❄ ↔ 6–10 ft (1.8–3 m)
↕ 6–8 ft (0.6–2.4 m)

This is a very hardy group of Old Roses that have light bluish green foliage and very fragrant pale-colored flowers that are usually double or semi-double. They flower only once during mid-summer. Most varieties grow 6–8 ft (1.8–2.4 m) tall. **'Alba Maxima'** (syns 'Bonnie Prince Charlie's Rose', 'Jacobite Rose', 'White Rose of York'), vigorous shrub, large, pure white, double flowers; **'Celestial'** (syn. 'Céleste'), heavily perfumed, semi-double flowers of soft pink; **'Chloris'** (syn. 'Rosée du Matin'), ancient rose, comparatively

thornless, darker leaves, double soft pink flowers; **'Félicité Parmentier'**, smaller shrub, flat double flowers, salmon pink, fading to pale pink; **'Great Maiden's Blush'**, vigorous shrub dating back to the fifteenth century or earlier, large, very double, blush pink flowers; **'Königin von Dänemark'** ★ (syn. 'Queen of Denmark'), smaller double flowers of a deeper pink than other Albas; **'Mme Plantier'**, rather flat, double, white flowers, buds often tinged reddish pink; **'Maiden's Blush'** fragrant, creamy white to very light pink, double flowers. Zones 4–10.

BOURBON ROSES

☀ ❄ ↔ 5–8 ft (1.5–2.4 m)
↕ 4–7 ft (1.2–2 m)

The first Bourbon Rose was a hybrid between *R. chinensis* and a Damask Rose that occurred naturally on the Ile de Bourbon. The majority are shrubs

of 4–7 ft (1.2–2 m); a few of climbing habit; highly perfumed, and many with repeat-flowering characteristics. The flowers may be semi-double or double, often cupped or with a quartered arrangement of petals. In humid areas they are susceptible to fungal diseases. **'Boule de Neige'**, globular, double, white blooms, sometimes with reddish purple tinge on petal edges; **'Commandant Beaurepaire'**, double flowers striped in shades of crimson, pink, purple, and white; **'Gros Choux d'Hollande'**, medium-sized, fragrant, pink flowers opening from rounded red buds; **'Honorine de Brabant'**, light pink cupped flowers, faint rose spotting on inner surfaces; **'Louise Odier'**, vigorous bush, very double bright rose pink flowers; **'Mme Isaac Pereire'**, one of the most heavily perfumed, large very double flowers of magenta-rose; **'Mme Pierre Oger'**,

cupped, double, translucent silvery pink flowers; **'Queen of Bourbons'**, semi-double, cupped, rose pink flowers, in summer; **'Reine Victoria'**, slender bush, cupped double flowers, silky textured, lilac-pink; **'Souvenir de la Malmaison'**, often grown in its climbing form, double flowers, flattened and quartered, palest flesh pink, quickly pulped by wet weather. Its sport, **'Souvenir de St Anne's'**, a semi-double form with prominent yellow stamens, survives bad weather; **'Zéphirine Drouhin'**, no thorns, rich pink, semi-double, fragrant flowers. Zones 6–10.

Rosa, Old Rose, Bourbon, 'Gipsy Boy'

Rosa, Old Rose, Bourbon, 'Souvenir de la Malmaison'

Rosa, Old Rose, Bourbon, 'Mme Pierre Oger'

Rosa, Old Rose, Bourbon, 'Zéphirine Drouhin'

Rosa, Old Rose, Bourbon, 'Gros Choux d'Hollande'

Rosa, Old Rose, Bourbon, 'Honorine de Brabant'

Rosa, Old Rose, Bourbon, 'Souvenir de Mme Auguste Charles'

Rosa, Old Rose, Bourbon, 'Souvenir de Mme Breuil'

Rosa, Old Rose, Bourbon, 'Mme Ernst Calvat'

Rosa, OR, B, 'Kathleen Harrop'

R., OR, Bourbon, 'Louise Odier'

Rosa, OR, B, 'Queen of Bourbons'

R., OR, Bourbon, 'Reine Victoria'

Rosa, OR, B, 'Mme Isaac Pereire'

R

Rosa, Old Rose, Centifolia, 'Fantin-Latour'

Rosa, Old Rose, Centifolia, 'Petite de Hollande'

Rosa, Old Rose, Centifolia, 'Petite Lisette'

Rosa, Old Rose, Centifolia, 'Reine des Centfeuilles'

Rosa, Old Rose, Centifolia, 'The Bishop'

Rosa, Old Rose, China, 'Archduke Charles'

Rosa, Old Rose, China, 'Fabvier'

Rosa, Old Rose, China, 'Gloire des Rosomanes'

Rosa, Old Rose, China, 'Green Rose'

Rosa, Old Rose, China, 'Hermosa'

Rosa, OR, China, 'Irène Watts'

Rosa, OR, China, 'Le Vésuve'

Rosa, OR, China, 'Mutabilis'

Rosa, OR, China, 'Old Blush'

R., OR, China, 'Sophie's Perpetual'

R., Old Rose, China, 'Cramoisi Supérieur'

Rosa, Old Rose, China, 'Fellenberg'

CENTIFOLIA ROSES

☼ ❄ ↔ 4–8 ft (1.2–2.4 m)
↑ 2–8 ft (0.6–2.4 m)

Many roses in this group are centuries old. Centifolia means "one hundred leaves" and refers to the crowded petals that form the large flowers. Centifolias, "rose of the painters," often feature in works by the Old Masters. The flowers come in shades of pink as well as white and, occasionally, purplish magenta shades. They generally flower only once in early summer. Bushes, often prickly and coarse with quite lax growth, vary in height from 2–8 ft (0.6–2.4 m). Smaller cultivars produce proportionally smaller blooms. '**Cabbage Rose**' (syn. 'Provence Rose'), rose of complex hybrid parentage, known in Europe since before 1600, grayish green leaves, deep pink flowers, very double and cupped, strong sweet perfume; '**Fantin-Latour**', highly fragrant, soft pink, double blooms; '**Petite de Hollande**', small, scented, double blooms of rose pink; '**Petite Lisette**', to 3 ft (0.9 m) tall, small, very fragrant, pink pompon flowers; '**Reine des Centfeuilles**', fragrant pink flowers, up to 2½ in (6 cm) across; '**Rose de Meaux**', to about 2 ft (0.6 m) high, small pink slightly frilly flowers, resemble those of *Dianthus;* '**The Bishop**', flowers slightly earlier than most, purplish magenta blooms; '**Tour de Malakoff**', tall lax bush, very fragrant purplish magenta blooms fade to lilac. Zones 5–10.

CHINA ROSES

☼ ❄ ↔ 3–6 ft (0.9–1.8 m)
↑ 3–6 ft (0.9–1.8 m)

When the first China Roses were introduced to Europe in the eighteenth century, their repeat-flowering characteristic was seized on by breeders who welcomed this new source with this attribute. Generally China Roses are low growing with airy, often spindly growth, and are rather sparsely foliaged. The flowers are usually quite small and semi-double or double in shades of pink, with some crimson and flame tints. Fragrance is usually light. '**Archduke Charles**', pink to crimson flowers mature to a deeper shade, banana-scented; '**Comtesse du Caÿla**', loosely semi-double, scented flowers in flame shades; '**Gloire des Rosomanes**', hardy rose, large, cup-shaped, semi-double, pink to crimson flowers, in spring–autumn; '**Green Rose**' (syn. 'Viridiflora') bears green leaf-like sepals with red-brown serrated edges, rather than colored petals; '**Le Vésuve**', large slightly fragrant flowers, can be pink or red, depending whether grown in sun or shade; '**Louis XIV**', scented almost-double flowers of a rich deep crimson, yellow stamens; '**Mutabilis**' ★, taller with single yellow flowers opening from buff red-streaked buds and changing in color through shades of pink and soft crimson; '**Old Blush**' (syns 'Common Monthly', 'Parsons' Pink'), one of the first China Roses, semi-double silvery pink flowers; '**Sophie's Perpetual**', few thorns, scented mid-pink flowers, darker pink shading on some outer petals. Zones 7–10.

DAMASK ROSES

☼ ❄ ↔ 5–8 ft (1.5–2.4 m)
↑ 3–7 ft (0.9–2 m)

Crusaders returning from the Middle East took the first Damask Roses back to Europe. Often untidy bushes, they grow 3–7 ft (0.9–2 m) tall, prickly, and with rather downy grayish leaves; the majority flower only once in spring or summer. The flowers are double or semi-double in paler shades of pink and white. Most are very fragrant, and Damask Roses have long been cultivated for making perfume. '**Autumn Damask**' (syn. 'Quatre Saisons'), highly fragrant mid-pink blooms; '**Blush Damask**', profuse summer-borne flowers, mid-pink in center, lighter pink towards outer petals; '**Celsiana**', clusters of semi-double clear pink flowers; '**Gloire de Guilan**', very double flowers, flattened and quartered when fully open; '**Ispahan**', longer flowering variety, intensely perfumed, clear pink, double flowers; '**Mme Hardy**', very double white flowers, petals arranged around a green "button" eye; '**Rose de Rescht**', deep pink double flowers; '**Summer Damask**', clusters of very fragrant, semi-double, pink flowers;

R

Rosa, Old Rose, Damask, 'Autumn Damask'

Rosa, Old Rose, Damask, 'Blush Damask'

Rosa, Old Rose, Damask, 'Botzaris'

Rosa, Old Rose, Damask, 'Celsiana'

Rosa, Old Rose, Damask, 'Gloire de Guilan'

Rosa, Old Rose, Damask, 'Leda'

Rosa, Old Rose, Damask, 'Mme Hardy'

Rosa, Old Rose, Damask, 'Professeur Emile Perrot'

Rosa, Old Rose, Damask, 'Rose de Rescht'

Rosa, Old Rose, Damask, 'York and Lancaster'

Rosa, Old Rose, Gallica, 'Tuscany'

Rosa, Old Rose, Gallica, 'Belle de Crécy'

Rosa, Old Rose, Gallica, 'Charles de Mills'

Rosa, Old Rose, Gallica, 'Duc de Guiche'

Rosa, Old Rose, Gallica, 'Duchesse d'Angoulême'

'York and Lancaster', unusual rose, semi-double flowers that can be white, blush pink, or two-toned. Zones 5–10.

GALLICA ROSES

☼ ❄ ↔ 4–6 ft (1.2–1.8 m)
↕ 4–6 ft (1.2–1.8 m)

This group are mostly compact plants growing to 4–6 ft (1.2–1.8 m) tall. Foliage is usually dark green, not very prickly. Most bear sweetly perfumed double or semi-double flowers in shades of pink or magenta-purple. They flower only once in spring or summer. 'Belle de Crécy', fragrant, rich pink and purple, double blooms; 'Belle Isis', double flowers, flattened when fully open, of clear flesh pink, fading to white near edges; 'Cardinal de Richelieu', scented, dark red-purple, double flowers; 'Charles de Mills' ★, very fragrant, rich purple, double flowers with a quartered arrangement

of the petals; 'Complicata', tall vigorous shrub, large single flowers of bright pink, paler at center, large stamens; 'Duc de Guiche', fragrant, deep pink-purple, double blooms; 'Duchesse d'Angoulême', summer-borne, semi-double to double, mid-pink flowers, highly fragrant; 'Duchesse de Montebello', small, fully double, very fragrant flowers of soft pink; 'Président de Sèze', scented double flowers, magenta to cerise at center, shading to lilac-pink at outer petals; 'Tuscany', extremely old and attractive variety, purple-red double flowers, prominent yellow stamens, 'Tuscany Superb', fragrant lilac flowers. Zones 5–10.

HYBRID PERPETUAL ROSES

☼ ❄ ↔ 3–6 ft (0.9–1.8 m)
↕ 4–7 ft (1.2–2 m)

Becoming prominent during the reign of Queen Victoria, this group has a

complex parentage involving several rose groups, including Bourbons and Chinas. Growing 4–7 ft (1.2–2 m) tall, they are repeat flowering, and bear large, double, usually fragrant blooms in shades of pink to red. 'Baron Girod de l'Ain', crimson flowers, petals edged in white; 'Baroness Rothschild', pink, very large, heavily scented flowers; 'Baronne Prévost', deep pink flowers, flattened when open; 'Champion of the World', large, pink, scented, double blooms; 'Comtesse Cécile de Chabrillant', rare rose, fragrant pink flowers; 'Frau Karl Druschki' (syns 'Reine des Neiges', 'Snow Queen', 'White American Beauty'), globular white blooms; 'Général Jacqueminot', fragrant, purple-red, double blooms on long stems; 'Henry Nevard', rich red, highly fragrant, double flowers, up to 30 petals each; 'Marchesa Boccella' ★, fragrant double flowers,

pink, almost white on outer petals; 'Maurice Bernardin', clusters of large, rich red, fragrant blooms; 'Paul Neyron', vigorous, mid-pink, cupped, fragrant flowers, up to 50 petals each; 'Reine des Violettes', sweetly scented purple to violet flowers; 'Souvenir du Docteur Jamain', deep ruby red semi-double flowers, full sun will scorch the petals; 'Sydonie', quartered mid-pink

R., OR, Hybrid Perpetual, 'Captain Hayward'

R., OR, HP, 'Baron Girod de l'Ain'

R., OR, HP, 'Général Jacqueminot'

Rosa, OR, HP, 'Georg Arends'

Rosa, OR, HP, 'Henry Nevard'

Rosa, OR, HP, 'Hugh Dickson'

Rosa, OR, Hybrid Perpetual, 'Comtesse Cécile de Chabrillant'

Rosa, OR, Hybrid Perpetual, 'Champion of the World'

Rosa, OR, Hybrid Perpetual, 'Marchesa Boccella'

Rosa, OR, Hybrid Perpetual, 'Maurice Bernardin'

Rosa, OR, Hybrid Perpetual, 'Mrs John Laing'

Rosa, OR, Hybrid Perpetual, 'Prince Camille de Rohan'

Rosa, OR, Hybrid Perpetual, 'Reine des Violettes'

Rosa, OR, Hybrid Perpetual, 'Souvenir du Docteur Jamain'

Rosa, OR, Hybrid Perpetual, 'Dr Andry'

Rosa, OR, Hybrid Perpetual, 'Paul Neyron'

Rosa, OR, Hybrid Perpetual, 'Ferdinand Pichard'

Rosa, OR, Hybrid Perpetual, 'Sydonie'

R., OR, Hybrid Perpetual, 'Ulrich Brunner Fils'

Rosa, OR, Hybrid Perpetual, 'Vick's Caprice'

Rosa, OR, Hybrid Perpetual, 'Victor Hugo'

flowers; **'Ulrich Brunner Fils'**, fragrant, cupped, pinkish red flowers open from rich red buds. Zones 5–10.

MOSS ROSES
☀ ❄ ↔ 5–8 ft (1.5–2.4 m)
↕ 3–7 ft (0.9–2 m)

The first Moss Rose occurred as the sport of a Centifolia. They are named for the mossy growth that arises on stems and buds. The degree and type of mossing varies, some being hard and prickly, others soft and downy. A small group, not widely grown, it is similar to the Centifolias, with large, double, fragrant blooms, flowering once in spring or summer. **'Alfred de Dalmas'** (syn. 'Mousseline'), semi-double creamy pink flowers; **'Catherine de Würtemberg'**, rare rose, slightly scented, rich pink flowers; **'Comtesse de Murinais'**, flattened double flowers opening soft pink, fading to white; **'Gloire des Mousseux'**, large light pink flowers; **'Henri Martin'**, deep pink-red semi-double blooms; **'Mme Louis Lévêque'**, warm pink silky-petalled flowers, double, cupped; **'William Lobb'**, semi-double purplish magenta flowers. Zones 5–10.

PORTLAND ROSES
☀ ❄ ↔ 3–5 ft (0.9–1.5 m)
↕ 2–4 ft (0.6–1.2 m)

A small group closely allied to the Damasks and Gallicas, foliage usually resembles one or the other. 'Autumn Damask' has given them the popular repeat-flowering characteristic. Small shrubs to 4 ft (1.2 m) tall, most bear fragrant double flowers in shades of pink to red. **'Duchess of Portland'** (syn. 'Portland Rose'), single or semi-double cerise-red flowers; **'Mme Knorr'**, large, heavily perfumed, rich pink, double flowers; **'Rose du Roi'**, heavily scented, rich red, double flowers. Zones 5–10.

Rosa, Old Rose, Moss, 'James Veitch'

Rosa, Old Rose, Moss, 'Catherine de Würtemberg'

Rosa, Old Rose, Moss, 'Salet'

Rosa, Old Rose, Moss, 'Shailer's White Moss'

Rosa, Old Rose, Moss, 'William Lobb'

Rosa, OR, Moss, 'Mme Louis Lévêque'

Rosa, Old Rose, Moss, 'Alfred de Dalmas'

Rosa, Old Rose, Moss, 'Communis'

Rosa, OR, Moss, 'Gloire des Mousseux'

Rosa, Old Rose, Portland, 'Duchess of Portland'

Rosa, Old Rose, Portland, 'Mme Knorr'

Rosa, Old Rose, Portland, 'Rose du Roi'

Rosa, Old Rose, Scots, 'Double White Burnet'

Rosa, Old Rose, Scots, 'Single Cherry'

Rosa, Old Rose, Scots, 'Stanwell Perpetual'

Rosa, Old Rose, Scots, 'Aïcha'

SCOTS ROSES

☀ ❄ ↔ 5–8 ft (1.5–2.4 m)
↕ 3–7 ft (0.9–2 m)

This group became prominent early in the nineteenth century when a breeding program began from seedlings of a malformed *R. spinosissima*. Scots Roses are quite tough plants, 3–7 ft (0.9–2 m) in height, with fern-like foliage and prickly stems. The flowers range from single to double in white and cream shades to yellow, and from light to deepest pink and red. Most flower only once in spring or summer. The hips are all unusually dark in color, a blackish maroon when fully ripe. '**Aïcha**', vigorous grower, large, semi-double, fragrant, yellow flowers; **Andrewsii** (syn. 'Andrew's Rose'), large, semi-double to double, mid-pink flowers, often cream toward the petal base; '**Double White Burnet**', highly fragrant white flowers, can be semi-double to double in form; '**Dunwich Rose**', soft yellow single flowers, prominent yellow stamens; '**Falkland**', fragrant, semi-double, cupped blooms of lilac-pink fading to white; '**Karl Förster**', lightly scented, creamy white, double flowers, prominent stamens when fully open, and repeat flowering; '**Single Cherry**', thorny stems, deep red single flowers, bright yellow stamens; '**Stanwell**

Perpetual', arching bush, grayish green foliage, very fragrant double flowers of soft pink, long flowering season; '**William III**', fragrant semi-double flowers of rich maroon, becoming lighter with age. Zones 4–10.

SWEET BRIAR ROSES

☀ ❄ ↔ 5–10 ft (1.5–3 m)
↕ 4–8 ft (1.2–2.4 m)

The apple-scented foliage of this group is inherited from its *R. eglanteria* parent and is its main distinguishing feature. The majority are large, rather untidy bushes, which are best suited for planting in hedgerows or wild gardens. The flowers are usually single or semi-double, and occur in shades of pink to deep red and white. '**Amy Robsart**', prolific flower bearer, almost-single, highly fragrant, deep pink blooms; '**Lady Penzance**', most strongly scented foliage of the group, single coppery pink flowers, prominent stamens; '**Magnifica**', dense scented foliage that can be pruned to form a hedge, and crimson semi-double flowers; '**Manning's Blush**', densely foliaged, large, fully double, white flowers flushed with pink; '**Meg Merrilies**', extremely vigorous and prickly rose, deep pink to bright crimson, semi-double, scented flowers. Zones 4–10.

TEA ROSES

☀ ❄ ↔ 3–6 ft (0.9–1.8 m)
↕ 3–7 ft (0.9–2 m)

Tea Roses arrived in Europe from Asia in the early nineteenth century. Their name is thought to come from being shipped on boats carrying tea rather than for a tea scent. With their repeat-flowering ability and the yellow coloring of some, they, together with the Chinas, revolutionized rose breeding. The foliage is large and glossy on plants ranging from 3–7 ft (0.9–2 m) tall. Their double flowers often have long pointed buds. Flower color varies from creamy yellows and white through to shades of pink and red. They grow better in warmer climates. '**Agnes Smith**', free-flowering, flowers rose pink in cooler weather, turning paler in hotter months; '**Catherine Mermet**', high-pointed buds opening to light salmon pink; '**Duchesse de**

Brabant' (syns 'Comtesse de Labarthe', 'Comtesse Ouwaroff'), free flowering, cupped, double, pink flowers; '**Francis Dubreuil**', velvety, dark red, double flowers; '**Freiherr von Marschall**', rich red, ageing to deep pink, fragrant, double flowers; '**Lady Hillingdon**', long, pointed, deep yellow buds open to loose, semi-double, buff-yellow flowers; '**Mme de Tartas**', lightly scented double blooms of blush pink; '**Mrs Reynolds Hole**', fragrant, rich purple-pink, double flowers; '**Monsieur Tillier**', rosy pink with salmon tonings, double flowers with darker shading; '**Niphetos**', double white flowers opening from creamy buds; '**Perle des Jardins**', very double, often quartered, sulfur yellow flowers; '**Rosette Delizy**', light pink to pale yellow petals, darker pink veins; '**Souvenir d'un Ami**', double flowers in shades of deep rose pink to salmon. Zones 7–11.

Rosa, Old Rose, Sweet Briar, 'Magnifica'

Rosa, Old Rose, Tea, 'Rosette Delizy'

Rosa, OR, Tea, 'Francis Dubreuil'

R., OR, T, 'Freiherr von Marschall'

Rosa, OR, Tea, 'Mme de Tartas'

R., OR, Tea, 'Mrs Reynolds Hole'

Rosa, OR, Tea, 'Monsieur Tillier'

MISCELLANEOUS OLD GARDEN ROSES

☼/❊ ❄ ↔ 20–48 in (50–120 cm)
↕ 2–6 ft (0.6–1.8 m)

In some instances the parentage of Old Roses is hard to establish or the plants simply do not seem to fit any particular category. This miscellaneous group is a mixed lot, though that in no way lessens their beauty. '**Duplex**' (syn. 'Wolly Dodd's Rose'), repeat-flowering, semi-double blooms; '**Dupontii**', plentiful grayish green leaves, sweetly perfumed single flowers, clear creamy white; '**Empress Josephine**', grayish green leaves, fragrant double flowers dark pink with darker veining, flushed with lilac and purple; '**Fortuniana**', of garden origin in China, dark green leaves, large, scented, double flowers creamy white; '**Harison's Yellow**' (the yellow rose of Texas), of garden origin in the USA, said to have been carried west by the pioneers and planted wherever they stopped, small double flowers, deep clear yellow; '**Mermaid**', fragrant, single, pale yellow blooms; '**Polliniana**', white flowers, sometimes flushed palest pink; '**The Garland**', scented semi-double blooms of pink, light yellow, and white. Zones 6–9.

OLD CLIMBING ROSES

Old Climbing Roses have a wide variety of growth habits. Most are hardy. Flowers may be single or double and are usually in shades of white, pink, and red. Some varieties are thornless, or nearly so. Flowering may occur in spring, summer, or recurrently. They are classified into a number of groups depending on parentage.

AYRSHIRE ROSES

☼ ❄ ↔ 10–20 ft (3–6 m)
↕ 5–10 ft (1.5–3 m)

Medium sized climbing or scrambling roses with *R. arvensis* parentage. The flowers are borne in clusters or singly; they may be single or double and vary in degree of fragrance. Flowers are white or in shades of pink. '**Ayrshire Queen**', semi-double purple-red blooms; '**Dundee Rambler**', pink-tinged white flowers; '**Ruga**', flowers open flesh-pink and age to ivory white. Zones 6–9.

BOURSAULT ROSES

☼ ❄ ↔ 8–12 ft (2.4–3.5 m)
↕ 8–12 ft (2.4–3.5 m)

A small group of nearly thornless climbing roses. Dark green foliage. Double flowers, in shades of light pink to deep red, mildly fragrant. '**Amadis**', deep red-purple semi-double flowers; '**Blush Boursault**', flowers blush pink, darker toward the center; '**Boursault Rose**' (syn. 'L'heritierana'), semi-double deep pink-purple flowers; '**Gracilis**', mid-red flowers, semi-double in form. Zones 6–10.

CLIMBING BOURBON ROSES

☼ ❄ ↔ 10–25 ft (3–8 m)
↕ 7–15 ft (2–4.5 m)

The climbing habit is present in only a few Bourbon Roses. They are repeat-flowering, highly perfumed, and no more than 15 ft (4.5 m) high. The flowers are in shades of light to dark pink. '**Mme Arthur Oger**', vivid pink double flowers. Zones 6–10.

CLIMBING CHINA ROSES

☼ ❄ ↔ 10–25 ft (3–8 m)
↕ 7–15 ft (2–4.5 m)

Only a few China Roses have a climbing habit. They grow to 15 ft (4.5 m) high. Small double blooms, usually in shades of pink, with varying fragrance. '**Climbing Cramoisi Supérieur**', small crimson flowers; '**Climbing Old Blush**', lightly scented, semi-double, mid-pink blooms; '**Climbing Pompon de Paris**', small pinkish red flowers, mild fragrance. Zones 7–11.

CLIMBING TEA ROSES

☼ ❄ ↔ 10–25 ft (3–8 m)
↕ 10–20 ft (3–6 m)

Most climbing Tea Roses are sports of the bush varieties. Best suited to warmer climates. Most varieties flower for long periods. They may be single or double and vary widely in fragrance. Colors are in all shades of white, pink, red, and yellow. '**Belle Lyonnaise**', pleasantly scented, large, yellow flowers, age to white; '**Gloire de Dijon**', scented double flowers, rich cream with hints of pink and old gold; '**Sombreuil**' ★, fragrant double flowers, ivory white, sometimes tinged pink or creamy yellow; '**Souvenir de Mme Léonie Viennot**', fragrant double flowers of pink and yellow tones. Zones 7–11.

LAEVIGATA ROSES

☼ ❄ ↔ 10–20 ft (3–6 m)
↕ 10–25 ft (3–8 m)

Vigorous sprawling or climbing roses with large, almost evergreen leaves. Large single flowers are usually white or in shades of pink. '**Cooper's Burmese**', single flowers of ivory white, scented. Zones 7–10.

NOISETTE ROSES

☼ ❄ ↔ 5–10 ft (1.5–3 m)
↕ 8–12 ft (2.4–3.5 m)

Vigorous climbing roses originally from a cross of China and Musk Roses. Double flowers are usually fragrant and recurring throughout the season. Flowers in shades of white, cream, yellow, and pink. '**Bouquet d'Or**',

Rosa, Old Rose, Miscellaneous, 'Empress Josephine'

Rosa, Old Rose, Noisette, 'Crépuscule'

Rosa, Old Rose, Noisette, 'Bouquet d'Or'

Rosa, Old Rose, Noisette, 'Duchesse d'Auerstädt'

Rosa, Old Rose, Boursault, 'Amadis'

Rosa, Old Rose, Boursault, 'Blush Boursault'

Rosa, Old Rose, Climbing Tea, 'Souvenir de Mme Léonie Viennot'

Rosa, OR, M., 'Harison's Yellow'

R., OR, Miscellaneous, 'Mermaid'

R., OR, Miscellaneous, 'Polliniana'

Rosa, OR, CT, 'Gloire de Dijon'

R., OR, Climbing Tea, 'Sombreuil'

Rosa, Old Rose, Noisette, 'Jaune Desprez'

Rosa, Old Rose, Noisette, 'Rêve d'Or'

Rosa, Old Rose, Noisette,
'Mme Alfred Carrière'

Rosa, Old Rose, Noisette,
'William Allen Richardson'

well perfumed, apricot-yellow, double flowers; '**Crépuscule**', fragrant blooms of soft apricot-yellow; '**Mme Alfred Carrière**' ★, perfumed double flowers of white with a hint of pink; '**Rêve d'Or**', scented, creamy yellow, double flowers. Zones 7–11.

SEMPERVIRENS ROSES

☀ ❄ ↔ 10–20 ft (3–6 m)
↑ 8–15 ft (2.4–4.5 m)

A group of usually evergreen, moderately vigorous climbers with lush foliage. These roses produce small double flowers, in shades of white and pink, borne in showy clusters. '**Adélaide d'Orléans**', lightly perfumed semi-double flowers of pale pink, almost white, emerge from pink buds; '**Félicité et Perpétué**', lightly scented double blooms open palest pink and age to white; '**Spectabile**', delicately scented rose pink flowers. Zones 7–10.

ROSCOEA

This genus of about 18 species of tuberous herbaceous perennials is a member of the ginger (Zingiberaceae) family. Summer growing, they are native to the Himalayas and China where they are found in grasslands, on the hills, and in lightly forested areas. They have often broad, heavily veined leaves sheathing the flower stems that support flowers almost orchid-like in their appearance. These exotic-looking plants are well suited to the front of a border or the rock garden, as well as to pot cultivation.
CULTIVATION: Grow in well-drained but humus-rich soil in a cool but not heavily shaded site. Plant the tubers about 6 in (15 cm) below the soil

surface in late winter. The tubers must not be stored dry. Propagation is by division or by freshly sown seed.

Roscoea alpina

☀ ❄ ↔ 4–5 in (10–12 cm)
↑ 10–12 in (25–30 cm)

Native to Nepal and Kashmir. Up to 4 leaves, to 4 in (10 cm) long, per tuber. Summer-produced flowers, pink or mauve, tend to be somewhat hidden among upper leaves. Zones 6–9.

Roscoea auriculata

☀ ❄ ↔ 4–6 in (10–15 cm)
↑ 12–20 in (30–50 cm)

From Nepal and Sikkim, India. Up to 10 broad lance-shaped leaves, to 10 in (25 cm) long. Purple flowers, late summer, 1½ in (35 mm) wide. Zones 6–9.

Roscoea 'Beesiana'

☀ ❄ ↔ 4–5 in (10–12 cm)
↑ 10–12 in (25–30 cm)

This hybrid is often said to be the result of a cross between *R. purpurea*

and *R. humeana,* but this is doubtful. The flowers can be yellow, red, pink, blue, or purple. Zones 6–9.

Roscoea cautleyoides

☀ ❄ ↔ 4–6 in (10–15 cm)
↑ 20–24 in (50–60 cm)

From China. Up to 4 narrow leaves, to 16 in (40 cm) long. Flowers held well above the leaves, usually yellow, can be purple or white, in early summer. Zones 6–9.

Roscoea humeana

☀ ❄ ↔ 5–6 in (12–15 cm)
↑ 8–10 in (20–25 cm)

Stocky Chinese species. Up to 3 leaves, not fully developed at flowering. Rich purple blooms, about 1½ in (4 cm) across, in early summer. Zones 7–9.

Roscoea purpurea ★

syn. *Roscoea procera*

☀ ❄ ↔ 5–6 in (12–15 cm)
↑ 12–16 in (30–40 cm)

From the Himalayas. Up to 8 leaves. Rich purple flowers, sometimes white or marked white, to 2½ in (6 cm) wide, in summer. Zones 6–9.

ROSMARINUS

ROSEMARY

This genus is part of the large mint (Lamiaceae) family, which includes many of the herbs we use for culinary and medicinal purposes. It contains just 2 species of evergreen shrubs. They have short linear leaves and their small 2-lipped flowers are usually pale blue and borne along the branches, which can become quite woody with age. Rosemary has been cultivated for centuries, being grown for the aromatic oil distilled from the shoots and leaves, and for use as a culinary herb. The ancient Greeks thought that rosemary strengthened memory and students wore sprigs of it; the herb has become a symbol of remembrance.
CULTIVATION: Rosemary likes a hot dry position and will grow in all sorts of soils but they must be well-drained, as it will not tolerate wet winter conditions. It should be pruned severely after flowering to maintain a bushy compact habit and is quite suitable for hedging. Propagation is usually from softwood or from half-hardened cuttings taken in summer.

Roscoea purpurea

Roscoea auriculata

Roscoea 'Beesiana'

Roscoea cautleyoides

Rosmarinus officinalis 'Blue Lagoon'

Rosmarinus officinalis 'Joyce DeBaggio'

Rosmarinus officinalis 'Majorca Pink'

Rosmarinus officinalis 'Tuscan Blue'

Rosmarinus officinalis var. *angustissimus* 'Benenden Blue'

Rosmarinus officinalis 'Prostratus'

Rosmarinus officinalis ★

ROSEMARY

☼ ❄ ↔6 ft (1.8 m) ↑7 ft (2 m)

Popular culinary, cosmetic, and medicinal herb native to Mediterranean regions. Variable in habit with erect ascending branches. Aromatic, dark green, linear leaves, leathery with rolled edges, silvery beneath. Small light blue flowers, in spring–early summer. *R. o.* var. *angustissimus* 'Benenden Blue', striking blue flowers, very narrow leaves; *R. o.* 'Blue Lagoon', narrow leaves, blue flowers; 'Joyce DeBaggio', lower and more compact; 'Majorca Pink', lilac-pink flowers; 'Miss Jessopp's Upright', tall and very erect; 'Roseus', pink flowers; 'Severn Sea', a cascading form, deep blue winter flowers; 'Silver Spires', white-edged light green leaves, blue flowers; 'Sissinghurst Blue', brilliant blue flowers, thin leaves; 'Tuscan Blue' ★, rich blue flowers. The **Prostratus Group** of low spreading forms, ideal for rock gardens or spilling over walls, includes 'Lockwood de Forest' and 'Prostratus'. Zones 6–11.

ROSSIOGLOSSUM

This is a small group of 6 different but similar Central American orchid species, which at one time were included under *Odontoglossum*. Due to their color and floral features they have become known as tiger or clown orchids. From the family Orchidaceae, members of this genus have a distinct somewhat flattened pseudobulb with up to 3 broad leathery leaves at the apex. The inflorescences generally appear from the leaf axil of the semi-matured new growth. They bloom only once from the pseudobulb.
CULTIVATION: These orchids like warm moist conditions and bright light during their main growing period, from late spring to autumn. Flower spikes will develop from late summer to autumn and blooming will take place during late autumn and winter.

During the winter months they need to be kept on the dry side and only watered enough to keep the pseudobulbs from shriveling. They are best grown potted, in a bark-based mix, under intermediate conditions. Propagate by division of large clumps.

Rossioglossum grande ★

☼/◑ ✢ ↔8–20 in (20–50 cm)
↑8–20 in (20–50 cm)

Well-known species from Mexico and Guatemala. Stiff spikes of up to 8 yellow flowers, 6 in (15 cm) across, chestnut brown bars across sepals, yellow and brown petals, in winter. Creamy labellum with dark red-brown markings. Zones 10–12.

Rossioglossum Rawdon Jester

☼/◑ ✢ ↔8–20 in (20–50 cm)
↑8–20 in (20–50 cm)

This cross between *R. grande* and *R. Williamsianum* (*R. grande* × *R. schlieperianum*) can be difficult to distinguish from robust forms of *R. grande*. Zones 10–12.

ROTHMANNIA

This is a genus of about 20 evergreen shrubs or small trees in the madder (Rubiaceae) family that are cultivated largely for their handsome glossy foliage, which is often deeply veined, and their bell-shaped or tubular flowers, which are often fragrant. They are native to Africa, Madagascar, and Asia. The fruits are brown pods containing seeds.
CULTIVATION: Although quite adaptable to most soils, *Rothmannia* species prefer well-composted neutral or slightly acid soil in a protected and sunny position. These plants are frost and drought resistant. Propagation is from seed sown in spring or from cuttings of half-hardened wood taken in early summer.

Rothmannia globosa

BELL GARDENIA, CAPE JASMINE, SEPTEMBER BELLS, TREE GARDENIA

☼ ⬙ ↔6–10 ft (1.8–3 m)
↑12–20 ft (3.5–6 m)

Native of South Africa. An evergreen shrub, similar to gardenia. Richly

Rossioglossum grande

Rossioglossum Rawdon Jester

Rothmannia globosa

textured, glossy green, elliptic to narrow leaves, distinctly veined with yellow, pink, or maroon. Fragrant, white, bell-shaped flowers, singly or in cymes, in spring. Zones 9–11.

ROYSTONEA
ROYAL PALM

This genus in the family Arecaceae consists of about 10 species of stately single-stemmed palms, the majority from the humid tropical Caribbean Islands and surrounding coastal regions. These pinnate or feather-leafed palms have a prominent crownshaft. Many species have majestic, smooth, gray-white trunks that may be swollen in the middle or base. Panicles of small, white, cup-shaped flowers appear from just below the crownshaft, followed by roundish, often deep purple berries. Most come from fertile low-lying forest areas near the sea, that are sometimes swampy. These attractive palms make useful landscape subjects in the tropics and subtropics, where they are popularly used to line roadways and paths or as specimen plantings.
CULTIVATION: *Roystonea* palms give best results in a moist, well-drained, fertile soil in full sun. They are moderately tolerant of seaside conditions. The genus is self-pollinating, and can be propagated from seed.

Roystonea borinquena
syns *Oreodoxa borinquena,*
Roystonea hispaniolana

PUERTO RICAN ROYAL PALM
☼ ☀ ↔ 15–20 ft (4.5–6 m)
↑ 50–60 ft (15–20 m)

Very fast growing palm from the West Indies. Grayish brown trunk, swollen above middle, about 24 in (60 cm) diameter at base. Huge crownshaft of

arching, feathery, divided, bright green leaves, up to 10 ft (3 m) long and 6 ft (1.8 m) across, with 2 crowded rows of leaflets with divided tips, up to 40 in (100 cm) long. Densely crowded clusters of yellow flowers emerge below the crownshaft, in summer. Pale brown oblong fruit, flat on one side. Zones 10–11.

Roystonea oleracea
CARIBBEAN ROYAL PALM
☼ ☀ ↔ 20 ft (6 m) ↑ 130 ft (40 m)

Tallest of the royal palms; occurs along the Caribbean coast of South America and on the Lesser Antilles islands of the West Indies. Grayish trunk swollen at base, bright shiny green crownshaft, dark green fronds held in one plane, appear flat. Zones 11–12.

Roystonea regia ★
syn. *Roystonia elata*
CUBAN ROYAL PALM
☼ ☀ ↔ 20 ft (6 m) ↑ 80 ft (24 m)

Native to Cuba. Attractive, smooth, whitish trunk, often thickened in the middle. Green feathery fronds, to 20 ft (6 m) long, plume-like, above long green crownshaft. Pendulous inflorescence of small white flowers. Purple-black fruits. Zones 11–12.

RUBUS

There are more than 250 species of climbing, low-growing, or upright shrubs, often with prickles on stems and leaves, within this genus from the rose (Rosaceae) family. Found throughout the world, they are cultivated for their ornamental value and as a useful food source. Most species have biennial stems or canes, which means they produce fruit only on second-year wood; leaves on first and second year's growth are often a different shape.
CULTIVATION: The wide distribution of this genus means it has a variety of habitats. Most species thrive in fertile, humus-rich, moist, free-draining soil.

Roystonea regia

Many grow in full sun to light shade, and some grow in deeper shade under deciduous trees. Propagate by dividing suckering species in spring or take half-hardened cuttings from evergreen species, or softwood or hardwood cuttings from deciduous species, or layer. Grow from stratified seed in spring.

Rubus allegheniensis
☼ ❋ ↔ 6 ft (1.8 m) ↑ 10 ft (3 m)
Native to North America. Deciduous shrub, slender arching stems, woolly tips, hook-shaped prickles. Double-toothed leaves, 3 to 5 leaflets, furry undersides. Long racemes of 5-petalled white flowers, in late spring. Black cone-shaped fruit. Zones 3–9.

Rubus arcticus
ARCTIC BRAMBLE, CRIMSON BRAMBLE
☼ ❋ ↔ 18–24 in (45–60 cm)
↑ 6–12 in (15–30 cm)

Herbaceous perennial, native to the boggy woods and marshes of the

higher latitudes of Europe, Asia, and North America. Compound leaves on long stalks, with 3 to 5 oval, smooth, toothed leaflets, on stems without prickles. Clusters of 1 to 3 pink or red flowers, up to 1 in (25 mm) across, purple stamens, in summer. Red globular fruit that is attractive to birds and people. 'Kenai Carpet' (nagoonberry), vigorous form, solitary pink flowers. Produces a minimal amount of fruit. Zones 1–7.

Rubus allegheniensis

Roystonea oleracea

R

Rubus biflorus

☼ ❄ ↔ 10 ft (3 m) ↑ 10 ft (3 m)

Deciduous shrub from China and the Himalayas. Prickly erect stems, white bloom on bare young stems. Leaves pinnate, 3 to 5 leaflets, dark green, white downy undersides. Flowers white, singly or in small clusters, in summer. Yellow edible fruit. Zones 7–9.

Rubus caesius

DEWBERRY

☼ ❄ ↔ 6–12 ft (1.8–3.5 m) ↑ 2–4 ft (0.6–1.2 m)

Creeping deciduous shrub from Europe and northern Asia. Slightly prickly stems. Aromatic, serrated-edged, rather downy, trifoliate foliage, leaflets with 2 to 3 lobes. Relatively large white flowers, in early summer. Edible black berries. Zones 5–9.

Rubus cockburnianus

☼ ❄ ↔ 8 ft (2.4 m) ↑ 8 ft (2.4 m)

Deciduous Chinese shrub. Upright prickly stems with white bloom during colder months. Dark green leaves with 9 egg-shaped leaflets, furry white

undersides. Saucer-shaped pale purple flowers, in racemes, in summer. Un-appetizing black fruit. Zones 6–10.

Rubus crataegifolius

KOREAN RASPBERRY

☼ ❄ ↔ 5 ft (1.5 m) ↑ 8 ft (2.4 m)

Deciduous shrub from temperate East Asia. Leaves deeply lobed, good color in autumn. Small white flowers. Large, juicy, bright red fruits. Uncommon in its own right, but crossed with the common raspberry (R. idaeus) to produce pest-resistant hybrids. Zones 5–9.

Rubus fruticosus

BLACKBERRY

☼ ❄ ↔ 10–25 ft (3–8 m) ↑ 3–6 ft (0.9–1.8 m)

Prickly, scrambling, woody perennial shrub, extremely variable in leaf shape and plant form, from the temperate Northern Hemisphere. Arching entangling stems, up to 25 ft (8 m) long, savage backward-pointing thorns and stout, branching, creeping underground roots. Stems root at tips to form new plants, and new stems grow from bases

Rubus caesius

Rubus crataegifolius

Rubus idaeus 'Heritage'

each year. Compound leaves, 3 to 5 toothed oval leaflets, prickly stalks and midribs. Many-flowered clusters of open, white to pink, 5-petalled flowers, in spring–summer. Red berries turning black when ripe. Can become invasive. Zones 4–7.

Rubus idaeus

RASPBERRY

☼ ❄ ↔ 4 ft (1.2 m) ↑ 5 ft (1.5 m)

Native to Europe, northern Asia, and North America. Deciduous erect shrub, prickly or bristly arching stems. Leaves pinnate, 7 oblong to egg-shaped

Rubus odoratus

Rubus idaeus 'Fallgold'

leaflets. White flowers on axillary or terminal racemes, in spring or summer. Red fruit. R. i. subsp. strigosus has more bristly stems. R. i. 'Amity', large dark red fruit; 'Aureus', low-growing cultivar, yellow fruit; 'Autumn Bliss', high yielding form, large red fruit; 'Chilcotin', large red fruit; 'Fallgold', popular for its early-ripening, large, bright yellow fruit, persisting over a long season, excellent for eating fresh; 'Glen Moy', red summer fruit; 'Heritage', late-bearing cultivar, crops heavily into early autumn, requires fewer hours of chilling than most other raspberries; 'Taylor', mid-sized red fruit. Zones 3–9.

Rubus loganobaccus

LOGANBERRY

☼ ❄ ↔ 2–3 ft (0.6–0.9 m) ↑ 4–6 ft (1.2–1.8 m)

Strongly growing herbaceous shrub developed in California in 1916 by Judge James Harvey Logan by crossing a blackberry, 'Aughinburgh', and a raspberry, 'Red Antwerp'. Vigorous prickly canes; leaves with 3 to 5 leaflets. Ruby red blackberry-shaped berries turn purplish red in early autumn when fully ripe. Zones 4–7.

Rubus occidentalis

BLACKCAP

☼ ❄ ↔ 10 ft (3 m) ↑ 10 ft (3 m)

Native to eastern and central North America. Deciduous shrub, prickly curved stems. Dark green leaves, 5 leaflets on non-flowering stems, 3 leaflets on flowering stems, white felty undersides. White flowers, in corymbs, in summer. Dark purple fruit. 'Brandywine', large purple-red fruit; 'Cumberland', large, glossy, black fruit; 'Jewel', vigorous grower, black fruit; 'Morrison', large black fruit; 'Munger', glossy black fruit; 'Sodus', vigorous form, purple fruit. Zones 3–9.

Rubus odoratus

PURPLE-FLOWERING RASPBERRY, THIMBLEBERRY

☼ ❄ ↔ 8 ft (2.4 m) ↑ 8 ft (2.4 m)

From eastern North America. Deciduous erect shrub, vigorous arching

Rubus biflorus

R

Rubus ulmifolius

Rubus phoenicolasius

stems, peeling bark. Toothed leaves, 5 lobes, hairy undersides. Fragrant lilac-pink flowers, in summer–autumn. Flat reddish orange fruit. '**Albus**', white flowers. Zones 3–9.

Rubus parviflorus
SALMON BERRY, THIMBLEBERRY
☼ ❄ ↔ 10 ft (3 m) ↑ 15 ft (4.5 m)
Native to North America. Robust deciduous shrub, upright stems, peeling bark, no prickles. New growth furry,

Rubus spectabilis

leaves mostly 5-lobed, edges unevenly toothed. White flowers, in corymbs, in summer. Red fruit. Zones 3–9.

Rubus pentalobus
syns *Rubus calycinoides,*
R. fockeanus of gardens
☼ ❄ ↔ 3–7 ft (0.9–2 m) ↑ 4 in (10 cm)
Taiwanese, evergreen, low-growing, spreading shrub. Dark green, 3- to 5-lobed leaves, wrinkled edges, heart-shaped base, paler and often woolly undersides. Solitary white flowers, in summer. Round red fruit. Zones 8–11.

Rubus phoenicolasius
☼ ❄ ↔ 10 ft (3 m) ↑ 10 ft (3 m)
Native to China, Korea, and Japan. Deciduous shrub, spreading stems featuring red bristles. Leaves have 3 leaflets, are broadly egg-shaped, coarsely toothed and lobed, with white felty undersides. Light pink flowers, in terminal racemes, in summer. Red cone-shaped fruit. Zones 5–9.

Rubus rosifolius
MAURITIUS RASPBERRY
☼ ❄ ↔ 10–15 ft (3–4.5 m)
↑ 7–8 ft (2–2.4 m)
Trailing shrub from East and Southeast Asia and Australia. Stems with a few scattered recurved thorns. Leaves divided, up to 7 sharply serrated leaflets. Solitary white flowers, in spring–summer. Small red fruit. '**Coronarius**', double white flowers. Zones 9–11.

Rubus spectabilis
SALMONBERRY
☼ ❄ ↔ 6 ft (1.8 m) ↑ 6 ft (1.8 m)
Native to North America. Deciduous shrub, upright stems, tiny thorns. Leaves have 3 egg-shaped leaflets. Pink to purple solitary flowers, in spring. Egg-shaped pale orange to yellow fruit. Can become invasive. *R. s.* var. *franciscanus*, name sometimes applied to coastal forms from California with hairier leaves. Zones 5–9.

Rubus thibetanus
☼ ❄ ↔ 6–8 ft (1.8–2.4 m)
↑ 6–8 ft (1.8–2.4 m)
Native to western China. Thicket-forming deciduous shrub, prickly stems with white bloom in winter. Leaves fern-like, dark green above, felty white underneath. Red-purple flowers, solitary or in small terminal

Rubus parviflorus

racemes, in summer. Round black fruit. '**Silver Fern**', twig shoots with white bloom, silver-gray leaves, purple flowers, red or black fruit. Zones 6–10.

Rubus tricolor
☼ ❄ ↔ 8–15 ft (2.4–4.5 m)
↑ 24 in (60 cm)
Native to western China. Low-growing evergreen or semi-evergreen shrub, bristly stems. Shiny, dark green leaves, 3-lobed, felty white beneath. White saucer-shaped flowers, singly or in sparsely flowered terminal racemes, in summer. Edible red fruit. Zones 7–9.

Rubus ulmifolius
BRAMBLE
☼ ❄ ↔ 10 ft (3 m) ↑ 8 ft (2.4 m)
Deciduous shrub from central and western Europe. Arching stems, leaves with 3 to 5 leaflets, downy beneath. White to pale pink flowers, in early summer. Purple-red fruits. Zones 7–10.

Rubus ursinus
☼ ❄ ↔ 3–10 ft (0.9–3 m)
↑ 20–36 in (50–90 cm)
Evergreen shrub, native to California, USA. Upright or prostrate habit. Leaves with 3 to 5 leaflets, hairy above, felty white underneath. Male and female flowers on separate plants, white, in prickly corymbs, in spring–summer. Black hairy fruit. Zones 7–9.

Rubus thibetanus cultivar

Rubus rosifolius '*Coronarius*'

Rudbeckia hirta

Rudbeckia fulgida

Rudbeckia fulgida var. *sullivantii*

Rubus Hybrid Cultivars

☀ ❉ ↔ 6–12 ft (1.8–3.5 m) ↕ 2–8 ft (0.6–2.4 m)

Most *Rubus* hybrids have been bred for fruit production, with an emphasis on flavor and vigor. '**Benenden**' ★ (syn. *R. × tridel*), deciduous shrub, vigorously arching canes, pure white flowers, in late spring–early summer; '**Navajo**', North American eating blackberry, bred for warmer climates, thornless canes, heavy crop of smallish black fruit; '**Silvan**', heavy yielding hybrid, large purple fruit; '**Tayberry**', heavy yielding hybrid, sweet, fairly large, highly perfumed fruit, dark red when ripe. Zones 6–9.

RUDBECKIA

BLACK-EYED SUSAN, CONEFLOWER

North American genus of 15 species of perennials in the daisy (Asteraceae) family. Popular in gardens for great hardiness, ease of cultivation, and valuable late-season flower display. Most are fairly bulky plants, over 4 ft (1.2 m) tall, and carry masses of large golden yellow daisies, usually with dark brown to black disc florets. Available in dwarf, double-flowered, and variously colored forms They flower from late summer until cut back by frost. Linnaeus named *Rudbeckia* to honor Olaus Rudbeck (1660–1740), a professor at Uppsala University, who employed the young Linnaeus as a tutor for his 24 children!

CULTIVATION: Plant in a sunny open position with moist well-drained soil. Deadhead to encourage continued blooming. Mildew can occur but usually only late in the season. Propagate by division, from basal cuttings or seed.

Rudbeckia fulgida

BLACK-EYED SUSAN, ORANGE CONEFLOWER

☀/◐ ❉ ↔ 24–48 in (60–120 cm) ↕ 40 in (100 cm)

Perennial from southeastern USA. Lance-shaped leaves, to over 4 in (10 cm) long, often bristly. Flowerheads to nearly 3 in (8 cm) wide, ray florets yellow to orange, disc florets dark purple-brown, in summer–autumn. Several natural varieties, including: *R. f.* var. *deamii*, 24 in (60 cm) tall, hairy pointed oval leaves; *R. f.* var. *speciosa*, 36 in (90 cm) tall, hairy elongated lance-shaped leaves; and *R. f.* var. *sullivantii*, 36 in (90 cm) tall, pointed oval leaves often downy, flowerheads to 4 in (10 cm) wide; '**Goldsturm**', to 24 in (60 cm) tall, slightly larger flowerheads. Zones 4–9.

Rudbeckia 'Herbstsonne'

syn. *Rudbeckia* 'Autumn Sun'

☀ ❉ ↔ 3 ft (0.9 m) ↕ 6 ft (1.8 m)

Vigorous *R. nitida* hybrid, strongly erect habit. Flowerheads to well over 4 in (10 cm) wide, yellow ray florets around a tall, yellow-green cone, in summer–autumn. Zones 3–10.

Rudbeckia hirta

BLACK-EYED SUSAN

☀/◐ ❉ ↔ 32–48 in (80–120 cm) ↕ 5–7 ft (1.5–2 m)

Biennial or short-lived perennial, native to central USA. Dwarf forms often treated as annuals. Narrow, 4 in (10 cm) long, lance-shaped leaves, toothed. Flowerheads to nearly 4 in (10 cm) wide, ray florets yellow, disc florets purple-brown, in summer–autumn. '**Becky Mix**', 10 in (25 cm) tall, mixed color dwarf seedling strain with yellow-, orange-, and red-flowered forms; '**Irish Eyes**' ★, olive green disc florets; '**Marmalade**', 18 in (45 cm) tall, golden orange ray florets; '**Rustic Dwarfs**', 24 in (60 cm) tall, warm shades of gold, orange, terracotta, and red-brown; '**Toto**', 10 in (25 cm) tall, golden yellow ray florets, large deep purple-brown disc florets. Zones 4–9.

Rudbeckia laciniata

CUT-LEAF CONEFLOWER

☀/◐ ❉ ↔ 3–7 ft (0.9–2 m) ↕ 7–10 ft (2–3 m)

Vigorous North American perennial. Leaves deeply lobed to pinnate, tending towards blue-green, often with hairy undersides. Flowerheads to over 5 in (12 cm) wide, ray floret yellow, disc florets yellow-green, in late summer–autumn. '**Goldquelle**' (syn. 'Gold Drop'), 30 in (75 cm) tall, large, yellow, fully double flowerheads; '**Hortensia**' (syn. 'Golden Glow'), 6 ft (1.8 m) tall, yellow double flowerheads. Zones 3–9.

Rudbeckia maxima

☀/◐ ❉ ↔ 24–40 in (60–100 cm) ↕ 3–5 ft (0.9–1.5 m)

Perennial found in central and southern USA. Leaves diamond- to lance-shaped, to over 4 in (10 cm) long. Flowerheads to around 3 in (8 cm) wide, golden yellow ray florets, prominent green and brown central disc, in late summer. Zones 7–10.

Rudbeckia nitida

☀/◐ ❉ ↔ 32–48 in (80–120 cm) ↕ 5–7 ft (1.5–2 m)

North American perennial. Leaves to 6 in (15 cm) long; deeply lobed, almost

Rubus, Hybrid Cultivar, 'Benenden'

to midrib. Flowerheads to 4 in (10 cm) wide, ray florets yellow, disc florets yellow-green, in late summer–autumn. Zones 3–9.

Rudbeckia occidentalis

☀/◐ ❉ ↔ 32–48 in (80–120 cm) ↕ 5–7 ft (1.5–2 m)

Perennial from western USA. Pointed oval leaves, to over 4 in (10 cm) long, sometimes toothed. Flowerheads to over 3 in (8 cm) wide, yellow ray florets, central cone brown-black, to over 2 in (5 cm) high, in summer. '**Green Wizard**', no ray florets but elongated bright green sepals around a large near-black disc. Zones 7–10.

Rudbeckia triloba

BROWN-EYED SUSAN

☀/◐ ❉ ↔ 24–40 in (60–100 cm) ↕ 3–5 ft (0.9–1.5 m)

Perennial from eastern central USA. Leaves 3- to 7-lobed, to over 4 in (10 cm) long, bristly. Flowerheads to about 3 in (8 cm) wide, ray florets golden yellow, disc florets brown to purple-black, in summer. Zones 5–9.

RUELLIA

Mostly from tropical and subtropical regions, with a few species in temperate North America, this is a genus containing some 150 species of evergreen perennials and soft-stemmed shrubs, belonging to the acanthus

Rubus, Hybrid Cultivar, 'Tayberry'

Rubus, Hybrid Cultivar, 'Navajo'

(Acanthaceae) family. They are grown either indoors or out for their showy funnelform flowers, usually red, pink, or mauve, that may occur singly, or in dense terminal panicles or axillary clusters. The attractive, smooth-edged, oblong to lance-shaped leaves have prominent veins.

CULTIVATION: Although some species from temperate America are quite frost hardy, most need a warm climate and a fertile, moist, well-drained soil in partial shade. In cooler areas they are grown indoors or in a greenhouse. Water potted specimens adequately during the growing season and keep just moist during winter. Trim excess growth regularly and especially after flowering to maintain density of foliage. Propagation is from seed or softwood cuttings in spring.

Ruellia brittoniana
COMMON RUELLIA

☼ ❄ ↔ 18–24 in (45–60 cm)
↑ 24–36 in (60–90 cm)

Upright evergreen perennial shrub from Mexico and southwestern USA.

Rumex hymenosepalus

Ruellia portellae

Purple fleshy stems; lower branches drooping over with age and taking root. The narrow, sword-shaped, serrated, dark green leaves have prominent purple veins. The funnel-shaped, purple or blue, petunia-like flowers, 2 in (5 cm) long, in leaf axils, last from mid-spring until the first autumn frosts. *R. brittoniana* dies back in winter and self-seeds aggressively. 'Alba' (syn. 'Clean White Katie'), a low-growing form, up to 8 in (20 cm) high, white flowers throughout summer; 'Chi Chi', 24–36 in (60–90 cm) tall, pale pink flowers throughout summer; 'Katie' (dwarf blue bells), low-growing form, 6–8 in (15–20 cm) high, purple flowers all summer; 'Texas Blue', up to 10 in (25 cm) tall, purple summer flowers. Zones 8–11.

Ruellia macrantha
CHRISTMAS PRIDE

☼ ❄ ↔ 20 in (50 cm) ↑ 6 ft (1.8 m)

This short-lived species is native to Brazil. Erect stems, rounded crown of hairy, dark green, oval to lance-shaped leaves. Large, deep pink, trumpet-shaped flowers, with spreading rounded lobes and darker veins, in winter. Zones 10–12.

Ruellia makoyana
MONKEY PLANT, TRAILING VELVET PLANT

☼ ✦ ↔ 15–18 in (38–45 cm)
↑ 6–12 in (15–30 cm)

Perennial native to Brazil. This species has a spreading habit with trailing branching stems. Variegated velvet-textured leaves are 2–3 in (5–8 cm) long, veined with white above and purple underneath. Brilliant reddish purple trumpet-shaped flowers, up to 2 in (5 cm) across, growing from leaf axils, appear all year round, but mostly from the autumn through to spring. Zones 10–12.

Ruellia macrantha

Ruellia peninsularis
DESERT RUELLIA

☼ ✦ ↔ 4–5 ft (1.2–1.5 m)
↑ 4–5 ft (1.2–1.5 m)

From southern half of Baja California peninsula and coastal Sonora state, northwest Mexico. Fast-growing evergreen shrub; rounded habit. Whitish gray stems; small glossy green leaves. Deep blue-purple flowers, 1 in (25 mm) in diameter, in spring–early summer, with occasional flowering throughout year. Zones 10–11.

Ruellia portellae

☼ ✦ ↔ 12–40 in (30–100 cm)
↑ 8–12 in (20–30 cm)

Prostrate annual or perennial from Brazil. Branching stems; glossy green white-veined leaves, 3 in (8 cm) long, reddish purple beneath. Pink bell-shaped flowers, 1½ in (35 mm) long, in spring–summer. Zones 10–12.

RUMEX
DOCK, SORREL

This genus of some 200 species of annuals, biennials, and often tap-rooted perennials belongs to the knotweed (Polygonaceae) family. Its members are found worldwide, in most countries with temperate climates. The leaves are usually basal and the normally small flowers are produced in terminal racemes or spikes. The seeds are enclosed in a papery membrane that allows them to float. Although some species are ornamental and some are edible, this genus also includes some dreadfully weedy species that have hitchhiked around the world with human travelers.

Ruellia peninsularis

CULTIVATION: Most species do best in a deep, fertile, and moist to even damp soil in full sun. Propagation is usually from seed, which will often self-sow; root cuttings are another option.

Rumex acetosa
GARDEN SORREL, SOUR DOCK

☼ ❄ ↔ 12–16 in (30–40 cm)
↑ 20–40 in (50–100 cm)

Clumping Northern Hemisphere perennia, can be weedy. Slightly succulent, bright green, spearhead-shaped leaves, to 6 in (15 cm) long, eaten as salad or cooked. Panicles of tiny red-brown flowers, in spring. Zones 3–10.

Rumex hymenosepalus
CANAIGRE, GANAGRA, TANNER'S DOCK, WILD RHUBARB

☼ ❄ ↔ 20–27 in (50–70 cm)
↑ 36–40 in (90–100 cm)

North American perennial. Spearhead-shaped leaves, to 12 in (30 cm) long, with slightly undulating edge. Flowers in upright panicles, turn from green to deep pink, in spring–summer. Brown seeds. Zones 6–10.

Rumex sanguineus

BLOODY DOCK, RED-VEINED DOCK

☀ ❄ ↔ 10–12 in (25–30 cm)
↑ 36–40 in (90–100 cm)

An attractive clumping species native to Europe, southwest Asia, and northern Africa. Dark stems, lance-shaped leaves, to 6 in (15 cm) long, beetroot red veins. Panicles of tiny green flowers, in early to mid-summer. Brown seeds. Zones 6–10.

Rumex scutatus

BUCKLER-LEAFED SORREL, FRENCH SORREL, GARDEN SORREL

☀ ❄ ↔ 12–16 in (30–40 cm)
↑ 16–18 in (40–45 cm)

Hardy clump-forming perennial native to Europe, western Asia, and northern Africa. Bright green spearhead-shaped leaves. Spikes of tiny green flowers, in summer. Brown seeds. Edible, and used in the famous sorrel soup. Zones 6–10.

Rumex vesicarius

☀ ❄ ↔ 6–8 in (15–20 cm)
↑ 8–10 in (20–25 cm)

Annual species from northern Africa and southwest Asia. Fleshy spearhead-shaped leaves, to ¾ in (18 mm) long. Produces tiny deep pink flowers, in panicles, in late spring. Creamy brown seeds. Zones 6–10.

Ruscus aculeatus

Rumex vesicarius (foreground), Docker River, Western Australia

RUMOHRA

This genus of 50 species of terrestrial or epiphytic ferns is sometimes placed in the haresfoot-fern (Davalliaceae) family, and sometimes in the shield-fern (Dryopteridaceae) family. Native to the Southern Hemisphere, they have creeping rhizomes covered in brown scales from which, at irregular intervals, they produce their large, finely divided, leathery fronds. They are often seen growing on the trunks of tree ferns in their native haunts.
CULTIVATION: In all but almost frost-free climates these ferns make good indoor or greenhouse pot or basket subjects. Given an aspect in light shade and a humid atmosphere with moist but not wet soil they will make quite large colonies. Propagation is by careful division of the rhizomes or by raising spores.

Rumohra adiantiformis

IRON FERN, LEATHER FERN, LEATHERLEAF FERN

☀ ⚘ ↔ 36–60 in (90–150 cm)
↑ 20–60 in (50–150 cm)

From tropical to temperate climates in Southern Hemisphere. Far-reaching brown rhizomes; fronds variable in size depending on conditions, to 24 in (60 cm) long, deep green with leathery triangular leaflets. Zones 10–11.

RUSCHIA

This large genus of about 400 perennial species, from the drier parts of southern Africa, belongs to the ice-plant (Aizoaceae) family. The plants are succulent shrubs or ground covers, with dark reddish brown internodes, some branches bearing spines derived from sterile portions of the flower-heads. Leaves in a pair are free to united, the free parts 3-angled to round in cross-section. Flowers may be solitary or in branched flowerheads; they have purple, pink, or sometimes white petals.
CULTIVATION: These plants need full sun and thrive in poor well-drained soils. Propagate from stem cuttings, which can be rooted at almost any time of year.

Ruschia caroli

PURPLE DEW PLANT

☀ ⚘ ↔ 12–18 in (30–45 cm)
↑ 8–12 in (20–30 cm)

Succulent ground-covering perennial from coastal western South Africa. Leaves up to 4 in (10 cm) long. Purple flowers, up to 1 in (25 mm) across, in early spring–summer. Zones 10–11.

Ruschia dichroa

ICE PLANT

☀ ⚘ ↔ 12–16 in (30–40 cm)
↑ 8–12 in (20–30 cm)

Succulent perennial from coastal western South Africa. Leaves up to 2½ in (6 cm) long. Purple, white, or pink flowers, 1¾ in (4 cm) across, in summer. Zones 10–11.

Ruschia perfoliata

☀ ⚘ ↔ 12–20 in (30–50 cm)
↑ 6–12 in (15–30 cm)

Succulent, perennial, cushion-forming ground cover, native to South Africa. Wiry branching stems. Fleshy thick leaves with sharp tips, sheathed at stems and united at base. Solitary, terminal, purple to pink, daisy-like flowers, 1 in (25 mm) wide, in early spring–summer. Zones 10–11.

Ruschia pulvinaris

☀ ❄ ↔ 10–18 in (25–45 cm)
↑ 4–10 in (10–25 cm)

Low growing, spreading, succulent subshrub from the mountains of South Africa. Small, fleshy, toothed, bluish green leaves. Red to rose pink daisy-like flowers, in summer. Zones 6–8.

RUSCUS

Genus of about 6 species of evergreen subshrubs from the Mediterranean region belonging to the asparagus

Ruschia caroli

Ruschia dichroa

Ruschia pulvinaris

(Asparagaceae) family. These plants form clumps, spreading slowly by underground rhizomes. Their leaves are more correctly called "cladodes," which are flattened stems that function as a leaf. The real leaf is a small protuberance on the surface of the cladode, from whence emerge the tiny greenish or white starry flowers. These are followed by red pea-sized fruits if both male and female plants are present. Some forms appear to be hermaphroditic. In former times, butchers used bunches of one species to sweep down their chopping blocks, hence the common name of butcher's broom.
CULTIVATION: These plants are very hardy and particularly good in dry shade. Grow in well-drained soil in full sun to half-sun. Propagate from seed or by division.

Ruscus aculeatus

BUTCHER'S BROOM

☀/◑ ❄ ↔ 40 in (100 cm)
↑ 30–40 in (75–100 cm)

Native to southern Europe and the Mediterranean region. Clumping subshrub spreading by rhizomes. Small, oval-shaped, dark green, leathery cladodes, ¾–1¼ in (18–30 mm) long, with prickly tips. Bright red berries appear in summer–winter. Zones 6–11.

Ruscus hypoglossum

☀/◑ ❄ ↔ 40 in (100 cm)
↑ 18–26 in (45–65 cm)

From southern Europe and elsewhere in the Mediterranean region. Clumping subshrub that spreads by rhizomes. Cladodes are oval-shaped, mid-green, to 4 in (10 cm) long. Arching stems. The green flowers and red fruit are borne on a cladode under a tongue-like leaf. Zones 7–11.

RUSPOLIA

The 4 species of evergreen shrubs in this genus, which is a member of the acanthus (Acanthaceae) family, are native to Africa. They have oval opposite leaves and bear spikes or panicles of flowers in shades of red or yellow with flaring petal lobes.
CULTIVATION: In cool climates, species of *Ruspolia* make attractive flowering shrubs for the conservatory or greenhouse where they should be shaded during the hottest part of the day. In very warm and tropical climates, grow outdoors in a humus-rich soil. Propagate from softwood cuttings taken in late spring.

Ruspolia hypocrateriformis

☀ ✦ ↔ 3 ft (0.9 m) ↕ 3 ft (0.9 m)
Small shrub from tropical and southern Africa; semi-trailing habit. Smooth leaves, to 3 in (8 cm) long. Tubular flowers, deep reddish pink, darker throat, in showy terminal panicles, over many months. Zones 10–12.

RUSSELIA

This genus of about 50 evergreen subshrubs and shrubs found from Mexico to Colombia is a member of the foxglove (Scrophulariaceae) family. The commonly grown species has arching stems, but *Russelia* species vary in habit and may be erect, arching, or spreading. They also vary in foliage, some species having much-reduced, scale-like leaves, others having heart-shaped leaves up to 4 in (10 cm) long. The flowers, however, are more distinctive, being flared pendulous tubes that appear through much of the year.
CULTIVATION: These plants are marginally frost tender and perform best in a mild climate. They flower most

Ruta graveolens

heavily when grown in full sun, and they prefer a gritty well-drained soil that can be kept moist in the warmer months. Trim lightly to encourage a neat bushy habit. Propagation is usually from cuttings or by removing self-rooted layers.

Russelia equisetiformis
CORAL PLANT

☀ ✤ ↔ 8 ft (2.4 m) ↕ 5 ft (1.5 m)
Native to Mexico. Arching weeping stems, leafless or nearly so, leaves reduced to small scales, closely held to wiry green stems. Small, bright red, tubular flowers, throughout the year. Great spillover plant for a wall or a bank. Zones 9–12.

RUTA

This genus of 8 species belongs to the rue (Rutaceae) family. Mostly subshrubs, some species can become shrubby in mild climates. The genus, found throughout temperate Eurasia, is the source of several herbs that since ancient times have been used both medicinally and in the manufacture of beverages. The foliage is a grayish blue-green and finely divided. Small yellow flowers in cymose heads appear in the summer and are followed by rather insignificant greenish seed heads.
CULTIVATION: These plants are very easily grown in any well-drained soil, preferably in full sun. Established plants may be trimmed to shape, but

Ruspolia hypocrateriformis

Russelia equisetiformis

Ruttya fruticosa 'Scholesii'

hard pruning is seldom necessary. Propagation is from seed or from half-hardened cuttings.

Ruta graveolens ★
COMMON RUE, HERB OF GRACE, RUE

☀ ✤ ↔ 15 in (38 cm) ↕ 20 in (50 cm)
Subshrub or shrub from southern Europe. Glaucous stems and leaves, finely divided foliage, rounded to lance-shaped leaflets, wavy edges. Heads of tiny greenish yellow flowers, in summer. *R. graveolens* has a strong, but rather musty, fragrance. During the Middle Ages, carrying sprigs of rue was believed to protect one from catching lice and diseases. Treat this species with caution as it is toxic and can become weedy. Several foliage cultivars include: 'Jackman's Blue' ★, very glaucous form; 'Variegata', creamy white-edged foliage. Zones 5–9.

RUTTYA

Genus in the acanthus (Acanthaceae) family containing 3 species of evergreen shrubs that are native to tropical areas of eastern Africa. They have oval opposite leaves and bear colorful tubular flowers on short spikes.

Ruttya fruticosa

CULTIVATION: In tropical and subtropical climates these plants are easily grown in a fertile well-drained soil, and are ideal for shrub borders. In cooler climates they make attractive flowering plants for the greenhouse or conservatory. Young plants should be pinched out to encourage bushiness. Propagation is from seed or from half-hardened cuttings.

Ruttya fruticosa
JAMMY-MOUTH

☀ ✤ ↔ 5 ft (1.5 m) ↕ 12 ft (3.5 m)
Bushy shrub native to eastern Africa. Leaves are oval. Flowers, which appear over several months, are in terminal spikes, with the petals fused into 2 lips; they are orangey red, the lower lip marked by a dark brown blotch. 'Scholesii' ★, yellow flowers, the lower lip marked with a black blotch. Zones 10–12.

R

S

Sabal palmetto

Sabal mexicana

Sabal bermudana

Sabal causiarum

Sabal uresana

SABAL

PALMETTO

This genus in the palm (Arecaceae) family consists of around 16 species found from southeastern USA to South America, the West Indies, and Bermuda. They mostly have tall erect trunks, but some species are stemless; some have old frond bases remaining, others are clean. All species have fan-shaped fronds that are deeply divided. The small cream flowers are bisexual, and are borne in long sprays growing from between the leaves; they are followed by small berries. The leaves of some species are used for making baskets, hats, and matting; the trunks are used to produce furniture and wharf piles. Most palmetto palms are found growing in swampy areas in the subtropics and tropics.

CULTIVATION: Most Sabal species are fairly adaptable palms that tolerate a range of soils, from wet to dry, as well as sandy; they even tolerate light frost. The best cultivation results, however, come from planting in a well-drained fertile soil in full sun, with adequate watering in the growth phase. Propagation is from seed.

Sabal bermudana

BERMUDA PALMETTO

☀ ❄ ↔ 10 ft (3 m) ↕ 40 ft (12 m)

Native to Bermuda, smaller in cultivation than the species. Fronds to 10 ft (3 m) wide, 24 in (60 cm) segments, central section around 12 in (30 cm) wide, undivided. Zones 10–11.

Sabal causiarum

PUERTO RICO HAT PALM

☀ ❄ ↔ 20 ft (6 m) ↕ 50 ft (15 m)

From West Indies islands of Anegada, Hispaniola, and Puerto Rico. Tall, stout, gray trunk. Heavy crown of bright green, sometimes dull blue-green fan-like fronds to 10 ft (3 m) wide. White flowers in sprays. Small, spherical, black fruits. Zones 9–12.

Sabal mexicana

MEXICAN PALMETTO, OAXACA PALMETTO, RIO GRANDE PALMETTO

☀ ❄ ↔ 12 ft (3.5 m) ↕ 60 ft (18 m)

Adaptable species from Texas, USA, and Mexico. Thick trunk, crown of light green fronds. Blades have deeply divided thread-like filaments. Inflorescence of small, white, fragrant flowers. Large black fruits. Zones 9–12.

Sabal minor ★

DWARF PALMETTO, SCRUB PALMETTO

☀ ❄ ↔ 12 ft (3.5 m) ↕ 10 ft (3 m)

From southeastern USA. May form large clump of fronds at ground-level, or above-ground trunk. Large, stiff, blue-green fronds, narrow segments. Flower stalk grows from clump, extending well above foliage. Zones 8–11.

Sabal palmetto ★

CABBAGE PALM, PALMETTO

☀ ❄ ↔ 15 ft (4.5 m) ↕ 80 ft (24 m)

From southeastern USA. Mature trunk bare. Large crown of twisted green to blue-green fan fronds, divided into segments, deeply lobed, thread-like filaments between. Inflorescences of small white flowers. Glossy brown to black fruits. Zones 8–12.

Sabal uresana

SONORAN PALMETTO

☀ ❄ ↔ 10 ft (3 m) ↕ 25 ft (8 m)

Eye-catching palm from Mexico. Large bluish green fan fronds, deeply divided into spreading segments; juvenile leaves bluer. Inflorescence as long as fronds. Brown fruits. Zones 8–12.

SACCHARUM

syn. Erianthus

This genus contains around 40 species of clumping or rhizomatous perennial grasses in the family Poaceae. Native to tropical and warm temperate regions worldwide, they grow by riversides and in rich soils in valleys. Their strong, cane-like, jointed stems are green to violet, with exposed roots near the base. Their long flat leaves are arranged in 2 ranks, and the tiny flowers are borne in attractive fluffy panicles. One species, S. officinarum, is a major crop from which several products are made, including sugar cane, rum, molasses, and wax. The genus is also host to a parasite, Aeginetia indica, which has purple flowers.

CULTIVATION: In cool temperate climates grow in the greenhouse in beds or large containers of rich damp loam. In warm regions grow outdoors in rich moist soil in full sun. These plants can be invasive in ideal conditions. Propagate from seed, or, more usually, from stem cuttings.

Saccharum officinarum

SUGAR CANE

☀ ❄ ↔ 3–6 ft (0.9–1.8 m) ↕ 12–20 ft (3.5–6 m)

Believed to have originated from New Guinea, where it hybridized and later spread to tropical Asia. Stout upright juicy canes to 2 in (5 cm) thick. Rich green leaves up to 6 ft (1.8 m) long have roughened edges. Tall flowering plumes in summer. Zones 9–12.

Saccharum ravennae

syn. Erianthus ravennae

PLUME GRASS, RAVENNA GRASS

☀ ❄ ↔ 40 in (100 cm) ↕ 10–15 ft (3–4.5 m)

Upright, decorative, dominant grass from southern Europe. Green leaf blades with a white stripe. Silver plumes, in late summer, turning gray with maturity. Do not plant in heavy clay soils. Zones 5–9.

Saccharum officinarum

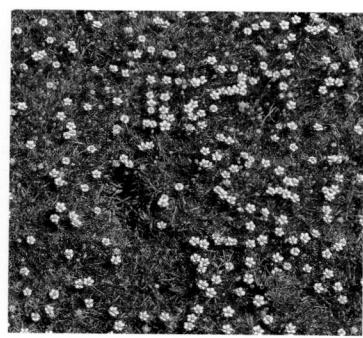

Sagina subulata

Sagina subulata 'Aurea'

SACCOLABIOPSIS

This genus contains about 8 mono-podial epiphytic species in the family Orchidaceae, related to *Sarcochilus*, from northern Australia, New Guinea, and Indonesia. They often grow on the edges of rainforests as twig epi-phytes, rarely on the trunks or main branches of trees. The small plants have leaves in 2 ranks and a network of coarse wiry roots. They produce short spikes of mainly green flowers that face the apex of the inflorescence. CULTIVATION: These plants resent having their roots covered, so are best mounted on long narrow sections of cork. They are ideally kept in a part-shaded position in a warm humid environment, with plenty of free cir-culating air. They are not easy to maintain in cultivation.

Saccolabiopsis armitii

☀ ✿ ↔ 2½–6 in (6–15 cm)
↑ 2½–8 in (6–20 cm)

From North Queensland, Australia. Pendent spikes, up to 50 tiny yellow-ish green blooms, crowded on in-florescence, in summer. Zones 11–12.

SADLERIA

This genus of 4 species of medium to large terrestrial ferns in the hard-fern (Blechnaceae) family is restricted to Hawaii, USA, and is generally found on lava in the wild. The stem is erect and trunk-like with age, with long, undivided scales. The fronds are pin-nate, lobed, or bipinnate; the leaf stalks have at least one groove. The leaf segments are firm, veined, ovate to tongue-shaped, with a scalloped to smooth edge, slightly recurved, and hairless or with scales beneath. The spore-bodies form continuous lines along both sides of the midrib. CULTIVATION: Grow in acid soils in frost-free humid sites, in shade, with no more than 6 hours' sun each day; keep moist year round. In temperate regions, grow under glass in a soil-less medium rich in crocks (although they are too big for all but the largest greenhouses). Propagate from spores.

Sadleria cyatheoides ★

☀ ✿ ↔ 2–4 ft (0.6–1.2 m)
↑ 2–5 ft (0.6–1.5 m)

Small tree fern, can form sizeable trunk with age. Emerging fronds pinkish red, becoming dark green and leathery. Leaflets have toothed margins. Zones 10–12.

SAGINA

PEARLWORT

This Northern Hemisphere genus contains approximately 20 species of annual and perennial, ground-covering, mat-forming plants, which grow on rocky outcrops. Members of the pink (Caryophyllaceae) family, many of the species in this genus are garden weeds, and can be extremely difficult to eradicate because of their highly developed reproductive system. Their fine linear leaves are arranged in pairs, and they quickly form dense mats of growth that cover both soil and rocky areas. CULTIVATION: Pearlworts do not like prolonged periods of hot dry weather; they prefer low temperatures and cool free-draining soils, with full sun or part-shade. Some of the golden forms of pearlwort will die if temperatures exceed 86°F (30°C). These plants can be propagated very easily, either from seed in spring or by division at any time of year.

Sagina subulata

GOLDEN PEARLWORT

☀/☀ ❄ ↔ 12 in (30 cm) ↑ 1 in (25 mm)

Mat-forming perennial from central Europe. The plants have soft foliage,

Saccolabiopsis armitii

and form dense ground-covering mounds, which bear solitary white flowers in summer. 'Aurea', lime green to canary yellow foliage. Zones 4–7.

SAGITTARIA

ARROWHEAD

This genus of some 30 mostly peren-nial species is distributed throughout the world, but particularly in the Americas. It belongs to the family Alismataceae. *Sagittaria* species are aquatic plants, usually with flowers of a single sex on the same plant. Some have rhizomes or runners; many have tubers, which are sometimes edible. The leaves are smooth-edged, and are borne below, on, or above the water. The flowerheads are erect, floating, or submerged, in racemes or panicles, rarely umbel-like. The 3-petalled flowers are white, sometimes with a pink spot. Fruits are compressed achenes, with a conspicuous dorsal wing and sometimes lateral wings. CULTIVATION: They are grown as marshy garden or pond-edge plants.

They can also be grown in deep fast-flowing water, and will tolerate light shade. Weighted tubers thrown into water to 24 in (60 cm) deep will grow well. Propagate by division in spring.

Sagittaria graminea

☀ ❄ ↔ 12 in (30 cm) ↑ 20 in (50 cm)

Cormous aquatic perennial from eastern USA. Narrow, strap-like, sub-merged leaves, emergent leaves being wider and pointed. Upright flowering stems bear whorls of white 3-petalled male flowers above small, green, petal-less female flowers. *S. g.* var. *platy-phylla*, flowers have longer beaks. Zones 6–12.

Sagittaria sagittifolia

ARROWHEAD

☀ ❄ ↔ 12 in (30 cm)
↑ 24–36 in (60–90 cm)

Aquatic perennial found throughout temperate Eurasia. Large arrowhead-shaped leaves, variable width, very long pointed lobes. White flowers, often purple basal spots. Cultivated in Asia for its edible tuber. Zones 7–12.

Sadleria cyatheoides

SAINTPAULIA

AFRICAN VIOLET

Discovered by Walter von Saint Paul, a botanically inclined soldier in the former German colony of Tanganyika in Africa. He sent the seeds to Germany where they were cultivated by his father and presented to the Royal Botanic Gardens at Herrenhausen. A genus of 20 perennials from tropical East Africa, it belongs to the African violet (Gesneriaceae) family. Only a few species are cultivated, most of those grown being cultivars or hybrids. They are soft-stemmed rosette-forming plants with finely hairy rounded leaves that have toothed edges and long stalks. The velvety 5-petalled flowers appear in clusters at the center of the rosettes throughout the year. CULTIVATION: Rarely grown outdoors, even in the tropics, African violets prefer constant temperatures, moderate to high humidity, and fertile, moist, humus-rich soil. They need bright but not sunny conditions. Propagate from leaf-petiole cuttings. The seed is very fine, and is cultured rather like orchid seed.

Saintpaulia ionantha

AFRICAN VIOLET, USAMBARA VIOLET

☀ ✿ ↔ 8–16 in (20–40 cm)
↕ 4–10 in (10–25 cm)

Tanzanian native perennial. Rounded to heart-shaped, downy, wavy-edged or softly toothed leaves. Flowers pale lavender to purple or white, with violet throat, in sprays above foliage, 8 to 10 blooms per head. Zones 11–12.

Saintpaulia shumensis

☀ ✿ ↔ 6–10 in (15–25 cm)
↕ 2–6 in (5–15 cm)

From Tanzania. Hairy, slightly glossy, rounded, serrated to toothed leaves, undersides often red-tinted. Heads of up to 5 flowers to over 2 in (5 cm) wide, white to pale mauve, sometimes with darker markings. Zones 11–12.

Saintpaulia Hybrid Cultivars

☀ ✿ ↔ 4–12 in (10–30 cm)
↕ 2–8 in (5–20 cm)

All the plants in this group are commonly known as hybrids, but most of the widely grown and popular African violets are in fact cultivars of *S. ionantha* (although some are true hybrids between *S. ionantha* and other species, such as *S. shumensis*). The attractive flowers of these compact, lavishly foliaged, long-flowering plants range in color from mainly pink to purple, but may also come in white, in near-red shades, and in yellow. 'Akira', lush dark foliage, deep crimson flowers; 'Chantiana', dwarf form, bright pink double flowers; 'Chimera Monique', dwarf form, white flowers with dark purple edges; 'Concord', deep maroon flowers, white edges; 'Diana', very dark foliage, deep red velvety flowers; 'Dorothy', pink flowers with fine white edges; 'Emi', very profuse pale mauve flowers with light edges; 'Hisako', deep purple-blue flowers with fine white edges; 'Irish Flirt', white flowers suffused with green, double; 'Jolita', dwarf form, lavender double flowers; 'Melodie Kimi', purple upper petal, white lower petals with broad purple edges; 'Milky Way Trail', pure white flowers; 'Optimara Colorado', bright purplish red flowers; 'Patty', purple-red and white flowers; 'Rococo Pink', dusky dark pink flowers, semi-double; 'Shades of Autumn', cream variegated foliage, ruffled pink and mauve flowers, semi-double; 'Zoja', purple-blue flowers with white edges, semi-double. Zones 11–12.

Saintpaulia, HC, 'Akira'

Saintpaulia, HC, 'Arctic Frost'

Saintpaulia, HC, 'Bellita'

Saintpaulia, HC, 'Blue Lagoon'

Saintpaulia, HC, 'Blush Pink'

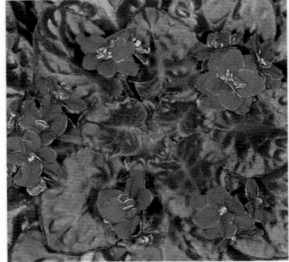
Saintpaulia, HC, 'Bob Serbin'

Saintpaulia, HC, 'Chantarolo'

Saintpaulia, HC, 'Chantiana'

Saintpaulia, HC, 'Classic Rock'

S., HC, 'Colonial Mr Remarkable'

S., HC, 'Colonial Port Fairy'

S., HC, 'Colonial Roseworthy'

Saintpaulia, HC, 'Crinkled Blue'

S., HC, 'Chimera Monique'

Saintpaulia, HC, 'Dorothy'

Saintpaulia, HC, 'Emi'

Saintpaulia, HC, 'Gundi'

Saintpaulia, HC, 'Harbor Blue'

Saintpaulia, HC, 'Hisako'

Saintpaulia, HC, 'I Feel Pretty'

S

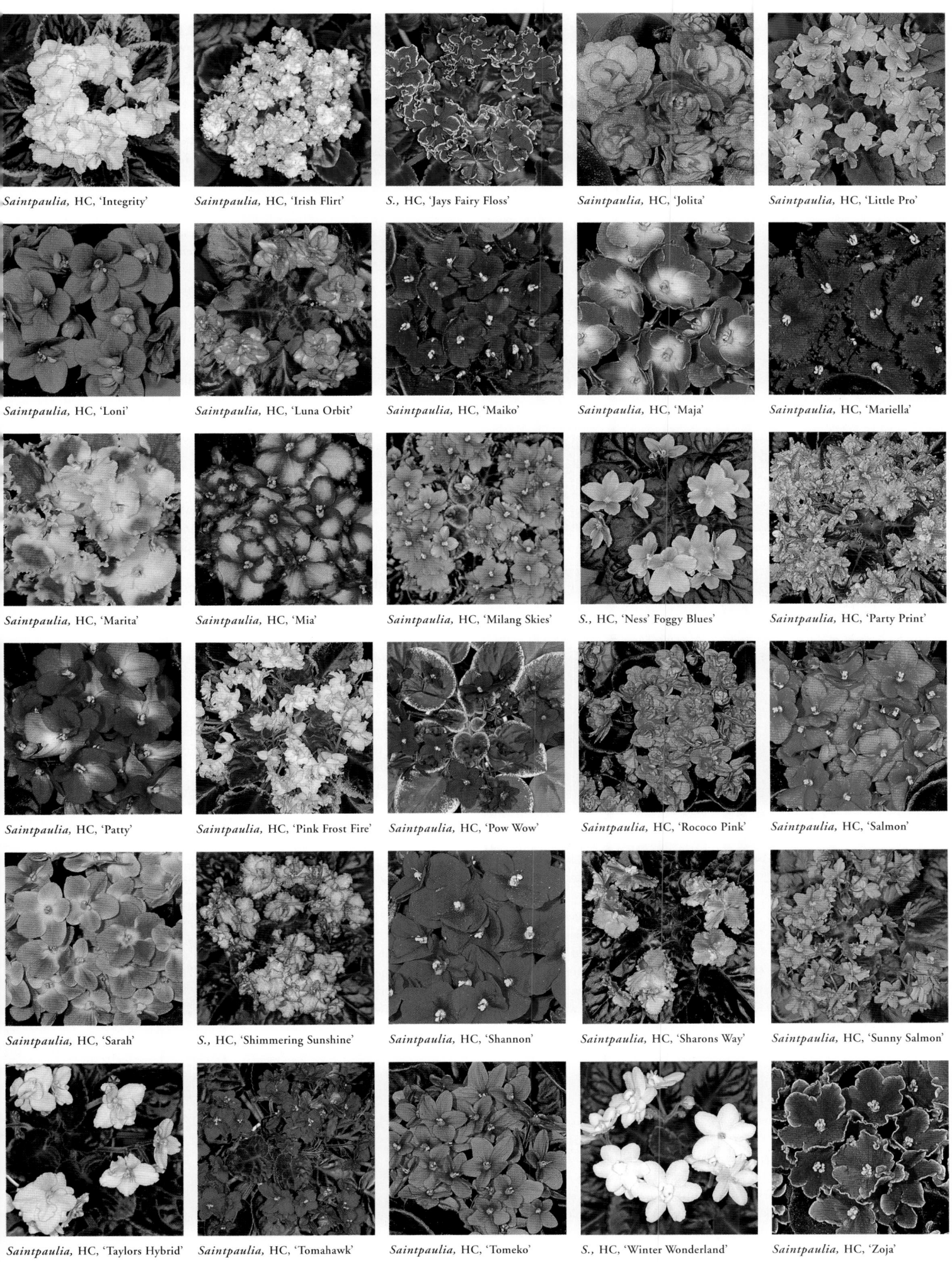

Saintpaulia, HC, 'Integrity'

Saintpaulia, HC, 'Irish Flirt'

S., HC, 'Jays Fairy Floss'

Saintpaulia, HC, 'Jolita'

Saintpaulia, HC, 'Little Pro'

Saintpaulia, HC, 'Loni'

Saintpaulia, HC, 'Luna Orbit'

Saintpaulia, HC, 'Maiko'

Saintpaulia, HC, 'Maja'

Saintpaulia, HC, 'Mariella'

Saintpaulia, HC, 'Marita'

Saintpaulia, HC, 'Mia'

Saintpaulia, HC, 'Milang Skies'

S., HC, 'Ness' Foggy Blues'

Saintpaulia, HC, 'Party Print'

Saintpaulia, HC, 'Patty'

Saintpaulia, HC, 'Pink Frost Fire'

Saintpaulia, HC, 'Pow Wow'

Saintpaulia, HC, 'Rococo Pink'

Saintpaulia, HC, 'Salmon'

Saintpaulia, HC, 'Sarah'

S., HC, 'Shimmering Sunshine'

Saintpaulia, HC, 'Shannon'

Saintpaulia, HC, 'Sharons Way'

Saintpaulia, HC, 'Sunny Salmon'

Saintpaulia, HC, 'Taylors Hybrid'

Saintpaulia, HC, 'Tomahawk'

Saintpaulia, HC, 'Tomeko'

S., HC, 'Winter Wonderland'

Saintpaulia, HC, 'Zoja'

S

Salix alba, Lake Tekapo, New Zealand

Salix amygdaloides

Salix babylonica f. *pekinensis*

SALIX

OSIER, WILLOW

This large genus in the willow (Salicaceae) family consists of around 400 species, most from cold and temperate Northern Hemisphere regions. The genus consists of trees through to creeping shrublets, mostly deciduous, with leaves often lance-shaped and toothed. The small flowers are usually insect-pollinated and are borne in a catkin, and male and female flowers often appear on separate trees. The capsular fruits contain wind-dispersed hairy seeds. Many willows are widely grown for their timber, used for basketry and cricket bats. The bark has been used medicinally, as it contains salicin, from which aspirin is derived.

They are valued ornamentally, particularly the weeping species, which are attractive when planted near water. CULTIVATION: Most are fairly adaptable if adequately watered during growth and the soil is well drained, not swampy. Propagate from seed, by layering, or from cuttings, which root easily even up to branch size.

Salix acutifolia

CASPIAN WILLOW, SHARP-LEAFED WILLOW

☼ ❄ ↔ 30 ft (9 m) ↑ 25 ft (8 m)

Shrubby willow, found from Russia to temperate East Asia. Gray bark, contrasting red-brown young twigs. Leaves narrow, dark green, bluish undersides. Conspicuous, silky, white catkins, in spring. '**Blue Streak**', dark

S. babylonica f. *pekinensis* '**Tortuosa**' (center rear)

branches, powdery blue-white bloom; '**Pendulifolia**', tree-like, to 20 ft (6 m) tall, pendulous branches. Zones 5–9.

Salix alba

WHITE WILLOW

☼ ❄ ↔ 30 ft (9 m) ↑ 80 ft (24 m)

Broadly columnar tree, native to western Asia and Europe. Drooping branch tips, dark gray deeply fissured bark. Narrow lance-shaped leaves, silky and white when young; dark green above, bluish green beneath with age. Thin catkins, with leaves, in spring. '**Vitellina**', bright yellow young shoots prominent in winter. Zones 2–10.

Salix amygdaloides

PEACH-LEAFED WILLOW

☼ ❄ ↔ 25 ft (8 m) ↑ 70 ft (21 m)

Tree, native to western North America. Young growth is smooth and yellow or reddish brown. The oval to lance-shaped leaves have finely serrated margins, are bluish or grayish green beneath, and downy when young. Female catkins to 4 in (10 cm). Zones 5–10.

Salix arctica

ARCTIC WILLOW

☼ ❄ ↔ 24–48 in (60–120 cm) ↑ 4 in (10 cm)

Creeping shrub, native to higher latitudes of Europe, Asia, and North America. Thick glossy twigs, leathery oval leaves networked with veins. Dark purple catkins. Zones 1–8.

Salix caprea '**Pendula**'

Salix babylonica

PEKING WILLOW, WEEPING WILLOW

☼ ❄ ↔ 35 ft (10 m) ↑ 40 ft (12 m)

Native to northern China; brought to Middle East via trade routes, then to Europe in the 1700s. Most planted trees belong to single female clone. Long vertically pendulous branches; leaves tapering to long fine point, finely toothed, smooth, bluish-gray beneath. Non-weeping ancestral Chinese trees are named *S. b. f. pekinensis* (syn. *S. matsudana*). They include: '**Crispa**', slow-growing, leaves twisted or spirally curled; '**Navajo**' (syn. *S. matsudana* '**Navajo**'), broad, umbrella-shaped dense crown, very large; '**Tortuosa**' (syn. *S. matsudana* '**Tortuosa**'), contorted shape, upright in habit, twigs twisted and curled, used in floristry; '**Umbraculifera**' (syn. *S. matsudana* '**Umbraculifera**'), broad rounded habit. Zones 5–10.

Salix 'Boydii'

☼ ❄ ↔ 24 in (60 cm) ↑ 36 in (90 cm)

Natural hybrid found in 1870s in Scotland. Slow-growing dwarf shrub, twigs persistently downy, gnarled appearance. Round gray leaves also downy. Small dark gray catkins, rarely produced. Zones 5–9.

Salix caprea

FLORIST'S WILLOW, PUSSY WILLOW

☼ ❄ ↔ 10–20 ft (3–6 m) ↑ 15–35 ft (4.5–10 m)

Small tree or shrub, occurs naturally from Europe to northeastern Asia. Elliptical to oblong leaves, slightly glossy, dark green above, gray and felted below, dull yellow in winter. Plump silky male catkins, in spring, harvested for decorations. '**Pendula**' (Kilmarnock willow) has weeping branches, yellow-brown shoots, and gray male catkins. Zones 5–10.

Salix caprea

Salix fragilis, in autumn

Salix fragilis, in winter

Salix fragilis, in spring

Salix cinerea

GRAY WILLOW

☼ ❄ ↔ 8 ft (2.4 m) ↑ 10 ft (3 m)

Shrubby species found from the UK and continental Europe to western Asia. Covered in fine gray down, remaining on twigs through second season. Narrow leaves dull green above, gray beneath. Silky catkins, appear before leaves. Zones 2–9.

Salix daphnoides

VIOLET WILLOW

☼ ❄ ↔ 20 ft (6 m) ↑ 35 ft (10 m)

Vigorous erect tree or shrub, native to Europe and central Asia to the Himalayas. Plum-colored bloom on young shoots. Long narrow leaves, glossy dark green above, bluish green below. Small, broad, silky male catkins, in late winter–spring. Zones 5–10.

Salix discolor

AMERICAN PUSSY WILLOW

☼ ❄ ↔ 15 ft (4.5 m) ↑ 25 ft (8 m)

Shrub or small tree native to North America. Purplish brown shoots, downy at first. Oval leaves taper at both ends, bright green above, bluish gray beneath. Catkins appear before leaves, to 3 in (8 cm) long, in late winter–spring. Zones 2–9.

Salix elaeagnos

HOARY WILLOW, ROSEMARY WILLOW

☼ ❄ ↔ 20 ft (6 m) ↑ 20 ft (6 m)

Shrub or small tree, native to central Europe, Turkey, and southwestern Asia. Twigs gray and downy, becoming smooth, reddish yellow to brown. Dark green leaves, long, narrow, and felted white beneath. Catkins appear before leaves, in spring. *S. e.* subsp. *angustifolia*, shrubby, creeping stems, thin narrow leaves, dark green above, silky gray beneath. Zones 4–9.

Salix exigua

COYOTE WILLOW

☼ ❄ ↔ 10 ft (3 m) ↑ 12 ft (3.5 m)

Tall erect shrub from North America. Long flexible stems, downy, becoming slender and smooth. Leaves silvery light green, narrow, silky at first. Oval catkins on long leafy stalks. Zones 2–9.

Salix fargesii

☼ ❄ ↔ 10 ft (3 m) ↑ 10 ft (3 m)

Chinese shrub, open habit. Large red winter buds. Leaves, serrated edges, glossy dark green above, dull green and silky below. Long slender catkins, with foliage, in spring. Zones 6–10.

Salix gracilistyla 'Melanostachys'

Salix 'Flame'

FLAME WILLOW

☼ ❄ ↔ 20 ft (6 m) ↑ 20 ft (6 m)

Large shrub or round-headed small tree, most likely a hybrid of *S. alba*. Young branches bright red. Leaves lance-shaped, downy when young, turn bright yellow, in autumn, contrasting with red twigs. Prune in spring to encourage bright new growth. Zones 5–9.

Salix fragilis

BRITTLE WILLOW, CRACK WILLOW

☼ ❄ ↔ 35 ft (10 m) ↑ 50 ft (15 m)

Broadly spreading tree native to Europe and northern Asia. Dark gray bark, deeply fissured, twigs break easily at joints. Long narrow leaves, silky, becoming dark green above, bluish green below. Slender catkins appear with leaves. Zones 6–10.

Salix gracilistyla

ROSEGOLD PUSSY WILLOW

☼ ❄ ↔ 10–15 ft (3–4.5 m) ↑ 10–15 ft (3–4.5 m)

Shrub native to eastern Asia. Oblong leaves 4 in (10 cm). Catkins before leaves, late winter; male catkins red, later orange, then yellow, female catkins silky gray. 'Melanostachys' ★ (syn. *S. melanostachys*), more upright male form; black catkins explode with red-tipped yellow stamens. Zones 6–10.

Salix fargesii

Salix elaeagnos

Salix hastata

HALBERD WILLOW

☼ ❄ ↔ 7 ft (2 m) ↑ 5 ft (1.5 m)

Dense erect shrub native to mountainous areas of central Europe and northeastern Asia. Twigs become purple in second year. Leaves variable, oblong to slightly rounded, dull green above, glaucous beneath. Small plump catkins appear with leaves, in spring. 'Wehrhahnii', attractive silvery catkins. Zones 6–9.

Salix helvetica

SWISS WILLOW

☼ ❄ ↔ 3 ft (0.9 m) ↑ 2–5 ft (0.6–1.5 m)

Shrub from European alpine regions. Forms a small spreading mound of densely interlaced twigs, larger in cultivation than the species. Red-brown stems, glossy green leaves with serrated edges and downy undersides. Smothered in small silver-gray catkins, in spring. Zones 5–9.

Salix hookeriana

☼ ❄ ↔ 3 ft (0.9 m) ↑ 3 ft (0.9 m)

Shrub native to northwestern North America. Prostrate habit. Branches occasionally shiny reddish brown in color. Leaves broadly oval, covered with whitish down when young, smooth, dark green above, bluish green beneath. Catkins on short leafy stalks. Zones 6–9.

Salix hookeriana

S

Salix integra
DAPPLED WILLOW, JAPANESE WILLOW

☼ ❄ ↔ 12 ft (3.5 m) ↕ 10–15 ft (3–4.5 m)

Slender shrub from Japan and Korea;
like *S. purpurea,* but leaves lighter
shade of green. Drooping, purplish
branches. Slender catkins before
leaves. 'Hakura Nishiki', pink leaf
buds and stems, light green leaves,
flecked pink and white. Zones 6–10.

Salix irrorata
ARIZONA WILLOW

☼ ❄ ↔ 10 ft (3 m) ↕ 10 ft (3 m)

Shrub from southwestern USA. Green
shoots become smooth and purplish
yellow with a waxy bloom in winter.
Narrow leaves glossy green above,
glaucous beneath. Red anthers of male
catkins age to yellow. Zones 5–10.

Salix laevigata
POLISHED WILLOW, RED WILLOW

☼ ❄ ↔ 25 ft (8 m) ↕ 50 ft (15 m)

Tree from southwestern USA. Smooth
red to yellow-brown shoots. Serrated-
edged leaves, light green above, glaucous below. Catkins to 4 in (10 cm)
long, with leaves. Zones 5–10.

Salix lanata
ARCTIC WILLOW, WOOLLY WILLOW

☼ ❄ ↔ 6 ft (1.8 m) ↕ 2–4 ft (0.6–1.2 m)

Slow-growing shrub native to northern areas of Europe. Stout branchlets,

Salix nakamurana

Salix miyabeana

densely woolly, gnarled with age. Oval
to rounded leaves covered in silvery
silky hairs, becoming dull green on
uppersurfaces. Bright golden catkins
after leaves, in spring. Zones 2–9.

Salix lindleyana

☼ ❄ ↔ 30 in (75 cm) ↕ 2 in (5 cm)

Alpine species found in the Himalayas. Low creeping plant forms dense
mats of small, green, rosemary-like
leaves on reddish stems. Leaves turn
attractive yellow in autumn. Tiny catkins appear with leaves. Ripened seed
like white cotton wool. Zones 5–10.

Salix lucida
SHINY WILLOW

☼ ❄ ↔ 15 ft (4.5 m) ↕ 25 ft (8 m)

North American tree. Glossy leaves,
yellowish brown twigs. Slender pointed
leaves, shiny green, paler beneath.
Golden catkins appear at same time
as leaves, in spring. Zones 2–9.

Salix magnifica

☼ ❄ ↔ 10 ft (3 m) ↕ 20 ft (6 m)

Tree native to China. Magnolia-like
foliage, smooth purplish shoots and

Salix nigra

buds. Blunt oval leaves, grayish green,
yellowish green midrib and veining.
Female catkins appear in spring with
leaves, to 10 in (25 cm). Zones 7–10.

Salix miyabeana

☼ ❄ ↔ 7–15 ft (2–4.5 m)
↕ 10–20 ft (3–6 m)

Ornamental species native to Japan;
resembles *S. purpurea.* Narrow leaves
to 7 in (18 cm) long. Small inconspicuous catkins. Branches have light
gray bark. Zones 6–10.

Salix nakamurana

☼ ❄ ↔ 36 in (90 cm) ↕ 12 in (30 cm)

Slow-growing dwarf shrub, native to
Japan. The stout arching stems eventually form a mound. Leaves are large
in relation to plant size, light green,
almost round, with silvery hairs.
Catkins also silvery. Zones 6–10.

Salix nigra
BLACK WILLOW

☼ ❄ ↔ 15 ft (4.5 m) ↕ 10–30 ft (3–9 m)

North American large shrub or small
tree. Rough bark, yellowish twigs.
Narrow, pointed, pale green leaves

Salix pentandra

Salix laevigata

with finely serrated margins. Catkins
on short downy shoots appear with
leaves in spring. Zones 4–10.

Salix pentandra
BAY WILLOW, LAUREL WILLOW

☼ ❄ ↔ 30 ft (9 m) ↕ 50 ft (15 m)

Shrub or tree native to a wide area of
Europe, naturalized in eastern USA.
Aromatic dark green foliage, glossy
brownish green twigs, yellow buds.
Male catkins bright yellow, with
foliage, in spring. Zones 5–10.

Salix purpurea
ALASKA BLUE WILLOW, ARCTIC WILLOW,
PURPLE OSIER WILLOW

☼ ❄ ↔ 15 ft (4.5 m) ↕ 15 ft (4.5 m)

Graceful shrub or small tree, native
from Europe to northern Africa, central Asia, and Japan. Arching purplish
shoots, narrow oblong leaves, bluish
green above, paler beneath. Red catkins, becoming purplish black, appear
in spring before leaves. 'Nana' (syn.
S. purpurea f. *gracilis*), compact cultivar, gray-green leaves, thin shoots;
'Pendula', thin pendulous branches.
Zones 5–10.

Salix purpurea 'Nana'

Salix irrorata

S

Salix sericea

Salix × *sepulcralis* 'Chrysocoma'

Salix repens
CREEPING WILLOW

☀ ❄ ↔ 5 ft (1.5 m)
↕ 8 in–5 ft (20 cm–1.5 m)

Creeping shrub from Europe, Turkey, southwestern Asia, and Siberia. Downy shoots become smooth. Small tapering leaves, green above, silvery below. Small catkins, spring. Zones 5–10.

Salix reptans
ARCTIC CREEPING WILLOW

☀ ❄ ↔ 18–36 in (45–90 cm) ↕ 2 in (5 cm)

Dwarf form from far northern Asia and European Russia. Reddish brown branches. Leaves green, wrinkled above, paler bluish beneath, dense long hairs, both surfaces. Erect catkins, long-haired black-tipped scales. Zones 2–8.

Salix reticulata
NET-LEAFED WILLOW

☀ ❄ ↔ 15 in (38 cm) ↕ 6 in (15 cm)

Dwarf creeping shrub from northern areas of Europe, North America, and Asia. Oval to rounded leaves, dark green, wrinkled above, white beneath. Small, erect, mauve-tipped catkins, after leaves, in spring. Zones 1–8.

Salix retusa

☀ ❄ ↔ 18 in (45 cm) ↕ 4 in (10 cm)

Prostrate species from the mountains of central Europe. Dense mat, stems root as they creep. Small, smooth, oblong leaves near branch tips. Erect catkins appear with foliage. Zones 2–9.

Salix × rubens

☀ ❄ ↔ 25 ft (8 m) ↕ 35 ft (10 m)

Naturally occurring hybrid between *S. alba* and *S. fragilis*, native to central

Europe. Olive twigs tinged yellow or red. Lance-shaped leaves, bright green above, glaucous beneath. Cylindrical catkins to 2 in (5 cm). Zones 6–10.

Salix × sepulcralis

☀ ❄ ↔ 40 ft (12 m) ↕ 40 ft (12 m)

Hybrid between *S. alba* and *S. babylonica*, of garden origin. Habit and foliage similar to but slightly less weeping than *S. babylonica*. Fissured bark. Slender catkins similar to *S. alba*. 'Chrysocoma' (syn. *S. alba* 'Tristis'), broadly weeping, thin golden twigs, bright green leaves. Zones 6–10.

Salix sericea
SILKY WILLOW

☀ ❄ ↔ 5–10 ft (1.5–3 m) ↕ 12 ft (3.5 m)

Shrub native to eastern USA. Gray bark, slender shoots, tinged purple. Lance-shaped leaves to 4 in (10 cm) long, silky beneath. Catkins appear before leaves, in spring. Zones 7–10.

Salix taxifolia

☀ ❄ ↔ 7–10 ft (2–3 m)
↕ 10–15 ft (3–4.5 m)

Shrub from southern North America and Mexico. Narrow leaves, branches slightly furry. Both male and female catkins inconspicuous. Zones 8–10.

Salix udensis

☀ ❄ ↔ 10 ft (3 m) ↕ 17 ft (5 m)

Shrub native to Japan and eastern Russia. Narrow lance-shaped leaves, dark green above, bluish green and slightly hairy beneath, sometimes with wavy edges. Small cylindrical catkins, in early spring. 'Sekka', upright branches. Zones 5–9.

Salix × *sepulcralis*, Queen Mary Gardens, London, UK

Salix viminalis
COMMON OSIER, HEMP WILLOW

☀ ❄ ↔ 15 ft (4.5 m) ↕ 8–20 ft (2.4–6 m)

Shrub native from Europe to north-eastern Asia and the Himalayas. Cultivated for use in basket making. Long flexible shoots, covered in thick gray hair when young. Narrow leaves are dull green above with silvery silky hairs beneath. Catkins appear before leaves, in spring. Zones 4–10.

SALPICHLAENA

A genus of only 3 species of unusual climbing ferns belonging to the hard-fern (Blechnaceae) family, and found in Central and South America and the Lesser Antilles Islands, West Indies, mostly in highland rainforests. From a creeping rhizome arise twining fronds that may be very elongated, growing continuously from their tips to as long as 50 ft (15 m). The fronds of the plants are bipinnate, their lateral segments looking like widely spaced pinnate fronds. The lower segments have broad leathery leaflets, and the upper ones have narrower spore-bearing leaflets. The tubular brown indusia (spore-concealing organs) on their undersides are soon shed, leaving apparently sterile leaflets.

CULTIVATION: *Salpichlaena* species have hardly ever been cultivated; they would require a spacious garden in the wet tropics or a large greenhouse in cooler climates, with support provided for their high-climbing habit. Propagation should be possible from rhizome division or from spores.

Salpichlaena volubilis

◐/☀ ⚘ ↔ 5–10 ft (1.5–3 m)
↕ 20–50 ft (6–15 m)

Native to Central and South America from Belize to Paraguay, and to the

Salpichlaena volubilis

eastern islands of the West Indies. Attractive fern with strong wiry stems, leathery leaflets to 1¼ in (3 cm) wide, glossy red-brown when young, soon turning deep green. Zones 10–12.

SALPIGLOSSIS

A genus of 2 species of annuals or short-lived perennials in the nightshade (Solanaceae) family. Natives of the southern and central Andes, they are small upright plants with alternate, simple linear to elliptical, dark green leaves with finely toothed edges. The stems and foliage are rather sticky to the touch. The flowers are funnel-shaped, 5-lobed; they are borne singly in the leaf axils near the stem tips, and are strikingly colored and patterned. Seedling strains in a range of sizes and colors are widely available. Named from the Greek *salpinx* (a trumpet) and *glossa* (a tongue), in reference to the flower shape.

CULTIVATION: Treated as an annual, *Salpiglossis* species are best grown in an area with cool moist summer conditions. Plant in a sunny position with fertile, moist, well-drained soil, and water well. In mild almost frost-free regions these species can be over-wintered. They are usually propagated by seed sown in situ.

Salix repens

Salix reptans

S

Salpiglossis sinuata, Casino Mixed (at rear), with *Salpiglossis sinuata*

Salvia argentea

Salpiglossis sinuata, Festival Strain

Salpiglossis sinuata

PAINTED TONGUE

☼/◑ ❄ ↔ 8–12 in (20–30 cm)
↕ 16–24 in (40–60 cm)

Annual, biennial, or short-lived perennial, usually treated as annual. Narrow, dark green, sticky leaves to 4 in (10 cm) long, often toothed, sometimes lobed. Heads of funnel-shaped flowers to 2 in (5 cm) wide, yellow to reddish purple, darker veins and markings. Mixed color seedling strains include: **Bolero Hybrids**, 12 in (30 cm) tall, wide color range; **Casino Mixed**, 12 in (30 cm) tall, wide color range with contrasting veining; **Emperor Royal Series**, 24 in (60 cm) tall, large petunia-like flowers, conspicuously veined; **Festival Strain**, dark red-maroon flowers. Zones 8–11.

SALVIA

SAGE

The largest genus in the mint (Lamiaceae) family, *Salvia* contains annuals, perennials, and softwooded evergreen shrubs. They grow in habitats from

coastal to alpine; over half the 900 or so species are native to the Americas. The leaves are opposite and carried on squared hairy stems, and are aromatic when crushed. The flowers are tubular, with the petals split into 2 straight or flaring lips. Colors may be shades of blue to purple and pink to red, as well as white and some yellows. CULTIVATION: The shrubby sages grow in a range of soil types but dislike heavy wet soils. Most do best in full sun; all require a well-drained situation. Prune in spring to remove straggly, bare, and frost-damaged stems. Propagate most shrubby

species from softwood cuttings taken throughout the growing season. Seed of all species can be sown in spring.

Salvia apiana

BEE SAGE, CALIFORNIA WHITE SAGE

☼ ❋ ↔ 3 ft (0.9 m) ↕ 4 ft (1.2 m)

Shrub from southwestern California, USA. Silvery covering of fine hairs. Leaves very aromatic. White or pale lavender flowers grow in loose whorls above foliage, in spring. Zones 9–11.

Salvia argentea

☼ ❄ ↔ 24–40 in (60–100 cm)
↕ 24 in (60 cm)

Perennial from southern Europe. Large, woolly, silvery-looking leaves, to 40 in (100 cm) long, grow on basal rosette of foliage. Tall candelabra-like stems of white flowers produced in second year. Zones 8–11.

Salvia aurea

syn. *Salvia africana-lutea*

BEACH SAGE, BROWN SALVIA, GOLDEN SAGE

☼ ❋ ↔ 3 ft (0.9 m) ↕ 3–5 ft (0.9–1.5 m)

Stiff well-branched shrub from coastal areas of South Africa. Small, aromatic, grayish green leaves. Whorls of large yellow flowers, fading to an orangey brown, in summer–autumn. Prominent greenish brown calyces. 'Kirstenbosch', dwarf cultivar. Zones 9–11.

Salvia aurita

AFRICAN BLUE SAGE

☼ ❋ ↔ 10 in (25 cm) ↕ 10 in (25 cm)

Suckering perennial with light blue flowers, from Africa. Long-flowering. Zones 9–11.

Salvia blepharophylla

EYELASH-LEAFED SAGE

◑ ❋ ↔ 20–27 in (50–70 cm)
↕ 8–12 in (20–30 cm)

Mexican mat-forming perennial, spreads by runners. Tiny hairs along

margins of glossy green oval leaves; orange-red flowers in early summer–late autumn. Zones 9–11.

Salvia buchananii

syn. *Salvia bacheriana* of gardens

BUCHANAN'S SAGE

◑ ↔ 12 in (30 cm)
↕ 12–20 in (30–50 cm)

Clumping perennial, most probably originating from Mexico. Lovely, rich, glossy, oval leaves ¾–2 in (18 mm–5 cm) long. Velvety hot magenta flowers appear mainly from summer to autumn. Zones 10–11.

Salvia bulleyana

syn. *Salvia flava* var. *megalantha*

◑ ❋ ↔ 16–24 in (40–60 cm)
↕ 20–40 in (50–100 cm)

Compact low-growing species from China. Bright green crinkled foliage. Yellow flowers with purplish brown lower lip and bright green calyx, in summer. Zones 9–11.

Salvia cacaliifolia

CACALIA SAGE

☼/◑ ❋ ↔ 12–20 in (30–50 cm)
↕ 36 in (90 cm)

Suckering perennial from Central America. Bright green arrowhead-like leaves. Royal blue flowers with green calyx. Blooms year round in mild climates, in mid-summer to autumn in cooler climates. Zones 10–11.

Salvia canariensis

CANARY ISLAND SAGE

☼ ❋ ↔ 3 ft (0.9 m) ↕ 4–7 ft (1.2–2 m)

Shrub native to the Canary Islands. The stems are covered in dense white hairs, and the soft arrowhead-shaped leaves are grayish green and hairy. The lilac-pink flowers emerge from showy purplish red calyces, in spring–summer. 'Alba', pink calyces, white flowers. Zones 9–11.

Salvia aurita

Salvia bulleyana

Salvia canariensis

Salvia coccinea

Salvia confertiflora

Salvia daghestanica

Salvia darcyi

Salvia dorisiana

Salvia candidissima

☀ ❄ ↔ 20–40 in (50–100 cm)
↑ 20–40 in (50–100 cm)

Subshrub from Greece, Turkey, and northern Iran. Wide silvery basal foliage, bright white flower spikes, 20 in (50 cm) long, mid-spring. Zones 8–11.

Salvia castanea

☀/◑ ❄ ↔ 24 in (60 cm) ↑ 36 in (90 cm)

Perennial from the Himalayas. Basal clump of narrow oval leaves with serrated margins and long stalks. Spikes of maroon-purple tubular flowers, 24 in (60 cm) long, tinged yellow below, in summer. Hardy. Zones 7–11.

Salvia chamaedryoides

syn. *Salvia chamaedryfolia*
GERMANDER SAGE

☀ ❄ ↔ 12–20 in (30–50 cm)
↑ 12–24 in (30–60 cm)

Suckering evergreen perennial from Mexico. Small silvery leaves, sky blue flowers, white throat markings, in spring–autumn. Zones 8–11.

Salvia chiapensis

CHIAPAS SAGE

☀/◑ ❄ ↔ 16–24 in (40–60 cm)
↑ 16–24 in (40–60 cm)

Perennial from Mexico. Glossy olive green leaves to 3 in (8 cm) long. Cerise-pink flowers, velvety green calyces. Long-flowering in mild climates. Zones 9–11.

Salvia clevelandii

CALIFORNIA BLUE SAGE, CLEVELAND SAGE

☀ ❄ ↔ 15–26 in (38–65 cm)
↑ 24–48 in (60–120 cm)

Shrub from California's dry chaparral. Aromatic, oval to lance-shaped, gray-green leaves, with toothed edges and wrinkled upper surfaces. Erect flower spikes, whorls of fragrant, lavender-blue, rarely white, flowers, in summer. 'Winifred Gilman' ★, compact and drought-tolerant, very dark flowers. Zones 8–10.

Salvia coccinea

syn. *Salvia coccinea* var. *pseudococcinea*
TEXAS SAGE, TROPICAL SAGE

☀ ❄ ↔ 20–32 in (50–80 cm)
↑ 40 in (100 cm)

Annual or short-lived shrub from tropical South America; in mild climates may be perennial, elsewhere treated as annual. Mostly triangular, hairy, green leaves, scalloped margins. Flowers usually scarlet, may be red, pink, or white. 'Lady in Red', slightly smaller, red flowers. Zones 9–12.

Salvia confertiflora

☀/◑ ❄ ↔ 24–40 in (60–100 cm)
↑ 40 in (100 cm)

Woody-based perennial from Brazil. Toothed, pointed, oval leaves to 8 in (20 cm) long, with tan to red-brown covering of hairs, especially on undersides; unpleasant scent when crushed. Flowerheads to 12 in (30 cm) long, bearing up to 15 downy deep red flowers, in summer. Zones 9–10.

Salvia daghestanica

DWARF SILVER-LEAF SAGE

☀ ❄ ↔ 8–12 in (20–30 cm)
↑ 12–18 in (30–45 cm)

Silver-leafed perennial from southern Russia. Violet-lavender flowers, in summer. Zones 5–8.

Salvia chiapensis

Salvia darcyi

syn. *Salvia oresbia*

☀ ❄ ↔ 4 ft (1.2 m) ↑ 3–4 ft (0.9–1.2 m)

Large clumping perennial from Mexico. Spreads slowly by runners. Flowers bright red with purplish green calyces, produced on spikes 12–24 in (30–60 cm) long, in summer–autumn. Zones 9–11.

Salvia discolor

ANDEAN SILVER SAGE

☀/◑ ❄ ↔ 32–40 in (80–100 cm)
↑ 32–40 in (80–100 cm)

Perennial from Peru. White, wiry, sprawling stems. Attractive leaves are green on top, silver beneath. Dark purple to navy blue flowers with green calyces and silver bracts, appear in late summer–early autumn. Zones 9–11.

Salvia dorisiana

FRUIT-SCENTED SAGE, PEACH SAGE

☀ ❄ ↔ 36 in (90 cm)
↑ 36–48 in (90–120 cm)

Hairy heavily branched plant from Honduras. Long velvety leaves. Spikes of bright pink loosely tubular flowers, 2 in (5 cm) long, in winter. Flowers and leaves scented; flowers attract hummingbirds. Zones 10–12.

Salvia castanea

Salvia clevelandii

Salvia candidissima

S

Salvia elegans
PINEAPPLE SAGE

☀ ❋ ↔ 3 ft (0.9 m) ↑ 6 ft (1.8 m)

Shrub from high mountain regions of Central Mexico and Guatemala. Crushed leaves have a distinctive pineapple aroma. Shorter habit in cold areas. Leaves soft and downy, with finely serrated edges. Narrow scarlet-red flowers in well-spaced whorls, in spring–autumn. Attracts hummingbirds. '**Scarlet Pineapple**' (syn. *S. rutilans*), stronger pineapple scent, larger flowers. Zones 8–11.

Salvia farinacea
MEALY SAGE

☀ ❖ ↔ 24 in (60 cm)
↑ 36–48 in (90–120 cm)

Popular perennial, often treated as an annual, from Texas and New Mexico, USA. Leaves oval, green and glossy. Flowers at ends of stems in shades of

Salvia elegans

Salvia gesneriiflora

Salvia fruticosa

blue, purple, or white, and dusted with a flour-like substance. '**Strata**', shorter habit, blue flowers, mealy white stem and calyces; '**Victoria**', blue flowers, blue stems and calyces; '**Victoria Blue**', shorter habit, flowers deeper blue, larger. Zones 9–11.

Salvia forskaohlii
syn. *Salvia forsskaohlii*

☀◐ ❋ ↔ 20 in (50 cm) ↑ 36 in (90 cm)

Hardy perennial from the Balkans. Abundant, thick, bristly, basal foliage. Flowers on tall stems, blue-mauve with white streaks on lower lip, in mid-summer. Zones 7–11.

Salvia fruticosa
GREEK SAGE, TRILOBA SAGE

☀ ❋ ↔ 24 in (60 cm) ↑ 36 in (90 cm)

Evergreen shrub with branching stems from the eastern Mediterranean region. Rough gray-green foliage. Spikes of small 2-lipped flowers, pink or mauve, at stem ends. May develop cherry-sized galls from insect sting. Zones 8–10.

Salvia fulgens
CARDINAL SAGE

☀ ❖ ↔ 30 in (75 cm) ↑ 48 in (120 cm)

Subshrub, native of Mexico. Woody-stemmed and shrubby in mild climates. Ovate to poplar-shaped leaves, cleft at base, toothed edges, downy undersides. Bright red flowers, 2 to 6, on spikes, in summer. Zones 9–10.

Salvia greggii

Salvia farinacea (purple flowers)

Salvia farinacea 'Victoria Blue'

Salvia gesneriiflora
☀ ❖ ↔ 10 in (25 cm) ↑ 26 in (65 cm)

Shrub or subshrub found from Mexico to Columbia. Dense mound of hairy, somewhat wrinkled, ovate leaves with toothed edges. Orange-red flowers, 2 in (5 cm) long, resembling those of *Columnea* species. Flower spikes to 8 in (20 cm) long appear in summer–autumn. '**Tequila**', large shrub, scarlet flowers, black calyx. Zones 9–11.

Salvia glutinosa
JUPITER'S DISTAFF

☀ ❋ ↔ 20 in (50 cm) ↑ 40 in (100 cm)

Small deciduous shrub from Europe and western Asia. Hairy spear-shaped leaves grow to 5 in (12 cm) long. The sticky flowers are pale yellow dotted with maroon on upper lip, with green calyces, and appear in early summer. Zones 6–10.

Salvia greggii 'Iced Lemon'

Salvia farinacea 'Strata'

Salvia farinacea 'Victoria'

Salvia greggii
AUTUMN SAGE

☀ ❖ ↔ 12–36 in (30–90 cm)
↑ 12–36 in (30–90 cm)

Variable species native to Texas, USA, and Mexico. Hybridizes freely with related *S. microphylla*. Small leathery leaves, usually smooth. Flowers usually red or shades of pink, purple, and white, in summer–late autumn. Cultivar names '**Alba**', '**Iced Lemon**', '**Peach**', and '**Raspberry Royale**' reflect flower colors. Zones 9–11.

Salvia guaranitica ★
syns *Salvia ambigens*, *S. concolor*
ANISE-SCENTED SAGE

☀ ❋ ↔ 16–27 in (40–70 cm)
↑ 4–5 ft (1.2–1.5 m)

South American perennial, suckering lightly to form large clumps. Flowers borne on 10 in (25 cm) long spike, true blue with green calyces, early summer–autumn. '**Black and Blue**', shorter, less spreading, blue flowers, almost black calyces; '**Blue Enigma**', shorter, earlier flowering, deep blue flowers, green calyces; '**Costa Rica Blue**', tall cultivar, violet-blue flowers, yellow-green calyces. Zones 8–11.

Salvia hians
☀ ❋ ↔ 24 in (60 cm)
↑ 24–40 in (60–100 cm)

Perennial from Kashmir and Pakistan. Basal green foliage, leaves to 10 in

Salvia involucrata

Salvia involucrata 'Bethellii'

Salvia × *jamensis,* pink form

(25 cm) long. Flowers fat, soft violet with brownish red calyx, borne in whorls on tall branching stems, in summer. Zones 7–11.

Salvia indica

☼ ✤ ↔ 24 in (60 cm)
↑ 24–36 in (60–90 cm)

Perennial from the Middle East. Gray leaves with scalloped margins form mound of basal foliage. Tall spikes of purple flowers with white markings on bottom lip, spring. May die down during warmer months. Zones 9–11.

Salvia involucrata

ROSELEAF SAGE

☼/◐ ✤ ↔ 5 ft (1.5 m) ↑ 5 ft (1.5 m)

Perennial from Mexico. Some wood at base. Purplish green leaves. Beetroot red flowers and calyces are borne in summer–autumn. **'Bethellii'**, more

compact, sometimes suckering, large heart-shaped leaves, flowers sugar pink. Zones 9–11.

Salvia × jamensis

☼ ✤ ↔ 27–40 in (70–100 cm)
↑ 27–40 in (70–100 cm)

Shrubby hybrid. A cross between *S. microphylla* and *S. greggii*, generally with glossy green oval leaves. Flowers in a range of solid colors, including reds, pinks, oranges, apricots, and yellows, also some bi-colored forms, in summer–autumn. **'Cinega de Oro'**, pale yellow flowers. Zones 9–11.

Salvia karwinskii

KARWINSKI'S SAGE

☼ ✤ ↔ 4 ft (1.2 m) ↑ 8 ft (2.4 m)

Large shrubby species from Central America. Large felted leaves. Bears abundant, large, showy heads of

Salvia indica

reddish pink flowers, in winter. Frost can nip it back, but it should recover. Zones 10–11.

Salvia lavandulifolia

syn. *Salvia hispanica*

SPANISH SAGE

☼ ✳ ↔ 18 in (45 cm) ↑ 18 in (45 cm)

From Spain and southern France. Builds some wood at base. Narrow grayish white leaves, scented like rosemary. Sparse short spikes of small pale lavender blue flowers, early summer. Zones 6–10.

Salvia leucantha

MEXICAN BUSH SAGE, VELVET SAGE

☼ ✤ ↔ 3 ft (0.9 m) ↑ 3 ft (0.9 m)

Spreading shrub, native to Mexico and tropical America. Stems very woolly. Soft, narrow, wrinkled leaves, dull green, thickly felted beneath. Spikes of white or purple flowers extend from showy, velvety, purple

Salvia × *jamensis,* yellow form

calyces, in late summer. **'Midnight'** (syn. 'Purple Velvet'), stunning purple flowers and calyces. Zones 9–11.

Salvia leucophylla

CHAPARRAL SAGE, GRAY SAGE, PURPLE SAGE

☼ ✳ ↔ 3 ft (0.9 m) ↑ 5 ft (1.5 m)

Well-branched shrub native to hot, dry, stony hillsides of California, USA. Attractive, whitish gray, hairy leaves. Whorls of pinkish purple flowers on pinkish stems, in autumn. **'Figuero'**, smaller, drought tolerant, silvery foliage; **'Point Sal Spreader'** ★, prostrate form, grayer leaves. Zones 8–11.

Salvia mexicana

MEXICAN SAGE

☼ ✤ ↔ 7 ft (2 m) ↑ 10 ft (3 m)

Vigorous grower native to Mexico. Smooth to slightly hairy leaves, almost heart-shaped, mid-green to grayish green. Spikes of deep purple flowers emerge from large green calyces, held well above foliage, in autumn. **'Black Sepals'**, deep green leaves with dark stems and calyces; **'Limelight'**, chartreuse stems and calyces. Zones 9–11.

Salvia leucantha

Salvia leucophylla

Salvia karwinskii

Salvia lavandulifolia

Salvia mexicana 'Limelight'

S

Salvia nemorosa

Salvia nemorosa 'Ostfriesland'

Salvia nemorosa cultivar

Salvia nemorosa 'Lubecca'

Salvia munzii

Salvia officinalis

Salvia officinalis 'Minor'

Salvia microphylla

LITTLE-LEAFED SAGE

☼ ❄ ↔ 3 ft (0.9 m) ↑ 4 ft (1.2 m)

Variable species, widespread in its native southern USA and Mexico. Slightly hairy serrated-edged leaves give off a blackcurrant-like aroma when crushed. Flowers variable in color, shades of pink, red, and deep purple, in summer–autumn.

S. m. var. *microphylla*, crimson flowers, heavily blooming; '**La Foux**', shrubby, glossy green, oval leaves, hot pink to red flowers with purple stems and calyces. *S. m.* '**Coral**', deep salmon pink flowers; '**Huntington Red**', bright scarlet flowers; '**Kew Red**', deep red flowers; '**La Trinidad Pink**', compact, bright pink to magenta flowers; '**Newby Hall**', vivid deep

scarlet flowers; '**Pink Blush**', magenta-pink flowers; '**San Carlos Festival**', continual display of crimson flowers. Zones 8–11.

Salvia munzii

MUNZ'S SAGE, SAN MIGUEL SAGE

☼ ❄ ↔ 3–5 ft (0.9–1.5 m)
↑ 3–7 ft (0.9–2 m)

Shrubby perennial from California, USA. Scented foliage. Spikes of lavender blue flowers with green calyces, in spring. Cold and drought tolerant. Zones 8–11.

Salvia nemorosa

BALKAN CLARY, STEPPE SAGE

☼ ❄ ↔ 12–24 in (30–60 cm)
↑ 24–36 in (60–90 cm)

Perennial from Europe to central Asia. Simple, oval to oblong, wrinkled, green leaves. Racemes of mauve to purple flowers, sometimes white to pink, summer–autumn. intensely blue flowers, tall, upright; '**Lubecca**' (syn.

S. × *superba* 'Lubecca'), dwarf cultivar, gray-green leaves, tall spikes of mauve flowers with rich burgundy bracts, in spring; '**Ostfriesland**' (syn. 'East Friesland'), vivid violet-blue flowers, slightly taller than 'Lubecca', in late spring. Zones 5–10.

Salvia officinalis ★

COMMON SAGE, GARDEN SAGE

☼ ❄ ↔ 36 in (90 cm) ↑ 30 in (75 cm)

Perennial shrub native to Spain, the Balkans, and northern Africa; naturalized in southern Europe. White hairy stems, oblong grayish green leaves, upper wrinkled, white-haired beneath, aromatic. Flowers white to pink and purple shades, in summer. Used for centuries for medicinal and culinary

Salvia microphylla

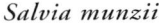

Salvia microphylla 'Pink Blush'

Salvia microphylla 'Coral'

S. microphylla 'Huntington Red'

S. m. var. *microphylla* 'La Foux'

S. microphylla 'La Trinidad Pink'

Salvia microphylla 'Newby Hall'

Salvia officinalis 'Tricolor'

Salvia przewalskii

purposes. **'Berggarten'** ★, rounded leaves, flowers less often; **'Extrakta'**, high-yielding medicinal oil; **'Icterina'**, attractive variegated leaves edged in pale yellow; **'Minor'**, dull green leaves, small violet-purple flowers; **'Purpurascens'**, reddish purple leaves; **'Purpurascens Variegata'**, purple leaves, splashed with white to cream; **'Purpurea'**, mauve flowers, purple leaves; **'Tricolor'**, dull green leaves edged with yellow and salmon pink. Zones 5–10.

Salvia pachyphylla

BLUE SAGE, MOUNTAIN DESERT SAGE, ROSE SAGE

☼ ❄ ↔ 40 in (100 cm) ↑ 40 in (100 cm)
Small evergreen shrub native to California, USA. Fragrant gray leaves. Large flowers borne in tight bunches, pink with hint of blue, with lavender bracts, in summer. Zones 5–11.

Salvia patens

GENTIAN SAGE

☼ ❄ ↔ 12–24 in (30–60 cm) ↑ 12–24 in (30–60 cm)
Perennial from Mexico. Dies back to tubers in winter. Oval green leaves to 8 in (20 cm) long. Bears spikes of gentian blue flowers, in pairs, 12 in (30 cm) long, with green calyces, in summer–autumn. **'Cambridge Blue'**, sky blue flowers. Zones 9–11.

Salvia regla

Salvia pratensis

MEADOW CLARY, MEADOW SAGE

☼ ❄ ↔ 12 in (30 cm) ↑ 36 in (90 cm)
Perennial of meadows across Europe. Basal clump of rich green wrinkled leaves with irregular margins. Violet flowers (also blue, pink, and white forms), brown calyces, green bracts, in spring. **Haematodes Group** (syn. *S. haematodes*), large erect sprays of pale lilac-blue flowers with reddish brown stems, in summer; **'Indigo'**, superb indigo blue flowers, in early summer. Zones 4–10.

Salvia przewalskii

☼ ❄ ↔ 12–24 in (30–60 cm) ↑ 12–24 in (30–60 cm)
Chinese species forming basal clump of yellow-green foliage. Some leaves grow to 12 in (30 cm) long. Flowers purple-red with reddish brown calyces, borne on much-branched stems, in summer. Zones 8–11.

Salvia regla

MOUNTAIN SAGE

☼ ❄ ↔ 3 ft (0.9 m) ↑ 4 ft (1.2 m)
Shrub found in Texas, USA, and Mexico. Erect woody habit, upper stems dark red-brown. Leaves roughly triangular with wavy edges. Large bright scarlet-red flowers, in autumn. **'Royal'**, tubular orange flowers; **'Huntington'**, orange-red flowers, tolerates hot dry conditions. Zones 9–10.

Salvia roemeriana

CEDAR SAGE

☼/❂ ❄ ↔ 12 in (30 cm) ↑ 12 in (30 cm)
Small perennial from Arizona and Texas, USA, and Mexico. Rounded,

Salvia pratensis

geranium-like, green leaves. Bright red flowers borne on 8 in (20 cm) long stalks, in summer. Zones 8–11.

Salvia sclarea

CLARY SAGE, CLEAR EYE

☼ ❄ ↔ 36 in (90 cm) ↑ 36–48 in (90–120 cm)
Perennial or biennial from southern Europe. Leaves are heart-shaped and puckered, 9–12 in (22–30 cm) long. Candelabra of small white-lilac or pale blue flowers are borne in prominent rosy pink or mauve bracts, in early summer. Long-blooming species with a strong musky aroma. **'Turkestanica'** ★, larger bluish or pinkish white flowers, violet bracts tinged with green. Zones 4–9.

Salvia sclarea

Salvia patens

Salvia sonomensis

CREEPING SAGE, SONOMA SAGE

☼ ❄ ↔ 3–7 ft (0.9–2 m) ↑ 12 in (30 cm)
Mat-forming perennial from California, USA. Leaves variable in shape and color, from long and narrow to short and round, green, yellow-green or gray-green. Flowers on short stalks, in various shades of lavender. **'Dara's Choice'**, slightly taller, more mounding, taller flower spikes, violet flowers, blue-green calyces. Zones 8–11.

Salvia roemeriana

Salvia sonomensis 'Dara's Choice'

Salvia pachyphylla, in the wild, Sierra San Pedro Mártir, Baja California, Mexico

S

Salvia splendens

Salvia transsilvanica

Salvia spathacea

CRIMSON SAGE, HUMMINGBIRD SAGE, PITCHER SAGE

☼/◐ ❄ ↔ 12–36 in (30–90 cm)
↕ 12–36 in (30–90 cm)

Suckering perennial from California, USA. Forms large mats. Large spear-shaped leaves. Flowers crimson-pink, prominent reddish black calyces and

Salvia × *sylvestris* 'Mainacht'

Salvia × *sylvestris* 'Blauhügel'

bracts, borne on tall stems, in early spring–summer. **'Powerline Pink'**, larger than the species, taller flower stems, pink flowers. Zones 8–11.

Salvia splendens

SCARLET SAGE

☼ ⚥ ↔ 8–32 in (20–80 cm)
↕ 8–48 in (20–120 cm)

Variable perennial, often treated as an annual. Many-branched. Oval green leaves, serrated margins. Flowers are usually red; many cultivars in other colors. **'Empire Purple'**, deep reddish purple flowers; **'Red Riches'** (syn. 'Ryco'), early-blooming, vivid scarlet flowers, dark green leaves; **'Scarlet King'**, traditional bedding variety, big dense spikes of scarlet flowers, dark green foliage; **Sizzler Series**, compact foliage, early-flowering, long-lasting, flowers burgundy, lavender, pink, red, salmon, white, and bi-colored;

Salvia thymoides

Salvia spathacea

'Vanguard', compact, early flowering, dark leaves, red flowers; **'Vista Salmon'**, compact, well-branched, dark green leaves, well-packed spikes of salmon flowers, pink inner petals. Zones 9–11.

Salvia stenophylla

☼ ⚥ ↔ 36 in (90 cm) ↕ 24 in (60 cm)

South African perennial. Tiny lance-shaped leaves and bright green stems, small mauve-blue flowers, in summer. Zones 10–11.

Salvia × superba

☼ ❄ ↔ 12–24 in (30–60 cm)
↕ 12–27 in (30–75 cm)

Hardy perennial hybrid between *S.* × *sylvestris* and *S. villicaulis*, of European origin. Many cultivars. Upright flower spikes in a range of colors, in summer. Zones 5–10.

Salvia × sylvestris

☼ ❄ ↔ 20–40 in (50–100 cm)
↕ 20–40 in (50–100 cm)

Very hardy and widespread European perennial. Small, narrow, green leaves

Salvia stenophylla

with stalks and scalloped margins. Flowers usually purple. **'Blauhügel'** (syns 'Blue Hills', 'Blue Mount'), deep blue flower spikes on low plants to 15 in (38 cm) high; **'Mainacht'** (syn. 'May Night'), midnight violet flowers, in early spring; **'Tänzerin'**, erect, deep violet flower spikes to 32 in (80 cm) long. Zones 5–10.

Salvia thymoides

☼ ⚥ ↔ 10 in (25 cm)
↕ 10 in (25 cm)

Perennial from Mexico. Small, gray-white, thyme-like leaves. Small violet-blue flowers, in mid-summer to autumn or early winter. Zones 9–11.

Salvia transsilvanica

☼/◐ ❄ ↔ 40 in (100 cm)
↕ 16–24 in (40–60 cm)

Leafy perennial from Russia and Romania. Many lax stems; leaves green with scalloped margin, large at base, decreasing in size along stem. Deep violet-blue flowers, in early summer–autumn. Zones 6–9.

Salvia splendens 'Empire Purple'

Salvia splendens 'Vista Salmon'

Salvia × *superba*

Salvia uliginosa

BOG SAGE

☼ ⬙ ↔ 3 ft (0.9 m) ↕ 3–6 ft (0.9–1.8 m)

Perennial from Brazil, Uruguay, and Argentina. Clump-forming, spreading by underground runners. Yellowish green lance-shaped leaves are carried on erect stems. Whorls of small sky blue and white flowers appear in late summer–autumn. Needs moist soil. Zones 9–11.

Salvia verticillata

LILAC SAGE

☼ ❋ ↔ 32 in (80 cm) ↕ 40 in (100 cm)

Perennial, widespread in Europe and western Asia; naturalized in North America. Leafy clump of hairy, pale green leaves. Branched inflorescences of whorls of lavender-violet flowers with green calyces, in summer. 'Alba', white flowers and lime green calyces; 'Purple Rain', slightly smaller than the species, dusky purple flowers and violet calyces. Zones 6–10.

Salvia uliginosa

Salvia verticillata 'Purple Rain'

Salvia viridis 'Tricolor Mixed'

Salvia viridis

syn. *Salvia horminum*

ANNUAL SAGE, PAINTED SAGE, PURPLE-TOP

☼ ❋ ↔ 12 in (30 cm)

↕ 12–24 in (30–60 cm)

Slender annual found from the Mediterranean across to Crimea, Ukraine. Tiny flowers bloom in the leaf axils; petal-like top bracts are purple, pink, or white with darker veining. Grow plants massed for best effect. 'Tricolor Mixed', improved form with blue, pink, or cream bracts. Zones 8–10.

Salvia wagneriana

syns *Salvia albopileata, S. tonduzii*

WAGNER SAGE

☼/◑ ⬙ ↔ 4 ft (1.2 m)

↕ 3–10 ft (0.9–3 m)

Shrub-like perennial from Central America. Yellowish green leaves. Flowers vary from red to pink and pale pink, with colored bracts and calyces, autumn–winter. Zones 10–11.

Salvia Hybrid Cultivars

☼/◑ ❋/⬙ ↔ 16–48 in (40–120 cm)

↕ 20–60 in (50–150 cm)

Salvia hybrids have been developed from a wide range of species—some are known crosses, others chance seedlings—and are a diverse group.

Salvia wagneriana

Salvia, Hybrid Cultivar, 'Hot Lips'

They are grown mainly for their flowers, but many cultivars also have attractive or unusual foliage. Many are probably perennial, but are often treated as annuals, especially in cold climates. 'Costa Rica Blue', vibrant green heart-shaped leaves and bright blue flowers; 'Hot Lips', white, red, and red/white flowers on the same plant; 'Indigo Spires' ★, deep violet flowers, double white bee-line, lower lip, dark purple calyces; 'Maraschino', cherry red flowers on sprawling plant, long-flowering; 'Phyllis's Fancy', white flowers, bluish tinge, calyces purple, long-flowering; 'Plum', flowers bright magenta, calyces deep reddish purple; 'Purple Majesty', flowers and calyces rich dark purple, growing in spikes 10 in (25 cm) long. Zones 6–10.

SAMBUCUS

ELDER, ELDERBERRY

This genus from the world's temperate areas encompasses around 25 species of perennials, shrubs, and small trees that are mostly deciduous, from the woodbine (Caprifoliaceae) family. Some are ornamental, others invasive

Salvia, Hybrid Cultivar, 'Plum'

weeds. Both flowers and fruits are used for making wines, jams, and jellies; the foliage is sometimes used medicinally. Elders have pinnate leaves, and the umbel-like heads of small white to creamy yellow flowers develop into quick-ripening berries, usually red to black.

CULTIVATION: Elders are not difficult to grow, and some species are only too easily cultivated; think twice before deliberately introducing *S. nigra* to your garden. They are not fussy about soil type as long as the ground remains fairly moist in summer, nor are they worried by brief periods of waterlogging in winter. Most species are very frost hardy, and will reshoot even when cut to the ground by frost. Prune trees to shape as necessary, and propagate from seed or cuttings.

S

Sanchezia speciosa

Sambucus canadensis

Sambucus canadensis 'Goldfinch'

Sambucus canadensis
AMERICAN ELDER, AMERICAN ELDERBERRY, SWEET ELDER

☼ ❀ ↔ 12 ft (3.5 m) ↕ 8–12 ft (2.4–3.5 m)

Deciduous shrub from eastern North America, sometimes suckering. Leaves usually have 7 leaflets with serrated edges, and may be smooth or rather woolly on the undersides. Cream flowers in summer, tiny purple-black berries. 'Goldfinch', lime green foliage, leaflets with incised edges, reddish young leaves. Zones 3–9.

Sambucus ebulus
DANE'S ELDER, DANEWORT, DWARF ELDER

☼ ❀ ↔ 3–7 ft (0.9–2 m) ↕ 5–7 ft (1.5–2 m)

Vigorous suckering perennial from southern Europe through northern Africa to Iran. Leaves divided, up to 9 leaflets to 6 in (15 cm) long. Tiny

flowers grow in flattish heads to 4 in (10 cm) wide, and are followed by black berries, in summer. Zones 5–10.

Sambucus nigra
BLACK ELDER, EUROPEAN ELDER

☼ ❀ ↔ 10–20 ft (3–6 m) ↕ 8–30 ft (2.4–9 m)

Deciduous shrub or small tree from Europe, North Africa, and western Asia. Self-sows and suckers freely. This species is a weed in many areas, but is cultivated for its edible flowers and fruits. Leaves have 3 to 9 dark green leaflets with serrated edges. Large heads of scented white flowers, in spring–early summer. Purple-black berries. 'Aurea', golden yellow foliage; 'Aureomarginata', paler variegated foliage, berries grow on pink stems; 'Guincho Purple', deep green leaves turn very dark purple; 'Laciniata', deeply dissected leaflets; 'Marginata', gold- to cream-edged foliage; 'Nana', loosely rounded form; 'Pulverulenta', cream and green mottled foliage and musk-scented flowers; 'Viridis', pale green flowers and fruits. Zones 5–10.

Sambucus racemosa
EUROPEAN RED ELDER, RED ELDERBERRY

☼ ❀ ↔ 12 ft (3.5 m) ↕ 12 ft (3.5 m)

Deciduous shrub found through most of temperate Eurasia, from the UK to

Japan. Leaves divided into 5 leaflets with coarsely serrated edges. Panicles of pale green to cream flowers appear in spring–early summer, followed by clusters of very small red berries. 'Plumosa Aurea', dissected yellow foliage; 'Sutherland Gold', deeply dissected golden foliage, turning copper-colored in spring (does best in partial shade, but can be grown in complete shade); 'Tenuifolia', dwarf, deeply cut foliage, purple new growth. Zones 4–9.

SANCHEZIA
Named after Josef Sanchez, an early Spanish professor of botany, this genus of about 20 species of soft-stemmed shrubs, climbers, and perennials from the acanthus (Acanthaceae) family is native to tropical America. *Sanchezia* species are grown for their attractive leaves, which are carried in opposite pairs, and for their showy tubular flowers, each with 5 lobes, and often with conspicuous colorful bracts. The fruits are oblong capsules containing 6 to 8 seeds.
CULTIVATION: Frost tender, these are warm-climate plants that need good soil and regular watering. They prefer well-drained soil, in full sun or bright

filtered light, in a position sheltered from wind. Water potted specimens adequately during the growing season, and keep just moist at other times. Plants can be kept neat and bushy by pinching out the growing tips. Propagate from cuttings taken in spring or summer.

Sanchezia speciosa
syn. *Sanchezia nobilis*

☼ ✿ ↔ 5 ft (1.5 m) ↕ 5 ft (1.5 m)

Bushy evergreen shrub from South America. Large, leathery, dark green, oblong-ovate leaves with prominent yellow or white veins. Tubular flowers, yellow with bright red bracts, on ends of spikes, in summer. Zones 10–12.

SANDERSONIA
A genus consisting of a single species of scrambling to climbing tuberous perennial, which is a member of the autumn-crocus (Colchiacaceae) family. Now rare in its native South African habitat of KwaZulu-Natal, the species is widely cultivated in gardens and for the cut-flower trade. It was named for John Sanderson (1820–91), honorary secretary to the Horticultural Society of Natal, and bears some similarities to the equally strange and surprising *Gloriosa rothschildiana* (glory lily).
CULTIVATION: Grow in full sun in a free-draining mix to which some well-rotted garden humus has been added.

Sambucus nigra

Sambucus nigra 'Laciniata'

Sandersonia aurantiaca

Poor soils are tolerated, and may even be preferable. Water well, and apply weak liquid feed every 10 days during the growth phase. Provide support for the climbing stems. Propagate from offsets in autumn, or by sowing ripe seed in a sandy mix in late winter.

Sandersonia aurantiaca ★
syn. *Sandersonia koetjape*
CHINESE LANTERN LILY, CHRISTMAS BELLS
☼ ⚘ ↔ 8 in (20 cm) ↑ 40 in (100 cm)
Deciduous perennial, tuberous and scrambling to climbing. Leaves are a soft green, growing alternately along the stems; tips often develop into tendrils by which the plant scrambles. Flowers are lantern-shaped, glowing golden orange, pendent, on downturned stalks, in summer. Zones 9–11.

SANGUINARIA
BLOODROOT, RED PUCCOON
This genus belonging to the poppy (Papaveraceae) family consists of a single species, found only in eastern North America. The plant is a hairless perennial that grows in woodlands. It has a branching rhizome, usually with a single palmately incised leaf. The small, white, starry flowers appear early, unfurling to reveal their rounded scalloped shape. The fruit capsules open from the middle to both the base and the apex. The many seeds have a juicy aril that is attractive to ants, which then help to disperse the seeds. This plant is an ephemeral and will die down by mid-summer—so mark its location. It will eventually spread to make a good woodland ground cover. The plant contains alkaloids, and has been used medicinally as an emetic.
CULTIVATION: Grow *Sanguinaria* in half-sun or shade in rich moist soil, and keep well watered. Prefers a damp

shaded area, where it can be left to spread. Sow seed when ripe, or divide rhizomes when the plant is dormant.

Sanguinaria canadensis
BLOODROOT, RED PUCCOON
☼/◑ ✻ ↔ 4 in (10 cm) ↑ 8 in (20 cm)
Perennial woodland plant from North America. Large green-gray leaves with deep indentations. White or pinkish flowers, 1 per stalk, in spring. Ephemeral, dies back in mid to late summer. Both 'Flore Pleno' and 'Multiplex' (syn. 'Plena') have showy double white flowers. Zones 2–8.

SANGUISORBA
syn. *Poterium*
BURNET
This genus, comprising about 10 species of shrubs and rhizomatous perennials found in temperate parts of Eurasia, North America, and the Canary Islands, is a member of the rose (Rosaceae) family. The spirally arranged leaves, divided into many leaflets with toothed edges, have a fern-like quality. The flowers are small, either unisexual or hermaphroditic, green, white, or pink, stalkless, and arranged in dense heads at the ends of stems, resembling bottlebrushes. The calyx tube has 4 petal-like lobes, and there are no petals. There are 4, rarely 12, stamens, and a single carpel. The fruits are leathery achenes. These plants are grown for their flower spikes and their attractive foliage. The rootstock has astringent qualities and was used to stop bleeding. Some species, such as *S. minor*, the salad burnet, have edible leaves.
CULTIVATION: Most *Sanguisorba* species are plants of damp meadowland, needing moist rich soils that do not dry out in summer. They are propagated by division in spring, or from seed sown in autumn or spring.

Sanguisorba canadensis
CANADIAN BURNET, GREAT BURNET
☼ ✻ ↔ 24–36 in (60–90 cm) ↑ 48–60 in (120–150 cm)
Clump-forming perennial from Newfoundland, Canada, through Michigan, and south to Georgia, USA. Bright green compound leaves with small regular indentations on edges. White bottlebrush-like flowers, in late summer. Zones 4–8.

Sanguisorba minor
GARDEN BURNET, SALAD BURNET
☼/◑ ✻ ↔ 12–16 in (30–40 cm) ↑ 30 in (75 cm)
Perennial from Europe and western Asia. Basal green leaves. Flowerheads

pink and rounded, in early to mid-summer. Young leaves give salads a cucumber flavor. Zones 3–8.

Sanguisorba officinalis
BURNET BLOODWORT, GREAT BURNET
☼ ✻ ↔ 24–36 in (60–90 cm) ↑ 30–36 in (75–90 cm)
Clump-forming perennial from temperate Eurasia. Medium green leaves, sometimes eaten when young. Deep red or dark purple flowers appear in summer. Zones 4–8.

SANSEVIERIA
BOWSTRING HEMP, MOTHER-IN-LAW'S TONGUE
A genus consisting of over 50 species of perennial plants in the dragon-tree (Dracaenaceae) family, all native to tropical and southern Africa and the East Indies. The thick fibrous leaves generally form a rosette, either lying nearly flat on the ground or stiffly upright up to 5 feet (1.5 m) tall. The flowers are held in a cluster or panicle on simple stems. The fiber from the leaves of *Sansevieria* species is traditionally used for making mats, rope, and bowstrings. These plants are generally cultivated for their decorative leaves, which may be variegated or mottled. They are important indoor plants in temperate climates.

Sanguinaria canadensis

Sanguinaria canadensis 'Flore Pleno'

CULTIVATION: Sansevierias are not tolerant of frost, and they need shade from the afternoon sun, and only moderate water in summer. Keep dry in winter. Propagation is by division of offsets or from leaf cuttings.

Sansevieria cylindrica
CYLINDER SNAKE PLANT
☼ ✦ ↔ 5 ft (1.5 m) ↑ 16 in (40 cm)
Native to southern tropical Africa. Long, arching, leathery leaves, cylindrical in section, forming low mound. Flowers white, flushed with pink, in raceme to 24 in (60 cm) long, held on stiff stem, in summer. Zones 10–11.

Sansevieria trifasciata
☼ ✦ ↔ 3 ft (0.9 m) ↑ 5 ft (1.5 m)
Native to tropical west Africa. Dense clump of stiffly upright straight leaves, pale to dark green transverse bands. White flowers in late spring. 'Bantel's Sensation', ivory to ocher, dark green variegated leaves; 'Golden Hahnii', yellow linear striations, can be weedy in warm moist conditions; 'Hahnii', dark green leaves, pale green transverse bands; 'Laurentii', dark green leaves, paler transverse bands, golden stripes along margins, can be weedy in warm moist conditions; 'Moonglow', compact, silver green leaves, edged dark green. Zones 10–11.

Sanguinaria canadensis 'Multiplex'

SANTALUM

This genus of around 25 species of evergreen shrubs and small trees of the sandalwood (Santalaceae) family comes from Southeast Asia, Australia, and some Pacific Islands. It includes a number of trees noted for their scented wood and oils. Some Australian species bear edible fruits, and have been researched as commercial food crops. They usually rely on the roots of other plants to supply their water and nutrients. The host may be another tree, a shrub, a dense ground-covering plant, or a well-established lawn with a vigorous root system. CULTIVATION: Grow in warm low-rainfall areas with full sun and light well-drained soils. *Santalum* species will tolerate saline soils and periods of dryness, but they resent root disturbance and poor drainage. They may

Santalum lanceolatum

Santalum acuminatum

be propagated from seed, but early growth is often slow, and grafted plants are preferred for orchard crops.

Santalum acuminatum
QUANDONG, SWEET QUANDONG

☀ ✂ ↔ 12 ft (3.5 m) ↑ 20 ft (6 m)

Large shrub or small tree, widespread in inland Australia. Spindly erect trunk, open crown of pale olive green lance-shaped leaves. Panicles of small whitish cream flowers at ends of stems, sporadically throughout year. Shiny, red, edible fruits. Zones 9–11.

Santalum lanceolatum
NORTHERN SANDALWOOD

☀ ✈ ↔ 15 ft (4.5 m) ↑ 20 ft (6 m)

Tall shrub or small tree from tropical Australia. Pendulous spreading branches, lance-shaped leaves. Cream or pale green flowers in leaf axils or in panicles at ends of branches, in spring–summer. Dark blue or purplish edible fruits. Zones 10–12.

SANTOLINA

This Mediterranean genus from the daisy (Asteraceae) family is composed of some 18 species of largely similar evergreen shrubs that form low hummocks. The slender stems are crowded with narrow leaves that have finely toothed or lobed margins. They are often clothed in silvery hairs, as are

the leaf stalks. Clusters of button-like flowerheads, usually bright yellow, appear in summer.
CULTIVATION: Fully to moderately frost hardy, these shrubs thrive in a warm sunny position and are ideal for dry banks and as border plants. They need perfect drainage and do not like overly wet winters, but are not fussy about soil type as long as it is reasonably loose and open. *Santolina* species respond well to regular trimming to keep the bushes neat and compact. It is also advisable to remove the dead flowerheads, as they are not attractive once they have dried. They can be propagated from small cuttings or by removing self-rooted layers.

Santolina chamaecyparissus
LAVENDER COTTON

☀ ❄ ↔ 4 ft (1.2 m) ↑ 24 in (60 cm)

Shrub from coastal southern Spain to the Adriatic region. Bright silvery gray foliage, almost white when young. Clusters of ½–¾ in (12–18 mm) wide flowerheads, early summer. *S. c.* var. *nana*, smaller, 12–24 in (30–60 cm) tall. *S. c.* 'Lemon Queen', soft yellow flowerheads; 'Pretty Carol', to 16 in (40 cm) tall. Zones 7–10.

Santolina rosmarinifolia
GREEN SANTOLINA

☀ ❄ ↔ 36 in (90 cm)
↑ 12–24 in (30–60 cm)

Bushy shrub native to southwestern Europe. Sparsely downy linear leaves have fine narrow teeth that are very closely spaced. Clusters of ¾ in (18 mm) wide bright yellow flower-

Santolina chamaecyparissus

Sanvitalia procumbens 'Aztec Gold'

Santolina rosmarinifolia

Sanvitalia procumbens

heads, in mid-summer. 'Morning Mist ★', compact form; 'Primrose Gem', light lemon flowers. Zones 7–10.

SANVITALIA

This genus of 7 species extends from southwestern USA through Central America to northwestern South America, and belongs to the daisy (Asteraceae) family. They are small ornamental shrubs or low-growing perennials or annuals. Leaves are opposite, with sheathing bases, and may be smooth-edged or lobed. The flowers resemble daisies. Outer florets have orange to yellow to white rays; disc florets are usually a deep purple.
CULTIVATION: Garden species are usually annuals, and are suited to an open sunny position in well-drained good soil. Propagate from seed sown in situ in spring or autumn.

Sanvitalia procumbens
CREEPING ZINNIA

☀ ❄ ↔ 12 in (30 cm) ↑ 6–8 in (15–20 cm)

Low spreading annual from southwestern USA and Mexico. Forms mats of hairy mid-green leaves. Many bright yellow to orange daisies, purple-black centers, in summer. 'Aztec Gold', bright yellow daisies, green centers; 'Gold Braid', double golden daisies; 'Mandarin Orange', bright orange flowers, black centers. Zones 6–11.

S

SAPINDUS

There are about 13 species in this tropical and subtropical genus of evergreen and deciduous trees, shrubs and climbers belonging to the soapberry (Sapindaceae) family. They are grown mostly as ornamental and shade trees. They have alternate simple or pinnate leaves, which in some species color attractively to shades of yellow in autumn. They bear clusters of small 5-petalled flowers with prominent hairy stamens in summer, and these are followed by a crop of fleshy berry-like fruits. These berries are rich in saponins (glycosides that foam in water solution), and are used to yield a soap substitute in some countries.
CULTIVATION: Most species are fairly adaptable, and will tolerate poor soil as long as it is well drained. They prefer a sheltered sunny position. Propagate from seed or cuttings.

Sapindus drummondii
WESTERN SOAPBERRY, WILD CHINA TREE
☀ ❄ ↔ 30 ft (9 m) ↑ 50 ft (15 m)
Deciduous tree from southern USA and Mexico, occupying harsh dry habitats. Spreading canopy of pinnate leaves, 18 mid-green leaflets, turning golden yellow in autumn. Small white flowers in panicles at ends of branches in summer. Rounded orange-yellow fruits. Zones 8–10.

Sapindus mukorossi
CHINESE SOAPBERRY
☀ ❄ ↔ 20 ft (6 m) ↑ 40 ft (12 m)
Deciduous tree found from India eastward through China to Japan. Pinnate leaves to 15 in (38 cm) long. White flowers bloom in panicles at the ends of branches in summer. The yellow to orange-brown fruits are used as a soap substitute; the black seeds are used for beads. Zones 8–11.

Sapindus mukorossi

Saponaria officinalis

SAPIUM

This is a genus of around 100 species of mainly deciduous trees and shrubs belonging to the euphorbia (Euphorbiaceae) family, from Southeast Asia and Central America. Some Sapium species are cultivated for commercially important products such as rubber, soap, and wax, but their sap can be poisonous. The leaves are simple and alternate. The monoecious flowers are borne in racemes at the ends of the branches, and are followed by hard-shelled capsular fruits.
CULTIVATION: They prefer full sun and well-drained soil, in moist temperate climates. Seeds can be collected in autumn and sown immediately, but the seedlings will vary considerably in quality. Young trees should be pruned every winter for several years until a shapely crown develops.

Sapium japonicum
syn. Neoshirakia japonica
☀ ❄ ↔ 15 ft (4.5 m) ↑ 25 ft (8 m)
Shrub or small tree from Korea, China, and Japan. Grayish hairless branches. Leaves smooth-edged, elliptical, or inversely egg-shaped; dark green, turning purplish red in autumn. Inconspicuous flowers on thin catkins, in mid-summer. Seed capsules 3-lobed. Zones 8–11.

Sapium sebiferum

Saponaria ocymoides

Sapium sebiferum
syn. Triadica sebifera
CHINESE TALLOW TREE
☀ ❄ ↔ 15 ft (4.5 m) ↑ 20 ft (6 m)
Attractive small tree from China and Taiwan. Round or oval sharply pointed leaves turn red, in autumn. Narrow racemes of green-yellow flowers. Fruits with waxy-coated seeds. Wax used to make candles in China. Zones 8–11.

SAPONARIA
SOAPWORT

This genus belonging to the pink (Caryophyllaceae) family contains some 20 species of temperate Eurasian annuals and perennials that contain saponin, a glycoside that forms a soapy colloidal solution when mixed with water. The roots in particular were once used as soap, and the extract is present in detergents and foaming agents. That use aside, these are pretty little plants that are well worth growing for their beauty alone. They are mainly low-growing, ranging from tufted mounds to fairly wide-spreading ground covers. They have blue-green linear to spatulate leaves, sometimes toothed, and in summer they are smothered in heads of small, starry, 5-petalled, pink flowers.
CULTIVATION: Mainly very hardy and easily grown, Saponaria species are most at home spilling over banks or in sunny perennial borders or rockeries with gritty, moist, humus-rich, free-draining soil. They will tolerate slightly alkaline soil. Propagate from cuttings or seed, or by layering.

Saponaria ocymoides
ROCK SOAPWORT
☀ ❄ ↔ 12–20 in (30–50 cm) ↑ 6–12 in (15–30 cm)
Summer-flowering, mound-forming, alpine perennial found from Spain to

Saponaria officinalis 'Rosea Plena'

the Balkans. Small, downy, lance-shaped leaves. Clusters of deep pink flowers, less commonly red or white, ½ in (12 mm) wide. 'Rubra Compacta' ★, dense mounding habit, deep crimson flowers. Zones 3–10.

Saponaria officinalis
BOUNCING BET, SOAPWORT
☀ ❄ ↔ 20–40 in (50–100 cm) ↑ 12–24 in (30–60 cm)

Perennial found over much of Europe. Large billowing mound of wiry stems, green to gray-green, with pointed oval leaves to ½ in (12 mm) long. Heads of 5 or more flowers to 1 in (25 mm) wide, usually bright pink, sometimes red or white, in late summer–autumn. 'Rosea Plena', tall, with pink double flowers; 'Rubra Plena', double flowers, crimson at opening, ageing to deep pink. Zones 4–10.

Saponaria × olivana
☀ ❄ ↔ 8 in (20 cm) ↑ 2 in (5 cm)
A dwarf cushion-forming hybrid, probably between S. caespitosa and S. pumilio, perhaps some S. ocymoides influence. Dense low mound, tiny green to gray-green leaves. Smothered in pink flowers, ¾ in (18 mm) wide, in late spring. Zones 3–10.

S

Sarcochilus, Hybrid, Armstrong

Sarcochilus, Hybrid, Bobby-Dazzler

Sarcochilus, Hybrid, First Light

Sarcochilus, Hybrid, Fitzhart

Sarcochilus, Hybrid, Velvet

Saraca cauliflora

Sarcochilus fitzgeraldii

Sarcochilus hartmannii

SARACA

A genus of about 70 species, these small evergreen trees from the cassia subfamily of the legume (Fabaceae) family come from the tropical forests of India, extending to China and Southeast Asia. They are grown for their dense upturned flower clusters in shades of yellow, orange, and red. Individual flowers have no petals; instead, they have 4 brightly colored sepals at the top of a tube with slender projecting stamens up to 8 in (20 cm) long. The leaves are pinnate with paired leaflets; they are soft, dangling, pinkish purple when young, maturing to a bright glossy green. These trees grow beneath taller trees in their natural habitat and therefore like to be in shade, preferably that of taller trees. CULTIVATION: Frost tender, they require a warm humid climate and a moist well-drained soil enriched with organic matter. In cooler areas, cultivate as greenhouse plants. Propagated from seed in autumn or winter.

Saraca cauliflora
syn. *Saraca thaipingensis*

☀ ✢ ↔25 ft (8 m) ↑30 ft (9 m)
Tree from Thailand to the Malay Peninsula. Compound leaves with 6 to 8 pairs of oblong leaflets, reddish when young. Night-fragrant yellow flowers, gradually deepening to red, appear at the beginning and end of tropical dry season. Narrow, oblong, leguminous fruits. Zones 11–12.

SARCOBATUS

Native to western North America, this genus contains only one species and belongs to the rose (Rosaceae) family. It is a dense spiny shrub with arching branches and narrow fleshy leaves. Male and female flowers appear on the same plant, and both are usually small, with the male flowers forming catkin-like spikes. The enlarging calyx of the female flowers develops into a leathery fruit with a broad papery wing toward the middle. CULTIVATION: Moderately frost hardy, this species grows best in a warm sheltered position in full sun and a well-drained soil. Propagation is from seed.

Sarcobatus vermiculatus
GREASEWOOD

❄ ❋ ↔7 ft (2 m) ↑6 ft (1.8 m)
Rounded spreading shrub with arching branches. Narrow, fleshy, gray-green leaves to 1½ in (35 mm) long. Spikes of male flowers up to 1¼ in (30 mm) long. The hard yellow wood is used for fuel. Zones 5–10.

SARCOCHILUS
FAIRY ORCHID

This genus contains about 20 diminutive monopodial species in the family Orchidaceae. They are native to eastern Australia and New Caledonia, and may be epiphytic or lithophytic. They grow in humid gullies and gorges, and in the fringes of rainforests. Mostly

spring- and summer-flowering, they have short inflorescences of showy blooms in many shapes and colors. Mainly cultivated are the lithophytic species, or rock dwellers. The tree-dwelling species often grow as twig epiphytes on the very outer branches of suitable shrubs and small trees. The lithophytes are clump-forming, whereas the epiphytes generally only have one growth. CULTIVATION: Lithophytic species are easily cultivated in pots, in a coarse mixture such as 2 parts medium-grade pine bark, one part pea-sized gravel, and a handful of perlite. Epiphytic species can be more temperamental, and should be grown on long narrow slabs of weathered timber or cork. They can succumb to crown rot almost overnight. They will take cool to cold conditions, but need at least 70 percent shade in a humid environment. Protect from frost and avoid excessive heat—keep them moist,

with good air circulation and high humidity. Clumping species may be propagated by division.

Sarcochilus fitzgeraldii

☀ ☷ ↔4–16 in (10–40 cm)
↑4–16 in (10–40 cm)

Australian lithophytic species that grows in cool heavily shaded situations. Up to 12 white blooms, 1¼ in (30 mm) wide, light pink to dark crimson spots or bands in center, in spring. Zones 9–11.

Sarcobatus vermiculatus, in winter

Sarcobatus vermiculatus, in summer

Saritaea magnifica

Sarcochilus hartmannii ★

☀ ⚘ ↔ 4–16 in (10–40 cm)
↑ 4–16 in (10–40 cm)

Variable, lithophytic orchid from Australia; often grows in strong light. Thick leaves. Upright to arching sprays of up to 25 pure white round flowers, 1 in (25 mm) wide, tiny labellum, may have reddish brown markings in center, spring. Zones 9–11.

Sarcochilus Hybrids

☀ ⚘ ↔ 4–16 in (10–40 cm)
↑ 4–16 in (10–40 cm)

Sarcochilus has been extensively line-bred and hybridized. Popular combinations link hardy lithophytic types such as *S. ceciliae*, *S. fitzgeraldii*, and *S. hartmannii* with smaller-flowered but colorful epiphytic species. The use of *S. hirticalcar* expanded both color range and flowering times of hybrids, so some bloom year round. Individual blooms range from ¾ in (18 mm) to 1½ in (35 mm) wide. **Armstrong**, orange toned blooms; **Bobby-Dazzler**, pink and purple flowers, blooms year round; **First Light ★**, brown and tan tones and spotting; **Fitzhart**, white blooms, bands and suffusions of purple; **Heidi**, backcross of *S. Fitzhart* and *S. hartmannii*; **Melba**, the primary hybrid between *S. falcatus* and *S. hartmannii*; **Velvet**, from pale to deep purples and pinks, blooms year round. Zones 9–11.

SARCOCOCCA

CHRISTMAS BOX, SWEET BOX
This genus within the box (Buxaceae) family consists of evergreen monoecious shrubs cultivated for their ornamental value. Their natural habitats are damp woods and dense forests in western China, the Himalayas, and the mountains of Southeast Asia. The male flowers can be recognized by their visible anthers, while the female flowers grow below the male flowers.

CULTIVATION: They grow best in neutral to alkaline soil, with plenty of humus added. Once established, they will tolerate drier conditions in shade. They can be grown in full sun, but will then need more moisture. Most will tolerate a variety of conditions, as well as years of negligence and air pollution. Propagation is from seed, by division of suckering species, or by taking half-hardened cuttings in late summer. Hardwood cuttings can be taken in winter and propagated in an area protected from winter frosts.

Sarcococca confusa

☀ ❄ ↔ 7 ft (2 m) ↑ 7 ft (2 m)

Attractive evergreen shrub, origin unknown. Leathery, dark green, elliptical to lance-shaped leaves with pale undersides. Clusters of cream flowers, female form very fragrant, in midwinter. Bright red berries turn black when ripe. Zones 6–10.

Sarcococca hookeriana

☀ ❄ ↔ 6 ft (1.8 m) ↑ 5 ft (1.5 m)

Evergreen thicket-forming often suckering shrub native to China. Lance-shaped deep green leaves. Clusters of scented white flowers, males with deep pink anthers, in late autumn to winter. Black fruits. *S. h.* subsp. *humilis* ★, ground cover, shiny bluish black fruit. *S. h.* var. *digyna*, slender leaves, off-white anthers. *S. h.* 'Purple Stem', young magenta shoots, pink-tinted flowers. Zones 6–10.

Sarcococca ruscifolia

☀ ❄ ↔ 3 ft (0.9 m) ↑ 3 ft (0.9 m)

Thick bushy suckering shrub native to western China and the Himalayas. Glossy, deep green, broadly lance-shaped leaves. Clusters of creamy white perfumed flowers in winter. Dark red fruits. Zones 8–10.

Sarcococca saligna

☀ ❄ ↔ 3 ft (0.9 m) ↑ 3 ft (0.9 m)

Suckering, evergreen, thicket-forming shrub native to the Himalayas from Nepal to Afghanistan. Narrow, lance-shaped, pale green leaves. Male flowers green, female flowers greenish white, in winter–early spring. Egg-shaped dark purple fruits. Zones 7–10.

SARITAEA

The single species in this genus, which belongs to the trumpet-vine (Bignoniaceae) family, is found in Ecuador and Colombia. The plant is a liane. The stems are almost round in cross-section, and are marked with longitudinal stripes. The leaves have 2 leaflets and a further 2 leaflet-like appendages at the base of the leaf stalk, plus a tendril at the tip. The large often showy flowers in shades of purple to red and rose pink are borne in panicles along or at the ends of the branches. Their nectar is collected by the male bees of the tropical genus *Euglossa*, which pollinate the flowers by brushing against the pollen and transferring it. The calyx is tubular, with an unlobed margin. The corolla is a tubular bell-shape, and is hairy inside around the bases of the stamens. The fruit is a long flattened capsule containing 2 winged seeds.
CULTIVATION: These plants prefer bright filtered light and well-drained moisture-retaining soil with plenty of humus; keep moist. Propagate from cuttings or seed.

Saritaea magnifica

syns *Arrabidaea magnifica*, *Bignonia magnifica*

☀/◑ ✈ ↔ 8–15 ft (2.4–4.5 m)
↑ 25 ft (8 m)

Evergreen climber with 2-part leathery leaves and oblong leaflets to 4 in (10 cm) long. Narrow, tubular, rosy purple flowers, flaring petals, showy heads, in summer. Zones 10–12.

SARRACENIA

AMERICAN PITCHER PLANT, TRUMPET PITCHER
The 8 species of *Sarracenia* are beautiful carnivorous American pitcher-plants in the family Sarraceniaceae. They hybridize easily, both in the wild and in cultivation. They are found in swamps, wetlands, and pine forest edges, mainly in southeastern USA. They are perennial, growing from a rhizome, and the leaves or pitchers form a basal rosette. Most have long tubular pitchers. Their stunning, nodding, scented flowers grow singly on tall leafless stalks. Inside, downward-pointing hairs prevent their prey—usually small insects—from escaping out of a well of digestive liquid.
CULTIVATION: Grow in full sun in peat moss or a mix of peat and sand. Water by tray, keeping level constant. Suits warmish temperate climate, with cold winters for the 3- to 5-month dormancy. Most will withstand light frosts. Propagate by division during winter dormancy. Divide and repot potted plants every 2 to 3 years.

Sarcococca ruscifolia

Sarcococca saligna

Sarracenia leucophylla, in the wild, Alabama, USA

Sarracenia flava, in the wild, Apalachicola, Florida, USA

Sarracenia alata ★

FLYCATCHER, PALE PITCHER PLANT

☼ ❄ ↔ 12 in (30 cm) ↑ 27 in (70 cm)

Pitcher plant from Texas, Louisiana, Mississippi, and Alabama, USA. Light green pitchers to 26 in (65 cm) high, sometimes red veined, red pitcher lid. Yellow to white flowers, 2 in (5 cm) wide, on long stalks, in spring.

S. a. × *S. flava* 'Maxima', vigorous, pitchers to 24 in (60 cm), flowers yellow to green. Zones 7–9.

Sarracenia × catesbaei

☼ ❄ ↔ 12 in (30 cm) ↑ 18 in (45 cm)

Popular hybrid of *S. purpurea* × *S. flava*. Tall pitchers, large frilled lid, red veined to fully red. Zones 7–9.

Sarracenia × exornata

☼ ❄ ↔ 12 in (30 cm) ↑ 14 in (35 cm)

Naturally occurring hybrid of *S. purpurea* × *S. alata*. Pitchers red veined to totally burgundy, frilled lid. Zones 7–9.

Sarracenia flava ★

YELLOW TRUMPET

☼ ❄ ↔ 12 in (30 cm) ↑ 30 in (75 cm)

Varied pitcher plant found along the Atlantic coastal plain of the USA. Tall pitchers, widening toward the mouth, large green lid. Yellow to greenish yellow flowers, spring. '**Red Veined**', red veined, red around throat. Zones 7–9.

Sarracenia 'Juthatip Soper'

☼ ❄ ↔ 12 in (30 cm) ↑ 18 in (45 cm)

Stunning award-winning cultivar of *S. mitchelliana* crossed with very pink form of *S. leucophylla*. Rich reddish purple pitchers. Zones 7–9.

Sarracenia leucophylla

WHITE TRUMPET

☼ ❄ ↔ 12 in (30 cm) ↑ 24 in (60 cm)

Pitcher plant found along Atlantic coastal plain of USA. Showy species,

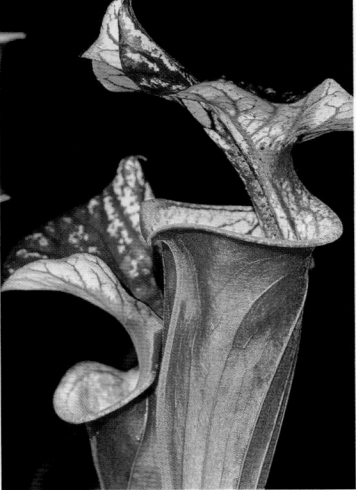

Sarracenia flava 'Red Veined'

beautiful pitchers, green at base, top white, red veined. Deep burgundy flowers, fragrant. *S. l.* × *S. oreophila*, robust, narrow, bright green pitchers, crimson veining. Zones 7–9.

Sarracenia minor

HOODED PITCHER PLANT

☼ ❄ ↔ 12 in (30 cm) ↑ 24 in (60 cm)

Pitcher plant found on floating sphagnum islands in North and South Carolina, Georgia, and Florida, USA. Pitchers are pale green to red, with the hood curling over pitcher mouth.

Sarracenia alata × *S. flava* 'Maxima'

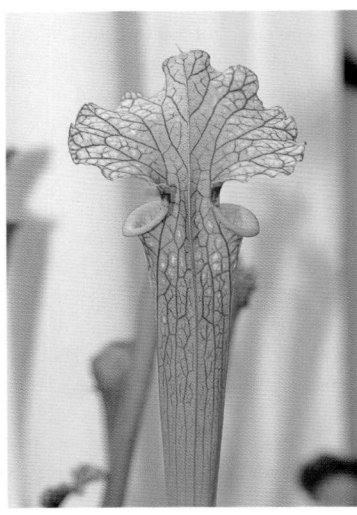

Sarracenia × *catesbaei*

Sarracenia × *exornata*

Sarracenia 'Juthatip Soper'

Sarracenia leucophylla × *S. oreophila*

S

Sarracenia purpurea

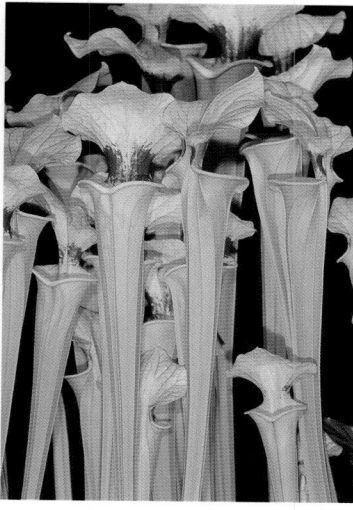

Sarracenia × moorei 'Brook's Hybrid'

Sarracenia × stevensii

Sarracenia × readii

The upper pitcher is covered with fenestrations ("windows" for admitting light). Bears yellow flowers in spring. Zones 7–9.

Sarracenia × mitchelliana

☼ ❋ ↔ 12 in (30 cm) ↑ 18 in (45 cm)
Pitcher plant, hybrid of *S. purpurea* and *S. leucophylla*. Curved pitchers, hood usually ruffled, lower parts green, red and white around top and hood. Zones 7–9.

Sarracenia × moorei

☼ ❋ ↔ 12 in (30 cm) ↑ 40 in (100 cm)
Pitcher plant, cross between *S. flava* and *S. leucophylla*. Very tall pitchers,

40 in (100 cm) or more. '**Brook's Hybrid**', red around throat, pink to red flowers. Zones 7–9.

Sarracenia oreophila

BUGLE GRASS, FROG BONNETS, GREEN PITCHER PLANT

☼ ❋ ↔ 12 in (30 cm) ↑ 24 in (60 cm)
Rare pitcher plant from Alabama, Georgia, and North and South Carolina, USA. Green pitchers, red veined to almost totally red, wide mouth, heart-shaped lid. Pale yellow fragrant flowers. Endangered species since 1979. Zones 7–9.

Sarracenia psittacina

LOBSTER POT, PARROT PITCHER PLANT

☼ ❋ ↔ 20 in (50 cm) ↑ 10 in (25 cm)
Unusual pitcher plant from the southeastern coastal plain of the USA. Pitchers grow upward and then fall back horizontally, forming a rosette with the pitcher openings facing the center of the plant. Pitchers green to red, puffed up hood. Red flowers. Prefers very wet soil, and can survive flooding, during which it preys on small swimming creatures. Zones 7–9.

Sarracenia purpurea ★

HUNTSMAN'S CAP, NORTHERN PITCHER PLANT, SIDESADDLE PLANT

☼ ❋ ↔ 24 in (60 cm) ↑ 10 in (25 cm)
Found east of Canadian Rockies and southward along coastal USA to Gulf of Mexico. Green to purple bulging pitchers 12 in (30 cm) high, prominent rib, hood ruffled or unruffled. Green, pink, or burgundy flowers. Grow in sphagnum moss. *S. p.* **subsp. venosa**, fat green to red pitchers. *S. p.* **f. heterophylla**, narrow, green, wide mouth pitchers, tolerates cool conditions, long winter frosts. Zones 2–9.

Sarracenia × readii

☼ ❋ ↔ 12 in (30 cm) ↑ 24 in (60 cm)
Naturally occurring cross between *S. leucophylla* and *S. rubra*. Bright green slender pitchers with ruffled lids that are white and veined with red. Zones 7–9.

Sarracenia × stevensii

☼ ❋ ↔ 12 in (30 cm) ↑ 24 in (60 cm)
The origins of this Dutch hybrid are disputed, but it is believed to be a cross between *S. rubra* and *S. leucophylla*. Pitchers are green and heavily veined with red. Zones 7–9.

Sarracenia minor

Sarracenia × mitchelliana

Sarracenia oreophila

S

Sassafras albidum

Sasa veitchii

SASA

Sasa is the Japanese word for bamboo, and this genus has 60 species of small to medium-sized bamboos native to southeastern Russia, southern China, northern Japan, and Korea. Members of the grass (Poaceae) family, they have running rhizomes and arching culms, and the stems have a waxy white bloom at the nodes. The broad finely toothed leaves wither in winter; those of *S. veitchii* create ornamental white margins of "false parchment," which lowers leaf maintenance yet still suppresses competition from weeds and protects buds from severe cold. The tropical appearance of these plants is illusory: when weighed down with snow, the thin flexible culms protect against severe cold winds.
CULTIVATION: Grow in a damp rich soil in part-shade. *Sasa* species spread rapidly, so careful siting is necessary, or the plants can be confined in a large container. Propagate in spring by coiling the mature rhizomes into pots and covering them with potting compost. Tidy plants by clearing away disheveled culms at the end of winter.

Sasa palmata
☀ ❄ ↔ 10–20 ft (3–6 m) ↑ 7 ft (2 m)
Native to Japan. Vigorous spreading species forms thick hedge. Stems may be streaked with purple. Palm-like foliage, long tapering leaves, bright shiny green all year, yellow midrib. 'Nebulosa', brown cloud-like markings on mature culms. Zones 7–11.

Sasa veitchii
KUMA ZASA
☀ ❄ ↔ 10–20 ft (3–6 m) ↑ 5 ft (1.5 m)
From Japan. Ground-covering foliage tolerates dark dry locations. Stems purple-lined, glaucous. Short tapering leaves wither in winter to broad, papery, white margins. Zones 6–11.

SASAELLA
This genus of around 10 species of bamboo from Japan belongs to the grass (Poaceae) family. It differs from the related *Sasa* in having multiple thinner canes and smaller narrow leaves on near-horizontal branches. The leaves are quite heavily textured, and often have longitudinal stripes or bands, as do the leaf sheaths. The widely cultivated colourful variegated forms are often low-growing and used as ground cover or ornamental shrubs.
CULTIVATION: Tolerant of fairly heavy frosts and able to grow in most exposures, they prefer warm humid summers and thrive in humus-rich soil. All species spread quite quickly through running roots, especially in moist loose soil, and can become invasive. Propagate by division whenever conditions are not extreme.

Sasaella masumuneana
syn. *Sasa masamuneana*
☀/❄ ❄ ↔ 3–10 ft (0.9–3 m)
↑ 3–7 ft (0.9–2 m)
Very fine canes, narrow leaves to 8 in (20 cm) long, purple-lined sheaths.

Rarely cultivated. Attractive 12–24 in (30–60 cm) tall cultivars include 'Albostriata', creamy striped leaves ageing to yellow; 'Aureostriata', golden yellow striped leaves. Zones 7–10.

SASSAFRAS
This genus includes just 3 species in the laurel (Lauraceae) family. They are deciduous trees with a rather scattered distribution, occurring in temperate East Asia and eastern North America. They have been cultivated for their aromatic oils, which repel pests and so are valuable in the furniture industry. *Sassafras* leaves may be smooth-edged or lobed, are downy on their undersides, and sometimes develop vivid autumn colors. Racemes of tiny, petal-less, yellow-green flowers appear in spring with the developing leaves, and are followed by blue-black drupes.
CULTIVATION: They are reasonably frost hardy. They prefer deep, fertile, well-drained soil, and will grow in sun or part-shade. They tend to produce multiple trunks, and pruning can be directed to encourage this habit or to produce a single-trunked tree, as the situation dictates. Propagate from seed, suckers, or root cuttings.

Sassafras albidum
SASSAFRAS
☀ ❄ ↔ 30 ft (9 m) ↑ 50 ft (15 m)
North American tree, may be many-trunked. Oval leaves, up to 3 lobes, dark green, downy undersides, turn gold and red in autumn. Elegant shape. The underbark is the source of sassafras oil. Zones 5–9.

SATUREJA
SAVORY
This genus of highly aromatic, small shrubs belonging to the mint (Lamiaceae) family, is native to dry stony hillsides in the Mediterranean, the woods of North America, and the Himalayas. Four-angled, woody stems bear small, hairy, round to oval leaves. Pale lilac to white flowers are borne in whorls on upright spikes throughout spring and summer. These are

Satureja montana

valuable plants for the rock garden and dry walls, and they attract bees and butterflies. It is a very fragrant herb, and the leaves of some species are used for herbal tea or as a seasoning.
CULTIVATION: Grow in any fertile well-drained soil. These plants require only minimal water through summer. Some species self-seed. Propagation is generally from cuttings or by removal of rooted shoots.

Satureja hortensis
SUMMER SAVORY
☀ ❄ ↔ 8 in (20 cm) ↑ 8 in (20 cm)
Annual from southern Europe. Erect hairy stems, long pointed leaves. Dense spikes of mauve to white flowers, in whorls, appear in spring–summer. Aromatic, it is widely used in cooking. Zones 5–9.

Satureja montana
WINTER SAVORY
☀ ❄ ↔ 12 in (30 cm)
↑ 20–36 in (50–90 cm)
Semi-evergreen shrublet from southern Europe and northern Africa. Small, highly fragrant, oblong leaves. Bears whorls of pale lilac flowers in summer. Leaves similar in flavor and scent to thyme (*Thymus vulgaris*) used for seasoning meat and vegetables. Zones 4–8.

SAURURUS
LIZARD'S TAIL
This genus of just 2 species—one from eastern Asia, one from eastern North America—gives its name to the lizard's-tail (Saururaceae) family. They are tall, erect, rhizomatous, perennials that grow in bogs. The leaves are undivided and spirally arranged. The leaf-base is kidney- to heart-shaped, and the stipules are joined to the stalk. The flowerhead is a dense raceme on the sides of the ends of branches. The ivory to white fragrant flowers are small, without sepals or petals, and have 6, rarely 8, stamens. They produce no nectar, but have a faint scent. The round fruit is warty with just a single seed.

Saururus cernuus

Saxegothaea conspicua

CULTIVATION: These are plants for bog gardens or damp woodlands. They are propagated by division, or from seed sown in pots kept moist.

Saururus cernuus
LIZARD'S TAIL

☀ ❄ ↔ 36 in (90 cm)
↑ 12–18 in (30–45 cm)

Water plant from eastern USA. Forms small colonies by underground runners. Leaves are arrow- or heart-shaped. Bottlebrush-like flower spikes arch above foliage. Bead-like seeds resemble lizard's tail. Zones 5–10.

SAXEGOTHAEA
This single-species genus of coniferous tree or shrub in the plum-pine (Podocarpaceae) family is native to southern Chile and adjoining parts of Argentina. Similar in some respects to yew *(Taxus)*, with its spreading and arching sprays of foliage, it is distinguished by its irregularly arranged leaves and in its fruits. In mild areas, especially in woodland, it will grow into a narrow-crowned upright tree. It is the only member of this family to have wingless pollen grains.
CULTIVATION: This species prefers well-drained moderately fertile soil in full sun or part-shade. In favorable locations, sheltered from cold winds, it will make a neat small tree or shrub. Propagate from half-hardened cuttings in late summer and early autumn.

Saxegothaea conspicua
PRINCE ALBERT'S YEW

☀ ❄ ↔ 15 ft (4.5 m)   ↑ 50 ft (15 m)
Slender, conical crown in mild areas, slow growing and bushy elsewhere. Bark is flaky and fluted. Deep green leaves, irregular, linear, or narrowly lanceolate, tapered to the base, pale green at margins. Male cones are egg-shaped. Zones 8–10.

SAXIFRAGA
This genus in the saxifrage (Saxifragaceae) family is very extensive, comprising a wide range of perennial, annual, or biennial ground-hugging plants, many of which are alpines. They are found throughout much of the temperate and subarctic zones of the Northern Hemisphere, with outposts in places such as Ethiopia, Mexico, and the Arctic. There are some 480 known species, as well as numerous garden hybrids. The 3 main sections that are of garden interest are the "mossies," the "silvers," and the Kabschia and Engleria subsections. A major attraction for many gardeners is that the plants are not only diverse in themselves but come from a variety of habitats, such as exposed mountains and moist woodlands.
CULTIVATION: Being shallow-rooted plants, they require free-draining relatively fertile soil in either sun or part-shade. Propagate by division at any time, or from seed in autumn.

Saxifraga andersonii
☀ ❄ ↔ 12 in (30 cm)   ↑ 4 in (10 cm)
Cushion-forming perennial from Nepal and Tibet. Loose rosettes of gray-green leaves. Clear white or pink flowers on 4 in (10 cm) tall stalks, in spring. Zones 6–8.

Saxifraga aretioides
☀/◐ ❄ ↔ 4–8 in (10–20 cm)
↑ 3–6 in (8–15 cm)
Cushion-forming perennial found from southern France to the Balkans. Tiny, blue-green, linear leaves with

Saxifraga andersonii

Saxifraga aretioides

white chalky coating at edges. Small heads of bright yellow flowers on wiry stems, in early summer. Zones 6–9.

Saxifraga californica
syn. *Heuchera rubescens*

☀ ❄ ↔ 6 in (15 cm)   ↑ 6 in (15 cm)
Clump-forming tufted perennial from western North America and Mexico. Rounded, kidney-shaped, mid-green leaves. Spikes of pale pink to white bell-shaped flowers, in summer. Zones 4–8.

Saxifraga callosa
syn. *Saxifraga lingulata*

☀ ❄ ↔ 8 in (20 cm)   ↑ 10 in (25 cm)
Evergreen perennial from western and eastern Spain, the southwestern alpine

Saxifraga callosa

areas of Europe, Sardinia, Sicily, and southern Italy. Rosettes of broad, round, silver-gray foliage growing in dense clumps. Star-shaped white flowers, ½ in (12 mm) wide, in early summer. Grows on limestone formations. Zones 7–9.

Saxifraga cochlearis
SNAIL SAXIFRAGE

☀ ❄ ↔ 6 in (15 cm)   ↑ 8 in (20 cm)
Very tight, dense, mat-forming cushion plant from the maritime Alps of France. Rosettes of mid-green spoon-shaped leaves. Clusters of red-spotted white flowers on 4 in (10 cm) tall hairy stems. 'Probynii', pure white flowers. Zones 7–8.

Saxifraga cochlearis 'Probynii'

S. californica, in the wild, Parque Nacional San Pedro Mártir, Baja California, Mexico

S

Saxifraga fortunei

syn. *Saxifraga cortusifolia* var. *fortunei*

☼ ❀ ↔ 12 in (30 cm) ↕ 20 in (50 cm)

Semi-evergreen to deciduous clump-forming perennial herb, native to Japan. Leaves are kidney-shaped and rounded, to 4 in (10 cm) long, with undersides of foliage frequently dark purple. White flowers appear on 20 in (50 cm) tall stems in late autumn. Zones 6–8.

Saxifraga × gaudinii

☼/◐ ❀ ↔ 6–12 in (15–30 cm) ↕ 4–6 in (10–15 cm)

Hybrid between *S. cotyledon* and *S. paniculata*. Forms low spreading clump of small spatula-shaped leaves. Purple-flecked white flowers appear in heads to 6 in (15 cm) tall from late spring. Zones 4–9.

Saxifraga hartii

Saxifraga maderensis var. *pickeringii*

Saxifraga globulifera

Saxifraga × geum

syn. *Saxifraga hirsuta × S. umbrosa*

☼ ❀ ↔ 8 in (20 cm) ↕ 8 in (20 cm)

Mat-forming perennial from the Pyrenees. Dark green rounded foliage forms dense rosettes. Clusters of star-shaped white flowers with red spots appear on 8 in (20 cm) tall stem, in summer. Zones 6–8.

Saxifraga globulifera

☼/◐ ❀ ↔ 8–12 in (20–30 cm) ↕ 6–8 in (15–20 cm)

Mounding perennial found on both sides of the Straits of Gibraltar. Short, leafy, erect stems, and rosettes of small 5-lobed leaves. White flowers to 6 mm wide appear in heads on stems to 6 in (15 cm) long in autumn–spring. *S. g.* var. *oranensis*, summer-dormant buds on long stalks. Zones 7–10.

Saxifraga hartii

syn. *Saxifraga rosacea* subsp. *hartii*

◐ ❀ ↔ 6–12 in (15–30 cm) ↕ 3–6 in (8–15 cm)

British species, now rare in the wild. Forms densely foliaged bright green cushions with a few trailing stems around the edges. Leaves are up to ¾ in (18 mm) long, cut at tips, usually into 5 segments. Short erect spikes carry heads of small white or pink flowers. Zones 7–9.

Saxifraga oppositifolia

Saxifraga spathularis

Saxifraga longifolia

PYRENEES SAXIFRAGE

☼ ❀ ↔ 8 in (20 cm) ↕ 27 in (70 cm)

From the Pyrenees. Single rosettes of silvery gray-green leaves form pyramid shape after 3 to 4 years of cultivation. Single flower panicle to 27 in (70 cm) tall, with about 80 white star-shaped flowers, in summer. Zones 6–7.

Saxifraga maderensis

☼/◐ ❀ ↔ 8–12 in (20–30 cm) ↕ 4–6 in (10–15 cm)

Cushion-forming perennial native of Madeira. Small kidney-shaped leaves with 5 lobes, themselves divided. Upright stems bear heads of white flowers in late spring. *S. m.* var. *pickeringii*, high-altitude form with larger rounder flowers. Zones 7–9.

Saxifraga oppositifolia

PURPLE MOUNTAIN SAXIFRAGE

☼/◐ ❀ ↔ 8 in (20 cm) ↕ 1 in (2.5 cm)

Very small, clumping and dense mat-forming perennial herb from arctic-latitude mountains of Europe, western Asia, and North America. Stiff, elliptical, dark green leaves grow in rosettes. Single, almost stemless, dark red to purple to pale pink flowers appear in summer. Zones 1–7.

Saxifraga longifolia

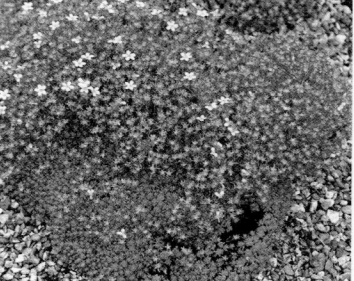

Saxifraga stansfieldii

Saxifraga paniculata

syn. *Saxifraga aizoon*

☼ ❀ ↔ 10 in (25 cm) ↕ 6 in (15 cm)

Mat-forming perennial from Canada, Norway, Greenland, and Iceland. Rosettes of narrow gray-green leaves, 2½ in (6 cm) long, lime-encrusted margins. Creamy white to pink flowers, in early summer. Zones 1–6.

Saxifraga spathularis

ST PATRICK'S CABBAGE

☼/◐ ❀ ↔ 6–8 in (15–20 cm) ↕ 8–12 in (20–30 cm)

Summer-flowering species from Ireland, Spain, and Portugal. Clumped rosettes of rounded, 1–2 in (25–50 mm) long, leathery, bright green leaves with coarsely toothed edges. Wiry stems bear sprays of tiny pinkish purple flowers in spring. Zones 5–9.

Saxifraga stansfieldii

☼/◐ ❀ ↔ 4–6 in (10–15 cm) ↕ 3–4 in (8–10 cm)

Thought to be a small European mountain species of rocky crevices and alpine troughs. Small toothed leaves forming rosettes. Clusters of soft pink flowers, in spring. Zones 5–9.

Saxifraga stolonifera

syn. *Saxifraga sarmentosa*

MOTHER OF THOUSANDS, STRAWBERRY BEGONIA

☼/◐ ❀ ↔ 12 in (30 cm) ↕ 16 in (40 cm)

Perennial from East Asia. Rounded, kidney-shaped, mid- to dark green, serrated leaves form dense mounds of foliage. Tall loose stems of white flowers, 16 in (40 cm) long and spotted with red or yellow, in summer. '**Eco Butterfly**', golden yellow leaves, green centers; '**Harvest Moon**', moon-shaped golden green to reddish leaves; '**Tricolor**', leaves edged in tones of red, white, and/or pink. Zones 5–10.

Saxifraga trifurcata
☼/◐ ❋ ↔ 8–16 in (20–40 cm)
↕ 8–12 in (20–30 cm)

Evergreen perennial native of northern Spain. Large open cushions of shiny, dark green, 3-lobed leaves, to ¾ in (18 mm) long. Wiry flower stems bear heads of up to 15 small white flowers, in summer. Zones 6–9.

Saxifraga umbrosa
☼ ❋ ↔ 12 in (30 cm) ↕ 12 in (30 cm)

Clump-forming perennial from the Pyrenees. Green foliage grows in stiff rosettes. Loose panicles of rose pink flowers, 10 in (25 cm) long, spotted with irregular red blotches, in late spring–early summer. Zones 1–5.

Saxifraga × *urbium*
syn. *Saxifraga umbrosa* 'London Pride'
LONDON PRIDE
☼ ❋ ↔ 18–36 in (45–90 cm)
↕ 12 in (30 cm)

Of garden origin, a quick-growing ground covering perennial with large rosettes of spoon-shaped, leathery, dark green leaves. Arching stems of

Saxifraga trifurcata

small pale pink flowers in summer. '**Aureovariegata**', gray-green and gold variegated leaves. Zones 6–7.

Saxifraga Hybrid Cultivars
☼/◐ ❋/❋ ↔ 6–18 in (15–45 cm)
↕ 3–12 in (8–30 cm)

Saxifraga species hybridize freely in the wild, and many garden plants are of indeterminate parentage. Nevertheless, their more carefully bred brethren are attractive little plants, at home in rock and alpine gardens. '**James Bremner**', 6 in (15 cm) tall, creamy white flowers; '**Purple Robe**', dense foliage cushion, many 4–6 in (10–15 cm) tall sprays of purple-pink flowers; '**Southside Seedling**' dark green spoon-shaped leaves in rosettes, arching panicles of white saucer-like flowers; '**Tumbling Waters**' (syn. *S. longifolia* 'Tumbling Waters'), dark green rosettes of foliage, and arching

Saxifraga, Hybrid Cultivar, 'Cloth of Gold'

Saxifraga, Hybrid Cultivar, 'James Bremner'

Saxifraga × *urbium* 'Aureovariegata'

Saxifraga umbrosa, cultivar

Scabiosa atropurpurea 'Chile Black'

Scabiosa atropurpurea 'Peter Ray'

racemes of star-shaped white flowers; '**Whitehill**', gray-green foliage with crusty white edges, white flowers on stems to 12 in (30 cm) tall. Zones 6–9.

SCABIOSA
SCABIOUS

An unpleasant sounding name, *Scabiosa* is derived from *scabies*, a Latin word for scurf or mange, which was said to be relieved by rubbing with the leaves of these plants. A member of the teasel (Dipsacaceae) family, the genus comprises around 80 species of annuals and perennials found in Europe, parts of Africa, and Japan. Most species form a spreading basal clump of light green to gray-green, rounded to lance-shaped leaves with deeply incised notches or lobes. A few species have an erect or branching habit. The flowers are individually

Saxifraga, Hybrid Cultivar, 'Purple Robe'

tiny, but occur in rounded to flattened composite heads on stems held clear of the foliage. White and pale yellow to soft pink or powder blue and mauve are the usual colors.
CULTIVATION: They are hardy and easily grown in any sunny position in fertile, moist, free-draining, slightly alkaline soil. Propagate annuals from seed and perennials from seed and basal cuttings, or by division.

Scabiosa atropurpurea
EGYPTIAN ROSE, MOURNFUL WIDOW, SWEET SCABIOUS
☼/◐ ❋ ↔ 16–30 in (40–75 cm)
↕ 16–36 in (40–90 cm)

Annual, biennial, or short-lived perennial herbs from southern Europe. Basal cluster of light green to gray-green, lobed or toothed leaves to 6 in (15 cm) long, upper leaves shorter and more deeply lobed, almost pinnate. Flowerheads crimson to deep purple-black, fragrant, to 2 in (5 cm) wide, in summer–early autumn. '**Blue Cockade**', 36 in (90 cm) tall, rounded, deep blue, double flowerheads; '**Chile Black**', 24 in (60 cm) tall, deep black-red flowers with minute flecks of lavender; '**Peter Ray**', 24 in (60 cm) tall, large purple-black flowerheads; '**Salmon Queen**', 36 in (90 cm) tall, deep salmon pink to light red double flowers. Zones 8–10.

S

Scadoxus multiflorus, in the wild, Masai Mara National Reserve, Kenya

Scadoxus multiflorus subsp. *katherinae*

Scabiosa caucasica

☀/◐ ❄ ↔16–18 in (40–45 cm)
↕20–36 in (50–90 cm)

Perennial from the Caucasus region. Leaves gray-green to blue-green, basal foliage lance-shaped, large, smooth-edged; upper leaves lobed almost to midrib. Powder blue flowers bloom in heads to 3 in (8 cm) wide, in summer–autumn. 'Alba', white flowers; 'Bressingham White', white flowers; 'Clive Greaves' ★, pale lavender blue flowers; 'Fama', bright blue flowers; 'Floral Queen', tall, vigorous, light blue flowers; 'Miss Willmott', tall, cream flowers; 'Nachtfalter', dark purple flowers; 'Pink Lace', bright pink flowers. Zones 4–10.

Scabiosa columbaria

☀/◐ ❄ ↔16 in (40 cm) ↕24 in (60 cm)
Biennial or short-lived perennial from temperate Eurasia and North Africa.

Stems and foliage gray-green, woolly; basal leaves smooth-edged to deeply lobed, upper leaves pinnate, often further divided. Lavender to purple-blue flowerheads to 1¾ in (40 mm) wide, summer. *S. c.* var. *ochroleuca*, 36 in (90 cm) tall, primrose flowerheads. *S.c.* 'Butterfly Blue', 28 in (70 cm) tall, lavender blue; 'Pink Mist', 24 in (60 cm) tall, light pink. Zones 6–10.

Scabiosa graminifolia

☀ ❄ ↔12–20 in (30–50 cm)
↕16 in (40 cm)

Southern European perennial. Short grassy leaves with dense covering of fine silver-gray hairs. Flowers lavender to purple-pink, flowerheads to 1¾ in (40 mm) wide, summer. 'Pinkushion', deep pink flowers. Zones 7–10.

Scabiosa incisa

☀/◐ ❄ ↔20–24 in (50–60 cm)
↕24–36 in (60–90 cm)

Perennial from the Cape region of South Africa. Gray-green deeply lobed leaves to 6 in (15 cm) long at plant base, upper leaves smaller. Large deep pink to lavender blue flowerheads in spring–early summer. Zones 7–10.

Scabiosa lucida

☀ ❄ ↔12–20 in (30–50 cm)
↕12 in (30 cm)

Low spreading perennial from central Europe. Deeply divided, hairy, dark

green to silvery leaves. Lavender-pink to purple-red flowerheads to 1¾ in (40 mm) wide, summer–autumn. 'Rosea', pale pink flowers. Zones 5–10.

Scabiosa minoana

☀/◐ ❄ ↔12–20 in (30–50 cm)
↕16–24 in (40–60 cm)

Evergreen shrub from southern Europe and the eastern regions of the Mediterranean, including the island of Crete, Greece. Rounded leaves with silver hairs. Small heads of lavender flowers in summer. Zones 7–10.

Scabiosa stellata

STARFLOWER

☀ ❄ ↔8–12 in (20–30 cm)
↕18 in (45 cm)

Annual found all the way around the Mediterranean. Short, toothed, gray-green, ferny, pinnate leaves. White flowers in heads over 1 in (25 mm) wide. Flowers fall, leaving enlarged calyces on the long-lasting heads, in summer. 'Drumstick', 12 in (30 cm) tall with rounded heads of light blue flowers and copper-colored calyces; 'Paper Moon', white to pale blue with bronze calyces. Zones 8–11.

SCADOXUS

BLOOD LILY

A member of the amaryllis (Amaryllidaceae) family, this genus of 9 perennial species comes from the tropical regions of Africa and the Arabian Peninsula. These plants are closely related to species belonging to the genus *Haemanthus,* to which they bear a striking resemblance, and they also share the common name, blood lily. However, *Scadoxus* species are

Scabiosa columbaria var. *ochroleuca*

distinguished by the form and arrangement of their leaves, which do not have obvious mid-veins and are arranged in a rosette. Moreover, *Scadoxus* has fleshy-stemmed bulbs, not true bulbs.
CULTIVATION: Plant bulbs in full sun or part-shade in fertile well-drained soil, with top of bulb above ground. When grown in containers, keep slightly damp while dormant in winter, and water well during their summer growth phase. In frost-prone areas, grow in the greenhouse. Propagate from seed or offsets in spring.

Scadoxus multiflorus

syn. *Haemanthus multiflorus*

BLOOD LILY

☀ ◗ ↔24 in (60 cm) ↕20 in (50 cm)
Perennial from southern Africa. Large bulb. Almost evergreen, large fresh-green leaves, lance-shaped to oval, growing in an upright arching rosette. Flowers glowing salmon-red, large rounded heads of star-shaped florets, narrow petals, whiskery stamens, in summer. *S. m.* subsp. *katherinae* ★ (syn. *Haemanthus katherinae*), wavy undulating leaves. *S. m.* 'Koning Albert' (syn. *Haemanthus* 'King Albert'), coral-red flowers. Zones 9–11.

Scabiosa incisa

Scabiosa minoana

Scabiosa caucasica 'Alba'

Scabiosa caucasica 'Clive Greaves'

Scabiosa caucasica 'Fama' (in bud)

Scabiosa caucasica 'Pink Lace'

S

Schefflera species, in fruit

Schefflera arboricola

Schefflera actinophylla

Schefflera arboricola 'Jacqueline'

SCAEVOLA

This genus from the Goodeniaceae family contains nearly 100 plants from Australia and islands in the Indian and Pacific Oceans, and includes shrubs, subshrubs, and perennials. Many have a ground-hugging habit, and provide reliable ground cover in temperate areas. The leaves of most are small, somewhat succulent, often hairy, and usually carried on short, often brittle stems. The foliage is covered in fan-shaped flowers in varying shades of blue, sometimes white, over a long period from midwinter onwards.
CULTIVATION: Full sun and freely draining soil are the main requirements. Many species are resistant to salt spray, making them ideal plants for coastal sites, but they do need a frost-free position. Propagate from cuttings taken in the warmer months.

Scaevola aemula

☼ ❄ ↔ 20 in (50 cm) ↑ 6 in (15 cm)
Perennial from southern and eastern Australia. Variable, usually prostrate habit; oblong, wedge-shaped, toothed leaves. Pale mauve-blue fan-shaped flowers, 1¼ in (30 mm) wide, along stems, in spring–summer. '**Blue Fan**', '**Blue Wonder**', and '**New Wonder**', more vigorous and upright; '**Mauve Clusters**' ★, mauve-pink flowers; '**Purple Fanfare**', large flowers over most of the year. Zones 9–11.

SCHAUERIA

This member of the acanthus (Acanthaceae) family has 8 species of evergreen shrubs and subshrubs, native to Brazil, and grown for their spikes of narrow tubular flowers; the bristly calyces give a brush-like appearance.
CULTIVATION: Outdoors in tropical climates, plant in a rich moist soil. In cool climates they are suitable for the conservatory or greenhouse, but need shading during the hottest part of the day. Propagate by softwood cuttings.

Schaueria flavicoma

☼ ❄ ↔ 24 in (60 cm) ↑ 36 in (90 cm)
Erect subshrub from Brazil. Glossy green leaves, with prominent pale veins and midribs. Narrow, soft yellow, tubular flowers with downy to bristly yellow-green calyces grow in dense spikes on ends of branches. Zones 10–12.

SCHEFFLERA

syns *Brassaia, Dizygotheca, Heptapleurum*

This large genus in the ivy (Araliaceae) family consists of around 900 species, occurring in tropical and subtropical regions throughout the world, usually in moist environments, with the majority found from Southeast Asia to the Pacific Islands. Mostly shrubs, trees, scrambling climbers, or epiphytes, they have leaves composed of usually rounded leaflets of similar sizes and arranged in whorls held on a long stalk. Small flowers are produced in umbels, panicles, racemes, or spikes, and are followed by small black or purple fruits. Cultivated for their ornamental foliage, they are suitable for the garden in frost-free climates, or they can be used as pot plants, both indoors and outside.
CULTIVATION: Most are fairly adaptable, tolerating full sun to semi-shade. They prefer a well-drained moderately fertile soil with adequate moisture during periods of growth. Propagate from seed, which is sown as soon as it is ripe, or from cuttings, or by aerial layering.

Schefflera actinophylla

syn. *Brassaia actinophylla*
OCTOPUS TREE, QUEENSLAND UMBRELLA TREE
☼ ❄ ↔ 12 ft (3.5 m) ↑ 30 ft (9 m)
Rainforest shrub or tree from New Guinea and northern and northeastern Australia. Many trunks, glossy light green leaflets. Radiating spikes of small red flowers on ends of branches in late summer–early spring. Fruits reddish black. Zones 10–12.

Schefflera arboricola

DWARF UMBRELLA TREE, HAWAIIAN ELF SCHEFFLERA
☼ ❄ ↔ 3 ft (0.9 m) ↑ 3–5 ft (0.9–1.5 m)
From Taiwan. Rounded shrub with palmate leaves, 7 to 11 glossy bright green leaflets. Small yellowish flowers appear on panicles near branch tips in spring–summer. Golden berries. Popular house plant. '**Jacqueline**', leaves irregularly splashed with pale yellow. Zones 10–12.

Schaueria flavicoma

Scaevola aemula

Scaevola aemula 'Blue Fan'

Scaevola aemula 'Purple Fanfare'

Scaevola aemula 'New Wonder'

S

Schefflera digitata
PATE

☼ ⧉ ↔ 8 ft (2.4 m) ↑ 10 ft (3 m)

New Zealand shrub or tree. Young branches and leaflet stalks reddish purple. Leaves have 7 to 10 oblong leaflets with finely serrated margins. Margins, veins, and midribs tinged with red. Panicles of tiny greenish white flowers in summer. White to purple berries. Zones 10–12.

Schefflera elegantissima
ARALIA, FALSE ARALIA

☼ ⧉ ↔ 10 ft (3 m) ↑ 50 ft (15 m)

Tree native to New Caledonia, smaller in cultivation. The juvenile stage is unbranched and well-foliaged, the

Schefflera umbellifera, Kirstenbosch National Botanical Garden, South Africa

leaves consisting of 7 to 11 long, narrow, deeply serrated leaflets. The lustrous dark green leaflets become wider and more broadly toothed with maturity. Black berries. Zones 10–12.

Schefflera umbellifera
BASTARD CABBAGE TREE, FOREST CABBAGE TREE

☼ ⧉ ↔ 25 ft (8 m) ↑ 30 ft (9 m)

Tree native to southern and southeastern Africa. Older specimens have dense rounded crowns and fissured resinous bark. Leaves comprising 5 oblong leaflets are crowded near branch tips on long stalks. Panicles of small yellowish green flowers. Black berries. Zones 10–12.

SCHIMA
There is just a single species of evergreen tree in this genus, which is a member of the camellia (Theaceae) family. Native to the area from India to Southeast Asia and Indonesia, it is

Schefflera elegantissima

Schima wallichii

an attractive small tree with glossy leaves and single white flowers that are borne in late summer.
CULTIVATION: This tree requires a sheltered frost-free environment and a humus-rich acid soil. In cool climates it can be grown in containers in the greenhouse or conservatory. Propagate from seed or half-hardened cuttings.

Schima wallichii
☼ ⧉ ↔ 20 ft (6 m) ↑ 25 ft (8 m)

Tree with a dense bushy head. The large, leathery, glossy, green leaves, bronze red when young, are arranged in spirals. White flowers, mildly fragrant with prominent yellow stamens, in late summer. Zones 9–11.

SCHINUS
Found in Central and South America, this genus from the cashew (Anacardiaceae) family includes some 30 species of evergreen shrubs and trees. They are notable for their attractive pinnate leaves, sometimes weeping branches, and their sprays of brown-red drupes. The fruits develop from racemes of tiny flowers—usually white, yellow-green, or pale pink—that open in spring or summer. There are separate male and female flowers, and these may occur on the same plants or on different plants.
CULTIVATION: Hardiness varies with the species, though no *Schinus* species is extremely frost tolerant and many are frost tender, preferring a warm climate. Most species are very drought tolerant once established, and are best grown in well-drained soil in full sun. Propagate from seed or cuttings.

Schinus molle
PEPPER TREE

☼ ⧉ ↔ 50 ft (15 m) ↑ 50–60 ft (15–18 m)

Spreading, evergreen tree from South America. Drooping branches, finely divided, pinnate leaves. Small yellow-white flowers, in spring. Clusters of pea-sized red berries. Street tree in southern Europe; can prove weedy in some conditions. *S. m.* var. *areira* (syn. *S. areira*), semi-weeping, dark

Schinus molle var. *areira*

Schinus terebinthifolius

green leaves have aromatic resin; pink to red-brown berries; drought and heat tolerant. Zones 9–11.

Schinus terebinthifolius
BRAZILIAN PEPPER TREE

☼ ⧉ ↔ 15 ft (4.5 m) ↑ 20 ft (6 m)

Shrub or small tree from southern Brazil, Argentina, and Paraguay. Leathery pinnate leaves with light undersides, covering of fine hairs when young. Small flowers open white from pale green buds. Bright red fruits. Zones 9–12.

SCHISANDRA
This genus, comprising some 25 species native to eastern Asia and eastern North America (where a single species is found), gives its name to the family Schisandraceae. They are aromatic woody lianes largely found in broad-leafed evergreen forests. The leaves are undivided and spirally arranged, with minutely toothed or scalloped edges. Small cup-shaped flowers are borne in clusters or as solitary blooms on the ends of branches. Male and female flowers can occur on the same plant or on separate plants. The brightly colored fruits are berry-like, each with 1 or 2 seeds. These plants are grown for their short-lived fragrant flowers and their conspicuous red or black fruits.
CULTIVATION: They need good soil, well-drained but moisture-retentive, and protection from the midday sun. Grow in subtropical gardens or greenhouses in temperate regions. They can tolerate some lime. Propagate from seed or long half-hardened cuttings, suckers, from root-cuttings taken in summer, or by layering in autumn.

Schisandra chinensis
☼/◑ ❉ ↔ 20 ft (6 m) ↑ 25–35 ft (8–10 m)

Vigorous woody twiner from China. Reddish young stems and rounded leaves. Cream to pale pink flowers, ¾ in (18 mm) wide. If both sexes are present, female flowers produce 6 in (15 cm) long drooping spikes of red or pink berries. Zones 4–10.

S

Schisandra rubriflora

☼/◐ ❄ ↔ 20 ft (6 m) ↑ 25–35 ft (8–10 m)

From northern India, Myanmar, and western China. Leaves 6 in (15 cm) long. Pendent red flowers to 1 in (25 mm) wide. On female plants, drooping 6 in (15 cm) long spikes of red berries. Zones 8–10.

SCHISTOSTYLUS

This monotypic genus in the family Orchidaceae, related to *Sarcochilus*, comes from eastern Australia. The small plants often grow as twig epiphytes on small branches overhanging water, rarely growing on the trunks or main branches of trees. They have leaves in two ranks and a network of coarse, wiry roots. They produce short spikes of mainly green flowers that face the apex of the inflorescence. CULTIVATION: These orchids do not like having their roots covered, so are best mounted on narrow but long sections of cork. They are best kept in a semi-shaded position in a humid environment, with plenty of free circulating air. This is not an easy genus to maintain in cultivation.

Schistostylus purpuratus

◐ ❀ ↔ 2½–5 in (6–12 cm)
↑ 2½–5 in (6–12 cm)

Restricted range in eastern Australia. Short pendent spikes of up to 6 reddish to green blooms, ¼ in (6 mm) wide, predominantly white labellum, in spring. Zones 10–11.

SCHIZAEA

COMB FERN, RUSH FERN

This genus, comprising some 30 species native to the tropics, to North America and southern temperate regions, gives its name to the comb-fern (Schizaeaceae) family. The plants are small to medium-sized terrestrial ferns with erect or creeping rhizomes covered with hairs. They are usually found growing on nutrient-poor soils, sometimes on decaying wood. The fronds are either undivided, sometimes consisting of only 2 wings of tissue along the midrib, or they may

Schistostylus purpuratus

branch repeatedly into two. Their spore-bodies are held in rows along the end segments of the fronds, and are often virtually covered by the incurved edge of the segment, though they are exposed when mature. CULTIVATION: They are very difficult to grow, and thus are rarely cultivated. Grow in shade in well-drained soil.

Schizaea dichotoma

BRANCHED COMB FERN, FAN FERN

☼ ❄ ↔ 2–3 in (5–8 cm)
↑ 4–14 in (10–35 cm)

A primitive grass-like fern growing in sandy soils in New Zealand; lives with kauri pines and fungi. Dependent for nutrition on rotting organic material. Stiff wiry stalks, brown at base, green and divided at top. Sterile fronds with many forks and fan-shaped laminae. Repeatedly branching fertile fronds, 2 divided rows of long, fine, brown hairs. Zones 6–8.

SCHIZANTHUS

POOR MAN'S ORCHID

This Chilean genus of 12 species of annuals and biennials is a member of the nightshade (Solanaceae) family, although the relationship is not an obvious one. The cultivated species are small upright plants around 12 in (30 cm) tall, with soft, green, ferny foliage, often covered with fine hairs. Flowers are borne in branching panicles that are held above the foliage. They are beautifully marked and shaped, with a prominent lower lip, hence the common name, poor man's orchid. Modern strains are available in a wide range of colors and sizes.

Schizaea dichotoma, sterile fronds; fertile fronds (inset)

The genus name is derived from the Greek *schizo* (divide) and *anthos* (flower), referring to the plant's deeply divided corolla. CULTIVATION: They are intolerant of cold, but are easily grown as annuals where summer temperatures are warm and consistent. Elsewhere they are best treated as greenhouse pot plants. Grow in a bright position in fertile, moist, well-drained soil. Raise from seed, with several sowings to ensure continued flowering. Pinch out growing tips when young to make bushy.

Schizanthus pinnatus

☼/◐ ❀ ↔ 8–16 in (20–40 cm)
↑ 8–20 in (20–50 cm)

Annual with bushy habit and lance-shaped, usually lobed, light green leaves. Tightly clustered heads of flat flowers, lobes almost evenly sized, in summer–autumn. White-throated deep pink flowers with yellow and black central markings. Garden forms come in many colors. Zones 9–11.

Schizanthus × *wisetonensis*

☼/◐ ❀ ↔ 12 in (30 cm)
↑ 12–20 in (30–50 cm)

Garden hybrid annual of *S. pinnatus* × *S. grahamii* parentage. Several cultivars resembling *S. pinnatus* in foliage and habit. Flowers in various colors, including white, pink to purple-brown, and blue. Zones 9–11.

SCHIZOPHRAGMA

This genus of 2 deciduous ornamental woody climbers in the hydrangea (Hydrangeaceae) family is native to woodlands and cliffs of China, Korea, and Japan. Both species climb by means of short, adhesive, aerial roots. Leaves are attractive, pointed, few- to many-toothed, sometimes turning yellow in autumn. Bark flakes off

older branches. Flowerheads consist of flat clusters of tiny fertile flowers and a ring of sterile, showy, outer florets, typically creamy white. The fruits are capsules. The vines can eventually grow very large, but can be slow to establish. They can be grown up trees, but need support until they develop their rootlets. CULTIVATION: Rich well-drained soil is ideal but will grow in nearly any soil. Tolerate a wide range of light conditions, including shade, but flower best in full sun if the roots are shaded. Propagate from softwood cuttings in early to mid-summer, or from half-hardened cuttings in late summer. Few pest or disease problems.

Schizophragma hydrangeoides

JAPANESE HYDRANGEA VINE

◐ ❄ ↔ 10 ft (3 m) ↑ 30 ft (9 m)

Deciduous, woody, self-clinging climber native to Korea and Japan. Pointed, toothed, dark green leaves. Flat clusters of creamy white flowers to 10 in (25 cm) wide, tiny fertile inner flowers, teardrop-shaped outer ones, in summer. 'Moonlight', blue-green foliage, pewter markings and deep green veins; 'Roseum', pale pink flowers intensifying to rose. Zones 5–9.

SCHIZOSTYLIS

KAFFIR LILY

Native to the damp meadows of southern Africa, this genus consists of a single highly variable species in the iris (Iridaceae) family. Recent studies indicate that *Schizostylis* should be included in the large African genus *Hesperantha*. Almost evergreen, these plants require some moisture throughout the year. They are valued for their bright flowers, which are borne in autumn, sometimes surviving into the winter months.

Schizanthus × *wisetonensis*

Schizanthus × *wisetonensis*

S

Schoenoplectus lacustris

Schlumbergera truncata cultivar

Schlumbergera truncata

CULTIVATION: Plant in a sunny place in permanently moist peaty loam, or use organic mulch to conserve moisture in a sandy loam. Propagate by division of clumps or from ripe fresh seed.

Schizostylis coccinea

syn. *Hesperantha coccinea*

☀◐ ❄ ↔ 12–24 in (30–60 cm)
↑ 12–24 in (30–60 cm)

Leaves mid-green, grassy, with distinct midribs. Cup-shaped flowers on spikes. Petals are narrow and pointed or wide and rounded, from red to pink or white. '**Jennifer**', robust pale pink flowers; '**Major**' ★ (syn. 'Grandiflora'), abundant, large, glossy, red flowers;

'**Sunrise**' ★ (syn. 'Sunset'), large salmon pink flowers; '**Viscountess Byng**', dainty, narrow-petalled, pale pink flowers. Zones 6–9.

SCHLUMBERGERA

syn. *Zygocactus*

A genus of 6 popular species in the family Cactaceae that grow on rocks or in trees in Brazil, where hummingbirds pollinate the red, purple, pink, or white flowers. Stems are segmented, flattened to round in cross-section, with weak or no spines. Fruits are berry-like, sometimes ribbed. Many cultivars, some with yellow flowers, which turn pink at low temperatures.

CULTIVATION: They are readily grown in heated greenhouses, on windowsills in small pots or hanging baskets in temperate regions, outdoors as epiphytes, or in rock gardens in warmer climates. They prefer slightly acidic humus-rich soils, with shade and high humidity all summer and reduced water in winter. Rest winter-flowering plants in late summer. Most species will grow from cuttings dried out for a week or so and then planted in humus-rich well-drained soil.

Schlumbergera × *buckleyi*

CHRISTMAS CACTUS

☀ ✶ ↔ 12–24 in (30–60 cm)
↑ 12 in (30 cm)

Garden hybrid between *S. truncata* and *S. russelliana*, long cultivated in northern Europe. Profuse cylindrical flowers with purple stigmas at stem tips, in winter. Zones 10–12.

Schlumbergera truncata

syn. *Zygocactus truncatus*

CRAB CACTUS

☀ ✶ ↔ 12–24 in (30–60 cm)
↑ 12 in (30 cm)

Stems scarcely woody at base. Stem segments to 3 in (8 cm) long, 2 to 4 forward-pointing teeth on each side. Flowers to 3 in (8 cm) long, variable colors, in autumn. Zones 10–12.

SCHOENOPLECTUS

This genus of some 50 tufted or creeping annuals or perennials found throughout the world belongs to the sedge (Cyperaceae) family. Perennial species are found in deep to shallow water, annuals in seasonal wet depressions. Leaves are usually represented merely by a sheath, less often by a strap-like blade. The reddish brown summer flowerheads are generally held on long slender stems, and usually comprise a few to many spikelets, each containing numerous flowers. The fruits are achenes. Many species are used for basketry and mat-making in various parts of the world.
CULTIVATION: They are easily grown in full sun or shade in any moist soil. Some may become invasive, so care should be taken if growing them in non-native areas. Easily propagated by division or raised from seed.

Schoenoplectus lacustris

syn. *Scirpus lacustris*

BULRUSH, CLUBRUSH, TULE

☀ ✶ ↔ 3–4 ft (0.9–1.2 m)
↑ 3–10 ft (0.9–3 m)

Grass-like annual or perennial, found throughout Europe, Asia, Africa, and northern South America. Slow-spreading, clump of circular rush-like stems. Dense rust-colored flowerheads made up of over 100 spikelets, in summer–autumn. Leaves used for making mats and baskets. *S. l.* subsp. *tabernaemontani*, shorter stems; its cultivar 'Zebrinus', less vigorous, usually less than 5 ft (1.5 m) tall, bands of yellow to ivory on stems. Zones 4–9.

SCHOENUS

This is a genus of some 100 species of tufted or rhizomatous perennials, rarely annuals, in the sedge (Cyperaceae) family. Found almost throughout the world, often in humid grassland or woodland, they are concentrated in the Malay Archipelago and Australia. The leaves are grass-like, often reduced to just a basal sheath. Flowering stems carry groups of small brown to black spikelets, each of 1 to 9 florets. The fruits are small and nut-like, and are concealed in the spikelet. Some species were valued in Europe for thatching.
CULTIVATION: These plants are easily grown in full sun or part-shade in any wet ground. They are easily increased by division or raised from seed.

Schoenus pauciflorus

BOG RUSH, BOG SEDGE

☀ ❄ ↔ 9–18 in (22–45 cm)
↑ 12–36 in (30–90 cm)

Tussock-forming aquatic perennial native to New Zealand. Narrow, stiff, grooved, upright leaves, long deep brown sheaths. Short lateral flower panicles of few spear-shaped dark brown spikelets, ¼ in (6 mm) long, each bearing 3 to 4 flowers. Paler, slanted, grooved stems. Zones 7–10.

Schizostylis coccinea

Schoenus pauciflorus

Schotia latifolia

Sciadopitys verticillata

SCHOMBURGKIA

This is a small sympodial genus in the family Orchidaceae, with about 20 species that resemble some of the closely related larger *Laelia* species. They are distributed from Mexico and the West Indies to Brazil. They have elongated pseudobulbs, sometimes hollow, with 2 or 3 rigid leathery leaves at the apex. Long inflorescences emerge from the most recently matured growth, and clusters of large, colorful, often waxy blooms make their appearance in summer and autumn.
CULTIVATION: They need high light levels and warm temperatures to grow and flower well. Rambling growth makes them difficult to contain in pots; often they will only bloom once they are pot bound or have grown out of their pots. They can be mounted on large slabs of cork or tree-fern. Some species can be grown in full sun in the tropics, but most appreciate protection from mid-summer heat, and light shading. They dislike temperatures below 50°F (10°C). They are propagated by division.

Schomburgkia tibicinis
☀/◐ ✛ ↔ 1–3 ft (0.3–0.9 m)
↕ 1–8 ft (0.3–2.4 m)
Central American species. Hollow pseudobulbs. Inflorescence to over 7 ft (2 m) tall. Bright pink, red, and yellow flowers, 3 in (8 cm), in early summer. Zones 11–12.

SCHOTIA

This small genus in the cassia subfamily of the legume (Fabaceae) family consists of 4 or 5 species from southern Africa. They are deciduous or semi-evergreen shrubs or trees with alternate leaves that have an even number of leaflets. The red or pink flowers have 5 petals, and are borne

in panicles that occur along or at the ends of branches or directly from older wood in spring. Fruit are pods, usually leathery, flat, and oblong; in some species the round flat seeds are high in protein and edible. These plants come from hot, dry, tropical and subtropical semi-desert regions, including deciduous woodland and scrub that may be rocky. They are grown for their handsome foliage and attractive flowers.
CULTIVATION: These plants perform best in warm frost-free areas in a well-drained soil and a sunny position protected from strong winds. Propagate from seed or cuttings.

Schotia brachypetala
AFRICAN WALNUT, TREE FUCHSIA
☀ ◈ ↔ 15–25 ft (4.5–8 m) ↕ 50 ft (15 m)
Deciduous large shrub or small tree native to Zimbabwe, Mozambique, and South Africa. Shiny, green, pinnate leaves and leaflets reddish when young. Fragrant crimson flowers, in large, showy, dense panicles, on leafless stems, in summer. Oblong bean-like pods, edible seeds. Zones 9–12.

Schotia latifolia
BEAN TREE, ELEPHANT HEDGE
☀ ◈ ↔ 25 ft (8 m) ↕ 50 ft (15 m)
Variable-shaped tree from eastern South Africa. Leaflets in pairs, 3 to

Schomburgkia tibicinis

5 per leaf, narrow rounded bases. Panicles of almost-stalkless pinkish flowers produced at ends of branches. Fruit a hard pod. Zones 9–12.

SCIADOPITYS

This remarkable conifer genus has its own family, Sciadopityaceae, and consists of a single species of evergreen tree endemic to the mountains of Japan. The most striking attribute of *Sciadopitys* is its foliage, as it features 2 kinds of leaves: brown scale-leaves arranged spirally on elongated intervals of stem, and long, green, leaf-like needles radiating in dense whorls of up to 30 at the end of each interval. Male and female cones are borne on the same tree. The seed cones are like small pine cones, and have broad thin scales recurving at their tips.
CULTIVATION: Plants are easily grown in cool climates as long as rainfall is adequate and summers are warm and humid. They prefer a reasonably sheltered position and deep fertile soil. Growth is slow but steady. Propagation is normally from seed, though germination is poor unless seeds are stratified and then chilled for 3 months before sowing.

Sciadopitys verticillata
JAPANESE UMBRELLA PINE, UMBRELLA PINE
☀ ✽ ↔ 20 ft (6 m) ↕ 70 ft (21 m)
Conifer tree, smaller in cultivation, habit neat, conical, branches to ground level. Young plants grown in shade are more elongated. Rich brown bark peels in vertical strips. Whorls of deep glossy green leaves. Zones 6–9.

SCILLA

BLUEBELL, SQUILL
A genus of 90 species of bulbs of the hyacinth (Hyacinthaceae) family, *Scilla* species are found from western Europe to Japan and in parts of Africa. They form clumps of grassy

or strappy bright green leaves, and some, for example *S. peruviana*, can cover a large area. Long flower stems carry conical heads of small, star-shaped, sometimes fragrant flowers. Flowering time varies with the species but is usually spring. While species often have mauve to purple flowers, cultivars occur in a wide color range. Extracts of squill bulbs have a long history of medicinal use, mainly as diuretics and expectorants.
CULTIVATION: They are mostly hardy and easily grown in full or half-sun with moist, humus-rich, well-drained soil. When the clumps become large, lift and divide as the foliage dies back in autumn. They can be raised from seed, but take longer to flower.

Scilla bifolia
TWO-LEAFED SQUILL
☀/◐ ✽ ↔ 3 in (8 cm)
↕ 3–6 in (8–15 cm)
From Europe. Each bulb produces 2, occasionally 3, green elongated leaves. Small deep blue-violet flowers, appear with leaves, in early spring. Zones 4–8.

Scilla hyacinthoides
HYACINTH SCILLA
☀ ✽ ↔ 12 in (30 cm) ↕ 36 in (90 cm)
Rare bulb from the Mediterranean. Strap-shaped green leaves. Strong stems each carry up to 100 small, violet-blue, star-shaped flowers, in mid-spring. Zones 8–11.

Scilla hyacinthoides

Schotia brachypetala

Scilla liliohyacinthus
PYRENEAN SQUILL

☼/◑ ❄ ↔ 4 in (10 cm) ↑ 4 in (10 cm)
From France and Spain. Leaves broad, strap-like, mid-green, lustrous. Flowers pale violet, deep purple anthers, mid- to late spring. Zones 6–8.

Scilla natalensis ★
BLUE SQUILL

☼/◑ ❄ ↔ 20 in (50 cm) ↑ 36 in (90 cm)
From South Africa. Short dark green leaves. Long-lasting, graceful, starry, blue plumes of flowers, 50 to 100 per stalk, in spring–summer. Zones 7–10.

Scilla peruviana
CUBAN LILY, HYACINTH-OF-PERU

☼ ❄ ↔ 18 in (45 cm) ↑ 12 in (30 cm)
From the Mediterranean. Broad-pointed, shiny, green leaves, fleshy

Scilla liliohyacinthus

Scilla natalensis

stems. Rounded cushion of indigo-blue star-shaped flowers in mid-spring–early summer. *S. p.* var. *venusta*, from Tunisia, mauve-blue flowers, leaves lie flat. Zones 8–11.

Scilla ramburei

☼ ❄ ↔ 4 in (10 cm) ↑ 6 in (15 cm)
From Spain and Portugal. Has 3 to 6, narrow, bright green curled, grasslike, leaves, and flattish nodding inflorescences of violet-blue flowers, ½–¾ in (12–18 mm) wide, spring. Robust, salt tolerant. Zones 7–10.

Scilla siberica
BLUE SQUILL, SIBERIAN SQUILL

☼/◑ ❄ ↔ 3 in (8 cm) ↑ 6 in (15 cm)
From Russia and southwest Asia. Strap-like, glossy, bright green leaves. Bright blue star-shaped flowers in groups of 3 to 5 per stem, in early spring. 'Spring Beauty', large blue flowers, taller. Zones 2–8.

Scilla tubergeniana ★
syn. *Scilla mischtschenkoana* 'Tubergeniana'

☼/◑ ❄ ↔ 4 in (10 cm) ↑ 5 in (12 cm)
From Iran and Russia. Cup-shaped white or pale blue flowers with deep blue veins in early spring. Shiny strap-like leaves follow flowers. Good in shady rock gardens. Zones 5–7.

Scilla siberica 'Spring Beauty'

Scleranthus biflorus

Scilla peruviana

SCLERANTHUS

This genus contains up to 10 species, and is a member of the pink (Caryophyllaceae) family, occurring naturally in Europe, Asia, Africa, South America, Australia, New Guinea, and New Zealand. Perennials or annuals, they have a densely tufted ground-covering habit. The small, linear, usually green leaves are joined at the base of the stems. The pale creamy green flowers are small, often less than ¼ in (6 mm), and are hard to see on some species. The plants are shallow-rooted, and generally all species creep along the ground, forming dense cushions.
CULTIVATION: They like sun or shade, but not long periods of dry or heavy wet weather. Propagate from stem cuttings in autumn or from fresh seed.

Scleranthus biflorus

☼ ❄ ↔ 12 in (30 cm) ↑ 2–4 in (5–10 cm)
Dense, perennial, mat-forming plant from New Zealand. Tiny, needle-like, bright green, sometimes lime green, foliage. Conspicuous pale creamy green flowers, in summer. Zones 5–9.

SCLEROCACTUS
syns *Ancistrocactus, Coloradoa, Glandulicactus, Toumeya*

This genus of 14 species and 7 subspecies of low-growing attractively

Scilla ramburei

Scilla peruviana var. venusta

spined members of the family Cactaceae is from southwestern USA and northern Mexico. The genus name comes from the Greek *scleros* (hard), referring to the hard or cruel spines of most members of the genus. Several species are listed in Appendix I of CITES. They are usually solitary, occasionally clustering, spherical to cylindrical, tubercled, and ribbed. Short, diurnal, funnel-form to bell-shaped flowers, in pink, purple, red, or yellow, are borne at the tips with naked pericarpels. Seed pods are oval to club-shaped and scaly. *Sclerocactus* now includes all species formerly classified as *Ancistrocactus, Coloradoa, Glandulicactus,* and *Toumeya,* but not *Echinomastus.*
CULTIVATION: Most need a well-drained mineralized soil and careful watering. Keep dry in winter and summer. They are difficult to propagate, and a challenge to all but expert growers. Propagate from seed, which may need to be scarified and exposed to heavy frosts to induce germination.

Sclerocactus scheeri
syns *Ancistrocactus megarhizus, A. scheeri*

☼ ❄ ↔ 1–4 in (2.5–10 cm) ↑ 1–6 in (2.5–15 cm)
Solitary spherical to cylindrical species from Mexico and southern Texas, USA. Covered with dense spines; 3 to 4 flattened white to gray centrals, lower one hooked, and 10 to 20 yellowish needle-like radials. Flowers greenish, funnel-form. Zones 8–10.

Sclerocactus uncinatus
syns *Ancistrocactus uncinatus, Glandulicactus uncinatus, Hamatocactus uncinatus*
BROWN-FLOWERED HEDGEHOG CACTUS, CAT'S CLAW CACTUS

☼ ❄ ↔ 1–4 in (2.5–10 cm) ↑ 1–6 in (2.5–15 cm)
Solitary, spherical to cylindrical, bluish green cactus from western Texas, USA, and Mexico. About 12 to 14 strong tubercled ribs. Spines, 1 to 5 hooked upward-pointing centrals, yellow, tipped with red, graying with age, and 8 to 15 radials, upper ones

S

creamy and flattened, and lower ones hooked and purplish. Flowers reddish brown. Zones 8–10.

SCLEROCARYA

There are 4 species of deciduous trees or shrubs in this genus in the cashew (Anacardiaceae) family from tropical and southern Africa. Their compound leaves are crowded towards the ends of the branches, and they bear panicles of small inconspicuous flowers in late winter and early spring, followed by berries, usually ripening in summer.
CULTIVATION: Frost tender, these are warm-climate plants needing full sun or part-shade in a well-drained soil. Propagate from seed.

Sclerocarya birrea
MAROOLA PLUM, MARULA
☀ ✤ ↔ 20 ft (6 m) ↑ 30 ft (9 m)
Deciduous tree found from Ethiopia to South Africa. Compound leaves, dark green oval leaflets. Inconspicuous flowers in spring. Large yellow berries, rich in vitamin C, eaten fresh or in drinks, jams, and jellies. Zones 10–12.

Sclerocarya birrea

Scolopia mundii, **Kirstenbosch National Botanical Garden, Cape Town, South Africa**

SCOLOPIA

Found from the tropics to the warm-temperate regions of Africa, Asia, and Australia, this genus from the governor's-plum (Flacourtiaceae) family contains around 35 species of shrubs and trees that are most notable for their sometimes spiny stems, their often scented flowers, and the fruits that follow. Their leaves are usually less than 4 in (10 cm) long, with smooth or wavy toothed edges. The tiny cream to pale greenish yellow flowers are conspicuous because they are massed in panicles. Berry-like fruits follow, often dark red and up to ½ in (12 mm) wide.
CULTIVATION: Found naturally over a wide range of climatic conditions, the cultivation requirements for these plants vary, though only a few species will tolerate frost. Species from the seasonally dry tropics will withstand droughts; otherwise plant in moist, humus-rich, well-drained soil in sun or part-shade. Trim to shape after the fruit has fallen. Propagate from seed or half-hardened cuttings.

Scolopia mundii
RED PEAR
☀ ⬡ ↔ 15 ft (4.5 m) ↑ 30 ft (9 m)
Erect bushy small tree, native to South Africa from the Cape region eastward. Glossy deep green foliage, trunk becoming fluted with age; young plants have spiny branches. Clusters of greenish flowers in autumn–winter. Bright orange and yellow fruits. Zones 9–11.

SCROPHULARIA
FIGWORT
The members of this genus of some 200 species in the foxglove (Scrophulariaceae) family are mainly perennials, with some being subshrubs. Often marsh-dwellers, they come mostly from temperate parts of the Northern

Scutellaria alpina 'Arcobaleno'

Hemisphere, although some species are found as far south as Central America. The stems are 4-angled; their leaves may be either simple or compound, and either alternate or opposite. The flowers are usually small, like tiny, fat, inflated foxgloves *(Digitalis)* with a lower lip, in bronze, copper, or dull red. Few species are of garden merit, and some are garden weeds. Some species were once thought to cure scrofulous tumors.
CULTIVATION: Most grow well in moist humus-rich soil in dappled shade; some are aquatic. Propagation is by seed sown in situ, or from basal cuttings taken in spring.

Scrophularia auriculata
syn. *Scrophularia aquatica*
WATER BETONY, WATER FIGWORT
☀ ❄ ↔ 36–48 in (90–120 cm)
↑ 36–48 in (90–120 cm)
Vigorous marginal aquatic species from western Europe. Slightly toothed opposite leaves to 10 in (25 cm) long. Open sprays of tiny, rounded, reddish brown flowers, drooping lip, yellowish green interior, in summer. 'Variegata', leaves, bold white edges. Zones 5–10.

SCUTELLARIA
HELMET FLOWER, SKULLCAP
This genus of about 300 species of annuals and perennials belongs to the mint (Lamiaceae) family. They are found mostly in temperate Northern Hemisphere regions, where they grow in scrub, open woodland, and grassland. The roots are often rhizomatous, and the plants are erect or sprawling, ranging from 6 in (15 cm) to 4 ft (1.2 m) high. The leaves are opposite and simple, sometimes pinnate or toothed. The 2-lipped tubular flowers emerge from hooded calyces, which give the genus its common names. The blue, white, or yellow flowers

Scutellaria alpina

appear in summer singly, in pairs, or on the ends of spikes. A number of species are grown ornamentally, and some are used in herbal medicine for their anti-spasmodic properties.
CULTIVATION: Plant taller species in borders and smaller species at the edges of borders or in rock gardens. Grow in full sun in any reasonable soil. Water well in dry summers. Propagate from seed or by division.

Scutellaria alpina
☀ ❄ ↔ 18 in (45 cm)
↑ 6–10 in (15–25 cm)
Sprawling perennial found in mountains from southern Europe to Siberia. Often roots at nodes. Mats of small oval leaves. Small flowers in crowded racemes, purple to pale pink, often with yellow on lower lip, in late spring to early summer. *S. a.* subsp. *supina*, soft lemon-colored flowers. *S. a.* 'Arcobaleno', bluish purple to white, rose, and pale yellow flowers, contrasting colors on lower lip. Zones 5–9.

Scutellaria baicalensis
☀ ❄ ↔ 8 in (20 cm) ↑ 16 in (40 cm)
Sprawling plant found from Siberia to Japan. Stems often suffused with purple. Small, narrow, slightly hairy leaves. Dense heads of velvety tubular flowers, purple with a white lower lip, in summer. Zones 5–9.

Scutellaria orientalis

Scutellaria barbata

Scutellaria incana

Scutellaria barbata

☼ ❈ ↔ 8 in (20 cm)
↑ 12–16 in (30–40 cm)

Annual or perennial from China, India, and Japan. Small oval or lance-shaped leaves. Blue tubular flowers along stems in spring–autumn. Used in Chinese herbal medicines; currently being researched as anti-cancer drug. **Zones 5–9.**

Scutellaria galericulata

☼ ❈ ↔ 8–12 in (20–30 cm)
↑ 12–24 in (30–60 cm)

Erect or spreading perennial from temperate Eurasia and North America. Pointed leaves to 2 in (5 cm) long. Lavender-blue flowers, white marks within; lower lip sometimes paler with dark blue speckling. **Zones 5–9.**

Scutellaria incana

DOWNY SKULLCAP

☼ ❈ ↔ 24 in (60 cm)
↑ 24–48 in (60–120 cm)

Bushy perennial native to eastern North America. Leaves grayish green, covered with minute hairs, oval, to 3 in (8 cm) long. Dense panicles of velvety purplish blue flowers appear on ends of stems in summer–autumn. **Zones 4–9.**

Scutellaria indica

☼ ❈ ↔ 12 in (30 cm) ↑ 6 in (15 cm)

Low-growing mat-forming perennial native to Japan, Korea, and China. Small, rounded, grayish green leaves, shallow toothed margins. Pale purplish blue flowers in dense racemes in summer. *S. i.* var. *parvifolia* ★, dark green leaves, relatively large lavender-blue flowers. **Zones 5–9.**

Scutellaria orientalis

☼ ❈ ↔ 6–10 in (15–25 cm)
↑ 12–18 in (30–45 cm)

Subshrub forming a low mound, native to southeastern Europe. Small oval leaves, dark green above, woolly gray beneath. Dense racemes of lemon yellow flowers, sometimes tinged or spotted with red. **Zones 7–10.**

SECHIUM

CHACO, CHAYOTE, CHOCHO

This genus, which belongs to the pumpkin (Cucurbitaceae) family, contains 6 to 8 species of climbing plants from the cooler mountain regions of tropical America. Their bright green leaves are long-stalked and palmately lobed, with heart-shaped bases. The star-shaped 5-lobed flowers are either male or female. The male flowers arise

Scutellaria indica var. *parvifolia*

in long racemes, while the females are borne singly or in pairs. The large, green, ridged, oval fruits are fleshy and have hairy, spiny, or smooth skin. They contain a single large seed that can germinate within the fruit. In tropical regions these plants are cultivated as a vegetable that is baked, boiled, or stewed.

CULTIVATION: In temperate regions grow *Sechium* species in the greenhouse with medium humidity and bright filtered light in a well-drained, fertile, gritty soil. Water and feed regularly. In warm climates, grow outdoors in free-draining soil enriched with compost. Propagate from cuttings or seed, planting the whole fruit if the seed has germinated within it

Sechium edule

CHAYOTE, CHOKO, CHRISTOPHINE

☼/❈ ⚬ ↔ 10–20 ft (3–6 m)
↑ 10 ft (3 m)

Tuberous-rooted climber native to Central America. Leaves have 3 to 5 lobes and a roughened surface. Pale yellow male flowers in racemes to 12 in (30 cm) long; greenish female flowers. Edible greenish yellow fruits to 7 in (18 cm) long. **Zones 9–12.**

SEDUM

STONECROP

This is a very diverse group of succulent species from the stonecrop (Crassulaceae) family, with many hybrids. Of Northern Hemisphere origins, with over 300 species they vary enormously in foliage and form. Some are shrubby, with flattened, oval, gray-green leaves; others are trailing, with succulent jellybean-like

Sechium edule

leaves; and some form very compact mats. Most produce small heads of tiny, bright yellow, 5-petalled flowers in summer and autumn. The autumn-flowering types have been reclassified, mainly to the genera *Hylotelephium* and *Rhodiola*. Their name is derived from the Latin *sedo* (to sit), referring to their low spreading habit. Some species have been used medicinally and as salad vegetables. Some, such as *S. spectabile,* are grown for their flowers; others, such as *S. rubrotinctum,* for their colorful plant bodies.

CULTIVATION: Plant in full sun in gritty well-drained soil. Most appreciate water at flowering time, but are otherwise drought tolerant. Propagate by division, from cuttings, or from seed, depending on the growth type.

Sedum acre

STONECROP, WALL PEPPER

☼ ❈ ↔ 12–24 in (30–60 cm)
↑ 2–4 in (5–10 cm)

Perennial native to Europe and North Africa. Spreading, slightly mounding mats of fine stems clothed with tiny, light green, overlapping, triangular leaves, often red-tinted in sun. Heads of small bright yellow flowers at the ends of stems in summer. 'Aureum', creamy yellow foliage variegations. **Zones 5–10.**

Sedum aizoon

☼ ❈ ↔ 20 in (50 cm) ↑ 16 in (40 cm)

Summer-flowering succulent native to temperate northern Asia. Upright stems, fleshy, toothed, 2–3 in (5–8 cm) long, lance-shaped leaves. Flat heads of golden yellow flowers, over ½ in (12 mm) wide. **Zones 7–10.**

Sedum aizoon

Sedum album

S

Sedum borissovae

Sedum confusum

Sedum album ★

☼ ❄ ↔ 8–20 in (20–50 cm)
↑ 2–4 in (5–10 cm)

Spreading mat-forming perennial from temperate regions of Eurasia and North Africa. Leaves ¼–¾ in (6–18 mm) long, often red-tinted, narrow and cylindrical. Heads of tiny white flowers appear during summer. '**Coral Carpet**', 2 in (5 cm) high cultivar, pink-tinted leaves, light pink flowers. Zones 6–10.

Sedum borissovae

☼ ❄ ↔ 12 in (30 cm) ↑ 2–4 in (5–10 cm)
Evergreen mat-forming perennial herb spread by runners, native to Ukraine. Spreading branching stems, minute overlapping leaves. Forked heads of tiny pale yellow flowers in summer. Zones 7–10.

Sedum cauticolum

syn. *Hylotelephium cauticolum*
☼ ❄ ↔ 8–20 in (20–50 cm)
↑ 4–6 in (10–15 cm)

Spreading ground cover, native to Japan. Wiry stems. Rounded, sometimes sparsely toothed, gray powder-coated, red-tinted leaves to 1 in (25 mm) long. Dense heads of small pink to near-red flowers in summer–early autumn. Zones 4–10.

Sedum confusum

☼ ❄ ↔ 12–16 in (30–40 cm)
↑ 12–24 in (30–60 cm)

Shrubby species of obscure origin, probably Mexican. Fleshy, shiny, bright green, lance-shaped leaves, 1–1½ in (25–35 mm) long. Small rounded heads of bright yellow flowers in spring. Zones 8–11.

Sedum dendroideum

Sedum dasyphyllum

☼ ❄ ↔ 8–16 in (20–40 cm)
↑ 2–4 in (5–10 cm)

Cushion-forming perennial from around the Mediterranean region, with some apparently natural forms found in southwestern parts of the USA. Spreading pink-tinted stems. Tiny overlapping leaves, grayish to bluish green. Few-flowered heads of tiny, pink-tinted, white flowers in summer. Zones 8–11.

Sedum dendroideum

☼ ❄ ↔ 12–16 in (30–40 cm)
↑ 6–12 in (15–30 cm)

Spring-flowering Mexican subshrub. Usually one main stem and many side branches that are tipped with rosettes of bright green spatula-shaped leaves to 1½ in (35 mm) long. Airy panicles of tiny yellow flowers appear in spring. Zones 8–11.

Sedum ewersii

syn. *Hylotelephium ewersii*
☼ ❄ ↔ 16–30 in (40–75 cm)
↑ 6–12 in (15–30 cm)

Perennial found from the Himalayas to Mongolia. Low spreading habit, branching stems. Broad blue-green leaves to 1 in (25 mm) long, smooth-edged or toothed. Dense heads of tiny purple-red flowers appear in summer–autumn. Zones 5–9.

Sedum hidakanum

syn. *Hylotelephium pluricaule*
☼ ❄ ↔ 12–24 in (30–60 cm)
↑ 4–6 in (10–15 cm)

Perennial from coastal areas of eastern Siberia. Forms clump of spreading stems with opposite pairs of small,

Sedum lucidum

rounded, gray-green leaves. Tiny purple-red flowers, densely clustered in small heads, in summer. Zones 7–10.

Sedum hispanicum

☼ ❄ ↔ 12–24 in (30–60 cm)
↑ 4–6 in (10–15 cm)

Low spreading annual to short-lived perennial from southern Europe to Iran. Wiry stems with small, narrow, fleshy, blue-green leaves, red-tinted in sun. Small heads of pink-tinted white flowers in summer. Zones 7–10.

Sedum kamtschaticum

KAMCHATKA STONECROP
☼ ❄ ↔ 16–24 in (40–60 cm)
↑ 4–12 in (10–30 cm)

Succulent native to Japan. Spreading by rhizomes. Low branching stems. Fleshy, coarsely toothed, deep green, lance-shaped leaves, under 2 in (5 cm) long. Flattish flowerheads of golden yellow blooms in summer. *S. k.* var. *ellacombeanum*, pale yellow flowers. *S. k.* '**Variegatum**', creamy white- and pink-variegated mid-green leaves, golden yellow flowers. Zones 7–10.

Sedum lucidum

☼ ❄ ↔ 12–20 in (30–50 cm)
↑ 12–18 in (30–45 cm)

Mexican evergreen subshrub. Low, spreading, branching stems. Leaves thick, fleshy, silver-green to bright green, pointed oval in shape, 1–2 in

Sedum kamtschaticum 'Variegatum'

(25–50 mm) long. Flowerheads of many small white blooms in late winter–spring. Zones 9–11.

Sedum lydium ★

☼ ❄ ↔ 6–12 in (15–30 cm)
↑ 2–4 in (5–10 cm)

Small tufted to cushion-forming Turkish perennial. Stems root as they spread, and bear ¼ in (6 mm) long, fleshy, red-tipped leaves. Heads of many tiny, pink-tinted, white flowers in summer. Zones 9–11.

Sedum moranense

☼ ❄ ↔ 12–16 in (30–40 cm)
↑ 4–6 in (10–15 cm)

Mexican perennial. Forms a bushy hummock of many wiry stems that are densely covered with minute bright green leaves. White flowers, sometimes red-tipped, around ¼ in (6 mm) wide, singly or in small clusters, in summer. Zones 9–11.

Sedum moranense

Sedum kamtschaticum

Sedum hispanicum

S

Sedum morganianum ★

BURRO'S TAIL, DONKEY'S TAIL

☼ ⁂ ↔ 4 ft (1.2 m) ↕ 20 in (50 cm)

Evergreen perennial of obscure origin, probably Mexican. Widely cultivated as hanging basket plant. Long trailing stems, and densely crowded, spiraly arranged, pointed cylindrical, blue-green leaves. Small long-stemmed flowerheads of pink blooms appear in spring–summer. Zones 9–11.

Sedum sieboldii 'Mediovariegatum'

Sedum rubrotinctum

Sedum niveum

☼ ❄ ↔ 20–24 in (50–60 cm)
↕ 2–4 in (5–10 cm)

Perennial native to southwestern California, USA. Mainly prostrate, short erect stems. Small rosettes of tiny, fleshy, pointed leaves. Flowers white, pink veins, to ½ in (12 mm) wide, few per head, in summer. Zones 8–10.

Sedum oreganum

☼ ❄ ↔ 12–16 in (30–40 cm)
↕ 6 in (15 cm)

Spreading North American perennial. Succulent, green, club-shaped leaves to ¾ in (18 mm) long, red-tinted in autumn. Small yellow flowers, singly or in flat heads, in summer. Zones 6–10.

Sedum praealtum ★

☼ ❄ ↔ 16–24 in (40–60 cm)
↕ 12–24 in (30–60 cm)

Surprisingly hardy shrub of Mexican origin. Shiny green, lance- to spatula-

Sedum oreganum

Sedum spathulifolium 'Cape Blanco'

shaped leaves to over 2 in (5 cm) long. Large panicles of bright yellow flowers in summer. *S. p.* subsp. *parvifolium*, compact habit, small leaves. Zones 6–10.

Sedum rubrotinctum

☼ ⁂ ↔ 12–24 in (30–60 cm)
↕ 10 in (25 cm)

Mounding evergreen subshrub of obscure origin, probably Mexican. The arching stems root where they touch ground. The leaves are thick and cylindrical, blunt-tipped, mid-green in color, red-tinted in sunlight. Loose heads of pale yellow flowers appear in spring. 'Aurora' ★, pale yellow-green leaves with a strong red tint. Zones 9–11.

Sedum rupestre

syn. *Sedum reflexum*

☼ ❄ ↔ 12–20 in (30–50 cm)
↕ 8–15 in (20–38 cm)

Spreading, somewhat mounding evergreen perennial native to central and southern Europe. Woody stems are crowded with small, narrow, fleshy, light blue-green leaves. Flowerheads of tiny bright yellow blooms appear in summer. Zones 7–10.

Sedum sediforme

☼ ❄ ↔ 12–24 in (30–60 cm)
↕ 8–24 in (20–60 cm)

Evergreen perennial herb from the Mediterranean region. Grows in a mounding hummock of woody-based stems. Leaves are small, fleshy, and lance-shaped. Erect flowering stems bear flowerheads of pale greenish yellow to gold flowers in summer. Zones 8–11.

Sedum spathulifolium

Sedum spathulifolium 'Purpureum'

Sedum sieboldii

syn. *Hylotelephium sieboldii*

☼ ❄ ↔ 12–20 in (30–50 cm)
↕ 4 in (10 cm)

Low spreading perennial from Japan. Leaves to ¾ in (18 mm), rounded, fleshy, long, gray- to blue-green, often tinted purple or red. Dense heads of tiny pale pink flowers in autumn. 'Mediovariegatum' ★, broad cream centered leaves; 'Variegatum', cream-mottled blue-green leaves. Zones 7–10.

Sedum spathulifolium ★

☼ ❄ ↔ 24 in (60 cm) ↕ 6 in (15 cm)

Clump-forming perennial from western North America. Spreads by long runners. Spatula-shaped fleshy leaves, often coloring to bronzy red, mainly clustered in rosettes at stem tips. Tiny flowers, bright yellow, in late spring–early summer. 'Cape Blanco', silver-gray leaves; 'Purpureum', foliage tinged purple-red. Zones 7–10.

Sedum niveum, in the wild, Parque Nacional San Pedro Mártir, Baja California, Mexico

Sedum praealtum

Sedum rupestre

S

Sedum spectabile ★

syn. *Hylotelephium spectabile*

ICE PLANT

↔ 16–32 in (40–80 cm)
↑ 27 in (70 cm)

Perennial from Korea and nearby parts of China. Erect thickened stems, opposite pairs or whorls of fleshy, toothed, elliptical leaves, 2–4 in (5–10 cm) long. Large 3-branched heads of small pink to red flowers in late summer–autumn. '**Brilliant**' ★, pink flowers; '**Iceberg**', white flowers, sometimes tinted with pink; '**Indian Chief**', deep pink to purple-red flowers. Zones 6–10.

Sedum spurium

↔ 12–20 in (30–50 cm)
↑ 6 in (15 cm)

Evergreen mat-forming perennial or subshrub, found from the Caucasus region to northern Iran. Spreading branches; opposite pairs of rounded, fleshy, toothed leaves, red-tinted in sunlight. Heads of small purple-red flowers, rarely white or pink, on erect stems, in summer. '**Dragon's Blood**', reddish pink flowers, sometimes red-tinged leaves; '**Variegatum**', leaves edged pink and cream. Zones 7–10.

Sedum telephium

syn. *Hylotelephium telephium*

LIVE-FOREVER, ORPINE

↔ 24–32 in (60–80 cm)
↑ 24 in (60 cm)

Perennial found from eastern Europe to Japan. Erect thickened stems; fleshy, toothed, pointed oval leaves, 1–3 in (2.5–8 cm) long. Showy heads of many purple-red flowers in late summer. *S. t.* subsp. *maximum*

Sedum spectabile

'**Atropurpureum**', deep purple-red foliage and red flowers. *S. t.* '**Matrona**', stems tinted with red, very pale pink flowers; '**Mohrchen**', deep red flowers, purple-red foliage. Zones 6–10.

Sedum treleasei

SILVER SEDUM

↔ 12–16 in (30–40 cm)
↑ 12 in (30 cm)

Mexican evergreen subshrub. Upright, branching habit. Succulent, upcurved, cylindrical to almost bead-like, pale blue-green leaves to ¾ in (18 mm) long. Long-lasting panicles of tiny soft yellow flowers in spring. Zones 8–10.

Sedum Hybrid Cultivars

↔ 12–24 in (30–60 cm)
↑ 12–24 in (30–60 cm)

Several popular interspecies garden hybrids are placed in the subgenus *Hylotelephium*; these are mainly autumn flowering, though the foliage is attractive throughout the growing season. '**Herbstfreude**' (syn. 'Autumn Joy') (*S. telephium* × *S. spectabile*) has blue-green foliage and salmon pink flowers ageing to bronze; '**Ruby Glow**' (*S. cauticolum* × *S. telephium*), purple-green foliage, often pink-edged,

Sedum telephium

Sedum telephium 'Matrona'

Sedum spectabile 'Brilliant'

Sedum spectabile 'Indian Chief'

Sedum spurium 'Dragon's Blood'

deep red flowers; '**Vera Jameson**' ('Ruby Glow' × *S. telephium* subsp. *maximum* 'Atropurpureum'), purple foliage, light pink flowers. Zones 6–10.

SELAGINELLA

This genus in the spikemoss (Selaginellaceae) family of about 700 species of evergreen, creeping, ground-covering plants is found in tropical and temperate regions right around the world. Distinctive to the genus is the dainty fern-like foliage that covers the slightly hairy ground-hugging stems. The long creeping branches of spikemoss species can travel some distance over soil, shrubs, and rocky areas.
CULTIVATION: Cultivate in an open moist soil rich in humus. Spores form on the ends of leafy spikes, and can be harvested when ripe in order to propagate new plants. Alternatively, divide the rhizomes in summer or the rooted stems in spring.

Sedum spurium 'Variegatum'

Selaginella kraussiana

TRAILING SPIKEMOSS

↔ 24–36 in (60–90 cm)
↑ 1 in (2.5 cm)

Perennial from tropical and southern Africa. Trailing stems of bright green foliage; forms dense mats. Ideal for hanging baskets. '**Aurea**', pale yellow to lime green foliage; '**Brownii**', dense dark green to brown foliage, compact plant; '**Variegata**', green foliage with creamy yellow streaks. Zones 10–11.

Selaginella lepidophylla

RESURRECTION FERN

↔ 8 in (20 cm) ↑ 3 in (8 cm)

Particularly unusual prehistoric plant found from Arizona and Texas, USA, to Peru. Apparently comes back from dead, hence its common name. Spreading habit, tufts of dark green leaves; when dried out it curls into dense ball; when soaked in water it opens out to a flat rosette. Zones 9–11.

Sedum, Hybrid Cultivar, 'Herbstfreude'

Sedum, Hybrid Cultivar, 'Ruby Glow'

Sedum, Hybrid Cultivar, 'Vera Jameson'

Selaginella plana

Selaginella martensii

Selenicereus wercklei

Selaginella martensii

☀ ✤ ↔ 8 in (20 cm), ↑ 6 in (15 cm)
Scrambling trailing perennial from Central America. Many-branched stems, glossy green leaves. Zones 10–11.

Selaginella pallescens

syn. Selaginella emmeliana

☀ ✤ ↔ 12 in (30 cm) ↑ 6 in (15 cm)
Multi-branched perennial from North America to northern Colombia and Venezuela. Densely tufted stems from base, very divided pale green leaves, white undersides. Zones 10–11.

Selaginella plana

☀ ✤ ↔ 12–24 in (30–60 cm)
↑ 6–12 in (15–30 cm)
Eastern Himalayan species. Spreading and semi-erect stems to 12 in (30 cm) long, bright green fern-like leaves to over 4 in (10 cm) long. Zones 9–11.

Selaginella uncinata

PEACOCK MOSS

☀ ❄ ↔ 18–36 in (45–90 cm)
↑ 2 in (5 cm)
From China. Delicate foliage with a trailing rooting system on its stems. The foliage has a distinctive gunmetal blue sheen. Zones 7–11.

SELENICEREUS

MOON CACTUS, QUEEN OF THE NIGHT

This genus of 28 species of thin-stemmed climbing plants in the family Cactaceae is from seasonal or tropical rainforests in the Americas. Named for Selene, the Greek moon goddess, in reference to its nocturnal flowers, this genus produces some of the largest of all cactus flowers. The floral tubes bear scales, bristles, and spines. Flowers are mainly white and perfumed, 5–16 in (12–40 cm) long, usually borne toward the end of the long, clambering, pencil-thick branches, which grow to 17 ft (5 m) long. Branches have 3 to 12 ribs, covered in short or bristly spines. To see a fully opened flower, one must wait until after midnight on the one day of the year when the plant blooms.
CULTIVATION: They are easily grown in a humus-rich well-drained soil, and are often grown on a frame or trellis, or in a hanging basket. Propagation is usually from cuttings that have been dried out for a few days. They may also be raised from seed. Rest the plants in winter.

Selenicereus anthonyanus

syn. Cryptocereus anthonyanus

☀/☀ ✤ ↔ 7 ft (2 m) ↑ 10 ft (3 m)
Distinctive clambering cactus from Mexico. Unusual stems and branches clustering from base; branches bright green, flat, zigzag-shaped, with deep lobes. Areoles small, 3 short spines. Fragrant flowers, cream with magenta pericarpels, in summer. Zones 9–12.

Selenicereus grandiflorus ★

☀/☀ ✤ ↔ 7–10 ft (2–3 m) ↑ 17 ft (5 m)
Widely cultivated cactus found in eastern Mexico and the Caribbean. Stems deep green, ½–1 in (12–25 mm) in diameter, with 5 to 8 low ribs. Spines 6 to 18, bristle-like, whitish to brownish. Flowers white, fragrant, with pale yellow to brown pericarpels, in summer. Seed pods oval, red. Zones 9–12.

Selenicereus wercklei

☀/☀ ✤ ↔ 3–7 ft (0.9–2 m)
↑ 3–7 ft (0.9–2 m)
Epiphytic much-branched cactus from Costa Rica. Aerial roots and slender, rounded, pale green stems. Ribs 6 to 12, low, spines absent. White flowers; spines on pericarpels and floral tubes. Seed pods oval, yellow, with brown spines in clusters. Zones 9–12.

SEMIAQUILEGIA

This genus, belonging to the buttercup (Ranunculaceae) family, contains 7 species of low perennial plants closely related to Aquilegia. They are native to Asia, where they grow in high mountain grassland and scrub in damp conditions. The lacy foliage resembles that of maidenhair fern (Adiantum), with leaves comprised of 3 leaflets. The nodding flowers are in shades of pink, red, and purple, often plump with many petals, but lacking the spurs typical of Aquilegia species.
CULTIVATION: Suitable for the rock garden, they should be grown in full sun to half-sun. They require a moist but well-drained soil. Propagate from seed or by division.

Semiaquilegia ecalcarata

☀/☀ ❄ ↔ 8–10 in (20–25 cm)
↑ 12 in (30 cm)
Perennial native to western China. Clumps of deeply divided ferny foliage, often with a purplish tinge. Nodding cup-like flowers, pink to purple, in loose panicles, in summer. Zones 6–9.

SEMIARUNDINARIA

This genus of bamboos is from Japan and contains 6 species, also found wild in China. This leptomorph bamboo is considered a natural bigeneric cross between Phyllostachys and Pleioblastus. Members of the grass (Poaceae) family, they are usually running plants but tend to be more clumping in cooler climates. The stems are comparatively short-lived, so should be regularly removed as they age to keep the plant tidy. The stems usually have 3 short principal branches and up to 7 branches at each node. Although they are regarded as shrubs, Semiarundinaria species can reach up to 40 ft (12 m) tall.
CULTIVATION: Plant in moist but not wet soils in partially shaded woodland situations. These plants are not particularly fussy about soil type, but they tend to prefer a humus-rich acid soil. Propagation is by division of the rhizomes in early spring.

Semiarundinaria fastuosa

syn. Arundinaria fastuosa

NARIHARA BAMBOO

☀/☀ ❄ ↔ 7–10 ft (2–3 m)
↑ 20–30 ft (6–9 m)
Erect clumping to running bamboo from Japan. Slender green stems, with purple-brown stripes in direct sun. Leaves to 6 in (15 cm) long, most numerous toward tops of stems. S. f. var. viridis, bushier growth habit, with narrower, non-fading, dark green leaves, easily propagated. Zones 7–10.

SEMPERVIVUM

HENS AND CHICKENS, HOUSELEEK

This genus in the stonecrop (Crassulaceae) family, containing about 40 species of perennials, comes from the mountains of central and southern Europe and eastward to Turkey and Iran, where it grows in rocks and crevices. The thick fleshy leaves may be dull or glossy, and are sometimes covered in a soft down of hairs. They form a flat crowded rosette and spread by offsets, in time becoming a dense tight mat. White, yellow, red, or purplish flowers are held in a cluster on stout fleshy stems in summer. Mainly grown for their colorful decorative leaves, these plants are excellent for rock gardens and pots.
CULTIVATION: These plants require sandy well-drained soil and dry conditions. Smaller species prefer to nest tightly in narrow crevices, while the larger species need a soil that is richer in humus. Sempervivum species are easily propagated from offsets, and they hybridize readily.

Semiaquilegia ecalcarata

Sempervivum arachnoideum subsp. *tomentosum*

Sempervivum calcareum 'Sir William Lawrence'

Sempervivum arachnoideum 'Cebanse'

Sempervivum arachnoideum ★

COBWEB HOUSELEEK

☼ ❋ ↔ 5–10 in (12–20 cm)
↑ 5 in (12 cm)

From the Pyrenees and the Carpathian mountains. Forms dense rosettes of green or reddish leaves, their pointed tips connected by fine, cobweb-like, white hairs. Bright rose red flowers appear in summer. *S. a.* subsp. *tomentosum,* particularly dense leaves with silvery cobwebbing and showy red flowers. *S. a.* 'Cebanse', larger rosettes. Zones 5–9.

Sempervivum calcareum

☼ ❋ ↔ 5–8 in (12–20 cm)
↑ 2–3 in (5–8 cm)

Native to the Pyrenees, closely related to *S. tectorum*. Rosettes of brown-tipped gray-green leaves. '**Mrs Giuseppi**', gray-green rosettes, red-tipped leaves darken in winter; '**Sir**

William Lawrence' ★, larger more globose rosettes, leaves with prominent reddish tips. Zones 5–9.

Sempervivum ciliosum

☼ ❋ ↔ 1–2 in (25–50 mm)
↑ ½–¾ in (12–18 mm)

From the Balkans and northwestern Greece. Somewhat globe-shaped tight rosette of gray-green incurving leaves. Grayish marginal hairs give the plant a furry appearance. Compact heads of starry greenish yellow flowers, in summer. Zones 6–9.

Sempervivum marmoreum

☼ ❋ ↔ 4 in (10 cm) ↑ 1–2 in (2–5 cm)

From the Balkans and eastern Europe. Flat open rosettes of reddish to purplish tinged leaves, softly hairy when young, becoming smooth and glossy. Star-shaped mauve flowers with white edges. Many cultivars have more red leaves, '**Brunneifolium**', pink-brown leaves; '**Rubicundrum**', red-tipped leaves; '**Rubrifolium**', bright red-tipped leaves. Zones 5–9.

Sempervivum montanum

☼ ❋ ↔ 1¼–1¾ in (30–40 mm)
↑ ¾ in (18 mm)

Native to mountains of Europe. Very variable; forms clustered mats of dense open rosettes, fleshy, softly furry green leaves, many offsets on fine stems. Violet-purple flowers,

in summer. *S. m.* subsp. *stiriacum*, larger, leaves with prominent brown-red tips. Zones 5–9.

Sempervivum pumilum

☼ ❋ ↔ 1–1¼ in (25–30 mm)
↑ ¾ in (18 mm)

Miniature species from the Caucasus region. Forms small rosettes of finely hairy green leaves. Mauve flowers with white margins, in summer. Zones 5–9.

Sempervivum tectorum ★

HEN AND CHICKENS, ST PATRICK'S CABBAGE

☼ ❋ ↔ 8 in (20 cm) ↑ 3–4 in (8–10 cm)

Found on mountains in Europe from the Pyrenees to the Balkans; naturalized in the UK. Vigorous and variable. Wide flat rosettes of very fleshy green leaves with reddish tips, many offsets on stout reddish stems. Mauve-red flowers in summer. Parent of many cultivars. Zones 5–9.

Sempervivum zeleborii

syn. *Sempervivum ruthenicum*

☼ ❋ ↔ 1½–2 in (35–50 mm)
↑ ¼–¾ in (6–18 mm)

From the Balkans. Produces small dense rosettes with fleshy, downy, slightly incurved leaves, occasionally with purple tips and offsets, on lax short stems. Bears yellow flowers in summer. Zones 6–9.

Sempervivum zeleborii

S. montanum subsp. *stiriacum*

Sempervivum marmoreum

Sempervivum pumilum

Sempervivum calcareum 'Mrs Giuseppi'

S

Sempervivum, HC, 'Booth's Red'

S., HC, 'Commander Hay'

Sempervivum, HC, 'Corona'

S., HC, 'Engle's Rubrum'

Sempervivum, HC, 'Hall's Hybrid'

Sempervivum, Hybrid Cultivar, 'White Eyes'

Sempervivum, HC, 'Raspberry Ice'

S., HC, 'Reginald Malby'

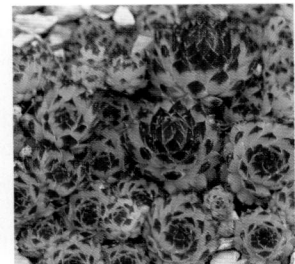

Sempervivum, HC, 'Reinhard'

Sempervivum, HC, 'Virgil'

Sempervivum Hybrid Cultivars

☼/◐ ❄ ↔ 4–16 in (10–40 cm)
↕ 4–8 in (10–20 cm)

Sempervivum species hybridize freely and garden forms vary. Mostly grown for their foliage, a few have showy flowers. 'Booth's Red', dense, neat, purplish red rosettes, symmetrically arranged, to over 3 in (8 cm) wide; 'Commander Hay', large mound of heavily red-tinted rosettes, each to over 6 in (15 cm) wide; 'Corona', many 1 in (25 mm) wide red-tinted rosettes, turning bright red in winter; 'Engle's Rubrum', 3 in (8 cm) wide gray-green rosettes heavily tinged with red; 'Hall's Hybrid', flat 3 in (8 cm) wide rosettes, flushed with red at the base; 'Raspberry Ice', tight symmetrical rosettes, red-tinted, fringed with white hairs; 'Reginald Malby', large flat rosettes of deep red-brown tinged leaves; 'Reinhard', many small rosettes with deep purple-red leaf tips, showy pink flowers; 'Virgil', 3 in (8 cm) wide gray-green rosettes, flushed purple-blue with darker tips; 'White Eyes', central part of rosette yellowish green. Zones 6–10.

SENECIO

There are 1,250 species in this cosmopolitan genus of trees, shrubs, lianes, annuals, biennials, perennials, and some succulent species in the daisy (Asteraceae) family; this is one of the largest genera of flowering plants. The leaves are lobed or smooth-edged, and the daisy-like flowers are usually arranged in clusters, with or without florets. The flowers are usually yellow, but can be purple, white, red, or blue. Many species are toxic to livestock. CULTIVATION: With such a large genus, cultivation requirements are diverse, so general guidelines only can be given. They grow in either moderately fertile well-drained soil in full sun, or in moderately fertile soil that retains moisture; a few will grow in bogs. Plants grown in pots in colder climates need fertile well-drained soil with added grit and leaf mold. They should be fed and watered moderately during the growing season. Propagation is from seed or cuttings.

Senecio articulatus

CANDLE PLANT

☼/◐ ⊰ ↔ 16–20 in (40–50 cm)
↕ 12 in (30 cm)

Shrubby succulent plant native to the Cape region of South Africa. The fleshy, jointed stems are grayish green, with inverted V-shaped markings below each leaf node. The bluish green leaves are flat and broadly triangular, soft and fleshy, and often purple on the undersides. The inflorescences grow at the ends of the branches; yellowish white florets with an unpleasant odor appear in winter. Zones 9–11.

Senecio cineraria

syn. *Cineraria maritima*

DUSTY MILLER, SEA RAGWORT

☼ ❄ ↔ 16 in (40 cm) ↕ 20 in (50 cm)

Mounding subshrub from southern Europe; naturalized in southern England. Leaves are deeply dissected and lobed, intensely silver-white. Small heads of yellow daisies appear in summer. 'Cirrus', rounded-lobed grayish blue leaves; 'Silver Dust' ★, broad, deeply cut, pewter leaves; 'Silver Lace', rounded leaves deeply lobed but less dissected; 'White Diamond', finely dissected white leaves, compact habit. Zones 7–10.

Senecio cineraria 'Cirrus'

Senecio cineraria 'Silver Dust'

Senna didymobotrya

Senna didymobotrya

Senna artemisioides subsp. *filifolia*

Senecio gregorii

☼ ❅ ↔ 6–12 in (15–30 cm)
↕ 6–12 in (15–30 cm)

Annual occurring widely in arid Australia, mostly in deep red sandy soil. Narrow, succulent, bluish green leaves to 3 in (8 cm) long. Bright golden yellow flowerheads to 1½ in (40 mm) across with 8 to 12 ray florets, in late winter–spring. Zones 9–11.

Senecio macroglossus

☼ ❅ ↔ 40 in (100 cm) ↕ 3–7 ft (0.9–2 m)

Slender twining climber from eastern South Africa, Zimbabwe, and Mozambique. Ivy-shaped, slightly succulent, shiny green leaves. Long-lasting cream to pale yellow daisies, in spring–summer. 'Variegatus', dark green leaves marked with cream. Zones 9–12.

Senecio rowleyanus ★

STRING OF BEADS
☼/◐ ❅ ↔ 8–12 in (20–30 cm)
↕ 20–32 in (50–80 cm)

Succulent perennial from Eastern Cape, South Africa. Creeping or pendent habit; thick mat of near-spherical leaves on thin bluish green stems, narrow "window" on uppersurface from tip to base. Single flowerheads at ends of branches. Lacks ray florets; white disc florets, mauve anthers, violet style, cinnamon perfume. Zones 9–10.

Senecio serpens ★

syn. *Kleinia repens*
BLUE CHALKSTICKS
☼ ❅ ↔ 24 in (60 cm) ↕ 12 in (30 cm)

Spreading South African shrub. Narrow, succulent, glaucous leaves with powdery white coating. White flowers in small heads in late spring; best removed to keep plant more lushly foliaged. Zones 9–11.

Senecio smithii

☼ ❆ ↔ 2 ft (0.6 m) ↕ 2–4 ft (0.6–1.2 m)

Perennial native to Chile and Argentina. Clumps of long-stemmed, large, oval leaves, white-haired beneath. Tall flowering stems with showy flowerheads of yellow-centered white daisies in summer. Zones 7–10.

Senecio vira-vira

syn. *Senecio leucostachys*
DUSTY MILLER
☼ ❆ ↔ 12–24 in (30–60 cm)
↕ 16–24 in (40–60 cm)

Shrubby perennial from Argentina. Covered in dense white hairs. Lacy effect of finely divided, soft, silvery gray leaves. Small, creamy, button-like flowers in summer. Zones 8–11.

SENNA

This genus contains about 350 species of tropical and warm-temperate trees, shrubs, and a few climbers, most from the Americas, Africa, Australia, and Asia. It is a member of the cassia subfamily of the legume (Fabaceae) family. All species have pinnate leaves, and almost all are evergreen. Most have yellow flowers, a few have pink flowers, but all are very showy when in flower. Many are the source of chemical compounds used medicinally. Fruits are long, flat, or rounded pods. Many species have become invasive weeds in countries where they have escaped from cultivation.
CULTIVATION: Many species are frost tender. Grow in well-drained soils in open sunny positions. Species that originate from low-rainfall desert regions appear to be more frost hardy. Propagation is usually from seed, which germinates readily after pretreatment, or from cuttings.

Senna alata

syn. *Cassia alata*
RINGWORM CASSIA
☼ ✦ ↔ 15 ft (4.5 m) ↕ 30 ft (9 m)

Shrub or tree native to the American tropics; has naturalized elsewhere. Leaves large, to 3 ft (0.9 m) long, 20 pairs of leaflets. Spikes of bright yellow flowers in late summer–early autumn. Green winged pods turn brown as they mature. Zones 10–12.

Senna artemisioides

syn. *Cassia artemisioides*
FEATHERY CASSIA, SILVER CASSIA
☼ ❅ ↔ 7 ft (2 m) ↕ 7 ft (2 m)

Occurs throughout the arid inland of mainland Australia. Many forms.

Typical subspecies, round shrub, silvery gray leaves, 2 to 6 pairs of narrow leaflets. Yellow flowers in the leaf axils in spring–autumn. Narrow flat pods. *S. a.* subsp. *filifolia* (syns *S. eremophila*, *S. nemophila*), pinnate leaves, 1 to 4 pairs of very narrow leaflets, leaf stalk flattened. Less frost tolerant than other forms. *S. a.* subsp. *sturtii*, bright yellow flowers year-round. Zones 9–11.

Senna corymbosa

syn. *Cassia corymbosa*
☼ ❄ ↔ 8 ft (2.4 m) ↕ 10 ft (3 m)

Native to Uruguay and Argentina; naturalized in southern USA. Shrub or small tree with a spreading habit. Long, light green, pinnately divided leaves with oval leaflets. Racemes of golden yellow flowers appear from spring–autumn. Zones 8–11.

Senna didymobotrya

syn. *Cassia didymobotrya*
☼ ❅ ↔ 10 ft (3 m) ↕ 10 ft (3 m)

Large evergreen shrub, originally from tropical Africa to Southeast Asia, now widely naturalized. Large leaves, leathery leaflets, downy when young. Erect flower spikes, golden yellow flowers emerging from blackish buds. Downy seed pods. Zones 10–12.

Senecio gregorii, in the wild, Mungo National Park, New South Wales, Australia

Senecio serpens

S

Senna hebecarpa
WILD SENNA

☼ ❄ ↔ 24 in (60 cm)
↑ 4–6 ft (1.2–1.8 m)

Well-foliaged perennial native to eastern USA, endangered in some states. Pinnately divided leaves. Bears large racemes of yellow flowers in summer. Long black seed pods. Zones 4–9.

Senna odorata
syn. *Cassia odorata*

☼ ❀ ↔ 7 ft (2 m) ↑ 8 ft (2.4 m)

Australian shrub found from southern Queensland southward to New South Wales. Leaves dark green and pinnate with 6 to 12 pairs of leaflets. Small clusters of yellow flowers appear in spring–autumn. Fruits are flat pods. Prostrate form occurs. Zones 9–11.

Senna pendula
syns *Cassia bicapsularis* of gardens, *C. coluteoides*

☼ ❀ ↔ 8 ft (2.4 m) ↑ 10 ft (3 m)

Spreading shrub or small tree from South America. Mature trunks have brown corky spots. Light green pinnately divided leaves, oblong leaflets.

Senna hebecarpa

Showy panicles of yellow flowers in autumn. Drooping cylindrical seed pods. Zones 9–11.

Senna polyphylla
syn. *Cassia polyphylla*

☼ ✈ ↔ 12 ft (3.5 m) ↑ 25 ft (8 m)

Shrub or small tree found in the Caribbean region. Stiff branches clothed with small leaves, 13 pairs of olive green leaflets with slightly downy undersides. Clusters of golden yellow flowers. Pendulous flattened seeds. Zones 10–12.

SEQUOIA

This genus from the cypress (Cupressaceae) family contains a single species of coniferous tree native to the coastal areas of Oregon and California, USA. It is the tallest plant species in the world, with plants in the wild growing to over 360 ft (110 m) high.
CULTIVATION: This tree is suitable only for parks and large gardens, as it can reach 90 ft (27 m) in 20 years. It does not grow well in cities as it dislikes pollution. Any good well-drained soil will suit it, but it does best in cool

Senna odorata

Sequoia sempervirens, in the wild, Redwood State Park, California, USA

Sequoia sempervirens, in the wild, John Muir Woods, San Francisco, California, USA

humid areas. It will coppice from the stump of a felled tree. Propagate from seed or from heeled cuttings.

Sequoia sempervirens
CALIFORNIAN REDWOOD, COAST REDWOOD

☼ ❄ ↔ 15–25 ft (4.5–8 m) ↑ 150 ft (45 m)

Tree develops a conical shape. Bark deeply ridged, reddish brown, very thick, spongy, exfoliating in strips. Dark green needle-like leaves grow in ranks along stems. Bears small, reddish brown, barrel-shaped cones. 'Adpressa', slow-growing dwarf cultivar, grayish green leaves, will reach 90 ft (27 m) tall in about 100 years. Two cultivars have almost horizontal branches: 'Aptos Blue', teal foliage with drooping tips, site carefully as it sets abundant seed; 'Soquel', greener foliage with curling tips. Zones 8–10.

SEQUOIADENDRON

There is just a single species of coniferous tree in this genus from the cypress (Cupressaceae) family, which was formerly included in *Sequoia*. It is found in small groves in the Sierra

Nevada foothills in California, USA. This species is the largest living organism (though *Sequoia* is taller), with trees acquiring massive bulk; the biggest existing specimen is named "General Sherman," and is estimated to weigh 2,460 tons (2,500 tonnes). It is also one of the longest living trees, with specimens in the range of 1,500 to 3,000 years old.
CULTIVATION: With its enormous bulk, this tree is suitable only for parks and similar situations. For planting in lines or avenues, trees should be spaced at least 70 ft (21 m) apart. They will grow in a wide range of conditions but dislike pollution. Propagate from seed or cuttings.

Sequoiadendron giganteum
syn. *Wellingtonia gigantea*
BIG TREE, GIANT SEQUOIA, SIERRA REDWOOD

☼ ❄ ↔ 20–35 ft (6–9 m)
↑ 150–165 ft (45–50 m)

Often confused with *Sequoia sempervirens*. Similar conical shape, very thick, reddish brown, spongy bark. Branches curve downward, then up

Senna pendula

Senna polyphylla

S

at tips. Leaves compressed, scale-like, spiraly arranged on stems. Cones are larger than those of *Sequoia*. '**Pendulum**', hanging branches. Zones 7–10.

SERENOA

This genus of palms in the family Arecaceae consists of a single species from southeastern USA, where it forms large colonies, particularly in coastal areas. It is short and has fan-shaped fronds. Branching flowerheads arise from within the foliage.
CULTIVATION: This adaptable palm grows in a range of soils and climates, including coastal areas, where it tolerates salt-laden winds. It does best in warm subtropical areas, and should be grown in a sunny situation. In cool climates it can be grown in pots in the greenhouse. Propagation is from seed.

Serenoa repens ★
SAW PALMETTO

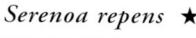

☼ ❄ ↔ 7 ft (2 m) ↑ 3–15 ft (0.9–4.5 m)
Branching subterranean trunk, forms dense clumps. Fan-shaped fronds, deeply divided into stiff segments, on very thorny stalks, from yellowish green to bluish and silvery green. Fragrant cream flowers on branching woolly flowerheads. Zones 8–11.

SERIPHIDIUM

This genus is a member of the large daisy (Asteraceae) family and is doubt-

Serenoa repens

Sequoiadendron giganteum cultivar

fully distinct from *Artemisia*. It contains about 60 species of aromatic annuals, perennials, and shrubs found in northern temperate regions. They have deeply dissected alternate leaves. The small flowers are of little interest. These plants are grown primarily for their silvery or gray foliage.
CULTIVATION: These plants tolerate a wide range of soils, including those with low fertility. They are useful for growing in difficult dry areas, and do best in a warm sunny position. Propagation of the shrubby species is from softwood or half-hardened cuttings taken in summer.

Seriphidium tridentatum
syn. *Artemisia tridentata*
BIG SAGEBRUSH

☼ ❄ ↔ 8 ft (2.4 m) ↑ 10 ft (3 m)
Shrub native to southwestern North America. Short trunk or stems are densely covered in white hairs, and later clad in pale shredded bark.

Sequoiadendron giganteum

Attractive foliage, fine, 3-lobed, aromatic leaves with a silvery hue, slightly sticky. Zones 8–11.

SERISSA

The sole species in this genus from the madder (Rubiaceae) family is a small, densely branched, evergreen shrub from warm-temperate Southeast Asia. It is a neat little bush with tiny leaves that emit an unpleasant smell when crushed. It produces small white flowers followed by berries, but it is often grown as a foliage plant, as there are several variegated cultivars.
CULTIVATION: Apart from being somewhat frost tender, *Serissa* is easily grown. It likes a warm, moist, humid

climate and a rich soil with plenty of humus. In areas where it cannot be grown outdoors it makes an excellent greenhouse or conservatory plant. Propagate from cuttings or from self-layered pieces.

Serissa japonica
syn. *Serissa foetida*

☼ ❄ ↔ 18 in (45 cm) ↑ 18 in (45 cm)
Attractive shrub, easily accommodated in most gardens. White flowers in spring–autumn. '**Flore Pleno**', very compact bush with double flowers; '**Mount Fuji**', very compact, leaves edged and striped with white; '**Variegata Pink**', pink flowers, white-edged leaves. Zones 9–11.

Seriphidium tridentatum (at rear), in the wild, Grand Teton National Park, Wyoming, USA

Serissa japonica, bonsai

Serissa japonica 'Flore Pleno'

Serruria 'Sugar 'n' Spice'

Sesbania punicea

SERRURIA

One of the many southern African genera in the protea (Proteaceae) family, *Serruria* encompasses some 55 species of evergreen shrubs, which are notable for their delicate inflorescences that often make excellent and very popular cut flowers. Most species have leaves that are very finely dissected, often so finely as to resemble needle-like foliage. A few species have simple undivided leaves. The flowerheads, which may be clustered or carried singly, are usually composed of several small hairy flowers that are largely concealed within showy bracts. Hard nut-like fruits follow.

CULTIVATION: Often tricky to cultivate outside their natural range, these species tend to be short-lived. They have the typical protea requirements: low-phosphate, slightly acidic, gritty,

very well-drained soil, a position in sun or part-shade, and good ventilation. If exposed to damp cool conditions in winter they tend to rot. They are also marginally frost hardy. Propagation is from seed or from cuttings, which are often slow to strike and prone to collapse.

Serruria 'Sugar 'n' Spice'
☼ ❀ ↔ 4 ft (1.2 m) ↑ 4 ft (1.2 m)
Originated as a hybrid between *S. florida* and *S. rosea*. Combines the large flowerheads and broad bracts of the first species with the richer pink coloring of the second. Zones 9–10.

SESAMUM

There are about 15 species of annuals and perennials in this genus in the sesame (Pedaliaceae) family. They are native to Africa, India, and Sri Lanka. The leaves are simple or divided, opposite or alternate. The flowers are white, pink, or purple, bell-shaped, and 2-lipped, similar to foxgloves (*Digitalis*). The seed pods are oblong to cylindrical and are split longitudinally. *S. orientale*, which is one of the earliest plants known to have been grown for its seeds, has been cultivated for thousands of years. It is widely grown in tropical and subtropical areas, the nutritious seeds have a variety of uses, including being used whole in cooking, ground to a paste for tahini, pressed for oil, and incorporated in stock feed.

CULTIVATION: Grow in tropical and subtropical areas in full sun in a rich, moist, but well-drained soil. Seed

pods explode and disperse their seed, so they should be harvested before they dry out. Propagate from seed.

Sesamum orientale
syn. *Sesamum indicum*
BENNE, GINGELLY, SESAME
☼ ✤ ↔ 1–2 ft (0.3–0.6)
↑ 2–6 ft (0.6–1.8 m)
Annual, originally from Africa. Hairy lance-shaped to oval leaves. Attractive white to pink tubular flowers, borne in leaf axils. When left on plant, dry seed pods explode, releasing numerous small seeds. Zones 10–12.

SESBANIA

Widespread throughout the tropics and subtropics, this genus from the pea-flower subfamily of the legume (Fabaceae) family encompasses some 50 species of evergreen and deciduous leguminous herbs, shrubs, and trees. They have pinnate leaves that can be quite large, but their main feature is their racemes of pea-flowers. These develop in the leaf axils and usually open in summer. Angular seed pods follow, and should be removed to prolong the flowering.

CULTIVATION: Demanding a warm climate, most *Sesbania* species, even the trees, are both quick growing and short lived. They can look rather rank and untidy unless they are kept neatly trimmed, but usually make up for it with a colorful display of flowers. They thrive in a moderately fertile, deep, well-drained soil, and a position in full sun or part-shade. Water well during the flowering season, but keep dry during the cooler months. Propagation is from seed or from half-hardened cuttings.

Sesbania punicea
ORANGE WISTERIA SHRUB
☼ ❀ ↔ 4 ft (1.2 m) ↑ 6 ft (1.8 m)
Shrub found throughout southern Brazil, Argentina, and Uruguay; naturalized in southeastern USA. Mid- to dark green leaves, 6 to 20 pairs of 1 in (25 mm) long leaflets. Vivid orange flowers, in racemes up to 4 in (10 cm) long. Zones 9–11.

SESLERIA
MOOR GRASS
This genus of about 35 low-growing, mounding, perennial grasses from the family Poaceae is native to Europe and western Asia. They have narrow leaf blades and dense rounded to cylindrical panicles of flower spikes.
CULTIVATION: Moor grasses prefer rocky well-drained soils in an open sunny position. Propagate by division.

Sesleria tatrae
☼/◐ ❄ ↔ 6–8 in (15–20 cm)
↑ 6–10 in (15–25 cm)
Tufted or clump-forming perennial grass from around the snowline in the Tatra Mountains, Poland. Forms a dense clump of very fine deep green leaves. Short flowerheads on stocky stems, in summer. Zones 3–8.

SHEPHERDIA
There are only 3 species of deciduous or evergreen shrubs in this genus from the oleaster (Elaeagnaceae) family. They are native to North America, where they grow on exposed slopes and dry rocky sites. They have simple opposite leaves and bear small petalless flowers; male and female flowers are produced on separate plants.
CULTIVATION: These shrubs will grow in a range of conditions, and can tolerate poor dry sites. They like full sun and free-draining soil. Propagation is from seed or cuttings.

Shepherdia argentea ★
BUFFALO BERRY, SILVER BUFFALO BERRY, SILVERBERRY
☼ ❄ ↔ 12 ft (3.5 m) ↑ 12 ft (3.5 m)
Well-branched shrub with spiny branches and silvery oblong leaves. Small yellowish white flowers in spring. Female plants produce glossy, red, pea-sized fruits. Zones 2–9.

Shepherdia canadensis
BUFFALO BERRY
☼ ❄ ↔ 8 ft (2.4 m) ↑ 8 ft (2.4 m)
Spreading shrub. Leaves dark yellowish green above, white below. Creamy yellow flowers. Fruits are yellow to red. Zones 2–9.

Sesleria tatrae

Shepherdia argentea

Sidalcea malviflora

Sidalcea oregana

SHOREA
BALAU, MERANTI

This genus, comprising more than 200 species that are found from Sri Lanka to southern China and Indonesia, belongs to the dipterocarp (Dipterocarpaceae) family. Huge trees that raise their crowns way above the forest canopy, they grow in lowland to mountain rainforest, deciduous forest, and savanna woodland. The resinous trunks generally have large buttresses. The leaves are simple, prominently veined, and spirally arranged. The scented flowers have 5 sepals and 5 petals, and are held in panicles. The persistent sepals act as propellers in dispersal of the fruits, which hold a single seed. Most *Shorea* species flower and fruit at long intervals. The most important timber trees of tropical Asia, some were formerly exploited for resin exudates used in varnishes. The seeds of many are rich in oil used in soaps, food-processing, and cosmetics.
CULTIVATION: These trees prefer full sun but because of their size they are rarely cultivated as ornamentals.

Shorea robusta
SAL

☼ ⚓ ↔ 30–50 ft (9–15 m) ↑ 50–100 ft (15–30 m)

Hardwood tree from the eastern Himalayas to Myanmar. Fissured bark. Rough, leathery, oval leaves. Panicles of small, creamy, aromatic, downy flowers, in summer. Resin burnt as incense. Zones 10–12.

SHORTIA
syn. *Schizocodon*

This genus in the family Diapensiaceae comprises 6 dainty, rhizomatous, clumping, evergreen perennials. Five are native to East Asia, the other to the woodlands of southeastern USA. Their leaves are heart-shaped, rounded, or elliptical, and are toothed and leathery, usually glossy dark green, often turning red in winter. In early spring they bear bell-, trumpet-, or funnel-shaped white to deep pink flowers with toothed or fringed petals.

CULTIVATION: All appreciate humus-rich, acidic, moist but well-drained soil and part- to full shade. They are a challenge to grow in dry regions, even with adequate water; regions with cool damp summers are preferred. If available, sow seed when ripe in autumn, or propagate by basal cuttings in early summer or runners in mid-summer. These plants do not like root disturbance.

Shortia galacifolia
OCONEE BELLS

◐ ❄ ↔ 10 in (25 cm) ↑ 6 in (15 cm)

Perennial native of southeastern USA. Sizeable clump of roundish glossy green leaves with scalloped edges, bronze-red in winter. Nodding, 1 in (25 mm), rose-flushed white bells, toothed edges, in spring. Zones 6–9.

Shortia soldanelloides
FRINGE BELLS, FRINGED GALAX

◐ ❄ ↔ 10 in (25 cm) ↑ 6 in (15 cm)

Perennial evergreen species from Japan. Round coarsely toothed leaves. Pinkish rose flowers, deeply fringed, whitish edges, in spring. *S. s.* var. *ilicifolia*, smaller, with smaller sparsely and coarsely toothed leaves, white or occasionally pink flowers. Zones 6–9.

SIBIRAEA

From Asia and southeastern Europe, this is a genus of 2 species of ornamental deciduous shrubs belonging to the rose (Rosaceae) family. They are grown for their attractive foliage and for their small, 5-petalled, cup-shaped flowers, which are borne at the ends of dense panicles in summer.
CULTIVATION: Grow in a well-drained moderately fertile soil in a sunny position. Prune to remove old or damaged wood, and trim to shape after flowering. Frost hardy, they are propagated from seed or cuttings.

Sibiraea altaiensis
syn. *Sibiraea laevigata*

☼ ❄ ↔ 5 ft (1.5 m) ↑ 5 ft (1.5 m)

Shrub from western China, Siberia, and the northern parts of the Balkans.

Leaves are oblong and bluish green, and grow to 4 in (10 cm) in length. Masses of small white flowers appear in panicles to 5 in (12 cm) long in early summer. Zones 5–9.

SIDALCEA
FALSE MALLOW

This genus of about 22 annual and perennial species in the mallow (Malvaceae) family is native to western parts of North America, where these plants grow on lime-free sandy grasslands along stream beds, and in damp mountain meadows. Resembling a small hollyhock (*Alcea rosea*) to which they are related, they have glossy, round, palmately lobed basal leaves and stiffly upright flower spikes that bear stalkless or short-stemmed, white, pink, or purple, open, cup-shaped flowers at the ends. These are popular and charming plants for perennial borders, and many improved varieties are bred for their color and length of flowering. They will flower freely throughout the summer if the spent flower spikes are removed.
CULTIVATION: They require a humus-rich free-draining soil in a sunny position, and they may be propagated by division or from seed.

Sibiraea altaiensis

Sidalcea candida

☼ ❄ ↔ 20 in (50 cm) ↑ 24–36 in (60–90 cm)

From Utah, New Mexico, Wyoming, and Colorado, USA. The roundish, 7-lobed, glossy leaves grow on long stalks. Branching stems carry white flowers with bluish anthers, in early summer. Parent, with *S. malviflora*, of many modern cultivars. Zones 5–9.

Sidalcea malviflora
CHECKERBLOOM

☼/◐ ❄ ↔ 16–30 in (40–75 cm) ↑ 24–40 in (60–100 cm)

Perennial found from Oregon, USA, to Baja California, Mexico. Forms clump of erect stems carrying shallow-toothed 7- to 9-lobed leaves, 1–2 in (25–50 mm) long. Racemes of many 1–2 in (25–50 mm) wide pink to lavender flowers in spring–autumn. Zones 6–10.

Sidalcea oregana

☼ ❄ ↔ 20 in (50 cm) ↑ 48 in (120 cm)

From Washington to California and Nevada, USA. Round basal leaves, shallow-lobed, up to 6 in (15 cm) across, stem leaves shiny green and segmented. Small deep pink flowers in dense racemes in summer. Zones 5–9.

Shortia soldanelloides var. *ilicifolia*

Shorea robusta, in the wild, Chitwan, Nepal

S

Silene fimbriata

Silene laciniata

Sideritis macrostachys

Silene hifacensis

Sidalcea Hybrid Cultivars

☀/◐ ❄ ↔ 16–24 in (40–60 cm) ↑ 24–32 in (60–80 cm)

These hybrids, which mostly have *S. malviflora* in their parentage, are compact heavy-blooming plants that usually hold their flowers well above the foliage. **'Elsie Heugh'**, triangular ruffled leaves, dainty shell pink flowers; **'Little Princess'**, miniature, compact, soft pink flowers; **'Rose Queen'** ★, deep rose pink flowers on many dense spikes; **'Sussex Beauty'**, particularly large pale pink flowers; **'Monarch'**, taller cultivar, pink flowers. Zones 6–10.

SIDERITIS

This Mediterranean genus, also occurring on the Canary Islands and nearby islands in the Atlantic, is composed of around 100 species of annuals, perennials, subshrubs, and shrubs in the mint (Lamiaceae) family. They have downy stems and leaves, and whorls of tubular to bell-shaped flowers at ends of spikes with leafy bracts at their base. The leaves are usually a pointed oval with a heart-shaped base, and may be smooth-edged or irregularly toothed or notched.
CULTIVATION: These plants are easily grown in any reasonably fertile, light, well-drained soil in full sun or morning shade. They tolerate light frosts, but prefer dry winters because prolonged wet and cold conditions can cause the downy leaves to rot. Apart from a little tidying up, trimming is seldom necessary. Propagate from seed or half-hardened tip cuttings of non-flowering stems.

Sideritis macrostachys

☀ ❁ ↔ 3 ft (0.9 m) ↑ 2–4 ft (0.6–1.2 m)
Shrub native to the Canary Islands. Downy, sage-like, gray-green leaves, faintly notched edges. Upright, sometimes branched, flower spikes carry small white flowers, brown-tipped petals, thin covering of white down on bracts and calyces. Zones 9–10.

SILENE

CAMPION, CATCHFLY, CUSHION PINK
A large and very varied genus in the pink (Caryophyllaceae) family, *Silene* contains about 500 annuals and perennials widely distributed throughout the Northern Hemisphere and southern Africa. The smaller cushion types, some of them very challenging to grow away from their native habitat, are often used in rock gardens, while some of the taller species are good as garden, hedgerow, or wild garden plants. The flowers are 5-petalled, generally white or shades of pink, and may be solitary or borne in one-sided spikes. The leaves and stems of many are downy and sticky to the touch.
CULTIVATION: Good drainage is essential for cultivation of these plants, as is a light loamy soil in a sunny position. Propagation is by seed, division, or cuttings.

Silene acaulis

CUSHION PINK, MOSS CAMPION
☀ ❄ ↔ 4 in (10 cm) ↑ 2 in (5 cm)
Perennial from Eurasia and North America extending into higher mountain regions further south. Forms low, dense, tufted cushion of bright green linear leaves. Solitary deep pink to purple flowers sit just above the foliage. Numerous cultivars. Zones 2–8.

Silene alpestris

syns *Heliosperma alpestre*, *Silene quadrifida*
☀/◐ ❄ ↔ 12 in (30 cm) ↑ 6–12 in (15–30 cm)
From the southern European Alps to the Caucasus region. Low loose cushion of linear-lanceolate leaves. Starry flowers on long stems, white, rarely pink, with cleft or fringed petals, in summer. Zones 5–9.

Silene dioica

RED CAMPION
☀/◐ ❄ ↔ 12 in (30 cm) ↑ 24 in (60 cm)
Perennial from the woods, rocky hillsides, and cliffs of Europe. Rosettes of downy leaves. Tall, stiff, branching stems carry bright pink, rarely white, flowers, in summer. Double and semi-double forms. Zones 6–10.

Silene fimbriata

☀/◐ ❄ ↔ 24 in (60 cm) ↑ 40 in (100 cm)
Perennial from damp woodlands of the Caucasus region. Rosettes of dark green, hairy, oval leaves forming a mound. Open panicles of fringed white flowers with swollen globular calyces, in early summer. Zones 5–8.

Silene hifacensis

syn. *Silene mollissima*
☀ ❄ ↔ 8 in (20 cm) ↑ 12 in (30 cm)
Endangered perennial from the Iberian Peninsula. Dense rosettes of oval leaves. Upright, occasionally branched stems bear open panicles of rosy pink flowers with tubular calyces in early summer. Zones 8–10.

Silene laciniata

FRINGED INDIAN PINK, MEXICAN CAMPION
☀ ❄ ↔ 8 in (20 cm) ↑ 36 in (90 cm)
From California and New Mexico, USA, and Mexico. Narrow oval leaves to 2 in (5 cm) long. Upright, softly hairy stems bear 1 or 2 large, starry, crimson flowers. Zones 7–10.

Sidalcea, Hybrid Cultivar, 'Elsie Heugh'

Sidalcea, Hybrid Cultivar, 'Little Princess'

Sidalcea, Hybrid Cultivar, 'Monarch'

Sidalcea, Hybrid Cultivar, 'Sussex Beauty'

Silene schafta

☼ ❊ ↔ 8 in (20 cm) ↕ 4 in (10 cm)
Perennial from the Caucasus region.
Many upright stems; small, bright
green, linear leaves forming loose
mat. Bears profuse, star-shaped, rosy
magenta flowers with cleft petals, in
late summer–autumn. Easily grown
rock garden plant. Zones 5–9.

Silene uniflora

syn. *Silene vulgaris* subsp. *maritima*
BLADDER CAMPION, SEA CAMPION
☼ ❊ ↔ 4 in (10 cm) ↕ 4–8 in (10–20 cm)
Native to coasts of western Europe
and North Africa. Perennial with gray-
tinged oval to spathulate leaves. Upright stems of solitary white flowers
with a pronounced inflated calyx like
a small bladder, in summer. 'Robin
Whitebreast' (syn. 'Flore Pleno'),
double-flowers. Zones 5–9.

SILPHIUM

This genus, comprising 23 species of
coarse-leafed perennials native to central and eastern North America, is in
the daisy (Asteraceae) family. The
simple to deeply divided leaves are
opposite to whorled, the basal ones
forming a rosette, those on the inflorescence stalks spiraly arranged. The
daisy-like flowerheads are large and
have numerous outer rayed florets
growing in 2 or 3 rows, white or yellow, while the disc florets are small and
yellow. Rather unspectacular plants,
they are mostly suited to the wild
garden, though their size can impress.
CULTIVATION: They grow in full sun
or very light shade in any soil not too
nitrogen-rich. Seed is the best method
of propagation, because the deep root
system of larger species makes them
difficult to propagate vegetatively.

Silphium laciniatum

COMPASS PLANT
☼/◐ ❊ ↔ 3–4 ft (0.9–1.2 m)
↕ 5–10 ft (1.5–3 m)
From central USA. Strongly erect,
hairy, fern-like leaves, 4–16 in
(10–40 cm) long, aligned north–
south. Bears clusters of bright yellow

flowerheads, 2 in (5 cm) wide, in
summer. It has traditional medicinal
and culinary uses. Zones 4–9.

Silphium perfoliatum

CUP PLANT
☼/◐ ❊ ↔ 3 ft (0.9 m) ↕ 5 ft (1.5 m)
Perennial from damp woodlands and
prairies of eastern North America.
Forms large clump of rough, irregularly toothed, ovate leaves, upper
leaves stem-clasping. Stiffly upright
stems branching towards top carry
single yellow daisy flowers. Zones 5–10.

Silphium terebinthinaceum

PRAIRIE DOCK
☼/◐ ❊ ↔ 3–6 ft (0.9–1.8 m)
↕ 7–10 ft (2–3 m)
From southern Canada to southeastern USA. Dense clump of large, long-
stemmed basal leaves to over 12 in
(30 cm) long, heart-shaped at base,
toothed or lobed near tip. Erect red-
brown flower stems with summer-
borne sprays of 1–2 in (25–50 mm)
wide golden flowerheads with many
ray florets. Zones 4–9.

SILYBUM

This genus in the daisy (Asteraceae)
family contains just 2 species of
annual or biennial plants grown for
their ornamental foliage. They are
native to the Mediterranean region
and eastern Africa, where they grow
in sunny free-draining areas. They are
robust upright plants forming basal
rosettes from which the stout flowering stems arise. The long leaves are
lobed or pinnate with extremely spiny
margins. They have prominent white
veins or variegations. The purple thistle flowers are borne on tall stems in
spring or summer. *S. marianum* has
long been used to stimulate milk
supply in nursing mothers.
CULTIVATION: Grow in the border
in full sun and in free-draining soil.
To prolong the display of attractive
foliage, the flowering stem can be
removed. When allowed to flower,
seed will self-sow freely. Young plants
need protection from slugs and snails.

Silphium perfoliatum

Silene uniflora

Silene uniflora 'Robin Whitebreast'

Silybum marianum

BLESSED THISTLE, OUR LADY'S MILK THISTLE
☼ ❊ ↔ 2 ft (0.6 m) ↕ 4 ft (1.2 m)
Biennial, native to Europe; naturalized in the Americas. Basal rosette of
long, deeply lobed, dark green leaves
with prominent white veins and spiny
margins. Purplish thistle flowers in
spring and summer. Zones 6–10.

SIMMONDSIA

This genus has only one species,
S. chinensis, a common shrub native
to the desert regions of southwestern
USA and northern Mexico. It is the
sole genus of the jojoba (Simmondsia-
ceae) family, which is related to the
box (Buxaceae) family. Sometimes
cultivated in hot arid climates as an
ornamental plant and for erosion control, it is more widely known and
valued for its seeds, which are the
source of jojoba oil, a clear waxy oil
used in a range of products, including
cosmetics and soaps.
CULTIVATION: This species requires
a warm to hot climate and a well-
drained dry soil in full sun. It is very
drought tolerant. Lightly prune regularly to shape. Propagate from seed.

Simmondsia chinensis

GOAT NUT, JOJOBA
☼ ❊ ↔ 6 ft (1.8 m) ↕ 8 ft (2.4 m)
Evergreen shrub from the USA and
Mexico. Hairy young stems, small,
leathery, oblong, gray-green leaves.
Male and female flowers borne on
separate plants. Clusters of cup-
shaped, yellow, male flowers, or bell-
shaped, greenish, female flowers, in
leaf axils, in summer. Fruit capsules
contain a single seed. Zones 9–12.

SINAPIS

This genus containing 8 species of
mostly annual edible herbs in the
cabbage (Brassicaceae) family, is native
to the Mediterranean region, and is
closely related to the genus *Brassica*.
The lower leaves form a rosette and
the upper leaves are stem-clasping.
Racemes of small yellow flowers
appear in summer. *S. arvensis* is a persistent weed of farmland, but is sometimes used for the oil obtained from
its reddish brown to black seeds.
CULTIVATION: These plants prefer
a sandy soil in sun. Raise from seed,
avoiding mid-summer sowing as they
run to seed when the weather is hot.

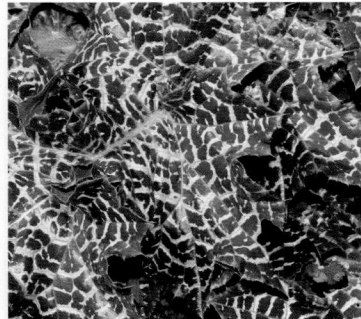
Silybum marianum

Simmondsia chinensis

Sinapis alba

WHITE MUSTARD

☀ ❄ ↔ 6 in (15 cm) ↕ 10–15 in (25–38 cm)

Annual with upright stems branching toward top. Ovate, downy, lobed leaves, bright green, sometimes spotted violet. Up to 50 small yellow flowers per raceme. Young seedlings used as a salad vegetable. Zones 7–11.

SINNINGIA

GLOXINIA

This genus belonging to the African violet (Gesneriaceae) family is made up of about 40 species of tuberous perennials and small shrubs distributed from Mexico to Argentina. The commonly cultivated species are perennials with large lance- to heart-shaped leaves made velvety by a dense covering of fine hairs. The well-known florist's gloxinia (*S. speciosa*) has large, upward-facing bell-shaped flowers; other species have tubular flowers, which are sometimes scented. CULTIVATION: Widely grown as indoor or greenhouse plants in pots, they are also raised successfully outdoors as a summer annual, or year-round in warm areas. The flower trumpets collapse if filled with water. Species of *Sinningia* prefer warm, humid conditions with a bright but not sunny exposure and moist, humus-rich, well-drained soil.

Sinningia cardinalis

Propagate by lifting and dividing the plants after the foliage has died back, or by seed or leaf-stalk cuttings. The tubers may be stored dry.

Sinningia aggregata

◑/☀ ✲ ↔ 16 in (40 cm) ↕ 24 in (60 cm)

From Brazil. Upright stems, opposite pairs of downy, strongly aromatic, bright green, pointed elliptical leaves. Orange tubular flowers to over 1 in (25 mm) long, in whorls on fine stems. Zones 11–12.

Sinningia canescens

◑/☀ ✲ ↔ 10 in (25 cm) ↕ 10 in (25 cm)

Tuberous perennial species native to Brazil. Heavy, thickened tubers, upright stems. Heart-shaped, velvety, deep green leaves, which are finely toothed.

Sinapis alba

Produces small heads of up to 5 long-stemmed, tubular, bright orange flowers. Zones 11–12.

Sinningia cardinalis

◑/☀ ✲ ↔ 12 in (30 cm) ↕ 8–12 in (20–30 cm)

Tuberous perennial from Brazil with paired, long-stemmed, rounded to heart-shaped, velvety deep green, finely toothed leaves. Bears red tubular flowers, with an overarching upper lip, in heads of many blooms, which are not all open at the same time. Zones 11–12.

Sinningia aggregata

Sinningia × pumila

◑/☀ ✲ ↔ 6–12 in (15–30 cm) ↕ 4–6 in (10–15 cm)

Low, mounding garden hybrid between *S. pusilla* and *S. eumorpha*. Short-stemmed, rounded, velvety leaves. Slightly flared, mauve, tubular flowers to 1¼ in (30 mm) long. Zones 11–12.

Sinningia speciosa

FLORIST'S GLOXINIA, GLOXINIA

◑/☀ ✲ ↔ 12–20 in (30–50 cm) ↕ 8–12 in (20–30 cm)

Brazilian species, popular house plant. Lush, deep green, velvety, soft-toothed,

Sinningia speciosa, Lawn Hybrid

S. s., Lawn Hybrid, 'China Rose'

S. speciosa, Lawn Hybrid, 'Sunset'

Sinningia speciosa, Lawn Hybrid

Sinningia speciosa, Lawn Hybrid

Sinningia speciosa, Lawn Hybrid

Sinningia speciosa, Lawn Hybrid

Sinningia speciosa, Lawn Hybrid

Sinningia speciosa, Lawn Hybrid

Sinningia speciosa, Lawn Hybrid

Sinningia speciosa, Lawn Hybrid

Sinningia speciosa, Lawn Hybrid

Sinningia speciosa, Lawn Hybrid

Sinningia speciosa, Lawn Hybrid

Sinningia speciosa, Lawn Hybrid

rounded to heart-shaped leaves. Upright flower stems, large bell-shaped flowers, mauve to purple with light center and contrasting spots. Cultivars have larger flowers and wider color range, including: '**Boonwood Yellow Bird**', yellow flowers; '**Buell's Queen Bee**', white flowers, 2 conspicuous pink blotches; '**Kiss of Fire**', many small bright red flowers. Seedling strains such as **Lawn Hybrids ★** available as individual colors or mixed. Zones 10–12.

SINOCALYCANTHUS

This genus from the family Calycanthaceae is closely related to the allspices (*Calycanthus*) and includes just one species, a deciduous shrub native to central and eastern China. It has variably sized elliptical leaves with a spicy aroma, and it produces miniature camellia-like flowers from midspring through to early summer. Hard seed capsules follow.
CULTIVATION: Relatively new to cultivation, *Sinocalycanthus* has proved quite hardy and appears to thrive in most well-drained soils. It is best grown in relatively cool conditions with full sun. In areas with hot summers it should be shaded from the hottest afternoon sun. Propagation is from seed or layers.

Sinocalycanthus chinensis
☼ ❋ ↔ 4–10 ft (1.2–3 m)
↑ 6–12 ft (1.8–3.5 m)
Rare in gardens, an ideal shrub for areas with cool moist summers. Lustrous dark green leaves taper abruptly to a point. White to cream camellialike flowers, pink-tinted yellow centers. Zones 5–9.

Sisyrinchium 'Biscutella'

SISYRINCHIUM

This genus has about 90 species of annuals and perennials from the iris (Iridaceae) family. These plants are native to North and South America, but have also been known to naturalize in other temperate countries. They produce clumps of stiff, upright, linear, or sword-shaped leaves, which arch out into a fan shape. During spring and summer, clusters of trumpet-shaped flowers appear on spikes that hold the flowers just above the top of the foliage.
CULTIVATION: These plants are happy in poor to moderately fertile, well-drained soil in full sun. *Sisyrinchium* species propagate readily from seed and the rhizomatous clumps divide easily in autumn and spring.

Sisyrinchium 'Biscutella'
☼ ❋ ↔ 6 in (15 cm) ↑ 12 in (30 cm)
Clumping evergreen perennial with mid-green linear leaves. Upright stems

Sisyrinchium 'Californian Skies'

bear short-lived, pale yellow flowers, dark brown to purple veining, in summer. Zones 7–9.

Sisyrinchium 'Californian Skies'
☼ ❋ ↔ 8 in (20 cm) ↑ 12 in (30 cm)
Hybrid with dark green lance-shaped foliage that supports sturdy flower stems. The mid-blue flowers appear in the summer through to late autumn. Zones 8–9.

Sisyrinchium californicum
syns *Sisyrinchium boreale*, *S. brachypus*
GOLDEN EYE GRASS
☼ ❋ ↔ 6 in (15 cm) ↑ 24 in (60 cm)
Semi-evergreen perennial found from California, USA, to British Columbia, Canada. Often short-lived. The linear to sword-shaped gray-green leaves are 4–6 in (10–15 cm) long. The starshaped yellow flowers, 1 in (25 mm) wide, are held on sturdy stems, in summer. *S. californicum* seeds freely. Zones 8–10.

Sisyrinchium graminoides
syns *Sisyrinchium angustifolium*, *S. bermudiana*
BLUE-EYED GRASS
☼ ❋ ↔ 8 in (20 cm) ↑ 20 in (50 cm)
Tight clump-forming perennial from North America. Rush-like dark green foliage year round. Stems of dark blue star-shaped flowers, each with a distinctive yellow center dot, in summer–autumn. Zones 5–10.

Sisyrinchium graminoides

Sisyrinchium idahoense
syns *Sisyrinchium bellum*, *S. birameum*
CALIFORNIAN BLUE-EYED GRASS
☼ ❋ ↔ 6 in (15 cm) ↑ 5 in (12 cm)
Semi-evergreen clump-forming perennial occurring from Washington and Idaho to California, USA. Narrow, sword-shaped, dark green foliage. The stiff upright stems support star-shaped violet-blue flowers with yellow throats, in summer. Zones 4–9.

Sisyrinchium palmifolium
YELLOW-EYED GRASS
☼/◑ ◗ ↔ 16–32 in (40–80 cm)
↑ 20–24 in (50–60 cm)
This large clumping species native to Argentina, Uruguay, and southern Brazil has long, narrow, strappy, blue-green leaves tapering to a fine point. The upright stems carry heads of bright yellow flowers that open in the evening; these appear from late spring. Zones 9–10.

Sisyrinchium idahoense

Sisyrinchium palmifolium

S

Skimmia japonica subsp. *reevesiana* 'Chilan Choice'

Skimmia laureola

Skimmia japonica 'Cecilia Brown'

Skimmia × confusa 'Kew Green'

Skimmia japonica 'Snow Dwarf'

leaves, compact height; '**Kew White**', narrow glossy leaves, fragrant, cream flowers; '**Nymans**', many large fruits; '**Robert Fortune**', pale leaves, dark green edge; '**Rubella**' ★, male cultivar with white flowers, yellow anthers; '**Snow Dwarf**', small prostrate cultivar with white flowers. Zones 7–10.

Skimmia laureola

☼ ❊ ↔ 3–10 ft (0.9–3 m)
↕ 2–40 ft (0.6–12 m)

Small spreading shrub or erect tree native to the Himalayas and western China. Dark green leaves. May be unisexual or have both male and female flowers on same plant. Flowers creamy white, fragrant, in spring. Black fruits. Zones 7–10.

Skimmia × confusa

Sisyrinchium striatum

syn. *Phaiophleps nigricans*

☼ ❊ ↔ 14 in (35 cm) ↕ 32 in (80 cm)

Clump-forming, upright perennial from Chile and Argentina. Attractive gray-green linear foliage. Sturdy spikes of pale yellow star-shaped flowers push up on stems through the foliage, in summer. '**Aunt May**', creamy yellow variegated foliage. Zones 8–10.

SKIMMIA

This genus of 4 slow-growing species belonging to the rue (Rutaceae) family is native to the Himalayas and eastern Asia. They are evergreen shrubs or small trees that will tolerate shade and seaside conditions in cool-temperate regions. The leaves are simple, smooth-edged, and mostly broad and glossy; they are slightly aromatic when crushed due to minute oil cavities. The small flowers are white, yellow or pink-tinged, and borne in short dense clusters at the branch tips. Some species

produce male and female flowers on different plants, so both sexes need to be grown in close proximity to ensure the production of the colorful winter-borne berries.

CULTIVATION: They are easily grown in cooler climates in soils that contain plenty of organic matter and have adequate drainage. The plants can be kept trimmed into compact shapes or as hedges. Propagation is best from tip cuttings; seeds can be used but the sex of plants cannot be predicted.

Skimmia × confusa

☼/◑ ❊ ↔ 4 ft (1.2 m)
↕ 2–10 ft (0.6–3 m)

Mound-forming shrub, hybrid between *S. anquetilia* and *S. japonica*. Pointed

leaves are aromatic. Perfumed off-white flowers are borne in large clusters, in late winter. '**Kew Green**' bears yellow to creamy white male flowers. Zones 7–10.

Skimmia japonica

☼ ❊ ↔ 20 ft (6 m) ↕ 20 ft (6 m)

Dense medium-sized shrub from Japan, shaped like a dome. Leathery leaves, flowers white, fragrant, in panicles, in spring. Clusters of red globular fruits. *S. j.* subsp. *reevesiana* bears male and female white flowers; dull pink berries; '**Chilan Choice**', fragrant flowers, red berries. *S. j.* '**Cecilia Brown**', bright green glossy leaves, large clusters of white flowers opening from red buds; '**Fructo Alba**', cream flowers, small

Sisyrinchium striatum (pale yellow flowers)

Sisyrinchium striatum, in winter

Sisyrinchium striatum, in summer

Sisyrinchium striatum, in autumn

Smilacina racemosa

Smilax glyciphylla

SMILACINA

FALSE SOLOMON'S SEAL, SOLOMON'S PLUME

There are 25 species of rhizomatous perennials in this genus, within the lily-of-the-valley (Convallariaceae) family. They come from Northern and Central America and Asia where they grow in shady and damp woodland areas. They are closely related to *Polygonatum*, Solomon's seal, and have similar alternately arranged lance-shaped leaves on unbranched upright to arching stems to 3 ft (0.9 m) tall. Unlike *Polygonatum* species, which bear their flowers along the stems, *Smilacina* species have panicles or racemes at the ends. The white flowers are small with 6 petals and are borne in spring or summer. The flowers are followed by small red berries.

CULTIVATION: Suitable for the woodland garden or shady border, grow these plants in deep fertile soil, moisture-retentive and neutral to slightly acid. Plants should not be allowed to dry out when in leaf. Propagation is usually by division.

Smilacina racemosa

FALSE SOLOMON'S SEAL, FALSE SPIKENARD, SOLOMON'S ZIGZAG

☀/◐ ✱ ↔ 24–48 in (60–120 cm)
↕ 36 in (90 cm)

From the USA and northern Mexico. Arching, downy, cane-like stems; several paired, pointed oval leaves to 6 in (15 cm) long. Panicles to 6 in (15 cm) long of tiny creamy white flowers, in summer. Red-tinted green berries. Zones 4–10.

Smilacina stellata

STAR-FLOWER, STAR-FLOWERED LILY OF THE VALLEY

☀ ✱ ↔ 18 in (45 cm) ↕ 24 in (60 cm)

Perennial native to North America and Mexico. Lance-shaped leaves to 6 in (15 cm) long on upright stems. Panicles of tiny starry white or greenish white flowers, in summer. Dark red or dark blue berries. Zones 3–9.

SMILAX

This genus of over 200 species of climbing plants gives its name to the sarsaparilla (Smilacaceae) family and is found throughout the world in temperate and tropical zones, but very few are found in cultivation. The stems are generally scrambling, wiry, often bearing spines; the plants support themselves with tendrils. They have handsome, glossy green, heart-shaped or triangular leaves. The insignificant small flowers are yellowish or greenish. The rootstock of *S. officinalis* is one of the sources of sarsaparilla, used in Western and Chinese herbal medicine for its tonic qualities, and in North America to flavor root beer.

CULTIVATION: In general *Smilax* species are planted to have their roots in shade while the upper part of the plant climbs to reach the sun.

Smilax aspera

☀ ✂ ↔ 24 in (60 cm) ↕ 10 ft (3 m)

Evergreen climber native to southern Europe, North Africa, and the Canary Islands. Angular, zigzag, prickly stems form dense tangle; leaves are ovate to heart-shaped, glossy and leathery. The small, fragrant, greenish flowers are followed by red fruits, in late summer. Zones 9–10.

Smilax glyciphylla

SWEET SARSAPARILLA

☀/◐ ✂ ↔ 5–10 ft (1.5–3 m)
↕ 5–10 ft (1.5–3 m)

Twining coastal eastern Australian species, also bearing tendrils. Elongated lance- to heart-shaped leaves to 6 in (15 cm) long, strongly pink-tinted when young. Sprays of tiny greenish white flowers, in summer, followed by black berries. Zones 9–11.

SMYRNIUM

This genus contains 7 species of biennial or monocarpic plants from western Europe and the Mediterranean region. They are tall rather coarse plants with leaves comprised of 3 broad leaflets. The small greenish yellow or yellow flowers are borne in umbels typical of the carrot (Apiaceae) family and are followed by shiny black or brown seeds, which readily self-sow. The botanical name *Smyrnium*, is derived from the Greek word *smyrna*, myrrh, which is a reference to the aromatic foliage. The leaves, roots, and stems of *S. olusatrum* taste like celery. This species was once widely cultivated as a vegetable and is still sometimes grown for this purpose.

CULTIVATION: Grow in an open, sunny position in a moisture-retentive but well-drained fertile soil. When growing *S. olusatrum* as a vegetable, it can be earthed up in spring to blanch the stems as for celery. Propagation is from seed sown in the late summer or early spring.

Smyrnium olusatrum

ALEXANDERS, BLACK LOVAGE, HORSE PARSLEY

☀ ✱ ↔ 18–36 in (45–90 cm)
↕ 3–5 ft (0.9–1.5 m)

Biennial with stout ridged stems, native to Europe, and widely naturalized elsewhere. Large, divided, shiny, dark green leaves, serrated margins. Umbels of small yellowish flowers, in spring. Shiny black seeds. Zones 6–10.

Smyrnium perfoliatum

☀ ✱ ↔ 18 in (45 cm) ↕ 36 in (90 cm)

Biennial, primarily grown for its foliage, found from southern Europe to the Czech Republic. Lower leaves, 2 to 3 oval leaflets. Upper leaves, popular for floral display, rounded, appear to surround stem. Zones 6–10.

SOBRALIA

A genus from the family Orchidaceae of about 100 species of leafy, terrestrial orchids native to tropical Central and South America. Very few are cultivated but availability is increasing. Popular species have huge *Cattleya*-like blooms, which are often short-lived, and produced from the top of the leafy cane-like growths in summer.

CULTIVATION: Pot into large, deep containers to accommodate extensive, thick roots. A well-drained terrestrial mix with bark added is ideal. Intermediate to warm conditions suit most species, with plants enjoying strong light, coupled with frequent watering and feeding during warmer months. During summer, sit plants in saucers of water, to 2 in (5 cm) deep. Keep dry in winter, when growth rate is reduced. Hardy species can be planted in gardens in frost-free climates providing a high percentage of organic matter has been worked into the soil. Propagate by division of large clumps in spring.

Sobralia macrantha

☀/◐ ✂ ↔ 1–4 ft (0.3–1.2 m)
↕ 1–7 ft (0.3–2 m)

Found from Mexico to Costa Rica. Stems can grow to 7 ft (2 m) tall, often less in cultivation. Very large rose-purple flowers, to 10 in (25 cm) wide. *S. m.* var. *alba*, pure white flowers. Zones 10–12.

Sobralia macrantha

Sobralia macrantha var. *alba*

Sobralia Mirabilis

☀/☀ ✲ ↔ 36 in (90 cm) ↑ 36 in (90 cm)

Hybrid grex, registered in 1903, the result of a cross between *S. macrantha* and the *Veitchii* grex. Original cross had white petals with faintest pink blush around a mid-pink, wavy-edged lip much elongated at base. Later forms vary, mainly in lip color. Zones 11–12.

Sobralia xantholeuca ★

☀/☀ ✲ ↔ 1–4 ft (0.3–1.2 m)
↑ 1–5 ft (0.3–1.5 m)

From Mexico and Guatemala. Similar growth habit to *S. macrantha*, can be hard to distinguish when not in bloom. Slightly nodding lemon yellow flowers, to 8 in (20 cm) wide. Zones 10–12.

SOLANDRA

CHALICE VINE

This genus of 8 species of showy vigorous climbers belongs to the night-shade (Solanaceae) family. They are native to tropical America where they grow in forests, often up buttressed trees near waterways. The alternately arranged simple leaves are usually leathery and shiny. The open trumpet-shaped flowers may be fragrant at night and are usually yellow or white, sometimes with purplish red stripes or markings. Some species were used by the Aztecs and other indigenous groups for their hallucinogenic properties, which are extremely dangerous and capable of causing death. **CULTIVATION:** In warm climates, grow against walls and fences or over pergolas in full sun in rich moist but well-drained soil. Grow in the greenhouse in cool temperate climates, Excessive watering will promote foliage growth at the expense of flowers. Prune to contain size. Propagate from seed or from cuttings.

Solandra longiflora

☀ ✲ ↔ 8–15 ft (2.4–4.5 m)
↑ 10–20 ft (3–6 m)

Vigorous climber native to the West Indies. Oval leaves to 4 in (10 cm) long. Fragrant white flowers, tinged purple, long corolla tube ending with flaring frilly-edged lobes. Zones 10–12.

Solandra maxima

syn. *Solandra hartwegii*

CUP OF GOLD

☀ ✲ ↔ 10–30 ft (3–9 m)
↑ 20–50 ft (6–15 m)

Rampant climber native to Mexico and Central America. Glossy green oval leaves to 7 in (18 cm) long. The large, golden yellow, funnel-shaped flowers are widely flared, with purple stripes along the center of each lobe. Zones 10–12.

Sobralia Mirabilis

Sobralia xantholeuca

Solandra maxima

Solanum aviculare

SOLANUM

syns *Cyphomandra*, *Lycianthes*

Distinguished by the humble potato (*S. tuberosum*) in its many forms, this genus in the nightshade (Solanaceae) family includes some 1,400 species of annuals, perennials, vines, shrubs, and trees with a cosmopolitan distribution, most from tropical America. The trees and shrubs may be deciduous or evergreen and many are armed with thorns. While variable, their flowers are all remarkably similar, being simple, small, 5-petalled structures carried singly or in clusters with a central cone of yellow stamens. Fleshy berries follow the flowers. The berries are usually somewhat poisonous and, because of their conspicuous color, may be attractive to children. **CULTIVATION:** Hardiness varies, although a few species are really frost tolerant, most are quite tender. They are generally easily grown in any well-aerated well-drained soil; some have become serious weeds in various parts of the world. Most species prefer sun or partial shade. Propagation is from seed or from cuttings, or in a few cases by division.

Solanum aviculare

KANGAROO APPLE, PORO PORO

☀ ❅ ↔ 3–12 ft (0.9–3.5 m)
↑ 3–12 ft (0.9–3.5 m)

Quick-growing, evergreen shrub native to Australia and New Zealand. Dark stems, leaves very dark green, tip end sometimes divided into 2 or 3 long lobes. Purple flowers. Egg-shaped fruits, green to purple to orange as they ripen. Zones 9–11.

Solandra longiflora

Solanum aviculare, fruit

Solanum ellipticum

Solanum betaceum

syn. *Cyphomandra betacea*

TAMARILLO, TREE TOMATO

☀ ❅ ↔ 7 ft (2 m) ↑ 10 ft (3 m)

Bushy evergreen shrub from the Andes in Peru. Light green, heart-shaped, large and floppy leaves, with an unpleasant smell. Pale pink bell-shaped flowers, in small clusters, at branch ends, in spring–summer. Fruits early autumn. Zones 9–11.

Solanum capsicastrum

FALSE JERUSALEM CHERRY

☀ ❅ ↔ 24 in (60 cm)
↑ 12–24 in (30–60 cm)

Brazilian native, evergreen shrub. The leaves, 2–3 in (5–8 cm) long, are often wavy-edged. White flowers. Small, orange to red, egg-shaped fruits. Often grown as a house or greenhouse plant. Zones 10–12.

Solanum crispum

CHILEAN POTATO VINE

☀ ❅ ↔ 8–15 ft (2.4–4.5 m)
↑ 10–20 ft (3–6 m)

Evergreen climbing plant native to Chile. Pointed oval to lance-shaped leaves, often wavy margins. Showy, crowded clusters, open, 5-lobed, purplish blue flowers, yellow stamens, in summer. 'Glasnevin', hardier, very free flowering. Zones 8–11.

Solanum ellipticum

BUSH TOMATO, VELVET POTATO BUSH, WILD GOOSEBERRY

☀ ❅ ↔ 3–7 ft (0.9–2 m)
↑ 3–7 ft (0.9–2 m)

Woody-based perennial from inland Australia. Low, hairy, prickly branches. Smooth dark blue-green leaves with

S

prominent veins. Racemes of 3 to 7 purple or blue flowers, yellow centers. Edible greenish fruits. Zones 9–11.

Solanum giganteum
AFRICAN HOLLY

☼ ⚘ ↔ 10 ft (3 m) ↑ 12 ft (3.5 m)

Large shrub or small tree found from tropical Africa to Sri Lanka. Spiny trunks, prickle-covered silvery white branches. Leaves lance-shaped, dark green, silvery white felting beneath. Flowers in panicles, open purple. Small, glossy, red fruits. Zones 10–12.

Solanum hispidum
DEVIL'S FIG

☼ ⚘ ↔ 6–8 ft (1.8–2.4 m) ↑ 10 ft (3 m)

Spiny-stemmed, spreading shrub from Mexico and Guatemala. Deeply lobed, spiny, dark green leaves, rusty hairs beneath. Dense racemes of starry white or mauve-blue flowers, in summer. Yellow berries. Zones 10–12.

Solanum jasminoides
POTATO VINE

☼ ⚘ ↔ 8–15 ft (2.4–4.5 m) ↑ 10–20 ft (3–6 m)

Evergreen Brazilian climber. Vigorous, twiggy-stemmed, well-foliaged. Oval, lance-shaped or lobed leaves. Clusters of long-lasting, starry, white flowers, tinged blue, in summer. 'Album', pure white flowers. Zones 9–12.

Solanum mauritianum

Solanum melongena 'Black Beauty'

Solanum laciniatum
LARGE KANGAROO APPLE, LARGE POROPORO

☼ ⚘ ↔ 6–10 ft (1.8–3 m) ↑ 6–10 ft (1.8–3 m)

Shrub native to Australia and New Zealand. It is similar to *S. aviculare*, but mostly larger. Leaves, very dark green, ovate or deeply lobed. The inflorescences of pale purple to deep indigo flowers appear in spring to summer, followed by orange-yellow berries. Zones 9–11.

Solanum mammosum
NIPPLE FRUIT

☼ ⚘ ↔ 3 ft (0.9 m) ↑ 5 ft (1.5 m)

Native of tropical America, this plant behaves as an annual or a shrubby perennial. The hair-covered stems are whippy and spiny, with angularly lobed or toothed leaves. Produces inflorescences of purple flowers. Orange fruits. Zones 10–12.

Solanum mauritianum
TREE TOBACCO, WILD TOBACCO

☼ ⚘ ↔ 6–10 ft (1.8–3 m) ↑ 6–10 ft (1.8–3 m)

Shrub or small tree from Argentina. Has become something of a weed in many areas. Branches powdery gray-green coating, dark green leaves, powdery green coating beneath. Flowers violet-blue, forming in heads. Fruits round, yellow, darkening to orange. Zones 10–12.

Solanum laciniatum

Solanum hispidum

Solanum melongena 'Ping Tung'

Solanum melongena 'Turkish Orange'

Solanum melanocerasum
GARDEN HUCKLEBERRY

☼ ⚘ ↔ 18 in (45 cm) ↑ 24 in (60 cm)

Bushy annual probably originating from western tropical Africa. Broadly oval leaves. Small white flowers. Black berries, ¾ in (18 mm) wide, through summer; edible if cooked. Zones 9–12.

Solanum melongena
AUBERGINE, EGGPLANT, JEW'S APPLE

☼ ⚘ ↔ 24 in (60 cm) ↑ 36 in (90 cm)

Bushy annual from southeastern Asia. Grown as a vegetable for its egg-shaped fruit. Stems are sometimes spiny. Leaves are downy, oval, and shallowly lobed. Violet to light blue flowers. White to purple-black fruit, to 8 in (20 cm) wide. 'Black Beauty' ★, nearly black oval fruit; 'Black Bell', purple-black round to oval fruit; 'Bonica', early maturing purple-black oval fruit; 'Ping Tung', clusters of long slender rich rosy mauve to

Solanum melongena 'Black Bell'

Solanum melongena 'Bonica'

purple fruit; and 'Turkish Orange', tiny squat orange-red fruits, which resemble tomatoes. Zones 9–12.

Solanum muricatum
PEPINO, MELON PEAR, MELON SHRUB

☼ ⚘ ↔ 36 in (90 cm) ↑ 36 in (90 cm)

Variable shrubby plant from the Andes. Flowers purple, or white, purple markings. Juicy, melon-flavored, white, green, purple, or striped, oblong to pear-shaped, edible fruit. 'Ecuadorian Gold', golden fruit, long fruiting season; 'El Camino', almost seedless variety; 'Golden Splendor', golden fruit. Zones 9–12.

Solanum rantonnetii

Solanum rantonnetii 'Royal Robe'

Solanum pseudocapsicum

Solanum pyracanthum

Solanum sessiliflorum

Solanum sessiliflorum

COCONA

☼ ✦ ↔ 4 ft (1.2 m) ↕ 7 ft (2 m)

Much-branched shrub from South America. Downy stems and large, oval, scallop-edged leaves, downy above, prominently veined beneath. Yellowish green flowers. Pear-shaped orangey red edible fruit, mild tomato flavor, in spring–summer. Zones 10–12.

Solanum tuberosum

POTATO

☼ ❄ ↔ 18 in (45 cm)

↕ 18–24 in (45–60 cm)

From South America, the potato was cultivated for 2,000 years before being introduced to Europe. Dark green leaves, white to pale violet flowers. Cultivars offer tubers of different texture, flavor, skin color, and maturing times. **'All Blue'** and **'Salad Blue'** have blue skin and lavender-blue flesh; **'Edzell Castle'**, white flesh, uniform

Solanum quitoense

Solanum quitoense

NARANJILLA

☼ ❄ ↔ 7 ft (2 m) ↕ 7 ft (2 m)

South American shrub, straggly growth habit. All parts have dense covering of fine hairs. Stems and leaves light green, purple toned; leaves angularly lobed. Clusters of white flowers. Tomato-like edible orange fruit, its green pulp makes a refreshing juice Zones 10–12.

Solanum pseudocapsicum

JERUSALEM CHERRY

☼ ❄ ↔ 4 ft (1.2 m) ↕ 3–6 ft (0.9–1.8 m)

Evergreen shrub from South America. Dark green leaves, wavy edges. Small white flowers, showy bright orange fruits. Many cultivars, variably colored fruit: cream, yellow, orange, and red. Fruit eaten by birds but poisonous to humans. Zones 9–11.

Solanum pyracanthum

☼ ✦ ↔ 2–3 ft (0.6–0.9 m)

↕ 3–6 ft (0.9–1.8 m)

Shrubby biennial or perennial from tropical Africa and Madagascar. Rust-colored felted stems. Lobed leaves; eye-catching long orange spines on midrib, which provide effective protection from herbivores. Bluish violet flowers are borne, in dense clusters, in summer. Zones 10–12.

Solanum seaforthianum

ST VINCENT LILAC

☼ ✦ ↔ 8–15 ft (2.4–4.5 m)

↕ 10–20 ft (3–6 m)

Attractive climber native to Trinidad and South America. Entire or pinnate leaves. Starry pale violet flowers, narrow widely spreading petals, in dense clusters, in summer. Small, shiny, bright red berries. Seeds dispersed by birds. Zones 10–12.

Solanum rantonnetii

syn. *Lycianthes rantonnetii*

BLUE POTATO BUSH, PARAGUAY NIGHTSHADE

☼ ❄ ↔ 7 ft (2 m) ↕ 6 ft (1.8 m)

Grown as scrambling shrub or semi-climber, long-flowering species from Argentina and Paraguay. Leaves, wavy edges. Fragrant purple to violet-blue flowers, in summer. Red fruit. Trim to keep plants compact. **'Royal Robe'**, long-blooming, rich purple flowers. Zones 9–11.

Solanum tuberosum 'Edzell Castle'

Solanum tuberosum 'Pentland Javelin'

Solanum tuberosum 'Salad Blue'

Solanum tuberosum 'Mimi'

Solanum tuberosum 'Red Duke of York'

Soldanella alpina

Soleirolia soleirolii

size; 'Mimi', red skinned, cherry size; 'Pentland Javelin' ★, white-skinned, white quite waxy flesh; and 'Red Duke of York' ★, red skin and yellow flesh. Zones 7–11.

Solanum vescum
GREEN KANGAROO APPLE, GUNYANG

☼ ❦ ↔ 3–6 ft (0.9–1.8 m) ↑ 3–6 ft (0.9–1.8 m)

Evergreen shrub from southeastern Australia. Edible cream to green fruit, otherwise similar to *S. aviculare*. Dark green leaves, sometimes lobed at tips, purple flowers, in spring–early winter. Zones 9–11.

Solanum wallacei
CATALINA NIGHTSHADE

☼ ❀ ↔ 3–5 ft (0.9–1.5 m) ↑ 3–7 ft (0.9–2 m)

Sparsely branched evergreen subshrub with an unpleasant smell, native to California, USA. Oblong leaves are covered in brownish hairs. Clusters of starry violet flowers, in summer. Dark purple berries to 1 in (25 mm) wide. Zones 8–11.

Solanum wendlandii
GIANT POTATO CREEPER, PARADISE FLOWER, POTATO VINE

☼ ✦ ↔ 5–10 ft (1.5–3 m) ↑ 15 ft (4.5 m)

Evergreen climber native to Costa Rica. Prickly scrambling branches. Glossy pinnate leaves. Lilac-blue flowers, to 2½ in (6 cm) wide, are produced in large showy clusters, in summer. Oval yellowish fruits to 4 in (10 cm) long. Zones 10–12.

SOLDANELLA

This genus, which belongs to the primrose (Primulaceae) family, contains 10 species of tiny alpine perennials native to the European Alps, the Carpathians, and the Balkans. They grow naturally in short damp turf and rocky places in the mountains. Plants form basal rosettes of leathery round or kidney-shaped leaves. The flowering stems often penetrate the snow cover in early spring. They bear heads of 1 to 6 hanging flowers in shades of blue to violet and white. The small funnel-shaped or bell-shaped flowers have fringed petals and are very dainty in appearance.

CULTIVATION: Grow in well-drained rich soil that in most cases should be neutral to slightly acid. Plant in an open cool position with protection from the hot midday sun. Protect from the winter wet and also from slugs at flowering time. Alternatively, grow in a cool greenhouse in a gritty soil mix in bright filtered light with good ventilation. Propagation is from seed or by division.

Soldanella alpina
ALPINE SNOWBELL

☼ ❀ ↔ 8 in (20 cm) ↑ 3–6 in (8–15 cm)

Perennial from the Pyrenees and Alps, Europe. Dark green, leathery, kidney-shaped to round leaves. Flowering stems to 6 in (15 cm) high, 2 to 4 fringed violet flowers, crimson markings inside, in spring–early summer. Zones 5–9.

Solanum wallacei

Soldanella carpatica

☼ ❀ ↔ 8 in (20 cm) ↑ 3–6 in (8–15 cm)

Perennial species from the Carpathian Mountains, Europe. Broad dark green leaves, to 2 in (5 cm) wide. During spring, flowering stems, to 6 in (15 cm) high, carry 2 to 5 small, fringed, violet flowers. Zones 5–9.

Soldanella villosa

☼ ❀ ↔ 8–12 in (20–30 cm) ↑ 6–12 in (15–30 cm)

Perennial from the Pyrenees, Europe. Round or kidney-shaped leaves to 2½ in (6 cm) wide, pale green beneath. Flowering stalks, to 12 in (30 cm) high, covered in short hairs, support 3 to 4 violet, fringed flowers, in early spring. Zones 5–9.

SOLEIROLIA
BABY'S TEARS, MIND-YOUR-OWN-BUSINESS

This monotypic genus, comprising an evergreen, mat-forming perennial native to the islands of the western Mediterranean, notably Corsica, and widely naturalized in warm countries, belongs to the nettle (Urticaceae) family. The branches are fine and root at the nodes. The tiny leaves are almost circular and spiraly arranged but appear alternate. The white flowers are pink-tinged, minute, solitary, 4-petalled, and held in the leaf axils.

CULTIVATION: Makes a neat ground cover in greenhouses, especially under staging, and in terraria, for temperate regions. Its invasive habit makes it less welcome in warmer climates. It needs humus-rich well-drained soil but can grow in crevices on almost bare ground, in paving, or against walls; it is intolerant of scorching midday sun. Easily propagated by division.

Soleirolia soleirolii
syn. *Helxine soleirolii*
ANGEL'S TEARS, BABY'S TEARS, MIND-YOUR-OWN-BUSINESS

☼/◐ ❧ ↔ 2–4 ft (0.6–1.2 m) ↑ 2–4 in (5–10 cm)

Creeping mat-forming perennial from Corsica and nearby islands, widely naturalized in Europe. Can be invasive. Tightly packed, small, rounded, bright green leaves. Tiny 4-petalled flowers, white tinged with pink, are produced in summer. 'Aurea', yellowish green leaves. Zones 9–12.

SOLENOSTEMON

This genus in the mint (Lamiaceae) family contains 60 species of shrubby plants native to tropical Africa and Asia. They may be erect, prostrate, or sprawling and are sometimes downy or succulent. Some of the species were previously included in the closely related genera *Plectranthus* and *Coleus*. Species of *Solenostemon* are grown for their colorful foliage that is often strikingly blotched or variegated, the leaves being pointed oval with toothed or scalloped margins. The flowers have little importance for their appearance, and are the typical tubular, 2-lipped flowers of the mint family.

CULTIVATION: In cool temperate climates, grow *Solenostemon* species in the conservatory, as house plants, or outdoors as annual bedding plants. In frost-free areas the plants can remain outdoors. Grow in any reasonable soil or potting mix in direct sunlight. Pinch back the growing tips regularly to maintain the plant's bushy shape and to prevent flowering. Propagation is easy from seed or from cuttings of desired plants.

Solanum wendlandii

S

Solenostemon scutellarioides
syns *Coleus blumei, C. scutellarioides, Plectranthus scutellarioides*

COLEUS, PAINTED NETTLE

☼/◐ ✦ ↔12–24 in (30–60 cm)
↑12–24 in (30–60 cm)

Shrubby plant from southeastern Asia. Square, semi-succulent, lightly downy stems. Pointed oval, scallop-edged leaves, extremely variable: green, red, purple, white, and yellow combinations. '**Cantigny Royale**', reddish purple leaves; '**Crimson Ruffles**', crimson leaves, lighter veins, ruffled margins; '**Crinkly Bottom**', deep blue-purple leaves, bright green edges; '**Display**', burnt orange leaves, bright green edges; **Dragon Series**, large serrated-edged leaves, scarlet to purple and black, gold edging; '**Frogsfoot Purple**', magenta leaves with deep purple edges; '**Jupiter**', beet red crinkly leaves, edged pale green; '**Kiwi Fern**', deeply serrated crimson leaves, edged lemon; '**Lemon Dash**', brilliant green leaves, yellow center; '**Muriel Pedley**', blood red leaves, splashed yellow, bright green edges; '**Pineapple Beauty**', deep maroon splashed, golden green leaves; **Rainbow Series**, variegated in greens, creams and purples, irregularly marked leaves of yellow, red, copper, purple, and green, including '**Rainbow Fringed Mix**', cut frilly edged leaves; '**Solar Eclipse**', serrated edge; '**Walter Turner**', red to dark red leaves, bright green edges; '**White Pheasant**', serrated-edged rich green leaves, pale lemon center; '**Winsley Tapestry**', highly serrated bright green leaves, beet red center; '**Winsome**', vivid green leaves, vivid red to black centers. Zones 10–12.

SOLIDAGO

GOLDENROD

Although a few species are found in other temperate regions, this genus of around 100 species of perennials is primarily North American, and belongs to the daisy (Asteraceae) family. These plants form clumps of upright, sometimes branching stems, the upper half of which develops panicles of tiny golden yellow flowers. The leaves may be linear, lance-shaped, or pointed oval, and usually have toothed edges. Often, by the time flowering starts in late summer, many of the lower leaves have withered somewhat. This late-flowering habit was used in the past by Native Americans as a kind of floral calendar, guiding them to when the corn would be ripe for harvest.

Solenostemon scutellarioides Dragon Series, 'Black Dragon'

Solenostemon scutellarioides 'Crinkly Bottom'

S. s. 'Cantigny Royale'

S. s. 'Crimson Ruffles'

S. scutellarioides 'Display'

S. s. 'Frogsfoot Purple'

S. scutellarioides 'Gloriosus'

S. scutellarioides 'Jupiter'

S. scutellarioides 'Kiwi Fern'

S. scutellarioides 'Lemon Dash'

S. scutellarioides 'Muriel Pedley'

S. s. 'Pineapple Beauty'

S. scutellarioides 'Solar Eclipse'

S. scutellarioides 'Walter Turner'

S. s. 'White Pheasant'

S. scutellarioides 'Winsome'

S. s. 'Winsley Tapestry'

CULTIVATION: They are very hardy plants and easily grown in full or half-sun in any position, provided the soil is reasonably fertile, moist, and well-drained. All *Solidago* species will grow in poor soil and withstand drought but will not flower well or reach maximum size with such conditions. Propagate from seed, basal cuttings, or by division. May self-sow.

Solidago bicolor
SILVERROD

☼/☀ ✳ ↔ 24 in (60 cm)
↑ 40 in (100 cm)

Perennial native to eastern and central North America. Broad lance-shaped leaves, smooth-edged or toothed, to 8 in (20 cm) long. The white to pale yellow flowerheads, occur in upright spikes, sometimes widely spaced, in the late summer and through autumn. Zones 4–9.

Solidago californica
CALIFORNIA GOLDENROD

☼/☀ ✳ ↔ 24–32 in (60–80 cm)
↑ 40–48 in (100–120 cm)

Perennial species from southwestern USA east to New Mexico and south to Mexico. The upright stems are coarsely toothed with narrow, pointed oval leaves to over 4 in (10 cm) long. Flowerheads, which are deep yellow and massed in slightly overarching spikes, appear in autumn. Zones 8–10.

Solidago canadensis

☼/☀ ✳ ↔ 40 in (100 cm)
↑ 60 in (150 cm)

Erect species widespread throughout North America. The narrow lance-shaped leaves, to 4 in (10 cm) long, have serrated edges. Short panicles of golden yellow flowers are borne in late summer–autumn. *S. c.* subsp. *elongata*, minutely bristly stems and leaves. Zones 3–9.

Solidago canadensis

Solidago confinis
YELLOW BUTTERFLY WEED

☼/☀ ✳ ↔ 20–32 in (50–80 cm)
↑ 24–40 in (60–100 cm)

From California and Mexico. Small leaves, compact growth habit. Large golden yellow flowerheads, in late summer–autumn. Hardiness and drought tolerance both excellent. Zones 4–10.

Solidago flexicaulis
ZIGZAG GOLDENROD

☼/☀ ✳ ↔ 24–40 in (60–100 cm)
↑ 100–48 in (100–120 cm)

Eastern North American native perennial. Sparsely hairy, toothed, pointed oval to elliptical leaves to 6 in (15 cm) long. Flowerheads in small clusters on alternate sides up flower stem, golden yellow, 3 or 4 ray florets, in summer–autumn. Zones 4–9.

Solidago rugosa
ROUGH-STEMMED GOLDENROD

☼/☀ ✳ ↔ 40 cm (100 cm)
↑ 60 in (150 cm)

Species from Eastern North America species. Forms densely foliaged basal

Solidago confinis, in the wild, Parque Nacional San Pedro Mártir, Baja California, Mexico

Solidago californica, in the wild, Parque Nacional San Pedro Mártir, Baja California, Mexico

clump of bristly, toothed, broad lance-shaped leaves to over 5 in (12 cm) long. Bears massed branching, arching panicles of small bright yellow flowerheads, in late summer. 'Fireworks', 48 in (120 cm) tall, very heavy flowering, produces starburst-like array of panicles. Zones 3–9.

Solidago virgaurea

☼/☀ ✳ ↔ 24 in (60 cm) ↑ 40 in (100 cm)

Native European species. Downy, finely toothed, broad lance-shaped leaves to 4 in (10 cm) long near plant base, and smaller higher up. Elongated branching sprays of yellow flowers are produced during summer and autumn. Zones 5–9.

Solidago Hybrid Cultivars

☼/☀ ✳ ↔ 12–48 in (30–120 cm)
↑ 24–60 in (60–150 cm)

Goldenrods, especially the hardier species from northern North America, interbreed freely, often producing vigorous heavy-flowering hybrids that generally make better garden plants. These include: 'Golden Wings', 60 in (150 cm) tall, toothed lance-shaped leaves and feathery bright yellow panicles; 'Goldenmosa' ★, 40 in (100 cm) tall, with strongly erect cane-like stems and small, overarched, bright yellow plumes; and 'Summershine', golden yellow panicles. Zones 4–9.

Solidago, Hybrid Cultivar, 'Summershine'

× SOLIDASTER

This is a hybrid genus, arising in cultivation, of a single clump-forming perennial. It is probably a cross between *Solidago canadensis* and *Aster ptarmicoides*, members of the daisy (Asteraceae) family, and was found in 1910 in a nursery in Lyons. It bears tiny daisy flowers from late summer into autumn; they are attractive in the border and make good cut flowers.
CULTIVATION: It grows well in a sunny well-drained border with moist but not wet soils and prefers a non-humid Mediterranean climate. Propagation is by dividing dormant plants throughout the winter or from basal cuttings taken in spring.

× Solidaster luteus
syn. × *Solidaster hybridus*

☼ ✳ ↔ 12–15 in (30–38 cm)
↑ 32–36 in (80–90 cm)

Erect clumping perennial with leaves to 6 in (15 cm) long. Summer sprays of tiny soft yellow daisies. 'Lemore', paler yellow flowers. Zones 6–10.

SOLLYA

This genus of 3 species of evergreen, climbing, or twining shrubs from the pittosporum (Pittosporaceae) family are closely related to *Billardiera*. The genus is named for the naturalist R. H. Solly. The plants are mainly found in southern Western Australia, and are established as a weed in parts of South Australia, Tasmania, and Victoria, Australia. Usually elliptical, the pale to dark green leaves in this genus can vary in shape; the stems twine around supporting structures such as other plants, trellises, or fences. These plants have found their way into cultivation for their attractive, star-shaped, bell-like flowers, which can range from blue to pale pink and white, and appear in summer.

Sophora japonica

Sophora japonica 'Pendula'

Sophora japonica 'Violacea'

Sophora davidii

CULTIVATION: *Sollya* species need full sunlight to provide the best show of flowers and prefer a well-drained fertile soil to thrive. Propagate from fresh seed in the spring or from softwood cuttings in late summer.

Sollya heterophylla

syn. *Sollya fusiformis*

BLUEBELL CREEPER

☼ ⚘ ↔ 3–5 ft (0.9–1.5 m)
↕ 5–7 ft (1.5–2 m)

Twining climber native to Western Australia. Mid- to dark green leaves. Can take time to fill out; often looks sparse. Intense blue flowers hang in groups, in summer. Can be invasive. *S. h.* subsp. *parviflora*, smaller, deeper blue flowers, vine habit. *S. h.* 'Alba', creamy white flowers. Zones 9–11.

SOPHORA

This widespread genus from the pea-flower subfamily of the legume

(Fabaceae) family includes more than 50 species of evergreen, deciduous, or briefly deciduous shrubs and trees. They have pinnate leaves, often composed of many tiny leaflets. The flowers are pea-like, usually cream or yellow, and frequently have a prominent keel; they are carried in racemes or panicles. Spring is the principal flowering season, though the tropical species tend to be less seasonal in their flowering. Woody winged seed pods follow the flowers.

CULTIVATION: While hardiness varies with the species, most adapt well to cultivation and thrive in any well-drained soil with a position in sun or light shade. Propagate from seed, cuttings, or, in some cases, from grafting. The seed is particularly moisture resistant and must be soaked in warm water to soften it before sowing. Its moisture resistance allows the seed to

Sophora prostrata

survive prolonged exposure to seawater and this feature accounts for the rather unusual distribution patterns of some *Sophora* species.

Sophora arizonica

ARIZONA MOUNTAIN LAUREL,
ARIZONA NECKLACE

☼ ❄ ↔ 8–10 ft (2.4–3 m)
↕ 10–15 ft (3–4.5 m)

Evergreen, slow-growing, spreading shrub or small tree from Arizona, USA. It has attractive silvery green pinnately divided leaves. Profuse wisteria-like bunches of fragrant violet flowers are produced in spring, and followed by bean-like seed pods, which are thought to be poisonous. Zones 8–10.

Sophora davidii

☼ ❄ ↔ 10 ft (3 m) ↕ 10 ft (3 m)

Deciduous shrub originating in China. Short leaves, to 20 small leaflets. The flowers are purple-blue with whitish tips to white, and are produced in short racemes at the stem tips, in summer. Zones 6–9.

Sophora japonica 'Regent'

Sophora japonica

CHINESE SCHOLAR TREE, PAGODA TREE

☼ ❄ ↔ 35 ft (10 m) ↕ 50 ft (15 m)

Deciduous tree from China and Korea, long cultivated in Japan. Smaller in cultivation. Leaves light to mid-green, 16 leaflets, downy undersides. Drooping panicles, 6–10 in (15–25 cm) long, fragrant creamy white flowers, in mid-summer. Weeping habit of flowers emphasized in 'Pendula', also weeping foliage, usually grafted on upright standard trunk; 'Princeton Upright' reaches 60 ft (18 m) tall; 'Regent' ★, white flowers; 'Violacea', pale mauve-pink flowers. Zones 5–9.

Sophora microphylla

KOWHAI

☼ ❄ ↔ 20 ft (6 m) ↕ 20–30 ft (6–9 m)

Evergreen or briefly deciduous tree native to New Zealand. Mass of fine twigs, sharply angled nodes, zigzag effect. Leaves small, tiny olive green leaflets. Pendulous clusters of golden yellow flowers, in spring. Brown seed pods. Zones 8–10.

Sophora prostrata

DWARF KOWHAI

☼ ❄ ↔ 7 ft (2 m) ↕ 6 ft (1.8 m)

New Zealand evergreen shrub, prostrate in windswept locations. Densely interlaced branches. Small leaves, 8 tiny deep green leaflets. Flowers deep yellow to light orange, in late winter, often hidden among the branches. 'Little Baby', bizarre branching habit, tiny leaves. Zones 8–10.

Sophora secundiflora

FRIJOLITO, MESCAL BEAN, TEXAS
MOUNTAIN LAUREL

☼ ❄ ↔ 15 ft (4.5 m) ↕ 30 ft (9 m)

Evergreen shrub or small tree, native of Texas and New Mexico, USA, and

Sophora prostrata

× *Sophrocattleya* Lana Coryell

× *Sophrolaelia* Gratrixiae

nearby parts of Mexico. Leaves with 3 to 5 pairs of leaflets. Racemes of fragrant violet-blue flowers, wisteria-like, in early spring. Silver-gray seed pods. Zones 8–11.

Sophora tetraptera
KOWHAI, YELLOW KOWHAI

☀ ❊ ↔ 15 ft (4.5 m) ↑ 15–40 ft (4.5–12 m)
National flower of New Zealand, also found in Chile, evergreen. Leaves with 20 to 40 tiny leaflets. Young leaves, branches, and flower buds covered in fine brown down. Racemes of golden yellow flowers, in spring. Zones 8–10.

Sophora tomentosa
SILVERBUSH

☀ ❊ ↔ 8 ft (2.4 m) ↑ 30 ft (9 m)
Large deciduous shrub or small tree from tropical Asia and Africa. Leaves with 18 leaflets. Leaves and young branches, silver-gray down. Flowers in racemes, unusual light yellow-green shade, in spring–summer. Zones 10–12.

Sophora toromiro
EASTER ISLAND SOPHORA

☀ ❊ ↔ 8 ft (2.4 m) ↑ 15 ft (4.5 m)
Extinct in wild, small evergreen tree most closely related to widely cultivated *S. tetraptera* of New Zealand and Chile. Small leaflets, hairy undersides. Flowers yellow, white-felted buds and 4 in (10 cm) long seed pods. Zones 10–12.

× *SOPHROCATTLEYA*

× *Sophrocattleya* is a bigeneric orchid hybrid (family Orchidaceae) between the sympodial genera *Sophronitis* and *Cattleya*. Most of these hybrids have the cool-growing *Sophronitis coccinea* in their background. The introduction of this species leads to smaller growing plants, flowers that have a more filled-in shape, and many of the red tones. The yellow-flowered hybrids often have *Cattleya luteola* in their lineage. They are mostly spring and summer blooming, with some flowering in autumn. CULTIVATION: These hybrids enjoy bright light and cool to warm temperatures. They require a cooler and drier rest in winter when the plants are in a dormant state. They must all have

unimpeded drainage and a coarse bark-based medium. They grow best in plastic or terracotta pots and must dry out between waterings. Healthy plants will develop an extensive system of thick white roots, which are long lived and freely branch. Propagate by division.

× *Sophrocattleya* Beaufort

☀/◐ ☂ ↔ 4–16 in (10–40 cm)
↑ 4–16 in (10–40 cm)
Very popular miniature primary hybrid between *Sophronitis coccinea* and *Laelia luteola*. Generally has bright yellow blooms, some clones in orange tones. Zones 10–12.

× *Sophrocattleya* Lana Coryell ★

☀/◐ ☂ ↔ 4–16 in (10–40 cm)
↑ 4–16 in (10–40 cm)
Popular compact-growing hybrid between × *Sophrocattleya* Beaufort and *Cattleya walkeriana*. Disproportionally large salmon pink to purple flowers. Has received many awards. Zones 10–12.

× *SOPHROLAELIA*

A bigeneric orchid hybrid in the family Orchidaceae combining the sympodial genera *Sophronitis* and *Laelia*. Generally brightly colored hybrids with long thin pseudobulbs and a single leathery leaf, bearing small clusters of flowers in spring–autumn. Called "cocktail

Sophora tetraptera

orchids," on account of their diminutive size, and the bright reds, oranges, and yellows that are produced. CULTIVATION: They enjoy bright light and cool to warm temperatures. Need a cooler and drier rest in winter when dormant. They must have unimpeded drainage and like to dry out between waterings. They are best grown in a coarse bark-based medium, and do well in pots, enjoying being potbound. They look best grown into specimen plants, producing a mass of flowers. Propagate by division.

× *Sophrolaelia* Gratrixiae

☀/◐ ☂ ↔ 4–16 in (10–40 cm)
↑ 4–16 in (10–40 cm)
This red-flowered primary hybrid between *Sophronitis coccinea* and *Laelia tenebrosa* was registered over 100 years ago. Zones 10–12.

× *Sophrolaelia* Orpetii

☀/◐ ☂ ↔ 4–16 in (10–40 cm)
↑ 4–16 in (10–40 cm)
Popular compact-growing and purple-flowered primary hybrid between *Sophronitis coccinea* and *Laelia pumila*. Zones 10–12.

Sophora secundiflora

× *SOPHROLAELIO-CATTLEYA*

This is a 3-way orchid hybrid (family Orchidaceae) from 3 sympodial genera: *Sophronitis*, *Laelia*, and *Cattleya*. Most of these hybrids have the cool-growing *Sophronitis coccinea* somewhere in their background, using its influence for shapely red blooms as well as its compact to miniature growth habit. The introduction of this species leads to smaller plants, flowers with a more filled-in shape, and many of the red tones. Yellow-flowered hybrids often have *Cattleya luteola* in their lineage. CULTIVATION: These hybrids do well in bright light and cool to warm temperatures. Give them a cooler and drier

Sophora tomentosa, seed pods

S

× *Sophrolaeliocattleya*, Hybrid, Ann Komine

× *Sophrolaeliocattleya*, Hybrid, Fire Lighter

× *Sophrolaeliocattleya*, Hybrid, Hazel Boyd 'Apricot Glow'

× *Sophrolaeliocattleya*, Hybrid, Sunset Nugget

× *Sophrolaeliocattleya*, Hybrid, (Bright Angel × Mahalo Jack)

× *Sophrolaeliocattleya*, Hybrid, Trizac

× *Sophrolaeliocattleya*, Hybrid, Jeweler's Art

× *Sophrolaeliocattleya*, Hybrid, Mahalo Jack

rest in winter when the plants are in a dormant state. They require excellent drainage and a coarse bark-based medium. Best grown in plastic or terracotta pots and allowed to dry out between waterings. Healthy plants will develop an extensive system of thick white roots, which are long lived and freely branch. Propagate by division.

× *Sophrolaeliocattleya* Hybrids

☀/◐ ✿ ↔ 4–16 in (10–40 cm)
↑ 4–16 in (10–40 cm)

Flower size varies in the many hybrids, from 1½ in (35 mm) to 6 in (15 cm) across petals. Mostly spring and summer blooming, some flower in autumn. **Ann Komine**, glossy claret colored blooms; (**Bright Angel × Mahalo Jack**), unregistered hybrid, deep salmon pink to red flowers; **Fire Lighter**, blooms readily off young plants, likes small pots, purplish red blooms; **Hazel Boyd 'Apricot Glow' ★** very popular clone of this successful American-bred hybrid between × *Sophrolaeliocattleya* California Apricot and × *Sophrolaeliocattleya* Jewel Box; **Jannine Louise**, popular orange- to red-flowered hybrid between × *Sophrolaeliocattleya* Kauai Starbright and × *Sophrolaeliocattleya* Hazel Boyd; **Jeweler's Art**, 5 in (12 cm) wide blooms, unusual orange-pink shades; **Mahalo Jack**, deep pink hybrid between × *Sophrolaelia* Orpetii and *Cattleya walkeriana*; **Sunset Nugget**, burnt orange blooms, overlaid with fine red flecking, deep red labellum; **Trizac**, older hybrid, purple blooms, darker labellum. Zones 10–12.

SOPHRONITIS

A small genus of brightly colored, sympodial, epiphytic orchids in the family Orchidaceae from Brazil and

Bolivia. They are closely related to the genus *Laelia*, in particular the Section *Hadrolaelia*, which includes species such as *L. dayana* and *L. pumila*. These laelias and *Sophronitis* share similarities in having single colorful blooms, and an inflorescence without a sheath but the young leaf folds around the buds. CULTIVATION: They are best grown in cool to intermediate conditions, in pots, using sphagnum moss for smaller plants and a bark-based mix for larger ones. Repot every other year as they lose their roots in stale mix. They need medium light levels, a humid and part-shaded environment, and fresh air, and will not tolerate stagnant conditions. Reduce watering in winter. *Sophronitis* have been extensively used within the *Cattleya* alliance, creating compact plants and brightly colored full blooms. Propagate by division.

Sophronitis cernua

☀/◐ ✿ ↔ 2½–7 in (6–18 cm)
↑ 1½–3 in (3.5–8 cm)

Creeping orchid native to Brazil and Bolivia. Groups of up to 6, ½ in (12 mm) wide blooms, on short nodding sprays, bright tangerine-orange, some yellow on the labellum, in the autumn. Will not tolerate cold, grow on cork mounts, intermediate to warm climate. Zones 11–12.

Sophronitis coccinea

syn. *Sophronitis grandiflora*

◐ ✿ ↔ 2½–8 in (6–20 cm)
↑ 1½–5 in (3.5–12 cm)

Magnificent Brazilian orchid. Large, to 3 in (8 cm) wide, round, flat blooms, bright orange to scarlet-red. Very narrow labellum, often yellow and orange markings, in autumn to winter. Clones such as 'Jannine' display improved vigor. Zones 9–11.

SORBARIA

This genus, native to Asia, is a member of the rose (Rosaceae) family and is

commonly called false spirea as the flowers are similar to *Spiraea*. There are 4 species of deciduous, usually suckering shrubs with pinnate leaves. They produce large panicles of small white flowers in summer followed by masses of small brownish seed capsules that often persist into winter. CULTIVATION: These attractive plants are grown for both their foliage and flowers. They prefer a fertile moisture-retentive soil in sun or part-shade and should be planted in a position with protection from strong winds, which may damage the foliage. Cut back in

Sophronitis coccinea 'Jannine'

Sorbaria grandiflora

early spring and remove any old weak branches at ground level. Propagation is by removal of suckers or from cuttings taken in summer.

Sorbaria grandiflora

☀ ❄ ↔ 36 in (90 cm)
↕ 12–36 in (30–90 cm)

Small shrub, native to eastern Siberia. Downy reddish gray shoots, exfoliating bark. Fine pinnate leaves, up to 8 in (20 cm) long. White flowers in flattened clusters, in summer. Zones 5–9.

Sorbaria kirilowii

syn. *Sobaria arborea*

TREE FALSE SPIREA, URAL FALSE SPIREA

☀ ❄ ↔ 20 ft (6 m) ↕ 17 ft (5 m)

Large, deciduous, spreading, Chinese shrub with slender pointed leaflets. White flowers on long panicles to 12 in (30 cm) in mid-summer. If deadheaded, continues blooming till frosts arrive. Spicy fragrance. Zones 5–7.

Sorbaria sorbifolia

FALSE SPIREA

☀ ❄ ↔ 10 ft (3 m) ↕ 10 ft (3 m)

Suckering shrub native to Asia, stiff erect stems. Pinnate leaves, finely serrated margins; colorful autumn foliage. White flowers in large plumes, in summer. Zones 2–9.

Sorbaria tomentosa

☀ ❄ ↔ 15 ft (4.5 m) ↕ 20 ft (6 m)

Wide-spreading, branching, Himalayan shrub. Pinnate leaves, to 21 narrow finely serrated leaflets. Yellowish white flowers, large panicles, in summer. *S. t.* **var. angustifolia** (syn. *S. aitchisonii*), purplish brown branches. Zones 6–10.

SORBUS

MOUNTAIN ASH

The 100-odd species of deciduous shrubs and trees in this genus from the northern temperate zones belong to the rose (Rosaceae) family. The

Sorbaria sorbifolia, in winter

foliage is usually pinnate with serrated-edged leaflets, but may be simple and oval to diamond-shaped. Clusters of white or cream, sometimes pink-tinted, spring flowers, somewhat unpleasantly scented, are followed by heads of berry-like pomes that ripen through summer and autumn. Some species develop russet to red toned foliage in autumn.
CULTIVATION: Most *Sorbus* species are very hardy and prefer a cool climate, suffering in high summer temperatures. They are best grown in moderately fertile, deep, humus-enriched soil with ample summer moisture, but adapt well to most conditions. Plant in sun or partial shade, prune to shape in the

Sorbus aria 'Lutescens'

autumn or winter and propagate from stratified seed or by grafting. Fireblight can cause significant damage.

Sorbus alnifolia

KOREAN MOUNTAIN ASH

☀ ❄ ↔ 25 ft (8 m) ↕ 50 ft (15 m)

From Japan and Korea. Leaves with heavily serrated edges; orange and red in autumn. Young stems red-brown, bright green young foliage. Flowers white; fruit red or yellow. Zones 6–9.

Sorbus americana ★

AMERICAN MOUNTAIN ASH

☀ ❄ ↔ 20 ft (6 m) ↕ 20–30 ft (6–9 m)

Sometimes shrubby tree from central and eastern USA. Leaves, 17 bright green leaflets, gray-green undersides, turn yellow, in autumn. Resinous buds, white flowers, in spring. Bright red fruit. Zones 2–9.

Sorbus alnifolia

Sorbus aria

WHITEBEAM

☀ ❄ ↔ 25 ft (8 m) ↕ 20–40 ft (6–12 m)

Tall broad-crowned tree from Europe. Broad, elliptical leaves, deep green, coated in white felt when young. White flowers, in spring. Orange-red fruit. Can be trained as an arbor. 'Chrysophylla', golden yellow foliage; 'Lutescens', conical growth habit, light green foliage; 'Majestica', very broad crown, large leaves. Zones 5–9.

Sorbus × arnoldiana

☀ ❄ ↔ 20 ft (6 m) ↕ 15–40 ft (4.5–12 m)

Garden hybrid of temperate Eurasian *S. aucuparia* and *S. discolor*. Similar to *S. aucuparia*, smaller darker green leaflets, gray-green beneath. Small cream flowerheads. Pink berries. 'Carpet of Gold', erect slender branches, golden yellow fruit, speckled red. Zones 5–9.

Sorbus × arnoldiana 'Carpet of Gold'

Sorbus aria

S

Sorbus aucuparia

EUROPEAN MOUNTAIN ASH,
MOUNTAIN ASH, ROWAN

☼ ❄ ↔ 20 ft (6 m) ↕ 15–40 ft (4.5–12 m)

This hardy tree is found over much of northern Eurasia. Dark green to bronze pinnate leaves, coarsely serrated leaflets, turning orange and red, in the autumn. Flowers have an unpleasant scent. Bears orange berries, which are both ornamental and a rich source of vitamin C; their juice is used as a flavoring. 'Aspleniifolia' has deeply cut leaves with hairy undersides; 'Black Hawk' is an upright, narrow tree; 'Cardinal Royal' has a very upright habit and dark red fruit; 'Fastigiata', a narrow crown, stiff upright shoots, and large fruit; 'Fructu Luteo', spreading habit; 'Xanthocarpa', golden yellow fruit. Zones 2–9.

Sorbus cashmiriana

Sorbus cashmiriana

☼ ❄ ↔ 20 ft (6 m) ↕ 30 ft (9 m)

Tree native to the Kashmir region of the Himalayas. Young branches red, dark green pinnate leaves, composed of 19 serrated leaflets with light green undersides. Pink-tinted white flowers, in spring, from deep pink buds. White to yellow-green fruits. Zones 5–9.

Sorbus chamaemespilus

DWARF WHITEBEAM

☼ ❄ ↔ 3–6 ft (0.9–1.8 m)
↕ 3–6 ft (0.9–1.8 m)

Shrub from central Europe. Simple, 1–3 in (25–80 mm) long, dark green leaves, finely serrated edges, yellowish, sometimes felted, undersides. Flowers deep pink. Red fruit. Zones 6–9.

Sorbus commixta

JAPANESE ROWAN

☼ ❄ ↔ 20 ft (6 m) ↕ 20–30 ft (6–9 m)

Native to Korea and Japan. Attractive pinnate leaves, 15 leaflets, open from sticky red buds, first bronze, then light green, glaucous undersides; yellow to red, in autumn. Flowers are white, fruit is red. 'Embley', red autumn foliage lasts into winter; 'Ethel's Gold', bright green leaves, golden yellow fruit; 'Jermyns', vividly colored autumn foliage, large clusters of orange-red fruit. Zones 6–9.

Sorbus commixta

Sorbus decora

SHOWY MOUNTAIN ASH

☼ ❄ ↔ 15 ft (4.5 m) ↕ 30 ft (9 m)

Often small and shrubby tree found in northeastern North America. Leaves, 17 leaflets. Loose white flowerheads, in spring. Clusters of small red fruits. Zones 2–8.

Sorbus domestica

SERVICE TREE

☼ ❄ ↔ 30 ft (9 m) ↕ 30–50 ft (9–15 m)

From southern Europe, North Africa, and western Asia, pinnate leaves, serrated edges, downy undersides. White flowers. Edible large berries yellow-green, ripening to red; sometimes used in jams and jellies. Zones 6–10.

Sorbus esserteauiana

☼ ❄ ↔ 35 ft (10 m) ↕ 50 ft (15 m)

Tree with impressive foliage native to western China. Leaves, open from red buds, 13 bright green leaflets, downy undersides, turning red in autumn. Massed panicles of white flowers. Red fruit. Zones 6–9.

Sorbus forrestii

Sorbus folgneri

☼ ❄ ↔ 25 ft (8 m) ↕ 30 ft (9 m)

Tree native to China. Young stems whippy, often arching, covered with a white down. Simple, lance-shaped leaves, white down, beneath. Flowers are white. Fruit is red, rarely yellow. Zones 6–9.

Sorbus forrestii

☼ ❄ ↔ 20 ft (6 m) ↕ 25 ft (8 m)

Similar species to the commonly grown *S. hupehensis*, but with larger fruit. This is pure white when ripe, and persists well into winter after the leaves have fallen. Zones 7–9.

Sorbus aucuparia 'Fructu Luteo'

Sorbus aucuparia

Sorbus decora

Sorbus hedlundii

☀ ❄ ↔ 25 ft (8 m) ↕ 30 ft (9 m)

Very like *S. vestita*, but this species has distinctly silvery undersides to its leaves. Prominent veins on undersides of the leaves are a distinguishing feature. Zones 8–10.

Sorbus × hostii

☀ ❄ ↔ 10 ft (3 m) ↕ 12–15 ft (3.5–4.5 m)

A hybrid between *S. chamaemespilus* and *S. mougeotii*, very similar to *S. mougeotii* except leaves a little longer, somewhat sharper teeth. Flowers pink to pale red, like those of *S. chamaemespilus*. Red fruits follow. Zones 6–9.

Sorbus hupehensis

☀ ❄ ↔ 20 ft (6 m) ↕ 30 ft (9 m)

Tree from central and western China. Pinnate leaves, dull gray-green above, lighter below, turn strong pink tones, redden then fall, in autumn. White flowers, in spring. Small white berries, blush pink as they ripen. ***S. h.* var. obtusa** (syn. *S. h.* 'Rosea'), up to 25 ft (8 m) tall. ***S. h.* 'Coral Fire'**, red bark, red autumn foliage, pinkish red fruit. Zones 6–9.

Sorbus insignis

☀ ❄ ↔ 15 ft (4.5 m) ↕ 15–20 ft (4.5–6 m)

Small tree native to Sikkim in the Himalayas. Pinnate leaves, shallowly toothed leaflets. Buds covered in fine rusty red hairs, white flowers. Pink fruit. **'Bellona'**, small deciduous tree, shrubby habit, compound leaves, small coral red fruits. Zones 8–10.

Sorbus intermedia

SWEDISH MOUNTAIN ASH,
SWEDISH WHITEBEAM

☀ ❄ ↔ 20 ft (6 m) ↕ 20–30 ft (6–9 m)

Usually small, sometimes shrubby, Scandinavian native. Felted young

Sorbus koehneana

stems, simple, oval leaves, small basal lobes. Densely branched heads of small flowers are borne in spring. Orange-red berries. **'Brouwers'**, compact, upright habit, small clusters of dark red berries. Zones 5–9.

Sorbus keissleri

☀ ❄ ↔ 20 ft (6 m) ↕ 30 ft (9 m)

Large shrub or small tree native to China. Simple shallowly toothed leaves, dark green and waxy above, lighter, slightly hairy below. Creamy white flowers, woolly buds. Fruit green, develops a red blush. Zones 6–9.

Sorbus koehneana

☀ ❄ ↔ 20 ft (6 m) ↕ 15 ft (4.5 m)

Medium-sized shrub or small tree native to China. Pinnate leaves, 25 or more dark green leaflets. White flowers followed by small shiny white fruit. Zones 6–8.

Sorbus latifolia

FONTAINEBLEAU SERVICE TREE

☀ ❄ ↔ 20 ft (6 m) ↕ 30–50 ft (9–15 m)

Strong-growing European tree, conical growth, bronze young branches. Oak-like lobed leaves, serrated edges, dark green above, yellowish felting on the undersides. Woolly heads of creamy white flowers. Green fruits speckled with brown. Zones 5–9.

Sorbus mougeotii

Sorbus insignis 'Bellona'

Sorbus intermedia

Sorbus megalocarpa

LARGE-FRUITED WHITEBEAM

☀ ❄ ↔ 8 ft (25 m) ↕ 30 ft (9 m)

Shrub or tree native to China. Simple wavy- to shallowly toothed-edged leaves. Creamy white flowers form in dense clusters. Rusty brown pomes. Zones 6–9.

Sorbus mougeotii

☀ ❄ ↔ 15 ft (4.5 m) ↕ 40 ft (12 m)

Large shrub or small tree found in the mountains of northern Europe. Simple, broad, ovate leaves, shallow lobes, pale gray down, beneath. Small heads of cream flowers. Green fruits become red as they ripen. Zones 6–9.

Sorbus pohuashanensis

☀ ❄ ↔ 20 ft (6 m) ↕ 70 ft (21 m)

This tree is native to the mountains of northern China, smaller in cultivation. Round-headed tree, pinnate leaves, felted undersides. Woolly clusters of cream flowers. Orange-red to red fruit. Zones 5–9.

Sorbus pseudofennica

ARRAN SERVICE TREE

☀ ❄ ↔ 30 ft (9 m) ↕ 30–50 ft (9–15 m)

Tree allied to *S. domestica*, possibly a hybrid between *S. arranensis* and *S. aucuparia*, and extremely rare. About 500 trees survive in Glen Diomhan Reserve, Isle of Arran, Scotland, on the bank of a stream among steep granite crags. Zones 6–9.

Sorbus hedlundii

Sorbus hupehensis

Sorbus pseudofennica

S

Sorbus vilmorinii

Sorbus randaiensis

Sorbus reducta 'Gnome'

Sorbus sargentiana

Sorbus randaiensis

☼ ❄ ↔ 10 ft (3 m) ↑ 20 ft (6 m)

Small tree native to the mountains of Taiwan. Species has an erect growth habit. Sticky leaf buds, pinnate leaves with 19 finely tapered, sharply toothed leaflets, downy gray undersides. Produces small clusters of white to cream flowers, followed by showy tiny red fruits in autumn, which persist into winter. Zones 7–10.

Sorbus reducta

DWARF CHINESE MOUNTAIN ASH

☼ ❄ ↔ 6 ft (1.8 m) ↑ 15 in (38 cm)

Low shrubby species from western China and Myanmar. Clump of suckering stems, bristly young stems. Pinnate leaves, reddish stalks. Flowers not abundant; fruit, cherry red. 'Gnome', smaller, compact form. Zones 6–10.

Sorbus sargentiana

SARGENT'S ROWAN

☼ ❄ ↔ 20 ft (6 m) ↑ 20–30 ft (6–9 m)

Western Chinese ornamental. Pinnate leaves, sticky buds, leaflets bright green, slightly serrated edges, lighter, downy beneath, vivid autumn foliage. Flower clusters; small red berries. Zones 6–9.

Sorbus scalaris

☼ ❄ ↔ 20 ft (6 m) ↑ 20 ft (6 m)

Large shrub or small tree from China. Leaves, up to 37 leaflets, with slightly

Sorbus × thuringiaca

toothed edges, pale gray felting beneath, deep red to purple, in autumn. Flowerheads quite large and downy, in spring. Tiny red fruits. Zones 5–9.

Sorbus thibetica

☼ ❄ ↔ 30 ft (9 m) ↑ 50 ft (15 m)

Wild form of Chinese S. thibetica seldom seen cultivated. Most known as such are cultivar 'John Mitchell' (syn. S. 'Mitchellii'), a broad-headed tree. Simple, rounded, bright green leaves, white-felted undersides. Flowers creamy white, fruit orange-red. Zones 8–10.

Sorbus × thuringiaca

OAK-LEAFED MOUNTAIN ASH

☼ ❄ ↔ 25 ft (8 m) ↑ 30–40 ft (9–12 m)

Hybrid between 2 European species, S. aria and S. aucuparia. Pinnate leaves, finely serrated leaflets. Flowers develop into small red fruits. 'Fastigiata', strong upright growth, very dark green foliage; 'Leonard Springer', leaves of only 9 to 11 heavily serrated leaflets, red stalks. Zones 6–9.

Sorbus torminalis

CHEQUER TREE, WILD SERVICE TREE

☼ ❄ ↔ 25 ft (8 m) ↑ 30–50 ft (9–15 m)

From Europe, western Asia and North Africa. Rounded crown, green-brown bark. Leaves bright green, simple, pronounced lobes, serrated edges, redden in autumn. Lax spring flower clusters, brown-speckled olive fruit. Zones 6–10.

Sorbus torminalis

Sorbus vestita

syns Sorbus cuspidata, S. lanata

HIMALAYAN WHITEBEAM

☼ ❄ ↔ 20 ft (6 m) ↑ 30 ft (9 m)

Tree native to the Himalayas. Bright green elliptical leaves, silvery white undersides. Fruit, rounded to pear-shaped, under 1 in (25 mm), green with brown spotting to warm russet tone. Zones 7–9.

Sorbus vilmorinii

☼ ❄ ↔ 15 ft (4.5 m) ↑ 20 ft (6 m)

Spreading shrub or small tree native to western China. Buds, young branches, warm red-brown shade, leaves pinnate, serrated edges, gray-green undersides. Loose open flower clusters, pink or pink-flushed white fruit. 'Pearly King', good autumn foliage color, larger fruit. Zones 6–9.

Sorbus wardii

☼ ❄ ↔ 15–25 ft (4.5–8 m) ↑ 50 ft (15 m)

Strongly upright tree found in the Himalayas. The leaves are downy when young, elliptical to rounded, a bright green shade. Flowers are creamy white. Large amber to orange-red fruits, which are often speckled with olive to brown. Zones 8–10.

Sorbus wilsoniana

☼ ❄ ↔ 20 ft (6 m) ↑ 20–30 ft (6–9 m)

Strongly built stocky tree occurring in central China. Leaves, 15 lance-shaped leaflets, pale undersides. Silvery white

Sorbus vestita

Sorbus wilsoniana

Sorbus, Hybrid Cultivar, 'Coral Beauty'

Sorbus, Hybrid Cultivar, 'Sunshine'

downy buds, flower clusters are followed by the near-spherical carmine fruits. Zones 6–9.

Sorbus Hybrid Cultivars

☀/◐ ❄ ↔ 7–15 ft (2–4.5 m)
↕ 10–25 ft (3–8 m)

Sorbus hybrids range in size, including dwarf forms, most seen in gardens are tree-like. Foliage type and fruit color vary, all tend to be heavy cropping, and are often have bright foliage in autumn. 'Coral Beauty', strong *S. aucuparia* influence, brilliant orange-scarlet fruits. 'Joseph Rock', probable hybrid, 20–30 ft (6–9 m) tall, pinnate leaves, deeply serrated leaflets, turn orange or purple-red, in autumn; flowers white; fruit, initially cream, ripens to golden yellow. 'Pearly King', pale pearl pink fruits; 'Sunshine', yellow fruit. Zones 6–9.

SORGHASTRUM

Genus of around 16 species of annual and perennial grasses in the family Poaceae from the American and African tropics. They can form open, rather airy sprays or strong, densely-foliaged clumps of long, very narrow leaves, often rolled along the midrib. Large feathery panicles, usually from late summer, are borne on long stems that hold them well clear of the foliage. CULTIVATION: They are easily grown in any reasonably sunny position with moist, well-drained soil. Drought tolerant once established. Hardiness varies with the species. Propagate by seed; perennials will also grow from division.

Sorghastrum nutans

INDIAN GRASS, WOOD GRASS

☀/◐ ❄ ↔ 16–32 in (40–80 cm)
↕ 5–7 ft (1.5–2 m)

Perennial grass from central and eastern USA. Narrow leaves to 24 in (60 cm) long. Pale to golden brown panicles, to over 12 in (30 cm) long. atop erect, wiry stems, in autumn. Zones 5–10.

SORGHUM

MILLET, SORGHUM

This genus of about 20 quick-growing, broad-leafed, annual or perennial grasses, members of the family Poaceae originates from tropical and subtropical Africa, Asia, and Australia, except for 1 species native to Mexico. The stems are quite robust, usually upright, and form clumps. The leaves have flat or wavy margins in 2 ranks and these overlap the waxy sheaths encircling the stem. Branching, finely hairy, usually upright, conical to oval-shaped panicles of flower spikelets, which yield round bluntly pointed seed, partly covered by glumes. *Sorghum* species are grown for grain and forage and for the sweetening syrup extracted from the stalks of *S. vulgare* var. *saccharatum.* CULTIVATION: Sorghum tolerates a wide range of fertile well-drained soils in an open sunny position. Propagate from seed.

Sorghum bicolor

GREAT MILLET, SORGHUM

☀ ❄ ↔ 2–3 ft (0.6–0.9 m)
↕ 10–20 ft (3–6 m)

Widely cultivated in warm climates; believed to be of African origin. Narrow strap-like leaves, to 36 in (90 cm) long, white midrib. Large dense panicles, to 24 in (60 cm) long, fertile spikelets to ½ in (12 mm), in summer. Large variously colored grains, which provide the staple diet for the people of many countries. Zones 9–12.

SPARAXIS

HARLEQUIN FLOWER

Under suitable conditions, this South African genus of 6 species of corms in the iris (Iridaceae) family will naturalize and form large drifts. The leaves are grassy to sword-shaped, with prominent ribbing, developing quickly from late winter. They are soon followed by wiry spikes carrying just a few blooms or fan-like sprays of ¾ in (18 mm) wide, 6-petalled, funnel-shaped flowers. These may be white, yellow, or shades of pink to orange and red, usually with a yellow center and contrasting dark colors in the throat. The name comes from the Greek *sparasso,* to tear, referring to the lacerated bracts at the base of the flowers. CULTIVATION: They are not hardy where the soil freezes but otherwise are easily grown in full sun in fertile, moist, well-drained soil. In cold areas, they can be lifted in the autumn and replanted in the early spring for a late flower show. Propagation is from seed or by division.

Sparaxis fragrans

☀/◐ ⚘ ↔ 6–12 in (15–30 cm)
↕ 8–18 in (20–45 cm)

Grassy leaves to ½ in (12 mm) long. Unbranched flower stems, spikes of variably colored, fragrant flowers to over 2 in (5 cm) wide. Flowers yellow, often purple-red or black sectors and dark streaks. *S. f.* subsp. *acutifolia,* pointed golden yellow flowers. *S. f.* subsp. *grandiflora,* fragrant yellow-centered white flowers. Zones 9–10.

Sparaxis tricolor ★

VELVET FLOWER

☀/◐ ⚘ ↔ 6–10 in (15–25 cm)
↕ 8–16 in (20–40 cm)

Narrow sword-shaped leaves and 1 to 5 flower stems per corm, each with up to 5 darkly marked, yellow-centered, orange to red flowers to over 1 in (25 mm) wide. Readily naturalizes in suitable climates. Zones 9–10.

SPARMANNIA

AFRICAN HEMP, HOUSE LIME

This genus of 3 to 7 species of evergreen large shrubs or small trees comes from the linden (Tiliaceae) family, and occurs in woodland areas of southern Africa and Madagascar. Much cultivated as house plants, they will stand some neglect and continue to flower regularly in temperate climates. The simple or palmate leaves are toothed and covered in soft hairs, as are the stems. The flowers, which are produced on umbels, are usually white, or sometimes purple or pink, with prominent stamens. The seed capsule contains several seeds and is prickly on the outside. In warm climates, this is a useful border plant. CULTIVATION: These plants require full sun and a rich well-drained soil. They need regular pruning to maintain their shape if grown in pots. Water very little during the dormant winter months. Propagate by sowing seed or air layer in the spring; half-hardened cuttings can be rooted in summer, but they require heat from beneath in cooler climates.

Sparaxis tricolor

Sparaxis fragrans subsp. *acutifolia*

Sparaxis fragrans subsp. *grandiflora*

Sparmannia africana
AFRICAN LINDEN, CAPE STOCK ROSE

☀ ⬨ ↔ 10 ft (3 m) ↕ 20 ft (6 m)

Large shrub or small tree, native to South Africa. Hairy stems, light green hairy leaves, shallow lobes. White flowers, bright yellow or reddish purple stamens, are produced in late spring–summer. '**Flore Pleno**' (syn. 'Plena') has double white flowers; '**Variegata**', variegated leaves, large white flowers. Zones 9–11.

SPARTINA
CORD GRASS, MARSH GRASS

This genus of 15 perennial species, members of the grass (Poaceae) family, is native to western and southern Europe, the Americas, northwestern and southern Africa, and the South Atlantic islands. These plants grow from rhizomes, with rigid upright stems and tough flat or folded leaves with finely hairy ligules. The flower-heads are stalkless spikelets, held close or spreading out. The name comes from the Greek word *spartine*, a cord, referring to the plant's tough flowering stems.

CULTIVATION: Marsh grasses prefer a position in full sun and thrive in salty coastal marshes and sand flats, but can adapt to any moist soil. Propagate by division or from seed planted in the autumn.

Sparmannia africana

Spartina pectinata
FRESHWATER CORD GRASS, MARSH GRASS, SALT GRASS

☀ ❄ ↔ 18–24 in (45–60 cm) ↕ 3–10 ft (0.9–3 m)

Aggressively spreading perennial grass native to the wet prairies of North America. Narrow, arching, leathery, flat leaves, to 4 ft (1.2 m) long; change from green to yellow to fawn. Feathery columnar flowerheads, masses of tiny purple flowers, in autumn–winter. '**Aureomarginata**' (syn. 'Variegata') arching olive green leaves, edged with golden yellow, purplish, hanging stamens. Zones 4–5.

SPARTIUM

All but one species in this genus of brooms from the pea-flower subfamily of the legume (Fabaceae) family have now been transferred, most of them to *Genista*. The one remaining species is a deciduous shrub native to the Mediterranean region and southwestern Europe. Leafless for much of the year, but green-stemmed, it produces a few small leaves in spring, usually as it comes into bloom. A yellow dye is extracted from the flowers.

CULTIVATION: Spanish broom is easily grown in any well-drained soil with a position in full sun. It can be cut back hard after flowering to encourage bush-iness. Pruning also helps to prevent

Spartina pectinata

Spathiphyllum phrynifolium, in the wild, Cahuita, Costa Rica

excessive self-sowing, which can be a problem if too many seed pods are left to ripen. Propagation is from seeds or from cuttings.

Spartium junceum
SPANISH BROOM

☀ ❄ ↔ 10 ft (3 m) ↕ 10 ft (3 m)

Many-stemmed shrub, smothered in flowers, in spring–early summer, later in cool climates. Strongly scented, bright yellow, pea-flowers are produced in large racemes on new growth. Flat dark brown seed pods split open when ripe. Zones 8–10.

SPATHIPHYLLUM
PEACE LILY

This genus of 36 species of evergreen perennials in the arum (Araceae) family originates mainly in the American tropics. They are large clump-forming plants with strong rhizomes, from which emerge lush, dark green, long-stemmed leaves that taper to a fine point and have a prominent midrib and veining. The tiny flowers, usually cream, are borne on an upright spike backed and partially enclosed by a large leafy spathe, which is often pure white but may be cream or pale green.

CULTIVATION: In recent years peace lilies have gained a reputation for their ability to remove vaporized solvents from the atmosphere. Because of this, along with their ability to flower with fairly low light levels, they are widely used as pot plants in shopping malls and offices. They do best in a warm humid environment with fertile, deep, moist, humus-rich, well-drained soil. Water and feed well. Propagate by division.

Spathiphyllum cannifolium

☀ ✦ ↔ 40 in (100 cm) ↕ 40 in (100 cm)

Originating in tropical South America and Trinidad. Long-stemmed leaves, lighter colored, less heavily veined than most species, on long stalk. The spathe is usually folded back, white inside, and with a green-tinted exterior. The spadix is white to pale gray-green. Zones 11–12.

Spathiphyllum wallisii

Spathiphyllum phrynifolium

☀ ✦ ↔ 24–32 in (60–80 cm) ↕ 40 in (100 cm)

From Panama and Costa Rica. Dark green, heavily veined, lance-shaped leaves to 20 in (50 cm) long. Spathes, short-stemmed, up to 10 in (25 cm) long, pale yellow-green to cream. The spadix is white, turning golden when the flowers open. Zones 11–12.

Spathiphyllum wallisii

☀ ✦ ↔ 20–40 in (50–100 cm) ↕ 24–48 in (60–120 cm)

From Panama and Costa Rica. Dark green, heavily veined, lustrous, lance-shaped leaves to 14 in (35 cm) long. Spathes white, ageing to green. White spadix, fragrant flowers. '**Clevelandii**', large spathes, deeply veined, glossy, drooping leaves to 16 in (40 cm) long, flowers indoors. Zones 11–12.

Spathiphyllum Hybrid Cultivars

☀ ✦ ↔ 12–60 in (30–150 cm) ↕ 12–72 in (30–180 cm)

Several hybrid peace lilies have been raised, ranging from the fairly compact, heavy-flowering '**Tasson**', to the largest hybrid cultivar in general cultivation, '**Sensation**', over 6 ft (1.8 m) tall. Zones 11–12.

SPATHODEA

The sole species in this genus from the trumpet-vine (Bignoniaceae) family is an evergreen tree found in the warmer areas of Africa. It has a domed crown, dark green compound leaves, and large bell-shaped flowers with a spathe-like calyx. Flowers are yellow at the base on the outside, becoming bright red near the mouth. They are a bright orange inside, merging to orangey red on the lobes.

CULTIVATION: It is best grown in fertile well-drained soil containing plenty of organic matter, which helps keep

Spartium junceum, Provence, France

the soil moist during hot summers; raised ground is ideal as it allows rapid air drainage. It is frost tender and needs shelter from wind, especially salt-laden wind. The strongest leading shoot should be kept free of competition until the trunk is 7 ft (2 m) or more tall, when the crown may be allowed to develop naturally. Seeds can be sown in spring in a warm environment.

Spathodea campanulata
syn. *Spathodea nilotica*
AFRICAN TULIP TREE
☼ ✛ ↔ 25 ft (8 m) ↑ 25–35 ft (8–10 m)
Evergreen tree native to tropical central and western Africa. Broad-domed crown. Leaves are compound on short stalks, leaflets are shiny, dark green, paler and dull underneath. Bell-shaped flowers, in racemes, in late spring–mid-summer. Fruit, slender capsule. Zones 11–12.

SPATHOGLOTTIS
This group of 40 evergreen to semi-deciduous, tropical, terrestrial orchids in the family Orchidaceae is from Southeast Asia, New Guinea, and northern Australia to nearby islands of the Pacific. They grow in grasslands and open forests in moist places. They have small, conical, and somewhat flattened pseudobulbs on or just below the soil surface. A few large pleated leaves and tall inflorescences of mainly pink and purple, occasionally yellow or white, showy flowers are produced. They bloom throughout the year in the tropics, and during warmer months in greenhouses in temperate climates. CULTIVATION: They are best in bright light. Warm conditions throughout the year are required as they dislike temperatures below 50°F (10°C). Grow in deep pots in a well-drained medium incorporating pine bark, sand, and peat moss. Keep moist—pots can be placed in a saucer of water, about 2 in (5 cm) deep, during the period of active growth in the summer. Reduce watering during the winter when the plants are semi-dormant. Propagation is by division.

Spathoglottis plicata
☼ ✛ ↔ 8–48 in (20–120 cm)
↑ 12–40 in (30–100 cm)
From Southeast Asia, Australia, and nearby Pacific Islands, naturalized in Hawaii, USA, where it is marketed as a native! Erect spikes of up to 20 pink to purple, 1½ in (35 mm) wide blooms. Zones 11–12.

Spathoglottis vieillardii
☼/☀ ✛ ↔ 8–48 in (20–120 cm)
↑ 12–40 in (30–100 cm)
From the southern Pacific Islands. Very closely related to *S. plicata*, some botanists consider that they belong to the same species. Zones 11–12.

SPHAERALCEA
syn. *Iliamna*
FALSE MALLOW, GLOBE MALLOW
This genus consists of 60 species belonging to the mallow (Malvaceae) family. Deciduous or evergreen perennials, subshrubs, and shrubs, they are native to the dry, even volcanic, mountain slopes of the warmer areas of North America, South America, and South Africa. The leaves are arranged in spirals, have a variety of shapes, and are usually toothed and downy. The saucer-shaped flowers are red, pale purple, pink, white, orange, or yellow and are produced singly in clusters or inflorescences. CULTIVATION: Grow outdoors in full sun in well-drained moderately fertile soil and provide protection from winter moisture. If grown in pots, provide added grit to loam-based compost and feed and water moderately. Propagate by sowing seed in spring and dividing perennials at the same time. In areas with heavy winter rain, they are best protected in a cool greenhouse as excess wet, rather than cold, often kills the hardier species.

Sphaeralcea ambigua
DESERT MALLOW
☼ ✻ ↔ 12–24 in (30–60 cm)
↑ 24–36 in (60–90 cm)
Upright shrubby perennial from southern USA and Mexico. Whiteish green or yellow felted stems. Thick, gray, shallowly lobed leaves. Small salmon to orange saucer-shaped flowers, in loose clusters, in spring–autumn. Zones 4–9.

Sphaeralcea coccinea
syn. *Malvastrum coccineum*
GLOBE MALLOW, PRAIRIE MALLOW, RED FALSE MALLOW
☼ ✻ ↔ 6–12 in (15–30 cm)
↑ 6–18 in (15–45 cm)
Well-branched perennial found from southern Canada to Arizona, USA. White or gray felted stems. Pinnately parted leaves, rough-textured, grayish green. Short racemes of orange to red flowers, in summer. Zones 4–9.

Sphaeralcea munroana
☼ ✻ ↔ 12–27 in (30–70 cm)
↑ 8–36 in (20–90 cm)
Short-lived perennial native to western North America. Felted gray stems. Small, deeply toothed, 5-lobed, hairy leaves. Apricot-pink to red or orange saucer-shaped flowers, in summer. Zones 4–9.

SPILOXENE
This genus of southern African corms of the star-flower (Hypoxidaceae) family with some 20 species has been the subject of considerable revision over the years, particularly concerning its relationship with *Hypoxis*. They form clumps of grassy foliage and produce starry flowers to around 2 in (5 cm) wide, often greenish white to creamy yellow with dark centers, at varying times. Some species are summer dormant, flowering in winter, while others bloom in spring, summer, or autumn. CULTIVATION: They are very easily grown in any sunny position with a moist, well-drained soil. The bulb will survive reasonably cold conditions provided the soil does not freeze solid. When dormant, the bulbs can be lifted and stored dry. Propagate by seed or natural offsets. May naturalize and become slightly invasive.

Spiloxene aquatica
☼ ⚶ ↔ 8–20 in (20–50 cm)
↑ 12–16 in (30–40 cm)
Can withstand very wet winter conditions, but prefers to dry off in the summer. Foliage very fine and grassy. Pure white flowers, with conspicuous yellow stamens, open in the wild with the arrival of the first rains in late summer. Zones 9–10.

Spathodea campanulata

Sphaeralcea ambigua

Spiloxene aquatica, in the wild, Niewondsville, South Africa

Spathoglottis plicata

Spathoglottis vieillardii

Spiraea blumei

Spinacia oleracea 'Space'

Spinacia oleracea 'Viking'

Spinacia oleracea 'Triathlon'

SPINACIA
SPINACH

Native to central Asia, this genus of 3 species of annuals or biennials lies within the goosefoot (Chenopodiaceae) family. Their leaves are large and flat and the small flowers are either male or female, the males borne on densely packed spikes and the females in the leaf axils. *S. oleracea*, the commonly cultivated species grown for its edible leaves, has a long history of cultivation, being introduced to Europe during the Middle Ages and grown in China since at least the seventh century. CULTIVATION: Grow *S. oleracea* in deep rich soil to accommodate the taproot. A top-dressing of nitrogen will encourage rapid growth. Water well throughout the growing period. Plants are best suited to cool season growing in spring and autumn. They are susceptible to downy mildew and leaf spot. Propagate from seed.

Spinacia oleracea
SPINACH

☼/◐ ❀ ↔ 12–18 in (30–45 cm) ↕ 24–36 in (60–90 cm)

Annual of uncertain origin, possibly from southwestern Asia. Large, bright green, oval to triangular, smooth or wrinkled leaves. Young leaves eaten raw in salads, older leaves cooked. 'Space', smooth-leafed, good mildew resistance; 'Triathlon' ★, vigorous, fast-growing; 'Viking', large leaves, slow to bolt. Zones 6–9.

SPIRAEA
BRIDAL WREATH, SPIREA

This genus has about 70 species of mainly deciduous, sometimes semi-evergreen, flowering shrubs in the rose (Rosaceae) family. It is valued for its flowering and foliage qualities. Leaves are simple and alternate, variously toothed and lobed. The genus is found in many northern temperate areas, mainly in eastern and southeastern Asia and in North America. CULTIVATION: They thrive in most soils, though some grow poorly on chalk, and prefer a sunny position and cool moist conditions. They fall into 2 groups for pruning: those that flower on the current year's growth, which can be hard pruned in spring, and those that flower on the previous year's growth, which should have the old flowering shoots removed just after

Spiraea alba var. *latifolia*

Spiraea betulifolia var. *aemiliana*

flowering. Propagation is from soft-tip or half-hardened cuttings during the summer months.

Spiraea alba
MEADOWSWEET

☼ ❀ ↔ 5 ft (1.5 m) ↕ 5 ft (1.5 m)

Shrub from eastern North America. Upright or slightly overarching spreading habit. Young stems coated with fine red-brown hairs. Leaves, pointed oblong shape, serrated edges. Large conical panicles of white, rarely pink, flowers, in summer. *S. a.* var. *latifolia*, noticeably broader leaves. Zones 5–9.

Spiraea 'Arguta'
BRIDAL WREATH

☼ ❀ ↔ 4 ft (1.2 m) ↕ 5–7 ft (1.5–2 m)

Dense shrub. Thin branches, hairless, inversely lance-shaped to oval leaves,

smooth edges or a few teeth. Clusters of white flowers along the branches, in spring. Zones 4–10.

Spiraea betulifolia
BIRCHLEAF SPIREA

☼ ❀ ↔ 3 ft (0.9 m) ↕ 3 ft (0.9 m)

A dwarf shrub found in Japan and northeastern Asia. Forms mound of brown hairless shoots, round to egg-shaped leaves. Flowers are white, in closely packed corymbs, appearing in mid-summer. *S. b.* var. *aemiliana*, to 12 in (30 cm) high, broad rounded leaves. Zones 5–10.

Spiraea × billardii

☼ ❀ ↔ 7 ft (2 m) ↕ 7 ft (2 m)

Spreading shrub, hybrid between *S. douglasii* and *S. salicifolia*. Hairy upright stems. Oblong to lance-shaped leaves, sharp teeth, gray downy undersides. Red flowers in densely packed panicles, in summer. 'Triumphans', small leaves, slightly downy undersides, flowers deep pink, sometimes hint of purple. Zones 4–10.

Spiraea blumei

☼ ❀ ↔ 6 ft (1.8 m) ↕ 4–6 ft (1.2–1.8 m)

This spreading shrub, native to Japan. has heavily toothed, 1 in (25 mm) long, blue-green leaves. Heads of ¼ in (6 mm) wide white flowers, in summer. Zones 6–9.

Spiraea × brachybotrys

☼ ❀ ↔ 6 ft (1.8 m) ↕ 8 ft (2.4 m)

Vigorous shrub, hybrid between *S. canescens* and *S. douglasii*. Arching branches, egg-shaped to oblong leaves, teeth at the tip, velvety gray undersides. Light red flowers in dense panicles, in summer. Zones 4–10.

Spiraea canescens

☼ ❀ ↔ 6 ft (1.8 m) ↕ 8 ft (2.4 m)

Shrub from the Himalayas. Velvety angular branches, egg-shaped to oval leaves, toothed at tip, felted gray beneath. White flowers in corymbs, in mid-summer. Zones 4–10.

Spiraea canescens

Spiraea fritschiana

Spiraea × cinerea 'Compacta'

Spiraea × cinerea 'Grefsheim'

Spiraea cantoniensis
REEVES' SPIREA

☼ ❄ ↔ 8 ft (2.4 m) ↑ 6 ft (1.8 m)
Deciduous or semi-evergreen shrub, native to China. Arching hairless branches. Diamond-shaped leaves have glaucous undersides, and are conspicuously toothed or 3-lobed. White flowers are borne in spherical clusters, in mid-summer. '**Flore Pleno**' (syn. 'Lanceata'), double flowers, the most popular form of *S. cantoniensis* in cultivation. Zones 5–11.

Spiraea chamaedryfolia
GERMANDER SPIREA

☼ ❄ ↔ 6 ft (1.8 m) ↑ 6 ft (1.8 m)
Suckering, densely branched shrub found from the eastern Alps to Siberia. Dark green, pointed, oval leaves. Puts on a showy display of small white flowers, in crowded domed clusters, in spring. Zones 5–9.

Spiraea × cinerea
GREFSHEIM SPIREA

☼ ❄ ↔ 5 ft (1.5 m) ↑ 5 ft (1.5 m)
Garden hybrid between *S. hypericifolia* and *S. cana*. Small, rather pale green leaves. Branch tips covered with tiny white flowers, a few in leaf axils of lower branches, in spring. '**Compacta**' is under 3 ft (0.9 m) tall, with arching branches; '**Grefsheim**', early-flowering, with slightly pendulous branches, and narrower leaves. Zones 5–9.

Spiraea decumbens

☼ ❄ ↔ 18 in (45 cm) ↑ 10 in (25 cm)
Low shrublet from the southeastern Alps. Prostrate branches from which wiry flowering stems arise. Small oval leaves, coarsely toothed near the tips. Small white flowers in clusters to 2 in (5 cm) wide, in summer. Zones 5–9.

Spiraea douglasii
WESTERN SPIREA

☼ ❄ ↔ 6 ft (1.8 m) ↑ 6 ft (1.8 m)
Suckering shrub mainly from northwestern USA, and naturalized in parts of Europe. Forms a thicket of red shoots. Oblong leaves have downy

Spiraea douglasii

Spiraea hypericifolia

gray undersides. Produces purplish pink flowers in panicles, in mid-summer. Zones 4–10.

Spiraea fritschiana
KOREAN SPIREA

☼ ❄ ↔ 5 ft (1.5 m) ↑ 3 ft (0.9 m)
This mounding shrub is a native of Korea. Rather glaucous foliage, develops purplish tones in autumn. Large clusters of white flowers sometimes tinged pink, are borne in summer. Zones 4–9.

Spiraea henryi

☼ ❄ ↔ 8 ft (2.4 m) ↑ 10 ft (3 m)
Robust shrub, native to central China. Arching red-brown branches. Leaves normally oblong or inversely lance-shaped. Produces white flowers, in spherical corymbs, during summer. Zones 4–10.

Spiraea cantoniensis 'Flore Pleno'

Spiraea cantoniensis

Spiraea hypericifolia

☼ ❄ ↔ 6 ft (1.8 m) ↑ 6 ft (1.8 m)
Shrub found from Europe to central Asia. Erect to arching and somewhat downy stems. Small leaves, bluish green, conspicuously veined beneath. Tiny creamy white flowers in small clusters, in spring. Zones 5–9.

Spiraea japonica
JAPANESE SPIREA

☼ ❄ ↔ 4 ft (1.2 m) ↑ 6 ft (1.8 m)
Upright shrub from Japan, China, and Korea. Lance- to egg-shaped leaves. Pink flowers, in clusters, in summer. *S. j.* var. *albiflora*, pale green leaves, white flowers. *S. j.* '**Anthony Waterer**', purplish red flowers; '**Bullata**', dwarf slow-growing shrub, deep pinkish red flowers; '**Bumalda**', dwarf form, leaves can be variegated pink and off-white;

Spiraea japonica 'Crispa'

Spiraea japonica var. *albiflora*

S

Spiraea japonica 'Fire Light'

S. japonica 'Golden Princess'

Spiraea japonica 'Goldflame'

Spiraea japonica 'Neon Flash'

Spiraea japonica cultivar

Spiraea japonica 'Dart's Red'

'**Crispa**', purplish pink flowers; '**Dart's Red**', bright pink flowers; '**Fire Light**', ovate leaves, purple-pink flowers; '**Gold Charm**', golden to chartreuse leaves; '**Gold Mound**' ★, golden leaves turn chartreuse; **Golden Princess**/'**Lise**', foliage ages from bronze to yellow; '**Goldflame**', orange autumn leaves, red flowers; '**Limemound**', leaves initially yellow, becoming lime green, russet in autumn, pink flowers; '**Little Princess**', pink flowers; **Magic Carpet**/ '**Walbuma**', bronze-red leaves turn chartreuse, pink flowers; '**Monhub**', dwarf shrub, light green leaves; '**Nana**', dwarf, dark pink flowers; '**Neon Flash**', lance-shaped leaves, pink flowers; '**Shirobana**', red buds open to deep pink and white flowers. Zones 3–10.

Spiraea miyabei

☼ ❋ ↔ 3 ft (0.9 m) ↑ 3 ft (0.9 m)
Small upright shrub, native to Japan. Somewhat angled branches. Pointed oval, deep green leaves. Small white flowers borne in crowded heads, in summer. Zones 6–9.

Spiraea mollifolia

☼ ❋ ↔ 7 ft (2 m) ↑ 6–8 ft (1.8–2.4 m)
From western China. Leaves and young stems covered in silky down.

Spiraea miyabei

Branches nod slightly at tips, elliptical to oblong leaves. Small umbels of white flowers on short side shoots, in summer. Zones 6–9.

Spiraea nipponica

NIPPON SPIREA
☼ ❋ ↔ 6 ft (1.8 m) ↑ 6 ft (1.8 m)
This vigorous bushy shrub is native to Japan. The leaves are oval or inversely egg-shaped, with teeth at tip. White flowers borne in clusters at the ends of the branches, in mid-summer. *S. n.* **var. *tosaensis***, smaller leaves; many sold under this name are the cultivar '**Snowmound**'. *S. n.* '**Halward's Silver**', smaller form than species, produces abundant white flowers; '**Rotundifolia**', broader leaves, rather larger flowers than most of other cultivars; and '**Snowmound**', green leaves, tinted blue. Zones 5–10.

Spiraea, 'Snow White'

Spiraea prunifolia

BRIDAL WREATH SPIREA,
SHOE BUTTON SPIREA
☼ ❋ ↔ 7 ft (2 m) ↑ 7 ft (2 m)
Rounded bush, native to China. Usually grown in the form '**Plena**', dense shrub with egg-shaped leaves, edged with very small teeth, which turn reddish orange in autumn. Double white flowers, in closely packed clusters, in spring. Zones 4–10.

Spiraea 'Snow White'

SNOW WHITE SPIREA
☼ ❋ ↔ 7 ft (2 m) ↑ 6 ft (1.8 m)
Vigorous shrub, arching branches. Pale green foliage developing attractive yellow tones, in autumn. Smothered in white flowers, in late spring. This cultivar is believed to have originated as a cross between *S. trichocarpa* and *S. trilobata*. Zones 3–9.

Spiraea nipponica 'Snowmound'

Spiraea nipponica 'Rotundifolia'

Spiraea mollifolia

Spiraea × *vanhouttei*

Spiraea tomentosa

Spiraea thunbergii

THUNBERG SPIREA

☼ ❋ ↔ 7 ft (2 m) ↑ 5 ft (1.5 m)

Shrub, native to China, extensively naturalized in Japan. Thin hairy stems, narrow hairless leaves, toothed margins. White flowers in small clusters, occur in spring. '**Okon**', early flowering, the pale yellow leaves fading to pale green. Zones 4–10.

Spiraea tomentosa

HARD HACK, STEEPLEBUSH

☼ ❋ ↔ 7 ft (2 m) ↑ 7 ft (2 m)

Robust, thicket-forming, upright shrub from eastern USA. Young stems, with brown velvety coating; tooth-edged leaves, downy yellow-gray undersides. Crimson flowers, in dense panicles, in late summer. Zones 4–10.

Spiraea trichocarpa

KOREAN SPIREA

☼ ❋ ↔ 4 ft (1.2 m) ↑ 6 ft (1.8 m)

This species is native to Korea. Shrub with stiff spreading branches, pointed leaves, few teeth toward the tip, and bluish undersides. Rounded dense clusters of white flowers are crowded along the outer branches, in summer. Zones 5–9.

Spiraea trilobata

THREE-LOBED SPIREA

☼ ❋ ↔ 4 ft (1.2 m) ↑ 4 ft (1.2 m)

Spreading shrub, ranging from Central Asia to northern China and Siberia. Dense twiggy habit. Small rounded leaves, coarsely toothed, bluish green. Tight umbels of small white flowers dot branches profusely, in summer. '**Fairy Queen**', more compact, floriferous, leaves more lobed; '**Swan Lake**', compact shrub, attracts butterflies. Zones 6–9.

Spiraea × vanhouttei

BRIDAL WREATH SPIREA, VAN HOUTTE SPIREA

☼ ❋ ↔ 4 ft (1.2 m) ↑ 6 ft (1.8 m)

Robust form, a hybrid shrub between *S. cantoniensis* and *S. trilobata*. Leaves inversely egg-shaped to diamond-shaped, lobed toothed edges. White flowers in dense umbels, in midsummer. Zones 5–11.

Spiraea veitchii

☼ ❋ ↔ 8 ft (2.4 m) ↑ 10 ft (3 m)

Vigorous shrub with arching branches found in central and western China.

Spiraea wilsonii

Spiraea trilobata 'Fairy Queen'

Oblong smooth-edged leaves, 1–3 in (25–50 mm) long. White flowers in dense corymbs, in summer. Zones 4–10.

Spiraea wilsonii

☼ ❋ ↔ 5–7 ft (1.5–2 m) ↑ 5–7 ft (1.5–2 m)

Arching shrub with purplish branchlets, native to central and western China. Foliage slightly hairy, dull green above, grayish green beneath. White flowers in dense domed clusters, in summer. Zones 6–9.

SPOROBOLUS

DROPSEED, RUSHGRASS

This genus of about 100 perennial or annual species, widely distributed and naturalized, belongs to the grass

Spiraea thunbergii

Spiraea thunbergii 'Okon'

(Poaceae) family. Finely textured, hairlike, medium green leaves, 8–24 in (20–60 cm) long, typically form a dense arching mound, to 15 in (38 cm) tall and 18 in (45 cm) wide. The leaves turn golden to orange in autumn, fading to light bronze in winter. Open branching panicles, 12–27 in (30–70 cm) long, of small stalked spikelets, carry a single fragrant flower with pink and brown tints, on slender stems that rise well above the foliage, from late summer to autumn. Tiny spherical seeds drop from their hulls in autumn. Cultivated as ornamentals and for livestock and wildlife feed. CULTIVATION: They are slow to establish but easily grown in a wide range of dry to medium-wet, well-drained soils in full sun. They are tolerant to drought. Propagate from seed.

Sporobolus heterolepis

PRAIRIE DROPSEED

☼ ❋ ↔ 12–16 in (30–40 cm) ↑ 24–36 in (60–90 cm)

North American prairie grass. Very fine bright green leaves, vivid orange in autumn. Airy, open, buff flower plumes on wiry stems, in summer. Drought tolerant once established. Zones 3–9.

Spiraea trichocarpa

SPREKELIA

This single-species genus in the amaryllis (Amaryllidaceae) family is native to the dry winter/wet spring and summer climates of Central and South America. In cultivation, however, these bulbous perennials seem quite happy to sit in damp but well-drained situations during the winter months. These highly adaptable plants are easily grown and will adjust their lifestyles to many different conditions, thriving on neglect and producing a generous supply of large red flowers in almost frost-free climates.
CULTIVATION: They flower best in well-established clumps and resent root disturbance. In frost-prone climates, *Sprekelia* can be pot-grown, providing the pots are moved into protected conditions during the colder months. When in growth they should be well drained, watered regularly, and given a weak liquid feed every 10

Sprekelia formosissima

Sprengelia incarnata

days. Propagate from offsets taken in autumn, and by sowing seeds as soon as they ripen.

Sprekelia formosissima ★
AZTEC LILY, JACOBEAN LILY, ST JAMES LILY
☼/◐ ❄ ↔ 8 in (20 cm) ↕ 12 in (30 cm)
Winter dormant or almost evergreen depending on conditions. Leaves straplike, forming dense clumps. Flowers showy, solitary, 6-petalled, 3 upright and 3 pointing downward, dark red to orange-red. Flowering varies between late winter and summer. Zones 7–10.

SPRENGELIA

Named in honor of German botanist Christian Sprengel (1750–1816) who studied the relationship between insects and the pollination of plants, this genus of 4 species of wiry-stemmed evergreen shrubs is native to southeastern Australia and belongs to the epacris (Epacridaceae) family of Australian heaths. They have spiraly arranged and overlapping leaves, tapering to a sharp tip and with broad bases that wrap around the stem. The white or pink star-shaped flowers are densely crowded at the stem tips or are borne singly in the upper leaf axils. Species of *Sprengelia* grow in heathland in acid boggy soil or cling tenaciously to sandstone rock-faces.
CULTIVATION: Like other Southern Hemisphere heaths, they are not easily cultivated unless their soil requirements are met. The soil should have a high proportion of coarse sand and well-aged peat and must remain at a fairly constant moisture level. Fertilizers should be used sparingly and should be low in phosphorus. Propagate from half-hardened cuttings or from seed if it is obtainable.

Stachys byzantina

Sprengelia incarnata
PINK SWAMP HEATH
☼ ⅃ ↔ 18 in (45 cm) ↕ 36 in (90 cm)
Erect slender shrub with few branches from moist coastal areas and adjacent ranges of mainland southeastern Australia. Leaves stiff, papery texture. Flesh pink starry flowers in dense conical clusters at branch tips, in winter–spring. Zones 9–10.

STACHYS
BETONY, HEDGE NETTLE, WOUNDWORT
About 300 species are in this genus in the mint (Lamiaceae) family, and they range from stoloniferous and rhizomatous perennials through to a few evergreen shrubs. In the wild these plants can be found in a range of situations, from dry mountain areas through to scrub areas, wastelands, meadows, and streamsides, particularly in northern temperate zones. The hairy, soft to touch, lance-shaped sometimes round leaves vary in color from pale silvery grays to greens. Flowers are tubular, sometimes hooded, and vary from red, pink, and purple through to white and yellow. The foliage is often aromatic, lending itself to many uses in the ornamental garden. *S. officinalis,* known then as wood betony, was revered for its curative properties by ancient Greek physicians and in the Middle Ages.
CULTIVATION: *Stachys* species require well-drained open soil in full sun. They will not cope very well in shade or humid areas. Propagate from seed in spring and autumn or softwood cuttings when material is available.

Stachys affinis
CHINESE ARTICHOKE
☼ ❄ ↔ 36 in (90 cm) ↕ 20 in (50 cm)
Tuberous perennial from China. Upright stems, crinkly leaves. Small white

Stachys byzantina 'Cotton Boll'

Stachys candida

or pink flowers, in summer. Many small, white, edible root tubers. Widely cultivated in Japan. Zones 4–8.

Stachys albotomentosa
☼ ❄ ↔ 16 in (40 cm) ↕ 27 in (70 cm)
Low-growing shrubby perennial from Mexico. Distinctly textured, elongated, heart-shaped leaves; the undersides of the foliage and stems covered in fine white down. Produces salmon-orange flowers, in summer. Zones 8–10.

Stachys byzantina
syns *Stachys lanata, S. olympica*
LAMBS' EARS, WOOLLY BETONY
☼ ❄ ↔ 24 in (60 cm) ↕ 18 in (45 cm)
Ground-hugging perennial found from the Caucasus region to Iran. Oblong to elliptical gray-green leaves covered in silvery white down. Soft to touch, with upright stems of pink to purple flowers, in late spring–early summer. 'Cotton Boll' ★ (syn. 'Sheila McQueen'), longer leaves, modified cottonball-like flowers. Zones 4–8.

Stachys candida
☼ ❄ ↔ 12 in (30 cm) ↕ 6 in (15 cm)
Low-growing subshrub from southern Greece. White-felted, gray-green, rounded leaves, 1 in (25 mm) long. Hooded flowers, white striped with cerise-purple, in summer. Zones 5–8.

Stachys citrina

☼ ❄ ↔ 12 in (30 cm) ↑ 8 in (20 cm)

This spreading, low-growing, woody perennial is a native of Turkey. Ovate, minutely serrated, delicately downy, soft green leaves. The yellow flowers, to 1 in (25 mm) wide, are borne on spikes, in summer. Zones 5–7.

Stachys coccinea

SCARLET HEDGE NETTLE

☼ ❄ ↔ 18 in (45 cm) ↑ 24 in (60 cm)

Mounding perennial species found from Arizona and Texas, USA, to Mexico. Ovate to lance-shaped, slightly downy, crinkly, mid-green leaves. Upright stems of scarlet-pink flowers, are produced from mid-spring through to late autumn. Zones 7–9.

Stachys macrantha

syns *Stachys grandiflora*, *S. spicata*

BIG BETONY

☼ ❄ ↔ 12–18 in (30–45 cm)
↑ 18–24 in (45–60 cm)

Upright hairy perennial from northeastern Turkey and northwestern Iran. Rosettes of wide, ovate, crinkly, veined, dark green leaves, to 3 in (8 cm) long. The spikes of hooded dark cerise-purple flowers, 1¼ in (3 cm) wide, are produced on erect stems, in summer. The cultivar 'Superba' has bright cerise-purple flowers. Zones 5–7.

Stachyurus chinensis

Stachys officinalis 'Rosea Superba'

Stachys coccinea

Stachys officinalis

syn. *Stachys betonica*

BISHOP'S WORT, WOOD BETONY

☼ ❄ ↔ 18–36 in (45–90 cm)
↑ 12–36 in (30–90 cm)

Perennial from Europe. Upright, almost completely hairless, oblong, wrinkled, mid-green leaves to 5 in (12 cm) long. Erect stems of oblong flower spikes carrying purple, reddish pink, or white flowers are produced in early summer–early autumn. 'Alba', white flowers; 'Rosea Superba', rose pink flowers. Zones 5–8.

Stachys sylvatica

HEDGE WOUNDWORT

☼ ❄ ↔ 16–48 in (40–120 cm)
↑ 36 in (90 cm)

A creeping perennial from western Asia. Not widely used in gardens owing to its unpleasant smell. Hairy green leaves and stems. White flowers, with reddish purple markings, in summer–autumn. Zones 5–8.

STACHYURUS

Subject to recent revisions, this genus includes 6 to 10 species of deciduous shrubs and trees from the Himalayan and temperate East Asian region. While generally not spectacular plants and somewhat like *Corylopsis*, though in a different family—the Stachyuraceae—they have the attraction of blooming

Stachyurus praecox

Stachys citrina

Stachys macrantha

in late winter and early spring, before or just as the leaves are developing. They produce drooping racemes of small cream to pale yellow flowers at every leaf bud. The leaves are lance-shaped and are usually around 6 in (15 cm) long.

CULTIVATION: *Stachyurus* species prefer a humus-rich, well-drained, acidic soil in sun or light shade. They are not hardy in the coldest regions but thrive in areas with distinct yet relatively mild winters. Hard late spring frost may damage the flowers and young leaves. Propagate from seed or from half-hardened cuttings.

Stachyurus chinensis

☼ ❄ ↔ 8 ft (2.4 m) ↑ 8 ft (2.4 m)

Deciduous shrub, native to China. The leaves, 2–6 in (5–15 cm) long ovals, taper at the tip. The pale yellow flowers are produced in racemes, in early spring. 'Magpie', light green, cream, and pink variegated foliage. Zones 7–9.

Stachyurus himalaicus

☼ ❄ ↔ 10 ft (3 m) ↑ 10 ft (3 m)

Found from western China to Taiwan, this shrub has red-stemmed lance-shaped leaves with serrated edges. The deep pinkish red flowers, on 2 in (5 cm) long racemes, are produced in spring. Zones 8–10.

Stachys macrantha 'Superba'

Stachys officinalis 'Alba'

Stachyurus praecox

☼ ❄ ↔ 6–12 ft (1.8–3.5 m)
↑ 6–12 ft (1.8–3.5 m)

Shrub, native of Japan. Branches somewhat tiered, reddish-brown stems bear 6 in (15 cm) long leaves, which color slightly in autumn. Gracefully drooping racemes of small pale yellow flowers, in late winter–early spring, before the foliage. Zones 7–10.

STANHOPEA

UPSIDE-DOWN ORCHID

This large popular genus of about 70 epiphytic orchids in the family Orchidaceae is found from Mexico to Brazil. They are grown for their large, bizarre, and colorful blooms and amazing labellum structure. The fragrant waxy blooms last only a few days.

CULTIVATION: Grow these orchids in baskets to allow their pendent

S

Stapelia gigantea

Stapelia leendertiziae

Stapelianthus decaryi

spikes to spear through the medium and burst into bloom. Use *Cymbidium* compost, sphagnum moss, fine grade pine bark, or a combination. Mounted plants rarely stay moist enough, resulting in a bunch of shriveled and yellowish back-bulbs. They appreciate constant moisture throughout the year and grow best in a part-shaded position. Leaves will burn in very strong light and low humidity. There are species suitable for cool to tropical climates, which flower over several months. Propagate by division.

Stanhopea embreei

☼ ✤ ↔ 8–20 in (20–50 cm) ↑ 8–20 in (20–50 cm)

From Ecuador. Up to 5, white, 5 in (12 cm) wide flowers, random dark red spots and deep purple spotting on white and yellow labellum, in summer. Zones 10–12.

Stanhopea nigroviolacea ★

☼ ⚘ ↔ 8–24 in (20–60 cm) ↑ 8–20 in (20–50 cm)

From Mexico, the most common species in cultivation. Pairs of yellowish green, 7 in (18 cm) wide blooms, heavily blotched with dark reddish brown, in summer. Pleasant powerful vanilla fragrance, often detected before sighting blooms. Zones 9–12.

Stanhopea oculata

☼ ✤ ↔ 8–20 in (20–50 cm) ↑ 8–20 in (20–50 cm)

Elegant, variable orchid found from Mexico to Brazil. Up to eight, ½ in (12 mm) wide flowers, pale yellow overlaid with red-purple circular spots. The cream labellum marked with fine reddish pepper spotting, has a bright orange base. Flowers in late summer–autumn. Zones 10–12.

Stanhopea wardii

☼ ✤ ↔ 8–20 in (20–50 cm) ↑ 8–20 in (20–50 cm)

Variable orchid found in Nicaragua, Costa Rica, Panama, Colombia, and Venezuela. Produces up to 10, bright yellow to orange, 5 in (12 cm) wide blooms, with fine maroon spotting,

Stanhopea wardii

in summer or autumn. They are distinguished by a very dark purple patch at the labellum base. Zones 10–12.

STAPELIA

CARRION FLOWER, STARFISH FLOWER

This genus belonging to the milkweed (Asclepiadaceae) family contains 99 species of succulent perennials. They are known as carrion flowers because of their putrid smell, which attracts flies for pollination. Most species are native to Africa where they grow in arid areas, often in the shade of scrub, grass, or rocks. Leaves are absent or short-lived on angular, thick, fleshy, toothed stems. The fleshy flowers, usually borne at the plant base, are flat and circular with 5 often pointed lobes, hence the common name of starfish flower. They are somewhat muted in shades of yellow, brown, purple, and red, and are often marked transversely with ridges or stripes of different colors.
CULTIVATION: In hot dry regions grow outdoors in full sun or part-shade. Elsewhere grow in the greenhouse in well-drained gritty potting mix with low humidity and bright filtered light. Withhold water in winter. Propagate from seed or stem cuttings.

Stapelia gigantea ★

GIANT STAPELIA

☼ ✤ ↔ 8 in (20 cm) ↑ 8–10 in (20–25 cm)

Found from South Africa to Tanzania. Upright, 4-ridged, pale green, fleshy stems, small teeth along angles. Flowers up to 14 in (35 cm) wide, cream to yellow, with transverse crimson lines. Zones 10–12.

Stapelia hirsuta

HAIRY STARFISH FLOWER

☼ ✤ ↔ 6–8 in (15–20 cm) ↑ 8 in (20 cm)

From the Cape region of South Africa. Upright, dull green, leafless stems,

Stanhopea oculata

fleshy, 4 spiny-edged angles. Starry flowers, to 5 in (12 cm) wide, very hairy, transverse lines of yellow and brownish red. Zones 10–12.

Stapelia leendertiziae

☼ ✤ ↔ 6–8 in (15–20 cm) ↑ 8 in (20 cm)

From northern South Africa. Narrow, branching, hairy stems with small teeth. Dark purple cup-shaped flowers, downy outside, wrinkled interior surface. Zones 10–12.

STAPELIANTHUS

This genus, which belongs to the milkweed (Asclepiadaceae) family, contains 9 species of small succulent perennials confined to arid areas of southern Madagascar where they grow in the shade and shelter of forests. No more than 8 in (20 cm) tall, they are similar to the related *Huernia* and *Stapelia*. Their fleshy stems branch at the base, are upright or prostrate with 4 to 8 angles, and are sometimes spiraling. Small leaves drop quickly. The flowers, in shades of purplish or reddish brown, are bell-shaped or flat and open with a prominent corona and 5 starry triangular lobes.
CULTIVATION: In hot dry regions grow outdoors in full sun or part-shade. Elsewhere grow in the greenhouse in well-drained gritty potting mix with low humidity and bright filtered light. Withhold water in winter. Propagate from seed or from stem cuttings.

Stapelianthus decaryi

☼ ✤ ↔ 8 in (20 cm) ↑ 8 in (20 cm)

Succulent species with creeping habit. Forms clumps of ½ in (12 mm) wide fleshy stems, up to 8 angles. The bell-shaped flowers, with recurving triangular lobes of cream covered in short red hairs, usually arise from the base. Zones 10–12.

Stanhopea nigroviolacea

Stauntonia hexaphylla

Stellaria holostea

STAPHYLEA
BLADDERNUT

This genus, belonging to the bladdernut (Staphyleaceae) family, of around 11 species of deciduous shrubs and small trees, is found over much of the northern temperate zone. They have large trifoliate to pinnate leaves, and long leaflets with serrated edges tapering to a point. Panicles of pale pink to white flowers are produced at the ends of branches, mainly in spring, followed by the 2- to 3-lobed inflated seed pods that give the genus its common name. The seed pods dry and brown as they ripen. The foliage may develop attractive autumn tones.
CULTIVATION: Mostly very hardy, bladdernuts thrive in nearly all well-drained moist soils in full sun or partial shade. The bushes tend to form a thicket, or if pruned after flowering they can be thinned to one or a few main stems and made tree-like. Propagate from seed or summer cuttings; rooted suckers can sometimes be removed and grown on.

Staphylea bumalda
JAPANESE BLADDERNUT

☀ ✽ ↔ 6 ft (1.8 m) ↑ 7 ft (2 m)
Deciduous shrub, native to Japan. Leaves trifoliate, lance-shaped leaflets, sharply serrated edges, down on underside veins. Panicles of white flowers, in spring. Pods are 1 in (25 mm) wide, 2-lobed. Zones 4–9.

Staphylea colchica
CAUCASIAN BLADDERNUT

☀ ✽ ↔ 10 ft (3 m) ↑ 10–15 ft (3–4.5 m)
Deciduous shrub from the Caucasus region. Leaves with 3 to 5 glossy green, finely toothed leaflets. Flowers to ½ in (12 mm) wide, white, fragrant. Seed pods are 3-lobed, 3 in (8 cm) across. 'Colombieri', ovate, finely serrated, light green leaves. Zones 6–9.

Staphylea holocarpa
CHINESE BLADDERNUT

☀ ✽ ↔ 10 ft (3 m) ↑ 15 ft (4.5 m)
Chinese native, shrub or tree. Trifoliate leaves, leaflets with hairy under-

sides. Flowers, in drooping panicles, open white from pink buds. Pods around 2 in (5 cm) wide. Zones 6–9.

Staphylea pinnata
EUROPEAN BLADDERNUT

☀ ✽ ↔ 15 ft (4.5 m) ↑ 15 ft (4.5 m)
Temperate Eurasian shrub. Leaves with 3, 5, or 7 leaflets taper to a fine point, serrated edges, glaucous undersides. Flowers white, red-tipped sepals, in late spring. Seed pods 1 in (25 mm) wide. Zones 6–9.

Staphylea trifolia
BLADDERNUT, EASTERN BLADDERNUT

☀ ✽ ↔ 15 ft (4.5 m) ↑ 15 ft (4.5 m)
Shrub from the eastern USA. Leaves trifoliate, 2–3 in (5–8 cm) long leaflets, finely pointed, sharply serrated edges, fine hairs beneath, change color in autumn. White flowers 1½ in (35 mm) wide, borne in short panicles; 3-lobed fruit. Zones 5–9.

STAUNTONIA

Genus of up to 16 species of evergreen and deciduous twining and climbing plants, belonging to the chocolate-vine (Lardizabalaceae) family. From East Asia, these plants are now naturalized in many other countries. Quick-growing and very ornamental plants,

they are frequently chosen for their handsome palmate foliage and fragrant bell-like flowers. They are only hardy outdoors in milder areas, tolerating temperatures down to about 15°F (–10°C) when fully dormant. The young growth in spring, however, can be damaged by late frosts. They are cultivated for their edible fruits in some countries, such as Japan.
CULTIVATION: They require a well-drained, moisture-retentive soil in a sheltered position and grow best if the roots are in a shady position and the top is grown into the sun. Propagate from seed in early spring, but note that seed can take 18 months to germinate.

Stauntonia hexaphylla ★

☀/◑ ✤ ↔ 10–17 ft (3–5 m) ↑ 35 ft (10 m)
Quick-growing climber from South Korea and Japan. Dark green leathery leaves. Fragrant white flowers tinged with violet, appear in spring–summer. Zones 10–11.

STELLARIA
CHICKWEED, STITCHWORT

This is a large genus of plants in the pink (Caryophyllaceae) family which also contains the carnation (*Dianthus*), though *Stellaria* has none of its popular relative's gardenworthiness. About 120 species are distributed worldwide; they are annuals and perennials with brittle stems and generally tiny white flowers. Some species, such as *S. media*, commonly known as chickweed, are weeds. Species with some ornamental value are only suitable in wild gardens, as fillers under large shrubs or as light airy plants among bolder woodland perennials.
CULTIVATION: Grow these plants in humus-rich soil in half-sun and propagate by division or from seed.

Stellaria holostea
GREATER STITCHWORT

☀ ✽ ↔ 3–7 ft (0.9–2 m)
↑ 20–24 in (50–60 cm)
Suckering perennial from Europe, North Africa, and western Asia. Narrow leaves to 3 in (8 cm) long. Open airy sprays of dainty white flowers, in spring–early summer. Zones 5–10.

STENOCACTUS
syn. *Echinofossulocactus*

Genus of 10 to 13 species of small low-growing cacti in family Cactaceae from the Chihuahua Desert region of northern and central Mexico. The name comes from the Greek *stenos*, narrow, referring to the thin wavy ribs that characterize most species. Usually solitary and spherical to cylindrical with age, most species have many narrow, often wavy ribs. The spines are well spaced along the ribs, straight, or upright and incurving, never hooked; the centrals are always uppermost in the spine cluster, the large and often dagger-like radials are always smaller and lower. The flowers are numerous, small, bell-shaped to funnel-form, white to yellow, pink, or purple, with a red, purple, or brown mid-stripe. The seed pods are spherical and uniformly small in all species.

Staphylea colchica 'Colombieri'

Staphylea bumalda

Staphylea pinnata

Stenocactus crispatus

Stenocarpus salignus

CULTIVATION: Grow in a rich well-drained soil. Propagate from seed. Rest in winter. This is an ideal plant for inexperienced cactus growers.

Stenocactus coptonogonus ★

☀ ❄ ↔ 3–5 in (8–12 cm)
↑ 2–4 in (5–10 cm)

Solitary spherical cactus from Mexico. Dark green, 10 to 15 stout ribs, depressed at spine cluster. Distinctive spines, 3 to 7, upper 3 to 5 broad flattened centrals, pointed upward, remainder all downward-pointing radials. White flowers with purple mid-stripe. Zones 8–10.

Stenocactus crispatus

syns *Echinofossulocactus flexispinus, E. multiareolatus*

☀ ❄ ↔ 3–5 in (8–12 cm)
3–5 in (8–12 cm)

Solitary, flattened spherical, yellow green to dark green cactus from Mexico with 25 to 60 wavy ribs. Spines variable; straight, yellow or brown, 1 to 4 upward-pointing centrals,

2 to 10 downward-pointing radials. Bright pink-red flowers are borne in spring. Zones 8–10.

Stenocactus multicostatus

syns *Stenocactus lloydii, S. zacatecasensis*
BRAIN CACTUS

☀ ❄ ↔ 4 in (10 cm) ↑ 3–5 in (8–12 cm)

Flattened spherical cactus from Mexico. Up to 120 very thin, sharp-edged, wavy ribs. Long, flexible, sword-like central spines, glassy, straight to curved radials. Flowers white, purple mid-stripe. Zones 8–10.

STENOCARPUS

Genus of 25 species of evergreen trees or large shrubs, in the protea (Proteaceae) family, from Southeast Asia, the Malay Peninsula to New Caledonia, and Australia. They feature simple alternate leaves. Tubular flowers, usually red to orange, are borne in umbels, sometimes partly hidden by foliage. The fruit is a narrow follicle containing winged seeds.

Stenocereus alamosensis

CULTIVATION: *Stenocarpus* species need a warm site, preferably near the coast but with shelter from salt-laden winds. They prefer a light, sandy, well-drained soil with plenty of organic matter, as well as plentiful summer water. Seeds sown as soon as ripe in winter germinate readily in a warm environment; clonal varieties may be grafted on seedling understocks. These species require little or no pruning.

Stenocarpus salignus

RED SILKY OAK, SCRUB BEEFWOOD

☀ ⚘ ↔ 10–15 ft (3–4.5 m) ↑ 100 ft (30 m)

Tree growing in warm rainforest on the coast and in adjacent ranges of northeastern Australia. Dark brown scaly bark. Leaves ovate to lanceolate, leathery, paler beneath. Creamy white flowers in umbels of 10 to 20 blooms, in spring–summer. Zones 9–12.

Stenocarpus sinuatus

FIREWHEEL TREE, QUEENSLAND FIREWHEEL TREE

☀ ⚘ ↔ 15 ft (4.5 m) ↑ 120 ft (36 m)

Attractive tree found in warm rainforests near the coast and in the adjacent ranges of eastern Australia. Gray to brown bark. Leathery leaves, shiny green above, duller beneath. Orange-scarlet flowers in umbels of 15 to 20 blooms in the upper axils. Zones 9–12.

STENOCEREUS

A genus of 23 disparate species of columnar to tree-like cactus (Cactaceae) family members from southwestern USA, Central America, the Caribbean, Venezuela, and Colombia. The name comes from the Greek *stenos*, narrow, and refers to the many thin ribs of many of the species. The genus now includes all species previously classified as *Rathbunia* and *Machaerocereus*, and most of *Lemaireocereus*. These plants have stout, cylindrical, mostly

green stems with numerous ribs. They may or may not have tubercles and the areoles may be woolly, but a common feature is very strong spines. Flowers are bell-shaped to funnelform, opening at night, lasting into the next day. Pericarpels are short, with many areoles, often spiny. Seed pods are spherical, fleshy, with deciduous spines.

CULTIVATION: Grow in a rich well-drained soil. Propagate from seed or cuttings dried out for a week or two. Rest in winter.

Stenocereus alamosensis

☀ ⚘ ↔ 15–20 ft (4.5–6 m)
↑ 7–15 ft (2–4.5 m)

Large Mexican shrub. Profusely branching from base, vertical to arching green stems, reddish initially, 5 to 8 tubercled ribs. Spines have 1 to 4 straight gray to whitish centrals, 11 to 18 whitish radials. Diurnal flowers, tubular, red, recurved petals. Green to reddish seed pods. Zones 9–10.

Stenocereus beneckei

syns *Lemaireocereus beneckei, Rathbunia beneckei*

☀ ⚘ ↔ 20–40 in (50–100 cm)
↑ 7–10 ft (2–3 m)

Upright to arching, thin, columnar cactus native to Mexico. Occasionally branching from base, white powdery stems. Ribs 7 to 9, widely separated, straight black central spine, 2 to 5 grayish radials. White nocturnal flowers, brown, naked, scaly pericarpels. Zones 9–10.

Stenocereus eruca

syns *Lemaireocereus eruca, Rathbunia eruca*

CATERPILLAR CACTUS, CREEPING DEVIL

☀ ⚘ ↔ 17–20 ft (5–6 m)
↑ 3–10 ft (0.9–3 m)

Prostrate plant from Mexico. Forms tangled mats of heavily spined dark

Stenocarpus sinuatus

Stephanandra incisa

Stephanandra chinensis

green stems, 10 to 12 ribs. Spines have 1 to 3 stout, flattened, dagger-shaped, gray centrals, 10 to 15 rounded, whitish radials. Flowers few, nocturnal, salverform, pinkish white to cream. Seed pods spherical. Zones 9–10.

Stenocereus thurberi
syns *Lemaireocereus thurberi*, *Marshallocereus thurberi*, *Rathbunia thurberi*

ORGAN PIPE CACTUS
☼ ✣ ↔ 3–15 ft (0.9–4.5 m)
↑ 3–25 ft (0.9–8 m)

Large cactus from the USA and Mexico. Numerous columnar gray-green branches, 10 to 20 ribs, usually lacking trunk. Spines have 1 to 3 gray centrals, 7 to 9 gray radials. Flowers nocturnal, funnelform, white. Seed pods edible. Zones 9–10.

STENOMESSON
There are about 30 species of bulbous perennials in this genus, which belongs to the amaryllis (Amaryllidaceae) family. Most are uncommon in cultivation. They come from South America where they are found on high rocky slopes and in the meadows of the Andes in

Stephanandra incisa 'Crispa'

Peru, Bolivia, and Ecuador, where snow sometimes provides the protection from frost that these plants require. The genus name comes from the Greek *stenos*, narrow, and *mesos*, middle, referring to the plant's narrow perianth.
CULTIVATION: Easily grown outside in frost-free climates, these plants can be cultivated under glass in colder climates provided temperatures do not fall below 44–50°F (7–10°C). Bulbs should be kept slightly moist when dormant in winter. Propagate from offsets or fresh seed sown ripe in sand.

Stenomesson miniatum ★
☼ ✳ ↔ 6 in (15 cm) ↑ 12–16 in (30–40 cm)
Almost evergreen in some conditions or winter dormant. Leaves dark green, narrow, strap-like. Flowers orange to red, umbels of drooping tubular bells, on straight stalks, in spring–summer. Anthers creamy yellow, protruding. Zones 8–10.

STENOTAPHRUM
This genus of 7 annual or perennial mat-forming species is native to tropical or subtropical regions. These members of the grass (Poaceae) family have creeping or rising stems, rooting at the nodes. Short flattened racemes at the ends of stems, growing from the leaf axils, bear spikelets of 2 stalkless flowers on upright or sprawling, solid, flattened stems. The leaves can be thick, flat, or folded, and narrow to

sword-shaped. They grow from the stems with a sheath at the base, with the leaf blade held at right angles to the stem. One species, *S. secundatum*, is used widely for lawns in the southern USA.
CULTIVATION: These plants prefer partial shade and moist soil. Propagate from cuttings.

Stenotaphrum secundatum
BUFFALO GRASS, GRAMA, ST AUGUSTINE GRASS

☼/☀ ✣ ↔ 2–16 in (5–40 cm)
↑ 2–16 in (5–40 cm)

Hardy creeping perennial grass, native to tropical regions. Widely grown as a warm-season lawn grass. Forms fans of smooth, flat, or folded, narrow, oblong leaves, to 6 in (15 cm) long. Stiff one-sided spikes, to 6 in (15 cm) long, green stalkless spikelets. 'Variegatum', leaves striped pale green and ivory, suited to indoor culture. Zones 9–11.

STEPHANANDRA
Genus of 4 species of deciduous shrubs in the rose (Rosaceae) family, allied to *Spiraea*, and native to eastern Asia. Valued for their attractive, soft green, toothed and lobed leaves, which often have rich orange autumn tones. Panicles of white or pale green flowers, shaped like tiny stars, with a profusion of stamens, borne in summer.

Stenomesson miniatum

CULTIVATION: They will grow in most soils in sun or part-shade, but prefer moist loam. Maintain shape by hard pruning in spring. Propagate in the autumn from cuttings or by division.

Stephanandra chinensis
☼ ✳ ↔ 8 ft (2.4 m) ↑ 10 ft (3 m)
Graceful deciduous shrub, native to China. Attractive, bright green, serrated leaves to 2½ in (6 cm) long, turning yellow-orange in autumn. Smooth pale brown branchlets are crowded with racemes of tiny white flowers. Zones 7–9.

Stephanandra incisa
CUTLEAFED STEPHANANDRA, LACE SHRUB
☼ ✳ ↔ 10 ft (3 m) ↑ 6 ft (1.8 m)
Dense shrub originating in Japan and Korea. Thin angular stems. Egg-shaped, deeply toothed, lobed leaves fade to yellow-green in autumn. Flowers in densely packed panicles, pale green to white, in mid-summer. 'Crispa' ★, mound-forming dwarf, small wrinkled leaves, ideal ground cover. Zones 4–10.

Stenocereus thurberi

Stenocereus eruca

Stephanandra tanakae

☼ ❀ ↔ 8 ft (2.4 m) ↑ 10 ft (3 m)

Shrub with arching branches, native to Japan. Deeply toothed leaves, egg-shaped to triangular, 5 lobes, pink-brown when young. Bears small white flowers, in summer, which are not a feature. Zones 4–10.

STERCULIA

This is a tropical genus of around 150 species of deciduous or evergreen trees or shrubs that gives its name to the family Sterculiaceae. They have broad, dark green, smooth-edged or lobed leaves and are grown mostly as ornamental shade trees. Small flowers are produced in racemes or panicles that are often pendulous. Individual flowers are without petals but the urn-shaped calyx with 4 or 5 spreading lobes is usually colorful. The decorative fruit consists of up to 5 boat-shaped woody or leathery follicles, usually pink to red when ripe, that open at an early stage of development to display shiny black seeds.

Sterculia apetala

Stephanandra tanakae

CULTIVATION: Usually fast growing, these plants need a warm climate and a fertile moist soil that is well drained. They grow best in full sun and like protection from winds. Water regularly when small. Propagate from fresh seed.

Sterculia apetala

BELLOTA, PANAMA TREE

☼ ✈ ↔ 30–50 ft (9–15 m)
↑ 50–100 ft (15–30 m)

Deciduous tree from tropical America. Umbrella-like crown of long-stemmed roughly heart-shaped leaves, 5 deep lobes, downy when young. Flowers, clustered in branched heads near stem tips, cream, pink tints, red throats. Pear-shaped fruit. Zones 11–12.

Sterculia murex

LOWVELD CHESTNUT

☼ ❧ ↔ 10–20 ft (3–6 m)
↑ 20–40 ft (6–12 m)

South African deciduous tree. Spreading branches; gray-brown, nearly black, cracked bark. Compound leaves, 5 to 10 oblong to lance-shaped leaflets, to 4 in (10 cm) long. Waxy yellow flowers with brown or red-pink marks, in spring. Woody fruit, stinging hairs irritate skin or eyes. Zones 9–11.

Sterculia quadrifida

PEANUT TREE

☼ ❧ ↔ 20 ft (6 m) ↑ 40 ft (12 m)

Bushy tree, open rounded crown, from northern Australia and New Guinea. Ovate to heart-shaped leaves. Scented, greenish yellow, bell-shaped flowers in racemes, in late summer. Leathery scarlet follicles; black, peanut-sized, edible seeds. Zones 10–12.

STERNBERGIA

AUTUMN CROCUS, AUTUMN DAFFODIL

There are 7 to 8 species in this genus

Sterculia murex

of bulbous perennials, which belong to the amaryllis (Amaryllidaceae) family. They come from the sparse woodlands and winter-rainfall climates of southern Europe and central Asia. Often confused with *Crocus*, they can be distinguished by their leaves, which do not bear the pale midrib of the true crocus. The goblet-like flowers, however, are recognizably crocus-like. The majority bloom in autumn. The genus take its name from Count Kaspar von Sternberg (1761–1838), a Austrian botanist and botanical author.

CULTIVATION: They do best when provided with sharp drainage, in summer heat, and a limy soil. While withstanding several degrees of short sharp frost, they are intolerant of wet soggy root conditions in frost-prone climates. In containers, use equal parts of loam, leaf mold, and sand. Water sparingly and only while in growth.

Sternbergia lutea ★

☼/◐ ❀ ↔ 3 in (8 cm) ↑ 6 in (15 cm)

Found from southern Europe to central Asia. Leaves black-green, linear, appear with flowers, persist until spring. Flowers large, bright yellow, goblet-like, in autumn. Zones 7–9.

Sternbergia sicula

☼/◐ ❀ ↔ 3 in (8 cm) ↑ 3–4 in (8–10 cm)

Vigorous species from Italy to southeastern Europe. Regarded by some as a subspecies of *S. lutea*, has a marked resemblance but smaller size and more open star-like flowers. Zones 7–9.

STETSONIA

The sole species in this genus from the family Cactaceae is an upright, branching, cylindrical-stemmed cactus from northwestern Argentina and southern Bolivia. Tree-like in habit, it is armed with formidable spines and can be difficult to deal with in cultivation. It bears 4–6 in (10–15 cm) long, funnel-shaped, white flowers that are up to 4 in (10 cm) wide at the throat. These open at night but are not noticeably scented.

CULTIVATION: As with most cacti, preferred conditions are light, gritty, very

Sternbergia lutea

Stetsonia coryne

well-drained soil and a position in full sun or morning shade. Although very drought tolerant, moisture is appreciated during the flowering season. Take care siting this species because it is known to be a source of the drug mescaline, making it a target for those interested in manufacturing homemade narcotics. Propagate by removing rooted offsets or by sowing seed.

Stetsonia coryne ★

TOOTHPICK CACTUS

☼ ❧ ↔ 3 ft (0.9 m) ↑ 30 ft (9 m)

Shrubby to tree-like organ-pipe-type cactus. Stems have up to 9 ribs, covered with clusters of 7 to 9 pale gray, needle-like spines, 1–6 in (2.5 cm–15 cm) long. Large white flowers open on summer nights. Zones 9–11.

STEWARTIA

Related to and resembling *Camellia* in their flowers, the 9 species in this genus are from the camellia (Theaceae) family. Deciduous trees and shrubs of eastern North America and temperate East Asia, they are cultivated for their spring flowers, bright autumn foliage, and beautifully marked and colored bark, often at its best in winter. The leaves, around 3 in (8 cm) long, are simple and short-stemmed with serrated edges. The flowers, usually white and about 2 in (5 cm) wide, are carried singly or occasionally in clusters of 2 or 3 blooms. The bark often flakes away to reveal a range of colors.

CULTIVATION: Generally preferring cool, moist, well-drained, humus-rich soil and a position in sun or partial shade, most species are adaptable and will grow well in any position that does not dry out in summer. If it becomes necessary, trim plants after flowering. Propagate from stratified seed or from summer cuttings.

Stewartia malacodendron
SILKY CAMELLIA, VIRGINIA STEWARTIA
☼ ❄ ↔ 10 ft (3 m) ↑ 15–30 ft (4.5–9 m)
Shrub or small tree found in southeastern USA. Young shoots and new leaves rather downy. Leaves with finely toothed edges, downy beneath, color well in autumn. Flowers carried singly, blue-gray anthers on purplish filaments, in summer. Zones 7–9.

Stewartia monadelpha
TALL STEWARTIA
☼ ❄ ↔ 20 ft (6 m) ↑ 50 ft (15 m)
Tree from Japan and Korea. Red-brown bark flakes to reveal lighter tones. Downy young shoots, leaves densely hairy on underside veins. Foliage turns vivid pinkish red in autumn. Flowers 1½ in (35mm) wide, violet anthers. Zones 6–9.

Stewartia ovata
MOUNTAIN STEWARTIA
☼ ❄ ↔ 15 ft (4.5 m) ↑ 15–20 ft (4.5–6 m)
Shrub occurring in southeastern USA. Leaflets with sparsely toothed edges, downy undersides, turn yellow in autumn. Flowers 2 in (5 cm) long. *S. o.* var. *grandiflora*, flowers to 5 in (12 cm) wide, purple anthers. Zones 5–9.

Stewartia pseudocamellia ★
JAPANESE STEWARTIA
☼ ❄ ↔ 15 ft (4.5 m) ↑ 20–50 ft (6–15 m)
Widely grown Japanese species. Light reddish brown bark flakes freely, leaves with serrated edges, downy undersides, bright red in autumn. Flowers with frilly-edged petals, golden anthers, in spring. *S. p.* var. *koreana*, broader leaves and larger flowers. Zones 5–9.

Stewartia pseudocamellia

Stewartia pteropetiolata
☼ ❄ ↔ 12 ft (3.5 m) ↑ 20 ft (6 m)
Shrub or small tree, native to southern China and Korea; evergreen in mild winters. Toothed-edged leaves, small wing-like bracts on their stalks. Small flowers, jagged-edged white petals, golden anthers, from mid- to late summer. Zones 5–9.

Stewartia sinensis
CHINESE STEWARTIA
☼ ❄ ↔ 20 ft (6 m) ↑ 15–30 ft (4.5–9 m)
From China. Flaking red-brown bark. Stems and leaves downy when young, leaves taper to fine point, serrated edges, purple-red in autumn. Fragrant flowers have yellow anthers. Zones 6–9.

STIGMAPHYLLON
A genus in the family Malpighiaceae, of about 100 species of mainly woody climbers, some shrubby, others perennial, mostly from Central and South America and the Caribbean. Twining species wind their stems around their supports. The leaves are usually opposite and smooth-edged. The 5-petalled

Stewartia pseudocamellia var. *koreana*

Stigmaphyllon ciliatum

yellow flowers occur in open sprays. The seeds are attractive, with wings like those of a maple seed.
CULTIVATION: These plants need frost-free conditions in well-drained soil and a sunny aspect. In frost-prone areas grow in a warm greenhouse. Propagation is by cuttings or layering. Seed, if available, should be sown fresh.

Stigmaphyllon ciliatum
GOLDEN VINE
☼ ⚊ ↔ 10–20 ft (3–6 m)
↑ 20–25 ft (6–8 m)
Evergreen twining climber found from Belize to Uruguay. Spearhead-shaped rich green leaves. Flowers flat, 1¾ in (4 cm) across, petal edges undulating, rich bright yellow, in late summer–autumn. Zones 10–12.

Stigmaphyllon littorale
☼ ⚊ ↔ 10–20 ft (3–6 m)
↑ 20–35 ft (6–10 m)
Tall Brazilian climber. Leaves to 5 in (12 cm) long, variable shape. Open sprays of bright yellow flowers to 1 in (25 mm) across, in late summer–autumn. Zones 10–11.

STILBOCARPA
One of the interesting "megaherb" genera found on the Australian and New Zealand subantarctic islands. Although this genus has traditionally been placed in the ivy (Araliaceae) family, this may

Stewartia sinensis

be changed as it is further studied. The genus currently includes 3 species; this may also change, especially if *S. lyallii* is reclassified under *Kirkophytum*. These plants spread by rhizomes and form clumps of thick, leathery, rounded, lobed leaves. They produce dense summer inflorescences of yellow flowers.
CULTIVATION: Not surprisingly, considering its origins, *Stilbocarpa* prefers constantly cool, moist conditions with no extremes of summer heat or winter cold. It has, however, proved surprisingly adaptable during its short period in cultivation and provided the soil is deep, moist, and humus-rich, it can withstand considerable summer heat. Propagate from seed or by division.

Stilbocarpa polaris
MACQUARIE ISLAND CABBAGE
☼/◐ ❄ ↔ 20–48 in (50–120 cm)
↑ 12–16 in (30–40 cm)
Found on Macquarie Island and many other subantarctic islands, where it gives shelter to nesting birds. Vigorous grower, strong rhizomes, large clumps of impressive, deeply veined leaves. Large inflorescences. Zones 7–9.

Stilbocarpa polaris (rear), with royal penguins, in the wild, Macquarie Island

Stipa tenuissima

Stipa arundinacea

Stipa gigantea

STIPA

FEATHER GRASS, NEEDLE GRASS, SPEAR GRASS

This is a wide and varied genus in the grass (Poaceae) family containing about 300 species of tufted evergreen and deciduous grasses. Originally found on slopes in the world's temperate and warm-temperate regions, these grasses are now widespread in ornamental gardens. They have fine-textured, linear, flat leaves that bear long panicles of feathery, often fluffy flowerheads. Some are grown for floral work, and they are often used in garden perennial borders and for roadside plantings. CULTIVATION: They need a fertile, medium to light soil in full sun. It is best to trim back deciduous species in winter to ensure good growth the next season. Propagate by division in summer or sow seed in containers in spring.

Stipa arundinacea
NEW ZEALAND WIND GRASS
☼ ❄ ↔ 4 ft (1.2 m) ↑ 3 ft (0.9 m)
Mid-sized New Zealand grass. Light green foliage, turns light orange with bronzy tones in sunlight. Spikelets of fluffy green flowers, tinted purple, in summer–autumn. Zones 8–10.

Stipa calamagrostis ★
syn. *Stipa lasiogrostis*
☼ ❄ ↔ 4 ft (1.2 m) ↑ 3 ft (0.9 m)
Deciduous perennial grass, native to southern Europe. Forms tufted clump.

Linear blue-green leaves arch slightly during the season. Bears creamy silver plumes of nodding feathery flowers, in summer. Zones 7–10.

Stipa gigantea ★
GIANT FEATHER GRASS, GOLDEN OATS
☼ ❄ ↔ 4 ft (1.2 m) ↑ 8 ft (2.4 m)
Striking large perennial grass from Spain and Portugal. Clump of green to gray-green foliage. Large loose panicles of flowers and seeds, in spring, become golden, persist through summer. Zones 8–10.

Stipa splendens
☼ ❄ ↔ 4 ft (1.2 m) ↑ 8 ft (2.4 m)
Deciduous perennial grass from Chile, central Asia, and Russia. Forms tufted mounded plant. Dark green leaves, slightly arching habit. Purple-tinted white flower spikes, in large loose panicles held above foliage, in summer. Zones 7–10.

Stokesia laevis 'Mary Gregory'

Stipa splendens

Stipa tenuissima
☼ ❄ ↔ 12 in (30 cm) ↑ 24 in (60 cm)
Perennial grass, native from Texas to Arizona, USA, Mexico, and Argentina. Almost hair-like, vertical, bright green stems and leaves, topped with soft feathery plumes of flowers and seeds that turn to straw yellow as they age. Zones 7–10.

STOKESIA
STOKES ASTER

Although there is just one species in this genus in the daisy (Asteraceae) family, it has been extensively developed in cultivation and is available in a wide range of plant sizes, flower colors, and forms. A late summer- to autumn-flowering perennial from the southeastern USA, the Stokes aster was named after Dr Jonathan Stokes, an English doctor and botanist. It arrived in England in 1766 and was in vogue in Victorian times, especially as a cut flower. It later fell from favor but is now happily popular in gardens again. It is an upright plant with 6–8 in (15–20 cm) long leaves and large cornflower-like heads of white, yellow, or mauve to deep purple-blue flowers. CULTIVATION: Plant in full sun or half-sun in light free-draining soil. Water and feed well. Watch for mildew, which may develop in late summer. Propagate by division near the end of the dormant period or they can be raised from seed.

Stokesia laevis
STOKES ASTER
◐/☼ ❄ ↔ 8–16 in (20–40 cm)
↑ 10–30 in (25–75 cm)
Found from South Carolina to Louisiana and northern Florida, USA. Narrow, deep green, lance-shaped leaves, smooth-edged, sometimes spiny-toothed at the base. Flowerheads to 4 in (10 cm) wide, occur solitary or in small clusters, usually mauve to purple. 'Blue Danube' ★, 16 in (40 cm) tall, deep blue with white center; 'Bluestone', 10 in (25 cm) tall, bright blue; 'Mary Gregory', pale yellow with a darker center; 'Purple Parasols', 20 in (50 cm) tall, deep violet-blue flowerhead to over 4 in (10 cm) wide; 'Silver Moon', 18 in (45 cm) tall, pure white; 'Wyoming', 20 in (50 cm) tall, very dark blue flowers. Zones 6–10.

STRELITZIA
Originating in South Africa, the 4 or 5 species in this genus are large evergreen perennials in the banana (Musaceae) family. Usually treated as shrubs or trees, they are clump-forming and have very long oblong to lance-shaped leaves that are borne on stout stems. A large bud or spathe borne at the end of the stem is usually held clear of the foliage; from it opens a succession of flowers, each with a long projecting corolla and wing-like calyces, often in a striking range of contrasting colors.

Stokesia laevis

Stokesia laevis 'Purple Parasols'

Strelitzia juncea

Strelitzia nicolai

CULTIVATION: They prefer full sun or partial shade, and are tender to all but the lightest frosts. Soil should be well-drained and moist, but most species will tolerate brief periods of drought once established and prefer to be kept on the dry side in winter. Roots are very strong, so take care when siting. Propagate from seed or by removing suckers. Division is possible.

Strelitzia juncea
syns *Strelitzia × kewensis* var. *juncea*, *S. reginae* var. *juncea*
☼ ❄ ↔ 3–5 ft (0.9–1.5 m) ↑ 5 ft (1.5 m)
Native to South Africa's Cape region. Thick, rush-like, grayish green leaves lack blades, tapering to point. Orange flowers emerging from beaked bract, like those of *S. reginae*. Zones 10–12.

Strelitzia nicolai
GIANT BIRD OF PARADISE, NATAL WILD BANANA
☼ ❄ ↔ 15 ft (4.5 m) ↑ 30 ft (9 m)
Found in KwaZulu-Natal and Eastern Cape, South Africa. Leaves and leaf stalks often over 4 ft (1.2 m) long. Flowers light greenish to purple-blue, white projecting corolla, open from red-brown spathes, in late spring–early summer. Zones 10–12.

Strelitzia reginae
BIRD OF PARADISE
☼ ❄ ↔ 3 ft (0.9 m) ↑ 4 ft (1.2 m)
Widely grown shrubby evergreen perennial. Leaves 12–30 in (30–75 cm) long, stems to 6 ft (1.8 m) tall. Flowers have orange calyces, deep purple-blue corolla, over 4 in (10 cm) long, in

winter–spring. 'Kirstenbosch Gold' and 'Mandela's Gold' ★, bright yellow calyces. Zones 10–12.

STREPTOCARPUS
CAPE PRIMROSE
Although widespread in the African and Asian tropics and subtropics, most of the cultivated plants in this genus of around 130 species of annuals and perennials are natives of southern Africa, and belong to the African violet (Gesneriaceae) family. A diverse lot, they range from the tiny, rosette-forming *S. saxorum* to *S. wendlandii*, which produces just one huge leaf. Despite this diversity of form they share some features. The leaves are velvety and heavily veined. The flowers are long-tubed, primrose-like and usually have 5 petals; they occur in heads on short upright stems. The name comes from the Greek *streptos*, twisted, and *karpos*, a fruit, referring to the spirally twisted fruits.
CULTIVATION: Cold tolerance varies, though none withstand more than the lightest frost. Plant in a bright but not sunny, warm, draft-free position, in fertile, moist, humus-rich, well-drained soil. Propagate by division, from leaf-stalk cuttings or from seed.

Streptocarpus baudertii
☼/☀ ✤ ↔ 16–20 in (40–50 cm) ↑ 12 in (30 cm)
Spring-flowering species native to South Africa. Forms rosettes of finely hairy, deeply veined leaves to 12 in (30 cm) long, usually held flat to the ground. The flower stems generally

support 2 pale-centered mid-pink to lilac flowers to over 1 in (25 mm) across. Zones 10–11.

Streptocarpus candidus
☼/☀ ✤ ↔ 10–16 in (25–40 cm) ↑ 12 in (30 cm)
South African species. Vertical carrot-like rhizome topped with rosettes of deep green, heavily veined, irregularly toothed leaves. Heads of up to 25 summer flowers long-tubed, white to pale mauve, usually fragrant. Zones 10–11.

Streptocarpus caulescens
☼/☀ ✤ ↔ 12–20 in (30–50 cm) ↑ 12–20 in (30–50 cm)
Erect to sprawling perennial with woody-based stems, native to Tanzania and Kenya. Broad, pointed oval leaves. Airy sprays of up to 12 white-centered purple flowers, in autumn–winter. Zones 11–12.

Streptocarpus cyaneus
☼/☀ ✤ ↔ 12–20 in (30–50 cm) ↑ 6–8 in (15–20 cm)
Species native to South Africa. Rosettes of toothed leaves to 16 in (40 cm) long. Produces dark-veined light pink to violet, funnel-shaped flowers to 3 in (8 cm) long, usually paired, on stems to 6 in (15 cm) long, in spring–summer. *S. c.* subsp. *polackii*, mauve-pink flowers, leaves and stalks red-tinted. Zones 10–11.

Streptocarpus formosus
☼/☀ ✤ ↔ 12–20 in (30–50 cm) ↑ 12 in (30 cm)
Native to South Africa. Dense rosettes of strappy leaves to over 12 in (30 cm) long. Flower stems to 12 in (30 cm) tall, few-flowered heads of funnel-shaped mauve-edged white flowers to over 2 in (5 cm) long, in spring–autumn. Zones 10–11.

Streptocarpus cyaneus subsp. *polackii*

Streptocarpus formosus

Strelitzia reginae 'Kirstenbosch Gold'

Strelitzia reginae 'Mandela's Gold'

Streptocarpus baudertii

Streptocarpus candidus

Strelitzia reginae

Streptocarpus glandulosissimus

☽/☀ ✛ ↔ 12–20 in (30–50 cm)
↑ 12–20 in (30–50 cm)

This is a Kenyan species with an upright to sprawling habit and weak stems. Downy pointed oval leaves to over 4 in (10 cm) long, often smaller. Bears airy sprays of widely flared, funnel-shaped, violet flowers, most of year. Zones 11–12.

Streptocarpus johannis

☽/☀ ✛ ↔ 8–20 in (20–50 cm)
↑ 6–12 in (15–30 cm)

Native to South Africa. Rosettes of finely hairy, deeply veined leaves to 14 in (35 cm) long. Flower stems are short, sometimes to 12 in (30 cm) tall, and usually support 2 white to pale mauve flowers, in spring. Zones 10–11.

Streptocarpus kirkii

☽/☀ ✛ ↔ 8–12 in (20–30 cm)
↑ 12–16 in (30–40 cm)

Native to Kenya and Tanzania. The erect stems become woody and trailing as they mature. Opposite pairs of sparsely hairy, pointed oval, serrated or smooth-edged leaves. In winter, produces airy sprays of up to 10 small violet-pink flowers, deep purple spots in throat. Zones 11–12.

Streptocarpus pentherianus

☽/☀ ✛ ↔ 8–14 in (20–35 cm)
↑ 4–6 in (10–15 cm)

South African native species. Produces a single large, velvety, heart-shaped leaf to over 12 in (30 cm) long. At the base of the leaf is a short flower stem carrying a few white to mauve, large-lobed funnel-shaped flowers. Zones 10–12.

Streptocarpus polyanthus

☽/☀ ✛ ↔ 8–20 in (20–50 cm)
↑ 8–12 in (20–30 cm)

Species native to South Africa. The plant often dies after blooming, but may live a few seasons. Usually 1 to 2 heavy-textured, hairy, deep green, heart-shaped leaves. Airy sprays of flat lavender flowers on short stems, in winter–summer. Zones 10–11.

Streptocarpus primulifolius

☽/☀ ✛ ↔ 12–24 in (30–60 cm)
↑ 10 in (25 cm)

This species is found in South Africa. Forms rosettes of strappy, heavily veined, downy, deep green leaves to 18 in (45 cm) long. The funnel-shaped mauve-blue flowers are produced, in heads of 1 to 4 on stems to 10 in (25 cm) tall, during the summer. Zones 10–11.

Streptocarpus johannis

Streptocarpus primulifolius

Streptocarpus saxorum

Streptocarpus saxorum

syn. *Streptocarpella saxorum*

☽/☀ ✛ ↔ 8–16 in (20–40 cm)
↑ 4–6 in (10–15 cm)

From Kenya and Tanzania. Compact, long-flowering. Low spreading clump of velvety pointed oval leaves to 1¼ in (30 mm) long. Relatively large, solitary or paired, white to pale mauve flowers, small upper lobes. Zones 10–12.

Streptocarpus wendlandii

☽/☀ ✛ ↔ 30 in (75 cm) ↑ 12 in (30 cm)

South African. Single, very large, heart-shaped, finely toothed, deep green leaf, to 30 in (75 cm) long, covered with fine hairs, red underside. Small, white to mauve, purple-marked flowers, in summer. Zones 10–12.

Streptocarpus Hybrid Cultivars

☽/☀ ✛ ↔ 12–20 in (30–50 cm)
↑ 12–20 in (30–50 cm)

Wide-ranging group of fancy-flowered, compact, rosette-forming hybrids developed by interbreeding mainly South African species. Flower most heavily

Streptocarpus wendlandii

from spring into summer, sometimes blooming sporadically year-round. Cultivated as house plants. 'Albatross', white flowers, yellow throat; 'Amanda', blue, dark-veined, white throat; 'Bethan', mauve, yellow throat; 'Blue Heaven', pale lavender, semi-double, white throat; 'Blushing Bride', white flushed pink, semi-double, long-tubed; 'Bristol's Very Best', magenta, double; 'Carys', mauve-blue, purple-blue throat and veining; 'Chorus Line', white with mauve-blue veining, double; 'Concord Blue', continual pale violet-blue flowers; 'Constant Nymph', blue, yellow throat; 'Crystal Ice', white, soft purple veining; 'Cynthia', magenta with darker lines, white tube; 'Emma',

Streptocarpus, Hybrid Cultivar, 'Bethan'

Streptocarpus, Hybrid Cultivar, 'Amanda'

Streptocarpus, HC, 'Blushing Bride'

Streptocarpus, HC, 'Blue Heaven'

Streptocarpus, Hybrid Cultivar, 'Crystal Ice'

Streptocarpus, HC, 'Carys'

Streptocarpus, HC, 'Chorus Line'

Streptocarpus, Hybrid Cultivar, 'Heidi'

Streptocarpus, Hybrid Cultivar, 'Jennifer'

Streptocarpus, Hybrid Cultivar, 'Concord Blue'

Streptocarpus, Hybrid Cultivar, 'Cynthia'

Streptocarpus, HC, 'Emma'

Streptocarpus, HC, 'Flexii White'

Streptocarpus, Hybrid Cultivar, 'Bristol's Very Best'

Streptocarpus, Hybrid Cultivar, 'Happy Snappy'

Streptocarpus, HC, 'Kim'

Streptocarpus, Hybrid Cultivar, 'Falling Stars'

Streptocarpus, HC, 'Lisa'

Streptocarpus, Hybrid Cultivar, 'Passion Pink'

Streptocarpus, HC, 'Lynette'

Streptocarpus, Hybrid Cultivar, 'Ruby'

Streptocarpus, HC, 'Megan'

Streptocarpus, HC, 'Melanie'

S., HC, 'Midnight Flame'

Streptocarpus, HC, 'Nymph'

Streptocarpus, HC, 'Rosebud'

Streptocarpus, HC, 'Tina'

Streptocarpus, Hybrid Cultivar, 'Sophie'

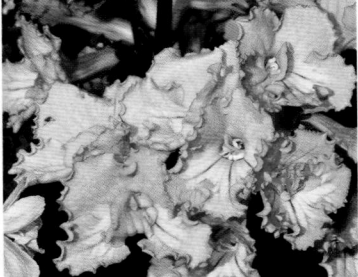

Streptocarpus, HC, 'Pink Souffle'

Streptocarpus, Hybrid Cultivar, 'Sian'

mid-pink, purple-red center; **'Falling Stars'**, pale lavender, white throat; **'Flexii White'**, white, dark purple veins; **'Happy Snappy'**, red, yellowish throat; **'Heidi'**, mauve-blue; **'Jennifer'**, dark blue, white throat; **'Kim'**, purple, white throat; **'Lisa'**, pink, white throat; **'Lynette'**, soft deep burgundy; **'Megan'**, deep purple, yellow throat; **'Melanie'**, mauve-blue, purple-pink veining; **'Midnight Flame'**, intense bright red;

'Nymph', bright purple, yellow throat; **'Party Doll'**, purple-edged, pale lavender, yellow throat; **'Passion Pink'**, deep pink with dark lines; **'Pink Souffle'**, frilly pink double; **'Rosebud'**, deep pink, double; **'Rosemary'**, light pink, double; **'Ruby'** ★, pure deep crimson; **'Sian'**, bright blue, white and yellow throat; **'Sophie'**, purple-red, dark throat; **'Tina'**, pale pink, dark pink center and veining. Zones 10–11.

Streptocarpus, Hybrid Cultivar, 'Party Doll'

Strombocactus disciformis

STREPTOSOLEN

This genus from the nightshade (Solanaceae) family is doubtfully distinct from *Browallia*. The single species is from tropical South America. It has a scrambling habit and simple alternate leaves. Popular in warm climates for its spectacular red to orange flowers.
CULTIVATION: Plant in a position in full sun with shelter from cold winds, in a light, fibrous, well-drained soil. This species should be well watered during dry weather. It is intolerant of frost. Frequent tip pruning in the first few years will help develop a densely foliaged bush and, thereafter, regular light pruning after flowering will maintain its shape. Soft-tip cuttings can be taken in late spring or summer, half-hardened cuttings in autumn.

Streptosolen jamesonii
syn. *Browallia jamesonii*
MARMALADE BUSH, ORANGE BROWALLIA
☀ ❉ ↔ 5 ft (1.5 m) ↑ 7 ft (2 m)
Evergreen shrub. Flexible branches, leaves simple, alternate, finely hairy, dark green, paler beneath. Inflorescence, dense panicle, 2 forms: one is a mixture of yellows and reds to orange, the other pure yellow flowers, in early to late spring. Zones 9–11.

STROBILANTHES

This genus of more than 250 species of evergreen or deciduous perennials and soft-stemmed shrubs is native to tropical Asia and Madagascar, and belongs to the acanthus (Acanthaceae) family. A few species are grown both indoors and out for their attractive tubular or funnel-shaped flowers, in varying shades of blue and purple. *Strobilanthes* species have colorful purplish foliage; the opposite paired leaves are frequently of unequal size.
CULTIVATION: Frost tender, these plants require a warm climate and prefer full sun or semi-shade in well-drained humus-enriched soil. Prune lightly to shape, or clip to form a hedge. The new growth has the most attractive coloring. Propagate from seed, cuttings, or by division.

Strobilanthes anisophyllus
GOLDFUSSIA
☀ ❉ ↔ 5 ft (1.5 m) ↑ 5 ft (1.5 m)
Bushy shrub native to Assam in northern India. Narrow silvery purple leaves in unequal-sized pairs. Tubular flowers, lavender-blue, 1 in (25 mm) long, ends of branches, in late summer–autumn. Zones 10–11.

Strobilanthes dyerianus
syn. *Perilepta dyeriana*
☀ ❉ ↔ 3 ft (0.9 m) ↑ 3 ft (0.9 m)
Originally a native of Myanmar. Evergreen shrub grown mostly as an indoor plant for its attractive foliage. Lanceshaped iridescent purple leaves, to 6 in (15 cm) long, toothed edges. Bears short spikes of funnel-shaped, pale blue flowers, above the leaves, in spring–summer. Zones 10–12.

Strobilanthes gossypinus
☀ ❉ ↔ 20–30 in (50–75 cm) ↑ 3–5 ft (0.9–1.5 m)
Shrubby species native to southern India and Sri Lanka. Green leaves, 2–4 in (5–10 cm) long, lance-shaped, tapering to a fine point, densely coated with cream hairs. Small heads of soft blue to lavender flowers clustered at the stem tip and in the upper leaf axils, in summer. Zones 10–12.

STROMANTHE

This genus of 15 species of leafy perennials growing 3–10 ft (0.9–3 m) high belongs to the arrowroot (Marantaceae) family. In their native Central and South America they grow on the forest floor where they are rampant and often weedy. Their appearance is similar to related plants such as *Ctenanthe* and *Maranta* with long oblong ornamental leaves, which emerge from sheathed stems. The leaves are often marked or veined with white or lighter or darker shades of green. Although they are grown as house plants for their foliage, the flowers often have showy colorful bracts, which add interest to their ornamental appeal.
CULTIVATION: In suitably warm climates grow in a shady and sheltered

Streptosolen jamesonii

position. In temperate climates they are widely cultivated as indoor plants. Grow in bright filtered light in a rich soil mix. During active growth, water moderately and apply liquid fertilizer fortnightly. Propagation is by division or cuttings.

Stromanthe sanguinea
☀/❉ ❉ ↔ 2–3 ft (0.6–0.9 m) ↑ 3–5 ft (0.9–1.5 m)
A handsome foliage plant that is native to Brazil. The large, thick, glossy oblong leaves, emerge from pinkish red sheaths, dark green above, purple beneath. Produces white flowers with showy red floral bracts. 'Stripestar' has leaves with distinctive white stripes. Zones 10–12.

STROMBOCACTUS
TOP CACTUS
A monotypic genus from Mexico in the cactus (Cactaceae) family whose botanical name comes from the Greek *strombo*, a spinning top, referring to the general shape of the plant. This plant has long fascinated botanists and collectors alike because of its small size and the spiral arrangement of its tubercles. *Strombocactus* is so rare in the wild that it has made it into the threatened list of plants in Appendix I of CITES.
CULTIVATION: This slow-growing rarity requires a purely mineralized soil and very careful watering. It is usually grown from seed since the plants are normally solitary but is also grafted to produce offsets, which can then be regrafted or grown on their own roots as cuttings that need to be dried out for several weeks before planting. The plants must be rested in winter. Cultivating *Strombocactus* is a challenge to all but experienced growers.

Strombocactus disciformis
☀ ❉ ↔ 1–3½ in (25–90 mm) ↑ ¾–5 in (18–120 mm)
Generally solitary cactus from Mexico. Olive green to bluish gray plant, spherical to flattened spherical, depressed woolly center. Ribs absent, tubercles close, in spirals, areoles on tips. Spines 1–4, weak, usually absent from the mature stems. Flowers funnel-form, cream to magenta, in summer. Seed pods magenta, elongated. Zones 9–10.

STRONGYLODON

This genus, comprising 12 species of vigorous evergreen or deciduous shrubs or twining climbers, is native to tropical areas from the island of Madagascar eastward to Polynesia but is especially numerous in the Philippines. It belongs to the pea-flower subfamily of the legume (Fabaceae) family. The compound leaves consist of 3 leaflets. Peaflowers are borne in long, spectacular racemes; the seed pods are large and do not split open at maturity.

Stromanthe sanguinea 'Stripestar'

Strobilanthes gossypinus

S

CULTIVATION: Grow outside in the tropics, in a heated greenhouse in temperate areas. Plants raised from seeds are slow to reach flowering size; air-layering or propagation by cuttings gives quicker results.

Strongylodon macrobotrys
EMERALD CREEPER, JADE VINE

☼/◑ ⚘ ↔ 5–10 ft (1.5–3 m)
↑ 20–40 ft (6–12 m)

Tall woody climber from the Philippines. Dark green 3-part leaves, open pinkish bronze. Large, waxy, claw-like flowers, luminous bluish green or jade, in pendulous racemes, to 40 in (100 cm) long, in spring. Zones 11–12.

STROPHANTHUS

This genus belongs to the dogbane (Apocynaceae) family and contains 38 species of evergreen shrubs and small trees found in tropical regions of Africa and Asia. These plants often have a semi-climbing habit and the stems contain a milky latex. The leaves may be opposite or whorled. The showy flowers are funnel-shaped, and in some species the petal lobes are long and narrow. Strophanthin, a drug that acts in a similar way to digitalis (a heart muscle stimulant), is extracted from the seeds of some species. It was

Strongylodon macrobotrys

Strophanthus gratus

introduced into medicine in 1890 by Sir Thomas Fraser, who discovered its digitalis-like action while he was studying African arrow poisons.
CULTIVATION: In subtropical and tropical climates these plants can be grown outdoors in a fertile soil that is moist but well drained. In cooler climates they can be grown in the greenhouse. Propagation is from seed or from hardwood cuttings taken in the spring.

Strophanthus gratus
CLIMBING OLEANDER, INDIA RUBBER VINE

☼ ❄ ↔ 10 ft (3 m) ↑ 10–15 ft (3–4.5 m)

Spreading semi-climbing shrub native to tropical western Africa. Leathery olive green leaves. Showy clusters of tubular white flowers, flushed pink or purple, rounded petal lobes have crimped edges. Zones 10–12.

Strophanthus speciosus
CORKSCREW FLOWER

☼ ❄ ↔ 10 ft (3 m) ↑ 10 ft (3 m)

Bushy spreading shrub from South Africa. Leaves in whorls of 3 to 4, leathery texture. Creamy yellow flowers marked with red, narrow petal lobes long and twisted, in summer–autumn. Ground seeds have been used for arrow-tip poison. Zones 10–12.

Strophanthus speciosus

Strychnos decussata

STRYCHNOS

This genus of around 150 species of woody climbers, shrubs, and small trees, from the logania (Loganiaceae) family, occurs mainly in tropical and subtropical regions of the world. Some species contain highly toxic alkaloids, most notably *Strychnos nux-vomica*, the chief source of the drug strychnine for rodent control. The plants have fairly large, smooth-edged, oval leaves borne in opposite pairs at right angles to each other, with 3 to 5 major veins originating from the base of the leaf. Often spines are present in the leaf axils. The creamy white, funnel-shaped or bell-shaped flowers, borne in small clusters at the ends of branches, are often perfumed, sometimes unpleasantly. The rounded berry-like fruit has a smooth hard rind or shell and fleshy juicy pulp.
CULTIVATION: Most species are suited to only warm-temperate to tropical climates and prefer well-drained acidic soils in a sunny to part-shaded position. Provide supplementary watering during extended dry periods. Propagate from seed or from cuttings.

Strychnos arborea
STRYCHNINE TREE

☼ ❄ ↔ 20 ft (6 m) ↑ 40 ft (12 m)

Tree from northeastern Australia. Broad oval leaves to 2½ in (6 cm) long. Clusters of small white flowers, dense fringe of hairs at mouth, in summer. Round orange-red fruit to about ½ in (12 mm) diameter. Zones 9–12.

Strychnos decussata
CAPE TEAK, CHAKA'S WOOD

☼ ⚘ ↔ 15 ft (4.5 m) ↑ 30 ft (9 m)

Small tree from eastern South Africa and tropical East Africa. Fluted trunk, smooth gray bark, smallish leaves glossy dark green. Small greenish white flowers in loose clusters, in spring to early summer. Globular orange or red berries. Zones 10–12.

Stylidium graminifolium

Strychnos spinosa
NATAL ORANGE

☼ ❄ ↔ 12 ft (3.5 m) ↑ 20 ft (6 m)

Spiny shrub or small tree native to Madagascar, and tropical and southern Africa. Leathery oval leaves. Greenish white star-shaped flowers in clusters, in spring. Yellow edible fruit, 4 in (10 cm) long. Zones 10–12.

STYLIDIUM
TRIGGERPLANT

This genus, belonging to the self-named triggerplant (Stylidiaceae) family, contains around 110 species of perennials. Most are native to Australia where they often grow in sandy coastal areas. The foliage is usually grass-like, sometimes with short leaves on narrow stems. Dainty flowers of white, pink, or yellow are borne on upright spikes in summer. Stamens and stigma are fused in a column; when an insect alights on the flower, they react like a trigger, hitting the insect's back and thereby transferring pollen. This trigger mechanism, which is only activated on warm sunny days, gives the genus its common name.
CULTIVATION: In very warm dry areas, plant in well-drained sandy soil, but these plants are better suited to pot culture. In cool temperate climates grow in the greenhouse in full light in a sandy potting mix. Water moderately when in growth but keep almost dry in winter. Propagate from seed, division, or cuttings.

Stylidium graminifolium
TRIGGERPLANT

☼ ❄ ↔ 10 in (25 cm)
↑ 10–20 in (25–50 cm)

Variable perennial from eastern and southern Australia where it is found from coastal to mountain regions. Stiff grass-like leaves. Pale pink to magenta flowers in spikes on hairy stems, in summer. Zones 9–11.

Stylidium lineare

☀ ❄ ↔ 4 in (10 cm) ↑ 6–12 in (15–30 cm)

Native to New South Wales, Australia. Small plant forming rosettes of short narrow leaves. Upright central stems bear spikes of pink flowers, in summer and autumn. Zones 9–11.

STYLOPHORUM

Genus, in the poppy (Papaveraceae) family, containing 3 species of hairy perennials, is native to eastern Asia and eastern North America where they grow in woodlands. When cut they ooze a yellow or red sap. The foliage is attractive, forming basal rosettes of long divided leaves, irregularly lobed and toothed. The stem leaves are much smaller and usually stalkless. Clear yellow or orange 4-petalled saucer-shaped flowers are borne in small clusters in spring. They are followed by narrow cylindrical seed pods covered in fine silvery hairs. The yellow sap from *S. diphyllum* was used by the American Indians in dye making.

Stylidium lineare

Stylidium lineare

CULTIVATION: *Stylophorum* species are woodland plants suitable for shady positions in the garden. Unlike most plants in the poppy family, which resent disturbance, these plants can be readily transplanted, and will grow in any reasonably fertile moist but well-drained soil. Propagate from seed or by division.

Stylophorum diphyllum
CELANDINE POPPY, WOOD POPPY

☀ ❄ ↔ 12 in (30 cm) ↑ 18 in (45 cm)

Downy perennial native to the eastern USA. Leaves deeply and irregularly lobed with scalloped or toothed margins. Simple yellow flowers, to 2 in (5 cm) wide, on delicate stems, in spring. Zones 5–9.

Stylophorum lasiocarpum
CHINESE CELANDINE POPPY

☀ ❄ ↔ 12 in (30 cm) ↑ 12 in (30 cm)

Perennial native to central and eastern China. Long irregularly lobed and toothed leaves rather like those of the dandelion (*Taraxacum* species). Clear yellow flowers, in clusters, 4–5 in (10–12 cm) wide, in spring. Zones 5–9.

STYPHELIA

This genus is a member of the epacris (Epacridaceae) family, with all 14 species occurring in Australia. Other species have been placed in this genus in the past, but are now correctly placed in other genera. All species are woody shrubs, often sparsely branched; some are small, some almost prostrate. Their leaves are stiff with parallel veins and a sharp point. The green, pink, or red flowers are long and tubular with the 5 petals rolled back, exposing the hairy interior and leaving the stamens protruding. CULTIVATION: These plants require acid soils that are free draining but do not dry out. Organic matter in the soil and mulching seem to improve the chances of success. Propagation is not easy, unfortunately; cuttings do not strike readily and seed germination is slow and erratic.

Styphelia tubiflora

Stylophorum diphyllum

Styphelia adscendens

☀ ❄ ↔ 12–24 in (30–60 cm) ↑ 8–18 in (20–45 cm)

Small shrub from heath habitats in southern states of Australia. Leaves lance-shaped, sharp point. Yellowish green flowers ½–¾ in (12–18 mm) long in leaf axils, in winter–spring. Not commonly cultivated. Zones 8–9.

Styphelia tubiflora

☀ ❄ ↔ 30 in (75 cm) ↑ 24 in (60 cm)

Straggly shrub, occurs only in New South Wales, Australia, on soils derived from sandstone. Leaves narrow, sharp point. Red flowers, 1 in (25 mm) long, in winter. Small berry-like fruits containing 5 seeds. Zones 8–9.

STYRAX

Found over much of the northern temperate and subtropical zones, this genus gives its name to the storax (Styracaceae) family. It includes some 100 species of deciduous and evergreen shrubs and trees. Foliage is usually a simple rounded leaf with serrated edges, obvious veins, and a pointed tip. The leaves are usually small to medium-sized, but a few species have attractive, large, felted leaves. The flowers, which are usually fragrant, hang in clusters beneath the foliage of the previous season's wood. They are white, occasionally with a flush of pink, and open in spring to be followed by 1- to 2-seeded drupes. CULTIVATION: They prefer a cool moist climate with clearly defined seasons that is not too cold in winter. Hardiness varies with species' native range. Propagate from seed, which often needs stratification to germinate well, or by taking cuttings in summer.

Stylophorum lasiocarpum

Styrax americanus ★

☀ ❄ ↔ 8 ft (2.4 m) ↑ 10 ft (3 m)

Deciduous shrub from southeastern USA. Gray-brown branches, thinly coated with golden down when young. Dark green leaves usually elliptical, serrated edges, pale, downy undersides. Pendulous clusters, up to 4 flowers, in late spring. Zones 6–10.

Styrax benzoin
BENZOIN

☀ ❄ ↔ 10–20 ft (3–6 m) ↑ 20 ft (6 m)

Evergreen tree, originating in the highlands of Sumatra, Indonesia. Stout trunk and main branches, heavy covering of resinous gray-brown bark. Leaves 4–6 in (10–15 cm) long, finely toothed along edges. Flower panicles carry up to 20 small white blooms. Zones 10–11.

Styrax dasyanthus

☀ ❄ ↔ 10–15 ft (3–4.5 m) ↑ 25 ft (8 m)

Large evergreen shrub or small tree; occurs naturally in south-central China. Dark gray bark; leaves with finely toothed edges. Racemes of white flowers, often partly hidden by the foliage, in late spring–early summer. Zones 9–10.

S

Styrax grandifolius
BIG-LEAFED SNOWBELL

☀ ❄ ↔ 15 ft (4.5 m) ↑ 15 ft (4.5 m)

Deciduous large shrub or small tree native to southeastern USA. The leaves are large, and like the young stems and flower buds, have a downy coating. The undersides of the leaves are gray, yellowish elsewhere. Fragrant flowers are produced in racemes in the spring. Zones 8–10.

Styrax japonicus
JAPANESE SNOWBELL, JAPANESE SNOWDROP TREE, SNOWBELL TREE

☀ ❄ ↔ 15 ft (4.5 m) ↑ 20–30 ft (6–9 m)

Deciduous tree from Japan. Lightly branched. Downy young stems. Leaves glossy dark green, shallowly toothed edges. Short pendulous flower clusters, are produced in late spring–early summer. 'Fargesii', vigorous cultivar with larger leaves; 'Pink Chimes', pale pink flowers. Zones 5–9.

Styrax obassia
BIG-LEAFED STORAX, FRAGRANT SNOWBELL

☀ ❄ ↔ 20 ft (6 m) ↑ 35 ft (10 m)

This is a beautiful tree native to Japan. Rounded oval leaves to 8 in (20 cm) long, dark green, very fine serrations, densely downy, beneath. Flowers, carried on 4–8 in (10–20 cm) long racemes, are produced in late spring. Zones 6–10.

Styrax japonicus 'Fargesii'

Styrax wilsonii

☀ ❄ ↔ 8 ft (2.4 m) ↑ 8–10 ft (2.4–3 m)

Deciduous shrub from western China, sometimes small tree. Leaves rarely over 1 in (25 mm) long, felted undersides, 3 to 5 small teeth. Small flowers, in clusters of 3 to 5 blooms, stud the branches, in early summer. Zones 7–10.

SUCCISA

This genus in the teasel (Dipsacaceae) family contains one species of perennial native to Europe, northern Africa, and western Asia, and naturalized in northeastern USA. Its natural habitat is wet grassy places in heath or open forest. The plant forms a basal rosette of oblong to lance-shaped leaves that are lightly downy. Slender flowering stems can be up to 40 in (100 cm) tall. The pincushion flowers are usually dark purple, occasionally pink or white, and appear in late summer to autumn.

Styrax japonicus

CULTIVATION: Grow in sun or part shade in moist soil. Suitable for planting informally in wildflower meadows. Mowing meadows should be delayed until late autumn to allow the plants to seed. Propagate by division or seed.

Succisa pratensis
DEVIL'S BIT SCABIOUS

☀/☀ ❄ ↔ 6–12 in (15–30 cm) ↑ 12–40 in (30–100 cm)

Perennial with short rootstock and basal rosettes of narrow oblong leaves. Stem leaves narrower and sometimes toothed. Flowerheads to 1 in (25 mm) wide, appear from axils of purple-tipped leafy bracts, in the summer to autumn. Zones 5–9.

SUTERA

This genus of about 130 perennials and annuals from the foxglove (Scrophulariaceae) family originates from South Africa. They have become well known in recent years as hanging basket plants. Breeders all over the world have been working to produce new colors of these reliable plants. Small, rounded, toothed, green leaves sit on thin stems that hug the ground. Starry white, mauve, lilac, pink, or blue flowers sit face-up on the foliage and the plants can flower for up to 10 months of the year.

Succisa pratensis

CULTIVATION: Require free-draining fertile soil and are adaptable to sun and shade. During the warmer months they need extra water to keep blooming. Propagate from stem cuttings in the autumn or by sowing seed in spring.

Sutera cordata
syn. *Bacopa cordata*

☀ ❧ ↔ 20 in (50 cm) ↑ 3 in (8 cm)

Low-growing, ground covering plant, pale green leaves throughout year. Pure white flowers with a delicate yellow eye appear almost year round in warmer climates. 'Snowflake' bears tiny white flowers in leaf axils. Zones 9–10.

Sutera grandiflora
PURPLE MORNING GLORY PLANT

☀ ❧ ↔ 24 in (60 cm) ↑ 40 in (100 cm)

Bushy perennial plant; elliptical green leaves. Lavender-blue flowers, white throat, in summer–autumn. Zones 9–11.

Sutera Hybrid Cultivars

☀ ❧ ↔ 27 in (70 cm) ↑ 4 in (10 cm)

Creeping perennials with dull green foliage. 'Blue Showers' has lilac to pale blue flowers, in early spring, continuing until the colder months; 'Lavender Showers', pale lavender star-shaped flowers; 'Snowstorm' ★, large pure white flowers, more compact plant habit. Zones 9–10.

Sutera, Hybrid Cultivar, 'Blue Showers'

Sutera, Hybrid Cultivar, 'Lavender Showers'

Sutera cordata

Sutera, Hybrid Cultivar, 'Snowstorm'

S

SUTHERLANDIA
BALLOON PEA

The 5 species of evergreen shrubs in this genus from the pea-flower sub-family of the legume (Fabaceae) family are natives of South Africa. They have pinnate leaves made up of many small finely hairy leaflets. The red to purple pea-flowers have a large keel, and are followed by inflated bladder-like seed pods, hence the common name.
CULTIVATION: Apart from being some-what susceptible to frost damage, *Sutherlandia* species are easily grown in any light well-drained soil in full sun. Seedlings grow quickly and will often flower in their first year; in cool winter areas with long summers it is possible to treat the plants as annuals. Cut back older plants to keep them compact. Propagate from seed, which germinates more evenly if soaked be-fore sowing, or from half-hardened summer cuttings.

Sutherlandia frutescens
BALLOON PEA, CAPE BLADDER PEA, DUCK PLANT

☀ ❄ ↔ 5 ft (1.5 m) ↑ 5 ft (1.5m)
Found in open areas and dry wood-lands of southern Africa. Softwooded shrub with drooping pinnate foliage, with 13 to 21, small, finely hairy leaflets. Pendulous clusters of orange-red flowers, in late winter. The inflated pale green, occasionally red-tinged, seed pods ripen quickly. Zones 9–11.

Sutherlandia montana
BERGKANKERBOSSIE

☀ ❄ ↔ 30 in (75 cm) ↑ 2–4 ft (0.6–1.2 m)
This South African shrub has silver-gray branches and small oblong leaves. Flowers bright red, in late spring. Able to withstand more cold if kept dry in winter. Zones 8–11.

Swainsona sejuncta

SWAINSONA

Around 50 species of perennials and subshrubs from the pea-flower sub-family of the legume (Fabaceae) family; all but one species in this genus are Australian natives. They are legumi-nous and have small racemes of ridged pea-flowers, often red or pink, but also occur in mauve- or white-flow-ered forms. The foliage is pinnate, usually with many small leaflets often gray-green and covered in fine downy hairs. The flowering season varies: some species bloom in winter, others in spring–summer, and those from very arid areas burst into bloom after rain.
CULTIVATION: Although some species tolerate very light frosts, most perform best in a mild frost-free climate in full sun. They vary in their soil require-ments; those from hot arid areas prefer to be dry over winter, while those from cooler zones require constant moisture. Good drainage is also most important. Propagation is from seed, which needs to be soaked before sowing, or from half-hardened summer cuttings.

Swainsona formosa

Swainsona formosa
syn. *Clianthus formosus*
GLORY PEA, STURT'S DESERT PEA

☀ ❄ ↔ 3–7 ft (0.9–2 m)
↑ 3–4 ft (0.9–1.2 m)
Sprawling subshrub. Silky, grayish green, pinnate leaves. The showy pea-flowers are borne in clusters of 5 to 6; flowers to 3 in (8 cm) long, black spot, brilliant red, from winter–summer. Zones 9–11.

Swainsona galegifolia

☀ ❄ ↔ 6 ft (1.8 m) ↑ 24 in (60 cm)
Upright or trailing perennial or soft-wooded shrub from eastern Australia. Gray- to dark green pinnate leaves, 25 tiny leaflets edged with fine hairs. Pink, mauve, purple, white, reddish purple pea-flowers, appear in spring–summer. Zones 9–11.

Swainsona sejuncta

☀ ✢ ↔ 5 ft (1.5 m) ↑ 3 ft (0.9 m)
Attractive small shrub from eastern Australia, rarely found in cultivation. Flowers occur in a range of colors: yellow, orange, pink, and white. They require light very well-drained soil. Zones 10–11.

SWIETENIA
MAHOGANY

From the tropical regions of Central America and the West Indies, this is a small genus of about 3 species of ever-green or semi-deciduous trees belong-ing to the mahogany (Meliaceae) family. Grown as shade and street trees in the tropics, they are highly prized for their reddish brown hard-wood timber, commercially known as mahogany, that is used in cabinetwork, paneling, and ship-building. Large pinnate leaves have smooth shiny leaf-lets. Small, 5-petalled, greenish white flowers are borne in panicles in the leaf axils or at the ends of branches. Woody capsules contain winged seeds.
CULTIVATION: Frost tender, they need a sunny protected position in a deep well-drained soil. Provide supplemen-tary watering during dry periods. Propagate from seed or cuttings.

Sutherlandia frutescens

S

Syagrus romanzoffiana

Swietenia macrophylla

Syagrus sancona

Swietenia macrophylla

HONDURAS MAHOGANY

☼ ✣ ↔ 25 ft (8 m) ↑ 150 ft (45 m)

Tall, straight, evergreen tree native to lowland tropical American forests, much shorter in cultivation. Pinnate leaves, 8 to 12 lance-shaped leaflets. Large, woody fruits, chestnut brown winged seeds. Cultivated for timber. Zones 10–12.

Swietenia mahogani

WEST INDIES MAHOGANY

☼ ✣ ↔ 15 ft (4.5 m) ↑ 80 ft (24 m)

Dome-shaped West Indian tree. Pinnate leaves, 4–8 in (10–20 cm) long, 4 or 5 oval leaflets. Small greenish yellow flowers, in clusters, in spring. Large woody fruits, 4 in (10 cm) wide. Provided the original mahogany for seventeenth-century European cabinetmakers. Zones 11–12.

SYAGRUS

syn. *Arecastrum*

This genus in the palm (Arecaceae) family consists of 32 species native to South America. Their fronds have a feathery appearance. Trunks may be single or clustered (some species are trunkless) and become smooth and ringed with age. Separate male and female flowers are produced in panicles on the same tree, followed by fibrous fleshy fruit. Some species are a source of palm kernel oil and wax. Most are suitable for growing in tropical and subtropical regions. *S. romanzoffiana* is suited to temperate areas. They may be grown as indoor plants but other palms from different genera are often better suited to indoor cultivation. CULTIVATION: Most are adaptable and very hardy once established. They perform best in a well-drained moderately fertile soil with adequate watering and added fertilizer. They tolerate seaside conditions and will grow in full sun to part-shade. Remove old fronds. Propagate from seed. These palms will transplant readily.

Syagrus flexuosa

ACUMA, PALMITO DO CAMPO

☼ ✣ ↔ 7–15 ft (2–4.5 m)
↑ 7–15 ft (2–4.5 m)

Solitary-trunked or clumping palm from Brazil. Crown of arching gray fronds. Narrow leaflets arranged in groups of 2 to 4 along stem. Flowering spikes borne within leaves. Zones 10–12.

Syagrus romanzoffiana ★

syns *Arecastrum romanzoffianum, Cocos plumosa*

COCOS PALM, QUEEN PALM

☼ ✤ ↔ 25 ft (8 m) ↑ 50 ft (15 m)

Palm native to Brazil. Gray trunk, thick head of deep green plume-like fronds to 15 ft (4.5 m) long. Cream flowers in panicles. The large heavy bunches of fat, orange, edible fruits, are highly favored by bats and insects. Zones 9–12.

Syagrus sancona

☼ ✤ ↔ 20 ft (6 m) ↑ 20–40 ft (6–12 m)

A rainforest palm native to South America. Single-trunked, with a graceful crown of arching fronds to 12 ft (3.5 m) long. Narrow leaflets arranged in groups of 2 to 4. Zones 10–12.

SYMPHORICARPOS

CORALBERRY, SNOWBERRY

Allied to the honeysuckles (*Lonicera*) the 17 deciduous shrubs in this genus from the woodbine (Caprifoliaceae) family are mainly found in North and Central America, with 1 species from China. They have opposite pairs of usually simple leaves with blunt rounded tips. The small white or pink flowers that appear in spring may be carried singly or in clusters. The fruit is really the dominating feature of most species. The berry-like drupes are near-spherical, and last well into the winter when they stand out clearly on the then leafless stems. CULTIVATION: Most species are very frost hardy and prefer to grow in a distinctly seasonal temperate climate. They are not fussy about soil type as long as it is well drained, but will crop more freely if fed well and watered during dry spells. Plant in sun or partial shade and prune or trim to shape in winter after the fruit has past its best. Propagation is most often from winter hardwood cuttings.

Symphoricarpos albus ★

COMMON SNOWBERRY, SNOWBERRY

☼ ❋ ↔ 4–6 ft (1.2–1.8 m) ↑ 4–6 ft (1.2–1.8 m)

Shrub with slightly differing varieties over most of North America. Wiry stems, suckering habit. Clusters of small pink flowers, in spring. Berries, pale green at first, ripen to a strikingly pure white. *S. a.* var. *laevigatus* (syn. *S. rivularis*) native to western North America, upright habit, forms dense thickets, fruits more heavily than eastern forms. Zones 3–9.

Symphoricarpos × chenaultii

CHENAULT CORALBERRY

☼ ❋ ↔ 5 ft (1.5 m) ↑ 6–8 ft (1.8–2.4 m)

This is a garden hybrid between *S. microphyllus* and *S. orbiculatus*. Deciduous shrub, downy young stems, dark green leaves, glaucous, slightly downy beneath. Small spikes of pink flowers near branch tips, in summer. Red-and-white spotted or mottled fruits. 'Hancock', low spreading habit, rarely exceeds 20 in (50 cm) high. Zones 5–9.

Symphoricarpos albus var. *laevigatus*

Symphoricarpos × chenaultii 'Hancock'

Symphoricarpos mollis

☼ ❄ ↔3 ft (0.9 m) ↑3 ft (0.9 m)

From western USA. Compact shrub, velvety new stems and young leaves. Foliage downy on undersides. Inconspicuous pinkish white flowers, in the spring. White berries, ¼ in (6 mm) in diameter. Zones 7–9.

Symphoricarpos orbiculatus

CORALBERRY, INDIAN CURRANT

☼ ❄ ↔6 ft (1.8 m) ↑6 ft (1.8 m)

From eastern USA and Mexico. Dark green leaves, gray undersides, red tints in autumn. Flowers white, flushed pink, in summer. Small berries ripen from dull white to deep red, various colors on bush at one time. Zones 3–9.

SYMPHYANDRA

RING BELLFLOWER

This genus, which comprises some 12 rather short-lived perennial species, occurs from the eastern Mediterranean region to central Asia, and belongs to the bellflower (Campanulaceae) family. They differ from *Campanula* merely in the anthers being united to form a collar around the style. The basal leaves are often heart-shaped and toothed, with long stalks. The flowers are held in racemes or panicles. The calyx has 5 long lobes. The corolla is bell-shaped with 5 lobes. There are 5 stamens with free filaments and united anthers. The fruit is a capsule. CULTIVATION: These plants suit the herbaceous border or rock garden in temperate areas. They grow best in good well-drained soils. Some die after flowering, though setting seed freely. They can be propagated by careful division of the fleshy rootstocks or by seed sown in autumn.

Symphyandra hofmannii

☼/❉ ❄ ↔6–12 in (15–30 cm) ↑12–24 in (30–60 cm)

Rosette-forming perennial from Bosnia and Herzegovina. Can be monocarpic in cultivation. Leaves oval to lance-shaped. Pendulous cream or pale yellow bell-flowers, borne in racemes, in summer. Zones 4–9.

SYMPHYTUM

COMFREY, KNITBONE

This genus contains 35 species of hardy perennials belonging to the borage (Boraginaceae) family. Of temperate Eurasian origin, they favor damp woodlands, streamsides, and wasteland. Plants are characterized by vigorous growth and prolific flowering. A basal rosette of coarse tapering leaves emerges from a fleshy tap root. Clusters of small bell-shaped flowers,

red-tipped in bud, reddish to blue in bloom, are arranged in 1-sided coils at the tips of branching stems. Hummingbirds are attracted to the flowers. Comfrey has a long history of use in the treatment of bruises and broken bones. If taken internally in quantity, it could be carcinogenic. CULTIVATION: Comfreys favor damp soil and will grow in full sun or partial shade. They are adaptable to dry conditions where their growth is restrained. They can be grown in full sun in cold climates if the soil is heavy and moisture-retentive. Control and propagate by chopping out extra growth; cut back after blooming.

Symphytum asperum

PRICKLY COMFREY

☼ ❄ ↔5–7 ft (1.5–2 m) ↑4–5 ft (1.2–1.5 m)

From Europe, the Caucasus region, and Iran. Oval bristly leaves to 10 in (25 cm) long. Tubular flowers to ¾ in (18 mm) long, start pink, ageing to blue or lilac, in summer. Zones 5–10.

Symphytum caucasicum

☼ ❄ ↔24–32 in (60–80 cm) ↑24–32 in (60–80 cm)

Native to the Caucasus region. Basal leaves mid-green, 10 in (25 cm) long. Flared trumpets of rich blue flowers to ½ in (12 mm) long, in summer. 'Eminence', smaller than the species leaves gray tinged, blue flowers produced in early summer. Zones 5–10.

Symphytum 'Goldsmith' ★

syns *Symphytum ibericum* 'Jubilee', *S. i.* 'Variegatum'

☼/❉ ❄ ↔12–20 in (30–50 cm) ↑10–12 in (25–30 cm)

Spreading bristly perennial. Leaves to 10 in (25 cm) long, irregularly and broadly edged with yellow. Drooping

blue and white flowers, to ¾ in (18 mm) long, open from pink buds, late spring–early summer. Zones 5–10.

Symphytum grandiflorum

☼ ❄ ↔20–24 in (50–60 cm) ↑15–16 in (38–40 cm)

From Europe and the Caucasus region. Bristly leaves to 10 in (25 cm) long. Trumpet shaped flowers open to pale yellow from red-tipped buds, in late spring–early summer. Zones 5–10.

Symphytum 'Hidcote Blue'

☼ ❄ ↔18–20 in (45–50 cm) ↑18–20 in (45–50 cm)

Hybrid with leaves to 10 in (25 cm) long. Red buds, pale blue trumpets, to ¾ in (18 mm) long, in late spring–early summer. Zones 5–10.

Symphytum ibericum

syn. *Symphytum grandiflorum* of gardens

☼/❉ ❄ ↔12 in (30 cm) ↑16 in (40 cm)

Creeping rhizomatous perennial native to Turkey and eastern Europe. Hairy oval leaves. Clusters of pendulous tubular cream flowers, in spring–summer. Can be invasive. Zones 5–10.

Symphytum officinale

COMFREY, COMMON COMFREY, ENGLISH COMFREY

☼/◉ ❄ ↔6 ft (1.8 m) ↑5 ft (1.5 m)

Vigorous plant with rangy habit from temperate Eurasia. Bell-shaped flowers in drooping clusters, rose-purple crimson, mauve crimson, white, in late spring–early summer. 'Variegatum', non-invasive, leaf margins are white. Zones 3–9.

Symphytum tuberosum

☼ ❄ ↔36–40 in (90–100 cm) ↑18–24 in (45–60 cm)

Tuberous perennial from Europe. Hairy stems. Leaves to 10 in (25 cm) long.

Drooping pale yellow flowers to ¾ in (2 cm) wide, long green sepals cover up to half of flower, in early summer. Zones 5–10.

Symphytum × *uplandicum*

syn. *Symphytum peregrinum*

RUSSIAN COMFREY

☼/◉ ❄ ↔4 ft (1.2 m) ↑6 ft (1.8 m)

Bristly plant of garden origin, may be a natural hybrid of *S. officinale* and *S. asperum*. Heavy clusters of rose-purple flowers, late spring–late summer. Use as a background plant. Has been used for cattle fodder. 'Variegatum', lilac flowers, yellow edged mid-green leaves. Zones 3–9.

SYMPLOCOS

This genus gives its name to the family Symplocaceae. It consists of 250 species of trees and shrubs, some evergreen and some deciduous, occurring in woodlands in Asia, Australasia, and North and South America, in tropical and warm-temperate regions. Their leaves are simple and alternate. Some of the species accumulate aluminum in their tissues and these have yellow-green leaves and blue fruits. Other species have egg-shaped fruits that are black, purple, or white. The flowers are yellow or white and are borne in a variety of inflorescences.

Symphytum officinale

Symphytum grandiflorum

Symphytum 'Goldsmith'

CULTIVATION: Well-drained, acid to neutral soils are required, in a full sun position. The species in cultivation respond well to regular feeding. The frost tolerance varies between species, depending upon the climate of their original habitat. Propagation is from fresh seed or cuttings, both methods are quite reliable.

Symplocos paniculata
SAPPHIRE BERRY

☀ ❄ ↔15 ft (4.5 m) ↕15 ft (4.5 m)

Deciduous, bushy spreading shrub or small tree from eastern Asia and the Himalayas. Oval, slightly hairy, dark green leaves, toothed margins. Small, white, sweet-smelling flowers in clusters, in late spring–summer. Egg-shaped blue fruits. Zones 7–9.

SYNADENIUM
This genus contains about 20 species of succulent shrubs and small trees native to central and east Africa and the Mascarene Islands. Belonging to the euphorbia (Euphorbiaceae) family, they are closely related to *Euphorbia* and similarly have smooth fleshy stems that contain a milky sap. A few species are grown for their ornamental leaves, which are alternate, lance-shaped or

Synadenium compactum 'Variegatum'

oval and rather fleshy. All parts of the plant are highly poisonous, and contact with the sap can irritate the eyes, mouth, and skin.

CULTIVATION: Most species prefer a warm dry climate. Grow in full sun in a moderately fertile well-drained soil. Water sparingly in winter and lightly prune in late winter to shape. Propagate from seed or from cuttings.

Synadenium compactum

☀ ⚘ ↔6 ft (1.8 m) ↕10–20 ft (3–6 m)

Small tree native to Kenya. Glossy green oval leaves, pronounced central rib. Very small greenish yellow flowers, near the ends of the stems, in autumn. 'Rubrum' (syn. *S. grantii* 'Rubrum'), lance-shaped to oval leaves, purple to rich bronze-red; 'Variegatum', interesting foliage with patches of bright green and dark olive to grayish green. Zones 9–12.

Synadenium grantii ★
AFRICAN MILKBUSH, GRANT'S MILKBUSH

☀ ⚘ ↔4 ft (1.2 m) ↕12 ft (3.5 m)

Erect succulent shrub native to tropical Africa, often smaller in cultivation. Fleshy light green leaves, finely toothed margins, spirally arranged near ends of stems. Small, bowl-shaped, deep red flowers are borne in the autumn. Zones 9–12.

SYNCARPHA
EVERLASTING

This genus of around 25 species of perennials and subshrubs endemic to the Cape region of South Africa belongs to the daisy (Asteraceae) family. They have a low, shrubby habit, usually with several erect stems densely covered with thickly downy leaves that are narrowly elliptical and

Syncarpha vestita, in the wild, Cape Point, South Africa

Syncarpha vestita

often semi-succulent. Showy, papery, "everlasting" flowerheads, usually white to cream with a small cluster of golden disc florets at the stem tips, can smother a small plant. Most species flower in spring or after rain.

CULTIVATION: These plants are tolerant of irregular light frosts and are also drought resistant once established. Plant in a sunny position with gritty soil that provides excellent drainage. A little added humus for moisture retention will help the plants through summer. Remove spent flowerheads but otherwise trim only very lightly to shape. Propagation is usually by seed, which, as with other plants frequently exposed to fires, has been found to germinate better if it is smoke treated.

Syncarpha vestita
syn. *Helichrysum vestitum*
CAPE EVERLASTING

☀ ⚘ ↔12–20 in (30–50 cm) ↕12–20 in (30–50 cm)

Found in the wild in rocky habitats. Makes clump of upright stems with mid-green leaves to 2 in (5 cm) long, densely covered with silvery white down. An abundance of creamy white flowerheads give the bush an overall silvery appearance. Zones 9–10.

SYNCARPIA
This genus in the myrtle (Myrtaceae) family contains 2 species found in the coastal areas of eastern Australia. Both are tall straight trees with simple opposite leaves with noticeable venation and thick fibrous bark. From the same family as the eucalypts, they have petalless flowers with numerous stamens and capsular fruits containing many seeds. These are important hardwood timber trees and make very good ornamental subjects for parks and large gardens. Wood from *S. hillii* was used for sidings in the building of the Suez Canal and for wharves in other countries.

CULTIVATION: These trees perform best in a moist well-drained soil in areas free from frost and protected from strong winds. Propagate from seed sown in a humid environment.

Syncarpia glomulifera
TURPENTINE

☀ ⚘ ↔25 ft (8 m) ↕100 ft (30 m)

Tall straight tree with dense crown, straight trunk, fibrous persistent bark. Ovate to narrow-ovate dull green leaves, whitish gray, hairy beneath, aromatic when crushed. Cream flowers, long stamens, in spring–summer. Multiple capsular fruits. Zones 9–12.

Symplocos paniculata

Syncarpia glomulifera, in the wild, Blue Mountains, New South Wales, Australia

Syncarpia hillii

SATINAY

☼ ❀ ↔ 15 ft (4.5 m) ↕ 200 ft (60 m)

This straight-trunked tree occurs only on Fraser Island and the adjacent mainland in Queensland, Australia. Bark rough and fibrous. Leaves opposite, dull on the uppersurface, whitish felty underneath. White flowers, elongated stamens, in spring–summer. Woody fruits. Zones 9–11.

SYNTHYRIS

KITTENTAILS

This genus belonging to the foxglove (Scrophulariaceae) family, contains 14 species of perennials from northern and western North America where they grow in woodland and alpine areas. Closely related to *Veronica*, they are low-growing, rhizomatous, tufted plants. The leathery leaves, which are heart-shaped, kidney-shaped, or deeply cut, become smaller and bract-like on the flowering stems. The flowers are blue or violet-blue with a short tube and 4 erect or spreading lobes.

CULTIVATION: Woodland species will tolerate quite poor soils such as those under deciduous trees but do best in a fertile well-drained soil with added organic matter in light shade. Alpine species require a sunny open site with protection from the hottest summer sun. Propagate from seed or division.

Synthyris platycarpa

Synthyris missurica

Syringa × *hyacinthiflora* 'Charles Nordine'

Synthyris missurica

◐/☼ ❄ ↔ 12 in (30 cm) ↕ 16–24 in (40–60 cm)

Tufted perennial native to northern and western North America. Dark green, leathery, heart-shaped to kidney-shaped, toothed leaves. Bright bluish purple tubular flowers in loose spikes are produced in spring–summer. 'Alba', white flowers. Zones 3–9.

Synthyris platycarpa

EVERGREEN KITTENTAIL

◐/☼ ❄ ↔ 6 in (15 cm) ↕ 6–12 in (15–30 cm)

Species native to Idaho, USA. Clumps of round leaves to 3 in (8 cm) wide, hairy with round-toothed margins. Flowering stems bear racemes of delicate, fringed blue flowers, in spring. Flattened, heart-shaped, capsular fruit. Zones 4–9.

Synthyris reniformis

SPRING QUEEN, SNOW QUEEN

◐/☼ ❄ ↔ 4 in (10 cm) ↕ 2–6 in (5–15 cm)

Species native to moist shady forest habitats in Washington and Oregon, USA. Round to heart-shaped leaves, shallowly lobed, paler beneath. Short racemes of bluish purple flowers, in early spring. Zones 6–9.

Synthyris stellata

☼ ❄ ↔ 6 in (15 cm) ↕ 10 in (25 cm)

Native to Washington and Oregon, USA. Round to heart-shaped deeply toothed leaves with starry appearance. Racemes of bluish purple tubular flowers are borne in spring–summer. Zones 6–9.

Synthyris missurica 'Alba'

Syringa × *hyacinthiflora*

SYRINGA

LILAC

This genus, which a member of the olive (Oleaceae) family, is made up of 23 species of vigorous, deciduous, flowering shrubs, most of them native to northeast Asia, with 2 species only in Europe. Of the European species one, *S. vulgaris*, the common lilac, is known to have been grown in the gardens of western Europe since the sixteenth century; today, it is represented by more than 1,500 named cultivars. The plants have simple pointed elliptical to heart-shaped leaves in opposite pairs and produce upright panicles of small 4-petalled flowers, usually in spring. The flowers may be single or double, and occur in conspicuous clusters. Almost all are strongly sweet smelling, although not every cultivar is noted for its fragrance. *Syringa* species are among the most popular of the cool-climate shrubs.

CULTIVATION: Their main requirements are a well-drained soil and a position in sun or light shade; they thrive in a sandy gravelly soil, preferably one that is slightly alkaline, but do not do well in heavy clay. Propagate from seed, but the results may be variable. They can be grown from cuttings of the current year's growth, or by layering.

Syringa × *chinensis*

CHINESE LILAC

☼ ❄ ↔ 12 ft (3.5 m) ↕ 12 ft (3.5 m)

This is the collective name for a group of hybrids between *S.* × *laciniata* and *S. vulgaris*. They are upright rounded bushes with slender branches, and oval medium to dark green leaves. Produce large panicles of flowers, white to pinkish lavender to reddish, highly fragrant, in late spring. 'Saugeana' ★, reddish mauve flowers. Zones 4–9.

Syringa × *hyacinthiflora* 'Laurentian'

Syringa emodi

HIMALAYAN LILAC

☼ ❄ ↔ 12 ft (3.5 m) ↕ 15 ft (4.5 m)

From western Himalayas. Upright branches, leaves oblong to elliptical, half main vein tinged purple. Flowers tinged pinkish mauve in bud, open to white, in early summer. 'Aurea', clear golden yellow leaves. Zones 4–9.

Syringa × *hyacinthiflora*

AMERICAN HYBRID LILAC, EARLY FLOWERING LILAC, HYACINTH LILAC

☼ ❄ ↔ 15 ft (4.5 m) ↕ 15 ft (4.5 m)

Hybrids of *S. oblata* and *S. vulgaris*. Strong-growing heavy-blooming plants, single or double flowers in early spring. Ovate leaves often reddish bronze, purplish red tones in autumn. 'Blue Hyacinth', pale purple to light blue flowers; 'Charles Nordine', lilac-pink flowers; 'Laurentian', rose pink buds. Zones 4–9.

Syringa × *josiflexa*

☼ ❄ ↔ 7 ft (2 m) ↕ 8–10 ft (2.4–3 m)

This is a hybrid between *S. josikaea* and *S. reflexa*. Erect shrub, broadly lance-shaped leaves, magenta flowers in early summer. 'Anna Amhoff' and 'Elaine', both with single white flowers; 'Bellicent', perfumed pink flowers; 'Lynette' and 'Royalty', both with single purple flowers. Zones 5–9.

S

Syringa julianae

Syringa pekinensis

Syringa komarowii

Syringa oblata

Syringa oblata subsp. *dilatata*

Syringa josikaea
HUNGARIAN LILAC

☼ ❋ ↔ 10 ft (3 m) ↑ 12 ft (3.5 m)
One of only 2 European lilacs, occurs in mountain regions of central to eastern Europe. Leaves leather-like, glossy green. Flowers dark blue-violet, in summer. Requires rich soil. Zones 5–9.

Syringa julianae
syn. *Syringa pubescens* subsp. *julianae*

☼ ❋ ↔ 10 ft (3 m) ↑ 5 ft (1.5 m)
Spreading shrub native of western China. Leaves dark green, pointed oval, fine hairs above, pale gray down beneath. Highly scented pink flowers in 4 in (10 cm) long panicles, in early summer. Zones 6–9.

Syringa komarowii

☼ ❋ ↔ 8–10 ft (2.4–3 m)
↑ 10–15 ft (3–4.5 m)
Chinese shrub, 6 in (15 cm) long, dark green, ovate to lance-shaped leaves.

Produces pendulous cylindrical panicles of deep pink flowers, in late spring–early summer Zones 5–9.

Syringa laciniata
CUT-LEAFED LILAC

☼ ❋ ↔ 10 ft (3 m) ↑ 12 ft (3.5 m)
Discovered in the Chinese Province of Gansu in 1915, one of the first of the oriental lilacs to be introduced into the West. Tall shrub, smooth-edged and cut leaves. Pale lavender flowers, small clusters along the branches, in spring. Zones 5–9.

Syringa meyeri
DWARF KOREAN LILAC, MEYER LILAC

☼ ❋ ↔ 4 ft (1.2 m) ↑ 5 ft (1.5 m)
Discovered in a garden near Beijing, China, in 1909, unknown in the wild. Low compact shrub, sturdy upright branches. Flowers, small clusters, pale lilac to lilac-purple, sometimes whitish lavender, in spring, repeat late summer

Syringa meyeri 'Palibin'

to very early autumn. '**Palibin**', smallest of all lilacs, around 4 ft (1.2 m) high, pinkish lavender flowers; '**Superba**', deep pink flowers, fade with age, long flowering season. Zones 4–9.

Syringa oblata
BROADLEAF LILAC

☼ ❋ ↔ 10 ft (3 m) ↑ 12 ft (3.5 m)
Native to China and Korea, like *S. vulgaris*, but flowers in mid-spring. Loose strongly fragrant panicles. *S. o.* subsp. *dilatata*, heart-shaped leaves, fragrant pale purple flowers. Zones 5–9.

Syringa pekinensis
syn. *Syringa reticulata* subsp. *pekinensis*
CHINESE TREE LILAC, PEKING LILAC

☼ ❋ ↔ 12 ft (3.5 m) ↑ 15 ft (4.5 m)
Tall shrub or tree collected in the Beijing area, China, in 1742. Dark green leaves. Tiny flowerheads, creamy white, in mid-summer. Bark peels into papery curls with age. Zones 5–9.

Syringa pinnatifolia

☼ ❋ ↔ 7 ft (2 m) ↑ 5–10 ft (1.5–3 m)
Western Chinese species. Light green pinnate leaves, up to 11 lance-shaped leaflets. Short slightly drooping panicles of tiny, tubular, pink-tinted white flowers, in mid–late spring. Zones 6–10.

Syringa potaninii
syn. *Syringa pubescens* subsp. *potaninii*

☼ ❋ ↔ 6 ft (1.8 m) ↑ 6–8 ft (1.8–2.4 m)
Discovered in the southern Gansu Province of China in 1885. Upright vase-like habit. Variable leaves, broadelliptic to oblong-elliptic, downy on both surfaces. Flowers light rose-purple to whitish purple, generally fading to near-white, in late spring. Zones 5–9.

Syringa × prestoniae
NODDING LILAC, PRESTON LILAC

☼ ❋ ↔ 12 ft (3.5 m) ↑ 12 ft (3.5 m)
Garden hybrid between *S. reflexa* and *S. villosa*. Dark green leaves, slightly

Syringa × *prestoniae*

Syringa laciniata, Syringa laciniata cultivar (inset)

Syringa reflexa

Syringa reticulata

Syringa tigerstedtii

glaucous, faintly downy, undersides. Slightly drooping panicles of scented soft pink to light purple flowers, in early summer. 'Desdemona', rich purple-pink to blue flowers; 'Elinor', purple tinged buds open to mauve flowers; 'James MacFarlane', soft pink flowers, spreading habit to over 8 ft (2.4 m) wide. Zones 4–9.

Syringa protolaciniata
syn. *Syringa afghanica*
AFGHAN LILAC
☼/☀ ❄ ↔ 40–48 in (100–120 cm) ↕ 40–48 in (100–120 cm)

Shrub native to northern Afghanistan and neighboring mountain areas. Dark slender stems, pinnate foliage. Narrow heads of small, fragrant, lavender flowers, in late spring. Zones 6–9.

Syringa pubescens
☼ ❄ ↔ 12 ft (3.5 m) ↕ 12 ft (3.5 m)
From China. Numerous slender branches. Flowers fragrant, buds, pale purple, mature to pale lilac with pinkish wash. *S. p.* subsp. *microphylla* (syn. *S. microphylla*), from western China, slightly shorter leaves, shorter panicles of more pinkish flowers in spring and earlier summer; 'Superba', heavy-flowering, slightly darker flowers over long season. *S. p.* subsp. *patula* (syn. *S. patula*) from northern China and Korea, larger leaves, purplish new growths; 'Miss Kim', darker pink

buds. *S. p.* 'Excellens', white flowers, pale flesh pink buds; 'Sarah Sands', very pale mauve-pink flowers, more compact clusters. Zones 5–9.

Syringa reflexa
☼ ❄ ↔ 12 ft (3.5 m) ↕ 12 ft (3.5 m)
Found in central China in 1901, used extensively in hybridizing. Erect stems, large ovate leaves. Flower buds deep bright red, opening to pale rose, in early summer. Flower clusters sometimes pendent like those of *Wisteria* species. Zones 5–9.

Syringa reticulata
JAPANESE TREE LILAC
☼ ❄ ↔ 15 ft (4.5 m) ↕ 30 ft (9 m)
Tree lilac native to Japan. Round top. Large plumes of feathery white blooms with their protruding yellow anthers, in summer, contrast well with the dark green foliage. Flowers have strong fragrance. Bark reddish brown,

Syringa pubescens subsp. *patula*

S. pubescens subsp. *patula* 'Miss Kim'

Syringa tomentella

peels on younger branches. 'Ivory Silk', abundant ivory flowers, blooms young. Zones 3–9.

Syringa × swegiflexa
☼/☀ ❄ ↔ 5 ft (1.5 m) ↕ 10 ft (3 m)
Garden hybrid between *S. reflexa* and *S. sweginzowii*. Upright shrub, pointed oval leaves, downy undersides. Slender, pendent, many-flowered, red to dusky pink panicles to over 6 in (15 cm) long, in late spring. Zones 6–9.

Syringa sweginzowii
☼ ❄ ↔ 6 ft (1.8 m) ↕ 10 ft (3 m)
Neat upright shrub probably found in northern Sichuan Province, China,

Syringa pubescens 'Excellens'

Syringa pubescens subsp. *microphylla*

around 1893. Small leaves. Brownish red stems covered with pink florets, in open clusters, in late spring–early summer. Spicy fragrance. Zones 3–9.

Syringa tigerstedtii
☼ ❄ ↔ 8 ft (2.4 m) ↕ 8 ft (2.4 m)
Slender shrub discovered in Sichuan Province, China, 1934. Widely spaced flower clusters, purplish pink to white, on inflorescences around 10 in (25 cm) long in summer. Zones 4–9.

Syringa tomentella
☼ ❄ ↔ 10 ft (3 m) ↕ 10 ft (3 m)
Neat compact shrub, first collected in Sichuan Province, China, in 1891. Smooth pale gray bark. Leaves elliptic to oblong, downy underside. Pink buds, paler pink flowers fade to white, in summer. Zones 4–9.

Syringa villosa
☼ ❄ ↔ 12 ft (3.5 m) ↕ 12 ft (3.5 m)
Chinese species discovered in the Beijing mountains. Round-topped dense habit. Leaves oval, broad-elliptic to oblong, hairy. Pink buds, flowers pale lavender tinged pink, in late spring–early summer. Zones 4–9.

Syringa pubescens 'Sarah Sands'

S

Syringa vulgaris

COMMON LILAC, FRENCH HYBRID LILAC

☼ ❄ ↔ 20 ft (6 m) ↑ 20 ft (6 m)

One of the 2 species native to Europe, with 14 subspecies reflecting geographic variations. Typical form has blue flowers, but cultivars can have deep purple and white flowers. Blooms appear in late spring–early summer.

Single-flowered cultivars include: 'Andenken an Ludwig Späth', dark reddish flowers; 'Charles X', crimson blooms in conical panicles; 'Congo', purple-red flowers, becoming lighter with age; 'Maréchal Foch', large bright purplish red flowers; 'Maud Notcutt', panicles of white blooms; 'President Lincoln', flowers are closest to true blue; 'Primrose', pale yellow flowers in small panicles; 'Sensation', purplish red blooms with white margins to the petals; 'Vestale', white flowers; 'Volcan', dark red to purple flowers.

Double-flowered cultivars include: 'Ami Schott', medium blue flowers with deeper tones; 'Ann Tighe', crimson-purple buds, pink flowers; 'Belle de Nancy', purplish red buds opening to pale purple-pink flowers; 'Charles Joly', dark purple-red blooms; 'Edith Cavell', pale yellow buds opening to white flowers; 'Madame Antoine Buchner', reddish pink to mauve flowers; 'Madame Lemoine', pale yellow buds opening to snow white flowers; 'Monique Lemoine', late-blooming white flowers; 'Mrs Edward Harding', deep purplish red flowers, shaded pink; 'Olivier de Serres', large panicles of lavender-blue flowers; 'Paul Thirion', red-purple buds becoming lovely lilac-pink flowers; 'Victor Lemoine', thin panicles of flowers ranging from lavender-pink to lilac-blue in color; and 'William Robinson', abundant pale pink flowers. Zones 4–9.

Syringa vulgaris 'Condorcet'

Syringa vulgaris 'De Miribel'

Syringa vulgaris 'Astra'

Syringa vulgaris 'Clyde Heard'

Syringa vulgaris 'Ami Schott'

Syringa vulgaris 'Congo'

Syringa vulgaris 'Duc de Massa'

S. v. 'Dwight D. Eisenhower'

Syringa vulgaris 'Edith Brown'

Syringa vulgaris 'Gaudichaud'

Syringa vulgaris 'Ann Tighe'

Syringa vulgaris 'Laplace'

S. vulgaris 'William Robinson'

Syringa vulgaris 'Georges Bellair'

S. vulgaris 'General Sherman'

S. vulgaris 'Mrs Edward Harding'

Syringa vulgaris 'Kardynal'

Syringa vulgaris 'Leon Gambetta'

S. vulgaris 'Mrs W. E. Marshall'

S. vulgaris 'Olivier de Serres'

Syringa vulgaris 'Priscilla'

Syringa vulgaris 'Pink Perfection'

Syringa vulgaris 'Président Grévy'

Syringa vulgaris 'Tita'

Syringa vulgaris 'Vestale'

Syringa vulgaris 'Victor Lemoine'

Syringa vulgaris 'Violet Glory'

Syringa vulgaris 'Volcan'

S. vulgaris 'Waldeck Rousseau'

Syringa vulgaris 'Zulu'

Syringa vulgaris 'Magellan'

S

Syringa wolfii

syn. Syringa formosissima

✺ ❄ ↔ 12 ft (3.5 m) ↑ 15 ft (4.5 m)

Tall shrub originally from northeastern China and Korea. Bright green elliptic leaves. Large pyramidal inflorescence, 12 in (30 cm) long, lilac-colored flowers, slightly fragrant, in late spring. Color may vary from pale lavender to darker purple. Zones 4–9.

Syringa yunnanensis

YUNNAN LILAC

✺ ❄ ↔ 8 ft (2.4 m) ↑ 10–12 ft (3–3.5 m)

Discovered in China's Yunnan Province in 1887, and still relatively unknown. Pinkish whitish rose-tinted flowers on shoots at ends of branches, in late spring. Poor grower, needs good soil. 'Rosea', pink flowers, fade with age. Zones 5–9.

Syzygium australe

SYZYGIUM

This large genus belonging to the myrtle (Myrtaceae) family consists of around 1,000 species, the majority occurring in Southeast Asia, Australia, and Africa. Mostly evergreen trees and shrubs, they have simple opposite leaves that are often smooth and hairless. The flowers, with numerous long stamens, usually occur in panicles along or at the ends of branches; petals and sepals are smaller than the stamens. The fruit is a succulent, mostly red, purple, blue, black, or white edible berry. Mostly tropical and subtropical species, they are cultivated for ornamental and medicinal uses, as well as for food and wood; many species are popular for hedging and topiary.
CULTIVATION: Syzygium species perform best in moist, well-drained, deep and fertile soil in sun or shade. Propagate from seeds sown as soon as they are ripe in spring or from cuttings in summer. In Australia, galls can disfigure the foliage. Scale may be a problem.

Syzygium australe

Syringa wolfii

Syzygium aqueum

WATER APPLE, WATER ROSE APPLE

✺ ⚕ ↔ 20 ft (6 m) ↑ 35 ft (10 m)

Tree from Malay Peninsula, Borneo, and New Guinea. Leathery leaves, dull light green. White, red, or dull purple flowers, in loose clusters, in summer. Glossy, pear-shaped, edible fruit, red or white. Zones 10–12.

Syzygium aromaticum

syn. Eugenia aromaticum

CLOVE

✺ ⚕ ↔ 15 ft (4.5 m) ↑ 50 ft (15 m)

Conical to columnar small tree from the Moluccas, Indonesia. Aromatic, mid-green, elliptical-shaped leaves, glossy above, paler beneath, pinkish when young. Late summer flowers are fragrant, pinkish yellow stamens darken with age. Purple berries. Flower buds exported as cloves. Zones 11–12.

Syzygium aromaticum

Syzygium aqueum

Syzygium australe

syn. Eugenia paniculata of gardens

BRUSH CHERRY, MAGENTA CHERRY

✺ ⚘ ↔ 20 ft (6 m) ↑ 25 ft (8 m)

Shrub or small tree native to coastal and highland rainforests of Australia. Upper stems are brownish green. Opposite rounded leaves, mid-green when mature. White flowers in small dense panicles, in summer. Large, red, fleshy edible berries. Zones 9–12.

Syzygium cumini

JAMBOLAN, JAMBU, JAVA PLUM

✺ ⚕ ↔ 30 ft (9 m) ↑ 70 ft (21 m)

Tropical tree native to Java and India. Rough scaly bark, smoother upward. Turpentine-scented, leathery, dark green leaves, elliptic or obovate shape. Clusters of white flowers are borne at the ends of branchlets, in summer. Produces ovoid-shaped, deep purple to black berries. Zones 11–12.

Syzygium francisii

GIANT WATER GUM

✺ ⚘ ↔ 70 ft (21 m) ↑ 80 ft (24 m)

Native to Australia. Medium to large tree, spreading crown of nearly horizontal branches, prominent buttressed trunk. Bark slightly flaky. Glossy, dark green leaves, ovate to elliptical, wavy edges. Panicles of flowers with cream stamens are produced in early–late summer, followed by violet-purple globe-shaped berries. Zones 10–12.

Syzygium francisii

Syzygium jambos
syn. *Eugenia jambos*
ROSE APPLE

☼ ⚘ ↔ 15 ft (4.5 m) ↑ 20 ft (6 m)

Large shrub or small tree from Malay
Peninsula and Indonesia. Leathery,
dark green, lance-shaped leaves, shiny
pink when new. Large showy flowers,
creamy white stamens, rich in nectar,
in summer. Fragrant, pink to yellow,
edible fruit. Zones 10–12.

Syzygium luehmannii
syn. *Eugenia luehmannii*
SMALL-LEAFED LILLYPILLY, RIBERRY

☼ ⚘ ↔ 30 ft (9 m) ↑ 50 ft (15 m)

Tree from rainforest of northeastern
Australia, smaller in cultivation. Glossy
dark green leaves are ovate to lance-
shaped, pale pink-red when young.
Panicles of small creamy white flowers,
in summer. Pink pear-shaped fruit.
Excellent shade, specimen, or screen
planting. Zones 9–12.

Syzygium luehmannii

Syzygium maire
syn. *Eugenia maire*

☼ ⚘ ↔ 15 ft (4.5 m) ↑ 20–35 ft (6–10 m)

New Zealand tree of swampy forests,
northern North Island. Smooth, gray,
buttressed trunk. Mottled leaves olive
green, blistered surface. Small white

Syzygium jambos

flowers, drop petals, leaving ring of
stamens, in autumn. Red berries follow.
Zones 9–11.

Syzygium malaccense
syn. *Eugenia malaccense*
MALAY APPLE

☼ ⚘ ↔ 15 ft (4.5 m) ↑ 40–80 ft (12–24 m)

Native to the Malay Peninsula. Soft
leathery, dark green leaves, paler undersurface, new growth wine red, then
pinkish. Clusters of cream or reddish
purple flowers occur on branches or
trunk, in summer. Edible red, pink, or
white fruit. Zones 10–12.

Syzygium oleosum
syn. *Syzygium coolminianum*
BLUE CHERRY, BLUE LILLYPILLY

☼ ⚘ ↔ 15 ft (4.5 m) ↑ 40 ft (12 m)

Australian species, shrub or small tree
from Queensland and New South
Wales. Flaky bark and glossy, green,
elliptic to lance-shaped leaves, paler
beneath. Flowers white, in panicles,
in summer. Globe to ovoid-shaped
blue fruit. Zones 9–12.

Syzygium luehmannii

Syzygium paniculatum
syn. *Eugenia paniculata*
AUSTRALIAN BRUSH CHERRY, MAGENTA
BRUSH CHERRY

☼ ⚘ ↔ 20 ft (6 m) ↑ 25 ft (8 m)

Native to coastal rainforests of eastern
Australia. Broadly pyramidal, dense
foliage, oblong to lance-shaped leaves,
glossy dark green, coppery brown when
young. Fluffy creamy white flowers in
panicles, in summer. Crimson-purple
berries. Useful hedge plant. Zones 9–12.

Syzygium pondoense
PONDO WATERWOOD

☼/◐ ⚘ ↔ 6–10 ft (2–3 m)
↑ 6–10 ft (2–3 m)

Rare shrub or small tree from South
Africa. New shoots and leaves, reddish.
Small, pointed, leathery leaves, shiny

Syzygium wilsonii

dark green, pale beneath, reddish veins.
Fluffy white summer flowers. Round
red–purple autumn fruits. Zones 10–12.

Syzygium samarangense
syns *Eugenia javanica*, *Syzygium javanica*
JAMBOSA, JAVA APPLE

☼ ⚘ ↔ 25 ft (8 m) ↑ 40 ft (12 m)

Small to medium, short-trunked tree
occurring from Malay Peninsula to the
Andaman and Nicobar Islands. Aromatic leaves, variable size and shape.
Panicles of fragrant yellow to white
flowers, in summer. Pear-shaped fruit,
shiny and waxy, red, green, or white.
Zones 11–12.

Syzygium wilsonii
POWDERPUFF LILLYPILLY

☼ ⚘ ↔ 7 ft (2 m) ↑ 6 ft (1.8 m)

Scrambling shrub from Queensland,
Australia, taller in wild. Smooth dark
green leaves, narrowly oval, bronze or
red new growth. Deep red flowers, in
spring–early summer. White berries.

Syzygium pondoense, Kirstenbosch National Botanical Garden, South Africa

Syzygium malaccense

S

T

Tabebuia rosea

Tabebuia chrysantha

TABEBUIA

GOLDEN TRUMPET TREE

This genus in the trumpet-vine (Bignoniaceae) family comprises 100 species of trees or shrubs native to tropical areas of the Americas and Caribbean. They may be briefly deciduous or evergreen and have simple or compound, 3- to 7-fingered leaves. They produce large crowded panicles of showy, frequently fragrant, trumpet-shaped flowers in a variety of colors, followed by bean-like pods. CULTIVATION: *Tabebuia* species are best grown in the greenhouse in cool-temperate climates. In tropical and subtropical areas they make attractive specimen trees and may produce flowers sporadically throughout the year. Propagate from seed, cuttings, or air layers.

Tabebuia chrysantha

↔ 20 ft (6 m) ↑ 20–50 ft (6–15 m)

This open-crowned tree grows naturally from Mexico to Venezuela. The gray bark becomes fissured and scaly. Leaves are 5-fingered, slightly hairy, in pointed oblong leaflets. The yellow trumpet flowers appear in large clusters, in spring. They are followed by long seed pods. Zones 11–12.

Tabebuia rosea

PINK POUI

↔ 30 ft (9 m) ↑ 90 ft (27 m)

Variable species found from Mexico to Colombia, and Venezuela, sometimes with a buttressed base. Leaves 3- to 7-fingered, in pointed oval leaflets. Flowers white to pale pink, with yellow throat, in loose clusters, in spring. Zones 11–12.

TABERNAEMONTANA

This genus of about 100 species of tropical and subtropical evergreen shrubs and small trees belongs to the dogbane (Apocynaceae) family and is grown for its gardenia-like flowers and attractive foliage. Found in the tropics and subtropics around the world, they have large glossy green leaves and waxy, usually white, funnel-shaped flowers with 5 wide-spreading curved petals. Flowers are borne throughout the warmer months and are fragrant, particularly at night. These plants have a milky sap and are recognized by the paired boat- to egg-shaped fruits joined to a common stalk. CULTIVATION: These warm-climate, frost-tender plants require regular watering. They need good soil that is well-drained but moisture-retentive, in full sun or bright filtered light, and shelter from wind. Plants can be kept neat and bushy by lightly trimming. Propagate from seed or cuttings.

Tabernaemontana catharinensis

syn. *Tabernaemontana australis*

SAPIRANGY, ZAPIRANDI

↔ 10 ft (3 m) ↑ 20 ft (6 m)

Large shrub or small tree, found from Bolivia and Argentina to southern Brazil and Uruguay. Glossy pointed leaves. White flowers, in spring. Twin reddish green warty fruits. Known in Bolivia as *huevo de perro* (dog's testicle). Zones 9–12.

Tacca integrifolia

Tabernaemontana divaricata

syns *Ervatamia coronaria, E. divaricata*

CRAPE GARDENIA, CRAPE JASMINE, PINWHEEL FLOWER

↔ 5 ft (1.5 m) ↑ 6 ft (1.8 m)

Tropical evergreen shrub found from India to Yunnan Province, China, and parts of northern Thailand. May grow into a small bushy tree. Leathery elliptic leaves. Large, waxy, fragrant white flowers, in small clusters, in summer. Perfume more noticeable at night. **'Flore Pleno'**, double flowers with crowded petals. Zones 11–12.

Tabernaemontana elegans

TOAD TREE

↔ 10 ft (3 m) ↑ 10–20 ft (3–6 m)

Deciduous shrub or small tree from southern Africa. Short single trunk, soft cork-like bark. Dense roundish crown of opposite, glossy, dark green, oblong leaves. Sweetly scented trumpet-shaped flowers in small panicles, in spring–summer. Fruit capsules egg-shaped or rounded. Zones 9–12.

TACCA

This genus, comprising 10 species native to the Asian and African tropics with 9 from the Malay Archipelago alone, is now a member of the yam (Dioscoreaceae) family, though it was formerly placed in Taccaceae. The plants are herbaceous perennials that arise from tubers. The leaves have long stalks bearing blades that are smooth and elliptical, or deeply dissected. The hermaphrodite flowers are regular, in cymes surrounded by a whorl of bracts and are pollinated by flies. The 6 tepals are petal-like, greenish to brown-purple. The fruit is a berry or more rarely a capsule with 10 to many seeds. These plants are found in semi-evergreen monsoon forests and are useful foliage plants in tropical gardens. They are used as flowering pot plants for indoor decoration in more temperate countries. The tubers are a source of starch for bread making, once the bitter substance taccalin has been removed. CULTIVATION: In the tropics these perennials are grown in shaded sites with humus-rich soils; in temperate regions they need a humid greenhouse. To maintain vigor such plants should be re-rooted and repotted every 2 years. They are propagated by division or from cuttings from old tubers. Seeds sown on the soil surface will yield flowering plants in 3 years.

Tabernaemontana elegans

Tacca integrifolia

BAT FLOWER, BAT PLANT, WHITE BAT FLOWER

↔ 24 in (60 cm)
↑ 24–48 in (60–120 cm)

Perennial from eastern India, southern China, and Indonesia. Large, broad, oblong or sword-shaped leaves emerging from a vertical rhizome. Long-stalked heads of nodding bat-like flowers, green to dark purplish black bracts (white in one popular form), green to dark purple bracteoles, in spring–summer. Zones 10–12.

Tabernaemontana catharinensis

Tagetes lucida

TAGETES

MARIGOLD

All but one of the 50-odd species of this genus in the daisy (Asteraceae) family originates in the American tropics and subtropics. They are mainly upright annuals or perennials with dark green, sometimes aromatic, pinnate leaves with toothed edges. Their flowers are usually yellow or orange, and often daisy-like, with obvious ray and disc florets. In some forms the disc florets are largely hidden. The genus name, referring to the marigold's habit of just popping

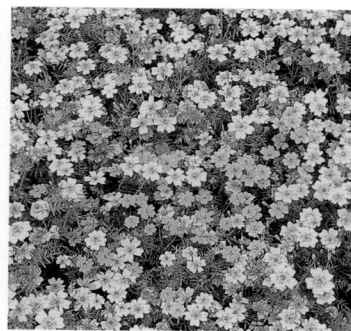

Tagetes tenuifolia 'Starfire'

up from seed, comes from Tages, an Etruscan deity, and grandson of Jupiter, who was said to have sprung from the plowed earth.
CULTIVATION: Marigolds prefer a warm sunny position in light, well-drained soil. Water well and feed if the foliage begins to yellow. Deadhead frequently to ensure continuous blooming. Propagate from seed, which is usually started indoors in early spring.

Tagetes lucida

MEXICAN MINT, SPANISH TARRAGON, SWEET MACE

☼/☀ ⚘ ↔ 16–32 in (40–80 cm)
↕ 16–40 in (40–100 cm)

This perennial comes from Mexico and Guatemala. It is woody-based, branching a little way up the stem.

The lance-shaped leaves are toothed and pleasantly aromatic. Small bright golden yellow flowerheads appear in late summer. Can be used as a tarragon substitute. Zones 9–11.

Tagetes patula

FRENCH MARIGOLD

☼ ⚘ ↔ 6–12 in (15–30 cm)
↕ 8–20 in (20–50 cm)

A compact bushy annual from Mexico and Guatemala. It has pinnate leaves with narrow, toothed, lance-shaped segments. Flowers solitary or in small clusters, usually yellow to orange in the wild, in early summer to autumn. Garden forms are available in many colors. Zones 11–12.

Tagetes tenuifolia

SIGNET MARIGOLD, STRIPED MARIGOLD

☼ ⚘ ↔ 12–24 in (30–60 cm)
↕ 12–32 in (30–80 cm)

This annual is found naturally from Mexico to Colombia. Sometimes narrowly upright, usually bushy, with fine branches. The pinnate leaves are many toothed, with narrow lance-shaped segments. Abundant bright yellow flowerheads with short ray florets, in early summer to autumn. 'Starfire' is a seedling mix which has various shades of yellow, orange, and red. Zones 11–12.

Tagetes Hybrid Cultivars

☼ ⚘ ↔ 6–12 in (15–30 cm)
↕ 8–12 in (20–30 cm)

Mainly derived from *T. patula,* these popular border marigolds make ideal summer bedding plants. They are usually marketed as seedling series, in mixed or individual colors; mostly double flowers with few visible ray florets, predominantly in yellow, orange, and red shades. **Antigua Series**, flowerheads up to 3 in (8 cm) wide; **Atlantis Series**, pompon-like flowerheads up to 4 in (10 cm) wide; **Bonanza Series**, crested flowerheads up to 2 in (5 cm) wide; **Boy Series**, crested flowerheads to 1½ in (35 mm) wide; **Crush Series**, flowerheads nearly 4 in (10 cm) wide; **Disco Series**, many single flowers up to 2 in (5 cm) wide; **Gate Series**, double flowerheads up to 3 in (8 cm) wide; **Girl Series**, dwarf, double flowerheads; **Inca Series**, flowerheads reach up to 5 in (12 cm) wide; **'Jolly Jester'**, red petals with yellow striping; **Little Hero Series**, double flowerheads up to 2 in (5 cm) wide; **'Naughty Marietta'** ★, single yellow flowers with red mid-band; **Safari Series**, double flowers to 3 in (8 cm) wide; **Zenith Series**, stocky and heavy foliage, double flowers to nearly 3 in (8 cm) wide. Zones 11–12.

Tagetes, Hybrid Cultivar, Little Hero Series, 'Little Hero Fire'

Tagetes, Hybrid Cultivar, Little Hero Series, 'Little Hero Yellow'

Tagetes, Hybrid Cultivar, Crush Series, 'Pineapple Crush'

Tagetes, Hybrid Cultivar, Safari Series, 'Safari Yellow'

Tagetes, Hybrid Cultivar, Antigua Series, 'Antigua Gold'

Tagetes, Hybrid Cultivar, Atlantis Series, 'Atlantis Primrose'

Tagetes, Hybrid Cultivar, Bonanza Series, 'Bonanza Bolero'

T., Hybrid Cultivar, Little Hero Series, 'Little Hero Orange'

Tagetes, Hybrid Cultivar, Boy Series, 'Harmony Boy'

Tagetes, HC, 'Jolly Jester'

T., HC, Girl Series, 'Girl Orange'

T., HC, Safari Series, 'Safari Queen'

T., HC, Safari Series, 'Safari Red'

T., HC, Safari Series, 'Safari Scarlet'

TAIWANIA

The single conifer species in this genus, which belongs to the cypress (Cupressaceae) family, is related to *Cryptomeria*. It is native to Taiwan, with a variety being found in south-western China and Myanmar. It is well known for the way the bark peels off in long strips. The foliage is bluish green, forming a rather cone-shaped crown on a very tall tree. The foliage becomes scaly with age and produces male and female cones in shades of brown. On some varieties, the cones can be in shades of gray and green.
CULTIVATION: This species prefers a sheltered sunny position in an acid soil that is moist but well drained. Propagate from seed.

Taiwania cryptomerioides

↔ 35 ft (10 m) ↑ 180 ft (55 m)
Tree much smaller in cultivation. Bark exfoliates in strips; conical or columnar crown. Variable bluish green foliage, narrow and pointed on juvenile plants, scale-like on adults. Small brown male and female cones, in summer.

Taiwania cryptomerioides

Tamarindus indica

T. c. var. *flousiana*, from China and Myanmar, cones grayish green stained with maroon. Zones 8–11.

TALINUM

A genus of over 40 species of succulent shrubs or herbs from Africa and the Americas, belonging to the purslane (Portulacaceae) family. The plants usually have deciduous leaves and branches arising from a perennial tuber or caudex. Leaves are alternate, often irregularly spaced, variously flat to cylindrical, more or less succulent and often soft and limp. Flowerheads are often solitary and usually held at the tips of the stems. The flowers come in various colors and open once, often for only a few hours, some setting seed without opening. The seed pod is a 3-chambered, spherical to oval capsule. Some have established themselves as introduced weeds.
CULTIVATION: These plants are extremely easy to grow in any well-drained soil. Most mature plants will readily set seed, which may germinate in surrounding pots or soil. Underground roots may be raised for display. Propagate from seed.

Talinum paniculatum

JEWELS OF OPAR
↔ 16–20 in (40–50 cm) ↑ 40 in (100 cm)
Variable perennial herb found from southern USA to central Argentina, naturalized throughout tropics and subtropics. Leaves elliptical to oblong. Flowerheads weakly branched; flowers small with 5 petals, pink, yellow, or white, in spring–summer. Seed pods yellow. Often a weed. Zones 9–10.

TAMARINDUS

There is one species of evergreen tree in this genus, which is a member of the cassia subfamily of the legume

(Fabaceae) family. Originally from tropical Africa, it is naturalized and cultivated in many other tropical areas. It has a wide crown, often spreading. The soft green leaves resemble fern fronds. The flowers are cream or yellowish, often with a red tinge. The seed pods are long and bean-like and are a dull brown when ripe. Apart from its ornamental value, the tree has many other uses. Its bean-like pods are used in a number of culinary ways, in curries, chutneys, drinks, and sweetmeats. Parts of the tree are also used medicinally.
CULTIVATION: This tree requires a sunny site in a tropical or subtropical climate. It will tolerate a range of soil types. In temperate climates it can be grown in the greenhouse but will not develop its full size. Propagate from seed or softwood cuttings.

Tamarindus indica

TAMARIND
↔ 35 ft (10 m) ↑ 90 ft (27 m)
Attractive tree originally from Africa but found in most tropical climates. Open spreading crown, fern-like bright green leaves. Racemes of small cream or orange-yellow flowers, flushed with red, in summer. Bean-like pods, to 6 in (15 cm) long, are brittle and grayish brown when fully ripe. Zones 11–12.

TAMARIX

TAMARISK SALT CEDAR
This genus consists of 50 species of deciduous shrubs and small trees belonging to the tamarisk family (Tamaricaceae), which are found in Europe, India, North Africa, and Asia. Most of the species occur on coastal flats, river estuaries, and on saline soil. They have dark-colored brown, deep red, and sometimes purple bark; the main feature is the mass of attractive drooping branches covered in fine foliage. The flowers come in shades of pink and appear in drooping panicles. *Tamarix* are often used as windbreak hedging for exposed gardens near the sea; some species are also grown to stop the

Tamarix chinensis

Tamarix parviflora

erosion of sand dunes. The galls of some species are used to tan leather.
CULTIVATION: In coastal areas they grow in well-drained soil in a sunny position, while in inland areas they prefer slightly moister soil and shelter from cold drying winds. Shrubs should be pruned regularly to prevent root movement in severe winds. Propagate from just-hardened seed sown in an area protected from frost, or half-hardened cuttings in summer, or hardwood cuttings in winter.

Tamarix chinensis

CHINESE TAMARISK, SALT CEDAR
↔ 10 ft (3 m) ↑ 15 ft (4.5 m)
Small tree or shrub, native to the temperate zones of eastern Asia. Densely branched with fine drooping branchlets. Bark brown to blackish, leaves bluish green. Drooping panicles of pink flowers, on current year's wood, in summer. Zones 7–10.

Tamarix gallica

FRENCH TAMARISK, FRENCH TREE, MANNA PLANT
↔ 10 ft (3 m) ↑ 12 ft (3.5 m)
Small tree or shrub, native to the Mediterranean area. Bark reddish brown to purple; blue-green stalkless leaves, small and narrow. Pink flowers in cylindrical racemes, on current year's wood, in summer. Larger in favorable conditions. Zones 5–10.

Tamarix hispida

KASHGAER TREE
↔ 2–3 ft (0.6–0.9 m) ↑ 3–15 ft (0.9–4.5 m)
A shrub or small tree found from the Caspian Sea to China. Bark is red-brown, branches are covered in fine hairs. Leaves are blue-green, egg to lance-shaped, and hairy. Pink flowers in dense racemes, forming terminal panicles, on current year's wood, in summer. Zones 6–9.

Tamarix parviflora

EARLY TAMARISK
↔ 20 ft (6 m) ↑ 15 ft (4.5 m)
This small tree or large shrub comes from Europe. Slender, arching, purple

T

branches have pointed narrow leaves. Racemes of pale pink flowers are produced on older wood, in late spring. Zones 5–9.

Tamarix ramosissima

syn. *Tamarix pentandra*

☀ ❊ ↔ 15 ft (4.5 m) ↑ 15 ft (4.5 m)

This shrub or small tree ranges from eastern Europe to central Asia. It has upright arching branches. Leaves are narrow, lance-shaped and pointed. Dense racemes of pink flowers, in late summer–late autumn. '**Pink Cascade**', deep pink flowers; '**Rubra**', magenta flowers, can become weedy. Zones 2–10.

Tamarix tetrandra

☀ ❊ ↔ 12 ft (3.5 m) ↑ 12 ft (3.5 m)

This shrubby species is from eastern Europe and western Asia. Fine pale green foliage on dark purple-brown branches. Pale pink flowers on old wood, below the newly developing foliage stems, in spring. Zones 6–10.

TANACETUM

This genus of about 70 annuals and perennials belonging to the daisy (Asteraceae) family originates in northern temperate regions. It includes plants with diverse foliage and forms that are suitable to grow in a variety of situations, from rock gardens and borders to naturalizing. Foliage is often strongly aromatic, sometimes silvery, and can be fringed, ferny, scalloped, or toothed. Flowers are daisy-like or rayless buttons, produced in a mass on vigorous plants of mounding, upright, or shrubby habit. Flower colors are dominated by yellow, white, and red. The genus name means "immortality," from the Greek, a reference to the flowers' habit of drying without wilting. CULTIVATION: These plants require well-drained, poor to moderately fertile soil, full sun, and dry growing conditions. Cut back plants after blooming to encourage new growth and to prevent prolific self-seeding of some types. Propagate by division or from seed in spring.

Tamarix ramosissima

Tanacetum camphoratum

Tanacetum balsamita

syns *Balsamita major, Chrysanthemum balsamita*

ALECOST, COSTMARY

☀ ❊ ↔ 18 in (45 cm) ↑ 36 in (90 cm)

A hardy mat-forming perennial found growing naturally from central Asia to Europe. Leaves are scalloped, silvery gray, slightly hairy, and aromatic. Prolific small, white, button-like flowers with a yellow eye bloom in late summer–autumn. Zones 6–10.

Tanacetum camphoratum

DUNE DAISY

☀ ❊ ↔ 20 in (50 cm) ↑ 27 in (70 cm)

This is a rare perennial from temperate zones of North America. Bright green serrated foliage all year round. Bright yellow button-like flowers, 1 in (25 mm) wide, are produced from summer to autumn. In some areas it can die back over the winter months. Zones 8–10.

Tanacetum cinerariifolium ★

syns *Chrysanthemum cinerariifolium, Pyrethrum cinerariifolium*

DALMATIA PYRETHRUM, INSECT FLOWER, PYRETHRUM

☀ ❊ ↔ 12 in (30 cm) ↑ 12–24 in (30–60 cm)

This perennial grows naturally in the Balkans. It features finely cut, silvery gray foliage on slender stems. The daisy-like flowers with white rays and a yellow center appear from late summer to autumn. Mulch where winters are severe. It needs hot dry conditions. The source of insecticidal pyrethrum. Zones 6–10.

Tamarix ramosissima 'Pink Cascade'

Tanacetum parthenium (left foreground, right center)

Tanacetum parthenium cultivar

Tanacetum coccineum

Tanacetum coccineum

syns *Chrysanthemum coccineum, Pyrethrum coccineum*

PAINTED DAISY, PYRETHRUM

☀ ❊ ↔ 18 in (45 cm) ↑ 18–30 in (45–75 cm)

Compact low-growing perennial from southwest Asia and the Caucasus. Fern-like, elliptical to oblong, silver-gray, aromatic foliage. White, pink, or red daisy flowers, yellow eye, in early summer–late autumn. Oils of leaves used to deter pests. '**Brenda**', bright cerise-pink flowers with yellow eye; '**Eileen May Robinson**', larger pale pink flowers with soft yellow eye; '**James Kelway**' ★, vibrant crimson-pink flowers. Zones 5–9.

Tanacetum corymbosum

☀ ❊ ↔ 18 in (45 cm) ↑ 36 in (90 cm)

Clumping, woody perennial from southern and central Europe. Leaves mid-green, elliptical to oblong, aromatic. Clusters of white flowers, early summer–late autumn. *T. c.* subsp. *clusii*, white daisy-like flowers with drooping petals. Zones 6–9.

Tanacetum niveum

SILVER TANSY

☀ ❊ ↔ 24 in (60 cm) ↑ 36 in (90 cm)

Superb species from southern and central Europe. Deeply cut, fragrant

Tanacetum corymbosum subsp. *clusii*

leaves are a striking silver-gray. Plant forms a mound and bears hundreds of *Chrysanthemum*-like white flowers in late spring–summer. Zones 6–9.

Tanacetum parthenium

syn. *Chrysanthemum parthenium*

FEVERFEW

☀/◑ ❊ ↔ 12 in (30 cm) ↑ 24 in (60 cm)

A short-lived perennial from southern Europe to the Caucasus. Branched sprays with ferny foliage. Flowers with a flat yellow center surrounded by short, stubby, white petals appear in summer. For rock garden, ground cover, or border. '**Aureum**', bright golden foliage with single yellow-tinted white flowers; '**Santana Lemon**', yellow button flowers, thinly rayed; '**Snowball**', tight ivory buttons; '**White Stars**', white starry flowers. Zones 4–9.

Taraxacum officinale

Tanacetum vulgare

GOLDEN BUTTONS, TANSY

☼/☀ ❄ ↔ 36–48 in (90–120 cm)
↑ 36–48 in (90–120 cm)

A perennial from Europe. Creeping roots and finely divided ferny foliage all along the stem. Flower clusters 4 in (10 cm) across, bright yellow, in spring to summer. Strong camphor scent. *T. v.* var. *crispum*, attractive arching foliage. *T. v.* 'Goldsticks', longer stems, larger flowers. Zones 4–9.

TANQUANA

These 3 small compact succulents, belonging to the iceplant (Aizoaceae) family, are from the Karoo area of Western Cape, South Africa. Plants are small, compact, branched or unbranched, with persistent green to purplish leaves on very short stalks and rounded at the tips. Daisy-like flowers with 50 to 70 petals are sweet scented, with 5 or 6 bracts, and open in the afternoon. Seed pods are pale brown with a funnel-shaped base. All were formerly included in *Pleiospilos* because of their spotted leaves, but their leaves are unkeeled and rounded, not rock-like as in *Pleiospilos*.
CULTIVATION: They need a mostly mineralized, slightly chalky, well-drained soil, in full sun, with plenty of fresh air and a rest both in winter and mid-summer. Water carefully at other times. Propagate from seed.

Tanquana hilmarii

syn. *Pleiospilos hilmarii*

☼/☀ ❄ ↔ 2 in (5 cm) ↑ 1¾ in (4 cm)

From Western Cape, South Africa. Usually single-bodied, superficially resembling *Lithops*. Leaves green to purplish, variable, narrowing slightly toward tip, slightly convex above, semi-cylindrical to rounded below, drawn forward over upperside. Golden yellow flowers in summer. Zones 8–10.

TAPEINOCHILUS

This genus is a member of the ginger (Zingiberaceae) family and contains about 15 species of perennial herbs found in Southeast Asia, Indonesia, New Guinea, and Australia. Like the related *Costus*, they are plants of the forest floor and have spirally arranged leaves. As is typical of the ginger family, the flowers are of less significance than the colorful showy bracts that surround them, which are usually red. The flowerheads may be on leafy shoots or a separate flowering stem.
CULTIVATION: In tropical areas plants can be grown in a shady border in rich, moist but well-drained soil. In cool-temperate climates, grow in the greenhouse in a rich soil-based mix, providing high humidity, plenty of water, and fortnightly feeding in summer. Water sparingly in winter and reduce humidity. Propagate from seed or bulbils or by division.

Tapeinochilus ananassae

☀ ⚘ ↔ 2–3 ft (0.6–0.9 m)
↑ 5–7 ft (1.5–2 m)

Rhizomatous perennial found from Malaysia to Australia. Cane-like stems; spirally arranged, bright green, oblong leaves. Yellow flowers held within a cone-like structure of densely packed overlapping red bracts, in summer. Zones 11–12.

TARAXACUM

DANDELION

Dandelions form a worldwide group of about 60 perennial or biennial weeds belonging to the daisy family (Asteraceae). They grow almost all over the Northern Hemisphere and different species are common in most parts of the world. They all share a sturdy tap root, hollow stems with milky sap, toothed green leaves, and bright yellow flowers. Considered by many to be a nuisance lawn weed, dandelions have a long history of use. All parts of the plant are edible and young leaves are high in vitamin A. Young leaves can be eaten raw while older leaves can be used as pot herbs, boiled or wilted. The common name is a corruption of the French *dent de lion*, meaning lion's tooth, a reference to the plant's toothed leaves.
CULTIVATION: Dandelions grow as an annual, like other salad greens, in rich friable soil in a sunny site. To lessen the bitter flavor, blanch plants by heaping dirt around them or covering them with a board. Propagate from seed.

Taraxacum officinale

BLOWBALL, DANDELION, WET-A-BED

☼ ❄ ↔ 8 in (20 cm)
↑ 10–12 in (25–30 cm)

A common weed from the Northern Hemisphere. Leaves vary from broad to narrow, and from deeply cut edges, even fringed, to nearly smooth. Yellow ray flowers produce a ball of tufted seeds dispersed by wind, in spring to summer. Cultivated mainly in Europe. 'Thick-leaved Improved', tender fleshy leaves; 'Vert de Montagny', finely cut leaves, large compact head. Zones 3–10.

TAVARESIA

A genus of 4 small succulent shrubs, much branched from the base, that is a member of the milkweed (Asclepiadaceae) family, from Angola, Namibia, Botswana, Zimbabwe, and South Africa. They have cylindrical stems with 6 to 12 gray-green ribs that are covered in clusters of small weak bristles in some species. The bell- to funnel-shaped flowers are large and conspicuous, in shades of brown, yellow, or red, and are borne in clusters at the base of new stems. The genus is named after Jose Tavares de Macado, a Portuguese government official who gave permission to early plant collectors to explore Angola.
CULTIVATION: These plants are a challenge to grow, requiring dry heat, very sandy soil, good air circulation, and water only in really hot weather. They are very prone to rotting and are occasionally grafted onto *Stapelia* plants or the tubers of *Ceropegia*. Propagate from seed, which will germinate in less than 24 hours.

Tavaresia barkleyi

☼/☀ ⚘ ↔ 12–20 in (30–50 cm)
↑ 5 in (12 cm)

Succulent shrub from South Africa, Botswana, and Namibia. Tufted stems with 10 to 12 angles, 3 small bristle-like spines. Flowers pale yellow with small red spots, base purple, 5 triangular, tapering, spreading lobes, outside pale green with reddish spots and stripes, inside with downy hairs, at base of stems, in summer. Seed pods long, thin, pale brown. Zones 9–11.

TAXODIUM

This group of 3 species from North America and Mexico belong to the cypress (Cupressaceae) family. These deciduous or semi-deciduous trees are found growing in or near water. In these swampy conditions mature trees often produce aerial roots known as "knees" or pneumatophores, which allow the roots to breathe. These majestic conical trees bear foliage that resembles that of the yew (*Taxus*), after which they were named, with fissured peeling bark on buttressed trunks. Both male and female cones are held on the same tree, the small male cones held in pendulous groups, the female ones scattered along the branches.
CULTIVATION: These plants will grow in either a clay or sandy soil as long as it remains relatively moist. They can withstand very low winter temperatures where their foliage color turns to vivid rust tones before the leaves fall to reveal a fine tracery of branches. Propagate from seed, except for cultivars, which need to be grafted.

Tanquana hilmarii

Tapeinochilus ananassae

Taxodium distichum, in the wild, Minter City, Mississippi, USA

Taxodium distichum var. *imbricatum,* in the wild, The Everglades, Florida, USA

Taxodium distichum

BALD CYPRESS, SWAMP CYPRESS

☀ ❄ ↔ 20 ft (6 m) ↑ 75 ft (23 m)

This fast-growing tree is from North America. The deeply fissured fibrous bark exfoliates in long strips. Initially conical outline broadens, becomes irregular as the tree matures. Fine leaves light green, in spring, ageing to a deep green before turning rusty red, in autumn. *T. d.* var. *imbricatum* (syn. *T. ascendens*), distinctly conifer shape, clasping bright green leaves; 'Nutans', initially upright, pendulous tips with maturity. *T. d.* 'Shawnee Brave', compact bright green leaves, ideal for hedges. Zones 6–10.

Taxodium mucronatum

MEXICAN SWAMP CYPRESS, MONTEZUMA CYPRESS

☀ ❄ ↔ 50 ft (15 m) ↑ 100 ft (30 m)

Tree from Mexico and southern Texas, USA. Evergreen in warmer climates, semi-deciduous in cooler areas. Pendulous foliage very similar to *T. distichum*. Clasping leaves, bright green turning rusty brown in autumn. Cones long, often warty. Zones 8–11.

TAXUS

YEW

This small evergreen conifer genus belonging to the yew (Taxaceae) family, consists of around 7 species, occurring in cool-temperate regions of the Northern Hemisphere and some more tropical mountain regions, including the Philippines and Mexico. Most are small to medium trees, with sharply pointed, linear or slightly sickle-shaped leaves, often with prominent olive green midribs. Most species have separate male and female plants and flower in spring. The single seed found on the female plant is partly clothed in a red fleshy covering (or aril) that is sweet and edible; the rest of the plant, including the seed, is poisonous. The seeds are dispersed by birds. They make useful specimen or hedge plants, and handsome topiary subjects. Slow growing but long lived.
CULTIVATION: Most members of the genus are fairly adaptable in cool regions, tolerating sun or shade, frost, alkaline soils, exposure, and pollution.

Propagate these conifers from seed sown as soon as hardened, from cuttings, or by grafting.

Taxus baccata

COMMON YEW, ENGLISH YEW

☀ ❄ ↔ 25 ft (8 m) ↑ 50 ft (15 m)

Slow-growing tree from Europe, North Africa, and western Asia. Very long lived, dense many-branched head. Reddish brown bark, dark green linear leaves, paler yellowish green below. Male cones yellow and scaly. Female flowers on separate plants, in summer. **Aurea Group** (golden yew), golden yellow young growth turning greener with age; **'Dovastonii Aurea'**, male plant, low and spreading, dense foliage; **'Dwarf White'**, low and spreading moderately dense foliage, new growth whitish but soon turning green; **'Fastigiata'** (Irish yew), female plant, dark green leaves; **Fastigiata Aurea Group** (golden Irish yew), smaller than 'Fastigiata', golden yellow leaves; **'Nutans'**, to less than 20 in (50 cm) high, dark green leaves; **'Repandens'**, spreading female, to 36 in (90 cm) high, green leaves; **'Semperaurea'**, male, to 10 ft (3 m) high, ascending branches of bright yellow young growth changing to russet-yellow in winter; **'Standishii'**, female, golden leaves, columnar habit. Zones 5–10.

Taxus baccata

Taxus baccata, Aurea Group, 'Aurea' ★

Taxus baccata 'Dovastonii Aurea'

Taxus baccata 'Standishii'

Taxus baccata 'Nutans'

Taxodium mucronatum

Taxus chinensis

CHINESE YEW

☀ ❄ ↔ 15 ft (4.5 m) ↑ 20 ft (6 m)

A shrub from China with stiff, sharp, pointed leaves, tapering abruptly at the point. Glossy green leaves, curling outward on top, gray-green below, in 2 ranks. Pollen cones yellowish maturing to brown, appear in summer. Zones 6–10.

Taxus cuspidata

JAPANESE YEW

☀ ❄ ↔ 20 ft (6 m) ↑ 50 ft (15 m)

Erect tree from Japan, normally seen as a shrub in gardens. The horizontal or ascending branches have spiraly arranged, dark green, linear leaves. New shoots are red-brown, fleshy aril

Taxus chinensis

Taxus cuspidata 'Capitata'

Taxus × media

red when ripe, in summer. Suitable for hedging and topiary, tolerant of pollution. *T. c.* var. *nana* is a low-spreading shrub with dense growth. *T. c.* 'Capitata', strong upright foliage; 'Densa', female compact form with dark green leaves to 36 in (90 cm) high; 'Densiformis', dwarf, to 36 in (90 cm) tall. Zones 4–9.

Taxus × media

ANGLO-JAP YEW, HYBRID YEW

☀ ❄ ↔ 20 ft (6 m) ↑ 25 ft (8 m)

A hybrid between *Taxus baccata* and *T. cuspidata*. Tree or shrub suitable for hedging. Linear olive green leaves, prominent white midribs beneath. Seed partly covered by a scarlet aril, in summer. 'Brownii', to 10 ft (3 m) high, dark green leaves, spherical shape; '**Dark Green Spreader**', a shrub with very dense deep green foliage; 'Everlow', a low, rounded, up to 8 ft (2.4 m) high; '**Hatfieldii**', male columnar form to about 6 ft (1.8 m)

Taxus cuspidata var. nana

Taxus cuspidata

Taxus × media 'Brownii'

high; '**Hicksii**', columnar habit, dense growth, popular for hedges. '**Nigra**', compact dark green foliage. Zones 5–9.

TECOMA

syns *Stenolobium, Tecomaria*

YELLOW BELLS

There are 13 species of mostly evergreen trees and scrambling shrubs in this genus belonging to the trumpet-vine (Bignoniaceae) family. They are found from southern Arizona, USA, to Mexico, the West Indies, and as far south as northern Argentina. One species (*T. capensis*), is native to southern and eastern Africa. Pinnate leaves are borne in opposite pairs in leaflets with toothed edges. Funnel-shaped or narrowly bell-shaped flowers are borne in showy terminal clusters in yellow, orange, or red, with 5 unequal petals. The fruit is a small-ish pod splitting into 2 halves.

CULTIVATION: Fine ornamentals for the tropical and subtropical garden. In cool climates they can only be grown as potted shrubs in a greenhouse or conservatory. They like a sunny but sheltered position and reasonably fertile soil with good drainage. Propagate from fresh seed, or from tip cuttings or larger cuttings from the previous year's growth. Suckering species can be divided or layered.

Tecoma capensis

syns *Bignonia capensis, Tecomaria capensis*

CAPE HONEYSUCKLE

☀ ◗ ↔ 7 ft (2 m) ↑ 10 ft (3 m)

An adaptable shrub, partly climbing habit, from eastern and southern Africa. Glossy green pinnate leaves.

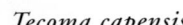

Tecoma capensis

Taxus × media 'Dark Green Spreader'

Taxus × media 'Nigra'

Orange-red to scarlet tubular flowers, in racemes at ends of branches, from spring to autumn. Tolerant of salt spray, drought, and wind. 'Aurea', golden yellow flowers. Zones 9–12.

Tecoma castaneifolia

☀ ◗ ↔ 8–12 ft (2.4-3.5 m) ↑ 15–25 ft (4.5–8 m)

Evergreen species, native to Ecuador. Upright tree, leathery elliptic leaves, very hairy undersides. Yellow flowers reach 2 in (5 cm) long, in spring to autumn. Beanpod-like capsules about 5 in (12 cm) long. Zones 10–12.

Tecoma stans

syns *Bignonia stans, Stenolobium stans*

SHRUBBY TRUMPET FLOWER, YELLOW BELLS, YELLOW ELDER

☀ ◗ ↔ 10 ft (3 m) ↑ 15–30 ft (4.5–9 m)

Small tree or large open shrub, native to southern USA and Central and

Tecoma capensis 'Aurea'

South America. Leaves oblong, lance-shaped, toothed, bright green leaflets. Yellow flowers, funnel-shaped, in terminal racemes or panicles, from late winter to summer. Fruit capsules ripen to brown. Zones 10–12.

TECOMANTHE

This genus of 5 species of vigorous climbing plants is a member of the trumpet-vine (Bignoniaceae) family. Its botanical name is derived from *Tecoma*, a genus to which it is closely related. Species are found in tropical and subtropical forests from Malaysia to New Zealand. The rich green leaves have 1 to 7 pairs of oblong leaflets with smooth or toothed edges. The plants are grown for their showy clusters of large funnel-shaped flowers, resembling foxgloves, in shades of cream, red, and purple.
CULTIVATION: In tropical and subtropical areas grow these plants in rich, moist but well-drained soil in partial shade. Provide a strong support such as an archway or trellis. In cool-temperate climates grow in the greenhouse in a free-draining soil mix enriched with organic material. Give them light shade in summer and water well when in growth. Propagate from seed or cuttings.

Tecomanthe speciosa ★
☀ ⬗ ↔ 5–10 ft (1.5–3 m)
↑ 20–30 ft (6–9 m)

A climber from Three Kings Islands, New Zealand with large, glossy, dark green leaves. Clusters of large, creamy, tubular flowers on old wood, from autumn to winter. Only one plant known in the wild. Zones 9–11.

TECOPHILAEA
BLUE CROCUS, CHILEAN CROCUS
Native to mountainous habitats in Chile, this genus of just 2 species of

Telanthophora grandifolia

cormous perennials has its own family (Tecophilaeaceae). It is rare to the point of extinction in the wild. However, collectors cherish them for their glamorous coloring, which varies between royal blue, gentian blue, and a pale true-blue. New growth occurs as the snows melt, and it is this protective blanket of snow that is thought to assist in the production of the spring-borne flowers.
CULTIVATION: Grow these plants in full sun in a well-drained soil. Snails are major predators. When grown under glass, use a sandy fertile potting mix and water only when in growth. Propagate from offsets or by sowing fresh ripe seed.

Tecophilaea cyanocrocus ★
CHILEAN CROCUS
☀ ❄ ↔ 2 in (5 cm) ↑ 4–5 in (10–12 cm)
Perennial from Chile. Leaves narrow, lance-shaped, emerging with flowers. Flowers are a heavenly blue, with 6 petals variously marked in white, in early spring. Dislikes soggy wet winters; likes dryish sunny summers. Zones 8–10.

TELANTHOPHORA

This genus, which is a member of the daisy (Asteraceae) family, was previously included in *Senecio* and contains 14 species of small evergreen trees and shrubs native to Central America. The stems are usually downy and have few branches and large leaves with wavy or toothed edges. The yellow flowers are daisy-like and carried in terminal clusters. They flower profusely from late spring through summer.
CULTIVATION: These are easily grown plants that tolerate a range of soils in sun or part-shade. They are frost tender and in cool-temperate climates will require greenhouse protection. Propagate from seed.

Telanthophora grandifolia
syn. *Senecio grandifolius*
☀ ⬗ ↔ 12 ft (3.5 m) ↑ 20 ft (6 m)
An attractive evergreen shrub or small tree native to Mexico. Downy stems, large oval leaves, with wavy, lobed or

Tellima grandiflora

Tecoma stans

toothed edges. Yellow daisies in large showy clusters, in late summer to early spring. Zones 9–11.

TELEKIA

This genus, comprising a single species native from central Europe eastward to the Caucasus region, belongs to the daisy (Asteraceae) family. The plant is a coarse perennial herb. Leaves are large and heart-shaped, deeply toothed, and hairy, with long stalks. The large flowerheads have ray florets and form loose terminal corymbs. The receptacle has scales, which persist after flowering. The whorl of bracts is cup-shaped and the bracts are heart-shaped and herbaceous. Ray florets are female, each with a very long, narrow, yellow petal. The dry fruits are linear and flattened.
CULTIVATION: This plant grows wild by streamsides and in wet woodlands up to the subalpine zone. It is easily grown in open or lightly shaded moist places in a garden but can readily become invasive. However, the statuesque forms of the larger ones in cultivation are always impressive. Propagate by division or from seed.

Telekia speciosa
syn. *Buphthalmum speciosum*
OXEYE DAISY, TELEKIA SUNFLOWER
☀ ❄ ↔ 4–6 ft (1.2–1.8 m)
↑ 4–6 ft (1.2–1.8 m)
A strongly scented perennial found from central Europe to Russia. Coarsely serrated leaves, finely hairy underneath. Clusters of 2 to 8 flowerheads, up to 35 tiny yellow ray florets, in summer. Zones 3–9.

TELLIMA

There is just the one species of perennial herb in this genus which belongs to the saxifrage (Saxifragaceae) family. It is native to western North America,

Tecoma castaneifolia

where it is found in cool moist woodland and rocky areas. The plant forms spreading clumps of hairy, heart-shaped or round leaves that are lobed and toothed. They are tinted with purple in some forms. In summer, tall wiry flowering stems bear spikes of small creamy flowers tinged with green and red. The flowers deepen in color as they age.
CULTIVATION: Fringecups are well suited for growing in cool woodland gardens, and in shady borders and rockeries. Grow in a moist humus-rich soil. Propagate by division in autumn or from seed sown in spring.

Tellima grandiflora
FRINGECUPS
☀ ❄ ↔ 24 in (60 cm) ↑ 24 in (60 cm)
This perennial is found growing from California to Alaska, USA. Clumps of almost round, lobed, hairy, basal leaves, up to 2–4 in (5–10 cm) wide. Delicate flowers with deeply fringed petals appear in summer. **Rubra Group** (syn. 'Purpurea') features rounder, scallop-edged leaves tinted bronze and green flowers fringed with pink. Zones 6–9.

Telopea speciosissima, in the wild, Australia

Telopea speciosissima 'Olympic Flame'

Telopea truncata, in the wild, central highlands, Tasmania, Australia

open, crimson flowerheads appear at branch ends from late spring to early summer. Zones 8–10.

Telopea oreades
GIPPSLAND WARATAH

☀ ⚘ ↔ 10 ft (3 m) ↑ 10–30 ft (3–9 m)

A waratah found naturally in sheltered wet forests of southeastern Australia. The smooth lanceolate leaves often have a glaucous underside. Globular deep crimson flowerheads, up to 3 in (8 cm) across, are produced in early summer. Zones 9–10.

Telopea speciosissima   ★
WARATAH

☀ ⚘ ↔ 5 ft (1.5 m) ↑ 10 ft (3 m)

Floral emblem of New South Wales, Australia. This erect slender shrub has toothed leathery leaves with prominent veins. The red dome-shaped flowerheads, surrounded by a ring of bright red bracts, appear in spring. This species is grown commercially for its high-quality cut flowers. 'Corroboree', vigorous growth with rather narrow leaves, large domed flowerheads with relatively inconspicuous bracts; 'Flaming Beacon', large very rich red bracts, red florets tipped white; 'Olympic Flame', released to mark the 2000 Sydney Olympic Games, a tall grower, exceptionally large high-domed flowerheads; and 'Wirrimbirra White', creamy white flowers. Zones 9–10.

Telopea truncata
TASMANIAN WARATAH

☀ ❄ ↔ 10 ft (3 m) ↑ 10 ft (3 m)

A species from Tasmania, Australia. Deep green smooth-edged leaves on new growth. Undersides of new leaves and unopened flowers usually covered with soft brown hairs. Slightly flattened red flowerheads, in late spring. Grows chiefly in subalpine mountainous country. Zones 8–10.

TEPHROCACTUS
syn. Opuntia

These 6 small shrubs from Argentina are members of the cactus (Cactaceae) family, and are related to opuntias. Characteristically, Tephrocactus grow by producing new stem segments that stack on top of each other and are

Telopea speciosissima 'Flaming Beacon'

Telopea mongaensis

CULTIVATION: Waratahs require a deep, well-drained, acidic soil in full sun or partial shade. They have a low resistance to alkaline soils and excessive phosphorus, and prefer not to be overfed. Frost tolerance varies with the species. Tip prune from an early age to encourage branching, and after flowering cut old flowered stems back to halfway. Propagate from seed in spring, or from cuttings.

TELOPEA
WARATAH

Known for their spectacular flowerheads in shades of red, there are just 5 species in this southeastern Australian genus of evergreen shrubs and small trees belonging to the protea (Proteaceae) family. They have dark green, prominently veined leaves with toothed or lobed edges and leathery pods up to 5 in (12 cm) long which contain many seeds. The flowerheads are large and waxy and have a ring of bright red bracts. The Australian Aboriginal name for T. speciosissima is "waratah," now the accepted common name for the genus. All species are highly ornamental and will make beautiful garden plants.

Telopea mongaensis

☀ ❄ ↔ 10 ft (3 m) ↑ 10 ft (3 m)

A multi-branched bushy shrub from southern New South Wales, Australia. Dark green, smooth, leathery leaves, smooth-edged or broadly lobed and yellowish green when young. Large,

Telopea speciosissima 'Wirrimbirra White'

Telopea speciosissima 'Corroboree'

Terminalia catappa, Parque Nacional Manuel Antonio, Quepos, Costa Rica

easily detached. The areoles are also distinctive, being sunken into the plant body. Spines are variable but generally flat and papery. Flowers appear from the growing tip in white, pink, yellow, or red. Seed pods are dry, without pulp. The name comes from Greek *tephra,* "ash," referring to the dull gray color of some species. CULTIVATION: These cacti are easy to grow in a rich well-drained soil. Rest in winter. Propagation is usually from the easily detached stem segments allowed to dry out for a week or two, but they may be grown from seed.

Tephrocactus articulatus
syns *Opuntia diademata, O. papyracantha, Tephrocactus strobiliformis*

PAPER-SPINED CACTUS, PAPER-SPINED CHOLLA

☼ ⧈ ↔ 36 in (90 cm) ↑ 36 in (90 cm)
Variable species from Argentina. Very long, flat, papery spines, sometimes not present. Usually upright, branching base and stems; stem joints oval to pear-shaped, prominent tubercles in spirals. Glochids red to purple-black, from few to copious. Flowers white to pink, in summer. Zones 9–11.

TEPHROSIA
Belonging to the pea-flower subfamily of the legume (Fabaceae) family, this genus contains about 400 species of usually evergreen perennials or shrubs native to tropical and subtropical areas throughout the world. They show considerable variation and may be erect or sprawling, with alternate leaves comprised of 1 to 41 leaflets. The flowers are borne in pairs or clusters. They are typical of those in the pea-flower family and range in color from orange to purple.
CULTIVATION: Most species are frost tender but if given a good protective mulch in winter in cooler areas they should resprout from the base in

spring. They will grow in any soil that is well drained and can tolerate quite arid conditions. Propagate from seed, which requires hot water treatment.

Tephrosia grandiflora
☼ ⧈ ↔ 3 ft (0.9 m) ↑ 2–5 ft (0.6–1.5 m)
A shrubby species, native to South Africa, naturalized in Jamaica. Stems are covered in white or rusty down. Pinnate leaves, 9 to 15 leaflets, white-hairy beneath. Clusters of purple-pink flowers, from spring to early summer. Zones 9–11.

TERMINALIA
The name of this genus of about 200 species of evergreen or deciduous trees

Tephrocactus articulatus

Tephrocactus articulatus

refers to the leaves, which are often clustered near the shoot tips. It is a member of the family Combretaceae. Found in tropical regions from Asia, India, Sri Lanka and south to Polynesia and parts of Australia. These trees often grow near the coast and their trunks are frequently buttressed. They are grown for the ornamental qualities of their large, handsome, often leathery leaves and sprays of flowers as well as for dyes, oils, nuts, and some medicinal purposes.
CULTIVATION: *Terminalia* species grow in any reasonably fertile soil that is well drained and in full sun. In cool areas they need to have greenhouse protection. Propagate from seed.

Terminalia arostrata
NUTWOOD
☼ ⧈ ↔ 6–10 ft (1.8–3 m) ↑ 17–35 ft (5–10 m)
Semi-deciduous drought-resistant tree from northern and western Australia. Upright trunk, drooping branches, fissured bark. A rounded crown and leathery, broadly oval-shaped leaves.

Spikes of inconspicuous creamy flowers, in summer. Berries dark purple or black, edible. Zones 9–11.

Terminalia catappa
INDIAN ALMOND, KOTAMBA
☼ ✈ ↔ 35 ft (10 m) ↑ 90 ft (27 m)
Tree found in tropical Asia, parts of Polynesia, and northern Australia. Broad spreading crown, tiered horizontal branches. Semi-deciduous; large oblong leaves turn brilliant red before falling. Small white flowers on spikes, in summer. Large greenish yellow and red edible fruits. Zones 11–12.

Tephrosia grandiflora

Terminalia arostrata, in the wild, Gregory National Park, Northern Territory, Australia

TERNSTROEMIA

This genus of 85 species of evergreen trees and shrubs is a member of the camellia (Theaceae) family. These plants are found in Asia, Africa, and the Americas. The large glossy leaves are leathery, sometimes with a serrated edge. The single white flowers are 5-petalled and appear in summer. The seed capsules are red.
CULTIVATION: These plants will grow well in a fertile, humus-rich, acid soil that is moisture retentive but well drained. Pinch out the shoot tips to encourage branching. Propagate from seed or from half-hardened cuttings in late summer.

Ternstroemia japonica ★

syn. *Ternstroemia gymnanthera*

☀ ❄ ↔ 10 ft (3 m) ↑ 12 ft (3.5 m)

A shrub or small tree, native to Japan. Well-branched; thick, leathery, glossy, oval leaves. Hanging clusters of small white flowers, lightly perfumed, are borne in summer. Round red fruits split to reveal red seeds. 'Variegata', dark green leaves marbled with gray, creamy white edges that turn pink in autumn. Zones 8–11.

TETRACENTRON

The single species of deciduous tree in this genus, belonging to the family Trochodendraceae, is found from Nepal to southwestern and central

Tetradium daniellii

Tetradium ruticarpum

China. It has an attractive form with smooth new shoots revealing oval leaves, sometimes heart-shaped. They have prominent veins and are mid-green changing to deep bluish red in autumn. The flowers are small and yellow and bloom on long spikes. This tree is often cultivated for its ornamental value.
CULTIVATION: This plant requires a moderately fertile soil in a sunny position and with shelter from cold winds. Although quite hardy, young shoots are susceptible to late spring frosts. Propagate from seed or half-hardened cuttings.

Tetracentron sinense

☀ ❄ ↔ 30 ft (9 m) ↑ 50 ft (15 m)

A tree found from southwestern and central China to Nepal. Dark smooth shoots, pale brownish orange buds. Leaves pointed oval to heart-shaped, prominent veins, bluntly toothed edges, color to a rich blue-red, in autumn. Small yellow flowers on pendulous spikes, in summer. Zones 6–9.

TETRACLINIS

This conifer genus, which belongs to the cypress (Cupressaceae) family, contains just one tree species. It is a native of northwestern Africa and southeastern Spain and is adapted to hot arid conditions. It is a very dense tree with a strong thick trunk that is crowded with branches. Typical of conifers, it has branchlets that are flat and splayed with slightly brittle thin leaves. Tiny erect cones appear at the tips of the branches.
CULTIVATION: This is a frost-tender species that requires greenhouse cultivation in cool climates. In mild climates it is a good choice for dry areas, being very drought tolerant. It should be planted in a well-drained soil. Propagate from seed or cuttings.

Ternstroemia japonica

Tetraclinis articulata

ALERCE, ARAR, JUNIPER GUM PLANT

☀ ❄ ↔ 25 ft (8 m) ↑ 50 ft (15 m)

Conifer from northwestern Africa and southern Spain. Broad conical crown, and a thick trunk with closely packed branches. Cypress-like foliage, branchlets arranged in flat open sprays, scale-like leaves in whorls of four. Small, erect, glaucous cones carried at branch tips, in summer. Zones 9–11.

TETRADENIA

Found in southern Africa and on the island of Madagascar, this genus of 5 deciduous or semi-deciduous shrubs belongs to the mint (Lamiaceae) family. Of these, just one is commonly cultivated. These shrubs are aromatic with semi-succulent stems that, along with the foliage, are often coated with a fine down. The light green to gray-green leaves are heart-shaped to rounded, usually with deeply lobed edges. The flowers are minute but are massed in whorled panicles that can smother the plant. They have a sweet honey scent.
CULTIVATION: Tolerating only the lightest frosts, *Tetradenia* species prefer a position in full sun or part-shade with a light well-drained soil. The plants will flower more freely if watered well during the growing season but will tolerate short periods of drought. Cut back after flowering to encourage a compact growth habit. Propagate from seed or cuttings.

Tetradenia riparia

syn. *Iboza riparia*

MOSCHOSMA, NUTMEG BUSH

☀ ❄ ↔ 8 ft (2.4 m) ↑ 8–10 ft (2.4–3 m)

A shrub from South Africa. Leaves are rounded, and light sage green due to velvety hairs covering them. Heads of scented pale pink to mauve flowers, in winter–early spring. Leaves and young stems emit a spicy aroma if crushed. Zones 10–11.

TETRADIUM

Native to the area from the Himalayas through to East and Southeast Asia, this small genus of about 9 species of

Tetraclinis articulata

Tetradenia riparia

deciduous and evergreen shrubs and trees belongs to the rue (Rutaceae) family. They are grown for their aromatic foliage, masses of small sweetly scented flowers, and the generous clusters of fruits. The capsular fruits contain dark red to black seeds and are poisonous in some species.
CULTIVATION: Most species are very frost hardy. To thrive, they need a fertile, moist but well-drained soil in full sun or partial shade. Prune to remove damaged foliage and spent flower-heads. Propagate from seed in autumn, or from cuttings in late winter.

Tetradium daniellii

syn. *Euodia daniellii*

KOREAN EUODIA

☀ ❄ ↔ 40 ft (12 m) ↑ 50 ft (15 m)

A large tree, native to southwestern China and Korea. The large pinnate leaves are composed of 11 ovate or lance-shaped, glossy, dark green leaflets that turn russet in autumn. Small, white, perfumed flowers in terminal dome-shaped sprays, from late summer to early autumn. Small pear-shaped fruits. Zones 8–10.

Tetradium ruticarpum

syn. *Euodia ruticarpa*

☀ ❄ ↔ 15 ft (4.5 m) ↑ 30 ft (9 m)

A small tree from China and Taiwan. Leaves are smooth, glossy, dark green above, greenish brown, densely hairy below. Sprays of small white or yellowish green flowers, in late summer. Round red to black fruit. Zones 9–11.

TETRAGONIA

This small genus has its own family, Tetragoniaceae, and is found in New

Zealand and Australia but is naturalized in many parts of the world. The few species are short-lived perennials with dark green fleshy leaves of variable shapes, from triangular to oblong with shiny undersides. The stems are succulent with small daisy-like flowers in shades of pale green, cream to yellow, appearing in spring. Fruits are square-shaped. The leaves of some species are edible. They are often considered weeds. The name comes from the Greek *tetra,* "four," *gonia,* "angle," referring to the 4-angled fruits.
CULTIVATION: These perennials are adaptable to most soils, but they do prefer sandy loam, in an open sunny or partly shaded position. Propagate from seed soaked in warm water before planting, and from cuttings.

Tetragonia tetragonioides
NEW ZEALAND SPINACH, WARRIGAL GREENS
☀ ✹ ↔ 24–40 in (60–100 cm)
↕ 8–12 in (20–30 cm)

A short-lived prostrate perennial from New Zealand and Australia but naturalized elsewhere. Dark green, oblong to triangular, pointed, fleshy leaves, shiny underneath, edible. Succulent stems. Small, greenish yellow, daisy-like flowers, usually blooming in spring. Sometimes weedy. Zones 7–9.

TETRAPANAX
The sole confirmed species in this genus, part of the ivy (Araliaceae) family, is a suckering clump-forming evergreen shrub or small tree from Taiwan. Known as rice-paper plant because a type of fine rice paper is made from the pith of its stems, it has large hand-shaped leaves that are

Teucrium cossonii

Teucrium fruticans

felted all over when young, although the covering soon wears from the uppersurfaces to reveal the underlying dark green coloration. Large panicles of creamy white flowers open from heads of woolly buds that develop at the stem tips in autumn.
CULTIVATION: Intolerant of drought or hard frosts, this species prefers to grow in a mild climate, with moist, humus-rich, well-drained soil in a position that is shaded from the hottest summer sun. It will also grow well in sandy soils near the coast. Old stems and spent flowerheads are best removed. Although rice-paper plant will grow from cuttings, these are large and unwieldy, so seed is more commonly used for propagation.

Tetrapanax papyrifer
RICE-PAPER PLANT
☀ ✹ ↔ 15 ft (4.5 m) ↕ 20 ft (6 m)
This evergreen small tree or shrub from Taiwan can sucker profusely to form a large clump. Downy palmate leaves, borne mainly at the stem tips, overlap to form a dense foliage canopy. Creamy white flowerheads appear in autumn. Clusters of purple-black berries. 'Variegata', cream-edged leaves. Zones 8–11.

TETRATHECA
BLACK-EYED SUSAN
This Australian genus is a member of the family Tremandraceae and comprises about 40 species. They are all low-growing evergreen shrubs and have fine green leaves held on slender stems. The nodding bell-like flowers are pink or purple with a black eye that is not readily seen. It is one of a number of plants with the common name of black-eyed Susan.
CULTIVATION: Give these shrubs a well-drained position in partial shade to make them trouble-free in both garden and pot culture. Propagate from half-hardened cuttings.

Tetratheca thymifolia ★
☀ ✹ ↔ 24 in (60 cm) ↕ 24 in (60 cm)
Mound-forming shrub from Australia. Small green leaves are held on dainty

Teucrium hircanicum

Tetratheca thymifolia

stems. Profusion of deep pink bell-like blooms, in spring. White-flowering forms are also available. Zones 9–11.

TEUCRIUM
GERMANDER
Members of this genus of about 100 species of herbs, shrubs, and sub-shrubs, part of the mint (Lamiaceae) family, occur in warm-temperate regions but particularly around the Mediterranean. The shrubs are attractive and often colorful flowering plants. All have characteristic squarish stems with opposite leaves that are usually downy or hairy, oval to lance-shaped, and have notched or slightly toothed edges. The summer flowers are borne in whorls on loose stems and are cream, purple, or pink. Some species are attractive to cats.
CULTIVATION: These plants require a sunny position and well-drained soil. They will tolerate the dry heat of the inland but do best in coastal areas. Lightly prune the ends of the branch-lets to remove spent inflorescences and stimulate lateral growth immediately after the summer-flowering period. Propagation is best from firm tip cuttings taken in summer.

Teucrium canadense
AMERICAN GERMANDER, WOOD SAGE
☀ ✹ ↔ 24–36 in (60–90 cm)
↕ 24–36 in (60–90 cm)

A perennial, native to North America. Stiff, erect, downy stems; leaves hairy, oval to lance-shaped, with notched edges. Spikes of cream, pink, or purple flowers, to 1 in (25 mm) wide, held in whorls, in summer. Zones 4–9.

Teucrium chamaedrys
GROUND OAK, WALL GERMANDER
☀ ✹ ↔ 24–36 in (60–90 cm)
↕ 12–24 in (30–60 cm)

A woody-based perennial from central and southern Europe but naturalized

Tetrapanax papyrifer

further north. Small oval leaves have toothed edges, and are shiny green above, downy below. Whorls of pink to purple flowers borne on terminal spikes in summer. Zones 5–10.

Teucrium cossonii
syns *Teucrium gussonei, T. majorcum*
☀ ✹ ↔ 24 in (60 cm) ↕ 8 in (20 cm)
Low-growing shrubby perennial from the Mediterranean island of Majorca, Spain. Small, narrow, gray leaves. Whorls of lavender flowers on short leafy spikes, almost year-round in warm climates. Zones 8–11.

Teucrium fruticans
BUSH GERMANDER, SHRUBBY GERMANDER
☀ ✹ ↔ 6 ft (1.8 m) ↕ 4 ft (1.2 m)
This small evergreen shrub is native to southern parts of Spain, Portugal, and Italy, as well as North Africa. Stems and undersides of the grayish leaves covered in dense white hairs. Flowers pale lilac-blue, in summer. 'Azureum', deep blue flowers. Zones 8–10.

Teucrium hircanicum
☀ ✹ ↔ 24 in (60 cm) ↕ 24 in (60 cm)
This woody-based perennial is from western Asia and the Caucasus region. The soft, green, and downy leaves are somewhat wrinkled on the upper-surface. Terminal spikes of closely packed whorls of small purple to reddish purple flowers are produced from summer to autumn. Zones 6–9.

Thalictrum delavayi 'Hewitt's Double'

Thalictrum delavayi

Teucrium polium
GOLDEN GERMANDER

☼ ❄ ↔ 6–12 in (15–30 cm)
↕ 4–16 in (10–40 cm)

A low mound-forming subshrub from the Mediterranean and western Asia. Woody-based, with downy stems; the small gray leaves have wrinkled surface. Small heads of white, yellow, pink, or purple velvety flowers appear in summer. Zones 7–10.

Teucrium pyrenaicum
☼ ❄ ↔ 16 in (40 cm) ↕ 3 in (8 cm)
A perennial from the Pyrenees. Forms mats of rounded leaves with notched edges. Dense terminal flowerheads, up to 1 in (25 mm) wide, bear 2-toned purple and cream flowers in summer. Zones 6–9.

Teucrium scorodonia
MOUNTAIN SAGE, WOOD GERMANDER, WOOD SAGE

☼/◗ ❄ ↔ 18 in (45 cm) ↕ 24 in (60 cm)
Downy rhizomatous perennial, native to southern and western Europe. The wrinkled, coarsely toothed, grayish

Thalictrum aquilegiifolium

green leaves resemble sage. Small yellowish green flowers borne in terminal spikes, in summer–autumn. '**Crispum Marginatum**', crimped, frilly-edged, green leaves. Zones 6–10.

THALIA
ALLIGATOR FLAG

This genus of 12 aquatic perennial herbs is a member of the arrowroot (Marantaceae) family, native to the tropical and subtropical Americas and tropical Africa. Growing from thick rhizomes, the overlapping, decorative, blue-green leaves have large oval- to sword-shaped blades that fold upward at night, and long stalks with sheaths at the base. Two ranks of tubular, often waxy flowers are produced in curving tassel-like branches on long-stalked panicles that extend beyond the leaves.
CULTIVATION: These plants grow in water 12–18 in (30–45 cm) deep, or in moist to wet loamy soil in an open sunny position. Propagate by division in spring.

Thalia dealbata
POWDERY ALLIGATOR FLAG, WATER CANNA

☼ ◖ ↔ 20–30 in (50–75 cm)
↕ 3–6 ft (0.9–1.8 m)

Erect perennial, native to southeastern North America, with unbranching stems. The large, textured, grayish green leaves with fine red edges are

powdery white underneath. Branching heads of 6-petalled, violet, waxy flowers are borne from late summer to early autumn. Zones 9–11.

THALICTRUM
MEADOW RUE

A member of the buttercup (Ranunculaceae) family, this genus of around 130 species of tuberous or rhizomatous perennials is found mainly in the northern temperate zone. They are upright plants with lacy, pinnate, blue-green leaves that are reminiscent of *Aquilegia* or *Adiantum* (maidenhair fern) foliage. Tall flower stems grow well above the foliage and from late spring to autumn, depending on the species, produce inflorescences of small fluffy flowers. Mainly in pink to mauve shades, but also white and yellow, the petal-less flowers sometimes gain color from their 4 or 5 petal-like sepals. The Romans favored meadow rue as a medicinal plant and also attached superstitions to it.
CULTIVATION: Usually very hardy, these plants are easily grown in temperate climates in full or half-sun in fertile, humus-rich, and well-drained soil. Propagate these perennials by division, as the cultivated plants are mainly selected forms.

Thalictrum aquilegiifolium
FEATHERED COLUMBINE, FRENCH MEADOW RUE

☼/◗ ❄ ↔ 20–40 in (50–100 cm)
↕ 60 in (150 cm)

Multi-stemmed perennial found from Europe to Japan. Blue-green aquilegia- or maidenhair fern-like foliage, leaves to 12 in (30 cm) wide. Panicles of greenish white through pink to purple flowers with inconspicuous sepals, in early summer. Zones 6–9.

Thalictrum delavayi
☼/◗ ❄ ↔ 16–24 in (40–60 cm)
↕ 4–5 ft (1.2–1.5 m)

A perennial native to the Himalayas. Dark-stemmed, blue-green, aquilegia- or maidenhair fern-like foliage. Erect showy heads of purple-pink, rarely white flowers, sepals similarly colored,

Teucrium pyrenaicum

large and long-lasting, in summer. '**Hewitt's Double**' ★, double flowers, slightly shorter. Zones 7–9.

Thalictrum dioicum
EARLY MEADOW RUE

☼/◉ ❄ ↔ 12–16 in (30–40 cm)
↕ 12–30 in (30–75 cm)

Species found in North America, from Ontario, Canada, to Tennessee, USA. Aquilegia-like blue-green foliage; tiny leaflets have deeply scalloped edges. The flowers have pendulous pink filaments below conspicuous pale green, sometimes purple-tinted sepals, said to resemble floating jellyfish, in summer. Zones 4–9.

Thalictrum flavum
FALSE RHUBARB, YELLOW MEADOW RUE

☼/◗ ❄ ↔ 16–20 in (40–50 cm)
↕ 40 in (100 cm)

A perennial found in southwestern Europe and North Africa, with finely divided, blue-green, aquilegia-like, pinnate foliage. Small heads of cream to yellow flowers with inconspicuous sepals, in summer. *T. f.* subsp. *glaucum* features intensely blue-green foliage. Zones 6–10.

Thalictrum kiusianum
◗ ❄ ↔ 12–20 in (30–50 cm)
↕ 6–12 in (15–30 cm)

A small species from Japan. Develops into a dense clump of short-stemmed, small, doubly trifoliate, blue-green leaves with 3- to 5-lobed segments. Abundant small heads of white to purple-pink blooms with inconspicuous sepals, in summer. Zones 8–10.

Thalictrum minus
☼/◗ ❄ ↔ 20–32 in (50–80 cm)
↕ 3–5 ft (0.9–1.5 m)

This erect species is found throughout Europe and Asia. Finely divided, blue-green, pinnate leaves. The panicles of

Thalia dealbata

Thalictrum orientale

Thalictrum rochebruneanum

yellow, sometimes purple-tinted flowers with inconspicuous sepals, are borne in summer. Zones 6–9.

Thalictrum orientale

☼/☀ ❄ ↔ 12–20 in (30–50 cm)
↑ 12 in (30 cm)

A small clump-forming species found from Greece to Iran. Leaves doubly trifoliate, 3-lobed rounded leaflets. Flat heads of small white to lavender flowers, with inconspicuous sepals, in late spring–early summer. Zones 7–10.

Thalictrum rochebruneanum

☼/☀ ❄ ↔ 16–20 in (40–50 cm)
↑ 40 in (100 cm)

From Japan. Finely divided foliage, smooth-edged or lobed leaflets, to over 1 in (25 mm) long. Airy sprays of small pendulous flowers with many yellow filaments and showy purple-pink sepals, in summer. 'Lavender Mist', large heads of tiny, bell-shaped, violet flowers. Zones 8–10.

THAMNOCHORTUS

This genus of 34 species of rush-like plants in the family Restionaceae is restricted to South Africa. The stems are green and the leaves are reduced to brown scales up the stems. Their tiny brown flowers are produced in tight heads at the top of the stems and are usually surrounded by brown to golden papery bracts that can be quite showy. Male and female flowers are borne on separate plants; in most cases the sexes look quite different and in earlier times they were often mistaken for different species. These plants are still used for thatching in South Africa.
CULTIVATION: They grow in a sunny site in almost frost-free climates. They enjoy moist, poor, sandy soils but are quite adaptable. Propagate them from smoke-treated seed sown in autumn.

Thamnochortus insignis

DEKRIET, THATCHING REED
☼ ❄ ↔ 6–7 ft (1.8–2 m)
↑ 6–7 ft (1.8–2 m)

This species is from the coastal areas of South Africa. The stiff deep green

stems have brown stem-clasping leaf bracts. The tiny brown flowers are surrounded by dark brown floral bracts, larger on the male plants, in summer. Zones 8–10.

THELOCACTUS

This is a genus of 12 small solitary to clustering members of the cactus (Cactaceae) family from the Chihuahua Desert, Mexico through to Texas, USA. The stems are spherical to columnar, to 10 in (25 cm) tall and 8 in (20 cm) in diameter. The ribs are vertical or spiraling, with tubercles usually prominent, rounded to conical, often with extra floral nectaries that attract ants. The spines are variable but persistent, usually straight, up to 2½ in (6 cm) long. Funnel-shaped flowers appear from the growing tip in various colors. Seed pods are spherical to oval, green to bright red, and can be dry to the touch. These plants are popular with collectors for their easy culture, showy spines, and large flowers.
CULTIVATION: These cacti are easily grown in a rich well-drained soil. Propagate from seed, or by division of older plants, or from cuttings allowed to dry out for a week or two. Rest them during winter.

Thelocactus conothelos

syn. *Thelocactus saussieri*
☼ ☀ ↔ 20 in (50 cm) ↑ 15 in (38 cm)
This usually solitary species from Mexico occasionally clusters. Spherical to short cylindrical stems are green to yellow-green; ribs indistinct, spiraling; tubercles delta-shaped. Spines red to reddish white, becoming gray. Flowers

Thelocactus conothelos

are produced in summer and can range from purple-magenta, white-yellow, to orange-yellow. Zones 9–11.

Thelocactus hexaedrophorus

syns *Thelocactus fossulatus, T. lloydii*
☼ ☀ ↔ 3–6 in (8–15 cm)
↑ 1¼–8 in (3–8 cm)

Usually solitary species from Texas, USA. Spherical to flattened-spherical stems. Ribs indistinct; tubercles compressed, rounded; areoles with grooves. Spines reddish, brownish, or grayish white. Flowers white, sometimes with a reddish mid-stripe, in summer. Seed pods green to magenta. Zones 9–11.

Thelocactus leucacanthus

☼ ☀ ↔ 32 in (80 cm) ↑ 2–6 in (5–15 cm)
Cactus from Texas, USA, and Mexico. It forms large clumps of stems to 2 in

Thelocactus hexaedrophorus

Thelocactus macdowellii

(5 cm) in diameter. Ribs are spiraling; tubercles conical, rounded at the tip; areoles have extra floral nectaries. Spines are yellowish to white to nearly black. The yellow, violet, or bright red flowers are produced in summer. Seed pods are green or yellowish green. Zones 9–11.

Thelocactus macdowellii

syns *Echinomastus macdowellii, Neolloydia macdowellii*
☼ ☀ ↔ 2–5 in (5–12 cm)
↑ 2–4 in (5–10 cm)

A solitary or clustering species from Texas, USA. Spherical stems, green to pale green, densely covered in spines. Ribs are indistinct; tubercles conical. Spines white to grayish white. The magenta flowers are borne in summer. Seed pods are dry. Zones 9–11.

Thamnochortus insignis, Kirstenbosch National Botanical Garden, South Africa

Thelocactus rinconensis ★

syns *Thelocactus lophothele, T. nidulans, T. phymatothelos*

☀ ❄ ↔ 3–8 in (8–20 cm) ↑ 6 in (15 cm)

Species from Texas, USA, and Mexico. Usually spherical stems, blue-green, often tinged purple. Ribs indistinct, numerous; tubercles conical, angled. Spines variable. Flowers white to light pink, in summer. Seed pods greenish yellow, slightly fleshy. Zones 9–11.

Thelocactus setispinus

syn. *Hamatocactus setispinus*

☀ ❄ ↔ 2–4 in (5–10 cm) ↑ 3–5 in (8–12 cm)

Solitary species from Mexico, rarely offsetting. Spherical to elongated

Thelymitra ixioides

Thelocactus tulensis

spherical stems, yellow-green. Ribs are conspicuous, thin, wavy; tubercles are absent; areoles with extra floral nectaries. Spines yellowish white to red, whitish, or reddish white. Flowers are yellow with a deep red throat, in summer. Seed pods are spherical, red, fleshy. Zones 9–11.

Thelocactus tulensis

☀ ❄ ↔ 2½–7 in (6–18 cm) ↑ 1–10 in (2.5–25 cm)

Solitary species from Texas, USA, and Mexico. Short cylindrical to hemispherical stems, with or without ribs; tubercles variable. Reddish brown spines, gray with age. Flowers white, yellow, purplish pink to magenta, in summer. Seed pods green, grayish magenta, to whitish brown. Zones 9–11.

THELYMITRA

SUN ORCHID

This large genus in the Orchidaceae family contains about 100 terrestrial orchid species, and is primarily from Australia with smaller outlying populations in New Zealand, New Guinea, New Caledonia, the Philippines, and Borneo. Plants produce a single thick and fleshy leaf and an upright inflorescence with a few to many flowers in late spring and summer, depending on the species. The un-orchid-like blooms have similar floral segments and lack the highly modified and specialized labellum seen on most orchid species.

Blues, pinks, and purples are the most common colors encountered, yet there are species with yellow, brown, and white flowers, some with additional spotting. However, it is the bright sky blue flowered species that has given these orchids international recognition. They are called sun orchids because the flowers will rarely open on cloudy days and evenings, relying on the bright sunlight and warm temperatures for the blooms to open. The plants are dormant throughout the hot and dry Australian summers, where they retreat to underground tubers.

CULTIVATION: These colorful sun orchids rely on a mycorrhizal fungus for their survival and have proved very difficult to maintain in cultivation, with the plants annually declining in vigor before fading away. Specialist growers of terrestrial orchids have had some success by growing some of the other species in a free-draining sandy mixture incorporating a small percentage of organic matter. Propagate by division of clumps.

Thelymitra ixioides

☀ ❄ ↔ 4–8 in (10–20 cm) ↑ 4–32 in (10–80 cm)

This robust species from Australia has strappy green leaves. The numerous flowers are pinkish blue to deep blue, up to 1¼ in (30 mm) wide, in spring. They often have some darker pepper spotting in the center of the flower. Zones 9–11.

THELYPTERIS

This genus gives its name to the wood-fern (Thelypteridaceae) family and contains 2 species of terrestrial ferns, 1 of which is native to the Northern Hemisphere, the other from the Southern Hemisphere. They are found in shaded, damp, marshy ground. Their creeping or upright rhizomes are covered with hair-like scales. The divided, sword-shaped or triangular, often glandular, frond blades are covered with fine gray hairs. Circular spore bodies are carried in rows on the undersides of the fronds. Different botanists have widely differing views as to how many species belong to this genus. At one extreme, 2 species are recognized, while acknowledging many other closely related genera. At the other extreme, 900 species are included in the genus.

CULTIVATION: These ferns prefer a shaded, protected position in a moist, well-drained, fertile soil. Propagation is from spores.

Theobroma cacao

Thelypteris palustris

syns *Dryopteris thelypteris, Thelypteris thelypteroides*

MARSH FERN

☀ ❄ ↔ 10–18 in (25–45 cm) ↑ 18–24 in (45–60 cm)

Found across temperate USA and Europe, Bermuda, Cuba, and Peru. Long creeping rhizome. Sterile frond blades sword-shaped, to 16 in (40 cm) long, oval segments, on smooth pale green stalks. Fertile fronds to 40 in (100 cm) long, narrower segments, on longer stalks, rows of spore bodies near midvein, in summer. Zones 6–11.

THEOBROMA

This genus from tropical America is a member of the cacao (Sterculiaceae) family and contains 20 species of evergreen trees; the best known is *T. cacao*, from which cocoa is obtained. They have alternately arranged simple leaves that are short lived. Flowers arise directly from the leaf axils after the leaves have fallen and are followed by large fleshy fruits that contain many seeds. It is the seeds that are used to manufacture chocolate.

CULTIVATION: Frost tender, they need a greenhouse in cool climates. In warm areas grow them in a sheltered position in a fertile soil that is moisture retentive but well drained. Water and feed regularly during the growing season. Propagate from seed, sown fresh, or by air layering.

Theobroma cacao

COCOA

☀ ❄ ↔ 10 ft (3 m) ↑ 25 ft (8 m)

Tree from Central and South America. Pointed oblong leaves, red and pendulous when young. Clusters of small, creamy pink, slightly fragrant flowers borne directly on the trunk and thick branches, in spring. Ribbed seed pods ripen to purplish brown. Zones 11–12.

THERMOPSIS
FALSE LUPIN

This genus, which belongs to the pea-flower subfamily of the legume (Fabaceae) family, contains 23 species of rhizomatous perennial herbs, native to North America, Siberia, and parts of Asia. They grow in habitats such as riverbanks and open woods. Attractive 3-part leaves are often silvery. Their nectar-rich, yellow or purple flowers are typical of the pea-flower family. They are borne in spring or summer in dense or loose terminal racemes, often resembling lupins *(Lupinus)*, a fact recognized in the common name applied to several species.
CULTIVATION: These plants are suitable for the border or for naturalizing in larger areas. Grow in full sun in any reasonably fertile soil that is moist but well drained. Some species spread rapidly by their rhizomes. Propagate from seed or by division, which must be undertaken carefully as these deep-rooted plants resent disturbance.

Thermopsis rhombifolia
FALSE LUPIN, GOLDEN BANNER

☼ ❄ ↔ 24 in (60 cm) ↑ 36 in (90 cm)
This species is found from the Rocky Mountains to New Mexico, USA. Broadly oval leaflets are hairy beneath. Yellow, softly hairy flowers, densely or loosely packed in racemes to 12 in (30 cm) long, are produced from spring to summer. The seed pods are upright and downy. Zones 4–9.

Thermopsis villosa
syn. *Thermopsis caroliniana*
CAROLINA LUPIN

☼ ❄ ↔ 2 ft (0.6 m) ↑ 3–5 ft (0.9–1.5 m)
A stout perennial from southeastern USA. Bluish green leaves are downy on the undersides. Yellow flowers are borne in terminal, downy, lupin-like racemes, from spring to summer. Seed pods are silky-hairy. Zones 6–9.

Thevetia peruviana

THEVETIA

This small genus belonging to the dogbane (Apocynaceae) family is made up of around 8 species native to tropical America. They are trees and shrubs with simple alternate leaves spiraly arranged. Their plentiful summer flowers are showy, often yellow, and funnel-shaped, and are produced at the ends of shoots. The fruit is squat and berry-like. The genus is closely related to *Nerium*, which includes the poisonous plants commonly known as oleanders. All parts of the plant are highly poisonous, including the milky sap.
CULTIVATION: Most members of this genus are fairly adaptable but will give the best results when planted in a mulched, well-drained, sandy soil with plenty of water during the summer months. They will tolerate full sun to part-shade. Propagate from seed or from cuttings.

Thevetia peruviana
syn. *Thevetia neriifolia*
LUCKY NUT, YELLOW OLEANDER

☼ ❀ ↔ 8 ft (2.4 m) ↑ 15 ft (4.5 m)
This upright shrub or small tree from Central America, Peru, and the West Indies has linear to narrowly lance-shaped leaves that are a shiny dark green. The fragrant funnel-shaped flowers, apricot-yellow, are borne in cymes, in summer. The fruit is fleshy. All parts of this plant are poisonous. Zones 10–12.

THRINAX
THATCH PALM

This genus, which is a member of the palm (Arecaceae) family, is made up of 7 species, the majority occurring in Florida, USA, the Caribbean Islands, Mexico, and Belize. Thatch palms are solitary-trunked fan palms with palmately lobed fronds on long unarmed stalks. The small flowers are cup-shaped and self-pollinating, borne in panicles from between the fronds and followed by fruit that is usually white. Members of this genus can be found growing in alkaline soils, from sea level to higher areas near the coast, including woodlands and mountain rainforests. They are very attractive palms, most being suited to tropical and subtropical regions although some are grown in warm-temperate zones. Thatch palms will make very handsome specimens or they can be used in garden bed plantings in combination with other species, or for tub planting.
CULTIVATION: These palms will give the best results when they are grown

Thrinax parviflora

Thrinax morrisii

Thrinax radiata

in well-drained soil in a warm sunny position that gives them protection from cold winds. In nature they grow in limestone soils. They are tolerant of salt winds. Propagation of these palms is from seed.

Thrinax morrisii
BRITTLE THATCH PALM, PEABERRY PALM

☼ ✈ ↔ 10 ft (3 m) ↑ 35 ft (10 m)
Small palm native to Cuba, the West Indies and Florida, USA. Smooth trunk swollen at base. Fan fronds blue-green, gray underside, small white dots. Arching panicles of tiny flowers, in summer. Clusters of small white fruit. Zones 11–12.

Thrinax parviflora
JAMAICAN FAN PALM, ROYAL PALMETTO

☼ ❁ ↔ 7 ft (2 m) ↑ 10–50 ft (3–15 m)
Variable small to medium palm from Jamaica. Green fan fronds, uneven surface. Fragrant cream to yellow flowers in panicles, in summer. Small white fruit. Zones 10–12.

Thrinax radiata
FLORIDA THATCH PALM

☼ ❁ ↔ 7 ft (2 m) ↑ 40 ft (12 m)
From the Caribbean to south Florida, USA. Fan fronds deep green, on stalks with base clothed in fibers. Upright panicles of small, white, fragrant, summer flowers. White fruit. Zones 10–12.

Thuja occidentalis 'Caespitosa'

T. o. 'Globosa Rheindiana'

T. occidentalis 'Golden Globe'

Thuja occidentalis 'Hetz Midget'

Thuja occidentalis 'Holmstrup'

Thuja occidentalis

Thuja occidentalis 'Columbia'

Thuja occidentalis 'Elegantissima'

Thuja occidentalis 'Lutea'

Thuja occidentalis 'Ohlendorffii'

Thuja koraiensis 'Glauca Prostrata'

THRYPTOMENE

This genus consists of approximately 40 species of evergreen shrubs from Australia. It is a member of the myrtle (Myrtaceae) family, and is allied to the genus *Baeckia*. These shrubs can reach 3–5 ft (0.9–1.5 m) tall, and have wiry stems and small linear leaves that are usually very aromatic when crushed. Their tiny starry flowers are white, pink-tinted, or pink and are abundant on every small side shoot, coloring the plant in late winter and spring. The flowers are rich in nectar, which gives them a honeyed scent.
CULTIVATION: *Thryptomene* species prefer a light well-drained soil, in full sun and will do best if kept free from frosts. These shrubs will not tolerate prolonged wet and cold conditions, but are otherwise easily grown. They make excellent cut flowers, and one of the best ways to keep the bush compact is to trim the flowering branches for use indoors. Propagation of *Thryptomene* species is from small tip cuttings of non-flowering stems.

Thryptomene calycina
GRAMPIANS THRYPTOMENE

☼ ❄ ↔ 8 ft (2.4 m) ↑ 4–6 ft (1.2–1.8 m)
Evergreen shrub from the Grampian Mountains of western Victoria, Australia. Branches carry somewhat flattened sprays of dark green foliage. A prolific display of star-shaped white flowers that open from pink buds, in winter to spring. Trim lightly during and after flowering. Zones 9–11.

Thryptomene saxicola
ROCK THRYPTOMENE

☼ ❄ ↔ 5 ft (1.5 m) ↑ 3–5 ft (0.9–1.5 m)
Shrub found naturally on rocky hillside outcrops in most of southern Australia. A mass of wiry stems, sprays of small rounded leaves. White or pale pink flowers bloom from late winter to spring. Give it a light annual trim after flowering. Prefers well-drained conditions. Zones 9–10.

THUJA
syn. *Platycladus*

ARBORVITAE, RED CEDAR, WHITE CEDAR
This genus consists of 5 coniferous evergreen trees within the cypress (Cupressaceae) family. Their natural habitat is North America and East Asia, in high rainfall woodland or damp, cold, coastal and lowland plains. The bark is reddish brown and comes off in long vertical strips on mature trees. The leaflets are flattened and scale-like. Solitary male cones grow on the ends of branchlets and the solitary female cones, with 6 to 12 overlapping scales, grow lower down. These are important timber trees as

well as being used often for hedging and the greenery for floristry. The aromatic foliage can cause skin allergies.
CULTIVATION: Young trees do well in full sun in deep, moist, well-drained soil, but need shelter from cold drying winds. *Thuja* species will survive boggy areas that are too wet for other conifers. Propagate by sowing seed in winter in an area protected from frosts, or by rooting half-hardened cuttings in late summer.

Thuja koraiensis
KOREAN ARBORVITAE

☼ ❄ ↔ 12 ft (3.5 m) ↑ 30 ft (9 m)
A small tree, native to northeastern China, as well as northern and central Korea. Conical shape with branchlets that often trail. Mid-green scale-like leaves are bright silver below. Female cones have 4 pairs of scales, during summer. 'Glauca Prostrata', very low growing with bluish foliage. Zones 5–9.

Thuja occidentalis
AMERICAN ARBORVITAE, EASTERN ARBORVITAE, WHITE CEDAR

☼ ❄ ↔ 15 ft (4.5 m) ↑ 30–70 ft (9–21 m)
Large conifer, native to eastern North America. Conical form, rounded at the top with dense foliage. Bark hangs in orange-brown strips. Crowded, flattened, dull green branchlets, with grayish green undersides. The female cones have 8 to 10 pairs of smooth scales, in summer. 'Caespitosa', round slow-growing shrub, 12 in (30 cm) high; 'Filiformis', thin pendent branchlets, grows to 25 ft (8 m) high, golden yellow leaves; 'Golden Globe', height and width of 3 ft (0.9 m); 'Nigra', grows up to about 30 ft (9 m) high, narrowly conical form with branches down to ground, compact, very dark green foliage that retains its color through winter; 'Ohlendorffii', retains juvenile foliage; 'Pyramidalis Compacta', a column of fairly dense,

Thryptomene calycina

Thryptomene saxicola

Thuja occidentalis 'Silver Queen'

Thuja occidentalis 'Smaragd'

Thuja occidentalis 'Little Gem'

Thuja occidentalis 'Tiny Tim'

Thuja occidentalis 'Wareana Lutescens'

Thuja occidentalis 'Woodwardii'

compact, bright green foliage to about 12 ft (3.5 m) high but no more than 4 ft (1.2 m) wide, tapering to pointed leader, fast-growing, good for screens and hedges; '**Rheingold**', pink tints when young, turns golden bronze in cold winters; '**Silver Queen**', green-yellow foliage; '**Smaragd**', conical, bright green foliage; '**Tiny Tim**', dwarf form with rust-colored winter foliage; '**Wintergreen**', broadly conical; '**Woodwardii**', compact shrub with light green foliage. Zones 2–10.

Thuja plicata
GIANT ARBOR, WESTERN RED CEDAR
 ↔ 15 ft (4.5 m)
↕ 70–120 ft (21–36 m)

Tall columnar tree, native to western North America, often with buttressed bole. Flattened horizontal sprays of foliage, mid- to dark green, pale green to gray-white underneath. The female cones have 4 to 5 pairs of scales, each one with a tiny hook, in summer.

'**Atrovirens**', dark green, makes a good compact hedge; '**Aurea**', narrow conical habit, gold-tipped shoots which soon revert to yellowish green; '**George Washington**', broadly conical habit with long leading shoot; '**Hillieri**',

dwarf, height and spread of 6–10 ft (1.8–3 m), and bluish green foliage; '**Stoneham Gold**', young leaves golden, ageing to green; '**Sunshine**', yellow-green foliage; '**Virescens**', dark green foliage; '**Zebrina**', conical, green leaves with yellow stripes. Zones 5–10.

Thuja standishii
JAPANESE ARBORVITAE
 ↔ 20 ft (6 m) ↕ 100 ft (30 m)
A large tree, native to Japan, with split reddish brown bark. The crown is open, broadly conical with irregular branches. Flattened branchlets are green above, white on the undersides. Female cones have 4 pairs of scales, in summer. Zones 6–9.

Thuja sutchuenensis
☼ ❉ ↔ 10–20 ft (3–6 m)
↕ 10–60 ft (3–18 m)

This endangered species is native to northeast Sichuan, China. It forms a shrub or tree with bright green leaves. Female cones have 4 pairs of scales, minute bract at apex of each, in summer. Probably now extinct, last collected in the wild in 1900; may not occur in cultivation. Zones 6–9.

THUJOPSIS
The single species of conifer tree in this genus is a member of the cypress (Cupressaceae) family and is native to Japan. It resembles the better known *Thuja* but has broader and flatter

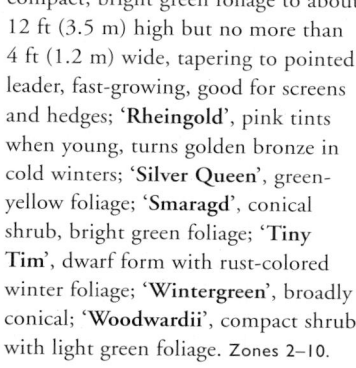

Thuja standishii

Thuja plicata 'Atrovirens'

Thuja plicata

T. plicata 'George Washington'

Thuja plicata 'Hillieri'

Thuja plicata 'Stoneham Gold'

Thuja plicata 'Virescens'

Thuja plicata 'Zebrina'

branchlets which are almost horizontal with tips lifting. The bark is brownish often tending to red. The deep glossy green leaves are larger than those of *Thuja* species, which have silvery undersides. The single species is extremely slow growing.
CULTIVATION: This tree should be planted in a sheltered position in moisture-retentive soil. It is very hardy but must have high humidity. Propagate from seed or cuttings.

Thujopsis dolabrata
DEERHORN CEDAR, FALSE ARBORVITAE, HIBA, HIBA CEDAR

☼ ❄ ↔ 20 ft (6 m) ↑ 100 ft (30 m)
This conifer is from Japan. Conical crown, almost horizontal branches, upswept at tips. Reddish brown bark exfoliates in strips. Leaves deep glossy green with silvery undersides. Slow growing, just 8 ft (2.4 m) after 5 to 10 years in the garden. 'Nana', dwarf, spreading flat-topped bush, grows to about 30 in (75 cm) high. Zones 6–10.

THUNBERGIA
From tropical Asia and Africa, and also found in South Africa and Madagscar, containing around 100 species of annuals, perennials, and

Thunbergia alata

Thujopsis dolabrata 'Nana'

shrubs that are members of the acanthus (Acanthaceae) family. They form an enormously varied group with many being vigorous twining climbers, others are shrubby in habit. Their leaves are usually pointed oval to heart-shaped, sometimes lobed or toothed. Flowers occur in a wide color range, but most often yellow, orange, and purple-blue shades, borne singly or in racemes and are generally long-tubed trumpets with 5 large lobes. Named after Carl Peter Thunber (1743–1828), a Swedish physician and botanist employed by the Dutch East India Company.
CULTIVATION: These plants are mostly frost tender or tolerant only of very light frosts. Plant in a warm sheltered position in moist, humus-rich, well-drained soil. Many species are quite drought tolerant but generally perform best with frequent watering and feeding. Propagate from cuttings or seed, rarely by division.

Thunbergia alata
BLACK-EYED SUSAN VINE

☼/◐ ☽ ↔ 10 ft (3 m) ↑ 10 ft (3 m)
A twining annual or perennial from tropical Africa. Quick-growing, with many long stems. Leaves are heart-shaped, toothed. Flowers numerous, usually orange with near-black throat, sometimes cream to yellow and/or evenly colored, in early summer. Suits hanging baskets. Zones 10–12.

Thunbergia erecta
BUSH CLOCK VINE, KING'S MANTLE

☼ ☽ ↔ 7 ft (2 m) ↑ 6–8 ft (1.8–2.4 m)
Erect freestanding or twining shrub found from tropical western Africa to South Africa. Toothed ovate leaves to 2 in (6 cm) long. In summer, solitary, cream-centered, violet-blue flowers that follow the sun. Zones 10–12.

Thunbergia togoensis

Thunbergia grandiflora
BENGAL CLOCK VINE, BLUE TRUMPET VINE, SKY VINE, SKYFLOWER

☼/◐ ☽ ↔ 15 ft (4.5 m) ↑ 15 ft (4.5 m)
Vigorous twining perennial, native to northern India. Downy pointed oval leaves, sometimes lobed or toothed. In summer, sky blue to violet flowers, to 3 in (8 cm) wide, occasionally solitary, usually in racemes. Zones 10–12.

Thunbergia gregorii
ORANGE CLOCK VINE

☼/◐ ☽ ↔ 6 ft (1.8 m) ↑ 6 ft (1.8 m)
Perennial twiner from tropical Africa, often cultivated as an annual. Toothed, coarsely hairy, triangular leaves. The flowers are solitary but abundant, bright orange, in summer. Zones 10–12.

Thunbergia mysorensis

☼/◐ ☽ ↔ 20 ft (6 m) ↑ 20 ft (6 m)
A strong-growing, twining, woody-based perennial or shrub from India. Simple, often toothed, narrowly elliptic leaves. Spectacularly long pendulous racemes of yellow and red-brown flowers, in late spring. Zones 10–12.

Thunbergia togoensis

☼/◐ ☽ ↔ 20 ft (6 m) ↑ 20 ft (6 m)
Vigorous, twining, climbing perennial, native to tropical Africa. Bright green lance-shaped leaves, to 3 in (8 cm) long. In summer, panicles of yellow-centered, intense purple-blue flowers, 3 in (8 cm) wide. Zones 10–12.

THYMUS
THYME
Well known as the source of one of the most widely used culinary herbs,

Thunbergia gregorii

Thunbergia mysorensis

this genus in the mint (Lamiaceae) family is composed of around 350 species of mainly evergreen, aromatic perennials and subshrubs, many of which become quite shrubby. They occur in most parts of Europe, temperate Asia, and northwest Africa but with the highest concentration around the Mediterranean and in the Middle East. Small wiry-stemmed plants, they have tiny, often downy leaves and heads of equally small mauve, pink, or sometimes white flowers that are very attractive to bees. Late spring to mid-summer is the main flowering season.
CULTIVATION: Frost hardiness varies with the species, though most will withstand moderate frosts. Thyme grows best in light, rather gritty soil that has been enriched with humus for moisture retention. Plant in full sun and trim lightly after flowering to keep the plants compact and well-foliaged. Propagate from seed, by removing naturally formed layers, or by taking half-hardened cuttings.

Thymus caespititius

☼ ❄ ↔ 15 in (38 cm) ↑ 2 in (5 cm)
This dwarf mat-forming shrub is found in Portugal and nearby parts of Spain, also Madeira and the Azores. Narrow, tiny, paddle-shaped leaves, edged with fine hairs. Flowers deep pink, lavender, or white, in late spring. Zones 7–10.

Thymus camphoratus
CAMPHOR THYME

☼ ❄ ↔ 8 in (20 cm) ↑ 8 in (20 cm)
A small woody shrub from western Europe, the western Mediterranean, and southern Portugal. Round, dark green, camphor-scented leaves. Unusual and attractive purplish leafy bracts surround the flowers. Rich rosy pink flowers, in summer. Zones 7–9.

T

Thymus praecox

Thymus praecox 'Albiflorus'

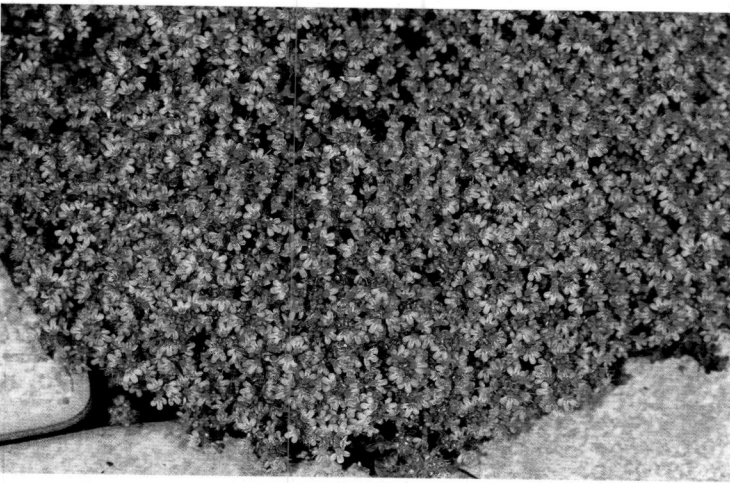

Thymus polytrichus subsp. *britannicus*

Thymus × *citriodorus*

LEMON-SCENTED THYME, LEMON THYME

☼ ❄ ↔ 24 in (60 cm)
↑ 6–12 in (15–30 cm)

This is a hybrid of garden origin between *Thymus pulegioides* and *T. vulgaris*. It is an erect subshrub with branching stems and glossy dark green leaves. Dense lavender-pink flower-heads are borne in summer. Strong lemon scent. **'Aureus'**, an upright, spreading plant with gold-splashed leaves; **'Bertram Anderson'** (golden lemon thyme) has gray-green leaves suffused with gold, new growth tinged red; **'Lime'**, low, creeping, lime green foliage, white flowers; **'Silver Queen'**, silver-green to cream marbled foliage. Zones 5–10.

Thymus Coccineus Group

☼ ❄ ↔ 14 in (35 cm) ↑ 3–4 in (8–10 cm)
Mat-forming creeper of garden origin, possibly forms of *T. serpyllum*. Tiny dark green leaves. Magenta flowers are

Thymus Coccineus Group

Thymus, Coccineus Group, 'Coccineus Minor'

borne in terminal clusters, in summer. **'Coccineus Minor'**, dwarf form, tiny leaves and pink flowers. Zones 4–9.

Thymus herba-barona

CARAWAY THYME

☼ ❄ ↔ 24 in (60 cm) ↑ 4 in (10 cm)
Wide-spreading species from Corsica and Sardinia. Carpet of glossy dark green leaves with a spicy scent. Loose clusters of pink-mauve flowers are produced in mid-summer. Makes a useful ground cover. Zones 7–9.

Thymus mastichina

☼ ❄ ↔ 16 in (40 cm)
↑ 6–12 in (15–30 cm)

An upright perennial from Spain and Portugal. Hairy shoots and leaves. Elliptical green leaves are aromatic. Clusters of white flowers, in summer. Zones 7–10.

Thymus membranaceus

☼ ❄ ↔ 10 in (25 cm) ↑ 10 in (25 cm)
Spreading mounding small shrub from southeastern Spain. Downy, grayish, linear leaves. Flowers and small bracts are white, in mid-summer. Zones 7–10.

Thymus pallasianus

☼ ❄ ↔ 8 in (20 cm) ↑ 6 in (15 cm)
Mounding species from the Caucasus region, with a spreading habit. Leaves grayish green, relatively large, up to ¾ in (18 mm) long. Flowers pale pink, in mid-summer. Zones 7–10.

Thymus pulegioides

Thymus pulegioides 'Foxley'

Thymus polytrichus

Thymus herba-barona

Thymus polytrichus

☼ ❄ ↔ 24 in (60 cm) ↑ 2 in (5 cm)
A tight mat-forming species from southern Europe. Creeping form; dark green oval leaves. Flowers are pale to deep purple splashed with white, in summer. *T. p.* **subsp.** ***britannicus***, dark pink flowers on slightly downy foliage; **'Minor'**, dwarf habit, tiny pink and white flowers; **'Thomas's White'** (syn. *T. praecox* subsp. *arcticus* 'Albus'), compact, crisp clear white flowers. Zones 5–9.

Thymus praecox ★

CREEPING THYME

☼ ❄ ↔ 24 in (60 cm) ↑ 2–4 in (5–10 cm)
Mat-forming creeper from southern, western, and central Europe. Tiny, slightly rounded leaves. Mauve-purple flowers, occasionally white, appear in terminal clusters with prominent purple bracts, in summer. **'Albiflorus'** produces white flowers on dark green foliage. Zones 4–9.

Thymus pseudolanuginosus

syn. *Thymus lanuginosus*

WOOLLY MOTHER-OF-THYME, WOOLLY THYME

☼ ❄ ↔ 24 in (60 cm) ↑ 1–3 in (2.5–8 cm)
This species is of unknown origin. It forms a low-spreading mat of woolly leaves. Scentless pink flowers in early summer. Sparse flowering. Must have sharp drainage. Plant between rocks. Zones 5–9.

Thymus pulegioides

LARGE THYME

☼ ❄ ↔ 12 in (30 cm) ↑ 10 in (25 cm)
This low-growing spreading subshrub is widely distributed throughout Europe. Pretty, mid-green, fragrant, oval leaves on a compact mounded plant. Pink and purple flowers, from spring to summer. **'Foxley'**, deep pink flowers, large variegated cream and dark green leaves; **'Sir John Lawes'**, cerise-pink flowers on a more compact plant. Zones 4–9.

Thymus serpyllum 'Snow Drift'

Thymus serpyllum 'Pink Chintz'

Thymus serpyllum 'Russetings'

Thymus serpyllum

CREEPING THYME, MOTHER-OF-THYME,
WILD THYME

☀ ❄ ↔ 36 in (90 cm) ↕ 1–4 in (2.5–8 cm)
Variable, wide, mat-forming perennial
found naturally from northern Europe
to northwestern Spain. Grows close
to ground from woody base. The tiny
lavender-purple flowers bloom prolifically, in early summer. 'Annie
Hall', old reliable cultivar, very early-
blooming, fragrant, pink flowers;
'Pink Chintz', gray-green leaves, pale
pink flowers; 'Rainbow Falls', more
upright form with gold-splashed deep
green foliage, pink mid-summer
flowers; 'Russetings', bronze-tinted
foliage, bright pink flowers; 'Snow
Drift', pure white flowers over a
spreading mat; 'Vey', compact form,
pale salmon pink flowerheads, darker
in bud. Zones 4–9.

Thymus vulgaris

COMMON THYME

☀ ❄ ↔ 10 in (25 cm) ↕ 12 in (30 cm)
Woody-based perennial or subshrub
found naturally around the western
Mediterranean. Tiny lance-shaped
leaves, downy undersides. White to
pinkish purple flowers, in summer–
autumn. The thyme most often used
in cooking. 'Argenteus', silver-edged
foliage, contain in pots as it spreads;
'Aureus', golden yellow foliage, reddish purple flowers; 'Compactus', a

dwarf, dense mound of gray-green
leaves; 'Erectus', upright growth with
very aromatic, conifer-like, gray-green
needle leaves, white flowers; 'Silver
Posie', white-edged foliage maintained throughout season, pale pink-
mauve flowers. Zones 7–10.

TIARELLA

This genus in the saxifrage (Saxifragaceae) family is made up of 5
perennials, 4 from North America
and 1 found from the Himalayas to
Japan. They spread by rhizomes or an
underground network of thin fleshy
stems, forming clumps of lobed heart-
shaped leaves with long stalks. The
flower stems carry airy open racemes
of tiny white and/or pink to red, 5-
petalled flowers, in late spring and
summer. Foliage and flower stems are
covered in fine hairs. *Tiarella* has been
crossed with *Heuchera* to produce the
intergeneric hybrid × *Heucherella*.

Thymus serpyllum 'Vey'

CULTIVATION: They are very hardy,
especially the American species, and
easily grown in woodlands or perennial borders; spreading but seldom
invasive. Plant in half or full shade in
humus-rich, moist, well-drained soil.
Propagate by division in late winter
to early spring or from seed.

Tiarella cordifolia

FOAMFLOWER

◑/☀ ❄ ↔ 16–20 in (40–50 cm)
↕ 12 in (30 cm)

This perennial is found naturally in
eastern North America; spreading by
underground stems. Leaves hairy,
lobed, toothed, heart-shaped, up
to 4 in (10 cm) long. Airy sprays
of tiny, often pink-tinted flowers on
fine stems, in early summer. 'Major'
has salmon pink flowers that darken
with age. Zones 3–9.

Tiarella polyphylla

◑/☀ ❄ ↔ 16–20 in (40–50 cm)
↕ 12–18 in (30–45 cm)

Species found from the Himalayas to
Japan. Toothed, 5-lobed, heart-shaped
leaves, to nearly 3 in (8 cm) long and
wide. Sturdy purple-red-tinted flower
stems with branching sprays of small,

Tiarella, Hybrid Cultivar, 'Dark Star'

pink-tinted, cream flowers, from late
spring to early summer. 'Rosea', deep
pink flowers. Zones 7–9.

Tiarella wherryi

◑/☀ ❄ ↔ 16–20 in (40–50 cm)
↕ 8–12 in (20–30 cm)

Perennial from North America, closely
allied to *T. cordifolia*. Leaves usually
have 5 pronounced lobes, reddening
in autumn. Racemes of narrow, cream
flowers open from base upward from
pink to maroon buds, in summer.
'Bronze Beauty', red-brown leaves,
pink flowers; 'Oakleaf' ★, leaves dark
center and more pronounced lobes,
flowers strongly pink-tinted. Zones 5–9.

Tiarella Hybrid Cultivars

◑/☀ ❄ ↔ 16–20 in (40–50 cm)
↕ 12–18 in (30–45 cm)

The North American foamflowers
interbreed freely and intermediate
forms are common. Hybridizers have
developed these into a range of attractive garden forms, including: 'Crow
Feather', foliage with a dark central
feather marking intensifying in winter,
cream to pink flowers on spikes; 'Dark
Star', bright green leaves with a dark
center, pink-tinted white flowers;
'Elizabeth Oliver', deep maroon-
veined foliage, maroon-tinted flowers;
'Spring Symphony', long-lobed, dark-
centered leaves, pale pink flowers from
dark buds; 'Tiger Stripe', dark-veined
bronze foliage, reddening in autumn,
pink-tinted cream flowers. Zones 6–9.

Tiarella, Hybrid Cultivar, 'Tiger Stripe'

Tiarella, Hybrid Cultivar, 'Crow Feather'

Tiarella, Hybrid Cultivar, 'Elizabeth Oliver'

Tiarella, HC, 'Spring Symphony'

T

Tibouchina urvilleana

TIBOUCHINA

syns *Lasiandra, Pleroma*
GLORY BUSH, LASIANDRA

This large genus belonging to the meadow-beauty (Melastomataceae) family consists of around 350 species, most from tropical South America. They are mostly shrubs or small trees, perennials, and scrambling climbers with large, hairy, prominently veined, simple leaves, oppositely arranged, often on square stems. The large, showy, 5-petalled flowers are violet, purple, pink, or white and may be borne singly or in panicles at the ends of branches followed by capsular fruit containing spiraly curved seeds. They are generally only suitable for warm to hot areas that are frost free, although well-established plants that are properly acclimatized may tolerate light frosts. Tibouchinas make very attractive horticultural subjects.
CULTIVATION: Most are fairly adaptable but perform best in warm areas in a light well-drained soil with a high organic content in full sun with plentiful water during the summer. Protect from strong winds and prune after flowering. Propagate from seed or cuttings taken in late spring or summer.

Tibouchina granulosa

GLORY BUSH
☀ ✷ ↔ 10 ft (3 m) ↑ 12–35 ft (3.5–10 m)
A large shrub or small tree, native to southeastern Brazil. Thick branching stems, lance-shaped to oblong leaves, shiny dark green, hairy underneath. Variable-colored flowers, violet to rose-purple or pink, in panicles at the ends of branches, in autumn. '**Rosea**' bears smaller purple to rosy magenta flowers. Zones 10–12.

Tibouchina heteromalla

☀ ✷ ↔ 4 ft (1.2 m) ↑ 3 ft (0.9 m)
This small spreading shrub comes from Brazil. Many erect stems, with broadly ovate velvety leaves, bright green; whitish green and very hairy beneath. Violet flowers, in erect panicles at the ends of branches, from summer to autumn. Zones 10–12.

Tibouchina 'Noeline'

Tibouchina 'Jules'

☀/✷ ✷ ↔ 24 in (60 cm) ↑ 24 in (60 cm)
A slow-growing compact hybrid that has become very popular because of its small size. Small bright purple-blue flowers throughout the year, most heavily in late summer to autumn. An excellent plant for city gardens or containers. Zones 9–12.

Tibouchina laxa

☀ ✷ ↔ 2 ft (0.6 m) ↑ 5 ft (1.5 m)
This sparse medium-sized shrub is native to Peru. It has weak branches and broadly ovate, bright green leaves, paler on the undersides. Violet-purple flowers, in clusters from the branch ends, appear from autumn to winter, over a longer period in warmer areas. Regular tip pruning will result in a tighter denser plant. Zones 10–12.

Tibouchina lepidota

GLORY BUSH
☀ ✷ ↔ 10 ft (3 m) ↑ 12 ft (3.5 m)
A bushy shrub, native to Ecuador and Colombia, that is taller and more tree-like in its natural environment. Ovate-oblong to oblong lance-shaped leaves are dark green, paler on the undersides. Panicles of violet-purple flowers, with violet-purple stamens, bloom from late summer to early winter. '**Alstonville**', prolific display of vibrant purple flowers. Zones 10–12.

Tibouchina macrantha

LARGE-FLOWERED GLORY BUSH
☀ ✷ ↔ 8 ft (2.4 m) ↑ 10 ft (3 m)
Shrub or small tree from Brazil. Dark green leaves, with a bumpy surface, paler beneath. Large violet to purple

Tibouchina laxa

flowers, around 4–6 in (10–15 cm) across, at the ends of branches, from late summer to spring. Zones 10–12.

Tibouchina 'Noeline'

☀ ✷ ↔ 10 ft (3 m) ↑ 20 ft (6 m)
A large shrub or small rounded tree. Leaves strongly veined, glossy. Short terminal sprays of flowers that open white and fade to mauve-pink, in autumn. '**Noeline**' is the name under which it has been sold in Australia but it is an unidentified species from South America. Zones 9–11.

Tibouchina urvilleana

syns *Lasiandra semidecandra, Tibouchina semidecandra*

GLORY BUSH, PRINCESS FLOWER
☀ ✷ ↔ 10 ft (3 m) ↑ 15 ft (4.5 m)
Fast-growing shrub from Brazil. Dense rounded form with red hairy stems. Oblong-ovate leaves, dark green with serrated edges. Purple-violet flowers with purple stamens, appear singly or in panicles, in summer. '**Edwardsii**', similar to the species but with somewhat larger flowers. Zones 9–12.

Tibouchina 'Jules'

TIGRIDIA

JOCKEY'S CAP, TIGER FLOWER

This bulbous genus in the iris (Iridaceae) family comprises 23 species found in Mexico and Guatemala. They have sword- to lance-shaped leaves with pronounced longitudinal ribbing. Upright, sometimes-branched flower stems appear from late spring through summer, carrying interestingly shaped and colored blooms with a bold tiger-stripe patterned central cup surrounded by 3 large lobes with 3 small lobes in between. Individual flowers last only one day and occur in a range of shades.
CULTIVATION: Considering their origins, these are surprisingly hardy bulbs that will thrive anywhere the soil does not freeze to bulb depth. Elsewhere they can be lifted for winter and replanted in spring. Propagate from offsets or from seed.

Tibouchina macrantha

Tibouchina lepidota 'Alstonville'

Tigridia pavonia ★

☼ ⚘ ↔ 12–20 in (30–50 cm)
↑ 24–48 in (60–120 cm)

This long-flowering species is native to Mexico. Basal leaves grow 12–20 in (30–50 cm) long. The flower stems are usually about 24 in (60 cm) long, sometimes considerably longer. The flowers are yellow to red with heavily red-marked yellow cup, from spring to summer. Zones 9–10.

TILIA

BASSWOOD, LINDEN

Tilia has been revised down to just 45 species of deciduous trees belonging to the linden (Tiliaceae) family. They occur in eastern and central North America, Europe, as well as most of temperate Asia. They are upright single-trunked trees with a rounded to conical crown of foliage. The bark is silver-gray and smooth and with great age it becomes fissured. The leaf shape is usually oval to heart-shaped with serrated edges, tapering to a fine point. The foliage is usually mid-green but develops vibrant yellow tones in autumn. Small, cream, scented, separate male and female flowers with large bracts are produced in small clusters from late spring. These trees produce conspicuous pale green fruits.
CULTIVATION: These very hardy trees prefer a temperate climate with 4 distinct seasons. They thrive in deep well-drained soil and should be given plenty of moisture in summer. Young trees should be trimmed to shape. Propagate from the copiously produced seed, which needs stratification; from cuttings or layers; or, for special forms, by grafting.

Tilia americana var. *caroliniana*

Tilia americana

AMERICAN LINDEN, BASSWOOD

☼ ❄ ↔ 40 ft (12 m) ↑ 100 ft (30 m)

Broad-crowned tree found in central and eastern North America. Leaves up to 6 in (15 cm) long and almost as broad, with serrated edges, paler green beneath, tapering abruptly to a point. In mid-summer, clustered, pale yellow, fragrant flowers are produced. This species is complex, with many regional variations. *T. a* var. *caroliniana* (syns *T. australis*, *T. caroliniana*), leaves generally smaller, more heavily serrated, blue-green on undersides. *T. a.* var. *heterophylla* (syn. *T. heterophylla*), leaves are white-felted on the undersides, sometimes sparsely. *T. a.* 'Ampelophylla' has large-lobed leaves; 'Fastigiata' has a narrow conical habit; 'Macrophylla' features very large leaves; and 'Redmond' has a conical growth habit. Zones 3–9.

Tilia amurensis

AMUR LINDEN

☼ ❄ ↔ 35 ft (10 m)
↑ 50–100 ft (15–30 m)

This large tree is found naturally in Russia, Korea, and in nearby parts of China. It has very thin bark, and dark green rounded leaves with narrow tips and serrated edges. The flowers are cream, fragrant, borne in clusters, in summer. Very similar to the far more commonly grown small-leafed lime (*T. cordata*). Zones 4–9.

Tilia cordata 'Greenspire'

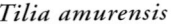

Tilia americana var. *heterophylla*

Tilia cordata 'Rancho'

Tilia cordata

Tilia cordata

LITTLE-LEAF LINDEN, SMALL-LEAFED LIME

☼ ❄ ↔ 40 ft (12 m)
↑ 80–100 ft (24–30 m)

This wide-crowned tree is found over most of temperate Europe from Wales, UK, to western Russia. Dark green rounded leaves, serrated, taper to a narrow tip. Clusters of 5 to 7 fragrant cream flowers, in summer. 'Greenspire' ★, strong-growing form with narrow crown; 'Rancho', conical habit, glossy leaves. Zones 3–9.

Tilia × *euchlora*

☼ ❄ ↔ 40 ft (12 m) ↑ 70 ft (21 m)

Hybrid most likely of *T. cordata* × *T. dasystyla* parentage. Arching branches,

Tilia americana 'Redmond'

Tigridia pavonia

Tilia japonica

Tilia × *europaea*

become increasingly more pendulous with age. Leaves deep glossy green, pale blue-green hairy beneath. Cream flowerheads, relatively large, attractive to bees, in summer. Zones 4–9.

Tilia × *europaea*

syn. *Tilia* × *vulgaris*

COMMON LIME, EUROPEAN BASSWOOD

☼ ❄ ↔ 40 ft (12 m) ↑ 100 ft (30 m)

This *T. cordata* × *T. platyphyllos* hybrid is much planted in parks and city avenues. Tall, broad, conical crown, branches well down trunk. Leaves dark green, heart-shaped, hairy underside veins. Yellow autumn color. Cream flowers, in clusters, in summer, attractive to bees. '**Pallida**', strongly upright growth with pale green leaves, ideal street tree; '**Wratislaviensis**', golden yellow leaves when young. Zones 5–9.

Tilia henryana

☼ ❄ ↔ 25 ft (8 m) ↑ 50 ft (15 m)

Tree from central China. Leaves broad, taper abruptly to a point, serrations reduced to bristles, hairs on veins of both surfaces, undersides tufted and brown. Flowers yellow, about 20 per cyme, in summer. Zones 7–10.

Tilia × *euchlora*

Tilia japonica

JAPANESE LIME

☼ ❄ ↔ 20 ft (6 m) ↑ 50 ft (15 m)

This tree is found in Japan and nearby parts of China. Small pointed leaves have somewhat glaucous undersides. Fragrant creamy yellow flowers, in summer. Its relatively small size and upright growth habit make it an attractive specimen for avenue planting. Zones 6–10.

Tilia mongolica

MONGOLIAN LIME, MONGOLIAN LINDEN

☼ ❄ ↔ 35 ft (10 m) ↑ 50 ft (15 m)

This native of Mongolia is rare in cultivation. Gray bark becomes fissured and purple-tinted with age. The small

Tilia mongolica

leaves have pointed tips and are red-tinted. They mature to dark green, roughly triangular to heart-shaped leaves that have 3 to 5 maple-like lobes and coarse triangular teeth. The cream flowers, 6 to 10 in each cyme, bloom in mid-summer. Zones 3–9.

Tilia oliveri

OLIVER'S LIME

☼ ❄ ↔ 30 ft (9 m) ↑ 100 ft (30 m)

A tall tree, native to western China. Particularly large leaves, light to mid-green, silver-white undersides, leaves tend to be held horizontally. Clusters of 7 to 10 flowers, in summer. Very beautiful tree—a superb specimen for any collector or arboretum. '**Chelsea**

Tilia oliveri 'Chelsea Sentinel'

Sentinel', forms a densely foliaged, broad, upright column with weeping branches. Zones 6–9.

Tilia platyphyllos

BROAD-LEAFED LIME

☼ ❄ ↔ 50 ft (15 m) ↑ 100 ft (30 m)

This dome-shaped tree is found in various forms from western Europe to southwest Asia. Stems are distinctive, very hairy when young. Small clusters of pale yellow flowers are produced in early summer. Fruits persist after the leaves have fallen. It is smaller in cultivation. '**Laciniata**' develops a pretty dome shape, and bears yellow flowers from the crown; '**Orebro**' is shorter and broader, with slightly deeper green foliage. Zones 5–9.

Tilia platyphyllos 'Laciniata'

Tilia platyphyllos 'Orebro'

Tilia platyphyllos

Tilia sibirica

SIBERIAN LIME

☀/☀ ❄ ↔ 10–35 ft (3–10 m)
↕ 4–70 ft (1.2–21 m)

Rarely cultivated species, a native of
northern Asia, especially western
Siberia. Often narrow and strongly
erect, but can develop a broad crown
with great age. Bark is pewter gray;
small heart-shaped to deltoid leaves,
bright green when young, golden in
autumn. Flowers pale yellow, insignificant ornamentally but popular
with bees, in summer. Zones 3–8.

Tilia tomentosa

EUROPEAN WHITE LIME, SILVER LIME,
SILVER LINDEN

☀ ❄ ↔ 50 ft (15 m)
↕ 80–100 ft (24–30 m)

A dense conical to dome-shaped tree
found in areas around the Black Sea.
Rounded heart-shaped leaves, very
dark green, coarsely serrated edges,
fine gray down beneath. Dull white
summer flowers. **'Brabant'**, broadly
conical; **'Nijmegen'**, mottled gray
bark, heart-shaped leaves. Zones 6–9.

Tilia tuan

☀ ❄ ↔ 25 ft (8 m) ↕ 50 ft (15 m)
Tree from central China. Broad ovate
leaves, to 5 in (12 cm) long, tapered

Tilia sibirica

Tillandsia crocata

tips, serrated edges, gray down on the
undersides. Heads of up to 20 pale
yellow flowers, in summer. Zones 6–9.

TILLANDSIA

AIR PLANT

This large genus of over 500 mostly
epiphytic species in the bromeliad
(Bromeliaceae) family extends from
southern USA to southern Argentina.
Plants vary from minute to 15 ft
(4.5 m) tall in flower. The leaves of
some species are covered with gray-
white moisture-absorbing hairs, while

Tillandsia cyanea

others have green strap-like leaves.
The flowerheads are usually globular
or pyramidal, with side-branches and
prominent bracts that are showy and
colorful. Flowers are mostly tubular,
sometimes scented, and are bluish,
pink, white, or yellow. The seed has
a feathery parachute.
CULTIVATION: Gray-leafed forms are
usually grown attached to a substrate.
Mist-spray weekly in cooler months,
as often as daily (early morning) in
warmer periods. They like some air
movement. Green-leafed forms are
generally grown in pots. Grow them
indoors in light and airy situations,
in a greenhouse or conservatory in
cool-temperate areas, outdoors with
protection from direct sunlight and
extremes of rain in warm areas. Propagation is mainly by offsets.

Tillandsia aeranthos

☀ ✈ ↔ 6 in (15 cm) ↕ 6 in (15 cm)
Clump-forming species found from
northeastern Argentina to southern
Brazil. Leaves are narrow triangular,
forming an elongated rosette. Flower
stem red, a little taller than the leaf
rosette. The flowerhead is egg-shaped,
mainly red, large dark blue petals, in
summer. Zones 11–12.

Tillandsia bergeri

☀ ✈ ↔ 6 in (15 cm) ↕ 6 in (15 cm)
Clump-forming species from southeastern Argentina. Leaves are narrow
triangular, gray-green, forming an
elongated rosette. Flower stem a little
taller than leaf rosette, pale red. The
flowerhead egg-shaped, mainly pale
red with large, wavy, pale blue petals,
in summer. Zones 11–12.

Tillandsia butzii

☀ ✈ ↔ 4 in (10 cm) ↕ 12 in (30 cm)
A tall clump-forming species found
from southern Mexico to Panama.

Tilia tuan

Tilia tomentosa 'Brabant'

Tilia tomentosa 'Nijmegen'

Base of leaves forms a dense globular
bulb, gray-green with darker spots
and broken lines, upper parts almost
tubular, contorted, spreading. Flower
stem red, slender. Flowerhead with
few sword-shaped spikes, petals blue-
violet, rolled into a tight tube, in
summer. Zones 11–12.

Tillandsia crocata

☀ ✈ ↔ 6 in (15 cm) ↕ 8 in (20 cm)
This tiny clump-forming species is
found from Bolivia to southern Brazil.
Leaves are narrow, almost cylindrical,
furry gray, in opposite rows on a
single plane. The flowerhead is short
sword-shaped, furry, gray, on a slender
stem, with wide-spreading petals
bright yellow, in summer. Delightful
scent. Zones 11–12.

Tillandsia cyanea

☀ ✈ ↔ 10 in (25 cm) ↕ 10 in (25 cm)
Small shrub from Ecuador. Closely
linked with *Tillandsia lindenii,* often
hybridizing. Leaves narrow triangular,
green, often with red lines underneath, forming an open rosette.
Flowerhead sword-shaped, fragrant,
petals deep violet, sometimes white
eye in center, in summer. Zones 11–12.

Tillandsia dyeriana

☀ ✈ ↔ 6 in (15 cm) ↕ 6 in (15 cm)
A tiny species from Ecuador. Leaves
strap-like, green and purple spotted,

Tillandsia butzii

T

forming a funnel-shaped rosette. The flower stem is slender, soon hanging. Flowerhead is sword-shaped, single or cluster of several branches, bright reddish orange, petals white, spreading wide, just emerging from bracts, in summer. Zones 11–12.

Tillandsia fasciculata
☀ ✛ ↔ 20 in (50 cm) ↕ 40 in (100 cm)
A large varied species from Mexico, Central America, and the West Indies. Leaves are narrow triangular, gray-green, rigid, forming an open rosette. Flowerhead spectacular, simple sword-shaped spike or cluster of up to 10 spikes, wholly red or yellow, or yellow and red, petals purple, rolled into tube, in summer. Eight varieties are recognized. Zones 11–12.

Tillandsia fuchsii
☀ ✛ ↔ 4 in (10 cm) ↕ 8 in (20 cm)
This small species is found naturally in Mexico. Leaves are almost tubular, very thin, and grayish, bottom part forming a tight bulb, upper part spreading, forming a globular rosette. The flower stem is dark wine red. The flowerhead is cylindrical, wine red, petals violet, rolled into a tight tube, in summer. Zones 11–12.

Tillandsia imperialis
☀ ✛ ↔ 16 in (40 cm) ↕ 20 in (50 cm)
This large species is native to Mexico. Leaves are green, narrow triangular, forming a spreading rosette. Flowerhead is cone-shaped, with many red overlapping bracts, tip bending outward and sometimes green, emerging petals violet, rolled tightly into a tube, in summer. Zones 11–12.

Tillandsia fuchsii

Tillandsia ionantha

Tillandsia magnusiana

Tillandsia ionantha
BLUSHING BRIDE
☀ ✛ ↔ 3 in (8 cm) ↕ 2 in (5 cm)
This variable clump-forming species is from Mexico and Central America. The leaves are narrow triangular, gray-green, erect, tips bent outward, almost forming a ball. Flowerhead is hidden, globular, with up to 5 flowers, petals violet, forming a tight tube, appearing in summer. Center leaves turn bright red at flowering. 'Druid' is an albino form. Zones 11–12.

Tillandsia leiboldiana
☀ ✛ ↔ 10 in (25 cm) ↕ 24 in (60 cm)
Tall species from Mexico and Central America. Leaves are strap-like, green, forming funnel-shaped rosette. Flower stem is erect to curved. Flowerhead is bright red, narrow pyramidal, up to 12 side branches with large red bract below each, petals violet, rolled into tight tube, in summer. Also variegated form. Zones 11–12.

Tillandsia lindenii
☀ ✛ ↔ 16 in (40 cm) ↕ 27 in (70 cm)
This tall species is from Ecuador and northern Peru. Narrow triangular green leaves, striped red underneath, forming an open rosette. Flower stem is tall. Flowerhead is fragrant, sword-shaped, petals opening wide, deep blue, white eye in center, appearing in summer. Zones 11–12.

Tillandsia streptophylla

Tillandsia leiboldiana, in the wild, Monumento Nacional Guayabo, Costa Rica

Tillandsia tectorum

Tillandsia magnusiana
☀ ✛ ↔ 6 in (15 cm) ↕ 6 in (15 cm)
Tiny species from southern Mexico to El Salvador. Leaves very thin, almost tubular, gray-green, furred, forming globular rosette. Flowerhead almost globular, violet petals rolled into tight tubes emerging above the leaves, in summer. Zones 11–12.

Tillandsia recurvata
BALL MOSS
☀ ✛ ↔ 2½–8 in (6–20 cm) ↕ 4 in (10 cm)
Minute clump-forming species from southern USA to Argentina. Stemmed leaves almost tubular, gray-green, furred, opposite rows on single plane. Flowerhead, 1 or 2 flowers; petals pale violet or white, in summer. Zones 11–12.

Tillandsia streptophylla
☀ ✛ ↔ 8 in (20 cm) ↕ 18 in (45 cm)
Tall species from southern Mexico to Honduras. Leaves narrow triangular, gray-green, bottom part forms erect bulb, top part bends downward, contorted, spiraling. Flowerhead pyramidal, up to 10 narrow sword-shaped side branches, gray-green; center axis and large bracts below branches bright red, petals purple, rolled into a tube, in summer. Zones 11–12.

Tillandsia stricta
☀ ✛ ↔ 6 in (15 cm) ↕ 8 in (20 cm)
A widespread species, especially in eastern South America. Leaves narrow

Tillandsia recurvata

triangular, green-gray, forming an open rosette, sometimes with leaves pointing in the same direction. Flower stem curving downward. Flowerhead egg-shaped, with many overlapping red bracts, petals blue, in summer. Zones 11–12.

Tillandsia tectorum
☀ ✛ ↔ 12 in (30 cm) ↕ 20 in (50 cm)
Larger species found in Ecuador and northern Peru. Sometimes stemmed leaves, narrow triangular, gray with long gray wool, forming open rosette. Flowerhead with up to 5 sword-shaped spikes, reddish gray, petals blue with white band, in summer. Dislikes wet conditions. Zones 11–12.

Tillandsia tenuifolia
☀ ✛ ↔ 6 in (15 cm) ↕ 6 in (15 cm)
This tiny species comes from eastern South America. Sometimes stemmed leaves are narrow triangular, gray-green, forming an open rosette but sometimes pointing in one direction. Flowerhead is egg-shaped, red overlapping bracts, petals white or blue, in summer. Zones 11–12.

Tillandsia usneoides, hanging from *Quercus virginiana*, Fontainebleau State Park, New Orleans, Louisiana, USA

Tillandsia usneoides

OLD MAN'S BEARD, SPANISH MOSS

☀ ☀ ✣ ↔ 4 in (10 cm) ↕ 24 in (50 cm)

This tall narrow species is found from southern USA to Argentina. It forms large clumps. The leaves are clothed in woolly hairs, gray, opposite and on the same plane, forming long strands that twist and twine. The flowerhead is single, with green petals, and is fragrant. This species blooms in summer. Zones 11–12.

Tillandsia Hybrid Cultivars

☀ ✣ ↔ 4–24 in (10–60 cm) ↕ 4–36 in (10–90 cm)

Cultivars in this genus are extremely varied in size. However, they all produce showy and colorful flowers. 'Anita' has links with *Tillandsia cyanea* and *T. lindenii*, and is a striking lavender instead of the more usual light pink, with large, cinnamon-scented flowers; 'Creation', a hybrid between *T. platyrhachis* and *T. cyanea*, flowerhead erect; many spreading branches with sword-shaped spikes in pink to dark rose, spreading violet-blue flowers; 'Curly Slim', leaves narrow triangular, gray-green, flowerhead pyramidal, gray-green with a pinkish tinge, central axis dull red, petals purple; 'Curra', flowerhead is conical, with many overlapping bright red bracts and emergent violet petals, the numerous inner leaves turn red at flowering; 'Eric Knobloch', leaves are gray-green, forming a bulbose base, flowers pointing upward; petals violet; at flowering, upper half of plant blushes yellow-orange, orange-scarlet, then deep rosy red; and 'Wildfire', the flower stem appears to be an extension of the plant, with up to 25 green bracts taking the place of the leaves; a brilliant red sword-shaped spike emerges from each bract, petals are purplish. Zones 11–12.

TIPUANA

From northern South America, this genus, which is a member of the pea-flower subfamily of the legume (Fabaceae) family, consists of a single species. It is an evergreen tree widely grown for its outstanding floral display and overall attractive appearance. It has a wide flat crown covered in dark green foliage. In spring, the tree bursts into a profusion of deep yellow flowers at the tips of the branches. It has become a favorite shade and avenue tree in subtropical regions of the world. In cool or dry conditions it may be deciduous, but is bare for only a short period.

CULTIVATION: This tree needs a warm climate and a fertile, moist but well-drained soil in full sun. Pruning is rarely necessary, but young specimens may be shaped in late winter. It is sensitive to frost. Propagate from scarified seed in spring, which must be pre-treated by rubbing them briefly on sandpaper and soaking in cold water.

Tipuana tipu

syn. *Tipuana speciosa*

PRIDE OF BOLIVIA, TIPU TREE

☀ ❄ ↔ 25 ft (8 m) ↕ 100 ft (30 m)

This fast-growing slender tree from northern South America develops a spreading, slightly flattened crown. Dark green pinnate leaves, composed of 11 to 21 glaucous, green, oblong leaflets. Profuse racemes of orange-yellow flowers, at the branch tips, in spring. Woody winged seed pods. Smaller under cultivation. Zones 9–12.

Titanopsis calcarea

TITANOPSIS

This genus of 5 species is a member of the iceplant (Aizoaceae) family, from Namibia and South Africa. They are small succulents making rosettes of 6 to 8 tightly packed, very warty leaves. The leaves are broad, spoon-shaped, with a triangular widening at the tip, in shades of white, gray, pink, red, and brown. The daisy-like, yellow to orange flowers are honey-scented, opening in the afternoon, closing by dusk, and are stemless or with a short stem. The seed pods have from 5 to 10 chambers, but usually 6 chambers. The name, from the Greek *titanos*, "chalk," *opsis*, "appearance," refers to the calcium-filled warts on the ends of the leaves.

CULTIVATION: These plants are relatively easy to grow in a mineralized well-drained soil. They should not be overwatered and should be given a distinct rest in the winter. They are usually propagated from seed, but may also be grown by careful division of older clumps.

Titanopsis calcarea

☀/◑ ❄ ↔ 20 in (50 cm) ↕ ¾–1¾ in (18–40 mm)

This tiny succulent is found among limestone rocks throughout Northern, Western, and Eastern Cape in South Africa. Rosettes of spoon-shaped leaves with truncated ends densely covered in reddish or gray-white tubercles, giving a greenish to bluish hue that mimicks its habitat. Flowers golden yellow to orange, in summer. Zones 8–10.

TITHONIA

MEXICAN SUNFLOWER

This genus is made up of 10 species of annuals, perennials, and shrubs that are native to Mexico and Central America. It is a member of the daisy (Asteraceae) family. Quite shrubby species, they are robust plants, sometimes with hairy stems, and have alternate leaves that are often lobed. They bear large daisy flowers in shades of yellow and orangey scarlet.

CULTIVATION: These plants are useful for providing a bright spot in the garden in late summer and autumn. Grow in a well-drained, moderately fertile soil in full sun. Propagate from seed or from cuttings.

Titanopsis calcarea

Tipuana tipu

Tithonia rotundifolia 'Torch'

Tithonia rotundifolia

syn. *Tithonia speciosa*
MEXICAN SUNFLOWER

☀ ◐ ↔ 2 ft (0.6 m) ↑ 3–6 ft (0.9–1.8 m)
This annual from Mexico and Central America is a rapidly forming, large, many-branched plant. Velvety-hairy leaves, to 12 in (30 cm) long. Orange ray flowers with tufted yellow centers, from summer to autumn, or first frost. '**Aztec Sun**', 4 ft (1.2 m) tall, golden flowers; '**Fiesta del Sol**', an earlier-blooming dwarf, to 3 ft (0.9 m) tall; '**Goldfinger**', a bushy selection with deep orange flowers; '**Torch**', orange-red flowers. Zones 9–10.

TOLMIEA

Native to the coastal mountains of western North America, from northern California and north to Alaska, USA, this monotypic genus in the saxifrage (Saxifragaceae) family is a mat-forming herbaceous perennial with shallowly lobed pale green leaves that are sometimes evergreen. Young plants are borne on the leaves where the leaf stalk and leaf blade meet.
CULTIVATION: They prefer neutral to acidic, cool, moist, humus-rich soil in partial to deep shade. Sun can scorch the leaves, particularly the variegated form. They are sometimes grown as a house plant, requiring cool temperatures and filtered light. Propagate by division in spring, or from seed in autumn. Plantlets may also be removed from leaves in mid- to late summer and potted up.

Tolmiea menziesii

PICKABACK PLANT, PIGGYBACK PLANT, THOUSAND MOTHERS

☀ ❄ ↔ 3–6 ft (0.9–1.8 m)
↑ 18–24 in (45–60 cm)
Shade-loving perennial from the west coast of North America. Shallowly lobed leaves, slightly hairy, medium green. Small, inconspicuous, reddish brown flowers are borne on top of 12–24 in (30–60 cm) stems, from late spring to summer. '**Taff's Gold**' (syns '**Maculata**', '**Variegata**') has leaves splashed with gold in spring; foliage fades somewhat in summer. Zones 6–9.

TOONA

syn. *Cedrela*
This small genus in the mahogany (Meliaceae) family consists of 4 or 5 species occurring from southern and eastern Asia to eastern Australia that were once included in the genus *Cedrela*. All are evergreen or deciduous trees with pinnate leaves. They are valuable timber trees, particularly *T. ciliata* which is suitable for temperate to tropical regions. *T. sinensis* suits cooler areas.
CULTIVATION: These plants achieve best results when grown in a deep, well-drained, and fertile soil in full sun with plentiful watering. Grow them in a moist climate and protect them from strong winds. Propagate from seed or suckers.

Toona ciliata

syns *Cedrela toona, Toona australis*
AUSTRALIAN RED CEDAR, RED CEDAR

☀ ◐ ↔ 20 ft (6 m) ↑ 120 ft (36 m)
Beautiful tree occurring in moist rainforests from northeastern Queensland to southeastern New South Wales, Australia. A deciduous tree with a spreading crown, glossy green pinnate leaves, composed of ovate leaflets. New foliage bronzy red color, in late spring. Small, fragrant, white or pink flowers, in spring. Zones 9–12.

Toona sinensis

syn. *Cedrela sinensis*
CHINESE TOON

☀ ❄ ↔ 30 ft (9 m) ↑ 40 ft (12 m)
A variable deciduous tree from China and Southeast Asia, with dark green pinnate leaves, with 8 to 12 pairs of leaflets, turning orange-yellow, in autumn, and rosy pink new growth. Hanging panicles of perfumed, small, white flowers, in spring. '**Flamingo**', suckering growth to 20 ft (6 m) high, new leaves bright pink changing to creamy yellow then green. Zones 6–11.

TORENIA

WISHBONE FLOWER
This is a genus of up to 50 species of low-growing, spreading, bushy annual

Toona sinensis 'Flamingo'

and perennial plants from tropical parts of Africa and Asia. They are members of the foxglove (Scrophulariaceae) family. These plants are noted for their ability to bloom well in both shady and sunny conditions. The toothed oval leaves, to 4 in (10 cm) long, cover the pale creamy green stems. The flowers are pale violet with dark blue-purple lower lips and a yellow throat blotch. A pair of stamens unites at the anthers in a shape resembling the wishbone of a chicken, hence the common name. The flowers generally appear from late spring and finish once the first frosts start. They make excellent edging plants for beds, borders, and shade or woodland gardens, as well as for containers or window boxes.
CULTIVATION: These plants need a warm spot to flourish and will not cope with frost, cold persistent winds, or cold wind-chill factors. They are best grown in consistently moist, organically rich, well-drained soils in part-shade to full sun. Propagate from seed in spring, or once the last of the frosts has finished.

Torenia fournieri

BLUEWINGS, WISHBONE FLOWER

◐/☀ ✛ ↔ 10 in (25 cm) ↑ 12 in (30 cm)
Small bushy species from tropical Asia. Pale green lightly serrated leaves, 2 in (5 cm) long, form mounds on stems. Flowers pale purple, from summer to autumn. Ideal hanging basket plant. '**Blue Panda**', compact habit, lilac-blue flowers; **Clown Series**, mix containing several colors, some with a contrasting rim to each flower. Zones 11–12.

Torenia fournieri 'Blue Panda'

Toona ciliata

Torenia Hybrid Cultivars

☼/◐ ✦ ↔ 10 in (25 cm)
↕ 12–15 in (30–38 cm)

Cultivars expand the range of flower colors to include shades of burgundy, pink, rose, lavender, as well as white. 'Duchess Deep-blue', deep purplish blue flowers with orange spotting; 'Duchess White and Blue' ★, white flowers with very deep blue blotches; 'Duchess White and Pink', white flowers with deep magenta markings. Zones 11–12.

TORREYA

This genus consists of 7 species of evergreen coniferous shrubs or trees belonging to the yew (Taxaceae) family. It is native to North America and Asia, and is found in sheltered woodland and moist riverside situations. The species vary from shrubs to trees with a wide-open crown. The leaves are glossy, fine, sharp needles, yew-like, with paler undersides. Some of the leaves will emit a scent when crushed. The fruit is a seed, smooth

Torreya californica

or furrowed, dull green to purplish in color. *Torreya nucifera*, the kaya nut of Japan, is edible and the oil is used for cooking in that country. The timber of *T. taxifolia* is used for fencing; however, this is an endangered species surviving in the wild in only a few small areas in the States of Florida and Georgia, USA.
CULTIVATION: These plants require shelter from cold or drying winds and grow in moist fertile soil with good drainage in full sun or part-shade. Propagate from half-hardened cuttings in late summer, or sow seed as soon as it is ripe in an area protected from frost. Label well as germination may take up to 2 years.

Torreya californica
CALIFORNIA NUTMEG, CALIFORNIA NUTMEG YEW

☼ ❄ ↔ 25 ft (8 m) ↕ 80 ft (24 m)
A tall tree, native to California, USA, only species to adapt to cool seaside climates. Open crown, broadly conical, and somewhat pendulous shoots. Leaves yew-like, dark green needles, paler on the underside, scented when crushed. Greenish purple female cones appear in summer. Zones 7–10.

Torreya nucifera
JAPANESE NUTMEG YEW, KAYA NUT

☼ ❄ ↔ 25 ft (8 m) ↕ 50–80 ft (15–24 m)
Tree or shrub, native to Japan. Leaves dark green glossy above, blue-white stomatal bands beneath, scented when crushed. Olive green female cones have an edible kernel. Considerably smaller in cultivation. Zones 7–10.

TOWNSENDIA

This genus of about 21 annual or perennial herbs is a member of the daisy (Asteraceae) family, and is native

Torenia, Hybrid Cultivar, 'Duchess Deep-blue'

to western North America. It features soft gray-green spatula-shaped leaves that are covered in very fine hairs. The flowers are very daisy-like with wide discs surrounded by pointed ribbed petals in grayish pink, pinkish white, and mauve. The disc florets are yellow. They produce a showy display throughout summer.
CULTIVATION: These plants prefer a sunny position with deep well-drained soil. Propagate from cuttings in spring or from seed when ripe.

Townsendia formosa

☼ ❄ ↔ 10–12 in (25–30 cm)
↕ 12–16 in (30–40 cm)

This tufting rhizomatous perennial is from dry stony grasslands of southwestern USA. Spatula-shaped leaves, with midribs and edges finely hairy. The flowers have purple or white ray florets and yellow disc florets, and are borne in summer. Zones 8–10.

Townsendia hookeri
syn. *Townsendia nuttallii*
EASTER DAISY

☼ ❄ ↔ 1½–2 in (35–50 mm)
↕ 1½–2 in (35–50 mm)

Tiny clumping perennial. Grows on the dry rocky slopes of the Rocky Mountains in Canada and the USA. Rosettes of narrow silky-hairy leaves,

Torenia, Hybrid Cultivar, 'Duchess White and Blue'

Torenia, HC, 'Duchess White and Pink'

curling edges. Ray florets pinkish white and mauve, disc florets yellow or pinkish, in late spring. Zones 4–8.

Townsendia parryi
PARRY'S TOWNSENDIA

☼ ❄ ↔ 10–15 in (25–38 cm)
↕ 10–15 in (25–38 cm)

Biennial or short-lived hairy perennial from northwestern North America. Spatula-shaped leaves. Large solitary flowerheads, ray florets bluish purple or violet, disc florets yellow, in early summer. Prefers subalpine to alpine habitats. Zones 5–8.

TOXICODENDRON

Widely distributed in temperate and subtropical regions of North America and East Asia, this is a genus of 6 to 9 species of trees, shrubs, and woody climbers belonging to the cashew (Anacardiaceae) family. It is closely related to *Rhus* and some highly noxious species that were previously included in *Rhus* have now been transferred to this genus, including the poison ivy of North America, *Toxicodendron radicans*. The cultivation of a few species is prohibited in some places; however, when *Toxicodendron* species are cultivated they are grown mainly for their brilliantly colored autumn foliage and sometimes ornamental fruit. They all contain a milky or resinous sap that is highly caustic and capable of producing dermatitis or a severe allergic reaction in susceptible people.
CULTIVATION: Frost hardy, these plants all require full sun and a well-drained soil. Locate as background plants away from lawns or walkways,

Townsendia parryi, in the wild, San Juan National Forest, Colorado, USA

Townsendia hookeri

where people are least likely to touch them. Propagate them from seed in summer, or from cuttings.

Toxicodendron diversilobum
syn. *Rhus diversiloba*
CALIFORNIAN POISON OAK, WESTERN POISON OAK

☼ ❄ ↔ 7 ft (2 m) ↑ 8 ft (2.4 m)

An erect, occasionally climbing shrub from western USA. Compound leaves, leaflets smooth-edged or lobed, hairy undersides. Panicles of greenish white flowers, in summer. Creamy white fruit. Contact can produce severe dermatitis. Not recommended for home garden situations. Zones 5–10.

Toxicodendron succedaneum
syn. *Rhus succedanea*
POISON SUMAC, RHUS TREE, WAX TREE

☼ ❄ ↔ 20 ft (6 m) ↑ 30 ft (9 m)

This large deciduous shrub or small spreading tree is from eastern parts of Asia. Compound leaves of 9 to 15 oval pointed leaflets, shiny green, orange-red to scarlet, in autumn. Tiny pale yellow flowers, in early summer. Waxy yellowish brown drupes. Highly poisonous and not recommended for home gardens. Zones 5–10.

Toxicodendron vernix
syn. *Rhus vernix*
POISON ELDER, POISON SUMAC

☼ ❄ ↔ 10 ft (3 m) ↑ 10 ft (3 m)

Deciduous shrub or small tree from temperate eastern North America. Pinnate leaves, 7 to 13 oblong leaflets, smooth edges, color brilliantly, in autumn. Small yellow flowers, in early summer. May produce dermatitis on contact; rarely cultivated. Zones 3–9.

TRACHELIUM

A small genus of 7 species of perennial herbs belonging to the bellflower (Campanulaceae) family, native to Mediterranean regions, and usually found growing in rocky crevices. They range from tiny cushion-forming species to more robust, erect, woody-based plants. Their simple leaves are alternately arranged. The flowers, in

Toxicodendron diversilobum

Toxicodendron succedaneum

shades of purple and white, usually appear in clusters in summer. They are tubular with prominently protruding styles. *T. caeruleum,* which is suitable for border planting, is most commonly seen, flowering from seed in its first year or grown as an annual. CULTIVATION: Grow in a sunny position in reasonably fertile, well-drained soil. The small species, requiring perfectly drained, alkaline soil, are better suited to the rock garden, pots or alpine house. Provide protection from the hottest sun and from winter wet. Propagate from seed or cuttings.

Trachelium caeruleum ★
☼ ❅ ↔ 18 in (45 cm)
↑ 24–36 in (60–90 cm)

Upright perennial from the Mediterranean. Serrated-edged, pointed, oval leaves. Rounded clusters of tiny, starry, pleasantly perfumed, purple flowers, in summer. Very long protruding styles give flowerheads a soft fluffy appearance. Zones 9–11.

TRACHELOSPERMUM
CONFEDERATE JASMINE, STAR JASMINE

A genus of about 20 species of evergreen climbing and twining plants found originally in woodland areas from Japan to India, and part of the dogbane (Apocynaceae) family. The

attractive, glossy, oval leaves are pointed at both ends. The stems will climb over supports and cling to walls and hard surfaces with great ease and abandon. These plants are popular in the ornamental garden for covering fences and pergolas or to clamber up tree trunks. They are used to soften concrete and brick walls and absorb heat in urban landscapes. They work well as ground cover for larger areas and are effectively used in containers and urns, making great indoor or greenhouse specimens. When grown indoors, they will reward with fragrant blossoms if supplied with at least a few hours of sun in winter. CULTIVATION: These climbers are not particular as to soil but prefer well-drained situations with some organic matter. They will grow happily in sun or shade and require average amounts of water; however, they are somewhat drought tolerant once established. Propagate from half-hardened cuttings in summer.

Trachelospermum asiaticum
☼/☀ ❄ ↔ 10–17 ft (3–5 m) ↑ 20 ft (6 m)

A twining climber from Japan and Korea. The oval, dark green, glossy, leathery-looking leaves can grow up to 2 in (5 cm) long. Very fragrant, star-shaped, white flowers hang in clusters, in summer. Zones 8–10.

Trachelospermum jasminoides ★
syn. *Rhynchospermum jasminoides*
CONFEDERATE JASMINE, STAR JASMINE

☼/☀ ❅ ↔ 17–25 ft (5–8 m) ↑ 30 ft (9 m)

A twining climber from Korea, Japan, and China, with oval to elliptical, dark green, glossy leaves, up to 4 in (10 cm) long. Masses of very fragrant white flowers appear in clusters, from summer to mid-autumn. This species can be grown as a ground-cover plant.

Trachelium caeruleum

'Tricolor' ★, red, yellow, and green foliage; 'Variegatum' ★, with white-marked dark green foliage that can burn in hot sun. Zones 9–10.

TRACHYCARPUS

Originally found from southern China to the Himalayas, this is a genus of about 6 species grown for their attractive foliage and their cold tolerance. They are members of the palm (Arecaceae) family. The fan-shaped or circular fronds are up to 5 ft (1.5 m) across and divided almost to the base into stiff, narrow, pleated segments. The frond stalks are often armed with stout sharp teeth. The small fragrant flowers are followed by rounded or kidney-shaped dark purple or orange fruit. These palms are slow-growing and long-lived. They will make good indoor plants in areas that experience severe frosts. CULTIVATION: These palms will grow well in any well-drained soil that is reasonably fertile. They need plenty of water and do best in full sun or part-shade in a position that is sheltered from cold winds, especially when they are young. Potted specimens should be watered moderately during the growing season, much less in cooler weather. Propagate these palms from fresh seed in spring.

Trachelospermum jasminoides 'Tricolor'

T. jasminoides 'Variegatum'

Trachycarpus fortunei ★

CHINESE FAN PALM, CHINESE WINDMILL
PALM, CHUSAN PALM

☀ ❋ ↔ 12 ft (3.5 m) ↑ 35 ft (10 m)
Widely cultivated cold-tolerant palm
from northern Myanmar and central
and eastern China. Slender trunk
clothed in loose dark brown fibers
and old frond bases. Deep green fan-
shaped fronds, divided into many segments. Clusters of small yellow flowers,
in summer. Bluish fruits. Zones 8–11.

Trachycarpus martianus ★

HIMALAYAN FAN PALM

☀ ❆ ↔ 10 ft (3 m) ↑ 50 ft (15 m)
A slender-trunked species, native to
northern India and Myanmar. Fiber
on the trunk is confined to a region
near the crown. Large fan fronds are
dark green, evenly divided. Drooping
yellow flowers, in summer. Black
fruit. Zones 9–11.

Trachycarpus wagnerianus ★

☀ ❆ ↔ 8 ft (2.4 m) ↑ 10–20 ft (3–6 m)
Known only in cultivation, this fan
palm is probably a form of the far
more commonly grown *T. fortunei*.
Distinguished by its smaller and
stiffer fronds and by the very tightly
woven thatch that develops on its
trunk. Zones 9–10.

TRACHYSTEMON

RUSSIAN BORAGE

This small genus of only 2 species
of herbaceous perennials is a member
of the borage (Boraginaceae) family
and is native to eastern Europe. They
have large bristly leaves very like
those of comfrey (*Symphytum*) and
bright blue starry flowers in very early
spring as the leaves come up. Only
T. orientalis is in general cultivation.
CULTIVATION: These exceptionally
hardy plants do best in light to heavy
shade in moist humus-rich soil where
they will make large weed-smothering
clumps. Propagate by division when
dormant. Plants will self-seed.

Trachystemon orientalis

syn. *Borago orientalis*
RUSSIAN BORAGE

☀ ❋ ↔ 3–7 ft (0.9–2 m)
↑ 2–3 ft (0.6–0.9 m)
A coarse herbaceous perennial from
Europe. Paddle-shaped, bristly, green
leaves, to 12 in (30 cm) long. Open
sprays of bright blue starry flowers
with a white center to ¾ in (18 mm)
across, in late winter–early spring.
Zones 5–10.

TRADESCANTIA

SPIDER LILY, SPIDERWORT

This genus is made up of around 70
species of annuals and perennials from
the Americas is a member of the
spiderwort (Commelinaceae) family.
It includes a few species that, while
attractive as garden plants, have
become serious pests in some areas.
Tuberous or fibrous rooted and often
evergreen, they have rather succulent
stems and fleshy, pointed elliptical,
lance-shaped, or narrow leaves. The
clusters of small, 3-petalled flowers,
subtended by bracts, appear through
the warmer months. They are sometimes very bright magenta, though
white, soft pink, and blue to mauve
predominate. Variegated and colored
foliage forms are common.
CULTIVATION: Most of these plants
are tolerant of light to moderate frosts.
Some species prefer a sunny aspect and
are drought tolerant, but most prefer
part-shade and moist well-drained soil.
Propagate by division, or from self-
struck layers, tip cuttings or seed,
depending on the growth form.

Tradescantia Andersoniana Group

☀ ❋ ↔ 12–48 in (30–120 cm)
↑ 8–20 in (20–50 cm)
This group includes hybrids of several
species, not just one cross. Mainly
derived from *Tradescantia virginiana*,
it is a selection of mainly clumping
hybrids with the narrow foliage and
flowering habits of *T. virginiana*. This
group is often wrongly called *T. ×
andersoniana*. Popular hybrids include:
'**Bilberry Ice**', blue-green foliage, pale
silver-mauve flowers; '**Blue and Gold**'
(syn. 'Sweet Kate'), with long, narrow,
bright yellow leaves and vivid blue
flowers; '**Concord Grape**', blue-green
foliage and deep magenta flowers;
'**Innocence**', bright green foliage, pure
white flowers; '**Isis**', green foliage and
bright blue flowers; '**J. C. Weguelin**',
green foliage and striking sky blue
flowers; '**Little Doll**', very compact,
bright green foliage, soft mauve-blue
flowers; '**Osprey**', green foliage and
flowers white to palest mauve with a
mauve-blue center; '**Purple Dome**',
green foliage, deep purple flowers;
'**Zwanenburg Blue**', green foliage,
blue to violet flowers. Zones 7–10.

Tradescantia fluminensis

syn. *Tradescantia albiflora*
WANDERING JEW

☀/☀ ❆ ↔ 24–60 in (60–150 cm)
↑ 12–20 in (30–50 cm)
A somewhat invasive perennial from
South America and naturalized in
southern USA. Thick succulent stems,
closely spaced. Broadly lance-shaped

Trachycarpus fortunei

Trachycarpus martianus

Trachycarpus wagnerianus

Trachystemon orientalis

Tradescantia, AG, 'Bilberry Ice'

Tradescantia, AG, 'Blue and Gold'

Tradescantia, AG, 'Concord Grape'

Tradescantia, AG, 'Little Doll'

T., AG, 'Zwanenburg Blue'

fleshy leaves with lighter central area, to over 3 in (8 cm) long; large white flowers. Cultivated forms occur in wide range of foliage colors and patterns. Zones 9–11.

Tradescantia sillamontana
WHITE VELVET

☼/◐ ⚬ ↔ 40 in (100 cm)
↑ 6–32 in (15–80 cm)

A perennial from northern Mexico. Sometimes erect, or spreading and trailing. Fleshy lance-shaped leaves, to nearly 3 in (8 cm) long, purple-red tinted under a dense covering of silky silvery hairs. Small purple-magenta flowers, in summer. Zones 9–11.

Tradescantia spathacea
syn. *Rhoeo discolor*
BOAT LILY, CRADLE LILY, MOSES-IN-HIS-CRADLE

☼/◐ ⚬ ↔ 12–16 in (30–40 cm)
↑ 15 in (38 cm)

A short-stemmed clumping perennial from southern Mexico, Guatemala, and Belize. Rosettes of erect leaves, to 14 in (35 cm) long, broadly spear-shaped, dark green above, purple-red below. Small white flowers in boat-shaped bract near leaf base, all year. 'Vittata' ★ (syn. 'Variegata'), cream-and-pink striped foliage. Zones 10–12.

Tradescantia virginiana

☼ ❄ ↔ 20–48 in (50–120 cm)
↑ 12–20 in (30–50 cm)

Mounding spreading perennial from eastern USA. Narrow, rather grass-like leaves. Small heads of white, pink, mauve-blue, or purple flowers with similarly colored bracts, in summer. Widely hybridized to produce a range of garden forms. Zones 7–10.

Tradescantia zanonia
syn. *Campelia zanonia*

☼/◐ ⚬ ↔ 5 ft (1.5 m)
↑ 24–40 in (60–100 cm)

An erect to spreading perennial from Central and South America. Leaves simple lance-shaped, silvery beneath. Inflorescence to 8 in (20 cm) long, tiny magenta-tinted white flowers,

Tragopogon porrifolius

Tradescantia zanonia 'Mexican Flag'

large purple-tinted green bracts, in summer–winter. '**Mexican Flag**', leaves with broad cream stripes. Zones 10–12.

TRAGOPOGON
GOAT'S BEARD

This genus is a member of the daisy (Asteraceae) family and contains about 50 species of tap-rooted annual, biennial, or perennial herbs native to temperate Eurasia and the Mediterranean. Their alternate leaves are long and linear, like those of bulbous plants. The daisy flowers are yellow or purple and open in the morning, turning to face the sun before closing in the afternoon or in cloudy weather. Seed heads resemble thistledown. They are plants of grassland and wasteland, often seen along roadsides, and are seldom cultivated as ornamentals. The most commonly cultivated species is *T. porrifolius* (vegetable oyster or salsify), grown for its edible roots.
CULTIVATION: Easily grown in any soil in full sun, and best suited to wild areas where self-seeding is not a problem. Need deep soil to accommodate the tap root. Propagate from seed.

Tragopogon porrifolius
OYSTER PLANT, SALSIFY, VEGETABLE OYSTER

☼ ❄ ↔ 6–12 in (15–30 cm)
↑ 24–36 in (60–90 cm)

A biennial from the Mediterranean. Long, strap-like, bluish green leaves.

Trevesia palmata

Tradescantia virginiana

Tradescantia sillamontana

Tradescantia spathacea

Dusky purple daisy flowers appear in summer. Although the flowers are attractive, the plant is more commonly grown for its edible root. Zones 5–9.

TRAPA
WATER CHESTNUT

The members of this genus, part of the water-chestnut (Trapaceae) family, consist of about 15 floating, aquatic, perennial herbs found from central Europe to eastern Asia and Africa. Their submerged stems have feathery roots usually rooted in mud. Leaves clustered toward the tips of the stems form rosettes; the leaves are toothed, floating, oval-shaped, held on swollen spongy stalks. Heads of 4 small white flowers emerge from the leaf axils. The hardened, horned, nut-like fruits are edible once they have been treated to remove toxins. Named from the Latin, *trapa*, "trap."
CULTIVATION: These plants prefer shallow water or wet muddy soil in a protected, sunny position. Propagate from seed.

Trapa natans
BULL NUT, JESUITS' NUT, WATER CHESTNUT

☼ ❄ ↔ 2–4 ft (0.6–1.2 m)
↑ 3–5 ft (0.9–1.5 m)

Aquatic perennial found from central Europe to eastern Asia and tropical Africa, widely cultivated across Africa and Asia. Floating or prostrate stems; submerged leaves are narrow, linear;

floating leaves triangular, leathery, hairy, forming rosettes. Insignificant flowers, in summer. Large, fleshy, nut-like fruit with 4 sharp barbed spines. Very invasive. Zones 5–8.

TREVESIA

The 12 species of shrubs and trees in this genus, which is a member of the ivy (Araliaceae) family, are found from the Himalayas to southern China and Southeast Asia. Often forming dense clumps, they have thick stems that may be prickly. The large palmately lobed leaves are carried in clusters near the branch tips. Large terminal clusters of small creamy flowers are borne in summer.
CULTIVATION: Grown for their handsome foliage, *Trevesia* species require heated greenhouse or conservatory protection in cold climates. In humid tropical areas they will grow in a shrub border, where they'll need a sheltered, and partly shaded site in moisture-retentive, deep, fertile soil. Propagate from seed or softwood cuttings.

Trevesia palmata

☼ ⚬ ↔ 12 ft (3.5 m) ↑ 30 ft (9 m)

Species native from India to southern China and Southeast Asia. Can grow unbranched or can develop into a wide-crowned shrub or tree. Stout thorny stems and unusual palmately lobed leaves. Large clusters of off-white flowers, in spring. Zones 10–12.

T

Trichodiadema intonsum

Trichodiadema bulbosum

Tricyrtis affinis

TRICHODIADEMA

These 34 shrubby species are members of the iceplant (Aizoaceae) family, from Namibia and South Africa. Plants range from shrubby with long, slender, arched branches to short-stemmed subshrubs. Most species have woody to tuberous roots. Leaves are small, semi-cylindrical, uniquely tipped with a cluster of bristles, and usually glisten with tiny specialized water-storing cells. Small, solitary, daisy-like flowers are white, cream, yellow, or pink to purple, borne from winter into early summer. Seed pods usually contain 5 or 6 capsules. CULTIVATION: These plants are easy to grow in a mineral-rich well-drained soil. Protect them from excessive rain in summer if planted outside; give them a short rest from watering in mid-winter. Propagate from seed, or more usually from cuttings allowed to dry out for a few days.

Trichodiadema bulbosum

☼ ❄ ↔ 16–20 in (40–50 cm)
↕ 6 in (15 cm)

This tiny shrub comes from South Africa. Tuberous roots, often partially raised for display. Leaves are short, cylindrical, appearing gray-green due to the covering of short white hairs. Flowers are deep purple and are produced in early spring. Zones 8–10.

Trichodiadema densum

☼ ❄ ↔ 16–20 in (40–50 cm)
↕ 6 in (15 cm)

Shrub from South Africa. Thick fleshy roots; stems short. Leaves in tufts, densely crowded, green, covered with numerous, short, downy hairs and tipped with tuft of white bristles. The dark red flowers are borne in early spring. Zones 8–10.

Trichodiadema intonsum

☼ ❄ ↔ 8–12 in (20–30 cm)
↕ 4 in (10 cm)

A minute shrub from Eastern and Western Cape, South Africa. Leaves green, semi-cylindrical, slightly curved away from thin stems, narrowing to a point, downy gray hairs, tipped with dark brown bristles. White or pink flowers, in early spring. Zones 8–10.

TRICHOSANTHES

This genus of some 15 species found from tropical Asia through to northern Australia and the Pacific Islands belongs to the pumpkin (Cucurbitaceae) family. The plants are climbing or sprawling annuals or perennials. The tendrils are unbranched or with up to 5 branches. The leaves are simple or with 3 or 5 lobes, their edges smooth or toothed. The flowers are unisexual, males and females on the same plant or on different plants, with 5 white petals that are conspicuously fringed. The fruit is spherical to egg-shaped, fleshy, with a smooth surface. Many of the species are of local medicinal importance and some have tubers that are sources of edible starch. They are grown for their fringed flowers and brightly colored fruits. CULTIVATION: In temperate zones they are grown as greenhouse annuals, raised from seed sown in spring in a potting mix rich in organic matter. In the tropics they are easily grown up buildings or hedges in sunny fertile sites. Propagate from seed.

Trichosanthes cucumerina

syn. *Trichosanthes anguina*
CLUB GOURD, SERPENT CUCUMBER, SNAKE GOURD

☼ ⌀ ↔ 5–10 ft (1.5–3 m)
↕ 8–20 ft (2.4–6 m)

This annual is found naturally from southern Asia to northern Australia. Compound leaves, slightly toothed lobes. Fragrant white flowers, opening late or at night, are produced in spring. Narrow, twisting, cylindrical, edible fruit, to 6 ft (1.8 m) long. Zones 10–12.

TRICHOSTEMA

This genus of 16 species of aromatic annuals and small shrubs is a member of the mint (Lamiaceae) family and is found throughout most parts of North America. They have simple lance-shaped leaves that have a woolly underside. They produce blue, or occasionally pink or white, tubular flowers, which resemble those of the related *Salvia* genus, during most of spring and summer. CULTIVATION: The shrubby species should be grown in a well-drained soil of medium fertility. In cool climates they are best overwintered in the greenhouse. Propagate these plants from seed sown in spring, or from half-hardened cuttings in autumn.

Trichostema lanatum

BLUE CURLS, WOOLLY BLUE CURLS

☼ ❄ ↔ 2 ft (0.6 m) ↕ 2–5 ft (0.6–1.5 m)

Shrubby species from California, USA. Dark green lance-shaped leaves, woolly beneath, rolled edges. Woolly, tubular purple-blue flowers on 15 in (38 cm) spikes, in spring–summer. Zones 6–10.

TRICYRTIS

TOAD LILY

A genus of 16 graceful, rhizomatous, woodland perennials in the lily-of-the-valley (Convallariaceae) family, occurring in moist woodlands and on mountains and cliffs from the eastern Himalayas to the Philippines, and in Japan and Taiwan. Their oblong to lance-shaped, pointed, often glossy and sometimes spotted leaves clasp upright on arching stems. The star-, bell-, or funnel-shaped flowers are terminal or in upper leaf axils and can be pure white, golden yellow, lavender, or purple, usually spotted, with a somewhat waxen or iridescent quality. They usually bloom in late summer and autumn. CULTIVATION: These perennials need moist, well-drained, humus-rich soil, and part-shade to sun. In warmer areas, they will do best in part- to full shade. Some species may be propagated from seed in autumn. All may be divided in spring when dormant.

Tricyrtis affinis

◑/◐ ❄ ↔ 24 in (60 cm) ↕ 36 in (90 cm)

Hardy Japanese species. Arching stems and large, broadly oval leaves. White flowers, 1 in (25 mm) wide, speckled purple, from mid-summer to autumn. Prefers full to part-shade. Zones 5–9.

Trichostema lanatum

Trichosanthes cucumerina

Tricyrtis hirta

Tricyrtis formosana

Tricyrtis formosana
syn. *Tricyrtis stolonifera*
FORMOSA TOAD LILY
☼ ❄ ↔ 18 in (45 cm) ↑ 36 in (90 cm)
Erect species, native to Taiwan, spreading by runners. Green leaves mottled deeper green. Flowers borne mostly in terminal clusters; maroon or brown buds open to white or pale lilac, purple-spotted flowers tinged yellow, in mid-summer to autumn. Zones 5–9.

Tricyrtis hirta
HAIRY TOAD LILY
☼ ❄ ↔ 24 in (60 cm) ↑ 36 in (90 cm)
Upright species from Japan. Arching stems, slightly hairy, with soft green foliage. White flowers speckled with dark purple, along stems in leaf axils, in early to mid-autumn. 'Myazaki', smaller plant, arching habit, slightly larger purple-spotted pink to white flowers; 'Myazaki Gold', similar flowers to 'Myazaki', with gold-edged leaves. Zones 4–9.

Tricyrtis macrantha
☀ ❄ ↔ 24 in (60 cm) ↑ 30 in (75 cm)
Graceful species, native to Japan. Arching stems; glossy green, ovate-oblong, bamboo-like leaves.

Pendulous bell-like flowers held on brownish, slightly fuzzy stems, lemon yellow with chocolate spots inside, in early autumn. Prefers deep shade and moist soil. Zones 7–9.

Tricyrtis macropoda
syn. *Tricyrtis dilatata*
☀ ❄ ↔ 24 in (60 cm) ↑ 30 in (75 cm)
Handsome species from China. Oblong-ovate leaves on erect stems. Branched inflorescences of lavender flowers with darker purple spots, in mid- to late summer. Zones 5–9.

TRIFOLIUM
CLOVER
A vitally important component of the world's pastures, at the same time clover is far less welcome in lawns. A member of the pea-flower subfamily of the legume (Fabaceae) family, it is found naturally throughout the temperate and subtropical zones except Australasia and consists of around 230 species of annuals, biennials, and perennials. Typically trifoliate and bright green, the leaves may have up to 9 leaflets, sometimes darkly marked. The individual flowers in the rounded heads are very much like pea-flowers. Associated with Ireland ever since St Patrick used it to describe the Christian Trinity, the 3-part cloverleaf and the 4-leafed shamrock are today primarily seen as good-luck symbols.
CULTIVATION: Clover is usually hardy and quite easily grown but rarely deliberately cultivated in gardens. Plant in full sun or half-sun in moist well-drained soil. Propagate by division but usually self-sows.

Trifolium pannonicum
HUNGARIAN CLOVER
☼/☀ ❄ ↔ 8 in (20 cm) ↑ 8 in (20 cm)
Perennial from eastern Europe; upright bushy habit. Fine silky hairs cover the red-tinted stems and narrow elliptical leaflets. Inflorescence erect, to 4 in (10 cm) long, with soft creamy yellow flowers, in summer. Zones 5–9.

Trifolium repens
WHITE CLOVER
☼/☀ ❄ ↔ 8–16 in (20–40 cm)
↑ 2 in (5 cm)
Low-growing widely naturalized perennial from Europe with creeping rhizomes. Leaves usually trifoliate, leaflets rounded, finely serrated, deep green with darker chevron markings. Flowers are fragrant, tiny, white or soft pink, in summer. 'Atropurpureum', red-bronze leaves, variable green edge; 'Green Ice', 2-tone gray-green foliage; 'Purpurascens', vigorous, leaflets with central purple-red zone; 'Purpurascens Quadrifolium', purplish brown leaves with 4 leaflets. Zones 4–10.

Trifolium rubens
☼/☀ ❄ ↔ 18–24 in (45–60 cm)
↑ 12–24 in (30–60 cm)
This bushy perennial is from southern Europe. Silver-haired, deep green, trifoliate leaves with elliptical leaflets. In summer, large conical heads of crimson flowers. Zones 7–10.

Trifolium uniflorum ★
ONE-FLOWERED CLOVER
☼/☀ ❄ ↔ 8–16 in (20–40 cm)
↑ 2–4 in (5–10 cm)
A trailing rhizome-rooted perennial found from Sicily to the eastern

Mediterranean. Trifoliate leaves, leaflets rounded, often downy undersides. White flowers, sometimes flushed with pink, solitary or in heads of up to 3, in spring–summer. Zones 7–10.

TRIGONELLA
This genus of some 50 species from the Mediterranean region, the islands of the subtropical North Atlantic, and South Africa, with just one species in Australia, belongs to the pea-flower subfamily of the legume (Fabaceae) family. These perennial or annual herbs are often strongly aromatic. The leaves have 3 toothed leaflets and the stipules are joined to the stalk. The 5-petalled flowers are in dense axillary racemes, umbels, or heads, rarely solitary, with small bracts. The calyx tube is short and bell-shaped with 5 lobes. The beaked fruit is obovate, flattened or round in cross-section. Some are fodder crops, some are grown as "bean sprouts," some for their strong flavor or for medicinal purposes. Species with flowers that "explode" on pollination are now referred to *Medicago*.
CULTIVATION: These plants are best grown in well-drained soil in full sun. Propagate from seed in situ.

Trigonella foenum-graecum
FENUGREEK, GREEK CLOVER, GREEK HAY
☼ ⚘ ↔ 8–12 in (20–30 cm)
↑ 12–24 in (30–60 cm)
Annual herb from southern Europe and the Mediterranean. Compound leaves, 3 toothed oval-shaped leaflets. Ivory to yellow pea-flowers, singly or in pairs from leaf axils, in summer. Foliage and flowers bitter. Aromatic seeds edible. Zones 9–11.

Trifolium pannonicum

T. repens 'Purpurascens Quadrifolium'

Trifolium rubens

Trifolium uniflorum

TRIGONIDIUM

This genus in the family Orchidaceae contains about 20 sympodial, epiphytic and semi-terrestrial orchid species from Central and South America. They have small clustered pseudobulbs topped with 2 or 3 long strap-like leaves. The flowers are produced singly on long peduncles, and have a most unusual shape with the 3 reflexing sepals dominating the bloom. The petals and labellum are disproportionally smaller. These spring-flowering orchids are rarely seen in cultivation, being found in specialist collections and botanical gardens. CULTIVATION: These orchids will grow well in pots using a bark-based medium. They appreciate regular watering and fertilizing and enjoy humid conditions combined with high light and intermediate to warm temperatures throughout the year, disliking periods that drop below 50°F (10°C). Propagate by division.

Trigonidium egertonianum

☀/◐ ✿ ↔ 8–24 in (20–60 cm)
↕ 8–20 in (20–50 cm)

Found from Mexico to Colombia. Mid-green strap-like leaves. Cup-shaped, pale yellow to pinkish tan, 1½ in (35 mm) wide blooms that also have finer and darker striping over the flower, in spring. Zones 11–12.

Trigonidium egertonianum

TRILLIUM

WAKE ROBIN, WOOD LILY

This group of 30 rhizome-rooted, spring-flowering, woodland perennials from North America and temperate Asia is the type genus for the wake-robin (Trilliaceae) family. Ranging from the tiny *T. rivale*, to 2 in (5 cm) high, to species 24 in (60 cm) tall in flower, the genus is remarkably consistent in form. The leaflets are bright green, often mottled and usually broadly oval, tapering to a point. At the center of the 3-leafed cluster is a simple 3-petalled flower that may be white, cream, pink, or deep maroon-red. The common name comes from their early flowering habit—the plant that wakes the robin in spring. CULTIVATION: Plant in part- or full shade in a cool, moist, humus-rich, well-drained soil. All species die back completely in autumn but race into growth in early spring. Propagate by division or from seed.

Trillium chloropetalum

Trillium erectum

Trillium cuneatum

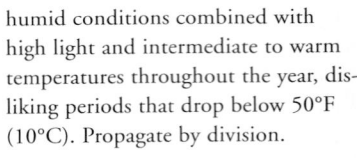

Trillium flexipes

Trillium albidum

☀/◐ ❁ ↔ 20 in (50 cm) ↕ 20 in (50 cm)

Species native to western USA, allied to *T. chloropetalum*. Leaves rounded, often silver mottled, making a complete ruff behind the flowers. Flowers fragrant, white with a pink base, with erect, slightly reflexed petals, in early spring. Zones 6–9.

Trillium chloropetalum

☀/◐ ❁ ↔ 20 in (50 cm) ↕ 20 in (50 cm)

Perennial from California, USA. Thick stems; rounded, often maroon-mottled leaves developing rapidly from early spring to form a full ruff behind the flowers. Fragrant, white to greenish white, soft yellow or maroon flowers with slightly reflexed petals, in early spring. *T. c.* var. *giganteum*, robust, usually dark red-flowered form, with maroon-mottled foliage. Zones 6–9.

Trillium cuneatum

SWEET BETSY, TOAD SHADE

☀/◐ ❁ ↔ 16 in (40 cm) ↕ 24 in (60 cm)

Variegated species native to south-eastern USA. Mottled gray-green and olive foliage said to resemble pattern of a toad's skin. Leaves pointed oval, not quite making a full circle. Flowers burgundy to yellowish green, musk-scented, in early spring. Zones 6–9.

Trillium kamtschaticum

Trillium grandiflorum f. *roseum*

Trillium grandiflorum 'Flore Pleno'

Trillium erectum ★

BETHROOT, BIRTHROOT

☀/◐ ❁ ↔ 20 in (50 cm) ↕ 20 in (50 cm)

Woodland perennial, native to eastern North America. Large, light textured, bright green leaves, sometimes making a complete ruff. Flowers unpleasantly scented, sitting at or slightly above foliage level, dark velvety red, rarely white, narrow petals, in early spring. Zones 4–9.

Trillium flexipes

BENT TRILLIUM

☀/◐ ❁ ↔ 12 in (30 cm) ↕ 16 in (40 cm)

Attractive species from northern USA. Pointed oval leaves. Distinctive nodding flowers on slender stems, white to pale pink, rarely maroon, petals and sepals reflexed or sometimes nearly horizontal, to 2 in (5 cm) long, in early spring. Zones 4–9.

Trillium grandiflorum

GRAND TRILLIUM, SHOWY TRILLIUM

☀/◐ ❁ ↔ 20 in (50 cm) ↕ 18 in (45 cm)

Late-flowering species from eastern North America. Rounded to pointed oval leaves, sometimes overlapping to form a full circle. Flowers opening white, ageing to pink, with narrow to broad petals to 3 in (8 cm) long, in early summer. *T. g.* f. *roseum* ('Roseum'), flowers pink, ageing to a deep dusky shade. *T. g.* 'Flore Pleno', double flowers. Zones 5–9.

Trillium kamtschaticum

☀/◐ ❁ ↔ 12 in (30 cm) ↕ 12 in (30 cm)

A clumping species from temperate East Asia. Short-stemmed pointed oval to rhomboidal leaves. Flowers white ageing to pale purple, petals

T

Trillium luteum

Trillium ovatum

Trillium pusillum

reflexed to almost horizontal, with similarly sized dark green sepals, in early spring. Zones 5–9.

Trillium luteum
WOOD TRILLIUM, YELLOW WAKE ROBIN
☀/◐ ❄ ↔ 18 in (45 cm) ↕ 18 in (45 cm)
Native to southeastern USA. Broad pointed oval, mottled leaves, not over-lapping. Yellow to yellow-green, very fragrant flowers with erect petals to over 3 in (8 cm) long, in early spring. Zones 5–9.

Trillium ovatum
WESTERN TRILLIUM, WAKE ROBIN
☀/◐ ❄ ↔ 20 in (50 cm) ↕ 20 in (50 cm)
Erect species, native to Oregon, USA. Conspicuously veined, deep green, pointed oval to rhomboidal leaves. Flowers held above foliage level on erect stems, white petals held almost horizontally, ageing to pink, musk-scented, in early spring. Zones 5–9.

Trillium pusillum
DWARF WAKE ROBIN
☀/◐ ❄ ↔ 6–8 in (15–20 cm)
↕ 6 in (15 cm)
A small woodland species from south-eastern USA. Narrow leaflets, to 2 in (5 cm) long, sometimes slightly blue-green. White flowers, nearly horizon-tal petals to 1 in (25 mm) long, sepals conspicuous, slightly larger, in early spring. Zones 6–9.

Trillium rivale
BROOK WAKE ROBIN
☀/◐ ❄ ↔ 6 in (15 cm) ↕ 4 in (10 cm)
A small species from the Siskiyou Mountains of California and Oregon,

USA. Leaves up to 1¼ in (3 cm) long, leaf stems slightly shorter. Flowers are white, held above the foliage, often flushed pink with purple-pink spotting, in early spring. Zones 5–9.

Trillium sessile
TOAD SHADE
☀/◐ ❄ ↔ 12–16 in (30–40 cm)
↕ 12 in (30 cm)
Native to northeastern USA. Elliptical to rounded leaves with dark mottling, often slightly drooping, leaves encircle flower but seldom overlap. Flowers musk-scented, petals deep purple-red, sepals green tinted purple-red, in early spring. Zones 4–9.

Trillium sulcatum
FURROWED WAKE ROBIN, SOUTHERN RED TRILLIUM
☀/◐ ❄ ↔ 20 in (50 cm) ↕ 16 in (40 cm)
A tall species found in central eastern USA. Large, light-textured, bright green leaves, making a complete ruff. Flowers held above the foliage on long stems, red-brown, to around 3 in (8 cm) wide, slightly malodorous, in early spring. Zones 5–9.

Trillium tschonoskii
☀/◐ ❄ ↔ 8–12 in (20–30 cm)
↕ 8 in (20 cm)
This small species is found from the Himalayas to Japan. Resembles *T. kamtschaticum*, forming small clump of short-stemmed pointed oval leaves, to 6 in (15 cm) long. Small greenish white flowers ageing to pink and mauve, in early spring. Zones 5–9.

TRISTANIA
This is a single-species genus from Australia and is a member of the myrtle (Myrtaceae) family. Several closely related species were included in this genus in the past, but have now been placed in other genera. A shrub or small tree, it has smooth sometimes flaking bark. The leaves are opposite, lance-shaped, with obvious oil glands. It flowers in summer, pro-ducing small yellow, rather insignifi-cant flowers that appear in bunches, giving it a more heavily flowered

Trillium sessile

Trillium tschonoskii

appearance. It produces a 3-celled fruit capsule. *Tristania* is limited in its distribution, occurring from just north of Sydney to just south and west, along the banks and beds of streams.
CULTIVATION: *Tristania* adapts par-ticularly well to garden situations. Well-drained sandy soils, acid to neutral pH, and water during dry periods are required for good growth. It is somewhat frost tender and seems to grow best in full sun. Propagate from seed or cuttings.

Tristania neriifolia
DWARF WATER GUM, WATER GUM
☀ ♦ ↔ 7 ft (2 m) ↕ 15 ft (4.5 m)
A shrub or small tree from the mid-coast of New South Wales, Australia. Smooth or flaking bark. Leaves are opposite, narrow, lance-shaped with numerous prominent oil glands. Small yellow flowers, in bunches in the upper axils, in summer. Zones 10–11.

TRISTANIOPSIS
This genus, a member of the myrtle (Myrtaceae) family, consists of 40 species, the majority of which are found in the moist forest areas of

eastern Australia, in New Caledonia, Indonesia, and parts of Southeast Asia. Most are shrubs or trees with simple alternate leaves without any obvious venation. Small clusters of cymes occur along the branches, composed of 5-petalled flowers that are yellow to white, often with many stamens. The fruit is a capsule that contains mostly winged seeds. This group of plants was once included in the closely related genus *Tristania*. Many species make useful screen or hedge plants.
CULTIVATION: Most species are fairly adaptable but perform best in warmer climates in a moist well-drained soil in full sun or part-shade. Prune to shape. Propagate from seed.

Tristaniopsis exiliflora
NORTHERN WATER GUM
☀ ♦ ↔ 20 ft (6 m) ↕ 35 ft (10 m)
This small tree comes from northern Queensland, Australia. It branches from near the base; the smooth bark peels off as it ages. The leaves are alternate, narrow, and elliptic, and turn red with age. In summer tiny white-petalled flowers are produced in bunches toward the ends of the branches. Zones 10–12.

Tristania neriifolia

Tristaniopsis laurina

Tristaniopsis glauca, in the wild,
Chute de la Madeleine, New Caledonia

Tristaniopsis glauca

☀ ✤ ↔ 5–10 ft (1.5–3 m)
↑ 5–15 ft (1.5–4.5 m)

One of 6 species endemic to New
Caledonia. Spreading woody shrub
with thick blue-green leaves up to
about 6 in (15 cm) long. Small white
to yellow flowers, in summer. Grows
in red, very iron-rich soils in shrub-
lands along stream banks. Zones 11–12.

Tristaniopsis laurina

syn. *Tristania laurina*

KANUKA BOX, WATER GUM

☀ ❋ ↔ 20 ft (6 m) ↑ 60 ft (18 m)

Tall tree, native to eastern Australia.
Dense canopy of oblong to lance-
shaped leaves, glossy dark green
above, paler beneath. Nectar-rich,
small, yellow flowers, in cymes along
the branches, in summer. Round
fruiting capsules. Smaller in cultivation. Tolerates medium frosts and
compacted wet soils. Zones 10–12.

TRITELEIA

The name of this genus of 15 species
of corms from western North America
was bestowed because the flowers are
arranged in threes. Members of the
onion (Alliaceae) family, they form
clumps of long, narrow, rather grass-
like leaves that are often starting to
fade or may have died away before the

upright flower stems appear. Usually
12–24 in (30–60 cm) tall and borne
in late spring, they carry heads of
funnel-shaped white, blue, or purple,
rarely yellow, flowers. The corms of at
least one species, *T. hyacinthina*, have
been used as vegetables by Native
Americans, eaten boiled and mashed.
CULTIVATION: These plants require
full sun and fertile well-drained soil.
Water them well during the growing
season but allow them to dry off after
flowering. Most species are very hardy
provided the soil does not become
waterlogged in winter. Propagate by
breaking up established clumps after
flowering, or from seed.

Triteleia grandiflora

DOUGLAS'S TRITELEIA, HOWELL'S TRITELEIA

☀/◑ ❋ ↔ 8–12 in (20–30 cm)
↑ 12–24 in (30–60 cm)

Clumping species found from British
Columbia, Canada, to Utah, USA.
Fine grass-like foliage. Each wiry
flower stem bears a head of mauve
to blue, rarely white, funnel-shaped
flowers with widely flared lobes, in
summer. Zones 5–9.

Triteleia hyacinthina

☀/◑ ❋ ↔ 8–12 in (20–30 cm)
↑ 18–24 in (45–60 cm)

Found from British Columbia,
Canada, to California, USA. Foliage

Triteleia ixioides

grass-like. Usually several wiry flower
stems with heads of around 10 white
to lavender, bowl-shaped flowers, to
1 in (25 mm) wide, in summer.
Zones 4–9.

Triteleia ixioides

GOLDEN BRODIAEA, PRETTY FACE

☀/◑ ❋ ↔ 8–12 in (20–30 cm)
↑ 18–24 in (45–60 cm)

A species widespread in western USA.
Grass-like foliage. Usually just 1 or 2
wiry flower stems with heads of around
10 golden yellow, widely flared, and
funnel-shaped flowers, in summer.
'Starlight', shorter flower stems, pale
yellow flowers, may be a form of *T. i.*
subsp. *scabra*. Zones 7–10.

Triteleia laxa

GRASSNUT, TRIPLET LILY

☀/◑ ❋ ↔ 8–12 in (20–30 cm)
↑ 24–30 in (60–75 cm)

This very commonly cultivated
species is widespread in western USA.
The flower stems are sturdy, with
heads to 6 in (15 cm) wide. Flowers
are funnel-shaped, lavender blue to
white, around 2 in (5 cm) long, and
are produced in summer. 'Koningin
Fabiola' (syn. Queen Fabiola) is vigorous, with stronger, more numerous
flower stems. Zones 6–9.

Triteleia lilacina

GLASSY HYACINTH

☀/◑ ❋ ↔ 6–10 in (15–25 cm)
↑ 12–20 in (30–50 cm)

Very grassy species from California,
USA, with very fine foliage and wiry
flower stems. Small lilac flowers with
glassy, finely textured interior, in
summer. Zones 7–10.

TRITICUM

WHEAT

This genus of about 30 annual clumping grasses, from temperate regions of
the Middle East and North Africa, is a
member of the grass (Poaceae) family,
and is particularly important as it
belongs to the cereals group. They
have flat, strap-like leaves. Their
upright or sprawling, solid or hollow,
cylindrical stems bear cylindrical or
flattened spikelets of 3 to 7 florets
with 3 stamens and yellow anthers,
appearing in summer. The ripe seed
heads of *T. aestivum,* the world's most
important cereal crop, are used for
making bread flour. *T. durum* is also
important as source of flour for pasta
and is widely cultivated. There are
more than 40,000 varieties of wheat.
CULTIVATION: Attractive though not
often grown as a garden plant, wheat
is adaptable to most soils in an open
sunny position. Propagate from seed.

Triticum aestivum

BREAD WHEAT

☀ ❊ ↔ 12–20 in (30–50 cm)
↑ 3–5 ft (0.9–1.5 m)

Found across the plains of the world
wherever cereal crops are grown. Flat,

Triteleia lilacina

Triteleia ixioides 'Starlight'

Tritonia crocata

Trochodendron aralioides

rough, narrow, strap-like leaves. Smooth hollow flower stem. Flowers in dense, somewhat flattened, stalkless spikelets, in summer. Bearded seed heads of oval kernels, usually yellowish brown, also red, white, blue, or purple. Flour ground from seeds used to make cereals and bread. Zones 9–11.

Triticum durum
DURUM WHEAT, EMMER WHEAT
☼ ⬧ ↔ 12–20 in (30–50 cm)
↕ 3–5 ft (0.9–1.5 m)
Grown across the flat plains of the world. Flat, rough, narrow, strap-like leaves. Smooth hollow flower stem. Flowers in dense, somewhat flattened, stalkless spikelets, in summer. Seed heads usually bearded; hard, oval-shaped, white, red, yellowish brown, or purple kernels ground to produce flour used to make pasta. Zones 9–11.

TRITONIA
This genus of 28 species of cormous deciduous perennials is a member of the iris (Iridaceae) family and comes from the grassy and stony hillsides of southern Africa. They are closely related to *Chasmanthe, Crocosmia, Ixia,* and *Montbretia,* with which they are often confused. To add to the confusion, many now nameless cultivars and hybrids survive in old gardens. These clump-forming plants have reed-like leaves and their flared trumpet flowers are usually arranged in rows along single or branching stems. CULTIVATION: These plants require dry summers and wet winters coupled with nutrition during growth. Sharp drainage will ensure good growth and plentiful increase. Some species may become weedy in the appropriate conditions. Propagate from offsets or by sowing fresh ripe seed.

Tritonia crocata
syn. *Tritonia hyalina*
BLAZING STAR
☼ ❋ ↔ 4 in (10 cm)
↕ 10–18 in (25–45 cm)
This variable summer-dormant species from Africa is widespread in

cultivation, but rare in the wild. Leaves are erect and grass-like, stems are wiry. Open-cupped flowers, up to 10 per spike, are produced in bright orange, tawny red, or salmon red shades, in spring. 'Princess Beatrix' has brilliant red-orange flowers. Zones 8–10.

TROCHODENDRON
This genus, a member of the family Trochodendraceae, contains a single species of evergreen tree or shrub that has attractive tiered branches and is native to Japan, Korea, and Taiwan. The leaves are glossy and bright green and grow spirally near the tips of the stems. The green and petal-less flowers are produced in upright clusters from late spring. The genus name means "wheel tree," which refers to the spoke-like arrangement of the flower stamens. In the wild this plant will often start life as an epiphyte growing on *Cryptomeria japonica.* Its wood resembles that of coniferous trees and it is thought to be a quite primitive plant. CULTIVATION: Although interesting and attractive, this species is very slow-growing in cultivation. It requires a fertile moisture-retentive soil in part-shade with protection from cold winds. Propagate from seed or half-hardened cuttings.

Trochodendron aralioides
WHEEL TREE
◑ ❋ ↔ 25 ft (8 m) ↕ 70 ft (21 m)
A tall tree from Japan, Korea, and Taiwan; in cultivation it will slowly grow to about 15 ft (4.5 m) high. Tiered branches bear simple glossy green leaves in spirals near the stem tips. Upright clusters of 10 to 12 small, green, petal-less flowers, in late spring. Zones 8–10.

TROLLIUS
GLOBE FLOWER
There are approximately 31 species of perennial herbs in this genus, which is a member of the buttercup (Ranunculaceae) family. They are found in

almost all northern temperate regions from the Himalayas to Turkey, China, Europe, and North America. The roots are thick and fibrous and the plants form basal tufts or rosettes of palmately lobed and divided leaves with toothed edges. The flowers, often cupped, are up to 3 in (8 cm) wide, and have spiraly arranged sepals and petals of white, yellow, or orange, sometimes tinged with red or lilac. They grow in damp sunny meadows and on stream banks, often in heavy soils. The many cultivars of *T. × cultorum* have a more refined bushy habit and will fit easily into the garden border. CULTIVATION: These plants will grow best in full sun or part-shade in permanently moist soil or in boggy areas beside water. Propagate from seed or by division.

Trollius chinensis
syn. *Trollius ledebourii*
☼/◑ ❋ ↔ 18 in (45 cm) ↕ 36 in (90 cm)
This clumping species can be found growing naturally in northern China. It has deeply lobed and finely toothed leaves. The flowers are bowl-shaped, golden yellow, and have prominent stamens. They are produced on tall stems, held well above the foliage, during summer. 'Golden Queen' ★, deep orange-yellow flowers. Zones 5–9.

Trollius × cultorum
☼/◑ ❋ ↔ 18 in (45 cm)
↕ 24–36 cm (60–90 cm)
This group of garden hybrids includes crosses between *T. asiaticus, T. chinensis,* and *T. europaeus.* They show characteristics intermediate between the parents with attractive, finely divided foliage and flowers in colors ranging from lemon to orange, in summer. 'Cheddar', palest lemon to almost white flowers; 'Feuertroll', rich orangey yellow flowers; 'Orange Princess', orange flowers tinted with yellow. Zones 5–9.

Trollius europaeus
COMMON GLOBE FLOWER
☼/◑ ❋ ↔ 18 in (45 cm) ↕ 24 in (60 cm)
This variable species is found growing naturally in Europe, northern Asia, and far northern North America. Leaves 3- to 5-lobed, much-divided, and toothed. Globular lemon yellow flowers, to 2 in (5 cm) wide, in spring–summer. Zones 5–9.

Trollius pumilus
☼/◑ ❋ ↔ 12 in (30 cm)
↕ 4–10 in (10–25 cm)
This alpine species is found from the Himalayas eastward to China. It has deeply lobed glossy leaves. Small, open, yellowish orange flowers are borne in summer. Zones 5–9.

Trollius chinensis 'Golden Queen'

Trollius × cultorum 'Cheddar'

Triticum aestivum, **Provence**

TROPAEOLUM
CANARY BIRD VINE, FLAME CREEPER, NASTURTIUM

The type genus for the nasturtium (Tropaeolaceae) family, this group of over 80 species of sometimes tuberous annuals and perennials is found from southern Mexico to the southern tip of South America. Many climb using their twining leaf stalks. Though variable, the leaves are often shield-shaped and tinted blue-green. All have long-spurred 5-petalled flowers in a wide range of mainly warm shades. The name comes from the Greek *tropaion*, "trophy," a term used for the tree trunk on which were hung the shields and helmets of defeated enemies. CULTIVATION: Hardiness varies considerably in these species. Plant in full sun or half-sun in moist well-drained soil. May need trimming back occasionally. Propagate by division, from basal cuttings or seed.

Tropaeolum majus

Tropaeolum majus 'Empress of India'

Tropaeolum ciliatum
☼/◑ ✽ ↔ 20 ft (6 m) ↑ 20 ft (6 m)

Vigorous, climbing, herbaceous perennial from Chile. Leaves mid-green, with 5 to 7 lobes. Bright golden yellow trumpet-shaped flowers have deep red center and veining, in summer. Capable of covering large area in one season. Zones 8–10.

Tropaeolum majus
NASTURTIUM
☼/◑ ⧓ ↔ 10 ft (3 m) ↑ 10 ft (3 m)

Annual climber or scrambler found from Colombia to Bolivia. Near round, dull green leaves, sometimes shallowly lobed. Flowers to over 2 in (5 cm) wide, long-spurred, in shades of yellow, orange, and red, in summer. Now grown mainly in the form of seed-raised cultivars in various colors, some double-flowered; it is possible that some cultivars are of hybrid origin, with other annual species such as *T. minus* and *T. peltophorum* in their parentage, but breeders have not revealed their history. **Alaska Series ★**, white-variegated foliage, most flower colors; '**Empress of India**', green to bluish green leaves, vivid red flowers; **Gleam Hybrids**, mixed or individual colors; '**Hermine Grashoff**', shallowly lobed leaves and orange-red double flowers; **Jewel Series ★**, white foliage variegation, in most flower colors; '**Margaret Long**', shallowly lobed

T. m., Gleam Hybrid, 'Gleaming Lemons'

Tropaeolum majus, Whirlibird Series, 'Whirlibird Cherry Rose' ★

leaves and golden yellow shading to pink double flowers; '**Peach Melba**', pale yellow flowers with orange blotch on each petal; '**Peach Schnapps**', pinkish orange with orange veining on each petal; '**Red Wonder**', low, slightly spreading, purple-blue leaves, deep red flowers; **Whirlibird Series**, low and spreading, in most flower colors. Zones 9–11.

Tropaeolum pentaphyllum
☼/◑ ✽ ↔ 20 ft (6 m) ↑ 20 ft (6 m)

Extremely vigorous tuberous-rooted climber widespread in South America. Small 5-lobed leaves with purple leaf stalks. Leaves often obscured by pendent masses of dusky coral red to scarlet tubular flowers, in summer. Zones 8–11.

Tropaeolum peregrinum
CANARY CREEPER
☼/◑ ⧓ ↔ 8 ft (2.4 m) ↑ 8 ft (2.4 m)

A quick-growing perennial climber from Peru and Ecuador, often treated as an annual. Light green, 5-lobed leaves. Clusters of long-stemmed, 1 in (25 mm) wide, sulfur yellow to gold flowers, cut-edged petals, in summer–autumn. Zones 9–11.

Tropaeolum polyphyllum
WREATH NASTURTIUM
☼/◑ ✽ ↔ 10 ft (3 m) ↑ 10 ft (3 m)

Annual or perennial trailer or climber from Chile and Argentina. Gray-green to blue-green leaves are 5- to 7-lobed; some forms have near-circular leaves. Clusters of bright yellow funnel-shaped flowers, partly contained in large calyces, appear in summer. Zones 8–11.

Tropaeolum polyphyllum

Tropaeolum majus 'Peach Schnapps'

Tropaeolum tricolor

Tropaeolum speciosum
FLAME CREEPER, FLAME FLOWER, FLAME NASTURTIUM
◑/◑ ✽ ↔ 10 ft (3 m) ↑ 10 ft (3 m)

Perennial climber from Chile. Mid-green to blue-green, palmate, 5- to 7-lobed leaves, often downy. Clusters of brilliant red, 1 in (25 mm) wide flowers, in summer–autumn. Blooms well in shade. Zones 8–10.

Tropaeolum tricolor
☼/◑ ✽ ↔ 7 ft (2 m) ↑ 7 ft (2 m)

Tuberous trailing or climbing perennial from Bolivia and Chile. Small, mid-green to blue-green, palmate leaves. Clusters of pendulous conical flowers, black-tipped red spurs, short cream to yellow petals, from spring to summer. Zones 8–11.

Tropaeolum tuberosum
☼/◑ ✽ ↔ 10 ft (3 m) ↑ 10 ft (3 m)

Tuberous-rooted perennial climber from central Andes. Gray-green leaves. Solitary long-stemmed flowers, spur red, petals golden yellow to red, in summer. The large purple-marked yellow tubers are used as a vegetable in its native range. *T. t.* var. *lineamaculatum* '**Ken Aslet**', orange flowers. Zones 8–10.

TRUDELIA

This small genus in the family Orchidaceae contains 6 different monopodial epiphytic orchid species that were previously included in *Vanda*. They are found from northern India and Nepal across Southeast Asia to Java, Indonesia. They are erect-growing, with thick, strap-like, channeled leaves, in 2 ranks. Larger plants may branch at the base, and have many, very thick, cord-like roots. Inflorescences appear from the base of the leaf stem. They are smaller plants and like cooler conditions than most *Vanda* species and have a different labellum structure, which is very fleshy. They are uncommon in cultivation and bloom in spring or summer. CULTIVATION: They grow in brightly lit situations, and require year-round humid intermediate conditions. They do best in wooden baskets, with the thick fleshy roots attaching to the timber and being allowed to ramble, as the roots require unimpeded air circulation and must dry out quickly after watering. Propagate by division.

Trudelia cristata
syn. *Vanda cristata*
☼/◐ ✼ ↔ 8–24 in (20–60 cm)
↑ 8–20 in (20–50 cm)

Found from Nepal to China. Green leaves. Greenish yellow, 2 in (5 cm) wide blooms, in summer. The blood-red-marked labellum is divided into 2 lobes at its tip. Zones 11–12.

Trudelia pumila
syn. *Vanda pumila*
☼/◐ ✼ ↔ 8–24 in (20–60 cm)
↑ 8–20 in (20–50 cm)

An erect species found from India to Indochina. Leaves narrowly lance-shaped. Flowers cream, 2 in (5 cm) wide, with red and white-marked labellum, in summer. Zones 11–12.

Trudelia cristata

TSUGA
HEMLOCK SPRUCE

These 10 or 11 evergreen, monoecious, coniferous trees from North America and Asia belong to the pine (Pinaceae) family. It grows in mountainous areas in its southern distribution, and in wet cool coastal areas and plains in the north. Most young trees are shade tolerant. They have flattened linear leaves with whitish silver bands on the undersides. The female cones become pendent as they ripen and drop off in the second year. Grown mainly for its timber and ornamental cultivars.
CULTIVATION: *Tsuga* grows in humus-rich, slightly acid, neutral to marginally alkaline soil in shade to sun. All need moist well-drained soil and shelter from cold winds. In poor dry soil these plants make weedy specimens. Propagate by sowing seed in pots in an area protected from winter frosts, or by rooting half-hardened cuttings in late summer to autumn.

Tsuga canadensis
CANADIAN HEMLOCK, EASTERN HEMLOCK
☼ ✼ ↔ 30 ft (9 m) ↑ 80–120 ft (24–36 m)

An evergreen tree, native to eastern North America, in cultivation often

Tsuga canadensis 'Jacqueline Verkade'

Tsuga canadensis

Tsuga canadensis 'Bennett'

Tsuga canadensis 'Gracilis'

Tsuga canadensis 'Minuta'

Tsuga heterophylla, in the wild, North Cascades National Park, Washington, USA

smaller, multi-stemmed. Gray hairy young shoots, linear leaves arranged in 2 rows. Leaves toothed, mid-green above, silver underneath. Female cones brown, grow on end of branchlets. 'Aurea', grows to 25 ft (8 m) tall, young foliage is golden, turning green as it matures; 'Bennett', a dwarf cultivar with lighter green leaves; 'Cole's Prostrate', low-growing ground cover that reaches up to 12 in (30 cm) tall; 'Gracilis', a slow-growing dwarf; 'Jacqueline Verkade', dwarf cultivar of globular form; 'Minuta', a very compact form; 'Pendula ★', a mound-forming slow-growing shrub with pendent branches that reaches 12 ft (3.5 m) in height. Zones 4–9.

Tsuga diversifolia
NORTH JAPANESE HEMLOCK
☼ ✼ ↔ 25 ft (8 m) ↑ 50 ft (15 m)

Large dense tree from northern Japan; rounded habit. Retains leaves for up to 10 years before shedding. Young branchlets are reddish brown; needles notched; cones dark brown, appearing in summer. Often seen as a shrub in cultivation. Zones 5–8.

Tsuga dumosa
☼ ✼ ↔ 25 ft (8 m) ↑ 150 ft (45 m)

A tall spreading tree, native to the Himalayas, from northwest India and Nepal to Yunnan and southwest

Tsuga canadensis 'Pendula'

Tsuga mertensiana

Sichuan in China. Foliage blue-green above, 2 vivid white bands beneath. Stalkless egg-shaped cones. Smaller in cultivation with more spreading branches. Zones 8–10.

Tsuga heterophylla
WESTERN HEMLOCK
☼ ✼ ↔ 20–30 ft (6–9 m)
↑ 60–120 ft (18–36 m)

A large tree, native to western North America. Horizontal branches have pendent tips, glossy dark green leaves. Egg-shaped female cones. Shade tolerant, needs protection from wind. Timber and bark used commercially. 'Argenteovariegata', white young shoots; 'Laursen's Column', dwarf, narrow and columnar. Zones 6–10.

Tsuga mertensiana
MOUNTAIN HEMLOCK
☼ ✼ ↔ 20 ft (6 m) ↑ 50 ft (15 m)

Slow-growing tree, native to western North America. Blue-green leaves, blunt tips. Young cones purple, mature to dark brown, in summer. 'Glauca Nana', to 10 ft (3 m) high, silver-gray foliage. Zones 4–9.

Tsuga sieboldii

Tulbaghia cominsii

Tulbaghia natalensis

Tulbaghia violacea

Tsuga sieboldii

SOUTHERN JAPANESE HEMLOCK

☼ ❄ ↔ 25 ft (8 m) ↑ 50–100 ft (15–30 m)

This multi-stemmed tree is native to southern Japan. It has shiny tan young shoots and leaves with notched tips. Leaves dark glossy green above, pale green to white undersides. Shiny yellowish tan young cones ripen to brown, in summer. Zones 6–10.

TULBAGHIA

SOCIETY GARLIC, WILD GARLIC

This genus, which is a member of the onion (Alliaceae) family, is known for its flowering habit. These bulbous perennials come from summer-rainfall areas in southern Africa, and those in cultivation adapt well to irrigated beds in dry-summer climates. They also pick well, pot well and, generally speaking, lead clumping trouble-free lives. The umbels of starry flowers are held well above the leaves. Many species carry a persistent stale garlic scent when crushed. The flowers of these garden-grown members are dainty to look at and perform well over extended periods, and some will even put on two flowery displays in a single year, depending on the local conditions. CULTIVATION: Grow in full sun in well-drained soils and water well while in growth. Provide a sheltered spot in cool climates. Propagate from offsets or by sowing fresh ripe seed.

Tulbaghia alliacea

☼ ❄ ↔ 16–20 in (40–50 cm)
↑ 18–20 in (45–50 cm)

A semi-evergreen perennial from Zimbabwe and South Africa. Green strappy leaves. Clusters of ½ in (12 mm) wide, green, slightly scented flowers with an orange center, up to 10 per stem, in summer. Zones 8–10.

Tulbaghia capensis

☼ ❄ ↔ 10–12 in (25–30 cm)
↑ 20–24 in (50–60 cm)

Clump-forming perennial from South Africa. Green strappy foliage. Dull green flowers with a purplish center, to ¾ in (18 mm) across, in clusters of 6 to 8 blooms, in summer. Zones 8–10.

Tulbaghia cominsii

☼/◐ ❄ ↔ 6 in (15 cm)
↑ 6–10 in (15–25 cm)

Sweetly scented perennial from South Africa. Foliage tidy, narrow, linear, grooved, with stale garlic scent when crushed. Flowers pale lilac to white to cream, purplish throat, from spring to summer. Recent introduction to cultivation. Good container specimen. Zones 8–10.

Tulbaghia natalensis ★

☼/◐ ❄ ↔ 6 in (15 cm)
↑ 8–12 in (20–30 cm)

Small perennial from Zimbabwe and South Africa. Leaves are linear, light green, with stale garlic scent when

crushed. Flowers are dark purple or white, slightly fragrant, in early to late summer. Good container specimen. Zones 8–10.

Tulbaghia simmleri

syns *Tulbaghia fragrans, T. pulchella*
PINK AGAPANTHUS, SWEET GARLIC

☼ ❄ ↔ 10–12 in (25–30 cm)
↑ 20–24 in (50–60 cm)

A bulbous semi-evergreen perennial from South Africa. Comparatively broad gray-green leaves. Clusters of up to 40 scented mauve flowers, from spring to summer. 'Alba' (syn. *T. fragrans* 'Alba') is a pure white form. Zones 8–10.

Tulbaghia violacea ★

☼/◐ ❄ ↔ 12 in (30 cm)
↑ 12–16 in (30–40 cm)

Vigorous clump-forming plant from South Africa, with gray-green foliage. Clusters of up to 20 pink-mauve flowers produced almost year-round where frost is minimal. The whole plant has a strong garlic smell when crushed. Can become a weed if neglected. 'Silver Lace' (syn. 'Variegata'), slightly smaller variegated form with cream stripes. Zones 8–10.

TULIPA

TULIP

This genus, a member of the lily (Liliaceae) family, contains approximately 100 species of bulbs occurring naturally in northern temperate regions, especially in central Asia. Cultivated for at least 3,000 years, they reached Europe from Turkey in 1554. The Dutch "tulipomania" of the 1630s established tulips in folk-

lore as well as gardens. The foliage is gray-green to blue-green and may be grass-like or quite broad, with contrasting markings. The flowers vary widely. The numerous hybrids and cultivars are divided into 15 groups based mainly on parentage and flower type. *Tulipa* species generally fall into the Miscellaneous Group (Group 15); any exceptions to this rule are indicated in their individual entry. CULTIVATION: Tulips require a temperate climate and winter chilling, preferring a sunny position that does not bake in summer. Plant at around 6 in (15 cm) depth in autumn, watering well once foliage appears. Propagate hybrids and cultivars from offsets; species also from seed.

Tulipa acuminata

HORNED TULIP

☼ ❄ ↔ 2–4 in (5–10 cm) ↑ 18 in (45 cm)

A narrow species from Turkey. The gray-green foliage has undulating edges. The narrow, 3–5 in (8–12 cm) long flowers, scarlet and yellowish with curious, narrow, twisted tips, are borne in late spring. Zones 3–8.

Tulipa aucheriana

☼ ❄ ↔ 2–4 in (5–10 cm)
↑ 2–4 in (5–10 cm)

Tiny species from Iran and Syria. Charming dwarf plant with strap-like, deep green, almost prostrate leaves with wavy edges. The flowers are star-shaped, 1 to 3 per stem, deep rose pink with a yellow basal blotch, borne in mid-spring. Zones 5–8.

Tulipa clusiana

CANDY-STICK TULIP, LADY TULIP

☼ ❄ ↔ 2–4 in (5–10 cm)
↑ 8–12 in (20–30 cm)

From Iran, Iraq, and Afghanistan, this species has linear gray-green leaves with a soft bloom. The flowers open flat and star-shaped. They have a white interior, a dark blue base, and the outer petals are red edged white, in mid- to late spring. *T. c.* var. *chrysantha* (syn. *T. chrysantha*) has bright golden tepals with a red or purple-brown exterior. Zones 3–8.

Tulbaghia simmleri

Tulbaghia simmleri 'Alba'

Tulipa hageri

T. linifolia, Batalinii Group, 'Bronze Charm'

Tulipa orphanidea, Whittallii Group, cv

Tulipa iliensis

T. linifolia, Batalinii Group, 'Yellow Jewel'

spring. **Whittallii Group** (syn. *T. whittallii*) bears star-shaped flowers, orange to red-brown, with black basal markings inside and greenish tinge outside. Zones 5–9.

Tulipa praestans

☼/☀ ❇ ↔ 6–8 in (15–20 cm)
↑ 6–20 in (15–50 cm)

From central Asia. Leaves blue-green, 4 to 6 per bulb. Goblet-shaped, bright red flowers to 3 in (8 cm) wide, 1 to 5 per stem, in early to mid-spring. 'Fusilier', up to 4 orange-red flowers per stem; 'Unicum', similar flowers but distinctive cream-edged foliage. Zones 5–9.

Tulipa fosteriana

☼ ❇ ↔ 4–6 in (10–15 cm)
↑ 12–16 in (30–40 cm)

Outstanding species from eastern Uzbekistan. Oblong to broadly ovate, glossy green leaves. Faintly scented, vivid scarlet flowers with black basal blotch edged yellow, in early to mid-spring. Mostly used in hybridizing. Group 13. Zones 5–8.

Tulipa greigii

☼ ❇ ↔ 4–6 in (10–15 cm)
↑ 6–10 in (15–25 cm)

Small species from central Asia. Lance-shaped to oblong leaves with a soft bloom, mottled and striped purple-brown. Solitary, cup-shaped, scarlet, yellow, or multicolored flowers with black or red blotch on a yellow base, in mid-spring. Group 14. Zones 5–8.

Tulipa hageri

☼/☀ ❇ ↔ 6–8 in (15–20 cm)
↑ 6–10 in (15–25 cm)

From the eastern Mediterranean. Each bulb has 2 to 7 grass-like leaves and 3 to 5 wide open, red flowers, contrasting buff exterior, about 2 in (5 cm) wide, in mid-spring. Excellent rockery or alpine-garden plant. Zones 5–9.

Tulipa humilis

syns *Tulipa pulchella, T. violacea*

☼ ❇ ↔ 2–4 in (5–10 cm)
↑ 4–6 in (10–15 cm)

Popular variable species from south-eastern Turkey, Iraq, and Azerbaijan. Linear gray-green leaves with a soft bloom. Flowers bright rose pink to violet, basal blotches pink, purple to

black, yellow, or blue, in early spring. **Violacea Group**, deep violet, yellow center, slightly smaller plant. Zones 3–8.

Tulipa iliensis

☼ ❇ ↔ 2–4 in (5–10 cm) ↑ 8 in (20 cm)

Erect species from central Asia, with channeled undulate leaves with a soft bloom. Clusters of 1 to 5 yellow flowers with red and dull green reverse, in early spring. Zones 6–8.

Tulipa kaufmanniana

WATERLILY TULIP

☼ ❇ ↔ 4–6 in (10–15 cm)
↑ 6–10 in (15–25 cm)

Broad-flowered species from central Asia. Slightly narrow, wavy-edged, gray-green foliage. Flowers open flat, star-shaped, creamy white with yellow base, outer segments streaked with red; also pink, orange, and red forms, often scented, in early spring. Group 12. Zones 3–8.

Tulipa linifolia

☼ ❇ ↔ 2–4 in (5–10 cm)
↑ 4–6 in (10–15 cm)

A variable species from central Asia, northern Iran, and Afghanistan. Lance-shaped, undulating, red-edged, gray-green leaves in rosette. Shiny red flowers with a cream-edged jet black blotch, in late spring. **Batalinii Group** (syn. *T. batalinii*), formerly listed as a separate species, single soft yellow to apricot flowers, to 3 in (8 cm) across; 'Bright Gem', yellow tinged with orange; 'Bronze Charm', yellow with bronze markings; 'Yellow Jewel', pink-tinted pale yellow. Zones 5–9.

Tulipa montana

IRANIAN TULIP, MOUNTAIN TULIP

☼/☀ ❇ ↔ 4–6 in (10–15 cm)
↑ 2–6 in (5–15 cm)

This small showy species is found naturally in northern Iran and central Asia. Narrow purple-tinted blue-green leaves, to 6 in (15 cm) long, 3 to 6 per bulb. Comparatively large, bright red, goblet-shaped flowers, in late spring. Makes a wonderful rockery plant. Zones 6–9.

Tulipa orphanidea

☼/☀ ❇ ↔ 6 in (15 cm)
↑ 6–15 in (15–38 cm)

This is a variable species from Turkey. Grass-like leaves, 2 to 7 per bulb. Flowers are orange to red with a contrasting buff exterior, often green- or purple-tinted, 1 to 4 per bulb, in

Tulipa montana

Tulipa praestans

Tulipa praestans 'Fusilier'

Tulipa linifolia, Batalinii Group, 'Bright Gem'

Tulipa primulina

☀ ❋ ↔ 2–4 in (5–10 cm) ↑ 8 in (20 cm)

An extremely rare species from north-western Algeria, difficult to obtain. Gray-green leaves. Nodding flowers are held singly or in pairs, ivory to pale yellow tepals with rose pink or light green exterior, in mid-spring. Zones 5–8.

Tulipa saxatilis

CANDIA TULIP

☀ ❋ ↔ 4–6 in (10–15 cm) ↑ 6–10 in (15–25 cm)

Popular species from Crete, Greece, and western Turkey. Network of thin fleshy stems; linear glossy leaves, occasionally with soft bloom. Flowers pale lilac-pink with large deep yellow blotch, cupped, fragrant, in early spring. **Bakeri Group** (syn. *T. bakeri*), lightly fragrant flowers, deep pink-purple with yellow base, opening flat, 3 or 4 per stem, in early spring; '**Lilac Wonder**', broad glossy green leaves,

Tulipa turkestanica

Tulipa undulatifolia

Tulipa tarda

up to 4 lavender-pink flowers with a bright yellow center that opens almost flat in the sun. Zones 6–8.

Tulipa sylvestris

☀ ❋ ↔ 4–6 in (10–15 cm) ↑ 10–18 in (25–45 cm)

A tall species, naturalized in Europe, Iran, and North Africa. Network of thin fleshy stems. Narrow dark green leaves with a soft bloom. Fragrant flowers, clear yellow, exterior occasionally tinged green or red, petal tips reflexed, in spring. Zones 3–8.

Tulipa tarda

☀/◐ ❋ ↔ 6–8 in (15–20 cm) ↑ 4–6 in (10–15 cm)

This small species comes from central Asia. Leaves are narrow, deep green to blue-green. The flowers are small, fragrant, starry, cream to yellow with a maroon- to green-tinted exterior, 1 to 8, rarely to 15, blooms per stem, in spring. Zones 5–9.

Tulipa urumiensis

Tulipa species, Washington, USA

Tulipa primulina

Tulipa turkestanica

☀/◐ ❋ ↔ 6–10 in (15–25 cm) ↑ 8–10 in (20–25 cm)

Slightly clumping species from central Asia. Narrow blue-green foliage, 2 to 4 leaves per bulb. The small, starry, yellow-centered white to cream flowers, up to 12 per stem, are borne in spring. The flower stem is shorter than the foliage. Zones 5–9.

Tulipa undulatifolia

syn. *Tulipa eichleri*

☀/◐ ❋ ↔ 6–10 in (15–25 cm) ↑ 12–20 in (30–50 cm)

This narrow species from the Balkans, Turkey, Greece, Iran, and central Asia has wavy-edged blue-green leaves, fringed with very short hairs. Flower stems are wiry, with 1 flower per stem. The bright red flowers, with a dark central zone, are an open goblet shape, in late spring. Zones 5–9.

Tulipa urumiensis

☀ ❋ ↔ 4–6 in (10–15 cm) ↑ 4–6 in (10–15 cm)

An easy growing species from north-western Iran and eastern Turkey that naturalizes readily. Mostly subterranean stem; rosettes of linear leaves with soft bloom. Flowers cup-shaped, opening to bright golden yellow star, bronze-streaked reverse, in mid- to late spring. Zones 3–8.

Tulipa vvedenskyi

☀/◐ ❋ ↔ 6–16 in (15–40 cm) ↑ 6–8 in (15–20 cm)

A small species from central Asia. Undulating, downy, blue-green, sometimes purple-tinted leaves, held near horizontally at ground level. Flowers

Tulipa vvedenskyi

T. saxatilis, Bakeri Group, 'Lilac Wonder'

vivid orange-red, single, with broad buff to pale green exterior mid-stripes, in mid-spring. Zones 3–9.

Tulipa Hybrid Cultivars

☀/◐ ❋ ↔ 4–12 in (10–30 cm) ↑ 4–30 in (10–75 cm)

Tulip hybrids are divided into 15 groups according to flower type. The flowers come in a bewildering array of forms and colors and include the Parrot Group with deeply cut petals, Viridifloras with green markings and those with broad splashes or "flames" of a contrasting color. Zones 6–9.

SINGLE EARLY GROUP (GROUP 1)

Single-flowered, single or multi-colored forms 12–18 in (30–45 cm) tall, generally blooming within a month after spring equinox. '**Apricot Beauty**', apricot-pink suffused soft orange, mild scent; '**Christmas Dream**', bright pink; '**Christmas Marvel**', very deep pink with pale edge; '**Diana**', pure white, mild scent; '**Kiezerkroon**', a Rembrandt Group look-alike, golden yellow with broad red flame; '**Merry Christmas**', bright deep red; '**Van der Neer**', bright purple, in cultivation since 1860.

DOUBLE EARLY GROUP (GROUP 2)

Fully double-flowered forms 12–16 in (30–40 cm) tall, generally blooming within a month after spring equinox. '**Baby Doll**', golden yellow; '**Double Price**', lavender-pink; '**Monte Carlo**', bright yellow; '**Murillo**', deep pink; '**Orange Nassau**', deep red with lighter zones; '**Peach Blossom**', deep pink flamed and flecked with white.

TRIUMPH GROUP (GROUP 3)

These single-flowered hybrids between single early and Darwin tulips, from

Tulipa, Hybrid Cultivar, Double Early, 'Peach Blossom'

Tulipa, Hybrid Cultivar, Double Early, 'Baby Doll'

Tulipa, Hybrid Cultivar, Double Early, 'Double Price'

Tulipa, Hybrid Cultivar, Double Early, 'Murillo'

Tulipa, Hybrid Cultivar, Double Early, 'Monte Carlo'

Tulipa, Hybrid Cultivar, Single Early, 'Apricot Beauty'

Tulipa, Hybrid Cultivar, Single Early, 'Christmas Dream'

Tulipa, Hybrid Cultivar, Single Early, 'Diana'

Tulipa, Hybrid Cultivar, Single Early, 'Merry Christmas'

Tulipa, Hybrid Cultivar, Single Early, 'Van der Neer'

Tulipa, HC, Single Early, 'Christmas Marvel'

Tulipa, Hybrid Cultivar, Triumph, 'Abra'

Tulipa, HC, Triumph, 'African Queen'

Tulipa, HC, Triumph, 'Annie Schilder'

Tulipa, HC, Triumph, 'Abu Hassan'

Tulipa, HC, Triumph, 'Attila'

T., HC, Triumph, 'Bing Crosby'

Tulipa, HC, Triumph, 'Blenda'

T., HC, Triumph, 'Couleur Cardinal'

T., HC, Triumph, 'Garden Party'

T., HC, T, 'Guus Papendrecht'

Tulipa, HC, Triumph, 'Ice Follies'

Tulipa, HC, Triumph, 'Inzel'

Tulipa, HC, Triumph, 'Kees Nelis'

T., HC, Triumph, 'Lustige Witwe'

T., HC, T, 'Meissner Porzellan'

Tulipa, HC, Triumph, 'Negrita'

Tulipa, HC, Triumph, 'Negrita'

T., HC, Triumph, 'New Design'

Tulipa, Hybrid Cultivar, Triumph, 'Orange Bouquet'

Tulipa, Hybrid Cultivar, Triumph, 'Orange Monarch'

Tulipa, Hybrid Cultivar, Triumph, 'Palestrina'

Tulipa, Hybrid Cultivar, Triumph, 'Prinses Irene'

Tulipa, Hybrid Cultivar, Triumph, 'Prominence'

Tulipa, HC, Triumph, 'Rosalie'

Tulipa, HC, Triumph, 'Silentia'

Tulipa, HC, Triumph, 'Shirley'

T., HC, Triumph, 'White Dream'

T., HC, Triumph, 'Yokohama'

15–20 in (38–50 cm) tall, often have contrastingly colored petal edges or flecks, generally bloom after spring equinox. 'Abra', red-brown with yellow edges; 'Abu Hassan', deep red with a yellow edge; 'African Queen', purple-red with feathered white edge; 'Annie Schilder', bright orange with darker flame; 'Attila', pinkish purple; 'Couleur Cardinal', bright red with purple-tinted base; 'Don Quichotte', mauve-pink; 'Ice Follies', Rembrandt Group look-alike, white with red flaming; 'Leen van der Mark', cherry red with yellow edges ageing to white; 'Meissner Porzellan', white with broad feathered pink edge; 'Negrita' ★, deep purple; 'New Design', white with pink edge, white-edged foliage; 'Palestrina', salmon pink with green flame; 'Prinses Irene', yellow-orange with purple flame; 'White Dream', pure white; 'Yokohama', bright yellow.

DARWIN HYBRID GROUP (GROUP 4)

Single-flowered hybrids between single late (Group 5) tulips and *T. f osteriana* and/or similar closely related species. They are 20–27 in (50–70 cm) tall, and in cool areas flower more than a month after spring equinox; also called Cottage tulips. 'Ad Rem' has orange-red blooms with a gold edge; 'Apeldoorn', deep red with a yellow center; 'Apeldoorn's Elite', red, edged with yellow; 'Daydream', irregular mix of yellow, orange, and apricot; 'Elizabeth Arden', orange-pink to red, yellow base; 'Golden Parade', deep yellow blooms; 'Golden Apeldoorn', deep yellow; 'Ollioules', dark pink with paler edges; 'Olympic Flame', Rembrandt Group look-alike, yellow with red flame; 'Pink Impression', soft pink ageing to rose with cream edge.

SINGLE LATE GROUP (GROUP 5)

These single-flowered forms, 18–30 in (45–75 cm) tall, usually flower more than a month after spring equinox.

Tulipa, Hybrid Cultivar, Darwin Hybrid, 'Ad Rem'

Tulipa, HC, Darwin Hybrid, 'Daydream'

Tulipa, Hybrid Cultivar, Darwin Hybrid, 'Apeldoorn'

Tulipa, Hybrid Cultivar, Darwin Hybrid, 'Elite'

Tulipa, Hybrid Cultivar, Darwin Hybrid, 'Elizabeth Arden'

Tulipa, Hybrid Cultivar, Darwin Hybrid, 'French Impression'

Tulipa, Hybrid Cultivar, Darwin Hybrid, 'Ollioules'

Tulipa, HC, DH, 'Golden Parade'

T., HC, DH, 'Golden Apeldoorn'

Tulipa, HC, DH, 'Olympic Flame'

T., HC, DH, 'Pink Impression'

T., HC, DH, 'World's Favourite'

'**Bleu Aimable**', purple suffused with lavender; '**Candy Club**', pale pink with dark central "kiss;" '**Dordogne**', soft orange edges, deepening to center; '**Douglas Bader**', soft pink; '**Dreamland**', deep pink, light edges, white base; '**Halcro**', deep red; '**Maureen**', pure white; '**Mrs John T. Scheeper**', massive deep yellow flowers; '**Perestroyka**', white with purplish red markings; '**Purple Prince**', light purple; '**Queen of Night**', deep black-purple;

'**Sorbet**', white flowers flamed cherry red; '**Sweet Harmony**', pale yellow; '**Union Jack**', Rembrandt Group look-alike, white flowers flamed and edged deep red; '**World Expression**', white ageing to cream with dark red flame.

LILY-FLOWERED GROUP (GROUP 6)

Long 2-toned flowers tapering at the center to distinct waist. Lily-flowered tulips are 15–24 in (38–60 cm) tall,

Tulipa, HC, Lily-Flowered, 'Aladdin'

Tulipa, HC, Lily-Flowered, 'Ballerina'

Tulipa, HC, Single Late, 'Blushing Bride'

Tulipa, HC, Single Late, 'Big Smile'

Tulipa, HC, Single Late, 'Colour Spectacle'

Tulipa, HC, Single Late, 'Douglas Bader'

T., HC, Single Late, 'Bleu Aimable'

T., HC, Single Late, 'Dordogne'

T., HC, Single Late, 'Dreamland'

T., HC, SL, 'Gander's Rhapsody'

T., HC, Single Late, 'Georgette'

T., HC, Single Late, 'Grand Style'

T., HC, SL, 'Ile de France'

T., HC, SL, ' Landseadel's Supreme'

T., HC, SL, 'Lemon Grove'

T., HC, Single Late, 'Maureen'

T., HC, Single Late, 'Patriot'

T., HC, Single Late, 'Perestroyka'

T., HC, Single Late, 'Picture'

T., HC, SL, 'Pink Diamond'

T., HC, Single Late, 'Primavera'

T., HC, SL, 'Queen of Night'

Tulipa, HC, Single Late, 'Sorbet'

T., HC, SL, 'Sweet Harmony'

T., HC, SL, 'World Expression'

T., HC, SL, 'Zomerschoon'

Tulipa, Hybrid Cultivar, Lily-Flowered, 'China Pink'

Tulipa, Hybrid Cultivar, Lily-Flowered, 'Elegant Lady'

Tulipa, Hybrid Cultivar, Lily-Flowered, 'Jacqueline'

Tulipa, Hybrid Cultivar, Lily-Flowered, 'Mariette'

Tulipa, Hybrid Cultivar, Lily-Flowered cultivar

T., HC, Lily-Flowered, 'Marjolein'

T., HC, Lily-Flowered, 'Maytime'

T., HC, L-F, 'Queen of Sheba'

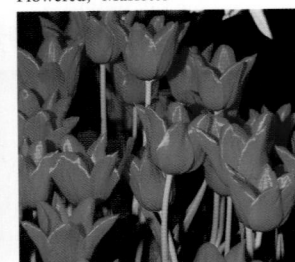

T., HC, Lily-Flowered, 'Red Shine'

T., HC, Lily-Flowered, 'West Point'

T., HC, Lily-Flowered, 'White Triumphator'

and have a variable flowering time. 'Aladdin', bright red with yellow edge and center; 'Ballade', violet edged with white; 'Ballerina', orange suffused with red; 'China Pink', deep pink with light tips and center; 'Elegant Lady', soft gold turning to pink near tips; 'Marilyn', white flamed with red; 'Queen of Sheba', red with golden orange edge; 'West Point', bright golden yellow; 'White Triumphator', pure white.

FRINGED GROUP (GROUP 7)

The flowers in this group have fringed edges, with the fringe itself often in a contrasting color to the rest of the flower and usually with a crystalline texture, 18–26 in (45–65 cm) tall. 'Arma', deep red with crystalline fringe; 'Blue Heron', dusky purple and mauve with white fringe; 'Burgundy Lace' ★, wine red with crystalline edge; 'Maja', bright yellow with crystalline fringe.

VIRIDIFLORA GROUP (GROUP 8)

The tulips in this group are around 12–20 in (30–50 cm) tall and have either strong green coloration in the base or an external flare up the center of each petal. 'Artist', salmon suffused with orange and purple, and a green flame; 'China Town', dusky light pink, with darker edges and green flame; 'Golden Artist', deep golden yellow, with a green flame that is edged with red; 'Groenland', mid-pink, a narrow green flame with a broad pale pink edge; 'Hollywood', red with darker flame; 'Spring Green', cream with a narrow green flame.

REMBRANDT GROUP (GROUP 9)

Fancy-flowered, often multi-colored tulips with contrasting flares, flecks, and veining, usually on a base color of yellow, red, or white, patterns originating from a viral disease that led to

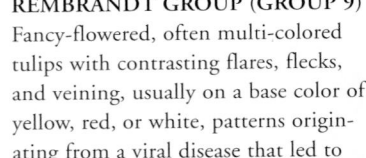

Tulipa, Hybrid Cultivar, Viridiflora, 'Artist'

T., HC, Viridiflora, 'China Town'

T., HC, Viridiflora, 'Golden Artist'

T., HC, Viridiflora, 'Groenland'

T., HC, Viridiflora, 'Hollywood'

T., HC, Viridiflora, 'Spring Green'

Tulipa, HC, Fringed, 'Arma'

T., HC, Fringed, 'Blue Heron'

T., HC, Fringed, 'Burgundy Lace'

Tulipa, HC, Fringed, 'Maja'

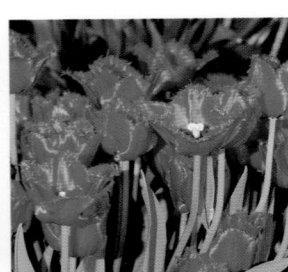

T., HC, Fringed, 'Red Wing'

T

T., HC, Parrot, 'Bird of Paradise'

Tulipa, HC, Parrot, 'Blue Parrot'

T., HC, Parrot, 'Karel Doorman'

T., HC, Parrot, 'Professor Röntgen'

T., HC, Parrot, 'Weber's Parrot'

Tulipa, HC, Parrot, 'Snow Parrot'

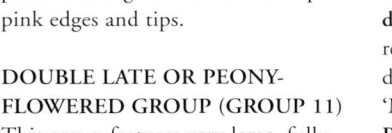

Tulipa, Hybrid Cultivar, Parrot, 'Fantasy'

Tulipa, Hybrid Cultivar, Parrot, 'Salmon Parrot'

the plants' slow decline; cultivars with such viral patterning are now banned from sale. Members of other groups can show similar color patterns. Modern Rembrandt look-alikes that fall into other groups include: '**Ice Follies**' (Triumph Group); '**Kiezerkroon**' (Single Early Group); '**Olympic Flame**' (Darwin Group); and '**Union Jack**', (Single Late Group).

Tulipa, HC, Kaufmanniana, 'Ancilla'

PARROT GROUP (GROUP 10)

The hybrids in this group, commonly 18–22 in (45–55 cm) tall, largely result from sports within other groups and are notable for their deeply cut petals, often bi-colored. '**Bird of Paradise**' has deep red flowers edged with gold; '**Blue Parrot**' is a deep mauve; '**Fantasy**', deep pink with purple-green flame near tips; '**Karel Doorman**', bright red edged with gold; '**Professor Röntgen**', orange-red flowers with a green-gold flame; '**Weber's Parrot**', twisted pale pink petals with a green flame and deep pink edges and tips.

DOUBLE LATE OR PEONY-FLOWERED GROUP (GROUP 11)

This group features very large, fully double flowers that are produced on stems 15–24 in (38–60 cm) tall. Impressive tulips, they usually bloom well after the spring equinox, and include: '**Allegretto**', red flowers with a golden edge; '**Angélique**', pink flowers with a pale exterior; '**Carnaval de Nice**', white flowers with narrow red striping; '**Lilac Perfection**', lilac deepening to purple center, fragrant; '**Maywonder**', deep pink; '**Orange Princess**', a deep orange center, lightening at the edges, tipped with green; and '**Wirosa**', deep pink blooms with a broad cream edge.

KAUFMANNIANA GROUP (GROUP 12)

This group are very early-flowering cultivars and hybrids of *T. kaufmanniana* growing to around 10 in (25 cm) tall. The flowers open flat and are sometimes known as waterlily tulips; leaves may be plain or mottled; flowers usually bi- or multi-colored in a variety of patterns. '**Ancilla**', white with orange-red-edged yellow center; '**Shakespeare**', dusky salmon pink.

T., HC, Double Late, 'Allegretto'

T., HC, DL, 'Lilac Perfection'

T., HC, DL, 'Orange Princess'

T., HC, Double Late, 'Maywonder'

Tulipa, Hybrid Cultivar, Double Late, 'Angélique'

Tulipa, HC, Fosteriana, 'Madame Lefeber'

Tulipa, HC, Fosteriana, 'Orange Emperor'

Tulipa, HC, Fosteriana, 'Princeps'

Tulipa, HC, Fosteriana, 'Purissima'

Tulipa, Hybrid Cultivar, Greigii, 'Plaisir'

Tulipa, Hybrid Cultivar, Greigii, 'Toronto'

FOSTERIANA GROUP (GROUP 13)

Variably sized cultivars and hybrids of *T. fosteriana*, 8–24 in (20–60 cm) tall; foliage may be plain, mottled, or variegated; flowers tend be very boldly colored. '**Madame Lefeber**' (syn. 'Red Emperor') is bright red; '**Orange Emperor**' is bright orange blending to a yellow base; '**Princeps**' bears large bright red flowers; '**Purissima**' (syn. 'White Emperor') is white with a creamy yellow center.

GREIGII GROUP (GROUP 14)

Sometimes known as rock or rockery tulips, these cultivars and hybrids of *T. greigii* rarely exceed 12 in (30 cm) tall and are widely grown. They are easily recognizable by their purple-red marbled gray-green foliage, and commonly simple single flowers in one or two colors. '**Cape Cod**', orange with gold edge; '**Oriental Splendour**', deep yellow with red flame; '**Plaisir**', cream with red flame; '**Red Riding Hood**', bright red; '**Toronto**' ★, bright salmon to orange; '**Yellow Dawn**', deep pink with yellow edge.

MISCELLANEOUS GROUP (GROUP 15)

This is a catch-all group for species and their cultivars which are otherwise ungrouped (*see* individual species).

TURBINICARPUS

A genus of 24 species of tiny cactus in the family Cactaceae, most from limited habitats in northern Mexico. The plants are usually unbranched, spherical to slightly depressed spherical. Ribs are replaced by tubercles, sometimes indistinct. The areoles are at the tubercle tips and are often woolly and white. There are generally few spines but those that exist are flexible and not usually sharp. Growing from the stem tips, flowers are funnel-shaped, diurnal, in white, rose, or magenta. Seed pods are spherical. Many species have had several name changes; some botanists argue that *Turbinicarpus*

Tulipa, HC, Greigii, cultivar

species originated as stabilized juvenile forms of *Neolloydia* and should be included in that genus.

CULTIVATION: Easily grown in well-drained, purely mineral soil or soil with very little organic material. Rest in winter, again in heat of summer. Less than average water in spring and autumn. Propagate from seed.

Turbinicarpus horripilus

syns *Gymnocactus goldii*, *Pediocactus horripilus*

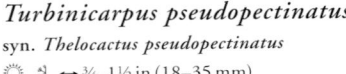
☼ ⚘ ↔ 10–20 in (25–50 cm)
↑ 3–7 in (8–18 cm)

Clustering species from northern Mexico. Olive green stems, spherical to short cylindrical; tubercles prominent, conical. Spines with reddish brown tips. Flowers magenta, sometimes white throats, in summer. Seed pods oval, greenish red. Zones 9–11.

Turbinicarpus pseudomacrochele

syn. *Strombocactus pseudomacrochele*
☼ ⚘ ↔ 1–1½ in (25–35 mm)
↑ ¾–1¾ in (18–40 mm)

This solitary, occasionally clustering species from Mexico has spherical to

short cylindrical stems, pale green to dark blue-green with woolly tips; tubercles low, tapering. Spines yellowish brown turning gray. Flowers are white, reddish purple, yellowish green, or magenta, in late spring. Seed pods are green and spherical. *T. p.* subsp. *krainzianus* (syn. *Neolloydia krainziana*), dark green stems, smaller magenta to cream flowers. Zones 9–11.

Turbinicarpus pseudopectinatus

syn. *Thelocactus pseudopectinatus*
☼ ⚘ ↔ ¾–1½ in (18–35 mm)
↑ ¾–1¼ in (18–30 mm)

A solitary species from northern Mexico. Bluish green stem obscured by tiny, dense, white spines; tubercles elongated vertically. Radial spines arranged like 2 tiny combs. Flowers are white with reddish or magenta mid-stripes, in summer. Seed pods spherical, greenish. Zones 9–11.

Turbinicarpus valdezianus

syn. *Pelecyphora valdeziana*
☼ ⚘ ↔ ½–1 in (12–25 mm)
↑ ½–1 in (12–25 mm)

This solitary species from Mexico has depressed spherical to hemispherical stems, green color obscured by dense feathery spines; tubercles flattened. Flowers white with magenta midstripe, in summer. Seed pods dark greenish brown, spherical. Zones 9–11.

T. pseudomacrochele. subsp. *krainzianus*

Turbinicarpus valdezianus

Tweedia caerulea 'Heaven Bow'

Turraea obtusifolia

Turraea obtusifolia

TURRAEA

There are about 70 species of trees and shrubs in this genus, which is a member of the mahogany (Meliaceae) family, found in tropical areas of Africa, Asia, and Australia. The leaves are simple and glossy and sometimes bluntly lobed. The flowers have a sweet fragrance and a starry appearance with 5 long strap-shaped petals.
CULTIVATION: *Turraea* species can be grown outdoors in a warm frost-free climate. They require a moderately fertile soil that is well drained. In cold areas they are better suited to the greenhouse or conservatory. Prune after flowering to maintain size and pinch out young plants to encourage branching. Propagate from seed or half-hardened cuttings.

Turraea floribunda
WILD HONEYSUCKLE
☼ ❄ ↔ 2 ft (0.6 m) ↕ 4 ft (1.2 m)
This deciduous shrub is a native of South Africa, with oval leaves. Fragrant flowers, on densely downy stalks, yellowish green, in groups of 2 to 3 blooms near the branch ends, in spring. Zones 10–12.

Turraea obtusifolia
LESSER HONEYSUCKLE TREE, SMALL HONEYSUCKLE TREE
☼ ❄ ↔ 5 ft (1.5 m) ↕ 6–10 ft (1.8–3 m)
Deciduous shrub or small tree, native to South Africa. Glossy green leaves,

oval, sometimes bluntly 3-lobed. Showy, white, fragrant flowers, with narrow reflexed petals, are borne along the stems in groups of 1 to 3 blooms, in spring. Zones 10–12.

TWEEDIA
This genus in the milkweed (Asclepiadaceae) family, contains a single species of twining or scrambling shrub, native to subtropical South America. It is sparsely branched with softly hairy stems and foliage. Oblong to heart-shaped leaves are up to 10 in (25 cm) long. Starry pale blue flowers are borne in summer and autumn. They are long-lasting when cut.

CULTIVATION: These plants flower from seed in the first year so can be grown as an annual in cool-temperate zones or, alternatively, they can be grown under glass. In frost-free areas grow in full sun in well-drained, moderately fertile soil. Pinch back when young to encourage bushier growth. Propagate from seed or cuttings.

Tweedia caerulea
syn. *Oxypetalum caeruleum*
☼ ❄ ↔ 36 in (90 cm) ↕ 36 in (90 cm)
Twining or scrambling shrub, a native of southern Brazil and Uruguay with lightly hairy grayish green leaves. Flowers starry pale blue, darken to lilac as they age, for long periods from summer. 'Heaven Bow', pretty pale blue to lilac flowers, look almost painted. Zones 10–12.

TYPHA
BULRUSH, CAT-TAIL, REED MACE
This genus, comprising some 10 to 12 species found almost throughout the world, makes up the family Typhaceae. These often very large perennials are from marshlands, where they can form extensive stands. The leaves arise from rhizomes and have sheathing bases; the leaf blade is very elongated and linear, flat or concave, with spongy internal tissue. Flowering stems are erect and spear-like, bearing dense cylindrical spikes of tightly packed wind-pollinated flowers. The male and female flowers are separate but on the same plant, the males borne in an upper distinct part, often differently colored. The fruits are tiny and plumed, like thistledown. They are released by disintegration of the female spike and float away on the breeze in vast numbers. The starch-rich rhizomes, and even the pollen, provide emergency food. The leaves

are used in matting and chair-seating ("rush") and have been tried for paper-making. The plush formed by the female flowers has been used as a substitute for kapok.
CULTIVATION: Cultivation is easy in any moist soil. They grow in water to 24 in (60 cm) or so deep, although seed germination takes place on damp mudbanks. Except for some of the smallest species, they are too invasive for use as aquatics in any but the largest ponds or artificial lakes. Propagate from seed or by rhizome division.

Typha minima
☼ ❄ ↔ 1¼–2 in (3–5 cm)
↕ 2½–3 in (6–8 cm)
Perennial from Europe, the Caucasus region, and Asia with narrow, sword-shaped, green leaves. Flower stalks shorter than leaves, bearing oblong, dark brown, terminal heads of scaly, finely hairy, upright, catkin-like flowers, in summer. Zones 3–11.

Typha orientalis
BROAD-LEAF CUMBUNGI, BULRUSH
☼ ❄ ↔ 12–20 in (30–50 cm)
↕ 3–8 ft (0.9–2.4 m)
A vigorous reed-like perennial found from northern Australia to the Philippines. Branching rhizomes; stout upright stems. Long narrow leaves. Cylindrical spikes of chestnut brown flowers produce masses of fluffy seed, in summer. Potentially invasive. Zones 9–11.

Typha shuttleworthii
☼ ❄ ↔ 1–3 ft (0.3–0.9 m)
↕ 3–5 ft (0.9–1.5 m)
Aquatic or marginal perennial herb native to southern Europe, with open sheathed leaves. Flowers brown to silvery gray, finely hairy, on short stalks, in summer. Zones 5–8.

Typha shuttleworthii

Typha orientalis, New Zealand

UV

Ulex europaeus 'Flore Pleno'

Ulex europaeus

Ugni molinae

Uebelmannia pectinifera

UEBELMANNIA

This is a genus of 3 small, globular members of the family Cactaceae, all from Brazil. The genus was named after Werner Uebelmann, a Swiss nurseryman. The plants are solitary, spherical to short cylindrical with distinct ribs, to 30 in (75 cm) tall. The numerous ribs are deep and divided into tubercles. The areoles have well-developed spines. The 2 to 7 straight or slightly curved spines are erect, and spreading to comb-like. Flowers appear from near the top, and are small, yellow, diurnal, and funnel-form. Seed pods are spherical to short cylindrical, yellow or red, with wool and bristles near the tip, naked below. All species are rare and have suffered from over-collection in their restricted habitats. All species of *Uebelmannia* are listed in Appendix I of CITES.
CULTIVATION: These cacti are a challenge and growers usually attempt to emulate the growing conditions of the Brazilian rainforest habitat where the plants grow in clearings in the forest,

in quartz soils. Add some quartz and humus to a well-drained standard cactus mix. Some growers choose to graft these species onto other cactus species. Avoid over-watering and low temperatures.

Uebelmannia pectinifera
☀ ✣ ↔ 6 in (15 cm) ↕ 30 in (75 cm)
From Minas Gerais, Brazil. Spherical to cylindrical, dark reddish brown and covered with minute white, waxy scales. Areoles almost run together, bearing brownish gray felt. Spines 1 to 4 brown to black, erect, often interlacing but in some clones comb-like. Flowers narrowly funnelform, to 15 mm long. Seed pods club-shaped to cylindrical, violet-red. Zones 9–10.

UGNI

Once included in the genus of the true myrtles *(Myrtus)*, this variable group of approximately 10 species of evergreen shrubs from the temperate Americas is now in a genus of its own within the myrtle (Myrtaceae) family. They have simple oval leaves that are usually tough, leathery, and small. Their flowers are carried singly, in the leaf axils; they have 5 petals and tend to hang downwards. Fleshy berries, sometimes edible, but not particularly flavorsome, follow the flowers and can become very aromatic as they near ripeness.
CULTIVATION: Apart from being a little frost tender when young, the only cultivation problem is a dislike

of lime. Grow in cool, moist, humus-rich, well-drained soil in sun or part-shade. An annual trim, after either flowering or fruiting, will keep the growth compact. Propagate from seed, cuttings or by removing naturally formed layers.

Ugni molinae ★
CHILEAN CRANBERRY, CHILEAN GUAVA
☀ ❄ ↔ 3 ft (0.9 m) ↕ 6 ft (1.8 m)
This is a native of Chile and western Argentina. It is a wiry-stemmed shrub with glossy deep green leaves on red stems. The flowers are cream flushed with pink, with a cluster of 40 to 60 tiny stamens at the center. Flowering time is spring to early summer. Red berries follow the flowers. Zones 8–10.

ULEX

Cultivated as ornamentals in some areas, but among the worst of weeds in others, gorses can provoke quite extreme reactions when gardeners meet farmers. This genus from the peaflower subfamily of the legume (Fabaceae) family is from North Africa and western Europe, and is made up of some 20 species of densely branched, fiercely spiny shrubs. Young plants have fuzzy trifoliate leaves but the foliage is reduced to a chlorophyll-bearing spine in adults. The flowers, borne singly or in small clusters, are fragrant and range in color from pale yellow to gold.
CULTIVATION: Gorses are tough and adaptable plants that thrive under a wide range of growing conditions. Generally they prefer a moist, light, well-drained soil, but they will tolerate winter damp and grow well on sandy soils near the coast. In New Zealand, where common gorse (*U. europaeus*) is a seemingly unstoppable weed, farmers often tame it and use it for roadside hedging.

Ulex europaeus
COMMON GORSE, FURZE, GORSE, WHIN
☀ ❄ ↔ 7 ft (2 m) ↕ 8 ft (2.4 m)
Most associated with Scotland but found over much of western Europe. Dense many-branched shrub covered with fine hairs, vicious ½ in (12 mm) long spines. Flowers fragrant golden yellow, in late winter–spring, 'Flore Pleno', double-flowered sterile form, preferable for cultivation. Zones 6–10.

ULMUS
ELM
There are 45 species of elms (family Ulmaceae). Most are trees, some very large, but a few are shrubs. Although most are deciduous and very hardy, a few are semi-evergreen and not so tough. They occur in northern temperate zones and even extend into the subtropics. They are generally round-headed trees with bark often furrowed or fissured though seldom corky, except on young shoots. Leaves are usually elliptic with conspicuous veins and serrated edges. Flowers are inconspicuous but the papery winged fruits (samaras) that follow can be showy.
CULTIVATION: In the main, elms are tough plants that adapt well to cultivation, growing successfully in a range of soils provided the drainage is good. However, in some areas populations have been decimated by Dutch elm disease, a fungal infection carried by small beetles with wood-boring larvae. Propagate from seed or by grafting.

Ulmus americana
AMERICAN ELM, WHITE ELM
☀ ❄ ↔ 100 ft (30 m) ↕ 100 ft (30 m)
Largest of the North American elms. Impressive tree, deep gray furrowed bark, and large leaves that turn bright yellow, in autumn. 'Augustine', vigorous grower, columnar habit; 'Columnaris', columnar habit. Zones 3–9.

Ulmus americana 'Columnaris'

Ulmus carpinifolia 'Variegata'

Ulmus glabra 'Pendula', in spring

Ulmus glabra 'Pendula', in summer

Ulmus carpinifolia

syn. *Ulmus minor*

FIELD ELM, SMOOTH-LEAFED ELM

☼ ❄ ↔ 70 ft (21 m) ↑ 50–70 ft (15–21 m)

Species native to central and southern Europe, including Britain. Leaves are 2–4 in (5–10 cm) long, with serrated edges, develop golden orange autumn tones. Many cultivars. '**Variegata**', white-speckled leaves. **Zones 5–10.**

Ulmus castaneifolia

☼ ❄ ↔ 20 ft (6 m) ↑ 70 ft (21 m)

A Chinese species unknown in cultivation in the West until recently. Botanical institutions began conducting trials of all east Asian elm species as replacements for the American and European elms that have mostly been wiped out by Dutch elm disease over the last 50 to 60 years. **Zones 6–9.**

Ulmus 'Coolshade'

☼ ❄ ↔ 20–30 ft (6–9 m) ↑ 20–35 ft (6–10 m)

This *Ulmus pumila* and *U. rubra* hybrid is a broad-headed and slow-growing tree that closely resembles *U. pumila*. However, it has a lusher head of foliage. Weeps slightly, so is resistant to snow damage. **Zones 3–9.**

Ulmus crassifolia

CEDAR ELM

☼ ❄ ↔ 40 ft (12 m) ↑ 70–100 ft (21–30 m)

Found in southern USA. Young twigs edged with "wings" of bark. Rather stiff leaves, about 2 in (5 cm) long, have toothed edges and downy undersides. **Zones 7–10.**

Ulmus glabra

SCOTCH ELM, WYCH ELM

☼ ❄ ↔ 70 ft (21 m) ↑ 100 ft (30 m)

This large tree is found from northern Europe to western Asia. The deeply toothed, dark green, rounded, 2–6 in (5–15 cm) leaves are sometimes lobed at the base, and they turn yellow in autumn. The bright lime green fruits are an attractive spring feature. Cultivars include: '**Camperdownii**' ★, a low-growing form with a dense spreading crown of weeping branches; '**Exoniensis**', with a low-growing, erect conical habit; and '**Pendula**', (syn. 'Horizontalis') which features horizontal spreading branches. **Zones 5–9.**

Ulmus × *hollandica*

DUTCH ELM

☼ ❄ ↔ 80 ft (24 m) ↑ 100 ft (30 m)

This is a naturally occurring hybrid between *U. glabra* and *U. carpinifolia*. Strong, heavily veined, serrated, deep green leaves turn a yellow tone in autumn months. Cultivars include: '**Groenveldt**', tall, vigorous, and disease-resistant; '**Jacqueline Hillier**', densely branched, shrubby to around 8 ft (2.4 m) tall; '**Major**', with a wide-spreading crown and broad leaves; '**Modolina**', tall and vigorous with a somewhat vase-shaped crown; and '**Vegeta**' (syn. *U.* × *vegeta*), a vigorous grower to 120 ft (36 m) tall. **Zones 5–9.**

Ulmus crassifolia

Ulmus × *hollandica* 'Vegeta'

Ulmus × *hollandica* cultivar, in winter

Ulmus × *hollandica* cultivar, in autumn

Ulmus × *hollandica* 'Modolina'

U

Ulmus japonica

☼ ❋ ↔ 60 ft (18 m) ↑ 100 ft (30 m)

A large broad-headed tree native to Japan and nearby parts of temperate northeastern Asia. Young stems have corky yellow-brown bark, roughly oval leaves taper abruptly to a point, coarsely toothed edges. Small purplish flowers, pale green fruits. **Zones 5–9.**

Ulmus laevis

RUSSIAN ELM

☼ ❋ ↔ 30 ft (9 m) ↑ 70 ft (21 m)

From France to eastern Europe and the Caucasus. Dark gray to brown bark, open spreading crown. Broad rough-textured leaves, 4 in (10 cm) long, gray hairs beneath. **Zones 4–9.**

Ulmus macrocarpa

☼ ❋ ↔ 20 ft (6 m) ↑ 30 ft (9 m)

Large shrub or small tree from northeastern Asia. Downy young stems, eventually covered with corky bark. Leaves, heavily serrated, pointed tips, downy undersides. Large, bristly, slightly notched fruits. **Zones 5–9.**

Ulmus parvifolia

CHINESE ELM

☼ ❋ ↔ 30 ft (9 m) ↑ 70 ft (21 m)

A disease-resistant tree from Japan, Korea, and China, near-evergreen in mild climates. Round crown, smooth

Ulmus 'Sapporo Autumn Gold'

Ulmus procera, in winter

flaking bark, fine branches. Mature fruit in autumn. '**Catlin**', slow grower, gracefully drooping branch tips; '**Frosty**', compact shrub, white-toothed leaves; '**Hansen**', vigorous upright growth; '**King's Choice**', larger bright green leaves, peeling bark, vigorous open growth habit; '**Pendens**', weeping branches; '**True Green**', reliably evergreen in mild winters. **Zones 5–10.**

Ulmus procera

ENGLISH ELM

☼ ❋ ↔ 50 ft (15 m) ↑ 70–100 ft (21–30 m)

Stately English tree now rare due to Dutch elm disease. A straight-trunked

Ulmus laevis

tree with broad crown of deep green, serrated-edged leaves that become bright yellow in autumn. Pale green fruits, most of them sterile, in spring. '**Argenteovariegata**', white-speckled leaves; '**Louis van Houtte**', a very popular yellow-leafed cultivar that is especially bright in autumn; and '**Purpurea**', with a slight purplish tint to the young foliage. **Zones 4–9.**

Ulmus pumila

CHINESE ELM, SIBERIAN ELM

☼ ❋ ↔ 20–30 ft (6–9 m) ↑ 20–35 ft (6–10 m)

This native of cool-temperate Asia has coarsely textured, serrated leaves that color slightly in autumn. '**Den Haag**', disease-resistant tall form, with open crown. **Zones 3–9.**

Ulmus 'Sapporo Autumn Gold'

☼ ❋ ↔ 35 ft (10 m) ↑ 50 ft (15 m)

A hybrid notable for its resistance or tolerance of Dutch elm disease. It has a strongly upright habit when young, eventually develops a broad crown. New spring foliage, soft yellow-green, matures to lime green, golden yellow autumn foliage. **Zones 4–9.**

Ulmus procera, in spring

Ulmus procera, in summer

Ulmus procera, in autumn

Ulmus 'Sarniensis'

JERSEY ELM, WHEATLEY ELM

☼ ❋ ↔ 23–25 ft (7–8 m) ↑ 75–80 ft (23–24 m)

This is a hybrid between *Ulmus carpinifolia* and *U.* × *hollandica.* It has a very erect upright habit, with a broad-based conical crown. Heavily serrated dark green leaves grow up to 4 in (10 cm) long. It sets copious quantities of fruits, most of which are sterile. This elm will make a good lawn tree. **Zones 7–10.**

Ulmus parvifolia

Ulmus japonica

Ulmus macrocarpa

Ulmus thomasii

CORK ELM, ROCK ELM

☀ ❄ ↔ 40 ft (12 m) ↑ 100 ft (30 m)

Native to eastern North America.
Upright tree, narrow rounded crown.
Young branches with distinctly corky
bark. Leaves 2–4 in (5–10 cm) long,
heavily serrated. Seldom color much
in autumn. Zones 2–9.

UMBELLULARIA

Related to the laurels (*Laurus*), the sole
species in this genus from the family
Ulmaceae is an aromatic evergreen tree
found in Oregon and California, USA.
It has tough leathery leaves and male
and female flowers carried on separate
flowerheads. The foliage is so strongly
aromatic that crushing it in the hand
and sniffing it can cause an instant
though usually brief headache. It was
widely used medicinally by native
North Americans. Its timber is quite
dense and used in woodturning for
mainly ornamental objects or utensils.
CULTIVATION: Tolerant of light to
moderate frosts and not particularly
fussy about the soil type, California
laurel grows best in deep, moist,
humus-enriched, well-drained soil
with a position in full sun or partial
shade. Propagate from seed or half-
hardened cuttings.

Umbellularia californica

CALIFORNIA LAUREL, HEADACHE TREE

☀ ❄ ↔ 35 ft (10 m) ↑ 50–70 ft (15–21 m)

Densely foliaged spreading crown,
scaly red-brown bark. Strongly aromatic, glossy deep green, oval to
lance-shaped leaves. Clusters of small
yellow flowers open at the branch
tips, in spring. Purplish, olive-like
berries 1 in (25 mm) long. Zones 8–10.

UNCINIA

HOOK SEDGE

This is a genus of about 40 species
of evergreen tuft-forming grasses
from southern temperate zones
throughout the world, except South
Africa. They are members of the sedge
(Cyperaceae) family. These grasses are
identified by their smooth, cylindrical
stems that arch as they mature. They
vary in color from rich oranges and
reds through to plums, dark browns,
and dull greens. Now popular garden
specimens, they are often chosen
because of their striking year-round
foliage color. The flowers appear in
summer and the mature seed head
spikes are distinctive because they
have barb-like hooks on them as they
mature. The hooks attach themselves
to passing animals and people, which
aids in the dispersal of the seed.

CULTIVATION: *Uncinia* species need
free-draining soils with plenty of natural light, in areas that do not have
extreme cold periods. They will not
tolerate long periods of wet weather;
too much water can kill them. Propagate by division in autumn or by
sowing fresh seed in spring.

Uncinia egmontiana

ORANGE HOOK SEDGE

☀ ❄ ↔ 16 in (40 cm) ↑ 12 in (30 cm)

From New Zealand. Colorful, perennial, ornamental grass that forms
tight, compact, erect clumps of
orange-bronze (color varies both
between seedlings and seasons) blades.
Flower spikes are followed by interesting black, sharply hooked seed heads,
in summer. Zones 8–11.

Uncinia rubra

RED HOOK SEDGE

☀/◑ ❄ ↔ 14 in (35 cm) ↑ 12 in (30 cm)

From New Zealand. Perennial, tuft-
forming grass with shiny, red-brown,
sharply pointed, narrow, flat leaves all
year round. Spikes of dark brown
flowers sit just above the foliage in
late summer. Zones 8–11.

URTICA

STINGING NETTLE

This genus of 100 annual or perennial
herbs, giving its name to the nettle
(Urticaceae) family, is widely spread
in temperate regions of the Northern
Hemisphere. The leaves and stems of
many species are covered with stinging hairs. The opposite, coarsely
toothed, sword- to heart-shaped leaves
have 3 to 5 prominent veins. Panicles
or racemes of 4 small, inconspicuous
flowers with no petals but 4 green
sepals grow from the leaf axils in
summer. They can become invasive
weeds. The young shoots of some
species can be used as a cooked vegetable. Several species have long been
used in traditional medicine.
CULTIVATION: These plants are
adaptable to most soils and positions
in sun or shade. Propagate from seed
or cuttings.

Urtica dioica

syn. *Urtica urens*

BIG STRING NETTLE, COMMON NETTLE,
STINGING NETTLE

☀ ❄ ↔ 3–6 ft (0.9–1.8 m)
↑ 2–8 ft (0.6–2.4 m)

Perennial herb, widely naturalized.
Square, bristly stems and leaves to
6 in (15 cm) long, downy underneath,
covered with stinging hairs. Leaves
used as food; stem fibre in rope, cloth,
and paper. Zones 3–9.

Ulmus 'Sarniensis'

Ulmus thomasii

Umbellularia californica

UTRICULARIA

BLADDERWORT

This genus in the bladderwort (Lentibulariaceae) family has around 200
species of small carnivorous plants.
Highly adaptable, these plants grow in
areas of perennial or seasonal wetness
in a wide range of environments.
Having no real root system, they form
rhizomes or stolons with green leaves
of varying size and shape and/or tiny
stalked bladders, spreading rapidly in
the growing season. Most have attractive 2-lipped flowers on slender scapes
from spring to early summer. The
genus name comes from the Latin
word for "bagpipes," referring to the
traps found on the stems or runners
which have tiny trigger hairs that
"vacuum" insects into the bladder.
CULTIVATION: Growing conditions
can be divided into 4 main groups.
All can be grown in a peat/sand mix
(4:1). Grow terrestrial species in part-
shade in permanently wet peat soil
occasionally flooded with shallow
water. Allow seasonal species to dry
out, then put in a shallow tray of
water in the growing season.
Tropical/epiphytic species prefer
warm, wet, humid conditions in part-
shade. Grow aquatic species in full
sun in a small tank of water with a
peat base, taking care to prevent algae
from forming. Propagate by division
in the growing season or from seed.

U

Utricularia reniformis

Utricularia alpina

Utricularia inflata

Utricularia bisquamata

Utricularia uniflora

Utricularia praelonga

Utricularia alpina
ALPINE BLADDERWORT

☀ 🌢 ↔ 6 in (15 cm) ↑ 12 in (30 cm)

Perennial tropical epiphyte or ground species from highland rainforests of Central and South America and the West Indies. Oval leaves, 6 in (15 cm) long, arise from tuberous root stock. Up to 4 white and yellow flowers, to 2 in (5 cm) wide. Zones 9–11.

Utricularia bisquamata
syn. *Utricularia capensis*

☀ 🌢 ↔ 3 in (8 cm) ↑ 2 in (5 cm)

Terrestrial species from South Africa. Profuse small flowers on scapes to 1 in (25 mm) long, in a color combination of violet, orange, white, and yellow. Spreads by seed. Zones 9–11.

Utricularia calycifida

☀ 🌢 ↔ 4 in (10 cm) ↑ 6 in (15 cm)

This tropical species is from Guyana, Venezuela, and Surinam. It features

teardrop-shaped leaves with purple streaks. Several purple flowers with a yellow center are borne on scapes to 6 in (15 cm) tall. Zones 10–11.

Utricularia dichotoma ★
FAIRY APRONS

☀ 🌢 ↔ 8 in (20 cm) ↑ 6–18 in (15–45 cm)

Tropical and temperate terrestrial species from New Zealand and temperate Australia. Leaves to 1 in (25 mm) long. Each scape bears 1 to 2 pairs of pale pink to purple flowers with white to yellow centers. Zones 9–11.

Utricularia inflata
syn. *Utricularia ceratophylla*
FLOATING BLADDERWORT

☀ 🌢 ↔ 12 in (30 cm) ↑ 12 in (30 cm)

North American tropical and subtropical perennial aquatic. Leaves 7 in (18 cm) long. Star-shaped whorl of 5 to 7 hollow tubes make it float. To 17 yellow flowers per scape. Zones 9–11.

Utricularia menziesii
REDCOAT

☀ 🌢 ↔ 2 in (5 cm) ↑ 3 in (8 cm)

From southwestern Western Australia. Leaves to 2 in (50 mm) long. Single orange to burgundy flower with a yellow center. Forms a tuber during hot dry summer months. Zones 9–11.

Utricularia praelonga

☀ 🌢 ↔ 12 in (30 cm) ↑ 18 in (45 cm)

Tropical and subtropical Brazilian species. Forms 2 types of leaves: long, thin; circular, flat on ground. Large yellow flowers on long stems. Zones 10–11.

Utricularia reniformis ★

☀ 🌢 ↔ 18 in (45 cm) ↑ 18 in (45 cm)

Tropical terrestrial species from Venezuela and Guyana. Thick fleshy rhizomes bearing traps. Large kidney-shaped leaves. Tall spikes of long-lasting, large, pinkish violet flowers. Zones 10–11.

Utricularia uniflora

☀ 🌢 ↔ 3 in (8 cm) ↑ 8 in (20 cm)

Perennial terrestrial found in the wet sandy soil of streams and on waterfall rockfaces of the Australian east coast. Small egg-shaped leaves; 1 to 2 mauve flowers on each slim stalk. Zones 9–11.

UVULARIA
BELLWORT, MERRYBELLS

This genus contains 5 species of easy-to-grow herbaceous perennials in the

lily-of-the-valley (Convallariaceae) family. From eastern North America, they are found in moist, well-drained, deciduous woodlands. Stems are erect or arching; the lance-shaped leaves are a bright green. Leaves are perfoliate (wrapping around the stem at the base) on all species except *U. sessilifolia*. Yellow bell-shaped flowers dangle from the stem and have long, slender, pointed, slightly twisted petals. Blooms last for 2 to 3 weeks in early spring to mid-summer, depending on species, but foliage remains visible all summer.
CULTIVATION: Grow in shade in deep, moist, slightly acid soil. Propagate by dividing clumps in spring or autumn, from ripened seed in late summer, or by transplanting underground stems, which spread easily.

Uvularia grandiflora
BIG MERRYBELLS, GREAT MERRYBELLS, LARGE-FLOWERED BELLWORT

☀ ❄ ↔ 12–24 in (30–60 cm)
↑ 12–24 in (30–60 cm)

From Quebec to Ontario, Canada, south to Minnesota, Georgia, Tennessee, and Kansas, USA. Light green foliage, arching stems. Bright yellow, drooping, bell-shaped flowers, mid-spring to early summer. Fruit a small triangular capsule. *U. g.* var. *pallida*, pale sulfur yellow flowers. Zones 3–9.

Uvularia perfoliata
PERFOLIATE BELLWORT, STRAW BELL, WOOD MERRYBELLS

☀ ❄ ↔ 12–18 in (30–45 cm)
↑ 16 in (40 cm)

From Quebec to Ontario, Canada, south to Florida and Mississippi, USA. Flowers pale yellow from mid-spring to early summer. Zones 3–9.

Uvularia sessilifolia
LITTLE MERRYBELLS, SESSILE BELLWORT, STRAW LILIES, WILD OATS

☀ ❄ ↔ 12–18 in (30–45 cm)
↑ 6–12 in (15–30 cm)

From moist woods from Ontario and New Brunswick, Canada, west to Minnesota, south to Georgia, Arkansas, USA. Flowers pale green-yellow, late spring to early summer. Zones 3–9.

Uvularia grandiflora var. *pallida*

Uvularia grandiflora

Vaccinium corymbosum

Vaccinium corymbosum

VACCINIUM

BLUEBERRY

This genus of around 450 species of evergreen and deciduous shrubs, small trees and vines includes the blueberries, cranberries, and huckleberries. Members of the heath (Ericaceae) family, they occur over much of the Northern Hemisphere, with a few species found in South Africa. Their main feature is the small but colorful edible fruits. Their flowers can be attractive, usually small, urn-shaped and downward-facing, carried singly or in clusters. The leaves are usually simple, oval to lance-shaped, often pointed at the tip and sometimes serrated around their edges.
CULTIVATION: As with most plants of the heath family, *Vaccinium* species prefer cool, moist, humus-rich soil that is acidic and well drained, with shelter from the hottest summer sun. In cultivation the type of conditions preferred by *Camellia* and *Rhododendron* tend to give the best results. Shrubbier species should be pruned to shape: after flowering if the fruit is not required, otherwise at harvest. Propagate from seed, cuttings, layers, and in some cases, by division.

Vaccinium ashei

RABBIT-EYE BLUEBERRY

☀ ❄ ↔ 7 ft (2 m) ↕ 3–15 ft (0.9–4.5 m)
Shrub from southeastern USA. Usually deciduous, sometimes near-evergreen in mild winters. Broad, serrated-edged leaves. White to light red flowers, in spring. Edible, ½ in (12 mm) wide, purple-black fruit. Zones 8–10.

Vaccinium bracteatum

☀ ❄ ↔ 2–3 ft (0.6–0.9 m)
↕ 2–3 ft (0.6–0.9 m)
Neat evergreen shrub from China and Japan. Small elliptical leaves with tiny teeth. Small clusters of tiny, white, late spring flowers. Berries red. Zones 7–10.

Vaccinium caespitosum

DWARF BILBERRY

☀ ❄ ↔ 24 in (60 cm)
↕ 4–10 in (10–25 cm)
Species found near the Arctic Circle in northern North America. Deciduous shrub. Small leaves, sometimes with serrated edges. Flowers pink to cream, late spring. Edible, blue-black fruit, ¼ in (6 mm) wide. Zones 2–8.

Vaccinium calycinum

☀ ❄ ↔ 2–6 ft (0.6–1.8 m)
↕ 3–10 ft (0.9–3 m)
Subtropical to tropical evergreen shrub from the mountains of Hawaii, USA. Leathery, deep green leaves, heavily serrated edges. Flowers white to pale pink, in small clusters at branch tips. Relatively large deep pinkish red berries. Zones 9–11.

Vaccinium corymbosum

BLUEBERRY, HIGHBUSH BLUEBERRY

☀ ❄ ↔ 5 ft (1.5 m) ↕ 3–6 ft (0.9–1.8 m)
Deciduous shrub from eastern USA widely cultivated for its edible fruit. Lance-shaped leaves develop fiery orange tones, in autumn. Flowers, white, sometimes with a red tint, in clusters, in spring. Edible, blue-black berries. 'Earliblue' is a tall vigorous cultivar with large fruit. Zones 2–9.

Vaccinium crassifolium

CREEPING BLUEBERRY

☀ ❄ ↔ 3 ft (0.9 m) ↕ 15 in (38 cm)
From southeastern USA. Low evergreen shrub takes root as it spreads. Tiny leaves, thick and leathery, finely serrated edges. Flowers very small, white, white with pink markings or pink, in small clusters, in late spring. Purple-black fruit. Zones 7–10.

Vaccinium glaucoalbum

☀ ❄ ↔ 36 in (90 cm)
↕ 12–36 in (30–90 cm)
Evergreen shrub from Himalayan India. Oblong leaves, bristly edges, hairs on underside veins. Flowers white, pink tints, in late spring. Berries purple-black. Zones 9–10.

Vaccinium macrocarpon

CRANBERRY

☀ ❄ ↔ 5–10 ft (1.5–3 m) ↕ 3 ft (0.9 m)
Native of eastern North America and northern Asia. Low-growing evergreen shrub, takes root as it spreads. Leaves dark green, lighter undersides. Flowers mauve with stamens extending beyond the petals. Fruit is red. Zones 2–9.

Vaccinium myrtillus

BILBERRY, BLAEBERRY, WHORTLEBERRY

☀ ❄ ↔ 36 in (90 cm) ↕ 18 in (45 cm)
Semi-deciduous shrub found from Europe to the cold near-Arctic of

Vaccinium nummularia

northern Asia. The 1 in (25 mm) long leaves have finely serrated edges, and hairs on the underside veins. Flowers are borne in small clusters, opening green and turning red with age. Edible blue-black berries. Zones 3–9.

Vaccinium nummularia

☀ ❄ ↔ 12–15 in (30–38 cm)
↕ 12–15 in (30–38 cm)
Small evergreen shrub found in the Himalayas, in Bhutan and the northeastern Indian province of Sikkim. Rounded, finely serrated leaves ¾ in (18 mm) long. Small clusters of tiny pink flowers. Edible, deep blue-black berries. Zones 7–10.

Vaccinium ovatum

BOX BLUEBERRY, EVERGREEN HUCKLEBERRY

☀ ❄ ↔ 3–5 ft (0.9–1.5 m)
↕ 3–5 ft (0.9–1.5 m)
Found naturally in western North America, this evergreen shrub has 1 in (25 mm) long oval leaves with finely serrated edges. Clusters of small white to pale pink flowers, tinted with red, are produced in spring. The fruit is blue-black. Zones 7–10.

Vaccinium bracteatum

Vaccinium calycinum

Vaccinium corymbosum 'Earliblue'

Vaccinium ovatum

V

Vaccinium parvifolium
RED HUCKLEBERRY, RED WHORTLEBERRY

☀ ❄ ↔ 6 ft (1.8 m) ↑ 6 ft (1.8 m)

Found from Alaska to California, USA. A deciduous shrub with small leaves, 1 in (25 mm) long. Flowers ¼ in (6 mm) wide, green with red tints, in late spring. Translucent, edible, pinkish red berries. Zones 6–10.

Vaccinium stamineum
DEERBERRY

◐ ❄ ↔ 3 ft (0.9 m) ↑ 5 ft (1.5 m)

Deciduous shrub found in eastern and southern USA. Leaves smooth-edged, covered with minute hairs, develop good autumn color. Sprays of small white to cream flowers are borne in spring. Greenish yellow to blue-green berries. Host for the blueberry maggot fly. Zones 5–9.

Vaccinium vitis-idaea
COWBERRY

◐ ❄ ↔ 2–4 ft (0.6–1.2 m) ↑ 6 in (15 cm)

Creeping evergreen shrub found over much of the cool-temperate Northern Hemisphere. The tiny oval leaves are deep green, with black spotting on undersides; they develop bronze tones in winter. Clusters of white to pink flowers appear in late spring. Bright red berries, in autumn. Zones 2–8.

Valeriana montana

Vaccinium Hybrid Cultivars

◐ ❄ ↔ 3–6 ft (0.9–1.8 m) ↑ 2–5 ft (0.6–1.5 m)

There are many popular hybrids and cultivars, some of indeterminate origin. 'Beckyblue', red-green stems, medium-sized blue fruit; 'Elliott', to 8 ft (2.4 m) tall, with a long-lasting display of orange-red autumn color; 'Lingonberry', reddish pink tints; 'Ornablue', narrow leaves turn bright red in autumn; 'Sharpeblue' ★, low-chill tetraploid variety, produces smallish sweet fruit. Zones 2–9.

VALERIANA
VALERIAN

This is a widely distributed (excluding Australasia) genus of vigorous annuals, hardy perennials, and small shrubs in the Valerianaceae family that favor moist habitats in woodlands, meadows, and mountainous regions. They are suited to informal cottage garden plants and naturalizing. These plants are creeping or tap-rooted, and their leaves vary from simple to lobed, pointed or deeply divided, sometimes arranged along the stems like the rungs of a ladder, disappearing near the top of the plant. Small flowers are produced, often in clusters, in pink, lavender-pink, white or yellow shades.

Valerianella locusta var. *olitoria*

Vaccinium vitis-idaea

The genus name means "healthy," a reference to the plants' medicinal properties.
CULTIVATION: Plants will grow best in moist soil and full sun or partial shade. Seeds should be sown in autumn or early spring. Cut back spent plants and take cuttings from the base of the plant to make new plants. Types with creeping roots will need to be divided often.

Valeriana montana

◐ ❄ ↔ 10 in (25 cm) ↑ 10 in (25 cm)

From the Alps and the Caucasus region. Alpine species suitable for the rock garden. Clumps of oval to round leaves. Small rounded clusters of lilac, pink, or white flowers in early summer. Zones 4–9.

Valeriana officinalis
GARDEN HELIOTROPE, TRUE VALERIAN, VALERIAN

◐/☀ ❄ ↔ 16–32 in (40–80 cm) ↑ 4–6 ft (1.2–1.8 m)

From western Europe. Musk-scented flowers borne in 2–4 in (5–10 cm) wide pinkish white heads atop stems with paired deeply cut leaves in early summer. Sometimes confused with *Heliotropium* species because of its scent. A famous sedative. Zones 3–10.

Valeriana phu

☀ ❄ ↔ 18 in (45 cm) ↑ 36 in (90 cm)

Native to Europe and the Caucasus. Tall perennial very like *V. officinalis* but differing in its basal leaves being mostly undivided. Tiny white flowers, in clusters, in summer. 'Aurea' has leaves that are yellow when young. Zones 3–9.

VALERIANELLA
CORN SALAD

This genus in the valerian (Valerianaceae) family contains 50 annual and biennial herbs occurring in North America, Europe, North Africa, and Asia. They have upright, branching stems with simple, smooth-edged or toothed, succulent leaves, often held in a rosette. The dense, paired,

Vaccinium, Hybrid Cultivar, 'Lingonberry'

Vaccinium, Hybrid Cultivar, 'Sharpeblue'

terminal heads of flowers with bracts have a minute or non-existent calyx, and a small, 5-lobed, saucer-shaped to tubular corolla with 2 or 3 stamens. Some species are grown as winter salad vegetables; others can become invasive weeds.
CULTIVATION: These are adaptable plants, growing well in most soils and positions, but they dislike lengthy dry periods. Propagate from seed, sown where they are to be grown from early spring to late summer.

Valerianella locusta
COMMON CORN SALAD, FETTICUS, LAMB'S LETTUCE

☀ ❄ ↔ 6–8 in (15–20 cm) ↑ 4–12 in (10–30 cm)

An annual native to Europe, northern Africa, and western Asia. Forms large rosette of slightly succulent, smooth-edged or slightly toothed, spoon-shaped to round, dark green leaves. Branched flower stalk with smaller stem leaves topped with rounded clusters of small, bluish mauve or white flowers with no sepals, in spring. Grown as a salad vegetable. *V. l.* var. *olitoria* has bright green leaves; 'Blonde Shell' has gold leaves; 'Broad Leaved', heat tolerant; 'Coquille de Louviers', spoon-shaped leaves, and a strong flavor; 'Grosse

Valeriana officinalis

'Graine' is larger than species; '**Verte de Cambrai**', slow-growing, very cold tolerant; '**Verte d'Etampes**', wrinkled leaves. Zones 5–9.

VANCOUVERIA

This genus is made up of 3 species of herbaceous creeping perennials that are native to the woodlands of northwestern North America. Like *Epimedium*, they are members of the barberry (Berberidaceae) family and are useful ground covers in shady areas, but they will not do well in dry soil. Their leathery divided leaves grow on wiry stems from crowns arising from branched underground rhizomes. The small and pendulous flowers are held above the foliage. Given ideal conditions they will spread quickly. The genus is named after Captain George Vancouver, an eighteenth-century English naval officer who explored the west coast of North America.
CULTIVATION: Grow in partial shade in cool, moist, organic, acid soil. Additions of leaf mold or humus will ensure success. They will not grow well in areas with hot dry summers. Propagate by dividing the rhizomes in spring or autumn.

Vancouveria chrysantha
☀ ❄ ↔ 12 in (30 cm) ↑ 12 in (30 cm)
From Oregon, USA. A creeping evergreen with stiff green leaves tinged with bronze. The small golden yellow flowers are produced in early summer. Zones 7–9.

Vancouveria hexandra ★
AMERICAN BARRENWORT
☀/☀ ❄ ↔ 12 in (30 cm) ↑ 12 in (30 cm)
Found from Washington to California, USA. Pale green deciduous foliage, similar to maidenhair fern (*Adiantum*). Drooping white flowers from late spring to early summer. Zones 7–9.

Vanda sanderiana var. *albata*

VANDA

This is a group of about 50 species of sturdy, monopodial orchids (family Orchidaceae) with representatives from Sri Lanka and India, across Southeast Asia to New Guinea and northeastern Australia. They are erect-growing, with strap-like, channeled leaves, in 2 ranks. Larger plants may branch at the base, and have numerous, very thick, cord-like roots. The inflorescences appear from the stem at the base of the leaf. They have showy, long-lasting blooms, which come in a range of colors and combinations. What were previously known as the "terete-leafed vandas" have since been transferred to the genus *Papilionanthe*, but in horticulture they continue to be known by their well-known, earlier name. This is one of the most important genera of plants for cut flower production in Thailand and Singapore. A large export industry has developed using a handful of species in an extensive hybridizing program, both within *Vanda* and combinations with related genera.
CULTIVATION: Vandas are readily grown in wooden baskets, with the majority thriving in bright, humid, and intermediate to warm conditions, and are suited to tropical gardens and greenhouses in climates away from the tropics. They are best grown in pots using a course grade of pine bark as the potting medium. The thick roots will often venture outside the confines of the pot or basket, and this culture should be encouraged as the roots require unimpeded air circulation and must dry out quickly after watering. In the tropics many species and their hybrids bloom throughout the year, with a peak in spring and summer. Propagate from cuttings with at least 3 roots attached.

Vanda coerulea ★
☀/☀ ❄ ↔ 4–10 in (10–25 cm) ↑ 6–36 in (15–90 cm)
This mountainous species from India to China is one of the best known in cultivation. Large, flat, spectacular pale to deep lilac-blue, tessellated, 4 in (10 cm) flowers are borne on erect spikes, frequently with over 12 blooms, in spring and summer. Cool- to intermediate-growing species, many improved clones in cultivation. Zones 9–11.

Vanda hindsii
☀/☀ ✛ ↔ 8–16 in (20–40 cm) ↑ 8–48 in (20–120 cm)
This is a spring-flowering species from Australia and New Guinea. Up to 10

Vanda coerulea

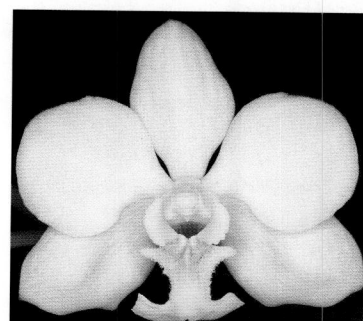
Vanda javierae

Vanda tricolor

shiny brown, 1¼ in (35 mm) blooms with yellow margins on the segments. The Philippine **V. merrillii** is a very similar species. Zones 11–12.

Vanda javierae
☀ ❄ ↔ 7–12 in (18–30 cm) ↑ 8–36 in (20–90 cm)
From the Philippines. Rare and spectacular, recently discovered spring bloomer. Up to 8 white, 2½ in (6 cm) flowers with wide segments. Related to *V. roeblingiana*, and has similar labellum structure, but is white with faint pink and brown markings at base. Likes cooler temperatures and heavier shade than most vandas. Zones 9–11.

Vanda luzonica
☀/☀ ✛ ↔ 8–20 in (20–50 cm) ↑ 8–40 in (20–100 cm)
From the Philippines. Attractive, white, 2½ in (6 cm) flowers, pink to purple splashing and blotching on the petals and sepals. Zones 11–12.

Vanda roeblingiana
☀ ❄ ↔ 7–12 in (18–30 cm) ↑ 8–36 in (20–90 cm)
From the Philippines. Distinctive species, brown, 2 in (5 cm) flowers in various shades and a bizarre anchor-shaped labellum. Summer-flowering orchid, enjoys cooler conditions than most species. Zones 9–11.

Vanda sanderiana
syn. *Euanthe sanderiana*
☀/☀ ✛ ↔ 8–20 in (20–50 cm) ↑ 8–48 in (20–120 cm)
From the Philippines. One of the most magnificent orchid species. A warm-growing epiphyte that has been used, like *V. coerulea*, extensively in hybrids. Up to ten, 4 in (10 cm) round blooms, pink with dark reddish brown suffusions and tessellations on the lateral sepals. Albino form, *V. s.* var. *albata*, green and white flowers. Zones 11–12.

Vanda testacea
syn. *Vanda parviflora*
☀/☀ ✛ ↔ 5–10 in (12–25 cm) ↑ 6–24 in (15–60 cm)
From Sri Lanka and India through to Thailand. A compact-growing, small-flowered species with numerous light yellow, 1 in (25 mm) wide blooms and a dark mauve-blue labellum. Zones 11–12.

Vanda tricolor
☀/☀ ✛ ↔ 8–20 in (20–50 cm) ↑ 8–48 in (20–120 cm)
From Java, Indonesia. Distinctive and common species, found on rocks or trees on the fringes of lowland forest. Perfumed, white, 2½ in (6 cm) wide flowers with dark reddish brown spots. Purple labellum, with yellow and white patches at its base. Zones 11–12.

Vanda, Hybrid, Pat Delight

Vanda, Hybrid, Bangkok Pink

V., Hybrid, (Gold Spots × *insignis*)

Vanda, Hybrid, Gordon Dillon

Vanda, Hybrid, Lumpini Red 'AM'

Vanda, Hybrid, Manisaki

Vanda, Hybrid, Marlie Dolera

Vanda, Hybrid, Miss Joaquim

Vanda, Hybrid, Miss Joaquim

V., H, (Pranerm Prai × Seeprai)

V., H, Reverend Masao Yamada

Vanda, Hybrid, Robert's Delight

Vanda, Hybrid, Rothschildiana

Vanda, Hybrid, Sansai Bluea

Vanda, Hybrid, Tailor Blue

Vanda Hybrids

☼/◐ ✿ ↔ 8–20 in (20–50 cm)
↕ 8–48 in (20–120 cm)

Thousands of *Vanda* hybrids have been produced over the past century. Most of the breeding has been centered on 2 important and spectacular species, *V. coerulea* and *V. sanderiana*. *V. coerulea* is behind all of the "blue" hybrids, many of which have darker tessellations throughout the bloom. It has also made these hybrids more adaptable to cooler growing conditions. *V. sanderiana* has passed its large round flowers onto its progeny, responsible for many of the pink- and brown-flowered combinations. The albino form has also been used to produce many of the green and yellow hybrids. The individual blooms of the hybrid flowers vary in size from 1½ in (35 mm) to 4 in (10 cm). **Bangkok Pink**, pinkish to purple blooms with fine spotting over the flower; (**Gold Spots** × *insignis*), unregistered hybrid with mustard-colored blooms, prominently spotted with brown; **Gordon Dillon**, round and very dark black-blue tessellated flowers; **Manisaki** has 4 different species in its background, *V. dearei*, *V. tricolor*, *V. luzonica,* and *V. sanderiana*; **Marlie Dolera**, a cross between a terete-leafed vandas and *V. sanderiana*, needs strong light to bloom well; **Miss Joaquim ★**, the national flower of Singapore, an important florist's flower and is a primary hybrid between *V. hookeriana* and *V. teres*; **Pat Delight**, deep pink blooms overlaid with prominent red markings; **Reverend Masao Yamada**, a well-shaped, colorful hybrid whose characteristics have come from *V. sanderiana*; **Robert's Delight** is a hybrid with heavy influence from *V. sanderiana*; **Rothschildiana ★**, popular blue to purple flowered vanda, it is a primary hybrid between *V. sanderiana* and *V. coerulea*; **Sansai Blue**, deep blue hybrid with heavy influence from *V. coerulea*. Zones 11–12.

VANILLA

The genus *Vanilla* consists of about 100 orchid species, members of the family Orchidaceae, which are found throughout the tropical regions of the world. They are unusual in having a vine-like growth habit, with adventitious roots being produced along nodes of the stem, adjacent to the succulent leaves. Many species start life as terrestrials before becoming epiphytic in their habit. The flowers bear a similarity to the unrelated *Cattleya*, and can be quite showy, but generally only last a day. In heavy flowerings, fresh blooms are produced daily from the short racemes.

CULTIVATION: They need plenty of room to grow to their full potential. In fact, many of the species refuse to bloom unless they have made it to the roof of the greenhouse! Commercially, they are often grown in pots with very long totems supporting the orchids' climbing habit, the roots adhering to the substrate. In private collections, they are often in hanging baskets in an attempt to control their growth habit, with many of the flexible stems manually turned back into the centre of the plant. They require bright light and warm conditions, in a very humid environment, throughout the year.

Vanilla planifolia

VANILLA

☼ ✿ ↔ 1–10 ft (0.3–3 m)
↕ 1–10 ft (0.3–3 m)

Native to Central and South America. This is the species from which vanilla

Veitchia arecina

Veitchia winin

essence is extracted, from the seed capsules. It is often grown as a conversation piece in botanical gardens and enthusiasts' collections. Pale yellow-green, 2½ in (6 cm) flowers, with a trumpet-like labellum. There is a variegated leafed form in cultivation. Zones 11–12.

VEITCHIA

This is a genus of 18 palms in the Arecaceae family, found in Vanuatu, the Philippines, and Fiji. They have single ringed trunks, conspicuous crownshafts and long feather-like fronds. The flowers hang below the crownshaft and are followed by clusters of red to orange-red fruit.
CULTIVATION: These palms are best suited to planting in humid tropical areas where they should be grown in a rich, moist but well-drained soil. Most require a partly shaded situation when young, becoming more tolerant of sun as they mature. Some make good potted plants for the house or greenhouse in cool climates. Propagate from fresh seed.

Veitchia arecina
☀/☀ ✦ ↔ 20 ft (6 m) ↑ 35 ft (10 m)
Native to coastal and lowland forests of Vanuatu. Palm with slender gray trunk. Prominent whitish crownshaft is topped with a rather flat crown of finely divided fronds. Showy clusters of crimson fruit below crownshaft. Zones 10–12.

Veitchia winin
☀ ✦ ↔ 10 ft (3 m) ↑ 50 ft (15 m)
Native to Vanuatu. A relatively fast growing and flowering palm with a very slender trunk, pale green crownshaft, stiff dark green arching fronds. Masses of white flowers. Bright red fruit. Zones 10–12.

VELLA

This genus in the cabbage family (Brassicaceae) is made up of 4 small cruciferous shrubs found in the western Mediterranean region. They are intricately branched with simple leaves and loose racemes of 4-petalled yellow flowers that are sometimes purple-veined.
CULTIVATION: Very much plants for sunny, rather dry positions, *Vella* species are interesting rather than very beautiful and are prone to damage from heavy frosts. Pruning, other than a post-winter tidying, is seldom necessary and they should not be cut back to the old wood or they may not reshoot. Propagate from seed or half-hardened cuttings.

Vella pseudocytisus
☀ ❄ ↔ 12 in (30 cm) ↑ 12 in (30 cm)
This evergreen species from central and southern Spain has small, lance-shaped, rather leathery leaves that are covered with short hairs. Small heads of ½ in (12 mm) wide, pure yellow flowers are borne in early summer. Zones 8–10.

VELTHEIMIA

This genus of the hyacinth (Hyacinthaceae) family consists of 2 species that are found on the grassy and rocky

Vella pseudocytisus

hillsides of southern Africa. The huge papery bulbs protruding from the soil's surface are decorative in their own right, as are the glossy undulating leaves, the well-held flowers, and the shimmering papery seed pods that follow the flowers.
CULTIVATION: These plants are easily grown outside in temperate climates and do well in wet-summer areas and in summer-irrigated beds. In other climates they are not so obliging. They resent root disturbance. Propagate by removing and replanting offsets while the plant is dormant, or by sowing fresh ripe seed. Alternatively, mature leaves can be taken from the base of the bulb, set in sand and grown on in a mild even temperature.

Veltheimia bracteata ★
syn. *Veltheimia capensis*
FOREST LILY, TORCH LILY
☀ ✦ ↔ 12 in (30 cm)
↑ 16–18 in (40–45 cm)

This robust, very variable, summer-dormant perennial bears long-lasting flowers in warm coral-red, pinkish purple, or murky white shades. The flowers are held in terminal racemes on straight mottled stems in spring. Decorative seed pods follow. Leaves are dark green, very glossy, forming a decorative rosette. As a container plant, place the bulb with top two-thirds protruding, water sparingly, and feed with a low-strength, low-nitrogen liquid feed when in growth. **'Yellow Flame'** produces pale yellow flowers. *V. capensis* is sometimes listed as a separate species, but is now considered by many to be a form of *V. bracteata*. It bears muted yellow, flesh pink, or murky white blooms, has very wavy leaves, and is smaller and slightly less robust than the common forms. Zones 9–11.

Veltheimia bracteata 'Yellow Flame'

Veltheimia bracteata

VEPRIS

This genus of some 15 species from tropical and southern Africa, Madagascar, and the Mascarene Islands belongs to the rue (Rutaceae) family. The plants are unarmed trees or shrubs, sometimes scrambling. The leaves are generally spirally arranged; they have 1 to 3 leaflets, dotted with transparent oil glands. The inflorescences are axillary or terminal panicles, racemes, or clustered cymes. Flowers are hermaphrodite or unisexual with rudiments of the opposite sex. The calyx is cup-shaped and generally has 4 lobes. There are usually 4 oblong petals. The fruit is a drupe with 2 to 4 compartments.
CULTIVATION: These plants are very rarely cultivated, but need full sun and well-drained soil.

Vepris lanceolata
syns *Boscia unulata*, *Toddalia lanceolata*
WHITE IRONWOOD
☼ ⚘ ↔ 20 ft (6 m) ↑ 20–40 ft (6–12 m)
A slow-growing evergreen shrub or small tree from southern Africa. Fine, narrow, wavy, oblong to sword-shaped leaves. Terminal panicles of small white flowers, followed by spherical black berries ripening over a long period. Zones 9–12.

Vepris lanceolata, Kirstenbosch National Botanical Garden, South Africa

VERATRUM
FALSE HELLEBORE

This genus of rhizomatous herbaceous perennials in the bunchflower (Melanthiaceae) family includes 20 species distributed throughout temperate Europe, North Africa, Asia, and North America and usually found in damp meadows and open woodlands. They have alternate, pleated, prominently veined, mid- to dark green leaves and numerous tiny flowers in white, green, brownish, or purple-black, held in terminal panicles. They are typically grown for their foliage. All parts, particularly the thick black rhizomes, are extremely toxic. The name is from Latin *vere*, "truly," *ater*, "black," referring to the rootstock.
CULTIVATION: Generally frost tolerant, they prefer moisture-retentive, rich soil in full sun or light shade. A few tolerate dry summer conditions. Propagate from root cuttings in spring or by division or from seed in autumn. It may take a decade for them to flower from seed.

Veratrum album
WHITE FALSE HELLEBORE
☼ ❄ ↔ 24 in (60 cm) ↑ 24 in (60 cm)
A rhizomatous herb that is native to Europe, North Africa, and northern

Verbascum acaule

Asia. It has large, oblong or elliptic, pleated leaves and dense racemes of green and white flowers, in summer. Zones 5–9.

Veratrum nigrum
BLACK HELLEBORE
☼ ❄ ↔ 24 in (60 cm)
↑ 24–48 in (60–120 cm)
Occurring from southern Europe to Siberia and Asia, this species has pleated, broadly elliptic to linear or lance-shaped leaves and numerous purple-black summer flowers in dense racemes. Zones 6–9.

VERBASCUM
MOTH MULLEIN, MULLEIN

This genus of some 300 species of annuals, biennials, perennials, and subshrubs in the foxglove (Scrophulariaceae) family includes cultivated plants and many that have become weeds outside their natural temperate Eurasian and North African range. The commonly cultivated species usually form basal rosettes of large elliptic leaves, often heavily veined and sometimes felted. Tall upright flower spikes emerge from the rosettes, carrying massed, small, 5-petalled flowers, usually in white, yellow, or pink to lavender shades. *Verbascum* was described by the Roman writer Pliny as attractive to moths: he called the plants moth mulleins. It also featured as a protection against evil in Greek legends and was used as an everyday medicinal plant to treat a variety of ills.
CULTIVATION: Hardiness varies with the species, but the majority prefer a sunny position with light, gritty, free-draining soil. They can tolerate summer drought but need moisture until after flowering. Propagate by division or from seed, depending on the growth form.

Verbascum acaule
☼/◐ ❄ ↔ 4 in (10 cm) ↑ 4 in (10 cm)
Tiny species native to the Peloponnesian region of Greece. Forms a tight rosette of dark green, toothed, elliptic leaves and produces

Verbascum adzharicum

glowing yellow flowers throughout the warmer months. Ideal for alpine troughs. Zones 7–10.

Verbascum adzharicum
☼/◐ ❄ ↔ 8–16 in (20–40 cm)
↑ 36 in (90 cm)
This summer-flowering biennial or short-lived perennial is endemic to the forests and alpine meadows of the Caucasus region. Rosettes of felted gray-green leaves. Leafy flower stems bear spikes of bright yellow flowers with purple filaments from early summer. Zones 4–9.

Verbascum blattaria
MOTH MULLEIN
☼/◐ ❄ ↔ 12–20 in (30–50 cm)
↑ 5–6 ft (1.5–1.8 m)
Widely naturalized temperate Eurasian biennial with basal rosettes of downy, toothed, lance-shaped, green leaves, up to 10 in (25 cm) long. Strong, erect, leafy flower stems, with many ¾ in (18 mm) wide, white, sometimes pale yellow or pink flowers. Cultivated forms may have considerably larger flowers. Zones 6–10.

Verbascum bombyciferum
☼/◐ ❄ ↔ 24–40 in (60–100 cm)
↑ 6–8 ft (1.8–2.4 m)
A western Asian summer-flowering biennial that forms large rosettes of broadly oval, wavy-edged, white-felted leaves, to 20 in (50 cm) long. Flower stems to over 6 ft (1.8 m) tall, leafy at the base but leafless from where the flowers start. Stems and buds woolly, sometimes branching, flowers deep yellow, to over 1¼ in (30 mm) wide. 'Polarsommer' (syn. 'Arctic Summer') is yellow flowered, deriving its name from the especially heavy silver felting on its leaves. Zones 6–10.

Verbascum chaixii

NETTLE-LEAFED MOTH MULLEIN

☼/◐ ❋ ↔ 12–24 in (30–60 cm)
↑ 36–48 in (90–120 cm)

A summer-flowering perennial found from central Europe to Spain and east to Russia. Forms a clump of rosettes of deeply veined, toothed, gray-green to dark green, downy leaves, to 12 in (30 cm) long. Narrow erect flower stems with flowers under 1 in (25 mm) wide, bright yellow with purple-red stamens. 'Album' ★ grows up to 33 in (85 cm) tall and bears white flowers with mauve stamens. Zones 5–9.

Verbascum dumulosum

☼/◐ ❋ ↔ 12–16 in (30–40 cm)
↑ 8 in (20 cm)

Turkish summer-flowering perennial that makes a dense clump of velvety, toothed, soft green, basal leaves to 2 in (5 cm) long, then produces many 10- to 35-flowered heads of bright yellow, ½ in (12 mm) wide blooms to develop into a small mound of color. Zones 8–10.

Verbascum olympicum

☼/◐ ❋ ↔ 20–40 in (50–100 cm)
↑ 5–6 ft (1.5–1.8 m)

A Turkish summer-flowering biennial or short-lived perennial that makes a dense basal foliage clump with

Verbascum thapsus

Verbascum, HC, 'Cotswold Beauty'

smooth-edged, lance-shaped, white, woolly leaves, around 12 in (30 cm) long, sometimes more than 24 in (60 cm) long. Branching leafy-based stems with dozens of 1 in (25 mm) wide bright yellow flowers. Zones 6–10.

Verbascum phoeniceum

PURPLE MULLEIN

☼/◐ ❋ ↔ 12–16 in (30–40 cm)
↑ 8–16 in (20–40 cm)

Southern Eurasian summer-flowering biennial or short-lived perennial. Usually one large rosette of sparsely hairy, dark green, wavy-edged or finely toothed, pointed oval leaves, to 6 in (15 cm) long. Simple or few-branched stems with mauve to purple, rarely white, pink, or yellow flowers, around 1 in (25 mm) wide. Zones 6–10.

Verbascum thapsus

AARON'S ROD

☼/◐ ❋ ↔ 20–32 in (50–80 cm)
↑ 6–7 ft (1.8–2 m)

This extremely vigorous, widely natu-ralized, summer-flowering, temperate

Verbascum, HC, 'Gainsborough'

Verbascum, Hybrid Cultivar, 'Letitia'

Eurasian biennial forms large rosettes of woolly white to gray leaves, up to 20 in (50 cm) long. The flower stem is strong and erect, usually leafy at the base, carrying many ½–1¼ in (12–30 mm) wide, deep yellow flowers. Zones 3–9.

Verbascum wiedemannianum

☼/◐ ❋ ↔ 10–20 in (25–50 cm)
↑ 24–48 in (60–120 cm)

A western Asian summer-flowering biennial. Rosettes of elliptic, toothed, finely hairy, 4–8 in (10–20 cm) long leaves with white web-like hair,

Verbascum, HC, 'Helen Johnson'

Verbascum, Hybrid Cultivar, 'Mont Blanc'

especially beneath. Stems simple or few-branched, with purple flowers to 1¾ in (40 mm) wide. Zones 7–10.

Verbascum Hybrid Cultivars

☼/◐ ❋ ↔ 12–20 in (30–50 cm)
↑ 12–60 in (30–150 cm)

Moth mulleins hybridize freely, and British breeders in particular have produced a range of hybrids that combine lush velvety foliage with beautifully shaded flowers. Some of the best include members of the **Cotswold Group** such as '**Cotswold Beauty**', to 48 in (120 cm), with buff to apricot-pink flowers, purple-pink anthers; '**Gainsborough**', to 48 in (120 cm), bright yellow flowers, gray felted foliage; '**Mont Blanc**', to 36 in (90 cm), pure white flowers, gray felted foliage; and '**Pink Domino**', to 48 in (120 cm), bright pink with a dark center. Other excellent cultivars include '**Helen Johnson**', 24–32 in (60–80 cm), variable dusky apricot-pink shades, gray-felted foliage; '**Jackie**', to 24 in (60 cm), dusky pink with deep magenta center; '**Letitia**', to 12 in (30 cm), shrubby habit, many bright yellow flowers. Zones 6–10.

VERBENA

VERVAIN

This member of the self-named vervain (Verbenaceae) family contains 250 species of annuals, perennials,

Verbascum chaixii 'Album'

Verbascum dumulosum

Verbascum olympicum

Verbena gooddingii

Verbena bonariensis

Verbena rigida

Verbena hastata

and subshrubs native to tropical and subtropical America. Plants are sprawling to erect. Leaves are opposite and variously divided. Terminal flower-heads range from narrow and overlapping to broader, rounder clusters. Individual flowers are tubular with flaring, sometimes notched, lobes and flowers come in shades of purple, pink, red, and white. Some botanists, particularly in North America, recognize the genus *Glandularia* as distinct from *Verbena*. As such, *Glandularia* includes most lower-growing verbenas with more colorful flowers in short, broad heads, in contrast to the erect slender spikes of flowers that characterize *Verbena* in the narrower sense.
CULTIVATION: Grow these plants in the border in full sun in moderately fertile, moist but well-drained soil. A number of cultivars are suitable for hanging baskets. Propagate annuals from seed and perennials from seed, cuttings, or by division.

Verbena bipinnatifida
syn. *Glandularia bipinnatifida*
☀ ❄ ↔ 36 in (90 cm) ↑ 12 in (30 cm)
Bristly stemmed perennial, native to North America. Forms mats of finely divided hairy leaves. Small lavender, pink, or purple flowers, notched petals, in summer. Zones 3–9.

Verbena bonariensis
PURPLE TOP, SOUTH AMERICAN VERVAIN, TALL VERBENA
☀ ❄ ↔ 24 in (60 cm) ↑ 3–5 ft (0.9–1.5 m)
South American perennial; also grown as annual. Erect, square, rough stems. Sparsely foliaged, lance-shaped serrated leaves. Tiny purple flowers in flat-topped clusters. Self-sows. Zones 7–10.

Verbena canadensis
syn. *Glandularia canadensis*
CREEPING VERVAIN, ROSE VERVAIN
☀ ❄ ↔ 16 in (40 cm) ↑ 8 in (20 cm)
From North America. Semi-prostrate perennial rooting at the nodes. Leaves toothed, deeply divided. Small showy heads of fragrant rosy pink to purple flowers, in spring to autumn. Zones 4–9.

Verbena gooddingii
syn. *Glandularia gooddingii*
☀ ❄ ↔ 24 in (60 cm) ↑ 24 in (60 cm)
Erect or spreading perennial from Mexico and southern USA. Pinnate leaves. Bluish purple, lavender, or pink flowers, in summer. Zones 9–11.

Verbena hastata
BLUE VERVAIN, SIMPLER'S JOY
☀ ❄ ↔ 12–24 in (30–60 cm)
↑ 3–5 ft (0.9–1.5 m)
Native to eastern and central USA. Perennial with stiff upright stems and lance-shaped, toothed, and roughened leaves. Small violet-blue flowers in spiky clusters in summer to autumn. Used in herbal remedies. Zones 3–9.

Verbena officinalis
COMMON VERBENA, COMMON VERVAIN
☀ ❄ ↔ 24–36 in (60–90 cm)
↑ 24–36 in (60–90 cm)
Southern European perennial, naturalized worldwide, can be invasive. Stiff, branching, 4-angled stems and opposite, oblong to sword-shaped leaves, deep cleft at base. Spikes of white, pale pink, or lilac flowers from spring to summer. Zones 4–8.

Verbena rigida
syn. *Verbena venosa*
VEINED VERBENA
☀ ❄ ↔ 12 in (30 cm)
↑ 24–36 in (60–90 cm)
Native to South America. Creeping perennial with stiff upright stems bearing stalkless oblong leaves, rough and irregularly toothed. Vivid purple to magenta flowers are borne in clusters in summer. 'Polaris' has silver-blue flowers. Zones 8–10.

Verbena stricta
HOARY VERVAIN
☀ ❄ ↔ 30–40 in (75–100 cm)
↑ 30–40 in (75–100 cm)
Perennial from western North America. Upright, stems densely covered with soft, fine hairs. Leaves rough, serrated, elliptic to nearly circular. Compact, upright spikes of deep purple, lavender, or white flowers. Zones 4–8.

Verbena tenera
syn. *Glandularia tenera*
☀ ❄ ↔ 12–20 in (30–50 cm)
↑ 12–20 in (30–50 cm)
Shrubby, clumping perennial, native from Brazil to Argentina. Sprawling stems rooting at the nodes and small, finely hairy, divided leaves. Elongated spikes of purplish or rose violet flowers. *V. t.* var. *maonetti* has reddish violet flowers edged with white; *V. t.* var. *pulchella* produces spikes of rose-violet flowers. *V. t.* 'Kleopatra', crimson-pink flowers. Zones 9–11.

Verbena tenuisecta
syn. *Glandularia tenuisecta*, *Verbena pulchella gracilior*
MOSS VERBENA
☀ ❄ ↔ 12–20 in (30–50 cm)
↑ 12–20 in (30–50 cm)
South American annual or perennial. Prostrate, sprawling, aromatic stems, square in cross-section. Leaves have 3 narrow, toothed leaflets. Spikes of broad-lobed lilac, mauve, purple, blue, or white flowers. Zones 9–11.

Verbena tenuisecta

Verbena tenera 'Kleopatra'

Verbena Hybrid Cultivars

syn. *Glandularia* Hybrid Cultivars

☼ ❄ ↔24–40 in (60–100 cm)
↑12–24 in (30–60 cm)

Fragrant perennials flowering from summer to autumn. '**Homestead Purple**', vigorous, trailing dark green foliage, purple flowers; '**Imagination**', violet-blue flowers; '**Peaches and Cream**', peach and cream flowers; '**Quartz Burgundy**', dwarf form, deep wine red flowers with tiny white eyes; '**Quartz Scarlet**', vigorous, scarlet flowers; '**Silver Ann**', vigorous, pale and deep pink flowers; '**Sissinghurst**', mat-forming, magenta pink flowers, can be invasive; **Tapien Series**, low-growing, long-blooming, heat-resistant forms, in blue, violet-blue, lavender, and pink; **Temari Series**, low-growing, trailing, long-flowering, dense mats of fern-like foliage, large flowerheads in pink, burgundy, blue, and scarlet. Zones 7–10.

VERONICA

BIRDSEYE, SPEEDWELL

This figwort (Scrophulariaceae) family genus of 250 species of annuals and perennials is widespread in northern temperate zones. Most are creeping mat-forming plants that sometimes strike root as they spread. Their leaves tend to be small, oval to lance-shaped, often shallowly toothed, and rarely pinnately lobed. A few species have solitary flowers, but more often many-flowered upright spikes develop in spring and summer. The color range is mainly in the white and pink to purple-blue shades, including some striking deep blue flowers. Probably named in honor of St Veronica, or because the floral markings of some species resemble the marks left on Veronica's sacred handkerchief or veil, with which she wiped Christ's face as he carried the cross.

CULTIVATION: They are mostly very hardy and easily grown in full to half-sun, with moist well-drained soil. Some are superb rock garden plants, others are better suited to borders. Propagate from cuttings or seed, or by self-rooted layers or division.

Veronica alpina

☼/◑ ❄ ↔8–16 in (20–40 cm)
↑2–6 in (5–15 cm)

This creeping, Arctic and temperate Eurasian, summer-flowering perennial forms a clump of wiry stems with 1 in (25 mm) long, faintly toothed, sparsely hairy, and pointed oval leaves. It produces short erect spikes with few light-centered, ¼ in (6 mm) wide, purple flowers, in spring and summer. '**Alba**' is a white-flowered form but the name *Veronica alpina* 'Alba' is sometimes used in the nursery trade to refer to *Veronicastrum virginicum* 'Album', which is a completely different plant. Zones 2–9.

Verbena, Hybrid Cultivar, Temari Series, 'Temari Patio Blue'

Verbena, Hybrid Cultivar, 'Silver Perlena'

Verbena, Hybrid Cultivar, Temari Series, 'Temari Bright Pink'

Verbena, Hybrid Cultivar, 'Pale Mauve'

Verbena, HC, Tapien Series, 'Tapien Lavender'

Verbena, HC, Temari Series, 'Temari Patio Rose'

Verbena, HC, Tapien Series, 'Tapien Blue Violet'

Verbena, HC, Temari Series, 'Temari Burgundy'

Verbena, HC, Temari Series, 'Temari Scarlet'

Verbena, HC, 'Maurena'

Verbena, HC, 'Lawrence Johnston'

Verbena, HC, 'Quartz Scarlet'

Verbena, HC, 'Homestead Purple'

Verbena, Hybrid Cultivar, 'Lilla'

Verbena, HC, 'Quartz Burgundy'

Verbena, Hybrid Cultivar, Tapien Series, 'Tapien Blue'

V

Veronica austriaca

☀/◐ ❋ ↔ 10–24 in (25–60 cm)
↕ 6–16 in (15–40 cm)

A spreading, late spring- to summer-flowering European perennial with wiry stems, sparsely hairy, narrow lance-shaped, ½ in (12 mm) long leaves, and upright spikes of many bright purple-blue flowers. *V. a.* subsp. *teucrium* has broader, more deeply toothed leaves, a parent of the best garden forms, such as 'Crater Lake Blue' ★, 10 in (25 cm) tall, compact, intense blue flowers; and 'Shirley Blue', 10 in (25 cm) tall, bright mid-blue flowers. Zones 6–10.

Veronica beccabunga

BROOKLIME

☀/◐ ❋ ↔ 8–20 in (20–50 cm)
↕ 4–6 in (10–15 cm)

Summer-flowering Eurasian perennial with fleshy often red-tinted stems upturned at the tips. Oval leaves, usually

V. austriaca subsp. *teucrium* 'Shirley Blue'

Veronica chamaedrys

Veronica macrostachya

finely toothed, 1¾ in (40 mm) long. At stem tips and nearby axils, small clusters of lilac to purple flowers, about ¼ in (6 mm) wide. Zones 5–9.

Veronica caucasica

☀/◐ ❋ ↔ 10–18 in (25–45 cm)
↕ 2–6 in (5–15 cm)

Caucasian perennial flowering from early summer. Spreading stems, generally with upturned tips. Leaves to around ¾ in (18 mm) long, bright mid-green, shallowly toothed. Flowers appear in small, mainly terminal heads, white, often with small blue flecks or streaks. Zones 6–10.

Veronica chamaedrys

ANGELS' EYES, BIRD'S EYE, GERMANDER SPEEDWELL

☀/◐ ❋ ↔ 12–20 in (30–50 cm)
↕ 6–10 in (15–25 cm)

A late spring- to summer-flowering temperate Eurasian perennial widely

Veronica caucasica

Veronica gentianoides

naturalized in North America. Forms a small mounding clump of bright green, sparsely hairy, and toothed, ½–1¾ in (12–40 mm) long, oval leaves. Flowers tiny, bright blue, white center, held above the foliage in airy sprays of up to 30 blooms. Zones 3–9.

Veronica cinerea

☀/◐ ❋ ↔ 6–10 in (15–25 cm)
↕ 2–4 in (5–10 cm)

Summer-flowering perennial from the Middle East and western Asia. Forms a dense cushion with ½ in (12 mm) long, sometimes toothed leaves that are covered with silver-gray hairs. Foliage color contrasts well with the short spikes of light-centered deep blue to purple-blue flowers. Zones 5–9.

Veronica gentianoides

☀/◐ ❋ ↔ 12–24 in (30–60 cm)
↕ 12–24 in (30–60 cm)

This spreading, summer-flowering, Caucasian and western Asian perennial forms a dense clump of upright stems with narrow, toothed, pointed oval leaves, to nearly 3 in (8 cm) long at the base of the clump. Usually pale blue flowers in erect spikes to 12 in (30 cm) long, in spring and summer. 'Tissington White' has white flowers; and 'Variegata' produces pale blue flowers and has attractive cream-variegated foliage. Zones 4–9.

Veronica cinerea

Veronica longifolia 'Pink Damask'

Veronica officinalis

Veronica longifolia

☀/◐ ❋ ↔ 16–30 in (40–75 cm)
↕ 20–48 in (50–120 cm)

Erect summer- to autumn-flowering perennial found over much of continental Europe and widely naturalized in northeastern North America. The foliage is narrow, lance-shaped, and toothed, sometimes sparsely hairy. Basal leaves to over 4 in (10 cm) long, upper leaves much smaller. Terminal flower spikes to 10 in (25 cm) long, with numerous tiny blue to lavender flowers. 'Blauriesin' (syn. 'Blue Giantess'), to 32 in (80 cm) tall, bright blue flowers; 'Pink Damask', to 36 in (90 cm) tall, soft pastel pink flowers. Zones 4–9.

Veronica macrostachya

☀/◐ ❋ ↔ 8–10 in (20–25 cm)
↕ 6–12 in (15–30 cm)

Turkish alpine species that forms a spreading evergreen mound of narrow, glossy, toothed leaves, 1 in (25 mm) long. From mid-spring to early summer foliage is hidden by sprays of tiny sky blue flowers. Zones 6–9.

Veronica officinalis

COMMON SPEEDWELL, GYPSY WEED

☀/◐ ❋ ↔ 12–20 in (30–50 cm)
↕ 8–20 in (20–50 cm)

This late spring- to early summer-flowering perennial is widespread in

Europe. Spreading or upright habit with downy to hairy stems and foliage. Leaves are toothed, broadly oval, ½–2 in (12–50 mm) long. Flowerheads to more than 2 in (5 cm) long, with ¼ in (6 mm) wide lilac flowers. Zones 3–9.

Veronica oltensis

☼/◐ ✱ ↔ 8–12 in (20–30 cm)
↑ 1–2 in (25–50 mm)

This is an alpine perennial from northern Turkey. It develops into a dense-foliaged ground-hugging mat with tiny pinnate leaves that in early summer disappear under clusters of ¼ in (6 mm) wide, pale to bright blue flowers. This species can make a marvelous rock garden specimen. Zones 6–10.

Veronica pectinata

☼/◐ ✱ ↔ 12–16 in (30–40 cm)
↑ 2–6 in (5–15 cm)

An evergreen southern Eurasian subshrub that flowers from late spring. Makes a mat of hairy, deeply toothed or cut leaves around 1 in (25 mm) long. Racemes, up to 8 in (20 cm) long, form in the leaf axils and carry numerous light-centered deep blue flowers that can reach to nearly ½ in (12 mm) wide. Zones 3–9.

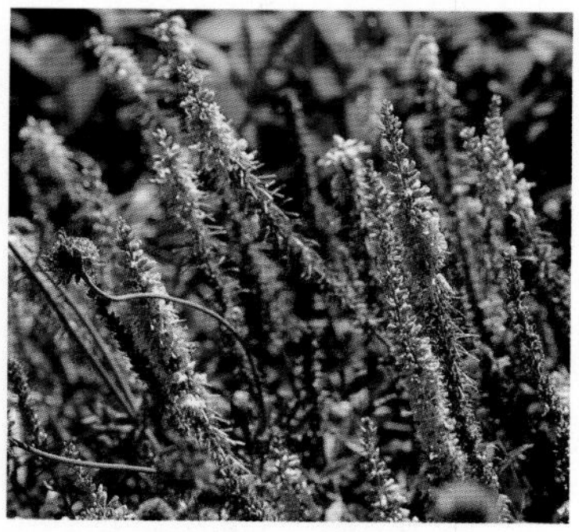

Veronica spicata 'Barcarolle'

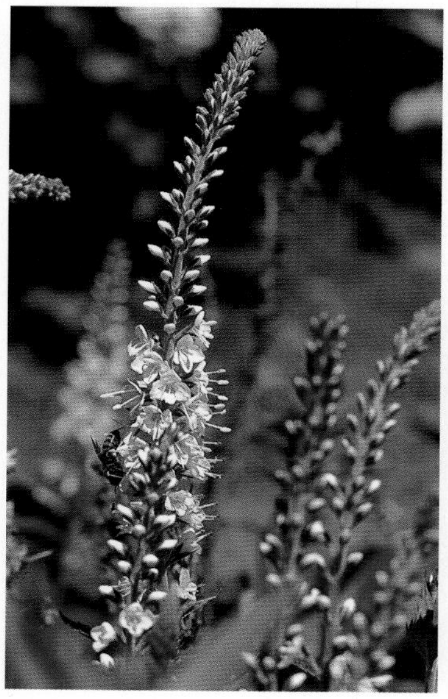

Veronica spicata 'Icicle'

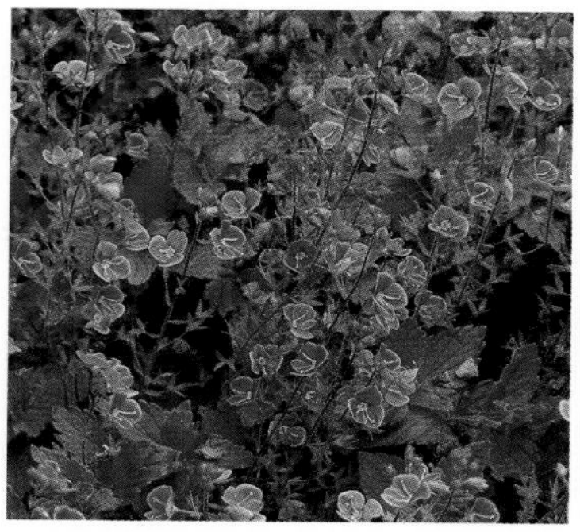

Veronica pectinata

Veronica peduncularis

☼/◐ ✱ ↔ 8–20 in (20–50 cm)
↑ 2–6 in (5–15 cm)

A late spring- to summer-flowering perennial found in the Caucasus, southern Russia, and western Asia. Forms a carpet of wiry stems with upturned tips and ¼–1 in (6–25 mm) long, dark green, toothed, lance-shaped leaves. Flowers are bright blue, sometimes pink or white, in small racemes. **'Georgia Blue'** has vivid mid-blue flowers. Zones 6–10.

Veronica petraea

☼/◐ ✱ ↔ 8–12 in (20–30 cm)
↑ 4–6 in (10–15 cm)

This Caucasian summer- to autumn-flowering perennial forms a small tuft of wiry, often purple-tinted stems with downy, sometimes toothed leaves, to ¾ in (18 mm) long. Stem tips are usually erect, with heads of up to 20 tiny blue or pink flowers at tips and in nearby leaf axils. **'Madame Mercier'**, lilac-blue flowers. Zones 6–9.

Veronica prostrata

☼/◐ ✱ ↔ 8–16 in (20–40 cm)
↑ 2–4 in (5–10 cm)

Flowering from late spring to summer, this European perennial forms a small mat of wiry stems with toothed, narrow pointed oval leaves, to 1 in (25 mm) long. Flower spikes in the leaf axils, with many small pale to deep blue flowers. Dainty rock garden plant. **'Heavenly Blue'**, intense bright blue; **'Spode Blue'**, deepest blue; **'Trehane'**, golden leaves and violet-blue flowers. Zones 5–9.

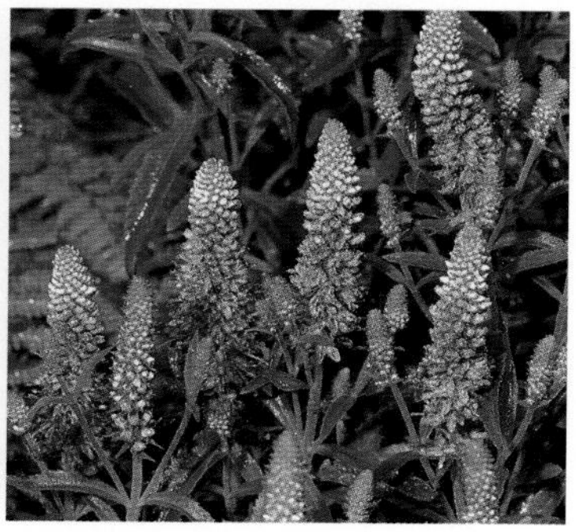

Veronica spicata 'Heidekind'

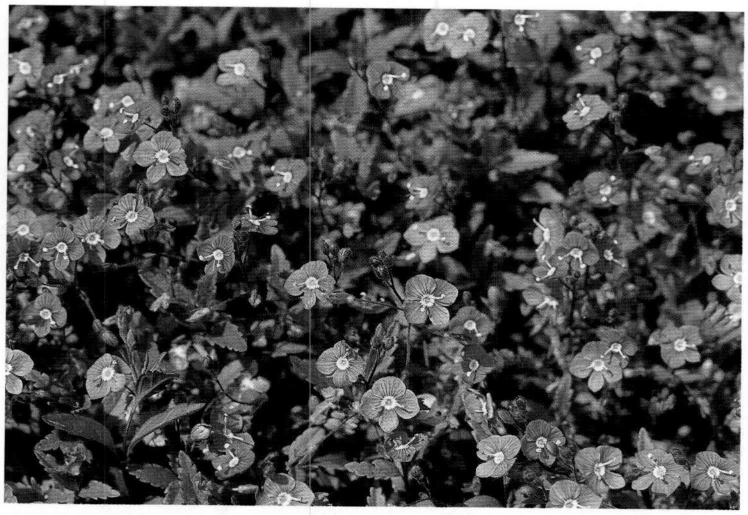

Veronica peduncularis 'Georgia Blue'

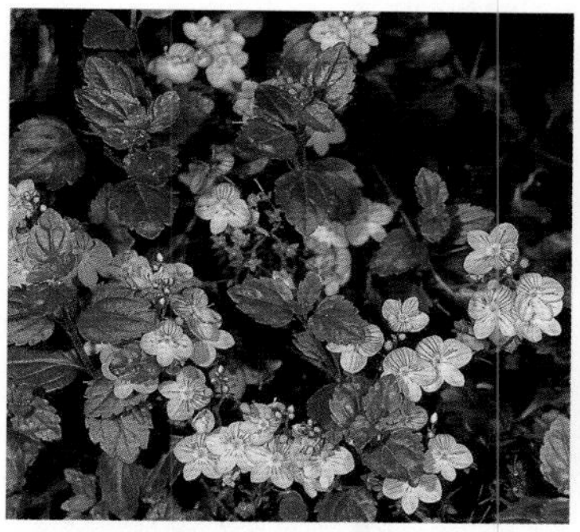

Veronica petraea 'Madame Mercier'

Veronica repens

CREEPING SPEEDWELL

☼/◐ ✱ ↔ 12–18 in (30–45 cm)
↑ 2–4 in (5–10 cm)

This low, spreading, late spring- to summer-flowering perennial is from Spain and Corsica. Foliage is bright green to yellow-green, pointed oval, sometimes toothed, less than ½ in (12 mm) long. Flowers are a little over ¼ in (6 mm) wide, pink, white, or blue, solitary or in heads of up to six. Zones 5–10.

Veronica spicata

☼/◐ ✱ ↔ 12–32 in (30–80 cm)
↑ 12–24 in (30–60 cm)

European summer-flowering perennial forming a clump of erect stems with downy, finely toothed, narrow lance-shaped, 1–3 in (25–80 mm) long leaves. Terminal spikes densely packed with ¼ in (6 mm) wide deep blue flowers. *V. s.* **subsp. *incana*,** velvety silver-gray to white flowers, sometimes classified as a distinct species. Its cultivars include: **'Rotfuchs'** (syn. 'Red Fox'), deep reddish pink flowers; **'Silbersee'**, a low spreading foliage carpet, spikes of dark blue flowers; **'Wendy'**, gray-green foliage and an open growth habit. *V. s.* **'Barcarolle'**, bright pink; **'Heidekind'**, short spikes of purple-red flowers; **'Icicle'**, long spikes of white flowers; **'Rosea'**, deep

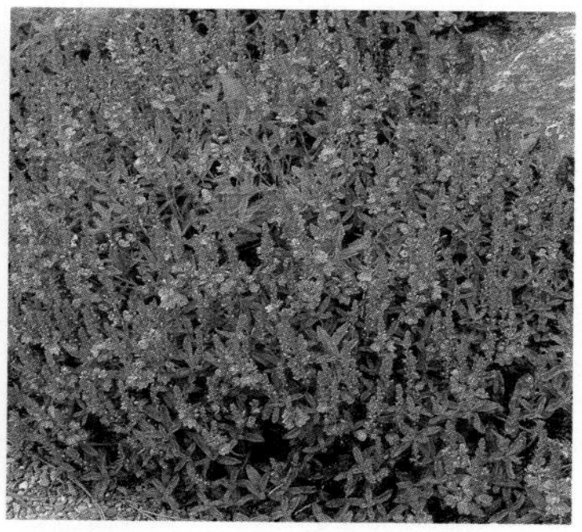

Veronica prostrata

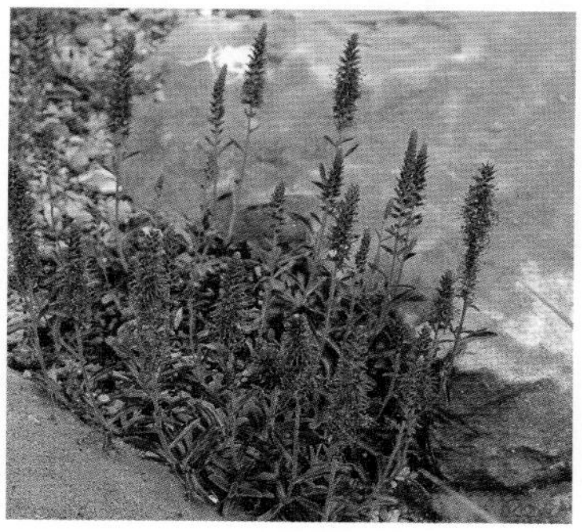

Veronica wormskjoldii

pink; and **'Sunny Border Blue'**, dark violet-blue flowers over a long season. Zones 3–9.

Veronica wormskjoldii

AMERICAN ALPINE SPEEDWELL

☼/◐ ✱ ↔ 8–20 in (20–50 cm)
↑ 4–12 in (10–30 cm)

Summer-flowering perennial found in North America and the southern tip of Greenland. It spreads by rhizomes to form a clump of erect sparsely hairy stems with sometimes toothed, pointed elliptic leaves to 2 in (5 cm) long. Tiny violet-blue blooms, in few-flowered terminal heads. Zones 4–9.

VERONICASTRUM

This genus of 2 upright perennials, in the foxglove family (Scrophulariaceae), is from northeastern Asia and northeastern North America. The plants

Verticordia grandis, in the wild, southwest Western Australia

Verticordia plumosa

have whorls of simple leaves and a terminal raceme of spikes of flowers with a calyx with 4 to 5 lobes, and saucer-shaped corolla with 2 stamens.
CULTIVATION: These perennials like moist, humus-rich soil and will grow in full or half-sun. Propagation is from seed, or by division.

Veronicastrum virginicum
syns Leptandra virginica, Veronica virginica
BLACKROOT, BOWMAN'S ROOT, CULVER'S ROOT
☼ ❄ ↔ 1–3 ft (0.3–0.9 m) ↕ 2–6 ft (0.6–1.8 m)
This perennial, native to northeastern America, has whorls of 4 to 7 simple, smooth, sword-shaped, serrated leaves. Dense, slender spikes, to 12 in (30 cm) tall, of tiny pale blue or white flowers in summer. V. v. var. sibiricum, narrow spikes of lilac flowers. V. v. 'Album', white flowers; 'Pointed Finger', lilac flowers; 'Roseum', soft pink flowers. Zones 3–6.

Verticordia chrysantha

VERSCHAFFELTIA
This monotypic genus in the palm (Arecaceae) family is native to the Seychelles on steep slopes and in gorges, putting out aerial roots for extra anchorage. A single-stemmed spiny palm with smooth-edged leaves that are pinnately ribbed and have a prominently notched apex.
CULTIVATION: This species is suitable for growing in humid tropical areas where it should be given shelter from strong winds. In cool climates, young plants make interesting potted specimens for the house or greenhouse. Propagation is from fresh seed.

Verschaffeltia splendida
☼ ✈ ↔ 8 ft (2.4 m) ↕ 70 ft (21 m)
Trunk ringed with long black spines, base has stilt-like aerial roots. Bright green leaves, undivided and pleated at first, later split and appear to be pinnate. Flowerheads arise within the leaves. Round fruits are olive green. Zones 10–12.

VERTICORDIA
This genus from the myrtle (Myrtaceae) family is endemic in Australia; most of its 97 species occur in the southwest of the country. All are woody shrubs. The small leaves are opposite in alternating pairs, and have

oil glands. The flowers are the attractive feature, with colors ranging from white to yellow, mauve and red and with the calyx of each flower deeply divided and appearing feathery. The petals of some species are also divided or lobed. Habitats are generally heaths and low scrubs, on sandy or gravelly soils that have an acid pH.
CULTIVATION: The majority do not do well in regions where summer rainfall is high or frequent. Propagate from seed and cuttings. Seeds are few and fertility is usually low. While cuttings are not always reliable, some species do strike readily. Grafting onto rootstocks of related genera that have proved reliable in a variety of garden situations has been successful with some species.

Verticordia chrysantha
☼ ❄ ↔ 24 in (60 cm) ↕ 24 in (60 cm)
Erect shrub from the southern sandplains of Western Australia. Small linear leaves, feathery flowers in dense yellow heads, in spring. Grafting onto rootstocks of Darwinia citriodora has also been successful. Zones 8–9.

Verticordia grandis
☼ ❄ ↔ 3 ft (0.9 m) ↕ 7 ft (2 m)
From sandheaths to the north of Perth in Western Australia. Straggling shrub with opposite, almost circular, grayish

Vesselowskya rubifolia

green leaves. Few brilliant scarlet flowers, 1 in (25 mm) across, in the upper leaf axils, in spring. Zones 8–9.

Verticordia plumosa
☼ ❄ ↔ 20 in (50 cm) ↕ 20 in (50 cm)
Variable species, with gray-green leaves about ¼ in (6 mm) long. Dense terminal heads of pinkish flowers, in spring. Propagation successful from seeds and cuttings. Most commonly cultivated Verticordia. Zones 8–9.

VESSELOWSKYA
This genus, endemic to Australia, contains a single species of evergreen shrub or small tree. It is a member of the family Cunoniaceae, restricted in distribution to moist forests and rainforests of northern New South Wales.
CULTIVATION: Can be grown in well-drained, moist, organically rich soils in sheltered positions. Extra water is needed during dry periods. Due to its attractive foliage, V. rubifolia is sometimes used as a potted plant indoors, but it requires high levels of humidity. Propagate from seeds and cuttings.

Veronicastrum virginicum 'Pointed Finger'

Veronicastrum virginicum var. sibiricum

Vestia foetida

Vesselowskya rubifolia
SOUTHERN MARARA

☼ ❄ ↔10 ft (3 m) ↕25 ft (8 m)

Tall shrub or small tree with reddish new shoots. Leaves compound, 3 to 5 hairy leaflets elliptic, toothed margins. Small cream flowers in dense clusters in leaf axils, in spring–summer. Red, 2-celled fruits. Zones 8–11.

VESTIA

The single species in this genus within the nightshade (Solanaceae) family is an evergreen shrub growing in the Chilean woodland. It is mainly grown for its flowers and foliage; the alternate, shiny, deep green leaves emit an unpleasant smell when crushed. The yellow-green flowers are pendent. CULTIVATION: Prefers well-drained soil in a site sheltered from full sun and frost. Water and feed moderately throughout the growing season, and reduce watering in the dormant period. Propagate from cuttings in summer, or sow seed in autumn or spring.

Vestia foetida
syn. *Vestia lycioides*

☼ ❄ ↔5 ft (1.5 m) ↕6 ft (1.8 m)

Erect evergreen shrub native to Chile. Thin, glossy, green leaves. Pale yellow, tubular, pendent flowers, in spring to late summer. Green seed capsules turn pale brown. Zones 9–10.

VIBURNUM

This genus in the woodbine family (Caprifoliaceae) consists of easily grown, cool-climate, deciduous, semi-evergreen or evergreen, shrubby plants that are grown for their pretty flowers, autumnal leaf color, and berries. Most have erect branching stems, paired leaves, a spread about two-thirds their height, and display their small white flowers in dense clusters. (Those plants that resemble the lace-top *Hydrangea* species bear sterile florets at the outer edges of the cluster.) The buds and petals, particularly in cultivars, may be softly colored in tints of pink, yellow, and green.
CULTIVATION: Light open positions and light well-drained soils are preferred. Many are drought tender. Prune the evergreens by clipping in late spring and the deciduous species by removing entire old stems after flowering. For a good berry display grow several in the same area. Propagate from cuttings taken in summer, or from seed in autumn.

Viburnum betulifolium

☼ ❄ ↔10 ft (3 m) ↕10 ft (3 m)

Upright, arching, deciduous shrub, native to western China. Bark is smooth, purple-brown. Bright green roundly oval leaves, glossy undersides. Tiny white flowers in flat-topped clusters, in early summer. Persistent, glowing, round, red berries. Zones 6–8.

Viburnum bitchiuense

☼ ❄ ↔10 ft (3 m) ↕10 ft (3 m)

Sometimes listed as *V. carlesii* var. *bitchiuense*. Bushy deciduous shrub, native of Korea. Smooth leaves have longer stems, are narrower than *V. carlesii*. Fragrant flowers, in open rounded clusters in early summer, pink on opening, fade to white. Egg-shaped red fruit. Zones 6–8.

Viburnum × bodnantense

☼ ❄ ↔7 ft (2 m) ↕10 ft (3 m)

Large, upright, deciduous shrub, a hybrid of *V. farreri* and *V. grandiflorum*. Long, oval, mid-green leaves, paler beneath, noticeably veined, color in autumn. Persistent, pinkish white to red, fragrant flowers, in dense clusters on bare wood, in late autumn–early spring. 'Charles Lamont' large bright pink flowers; 'Dawn', distinctive, deep pink, fragrant flowers that fade with age. Zones 7–9.

Viburnum × burkwoodii
BURKWOOD'S VIBURNUM

☼ ❄ ↔8 ft (2.4 m) ↕8 ft (2.4 m)

Open bushy shrub, an English hybrid of *V. carlesii* and *V. utile*. Evergreen dark leaves, shiny above, felted below, bronze when young, turn yellow. Flowers are produced in rounded clusters, intense fragrance, in early spring, pink in bud, white on opening. 'Anne Russell', deciduous, valued for its small size, neat compact habit; 'Park Farm Hybrid', featuring red autumnal foliage. Zones 6–9.

Viburnum × carlcephalum
FRAGRANT SNOWBALL VIBURNUM

☼ ❄ ↔8 ft (2.4 m) ↕8 ft (2.4 m)

Deciduous shrub, a garden hybrid between *V. carlesii* and *V. macrocephalum* f. *keteleeri*. Lustrous leaves redden in autumn. Pink, 6 in (15 cm) wide buds appear in spring, opening to reveal mildly scented pink flowers that lighten with age. Zones 5–9.

Viburnum carlesii
KOREAN SPICE VIBURNUM

☼ ❄ ↔7 ft (2 m) ↕8 ft (2.4 m)

From the open scrub of Korea and Japan, a dense, deciduous, rounded shrub. The mid-green leaves, paler beneath, oval shape, bronze-tinted when young, purple-red in autumn. Clustered crimson-pink buds open to reveal pink flowers that fade to white. 'Aurora' ★ features light acid green young leaves, red buds, and pink flowers; 'Diana' has bronzed new growth, and red flowers that fade to

Viburnum bitchiuense

Viburnum × burkwoodii

Viburnum × bodnantense

Viburnum carlesii

Viburnum cassinoides
WILD RAISIN, WITHE-ROD

☀ ❋ ↔ 10 ft (3 m) ↑ 12 ft (3.5 m)

Deciduous shrub from eastern North America, noted for deep bronze new growth and scarlet autumn coloring. Oval leaves thick, dull green, finely toothed. Flowers white or yellowish white, in summer. Red fruit, ripening to deep blue and black. Zones 2–6.

Viburnum 'Cayuga'

☀ ❋ ↔ 6 ft (1.8 m) ↑ 6 ft (1.8 m)

Hybrid between *Viburnum carlesii* and *V. × carlcephalum*. Leaves develop soft orange tones in autumn. Flowers pleasantly scented, open from pink buds, outer flowers a similar pink shade, those in the center, white. Fruit deep purple-red to black. Zones 8–10.

Viburnum cylindricum

☀ ❋ ↔ 12 ft (3.5 m) ↑ 12 ft (3.5 m)

Evergreen Chinese shrub with dark green leaves. The flowers are white, in rayed clusters, appearing in summer. Black fruits. Zones 6–8.

Viburnum davidii

☀ ❋ ↔ 4 ft (1.2 m) ↑ 4 ft (1.2 m)

This low-growing, dense, evergreen, mound-forming shrub is from the

Viburnum cylindricum

woods of western China. Glossy green leather-like leaves, 3 distinctive main veins. Small off-white flowers in stiff well-spaced clusters, are produced in late spring. Bright, oblong, midnight blue berries. Zones 6–8.

Viburnum dentatum
ARROWWOOD, SOUTHERN ARROWWOOD

☀ ❋ ↔ 10 ft (3 m) ↑ 10 ft (3 m)

This dense, deciduous, bushy shrub is found naturally across North America. Stems are erect and branching, leaves broadly oval, coarsely toothed, redden in autumn. Flat clusters of tiny white flowers, from late spring through to early summer. Dark blue oblong fruit. 'Ralph Senior' has a vigorous bushy habit and large leaves. Zones 2–6.

Viburnum davidii

Viburnum 'Eskimo'

Viburnum dentatum

Viburnum dilatatum
LINDEN VIBURNUM

☀ ❋ ↔ 8 ft (2.4 m) ↑ 10 ft (3 m)

A deciduous bushy shrub from China and Japan. Large, oval, coarse leaves, roundish, toothed, dark green, good autumn coloring. Tiny, creamy white, star-shaped flowers, in clusters, in late spring or summer. Oval scarlet fruits persist. 'Catskill', broad low-growing habit, smaller leaves than the species, good autumn coloring; 'Erie', pink fruit, rich autumn colors; 'Iroquois', shorter than the species, with reddish yellow fruits. Zones 5–8.

Viburnum erubescens

☀ ❋ ↔ 10 ft (3 m) ↑ 20 ft (6 m)

Found from the Himalayan region southwards to Sri Lanka, this is a deciduous to near-evergreen shrub or small tree. Elliptic leaves have serrated edges and downy undersides. Small pendulous clusters of pink-tinted white flowers are borne in summer. Red fruits ripen to black. Zones 6–11.

Viburnum dilatatum

Viburnum 'Eskimo'

☀ ❋ ↔ 4 ft (1.2 m) ↑ 4 ft (1.2 m)

Attractive hybrid between *V.* 'Cayuga' and *V. utile*. Dwarf shrub, mounding growth habit. Semi-evergreen, glossy, dark green leaves. Flowers, white opening from pink-tinted buds, small carried in rounded heads. Zones 8–10.

Viburnum farreri
syn. *Viburnum fragrans*

☀ ❋ ↔ 8 ft (2.4 m) ↑ 10 ft (3 m)

Upright, deciduous shrub, native of northern China. Leaves oval, veined, tapering, bronze when young, red when old. Sweetly scented persistent flowers pale pink or white, appear before the leaves, from mid-autumn to spring. Edible scarlet berries with poisonous stones. Zones 6–9.

Viburnum foetidum

☀ ❋ ↔ 10 ft (3 m) ↑ 12–15 ft (3.5–4.5 m)

Evergreen shrub from western China and the Himalayas. Dark green, ovate leaves, with smooth or toothed edges, often 3 small lobes near the leaf tip.

Viburnum cassinoides

Viburnum farreri

Heads of tiny white flowers. Showy, red, egg-shaped to rounded fruits. Zones 9–10.

Viburnum × globosum

☼ ❄ ↔ 3–4 ft (0.9–1.2 m) ↕ 3–4 ft (0.9–1.2 m)

Evergreen *V. davidii* × *V. lobophyllum* hybrid usually seen as selected form '**Jermyn's Globe**', neat rounded shrub. Lustrous, leathery, heavily veined, red-stemmed leaves. Heads of massed small white flowers open from red-tinted buds. Small dark blue fruit. Zones 7–10.

Viburnum grandiflorum

☼ ❄ ↔ 7 ft (2 m) ↕ 6 ft (1.8 m)

Dense, deciduous, stiff shrub from the Himalayas and western China. Dark green leaves, oblong, turn dark purple in autumn. Flowers white, fading to pink, in terminal clusters in late winter to early spring on bare wood. Purple-black oval berries. Zones 7–9.

Viburnum macrocephalum

Viburnum lantana 'Versicolor'

Viburnum henryi

☼/◐ ❄ ↔ 6 ft (1.8 m) ↕ 8 ft (2.4 m)

Native to China. Evergreen tree-like shrub. Narrow, oval, shiny, dark green leaves. Stiff pyramidal panicles of small white flowers in summer. The ensuing berries are red, turning to black. Zones 7–10.

Viburnum × hillieri

☼ ❄ ↔ 7 ft (2 m) ↕ 6–8 ft (1.8–2.4 m)

English-raised hybrid, cross between *V. erubescens* and *V. henryi*. Evergreen shrub with elliptic leaves, shallowly, irregularly serrated edges. In summer, small panicles of white flowers. Red fruits ripen to black. Typical form usually sold as '**Winton**'. Zones 6–10.

Viburnum japonicum

☼ ❄ ↔ 8 ft (2.4 m) ↕ 8 ft (2.4 m)

Robust evergreen shrub from Japan. Long, leathery, lustrous leaves, oval, dark green above, paler beneath. Tiny, white, strongly scented flowers in clusters, in early summer. Berries red, persist through the winter. Zones 7–9.

Viburnum × juddii

JUDD VIBURNUM

☼ ❄ ↔ 7 ft (2 m) ↕ 6 ft (1.8 m)

Deciduous *V. bitchiuense* and *V. carlesii* cross. Bushy spreading habit. Sweetly fragrant, pink budded, white starry flowers in rounded clusters, in mid–late spring. Elongated oval foliage, dull dark green. Zones 5–9.

Viburnum lantana

WAYFARING TREE

☼ ❄ ↔ 12 ft (3.5 m) ↕ 15 ft (4.5 m)

Robust deciduous shrub or small tree, native of Europe and northwest Asia.

Viburnum foetidum

Viburnum × globosum 'Jermyn's Globe'

Oblong-oval dull green leaves sometimes turn rusty crimson in autumn. Creamy white flowers in terminal clusters, in late spring–early summer. Red oblong fruits mature to black. Grows best on alkaline soils. Darker-leafed '**Mohican**' ★ has reddish orange fruit, maturing to black; '**Versicolor**' has light yellow new leaves ageing to golden yellow. Zone 3–6.

Viburnum lantanoides

syn. *Viburnum alnifolium*

HOBBLE BUSH

☼/◐ ❄ ↔ 15 ft (4.5 m) ↕ 15 ft (4.5 m)

Deciduous bushy shrub native to North America. Spreading suckering branches, downy when young. Large leaves clearly veined, broadly oval, turn yellow and claret red in autumn. Large white flowers in lace-top clusters, in late spring–early summer. Oblong purple-black fruit. Zones 3–6.

Viburnum lantana

Viburnum henryi

Viburnum lentago

NANNYBERRY, SHEEPBERRY, WILD RAISIN

☼/◐ ❄ ↔ 10 ft (3 m) ↕ 20 ft (6 m)

Slender, branching, vigorous, deciduous shrub or small tree from North America. Broadly oval, lustrous, dark green leaves, attractive autumn hues. Creamy white, fluffy flowers, similar to elderberry (*Sambucus*) species, in clusters, from spring to early summer. Oval bluish black berries. Zones 2–5.

Viburnum macrocephalum

CHINESE SNOWBALL BUSH/TREE

☼ ❄ ↔ 15 ft (4.5 m) ↕ 15 ft (4.5 m)

A Chinese species with spreading branches. Showy pompon-like clusters of white flowers, opening from almost luminous green buds, in spring. May be semi-evergreen in mild winters. Dark green oval-oblong leaves, downy on the undersides. *V. m.* f. *keteleeri* has attractive lacecap-like flowers. *V. m.* '**Sterile**', sterile and berryless, is a popular cultivar for mild-climate gardens. Zones 6–9.

Viburnum mongolicum

☼ ❄ ↔ 4 ft (1.2 m) ↕ 6–8 ft (1.8–2.4 m)

Found naturally in eastern Siberia and Mongolia. A deciduous shrub with 2½ in (6 cm) long, serrated-edged leaves, downy undersides. Small, flat, open heads of white flowers are borne in spring. Clusters of red berries, ripening to black. Zones 4–9.

V

Viburnum opulus 'Notcutt's Variety'

Viburnum opulus 'Aureum'

Viburnum opulus

Viburnum nudum

Viburnum opulus 'Roseum'

Viburnum nudum

POSSUM-HAW VIBURNUM, SMOOTH
WITHE-ROD

☼ ❄ ↔ 6 ft (1.8 m) ↑ 10 ft (3 m)
Native to eastern USA and Canada.
Deciduous erect shrub. Oval glossy
leaves, prominent veins, minutely
toothed edges, turn reddish purple in
autumn. Flowers are white or pale
yellow, in summer. Fruit is blue-black.
Zones 6–9.

Viburnum opulus

COMMON SNOWBALL, EUROPEAN CRAN-
BERRY, EUROPEAN SNOWBALL, GUELDER ROSE

☼ ❄ ↔ 15 ft (4.5 m) ↑ 15 ft (4.5 m)
Vigorous parent plant to many popular deciduous garden shrubs. Native

hedgerow habitat from Siberia to
Algeria. Deep green vine-like leaves,
paler downy undersides, redden in
autumn. Lace-top clusters of white
flowers, in early summer. Lustrous,
semi-translucent, red fruits. '**Aureum**',
bright yellow spring foliage, yellow-
green in summer, easily scorched by
sun; '**Nanum**', dwarf cultivar of dense
multi-stemmed habit, to about 2 ft
(0.6 m) tall, with small crowded
leaves, rarely flowers; '**Notcutt's
Variety**', tall vigorous shrub to about
12 ft (3.5 m) high with fine foliage
color in autumn, large red fruits last
into winter; '**Roseum**' (syn. 'Sterile'),
showy, snowball-like, greenish white
flower clusters, in mid-spring with the

leaves; '**Xanthocarpum**', white flowers,
mid-green leaves, glossy, partly translucent, yellow berries. Zones 3–9.

Viburnum plicatum

syn. *Viburnum plicatum* var. *tomentosum*
DOUBLEFILE VIBURNUM, JAPANESE SNOWBALL

☼ ❄ ↔ 10 ft (3 m) ↑ 8 ft (2.4 m)
From China and Japan. A vigorous,
deciduous, spreading shrub with tiered
branches. Leaves with pleated surface,
bright green in spring, mid-green in
summer, burgundy-red in autumn.
Profuse flat umbels of small, cream,
fertile flowers, in late spring to early
summer, ringed by larger, white, sterile flowers. Small red fruits. '**Fireworks**', reddish black fruits, purple-

red autumn foliage; '**Grandiflorum**',
white flowers turn pink; '**Lanarth**',
spreads to 15 ft (4.5m); '**Mariesii**',
horizontal overlapping branches, large
flat heads of mainly sterile flowers,
rarely fruiting; '**Nanum Semperflorens**'
(syn. *V. watanabei*), slow-growing,
small flowerheads during the warmer
months; '**Pink Beauty**', white flowers
ageing to pink; '**Roseum**', flowers age
from white to deep pink; '**Shasta**', 7 ft
(2 m) tall, deep purple-red autumn
foliage, large white flowers followed by
dark red fruit; '**Summer Snowflake**',

Viburnum plicatum 'Mariesii'

Viburnum plicatum 'Grandiflorum'

Viburnum plicatum 'Lanarth'

Viburnum plicatum, in winter

Viburnum plicatum, in spring

Viburnum plicatum, in summer

Viburnum plicatum, in autumn

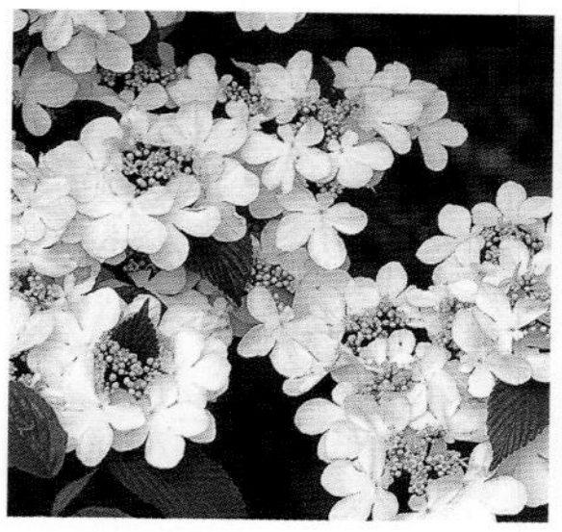

Viburnum plicatum 'Pink Beauty'

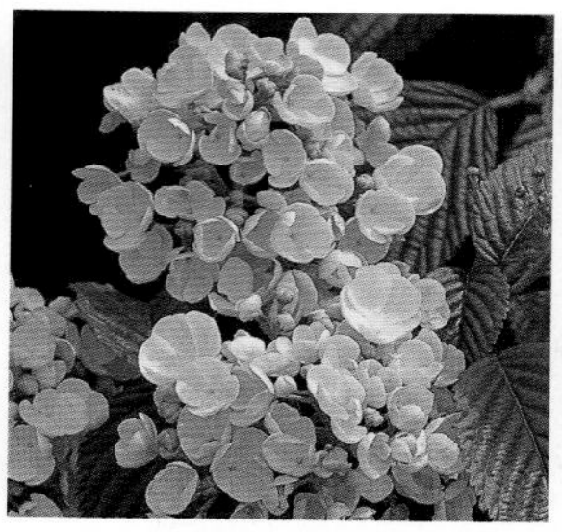

Viburnum plicatum 'Popcorn'

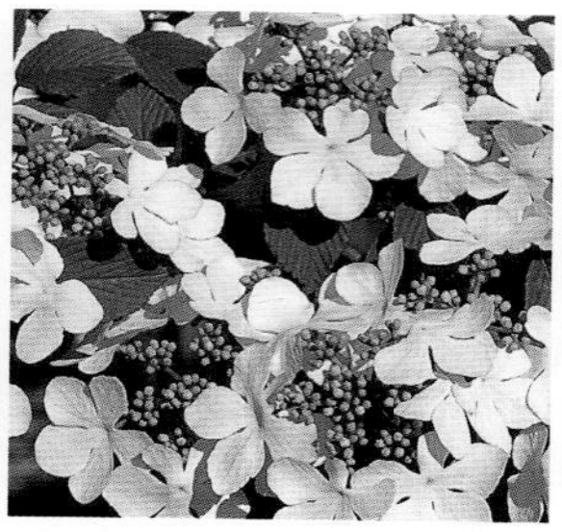

Viburnum plicatum 'Roseum'

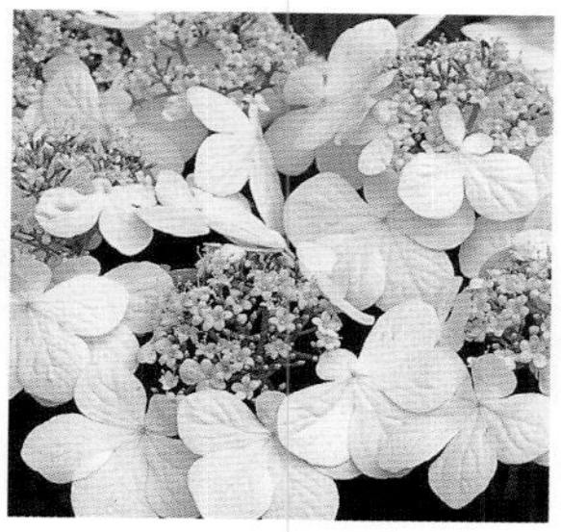

V. plicatum 'Summer Snowflake'

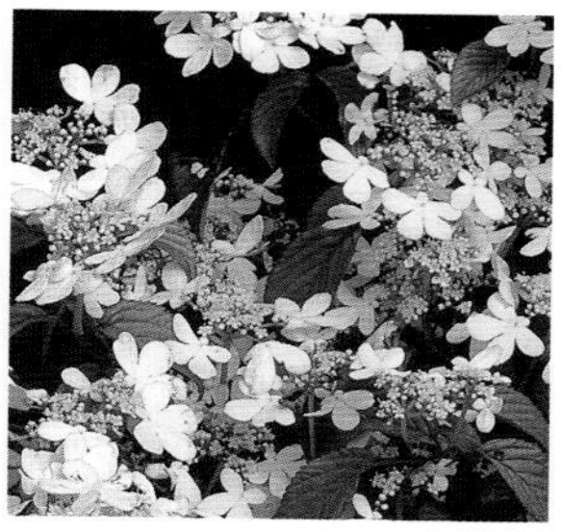

V. p. 'Nanum Semperflorens'

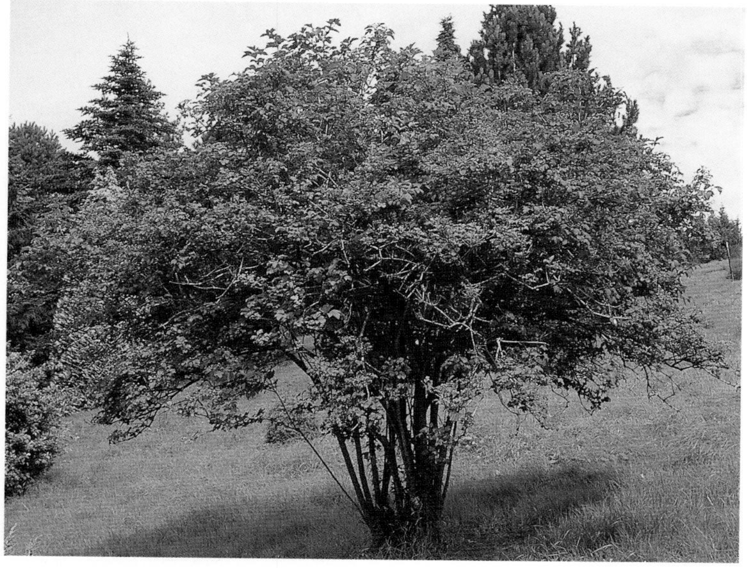

Viburnum sargentii

compact shrub with strongly tiered branches, long-lasting white flowers, purple-red autumn foliage. Zones 4–9.

Viburnum prunifolium

BLACK HAW

↔ 12 ft (3.5 m) ↑ 20 ft (6 m)

Spreading deciduous shrub or small tree from eastern parts of North America. Leaves roundish oval, finely and sharply toothed. Reddish buds open to small, white, flat-topped clusters of flowers, in spring to early summer. Yellow-green berries ripen to blue-black. Zones 3–9.

Viburnum × *rhytidophylloides*

↔ 15 ft (4.5 m) ↑ 20 ft (6 m)

Of garden origin, a hybrid between *V. rhytidophyllum* and *V. lantana.* Deciduous in cold climates, densely upright shrub or small tree. Long oval leaves, shiny dark green, paler on the undersides. Flowers a dull yellowish to pinkish white, in spring to summer. Red berries ripen to black. Zones 5–9.

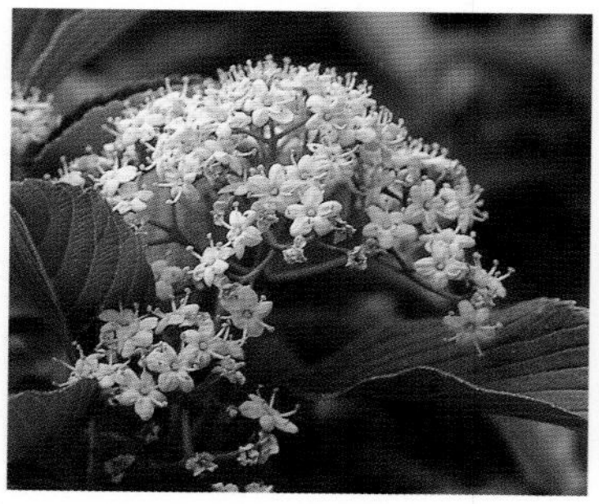

Viburnum sieboldii 'Seneca'

Viburnum rhytidophyllum

↔ 8 ft (2.4 m) ↑ 10 ft (3 m)

Stout, upright, fast-growing, evergreen shrub. Long, narrow, wrinkled, veined, leathery, dark green leaves, gray or yellow woolly beneath. Terminal clusters of small, fluffy, yellowish to pinkish white flowers, in early summer. Oval red fruit darkens to black. **'Aldenhamense'**, leaves with sulfur yellow tinges; **'Roseum'**, deep pink flowers turn lighter with age. Zones 6–8.

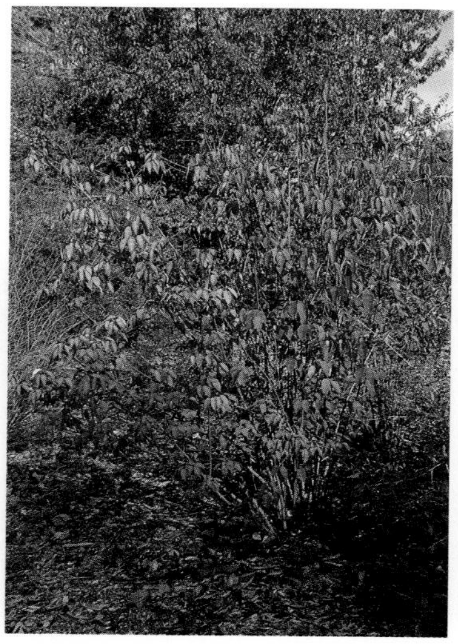

Viburnum setigerum

Viburnum sargentii

SARGENT VIBURNUM

↔ 10 ft (3 m) ↑ 10 ft (3 m)

Large deciduous shrub from Siberia, China, and Japan. Thick, dark gray, fissured, corky bark. Leaves large, long, maple-like, turn yellow-orange and scarlet in autumn. Creamy white lacecap flowers, early summer. Semi-translucent, light red, round berries. **'Onondaga'** has bronze red young growth. **'Susquehanna'** is smaller than the species, with a rounded growth habit. Zones 5–9.

Viburnum setigerum

↔ 7 ft (2 m) ↑ 5–12 ft (1.5–3.5 m)

Deciduous shrub variable in height, depending on climate and clone. Large oblong-oval leaves dark green above, paler, slightly woolly beneath, color well in autumn. Flowers are insignificant. Spectacular, gleaming, golden orange and bright red, oval fruits. Zones 5–9.

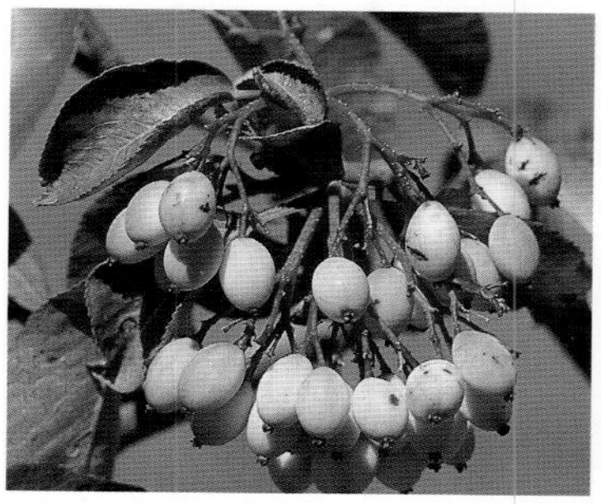

Viburnum prunifolium

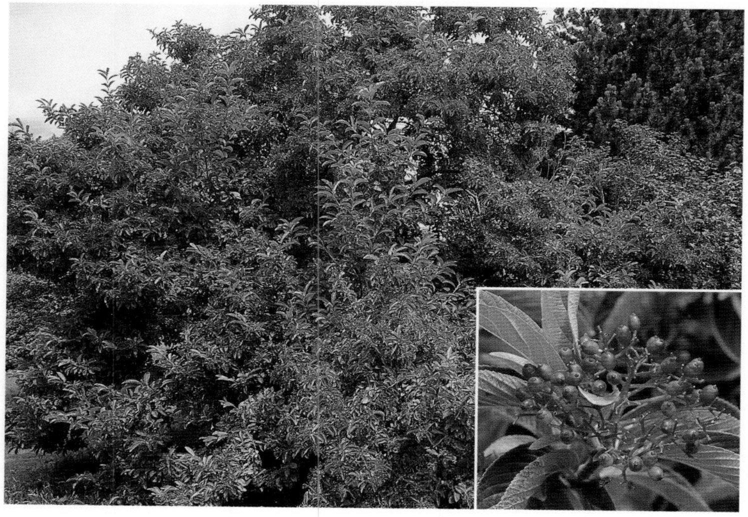

Viburnum sieboldii

Viburnum sieboldii

↔ 15 ft (4.5 m) ↑ 10 ft (3 m)

From Japan. Spreading deciduous shrub. Young growth downy. Large prominently veined leaves, oblong-oval, glossy, dark green above, paler beneath. Panicles of tiny creamy white flowers, in late spring–early summer. Fruits red when young, ripen to black. **'Seneca'**, reaching up to 30 ft (9 m) high, has clusters of white flowers followed by persistent red fruit, ripening to almost black. Zones 4–8.

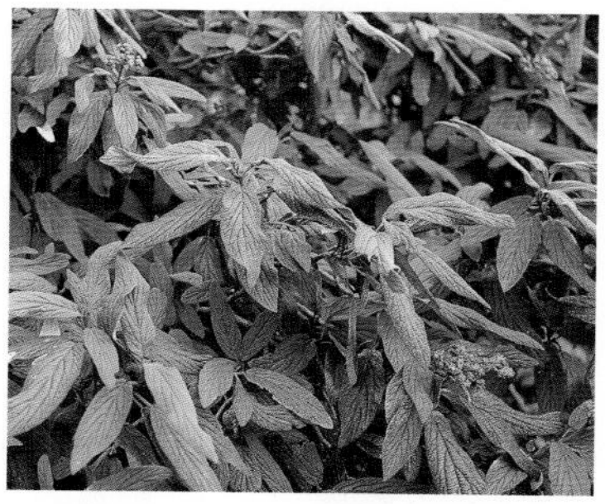

Viburnum rhytidophyllum

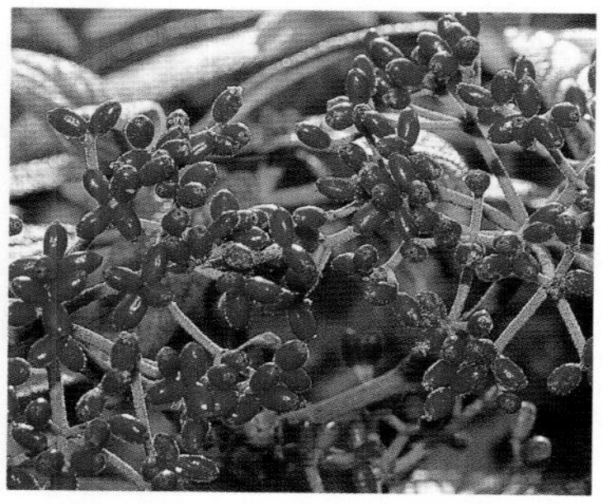

Viburnum rhytidophyllum 'Aldenhamense'

Viburnum tinus
LAURUSTINUS

☀ ❄ ↔ 8–10 ft (2.4–3 m)
↑ 8–10 ft (2.4–3 m)

Native of the Mediterranean region. A dense evergreen shrub that has been popular for centuries as a hedging plant. The dark green glossy leaves are oblong-oval and pointed. Flattened heads of white, pink or pinkish white flowers, strongly fragrant. Blue-black berries. Several named forms grow in sun or shade, tolerate coastal conditions, and are semi-tolerant of summer drought. '**Eve Price**', elongated leaves and light pink flowers; '**Lucidum**', particularly glossy leaves; '**Purpureum**', bronzed new growth; '**Robertson**', small whitish flowers; and '**Variegatum**', leaves margined in yellow. Zones 7–9.

Viburnum tinus

Viburnum tinus 'Eve Price'

Viburnum veitchii

Viburnum trilobum, in winter

Viburnum trilobum
syns *Viburnum americanum*, *V. opulus* var. *americanum*

AMERICAN HIGHBUSH CRANBERRY, CRANBERRY BUSH

☀ ❄ ↔ 10 ft (3 m) ↑ 10 ft (3 m)

Deciduous shrubby plant from North America. Dark leaves, broadly oval, deeply serrated, redden in autumn. Showy, flat-topped, white flowerheads, in early summer. Bright scarlet edible berries. '**Bailey Compact**' and '**Compactum**' have attractive autumn foliage; '**Wentworth**', vigorous cultivar, tolerant of damp soils, very brightly colored long-lasting fruit. Zones 2–8.

Viburnum tinus 'Robertson'

Viburnum trilobum, in summer

Viburnum utile

☀ ❄ ↔ 5 ft (1.5 m) ↑ 6 ft (1.8 m)

From China. Evergreen, slender, open shrub with dark shiny leaves. Flowers white, in dense rounded clusters, in spring. Oval berries. Zones 7–9.

Viburnum veitchii
CHINESE WAYFARING TREE

☀ ❄ ↔ 5 ft (1.5 m) ↑ 5 ft (1.5 m)

From central China. This deciduous upright shrub has sharply toothed mid-green leaves. White flowers, in flat rayed clusters, red berries ripen black. Zones 5–9.

Viburnum wrightii

☀ ❄ ↔ 10 ft (3m) ↑ 12 ft (3.5 m)

Deciduous shrub from Japan. Broad, bright green, oval leaves turn red in autumn. Flowers white, in flat rayed clusters, in late spring–early summer. Glistening red fruit. Zones 6–8.

VICIA
VETCH

The members of this genus within the pea-flower subfamily of the legume (Fabaceae) family include around 140 mostly sprawling, annual or perennial herbaceous vines that often climb by tendrils at the tips of the leaves. The species are widely distributed across temperate regions of the Northern Hemisphere. They have divided leaves and butterfly-like flowers of lavender, white, or purple, occasionally yellow, followed by seed carried in long pods.

Viburnum trilobum 'Bailey Compact'

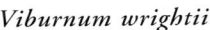

Viburnum trilobum, in autumn

Vicia faba 'Red Epicure'

Several species are grown as food crops, others as animal forage, and some as ornamentals.
CULTIVATION: These plants prefer open sunny positions, and are adaptable to most soils. Propagate from seed. Care should be taken in positioning, as some species self-seed readily and can become invasive.

Vicia faba
BROAD BEAN, HORSE BEAN

☀ ❄ ↔ 12 in (30 cm)
↑ 3–6 ft (0.9–1.8 m)

An upright annual, native to northern Africa and southwest Asia. Divided leaves without tendrils. Flowers are white with a dark purple blotch, in the leaf axils. Oblong seed pods, up to 12 in (30 cm) long, are edible. '**Red Epicure**', red flowers. Zones 8–10.

Viburnum trilobum 'Wentworth'

VICTORIA

GIANT WATER LILY

The 2 species of aquatic perennials in this genus, members of the waterlily (Nymphaeaceae) family, are native to tropical South America where they grow in slow-moving or still water. These giant plants are grown for their large flat leaves, reputed to be able to bear the weight of a small child, and for their beautiful perfumed flowers. Arising from stout rhizomes, they produce floating round leaves, to 7 ft (2 m) wide, with upturned rims. The many-petalled flowers open at night, white at first deepening to pink on the second day, and purple on the third day before dying.

CULTIVATION: These are spectacular plants for large warm pools in tropical greenhouses. They are usually grown as annuals because of their rapid growth rate. Propagate from seed and gradually increase pot size and water depth as plants grow. Grow in full sun.

Victoria amazonica

syn. *Victoria regia*

AMAZON WATER LILY, ROYAL WATER LILY

☼ ✚ ↔ 15–20 ft (4.5–6 m)
↑ 10–12 in (25–30 cm)

Native to the Amazon region. Leaves to 7 ft (2 m) wide with upturned rim to about 6 in (15 cm) high. The leaf underside is reddish purple and spiny. Perfumed flowers arise in summer and autumn. Zones 10–12.

Victoria amazonica

Victoria amazonica

Vigna caracalla

Victoria 'Longwood Hybrid'

☼ ✚ ↔ 12–40 ft (3.5–12 m)
↑ 10–12 in (25–30 cm)

A vigorous hybrid of *V. amazonica* and *V. cruziana* raised at Longwood Gardens, Philadelphia. Its leaves grow to 8 ft (2.4 m) wide and flowers open earlier in the evening. It is a little hardier. Zones 10–12.

VIGNA

This genus, comprising some 150 species native throughout the tropics, but particularly in the Americas, is a member of the pea-flower subfamily of the legume (Fabaceae) family. The plants are erect or twining herbs. They usually have woody or tuberous rootstocks. The leaves have 1 to 3 elliptic to ovate leaflets. The flowers are in racemes or clustered together, often on long stalks. The calyx is 2-lipped. The yellow, blue, or purple corolla has an upper petal generally with 2 to 4 appendages; the inner petals forming the keel are often beaked, the beak can be incurved up to 360 degrees. The pod is cylindrical or flattened, straight or curved. The seeds are often kidney-shaped and sometimes have an aril.

CULTIVATION: These are important pulses and many provide valuable green manure. They are also grown as "bean sprouts." Frost tender. In tropical regions grow in full sun in fertile well-drained soil; in cooler climates grow in the greenhouse. Propagate from seed in spring.

Vigna caracalla

syn. *Phaseolus caracalla*

CORKSCREW FLOWER, SNAIL BEAN, SNAIL FLOWER

☼ ✚ ↔ 10 ft (3 m) ↑ 12–20 ft (3.5–6 m)

A twining perennial from tropical South America. Finely hairy leaves with 3 oval-shaped leaflets. Fragrant white or yellow flowers, up to 2 in (5 cm) across, with pinkish purple wings. Coiled keel resembles a snail shell. Zones 10–11.

Vigna mungo

syn. *Phaseolus mungo*

BLACK GRAM

☼ ✚ ↔ 24–36 in (60–90 cm)
↑ 12–24 in (30–60 cm)

A spreading annual from Asia, with compound leaves. Pointed, oval-shaped leaflets and yellow, pea-like flowers. Seed pods up to 2 in (5 cm) long, containing small oblong seeds. *V. m.* var. *radiata* has stems and seed pods covered with fine, short reddish hairs. Zones 10–12.

Vigna radiata

syns *Phaseolus aureus*, *P. radiatus*

GOLDEN GRAM, GREEN GRAM, MUNG BEAN

☼ ✚ ↔ 8–12 in (20–30 cm)
↑ 5–6 ft (1.5–1.8 m)

This annual vine is native to India, Indonesia, and Southeast Asia. It is finely hairy, with slender, twining stems and divided leaves. Yellowish purple, pea-shaped flowers. Finely hairy seed pods. Sprouted seeds are edible. Zones 10–11.

VIGUIERA

This genus of about 150 annual or perennial herbs and shrubs, members

Viguiera multiflora, in the wild, Theodore Roosevelt National Park, North Dakota, USA

Viguiera laciniata

of the daisy (Asteraceae) family, is native to North and South America. Several stems grow from a central base. The leaves are simple, alternate or opposite. Solitary flowerheads, about 2 in (5 cm) across, are borne on long stalks, usually with yellow daisy-like flowers.

CULTIVATION: *Viguiera* species prefer a position in full sun, in most well-drained soils. Propagate from seed.

Viguiera laciniata

SAN DIEGO COUNTY VIGUIERA

☼ ✚ ↔ 3–6 ft (0.9–1.8 m)
↑ 3–4 ft (0.9–1.2 m)

Roughly hairy shrub from western California and northwestern Mexico. All parts covered with a varnish-like resin. Alternate, triangular to sword-shaped, toothed leaves, arrow-shaped base, prominent veins. Flat-topped heads of yellow daisy-like flowers in summer. Zones 10–12.

Viguiera multiflora

☼ ✚ ↔ 30–40 in (75–100 cm)
↑ 30–40 in (75–100 cm)

Resinous perennial herb native to southern, central, and western USA, and south to Mexico. Smooth-edged or sparsely toothed leaves, narrowly oval- to sword-shaped. Yellow daisy-like flowers, in summer. Zones 10–12.

V

Vinca minor

Vinca minor 'Alba'

Vinca minor 'Atropurpurea'

Vinca minor 'Gertrude Jekyll'

Vinca minor cultivar

Vinca minor 'Ralph Shugert'

Vinca minor 'Illumination'

VINCA
PERIWINKLE

This genus of 7 species of evergreen groundcovering perennials found in woodland areas of North Africa, central Asia, and Europe, is part of the dogbane (Apocynaceae) family. These plants are distinctive for their opposite, simple, lance-shaped leaves that cover the slender, often cream or pale green, ground-hugging stems. The foliage varies in color from pale to dark green and many variations occur with attractive variegations. The star-shaped flowers are produced from spring through to late autumn, and will vary in color from dark purple to blue and white.
CULTIVATION: Ideally, these plants like a free-draining light soil with a reasonable level of organic matter. They will spread indefinitely and in some areas they can become invasive if neglected. Plant in sun or shade. The plant spreads by sending out long trailing and rooting shoots, which make new plants. Propagation is easy any time of year by separating the new offshoots or by layering new shoots.

Vinca difformis
☀/☀ ❄ ↔ 5–10 ft (1.5–3 m)
↕ 12 in (30 cm)

From North Africa, and southern and western Europe. A low-growing perennial with narrowly lance-shaped, glossy, dark green leaves up to 3 in (8 cm) long. In early spring, soft blue flowers appear that fade to white as the season develops. Zones 8–9.

Vinca major
BLUE BUTTONS, GREATER PERIWINKLE
☀/☀ ❄ ↔ 5–10 ft (1.5–3 m)
↕ 18 in (45 cm)

From western parts of Mediterranean. Mounding plant with dark green leaves, 3½ in (9 cm) long, on arching stems. Rich violet-blue flowers, 2 in (5 cm) across, from early spring to late autumn. 'Variegata' (syn. 'Elegantissima') has creamy white streaked green leaves. Zones 7–11.

Vinca minor
CREEPING MYRTLE
☀/☀ ❄ ↔ 5–10 ft (1.5–3 m)
↕ 8 in (20 cm)

From Europe, southern Russia, and northern Caucasus. This tight mat-forming, evergreen perennial has dark green leaves, to 2 in (5 cm) long. The star-shaped violet-blue flowers, 1¼ in (3 cm) across, appear from early spring to mid-autumn. It is ideal for hanging baskets. 'Alba' bears white flowers; 'Argenteovariegata' (syn. 'Variegata'), creamy white stripes on foliage with pale lavender flowers; 'Atropurpurea', dark plum colored flowers; 'Azurea Flore Pleno', pale blue, frilly, double flowers; 'Bowles' Variety', with pale lavender-blue flowers; 'Gertrude Jekyll', a compact plant with plenty of white flowers; 'Illumination', variegated leaves, mainly yellow, with some green marking; 'Multiplex', double, red wine colored flowers; 'Ralph Shugert', deep green leaves outlined in white variegations. Zones 4–9.

Vinca Hybrid Cultivars
☀/☀ ❄ ↔ 12 in (30 cm) ↕ 16 in (40 cm)
Plants have an upright habit and branch early in the growing season. Quite tolerant of cool wet growing conditions. 'Cooler Raspberry Red', dark green leaves and large, overlapping flower petals of bright red with a white eye; 'Merlot Mix', large flowers displaying rich shades of burgundy, orchid, rose, and white; 'Pacific Red', carmine red; 'Pacific White', pure white. Zones 10–11.

VIOLA
HEARTSEASE, PANSY, VIOLET

The type genus for the family Violaceae, *Viola* includes some 500 species of annuals, perennials, and subshrubs found in all the world's temperate zones from the mountains of New Zealand to the subarctic. Most species are small clump-forming plants with lobed, elliptic, kidney- or heart-shaped leaves. All violas have remarkably similarly shaped 5-petalled flowers, with the lower petal often carrying dark markings. White, yellow, and purple predominate but the flowers occur in every color, at least among the garden forms. The plants have been used medicinally in several ways, and also symbolically: *V. tricolor* was a symbol of Athens and was also used by Napoleon.
CULTIVATION: They are mostly very hardy and easily grown in sun or shade. The woodland species prefer a humus-rich soil, while the rock-garden types like something grittier, but most do perfectly well in any moist well-drained soil. Propagation is from seed or basal cuttings or by division, depending on the growth form.

Viola adunca
HOOKED-SPUR VIOLET, PURPLE VIOLET, WESTERN DOG VIOLET
☀/☀ ❄ ↔ 12–16 in (30–40 cm)
↕ 2–4 in (5–10 cm)

Spreading spring-flowering perennial found across northern USA. Rounded to heart-shaped leaves, up to 1¾ in (40 mm) long. Spurred lavender to violet flowers, ½ in (12 mm) wide, deepen in color with age. Zones 4–9.

Viola biflora
☀ ❄ ↔ 6–10 in (15–25 cm)
↕ 4–8 in (10–20 cm)

Mounding spring-flowering perennial widespread in the mountains of temperate Eurasia and North America. Shallowly toothed, faintly downy, heart- or kidney-shaped leaves, to over 1¼ in (30 mm) long. Unscented, ¾ in (18 mm) wide, yellow flowers with dark streaks. Zones 3–9.

Viola blanda
SWEET WHITE VIOLET, WILLDENOW VIOLET, WOODLAND WHITE VIOLET
☀/☀ ❄ ↔ 12–20 in (30–50 cm)
↕ 3–6 in (8–15 cm)

A stemless, spring-flowering, North American perennial spreading by runners to form a clump of shallowly toothed, sparsely downy, deep green, heart-shaped leaves, to more than 2 in (5 cm) long. Unscented, about ½ in (12 mm) wide, white flowers with dark central veining. Zones 2–9.

Vinca major

Viola canina

HEATH DOG VIOLET, HEATH VIOLET

☀ ❋ ↔ 12–20 in (30–50 cm)
↕ 4–12 in (10–30 cm)

A summer-flowering perennial found over much of the northern temperate Eurasian region. Usually low and spreading, sometimes more upright. The deep green, shallowly toothed, pointed oval to heart-shaped leaves, grow to 1 in (25 mm) long. Mauve, purple, or white flowers, up to ¾ in (18 mm) wide, with a pale yellow spur, on erect stems. Zones 6–9.

Viola cornuta

BEDDING PANSY, HORNED VIOLET

☼/☀ ❋ ↔ 8–14 in (20–35 cm)
↕ 6–12 in (15–30 cm)

From the Pyrenees and northern Spain. A late spring- to summer-flowering, rhizome-rooted perennial, initially prostrate then more mounding. Oval, 1 in (25 mm) long, shallowly toothed leaves and spurred, broad-petalled, ¾ in (18 mm) wide, violet flowers with darker veining and yellow center. **Alba Group**, white-flowered forms of various sizes and degree of color purity; **'Belmont Blue'** (syn. 'Boughton Blue'), 1 in (25 mm) wide lilac flowers; **'Jewel White'**, very compact habit, white flowers to 1¾ in (40 mm) wide; **'Magnifico'**, white flowers with broad mauve border; **'Pat Kavanagh'**, pale lemon yellow, forms large clumps; **'Victoria's Blush'**, mid-pink narrow-petalled flowers. Also many mixed color seedling strains, such as **Penny Series** and **Princess Series**. **Sorbet Series** includes **'Sorbet Black Delight'**, deep velvet inky purple, almost black; and **'Sorbet Coconut'**, pure white with faint yellow center. Zones 7–10.

Viola cornuta, Sorbet Series, 'Sorbet Magnifico'

Viola cornuta 'Jewel White'

Viola cornuta, Sorbet Series, 'Sorbet Black Duet'

Viola cornuta, Sorbet Series, 'Sorbet Red Wing'

Viola cornuta, Princess Series, 'Princess Lavender and Yellow'

Viola cornuta 'Magnifico'

Viola cornuta 'Pat Kavanagh'

Viola cornuta, Penny Series, 'Penny Orange'

V. cornuta, Penny Series, 'Penny Orange Sunrise'

Viola cornuta, Penny Series, 'Penny Orchid Frost'

Viola cornuta, Penny Series, 'Penny Violet Beacon'

Viola cornuta, Princess Series, 'Princess Purple and Gold'

Viola cornuta, Sorbet Series, 'Sorbet Sunny Royale'

V. c., SS, 'Sorbet Beaconsfield'

V. c., SS, 'Sorbet Blueberry Cream'

Viola cornuta 'Victoria's Blush'

Viola cucullata
syn. *Viola obliqua*
MARSH BLUE VIOLET
☼/❁ ❄ ↔ 8–16 in (20–40 cm)
↑ 4–6 in (10–15 cm)

This is a North American spring- to early summer-flowering perennial. It develops a low spreading habit and has shallowly toothed, broad, pointed oval to kidney-shaped leaves, to over 3 in (8 cm) wide. The 5-petalled, short-spurred flowers, up to 1¼ in (30 mm) wide, are white washed with mauve to purple, sometimes heavily. Zones 4–9.

Viola glabella
STREAM VIOLET
❁ ❄ ↔ 8–16 in (20–40 cm)
↑ 6–10 in (15–25 cm)

This spring-flowering perennial can be found growing naturally on both sides of Bering Strait, southwards to Japan and western USA. It forms a dense clump of bright green, broad, pointed oval to heart-shaped leaves, up to a little over 1 in (25 mm) long. This species produces bright yellow, sometimes green-tinted, 5-petalled flowers that can reach about ½ in (12 mm) wide. Zones 5–9.

Viola glabella

Viola jooi

Viola pyrenaica

Viola hederacea
AUSTRALIAN VIOLET, TRAILING VIOLET
❁ ❄ ↔ 6–12 in (15–30 cm)
↑ 2–3 in (5–8 cm)

This small creeping perennial is native to southeastern Australia. Its broad, oval to kidney-shaped, sometimes shallowly toothed leaves grow to over 1¼ in (30 mm) wide. Throughout the warmer months, it produces dark-centered pale lavender or white flowers, approximately ¾ in (18 mm) wide. Zones 8–10.

Viola jooi
☼/❁ ❄ ↔ 8–14 in (20–35 cm)
↑ 2–4 in (5–10 cm)

A native of southeastern Europe, this is a spring- to summer-flowering perennial. It has a stemless habit, spreading by runners, with shallowly toothed heart-shaped leaves, to 3 in (8 cm) long, and short-spurred, ½ in (12 mm) wide, dark-streaked, mauve flowers. Zones 5–10.

Viola odorata
SWEET VIOLET
☼/❁ ❄ ↔ 12–24 in (30–60 cm)
↑ 4–6 in (10–15 cm)

A spring- to early summer-flowering southern and western European perennial that spreads by runners. Its heart-shaped dark green leaves, grow to over 2 in (5 cm) long and wide. The highly fragrant, spurred, 1 in (25 mm) wide flowers are lavender, purple, yellow, or white. Can be weedy. Numerous cultivars are available, with single or double flowers in a range of colors. '**Purple Robe**' ★ has a low spreading habit and masses of deep purple flowers. Zones 7–10.

Viola riviniana '**Purpurea**'

Viola selkirkii f. *variegata*

Viola tricolor

Viola pedata
BIRD'S FOOT VIOLET, PANSY VIOLET
❁ ❄ ↔ 8–16 in (20–40 cm)
↑ 4–6 in (10–15 cm)

Stemless, spring-flowering, eastern North American perennial, spreads by runners. Foliage different from most other violets: palmate with up to 5 narrow lobes. Spurred 1¼ in (30 mm) wide flowers with faintly downy petals. Flowers lavender, with darker upper petals and veining. Zones 4–9.

Viola pyrenaica
PYRENEAN VIOLET
☼/❁ ❄ ↔ 6–8 in (15–20 cm)
↑ 4 in (10 cm)

Small spring-flowering perennial found in southern Europe, from Spain to Bulgaria. Develops into a clump of shallowly toothed, pointed oval leaves, to 1¼ in (30 mm) long, with short-spurred purple flowers, about ¾ in (18 mm) wide. Zones 6–9.

Viola riviniana
DOG VIOLET, WOOD VIOLET
☼/❁ ❄ ↔ 8–24 in (20–60 cm)
↑ 4–6 in (10–15 cm)

European and North African spring- to early summer-flowering perennial. Develops into a dense clump of broad, pointed oval to rounded, toothed, often purple-tinted leaves, about 2 in (5 cm) long. Short-spurred lavender-blue flowers, 1 in (25 mm). '**Purpurea**', foliage with purplish tints. Zones 5–9.

Viola selkirkii
GREAT-SPURRED VIOLET
❁ ❄ ↔ 8–16 in (20–40 cm)
↑ 2–6 in (5–15 cm)

A North American spring-flowering perennial with shallowly lobed, heart-

Viola sororia '**Freckles**'

shaped to rounded, to 1 in (25 mm) wide leaves. Flowers are bright light purple, ½ in (12 mm) wide, with a pale center, dark veining, conspicuous broad spur. *V. s.* f. *variegata*, smaller form, variegated leaves. Zones 5–9.

Viola sempervirens
EVERGREEN VIOLET, REDWOOD VIOLET
☼/❁ ❄ ↔ 8–18 in (20–45 cm)
↑ 2–4 in (5–10 cm)

Very low-growing, slowly spreading, spring-flowering perennial found in western North America. The broad, pointed oval, evergreen foliage is faintly downy, toothed, and around 1¼ in (30 mm) long and wide. Flowers yellow with brown veining, to 1 in (25 mm) wide. Zones 6–9.

Viola septentrionalis
NORTHERN BLUE VIOLET
❁/☼ ❄ ↔ 6–16 in (15–40 cm)
↑ 4–6 in (10–15 cm)

A spring- to early summer-flowering North American perennial that spreads by rhizomes. Pointed oval to rounded heart-shaped leaves, to 2 in (5 cm) long, edged with fine hairs. Downy, 1 in (25 mm) wide, dark-veined flowers, lavender, less commonly purple or white. Zones 4–9.

Viola sororia
❁/☼ ❄ ↔ 6–16 in (15–40 cm)
↑ 2–6 in (5–15 cm)

Eastern North American spring- to early summer-flowering perennial Leaves broad, rounded, toothed, light-textured, downy, up to 4 in (10 cm) long, often smaller. Light-centered violet flowers, to 1 in (25 mm) wide, less commonly white with purple veining. '**Freckles**', white flowers heavily purple-spotted; '**Priceana**', flowers white, deep blue center. Zones 4–9.

Viola tricolor
HEARTSEASE, JOHNNY JUMP-UP, LOVE-IN-IDLENESS
☼/❁ ❄ ↔ 6–16 in (15–40 cm)
↑ 4–14 in (10–35 cm)

A temperate Eurasian spring- to early summer-flowering annual, biennial, or perennial that is usually treated as an annual. It often self-sows and

Viola tricolor '**Bowles' Black**'

naturalizes. Pointed oval to lance-like, shallowly lobed or toothed leaves and small bi- or multi-colored pansy flowers, often with a face-like pattern. Many cultivars and seedling strains, including: **'Bowles' Black'** (syn. 'E. A. Bowles'), intense velvety black flowers to 1¼ in (30 mm) wide, with small yellow center; **'Czar Bleu'**, pink to purple; and **Tinkerbelle Series**, small flowers in various pure shades and combinations. Zones 4–10.

Viola Hybrid Cultivars

PANSY, VIOLA

☼/◐ ❄ ↔ 8–16 in (20–40 cm)
↕ 6–12 in (15–30 cm)

Annual or short-lived perennial garden hybrids developed from *V. cornuta, V. tricolor, V. corsica,* and other mainly European species. Mostly neat, slowly spreading clumps of fleshy, dark green, shallowly lobed, ½–2 in (12–50 mm) long, pointed oval to lance-shaped leaves. Flowers variably sized from small to giant styles nearly 3 in (8 cm) wide. Virtually all colors and many beautiful combinations and patterns. **Baby Face Series**, bi- to multicolored flowers with central "face" markings; **Banner Series**, vigorous plants with massed display of mainly bright clear colors; **Crystal Bowl Series**, large flowers, bright pure colors; **Delta Series**, large flowers, wide color range in pure and bi-color; **Dynamite Series**, large flowers, pure colors and several multi-tone forms; **Fama Series**, semi-trailing habit, abundant mid-sized flowers, usually selfs but some pastel blends; **Imperial Series**, similar colors to 'Antique Shades' but larger flowers, such as **'Imperial Antique Shades'**, large heat-tolerant flowers in delicate pale creams, mauves, peachy apricots, blues, rosy pinks; **Joker Series**, boldly patterned mid-sized flowers usually combining blue and another color; **Panola Series**, narrow

Viola, Hybrid Cultivar, 'Antique Shades'

Viola, HC, Crystal Bowl Series, 'Crystal Bowl Supreme Sky Blue'

Viola, Hybrid Cultivar, Imperial Series, 'Imperial Frosty Rose'

Viola, Hybrid Cultivar, 'Fanfare Blue Centre'

V., HC, Baby Face Series, 'Baby Face Light Blue and White'

Viola, Hybrid Cultivar, Banner Series, 'Banner Clear Red'

V., Hybrid Cultivar, Banner Series, 'Banner Violet with Blotch'

Viola, Hybrid Cultivar, Fama Series, 'Fama Blue Angel'

Viola, Hybrid Cultivar, 'Comtessa White Blotch'

Viola, HC, Crystal Bowl Series, 'Crystal Bowl Orange'

V.iola, HC, Crystal Bowl Series, 'Crystal Bowl Supreme White'

V.iola, HC, Crystal Bowl Series, 'Crystal Bowl True Blue'

Viola, Hybrid Cultivar, Delta Series, 'Delta Pure Rose'

Viola, Hybrid Cultivar, Delta Series, 'Delta True Blue'

Viola, Hybrid Cultivar, Dynamite Series, 'Dynamite White'

Viola, Hybrid Cultivar, Dynamite Series, 'Dynamite Blue Blotch'

Viola, Hybrid Cultivar, Dynamite Series, 'Dynamite Light Blue'

Viola, Hybrid Cultivar, Dynamite Series, 'Dynamite Scarlet'

Viola, Hybrid Cultivar, Joker Series, 'Joker Poker Face'

Viola, HC, 'Black Moon'

V., HC, Imperial Series, 'Imperial'

Viola, HC, 'Elaine Quin'

V., HC, Viola Group, 'Nora Leigh'

Viola, Hybrid Cultivar, 'Panola'

V

Viola, Hybrid Cultivar, Panola
Series, 'Panola True Blue'

Viola, Hybrid Cultivar,
'Patience'

Viola, Hybrid Cultivar,
'Perry's Pride'

Viola, Hybrid Cultivar, Turbo
Series, 'Turbo Blue Wings'

Viola, Hybrid Cultivar, Turbo
Series, 'Turbo Orange'

Viola, HC, Turbo Series,
'Turbo Purple Yellow'

Viola, HC, Turbo Series,
'Turbo Red with Blotch'

Viola, HC, Turbo Series,
'Turbo True Blue'

Viola, Hybrid Cultivar,
Turbo Series, 'Turbo White'

Viola, HC, Turbo Series,
'Turbo Wine Bicolor'

Viola, HC, Ultima Series,
'Ultima Baron Coronation Coat'

Viola, HC, Ultima Series,
'Ultima Baron Purple'

Viola, HC, Ultima Series,
'Ultima Baron Red'

Viola, Hybrid Cultivar, Velour
Series, 'Velour Blue'

Viola, HC, Velour Series,
'Velour Blue Bronze'

V., HC, Viola Group, 'Baby Lucia'

V., HC, Viola Group, 'Columbine'

V., HC, Viola Group, 'Desdemona'

V., HC, Viola Group, 'Elizabeth'

V., HC, Viola Group, 'Fiona'

V., Hybrid Cultivar, Viola Group,
'Gemini Purple Yellow'

V., Hybrid Cultivar, Viola Group,
'Gemini Twins'

V., Hybrid Cultivar, Viola Group,
'Irish Molly'

V., Hybrid Cultivar, Viola Group,
'Martin'

V., Hybrid Cultivar, Viola Group,
'Molly Sanderson'

V., HC, Viola Group, 'Myfawnny'

V., HC, Viola Group, 'Pat Creasy'

Viola, HC, VG, 'Purple Wings'

Viola, HC, VG, 'Winifred Jones'

V., HC, Violetta Group, 'Bryony'

Viola, HC, Violetta Group, 'Dawn'

Viola, HC, Violetta Group, 'Melinda'

leaves and abundant small flowers with dark faces; **Penny Series**, including 'Penny Primrose', creamy white upper petals, pale yellow lower petals; 'Penny Violet Flare', deep violet petals; **Turbo Series**, hardy plants, bright colors; **Ultima Series**, fast-growing, large flowers, wide color range, including selfs, blotched and pastel types in lavender, scarlet, yellow, bronze-apricot, pale salmon orange, including **Ultima Supreme**, compact form bred to withstand very cold temperatures, with mid-sized early-flowering blooms; **Universal Series**, tolerant of hot and cold weather, 18 prolific bloomers, masses of early-flowering blooms with 13 clear colors, including blue, white, burgundy, orange, purple and yellow, or the typical pansy face; **Velour Series**, medium to large, velvet-textured flowers in intense shades, often with dark markings. Other cultivars include 'Antique Shades', mid-sized, dusky pink and apricot pastel tones; 'Black Moon', rich black petals; and 'Elaine Quin', deep velvety rosy mauve with cream stripes, giving a marbled effect.

Viola Group, more compact pansies, usually fragrant, flowers often patterned. 'Baby Lucia', clear blue blooms, 6 in (15 cm) high mounding plant, heavy bloomer, cold tolerant; 'Etain', cream-yellow petals edged with lavender, refreshing scent; 'Fiona', sweet scent, creamy white flowers, suffused with lavender-blue; 'Irish Molly' ★, gold-bronze yellow petals, dark maroon eye; 'Jackanapes', lower sections bright yellow, upper chocolate brown; 'Maggie Mott', a silvery mauve with creamy center and golden eye; 'Martin', violet flowers with a creamy center; 'Masterpiece', large ruffled flowers, purple-blue with bronze; 'Molly Sanderson', long-lasting, nearly black, velvety flowers with purple veins and a golden eye, green heart-shaped leaves; 'Nellie Britton', originally called 'Haslemere', rosy pink; 'Vita', small dainty flowers, with delicate lavender-pink petals and a creamy eye.

Violetta Group, similar to Viola Group but smaller, more compact fragrant flowers. 'Dawn', pale cream flowers deepening to gold; 'Melinda', white with mauve-blue edges and gold centers. Zones 7–10.

VIRGILIA

This is a small South African genus of evergreen trees in the pea-flower subfamily of the legume (Fabaceae) family, named after Virgil, the classical Latin poet (70–19 BC). They are popular for their attractive fern-like foliage, showy flowers and extremely rapid growth rate, although they have a rather short life span, especially in warm moist climates. The fruits are flat pods typical of legumes.
CULTIVATION: These trees thrive in well-drained light soils with adequate summer moisture, but are likely to fall over in heavy shallow soils. While they are adaptable to many situations, they require shelter from frost when young. Sow seeds in spring in a position protected from winter frosts. Pre-soak seeds for a day before sowing.

Virgilia oroboides
syn. *Virgilia capensis*
CAPE LILAC, TREE-IN-A-HURRY
☼ ⬤ ↔ 15 ft (4.5 m) ↕ 30 ft (9 m)
Erect evergreen tree, broadly conical crown, native to South Africa. A fast-growing but often short-lived species. Leaves are alternate, with 11 to 31 leaflets. Lightly perfumed pea-flowers, pink-purple with dark burgundy veins, are produced from spring to summer. Zones 9–11.

VITEX

This unusual genus that encompasses several seemingly very different species is made up of some 250 species of evergreen and deciduous shrubs in the Verbenaceae family, and has a widespread distribution in the tropical, subtropical, and warm-temperate zones. The foliage is usually digitately divided with up to 7 leaflets, and may be smooth-edged or toothed. The flowers are clustered in panicles, racemes, or cymes, and come in a wide range of colors.
CULTIVATION: As expected of a genus with tropical members, many species of *Vitex* are frost-tender, but some are quite hardy and will tolerate moderate frosts. In general, *Vitex* species prefer to avoid the extremes of soil moisture, being tolerant of neither drought nor waterlogging. Plant them in moist, fertile, well-drained soil and water them well in summer. Most grow best with at least half-sun. Hard pruning is seldom required but trim to shape as necessary. Propagate from seed or cuttings.

Vitex agnus-castus ★
CHASTE TREE
☼ ❄ ↔ 15 ft (4.5 m) ↕ 15 ft (4.5 m)
This aromatic shrub or small tree is found from southern Europe through to western Asia, naturalized in mild areas. The gray-green leaves have 5 to 9 narrow leaflets, and downy undersides. Dusty white panicles of buds open to scented lilac flowers, from summer to autumn. Purple drupes. Zones 7–10.

Vitex lucens
PURIRI
☼ ⬤ ↔ 10–15 ft (3–4.5 m) ↕ 30–50 ft (9–15 m)

An evergreen tree from New Zealand. Lustrous deep green leaves, with 3 to 5 wavy-edged leaflets. Sprays of 1 in (25 mm) long pink to red flowers, from autumn to winter. Pinkish red drupes. Host of the puriri moth, which has a wingspan of 6 in (15 cm). Zones 9–11.

VITIS
GRAPE

This is a genus of 65 species of woody deciduous vines which are indigenous to the Northern Hemisphere, particularly North America, giving its name to the grape (Vitaceae) family. The vines climb by tendrils; the leaves are mostly simple, toothed or lobed and the bark often peels from the stems in strips. Flowers are small, sometimes fragrant. Berries can be small and unpalatable or large and sweet and are often produced in bunches. There are hundreds of cultivars, particularly of *Vitis vinifera*, the European wine grape. Asian species are primarily grown for their attractive foliage and autumn color.
CULTIVATION: These vines prefer to be cultivated in deep, moderately fertile, well-drained, often chalky, alkaline soil. Full sun and warmth are necessary for best fruit ripening. Most commercial *Vitis vinifera* grapes are grafted onto *Phylloxera*-resistant American species rootstock. Propagate most species from hardwood cuttings in late winter; propagate *V. coignetiae* by layering or from seed.

Virgilia oroboides

Vitex agnus-castus

Vitex lucens

Vitis vinifera 'Cabernet Sauvignon'

Vitis vinifera 'Chardonnay'

Vitis vinifera 'Pinot Noir'

Vitis vinifera 'Merlot'

Vitis vinifera 'Gelber Muskateller'

Vitis amurensis ★

AMUR GRAPE

☼ ❄ ↔ 10–20 ft (3–6 m) ↑ 50 ft (15 m)
Vine or strong-growing shrub from
northeast Asia. Reddish young shoots.
Large, 3- to 5-lobed leaves turning
rich red, orange, yellow, and purple in
autumn months. Fruit is oval, black,
usually bitter, and produced in late
summer. Zones 4–9.

Vitis californica

CALIFORNIA WILD GRAPE

☼ ❄ ↔ 15–30 ft (4.5–9 m) ↑ 30 ft (9 m)
Native western North American vine
with large, rounded to heart- or
kidney-shaped, occasionally 3-lobed
leaves turning rich red in autumn.
Small black fruit enjoyed mainly by
birds. 'Roger's Red', brilliant red
autumn color, gray-green summer
foliage; 'Walker Ridge' more compact, bright red and orange autumn
color. Zones 7–9.

Vitis coignetiae

CRIMSON GLORY VINE

☼ ❄ ↔ 10–20 ft (3–6 m) ↑ 50 ft (15 m)
A native of Japan and Korea. This
fast-growing, vigorous vine has large,
rounded, toothed, 3- or 5-lobed,
thickly textured, somewhat puckered
leaves, becoming bronze, fiery red,
and scarlet in the autumn months.
The purple-black fruit is inedible.
Zones 5–9.

Vitis riparia

FROST GRAPE, RIVERBANK GRAPE

☼ ❄ ↔ 10–20 ft (3–6 m) ↑ 40 ft (12 m)
Climbing or scrambling central North
American native. Leaves typically 3-
lobed, serrated, shiny green. Sweetly
fragrant flowers. Round, somewhat
tart but edible blackish purple fruit.
'Brant' has leaves turning purple and
red with yellow-green edged veins in
autumn. Fruit sweet, purple-black.
Zones 2–8.

Vitis rotundifolia

BULLACE, FOX GRAPE, MUSCADINE

☼ ❄ ↔ 10–20 ft (3–6 m) ↑ 100 ft (30 m)
From moist swampy areas in southeastern USA, this vigorous plant has
tight, non-shredding bark. Its glossy,
coarsely toothed, occasionally lobed,
rounded leaves turn a soft yellow
during the autumn months. The
large, round, greenish to purplish
fruit has a musky flavor. Zones 5–9.

Vitis vinifera

COMMON GRAPE VINE

☼ ❄ ↔ 15–30 ft (4.5–9 m) ↑ 35 ft (10 m)
From southern and central Europe.
High-climbing. Variably sized leaves,
rounded or palm-shaped, 3- to 7-lobed,
toothed, heart-shaped at base. Late
summer fruit. Source of most of the
world's wine and table grape cultivars,
including: 'Black Corinth' (syn. 'Zante
Currant'), tiny seedless black fruit,
tiny yields; 'Cabernet Sauvignon',
small, black, and very seedy fruit;
'Chardonnay', small round fruit, used
for white wines; 'Chenin Blanc',
medium-sized yellow-green fruit,
tough skin, juicy; 'Flame Seedless' ★,
medium-sized clusters of firm, crisp,
red fruit; 'Gelber Muskateller', small
green fruit; 'Golden Chasselas', firm,
sweet, juicy, greenish yellow fruit;
'Merlot', medium-sized blue-black
fruit yielding soft wines; 'Muller-
Thurgau', medium-sized fruit with
green to grayish skin; 'Muscat
Hamburg', large, sweet, black, seeded
fruit; 'Muscat of Alexandria', large,
seeded, green to amber fruit with
musky flavor and aroma; 'Pinot Gris',
distinctive gray-blue to brown-pink
seeded fruit; 'Pinot Noir', small to
medium black fruit; 'Purpurea' (syns
'Claret Vine', 'Tenturier'), ornamental, leaves dark purple in spring,
purplish green in summer, red-purple
in autumn; 'Schiava Grossa' (syn.
'Black Hamburg'), medium to large
fruit, dark purplish red to black, juicy,
sweet; 'Silvaner', medium sized blue
to yellow-green fruit; 'Sultana' (syns
'Sultanina', 'Thompson Seedless'),
small, seedless, greenish table fruit;
'Trebbiano' (syns 'Saint-Emilion',
'Trebbiano Toscano', 'Ugni Blanc'),
medium-sized, golden yellow fruit,
one of most widely planted grapes in
the world; 'Zinfandel', medium-large,
reddish black to black fruit. Zones 6–9.

Vitis 'Waltham Cross'

syns Vitis 'Dattier', V. 'Lady Finger'
☼ ❄ ↔ 15–30 ft (4.5–9 m) ↑ 35 ft (10 m)
This popular, older Middle Eastern
variety may be a pure V. vinifera cultivar. Large, oval, sweet, juicy, gold-
tinted white fruit. Zones 6–9.

VRIESEA

From Mexico, Central America, the
West Indies, and South America, this
genus of over 250 species and 650
listed hybrids in the bromeliad
(Bromeliaceae) family is closely related
to Tillandsia. Vriesea have mainly
green leaves, indicating they need
more shade, with only a few having
gray-green leaves, and they have 2
small appendages at the base of each
petal. Their leaves are spineless and
form a dense rosette capable of storing
water. Mainly medium-sized plants,
some can flower to 7 ft (2 m) tall.
The flowerhead is usually colorful.
CULTIVATION: Grow indoors or in
the greenhouse in cool-temperate
areas, or outdoors with protection
from prolonged sunlight and heavy
rain in warm-temperate, subtropical
and tropical areas. Water when potting mix is dry. A foliar feed high in
potash and low in nitrogen (other
than in the form of urea) will increase
flower size. Propagate from offsets.

Vriesea carinata

☀ ✣ ↔ 12 in (30 cm) ↑ 14 in (35 cm)
From Rio de Janeiro, Brazil. Leaves
strap-like, green, forming a funnel-
shaped rosette. Flower stem erect,
longer than the rosette. Flowerhead
sword-shaped, made up of mainly red
bracts with green edges. Petals tubular, yellow, green tipped. Zones 11–12.

Vriesea erythrodactylon

☀ ✣ ↔ 16 in (40 cm) ↑ 16 in (40 cm)
From Brazil. Leaves strap-like, green,
forming funnel-shaped rosette. Flower
stem is erect, shorter than the rosette.
Flowerhead is broadly sword-shaped,
center portion solid and green, outer
edges deeply notched and red, with
yellow tubular petals. Zones 11–12.

Vriesea erythrodactylon

Vriesea, Hybrid Cultivar, 'Mariae'

Vriesea fenestralis

☀ ✛ ↔ 28 in (70 cm) ↑ 40 in (100 cm)

From Brazil. Leaves strap-like, green with dark green, narrow, longitudinal lines and irregular, broken, thick crossbands, forming a broad rosette. Flower stem is sturdy, longer than the rosette. Flowerhead is sword-shaped, green bracts with red spots. Petals are greenish white. Zones 11–12.

Vriesea fosteriana

☀ ✛ ↔ 40 in (100 cm) ↑ 60 in (150 cm)

From Brazil. Leaves strap-like, rigid, green or purplish, with wavy broken crossbands in dark green, purple or white, forming a spreading rosette. Flower stem erect, longer than rosette. Flowerhead sword-shaped, yellowish bracts with red spots. Petals creamish purple. Zones 11–12.

Vriesea malzinei

☀ ✛ ↔ 16 in (40 cm) ↑ 32 in (80 cm)

From Mexico. Leaves strap-like, green above, red below, forming a funnel-shaped rosette. Flower stem erect, longer than rosette. Flowerhead cylindrical, red, pale green or yellow overlapping bracts and long white tubular petals with flared tips. Zones 11–12.

Vriesea saundersii

☀ ✛ ↔ 16 in (40 cm) ↑ 24 in (60 cm)

A native of Brazil. Leaves strap-like, dull green on top with small brown speckles below, forming broad funnel-shaped rosette. Flower stem is longer than the rosette, erect. Flowerhead is pyramidal, with 3 to 4 side-branches, mainly yellow. Petals are yellow and tubular. Zones 11–12.

Vriesea splendens

FLAMING SWORD

☀ ✛ ↔ 20 in (50 cm) ↑ 40 in (100 cm)

From Venezuela and the Caribbean Islands. Leaves strap-like, green, often with broad dark irregular crossbands, forming broad funnel-shaped rosette. Flower stem is erect, about equal in length to the rosette. The flowerhead is long, sword-shaped, and bright red. The petals are yellow and tubular. Zones 10–12.

Vriesea Hybrid Cultivars

☀ ✛ ↔ 8–20 in (20–50 cm) ↑ 16–36 in (40–90 cm)

These hybrids feature a larger flower spike and strongly patterned foliage. They include: 'Bananas', leaves form upright rosette, flower stem reddish, flowerhead sword-shaped at top, with up to 8 sword-shaped side-branches, mostly bright yellow but sometimes with reddish edges; 'Carlsbad', leaves pointed, green with red mottling, flushed red near base, flower stem red; 'Charlotte', flowerhead broad sword-shaped, with up to 7 side-branches, all red towards base, bright yellow above; 'Christiane', flowerhead bright red with yellow tubular petals; 'Eva', strap-like leaves, green tinged maroon, forming an open rosette; 'Grafton Sunset', flowerhead mainly golden orange suffused with red, petals yellow; 'Gunther', bright red flowerhead; 'Komet', overlapping, mainly red, yellow-tipped bracts, pale yellow petals; 'Likely Lad', flowerhead pyramidal with red side-branches, each with up to 5 flowers and a large red bract below each branch; 'Little Chief', flowerhead glossy orange tinted red; 'Mariae', petals tubular, yellow with green tips; 'Poelmanii', flowerhead sword-shaped, with up to 7 bright red branches, yellow petals; 'Purple Cockatoo', flowerheads purple, with deep serrations around the edge resembling a cockatoo's crest; 'Red Chestnut', yellowish bracts with small reddish spots and creamish purple petals; 'Splendide', flowerhead sword-shaped, with up to 4 bright red side-branches, pinkish yellow, tubular petals. Zones 11–12.

× VUYLSTEKEARA

This is a tri-generic sympodial orchid hybrid (family Orchidaceae) involving the genera *Cochlioda*, *Miltonia*, and *Odontoglossum*. Generally, the crossing of *Odontodia* with *Miltonia* has formed these colorful hybrids. They produce long, erect to arching inflorescences of shapely blooms that come in a range of colors and patterns.

CULTIVATION: × *Vuylstekeara* orchids do not like their roots to dry out, so plant in sphagnum moss or a fine bark mix. They are suitable for cool growing conditions, and need abundant water throughout the year and a part-shaded position. Give them a humid environment and plenty of air circulation. Propagate by division.

× Vuylstekeara Hybrids

☀ ◗ ↔ 4–20 in (10–50 cm) ↑ 4–24 in (10–60 cm)

Flowers range from 1½ in (35 mm) to 5 in (12 cm) across the petals. They are members of the *Odontoglossum* alliance. **Cambria** ★, a popular hybrid, mass-produced using modern tissue culture techniques, white and maroon blooms with a yellow blotch on the lip; **Edna 'Stamperland'**, medium-sized vibrant red and orange flowers on tall inflorescences; **Ephyra**, raspberry-colored blooms with white edging to the segments; **Everglades Promise**, showy pink and red blooms with a large flared labellum; **Linda Isler**, numerous claret blooms with a white lip; **Memoria Hanna Lassfolk** highlights the variation once 3 different genera become involved; **Memoria Mary Kavanaugh**, large purple flowers, a legacy of its parent *Miltonia spectabilis*. Zones 9–11.

× *V.*, Hybrid, Memoria Hanna Lassfolk

× *Vuylstekeara*, Hybrid, Ephyra

× *V.*, Hybrid, Edna 'Stamperland'

× *Vuylstekeara*, Hybrid, Cambria

× *V.*, Hybrid, Everglades Promise

× *V.*, Hybrid, Linda Isler

× *V.*, H, Memoria Mary Kavanaugh

WXYZ

Wachendorfia thyrsiflora (at front), Harold Porter National Botanical Garden, South Africa

Waldsteinia geoides

Waldsteinia ternata

Warszewiczia coccinea

WACHENDORFIA

This genus of some 25 species of mostly deciduous strappy-leafed perennials from South Africa is a member of the bloodroot (Haemodoraceae) family. The deciduous species have bright red tubers, and both deciduous and the single evergreen species have orange-red roots. The leaves are usually bright green and heavily pleated, with each leaf sheathing the next one in a flat fan arrangement. The flowers are yellow and star-shaped and produced in tall narrow spikes or, in the case of smaller species, in open clusters. These plants are considered to be weeds in southern Australia.

CULTIVATION: In more or less frost-free climates, grow in a sunny moist position; in other areas, protect from frost by growing *Wachendorfia* in large pots which can be overwintered in a greenhouse. Raise from fresh seed or by division in late winter.

Wachendorfia thyrsiflora

☼ ⚥ ↔ 36–40 in (90–100 cm)
↑ 7–8 ft (2–2.4 m)

The only evergreen *Wachendorfia*. Strongly pleated, rich green leaves to 40 in (100 cm) long. In early summer it produces tall upright spikes with star-shaped rich yellow flowers to 1¼ in (30 mm) across. Zones 10–11.

WALDSTEINIA

There are 6 species of creeping fleshy-stemmed perennials in this genus, which belongs to the rose (Rosaceae) family. They are native to northern temperate regions where they are inhabitants of woodland areas. Plants form low mats of lobed and toothed leaves that are similar to those of the related strawberry and cinquefoil (*Potentilla*). Their leaves sometimes take on bronze tones in winter. The saucer-shaped 5-petalled flowers are yellow and are carried for long periods in spring and early summer. They are often more prolific on new growth.

CULTIVATION: These plants are suitable for the rock garden, the front of a border or a woodland edge. Their creeping well-foliaged habit makes them useful ground covers. Grow in partial shade in moist but well-drained soils. Where soils remain moist in summer, they can be grown in full sun. Propagate by division of rooted runners or from seed.

Waldsteinia fragarioides

BARREN STRAWBERRY

☼/◐ ❄ ↔ 12–20 in (30–50 cm)
↑ 2 in (5 cm)

Mat-forming species native to eastern USA. Trifoliate bronze-green leaves with toothed, pointed oval leaflets to nearly 3 in (8 cm) long. From spring, clusters of up to 8 yellow, ¾ in (18 mm) wide flowers. Zones 3–9.

Waldsteinia geoides

◐ ❄ ↔ 18 in (45 cm) ↑ 8 in (20 cm)

Native to central and eastern Europe. Low creeping perennial, less vigorous than *W. ternata*. Broadly heart-shaped, hairy, lobed leaves. Flowers nearly 1 in (25 mm) wide borne in lax clusters, in spring. Zones 5–9.

Waldsteinia ternata ★

◐ ❄ ↔ 24 in (60 cm) ↑ 6 in (15 cm)

Found from Europe to China and Japan. A vigorous ground-covering plant with dark green, 3-lobed, toothed, somewhat hairy leaves. The flowers, nearly ¾ in (18 mm) wide, are borne in groups of 3 to 7 in spring and summer. Can become invasive. Zones 3–9.

WARSZEWICZIA

This genus in the madder (Rubiaceae) family contains 4 species of shrubs or trees native to tropical America. They are slightly hairy plants with opposite leaves and terminal panicles of small funnel-shaped flowers with showy bracts. Only *W. coccinea* is usually seen in cultivation.

CULTIVATION: In cool climates grow in a greenhouse. In warmer areas it can be grown outdoors in a moist well-drained soil in a sunny situation. Propagate from seed or from green-wood cuttings in spring.

Warszewiczia coccinea

☼ ⚘ ↔ 10 ft (3 m) ↑ 15 ft (4.5 m)

Leaves are oblong and from 6–24 in (15–60 cm) long. Terminal panicles, up to 20 in (50 cm) long, of small yellow flowers, 1 to 2 calyx lobes enlarged into showy, bright red, petal-like bracts, year round. Zones 10–12.

Washingtonia robusta, in the wild, Mexico

WASHINGTONIA

This genus in the palm (Arecaceae) family consists of 2 species from southwest USA and northwestern Mexico. These single-stemmed robust palms have fan leaves. The trunks are clothed in old leaf bases that hang like a skirt or petticoat. The leaves are deeply lobed with fibrous margins, while the small, bisexual, tube-shaped flowers can be creamy white or creamy apricot-pink, in slender hanging clusters among the leaves. The small fruits are drupes, and each contains a single seed. They come from desert areas where they obtain moisture from springs or streams, and can be seen cultivated in drier parts of tropical and subtropical regions as well as in temperate areas. They are useful for lining roadways and for planting in parklands.

CULTIVATION: These are very hardy and adaptable palms in a well-drained soil. They tolerate full sun, exposed conditions and, once established, drought. Both species grow very tall, so a large garden is a must; dispose of seed carefully, to avoid unwanted proliferation. Decaying foliage can be a fire risk and is best removed. Propagate from seed.

Washingtonia filifera ★

COTTON PALM, PETTICOAT PALM,
WASHINGTONIA PALM

☼ ⚥ ↔ 25 ft (8 m) ↑ 50 ft (15 m)

Heavy, gray trunk clothed in old leaves. Long spiny leafstalks, gray-green leaves, with thread-like filaments. Panicles of creamy white flowers. Hard blackish drupes. Zones 9–11.

Washingtonia robusta ★

COTTON PALM, MEXICAN WASHINGTONIA
PALM, THREAD PALM

☼ ⚥ ↔ 25 ft (8 m) ↑ 80 ft (24 m)

Native to northwestern Mexico and California, USA. This species differs

Washingtonia filifera

Watsonia borbonica subsp. *ardernei*

Watsonia meriana

Watsonia borbonica

from *W. filifera* in having a slender, taller, tapering trunk. Mature fan-shaped leaves brighter green, reddish brown spiny leaf stalks. The cottony threads are inconspicuous or absent on mature plants. Panicles of creamy apricot-pink flowers, in summer. Dark brown drupes. Zones 9–11.

WATSONIA
BUGLE LILY

This genus contains 52 species of sun-loving bulbous perennials from South Africa. Members of the iris (Iridaceae) family, they are cormous and clump forming, with the common garden-grown species holding their flowers well above the reed-like foliage. Species that flower in late spring–early summer are dormant during summer months and require wet-winter to dry-summer climates. Those that flower in summer and autumn are either evergreen or winter dormant, requiring damp-summer climates. Those with narrow tubular flowers are thought to be pollinated by honey-eating birds; those with open cupped flowers by bees. There are many cultivars and hybrids, and some confusion exists with the nomenclature. Named for Sir William Watson (1715–1787), a British scientist who helped introduce the Linnaean system of plant classification to the UK. CULTIVATION: Protect from frost in cold climates. They require sharp

drainage, an open sunny position and light liquid feed when grown on very poor soils. Propagate from seed in spring or from offsets just as the plants move into dormancy.

Watsonia borbonica
syn. *Watsonia pyramidata*
☼ ⚘ ↔ 4 in (10 cm) ↕ 3–7 ft (0.9–2 m)
Leaves narrowly sword-shaped. Flowers are lightly scented, pale or deep pink, appearing in spring–early summer. Corms ¾–1¾ in (18–40 mm) wide. *W. b.* subsp. *ardernei* (syn. *W. ardernei*) is white, occasionally light pink, with flared trumpets, flowering for an extended period in late spring. Can become invasive. Zones 9–10.

Watsonia meriana
☼ ⚘ ↔ 6 in (15 cm)
↕ 20–60 in (50–150 cm)
From southern Africa. Leaves are sword-shaped. The flowers are small, well-spaced, dull pink to bright rose-red, rarely red or white, on branched spikes, long tube with flared trumpet, in summer. Potentially invasive, particularly *W. m.* subsp. *bulbillifera*, which has dull apricot flowers and ruby stems. Zones 9–10.

Watsonia pillansii
☼ ❄ ↔ 4 in (10 cm)
↕ 20–48 in (50–120 cm)
Leaves dense, evergreen. The orange and red-orange flowers are held in dense racemes, from summer to autumn. Requires well-drained damp conditions in summer. Zones 7–10.

WEIGELA
CARDINAL BUSH, WEIGELA

The 10 or 12 species of this genus within the woodbine (Caprifoliaceae) family are deciduous long-lived shrubs with opposite oblong to elliptic leaves. Native to eastern Asia, their natural

habitat is scrubland and the edges of woods. Cultivated for their bell- or funnel-shaped flowers, produced in late spring and early summer, they have pink, red, white, or sometimes yellow blooms, growing on the previous year's wood.
CULTIVATION: They do well in moist but well-drained fertile soil in sun or partial shade. Remove older branches after flowering to encourage vigorous growth. Propagate by sowing seed in autumn in an area protected from winter frosts or from half-hardened cuttings in summer. Seed may not come true, as weigelas have a tendency to hybridize freely.

Weigela decora
☼ ❄ ↔ 5–7 ft (1.5–2 m)
↕ 10–15 ft (3–4.5 m)
Species native to Japan with leaves 4 in (10 cm) long. In spring–early summer bears white trumpet flowers to 1½ in (35 mm) long, ageing to cerise-red. Zones 6–10.

Weigela floribunda
☼ ❄ ↔ 8 ft (2.4 m) ↕ 10 ft (3 m)
Deciduous shrub native to Japan. The slender toothed leaves are slightly hairy above, white and woolly, beneath. Up to 3 dark red flowers are produced in each leaf axil, in spring to summer. Zones 6–10.

Weigela florida 'Alexandra'

Weigela florida
OLD-FASHIONED WEIGELA, WEIGELA
☼ ❄ ↔ 8 ft (2.4 m) ↕ 8 ft (2.4 m)
From East Asia, larger in the wild. Oblong leaves, pointed tips, toothed margins, felty undersides. Funnel-shaped dark pink to nearly white flowers, in spring–summer. 'Alexandra' (syn. 'Wine & Roses') recent cultivar with purple spring foliage becoming almost blackish and glossy in summer, flowers bright rose red, plant compact form, under 5 ft (1.5 m) in height; 'Foliis Purpureis', coppery foliage with dark pink flowers, compact habit to 3 ft (0.9 m); 'Java Red', purple-tinged foliage, dark pink flowers. Zones 5–10.

Weigela hortensis
☼ ❄ ↔ 10 ft (3 m) ↕ 10 ft (3 m)
Japanese native with 4 in (10 cm) long heavily serrated leaves, very downy undersides. Rose pink flowers 1½ in (35 mm) long, in clusters of 3 blooms, in mid-spring–early summer. 'Nivea', large white flowers. Zones 7–9.

Weigela japonica
☼ ❄ ↔ 10 ft (3 m) ↕ 10 ft (3 m)
Native to Japan, larger in the wild. Leaves dark green. Spring flowers are solitary or in pairs, white, turning red later. *W. j.* var. *sinica* taller than the species, with light pink flowers, turning a deeper pink. Zones 6–10.

Weigela japonica var. *sinica*

Weigela florida

Weigela middendorffiana

☼ ❄ ↔ 5 ft (1.5 m) ↑ 5 ft (1.5 m)

Erect shrub from eastern Asia has vivid green leaves. Solitary or paired blossoms, bell-shaped flowers pale yellow with orange or red throat markings, in summer. Protect from strong winds. Zones 4–10.

Weigela praecox

☼ ❄ ↔ 7 ft (2 m) ↑ 8 ft (2.4 m)

An erect densely branched shrub that is native to Korea, northeastern China, and Japan. Parent of numerous early-flowering cultivars. Leaves are dark green with hairy undersides. Fragrant, pink, funnel-shaped flowers with yellow throats, are produced in late spring–early summer. Zones 5–10.

Weigela, Hybrid Cultivar, 'Florida Variegata'

Weigela Hybrid Cultivars

☼ ❄ ↔ 5–8 ft (1.5–2.4 m)
↑ 5–12 ft (1.5–3.5 m)

Great plants for placing in borders, these are hybrids between a number of *Weigela* species. The range of cultivars to choose from is very extensive with many color possibilities. These include: **'Abel Carrière'**, dark green leaves, bell-shaped pink to red flowers; **'Bristol Ruby'**, carmine red flowers; **'Candida'**, vivid green leaves, bell-shaped white flowers; **'Chameleon'**, around 6 ft (1.8 m) tall, finely serrated mid-green leaves, pastel pink flowers, grows in sun or in part-shade; **'Eva Rathke'**, dark green leaves, funnel-shaped dark purple flowers; **'Florida Variegata'** (syn. *W. florida* 'Variegata'), cream-edged leaves and rich pink trumpets to 1¼ in (30 mm) long; **'Looymansii Aurea'**, yellowish leaves, rich pink flowers with paler pink center, foliage will scorch in hot sun, and lose its color in heavy shade; **'Madame Lemoine'**, pale pink flowers fading to white; **'Minuet'**, 30 in (75 cm) high with coppery oval leaves, bell-shaped magenta flowers; **'Newport Red'** ★ (syn. 'Vanicek'), tall, very hardy, with dark red flowers; **'Praecox Variegata'** (syn. *W. praecox* 'Variegata'), slightly scented pink trumpets with soft yellow center, leaves have creamy yellow margins turning white as they age; and **'Red Prince'**, lushly foliaged, long-lasting dark red flowers. Zones 5–10.

Weigela, Hybrid Cultivar, 'Newport Red'

Weigela middendorffiana

WEINMANNIA

This genus of 150 to 190 species of evergreen shrubs and trees in the family Cunoniaceae is widespread, from Central and South America, to the Pacific region and tropical Asia. The cultivated species are grown mainly for their dense dark foliage and their wand- or bottlebrush-like racemes of flowers, which are usually white or cream. The foliage is usually pinnate and made up thick leathery leaflets that are often toothed and which may differ in size and shape between juvenile and adult plants.
CULTIVATION: While hardiness varies somewhat with the species, none are extremely frost tolerant. They prefer relatively mild winter conditions and a moist, humus-rich, well-drained soil that does not dry out in summer. Plant in full sun or partial shade and trim plants lightly to shape after flowering. Propagation is from seed or from half-hardened cuttings.

Weinmannia racemosa

KAMAHI

☼ ❄ ↔ 8–15 ft (2.4–4.5 m) ↑ 30 ft (9 m)

New Zealand shrub or tree, taller in the wild. Leaves simple, dark green

Weigela, HC, 'Looymansii Aurea'

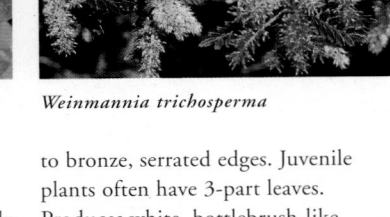

Weinmannia trichosperma

to bronze, serrated edges. Juvenile plants often have 3-part leaves. Produces white, bottlebrush-like blooms, in summer. Very attractive to bees and apiarists. Zones 9–10.

Weinmannia trichosperma

MADEN, TINEO

☼ ❄ ↔ 5–12 ft (1.5–3.5 m) ↑ 70 ft (21 m)

Large shrub or tree native to Chile and Argentina. Remains bushy for many years. Pinnate leaves, composed of 11 to 13 toothed leaflets, each 1 in (25 mm) long. Flowers creamy white, on long spikes. Zones 9–10.

WELDENIA

This is a single-species genus consisting of a very variable tuberous perennial that is found in the wilds of South America and in the summer-wet mountainous terrains of Mexico and Guatemala. A member of the spider-wort (Commelinaceae) family, it has long tuberous roots and tufts or rosettes of leathery lance-shaped leaves. Its cupped flowers are white with yellow anthers. It is named for L. von Welden (1780–1853), an Austrian soldier and student of alpine flora.
CULTIVATION: Grow in sharply drained gritty soil in full sun or in a cool greenhouse. Provide frost protection in harsh climates. Keep damp while in growth. Propagate from fresh ripe seed, from root cuttings taken in winter or by division in spring.

Weldenia candida

☼ ❄ ↔ 6 in (15 cm)
↑ 5–6 in (12–15 cm)

Large, leathery, lance-shaped leaves with wavy margins, rosette-forming. Flowers white, cupped, held among

Weigela, HC, 'Chameleon'

Weigela, HC, 'Bristol Ruby'

Weigela, HC, 'Madame Lemoine'

Weigela, HC, 'Abel Carrière'

Weigela, HC, 'Praecox Variegata'

the leaves, in late spring–early summer. Tubers elongated, necessitating a deep pot when container grown. Zones 8–9.

WELWITSCHIA

This genus, which makes up the family Welwitschiaceae, comprises just one species found in the deserts and nearby woodland of southwest Africa. It is a long-lived perennial (up to 1,500 years) with a short exposed stem which can reach 40 in (100 cm) wide, and a long tap root. There are just 2 parallel-veined leaves growing from the base. With time these become shredded and look like multiple leaves. Male and female flowers, on separate plants, are in red cones at the apex of the plant. *Welwitschia* is rarely grown except in botanic gardens for its curiosity value. CULTIVATION: It is cultivated from fresh seed under conditions suitable for cacti, with seedlings requiring careful watering to prevent rotting off. Often they are grown in clay drainpipes to accommodate the tap root, which is easily damaged.

Welwitschia mirabilis
syn. *Welwitschia bainesii*
☼ ✤ ↔ 10 ft (3 m) ↑ 4 ft (1.2 m)
Tree with more of its trunk below than above ground. Two strap-like olive green leaves arise from the top of the truncated stem, growing from the base. Male cones, brightly colored, possess stamens, female cones greenish yellow and reddish brown with a style-like structure present. Zones 9–10.

WESTRINGIA

This is an Australian genus in the mint (Lamiaceae) family consisting of

Weldenia candida

25 species. All are shrubs with angled stems and foliage usually arranged in whorls of 3 to 5 small leaves. The small tubular flowers are 2-lipped, the upper lip having 2 lobes and the lower lip 3 lobes, and are produced in the leaf axils over a long period. The fruit is divided into 4 tiny nutlets hidden in the persistent calyx. Most grow in coastal heathlands, scrublands, forests, and sandy or rocky areas. They are useful landscape subjects for regions with mild winters and are often seen as hedging or screening plants. CULTIVATION: Most are fairly adaptable in a well-drained soil with full sun, tolerating salty winds and exposed conditions. They require adequate water in summer. Prune after flowering to maintain a compact shape. Propagate from cuttings.

Westringia fruticosa
COASTAL ROSEMARY, NATIVE ROSEMARY
☼ ✤ ↔ 7 ft (2 m) ↑ 6 ft (1.8 m)
From eastern coastal Australia. Linear leaves gray above and felty white below, in whorls of 4 around the stems. White flowers, the lower lobe dotted brownish or purplish, for most of the year. Tolerant of wind, drought and salt winds. Zones 9–11.

Westringia glabra
VIOLET WESTRINGIA
☼/◐ ✤ ↔ 3 ft (0.9 m) ↑ 3 ft (0.9 m)
Small bushy shrub from eastern Australia. Narrow-elliptic to lance-shaped leaves in whorls of mostly 3, shiny dark green above, paler below. Pale purple to violet-lilac flowers dotted maroon year-round, peak display during spring. Zones 9–11.

Westringia fruticosa

Westringia glabra

Westringia 'Wynyabbie Gem'

Welwitschia mirabilis, in the wild, Namibia

Widdringtonia nodiflora, Kirstenbosch National Botanical Garden, South Africa

Westringia 'Wynyabbie Gem'
☼ ✤ ↔ 5 ft (1.5 m) ↑ 4 ft (1.2 m)
Popular hybrid between *W. eremicola* and *W. fruticosa*. Bushy shrub with fine dark green foliage. Small bluish pink flowers in groups at the branch tips, most of the year. May not be long-lived. Zones 9–11.

WIDDRINGTONIA

Genus in the cypress (Cupressaceae) family containing 3 species, 2 native to South Africa and 1 distributed more widely from tropical Africa south to Cape Town. All are evergreen shrubs or trees with fragrant timber. Timber cutting and bushfires have decimated the populations of these trees. Juvenile leaves are needle-like and spirally arranged on the young twigs. The adult leaves, are scale-like, arranged in an opposite or alternate pattern, and closely pressed against the stems. Male and female cones are borne on the same plant, the males are catkin-like, the female are woody. The seeds are egg-shaped with a thin wing. CULTIVATION: They do not adapt well to cultivation. Early growth is slow, and the plants sometimes languish and fail to thrive. Maintaining them as compact plants in a large pot may be a better option. They grow best in a humid mild climate. Propagation is from seed, which germinates readily, or from cuttings.

Widdringtonia schwarzii

Widdringtonia cedarbergensis
syn. *Widdringtonia juniperoides*
CLANWILLIAM CEDAR
☼ ✤ ↔ 17–35 ft (5–10 m) ↑ 70–100 ft (21–30 m)
From the Cedarberg Mountains of South Africa's Cape region. Upright to eventually spreading tree with small, scale-like adult foliage. Warty ball-shaped cones 1 in (25 mm) across. Threatened in the wild. Zones 9–11.

Widdringtonia nodiflora
MLANJE CEDAR, MOUNTAIN CEDAR, MOUNTAIN CYPRESS
☼ ✤ ↔ 6–12 ft (1.8–3.5 m) ↑ 40 ft (12 m)
Surviving only in relatively inaccessible sites. Grayish bark peels in long strips. Tiny leaves. Cones ripen early autumn, seeds black with red wing. Zones 9–11.

Widdringtonia schwarzii
WILLOWMORE CEDAR
☼ ❄ ↔ 15–30 ft (4.5–9 m) ↑ 120 ft (36 m)
Only known from a small area just east of Cape Town, South Africa. Bark flaky, leaves arranged in opposite pairs. Male cones catkin-like, female cones globular, dark brown. Seeds flattish with prominent wing. Zones 8–9.

× *Wilsonara*, Hybrid, Blazing Lustre

× *Wilsonara*, Hybrid, Firecracker

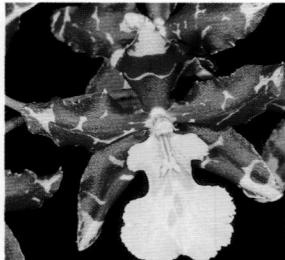

× *Wilsonara*, Hybrid, Athol Bell

× *Wilsonara*, Hybrid, Dorset Gold   × *W.*, Hybrid, Russiker Tiger

WIGANDIA

The 5 members of this genus belonging to the waterleaf (Hydrophyllaceae) family are evergreen shrubs from Central and South America. The large, alternate, oval to oblong leaves can be up to 18 in (45 cm) long. The undersurfaces of the deep green leaves are covered in white hairs, often stinging. Violet-blue flowers are borne from spring to autumn in large, terminal, 1-sided panicles.
CULTIVATION: These plants need moist but well-drained soil in the full sun. They are frost tender, and make good container specimens. Propagation is from seed or from cuttings taken in the spring.

Wigandia caracasana
syn. *Wigandia urens* var. *caracasana*
☼ ✿ ↔ 12 ft (3.5 m) ↑ 15 ft (4.5 m)
Found in the jungles of Mexico, Colombia, and Venezuela. Variable species, small spreading tree. Rough-textured deep green leaves, oval, with wavy edges and hairy white undersides. The flowers, violet to purple, with a white throat, form in long terminal clusters. Zones 10–12.

Wigandia urens
☼ ✿ ↔ 8 ft (2.4 m) ↑ 10 ft (3 m)
From Peru, similar to *W. caracasana*, but smaller. Leaves up to 12 in (30 cm) long. Violet-blue flowers are split into 2 lobes. Zones 10–12.

WIKSTROEMIA

The 50 or so species of evergreen trees or shrubs comprising this genus range from Australia throughout the Pacific region, and from Sri Lanka to southern China. In the mezereum (Thymelaeaceae) family, they are closely related to *Daphne* and have ovate to elliptic opposite leaves and tubular flowers in short terminal or axillary racemes that are followed by berry-like fruits.
CULTIVATION: Depending on the species, they are frost hardy to frost tender. They prefer a light soil with good drainage, full sun to partial shade and a position sheltered from cold winds, especially when young. Propagate from seed.

Wikstroemia indica
☼ ✿ ↔ 3 ft (0.9 m) ↑ 5 ft (1.5 m)
From Asia to the Pacific region and Australia. Small tree or erect shrub with ovate leaves to 2½ in (6 cm) long. White, cream, or greenish flowers in terminal heads, in late summer–early autumn. Zones 9–12.

× WILSONARA

This is a tri-generic orchid hybrid in the family Orchidaceae, which combines the sympodial genera *Cochlioda*, *Odontoglossum*, and *Oncidium*. Generally, the crossing of *Odontodia* with *Oncidium* has formed these colorful hybrids, which are more tolerant of higher temperatures than most of the pure *Odontoglossums*. They produce long, erect to arching inflorescences of shapely blooms that come in a range of colors and patterns.
CULTIVATION: These orchids do not like their roots to dry out, so the plants need to be potted in sphagnum moss or a fine bark mix. They are suitable for cool to intermediate growing conditions, and require abundant water throughout the year and a part-shaded position. The plants must be kept in a humid environment with plenty of air circulation. Propagate × *Wilsonara* by division.

× Wilsonara Hybrids
☼ ✿ ↔ 4–20 in (10–50 cm)
↑ 4–24 in (10–60 cm)
Individual flowers range in size from 1½ in (35 mm) to 3½ in (9 cm) across the petals. They are members of the *Odontoglossum* alliance. **Athol Bell**, pale cream blooms with caramel spotting on the edges of segments; **Blazing Lustre**, peach-colored flowers with darker maroon spotting with a contrasting white labellum; **Dorset Gold**, cream blooms heavily suffused in gold tones; **Firecracker**, orange to red blooms last for up to 2 months in good conditions; **Russiker Tiger**, brown and yellow hybrid heavily influenced by *Oncidium tigrinum*. Zones 9–11.

WISTERIA

Often seen covering verandahs and porches and capable of spreading a great distance, the 10 species of twining deciduous vines in this genus belong to the pea-flower subfamily of the legume (Fabaceae) family. They are native to China, Japan, and eastern USA. When young, the pinnate leaves are a soft bronze green but turn light green when mature. The flowers, primarily mauve in the species, occur in long racemes that start to open as the leaves expand. Cultivated forms range from white to various pink and purple tones. Named for Caspar Wistar (1761–1818), an anatomy professor at the University of Pennsylvania, USA.
CULTIVATION: Like *Clematis*, wisterias like their tops in sun and their roots in cool, moist, humus-rich, well-drained soil. These hardy, heavy-wooded, vigorous climbers need sturdy support and routine trimming. Propagate from cuttings or seed, by layering or grafting.

Wikstroemia indica

Wigandia caracasana

Wigandia urens

Wisteria species, in winter

Wisteria species, in spring

Wisteria species, in summer

Wisteria species, in autumn

Wisteria brachybotrys
syn. *Wisteria venusta*
SILKY WISTERIA
☼/◐ ❄ ↔ 30 ft (9 m) ↑ 30 ft (9 m)
Vigorous Japanese climber with stems twining anticlockwise, densely downy when young. Leaves to 14 in (35 cm) long with 9 to 13, downy, pointed oval leaflets to 4 in (10 cm) long. Pendulous racemes to 6 in (15 cm) long of white, very fragrant, 1 in (25 mm) wide flowers. 'Murasaki Kapitan' (syn. *W. venusta* 'Violacea'), clockwise-twining with purple-keeled mauve flowers; and 'Shiro-kapitan' (syn. *W. sinensis* 'Prematura Alba'), like the species but shorter, sometimes pink-tinted racemes. Zones 6–9.

Wisteria floribunda ★
JAPANESE WISTERIA
☼/◐ ❄ ↔ 25 ft (8 m) ↑ 25 ft (8 m)
Clockwise-twining Japanese climber with leaves to 14 in (35 cm) long, downy when young, 11 to 19 pointed oval leaflets to 3 in (8 cm) long. Pendulous racemes 16–40 in (40–100 cm) long, fragrant violet, purple, pink,

white, or magenta-red flowers to ¾ in (18 mm) wide. 'Alba' (syn. 'Shîro-nôda'), long racemes with more than 100 faintly scented white flowers; 'Kuchi-beni', dark-keeled pale pink flowers in racemes to 18 in (45cm) long; 'Multijuga' (syn. 'Macrobotrys'), extremely long racemes of light purple flowers; 'Violacea Plena', clustered racemes to 16 in (40 cm) long with many lavender and purple double flowers. Zones 5–10.

Wisteria × *formosa*
☼/◐ ❄ ↔ 30 ft (9 m) ↑ 30 ft (9 m)
Garden hybrid between *W. floribunda* and *W. sinensis*. Clockwise-twining stems and leaves to 14 in (35 cm) long, with 9 to 15 pointed oval leaflets to over 3 in (8 cm) long, silky when young. Dark-keeled violet flowers to

¾ in (18 mm) wide, very fragrant, all opening together on the raceme not in succession. 'Yae-kokuryû' (syn. 'Black Dragon'), lilac blooms. Zones 5–9.

Wisteria frutescens
AMERICAN WISTERIA
☼/◐ ❄ ↔ 40 ft (12 m) ↑ 40 ft (12 m)
Very vigorous clockwise-twining climber native to eastern USA. Leaves to 12 in (30 cm) long, with 9 to 15 pointed oval leaflets around 2 in (5 cm) long. Racemes to 4 in (10 cm) long, often held horizontally or semi-erect; flowers bright purple, mildly scented. Zones 5–9.

Wisteria macrostachya
KENTUCKY WISTERIA
☼/◐ ❄ ↔ 25 ft (8 m) ↑ 25 ft (8 m)
Anticlockwise-twining climber found from Louisiana to Illinois, USA. Leaves to 12 in (30 cm) long, with 7 to 11 leaflets, 2 in (5 cm) long, tapering to fine point. Pendulous, 6–12 in (15–30 cm) long racemes of small pale pink and lavender flowers opening from deep pink buds. Zones 5–9.

Wisteria sinensis ★
CHINESE WISTERIA
☼/◐ ❄ ↔ 35 ft (10 m) ↑ 35 ft (10 m)
Rapid-growing anticlockwise-twining climber native to China. Leaves to

Wisteria × *formosa*

35 cm (14 in) long, with 7 to 13 pointed elliptical leaflets to 3 in (8 cm) long. The flowers are lavender and purple-blue, strongly scented, to 1 in (25 mm) wide, in pendulous racemes, 6–12 in (15–30 cm) long . 'Alba' bears white flowers; 'Sierra Madre' has fragrant, lavender-keeled, white flowers. Zones 5–10.

Wisteria brachybotrys 'Shiro-kapitan'

Wisteria × *formosa* 'Yae-kokuryû'

Wisteria floribunda

Wisteria floribunda 'Kuchi-beni'

Wisteria floribunda 'Alba'

WITTROCKIA

This small genus of 6 species comes from southeastern Brazil, is related to *Canistrum,* and is a member of the bromeliad (Bromeliaceae) family. These medium-sized to large plants have strap-like leaves with strong teeth on the edges, forming a broad cup-shaped rosette. The flower stem varies in length. The flowerhead is globular, with many flowers, usually surrounded by bright red bracts around the bottom edge. Petals are yellow, red, or white.
CULTIVATION: Grow in a greenhouse or conservatory in cool-temperate areas, or outdoors with protection from prolonged sunlight and heavy rain in warm-temperate, subtropical, and tropical areas. Water when potting mix is dry. Extra fertilizer is not necessary if good quality potting mix has been used. Propagate from offsets.

Wittrockia superba

☀ ⚘ ↔ 55 in (140 cm) ↕ 16 in (40 cm)
Large plant from Rio de Janeiro, Brazil. Strap-like large-toothed leaves, dark green with a bright red tip, forming broad cup-shaped rosette. Flower stem very short. Flowerhead globular, with many flowers, surrounded by bright red bracts. Petals white. Zones 10–12.

WOLLEMIA

This genus belonging to the araucaria (Araucariaceae) family consists of a single species, endemic to the Wollemi

National Park, 150 kilometers northwest of Sydney, Australia. It comes from warm-temperate forests and emerges over coachwood and sassafras trees within sandstone canyons of the National Park. An extremely rare, endangered and remarkable conifer, it has spongy nodular bark and an unusual branching pattern producing a double crown effect. The old leaves do not fall individually—instead, the tree sheds whole branches. *W. nobilis* was discovered in 1994. The chance discovery reinforces the importance of conservation areas in preserving both plant and animal species. The tree yields the anti-cancer drug taxol.
CULTIVATION: Because this genus is so new to horticulture, cultivation information is limited. The pine can be seen growing at the Royal Botanic Gardens in Sydney. Propagation from seed, cuttings, and tissue culture has been undertaken and research in these and other areas continues.

Wollemia nobilis
WOLLEMI PINE

☀ ⚘ ↔ 4–10 ft (1.2–3 m) ↕ 120 ft (36 m)
Very rare majestic conifer. Fern-like juvenile leaves dark green and waxy on the underside, 4-ranked adult leaves yellow-green, stiff, long and narrow. Cylindrical male cones on separate branches to the globular female cones, which contain winged seeds. Zones 9–11.

WOODSIA

Widespread in the northern temperate and tropical zones, this group of some 25 species of ferns belongs to the shield-fern (Dryopteridaceae) family. Most species have short creeping rhizomes that are sometimes adapted for growing over rocks and in narrow crevices. The pinnate fronds, though not very finely divided, rarely grow more than about 16 in (40 cm) long. The more northerly species may be

deciduous or have greatly reduced fronds over winter. Many species have scaly red-brown stems and this coating can extend to the fronds, which tend to be slightly downy.
CULTIVATION: Those species that occur naturally on rocky outcrops, growing in crevices, will tolerate fairly sunny conditions, otherwise plant in half-sun or dappled light with moist, humus-rich soil. Water well during the growing season to encourage lush growth. Propagation is usually by division, which is easiest in early spring.

Woodsia × gracilis
LAWSON'S CLIFF FERN

☀ ❄ ↔ 12–20 in (30–50 cm)
↕ 4–10 in (10–25 cm)
Natural hybrid between *W. alpina* and *W. ilvensis.* Fronds to 8 in (20 cm) long with red scaled stems, scaling sometimes occurring sparsely on fronds, which can have a leathery texture. Zones 4–9.

Woodsia ilvensis
FRAGRANT WOODSIA, RUSTY WOODSIA

☀ ❄ ↔ 12–20 in (30–50 cm)
↕ 4–10 in (10–25 cm)
North American and Eurasian species often found growing in rock crevices. Fronds to 10 in (25 cm) long, often smaller, with red-brown scales extending to frond bases and sometimes quite vivid on stems. Zones 1–9.

× WOODWARDARA

A recently registered orchid genus (family Orchidaceae), which is a trigeneric hybrid between the sympodial *Pabstia* (previously known as *Colax*), *Neogardneria,* and *Zygopetalum.* They are compact-growing orchids that produce predominantly shapely green blooms with purple and brown markings over the broad floral segments, with up to 6 blooms on the inflorescence. The flowers are 2½–4 in (6–10 cm) across the petals. Their main flowering period is winter and spring, but mature plants may bloom at other times throughout the year. These orchids are members of the *Zygopetalum* alliance.

Wollemia nobilis, Mt Tomah Botanic Garden, New South Wales, Australia

CULTIVATION: They enjoy intermediate temperatures, under moist and shaded conditions. Avoid direct sunlight as the leaves are prone to scorch if exposed for even short periods. The plants must be in a humid environment and have plenty of air circulation, otherwise the leaf tips will dry off and the foliage may spot. Sphagnum moss or fine-grade bark is a suitable medium, and they must not be over-potted. Propagate by division.

× Woodwardara Adelaide Alive

☀ ❄ ↔ 4–16 in (10–40 cm)
↕ 6–24 in (15–60 cm)
This hybrid produces dark chocolate brown flowers with a bright purple labellum. Zones 9–11.

× Woodwardara Beverley Lou

☀ ❄ ↔ 4–16 in (10–40 cm)
↕ 6–24 in (15–60 cm)
This hybrid bears green flowers with petals and sepals, striped with deep maroon markings, and a white labellum suffused with lilac. Zones 9–11.

WOODWARDIA
CHAIN FERN

A mainly North American and Asian genus of some 10 species of ferns of the hard-fern (Blechnaceae) family. The rhizomes may be short and stocky or elongated and creeping, sometimes forming short trunks. The fronds, which are usually long, gracefully arching, and borne in a crown, most often occur in distinctly different fertile (spore-bearing) and sterile forms. Frequently the sterile fronds are simple pinnate structures that are not further divided, though a few species have feathery fronds. The fertile fronds tend to occur toward the center of

× *Woodwardara* Beverley Lou

× *Woodwardara* Adelaide Alive

Woodsia × *gracilis*

the crown and are more erect, and often with conspicuous spore-bearing organs (sporangia).

CULTIVATION: They are best grown in humid woodland conditions with humus-rich soil that is well-drained but which remains moist throughout the year. Hardiness varies considerably with the species. The hardier species are mainly deciduous. Propagation is mainly by division in early spring, though in suitable climates these ferns multiply freely from spores.

Woodwardia areolata
NETTED CHAIN FERN
◐/◉ ❄ ↔ 20–48 in (50–120 cm)
↑ 20–40 in (50–100 cm)

Tough deciduous species native to much of North America. Broad, simply divided pinnate sterile fronds to 32 in (80 cm) long. Fertile fronds erect, slightly longer, with twisted segments often darkened by sporangia. Both frond forms have dark stems. Zones 5–9.

Woodwardia fimbriata
GIANT CHAIN FERN
◐/◉ ❄ ↔ 3–7 ft (0.9–2 m)
↑ 3–7 ft (0.9–2 m)

Evergreen species from California and Arizona, USA. Fronds to 10 ft (3 m) long, frequently smaller. Sterile and fertile fronds do not differ greatly except for obvious sporangia on undersides of fertile fronds. May develop short trunk with age. Zones 8–10.

Woodwardia fimbriata

Woodwardia unigemmata
◐/◉ ⚘ ↔ 4–8 ft (1.2–2.4 m)
↑ 24–40 in (60–100 cm)

Evergreen species native to Southeast Asia and the Himalayas with broad, doubly divided fronds to nearly 4 ft (1.2 m) long. Young fronds are often vivid red if they are exposed to sun. Fertile fronds do not differ greatly. Can produce new plantlets at frond tips. Zones 9–12.

XANTHOCERAS
The one species of deciduous shrub or small tree in this genus is native to northern China and is a member of the soapberry (Sapindaceae) family. It has pinnate leaves clustered near the branch tips and bears clusters of 5-petalled flowers. The fruits are thick-walled green capsules resembling the fruit of chestnut trees.

CULTIVATION: Although quite hardy, this species needs a long hot growing season to flower well, so in cooler areas should be given the shelter of a warm wall. Grow in a well-drained fertile soil and prune to maintain a compact shape. Propagate from seed, cuttings or suckers.

Xanthoceras sorbifolium ★
☼ ❄ ↔ 10 ft (3 m) ↑ 25 ft (8 m)
Shrub or small tree with wide rounded habit, dark green pinnate leaves, and sharply toothed leaflets. The fragrant white flowers have a crimson blotch at their base, and are borne in sprays, in spring–summer. Zones 6–9.

XANTHOPHTHALMUM
This rather unwieldy genus name goes back to the nineteenth century but until recently was virtually forgotten. Its 2 species of annuals from Europe, temperate Asia, and North Africa in the daisy (Asteraceae) family were usually included in the genus *Chrysanthemum*, but that name is now

Xanthoceras sorbifolium

reserved for the florists' chrysanthemum and its close allies, mostly rather woodier perennials from Asia. *Xanthophthalmum* plants are branched near the ground into several to many erect stems bearing toothed or lobed hairless leaves and produce few daisy-like cream to yellow flowerheads at each branch tip. They are free-seeding and may become minor weeds of crops. In most countries of eastern Asia the tender young leaves, buds, and flowers of *X. coronarium* are eaten as vegetables, known in the West as "chop-suey greens."

CULTIVATION: Easily grown in almost any garden soil in full sun. For floral display a light soil is best, and fertilize sparingly. For use as a vegetable, apply a frequent light application of nitrogenous fertilizer and keep soil moist. Sow seed in spring.

Xanthophthalmum coronarium
syn. *Chrysanthemum coronarium*
CROWN DAISY
☼ ❄ ↔ 12–24 in (30–60 cm)
↑ 18–30 in (45–75 cm)

Occurs wild across the Mediterranean region. Vigorous annual. Lower leaves often narrowly lobed. Profuse flowerheads with broad cream ray florets and yellow disc, in spring–early summer. Young shoots and buds a popular green vegetable in Asia. Zones 8–11.

XANTHORRHOEA
Now classified in their own family—Xanthorrhoeaceae—there are around 30 species of grass trees found across Australia. They are slow-growing long-lived woody perennials with long narrow leaves which emerge in tufts from the extremities of the branches; there are also species that appear to be stemless because they grow directly from the soil, but which have substantial subterranean stems. White or

Xanthorrhoea australis, in the wild, Australia

cream flowers are clustered on long-stalked spikes, and usually appear in the spring or as a reaction to fire. Leathery capsular fruits are clustered along the spikes. Both flower spikes and foliage are used in floristry.

CULTIVATION: The young plants may take 20 years to develop stems and more than 100 years to flower, particularly in the absence of fire. They do not happily transplant. An open sunny situation with well-drained soil is preferred by most species. They are also excellent subjects for growing in containers. Propagation is from seed sown in the spring or autumn in a coarse free-draining mix.

Xanthorrhoea australis
SOUTHERN GRASS TREE
☼ ⚘ ↔ 3 ft (0.9 m) ↑ 3 ft (0.9 m)
From southeastern Australia. Dense rosette of narrow, arching leaves, finely hairy. A short trunk may develop with age. The fragrant spring flowers white or cream, cluster on long "spears," after many years. Crowded fruit capsules follow. Zones 9–11.

Xanthorrhoea johnsonii,
in the wild, Australia

X. johnsonii, with termite mound, in the wild, Cape York, Queensland, Australia

Xanthorrhoea preissii, in the wild, John Forrest National Park, Western Australia

X. glauca, in the wild, Australia

Xanthorrhoea quadrangulata, in the wild, Para Wirra Recreation Park, South Australia

Xanthorrhoea glauca
NARROW-LEAFED GRASS TREE

☼ ❄ ↔ 3 ft (0.9 m) ↑ 20 ft (6 ft)

Occurring in the Great Dividing Range country of New South Wales and southeastern Queensland, Australia. Branched blackish trunks, several foliage rosettes. Leaves are a bluish shade of green. Flower spike up to 7 ft (2 m) long. Zones 8–11.

Xanthorrhoea johnsonii
QUEENSLAND GRASS TREE

☼ ⚘ ↔ 3 ft (0.9 m) ↑ 7 ft (2 m)

With a fire-blackened trunk, this species has bright green clusters of grass-like leaves. Huge cylindrical spikes comprising hundreds of nectar-rich cream flowers. Zones 9–10.

Xanthorrhoea preissii ★
WESTERN AUSTRALIAN GRASS TREE

☼ ⚘ ↔ 4 ft (1.2 m) ↑ 15 ft (4.5 m)

From Western Australia. The stems are usually blackened from fire, and often have a twisted form. Arching leaves. Creamy yellow flower spikes reach 5 ft (1.5 m). Brown, leathery, capsular fruits. Zones 10–11.

Xanthorrhoea quadrangulata
SQUARE-LEAF GRASS TREE

☼ ⚘ ↔ 4–7 ft (1.2–2 m) ↑ 7–10 ft (2–3 m)

A drought-tolerant perennial from southern Australia. Trunk to 10 ft (3 m) tall with a spray of very narrow, tough, dark green leaves, quadrangular in section, to 24–36 in (60–90 cm) long. The narrow whitish flower spikes, 3–4 ft (0.9–1.2 m) tall, emerge from the foliage crown during the autumn. Aborigines make these into spears or pound them into flour. The soft bases of the leaves and roots are also edible. Zones 9–11.

XANTHOSOMA
YAUTIA, TANNIA

This arum (Araceae) family genus of around 50 species of tuberous-rooted perennials is native to tropical America. Their leaves are variable, often long and arrowhead-shaped but sometimes pointed, oval, or even divided into large segments. The flowerheads are usually short-stemmed, often concealed by the foliage, with a bulbous base and a green, white or creamy yellow spathe that partly encloses a short spadix. Within their native range several species are cultivated for their edible stems and tubers. One species, *X. saggittifolium,* has become a staple in many tropical areas.

CULTIVATION: These tropical aroids demand warm humid conditions with moist, humus-rich soil. They will not tolerate frosts or prolonged cold and outside the tropics they are mainly cultivated as house or greenhouse plants. Propagation is by seed or the division of well-established clumps.

Xanthosoma undipes

☼ ⚘ ↔ 7–10 ft (2–3 m) ↑ 7–10 ft (2–3 m)

Perennial herb from Mexico to Peru, and cultivated widely in the Caribbean. Stem to 7 ft (2 m) long. Broadly heart-shaped leaves, 20 in–7 ft (0.5–2 m) long, on stalks to 40 in (100 cm) long. The egg-shaped spathe tube, to 3 in (8 cm) long, is yellowish green inside, with a limb to 10 in (25 cm) long. Zones 10–11.

XANTHOSTEMON

The 45 or so evergreen trees and shrubs in this genus suited to warmer climates are members of the myrtle (Myrtaceae) family. They are native to the wet tropical and subtropical regions of northern Australia, New Caledonia, New Guinea, Indonesia, and the Philippines. The trunk is either solitary or has a branching habit with rough flaky bark. The smooth, leathery, oval-shaped leaves are crowded toward the ends of branches. Single flowers or clusters, with 5 petals and numerous yellow, red, or orange stamens, sometimes fragrant, grow from the leaf axils. The fruit is a spherical capsule which splits open to reveal a circle of flat seeds. The genus name comes from two Greek words: *xanthos,* yellow, and *stemon,* stamen, referring to the yellow stamens.

CULTIVATION: These plants prefer light to medium well-drained soils in an open sunny position, with regular watering. Propagate from seed or from cuttings taken in autumn.

Xanthostemon aurantiacum

☼ ✦ ↔ 15 in–6 ft (38 cm–1.8 m) ↑ 20 in–10 ft (50 cm–3 m)

Much branching evergreen shrub from New Caledonia. Smooth, leathery, oval leaves, 4–5 in (10–12 cm) long, slightly curled margins, silvery when young. Branching heads of up to 12 flowers, bright orange-red petals and massed yellow stamens, growing from leaf axils, in spring–summer. Woody capsular fruit. Zones 10–12.

XERANTHEMUM

This genus of 6 upright annual herbs in the daisy (Asteraceae) family originates from the Mediterranean region to southwestern Asia. They have alternate smooth leaves and solitary, terminal, disc-like flowerheads resembling daisy flowers, in white, mauve, rose, or lilac shades, with papery petal-like bracts. The genus name comes from the Greek *xeros,* dry and *anthemum,* flower, referring to the dry papery flowerheads that retain their shape and color for many years.

CULTIVATION: These plants prefer an open sunny position in most well-drained fertile soils. Propagation is from seed.

Xeranthemum annuum
COMMON IMMORTELLE

☼ ❄ ↔ 10–36 in (25–90 cm) ↑ 10–36 in (25–90 cm)

Annual herb found from southeastern Europe to the Caucasus and Iran, naturalized elsewhere. Upright branching stems with alternate, smooth, narrow, oblong leaves, covered with fine white hairs, denser underneath. Flowerheads have spreading, oblong, bright pink or white inner bracts and many florets, from summer–autumn. Zones 6–10.

XEROCHRYSUM
ALPINE EVERLASTING, ORANGE EVERLASTING

A small genus of 6 Australian species, formerly classified in the genus *Bracteantha.* They are members of the daisy (Asteraceae) family. The genus name comes from the Greek *xeros,* dry, and *chrysos,* golden, referring to the dry papery bracts, which are golden yellow in many species.

CULTIVATION: Grow these plants in full sun, in light well-drained soil. Propagate from seed.

Xerochrysum bracteatum
syns *Bracteantha bracteatum,*
Helichrysum bracteatum
GOLDEN EVERLASTING, STRAWFLOWER

☼ ❄ ↔ 16 in (40 cm) ↑ 3 ft (0.9 m)

Australian annual or short-lived perennial with often sticky, narrow, pointed

Xerochrysum bracteatum

Xerochrysum bracteatum 'Coco'

Xerochrysum bracteatum 'Golden Beauty'

Xerochrysum bracteatum 'Pink Sunrise'

lance-shaped leaves to over 4 in (10 cm) long. The flowerheads are nearly 3 in (8 cm) wide, and a deep golden yellow. Garden forms produce flowerheads in many colors, including: '**Bright Bikini**' strain in all shades except blue and mauve; '**Coco**', pale yellow flowers; '**Dargan Hill Monarch**' (syn. *Bracteantha bracteata* 'Dargan Hill Monarch'), buttery yellow flowers; '**Golden Beauty**', all-over deep golden yellow; '**Pink Sunrise**', orange and cream flowerheads opening from pink buds; and '**Princess of Wales**', compact habit, golden yellow flowerheads. Zones 8–10.

XERONEMA

This genus in the family Phormiaceae contains just 2 species of tender perennial herbs from New Caledonia and New Zealand's Poor Knights Islands. They form tight fan-like clumps of erect to arching, long, pointed, leathery

leaves. The flowering stems are tall and unbranched and the flowerhead, which is densely packed with small flowers, resembles a brush. It is very showy, with the flowers being bright red to crimson.

CULTIVATION: These plants can be difficult to grow and take a very long time to flower. In very warm areas grow outside in perfectly drained soil in full sun. They are suitable for growing in containers, and often perform better when rootbound. In cool climates grow under glass in free-draining sandy loam in a humid atmosphere and water well when in growth. Propagate from seed or by division.

Xeronema moorei

☼ ✿ ↔ 24 in (60 cm)
↕ 24–36 in (60–90 cm)

Native to New Caledonia. Leathery leaves with a distinct fold. Flowering stems bear one-sided crowded racemes

of bright crimson flowers, which appear in spring. The fruit ripens to deep purple. Zones 10–12.

YUCCA

Native to dry regions of North and Central America and the West Indies, there are about 40 species in this genus within the agave (Agavaceae) family, which include evergreen herbaceous perennials, as well as trees and shrubs. They have a strong bold form and strap- to lance-shaped leaves arranged in rosettes. Bell- to cup-shaped flowers are held on usually erect panicles. The inflorescence of *Y. whipplei* grows to 12 ft (3.5 m) in 14 days. Herbalists and traditional healers make a tea from boiled yucca roots. Native Americans still use parts of the yucca plant for craft tools, and as a dye to color fibers. CULTIVATION: All *Yucca* species grow best in loamy soil with good drainage, but they will tolerate poor sandy soil. In colder regions it is best to grow the tender species in large pots in loam-based potting compost and overwinter them indoors. Grown outdoors they need good light through summer, a monthly feed and careful watering. *Yucca* species range from frost hardy to frost tender. Propagation is by sowing seed in spring, or by taking root cuttings in winter, or by removing suckers in spring.

Xanthostemon aurantiacum

Yucca aloifolia

DAGGER PLANT, SPANISH BAYONET

☼ ❄ ↔ 10 ft (3 m) ↕ 25 ft (8 m)

Native to the West Indies, Mexico, and southeastern USA. Slow-growing shrub or small tree. Erect stem simple or branched, stiff, lance-shaped, toothed, gray-green leaves to 20 in (50 cm) long, sharply pointed. Bell-shaped, pendent, white flowers, on erect spikes, in summer to autumn. Fleshy fruit. '**Marginata**' ★, yellow leaf edges, but its spreading habit can pose problems; '**Tricolor**', leaves striped white or yellow in the center. Zones 8–11.

Yucca baccata

BANANA YUCCA, BLUE YUCCA, SPANISH BAYONET

☼ ❄ ↔ 4 ft (1.2 m) ↕ 5 ft (1.5 m)

Native to northern Mexico and southwestern USA. Can be single-stemmed or branched, spent leaves persist on the stem. Leaves green with yellow or blue tinges, fine hairs on leaf edges. Bell-shaped flowers, in panicles, cream sometimes tinged purple. Zones 9–11.

Yucca baccata

Xeronema moorei, in the wild, Monts Koghis, New Caledonia

Xanthostemon species, in the wild, New Caledonia

Yucca faxoniana, in the wild, Big Bend National Park, Texas, USA

Yucca glauca, in the wild, Montana, USA

Yucca gloriosa

Yucca elata, in the wild, White Sands National Monument, New Mexico, USA

Yucca brevifolia

JOSHUA TREE

☼ ❄ ↔ 5 ft (1.5 m) ↕ 30–40 ft (9–12 m)

Found from California to southwestern Utah, USA. Branching habit, bark gray or orange-brown forming plates. Leaves straight and narrow, finely toothed edges. Flower spikes bear unpleasant smelling greenish flowers, tinged with yellow or cream, in the late spring. Zones 7–10.

Yucca elata

PALMELLA, SOAP WEED

☼ ❄ ↔ 5 ft (1.5 m) ↕ 10 ft (3 m)

Found from Arizona to Texas, USA, and Mexico. Suckering shoots, multiple stems covered with dead leaves. New leaves light green, edged with fine hairs. Flower stalk is 6 ft (1.8 m) tall, flowers are creamy white, tinted pink or green. Zones 9–11.

Yucca elephantipes

syn. *Yucca guatemalensis*

GIANT YUCCA, SPINELESS YUCCA

☼ ❄ ↔ 10 ft (3 m) ↕ 30 ft (9 m)

Native to Central America and Mexico. Large erect shrub or small tree. Narrow, leathery, mid-green leaves, to 3 ft (0.9 m) long, finely toothed edges.

Yucca brevifolia, in the wild, Death Valley National Park, California, USA

White or cream flowers borne on 3 ft (0.9 m) tall stalks, in summer through to autumn. Zones 10–12.

Yucca faxoniana

☼ ❄ ↔ 7–10 ft (2–3 m) ↕ 10–17 ft (3–5 m)

Evergreen perennial shrub from southwestern USA and Mexico. Forms stout upright trunk, to 12 in (30 cm) in diameter. Rosette of stiff pointed leaves, to 3 ft (0.9 m) long, sharply pointed tips, reddish or sometimes black margins with curly threads. The old yellow leaves bend down to form a thick thatch. Terminal stalk emerges from the center of the leaf rosette, 3–4 ft (0.9–1.2 m) tall. Creamy white bell-shaped flowers. Reddish seed pods. Zones 8–10.

Yucca filamentosa ★

ADAM'S NEEDLE

☼ ❄ ↔ 5 ft (1.5 m) ↕ 3 ft (0.9 m)

From eastern USA. Usually trunkless, multiple suckering heads of 30 in (75 cm) long, filamentous, blue-green leaves. Flower stems up to 10 ft (3 m) tall bear masses of pendulous cream flowers, in summer. '**Bright Edge**' ★, dwarf cultivar with yellow-edged foliage, creamy flowers tinged with

Yucca elephantipes, in the wild, Costa Rica

green; '**Golden Sword**' ★, similar but larger; '**Ivory Tower**', creamy white flowers tinged with green. Zones 6–10.

Yucca flaccida

syn. *Yucca filifera*

☼ ❄ ↔ 17–35 ft (5–10 m)
↕ 17–35 ft (5–10 m)

Branching, evergreen, perennial North American shrub. Dark bluish green, flexible, narrowly sword-shaped leaves, to 22 in (55 cm) long, sharp tips, yellow serrated margins ending in straight threads. Cylindrical heads of creamy white bell-shaped flowers, to 2 in (5 cm) long, from summer–autumn. '**Golden Sword**', green leaves with yellow margins; '**Ivory**', freely flowering with spikes of ivory flowers. Zones 6–9.

Yucca filamentosa 'Bright Edge'

Yucca glauca

SPANISH BAYONET

☼ ❄ ↔ 36 in (90 cm) ↕ 24 in (60 cm)

From western and central USA. Clump-forming species, blue-green narrow leaves, thin straight filaments along the edges. Flower stalk to 3 ft (0.9 m) tall, bell-shaped off-white flowers, sometimes tinged green or red-brown, in summer. Zones 4–9.

Yucca gloriosa

CANDLE YUCCA, PALM LILY, ROMAN CANDLE

☼ ❄ ↔ 6 ft (1.8 m) ↕ 6–8 ft (1.8–2.4 m)

Found from North Carolina to Florida, USA. Usually unbranched tree-like species. Stiff, thin, lance-shaped, blue-green, age to dark green. White, pendent bell-shaped flowers, sometimes tinged green, pink or purplish red on tall panicles, in summer–autumn. '**Variegata**' ★, leaves with yellow-cream stripes and edges. Zones 7–10.

Yucca recurvifolia

WEEPING YUCCA

☼ ❄ ↔ 4 ft (1.2 m) ↕ 4–8 ft (1.2–2.4 m)

Native to southeastern USA. Robust shrub, may have multiple stems. Leathery, bluish to deep green, tapered leaves, recurved and drooping in some forms, but mostly straight in

Yucca filamentosa 'Bright Edge'

Yucca schidigera, Baja California, Mexico

Yucca whipplei

Yucca recurvifolia

Yucca whipplei subsp. *parishii*

others. Large, creamy white, bell-shaped flowers, tall panicles, in late summer–late autumn. Zones 8–11.

Yucca schidigera
syn. *Yucca mohavensis*
☀ ❄ ↔ 8 ft (2.4 m) ↑ 15 ft (4.5 m)
Native to southwestern USA. Tree-like, trunk is often branched. Leaves, smooth, thick edges carry fine filaments. Flower spikes to 4 ft (1.2 m) long, in late spring or after warm rain, carry waxy, cream flowers. Zones 8–10.

Yucca whipplei
OUR LORD'S CANDLE
☀ ❄ ↔ 4 ft (1.2 m) ↑ 3 ft (0.9 m)
Stiff-leafed stemless yucca ranges from southwestern USA into Baja California, Mexico. Rosettes of narrow, rigid, blue-green leaves, spiny tips, fine-toothed edges. The flowering panicle grows rapidly to 10–15 ft (3–4.5 m) high, with pendulous, small, white flowers, often green- or purple-tipped, from the late summer to early autumn. *Y. w.* subsp. *parishii* is an unbranched race. Zones 8–11.

YUSHANIA
Yushania (Chinese for "jade mountain") is a large genus of over 80 species in the grass (Poaceae) family. Technically, *Yushania* species are cold hardy pachymorph bamboos, but the rhizome neck is so long that the culms arise at considerable distances, so they

should be treated as spreaders. Found from China, Taiwan, and Southeast Asia to Madagascar and the mountains of East Africa. Typically shrubs, they are highly regarded as screens.
CULTIVATION: Propagation is by division, taken in winter with the culm and rhizome buds present.

Yushania anceps
☀ ❄ ↔ 15–30 ft (4.5–9 m) ↑ 15 ft (4.5 m)
Native to the Himalayan mountains of India. Erect culms, ¾ in (18 mm) in diameter, completely pendulous, bowed down by the weight of the foliage. Makes fine screens on steep banks. 'Pitt White', smaller foliage, more vigorous, double the height of species. Zones 7–10.

ZALUZIANSKYA
Genus of about 35 species of sticky-leafed annuals, perennials and subshrubs from southern and eastern Africa belonging to the foxglove (Scrophulariaceae) family. Their leaves are smooth or toothed and the flowers have 5 spreading notched petals at the end of a long tube. Most are night-scented and the outside color of the flowers is quite different from the inside. The genus is named after Adam Zaluziansky von Zaluzian, a sixteenth-century Bohemian botanist.
CULTIVATION: These plants like full sun and a well-drained soil in almost frost-free climates. Where frost is usual,

they can be grown in a cool greenhouse as a colorful filler. Keep almost dry in winter. Propagation needs to be regular as even the shrubby species are short-lived. Take tip cuttings in the summer or sow seed in spring with bottom heat.

Zaluzianskya ovata
☀ ❄ ↔ 20–24 in (50–60 cm) ↑ 8–10 in (20–25 cm)
Brittle-stemmed evergreen perennial from South Africa. Toothed leaves to 1¾ in (40 mm) long. Flowers are white inside with rich crimson on the petal backs, produced over a long period in summer–autumn. Zones 10–11.

ZAMIA
This genus in the zamia (Zamiaceae) family consists of more than 55 species, the majority occurring in South, Central, and North America. All have pinnate leaves and cylindrical or tuber-like stems that are usually subterranean but may be above ground. They are fern or palm-like in appearance, with the male and broader female cones borne on separate plants. Many species have highly toxic seeds. The spiraly arranged arching leaves have mostly smooth leaflets, and the margins can be smooth-edged, toothed or bumpy, and spiny in some species. They come from a range of habitats. These plants make useful landscape subjects. Most are best suited to tropical and subtropical regions that are free from frost.
CULTIVATION: Most are fairly adaptable in a well-drained soil. Tolerances vary; the understory types with softer lusher foliage usually are best in sheltered, more humid, semi-shaded positions, while the tougher-leafed species from more open habitats can usually tolerate more exposure and sun. Propagate from fresh seed.

Zamia fairchildiana ★
☀ ⚘ ↔ 5 ft (1.5 m) ↑ 8 ft (2.4 m)
From Costa Rica and western Panama. Attractive, with upright trunk. Leaves in whorls of 3 to 10, erect, thinly textured, papery green. Leaf stalk densely prickly. Male cones cream to yellow, female yellowish green to light brown. Zones 11–12.

Zamia furfuracea ★
CARDBOARD PALM
☀ ⚘ ↔ 7 ft (2 m) ↑ 3 ft (0.9 m)
From Mexico. Broad, hairy, stiff leaflets, attractive small to medium cycad, subterranean stem when young. Forms mound of spreading leaves, olive green leathery leaflets, on spiny stalks. Cones are pink to red. An excellent tub plant. Zones 11–12.

Zamia pumila
GUAYIGA
☀ ❄ ↔ 6 ft (1.8 m) ↑ 5 ft (1.5 m)
From islands of the Caribbean. Short, many-branched, subterranean stems from which emerge 4 to 12 erect dark green leaves with smooth leaf stalks. Cones red to red-brown. Zones 10–12.

Zamia furfuracea

Zaluzianskya ovata

ZANTEDESCHIA

ARUM LILY, CALLA LILY

The large calla lily *(Z. aethiopica)* is a plant that polarizes opinions. Some gardeners love it, while others cannot abide its funereal associations. Named after the Italian botanist Giovanni Zantedeschi (1773–1846), this genus in the arum (Araceae) family comprises 6 species of rhizome-rooted perennials from southern Africa, with large, upward-facing, elongated heart-shaped leaves that taper to a long tip and sometimes speckled with translucent spots. The flower spathe is funnel-shaped and also tapers to a tip. The spadix may be enclosed within the spathe or protrude slightly. Although the white form is the best known, modern hybrids cover a wide color range. Both leaves and the flowers are supported by strong stalks.

CULTIVATION: Cultivated callas withstand moderate frosts. They lose their foliage in cold winters but may retain some in milder conditions. Some prefer

Zantedeschia, HC, 'Scarlet Pimpernel'

Zantedeschia pentlandii, in the wild, South Africa

Zantedeschia aethiopica, in the wild, South Africa

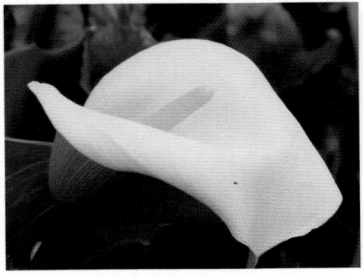

Zantedeschia aethiopica 'Crowborough'

Zantedeschia aethiopica 'Green Goddess'

damp almost boggy conditions, but most will grow in full or half-sun in any garden soil that does not dry out. Propagate by division, or from basal offsets or seed.

Zantedeschia aethiopica

ARUM LILY, CALLA LILY

☀/◐ ❄ ↔ 20–60 in (50–150 cm) ↕ 4–6 ft (1.2–1.8 m)

From South Africa and widely naturalized in mild areas, this evergreen or semi-evergreen species develops large rhizomes and can form impressive clumps of long-stemmed, 12–24 in (30–60 cm) long, arrowhead-shaped leaves. Tall flower stems topped with a white spathe, to 10 in (25 cm) long,

Zantedeschia, Hybrid Cultivar, 'Hercules'

around a yellow spadix. Can become invasive. 'Childsiana' ★, compact, small leaves, pink-tinted flowers last well when cut; 'Crowborough', 36 in (90 cm) tall; 'Green Goddess', 36 in (90 cm) tall, small greenish spathe, can be invasive. Zones 8–11.

Zantedeschia albomaculata

☀ ❀ ↔ 16–24 in (40–60 cm) ↕ 24–40 in (60–100 cm)

Perennial found from South Africa to tropical eastern Africa. Long-stemmed, white-spotted, arrowhead-shaped leaves, to 18 in (45 cm) long. Sturdy flower stems with cup-shaped spathe, to 5 in (12 cm) long, usually white to cream, sometimes yellow or pink. Spadix pale to deep yellow. Zones 9–11.

Zantedeschia elliottiana ★

GOLDEN CALLA

☀ ❀ ↔ 12–18 in (30–45 cm) ↕ 12–18 in (30–45 cm)

Unknown in the wild and possibly of hybrid origin. Heavily white-spotted, arrowhead-shaped leaves, 8–12 in (20–30 cm) long, deep yellow 4–5 in (10–12 cm) long spathes. Zones 9–11.

Zantedeschia pentlandii

☀ ❀ ↔ 12–16 in (30–40 cm) ↕ 12–24 in (30–60 cm)

South African species with usually unspotted, 6–8 in (15–20 cm) long, arrowhead-shaped leaves on long thin stems. Golden yellow cup-shaped spathe to over 4 in (10 cm) long, the spadix similarly colored. Interior of the spathe has a purple patch at base. Zones 9–11.

Zantedeschia rehmannii

☀ ❀ ↔ 12–20 in (30–50 cm) ↕ 16–20 in (40–50 cm)

Native of South Africa and Swaziland. Narrow, unspotted, lance-shaped leaves, to 16 in (40 cm) long. Flowerheads

Zantedeschia, Hybrid Cultivar, 'Flame'

often held below foliage level. Spathes white, pink, or purple-red, to over 4 in (10 cm) long. 'Superba', many deep pink spathes held just above foliage level. Zones 9–11.

Zantedeschia Hybrid Cultivars

☀ ❀ ↔ 1–5 ft (0.3–1.5 m) ↕ 1–6 ft (0.3–1.8 m)

Developed through crossing most of the smaller species, these hybrids are generally quite compact. White-spotted leaves, sturdy flower stems with showy spathes. 'Flame', 24 in (60 cm), red-flecked yellow spathes deepening with age; 'Hercules', 6 ft (1.8 m), giant-sized, white to very pale pink spathes; 'Kiwi Blush', 30 in (75 cm), white spathes heavily flushed pink; 'Scarlet Pimpernel' ★, 18–24 in (45–60 cm), bright red spathes. Zones 9–11.

ZANTHOXYLUM

This is a widespread genus of around 250 species of deciduous or evergreen spiny shrubs and trees with pinnate leaves and aromatic bark from North and South America, Africa, Asia, and Australia. They are members of the rue (Rutaceae) family, and are grown for their attractive habit and handsome aromatic foliage, and sometimes for their fruits, which are dried and used for spices. Some species have medicinal uses and others provide a fine timber.

Zea mays 'Cuties Pops'

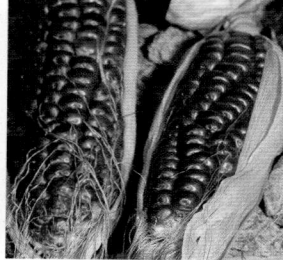
Zea mays 'Blue Jade'

Zea mays 'Earlivee'

Zea mays 'Indian Summer'

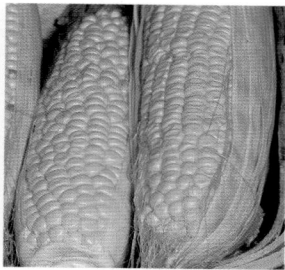
Zea mays 'New Excellence'

CULTIVATION: Depending on the species, they are frost hardy to frost tender. They need a fertile, moist but well-drained soil with a position in full sun or partial shade. Pruning is rarely necessary, but young specimens may be shaped in early spring. Propagate from seed, cuttings and rooted suckers.

Zanthoxylum americanum
NORTHERN PRICKLY ASH, PRICKLY ASH, TOOTHACHE TREE

☀ ❄ ↔ 15 ft (4.5 m) ↕ 25 ft (8 m)
Native to eastern North America. Deciduous large shrub or small tree, with spiny stems, and aromatic pinnate leaves. Very small yellow-green flowers occur in clusters, before the leaves, in spring. Fruit is a black berry. Zones 4–10.

Zanthoxylum piperitum
JAPANESE PEPPER

☀ ❄ ↔ 10 ft (3 m) ↕ 20 ft (6 m)
Deciduous, bushy, spiny shrub or small tree, native to China, Korea, and Japan.

Zanthoxylum planispinum

Aromatic, glossy, dark green, pinnate leaves are composed of many oval leaflets, which turn yellow, in autumn. Small yellow-green flowers in small clusters, in spring. Tiny orange-colored berries. Zones 7–10.

Zanthoxylum planispinum
☀ ❄ ↔ 8 ft (2.4 m) ↕ 12 ft (3.5 m)
Native to Japan, Korea, and China. A deciduous shrub with spreading prickly stems, pinnate leaves, stem-clasping leaflets to 4 in (10 cm) long. The pale yellow flowers appear in small clusters, in spring. Tiny, warty, red berries. Zones 7–10.

Zanthoxylum simulans
FLAT-SPINE PRICKLY ASH, PRICKLY ASH

☀ ❄ ↔ 7–25 ft (2–8 m) ↕ 7–25 ft (2–8 m)
Rounded, spreading, deciduous shrub or small tree, from China and Taiwan. Broad flattened spines on finely hairy branches. Compound leaves have 7 to 11 smooth, toothed, oval to oblong leaflets, to 2 in (5 cm) long, with a prickly midrib. Slender cymes of reddish green flowers in mid-summer, followed by red to black berries in autumn. Zones 5–8.

ZEA
This genus of 4 annual grasses, members of the grass (Poaceae) family, is native to Central America. Strong upright stems with broad, smooth, strap-like leaves. Male flowers are at tops of stems, female flowers grow from leaf

Zea mays cultivar, Montana, USA

axils, with solid spathe-like core enclosed within the leaves, in summer. Fruit forms as massed grains (cobs or ears) around the core in late summer–autumn. *Z. mays*, which is high in nutritional value, is grown throughout the world both as a food crop for humans and to fatten cattle. Ornamental cultivars are also available.
CULTIVATION: *Zea* species are adaptable to most soil types, and should be placed in an open sunny position. They can be propagated from seed.

Zea mays
CORN, MAIZE, MEALIE, INDIAN CORN, SWEET CORN

☀ ❄ ↔ 20–40 in (50–100 cm) ↕ 7–15 ft (2–4.5 m)
Upright, stout, robust stems and smooth strap-like leaves, to 36 in (90 cm) long, in 2 ranks, with pointed tips and sheathed bases. Feathery male flowers in terminal panicles; female flowers in heads to 8 in (20 cm) long, growing from leaf axils, maturing to shining, yellow, white, or black grains, to 10 mm across, enclosed within the leaves. 'Black Aztec', very old variety with white ears that turn black when dried; 'Blue Jade', dwarf bushy habit, with deep bluish black kernels; 'Cuties Pops', ornamental variety; 'Earlivee', compact, early-maturing,

yellow form, to 4 ft (1.2 m) high; 'Indian Summer' ★, dense ears, 8 in (20 cm) long, with mixed kernels of white, yellow, red, and purple; 'New Excellence', sweet yellow kernels. Zones 8–10.

ZELKOVA
Allied to the elms *(Ulmus)* but not troubled by Dutch elm disease, the 5 deciduous trees in this genus are members of the family Ulmaceae, and are found in China, Taiwan, and Japan, as well as in the Caucasus and Crete, Greece. They have simple, pointed, elliptical leaves with conspicuous veins and heavily serrated edges. The foliage often develops some attractive autumn colors. In some species the bark is an attractive feature, flaking to reveal interesting patterns and colors. The separate male and female flowers are largely inconspicuous, as are the small nut-like fruits.
CULTIVATION: Quite frost hardy, these spreading round-headed trees develop a better shape if sheltered from strong winds when they are young. They also benefit from pruning to encourage a strong single trunk. Plant in deep, fertile, well-drained soil in full sun. Propagation is from seed, from root cuttings of the young potted plants, or by grafting.

Zanthoxylum simulans

Z

Zingiber spectabile

Zelkova abelicea

CRETAN ZELKOVA

☀ ❄ ↔ 20 ft (6 m) ↕ 50 ft (15 m)

Large shrub from the island of Crete, Greece. Young branches covered in fine white down, similar hairs on undersides of the small leaves. Zones 8–10.

Zelkova carpinifolia

CAUCASIAN ZELKOVA

☀ ❄ ↔ 25 ft (8 m) ↕ 100 ft (30 m)

Native to the Caucasus. May develop several trunks. Round-headed tree, upright gray-barked branches, weep at the tips. Young stems very downy, veins on undersides of the serrated leaves. Flowers pleasantly scented. Zones 5–9.

Zelkova serrata

JAPANESE ZELKOVA

☀ ❄ ↔ 50 ft (15 m) ↕ 60–100 ft (18–30 m)

Widely cultivated, found in Japan, Taiwan, and eastern China. Wide-spreading crown, bark flakes to reveal range of colors and textures. Heavily toothed, veined leaves, fine hairs on underside veins. Foliage turns gold and russet, in autumn. 'Goblin', 3 ft (0.9 m) high dwarf cultivar; 'Green Vase' ★, vase-shaped form, brilliant green foliage; 'Village Green', fast-growing, rich green leaves. Zones 5–9.

ZENOBIA

The single species in this genus in the heath (Ericaceae) family is a deciduous or semi-evergreen shrub found in southeastern USA, on open heathland and in pine forest clearings. Notable for beautiful flowers and their pleasant scent. Foliage sometimes develops red tints in autumn.
CULTIVATION: This plant prefers cool, moist, humus-rich, acidic soil conditions. Very frost hardy; prefers partial shade. If necessary trim to shape after flowering. Propagate from seed or summer cuttings. Alternatively, try removing rooted layers or suckers.

Zigadenus fremontii

Zenobia pulverulenta ★

☀ ❄ ↔ 4 ft (1.2 m) ↕ 3–10 ft (0.9–3 m)

From southeast Virginia to South Carolina, USA. Retains much of its foliage in mild winters, deciduous elsewhere. Narrowly elliptical leaves, light green, covered with a powdery bluish bloom. Heads of bell-shaped, nodding, scented white flowers, in late spring. 'Quercifolia' retains shallowly lobed foliage often seen on juvenile plants. Zones 5–10.

ZIGADENUS

DEATH CAMAS, ZYGADENE

This genus of 18 bulbous or rhizomatous perennial herbs, members of the lily (Liliaceae) family, is native to temperate North America and northern Asia. Narrow, folded, and curved leaves grow from a central base. Terminal panicles or racemes of greenish white to yellowish white, bisexual flowers, with 6 free, spreading, petal-like tepals with green basal glands, appear in summer. Fruit is a capsule. All members of the genus are highly poisonous to humans and livestock.
CULTIVATION: Death camas prefer a position in full sun and are adaptable to most well-drained soils. Propagate by division of bulbs or rhizomes, or from seed.

Zigadenus fremontii

STAR LILY, STAR ZYGADENE

☀ ❄ ↔ 2–5 in (5–12 cm) ↕ 20–36 in (50–90 cm)

Perennial herb from southern Oregon, USA, to northern Baja California, Mexico. Grows from spherical bulbs, 1–1¼ in (25–30 mm) wide. Narrow, slightly rough, curved leaves, to 24 in (60 cm) long, grow from a central base. Open spreading panicles of off-white or ivory flowers, in summer, on smooth stems 16–36 in (40–90 cm) tall. Zones 5–10.

ZINGIBER

GINGER

This group of approximately 60 herbaceous and evergreen rhizomatous, clumping, perennial herbs gives its name to the ginger (Zingiberaceae) family. The leaves, usually narrow, are arranged in 2 ranks on upright stems. Inflorescences, often intensely colored and cone-like, with overlapping waxy-looking bracts, arise from the base of the plant in summer. Originating in Asia and northern Australia, most species are frost tender, although some prove surprisingly hardy in temperate gardens. The rhizome of *Z. officinale* is the source of culinary ginger root. A milky substance that is produced in the flower cones of *Z. zerumbet*, and traditionally used as a shampoo, is an ingredient of some modern commercial shampoos.
CULTIVATION: Most species prefer nutrient-rich, well-drained, moist soil and full sun to part shade in warm, humid conditions. Most are easily propagated by division in early spring.

Zingiber officinale

CANTON GINGER, COMMON GINGER, STEM GINGER

☀ ❀ ↔ 3 ft (0.9 m) ↕ 3–5 ft (0.9–1.5 m)

From tropical Asia, its exact origin is obscure. Narrow, glossy green leaves and small green inflorescences with white and maroon flowers. Various forms, most are sterile. *Z. officinale* is grown solely for its spicy aromatic root used in cooking and medicine. Zones 9–12.

Zingiber spectabile

BEEHIVE GINGER

☀ ❀ ↔ 3 ft (0.9 m) ↕ 5–7 ft (1.5–2 m)

Native to Malaysia. *Z. spectabile* has long deep green leaves with paler downy undersides. Long cylindrical inflorescences, yellow bracts turning to scarlet. Small creamy white flowers with 2-lobed dark purple lip with yellow spots, are produced in late summer. Zones 9–12.

Zingiber zerumbet

syn. *Zingiber americans*

AWAPUHI, PINE-CONE GINGER, SHAMPOO GINGER

☀ ❄ ↔ 3 ft (0.9 m) ↕ 6–8 ft (1.8–2.4 m)

From India. Upright, highly ornamental with shiny, dark green leaves on arching stems. Large cone-shaped inflorescences, pale green turning bright red. Flower white with pale yellow lip; late summer. Long-lasting as a cut flower. 'Variegatum' (syns *Z. darceyi*, *Z.* 'Darceyi'), smaller, more frost tender, leaves are striped with cream. Zones 8–12.

Zelkova carpinifolia

Zelkova serrata

Zelkova serrata 'Village Green'

ZINNIA

Named for Johann Gottfried Zinn (1727–1759), a German botany professor, this daisy (Asteraceae) family genus of around 20 species of annuals, perennials, and small shrubs is from south-central USA to Argentina, with its center in Mexico. Zinnias have soft light green leaves that range from linear to broadly spatula-shaped, depending on the species. While the flowers of the wild species are typically daisy-like with conspicuous ray and disc florets, modern seed strains are mainly doubles with the disc florets largely hidden or absent. The color range is very wide, though mostly warm tones: yellow, pink, orange, and red to mahogany.

CULTIVATION: Cultivated plants are mostly frost-tender summer annuals that should be grown in a sunny warm position sheltered from drafts. The soil should be moist and well-drained, but zinnias can withstand dry periods. Deadhead frequently to prolong the flowering. Propagate from seed.

Zinnia angustifolia

☀ ❄ ↔ 12–20 in (30–50 cm)
↕ 8–16 in (20–40 cm)

Erect summer-flowering annual from southeastern USA and Mexico. Needle-like to narrow lance-shaped leaves, to 3 in (8 cm) long. Flower-heads consist of up to 9 bright orange ray florets and orange disc florets, interspersed with dark hairs. Selected forms include: '**Classic**', which has 12 in (30 cm), white ray florets; '**Coral Beauty**', 12 in (30 cm), semi-double orange-pink; '**Crystal White**', 12 in (30 cm), white ray florets; '**Golden Eye**', 14 in (35 cm), white ray florets deepening to creamy yellow at the center; and '**Star White**', 12 in (30 cm), white ray florets arranged around a pure orange disc. Zones 9–11.

Zinnia elegans

syn. *Zinnia violacea*

☀ ❄ ↔ 8–18 in (20–45 cm)
↕ 8–40 in (20–100 cm)

These are popular garden flowers and some of the newer varieties are disease resistant. The numerous cultivars include: '**Aztek**', white flowers; '**Canary Yellow**', 30 in (75 cm), bright yellow flowers; **Dreamland Series**, 12 in (30 cm), double flowers, in many colors; '**Envy**', 30 in (75 cm), light green fully double flowers; '**Giant Purity**', 30 in (75 cm), fully double white flowers; '**Halo**', red flowers; **Mammoth Exhibition Series**, 30 in (75 cm), double flowers, large color range; **Oklahoma Series**, 36 in (90 cm) tall, semi-double and fully double flowers, wide color range; '**Polar Bear**', 30 in (75 cm), pure white double flowers; **Profusion Series**, 12 in (30 cm), single flowers, in red, orange, or white; '**Pulcino**', 16 in (40 cm), semi-double and fully double flowers, wide color range; **Ruffles Series**, 27 in (70 cm), double flowers in most colors; **Splendor Series**, 24 in (60 cm), fully double flowers in red, pink, orange, or yellow; **Sun Series**, 20 in (50 cm) tall, double flowers, in a variety of bright warm colors. Zones 9–11.

Zinnia angustifolia 'Coral Beauty'

Zinnia angustifolia 'Crystal White'

Zinnia elegans 'Aztek'

Zinnia elegans 'Canary Yellow'

Zinnia elegans, Dreamland Series, 'Dreamland Scarlet'

Z. elegans, Mammoth Exhibition Series, 'Mammoth Exhibition'

Zinnia elegans, Oklahoma Series, 'Oklahoma Pink'

Z. elegans, Oklahoma Series, 'Oklahoma Salmon'

Zinnia elegans, Oklahoma Series, 'Oklahoma White'

Zinnia elegans, Profusion Series, 'Profusion Cherry'

Zinnia elegans, Profusion Series, 'Profusion Orange'

Zinnia elegans, Ruffles Series, 'Cherry Ruffles'

Zinnia elegans, Ruffles Series, 'Pink Ruffles'

Zinnia elegans, Splendor Series, 'Pink Splendor'

Zinnia elegans, Sun Series, 'Desert Sun'

Zinnia elegans cultivar

Zinnia elegans 'Envy'

Zinnia elegans 'Halo'

Zinnia elegans 'Polar Bear'

Zinnia elegans 'Pulcino'

Z

Zinnia grandiflora
PRAIRIE ZINNIA

☀/◑ ❀ ↔ 24–32 in (60–80 cm)
↑ 12 in (30 cm)

Shrubby summer-flowering perennial from southern USA and northern Mexico. Narrow sparsely hairy leaves, to 1 in (25 mm) long. Very bright 1¾ in (40 mm) wide flowerheads with 3 to 6 broad golden yellow ray florets around an orange-red disc. Zones 9–11.

Zinnia haageana
syn. *Zinnia angustifolia* of gardens

☀/◑ ❀ ↔ 12–24 in (30–60 cm)
↑ 24 in (60 cm)

This species is an erect, bushy, summer-flowering annual from Mexico. Narrow, sparsely hairy to downy, lance-shaped leaves, to over 1¼ in (30 mm) long. Forms flowerheads with 8 to 9 golden to red-brown ray florets around an orange disc; fully double-flowered forms, such as 'Old Mexico', common in cultivation. 'Stargold', yellow-orange flowers. Zones 9–11.

Zinnia peruviana

☀ ❀ ↔ 12–16 in (30–40 cm)
↑ 36 in (90 cm)

Fast-growing summer-flowering annual found from southern USA to Argentina. Narrow, bright green, lance-shaped leaves, to nearly 3 in (8 cm) long. Flowerheads borne on broad stems held clear of the foliage, with up to 15 red, dusky tangerine, or yellow ray florets, to 1 in (25 mm) long, around a yellow to purple-black disc. 'Yellow Peruvian' has yellow flowerheads ageing to gold. Zones 9–11.

ZIZIPHUS

This tropical and subtropical genus consists of 80 or so species of evergreen or deciduous trees and shrubs in the buckthorn (Rhamnaceae) family. Some have spiny branches with double armaments—one hooked and one straight thorn at each node. They have alternate shiny green leaves, mostly with 3 prominent veins from the base. The insignificant flowers are small, greenish, white, or yellow and arranged in axillary clusters; they are followed by small fleshy fruits that are sometimes edible. The genus is best known in horticulture for *Z. jujuba*, the jujube, which has been cultivated in China since antiquity.
CULTIVATION: *Ziziphus* species are ideally grown in a deep moisture-retentive soil that is well drained. They prefer a sunny position. Shelter from strong winds and water regularly during the growing season. Tip prune to maintain compact growth. Propagate from seed or root cuttings. Improved fruiting varieties may be obtained from grafting.

Zinnia haageana 'Stargold'

Zinnia peruviana 'Yellow Peruvian'

Ziziphus jujuba
CHINESE DATE, CHINESE JUJUBE, COMMON JUJUBE

☀ ❀ ↔ 12 ft (3.5 m) ↑ 30 ft (9 m)

Widely distributed from southern Europe to China. Fast-growing, deciduous, spiny tree. Oval to lance-shaped serrated leaves. Axillary clusters of tiny creamy flowers, in late spring. Dark red plum-like fruits, eaten fresh, dried, preserved or candied. Zones 7–10.

Ziziphus mucronata
BUFFALO THORN

☀ ❀ ↔ 10–20 ft (3–6 m)
↑ 17–35 ft (5–10 m)

Evergreen tree from South Africa with crooked trunk and drooping branches, usually covered with pairs of spines, one curved and one straight. Glossy drooping leaves are conspicuously 3-veined from the base. Inconspicuous yellowish flower clusters. Roundish russet-colored fruit containing a dry meal-like pulp. Used in traditional medicine for many ailments. Zones 7–9.

ZOYSIA
ZOYSIAGRASS

This genus of 5 creeping, warm season, perennial grasses in the grass (Poaceae) family comes from Southeast Asia. These plants grow from both runners and rhizomes. Leaves are rounded to slightly flattened, stiff, and sharply pointed, with occasional hairs near the base, smooth margins and fine to coarsely textured surfaces. Short, slender, and sheathed terminal spikes or spikelets, each with 1 flower, on short stalks. This genus takes its name from the eighteenth-century Austrian botanist, Karl von Zois.
CULTIVATION: They are normally planted in the late spring and early summer for lawn turf as plugs. Adaptable to most soils in the full sun; they are also shade-tolerant.

Zoysia 'Emerald'

☀ ❀ ↔ 1–2 in (25–50 mm)
↑ 1–2 in (25–50 mm)

Developed for lawn turf use. Hybrid between *Z. japonica* and *Z. tenuifolia*. Creeping, fast-growing, dark emerald green, perennial grass growing from underground runners. Fine dense texture, cold- and drought-tolerant. Zones 1–9.

Zoysia tenuifolia ★
KOREAN VELVET GRASS, MASCARENE GRASS

☀ ❀ ↔ 1–2 in (25–50 mm)
↑ 1–2 in (25–50 mm)

Extremely slow-growing, creeping, ornamental, perennial grass from Southeast Asia. Spreads by underground rhizomes. Low-growing ground cover, forms clumps or mounds. Fine, short, wiry, dark green leaves, to 2 in (5 cm) long. Narrow oblong spikelets of green flowers, to 2 in (5 cm) long, in late summer. Zones 6–10.

× *ZYGOPABSTIA*
syn. × *Zygocolax*

× *Zygopabstia* is a hybrid combination between the sympodial orchid genera *Zygopetalum* and *Pabstia* (previously known as *Colax*), belonging to the family Orchidaceae. These are more compact plants than many of the zygopetalums, and have the advantage of blooming more than once a year. Until recently, the hybrid genus × *Zygopabstia* was well known as × *Zygocolax*. The individual flowers are 1½–3½ in (35–90 mm) across.
CULTIVATION: These plants enjoy intermediate temperatures, under moist and shaded conditions. Avoid direct sunlight, as the leaves are prone to scorching if exposed for even short periods. The plants must be in a humid environment with plenty of air circulation, otherwise the leaf tips will dry off and the foliage may spot. Sphagnum moss or fine-grade bark is a suitable medium, and they must not be over potted. Their main bloom period is winter and spring, but many of these hybrids will also bloom at other times of the year once a new growth is semi-mature. Propagation of these orchids is by division.

× *Zygopabstia* Gumeracha

☀ ❀ ↔ 4–20 in (10–50 cm)
↑ 8–24 in (20–60 cm)

A fourth generation hybrid with the species *Zygopetalum maxillare*, *Z. intermedium*, *Z. crinitum*, and *Pabstia jugosa* in its background. The blooms are green, overlaid with dark brown and maroon markings. The labellum is sometimes marked with white or cream. Zones 9–11.

Ziziphus mucronata, in the wild, Karoo, South Africa

Ziziphus jujuba

Zygopetalum, Hybrid,
Alan Greatwood

Zygopetalum, Hybrid,
Blanchetown

Zygopetalum, Hybrid,
Imagination

Zygopetalum, Hybrid,
Kiwi Dust

Zygopetalum, Hybrid,
Titanic

ZYGOPETALUM

This is a small genus of about 16 terrestrial and epiphytic sympodial orchids (family Orchidaceae) native to South America. They have tall spikes of large, showy, long-lasting and highly fragrant flowers. Zygopetalums are hardy orchids that enjoy similar conditions to cymbidiums, and are often grown with them. There have been many hybrids made, within both *Zygopetalum* and related genera, to produce compact plants and expand and intensify the color range of the blooms.
CULTIVATION: Most zygopetalums may be grown in commercially available "orchid composts," which are generally free draining but retain some moisture. Some growers use fine-grade pine bark, others make up their own combinations to suit their conditions and watering frequency. The epiphytic species prefer a mix incorporating a high percentage of coarse bark. They like deep pots to accommodate the vigorous root system. The plants respond to frequent watering and feeding, and like to be kept moist year-round, with increased watering and fertilizing from spring to autumn

× *Zygopabstia* Gumeracha

while actively growing. They need high humidity and good air circulation, or leaf tips will dry off and foliage may spot. Propagate by division.

Zygopetalum crinitum
☼/◐ ❄ ↔ 4–16 in (10–40 cm)
↕ 8–24 in (20–60 cm)

Winter- to spring-flowering species from Brazil, with upright inflorecences of up to 8 blooms, 3 in (8 cm) wide; yellow-green petals and sepals streaked with dark brown. Labellum is white with purplish red veins and covered in dense, fine, short hairs. Zones 9–11.

Zygopetalum intermedium
☼ ❄ ↔ 4–16 in (10–40 cm)
↕ 4–16 in (10–40 cm)

From Brazil. Similar to *Z. mackayi*. Fleshy, green petals and sepals blotched with deep maroon-purple. Labellum is fan-shaped and white with dark lilac veining. Up to 6 blooms, 3 in (8 cm) wide, appear on thick erect spikes, in autumn–winter. Zones 9–11.

Zygopetalum mackayi
☼ ❄ ↔ 4–16 in (10–40 cm)
↕ 4–16 in (10–40 cm)

From Brazil. Fleshy, green petals and sepals blotched with maroon-purple. Fan-shaped labellum is white with dark lilac veining. Up to 10 blooms, 3 in (8 cm) wide, are borne on thick erect spikes, in autumn–winter. Zones 9–11.

Zygopetalum maxillare
☼ ❄ ↔ 4–16 in (10–40 cm)
↕ 4–16 in (10–40 cm)

From Brazil and Paraguay. Climbing species with up to 6 bright green, 2½ in (6 cm) wide flowers with

Zygophyllum stapfii, in the wild, Namibia

varying degrees of red-brown blotches, in winter and spring. The labellum is bright bluish purple. Long, distinct rhizome between pseudobulbs and ascending habit, makes it suitable for slab culture using treefern as medium. Zones 9–11.

Zygopetalum Hybrids
☼ ❄ ↔ 4–16 in (10–40 cm)
↕ 4–16 in (10–40 cm)

Most of the hybrids have a heavy influence from *Z. mackayi*, and this has led to a similarity with many of the crossings. More compact plants have been obtained from using *Z. maxillare*, which may also bloom more than once a year. Flower size is 2½–3 in (6–8 cm) across the petals. **Alan Greatwood**, very shapely and round dark brownish maroon blooms with a distinctive greenish edge to the petals and sepals, the labellum white, with dark lilac veining; **Blanchetown**, light tan blooms with purple labellum that has darker

striping; **Imagination**, dark brown blooms with a deep purple labellum; **Kiwi Dust**, green blooms barred with maroon markings and a contrasting white and deep lilac labellum; and **Titanic**, robust hybrid, highly fragrant. Zones 9–11.

ZYGOPHYLLUM
CAPER BEAN

This genus of 80 herbs or shrubs with jointed branches, members of the twin-leaf (Zygophyllaceae) family, is found from the Mediterranean to central Asia, southern Africa, and Australia. The flowers grow from the leaf axils, solitary or in pairs, with overlapping fleshy sepals. Leaves are simple or sometimes divided into 2 fleshy leaflets with 2 spiny stipules. The fruit is a winged or angular capsule.
CULTIVATION: In cool areas, caper beans need the protection of a greenhouse. Propagation is from seed or by cuttings taken in spring.

Zygophyllum stapfii
DOLLAR BUSH
☼ ❄ ↔ 12–20 in (30–50 cm)
↕ 4–10 in (10–25 cm)

Very distinctive species from the Namib desert in southern Africa. Derives moisture from fog and dew condensation channeled to the roots from its flat, round, succulent leaves. Leaves also collect windblown sand. Sprays of tiny cream flowers appear sporadically. Zones 10–11.

Zygopetalum crinitum

Zygopetalum intermedium

Zygopetalum mackayi

Z

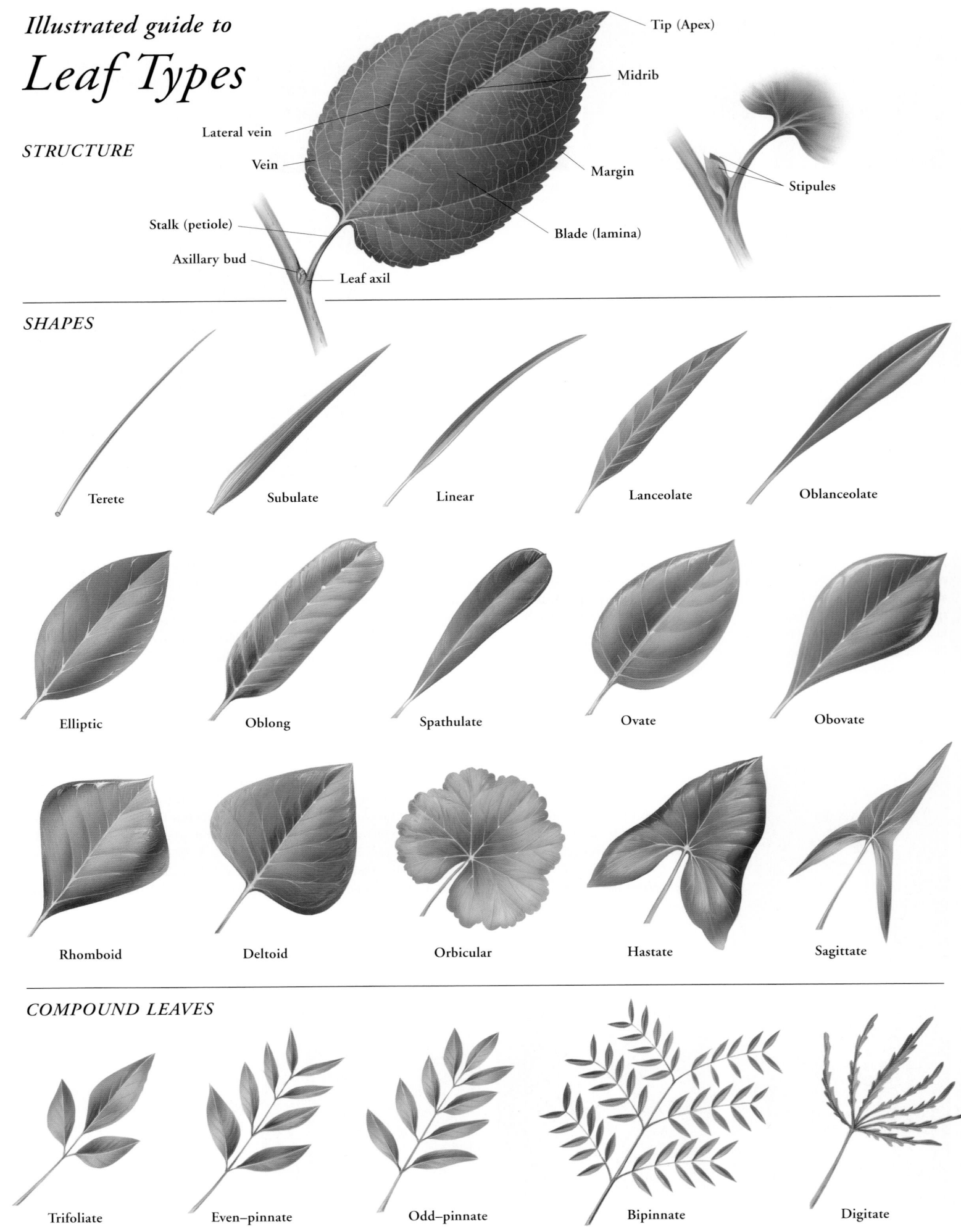

Illustrated guide to
Leaf Types

STRUCTURE

Tip (Apex)

Midrib

Lateral vein

Vein

Margin

Stipules

Stalk (petiole)

Blade (lamina)

Axillary bud

Leaf axil

SHAPES

Terete

Subulate

Linear

Lanceolate

Oblanceolate

Elliptic

Oblong

Spathulate

Ovate

Obovate

Rhomboid

Deltoid

Orbicular

Hastate

Sagittate

COMPOUND LEAVES

Trifoliate

Even–pinnate

Odd–pinnate

Bipinnate

Digitate

ARRANGEMENTS

Opposite
Decussate

Opposite
Distichous

Alternate
Distichous

Alternate
Spiral

Whorled

MARGINS

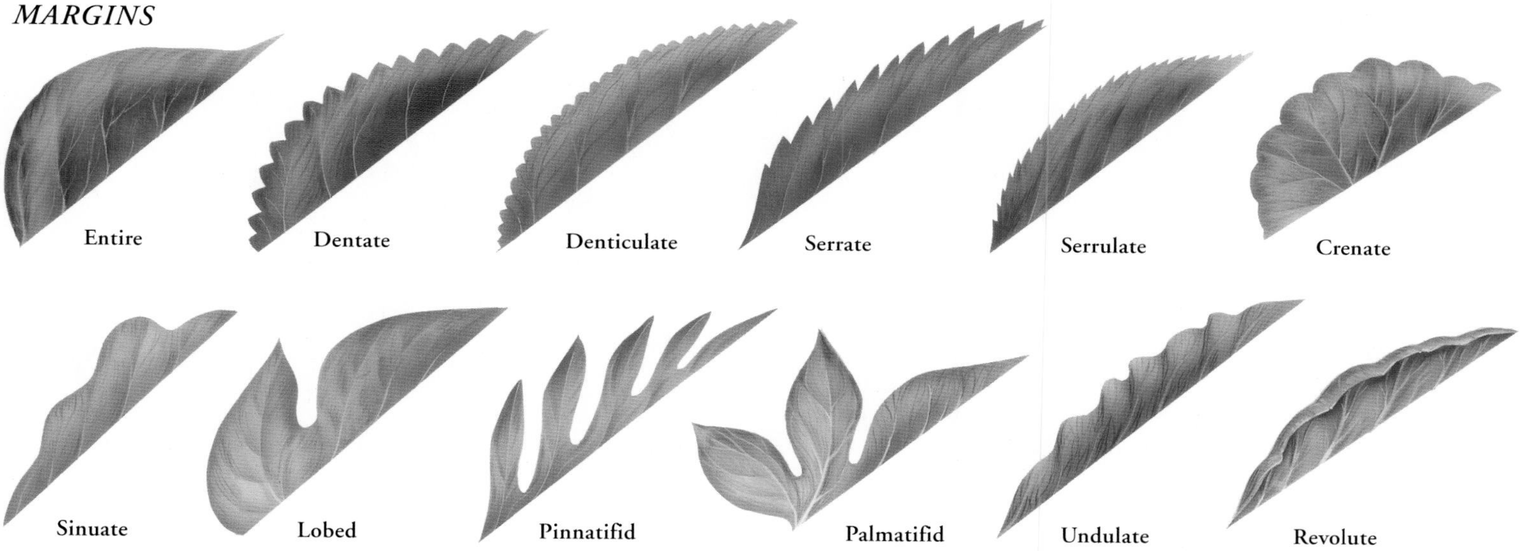

Entire

Dentate

Denticulate

Serrate

Serrulate

Crenate

Sinuate

Lobed

Pinnatifid

Palmatifid

Undulate

Revolute

BASES

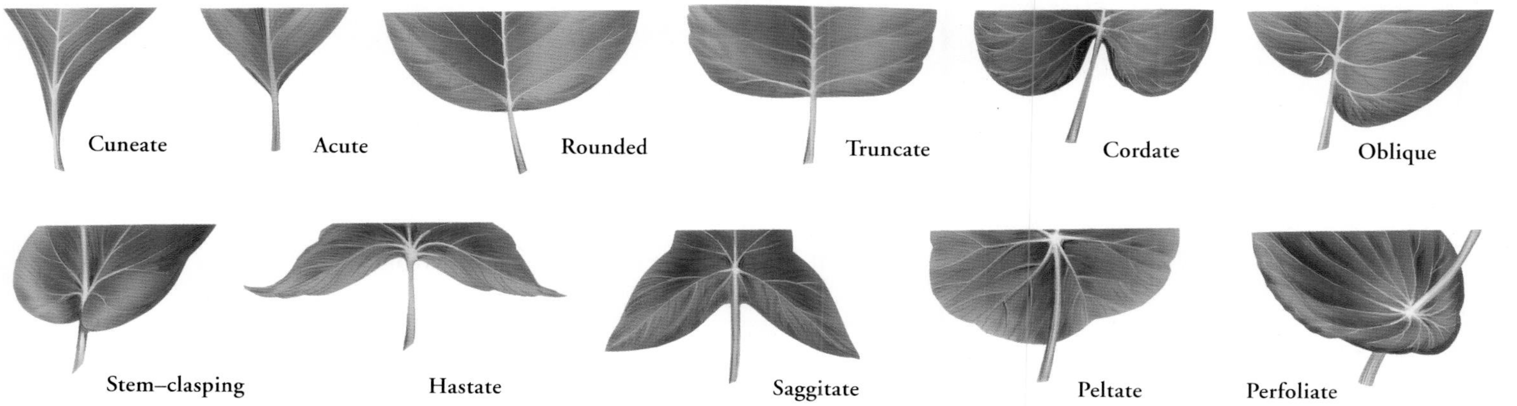

Cuneate

Acute

Rounded

Truncate

Cordate

Oblique

Stem–clasping

Hastate

Saggitate

Peltate

Perfoliate

TIPS

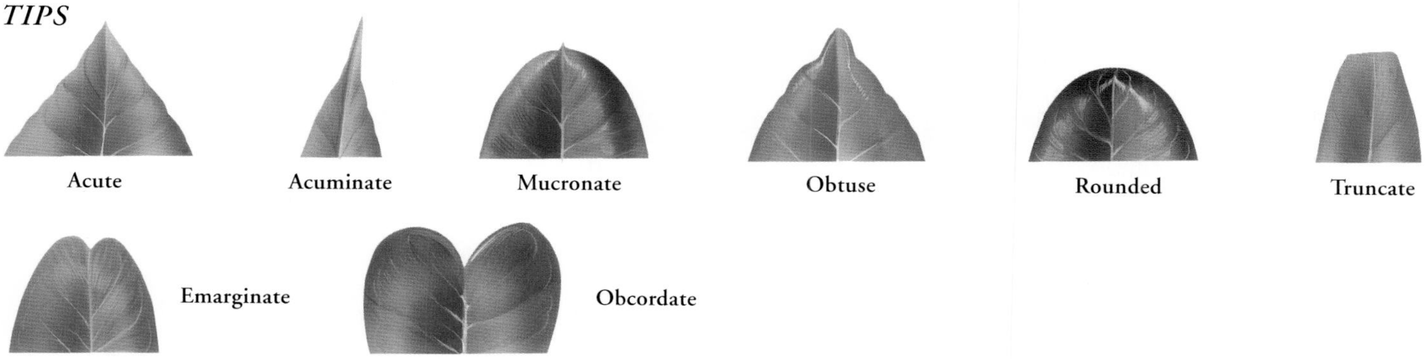

Acute

Acuminate

Mucronate

Obtuse

Rounded

Truncate

Emarginate

Obcordate

Illustrated guide to
Flower Types

STRUCTURE

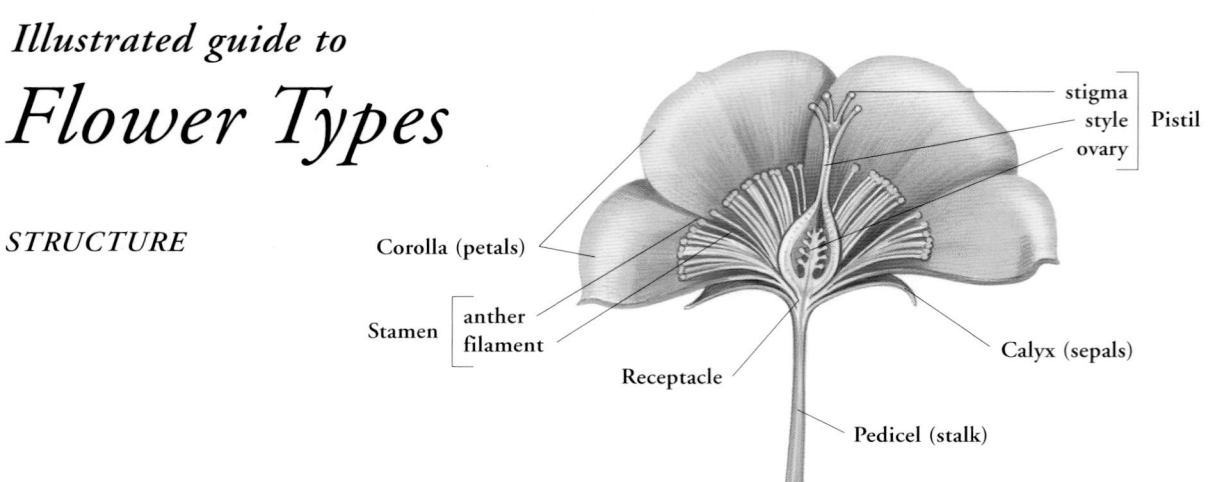

stigma
style — Pistil
ovary

Corolla (petals)

Stamen — anther
filament

Calyx (sepals)

Receptacle

Pedicel (stalk)

SHAPES

Star-shaped

Saucer-shaped

Cup-shaped

Bell-shaped

Tubular

Pitcher-shaped

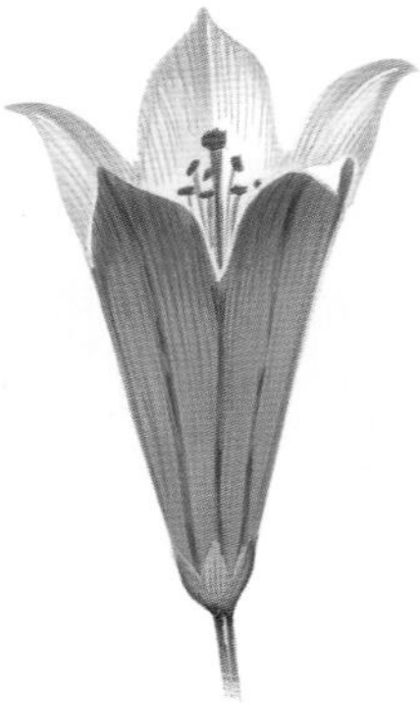

Funnel-shaped

Trumpet-shaped

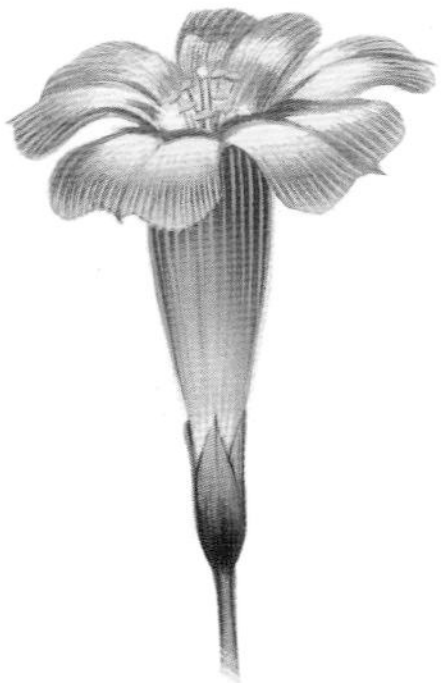

Salverform

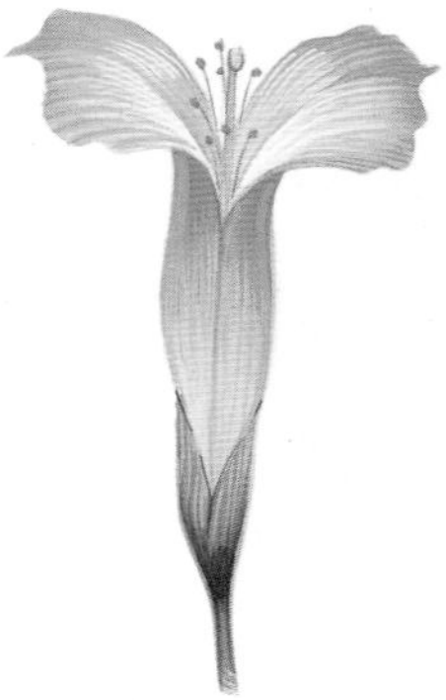

Two-lipped

ORIENTATION

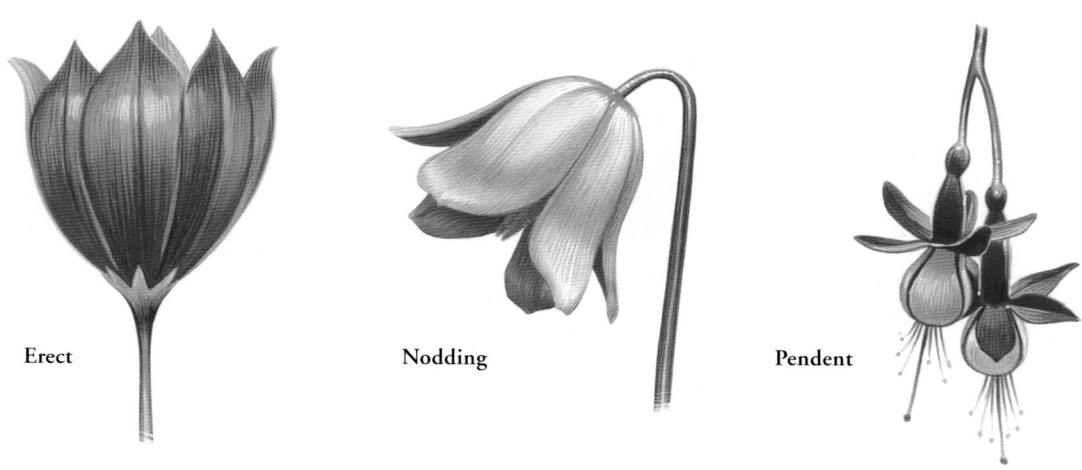

Erect

Nodding

Pendent

INFLORESCENCES

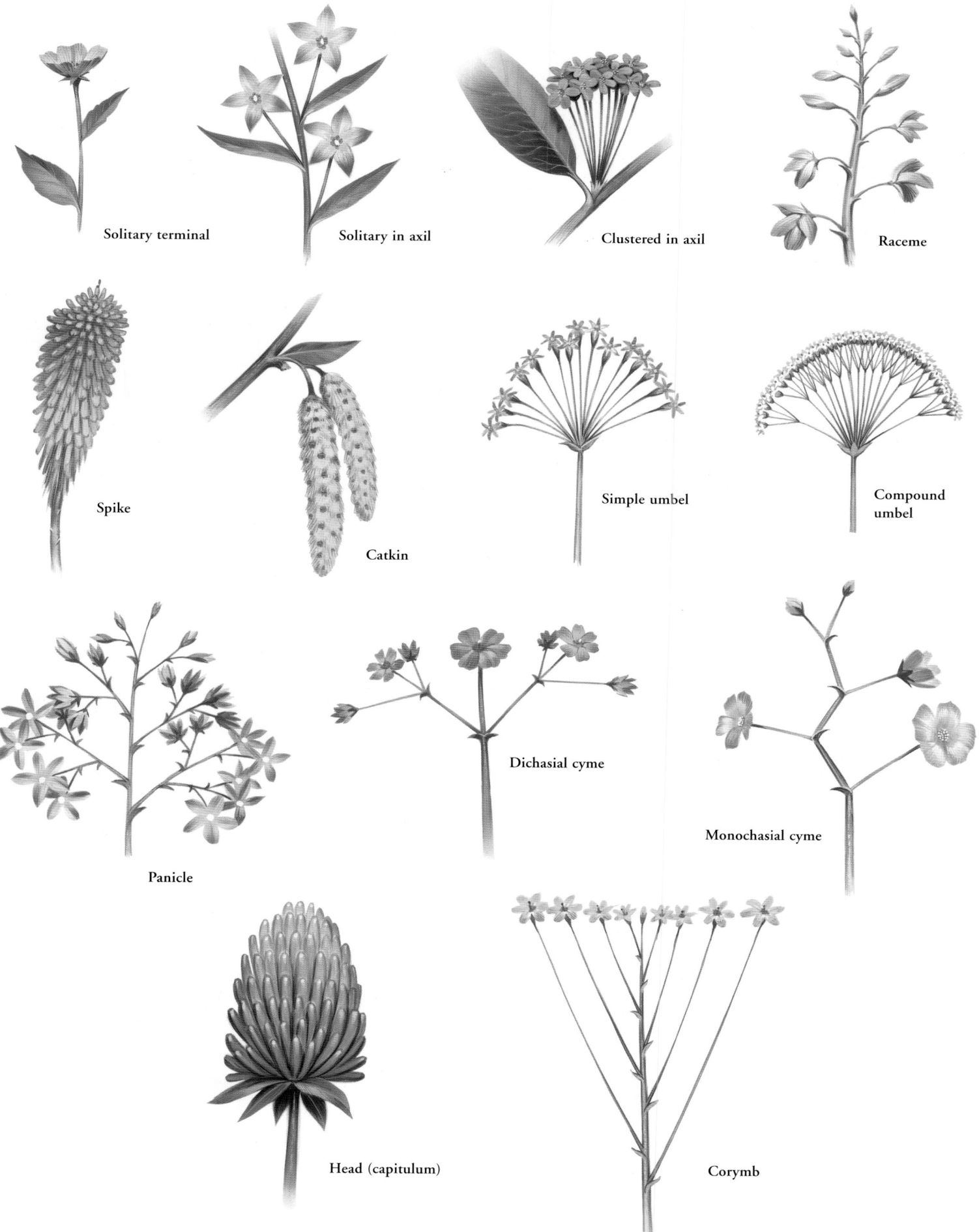

Solitary terminal

Solitary in axil

Clustered in axil

Raceme

Spike

Catkin

Simple umbel

Compound umbel

Panicle

Dichasial cyme

Monochasial cyme

Head (capitulum)

Corymb

Illustrated guide to
Fruit Types

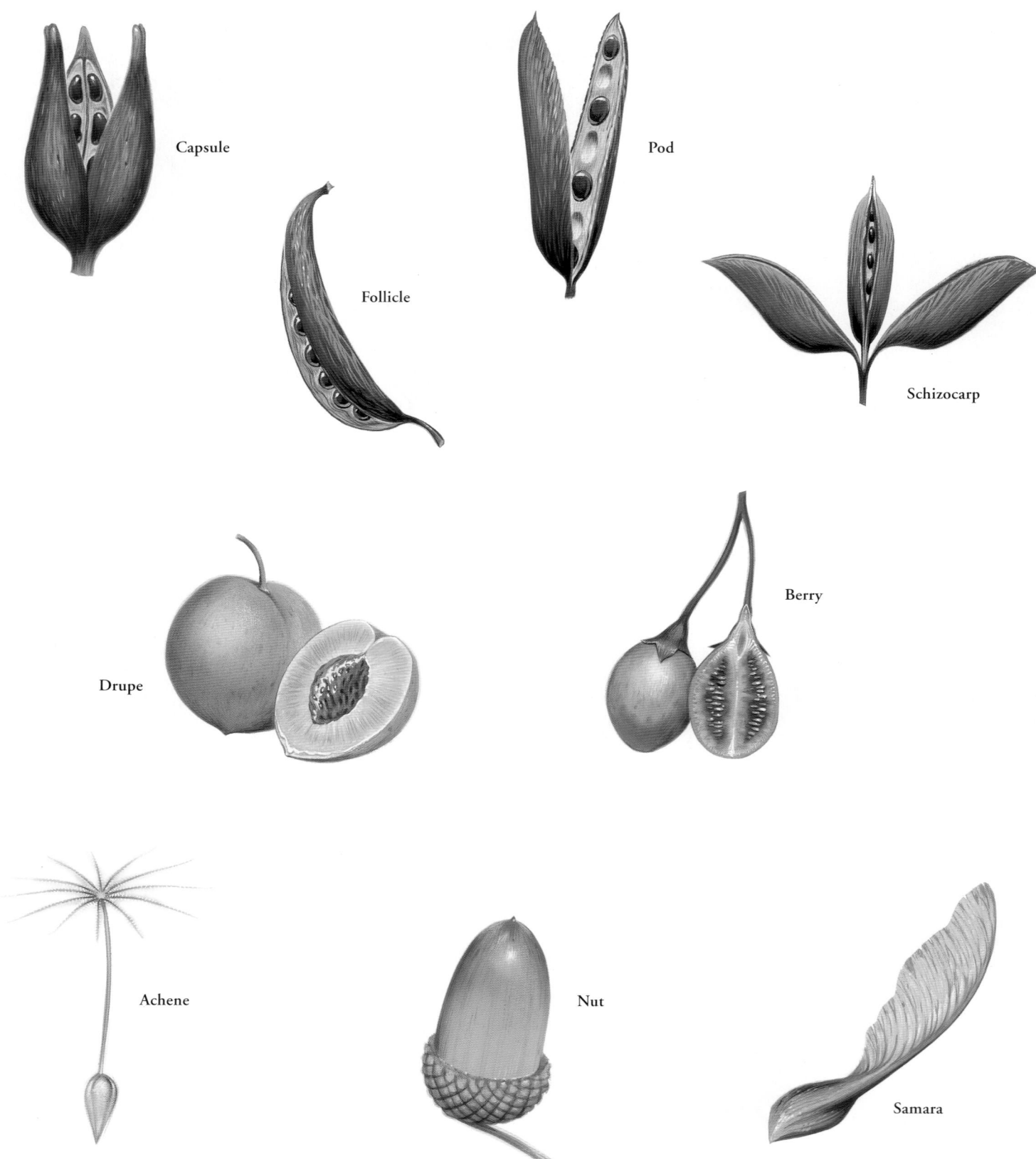

Capsule

Pod

Follicle

Schizocarp

Drupe

Berry

Achene

Nut

Samara

Glossary

Abscission Shedding of plant parts such as leaves by formation of a zone of weakness at their base, resulting in a clean break. The verb *abscise* is used, though *abscind* is historically correct.

Achene A small, dry, single-seeded fruit resulting from fertilization of a single carpel of a flower, as in *Potentilla*.

Acid (of soils) Having a pH below about 6. The more strongly acid soils are mostly high in organic materials such as peat; lime (calcium carbonate) is completely absent from them. Acid soils dominate in regions of higher rainfall. See also ALKALINE.

Acuminate (of leaf tips) With a drawn-out point, the convex margins changing to concave close to the point.

Acute (of leaf tips) Ending in a fine point, though not drawn out as in acuminate.

Adventitious (of roots or buds) Arising at various points along a stem rather than at base or apex or another such specific zone.

Aerial (of plant parts) Arising anywhere above the ground.

Aggregate fruit A head of separate fruitlets arising from the free carpels of a single flower, e.g., a blackberry.

Air layering A technique of propagation whereby a branch is stimulated to root by cutting the bark and wrapping a moisture-retentive medium such as sphagnum moss around the wound, the medium then wrapped in air-tight plastic. When roots form, the branch is cut off and planted in soil.

Alga (plural algae) Any of a large class of non-vascular plants including the seaweeds and many single-celled plants found in water, all containing photosynthetic pigments (not necessarily chlorophyll). In gardens algae are evident as green slime on damp paths, or as green filaments in ponds or scum on their surface. Copper sulphate is an effective algicide.

Alkaline (of soils) Having a pH above about 8. Alkaline soils usually contain lime in the form of calcium carbonate or calcium hydroxide. They occur naturally in regions of lower rainfall. See also ACID.

Alkaloid One of a large class of organic chemicals, mostly derived from plants, having strong, often toxic effects on humans and animals. The active principles of many well-known drugs, they include morphine, nicotine, cocaine, quinine, strychnine, and caffeine. Many poisonous plants contain alkaloids.

Alpine (of plants) Those adapted to high mountain environments where they are usually blanketed in snow during winter; they may be damaged by very severe frosts if not protected by snow, and in cold climates are therefore grown in "alpine houses" under glass. Alpine vegetation is the low herbs and shrubs growing above the treeline on high mountains.

Alternate (of the arrangement of leaves on a stem) Arising one from each node in a staggered formation. Many alternate leaf arrangements are also spiral, their points of attachment forming a spiral around the stem; others are alternate and DISTICHOUS, forming two rows more or less in the one plane.

Amphibious (of plant species) Able to grow either in water or on dry land.

Anemone-form (of a cultivar) Having a double flower with an outer circle of relatively flat petals around a dome of crowded inner petals or staminodes.

Angiosperms The flowering plants, now classified as DIVISION Magnoliophyta, defined by possession of true flowers and seeds fully enclosed in fruit. The vast majority of the world's larger land plant species are angiosperms, the main exceptions being the conifers, cycads and ferns.

Annual A plant species or variety with a life span of 1 year or less, within which time it flowers and fruits. Annuals depend entirely on seeds for reproduction.

Anther The pollen-containing part of a stamen, the other part being the filament (stalk).

Aphid Small sap-sucking insect of the family Aphididae, mostly wingless and translucent. Aphids feed on young foliage in large numbers and may weaken a plant. They excrete sugary droplets that attract ants.

Apical Positioned at the apex or outer end of a stem, branch, leaf, etc.

Apomict Plant that appears to reproduce by pollination and subsequent fruiting with viable seed, but in fact produces offspring with no genes from the pollen parent (nor, if self-pollinated, with any recombining of genes), so that offspring are effectively clones of the parent.

Appressed (adpressed) Lying flat against the part from which the organ arises, e.g., leaves appressed to the stem, leaf hairs appressed to the leaf.

Approach graft Type of graft where SCION plant is kept growing on its own roots and rootstock with its own foliage until the graft has "taken" (i.e. tissues have fused), the connections with scion roots and rootstock foliage then severed. In the case of trees this may require that a potted rootstock is raised up level with branch of scion tree.

Aquatic A plant species that grows in water for at least the greater part of its life cycle. Aquatics are divided into submerged, emergent, and floating.

Arboretum A park or similar area devoted to a collection of trees, for scientific study and/or horticultural trial.

Arboriculture The science and art of growing trees for ornament and amenity (if for timber the term *silviculture* is normally used)

Arborist Person trained in the maintenance and repair of trees, including control of diseases and pests; replacing the older term "tree surgeon."

Arctic (of climates) Those of lands above the Arctic Circle (latitude 66 deg 30 min North).

Areole Characteristic organ of the cacti (family Cactaceae) positioned at each stem node: a small area or point from which emerge spines, bristles, and hairs as well as leaves (often tiny or short lived) and potentially flowers. Botanists interpret areoles as highly modified SHORT SHOOTS.

Aril Attachment to a seed originating as an outgrowth of the seed stalk, fleshy and attractive to birds or animals who disperse the seed. The flesh of the lychee is an aril.

Aroid Any member of the MONOCOT family Araceae, consisting of tropical herbs, shrubs, and climbers such as *Philodendron* species as well as temperate perennials such as *Arum* and *Arisaema* species. All aroids have tiny flowers crowded onto a SPADIX which may be enclosed in bud by a SPATHE.

Aromatic As normally used, of plant smells; those of a spicy, resinous, or musky character, and often associated with foliage or fruit, in contrast to the sweet smells of flowers normally described as "fragrant."

Articulate (of a stem) Having constrictions (as in *Opuntia*); (of a leaf or leaflet) having a "joint," often swollen or constricted, in the stalk.

Ascending (of stems, branches, inflorescences) Rising at a steep angle but not vertical.

Aspect The way a slope faces, which determines how much sunshine it gets, and whether in morning, evening, or at midday; or more generally the outlook of a part of a house or garden especially in relation to sunlight.

Auricle Small ear-like lobe usually at or close to the base of an organ such as a leaf.

Auriculate (of leaves, etc.) Possessing AURICLES (usually paired).

Auxin A plant "hormone," any of a large range of organic chemicals occurring naturally in plant tissues in small traces, essential for the control of all growth processes including the differentiation of embryonic tissue into stem, roots, leaves, etc., the responses of the plant to light, temperature, and seasons, and the initiation of flowering. Artificially produced auxins can be used to promote rooting of cuttings, to initiate roots and shoots in laboratory tissue culture (see MERICLONE), to hasten or retard fruiting, and for various other purposes.

Awn A bristle-like projection from a plant organ, used mainly of fruiting structures, for example, the awns of a head of wheat.

Axil The inner angle between an organ such as a leaf and the organ that supports it, usually a stem.

Axillary (of buds, flowers, inflorescences) Arising from a leaf AXIL.

Axis General term for any STEM, RACHIS of INFLORESCENCE, or COMPOUND leaf, or center-line of a flower.

Backcross A hybrid resulting from crossing an existing hybrid with one of its parents, thereby increasing the proportion of genes from that parent.

Bamboo Member of the bamboo SUBFAMILY of the grass family (Poaceae), plants with long-lived aboveground stems, usually hollow, with thick strong walls and grass-like leaves.

Bark Outer layer of stem containing protective corky and fibrous tissues as well as the PHLOEM which conducts sugary sap downwards. Best developed in trees, often becoming very thick with age.

Basal At or near the base of a plant's trunk, stem, leaf, etc.

Basal offset A shoot sprouting from the base of larger shoot or stem, often easily detached and able to be used for propagation, e.g., of agaves or many bromeliads (where commonly called "pups").

Basal scales In *Lilium* and some other bulbous plants, the outer or basal scales of a bulb, which can be detached and used for propagation, with plantlets arising from their lower edges.

Bean Pod or plant of legume genera such as *Phaseolus*, *Vigna*, or *Lablab*, used as vegetables or pulses, or applied more loosely to various leguminous (or even non-leguminous) plants with bean-like fruits.

Bedding plants Mostly compact colorful plants used for ornamental effect when mass-planted in display beds; traditionally annuals, short-lived perennials, or bulbs, but more recently frost-tender foliage plants, shrubs, and grasses have become widely used for summer bedding.

Berry In botanical usage, a fleshy fruit in which seeds are embedded without being surrounded by a fibrous or hard layer (as in a DRUPE). Tomatoes and blueberries are examples. In popular usage, berries include such fruits as blackberries and mulberries which are quite different in structure.

Biennial A plant that completes its life cycle within two years and then dies. It may flower and fruit in each of the two years, or only in the second year.

Bifoliate Having only 2 leaves per shoot; used in particular for species and hybrids of the orchid genus *Cattleya* with 2 leaves per pseudobulb, as opposed to the unifoliates with only one.

Bigeneric hybrid Generic hybrid (especially of orchids) with genes from 2 different genera, as opposed to multigeneric hybrids with genes from 3 or more genera.

Binomial A scientific name consisting of two parts, the genus name and the specific epithet. *Homo sapiens* and *Rosa gallica* are both binomials.

Bipinnate (of compound leaves) Divided pinnately into leaflets (pinnae) that are themselves further divided into smaller leaflets (pinnules). *Gleditsia* and *Jacaranda* are examples.

Bipinnatifid (of leaves) Deeply lobed in a pinnate manner, with the lobes again lobed pinnately.

Bisexual (of plants) Having flowers or cones of both sexes on the one plant; (of flowers) having both functional male and functional female organs present.

Blade The flat part of a leaf, as opposed to the stalk.

Bloom General term for a flower or flower-like inflorescence such as a daisy; or, on leaf or fruit surfaces, a thin, delicate, white, or bluish film of wax, as on grapes or plums.

Blossom A flower, or flowers in mass as on orchard trees, or used to designate the part of a fruit bearing floral remains, as in the "blossom end" of a pumpkin or marrow (*Cucurbita*) as opposed to the "stalk end."

Bog garden Area of garden, often at edge of a pond, devoted to plants that love wet boggy soil.

Bole The trunk of a tree below the first branch.

Bolting (of leaf vegetables) Progressing too early from production of edible leaves or shoots to elongation of inflorescence, flowering, and seeding; a response to planting too late in the season or to interruptions in watering or fertilizing.

Bonsai The practice of dwarfing trees in containers in a style originated in Japan (contrast with Chinese PENJING).

Botanical name The internationally recognized name of a plant species, genus, family, etc., usually derived from Latin or Latinized Greek elements, and published in conformity with the *International Code of Botanical Nomenclature*.

Botany The scientific study of plants.

Bottom heat In plant propagation, gentle heat provided from below the medium, used for striking cuttings or germinating seed, now usually achieved with buried electric elements (cables) below a layer of gravel or other porous material on which the propagating containers rest.

Botrytis Botanically, a genus of microscopic fungi that cause rots in various flowers and fruits, perhaps best known when producing "noble rot" of wine grapes left too long on the vine, which when finally picked produce sweet wines of a remarkable flavor.

Bract A modified leaf associated with a flower or an inflorescence; not to be confused with a sepal, though in some plants bracts may mimic sepals.

Bracteole A small bract attached to a flower stalk (pedicel), usually between the bract and the flower.

Bristle A stiff outgrowth of a plant organ such as a stem, leaf, sepal, or fruit; intermediate between a hair and a prickle, as on the stems of some rose species.

Bromeliad Any member of the large MONOCOT plant family Bromeliaceae, in the wild virtually confined to the Americas, consisting of evergreen perennials and subshrubs, many of them EPIPHYTES often with leaf-bases forming a funnel-shaped "tank" that collects rainwater; inflorescences often with colorful bracts. Grown in quantity as indoor plants, collected by enthusiasts.

Bud The early stage of a flower or group of flowers, or of a leafy shoot (vegetative bud), before expanding or elongating.

Budding A propagation technique similar to grafting except that the scion is no more than a single vegetative bud sliced off with a sliver of bark, inserted in contact with the rootstock's CAMBIUM through a slit in its bark and bound securely until the tissues unite.

Bulb Storage organ of herbaceous perennials consisting of expanded fleshy leaf bases arranged in concentric layers. A bulb is tunicate if the leaf bases are all encircling, as in an onion, or scaly if they are narrower but with overlapping edges, as in a lilium.

Bulbil, bulblet Small bulb or bulb-like shoot developing from the base of a parent bulb or from various other parts of a plant, e.g., leaf axils in some *Lilium* species, inflorescence in some onions; readily used for propagation.

Burr Small, usually dry fruit (often perceived as a "seed") armed with spines or bristles that are usually hooked or barbed, allowing it to cling to animals' fur or skin (or human clothing), and its contained seed to be carried far from the parent plant—an effective means of distance dispersal and a feature of many WEEDS.

Buttress A flange-like projection at the base of a tree trunk. Mostly found on tropical trees, buttresses aid in spreading the connection between trunk and roots when thin or poorly aerated soils make for a very shallow root system that provides poor anchorage.

Cactus (plural cacti) Any member of the large American plant family, Cactaceae, consisting mainly of spiny, leafless, succulent plants. There are many other succulents that are not cacti, although the name is often carelessly applied to them.

Calcareous (of soils) Containing particles or nodules of calcium salts especially calcium carbonate. Calcareous soils are formed on chalk, coral, limestone, or dolomite but are also common in arid regions.

Callus A thickening or swelling of a stem or leaf stalk, in some cases a relic of an organ or connection that has almost disappeared in the course of evolution. Also used for cuttings, being the spongy mass of cells that precedes root development at the cut end, and in tissue culture for the similar mass of cells that first develops.

Calyx (plural calyces) The lowest or outermost of the layers attached to the receptacle of a flower. The calyx consists of SEPALS, that may be separate or partly or fully fused to one another and which are commonly green in contrast to the more colorful petals.

Cambium Layer of continuously dividing cells forming the boundary between wood and bark in the stems of dicotyledons and conifers. The dividing cells lay down tissues on either side, wood on the inner and bark on the outer, resulting in the stem increasing in diameter as long as growth continues.

Campanulate Bell-shaped, mostly referring to flowers with petals fused together, as in many campanulas.

Cane (in gardening) A long straight branch produced by one season's growth, as in raspberries. The cane of commerce comes from bamboos or climbing palms (rattans).

Canopy (of a tree) The whole of the foliage and outer parts of branches, being the part of the tree that shades the ground; (of a forest) the uppermost layer of tree crowns.

Capitate (of inflorescences) With flowers crowded into a head-like group at end of stem. Also used for a STYLE that broadens into a knob at the stigma end.

Capitulum (head) Inflorescence in which many flowers are crowded onto the end of a stem, and their individual stalks are all reduced to near-zero length.

Capsule A non-fleshy fruit derived from an ovary of two or more carpels that opens to release its seeds.

Carnivorous plants Plant species having the ability to catch living animals and extract nutrients from them. In practice nearly all such plants' prey are insects or other small arthropods, though some larger PITCHER PLANTS do occasionally catch small birds, mice, or lizards. Carnivorous plants use a variety of trapping mechanisms including sticky hairs and leaves modified into pitchers, but all digest prey by exuding enzymes that break down animal tissues into smaller molecules the plant can absorb.

Carpel The fundamental unit of a flower's gynoecium (female organ), usually differentiated into an OVARY containing OVULES (embryonic seeds), and a narrower STYLE tipped by a STIGMA which receives pollen. Carpels may be single or multiple in one flower, and multiple carpels are often fused together.

Catkin A type of spike, often pendulous, found mostly in wind-pollinated plants, with small flowers of reduced structure and usually of one sex only.

Caudex A more or less fleshy, long-lived, usually unbranched stem supporting a crown of fronds, as in cycads, or smaller branches and foliage in some desert plants.

Cauliflorous (of trees and shrubs) Producing flowers or inflorescences directly from the trunks and larger limbs rather than the smaller branches.

Cell One of the fundamental units, mostly of microscopic size, of which most tissues of higher plants are composed. Each cell contains a nucleus with chromosomes in which are encoded all of a plant's genetic information, hence the possibility of recreating a whole plant by laboratory culture of a small group of cells from various tissues.

Cellulose A complex carbohydrate, chemically a polymer of glucose, that forms most of the CELL walls of plants and is thus one of the most abundant organic chemicals in nature. It gives structural strength to plants (a role shared by LIGNIN in woody plants) and is the main component of dietary fiber. Cellulose is not broken down by the human digestive system and hence provides no energy, but many micro-organisms can convert it into useful food, as in the rumen of cattle.

Central spines In CACTI, the spines that stick straight out (more or less) from an AREOLE, in contrast to the RADIAL SPINES that radiate in a plane tangential to the plant body. Number, size, and other features of central and radial spines are often diagnostic for a cactus species.

Cephalium In CACTI, an area of stem, often at or near its apex but sometimes lower on stem, from which flowers emerge year after year from a dense mass of bristles and/or woolly hairs. A cephalium is a characteristic feature of certain genera, e.g., *Melocactus, Espostoa*. Some cactus specialists distinguish between a true cephalium and a PSEUDOCEPHALIUM, a lateral area of stem repeatedly producing flowers but with ribs not concealed.

Cereal The edible GRAIN harvested in quantity from certain GRASSES grown as CROPS, including wheat *(Triticum)*, barley *(Hordeum)*, oats *(Avena)*, rye *(Secale)*, maize *(Zea)*, and millet *(Setaria)*.

Chalk A porous lightweight form of limestone consisting almost entirely of calcium carbonate, occurring mainly in southern England, France, and parts of North America. It yields a powdery alkaline soil that greatly restricts a gardener's choice of plants.

Chaparral Characteristic vegetation of drier slopes of North America's west coast region, principally in California, consisting of dense scrub of evergreen shrubs and low trees, including species of *Quercus* and *Arctostaphylos*.

Chelate An organic chemical compound within whose molecule an element is tightly bound; in horticulture usually refers to iron chelates, in which iron, a major NUTRIENT element, is thus bound and prevented from recombining with other salts in the soil, so making it available to plants. Iron chelates are thus added where plants show symptoms of iron deficiency.

Chlorophyll The green pigment in plants, mainly in the leaves, that with the aid of light energy combines carbon dioxide from the air and water from the soil to create the sap sugars that are the building blocks of plant cell-wall materials such as cellulose and lignin. The process is called PHOTOSYNTHESIS.

Chlorosis Loss of chlorophyll resulting in yellow or white foliage, usually as a result of mineral deficiency or disease.

Chromosomes Microscopic thread-like bodies, a number present in the nucleus of each CELL of a plant and the site of nearly all of its genes. Rearrangement of chromosomes and portions of chromosomes during the creation of germ cells *(meiosis)* in pollen or ovules is what gives rise to variation in seedlings. A species or cultivar has a characteristic number of chromosomes per nucleus, normally in 2 matched sets in the vegetative plant—such a plant is termed a DIPLOID; if in 3 matched sets the plant is a TRIPLOID, if in 4, a TETRAPLOID, both resulting in abnormal breeding behaviour. The general term for a plants with more than 2 sets is POLYPLOID.

Circumpolar (of species' distributions) Occurring right around a hemisphere in arctic or cooler temperate regions. In practice this applies mainly to the Northern rather than the Southern Hemisphere. Circumpolar species occur in northern Europe, Asia, and North America and often also in Greenland, Iceland, and on higher mountains of the temperate zones such as the Alps, Pyrenees, Carpathians, Rockies, and Sierra Nevada.

Cladode A green stem or branch that has taken over the major part of a plant's photosynthetic function. Found on plants whose leaves fall at an early stage or are very small, e.g., the branches of *Spartium* or many cacti. See also CLADOPHYLL.

Cladophyll A cladode that is flattened and mimics a leaf, as in *Ruscus*.

Class One of the higher levels of plant classification: for example, the division Magnoliophyta (ANGIOSPERMS or flowering plants) is usually divided into 2 classes, the Liliopsida (MONOCOTYLEDONS) and the Magnoliopsida (DICOTYLEDONS). The content of a class or division is not fixed but may change as understanding of relationships progresses; for example, recent research has shown that the dicotyledons are an "unnatural" group in that the monocotyledons appear to have branched from them only *after* several "dicot" families had branched from the main lineage, and this will need to be reflected in any future classification that purports to be natural.

Claw In flowers, any basal narrowing of an organ such as a petal into a slender stalk-like portion (as in petals of *Lagerstroemia*), in which case the petal is said to be "clawed."

Clay Mineral substance forming the finest particles in most soils, swelling and becoming sticky when wetted. Clays consist mainly of hydrous aluminium silicates with smaller amounts of other minerals that are of major importance to plant nutrition.

Climber A plant species or variety able to climb to heights that its own stem could not support, allowing it to reach sunlight that might otherwise be blocked by competing plants. A variety of mechanisms enable climbers to support themselves on other plants, including spiraly twining stems, TENDRILS, clinging roots, hooked thorns, or even leaves with reflexed stalks.

Clone A group of plants that are genetically identical, usually resulting from propagation using cuttings, grafts, layers, division, or tissue culture. Most tree and shrub cultivars are single clones and repeated propagation can spread one clone around the world, for example *Rosa* "Iceberg."

Cloud forest Also called "mist forest," "elfin forest." Forest type occurring mainly on tropical mountains frequently enveloped in cloud throughout the year, with moisture-saturated air. Trees are evergreen, often low and crooked, with trunks and limbs draped in epiphytes such as mosses, lichens, ferns, orchids, bromeliads. Plants from these environments require high humidity and narrow temperature range, usually frost-tender.

Clubmoss Any primitive spore-bearing plant of family Lycopodiaceae, chiefly species of the genera *Lycopodium, Lycopodiella,* or *Huperzia*. Foliage moss-like but on a larger scale, spores borne in cone-like structures.

Column (in orchids) The fleshy structure in the flower's center consisting of fused style, stigma, and stamens. Similar structures are found in some other plant families.

Columnar (of growth habit) Shaped more or less like a column or cylinder.

Common name Name of a plant species that is not its botanical or scientific name and has no scientific status. Common names are generally in the language of the country where the plant is growing. A species may have many common names, or if obscure may never have acquired any.

Composite Any member of the very large DICOT family Asteraceae, the daisy family, from its alternative and more traditional name Compositae.

Compost Decayed or decaying ORGANIC matter used in gardening to improve SOIL or as a MULCH. Any plant material can be converted to compost by heaping it and keeping it moist, encouraging breakdown by fungi, bacteria, worms, and microfauna. Addition of animal MANURE or nitrogenous fertilizer will hasten the process. Other animal products such as meat or fish scraps can also be added, though with the disadvantage of bad smell or attraction of vermin. Good compost management and container design will promote spontaneous heating, which should kill weed seeds or bulbs as well as shortening composting time.

Compound (of a plant organ) Consisting of smaller units grouped together, so a compound leaf consists of two to many discrete leaflets, a compound inflorescence is a branched structure consisting of two or more basic units such as spikes, umbels, or heads.

Cone Reproductive organ of gymnosperms (conifers and cycads), consisting of scales arranged around a central axis; pollen cones have scales bearing tiny pollen sacs, while seed cones have scales with seeds attached to the surface.

Conifer Member of the largest group of gymno-sperms, the conifers, now classified as DIVISION Pinophyta; mostly trees with seeds and pollen borne in separate cones and leaves mostly needle-like or scale-like, containing resin. Largest conifer genera are *Pinus, Abies, Picea,* and *Cupressus.*

Conservatory An attachment to a house, glass-roofed or at least with glass external walls, in which cold-tender plants may be grown.

Container Any item in which a plant may be grown out of the ground. In the nursery industry container-grown plants are the major alternative to bare-rooted plants at point of sale. Common containers are tubes, pots, tubs, and hanging baskets.

Cool-temperate (of climatic regions) Those in the cooler half of the temperate zone, where winter frosts and snow are of regular occurrence; lands at sea level that lie approximately 40–60 degrees latitude.

Cordate (of leaves) Heart-shaped, with an indentation where the leaf stalk joins at the base; also used for the base only, regardless of overall shape.

Corm A swollen stem modified for the purpose of food storage and annual renewal, usually underground and upright, with a new corm or section of corm added above each growing season and an old one withering below.

Cormous (of a plant species) Having corms as its food-storage organ.

Corolla Collective term for the petals of a flower, which may be separate or wholly or partly fused into a tube, bell, or disc; the tubular part is then termed the corolla tube and the flared part the corolla LIMB, which may consist of corolla lobes (the free ends of the petals).

Corona A crown-like part of a flower, consisting of a ring of fused outgrowths from either the petals or stamens. Species of *Narcissus* have a prominent corona arising from the petals.

Corymb An inflorescence, usually a modified raceme, in which the stalks of the lower flowers are elongated to bring them to the same level as the upper flowers.

Cotyledon The first leaf produced by a germinating seed. Cotyledons of some plants (e.g., palms) remain enclosed in the seed; others are carried on the stem above the ground.

Creeper A plant species or variety that can rapidly spread horizontally over the soil surface to cover an area of ground (when alternatively called a PROSTRATE or GROUNDCOVER plant), or vertically to cover a wall or tree trunk, usually clinging by aerial roots or adhesive pads (as in *Parthenocissus* species, Virginia creeper). A vertical creeper may also be called a CLIMBER, but there are many climbers that are not creepers.

Crenate (of leaf margins) Scalloped, or with broadly rounded teeth separated by shallow indentations.

Crenulate As for crenate but with much smaller, more closely spaced teeth.

Crest (of irises) Ridge-like projection along the center-line of each of the fall (lower) petals near its base (in cacti and other succulents). A plant of any species with a growth aberration resulting in the growing point extending sideways into a line, which may become wavy or convoluted. Such plants can be propagated and appeal to some collectors. Sometimes termed CRISTATE.

Cristate Adjective for any plant organ of crest-like form. For cacti and succulents, see CREST.

Crop A planting of a single species or cultivar covering a large area and numbering usually thousands of plants, usually of annuals or biennials, and usually of edible plants. Common crop plants are the cereal grains (wheat, oats, barley, maize, etc.), pulses (soybean, field beans, chickpeas) and broad-acre vegetables such as potatoes or cabbages. Cropping usually involves ploughing and is often irrigated.

Cross A less formal term for hybrid, also applicable to plants resulting from cross-pollination of different races or cultivars within a species.

Cross-pollination The transmission of pollen from one plant to another plant that is not part of the same clone or cultivar, with resulting fertilization of its flowers.

Crown The part of a tree held up by the trunk, consisting of limbs, smaller branches, twigs, and foliage.

Crownshaft Part of some palms, formed by the sheathing frond bases wrapped around one another to form a smooth, usually green cylinder that forms an apparent continuation of the trunk.

Crozier (of ferns) An uncoiling new frond at the center of the shoot.

Cucurbit Any member of the DICOT family Cucurbitaceae, in particular of the genus *Cucurbita*, which includes pumpkins, marrows, squashes. and courgettes. Other important cucurbits are the melons (*Cucumis melo, Citrullus lanatus*), cucumbers (*Cucumis sativus*), and gourds (*Lagenaria*).

Culm The erect stem, usually hollow, of GRASSES including BAMBOOS and some other MONOCOTS such as SEDGES and RUSHES, as contrasted to the RHIZOME from which it arises. In most such plants it terminates in the INFLORESCENCE but in bamboos the culms may hardly ever bear flowers.

Culinary herb A HERB (in the popular not the botanical sense) grown for use in cooking, or more doubtfully in salads, rather than for its medicinal properties.

Cultivar A cultivated variety that has been given a distinguishing name. A cultivar is assumed to be constant in its horticultural qualities and able to be propagated with those qualities unaltered. Tree and shrub cultivars are nearly always single clones, selected either from the variation within a species or from hybrid seedlings between 2 or more species. Modern cultivars must be given names of non-Latin form. Their names are enclosed in single quotes and are capitalized, e.g., 'Golden Delicious.'

Cultivar group A group of cultivars sharing a common character or origin, e.g., *Prunus* Sato-zakura Group.

Cultivated (of a plant species) Established in culti-vation with its requirements known to gardeners.

Cuneate (of leaves) Wedge-shaped with stalk at narrowest end; also used for the leaf base alone.

Cupule (in oaks, *Quercus*) The small cup formed from fused bract scales that encloses the base of the acorn.

Cuticle The waxy outer coating of the surface layer of cells on a plant organ, especially on a leaf where its impervious nature prevents water loss by evaporation; instead water vapour moves through pores in the cuticle, or STOMATES, which can open and close as the plant requires.

Cutting A piece of plant stem (more rarely of leaf, root or rhizome) cut off the parent plant for purposes of propagation; its lower end is inserted in soil or a sterile medium such as sand until roots form and a new plant is obtained.

Cyathium (plural cyathia) Specialized unit of INFLORESCENCE in *Euphorbia* and some allied genera, consisting of a tiny UNISEXUAL flower surrounded by a ring of fleshy bracts, with NECTAR glands within. Cyathia are often grouped into larger CYMES, often with larger, colored, leafy bracts as in poinsettia (*Euphorbia pulcherrima*).

Cycad Member of the second largest group of GYMNOSPERMS after the CONIFERS, now classified as DIVISION Cycadophyta; plants with palm-like fronds and very large cones, the pollen and seed cones on separate plants. Largest genera are *Cycas, Encephalartos, Macrozamia,* and *Zamia.*

Cyme INFLORESCENCE in which each branch is terminated by a solitary flower, new flowering branches emerging laterally below the flower. If lateral branches are paired it is a dichasial cyme; if single, a monochasial cyme.

Daisy Flower, or correctly FLOWERHEAD, of family Asteraceae, more specifically those types with conspicuous RAY FLORETS radiating from the central mass of DISC FLORETS; for example, shasta and ox-eye daisies (*Leucanthemum*), though the original English daisy is *Bellis perennis*. Also used as a collective term for all plants of this family, although many of its genera do not have the daisy type of flowerhead.

Deadhead To remove spent and dead flowers on a regular, often daily basis, both for reasons of tidiness and to prolong flowering season by preventing the plant's food resources going into fruit and seed development.

Deciduous (of a plant species) Losing all leaves at a certain season of the year, usually winter in the case of cool-climate species, usually the dry season in the case of tropical species.

Decussate Arrangement of opposite leaves in which

each leaf pair is oriented at right angles to the next pair below it, resulting in four vertical ranks of leaves.

Dehiscent (of fruits) Splitting open at maturity to release seeds.

Deltoid (or deltate) (of leaves, bracts, etc.) More or less triangular in outline, though corners may be blunt.

Dentate (of leaf margins) With a row of more or less triangular teeth, their points directed outward rather than forward.

Denticulate Finely dentate, that is, with smaller and more closely spaced teeth.

Dicotyledon (or dicot) The larger of the two great classes into which the flowering plants (ANGIOSPERMS) are divided, the other being the MONOCOTYLEDONS. As the name implies, dicotyledons have two seed leaves and additionally they mostly have net-veined leaves, flower parts in multiples of four or five, and a CAMBIUM layer in the stems.

Digitate (palmate) Type of COMPOUND leaf in which the LEAFLETS are all attached to the apex of a common stalk, their individual stalks radiating like the spokes of an umbrella. Also used to describe a pattern of lobing in which the lobes appear to radiate from a central point, as in *Acer palmatum.*

Dimorphic Of 2 different shapes; in botany, most often describing leaves, for example in some AQUATICS where the emergent leaves may be quite different in shape from the submerged leaves.

Diploid Plant having 2 matching sets of chromosomes, as in most wild plants. See under CHROMOSOMES for more detail. Diploids reproduce sexually with greater freedom than POLYPLOIDS.

Dioecious (of a plant species) With male and female flowers borne on different plants, so that plants of both sexes need to be present for POLLINATION and fruit set. Flowers can be termed dioecious if of different sexes though borne on the same plant.

Disease Any kind of ill health or disfigurement of a plant caused by micro-organisms such as viruses, bacteria, fungi or nematodes, or by deficiency or excess of a particular nutrient element. Distinct from PESTS, a term applied to more visible insects or other fauna which attack the plant.

Disc floret One of the individual small flowers that make up the central disc of a DAISY flower (family Asteraceae), especially when these are different from the outer circle of longer-petalled RAY FLORETS, as in a sunflower.

Disjunct (of geographical distribution) Occurring wild in two or more widely distant areas; for example, the genus *Liquidambar* in eastern North America, Central America, China, and Turkey.

Dispersal The natural spread of a plant to new sites, usually by seed but sometimes by bulbs, pieces of stem or even detached leaves. A species' dispersal mechanism is the way it ensures this spread, e.g., by wind-carried seed, fruits eaten by birds which pass the seed, fruits that hook onto animal fur or human clothing.

Dissected (of leaves, bracts, petals, etc.) Deeply divided into many small or narrow segments, as in a carrot or parsley leaf.

Distichous (of leaf arrangement) Forming two rows or ranks, regardless of whether leaves are OPPOSITE or ALTERNATE; contrasted with spiral, DECUSSATE.

Diurnal (of a species' flowering habit) Opening its flowers during the daytime, generally in the morning; contrasted with NOCTURNAL, flowers opening late afternoon or at dusk.

Division The most simple means of propagation of most clump-forming perennials, usually achieved by lifting the whole plant out of the soil or its container and cutting through the root-crown or rhizomes with a sharp blade or, for some kinds of plants, simply pulling apart, into two or more pieces, which are then replanted. Also one of the higher levels of plant classification (see also CLASS); the flowering plants are now treated as the division Magnoliophyta.

Dolomite Type of rock similar to limestone but consisting of magnesium carbonate in addition to calcium carbonate; ground into powder it is used as an amendment for acid soils.

Domatium (plural domatia) Small cavities in leaves, usually on the underside adjacent to the midrib or in angles of main veins; found mostly in tropical rain-forest trees. Their function is not fully understood but they commonly provide shelter for minute fauna such as mites.

Dormant In a state of suspended growth of a plant, usually during winter or other adverse season, and usually in a leafless state.

Dorsal The side of a plant organ that, when it is expanding from the bud, faces away from the axis to which it is attached; thus in a normal leaf the dorsal side is the underside; in an ORCHID flower the apparent upper SEPAL is referred to as the dorsal sepal, but that is because the stalks of most orchid flowers are twisted through 180 degrees.

Double (of garden flowers) Having more than the regular number of petals occurring in the wild form, found mainly in cultivars.

Drainage (of soils or growing media) The means by which excess water is enabled to flow away by gravity, so opening up air spaces needed by the roots of most plants for absorption of gases, principally oxygen. In gardens, good drainage is ensured by raising of beds, improving soil texture, or inserting special drainage pipes and/or gravel beds beneath the soil. In container-grown plants drainage is achieved by adequate number and size of holes in the base, and sometimes by a layer of coarse, rot-resistant material (traditionally "crocks" from broken clay pots) below the growing medium, which itself should be open and free-draining.

Drupe A fleshy fruit in which the seeds are separated from the outer flesh by a hard inner layer of bony, woody or fibrous tissue, as in plums *(Prunus)* or olives *(Olea).*

Drupelet A tiny drupe, usually resulting from fertilization of a single carpel of a many-carpelled flower, as in blackberries *(Rubus).*

Elepidote Literally "without scales," used to refer to the major subdivision of the genus *Rhododendron* in which the young leaves and stems lack a coating of minute scales. Most of the common larger evergreen rhododendrons and their hybrids are elepidotes, other species being divided largely between the LEPIDOTES (including the VIREYAS) and the azaleas.

Ellipsoid (of three-dimensional organs such as fruits) More or less elliptical in outline, usually with the long axis running through the stalk.

Elliptic (of leaves, petals, etc.) In the shape of an ellipse but commonly with both ends more or less pointed, with the widest part at the mid-point of the length.

Emarginate (of leaf apex) Slightly indented, though not with a very large, broad indentation.

Embryo The part of a seed after fertilization but before germination that will develop into the new plant; distinct from the seed's ENDOSPERM or food storage, and its seed coat.

Endemic (of a species, genus, etc.) Occurring in the wild only in one readily defined geographical region, e.g., *Franklinia* is endemic to Georgia, USA; *Sorbus anglica* is a British endemic.

Endocarp The innermost layer of a fruit wall, enclosing the seed or seeds; most readily distinguished in a DRUPE, when it is thickened and often tough and fibrous or hard and stony.

Endosperm A unique type of tissue found in seeds in larger or smaller quantity; in some plant groups forming the seed's major food storage, containing starch and/or sugars, oils, or proteins providing a source of energy for the germinating embryo. Some plants have endosperm with no internal cell walls. Cereal grains and coconuts are among the many seed types with large amounts of endosperm.

Entire (of margins of leaves, leaflets, petals, etc.) Smooth, without indentations or projections such as teeth or lobes.

Ephemeral (of plant species) An annual able to germinate and run through its full life-cycle in a short season, as little as a few months or even weeks, taking advantage of temporarily favorable conditions, e.g., a good fall of rain in a desert region.

Epicormic (of new growths) Sprouting from anywhere on or beneath the bark of a trunk or branch of a tree or shrub, not only from visible leaf or branch axils.

Epiphyte (of a plant species) One that habitually grows in the wild on the branches or trunk of a tree, well above the ground. Epiphytes do not feed on living tissues of their host but on dead bark, leaf litter, and dust, often using a symbiotic fungus to extract nutrients from these. Most cultivated orchids are epiphytes.

Erect Directed vertically upward or almost so.

Ergot A fungal disease of cereals and other grasses that results in the grain being replaced by a sticky mass of black spores, highly toxic to humans and other animals. Cows eating ergot-infested grass often abort their calves, while people who ate rye bread made from ergot-infested rye have suffered a range of severe symptoms and often deaths. Lysergic acid derives its name from ergot, from which it was first isolated; this is best known in the form of its compound lysergic acid dimethylamide or LSD.

Escape (or garden escape) A plant that has dispersed from where it was planted to nearby places, usually by seed (see DISPERSAL) or sometimes from dumped garden waste, but which may not have become fully naturalized.

Espalier A tree or shrub trained into a single vertical plane along a trellis or against a wall.

Essential oil Highly aromatic oil present in various parts of certain plants, often in minute cavities (oil glands), in leaves, petals, or fruit (e.g., in lemon rind), or mixed with resins as a surface exudation (e.g., in pelargoniums). In many plants the oil is a mixture of several pure oils such as peppermint oil (piperitol), lemon oil (citral), or oil of thyme (thymol) in varying proportions. Originally termed "essential" oils because each was considered the essence of a particular perfume.

Even-pinnate Pinnate with an even number of leaflets, typically with leaflets all in pairs including a terminal pair.

Everlasting Mostly species of the daisy family (Asteraceae) with flowerheads surrounded by dry, colored, often translucent bracts, appearing from a distance like ray florets; often the bracts do not deteriorate as the flowerhead ages and dies, making the bloom "everlasting" and suitable for dried arrangements. All species of *Helichrysum, Xerochrysum, Xeranthemum,* and *Rhodanthe* are classed as everlastings.

Evergreen (of a plant species) Maintaining its foliage through all seasons, although old leaves may be shed in larger numbers in certain seasons.

Eurasia Term used for the combined continent of Europe and Asia, usually including their major islands such as the British Isles and Japan.

Exotic (of a plant species) One that is not native to the country or region in question.

Exserted (of floral organs such as stamens and styles) Longer than and protruding from their enclosing parts such as a flower's corolla, e.g., many species and cultivars of *Fuchsia.*

F1 hybrid The First Filial generation (hence the abbreviation) that results from a cross between 2 genetically different plants. In F1 plants the genes are mixed more or less uniformly so there is little variation among the seedlings. The next, or F2 generation, raised from the seed of F1 plants, shows more recombinations of genes and hence greater variation in PHENOTYPES. Some crop plant cultivars are F1 hybrids, produced afresh for each batch of seed by mass pollination of one parental cultivar with another; they are valued for both uniformity and HYBRID VIGOR.

Falcate (of leaves) More or less sickle-shaped in outline, with one concave margin and one convex.

Family The next major category above GENUS in plant classification. A family may contain a single genus (e.g., Cercidiphyllaceae) or many genera (e.g., Fabaceae with around 650 genera). In modern systems all family names end in -aceae though the *International*

Code of Botanical Nomenclature allows several traditional alternatives including Leguminosae (for Fabaceae) and Compositae (for Asteraceae). A family name is grammatically a plural.

Fan palm One of the two major types of PALM in terms of FROND structure, with a fan-shaped frond (leaf) in which segments radiate from the end of the frond stalk. See also FEATHER PALM.

Fancy Used for classes of cultivars of certain genera, mostly with multicolored foliage (as in *Pelargonium*, Zonal Hybrids, Fancy-leaf) or bi- or multi-colored flowers (as in *Dianthus*, Garden Pinks, Fancy).

Fascicle A narrow bundle of leaves or stems, e.g., the needles of *Pinus* which mostly occur in fascicles of two, three or five.

Fastigiate (of growth habit) With many upright stems or branches of roughly equal size and closely crowded together.

Feather palm The other major type of palm (see FAN PALM) in which frond segments or leaflets are arranged along either side of a midrib, the whole frond resembling a feather.

Female (of flowers) Possessing no functional male organs, only female; (of plants) producing only female flowers or cones.

Fern Member of the largest living group of pteridophytes, the Filicopsida, characterized by fronds bearing wind-carried spores which germinate to produce small, delicate, sexual plantlets (gametophytes) with male and female organs. These rely on water droplets for fertilization, producing a new spore-bearing plant.

Fertile (of soil) Having adequate amounts of the major and minor mineral nutrients for plant growth; (of plants or flowers) bearing viable sexual organs.

Fertilize (in gardening and agriculture) To add NUTRIENTS to soil; (in botany) to bring pollen to a stigma and effectively pollinate it so that the pollen nucleus combines with the egg nucleus in the ovule.

Fertilizer Any material added to the soil to provide NUTRIENTS for plants, including COMPOST, MANURE, manufactured chemicals such as urea, potassium sulfate, or superphosphate, and liquid extracts such as fish emulsion.

Filament The stalk of a stamen, bearing the anther at its tip.

Fimbriate Fringed with hairs or very narrow, fine lobes.

Fireblight A virulent disease of POME fruit trees, its main symptom blackening of flowers and foliage as though burnt. Caused by bacteria of the genus *Erwinia*, it was first recognized in the USA in the eighteenth century but did not reach Europe until the twentieth century. Strict quarantine barriers are in place in many countries to prevent its spread. It can only be controlled by removing and burning all infected branches or whole plants.

Floret Any one of the small flowers in a dense inflorescence such as a head.

Flower The reproductive organ of all members of the flowering plants (angiosperms) consisting typically of a PERIANTH which is often differentiated into CALYX and COROLLA, a group of STAMENS that release POLLEN, and one or more CARPELS containing OVULES that on fertilization develop into SEEDS. Many flowers are reduced in structure with some of these parts missing.

Flowerhead Any dense cluster of flowers of more or less regular size, including a head (CAPITULUM) in the strict botanical sense.

Flowering plant See ANGIOSPERM.

Fodder The cut foliage of plants used to feed livestock. It can include grains and pods of the plants.

Forage plants Plants grown for livestock to browse, or on which they feed as they wander in natural or semi-natural vegetation, including trees and shrubs as well as grasses and other herbs.

Forb Botanist's term for any HERB (in the botanical sense) that is not a grass, sedge, or rush, thus applied mainly to dicotyledonous herbs.

Foliage Leaves and twigs in mass, a term used only in the singular.

Follicle A fruit derived from a single carpel that splits open along one side or across its apex to release the seeds.

Forma A level in botanical classification below species, subspecies, and variety, normally applied to a variation in a single character that may recur in wild stands. Thus *Gleditsia triacanthos* forma *inermis* differs from typical *Gleditsia triacanthos* only in being thornless. Abbreviated as f., and referred to as "form" in English.

Formal (of garden style) With beds, paths, hedges, etc., laid out in straight lines and smooth curves, and with lawns close-mown, plants kept trimmed.

Free (of flower parts) Not fused to neighboring parts of the same whorl, e.g., petal to petal, nor to parts of the next outer whorl, e.g., stamen to petal.

Frame A miniature and usually unheated greenhouse, mostly used in cool climates for propagating frost-tender annuals early in the growing season, traditionally rectangular with low masonry walls and a low-pitched roof frame with glass panes, hinged at the upper edge and able to be propped open during the day and shut at night.

Frond Any large, much-divided or compound leaf that to a non-botanist might appear to consist of many leaves. Leaves of palms and tree-ferns are commonly called fronds.

Frost The condition of air temperature falling below the freezing point of water ($32°$ F or $0°$ C), resulting in formation of ice crystals if the air contains moisture. Because cold air sinks, frost may occur at soil level when temperature at standard meteorological measuring height (5 ft or 1.5 m) is several degrees above freezing. In dry air there may be no ice crystals (hoar frost) formed but plant foliage may be killed; such an event is known as a *black frost*.

Frost hardy (of plant species, varieties, or cultivars) Able to withstand exposure to frost without damage to foliage, stems, or whatever parts normally persist through winter. Frost hardiness is entirely relative to climate, for example, *Abutilon megapotamicum* survives the light frosts in the hills of southeastern Australia (Zone 8) but will not survive outdoors in the interior of Britain (Zone 7); and while *Araucaria araucana* tolerates winters in most parts of Britain, it is killed outright by winter frost in northeastern USA (Zone 5).

Fruit (in the botanical sense) The seed-containing organ of any of the flowering plants, whether fleshy or dry. Normally one fruit is developed from one flower; if derived from more than one flower it is termed a compound fruit or SYNCARP (e.g., in *Pandanus*, *Morus*); if derived from only one of several carpels of the flower it is termed a MERICARP, the mericarps resulting from all the carpels collectively called a SCHIZOCARP (e.g., in *Brachychiton*).

Fruit-fly Any of a number of species of small fly that lay their eggs beneath the skin of ripening fruit, their larvae then feeding on the flesh of the ripe fruit, usually hastening the entry of microorganisms causing ferment and rot. They can cause great economic loss to commercial growers and have often been the reason for quarantine restrictions on trade and movement of fruit.

Fungus (plural fungi) Any member of the large group of organisms, once regarded as plants but now considered members of a separate kingdom, that cannot photosynthesize and therefore need living or dead plant or animal matter on which to feed. Fungi may be single-celled (e.g., yeasts) but more often consist of fine filaments (hyphae) that spread through the soil or the materials they feed upon, and may from time to time concentrate and rise above the surface in the form of "fruiting bodies" that release millions of minute spores. Toadstools, mushrooms, puffballs, etc., are such fruiting bodies. Fungi are the main agents of decay in wood, plant litter, and compost heaps, releasing nutrients back into the soil; there are also many parasitic fungi, some of them significant causes of plant disease or fruit rot.

Fungicide A chemical applied for the control of fungal parasites of plants.

Funnelform (of flowers) Shaped like a funnel or inverted cone, with petals either fused or overlapping and usually joined into a short tube at the base.

Gene One of the ultimate units of inheritance in any living organism, in higher plants and animals mostly carried on the CHROMOSOMES in the nuclei of its CELLS (though some are transmitted in far smaller cell inclusions called "mitochondria") . Each gene influences some character of the plant or animal, though many characters are not externally visible but biochemical. In the normal DIPLOID plant, genes influencing a particular character lie in corresponding positions on the matched pairs of chromosomes; if producing the same state of that character, the plant is said to be "homozygous" for that gene; if producing different states, the plant is "heterozygous" for the character, in which case one state is usually dominant over the other.

Genome The totality of the GENES present in each cell of a particular organism and their arrangement on CHROMOSOMES and in mitochondria, thus also the totality of its inherited characteristics. See also GENOTYPE, PHENOTYPE.

Genotype The underlying genetic makeup of an individual plant or clone, regardless of the ways in which its size or growth-form may be influenced by its environment. In contrast its PHENOTYPE is its actual form, the result of interaction between genotype and environment.

Genus (plural genera) The next level of botanical classification above species. The genus name can stand by itself, e.g., *Quercus* (the oak genus) but it also forms the first part of a species name, e.g., *Quercus rubra* (the red oak).

Germination The emergence of a new plant from a seed, mostly requiring absorption of water by the seed and certain temperature and light levels.

Gesneriad Any member of the dicot family Gesneriaceae (African violet family), consisting mainly of tropical herbs, subshrubs, shrubs, and creepers, some epiphytic, mostly with colorful flowers, tubular in the lower part.

Ginger The fresh or dried rhizome of *Zingiber officinale*; but, as used by gardeners and plant collectors, any plant belonging to the medium-sized MONOCOT family Zingiberaceae—all tropical or subtropical RHIZOMATOUS plants with aerial PSEUDOSTEMS (less commonly true stems) bearing large leaves, and often colorfully bracted panicles or heads of ZYGOMORPHIC flowers.

Glabrous (of plant parts) Lacking any covering of hairs or scales.

Gland In its strict sense, any small appendage, protrusion, depression, or cavity, in or upon a plant organ, which exudes or contains some liquid or sticky substance such as sugar or resin. Most common are the nectar glands (nectaries) in the base of many flowers, exuding nectar to attract insects or birds that in return pollinate the flowers. Some glands on leaf margins or stalks are vestigial (in the evolutionary sense) and do not secrete anything.

Glaucous (of leaves, stems, fruits) Having a bluish cast due to a surface film of wax or a wax-impregnated cuticle, and so modifying the green color from the chlorophyll in the underlying tissues.

Globose Approximately spherical in form.

Glochid A barbed hair, most often encountered in some genera of CACTI, notably *Opuntia* and its relatives, found in tufts arising from the AREOLES, causing irritation when these cacti are handled.

Glume Small chaff-like bract in grasses and sedges, defined as one of the pair of bracts at the base of each spikelet in grasses, but in sedges used for any of the bracts enclosing single florets.

Grain The small dry fruit of any GRASS, though more popularly used for the cereals, grasses grown as food crops.

Grass In the botanical sense, any member of the very large MONOCOT family Poaceae (alternative name Gramineae), though in common use the taller members of the BAMBOO subfamily (Bambusoideae) are not generally called grasses. Most grasses are annuals or herbaceous perennials with linear leaves; they have greatly reduced flowers borne in specialized inflorescence units called spikelets. They include the major CROP plants wheat, oats, barley, rye, maize, sorghum, and millet, and also provide the main food of grazing animals around the world.

Graft   The joining of two different plants, one termed the STOCK (or ROOTSTOCK) with lower stem and roots, the other termed the SCION cut from a branch, so that their tissues fuse at the junction. The aim of grafting is to "borrow" vigor or disease resistance from the rootstock for the more desirable scion, or to enable vegetative propagation of a cultivar that is difficult to raise from cuttings. The stock must be compatible for grafting to succeed, belonging to a closely related cultivar, species, or genus—for example Hybrid Tea roses grafted onto *Rosa multiflora* stock, or *Syringa* onto *Ligustrum*. There are many different techniques of grafting. See also BUDDING.

Graft hybrid   A plant that results when the tissues of the SCION become mixed with those of the STOCK in a GRAFT, the shoots that arise from the area of union displaying characters of both types of plant though sometimes dominance of one "parent" can change to dominance of the other as the plant grows and branches. Among garden plants the best known graft hybrids are the intergeneric ones +*Laburnocytisus* and +*Crataegomespilus*. The "+" symbol is used to distinguish graft hybrids from the much more common sexual hybrids.

Greenhouse   An enclosed structure with roof of transparent or translucent material, traditionally glass but nowadays usually plastic, in which plants are grown, its purpose being to raise the temperature of their environment and so protect them from winter frost and/or promote faster growth even in summer in cool climates. Greenhouses may be heated artificially or unheated, relying on their capacity to absorb and trap solar radiation. In normal use a greenhouse is a high-roofed structure distinguished from a FRAME, cloche, tunnel, or "igloo." The term greenhouse is now preferred over both *glasshouse* and *hothouse*.

Green manure   Plants, usually fast-growing annuals, that are plowed into the soil (or otherwise incorporated) while still green and alive, thus returning their nutrients to the soil as well as improving its texture. LEGUMES are among the best sources of green manure, as their root nodules containing SYMBIOTIC bacteria can fix nitrogen from the air, thus enabling a net increase in this major NUTRIENT element in the soil without addition of any chemical fertilizer.

Grex   All the progeny of a cross between two species or two other grexes (or a species and a grex), regardless of when and where the crossing occurred; a concept applied in practice in only in a few groups of plants, notably orchid and rhododendron hybrids. A grex name is similar in form to a cultivar name but without quotation marks, and may precede a cultivar name, e.g., *Rhododendron* Avalanche "Alpine Glow." A single grex may include many named cultivars.

Ground cover   Any plant that can spread to effectively blanket an area of ground in a garden. Most ground covers used in landscaping are longer-lived PROSTRATE plants, but CREEPERS and many RHIZOMATOUS or STOLONIFEROUS plants (e.g., *Ophiopogon, Fragaria*) are often used as well.

Growing season   The season in which growth of a particular plant takes place, in cool-temperate climates nearly always between spring and the end of summer, in drier tropical climates nearly always the wet season.

Growth habit   The overall form or shape of a plant.

Gum   Chemically polysaccharides, exuded from various plants, mostly from bark of certain trees and shrubs, having a sticky or slimy feel when wet. Soluble in hot water, gums are distinguished from resins, which require organic solvents. They have various commercial uses, including the traditional gum on envelope flaps. Gum Arabic from *Acacia senegal* is one of the best known gums.

Gymnosperm   That large class of plants that reproduce from seeds but bear them more or less exposed on the scales of a cone, rather than fully enclosed in a fruit (as in the flowering plants or ANGIOSPERMS). Gymnosperms lack true flowers. They are now considered a stage of evolution rather than a natural group derived from a single common ancestor. The two major gymnosperm groups are the conifers and cycads. There are also four evolutionary "dead ends" with a single genus each, namely *Ginkgo, Ephedra, Gnetum, Welwitschia*.

Gynophore   A stalk at the base of a flower's ovary, extending it some way above the receptacle. It may be more obvious in the fruiting stage, as in *Capparis* or some legume pods.

Gypsum   Hydrated calcium sulfate, a compound occurring naturally in soils of many arid regions. Used in horticulture both as a fertilizer where soil deficiencies indicate, and to improve texture of stiff clay soils.

Habitat   (of a species) The sum of geographical location, soil, topography and vegetation type in which a species is normally found wild.

Hair   Any fine hair-like outgrowth from the surface of a plant part. If it is noticeably flattened it is usually termed a SCALE.

Half-hardened   Used of CUTTINGS to distinguish those taken from close to the tips of actively growing shoots, though not so close that they are still very soft and tender. An alternative term is "semi-ripened."

Half-hardy   (of plant species) Able to survive occasional light frosts, of down to around 25° F (–4° C), especially when in a state of dormancy.

Hardwood   (of tree species) Having a hard timber, though more traditionally signifying any dicotyledonous (broadleaf) tree as opposed to a SOFTWOOD or CONIFER, regardless of relative hardness or density of timber. (of cuttings). Taken from stems that are mature and more or less woody, whether from the last season's or the current season's growth.

Hardy   (of a species or cultivar) Able to survive and thrive in a hostile environment; but gardeners in colder climates have generally narrowed its meaning to FROST HARDY.

Hastate   (of leaves) Shaped like a spearhead, or more literally like a medieval halberd, with a sharp triangular point and two triangular basal lobes spreading almost at right angles from the leafstalk. Used also for the leaf base only.

Haustorium   The organ by which a parasite such as a mistletoe or even a microscopic fungus invades the tissues of a host plant and takes water and dissolved nutrients from its sap.

Haw   The fruit of *Crataegus* species (hawthorns). These are small pomes, mostly red, with few bony seeds.

Head   See CAPITULUM.

Heartwood   The inner WOOD of a tree's trunk or larger branches, in which the cells have died and which no longer conducts sap from roots to crown, a function that continues in the outer living cylinder of SAPWOOD. In many trees the heartwood darkens in color and so is visually distinguishable from the paler sapwood; its vessels become blocked by outgrowths from their walls, and tannin deposits make it unattractive to insects and wood-decaying fungi, hence making it more durable as timber.

Heath   Vegetation type dominated by low wiry shrubs, usually treeless, occurring on boggy, acid, infertile soils. Also shrubs of the genus *Erica*, or more generally any small-leafed shrub of family Ericaceae or its Australasian counterpart Epacridaceae.

Heel   In cuttings, a small sliver of the parent branch, retained at the base of the cutting. Including a heel is believed to help with callus and root formation in certain types of plants.

Hemisphere   One half of the earth's surface, most commonly the Northern or Southern hemisphere, divided by the equator, although historically Eastern and Western hemispheres were just as important, the latter centered on the Americas.

Herb   (in botany) A plant with non-woody stems; (in gardening and cookery) an edible plant that adds flavor rather than bulk to a cooked dish or salad; (in medicine) a plant believed to have healing or health-giving properties and used in medicinal preparations.

Herbaceous   (in botany) The adjectival form of HERB; (in gardening) usually taken to refer to perennials that die back each winter to a rootstock , rhizome, or tuber.

Herbal   (adjective) Indicating origin from HERBS in the third sense above, i.e., used for medicinal purposes; (noun) a book, usually first published several centuries ago, describing all plants used medicinally and detailing their uses.

Herbarium   (in botany) A collection of preserved (usually dried and pressed) plant specimens used for purposes of botanical classification and identification. Herbaria in former times were often privately owned but are now nearly all are held by public institutions, e.g., the botanical gardens of Kew and New York, the Smithsonian Institution, the British Museum. Under modern rules of nomenclature, every newly published botanical name must have a unique specimen, held in a recognized herbarium, nominated as its "type," thus giving a guide to the name's application in the event of the name's scope widening or narrowing in future interpretations.

Herbicide   Any poison used to kill plants, or more specifically weeds; nowadays nearly all being chemicals that have very low toxicity to humans. A selective herbicide is one that, at a prescribed dilution, kills one class of plants without harming another, e.g., broad-leafed weeds growing among lawn grasses.

Hermaphrodite   (of flowers) Having fully functional male and female organs present in the same flower.

Hip (or hep)   The fruit of roses *(Rosa)*, consisting of a fleshy hollowed-out receptacle that develops from the flower's receptacle, to the inner surface of which are attached the dry "seeds" (achenes or nutlets), each derived from a single carpel.

Hirsute   One of the kinds of hairiness of plant parts, consisting of long, rather tangled hairs.

Hispid   Clothed in very short, stiff hairs that give a harsh feel to a plant surface (usually of leaves or stems).

Hoary   (of leaves, stems, etc.) With a coating of white hairs resembling frost.

Horticulture   The practice of growing plants, and other aspects of gardening. Commercial horticulture (as opposed to agriculture) embraces the growing of fruit, nuts, and cut-flowers, as well as the nursery and landscape industries.

Houseplant   Any plant grown full-time for ornament inside a house, generally being a species or cultivar able to tolerate low light levels and other adverse environmental factors associated with house interiors.

Humus   The organic matter in soil, derived in nature from leaf and twig litter, dead roots, and decayed tree trunks; in gardens it can be added in the form of compost, manure, or peat. Humus greatly improves soil by retaining moisture and mineral nutrients and keeping the soil open and well aerated.

Hybrid   The progeny resulting from fertilization of a species, variety, or cultivar by a different species, variety, or cultivar, combining the genetic makeup of both. The progeny of hybrids continue to be hybrids. Botanical names of hybrids between 2 species are indicated by the multiplication sign "×" inserted in one of 2 positions, namely: (a) where no hybrid name has been published—between the names of the two parent species, e.g., *Freesia alba × F. leichtlinii*; (b) where a hybrid name has been published for a hybrid between 2 species—before the epithet, e.g., *Magnolia × soulangeana* [*M. denudata × M. liliiflora*]; Where 3 or more species are involved in a hybrid, the "×" sign is not used; the resulting hybrid may be given a grex name, as in rhododendrons, or a cultivar name is used directly following the genus name, as in modern roses. For hybrids involving different genera, see INTERGENERIC HYBRID.

Hybrid cultivar   A CULTIVAR selected and named from the progeny of cross. The variation found in hybrid progeny is greater than within wild species, thus giving more scope for selection of cultivars. In the case of a cultivar derived from a named cross between 2 species, the cultivar name may follow the epithet, e.g., *Magnolia × soulangeana* "Burgundy." If originating from 3 or more species and/or earlier hybrids, the cultivar name may follow directly after the genus name, e.g., *Rhododendron* "Markeeta's Prize," or sometimes after a GREX name, if one has been registered.

Hybrid vigor The phenomenon of increased size and growth-rate found in F1 hybrids in certain plants. An alternative term is "heterosis." The use of F1 hybrid seed for some crops such as maize takes advantage of hybrid vigor.

Imbricate (of leaves, petals) Overlapping the adjacent leaves or petals, like shingles on a roof.

Incised (of leaf or petal margins) With deep, narrow, finely pointed teeth.

Incurved (of leaves, etc.) With margins curved upwards and inwards, as opposed to RECURVED.

Indehiscent (of fruit types) Not splitting open at maturity to release their seed, as opposed to DEHISCENT. Most fleshy fruits are indehiscent.

Indusium In ferns, a small flap or hood of tissue that covers a SORUS, usually shrinking or folding back as the SPORANGIA are about to release their spores.

Indigenous (of plant species or subspecies) Forming part of the original natural flora of a country or region (though not necessarily endemic); thus, *Sorbus aucuparia* is indigenous to Britain.

Indoor In horticulture, general term for any enclosed growing environment, whether in a house, conservatory or GREENHOUSE.

Inflorescence Specialized flower-bearing branch of a plant, together with the flowers on it.

Informal (of garden flowers, mainly "double" cultivars) Having the petals (sometimes also stamens and staminodes) loosely and irregularly arranged.

Intergeneric hybrid HYBRID with species of 2 or more different genera in its parentage, most commonly created in ORCHIDS. Generally distinguished by a hybrid botanical name, formed in accordance with the following rules:(a) where published for hybrid between species of 2 different genera (a bigeneric hybrid), the name combines elements of the names of the parent genera and is preceded by a multiplication sign "×," e.g., × *Crataemespilus grandiflora* [*Crataegus* × *Mespilus*]; (b) where published for hybrid between 3 or more genera, the name is taken from a person's name followed by the suffix —*aa*, e.g., the orchid generic hybrid × *Wilsonara*, which has species of *Odontoglossum*, *Oncidium*, and *Cochlioda* in its parentage. Alternatively, so as to cover existing names such as × *Sophrolaeliocattleya*, the rule allows for names of trigeneric hybrids to be formed in the same way as bigeneric.

Insecticide A substance, nowadays usually of synthetic chemical origin, used to kill insect pests (see also PESTICIDE). Modern insecticides are mostly designed to target biochemical processes specific to insects or even particular types of insects, and to have low toxicity to humans and other vertebrate animals.

Internode The interval between two successive NODES in a plant stem or twig.

Introduced (of plant species) Not native (indigenous) to the country or region in question; usually implying deliberate introduction by humans.

Invasive (of a species or cultivar) Tending to spread well beyond the place where it was planted in the garden, whether by seeds or rhizomes, stolons, etc., and thereby becoming a nuisance.

Involucre A ring or cup of bracts beneath a flower or group of flowers, as in most members of the daisy family (Asteraceae).

Irregular (of flowers) Not having the petals, sepals, and/or stamens arranged regularly like spokes of a wheel and of equal shape and size in the one whorl. ZYGOMORPHIC flowers (having only one plane of symmetry) are irregular, e.g., *Salvia*, but so are flowers with no symmetry, e.g., *Canna*.

Juvenile (of leaves or leafy shoots) Showing the characteristics of seedling leaves; e.g., in mulberries (*Morus*) juvenile leaves are deeply lobed. The first shoots from lopped branches often revert to the juvenile type.

Keel (in flowers of the pea subfamily of legumes, Fabaceae) The two fused lower petals which usually project forward and enclose the stamens; (of leaves) having the midrib projecting like the keel of a boat or forming a sharp "V" in cross-section.

Labiate Any member of the large DICOT family Lamiaceae, the mint family, from its alternative and more traditional name Labiatae (meaning "lipped").

Labellum In an ORCHID flower, the usually large and distinctively shaped petal that commonly juts forward from the flower's center; it is technically the upper of the 3 petals (or inner perianth segments), but because most orchid flowers have stalks twisted through 180 degrees, it may appear to be the lower. The various protuberances and color patterns on an orchid labellum are nearly always adaptations to attract and guide pollinating agents, principally insects.

Laciniate (of leaf or petal margins) Divided into very deep, narrow, finely pointed lobes.

Lamina The flat part of a leaf, as opposed to its stalk (same as BLADE).

Lanceolate (of leaves) Fairly narrow and tapering to both ends, usually with the widest part a little below the middle; mostly applied to leaves whose length is between 4 and 8 times their width.

Lateral On the sides of a plant part such as a branch or leaf, as opposed to its apex or base.

Latex Sticky substance, usually white, found in the tissues of many plants (e.g., figs and euphorbias) and exuding from any cut or wound. Natural rubber is derived from a plant latex. Latexes are not poisonous in themselves but are associated with poisonous sap in some plant groups.

Lax Loose, open, or floppy in habit, as the branches of many trailing plants.

Layering PROPAGATION method by which branches are encouraged to produce ADVENTITIOUS roots and then detached to be grown as new plants. Most basically it is simply the mounding of soil or damp sand around bases of multiple stems or sucker growths; or lower branches are bent down and pegged against the ground, often with a slanting cut halfway through, until they take root. When a plant's lower branches spontaneously root where they touch the ground, it is said to be "self-layering." See also AIR LAYERING.

Leader The skyward-growing tip of a tree trunk, best developed in trees with a long-pointed crown, e.g., *Picea* species (spruces).

Leaf The plant organ that is primarily responsible for photosynthesis.

Leaflet One of the leaf-like parts that make up a compound leaf.

Legume Any member of the large plant family Fabaceae (alternative name Leguminosae), characterized by their fruits like peas or beans. Most have root nodules containing bacteria that can convert the air's nitrogen into a form that the plant can utilize. The family is divided into three subfamilies, the largest containing all the pea-flowered legumes, another containing mimosas and acacias, and the third containing cassias and bauhinias (among many other genera). In botany the term "legume" has also been used to describe the fruit type.

Lenticel A small corky outgrowth or rough patch on a plant surface, usually the bark, possibly for the purpose of allowing entry or exit of gases.

Leptomorph Of BAMBOO species, those with long-running RHIZOMES and widely spaced CULMS.

Lepidote Literally "having scales," used to refer to the major subdivision of the genus *Rhododendron* in which the young leaves and stems have a coating of minute scales. They are a large and diverse group of rhododendrons, though not including most larger evergreen species and hybrids of gardens, which are ELEPIDOTES.

Liane A high-climbing plant that develops thick woody stems, often hanging from trees in conspicuous loops; most abundant in tropical rainforests.

Lichen Member of a large group of somewhat moss-like plants that are in fact composed of fungal tissues within which dwell single-celled algae, the two organisms having a symbiotic relationship. Lichens grow on tree trunks, twigs, and even leaves as well as on rocks and the soil surface. On trees they are epiphytes not parasites.

Lignin Substance deposited in cell walls in WOOD, in combination with CELLULOSE giving it strength and density. Chemically it is a highly polymerized phenyl propene. A commercial by-product of lignin is artificial vanilla (vanillin).

Lignotuber A woody tuber, sometimes quite large, that persists at or below the soil surface for many years, found in some shrubs and small trees and capable of resprouting when the plant is defoliated, for example, by fire.

Ligule A flap of tissue projecting from the upper surface of a leaf stalk or base of blade, often wrapping around the stem; best developed in the grass family; also used for the fused and flattened petals of a ray floret in daisies.

Limb (of trees) The larger branches that spring directly from the trunk, as opposed to smaller branches and twigs; (of flowers) the part of an elongated corolla that spreads outwards, in contrast to the corolla tube.

Lime Mineral component of or additive to soil, always a form of the element calcium. Quick lime is calcium oxide, slaked or hydrated lime calcium hydroxide, crushed limestone calcium carbonate—all are alkaline or at least neutralize acidity in soils, making certain nutrients more available to plants, others less so.

Linear (of leaves) Narrow in relation to length, used for leaves whose length is more than about eight times their width.

Linnaean system The modern system of naming of plants and animals, in which each SPECIES is designated by the name of the GENUS it belongs in, followed by a specific epithet. These epithets first appeared as marginal annotations beside longer Latin phrase-names in Linnaeus' *Species Plantarum* of 1753, a work in which all plants known at that time were classified and described. Linnaeus also established a full hierarchy of levels of classification, though most of his higher-level names (family and above) have long since been replaced by more scientifically valid concepts.

Lip An upper or lower lobe, or group of several lobes, of the usually tubular COROLLA of a flower with a single vertical plane of symmetry (ZYGOMORPHIC). Most such flowers are 2-lipped, e.g., *Salvia*, *Nemesia*.

Lithophyte A plant species that habitually grows on rocks, virtually in the absence of soil. Many epiphytes are also capable of growing as lithophytes.

Liverwort Botanically any member of the subdivision Hepaticopsida of the DIVISION Bryophyta of green land plants, the other major subdivision being the Bryopsida, or MOSSES. Liverworts are low creeping plants, not differentiated into stems and leaves. Some can blanket moist soil and may be minor weeds, particularly of nursery pots and seed trays.

Loam A soil in which the proportions of clay, sand, and silt are fairly evenly balanced and the humus content is adequate. A clay loam is one with higher CLAY content, a sandy loam is one with more SAND.

Lobe (of leaves) A large projection of the margin, generally one that measures at least a third of the distance from the leaf's midrib to its outer edge.

Lyrate (of leaf shape) Pinnately lobed, usually with rather few, large lobes, and terminating in a rounded lobe larger than the lateral ones, e.g., leaf of watercress (*Rorippa*).

Male (of flowers or cones) Having only pollen-bearing organs, though in some male flowers non-functional (vestigial) female organs may be present as well; (of plants) producing only male flowers or cones.

Mallee One of a large group of Australian *Eucalyptus* species characterized by many stems of equal size springing from a large LIGNOTUBER. Most are between 6 ft (1.8 m) and 30 ft (9 m) in height, and some form extensive woodlands in semi-arid regions.

Mallow In narrowest sense, a species of *Malva*; in a broader sense, any member of the mallow tribe, e.g., *Alcea*, *Lavatera*; in the broadest sense any member of the mallow (Malvaceae) family, including such genera as *Hibiscus* and *Gossypium*.

Manure Any organic material used as FERTILIZER, though nowadays generally understood as the excreta of animals, in particular domestic herbivores such as cattle, horses, sheep, and also poultry.

Marcottage Another name for AIR LAYERING.

Margin (of a leaf) The edge.

Mealy Any white or gray, somewhat powdery coating of a leaf, stem, or fruit, consisting of very short white hairs, bubble-like surface cells, or fragments of wax.

Mealybug Small sap-sucking insects of the family Coccidae (to which scale-insects also belong), wingless, slow-moving, and covered in a whitish water-repellent powder. They infest and weaken plants, often hiding among leaf bases or underground parts, and may be difficult to control.

Mediterranean (of countries) Those bordering the Mediterranean Sea; (of climates) those of warm-temperate regions with hot dry summers and rainfall concentrated in the winter months—they occur on the west-facing coasts of the continents and include California, Chile, southwestern South Africa, and southwestern and southern Australia, as well as the Mediterranean itself.

Megaherb A pretentious term, ignorantly combining Greek and Latin elements, supposedly describing those herbaceous plants that produce exceptionally large leaves, e.g., *Musa* species (bananas).

Mericarp An apparent fruit but in fact only one segment of a SCHIZOCARP, the segmented fruit developing from separate carpels of one flower (e.g., the pod of *Brachychiton*).

Mericlone A plant resulting from the division of a selected CULTIVAR's MERISTEM tissue into minute pieces and culturing them in a sterile medium in a laboratory, using AUXINS to initiate root and shoot development. Mericloning allows rapid production of large numbers of identical and disease-free plants.

Meristem The zone of dividing CELLS where new plant tissues are created. The CAMBIUM is one kind of meristem, while the growing tips of shoots and roots all have APICAL meristems.

Mesocarp (of fruits) The softer flesh of a fruit wall, especially where the wall is composed of different layers; for example, in a plum *(Prunus × domestica)* the mesocarp is the juicy flesh between the exocarp (skin) and the endocarp (stone), the latter enclosing the seed.

Microclimate The climate of any small area as modified by local topography, vegetation, structures, or activities, in contrast to the regional climate. For example, the shelter of trees or masonry walls may create a frost-free microclimate in an otherwise frosty climate. Microclimates are an important part of plant habitats, both in gardens and in the wild.

Midrib A leaf's main central vein, usually thickened and slightly projecting on at least one surface.

Mildew Type of infestation characteristic of some fungi.

Mist In meteorological terms, the slow falling of water droplets much smaller than raindrops, light enough to be blown around by wind; often treated as synonymous with fog but, if there is a distinction, it's that fog is more vapor-like. In plant PROPAGATION and indoor growing, the use of fine nozzles that give a mist-like spray of water, achieving saturation of the air and gentle wetting of foliage (also called fogging).

Mist forest See CLOUD FOREST.

Mistletoe A PARASITIC flowering plant belonging (with few exceptions) to one of the 2 DICOT families Loranthaceae or Viscaceae, always growing aerially on the branches of trees or shrubs and attached to the host by HAUSTORIA. Mistletoes have their own PHOTOSYNTHETIC tissues and obtain from the host's sap-stream mainly water and dissolved NUTRIENTS. If attached in numbers they can weaken the host plant but rarely kill it. The original mistletoe is *Viscum album*.

Monocarpic (of a plant species) Fruiting only once before the whole plant dies. All annuals are monocarpic by definition, and most biennials, but there are also longer-lived monocarpic plants, e.g., all species of the palm genus *Corypha,* some *Agave* species.

Monocotyledon (or monocot) A plant belonging to

the smaller of the two great classes into which the flowering plants (angiosperms) are divided, the larger being the DICOTYLEDONS. As the name implies, monocotyledons have only one seed leaf and additionally they mostly have parallel-veined leaves, flower parts in multiples of three, and no cambium layer in the stems. Only a minority of monocotyledons are trees or shrubs, for example the palms, aloes, yuccas, dracaenas, and cordylines.

Monoecious (of species) Having both functional male and functional female organs present in the one plant, whether in the same flower or in separate male and female flowers. Contrasted with DIOECIOUS.

Monopodial (of a species' growth habit) Characterized by each shoot having a continuing apical growing point which, at least for a period of years, maintains dominance over the lateral shoots that branch from its leaf axils. Contrasted with SYMPODIAL, in which growth is always continued by lateral shoots. This distinction is important in ORCHID genera, which are always either monopodial (as in *Vanda* and its allies) or sympodial (as in *Cattleya*).

Monotypic Describes a TAXON, in particular a GENUS, FAMILY, ORDER, CLASS, or DIVISION, that has only one member at the next lower level in the hierarchy. Thus *Ravenala* is a monotypic genus, with only a single species, *R. madagascariensis*; Symplocaceae is a monotypic family, with only a single genus, *Symplocos* (though that contains numerous species).

Monsoonal (of climates) Having a long, very dry season terminated by the monsoon, a season of frequent thunderstorms and very heavy rains, these usually continuing for one to several months. Monsoonal climates are confined to the tropics and subtropics.

Moss Botanically a member of the subdivision Bryopsida of the division Bryophyta of green land plants. They lack true roots, their stems lack distinct conducting tissues, and their tiny leaves are membranous. Mosses are not to be confused with lichens, which are composed mainly of fungal tissues, nor with algae, which lack true stems and leaves.

Mucronate (of leaf tips) Having a very small point projecting from an otherwise rounded or obtuse apex.

Mulch (in gardening) Any material that can be spread over the soil surface for the purposes of preventing water loss, insulating from cold or heat, and suppressing weed growth. Mulches may consist of gravel, pebbles, plastic film, newspapers, straw, wood or bark chips, dead leaves, grass clippings, or COMPOST, to name the most common.

Mycorrhiza A fungus that invades the root tissues of a plant and forms a symbiotic relationship with it. The plant benefits because the fungus can digest organic matter that occurs in the surrounding soil, converting it to simpler molecules such as sugars that the plant can absorb more easily, while the fungus is assured of access to moisture.

Native (of a species) Forming part of the original wild flora of the country or region under consideration. See also INDIGENOUS.

Naturalized (of a species) Not originally native to the country or region under consideration but now established, reproducing itself freely and spreading into new areas without human aid. In gardening, naturalizing sometimes means letting a particular plant multiply and spread over successive seasons, with no need for cultivation.

Nectar Sugary liquid exuded by plants, mainly from nectar glands (nectaries) of flowers, being a food reward for insects or birds (sometimes even mammals) that in return carry away pollen to another flower.

Nectary (or nectar gland) A specialized area of surface tissue that exudes nectar, usually in flowers and located at bases of petals, stamens, ovaries; taking many forms including a tiny pit, a knob, or colored band (as in *Calochortus*); or an *extrafloral* nectary may be located on a stem, leaf, or petiole (as in many *Acacia* species).

Needle A leaf modified into needle-like form, as in the true pines *(Pinus)*.

New World Traditional term for all of the Americas, going back to Columbus's time. Contrasted with the OLD WORLD.

Neutral (of soils) Having a pH of 7 or very close to 7 (on a scale of 0–14), that is, neither acid (below 7) nor alkaline (above 7).

Nitrogen-fixing (of micro-organisms) The ability to absorb nitrogen from the atmosphere (of which it is the most abundant gas) and combine it with hydrogen and oxygen to form simple inorganic molecules such as ammonia and nitrous acid that higher plants can absorb. Nitrogen-fixing organisms such as the bacterium *Rhizobium* and some blue-green algae may form SYMBIOTIC relationships with higher plants (notably the legumes), allowing the latter to thrive in nitrogen-deficient soils.

Node The region of a stem to which a leaf or leaves are attached. If leaves are alternately arranged then there is only one leaf per node, but if opposite then there are two, and if whorled, three or more. Nodes alternate with INTERNODES on a stem.

Nodule Any small swelling on an organ, but in particular the root swellings on LEGUMES that contain NITROGEN-FIXING bacteria.

Noxious (of weeds) Any weed identified as a major threat to agriculture, horticulture, or natural environments and listed as such by government agencies responsible for weed control, usually with a range of legal requirements.

Nut Botanically, a fruit that is not fleshy but does not split open when ripe; in popular usage an edible seed, larger than a grain, that can be eaten raw or with minimal roasting.

Nutrient (of plants) The mineral elements that the plant absorbs from the soil or growing medium through its roots, in the form of salts dissolved in the water taken up. They are divided into the major or essential elements nitrogen, phosphorus, potassium, sulfur, calcium, and magnesium; and the minor or trace elements iron, manganese, copper, zinc, boron, and molybdenum. Plant nutrients do not themselves form the bulk of the plant, which is built essentially from air and water, but they are key components of molecules essential to plant metabolism.

Obcordate (of leaves) Shaped like an upside-down heart, with the notch at the apex.

Oblanceolate (of leaves) As for lanceolate but with the widest part slightly above the mid-point.

Oblong Having more or less parallel margins and with length about 2 to 8 times the width; the base and apex may be rounded or obtuse, not necessarily squared-off.

Obovate (of leaves) As for ovate but with the widest part above the mid-point.

Obovoid (of fruits or other three-dimensional organs) Egg-shaped but with the widest part above the middle, that is, furthest from the stalk.

Obtuse (of leaf apex) Blunt, that is, not acute, though not necessarily broadly rounded.

Ochrea (or ocrea) A sheath, usually an outgrowth from the base of a leaf stalk, that encircles the stem above the node.

Odd-pinnate (of leaves) Pinnate with an odd number of leaflets, though also implying that there is a single terminal leaflet.

Offset Any small basal shoot of a plant that can be detached and used for PROPAGATION.

Oilseed A plant species or cultivar grown as a crop or in a plantation, for the extraction of a natural oil or fat from its seeds, e.g., safflower (*Carthamus*), canola (*Brassica*), or oil palm (*Elaeis*). Some oilseed plants have multiple uses, e.g., peanuts (*Arachis*), sunflower (*Helianthus*).

Old World Traditional collective term for Europe, Asia, Africa, Australia, and all nearby islands, as contrasted to the NEW WORLD. The concept only arose following Columbus's discovery of the Americas.

Operculum A cap that encloses a flower in bud in certain plants, most notably *Eucalyptus* where it is formed from the fused petals, or both petals and sepals.

Opposite (of leaves) Attached to the stem in pairs, on opposite sides of a node.

Orbicular (of leaves) More or less circular in outline.
Orchid Any member of the very large MONOCOT family Orchidaceae, exceeded in number of species only by the dicot family Asteraceae (composites or daisies), occurring in most of the world's lands but most diverse in the tropics, where the great majority grow as EPIPHYTES. Orchids have ZYGOMORPHIC flowers of elaborate structure, CAPSULAR fruits containing vast numbers of minute seeds containing no food reserves, and roots that contain SYMBIOTIC fungal MYCORRHIZA, essential for the orchid's nutrition. They are little used by humans except as ornaments, but are grown and collected by a vast number of enthusiasts around the world, and their flowers are sold in every florist's shop.
Order The next major level of plant classification above FAMILY. The names of orders all end in *-ales.*
Organic (of substances) Being composed of molecules that originated in living things. Organic chemistry concerns itself with compounds in which carbon and hydrogen predominate; (in horticulture and agriculture) of plants and their produce grown without the use of any manufactured chemical FERTILIZERS or PESTICIDES (except simple inorganic chemicals such as lime, sulfur, etc.), based on the belief that such chemicals are harmful to the soil and to humans and animals who consume the produce.
Ornamental A plant grown primarily for ornament, as opposed to food, timber, fiber, drugs, and the like.
Ovary (in flowers) The swollen part of the female organ containing the ovules.
Ovate (of leaves, bracts, petals, etc.) Approximately egg-shaped in outline with the widest part toward the stalk end; it refers to the overall outline and the base or apex may be acute, obtuse or rounded.
Ovoid Egg-shaped (three-dimensionally), like some olive varieties, with the widest part toward the stalk end.
Ovule The future seed but before fertilization; in flowering plants enclosed in the ovary but in conifers and cycads borne on the scale of a cone.
Pachymorph Of BAMBOO species, those with short, fat RHIZOMES, resulting in closely crowded CULMS.
Palm Any member of the large MONOCOT family Arecaceae or Palmae, mostly tropical plants with large FRONDS (actually leaves) that are usually divided into many leaflets or segments folded along their midribs. Palm trunks may be tall and apparently woody but have no cambium layer.
Palmate See DIGITATE.
Palmatifid (of leaves) Deeply lobed with lobes radiating from the leaf stalk.
Panicle In the looser sense, any INFLORESCENCE that is repeatedly branched, though more strictly it is a branched RACEME.
Pantropical (of species or genera) Indigenous in the TROPICS of all the continents and major tropical islands.
Parasite A plant growing in or upon another plant with attachments to the host's tissues that allow it to steal some of the host's nutrients or water supply. Mistletoes are typical parasites.
Patent Of plants, the right of the breeder of a cultivar to propagate and sell it or to license others to do so. The term patent is used in the USA; in other countries these rights are called Plant Breeders' Rights, or Plant Variety Rights.
Pea In the narrow sense, the fruit or plant of *Pisum sativum;* in a broader sense, any of various LEGUMES with similar short pods, e.g., pigeon pea (*Cajanus*).
Pea-flower The type of flower characteristic of the largest SUBFAMILY (Faboideae) of the LEGUME family (Fabaceae, alternative name Leguminosae); the flowers are ZYGOMORPHIC, with a broad upper petal known as the STANDARD, two forward-pointing outer petals known as the "wings," and two partially fused lower petals that form the KEEL; held within these are a slender group of 10 stamens and a single carpel (which becomes the pod at the fruiting stage).
Peat The remains of dead plants that have been preserved in a wet acid environment for long periods (thousands, even millions of years), becoming

compressed and darkened. Large deposits are mined, the peat used for fuel, for soil improvement, and for horticultural potting media. The best peat is moss peat, derived largely from sphagnum moss, but sedge peat is also available.
Pedate (of compound or deeply lobed leaves) Similar to digitate but with leaflets or lobes arising from a broadened "foot," with the leaf's petiole attached at the middle.
Pedicel The stalk of an individual flower.
Peduncle The common stalk of a group of flowers or of a whole inflorescence.
Peltate (of leaves) Having the leaf stalk (petiole) joining the blade on its underside away from the margin.
Penjing The Chinese practice of maintaining miniature trees and shrubs, similar to the Japanese BONSAI.
Perennial (of species) In botanical usage, one that has an indefinite life span, or at least 3 years' life span. By this criterion all trees and shrubs are perennials. But gardeners tend to use the term to mean a herbaceous perennial, in contrast to trees and shrubs.
Perfoliate (of leaves) Having the plant stem pass through the leaf, away from the margin.
Perianth The parts of a flower that enclose the sexual organs in bud, normally the combined petals (corolla) and sepals (calyx). Used mainly for flowers where petals are not clearly distinguishable from sepals, e.g., palms, lilies, in which case they are all termed perianth-segments.
Persistent Lasting beyond one season on a plant, or into a different phase of reproduction, e.g., the sepals of a flower persistent on the fruit.
Pest (in gardening) Mostly insects or other small fauna that feed on plants, either weakening them or disfiguring them. Contrast with DISEASE.
Pesticide General term for chemicals used to kill undesirable organisms, whether weeds, fungi, insects, snails, etc.—though the more precise terms are herbicide, fungicide, insecticide, molluscicide, etc.
Petal One of the inner layer of the 2 layers of organs that surround the sexual organs of a flower, the outer being the SEPALS. Petals are often thin and brightly colored or white, and are seldom green like sepals. The petals of one flower are collectively termed the COROLLA. They may be fused into a tube, bell, or funnel, or may be absent.
Petiole The stalk of an individual leaf.
Petiolule The stalk of one leaflet of a compound leaf.
pH (in chemistry) The scale by which acidity and alkalinity are measured, applicable to soils, potting media, and water for irrigation. It runs from 0 (extreme acidity) to 14 (extreme alkalinity) with the midpoint 7.0 regarded as neutral. Most soils fall within a pH range of between 4 and 9.
Phenotype The whole set of features of an individual plant resulting from the interaction between its GENOTYPE and the environment in which it has developed from earliest embryo stage.
Phloem The conducting tissue found mainly in BARK (except in MONOCOTS), responsible for conducting synthesized products, such as sugars in solution, to various parts of the plant.
Photosynthesis The process that takes place in green leaves of plants. With the aid of the pigment CHLOROPHYLL and the sun's energy, water from the soil and carbon dioxide from the air are combined to produce the carbohydrates (initially sugars) essential to the formation of new tissues.
Phyllode A leaf stalk (petiole) that has become flattened and leaf-like, usually with loss of the leaf blade, and takes over the leaves' photosynthetic function. Most Australian *Acacia* species have phyllodes rather than true leaves in the adult state.
Phylum Alternative term for DIVISION, in the hierarchy of plant classification, adopted by those biologists who seek uniformity between the botanical and zoological systems of classification
Picotee Pattern of flower coloring in some groups of cultivars, principally in *Dianthus*, characterized

by petals having a narrow marginal zone of contrasting color.
Pilose (of leaf and stem hairs) Straight and soft but rather crowded.
Pine In the strict sense a member of the conifer genus *Pinus*, but often used rather loosely for any conifer.
Pinna (plural pinnae) A leaflet of a pinnate leaf.
Pinnate (of compound leaves) Having the leaflets attached in 2 rows to either side of a center stalk or RACHIS, in the manner of a feather.
Pinnatifid (of leaves) Deeply lobed in a feather-like form, with the lobes forming a row on either side.
Pinnule The ultimate leaflet of a BIPINNATE leaf, or of a leaf that is COMPOUND to any higher order such as tripinnate or quadripinnate.
Pioneer plant A plant species able to quickly colonize newly available habitats, such as landslip sites, sand or gravel banks in rivers, volcanic lava, or cinder slopes. Pioneer plants need to have effective dispersal mechanisms using mainly wind or water, a rapid rate of growth, and root systems able to extract nutrients efficiently from raw substrates.
Pistil A discrete unit of the female organs in a flower, either a single CARPEL or a group of fused carpels. A somewhat old-fashioned term in botany.
Pistillate (of a plant) Having flowers with functional female organs (pistils) but no functional male ones, or may apply to individual flowers of the one plant. Means much the same as FEMALE.
Pith The soft, usually whitish tissue in the center of a plant stem or twig.
Pitcher plants Species of CARNIVOROUS plant in which the trapping mechanism is of pitcher-like form, with a pool of digestive liquid in the bottom. The main pitcher plant genera are *Nepenthes, Sarracenia, Darlingtonia, Heliamphora,* and *Cephalotus.*
Plant Kingdom One of the major groups into which living organisms are divided, traditionally including algae, fungi, and bacteria as well as all green plants; but modern systems based on a fuller understanding of relationships have narrowed the scope of the Plant Kingdom to the green land plants plus the green algae only.
Plicate (of leaves) Folded or creased lengthwise, like the folds of a fan.
Plumose Like a plume, that is, feather-like but with the segments not in two neat rows.
Pneumatophore A root that emerges above the ground for the purposes of exchanging gases such as oxygen from the air, as in some mangroves.
Pod Any fruit that is hollow inside and eventually splits open to reveal its seeds or, in a narrower sense, the elongated fruit of legumes (family Fabaceae or Leguminosae) that splits along its top and bottom sides (or top only) to reveal a row of seeds.
Pollard A tree with trunk or limbs lopped, with resulting sprouting of many cane-like branches from the cut ends.
Pollen The dust-like material produced by the male organs of both flowering plants and gymnosperms, each tiny grain containing a male nucleus that combines with a female nucleus in an ovule to produce a seed. In flowering plants a pollen grain is received on the stigma and "germinates," producing an extremely fine tube that grows down through the style and into an ovule, the nucleus descending through this tube.
Pollination The mechanism by which POLLEN is transferred from STAMENS to STIGMA (or male cones to female cones in the CONIFERS), whether in the same flower or different flowers, or on different plants. Agents of pollination include wind, insects, and birds; pollen can be deliberately transferred by humans.
Polyploid A species, subspecies, or cultivar having more than 2 matching sets of CHROMOSOMES; includes triploids (3 sets), tetraploids (4 sets), and hexaploids (6 sets). Polyploids may show increases in size and vigor compared with the more usual wild DIPLOIDS, but often have impediments to normal sexual reproduction.
Pome The characteristic fruit type of that subfamily of the rose family that includes apples, pears, hawthorns, cotoneasters, and related genera. The

"flesh" of a pome derives from the floral receptacle; the true fruit containing several seeds is fused to the inner wall of the floral receptacle, with only its apex exposed in a small pit at the top.

Pome fruits The major commercial fruit species bearing a POME, namely apples, pears, quinces, and loquats.

Pot A CONTAINER for growing a plant in, in common usage being one of small to medium size (under about 12 in or 30 cm diameter) and usually tapering slightly from top to bottom, with a drainage hole or holes in the base. Smaller, more elongated containers are generally called *tubes*; broad, shallow containers for bulbs or orchids are *pans*; larger pots, heavy to lift, are *tubs*.

Potash Common name for the element potassium, one of the major NUTRIENTS of plants, traditionally available in the form of its carbonate and hydroxide salts obtained by extracting wood ash with hot water which was then evaporated. Nowadays it is mostly added in the form of potassium sulfate.

Potpourri A mixture of dried aromatic and fragrant plants, usually flowers.

Prickle In botany, a sharp-pointed, broad-based outgrowth of a stem, as in roses (*Rosa*) and blackberries (*Rubus fruticosus*), as opposed to a THORN or a SPINE.

Prairie Flat or undulating grasslands characteristic of a large inland area of cooler-temperate North America, from the Canadian provinces of Manitoba, Alberta, and Saskatchewan, south to northern Texas in the USA.

Procumbent (of a plant's growth habit) With branches tending to lie flat on the ground but with the growing tips more upward-pointing, rather than horizontally as for PROSTRATE.

Propagation The practice of multiplying plants artificially, whether by seed, cuttings, layers, grafts, divisions, or tissue culture.

Prostrate (of plants) With branches lying flat on the ground.

Prune To improve or maintain the shape of a plant, most commonly a shrub (e.g., rose bush) or woody climber (e.g., grape vine), by carefully cutting off some branches at the base and shortening others, often with the aim of increasing quantity or size of flowers or fruit. In a broader sense, any cutting back of a plant's branches, but when done uniformly over the whole foliage canopy (like a haircut) such cutting is more usually called trimming or clipping, or if of limbs of a tree, lopping.

Pseudobulb A bulb-like storage organ that is not a bulb, i.e., does not consist of concentrically arranged leaves modified for food storage. Used almost exclusively for the stems of SYMPODIAL ORCHID genera, based on the bulb-like form of some, e.g., *Cymbidium*, *Lycaste*, but among orchid growers its use has extended to some much more elongated or slender stems, as in many *Dendrobium* species.

Pseudocephalium See under CEPHALIUM.

Pseudostem An apparent stem that is actually formed from a group of concentrically furled sheathing leaf bases, as in bananas (*Musa*, *Ensete*), or in *Canna*—in both cases the true stem terminating in the INFLORESCENCE subsequently elongates through the center of the pseudostem, but in some genera of gingers, e.g., *Zingiber*, it arises separately from the rhizome.

Pseudowhorl An apparent whorl of leaves that, when examined more closely, is seen to consist of a group of spirally (or rarely oppositely) arranged leaves separated by very short internodes, with much longer internodes separating it from the previous pseudowhorl. Azaleas (*Rhododendron*) are a common example.

Pteridophyte Any spore-bearing (as opposed to seed-bearing) plant that has stems containing a well-differentiated vascular (conducting) system of tissues. Pteridophytes are now regarded as representing a stage of evolution of land plants, rather than forming a "natural" group with a single common ancestor. They comprise the DIVISIONS Psilophyta (*Psilotum* and *Tmesipteris*), Lycopodiophyta (*Lycopodium*, *Lycopodiella*, *Huperzia*, *Isoetes*, *Selaginella*),

Equisetophyta (*Equisetum*), and Polypodiophyta (the true FERNS, with some 350 genera).

Pubescence Any coating of hairs on plant parts such as leaf, stem, calyx, fruit.

Pubescent Having a coating of fairly short, soft hairs, whether sparse or dense.

Pulses Legume seeds harvested dry, removed from pods and used as food in a similar manner to CEREAL grains.

Punctate (of leaves, stems, petals, fruit, etc.) Having dots, sometimes raised or sunken, and of contrasting color to background color.

Pungent Very sharp-pointed, e.g., like the spines of a cactus. This is the literal meaning of pungent still used by botanists, though in popular use it has come to mean sharp-smelling.

Race Informally, any broad grouping within a species that may include a large population of individuals. A distinct geographic race may sometimes achieve formal recognition as a subspecies, or a cultivated race may be named as a cultivar group.

Raceme An unbranched inflorescence consisting of an elongated stem or RACHIS bearing a succession of stalked flowers, the youngest at the tip.

Rachis (rhachis) Any elongated stem other than a leafy shoot bearing organs distributed along its length, as in the central stalk of a pinnate leaf or the stem of a raceme.

Radial spines In CACTI, the spines that radiate (more or less) from an AREOLE in a plane tangential to the plant body. Contrasted to CENTRAL SPINES.

Rainforest Luxuriant forest with a completely closed canopy developed in areas of high rainfall. Tropical rainforest is characterized by a great diversity of tree species and abundance of lianes and epiphytes, while temperate rainforest may have only three to six tree species.

Ray (medullary ray) In wood, the bands of tissue that run across the grain from the inner core of a tree trunk to the outer boundary of the wood. Each ray runs along a radius in a cross-section of the trunk. They vary greatly in size from large and conspicuous as in oak timber, to fine and hardly visible as in pine.

Ray floret (in members of the daisy family, Asteraceae or Compositae) The outer ring of florets in a head, when these are distinct from the inner ones or DISC FLORETS. They usually have longer petals that are fused together side by side to form a flat strap, or LIGULE; such florets are termed ligulate.

Receptacle That part of a flower, at the apex of its stalk, to which all the other parts are attached, namely the sepals, petals, stamens, and carpels. In strawberries (*Fragaria*) it is the receptacle that develops into the fleshy part of the fruit.

Recurved (of leaves, flower stalks, petals, or sepals) Curved downward; (of a leaf margin) curved gently downward but not rolled.

Reed Name used loosely for a number of GRASSES, SEDGES, or RUSHES, generally with well-developed, flat leaves and growing in marshy areas or along stream banks. The common reed is the grass *Phragmites australis*, the giant reed is *Arundo donax*, also a grass. Reed-mace is one name for *Typha*.

Reflexed Like recurved but more sharply bent rather than curved.

Resin Class of AROMATIC substances exuded from some plant tissues, especially wood, bark, or fruit, in nature rendering them less edible to animals. Plant resins are insoluble in water and alcohol but soluble in organic solvents such as benzene or gasoline; they become liquid or semi-liquid when warm, hard when cold. Many plant exudates (e.g., of CONIFERS) are "oleoresins," resins mixed with ESSENTIAL OILS which make them more liquid but which gradually evaporate away when exposed, leaving the hard resin. Natural resins were once put to a wide range of industrial and domestic uses but for many of these they have been replaced by synthetic resins made from petroleum.

Resurrection plant A plant that is apparently capable of coming back to life after dying and shrivelling. Few flowering plants (in contrast to mosses and lichens) truly have this capacity, but there are some

"resurrection plants" that curl into tight balls when dead, and expand again when wetted.

Reticulate (of the veining of leaves) Forming a net-like pattern.

Retuse (of a leaf apex) Having a small notch.

Revolute (of a leaf margin) Rolled downward and inward, tightly curled.

Rhachis See RACHIS.

Rhizomatous (of a plant species) Having RHIZOMES as its form of food storage or mode of spread.

Rhizome A stem that runs horizontally along or below the soil surface, putting out roots along its length and sending up erect shoots at intervals; it may be swollen and behave as a storage or overwintering organ.

Rock garden A style of garden incorporating natural rocks, often large and carefully placed to produce a more or less natural effect, the aims of its design being both esthetic and to provide appropriate rooting conditions and microclimates for the selected plants, which usually originate from similar rocky wild habitats.

Rockery Much the same as a ROCK GARDEN but usually on a smaller scale and more humble in its esthetic ambitions.

Root The organ of absorption of water and mineral nutrients, as well as of anchorage to the soil, in the higher plants. Roots are distinguished from underground stems (such as rhizomes) by their anatomical structure.

Rooting powder A powder containing synthetic AUXINS or plant "hormones," in which the wetted ends of cuttings are dipped before inserting them in the rooting medium. The auxins stimulate and hasten the formation of CALLUS and roots.

Rootstock The base of a stem, from which the roots emerge. The underground overwintering stem bases of many herbaceous perennials are termed rootstocks. In grafting, the rootstock is the stem, usually grown from a seedling, onto which the SCION is grafted.

Rosette Any group of plant organs such as leaves that radiate out from a central point on a stem, e.g., the "stemless" yuccas or the short shoots of *Cedrus*.

Rotate (of a flower, or one whorl of a flower such as the corolla) With parts radiating more or less in one plane, like the spokes of a wheel, or forming a disc.

Rugose (of leaves) Having a wrinkled surface, usually due to the veins being impressed into the surface.

Runner Any horizontally spreading stem, usually fairly slender and fast-growing, capable of rooting where it touches the soil and sending up more erect shoots at intervals. Much the same as a STOLON.

Rush In the narrower sense, a species of the large MONOCOT genus *Juncus*, consisting of plants from boggy and marshy habitats, mostly with tufts of slender TERETE leaves and CULMS, and rather insignificant flowers. Wood-rushes (*Luzula*) in the same family (Juncaceae) have flat, hairy-edged leaves. Various members of the SEDGE (Cyperaceae) family are known as rushes, usually with a prefix, such as spike-rushes (*Eleocharis*), club-rushes (*Isolepis*). Flowering-rush is *Butomus*, in a family of its own; scouring-rushes are *Equisetum*, a quite unrelated group of PTERIDOPHYTES of rush-like appearance.

Rust fungus A FUNGUS of the order Uredinales, parasitic on plants, producing small spore-bodies that appear as fine yellow or orange dots on leaves. Most are specific to a host species or genus and can cause severe losses. Poplars and pines are often devastated by their specific rusts. They have very complex life cycles and may need to overwinter on an alternate host, for example wheat rust on *Berberis*.

Sagittate (of leaves) Shaped like an arrowhead, with 2 rearward-pointing basal lobes.

Salt The compound sodium chloride (common salt), toxic to most land plants when present in soil or irrigation water except in small concentrations. In the wider and more technical sense, any chemical compound resulting from the reaction between an acid and an alkali. Many common inorganic salts are water-soluble, e.g., ammonium sulfate, potassium nitrate. They include many popular sources of plant

NUTRIENT elements, both major and minor. Organic compounds can also form salts, e.g., nicotine sulfate.

Salverform (of flowers) With a corolla that opens out from a narrow tube into a flat disc, whether or not the petals are fully fused together.

Samara A dry fruit that retains its seed (does not split open) and is extended at the apex or on 1 side into a wing.

Sand The coarsest component of most soils, defined as having particles more than 0.5 mm but less than 2 mm in diameter (larger particles are classed as gravel). Sands are composed of hard minerals, in most cases predominantly quartz which is almost pure silica, extremely hard and virtually insoluble in water; but beach sands may also contain shell grit, which is chemically similar to limestone.

Sandstone A sedimentary rock formed from ancient sand deposits, the grains cemented together by clay minerals or by the slow dissolving of the minerals that form the grains. Some hard sandstones are composed almost entirely of quartz sand, and break down to sandy soils very deficient in plant nutrients; softer sandstones may contain a range of minerals, producing more fertile soils. Sandstones are often used as building stone and for garden construction.

Sap The water-based liquid that flows through the conducting tissues of plants, either through the SAPWOOD from roots to foliage, or through the inner BARK in the reverse direction. The upward-flowing sap carries dissolved mineral nutrients, which aid PHOTOSYNTHESIS in the foliage and other processes in which complex molecules are synthesized; the downward-flowing sap in the bark carries mainly sugars, used to create the structural materials that make up the plant's bulk, principally cellulose and lignin, and also providing energy for metabolic processes in the living cells.

Saprophyte A plant or fungus that is able to make use of dead organic matter (such as leaf litter, fallen logs, or straw) as its source of nutrition. A large proportion of the fungi are saprophytes, but saprophytic flowering plants require a symbiotic relationship with a lower organism, usually a fungus, in or around their roots.

Sapwood The outer cylinder of wood in the trunks of trees, consisting of live cells and which actively conducts SAP. It is often paler in color than the inner, dead HEARTWOOD and can vary greatly in thickness depending on species, age, and growing conditions. Its cells are usually rich in starch, the tree's principal stored food; this means sapwood is prone to destruction by wood-boring insects and rot fungi, in contrast to heartwood which is not only starch-free but contains deposits of tannins and other substances that help it resist such attack.

Savannah (savanna) A common vegetation type in the tropics consisting of grassland with sparsely scattered trees, occurring on plains in regions of highly seasonal rainfall.

Scale Minute organ found on leaves and other plant surfaces, like a hair but flattened and thin. Some closely appressed scales, e.g., on olive leaves, are attached by a stalk at their center and are termed peltate scales. Also that part of the cone in conifers and cycads to which the seeds or pollen sacs are attached.

Scale insect Any of a group of sap-sucking insect of the family Coccidae (to which MEALYBUGS also belong) that in its adult state covers itself with a layer of wax and becomes virtually immobile. Some scale insect species are garden pests and may cause major damage to commercial plantings, e.g., white wax scale of citrus.

Scale leaves Leaves that are reduced to a small size and pressed against the twig, usually overlapping one another, as in most *Cupressus* and *Juniperus* species.

Scape An elongated, more or less leafless stalk that supports a whole inflorescence (as in a yucca, or onion, *Allium*) or a single terminal flower (as in a tulip, *Tulipa*).

Scarify Literally to scratch; in agriculture meaning to draw a sharp-pointed implement across plowed ground to break up clods; in plant propagation, to scratch or abrade a hard impervious seed coat (e.g., of many

LEGUMES) so the seed can absorb the water necessary to begin germinating.

Schizocarp A fruit, developing from a single flower, that is deeply divided into segments each containing seeds, each segment (termed a MERICARP) usually deriving from one carpel and resembling a separate fruit. *Sterculia* and *Brachychiton* fruits are examples.

Scion That part of a graft that is the subject of propagation, usually a cut piece of branch or twig of the desired cultivar, which is grafted onto the ROOTSTOCK.

Sclerophyll Term describing a species whose leaves are somewhat harsh and rigid due to containing a high proportion of cellulose and woody tissues. Especially common among Australian shrubs, it is believed to be an adaptation to very infertile soils.

Scrub A term loosely used for any type of more or less-dense vegetation consisting of shrubs and sometimes also small trees.

Sedge Any member of the large monocot family Cyperaceae, of worldwide occurrence, and in particular members of its two largest genera, *Carex* and *Cyperus*. Sedges have grass-like leaves and spikelets of tiny but numerous flowers concealed among dry bracts that are often reddish to blackish; most grow in marshy ground. See also RUSH.

Seed Organ of reproduction and dispersal of flowering plants and gymnosperms (collectively called the seed plants), developing enclosed in the fruit of the former or on scales of female cones of the latter. A seed consists of a plant embryo, food storage tissue, and a protective seed coat. A seed may remain dormant for a long period before its germination is initiated by moisture and warmth.

Seed leaf See COTYLEDON.

Seedhead Any fruiting inflorescence of compact form, e.g., of sunflowers or wheat.

Segment One of the lobes of a deeply lobed leaf, or any similar structure.

Self (in plant breeding) Progeny resulting from a plant being fertilized by its own pollen or pollen from a plant of the same clone, in this sense mainly used by orchid breeders; (of flower color of cultivars) of the same color all over.

Self-seeding Used of any plant whose seed is shed and grows in the garden without aid from the gardener; applied more to desired plants than to weeds, which are almost self-seeding by definition.

Semi-double (of cultivars) Having flowers with more than the normal number of petals of the wild species, and usually forming more than one row, but with stamens still visible in the flower's center.

Sepal One segment of the CALYX of a flower. Sepals are usually green in contrast to the colored petals; they may be fused to one another, at least toward their bases.

Series (of cultivars) A group of cultivars with a common ancestry and often sold under the one name but with mixed colors, most usually encountered in annuals; (in botanical classification) a named group of closely similar species; series is lowest of the ranks between genus and species, the next higher being section and then subgenus.

Serrate (of leaf margins) Having sharp, forward-pointing teeth, like the teeth of a saw.

Serrulate Like serrate but with smaller, more closely spaced teeth.

Sessile (of flowers, leaves) Having no individual stalk; attached directly to the stem.

Sheath (of leaves) A leaf stalk or base of a sessile leaf that is expanded and wraps around the stem, as in many palms.

Shoot A leafy branch or stem that is in the process of growing and elongating.

Short shoot A lateral branch of limited growth with extremely short INTERNODES, arising like all branches from leaf axils on the parent branch; in some plants producing new leaves and potentially flowers year after year (as in apples, *Malus*), in others never producing more than its initial complement of leaves (as in the needle clusters of *Pinus*, an extreme example of short shoots). On fruit trees commonly known as spurs or SPUR SHOOTS.

Shrub A plant with permanent, woody, aboveground stems from which new growths arise, and one that is too small to be classed as a tree.

Silt The middle one of the three major constituents of soil, finer than sand and coarser than clay.

Simple (of leaves) Individual leaves without discrete leaflets.

Single (of cultivars) Having flowers with much the same number of petals as the wild species of the genus to which they belong, or at least having the petals forming a single row.

Sinuate (of leaf margins) Wavy, with the waves bending in and out in relation to the leaf midrib and in the same plane as the leaf blade.

Sinus Literally a bay; any indentation in the margin of a flat organ, such as between lobes of a leaf, or the gap between any 2 adjacent organs such as sepals that are fused to one another at the base.

Smoke treatment Promoting germination of certain seeds by exposing them to wood smoke or, more effectively, pre-soaking them in water in which wood smoke has been condensed. Based on recent research that has shown importance of smoke in breaking dormancy of seeds of many Australian and South African shrubs, difficult to germinate by other means.

Smut Any of a group of parasitic FUNGI of the order Ustilaginales that infect cereals and other grasses, replacing their florets and grains with dense masses of black spores resembling soot; smut of wheat is also called "bunt."

Soil The thin mantle of material covering most of the earth's lands, derived mainly from the chemical breakdown of bedrock over many centuries. It is composed of mineral particles of various sizes (see CLAY, SILT, SAND) as well as particles of dead organic matter from plant roots, leaves, and fallen logs, this organic matter often mixed into the soil by earthworms. Soil contains the moisture and mineral nutrients that plants need for growth.

Softwood (of tree species) Having a soft timber, though more traditionally signifying any CONIFER—as opposed to a HARDWOOD (flowering plant), regardless of relative hardness or density of timber; (of cuttings) Taken from stems at or near their growing tips of the current year's growth, where tissues have not fully hardened.

Solitary (of flowers) Borne singly, not grouped in an inflorescence. A flower may be solitary and terminal, borne at the tip of a branch, or solitary and axillary, borne in a leaf axil. (of palms) consisting of only a single trunk.

Sorus (in ferns) The cluster of numerous minute sporangia or spore sacs that forms a usually brown dot or patch on the underside of a mature frond.

Spadix A spike or dense panicle of flowers. It is a somewhat obsolete term among botanists except for its use for the specialized inflorescence of the arum family.

Spathe A large bract that encloses a whole inflorescence in bud. Like spadix, this is now most commonly used for the inflorescence of the arum family.

Spathulate (of leaves) Shaped like a spatula, or at least an old-fashioned one, that is, long and fairly narrow with a rounded tip and tapering gradually to the base.

Species (abbreviation sp., plural spp.) The basic unit of plant classification, usually consisting of a population of individuals that are fairly uniform in character and breed freely with one another over many generations without obvious change in their progeny. A species is normally unable to breed with another species or if it does, the resulting progeny do not remain constant or do not produce viable seed. The scientific name of a species consists of the name of the GENUS to which it belongs, followed by a name referred to as the specific epithet, somewhat like a person's given name—e.g., *Pinus contorta*.

Spermatophytes The seed plants, consisting of all the flowering plants and also the gymnosperms (mainly the conifers and cycads). The evolution of seeds was an important step in the colonization of the earth's land surfaces by larger plants, allowing their dispersal into environments where moisture was not constantly available.

Sphagnum   Mosses belonging to the genus *Sphagnum*, found in largest quantities in cooler regions of world where they grow in extensive bogs. Sphagnum can absorb and retain many times its own weight of water while remaining well aerated and is therefore valued in horticultural growing media. Peat, or at least moss peat, is mainly fossilized sphagnum.

Spike   (in botany) An unbranched inflorescence in which the flowers are sessile, that is, lacking individual stalks.

Spikelet   A small shortened spike of specialized structure forming one unit of a larger inflorescence. Used mainly for grasses and sedges.

Spine   In botany, a sharp needle-like organ that is a modification of some other organ such as a leaf, stipule, or sepal, though not of a branch, as that is a THORN.

Sporangium   (plural sporangia) A small receptacle on a spore-bearing plant in which SPORES are formed and from which they are released. In FERNS the sporangia are tiny, usually stalked sacs, barely visible to the naked eye, borne in more readily seen masses (SORI) of varying shape and size on the underside of the frond.

Spore   Minute reproductive bodies of FERNS, carried by wind and germinating in moist, shady places to produce the sexual plantlets (gametophytes) with male and female organs that on fertilization produce another spore-bearing plant. Mosses and fungi also have wind-borne spores.

Sporophyll   Botanical jargon for the scale or "leaf" that bears pollen or ovules, e.g., in conifer cones, or in fact the stamen or carpel in flowers, though these are spore-bearing only in the theoretical sense of a spore.

Sport   A spontaneous mutation in one branch of a plant, affecting such features as flower color, shape, or number of petals, and shape or variegation of leaves. Sporting is a common source of new cultivars in some groups of shrubs and trees, e.g., camellias, being perpetuated from cuttings or grafting, but they may have a tendency to mutate back again to the original type.

Spur   A backward projection from a petal or sepal in the shape of a spur or horn, usually hollow and containing nectar. A SPUR SHOOT is one of the short lateral branches of trees such as apples that bear the flower clusters.

Stalk   The part of a leaf (technically the PETIOLE) that attaches to the plant stem, at least when it is distinct from the leaf blade; likewise the organ (technically the PEDICEL) that supports an individual flower, or that supports a whole inflorescence (technically the PEDUNCLE).

Stamen   The male reproductive organ in a flower, consisting typically of a slender stalk (FILAMENT) and a pollen-sac (ANTHER), which opens by a slit or pore to release pollen. The stamens form the third row of organs from the outside of a flower, inside the sepals and petals.

Staminal column   A tubular or less commonly solid structure formed from the fused filaments of a flower's stamens, characteristic of certain plant genera, e.g., *Hibiscus*, in which it is a prominent feature.

Staminode   A non-functional stamen, often lacking an anther or the anther lacking pollen, and often flattened and imitating a petal, as in many "double"-flowered cultivars.

Standard   (in gardening) Usually a shrub (sometimes a tree) trained to have a long bare stem topped by a compact crown of foliage; or often a grafted plant with a tall unbranched rootstock; pendulous cultivars are usually grafted in this way; (of irises) term used for each of the 3 outer PERIANTH segments that in many species and cultivars stand erect, alternating with the 3 outer ones, the "falls," which are bent downward; (of PEA-FLOWERS) the upper and usually largest petal of the flower, usually standing erect and to the rear of the other petals, often marked with a basal blotch of contrasting color or with radiating lines.

Stellate hair   A kind of plant hair that divides near the base into several radiating branches, the resulting star-like structure sometimes visible even without magnification. Stellate hairs can be a feature of certain plant families, notably the mallow (Malvaceae) family.

Stem   The organ of a plant that supports leaves and flowers, and to which the roots attach; in the broadest sense, any shoot, trunk, branch, or twig is a stem. Distinguished from a STALK.

Sterile   (of flowers) Lacking functional reproductive organs; (of stamens) not containing pollen.

Stigma   The apical part of a CARPEL, or of two or more fused carpels, that is receptive to pollen, often separated from the OVARY by a slender STYLE.

Stilt-roots   (or prop-roots, strut-roots) Roots that emerge from a stem above the ground and grow out and down to the soil, stabilizing the plant by spreading its base in soft ground such as mud or sand. They are a feature of some MANGROVES and some pandanus and PALM species, among larger plants, but some quite small plants may also have stilt roots.

Stipe   A narrowed basal portion of an organ such as an ovary or petal that connects it to the flower's receptacle; in ferns, the stalk of a leaflet or pinnule.

Stipule   Appendage at base of a leaf stalk (PETIOLE), usually paired, sometimes tiny and scale-like, or modified into a spine, or even of similar size to the leaf itself (e.g., in *Bauera*).

Stock   See ROOTSTOCK.

Stolon   A slender horizontal stem that extends from a parent stem and forms a new plantlet at the end. This takes root and the process is often repeated, usually on top of the soil but may be below the surface. Much the same as RUNNER.

Stoloniferous   (of a species) Spreading by STOLONS.

Stomate   One of the minute pores in a leaf through which gases pass in, especially the carbon dioxide essential to photosynthesis, and water vapor passes out thereby drawing water up from the roots. Stomates are able to close up when water loss is excessive.

Stone cell   A cell or more often a small, grit-like group of cells with thickened, irregular walls, occurring scattered through softer tissues, as in the flesh of quinces (*Cydonia oblonga*) and some pear (*Pyrus*) cultivars.

Stone fruit   All those edible fruits produced by species (or hybrids) in the genus *Prunus*, all being DRUPES with a single seed enclosed in a very hard, ridged ENDOCARP or "stone."

Stool   An erect shoot of a shrub or tree arising from the base of the stem where the roots depart; can be detached as a means of propagation; much the same as a basal "sucker."

Strain   A group of cultivars that inherit some common features through several or many generations of breeding.

Stratification   Treatment of seeds to promote germination by breaking dormancy, usually by refrigerating for 2 to 4 months in a slightly moist medium, though traditionally achieved by layering in the medium in an outdoor location that experiences frosts and receives little sun. In nature the seeds lie in moist leaf litter over winter.

Striate   (of stems, leaves, seeds, etc.) Marked with fine longitudinal furrows, or even fine stripes of darker color.

Style   The slender portion of a carpel, or of several fused carpels, between the ovary and the stigma.

Subarctic   (of climates) Those characteristic of lands just outside the Arctic Circle.

Subgenus   A major subdivision of a genus, ranking higher than a section or series in the taxonomic hierarchy; usually recognized in genera with many species, e.g., *Pinus* is subdivided into subgenus *Pinus*, the "hard pines" and subgenus *Strobus*, the "soft" or "white pines."

Subfamily   In the hierarchy of botanical classification, a major subdivision of a plant FAMILY, higher in rank than TRIBE. Subfamily rank is indicated by the termination -oideae, and there will always be a "type" subfamily that takes the name of its family except for this change in ending. In the classifications of some smaller and even some larger families no subfamilies are recognized, only tribes, but in others there are subfamilies of significance to gardeners, e.g., the BAMBOO subfamily (Bambusoideae) of the GRASS family (Poaceae), or the PEA-FLOWER subfamily (Faboideae) of the LEGUME family (Fabaceae).

Subshrub   A low shrub that is not very woody at the base, and hence is somewhat intermediate between a shrub and a herbaceous perennial.

Subsoil   Deeper layer of soil that has developed more recently from bedrock than the topsoil, and which usually contains little or no organic matter. Trees may derive more mineral nutrients from the subsoil than from the topsoil, as soluble minerals are leached from the latter by rainwater.

Subspecies   A major division of a species, ranking above variety and forma, though used by some botanists instead of variety. A subspecies may be thought of as a species still in the process of evolving but not yet reproductively isolated from its related subspecies except by geography; there are usually intermediate plants where subspecies adjoin. The "type" subspecies takes the same epithet as the species, thus *Acer saccharum* is divided into 6 or more subspecies including subsp. *saccharum* and subsp. *grandidentatum*, each subspecies occurring in a different region of North America. Abbreviated to "subsp." or "ssp."

Substrate   Any material on or in which a plant is rooted, e.g., soil, sand, rock, bark.

Subtend   To include within the angle of, e.g., a leaf subtends a flower that arises from its axil.

Subtropical   (of climates) Those characteristic of lands just outside the tropical zones, generally warm and frost free, at least in coastal regions.

Subulate   (of leaves, mainly) Literally, shaped like an awl, that is, a thickened tapering needle with angled sides.

Succulent   (of a species, or its leaves or stems) Swollen and consisting of fleshy tissue that has a very high water content, as opposed to fibers and wood cells. Succulent plants occur in semi-arid regions mainly in Africa and the Americas; they include most of the cacti and many euphorbias.

Sucker   A vigorous erect shoot arising from the base of a shrub or the trunk or limb of a tree; also known as a stool or water shoot.

Symbiosis (symbiotic)   A relationship between 2 organisms, e.g., a FLOWERING PLANT and a FUNGUS, that is beneficial to both. Well-known examples are the *Rhizobium* bacteria in the root nodules of most LEGUMES, which supply the legume plant with nitrogen in exchange for moisture and sugars; or the combination of a fungus and single-celled ALGAE to form a LICHEN.

Sympodial   (of a species' growth habit) Characterized by each shoot having limited growth, stopping after one to several NODES are formed and often terminating in an inflorescence, with growth continuing from a lateral shoot, the process being repeated indefinitely and often following a seasonal rhythm. Contrasted with MONOPODIAL, the distinction being especially important between ORCHID genera.

Syncarp   An apparent fruit that is actually a number of fruits fused together, e.g., of *Maclura*, *Morus*, *Pandanus*.

Synonym   Any name referring to the same species or genus as another name, though usually taken to mean the name that is currently not accepted; thus *Pinus insignis* is a synonym of *Pinus radiata*, now the accepted name for the Monterey pine. When a genus has been merged with or split from another genus, the synonym is never the larger or older genus: for example, *Fortunella* is a synonym of *Citrus*, but *Citrus* is not a synonym of *Fortunella*.

Tannin   Bitter or astringent substance soluble in water, found in many parts of many plants but often most concentrated in the bark. Tannins have the property of coagulating animal proteins, hence their long use for tanning leather. Their role in nature is to make the plant less edible.

Taproot   A thick central root that goes vertically down into the soil; a carrot is an extreme example.

Taxon (plural taxa) In botanical classification, general term for any named group of plants at whatever rank in the taxonomic hierarchy. Thus if one needs to talk collectively about the genus *Rosa*, the species *Salix alba* and the subspecies *Cistus incanus* subsp. *creticus*, the term taxa is convenient.

Taxonomy The science and practice of classifying and naming living organisms.

Temperate (of climates) Those of lands lying between the Tropic of Cancer and the Arctic Circle, or between the Tropic of Capricorn and the Antarctic Circle—but climates close to the tropics (within about 10 degrees of latitude) are generally termed SUBTROPICAL, and those close to the Arctic Circle are termed SUBARCTIC. Temperate climates may also be found at high altitudes in the tropics. See also COOL-TEMPERATE and WARM-TEMPERATE.

Tendril A modified branch, leaf, stipule, or inflorescence that coils around twigs, wires, or other such objects to enable a plant to climb. Grape vines have tendrils.

Tepal Alternative term for PERIANTH-segment in flowers where PETALS and SEPALS are not strongly differentiated. Used mainly for plants in the lily group of MONOCOT families, e.g., *Tulipa, Lilium.*

Terete (of leaves or stems) Circular in cross-section.

Terminal (of flowers) Positioned at the apex of a stem or inflorescence branch and terminating its growth.

Terrarium Any small enclosed structure of glass or clear plastic in which delicate frost-tender plants can be grown, often in 100 percent humidity. Used also for a variant of an indoor aquarium or fish tank in which a lizard, tortoise, frog, etc., is kept, with a dry or partially dry floor of pebbles, rocks, etc., sometimes with plants as well.

Terrestrial (of a species) Normally found in the ground and on dry land, as opposed to EPIPHYTIC or AQUATIC.

Tessellated (of tree bark) Broken up into small squares or other angular shapes, like floor tiles.

Testa The hard or tough outer coat of a SEED.

Tetraploid (of a hybrid or cultivar) One with double the normal set of chromosomes of its DIPLOID wild relatives, i.e., with four matching sets of CHROMOSOMES instead of two sets. Tetraploids are sometimes created artificially by plant breeders and tend to be larger in all their parts—e.g., some *Forsythia* cultivars. See also POLYPLOID.

Thorn In botany, a branch or twig that terminates in a sharp point, as in hawthorns *(Crataegus).* Not to be confused with a PRICKLE or SPINE.

Thrips (plural thrips) Tiny, soft-bodied insects of the order Thysanoptera that may infest plant foliage and flower buds in large numbers, scraping with their mouth-parts through the epidermis and feeding on exuding sap. Can be a major pest of garden plants and vegetable crops (Latin *thrips,* the true plural *thripes).*

Throat (of flowers) The inside of the tube of a funnel-shaped or trumpet-shaped flower.

Tomentose (of leaves or stems) Coated with a dense, somewhat woolly layer of hairs.

Topiary The art of trimming densely-foliaged plants into geometric or fanciful shapes and maintaining the plants in those shapes indefinitely.

Trailing (of a plant's growth habit) With stems lying on the ground and spilling down slopes or over banks.

Transpiration The process that takes place in all plant foliage (unless submerged in water) whereby water evaporates through walls of cells beneath the STOMATES or minute pores, through which it then escapes to the surrounding air. Evaporation from the leaves creates negative pressure in the conducting tissues of leaves and stems, drawing water upward from the roots; this water and its dissolved nutrients are essential for PHOTOSYNTHESIS. Rate of transpiration varies with humidity, temperature, and air movement and is also controlled by opening and closing of the stomates.

Tree A woody plant of much greater height than the human figure, usually at least 15 ft (4.5 m) though shorter plants may be regarded as trees if they have a single, thick trunk.

Tree fern A fern with a long-lived vertical stem topped by a single crown of fronds, mostly species of *Cyathea, Cibotium,* or *Dicksonia.* Tree ferns are restricted to the tropics and warm-temperate areas where rainfall is high.

Tribe A subdivision of a family below the rank of SUBFAMILY but above genus. For example, the tribe Genisteae of the family Fabaceae contains all of the European brooms including the genera *Cytisus, Genista, Chamaecytisus, Laburnum,* and *Ulex.*

Trifoliate (of compound leaves) Having three leaflets—this can be a minimal case of either a pinnate or digitate (palmate) leaf. Trifoliolate is the more pedantic form.

Tripinnate (of leaves) Compound to the third order, with leaves divided pinnately into leaflets, these again divided pinnately, and yet again.

Tropical (of climates, species) Occurring in the tropics, that is, in lands between the Tropic of Cancer and Tropic of Capricorn.

Truncate (of leaf apex or base) Cut off more or less squarely.

Trunk The central stem of a tree that supports the crown; it may continue well above the lowest branches though where the trunk stops and the upper limbs start is a subjective judgment.

Truss Gardener's term for a group of crowded flowers such as the inflorescence of many *Rhododendron* species and cultivars.

Tuber A stem modified into a storage organ, either underground or at the soil surface. A potato is the archetypal tuber.

Tubercle Any small projection from a plant surface that is more or less bulbous in shape, the surface being then termed tuberculate.

Tuberous root A root that is swollen so as to resemble a TUBER (which is a swollen stem). Dahlias have tuberous roots, not true tubers.

Tumbleweed Type of growth habit and seed dispersal mechanism found in a number of plants, not necessarily related. Mostly annuals or biennials of spreading habit, they die as fruits mature and break off at the root, the branches drying and curving inward to give the whole plant a ball-like form. This is propelled by wind, bowling over plains sometimes for long distances, gradually disintegrating and shedding seeds. A well-known species of tumbleweed is *Boophone disticha.*

Tunic In bulbs and corms, the tough or membranous outer "skin" (a modified leaf base), as in an onion. It may be shredded into fibers or form a net in some plants.

Turbinate (of 3-dimensional plant organs, e.g., fruits) Shaped like a top, roughly OBCONICAL though more swollen.

Twig The ultimate branches of a tree or shrub's canopy, usually weak and slender.

Twiner A climber that gains its support from other plants by its stems twining spiraly around their stems. Any one species of twiner will (with few exceptions) spiral either in a clockwise or an anticlockwise direction (viewed from above).

Umbel An inflorescence in which the individual flower stalks (pedicels) radiate from the end of the common stalk (peduncle). It may be derived from either a raceme or a cyme, when internodes of the inflorescence are reduced to zero length.

Umbellifer Any plant belonging to the large DICOT family Apiaceae, taken from its traditional alternative name Umbelliferae. Mostly herbaceous and with deeply DISSECTED or COMPOUND leaves, they have numerous small flowers arranged in UMBELS, often compound, and small dry fruits that may be highly aromatic, as in caraway *(Carum)* and cumin *(Cuminum).* A number of well-known vegetables are umbellifers, notably carrots, parsnips, celery, and parsley.

Undulate (of leaf margins) Wavy, with the undulations at right angles to the plane of the leaf.

Unisexual (of a species) Dioecious, having only male or female flowers; (of flowers) having only male or female organs, not both in the one flower.

Urceolate (of flowers) Urn-shaped, with an inflated tube narrowed in at the mouth but slightly broadening again at the lip.

Vandaceous Those MONOPODIAL genera of orchids comprising *Vanda* and its close allies, frequently combined in generic hybrids.

Variegated (of leaves) Mottled, streaked, edged, or striped with colors (mostly white to yellow) other than the normal green of wild plants. They are mostly found in ornamental cultivars; less commonly applied to flowers, e.g., some *Camellia* cultivars.

Variety (in plant classification) A subdivision of a species, of lower rank than SUBSPECIES but higher than FORMA, though used by some botanists instead of subspecies. In a looser sense "variety" may refer to a cultivar.

Vascular (of plants) Having stems with specialized conducting tissues. The vascular plants comprise the ferns and fern-allies, the gymnosperms and the flowering plants.

Vegetative Pertaining to those parts of a plant not associated with flowers or fruits.

Vein A visible strand of conducting tissue in a leaf or a petal.

Venation The arrangement of the veins in a leaf or a petal.

Vine A climbing plant; in the original sense, the wine-grape plant *(Vitis vinifera).*

Vireya Member of the large, mainly tropical section *Vireya* of the genus *Rhododendron,* consisting of over 100 species found mostly in the Malay Archipelago, principally the islands of New Guinea and Borneo, with outliers extending to China and 2 species northeastern Australia. They are evergreen and repeat-flowering, with brilliantly colored flowers. Many Vireya hybrids have been raised.

Warm-temperate (of climates) Those of lands in the warmer halves of the temperate zones, at latitudes between about 25 and 40 degrees.

Weed A plant that is not wanted in a garden but multiplies nonetheless, robbing cultivated plants of light, moisture, and nutrients and appearing unsightly.

Whorled (of leaves) Arranged in groups of 3 or more at the 1 node, distributed equally around the node.

Winged (of stems or leaf stalks) Having one or more longitudinal thin flanges projecting; (of fruits or seeds) having a flat papery extension from one or more edges.

Witch's broom A malformation of the foliage of a tree branch, usually with leaves and twigs smaller and more crowded than on other branches; sometimes propagated from cuttings or grafts and named as cultivars, especially of conifers.

Wood The main conducting and supporting tissue in trees and shrubs, found only in dicotyledons, formed by the cambium layer on its inner side and termed xylem in plant anatomy. Sapwood, which is the outer living layer of xylem, conducts water and dissolved nutrients from the roots to the leaves. Heartwood is dead xylem and its function is merely support. Xylem cell walls are composed of the carbohydrates cellulose and lignin.

Woody (of plant species) Those developing wood in their stems and branches.

Xerophyte A plant adapted to dry climates and capable of surviving through droughts other than by seeds or bulbs.

Xylem See WOOD.

Zygomorphic (of flowers) Having only one, vertical plane of symmetry, e.g., as in snapdragons and nearly all ORCHIDS. Contrasted with "actinomorphic," in which a plane of symmetry passes through each petal and sepal.

Index

The page number in *italics*, usually the second page number, indicates a photograph.

Produced by Global Book Publishing Pty Ltd   Unit 1/181 High Street, Willoughby, NSW 2068, Australia   Ph +61 2 9967 3100 Fax +61 2 9967 5891   Email rightsmanager@globalpub.com.au

Photos and illustrations from the Global Photo Library © Global Book Publishing Pty Ltd 2003   Text © Global Book Publishing Pty Ltd 2003